Schroeder's Collectible
TOYS
Antique to Modern
Price Guide

Sixth Edition

Edited by Sharon and Bob Huxford

COLLECTOR BOOKS
A Division of Schroeder Publishing Co., Inc.

The current values in this book should be used only as a guide. They are not intended to set prices, which vary from one section of the country to another. Auction prices as well as dealer prices vary greatly and are affected by condition as well as demand. Neither the editors nor the publisher assumes responsibility for any losses that might be incurred as a result of consulting this guide.

On The Cover:

Front: Kiddy Cyclist windup, Unique Art, 1930s, NM, $450.00; Dakins Tweety Bird, 1969, M, $35.00; Erector Set #6½, 1951, MIB, $165.00; Shirley Temple Ideal doll in Wee Willie Winkie outfit, 1959, 15", $250.00 (photo courtesy Cindy Sabulis); Clash of the Titans action figure, Kraken Sea Monster, MIB, $190.00; Atom Friction Racer, Y, 16", NM, $1,150.00; Star Wars Obi-Wan Kenobi mug, California Originals, M, $175.00 (photo courtesy June Moon); Coca-Cola vending machine, Linemar, lithographed tin, NM, $450.00 (photo courtesy John Turney); Roy Rogers and Dale Evans lunch box, American Thermos Bottle Co., NM, $150.00 – 175.00.

Back: Robin Hood and Maid Marian paper dolls, Saalfield # 2748, 1956, uncut, M, $75.00 (photo courtesy Mary Young); Pyro Deluxe Classics model kit, VW Sun Roof Sedan, MIB, $60.00; Push-Button Puppets, Gabriel the Giraffe, Terry the Tiger, and Lucky the Lion, Kohner, 1960s, $12.00 each; Felix the Cat Walker, wooden, 1930s, 18", $550.00; Ludwig Von Drake Tiddly Winks, Whitman, EX (EX box), $35.00.

Editorial Staff:

Editors: Sharon and Bob Huxford

Research and Editorial Assistants: Michael Drollinger, Nancy Drollinger, Donna Newnum, Loretta Suiters

Cover Design: Beth Summers

Layout: Terri Hunter and Beth Ray

Searching For A Publisher?

We are always looking for knowledgeable people considered to be experts within their fields. If you feel that there is a real need for a book on your collectible subject and have a large comprehensive collection, contact Collector Books.

COLLECTOR BOOKS
P.O. Box 3009
Paducah, Kentucky 42002-3009

Introduction

It seems that every decade will have an area of concentrated excitement when it comes to the antiques and collectibles marketplace. What Depression glass was to the late sixties, Fiesta to the seventies, and cookie jars were to the eighties, toys are to the nineties. No one even vaguely involved in the field can have missed all the excitement toys have stirred up among many, many collectors. There are huge toy shows nationwide; scores of newsletters, magazines, and trade papers that deal exclusively with toys; cataloged toy auctions with wonderful color photographs and several hundred lots each; and more and more toy collectors' guides are appearing in the book stores each week.

If you've been using *Schroeder's Antiques Price Guide*, you know that we try very hard not to omit categories where we find even a minor amount of market activity — being collectors ourselves, we know how frustrating it can be when you are unable to find any information on an item in question. But that book is limited to a specific number of pages, and as we watched the toy market explosion taking place, we realized that if we were to do it justice, we would have to publish a companion guide devoted entirely to toys. And following the same convictions, we decided that rather than to try to zero in on only the larger, more active fields, we'd try to represent toys of all kinds, from the 19th century up to today. This is the format we chose to pursue.

Our concept is unique in the collectibles field. Though we designed the book first and foremost to be a price guide, we wanted to make it a buying/selling guide as well. So we took many of our descriptions and values from the 'toys for sale' lists of dealers and collectors around the country. In each of those listings we included a dealer's code, so that if you were looking for the particular model kit (or whatever) that (S5) had to offer, you'd be able to match his code with his name and address in the 'Dealer and Collector Codes' section and simply drop him a line or call him to see if it were still available. Our experiment has been very successful. Feedback indicates that many of our sellers do very well, making productive contacts with collectors who not only purchase items from them on their initial call but leave requests for other merchandise they are looking for as well.

Each edition contains about 24,000 listings, but even at that we realize that when it comes to the toy market, that only began to scratch the surface. Our intent is to provide our readers with fresh information, issue after issue. The few categories that are repeated in their entirety in succeeding editions generally are those that were already complete or as nearly complete as we or our advisors could make them. But even those are checked to make sure that values are still current and our information up to date.

When we initially began to plan our layout, we soon discovered that organizing toys is mind-boggling. Collectors were quick to tell us that toys generally can't be sorted by manufacturer, as we were accustomed to doing in our other price guides. So we had to devise a sort that would not only be easy to use but one that our staff could work with. With this in mind, we kept our categories very broad and general. On the whole this worked very well, but we found that the character section was so large (4,000 lines) it was overwhelming to our advisors. So even though our original approach was probably the most user-friendly, we have broken the character collectibles down into several groups of collectibles and genres and created specific categories for them. But you'll find 'See Alsos' in bold, cross-references within the description lines, and a detailed index to help you locate the items you're looking for with ease.

What we want to stress is that our values are not meant to set prices. Some of them are prices realized at auction; you'll be able to recognize these by the 'A' at the end of the description line. The listings that have neither the 'A' code nor the dealer code mentioned above were either sent to us for publication by very knowledgeable collectors who specialize in those specific types of toys or were originally dealer coded but altered at the suggestion of an advisor who felt that the stated price might be far enough outside the average market price range to be misleading (in which case, the dealer's code was removed). There are so many factors that bear on the market that for us to attempt to set prices is not only presumptuous, it's ludicrous. The foremost of these factors is the attitude of the individual collector — his personal view of the hobby. We've interviewed several by telephone; everyone has his own opinion. While some view auction prices as useless, others regard them as actual selling prices and prefer them to asking prices. And the dealer who needs to keep turning his merchandise over to be able to replenish and freshen his stock will of necessity sell at lower prices than a collector who will buy an item and wait for the most opportune time to turn it over for maximum profit. Where you buy affects prices as well. One of our advisors used this simple analogy: while a soda might cost you $2.50 at the ball park, you can buy the same thing for 39¢ at the corner 7 - 11. So all we (or anyone) can offer is whatever facts and information we can compile, and ask simply that you arrive at your own evaluations based on the data we've provided, adapted to your personal buying/selling arena, desire to own, and need to sell.

We hope you enjoy our book and that you'll be able to learn by using it. We don't presume to present it as the last word on toys or their values — there are many specialized books by authors who are able to devote an entire publication to one subject, covering it from 'A' to 'Z,' and when we're aware that such a text book exists, we'll recommend it in our narratives. If you have suggestions that you think will improve our format, let us hear from you — we value your input. Until next time — happy hunting! May you find that mint-in-the-box #1 Barbie doll or if you prefer that rare mechanical bank that has managed to so far elude you. But even if you never do, we hope that you'll find a generous measure of happiness and success, a treasure now and then, and new friends along the way.

— The Editors

Advisory Board

The editors and staff take this opportunity to express our sincere gratitude and appreciation to each person who has contributed their time and knowledge to help us. We've found toys to be *by far* the largest, most involved field of collecting we've ever tried to analyze, but we will have to admit, it's great fun! We've been editing general price guides for fifteen years now, and before ever attempting the first one, we realized there was only one way we would presume to publish such a guide — and that would be to first enlist the help of knowledgeable collectors around the country who specialized in specific areas. We now have more than 120, and we're still looking for help in several areas. Generally, the advisors are listed following each category's narrative, so if we have mentioned no one and you feel that you are qualified to advise us, have the time, and would be willing to help us out with that subject, please contact us. We'd love to have you on our advisory board. (We want to stress that even if an advisor is credited in a category narrative, that person is in no way responsible for errors. Errors are our responsibility.) Even if we currently list an advisor for your subject, contact us so that we'll have your name on file should that person need to be replaced. This of course happens from time to time due to changing interests or because they find they no longer have the time.

While some advisors sent us listings and prices, others provided background information and photographs, checked printouts or simply answered our questions. All are listed below. Most are followed by their code, see the section called *Dealer and Collector Codes* for an explanation of how these are used in the listings.

Matt and Lisa Adams (A7)
Geneva Addy (A5)
Diane Albert (T6)
Sally and Stan Alekna (A1)
Pamela E. Apkarian-Russell (H9)
Bob Armstrong (A4)
Richard Belyski (B1)
Larry Blodget (B2)
Bojo (B3)
Scott Bruce (B14)
Sue and Marty Bunis (B11)
Bill Campbell (C10)
Candelaine (Candace Gunther) (G16)
Casey's Collectible Corner (C1)

Brad Cassity (C13)
Mark Chase (C2)
Joel Cohen (C12)
Cotswold Collectibles (C6)
Marilyn Cooper (C9)
Cynthia's Country Store (C14)
Rosalind Cranor (C15)
Marl Davidson (D2)
Larry DeAngelo (D3)
Doug Dezso (D6)
Donna and Ron Donnelly (D7)
George Downes (D8)
Larry Doucet (D11)
Larry Egelhoff (E1)

Paul Fink (F3)
Steve Fisch (F7)
Mike and Kurt Fredericks (F4)
Fun House Toy Co. (F5)
Lee Garmon
Carol Karbowiak Gilbert (G6)
Mark Giles (G2)
Joan Stryker Grumbaugh (G8)
Bill Hamburg (H1)
Don Hamm (H10)
George Hardy (H3)
Ellen and Jerry Harnish (H4)
Amy Hopper
Tim Hunter (H13)
Dan Iannotti (I3)
Kerry and Judy Irwin (K5)
Terri Ivers (I2)
Ed Janey (J2)
Keith and Donna Kaonis (K6)
Ilene Kayne (K3)
David Kolodny-Nagy (K2)
Trina and Randy Kubeck (K1)
Tom Lastrapes (L4)
Kathy and Don Lewis (L6)
Val and Mark Macaluso (M1)
Helen L. McCale (M12)
John McKenna (M2)
Nancy McMichael (M18)
Michael and Polly McQuillen (M11)
Lucky Meisenheimer (M3)
Bill Mekalian (M4)
Steven Meltzer (M9)
Bruce Middleton (M20)
Gary Mosholder (G1)
Judith Mosholder (M7)
Peter Muldavin (M21)

Natural Way (N1)
Roger Nazeley (N4)
Dawn Parrish (P2)
Diane Patalano (P8)
Sheri and John Pavone (P3)
Pat Peterson (P1)
The Phoenix Toy Soldier Co. (P11)
Pat and Bill Poe (P10)
Gary Pollastro (P5)
Judy Posner (P6)
Michael Paquin (P12)
Lorraine Punchard (P13)
John Rammacher (S5)
Jim Rash (R3)
Robert Reeves (R4)
Charlie Reynolds (R5)
David Riddle (R6)
Cindy Sabulis (S14)
Scott Smiles (S10)
Carole and Richard Smythe (S22)
Steve Stephenson
Bill Stillman (S6)
Nate Stoller (S7)
Mark and Lynda Suozzi (S24)
Toy Scouts, Inc. (Bill Bruegman) (T2)
Richard Trautwein (T3)
Marcie and Bob Tubbs (T5)
Judy and Art Turner (H8)
Marci Van Ausdall (V2)
Norm Vigue (V1)
James Watson (W8)
Randy Welch (W4)
Dan Wells (W1)
Larry White (W7)
Mary Young (Y2)
Henri Yunes (Y1)

How to Use This Book

Concept. Our design for this book is two-fold. Primarily it is a market report compiled from many sources, meant to be studied and digested by our readers, who can then better arrive at their own conclusion regarding prices. Were you to ask ten active toy dealers for their opinion as to the value of a specific toy, you would no doubt get ten different answers, and who's to say which is correct? Quite simply, there are too many variables to consider. Where you buy is critical. Condition is certainly subjective, prices vary from one area of the country to another, and probably the most important factor is how badly you want to add the item in question to your collection or at what price you're willing to sell. So use this as a guide along with your observations at toy shows, flea markets, toy auctions, and elsewhere to arrive at an evaluation that satisfies you personally.

The second function of this book is to put buyers in touch with sellers who deal in the type of toys they want to purchase. We contact dealers all over the country, asking them to send us their 'for sale' lists and permission to use them as sources for some of our listings, which we code so as to identify the dealer from whose inventory list the price and description are taken. Even though by publication much of their merchandise will have been sold since we entered our data early last spring, many of them tell us that they often get similar or even the same items in over and over, so if you see something listed you're interested in buying, don't hesitate to call any of them. Remember, though, they're not tied down to the price quoted in the book, since their asking price is many times influenced by what they've had to pay to restock their shelves. Let us know how well this concept works out for you.

Toys are listed by name. Every effort has been made to list a toy by the name as it appears on the original box. There have been very few exceptions made, and then only if the collector-given name is more recognizable. For instance, if we listed 'To-Night Amos 'n' Andy in Person' (as the name appears on the box lid), very few would recognize the toy as the Amos 'n' Andy Walkers. But these exceptions are few.

Descriptions and sizes may vary. When we were entering data, we often found the same toy had sold through more than one auction gallery or was listed in several dealer lists. So the same toy will often be described in various ways, but we left descriptions just as we found them, since there is usually something to be gleaned from each variation. We chose to leave duplicate lines in when various conditions were represented so that you could better understand the impact of condition on value. Depending on the source and who was doing the measuring, we found that the size of a given toy might vary by an inch or more. Not having the toy to measure ourselves, we had to leave dimensions just as they were given in auction catalogs or dealer lists.

Lines are coded as to source. Each line that represents an auction-realized price will be coded 'A' at the end, just before the price. Other letter/number codes identify the dealer who sent us that information. These codes are explained later on. Additional sources of like merchandise will be noted under the narratives. These are dealers whose lists arrived at our office too late to be included in the lines themselves.

As we said before, collectors have various viewpoints regarding auction results. You will have to decide for yourself. Some feel they're too high to be used to establish prices while others prefer them to 'asking' prices that can sometimes be speculative. We must have entered about 8,000 auction values, and here is what we found to be true: the really volatile area is in the realm of character collectibles from the '40s, '50s, and '60s — exactly where there is most interest, most collector activity, and hot competition when the bidding starts. But for the most part, auction prices were not far out of line with accepted values. Many times, compared to the general marketplace, toys in less-than-excellent condition actually sold under 'book.' Because the average auction-consigned toy is in especially good condition and many times even retains its original box, it will naturally bring higher prices than the norm. And auctions often offer the harder-to-find, more unusual items. Unless you take these factors into consideration, prices may seem high, when in reality, they may not be at all. Prices may be driven up by high reserves, but not all galleries have reserves. Whatever your view, you'll be able to recognize and consider the source of the values we quote and factor that into your personal evaluation.

Categories that have priority. Obviously there are thousands of toys that would work as well in one category as they would in another, depending on the preference of the collector. For instance, a Mary Poppins game would appeal to a games collector just as readily as it would to someone who bought character-related toys of all kinds. The same would be true of many other types of toys. We tried to make our decisions sensibly and keep our sorts simple. But to avoid sending our character advisors such huge printouts, we felt that it would be best to pull out specific items and genres to create specific categories, thereby reducing the size of the character category itself. We'll guide you to those specialized categories with cross-references and 'See Alsos.' If all else fails, refer to the index. It's as detailed as we know how to make it.

These categories have precedence over Character:

Action Figures
Battery-Operated Toys (also specific manufacturers)
Books
Bubble Bath Containers
Celebrity Dolls (see Dolls)
Character and Promotional Drinking Glasses
Character Clocks and Watches
Character Bobbin' Heads
Chein
Coloring, Activity, and Paint Books
Corgi
Dakins
Disney
Fisher-Price
Games
Guns
Halloween Costumes
Lunch Boxes
Marx
Model Kits

Nodders
Paper Dolls
Pez Dispensers
Pin-Back Buttons
Plastic Figures
Playsets
Puppets
Puzzles
Radios
Records
Rock 'N Roll
Snow Domes
Sports Collectibles
Telephones
Trading Cards
Toothbrush Holders
View-Maste
Western
Windups, Friction, and Other Mechanicals

Price Ranges. Once in awhile, you'll find a listing that gives a price range. These result from our having found varying prices for the same item. We've taken a mid-range — less than the highest, a little over the lowest — if the original range was too wide to really be helpful. If the range is still coded 'A' for auction, all that were averaged were auction-realized prices.

Condition, how it affects value, how to judge it. The importance of condition can't be stressed enough. Unless a toy is exceptionally rare, it must be very good or better to really have much collector value. But here's where the problem comes in: though each step downward on the grading scale drastically decreases a toy's value, as the old saying goes, 'beauty is in the eye of the beholder.' What is acceptable wear and damage to one individual may be regarded by another as entirely too degrading. Criteria used to judge condition even varies from one auction company to the next, so we had to attempt to sort them all out and arrive at some sort of standardization. Please be sure to read and comprehend what the description is telling you about condition; otherwise you can easily be mislead. Auction galleries often describe missing parts, repairs, and paint touch-ups, summing up overall appearance in the condition code. When losses and repairs were noted in the catalog, we noted them as well. Remember that a toy even in mint restored condition is never worth as much as one in mint original condition. And even though a toy may be rated 'otherwise EX' after losses and repairs are noted, it won't be worth as much as one with original paint and parts in excellent condition. Keep this in mind when you use our listings to evaluate your holdings.

These are the conditions codes we have used throughout the book and their definitions as we have applied them:

M — mint. Unplayed with, brand new, flawless.
NM — near mint. Appears brand new except on very close inspection.
EX — excellent. Has minimal wear, very minor chips and rubs, a few light scratches.
VG — very good. Played with, loss of gloss, noticeable problems, several scratches.
G — good. Some rust, considerable wear and paint loss, well used.
P — poor. Generally unacceptable except for a filler.

Because we do not use a three-level pricing structure as many of you are used to and may prefer, we offer this table to help you arrive at values for toys in conditions other than those that we give you. If you know the value of a toy in excellent condition and would like to find an approximate value for it in near mint condition, for instance, just run your finger down the column under 'EX' until you find the approximate price we've listed (or one that easily factors into it), then over to the column headed 'NM.' We'll just go to $100.00, but other values will be easy to figure by addition or multiplication. Even though at auction a toy in very good to excellent condition sometimes brings only half as much as a mint condition toy, the collectors we interviewed told us that this was not true of the general marketplace. Our percentages are simply an average based on their suggestions.

G	VG	EX	NM	M
40/50%	55/65%	70/80%	85/90%	100%
5.00	6.00	7.50	9.00	10.00
7.50	9.00	11.00	12.50	15.00
10.00	12.00	15.00	18.00	20.00
12.00	15.00	18.00	22.00	25.00
14.00	18.00	22.50	26.00	30.00
18.00	25.00	30.00	35.00	40.00
22.50	30.00	37.50	45.00	50.00
27.00	35.00	45.00	52.00	60.00
32.00	42.00	52.00	62.00	70.00
34.00	45.00	55.00	65.00	75.00
35.00	48.00	60.00	70.00	80.00
40.00	55.00	68.00	80.00	90.00
45.00	60.00	75.00	90.00	100.00

Condition and value of original boxes and packaging. When no box or packaging is referred to in the line or in the narrative, assume that the quoted price is for the toy only. Please read the narratives! In some categories (Corgi, for instance), all values are given for items mint and in original boxes. Conditions for boxes (etc.) are in parenthesis immediately following the condition code for the toy itself. In fact, any information within parenthesis at that point in the line will refer to packaging. Collector interest in boxes began several years ago, and today many people will pay very high prices for them, depending on scarcity, desirability, and condition. The more colorful, graphically pleasing boxes are favored, and those with images of well-known characters are especially sought-after. Just how valuable is a box? Again, this is very subjective to the individual. We asked this question to several top collectors around the country, and the answers they gave us ranged from 20% to 100% above mint-no-box prices.

Advertising. You'll notice display ads throughout the book. We hope you will contact these advertisers if they deal in the type of merchandise you're looking for. If you'd like your ad to appear in our next edition, please refer to the advertising rate chart in the back of the book for information.

Listing of Standard Abbreviations

These abbreviations have been used throughout this book in order to provide you with the most detailed descriptions possible in the limited space available. No periods are used after initials or abbreviations. When two dimensions are given, height is noted first. When only one measurement is given, it will be the greater — height if the toy is vertical, length if it is horizontal. (Remember that in the case of duplicate listings representing various conditions, we found that sizes often varied as much as an inch or more.)

Am	American
att	attributed to
bl	blue
blk	black
brn	brown
bsk	bisque
c	copyright
ca	circa
cb	cardboard
CI	cast iron
compo	composition
dbl	double
dia	diameter
dk	dark
dtd	dated
ea	each
emb	embossed
EX	excellent
F	fine
fr	frame, framed
ft, ftd	feet, foot, footed
G	good
gr	green
hdl	handle, handled
hdw	hardware
illus	illustrated, illustration
inscr	inscribed
jtd	jointed
L	long, length
litho	lithographed
lt	light, lightly
M	mint
MBP	mint in bubble pack
mc	multicolored
MIB	mint in box

MIP	mint in package
mk	marked
MOC	mint on card
MOT	mint on tree
NM	near mint
NP	nickel plated
NRFB	never removed from box
NRFP	never removed from package
orig	original
o/w	otherwise
P	poor
Pat	patented
pc	piece
pg, pgs	page, pages
pk	pink
pkg	package
pnt	paint, painted
pr	pair
prof	professional
rfn	refinished
rnd	round
rpl	replaced
rpr	repaired
rpt	repainted
rstr	restored
sq	square
sz	size
turq	turquoise
unmk	unmarked
VG	very good
W	with, width, wingspan
wht	white
w/	with
w/up	windup
yel	yellow

Action Figures

Back in 1964, Barbie dolls had taken the feminine side of the toy market by storm. Hasbro took a risky step in an attempt to target the male side. Their answer to the Barbie doll craze was GI Joe. Since no self-respecting boy would admit to playing with dolls, Hasbro called their boy dolls 'action figures,' and to the surprise of many, they were phenomenally successful. Both Barbie and GI Joe were realistically modeled (at least GI Joe was) and posable 12" vinyl dolls that their makers clothed and accessorized to the hilt. Their unprecedented successes spawned a giant industry with scores of manufacturers issuing one 'action figure' after another, many in series. Other sizes were eventually made in addition to the 12" dolls. Some are 8" to 9", others 6", and many are the 3¾" figures that have been favored in recent years.

This is one of the fastest-growing areas of toy collecting today. Manufacturers of action figures are now targeting the collector market as well as the kids themselves, simply because the adult market is so active. You will find a wide range of asking prices from dealer to dealer; most of our listings are coded and represent only a sampling. Naturally, *where* you buy will also affect values. Be critical of condition! Original packaging is extremely important. In fact, when it comes to the recent issues, loose, played-with examples are seldom worth more than a few dollars. Remember, if no box is mentioned, values are for loose (unpackaged) dolls. When no size is given, assume figures are 3¾" or standard size for the line in question.

For more information we recommend *Collectible Action Figures*, 1st and 2nd edition, by Paris and Susan Manos; *Collector's Guide to Dolls in Uniform* by Joseph Bourgeois; and *Mego Toys* by Wallace M. Crouch (all published by Collector Books).

Advisors: George Downs (D8); Robert Reeves (R4), Best of the West.

Other Sources: B3, F5, H12, I2, J2, J5, J7, M15, M17, P3, S17.

See also Character Collectibles; Dolls, Celebrity; GI Joe; Star Trek; Star Wars.

A-Team, figure, Cobra, Python, Rattler or Viper, Galoob, 6½", MOC, M17, ea...$22.00

Action Boy, accessory, Aqua Lad, Robin or Superboy outfit, Ideal, complete, MIB, T2, ea from $800 to...........$1,000.00

Action Jackson, accessory, Aussie Marine outfit, Mego, MIB, J5 ....$15.00

Action Jackson, accessory, Fire Rescue Pack, Mego, MIB, F1 ....$15.00

Action Jackson, accessory, Surf & Scuba outfit, Mego, MIB, H4 ....$12.00

Action Jackson, figure, Action Jackson, dk bl jumpsuit, w/beard, Mego, 8", NMIB, J5 ....$35.00

Action Jackson, figure, Action Jackson, lt bl jumpsuit, Mego, 8", NMIB, J5...$35.00

Action Jackson, figure, Action Jackson, Mego, Army fatigues, red hair, 8", EX, H4 ....$20.00

Action Jackson, accessory, baseball, football, hockey or karate outfit, Mego, MIB, F1/H4, ea from $10 to $12.00

Adventures of Indiana Jones, accessory, Map Room, MIB, B5, $70.00. (Photo courtesy Martin and Carolyn Berens)

Adventures of Indiana Jones, accessory, Wells of the Soul play-set, MIB $100.00

Adventures of Indiana Jones, figure, Indiana Jones, Kenner, 4", NM, J5 ....$50.00

Adventures of Indiana Jones, figure, Indiana Jones, Raiders of the Lost Ark, Kenner, 12", MIB............................$350.00

Adventures of Indiana Jones, figure, Marion Ravenwood, Raiders of the Lost Ark, Kenner, 3¾", MOC..........$200.00

Adventures of Indiana Jones, horse, Arabian, Raiders of the Lost Ark, Kenner, 1982, MOC, J6, $145.00.
(Photo courtesy June Moon)

Aliens, accessory, Evac Fighter or Power Loader, Kenner, MIB, F1, ea...$30.00

Aliens, accessory, Queen Hive playset, Kenner, MIB.......$50.00

Aliens, figure, King, Queen, Swarm or Arachnid, Kenner, MOC, F1, ea $25.00

Aliens, figure, Queen, Flying Queen or Atax, Kenner, w/trading cards, MOC (European), F1, ea...................................$25.00

Batman (Animated Series), accessory, Batmobile, Kenner, NM...$30.00

Batman (Animated Series), accessory, Batmobile or Night-sphere, Kenner, complete w/figures, MOC, F1, ea.....$40.00

Batman (Animated Series), accessory, Joker Mobile, Kenner, MOC, F1 ....$30.00

Batman (Animated Series), accessory, Triple Attack Jet, Kenner, MOC, F1 ....$20.00

Batman (Animated Series), figure, Bane, Ras A Gual or Bruce Wayne, Kenner, MOC, F1, ea.........................$20.00

Batman (Animated Series), figure, Manbat, Kenner, MOC, F1 ....$25.00

Batman (Animated Series), figure, Poison Ivy, Killer Kroc, Clay-face or Scarecrow, Kenner, MOC, F1, ea...................$30.00

Batman Returns, accessory, Bruce Wayne's Custom Coupe, w/figure, Kenner, MIB, F1 ....$40.00

Batman Returns, accessory, Robin Jet Foil Cycle, Kenner, MIB, F1 ....$30.00

Batman Returns, carrying case, Tara Toy, triangular, holds 12 figures, EX, M17 ....$30.00

Batman, see also DC Comics Super Heroes, Legends of Bat-man, Marvel Super Heroes, Official World's Greatest Super Heroes and Super Powers

Battlestar Galactica, accessory, Colonial Scarab, Mattel, M (NM Canadian box) $60.00

Battlestar Galactica, accessory, Cylon Raider, Mattel, M (NM Canadian box) $60.00

Battlestar Galactica, figure, Colonial Warrior, Mattel, 12", VG, H4 ....$30.00

Battlestar Galactica, figure, Commander Adama or Cylon Cen-turian, Mattel, 3¾", MOC, J5, ea.............................$25.00

Battlestar Galactica, figure, Imperious Leader or Lieutenant Starbuck, Mattel, 3¾", MOC (unpunched), H4, ea..$30.00

Beetlejuice, accessory, Gross Out Meter, Kenner, 1990, MIB, P3...$15.00

Beetlejuice, accessory, Vanishing Vault, Kenner, 1990, MIB, P3...$15.00

Beetlejuice, figure, Showtime Beetlejuice, Spinhead Beetlejuice or Shishkebab Beetlejuice, Kenner, 1989, MOC, ea .$15.00

Best of the West, accessory, Circle X Ranch, Marx, MIB.$175.00

Best of the West, accessory, Jeep & Horse Trailer, Marx, MIB...$150.00

Best of the West, accessory, Johnny West Adventure Jeep, Marx, VG, H4.................................$40.00

Best of the West, accessory, teepee, Marx, complete, EX+, H4 ....$50.00

Best of the West, buffalo, Marx, NM, F5 ....$100.00

Best of the West, figure, Bill Buck, Marx, complete, M (EX box), H4, from $500 to.................................$650.00

Best of the West, figure, Captain Maddox, Marx, complete, M (VG Fort Apache Fighters box), H4.........................$100.00

Best of the West, figure, Chief Cherokee, Marx, complete, NM (NM box), F5 ....$160.00

Best of the West, figure, Fighting Eagle, Marx, complete, NM (NM box), F5 ....$275.00

Best of the West, figure, General Custer, Marx, complete, M (VG Fort Apache Fighters box), H4 ....$75.00

Best of the West, figure, Geronimo, Marx, complete, NM (EX box), F5 ....$140.00

Best of the West, figure, Geronimo, Marx, missing few acces-sories, EX (VG box), H4 ....$75.00

Best of the West, figure, Jaimie West, Marx, complete, M (NM box)...$85.00

Best of the West, figure, Jane West, Marx, missing few acces-sories, NM (NM box), F5 ....$90.00

Best of the West, figure, Jane West, Marx, missing few accessories, NM (VG box), $75.00.

Best of the West, figure, Jay West, Marx, complete, NM, F5 ....$55.00

Best of the West, figure, Jed Gibson, Marx, complete, NM (EX box)...$350.00

Best of the West, figure, Johnny West, Marx, complete, VG, H4 ....$40.00

Best of the West, figure, Josie West, Marx, complete, MIB...$75.00

Best of the West, figure, Josie West, Marx, missing few acces-sories, EX (VG box), H4 ....$50.00

Best of the West, figure, Princess Wildflower, Marx, complete, NMIB, H4/J5 ....$150.00

Best of the West, figure, Sam Cobra, Marx, missing few acces-sories, NM, F5 ....$110.00

Best of the West, figure, Sheriff Garrett, Marx, missing few accessories, EX (G photo box), H4 ....$175.00

Best of the West, figure, Zeb Zachary, Marx, complete, EX (EX box), minimum value $150.00

Best of the West, figure set, Geronimo & horse, Marx, EX, from $45 to $65.00

Best of the West, figure set, Jane West & Flame, Marx, missing few accessories, EX (EX box), H4 ....$175.00

Best of the West, figure set, Johnny West & Thunderbolt, Marx, missing few accessories, VG (VG box), H4 ....$100.00

Best of the West, figure set, Sheriff Garrett & Thunderbolt, Marx, complete, rare, NMIB, H4 ....$485.00

Best of the West, horse, Buckskin, Marx, dk brn, no accessories, NM, F5 ....$50.00

Best of the West, horse, Comanche, Marx, complete, EX (EX Fort Apache Fighters box), H4 ....$125.00

Best of the West, horse, Flame, Marx, palomino, complete, MIB, H4 ....$125.00

Best of the West, horse, Pancho, cream colored, complete, VG, H4 ....$30.00

Best of the West, horse, Pancho, Marx, complete, VG, H4.$25.00

Best of the West, horse, Pancho, Marx, palomino, no accessories, EX, F5 ....$20.00

Best of the West, horse, Thunderbolt, Marx, blk w/blk tack, complete, NM, from $50 to $70.00

Best of the West, horse, Thunderbolt, Marx, cream colored, complete, EX (VG box), H4 ....$80.00

Best of the West, horse, Thunderbolt, Marx, dk brn, complete, MIB, H4 ....$100.00

Big Jim, accessory, Jungle Vet outfit, Mattel, MIP............$15.00
Big Jim, accessory, Kung Fu Studio, Mattel, MIB, H4 ......$85.00
Big Jim, accessory, Motorized Dune Devil, Mattel, G (G box), H4 ....$35.00
Big Jim, accessory, Sports Camper w/Boat, Mattel, MIB, H4 .$50.00
Big Jim, accessory, tent, Mattel, MIB, H4 ....$70.00
Big Jim, figure, Dr Steel, Torpedo Fist, Warpath or Whip, Mattel, complete, EX, ea from $25 to $30.00
Bonanza, figure, Ben, Little Joe, Hoss or Outlaw, Am Character, 8", MIB, J6, ea from $200 to...............$250.00
Bonanza, horse, Am Character, complete, EX, H4 ....$30.00
Buck O'Hare, figure, Stormtoad Trooper, Commander Dogstar, Willy Duwitt, Dead-Eye Duck or Toadborg, Hasbro, MOC, F1, ea $10.00
Buck Rogers, accessory, Command Center, Mego, MIB, C1.$110.00
Buck Rogers, figure, Walking Twiki, Draco or Killer Kane, Mego, 3¾", M, F1, ea $25.00
Captain Action, accessory, Anti-Gravitational Power Pack, Ideal, complete, MIB, T2 ....$200.00
Captain Action, accessory, Inter-Galactic Jet Mortar, Ideal, complete, MIB, T2 ....$200.00
Captain Action, accessory, Silver Streak Amphibian Car, Ideal, 24", MIB, T2, from $2,000 to...............$3,000.00
Captain Action, accessory, Silver Streak Garage, Ideal/Sears, 24", NM, T2, from $650 to $750.00
Captain Action, accessory, Survival Kit, Ideal, complete, MIB, T2 ....$200.00
Captain Action, accessory, Weapons Arsenal, Ideal, complete, MIB, T2 ....$200.00
Captain Action, carrying case, Ideal/Sears, opens to reveal 2-room secret headquarters, vinyl, NM, from $400 to .$500.00
Captain Action, figure, Action Boy, Ideal, 12", complete, EX $400.00
Captain Action, figure, Aqualad, Ideal, 12", complete, EX, H4 ....$265.00
Captain Action, figure, Batman, Ideal, 12", complete, EX, H4 ....$200.00

Captain Action, figure, Captain Action, Ideal, 12", complete, EX, H4 ....$225.00
Captain Action, figure, Captain America, Ideal, 12", complete, VG, H4 ....$225.00
Captain Action, figure, Dr Evil, Ideal, 12", complete, NM (VG box)...............$450.00
Captain Action, figure, Lone Ranger, Ideal, 12", complete, EX (EX box) $450.00
Captain Action, figure, Robin, Ideal, 12", missing few accessories, EX, H4 ....$200.00
Captain Action, figure, Superman, Ideal, 12", MIB $950.00
Captain Action, outfit, Aquaman, Ideal, complete, MIB, T2, from $500 to $600.00
Captain Action, outfit, Buck Rogers, Ideal, complete, MIB, T2, from $600 to $800.00
Captain Action, outfit, Green Hornet, Ideal, complete, MIB, T2, from $2,000 to $3,000.00
Captain Action, outfit, Lone Ranger, Ideal, complete, MIB, T2, from $800 to $1,000.00
Captain Action, outfit, Sgt Fury, Ideal, complete, MIB, T2, from $400 to $500.00
Captain Action, outfit, Steve Canyon, Ideal, complete, MIB, T2, from $400 to...............$500.00
Captain Action, outfit, Tonto, Ideal, complete, MIB, T2, from $800 to...............$1,000.00
Captain Action & Action Boy, booklet, Ideal, 1967, NM, T2...............$25.00
Captain America, figure, Lakeside, bendable, 6", MOC, T2 ....$100.00
Captain Planet & the Planeteers, accessory, Eco Cycle, Kenner/Tiger, MIB, F1...............$15.00
Captain Planet & the Planeteers, accessory, GEO Cruiser, Kenner/Tiger, MIB, F1...............$25.00
Captain Planet & the Planeteers, accessory, Skumm Copter, Kenner/Tiger, MIB, F1 ....$25.00
Captain Planet & the Planeteers, accessory, Toxic Cannon or Toxic Dump, Kenner/Tiger, MIB, F1, ea $15.00
Captain Planet & the Planeteers, figure, any character, Tiger/Kenner, MOC, F1, ea...............$15.00
Captain Power, figure, any character, Mattel, MOC, F1, ea from $15 to $20.00
CHiPs, figure, Wheels Willy, Mego, 3¾", MOC, F1 ....$20.00
Chuck Norris, figure, Kung-Fu, Battle Gear, Undercover Agent, Tabe, or Ninja Warrior, Kenner, 6", MOC, M17, ea.$15.00
Cops, figure, any character, Hasbro, 1988, MOC, F1, ea..$15.00
Dark Knight, figure, Tec-Shield Batman, Shadow-Wing Batman, Iron Winch Batman or Bruce Wayne, Kenner, MOC, F1, ea...............$20.00
DC Comics Super Heroes, figure, Aquaman, Green Lantern, Hawkman or Two-Face, Toy Biz, 3¾", MOC, F1, ea ..$25.00
DC Comics Super Heroes, figure, Batman, Robin, Penguin, Joker, Riddler or Flash, Toy Biz, 3¾", MOC, F1, ea..$20.00
Dick Tracy, figure, any character except Flattop, Playmates, MOC, F1, ea $10.00
Dick Tracy, figure, Flattop, Playmates, rare, MOC, F1 .....$20.00
Dukes of Hazzard, figure, Bo, Luke, Daisy or Boss Hogg, Mego, 8", MOC, ea...............$35.00
Dukes of Hazzard, figure, Coy, Mego, 8", MOC, F1 ....$40.00

Dukes of Hazzard, figure, Daisy or Luke, Mego, 3¾", MOC, ea from $20 to...$25.00

Dukes of Hazzard, figure, Uncle Jesse, Mego, 3¾", MOC, B5 ...$35.00

Emergency, figure, John or Roy, 8", MOC, H4, ea............$70.00

Fighting Furies, figure, Hooded Falcon Adventure, Matchbox, MIB, J6...$95.00

Fighting Yank, figure, Mego, 12", MIB, M17 ....$50.00

Flash Gordon, figure set, Flash, Dr Zarkov & Thun, Mattel, MIB, H4..$40.00

Flash Gordon, figure set, Ming, Lizard Woman & Beastman, Mattel, MIB, H4 ....$40.00

Generation X, figure, any character except Marrow or White Queen, Toy Biz, MOC, F1, ea $15.00

Generation X, figure, Marrow or White Queen, Toy Biz, MOC, F1, ea $20.00

Ghostbusters, figure, Winston Zeddmore, Egon Spengler or Janine, Kenner, complete, NM, ea......................$40.00

Happy Days, figure, any character, Mego, 8", MOC, ea from $50 to $60.00

He-Man, figure, any character, Mattel, MOC, F1, ea.......$15.00

Hercules, figure, Hercules, Toy Biz, 3 different, MOC, F1, ea..$15.00

How the West Was Won, figure, Lone Wolf or Zeb Macahan, Mattel, 9", MIB, H4, ea from $40 to $50.00

Incredible Hulk, figure, Savage Hulk, Leader, Rampaging Hulk or She-Hulk, Toy Biz, MOC, F1, ea............................$15.00

Indiana Jones, see Adventures of Indiana Jones

James Bond, figure, Drax or Holly, Moonraker, Mego, 12", NMIB, ea $135.00

James Bond Jr, figure, Jaws, Hasbro, 1991, rare, MOC, F1.$15.00

Justice League of America, figure, Aquaman, Flash, Robin or Wonder Woman, Ideal, 3", EX, H4, ea from $65 to..$75.00

Justice League of America, figure set, Wonder Woman & Flash, Ideal, 4", MOC, T2, from $600 to............................$700.00

Karate Kid, figure, Sato, Remco, MOC, M17 ....$20.00

Kung Fu, figure, Kane, 6", MOC, H4 ....$60.00

Land of the Lost, accessory, Boulder Bobber Catapult Weapon, Tiger, MOC, F1 ....$10.00

Land of the Lost, accessory, Jeep, Tiger, MOC $20.00

Land of the Lost, accessory, SS Frisco Sailing Raft, Tiger, MOC, F1 ....$10.00

Land of the Lost, accessory, Villain Playset, Tiger, MOC..$20.00

Land of the Lost, figure, Talking Stink, Talking Annie or Talking Kevin, MOC, F1, ea.....................................$15.00

Land of the Lost, figure, Tom Porter, Annie Porter, Shung, Tasha or Kevin Porter, MOC, F1, ea $10.00

Last Action Hero, accessory, convertible, Mattel, EX (EX box), F1 ....$25.00

Legend of the Lone Ranger, figure set, Lone Ranger & Silver, Gabriel, 9", NRFB, H4 ....$150.00

Legends of Batman, figure, Crusader, Riddler, Firstmate, Laughing Man, Gladiator or Buccaneer, Kenner, MOC, F1, ea ..$10.00

Legends of Batman, figure, Flightpack, Silverknight, Catwoman or Joker, Kenner, MOC, F1, ea............................$20.00

Legends of Batman, figure, Ultimate Batman, Kenner, 15", MIB, F1 ....$50.00

Legends of Batman, figure set, Egyptian Batman & Catwoman, Kenner, MOC, F1 ....$25.00

Legends of Batman, figure set, Pirate Batman & Two-Face, Kenner, MOC, F1..$25.00

Legends of the Lone Ranger, figure, any character, Gabriel, 3¾", MOC, ea $20.00

Legends of the Wild West, figure, Buffalo Bill, Cochise, Wild Bill Hickok or Wyatt Earp, 9½", NMIB, ea from $45 to $55.00

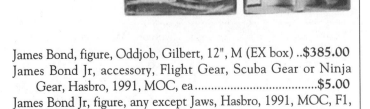

James Bond, figure, James Bond, Gilbert, with scuba gear, 12", NM (NM box), A, $800.00.

Lone Ranger Rides Again, accessory, Hopi Medicine Man, MIB, from $25.00 to $35.00. (Photo courtesy Lee Felbinger)

James Bond, figure, Oddjob, Gilbert, 12", M (EX box) ..$385.00

James Bond Jr, accessory, Flight Gear, Scuba Gear or Ninja Gear, Hasbro, 1991, MOC, ea......................................$5.00

James Bond Jr, figure, any except Jaws, Hasbro, 1991, MOC, F1, ea...$5.00

Lone Ranger Rides Again, accessory, Hidden Rattler Adventure, Gabriel, MIB, from $25 to $30.00

Lone Ranger Rides Again, accessory, Hidden Silver Mine, Gabriel, MIB, from $25 to $30.00

Lone Ranger Rides Again, accessory, Landslide Adventure, Gabriel, MIB, from $25 to $35.00

Lone Ranger Rides Again, accessory, Tribal Wigwam, Gabriel, NRFB, H4 ....$60.00

Lone Ranger Rides Again, figure, Butch Cavendish or Little Bear, Gabriel, 9", NRFB, H4, ea..............................$50.00

Lone Ranger Rides Again, figure, Lone Ranger or Tonto, Gabriel, EX, H4, ea...$20.00

Lost World of the Warlords, figure, any character, Remco, 6", MOC, H4, ea from $15 to $20.00

Love Boat, figure, any character, Mego, 3½", MOC, H4/J5, ea..$25.00

Major Matt Mason, accessory, Astro Trac Vehicle, Mattel, MIB, H4 ....$150.00

Major Matt Mason, accessory, Captain Laser instruction sheet, Mattel, EX+, H4 ....$10.00

Major Matt Mason, accessory, Cat Trak, Mattel, red or wht, EX, H4, ea $10.00

Major Matt Mason, accessory, crescent wrench, Mattel, EX, H4 ....$8.00

Major Matt Mason, accessory, Decontamination Gun, Mattel, complete, EX, H4 ....$10.00

Major Matt Mason, accessory, Firebolt Space Cannon, Mattel, M (EX+ box), H4 ....$90.00

Major Matt Mason, accessory, Gamma Ray Guard Pak, Mattel, MIB, D8 ....$95.00

Major Matt Mason, accessory, Jet Pack, Mattel, complete, EX, H4 ....$15.00

Major Matt Mason, accessory, moon suit, Mattel, VG, H4 ..$12.00

Major Matt Mason, accessory, Satellite Launch Pak, Mattel, EX, H4 ....$30.00

Major Matt Mason, accessory, Satellite Locker, Mattel, VG, H4..$22.00

Major Matt Mason, accessory, Space Bubble, Mattel, VG (VG+ box), H4 ....$50.00

Major Matt Mason, accessory, Space Crawler Action Set, Mattel, complete w/figure, MIB, H4 ....$150.00

Major Matt Mason, accessory, Space Shelter Pak, Mattel, MIB, D8..$95.00

Major Matt Mason, accessory, Space Station, Mattel, M (EX+ box), H4 ....$200.00

Major Matt Mason, accessory, Supernaut Power Limbs, Mattel, EX, H4 ....$25.00

Major Matt Mason, accessory, Talking Backpack, Mattel, VG+, H4 ....$30.00

Major Matt Mason, accessory, Talking Command Console, Mattel, MIB, H4..$85.00

Major Matt Mason, accessory, United & Space Bubble, Mattel, complete, EX, H4 ....$150.00

Major Matt Mason, accessory, Unitred Space Hauler, Mattel, M (VG+ box), H4 ....$65.00

Major Matt Mason, carrying case, vinyl spaceship, Mattel, 20", EX, J5 ....$65.00

Major Matt Mason, figure, Calisto, Mattel, complete, EX, H4..$75.00

Major Matt Mason, figure, Captain Lazer, Mattel, complete, 12", EX, $150.00.
(Photo courtesy Linda Baker)

Major Matt Mason, figure, Doug Davis, Mattel, w/helmet, EX, H4 ....$75.00

Major Matt Mason, figure, Jeff Long, Mattel, w/helmet, VG, H4...$100.00

Major Matt Mason, figure, Matt Mason on glider w/talking backpack, Mattel, MIB, H4.....................................$650.00

Major Matt Mason, figure, Scorpio, Mattel, complete, M, H4 ....$500.00

Major Matt Mason, figure, Sgt Storm on Cat Trac, Mattel, 1967, fully jtd, 7", NM (NM card) $665.00

Man From UNCLE, accessory, Uncle Husky car, Gilbert, MOC, H4 ....$225.00

Man From Uncle, figure, Illya Kuryakin, Gilbert, 12", VG (VG box), H4..$150.00

Marvel Super Heroes, accessory, Super Vator Playset, Mego, EX, H4 ....$50.00

Marvel Super Heroes, figure, any character, Toy Biz, MOC, F1, ea from $15 to $20.00

Marvel Super Heroes, figure, Aqualad, Mego, complete, NM, H4 ....$120.00

Marvel Super Heroes, figure, Aquaman, Mego, complete, EX, H4 ....$45.00

Marvel Super Heroes, figure, Batman, Mego, complete, NM, H4 ....$75.00

Marvel Super Heroes, figure, Captain America, Mego, complete, NMIB, H4...$195.00

Marvel Super Heroes, figure, Catwoman, Mego, complete, EX, H4 ....$125.00

Marvel Super Heroes, figure, Conan, Mego, complete, NM (NM box), H4...$225.00

Marvel Super Heroes, figure, Daredevil, 1st issue, Toy Biz, MOC, F1 ....$40.00

Marvel Super Heroes, figure, Daredevil, 2nd issue, Toy Biz MOC, F1 ....$15.00

Marvel Super Heroes, figure, Green Arrow, Mego, complete, EX, H4 ....$95.00

Marvel Super Heroes, figure, Green Goblin, Mego, complete, NMIB, H4..$200.00

Marvel Super Heroes, figure, Human Torch, Mego, complete, NMIB, H4..$90.00

Marvel Super Heroes, figure, Invisible Woman, Toy Biz, MOC, F1 ....$25.00

Marvel Super Heroes, figure, Iron Man, Mego, complete, NMIB, H4 ....$175.00

Marvel Super Heroes, figure, Joker, Mego, complete, NM (NM box), H4...$175.00

Marvel Super Heroes, figure, Lizard, Mego, wht jacket, complete, EX, H4 ....$95.00

Marvel Super Heroes, figure, Mr Fantastic, Mego, complete, NMIB, H4..$100.00

Marvel Super Heroes, figure, Mr Mxyzptlk, Mego, complete, NMIB, H4 ....$50.00

Marvel Super Heroes, figure, Penguin, Mego, complete, NM, H4..$40.00

Marvel Super Heroes, figure, Riddler, Mego, complete, MOC (unpunched), H4...$225.00

Marvel Super Heroes, figure, Spider-Man, Mego, complete, NMIB, H4 ....$50.00

Marvel Super Heroes Secret Wars, figure, Constrictor or Iceman, Mattel, 4", M (NM European card), ea.............$85.00

Marvel Super Heroes Secret Wars, figure, Dardevil & His Secret Shield, Mattel, 3¾", MOC....................................$40.00

Marvel Super Heroes Secret Wars, figure, Electro, Mattel, EX (EX European card), J5 ....$65.00

Marvel Super Heroes Secret Wars, figure, Magneto, Kang or Dr Doom, Mattel, MOC, F1, ea $15.00

Marvel Super Heroes Secret Wars, figure, Spider-Man, Mattel, VG (VG card), J5 ....$45.00

Marvel Super Heroes Secret Wars, figure, Wolverine, blk claws, Mattel, NM (EX card), J5 ....$175.00

Marvel Super Heroes Secret Wars, figure, Wolverine, silver claws, Mattel, NM (EX card), J5 ....$75.00

Mask, Firefly and figure, MIB, $35.00.
(Photo courtesy Martin and Carolyn Berens)

Masters of the Universe, accessory, Blasterhawk, Mattel, MIB, F1 ....$40.00

Masters of the Universe, accessory, Dragon Walker, Mattel, MOC, F1 ....$20.00

Masters of the Universe, accessory, Fright Zone playset, Mattel, MIB $85.00

Masters of the Universe, accessory, Jet Sled, Mattel, MOC, F1 ....$20.00

Masters of the Universe, accessory, Land Shark, Mattel, MOC, F1 ....$20.00

Masters of the Universe, accessory, Megalaser, Mattel, MOC, F1 ....$10.00

Masters of the Universe, accessory, Road Ripper, Mattel, MOC, F1 ....$20.00

Masters of the Universe, accessory, Slit Stalker, Mattel, MOC, F1 ....$10.00

Masters of the Universe, accessory, Spydor Evil Stalker, Mattel, MIB, H4 ....$40.00

Masters of the Universe, accessory, Weapon Pak, Mattel, MOC, F1 ....$50.00

Masters of the Universe, figure, Buzz-Off, Skeletor, Jitsu, Orko or Fisto, Mattel, MOC, H4, ea....................................$30.00

Masters of the Universe, figure, King Randor, Mattel, MOC, F1 ....$25.00

Masters of the Universe, figure, Moss Man, Two Bad, Roboto, Spikor or Sy-Klone, Mattel, MOC, H4, ea $20.00

Masters of the Universe, figure, Mousquitor, Dragstor, Clamp Champ, King Hiss, Rokkon or Rio Blast, Mattel, MOC, F1, ea......$15.00

Masters of the Universe, figure, Thunder Punch He-Man or Buzzsaw Hordak, Mattel, MOC, F1, ea $20.00

Micronauts, accessory, Neon Orbiter or Throium Orbiter, Mego, EX (EX box), J5, ea...$25.00

Micronauts, figure, Acroyear, Mego, 3¾", MOC, H4.......$50.00

Micronauts, figure, Repto, Mego, 3¾", MOC, H4..........$120.00

Mortal Combat, figure set, Goro Vs Johnny Cage, Hasbro, 1994, 4", complete w/Battle Arena, MIP, F1 ....$20.00

Mortal Kombat, accessory, Dragon Wing w/Shang Tsung figure, Hasbro, 1994, MIP, F1 ....$30.00

Mortal Kombat, accessory, Kombat Cycle w/Kano figure, Hasbro, 1994, MIP, F1 ....$15.00

Official Scout High Adventure, accessory, Avalanche at Blizzard Ridge, Kenner, complete, EX, H4 ....$25.00

Official Scout High Adventure, accessory, Balloon Race to Devils Canyon, Kenner, MIB, H4.................................$35.00

Official Scout High Adventure, figure, Steve Scout or Craig Cub, Kenner, NRFB, H4, ea....................................$30.00

Official World's Greatest Super Heroes, accessory, Amazing Spider Car, EX, H4 ....$15.00

Official World's Greatest Super Heroes, accessory, Amazing Spider Car, Mego, MIB, T2 ....$50.00

Official World's Greatest Super Heroes, accessory, Batcopter, Mego, NM (NM box), H4..$175.00

Official World's Greatest Super Heroes, figure, Aquaman, Mego, 8", EX, J6..$45.00

Official World's Greatest Super Heroes, figure, Aquaman, Mego, 8", M (NM box), H4 ....$175.00

Official World's Greatest Super Heroes, figure, Batman, Bend'n Flex, Mego, 5", NMOC $50.00

Official World's Greatest Super Heroes, figures, Bat-girl, Mego, 8", NM, J6, $300.00; Batman, Mego, removable mask, 8", NM, J6, $75.00. (Photo courtesy June Moon)

Official World's Greatest Super Heroes, figure, Batman, Mego, 12", MIB..$75.00

Official World's Greatest Super Heroes, figure, Captain American, Mego, 8", EX, J6...$50.00

Official World's Greatest Super Heroes, figure, Falcon, Mego, 8", M (EX+ box), H4 ....$85.00

Official World's Greatest Super Heroes, figure, Green Goblin, Mego, 8", EX, J6 ....$125.00

Official World's Greatest Super Heroes, figure, Human Torch, Mego, 8", MOC, D8 ....$50.00

Official World's Greatest Super Heroes, figure, Incredible Hulk, Mego, 8", MIB, T2..$100.00

Official World's Greatest Super Heroes, figure, Joker, Mego, 8", complete, M, D8...$55.00

Official World's Greatest Super Heroes, figure, Mr Mxyzptlk, Mego, 8", MOC (sealed), T2...........................$175.00

Official World's Greatest Super Heroes, figure, Mr Mxyzptlk (smiling version), Mego, 8", EX, J6.....................$45.00

Official World's Greatest Super Heroes, figure, Penguin, Mego, 8", MOC (sealed), T2..................................$125.00

Official World's Greatest Super Heroes, figure, Riddler, Fist Fighting, Mego, 8", M, D8.................................$150.00

Official World's Greatest Super Heroes, figure, Riddler, Mego, 8", complete, NM, D8.................................$95.00

Official World's Greatest Super Heroes, figure, Robin, Fist Fighting, Mego, 8", M, D8.................................$125.00

Official World's Greatest Super Heroes, figure, Shazam, Mego, 8", EX, J6..$50.00

Official World's Greatest Super Heroes, figure, Spider-Man, Mego, 8", EX, J6...$35.00

Official World's Greatest Super Heroes, figure, Spider-Man, Bend'n Flex, Mego, MOC $75.00

Official World's Greatest Super Heroes, figure, Spider-Man, Mego, 12", complete, M, D8.............................$35.00

Official World's Greatest Super Heroes, figure, Spider-Man, Mego, 12", NRFB...$80.00

Official World's Greatest Super Heroes, figure, Supergirl, Bend'n Flex, Mego, MOC (sealed), T2 ....$150.00

Official World's Greatest Super Heroes, figure, Superman, Bend'n Flex, Mego, MOC (sealed), T2............$150.00

Official World's Greatest Super Heroes, figure, Tarzan, Mego, 8", EX, J6..$45.00

Official World's Greatest Super Heroes, figures, Wonder Woman, Mego, 8", NM, J6, $150.00; Mr. Fantastic, Mego, 8", NM, J6, $125.00; Conan, Mego, 8", NM, J6, $150.00. (Photo courtesy June Moon)

Official World's Greatest Super-Gals, figure, Catwoman, Mego, 8", EX, J6..$95.00

Official World's Greatest Super-Gals, figure, Invisible Girl, Mego, 8", EX, J6...$35.00

Official World's Greatest Super Heroes, figures, Lizard, Mego, 8", NM, J6, $185.00; Human Torch, Mego, 8", M, J6, $30.00. (Photo courtesy June Moon)

Official World's Greatest Super-Gals, figure, Supergirl, Mego, 8", MOC, T2.................................$200.00

Official World's Greatest Super-Gals, figure, Wonder Woman, Mego, 8", MOC (sealed), T2.................$200.00

Our Gang, figure, Alfalfa, Spanky, Mickey or Porky, Mego, MOC (unpunched), H4, ea........................$40.00

Our Gang, figure, Buckwheat, Mego, MOC (unpunched), H4...$45.00

Pee Wee's Playhouse, figure, King of Hearts, Magic Screen, Ricardo or Reba, Matchbox, 6", MOC, ea.................$20.00

Pee-Wee's Playhouse, figure, Miss Yvonne, Matchbox, 6", MOC, H4...$30.00

Pee-Wee's Playhouse, figure, Pee-Wee, Matchbox, 6", MOC, H4...$25.00

Pirates of Dark Water, figure, Ren or Bloth, Hasbro, 1990, MOC, F1, ea..$10.00

Planet of the Apes, figure, Cornelius or Astronaut, Mego, 8", complete, EX, ea from $65 to $75.00

Planet of the Apes, figures, Dr. Zaius and Zira, Mego, bendable, 8", EX, $65.00 each. (Photo courtesy Pat Smith)

Planet of the Apes, figure, General Ursus, Mego, bendable, 8", NM (NM card)....................................$200.00

Planet of the Apes, figure, Peter Burke, Mego, 8", complete, EX, H4...$75.00

Planet of the Apes, figure, Soldier Ape, Bend'n Flex, Mego, 5", MOC..$65.00

Power Lords, figure, any character, Revell, MOC, M17, ea from $10 to..$15.00

Power Rangers, figure, any character, Bandai, MIB, H4, ea from $15 to..$20.00

Power Rangers, figure set, White Ranger & Tigerzoid, Bandai, MIB, H4.................................$50.00

Princess of Power, accessory, Crystal Castle, Mattel, complete, MIB.................................$120.00

Princess of Power, accessory, outfit, Mattel, several different, MOC, ea.................................$18.00

Princess of Power, figure, Angella or Bow, Mattel, MOC, ea ..$20.00

Princess of Power, figure, Entrapta, Peekablue or Starburst She-Ra, Mattel, MOC, ea.................................$25.00

Princess of Power, horse, Arrow, Mattel, MIB.................$25.00

Rambo, accessory, Weapons Pack, Coleco, MOC, F1 ....$5.00

Rambo, figure, Gripper, Sgt Havok or Turbo, Coleco, MOC, F1, ea.................................$20.00

Real Ghostbusters, accessory, Ghost Grab, Kenner, MOC, F1.................................$15.00

Real Ghostbusters, figure, any character except Stay Puft Man or Slimer, Kenner, MOC, F1, ea.................$15.00

Real Ghostbusters, figure, Slimer, Kenner, MOC, F1.......$25.00

Real Ghostbusters, figure, Stay Puft Man, Kenner, MOC, F1 ...$30.00

Robin Hood Prince of Thieves, figure, Azeem or Little John, Kenner, MOC, F1, ea.................................$15.00

Robin Hood Prince of Thieves, figure, Friar Tuck, Kenner, MOC, F1.................................$30.00

RoboCop, accessory, Robocycle or Skull Hog, Kenner, MOC, F1, ea.................................$10.00

RoboCop, figure, any character, Kenner, rare, MOC, F1, ea..$25.00

Robotech, figure, Lynn Minmei, Dana Sterling or Lisa Hayes, Matchbox, 12", MIB, F1, ea.................$30.00

Robotech, figure, Rook Bartley, Matchbox, MOC, D8 ....$25.00

Rookies, figure, any character, LJN, 8", MOC, ea.............$70.00

Saban's VR Troopers, figure, any character, Kenner, 1994, MOC, F1, ea.................................$10.00

Six Million Dollar Man, figure, Maskatron, Kenner, 12", NMIB, $100.00. (Photo courtesy Pat Smith)

Silverhawks, figure, Hardware, Steel Will, Moon Stryker, Windhammer or Condor, 2nd series, Kenner, 1986, MOC, F1, ea $15.00

Six Million Dollar Man, accessory, Bionic Mission Vehicle, Kenner, 20", EX $25.00

Six Million Dollar Man, accessory, Bionic Transport & Repair Station, Kenner, NMIB, J2..............................$60.00

Six Million Dollar Man, accessory, Mission Control Center, Kenner, NMIB, J2..$80.00

Six Million Dollar Man, accessory, Porta Communicator, Kenner, MIB, J2...$50.00

Six Million Dollar Man, figure, Bionic Bigfoot, Kenner, 12", complete, EX, H4..$70.00

Six Million Dollar Man, figure, Fembot, Kenner, 12", NRFB, H4 ....$125.00

Six Million Dollar Man, figure, Maskatron, Kenner, 12", NRFB, H4...$150.00

Sky Commanders, accessory, Cable Cannon Vehicle w/Pete Crane figure, Kenner, MIB, M17 ....$15.00

Sky Commanders, accessory, Rapid Development Vehicle w/Pete Crane figure, Kenner, MIB, M17....................$15.00

Space: 1999, accessory, Moon Base Alpha Deluxe Set, Mattel, complete, MIB..$300.00

Space: 1999, figure, Commander Koenig or Professor Bergman, Mattel, 9", MOC, ea.....................................$50.00

Space: 1999, figure, Dr. Russell, Mattel, 9", MOC, $50.00.

(Photo courtesy J. Michael Augustyniak)

Spawn, accessory, Spawn Alley, Todd Toys, MIB, F1 ......$40.00

Spawn, accessory, Spawnmobile, Todd Toys, MOC, F1 ...$30.00

Spawn, figure, Angela, Todd Toys, 13", MIB, F1.............$40.00

Spawn, figure, any character from 1st or 2nd series, Todd Toys, MOC, F1, ea $30.00

Spawn, figure, any character from 3rd or 4th series, Todd Toys, MOC, F1, ea $15.00

Spawn, figure, Violator, Todd Toys, 13", MIB, F1 ....$50.00

Spider-Man (Animated Series), figure, any character, Toy Biz, MOC, F1, ea $15.00

Spider-Man, see also Marvel Super Heroes and Offical World's Greatest Super Heroes

Star Raiders, figure, Coth, Grand or Wik, Tomland, 8", MOC, M17, ea $15.00

Starsky & Hutch, figure, any character, Mego, 8", MOC, ea from $40 to $50.00

Sting, figure, Sting, Galoob, 5", MOC, M17....................$30.00

Stony Smith, figure, Paratrooper, Marx, complete, 12", NM (NM box) $250.00

Super Human Samurai Syber Squad, figure, any character, Playmates, 1994, MOC, F1, ea $10.00

Super Mario Brothers, figure, any character, Ertl, 1993, MOC, F1, ea...$10.00

Super Powers, accessory, Darkseid Destroyer, Kenner, MIB, H4...$45.00

Super Powers, accessory, Justice Jogger, Kenner, MIB, J5.$25.00

Super Powers, accessory, Kalibak Boulder, Kenner, MIB, J5 ....$25.00

Super Powers, accessory, Lex-Soar 7, Kenner, MIB, J5.....$25.00

Super Powers, accessory, Supermobile, Kenner, MIB, J5 ..$25.00

Super Powers, figure, Batman, Kenner, MOC (unpunched), H4 ....$50.00

Super Powers, figure, Brainiac, Kenner, complete w/ID card & comic book, NM, H4...$30.00

Super Powers, figure, Cyborg, Kenner, MOC (Mexico Super Amigos), H4...$100.00

Super Powers, figure, DeSaad, Kenner, M (EX card), H4.$25.00

Super Powers, figure, Firestorm, Kenner, complete w/ID card & comic book, NM, H4...$25.00

Super Powers, figure, Flash, Kenner, complete w/accessories, NM, H4...$8.00

Super Powers, figure, Flash, Kenner, MOC, H4..............$15.00

Super Powers, figures, Mister Miracle, Kenner, MOC, J6, $125.00; Cyclotron, Kenner, MOC, J6, $75.00.

(Photo courtesy June Moon)

Super Powers, figure, Hawkman, Kenner, complete w/ID card & comic book, NM, H4....................................$35.00

Super Powers, figure, Joker, Kenner, complete w/ID card & comic book, NM, H4....................................$35.00

Super powers, figure, Kalibak, Kenner, MOC, H4 ....$15.00

Super Powers, figure, Lex Luther, Kenner, complete w/ID card & comic book, NM, H4....................................$15.00

Super Powers, figure, Mr Freeze, Kenner, complete, M, H4 .$40.00

Super Powers, figure, Orion, Kenner, MOC, J6 ....$55.00

Super Powers, figure, Penguin, Kenner, complete w/ID card & comic book, M, H4....................................$25.00

Super Powers, figure, Plastic Man, Kenner, MOC, J6.....$125.00

Super Powers, figure, Robin, Kenner, MOC (unpunched), H4....................................$50.00

Super Powers, figure, Samurai, Kenner, 3rd series, complete w/ID card & comic book, NM, H4..........................$60.00

Super Powers, figure, Steppenwolf, Kenner, complete w/ID card & comic book, NM, H4..........................$30.00

Super Powers, figure, Tyr, Kenner, MOC, H4 ....$60.00

Super Queens, figure, Mera (Aquaman's wife), Ideal, 1967, 12", MIB, T2, from $600 to $800.00

Supergirl, figure, Ideal, 1967, 12", scarce, from $2,000 to..$3,000.00

SWAT, figure, Hondo, Luca or Decon, LJN, 8", MOC, J5, ea .$25.00

Teenage Mutant Ninja Turtles, figure, any character, Playmates, MOC, F1, ea $15.00

Teenage Mutant Ninja Turtles, see also Toon Turtles

Terminator 2, figure, any character except John Conner, Kenner, MOC, ea $20.00

Terminator 2, figure, John Conner, Kenner, MOC $25.00

Thundercats, accessory, Luna-Lasher or Mutant Skycutter, LJN, MIB....................................$35.00

Thundercats, figure, any character, LJN, MOC, ea from $35 to....................................$45.00

Tigers Action, figure, Big Ears, Machine Gun Mike or Pretty Boy, Topper, 1970s, 8", complete, NM, J5, ea $35.00

Toon Turtles, figure, Toon Mike, Toon Don, Toon Ralph, or Toon Leo, Playmates, MOC, F1, ea $15.00

Toxic Crusaders, figure, Toxic Crusader, Playmates, 1991, 5", MOC, F1....................................$15.00

Universal Monsters, figure, Creature From the Black Lagoon, glow-in-the-dark, Remco, 3¾", MOC $45.00

Universal Monsters, figure, Dracula, Frankenstein or Phantom, glow-in-the-dark, Remco, 3¾", MOC, ea $35.00

Universal Monsters, figure, Mummy, glow-in-the-dark, Remco, 3¾", MOC....................................$75.00

V, figure, Enemy Visitor, 12", MIB....................................$75.00

Venom, figure, any character, 1st or 2nd series, Toy Biz, MOC, F1, ea....................................$15.00

Warrior Beasts, figure, Zardus, Remco, 1982, M (worn card), M17....................................$10.00

Welcome Back Kotter, accessory, Grease Machine, AHI, MOC, H4 ....$70.00

Welcome Back Kotter, figure, any character, Mattel, 9", MOC, ea from $45 to....................................$50.00

Wizard of Oz, accessory, Wizard of Oz & His Emerald City, Mego, complete, MIB....................................$300.00

Wizard of Oz, figure, Cowardly Lion, Mego, 8", M, D8 ....$25.00

Wizard of Oz, figure, Cowardly Lion, Mego, 8", MIB $45.00

Wizard of Oz, figure, Glinda the Good Witch, Mego, 8", MIB....................................$45.00

Wizard of Oz, figure, Scarecrow, Mego, 8", MIB, D8........$65.00

Wizard of Oz, figure, Tin Woodsman, Mego, 8", MIB, D8 .$35.00

Wizard of Oz, figure, Wicked Witch, Mego, 8", MIB, H4...$65.00

Wizard of Oz, figure, Wizard, Mego, 8", MIB, F1 ....$25.00

Wonder Woman, figure, Ideal, 1967, 12", MIB, T2, from $800 to....................................$1,000.00

Wonder Woman, figure, Nubia, Mego, 12", MIB, T2.......$75.00

Wonder Woman, figure, Queen Hippolyte, Mego, 12", MIB, T2....................................$75.00

Wonder Woman, figure, Steve Trevor, Mego, 12", MIB, T2 .$75.00

World Championship Wrestling, figure, Hulk Hogan, San Francisco Toymakers, yel shirt, MOC, F1 ....$15.00

World Championship Wrestling, figure, Jimmy Hart, San Francisco Toymakers, red suit & pants, MOC, F1 ....$20.00

World Championship Wrestling, figure, Johnny B Badd, San Francisco Toymakers, silver tights, MOC, F1 ....$15.00

World Championship Wrestling, figure, Kevin Sullivan, San Francisco Toymakers, bl tights, MOC, F1................$20.00

World Championship Wrestling, figure, Randy Macho Man Savage, San Francisco Toymakers, MOC, F1 ....$20.00

World Championship Wrestling, figure, Ric Flair, San Francisco Toymakers, gr tights & boots, MOC, F1 ....$15.00

World Championship Wrestling, figure, Sting, San Francisco Toymakers, pk & yel tights, MOC, F1 ....$15.00

World Championship Wrestling, figure, Vader, San Francisco Toymakers, blk & red, MOC, F1...............................$15.00

World Championship Wrestling, figure set, Hulk Hogan & Sting, San Francisco Toymakers, MOC, F1 ....$25.00

World Championship Wrestling, figure set, Nasty Boys, San Francisco Toymakers, orange outfits, MOC, F1.........$25.00

World Wrestling Federation, accessory, Monster Ring, Jakks, 1997, complete w/6 figures, MIB, F1 ....$30.00

World Wrestling Federation, figure, Adam Bomb, Hasbro, MOC (gr), D8....................................$28.00

World Wrestling Federation, figure, Ahmed Johnson or Yokozuna, Just Toys, Bend-Ems, 3rd series, MOC, F1, ea................$10.00

World Wrestling Federation, figure, Andre the Giant, Hasbro, MOC (bl), D8....................................$150.00

World Wrestling Federation, figure, any character, Just Toys, Bend-Ems, 5th or 6th series, MOC, F1, ea $8.00

World Wrestling Federation, figure, any from 1st to 5th series, Jakks, 6", MIP, F1, ea....................................$15.00

World Wrestling Federation, figure, any from Jakks Manager 2-Pack Series, MIP, F1, ea $20.00

World Wrestling Federation, figure, any from Jakks Signature Series, MOC, F1, ea....................................$15.00

World Wrestling Federation, figure, any from Jakks Stomp Series, MOC, F1, ea....................................$15.00

World Wrestling Federation, figure, any from Jakks Tag Team 2-Pack Series, MIP, F1, ea $20.00

World Wrestling Federation, figure, Bart Gunn or Billy Gunn, Hasbro, MOC (gr), D8, ea....................................$35.00

World Wrestling Federation, figure, Berzerker, Hasbro, MOC, F1 ....$15.00

World Wrestling Federation, figure, Big Boss Man #1 or #2, Hasbro, MOC, F1, ea....................................$15.00

World Wrestling Federation, figure, Big John Studd, LJN, bendable, MOC, D8 ....$15.00

World Wrestling Federation, figure, Billy Jack Haynes, Hasbro, MOC, J6......................$85.00

World Wrestling Federation, figure, Bobby Heenan, LJN, complete w/poster, M, D8 ....$35.00

World Wrestling Federation, figure, Brutus Beefcake, Hasbro, wht & blk outfit, MOC, F1 ....$30.00

World Wrestling Federation, figure, Bushwacker Luke, Hasbro, MOC, F1 ....$15.00

World Wrestling Federation, figure, Carlos Colon, Remco, M, D8......................$28.00

World Wrestling Federation, figure, Classie Freddie Blassie, LJN, complete w/poster, M, D8......................$35.00

World Wrestling Federation, figure, Crush, Hasbro, MOC, F1......................$25.00

World Wrestling Federation, figure, Crush, Hasbro, MOC (yel), D8......................$20.00

World Wrestling Federation, figure, Doink the Clown, Hasbro, MOC (purple), D8......................$16.00

World Wrestling Federation, figure, Dragon Steamboat, Hasbro, MOC, F1......................$15.00

World Wrestling Federation, figure, Earthquake, Hasbro, MOC (bl), D8 ....$35.00

World Wrestling Federation, figure, El Matador, Hasbro, M, D8 ....$15.00

World Wrestling Federation, figure, Giant Gonzalez, Hasbro, MOC, F1......................$15.00

World Wrestling Federation, figure, Goldust or Shawn Michaels, Just Toys, Bend-Ems, 3rd series, MOC, F1, ea..............$8.00

World Wrestling Federation, figure, Greg Valentine, Hasbro, MOC, F1 ....$30.00

World Wrestling Federation, figure, Hulk Hogan, Hasbro, 4", NM, $25.00. (Photo courtesy June Moon)

World Wrestling Federation, figure, Hackshaw Duggan #1 or #2, Hasbro, MOC, F1, ea......................$15.00

World Wrestling Federation, figure, Headshrinker Samu, Hasbro, MOC, F1......................$15.00

World Wrestling Federation, figure, Hillbilly Jim, LJN, complete w/poster, M, D8 ....$35.00

World Wrestling Federation, figure, Honky Tonk Man, Hasbro, MOC, F1......................$40.00

World Wrestling Federation, figure, Iron Sheik, LJN, 10", M (EX card w/poster), M17 ....$30.00

World Wrestling Federation, figure, Iron Sheik, LJN, bendable, MOC, D8......................$15.00

World Wrestling Federation, figure, Jake the Snake Roberts, Hasbro, MOC, F1......................$20.00

World Wrestling Federation, figure, Jesse Ventura, Hasbro, MOC, J6......................$45.00

World Wrestling Federation, figure, Jimmy Superfly Snukka, LJN, complete w/poster, M, D8......................$45.00

World Wrestling Federation, figure, Junk Yard Dog, LJN, 10", M (EX card w/poster), M17 ....$30.00

World Wrestling Federation, figure, Kamala, Hasbro, MOC, F1......................$25.00

World Wrestling Federation, figure, King Kong Bundy, LJN, complete w/poster, M, D8......................$35.00

World Wrestling Federation, figure, Koko B Ware, Hasbro, MOC (bl), D8......................$65.00

World Wrestling Federation, figure, Legion of Doom, Hasbro, MOC (bl), D8......................$50.00

World Wrestling Federation, figure, Lex Luger, Hasbro, MOC (red), D8......................$20.00

World Wrestling Federation, figure, Ludwig Borga, Hasbro, MOC (gr), D8......................$45.00

World Wrestling Federation, figure, Marty Genetti, Hasbro, M, D8......................$10.00

World Wrestling Federation, figure, Mean Gene, LJN, complete w/poster, M, D8 ....$25.00

World Wrestling Federation, figure, Mr Perfect, Hasbro, MOC (red), D8......................$20.00

World Wrestling Federation, figure, Mr Wonderful, LJN, complete w/poster, M, D8 ....$35.00

World Wrestling Federation, figure, Nailz, Hasbro, MOC, F1......................$25.00

World Wrestling Federation, figure, Owen Hart, Hasbro, MOC (yel), D8......................$20.00

World Wrestling Federation, figure, Randy Savage, Hasbro, Macho King w/Crown, MOC, F1 ....$30.00

World Wrestling Federation, figure, Razor Ramone, Hasbro, MOC (bl), D8......................$25.00

World Wrestling Federation, figure, Razor Ramone, Hasbro, MOC (yel), D8......................$28.00

World Wrestling Federation, figure, Repo Man, Hasbro, MOC, F1 ....$15.00

World Wrestling Federation, figure, Rick Rude, Hasbro, M, D8......................$25.00

World Wrestling Federation, figure, Rick Steiner, Hasbro, MOC (purple), D8 ....$14.00

World Wrestling Federation, figure, Ricky the Dragon Steamboat, LJN, complete w/poster, M, D8......................$35.00

World Wrestling Federation, figure, Roddy Piper, Hasbro, MOC, F1 ....$35.00

World Wrestling Federation, figure, Scott Steiner, Hasbro, MOC, F1 ....$15.00

World Wrestling Federation, figure, Sgt Slaughter, Hasbro, MOC, F1 ....$30.00

World Wrestling Federation, figure, Sid Justice, Hasbro, M, D8..$18.00

World Wrestling Federation, figure, Sid Justice, Hasbro, MOC (bl), D8 ....$45.00

World Wrestling Federation, figure, Sunny, Marc Mero, Psycho Sid or Vader, Just Toys, Bend-Ems, 4th series, MOC, F1, ea .$8.00

World Wrestling Federation, figure, Tatanka, Hasbro, MOC, F1 ....$15.00

World Wrestling Federation, figure, Ted Dibiase, Hasbro, blk suit, MOC, F1 ....$30.00

World Wrestling Federation, figure, Ted Dibiase, Hasbro, gr suit, MOC, F1 ....$20.00

World Wrestling Federation, figure, Texas Tornado, Hasbro, MOC, F1 ....$50.00

World Wrestling Federation, figure, Tito Santana, LJN, complete w/poster, M, D8 ....$35.00

World Wrestling Federation, figure, Typhoon, Hasbro, MOC, F1 ....$30.00

World Wrestling Federation, figure, Ultimate Warrior, Hasbro, purple trunks, MOC, F1 ....$50.00

World Wrestling Federation, figure, Ultimate Warrior, PVC, 3", EX, F1 ....$5.00

World Wrestling Federation, figure, Undertaker, Hasbro, MOC (red), D8 ....$25.00

World Wrestling Federation, figure, Undertaker or Bulldog, Just Toys, Bend-Ems, 2nd series, MOC, F1, ea $8.00

World Wrestling Federation, figure, Vince McMahon, LJN, 10", M (EX card w/poster), M17 ....$30.00

World Wrestling Federation, figure, Warlord, Hasbro, MOC (bl), D8 ....$45.00

World Wrestling Federation, figure, Yoko Zumo, Hasbro, MOC (gr), D8 ....$28.00

World Wrestling Federation, figure, Yoko Zumo, Hasbro, MOC (red), D8 ....$25.00

World Wrestling Federation, figure, 1-2-3 Kid, Hasbro, MOC (gr) D8 ....$75.00

World Wrestling Federation, figure, 1-2-3- Kid or Mabel, Just Toys, Bend-Ems, 2nd series, MOC, F1, ea $10.00

World's Greatest Super Heroes, see Official World's Greatest Super Heroes

Wyatt Earp, figure, Mego, Am West series, complete, 8", M (EX Sears box), F1 ....$50.00

X-Force, figure, any except Deadpool, Domino or The Blob, MOC, F1, ea $15.00

X-Force, figure, Deadpool, Domino or The Blob, MOC, F1, ea $20.00

X-Men (Animated Series), figure, any character, Toy Biz, MOC, F1, ea $15.00

X-Men (Flashback Series), figure, any character, Toy Biz, MOC, F1, ea $15.00

X-Men (Mutant Armor Series), figure, any character, Toy Biz, MOC, F1, ea from $15 to $20.00

X-Men Classics (Animated Series), figure, any character, Toy Biz, MOC, F1, ea $15.00

X-Men 2099, figure, any character, Toy Biz, MOC, F1, ea ..$15.00

Activity Sets

Activity sets that were once enjoyed by so many as children — the Silly Putty, the Creepy Crawlers, and those Mr. Potato Heads — are finding their way back to some of those same kids, now grown up, more or less, and especially the earlier editions are carrying pretty respectable price tags when they can be found complete or reasonably so. The first Thingmaker/Creepy Crawlers (Mattel, 1964) in very good but played-with condition will sell for about $65.00 to $75.00. For more information about Tinker Toys see *Collector's Guide to Tinker Toys* by Craig Strange (Collector Books).

Advisor: Bill Bruegman (T2).

See also Character, TV and Movie Collectibles; Coloring, Activity and Paint Books; Disney; Playsets; Western.

Abascus Tinker, Toy Tinkers, 1929-30, NMIB $100.00

Big Top Cotton Candy Machine, Hasbro, 1960s, unused, MIB, J2 ....$125.00

Boy's World Thingmaker, Mattel, 1968, Deluxe edition, NMIB, from $200 to $250.00

Cartoonist Stamp Set, 1960s, features Hanna-Barbera characters, complete, EX (G box), from $100 to................$125.00

Colorforms, 1950, 1st issue, complete w/100 geometric shapes, unused, rare, MIB, T2 ....$80.00

Coney Island Action Arcade, Gabriel, 1978, plastic w/vinyl figures, 19", EX...$20.00

Cooky Cucumber w/Her Friend Mr Potato Head, Hasbro, 1966, complete, EX (EX box), H4/M17.........................$50.00

Creative Clips, Fisher-Price, 1983-84, complete, EX, C13...$15.00

Creeple Peeple Thingmaker, Mattel, 1965, complete, MIB.$100.00

Creeple Peeple Thingmaker Pak, EX, T2.....................$50.00

Creative Stamper Caddy, Fisher-Price, 1984–86, MIB, $35.00. (Photo courtesy Brad Cassity)

Creepy Crawlers, Mattel, 1964, 1st issue, VG (VG box), from $65 to $75.00
Design-O-Marx Set, Marx, 1960s, scarce, unused, MIB, M17....$45.00
Doll-E-Dish Time, Amsco, 1955, complete, MOC..........$20.00
Drawing Teacher, Milton Bradley, complete, EX (EX box) ..$100.00
Easy-Bake Oven, Kenner, MIB, B5, from $75 to $85.00
Electric Mold Master, Kenner, MIB, B5...........................$40.00
Electro-Art, Hasbro, 1960s, complete, EX (EX box) $25.00
Famous Heroes Color 'N Play, Colorforms, 1970s, complete, MIB, J5...$25.00
FBI Jr Finger Print Set, Nasta, complete, MIB................$100.00
Federal Agent Fingerprint Outfit, Transogram, 1938, complete, MIB, A...$200.00
Fighting Men Thingmaker, Mattel, 1960s, complete, EX (EX box), J5 ....$50.00
Fireball XL5 Magic Wand, 1963, VG (VG box), J2, from $100 to...$150.00
Freeze Queen Ice Cream Maker, Kenner, 1966, complete, MIB..$75.00

Fulton Sign Writer, Fulton Specialty Co., complete, EX (EX box), from $40.00 to $50.00. (Photo courtesy Linda Baker)

Girl's World Thingmaker, Mattel, 1968, complete, NMIB...$50.00
Great Foodini Magic Set, Pressman, 1960, complete, rare, NMIB...$150.00
Hocus Pocus Magic Set, 1976, complete, NMIB $50.00
Incredible Edibles Gobble-Degoop, Mattel, 1966, MOC, J2/M17...$35.00
Incredible Edibles Kooky Kakes, Mattel, 1967, contents sealed, MIB, M17 ....$120.00
Junior Chef Poppity Corn Popper, Argo Industries, 1971, VG (VG box), M17....................................$20.00
Junior Chef See-It-Pop Corn Popper, Argo Industries, 1971, VG (VG box), M17....................................$20.00
Krazy Ikes, Whitman, 1964, complete, EX (EX canister), T2..$25.00
Lacing Shoe, Holgate, 1940s, wood, Old Woman Who Lived in a Shoe nursery rhyme printed on side, complete, EX.$50.00
Little Toy Town Grocery Store, Parker Bros, complete, EX (EX box), A..$250.00
Looney Tunes Cartoon-O-Craft Molding & Coloring Set, Warner Bros, complete, EX (EX box) $100.00

Magic Kit of Tricks & Puzzles, Transogram, 1960s, complete, EX (EX box), M17..........................$55.00
Magician Magic Set, TV Mystery Products, 1974, rare, NMIB, A $125.00
Mister Funny Face, Peerless Playthings Inc, 1953, complete, NM (NM box), M17.........................$100.00
Monster Machine, Gabriel, MIB, B5..............................$25.00
Moon Rocks, Hasbro, 1970, 3-D, EX (EX box), J2 ....$35.00
Mr & Mrs Potato Head, Hasbro, MIB, B5......................$85.00
Mr & Mrs Potato Head & Pets, Hasbro, complete, MIB, from $60 to $70.00

Mr. Potato Head, Hasbro/Romper Room, 1965, MIB, $25.00.

Mr Potato Head Frenchy Fry Set, Hasbro, complete, rare, EX (EX box) $85.00
Mr Potato Head Funny Face Kit, Hasbro, 1950s, EX (EX box), J2 ....$50.00
Mr Potato Head on the Moon, Hassenfeld, 1968, MIB, M17, from $175 to $250.00
Mr Wizard Science Lab, Handy Andy, 1950s, EX (EX box), from $100 to $125.00
Mystic Smoke, Adams, 1958, MOC, M17 ....$20.00
Mysto Magic Exhibition Set, Gilbert, 1920s, EX (EX box) $450.00
Mysto Magic Exhibition Set, Gilbert, 1938, complete, EX (EX box), A..$200.00
Play-Doh Fun Factory, 1960s, rare, MIB, from $40 to $50.00
Playstone Funnies Casting Kit, Allief Mfg, 1936, features Little Orphan Annie, Sandy, Skeezix, etc, EX (EX box) ..$150.00
Police Fingerprint Kit, 1940s?, contents in 16x11" blk metal attache case, EX, M17 ....$250.00
Pretzel Jetzel Factory, Transogram, 1965, complete, EX (G box) $50.00
Professional High Power Microscope Set, Quality Toys, 1970s, MOC, M17 ....$25.00
Royal Magic Chinese Sticks, Fun Inc, 1950s, EX (EX box), M17 ....$30.00
Shaker Maker Bugglies Set, Ideal, 1972, MIB...................$30.00
Shrink Machine, Wham-O, 1968, complete, EX (EX box) ..$70.00

Shrunken Head Apple Sculpture, Milton Bradley, 1975, complete, NM (NM box), $65.00. (Photo courtesy Martin and Carolyn Berens)

Small Fry Barber Set, MIB, $75.00. (Photo courtesy John Turney)

Simple Sewing Cards for Nimble Fingers, Milton Bradley, complete, EX (EX box) $150.00
Sneaky Pete's Magic Show, Remco, 1960s, complete, NMIB..$150.00
Space Scientist Drafting Set, 1950s, complete, EX (EX box), J2 ....$100.00
Spirofoil Set, Kenner, 1970, complete, EX (EX box) $25.00
Stacking Rings, Holgate, 1945, wood, complete w/12 rings & post, EX..$50.00
Stamps & Coloring Outfit, Baumgarten & Co, 1920s, w/12 Brownie & 12 animal stamps, ink pad & tablet, EX (EX box), A $135.00
Sugar Plum Quick Freeze, Hasbro, unused, NMIB, J2 ......$45.00
Super Adventure Colorforms Set, 1974, features Marvel Super Heroes, complete, EX (EX box), T2.........................$30.00
Super Powers Sunshiners, Craftmaster, 1985, complete, MIP, J5 ....$25.00

Suzy Homemaker Grill, Topper, 1960s, MIB, C17 ....$65.00
Suzy Homemaker Super Safety Oven, Topper, 1960s, MIB, M17..$50.00
Suzy Homemaker Sweet Shoppe Soda Fountain, Topper, 1960s, MIB, B5..$50.00
Tasket Basket Shape Sorter, Holgate, 1953, masonite-type material w/wooden ends & handle, 9", complete, EX........$30.00
Thingmaker Fright Factory, Mattel, MIB (sealed), J2 ....$150.00
Thingmaker Fun Flowers, Mattel, complete, complete, EX .$35.00
Tinker Fish, Toy Tinkers, 1927, complete w/pole, EX (worn box) $50.00

Tinker Spots, Toy Tinkers, late 1930s, EX (EX box), $60.00. (Photo courtesy Craig Strange)

Tinkerbeads No 4, Toy Tinkers, 1928, complete, EX (EX tin container) $80.00
Tinkerbeads No 6, Toy Tinkers, 1930-35, complete, EX (EX glass jar w/metal top) $60.00
Tinkerprints, Toy Tinkers, 1938, complete, EX (EX box)..$60.00
Tinkertoy Color Coded Dominoes, Spalding, 1967, complete, EX (EX container)..$25.00
Vac-U-Form Casting Set, Mattel, 1960s, MIB, from $65 to..$75.00

Weebles Tarzan Jungle Hut, Romper Room, MIB, from $35.00 to $40.00. (Photo courtesy Martin and Carolyn Berens)

Weebles Circus, Hasbro/Romper Room, MIB, B5 ....$25.00
Weebles Tumblin' Funhouse, Hasbro/Romper Room, complete, EX $25.00
Winky Dink Paint Set, Pressman, 1950s, complete, EX ...$75.00

Advertising

The assortment of advertising memorabilia geared toward children is vast — plush and cloth dolls, banks, games, puzzles, trucks, radios, watches, and much, much more. And considering the popularity of advertising memorabilia in general, when you add to it the crossover interest from the realm of toys, you have a real winning combination! Just remember to check for condition very carefully; signs of play wear are common. Think twice about investing much money in soiled items, especially cloth or plush dolls. (Stains are often impossible to remove.)

For more information we recommend *Zany Characters of the Ad World* by Mary Jane Lamphier; *Advertising Character Collectibles* by Warren Dotz; *Huxford's Collectible Advertising* by Sharon and Bob Huxford; *Cracker Jack Toys* and *Cracker Jack, the Unauthorized Guide to Advertising* both by Larry White; *Pepsi-Cola Collectibles*, *Vols I, II, and III*, by Bill Vehling and Michael Hunt; and *Collectible Coca-Cola Toy Trucks* by Gael de Courtivron.

Advisors: Michael Paquin (P12), Jim Rash (R3), advertising dolls; Larry White (W7), Cracker Jack.

See also Bubble Bath Containers; Cereal Boxes and Premiums; Character, TV, and Movie Collectibles; Dakins; Disney; Fast-Food Collectibles; Halloween Costumes; Pin-Back Buttons; Premiums; Radios; Telephones; Western; and other specific categories.

A&P Super Markets, truck, Marx, red- & silver-pnt pressed steel w/plastic mesh rear door, 19", NMIB, A..........$600.00
A&P Super Markets, truck, red & silver litho tin w/plastic wheels, 27½", VG, A $125.00
A&W Root Beer, bear, 1975, stuffed plush, 13", EX, from $25 to..$35.00
Aero Mayflower Transit Co, truck, Linemar, litho tin, friction, MIB, D10...$350.00
Alka-Seltzer, bank, Speedy, vinyl, 5½", EX, minimum value...$200.00
Alka-Seltzer, doll, Speedy, Canadian, pnt rubber, 5", EX, A $225.00
Alka-Seltzer, doll, Speedy, 1960, squeeze vinyl, 8", EX, from $500 to..$700.00
Allied Van Lines, doll, 1970s, stuffed cloth, 17", NM, minimum value...$25.00
Atlantic Oil, game, WWII giveaway, 1942, EX, V1.........$20.00
Aunt Hannah's Bread, jigsaw puzzle, 1932, boy fishing & girl eyeing loaf of bread, complete, EX $45.00
Aunt Jemima, doll, Breakfast Bear, bl plush w/chef's hat, apron & bandana, 13", M...$175.00
Aunt Jemima, doll, Diana, 1940-50 premium, stuffed oilcloth, 8½", EX, P6..$150.00
Aunt Jemima, Jr Chef Pancake Set, Argo Industries, 1949, EX..$150.00
Blue Bonnet Margarine, doll, Blue Bonnet Sue, 1980s, stuffed cloth w/yel yarn hair, NM, minimum value...............$20.00
Borden, doll, Elsie, plush w/vinyl head, brn w/yel hands & feet, yel bow w/plastic charm, 16", M $135.00
Borden, Elsie's Funbook Cut-Out Toys & Games, 1940s, EX, P6..$65.00
Borden, figure, Elsie, 1993, PVC, 3½", M, from $10 to....$20.00
Borden, punch-out train, Elsie's Good Food Line, 1940s, cb, unpunched, 24½x37", M (EX envelope), from $150 to.$200.00

Aunt Jemima, dolls, Uncle Moses, 1940–50, stuffed oilcloth, 12", EX, $150.00; Aunt Jemima, 1940–50, stuffed oilcloth, 11", EX, $200.00.

Borden, push-button puppet, Elsie the Cow, wood, EX, $125.00.

Bosco Chocolate, doll, Bosco the Clown, vinyl, NM, J6 ..$45.00
Brach's Candy, doll, Scarecrow, stuffed cloth, EX, minimum value..$35.00
Breck, doll, Bonnie Breck, Hasbro, 1972, orig outfit, 9", VG, M15..$40.00
Burlington Northern Lines, figure, wind-up walker, EX, P12 .$45.00

Campbell's Soups, doll, Campbell Girl, Ideal, 1955, rubber and vinyl with cloth outfit, 8", EX, minimum value, $125.00.

Campbell's Soups, doll, Campbell girl as cheerleader, 1967, vinyl, 8", EX..$75.00
Campbell's Soups, doll, Campbell girl in Scottish outfit, M, J6, from $85 to..$100.00
Campbell's Soups, dolls, Campbell Kids, 1970s, rag-type, MIB, pr..$125.00
Campbell's Soups, dolls, Campbell Kids in colonial outfits, vinyl w/cloth clothes, 9", MIB, H4, pr $50.00
Campbell's Soups, game, Campbell Kids Shopping Game, Parker Bros, 1955, scarce, NMIB, A......................$300.00
Campbell's Soups, tea set, Chilton, 1992, child's, porcelain, 9-pc set, MIB (recalled for high lead content)..................$20.00
Campbell's Soups, tea set, 1982, Campbell Kids image, 4 cups & plates w/tray, dish & utensils, MIB..........................$50.00
Campbell's Soups, trading cards, Collect-A-Card, 1995, set of 72, M1..$16.00
Canada Dry, truck, H/Japan, 1950s, lt gr w/yel & blk detail, friction, 8", EX+, A................................$160.00
Cap'n Crunch, doll, stuffed plush, 14", EX, from $20 to...$50.00
Cap'n Crunch, Island Adventure Game, Warren, 1987, complete, EX (EX box), minimum value $20.00
Caravelle Candy Bar, figure, Caravelle man on horse, bendable, M, from $125 to................................$175.00
Ceresota Flour, doll, Ceresota boy (Hecker's Flour boy), Chase Bag Co, 1972, stuffed cloth, EX, minimum value $30.00

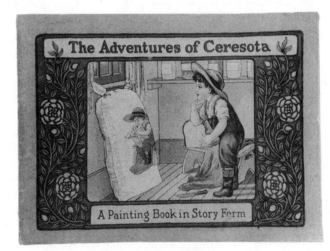

Ceresota Flour, paint book, VG, $30.00.

Chase & Sanborn's Coffees, jigsaw puzzle, Old Fashioned New England Country Store, 1910, 6x8", EX.................$50.00
Cheetos, doll, Cheetah, 1980s, stuffed plush, wearing tennis shoes & sunglasses, 20", EX, H4..........................$70.00
Chicken of the Sea, doll, mermaid, Mattel, 1974, stuffed printed cloth, 15", NM, C17................................$20.00
Chips Ahoy, figure, Nabisco, 1990s, rubber, 5", M...........$20.00
Chiquita Bananas, doll, Chiquita Banana girl, 1974 mail-in premium, stuffed cloth, NM, minimum value.................$40.00
Chocks Vitamins, doll, Charlie Chocks, 1970, stuffed cloth, 20", NM, minimum value $35.00
Chrysler, figure, Mr Fleet, 1970s, vinyl, all wht version, 10", VG, from $150 to $250.00

Citroen Motor Co, puzzle blocks, 30 paper-on-wood blocks in dovetailed wooden box, 6 different scenes, 11x9x2", EX+, A $200.00

Coca-Cola, bank, can shape, tin, EX..............................$10.00

Coca-Cola, baseball glove, 1930s, leather child's sz w/Drink Coca-Cola in Bottles emb on back, rare, G, A $575.00

Coca-Cola, bicycle light/radio, Hong Kong, red plastic w/logo, 6", EX..$50.00

Coca-Cola, boomerang, 1950s, EX $35.00

Coca-Cola, bus, Ashitoy, litho tin w/plastic windows, friction, 14", NM...$1,300.00

Coca-Cola, car, Ford Sedan, Taiyo, 1960s, litho tin, Refresh w/Zest on sides, friction, 9", EX...............................$200.00

Coca-Cola, car, Ford Taxi, Taiyo, litho tin, friction, 9", MIB..$400.00

Coca-Cola, cribbage board, 1940s, EX $45.00

Coca-Cola, dispenser, #16, w/4 plastic flared glasses, NMIB $135.00

Coca-Cola, dispenser, Linemar, 1950s, insert coin & Coke dispenses into cup, tin, battery-op, 9½", NM (EX box)..$950.00

Coca-Cola, Frozen Coca-Cola mascot, 1960s, stuffed cloth, NM $150.00

Coca-Cola, game, Age Cards, 1928, NM (orig envelope)...$550.00

Coca-Cola, game, Broadsides, Milton Bradley, 1940s-50s, Compliments of the Coca-Cola Co, EX+ $80.00

Coca-Cola, game, Down the Mississippi Race, saleman's incentive, 1956, EX+...$50.00

Coca-Cola, game, Horse Race, 1940s, EX, A..................$350.00

Coca-Cola, game, NFL Football, ca 1964, NM..................$15.00

Coca-Cola, game, Safety & Danger, 1938, cb, complete, EX+...$100.00

Coca-Cola, game, Santa Ring Toss, 1980s, VG................$10.00

Coca-Cola, game, Tic-Tac-Toe, EX (EX box).................$165.00

Coca-Cola, grocery cart, 1950s, litho metal, complete w/cb product boxes, EX...$400.00

Coca-Cola, jigsaw puzzle, Coca-Cola Pop Art, 1960, M (sealed canister) $20.00

Coca-Cola, jigsaw puzzle, Hawaiian Beach, rare, NMIB...$185.00

Coca-Cola, jigsaw puzzle, pictures several Coca-Cola items, 2,000 pcs, EX (EX box) $60.00

Coca-Cola, jigsaw puzzle, Teenage Party, NMIB............$100.00

Coca-Cola, jump rope, 1920s, whistle in 1 hdl, G..........$350.00

Coca-Cola, kite, Am Flyer, 1930s, bottle at end, EX......$400.00

Coca-Cola, magic kit, 1965, complete, EX $175.00

Coca-Cola, playing cards, 1970s, dbl-deck in 6-pack carton, EX..$65.00

Coca-Cola, pop gun, 1950s, cb & paper w/image of clown holding Compliments of Coca-Cola sign, M.....................$50.00

Coca-Cola, pop-gun, 1950s, cb & paper pistol w/G-Man logo & It's the Real Thing, M $75.00

Coca-Cola, ring toss, Santa face at top, VG $35.00

Coca-Cola, train set, Lionel, 1970s-80s, cars feature various Coke products, electric, NMIB $275.00

Coca-Cola, train set, Markatron, 1987, Express Limited #2, 27-gauge, unused, NMIB, A $200.00

Coca-Cola, truck, Buddy L, 1947-48, wood, yel w/red details, blk wheels, 19", VG+, A...$2,200.00

Coca-Cola, truck, Buddy L #5216, 1962, plastic, yel w/8 cases, 12", rare, M..$600.00

Coca-Cola, truck, Buddy L #5426, 1962-64, pressed steel, yel w/2-tiered divided bay, 15", NM, A........................$275.00

Coca-Cola, truck, Buddy L #5546, 1957, pressed steel, yel 2-tier w/8 cases & 2 hand trucks, 14", MIB $350.00

Coca-Cola, truck, Buddy L #5646, 1957-58, yel GMC w/conveyor belt, 8 cases & 2 hand trucks, 14", NMIB......$500.00

Coca-Cola, truck, Buddy L/Aiwa #591-1350, pressed steel, red w/see-through trailer, 11", rare, NMIB....................$85.00

Coca-Cola, truck, Budgie, 1950s, diecast, orange w/divided open bay, 5", EX..$125.00

Coca-Cola, truck, Hartoy, diecast, lights up & plays Coca-Cola song, 1/64th scale, MOC, M15.................................$20.00

Coca-Cola, truck, Lincoln Toy, 1950s, pressed steel, gray, w/12 wooden blocks, 16", NMIB $1,000.00

Coca-Cola, truck, Lincoln Toy, 1950s, pressed steel, red, w/12 wooden blocks, 16", NMIB $850.00

Coca-Cola, truck, Marusan, 1956-57, tin, yel & bl w/red detail, 2 removable bottle racks, friction, 8", NMIB...........$850.00

Coca-Cola, truck, Marx, metal, 1956-57, tin, yel w/red detail, open bay w/center ad panel, 7 cases of Coke, 17", G, A.......$350.00

Coca-Cola, truck, Marx, pressed steel, yel w/red detail, open-sided 2-tiered bed w/4 cases of Coke, 12½", MIB, A..........$1,000.00

Coca-Cola, truck, Marx, 1949, plastic, yel w/red decals, side panels lift up to reveal cases of Coke, 10", VG (VG box)......$700.00

Coca-Cola, truck, Marx, 1950-54, plastic, red & yel Chevy w/enclosed bed & top ad panel, 11", EX $800.00

Coca-Cola, truck, Marx, 1956-57, litho tin w/Sprite Boy logo, 17", NMIB $625.00

Coca-Cola, truck, Marx #991, 1950s, pressed steel, red cab w/yel stake bed, Sprite boy logo, 20", MIB, A................$1,100.00

Coca-Cola, truck, Marx #991, 1950s, pressed steel, yel, Sprite Boy logo, 20", MIB $550.00

Coca-Cola, truck, Metalcraft, pressed steel, red & yel w/10-bottle payload, 11", EX, A..$1,000.00

Coca-Cola, truck, Pyro Plastic Corp, 1950s, yel w/red lettering & blk tires, 5½", MIP $150.00

Coca-Cola, truck, Rico/Spain, 1970s, Sanson Jr, pressed steel, red w/lg contour logo, 13½", VG $45.00

Coca-Cola, truck, Sanyo, 1950s, tin, yel & wht w/red logo & detail, battery-op, 12½", EX (EX box mk Route Truck), A....$700.00

Coca-Cola, truck, Smith-Miller, 1953-54, pressed steel, yel GMC model w/red detail, 6 cases & 24 bottles, 14", NMIB, A.............$1,700.00

Coca-Cola, truck, Smith-Miller, pressed steel cab with wood body, red with wire load divider and wood blocks, 14", EX, A, $950.00.

Coca-Cola, truck, Taiyo, Big Wheel Van, plastic & tin, advances w/non-fall action, battery-op, 10", EX (EX box), A.....$125.00

Coca-Cola, truck set, Buddy L #4973, 1970s, 7 pcs, MIB, J6..$85.00

Coca-Cola, van, Van Goodies/Canada, 1970s, Denimachine, simulated wood w/red & wht contour logo, 12", rare, NM $125.00

Coca-Cola, VW Van, Taiyo, 1950s, litho tin, friction, 7½", EX $250.00

Coca-Cola, whistle, 1930, tin, red & yel w/Drink Coca-Cola logo, VG $125.00

Coca-Cola, whistle, 1950, plastic, Merry Christmas...Memphis Tenn, EX...$25.00

Consolidated Biscuit Co, dollhouse, 1932, 2-story litho cb biscuit box w/red roof, 9x9x5", EX+, A $85.00

Cracker Jack, book, Baby Bears, 1910, EX $80.00

Cracker Jack, book, Cracker Jack Riddles, paper w/Jack & Bingo on front, EX $95.00

Cracker Jack, book, Handy Andy, 1920, EX $75.00

Cracker Jack, charm, 1920, pot metal w/gold japan finish, various instruments, EX, ea...$12.00

Cracker Jack, doll, Cracker Jack boy, Ideal, 1917, compo head & hands w/cloth body, orig outfit, 14", EX $325.00

Cracker Jack, doll, Cracker Jack boy, Vogue, 1980, vinyl w/cloth clothes, MIP, minimum value $65.00

Cracker Jack, doll, Sailor, stuffed cloth w/yarn hair, EX, minimum value...$30.00

Cracker Jack, figure, skunk, squirrel, fish, etc, 1950, plastic, EX, ea from $7 to $10.00

Cracker Jack, game, Monkey Ring Toss, 1940, paper, red & gr, EX..$30.00

Cracker Jack, Goofy Zoo Wheel Game, 1940, red, brn & gr paper, EX...$40.00

Cracker Jack, horse & wagon, 1910, litho metal, EX, J6 .$200.00

Cracker Jack, magic kit, 1950s Sweepstakes Second Place Prize, complete, EX (EX box), A $100.00

Cracker Jack, magic slate, 1980, paper & plastic, EX..........$8.00

Cracker Jack, maze puzzles, 1980s, plastic & paper, 20 different, EX, ea $8.00

Cracker Jack, palm puzzle, plastic & paper w/rising moon image, EX...$85.00

Cracker Jack, puzzle books, 1910, 3 different, EX, ea......$100.00

Cracker Jack, ring, 1950, metal & plastic, split back w/colored faux jewel, EX $5.00

Cracker Jack, squeaker, 1910, paper bellows, Me For Cracker Jack w/several different designs, EX, ea......................$60.00

Cracker Jack, squirt gun, 1900s, metal & rubber, EX........$65.00

Cracker Jack, top, 1910, metal & wood, Always on Top, EX.$75.00

Cracker Jack, whistle, 1930, metal w/playing card face, EX $60.00

Curtiss Candy, bunny cart, Marx, plastic, NM (G box), A $65.00

Diaparene, figure, Diaparene Baby, 1980s, vinyl, orig diaper, M, from $50 to...$75.00

Dole Pineapple, doll, Bananimal Banabear, Trudy Toys, 1989, stuffed plush, orig tag, 10", M $15.00

Dow, figure, Scrubbing Bubble, 1989, vinyl, EX, C17 ......$20.00

Eskimo Pie, doll, Eskimo Pie Boy, Chase Bag Co, 1975, stuffed cloth, 15", NM $20.00

Fanny Farmer Candies, truck, Marx, 1950s, plastic, wht w/brn lettering, 10", NM (NM box), A $165.00

Ford Motor Co, St Bernard, stuffed plush, orig tag, M, minimum value...$15.00

Fruit Roll Ups, figure, Rollupo the Wizard, bendable, 6", EX, from $10 to $15.00

Gerber, boxcar, Bachmann, 1978, bl, HO scale, 5¾", MIB, G8..$95.00

Gerber, squeaker dolls, Atlanta Novelty, 1985, girl or boy, vinyl, 8", EX, G8, $20.00 each. (Photo courtesy Joan Stryker Grubaugh)

Gerber, teddy bear, Tender Loving Care Bear, Atlanta Novelty, 1978, plush w/red bow tie, 20", EX, G8.....................$25.00

Gerber, truck, Nylint, 1978, GMC 18-wheeler, pressed steel, 21½", M, G8..$85.00

Good Humor Ice Cream, truck, KTS, 1950s, friction, 11", NMIB, A, $1,500.00.

Goodrich Silvertown Tires, truck, red w/open wht bed, complete w/winch & 3 spare tires, 12", NM, A......................$650.00

Gordon's Farm Products, truck, MSK, 1950s, tin, wht van-type w/2 bottle carriers on top, friction, 6½", NMIB, A .$250.00

Green Giant, bank, Little Sprout, compo, musical, NM, S21 .$45.00

Green Giant, doll, Jolly Green Giant, Product People, vinyl, 9½", NRFB, from $125 to $175.00

Green Giant, doll, Little Sprout, 1970s-90s, vinyl, 6½", EX, from $10 to $20.00

Green Giant, figure, Little Sprout, 1970s, inflatable vinyl, 24", MIP, from $35 to $65.00

Green Giant, jump rope, Little Sprout hdls, MIP, from $10 to $20.00

Green Giant, kite, Jolly Green Giant, 1960s, thin plastic, 42x48", M, from $20 to...$30.00

Gulf Gasoline & Motor Oils, truck, Courtland-Reach, orange & bl litho tin, friction, 12½", NM, A $450.00

Hamburger Helper, doll, Helping Hand, plush, EX, C17 .$20.00

Hawaiian Punch, doll, Punchy, stuffed cloth, 20", NM $65.00

Heinz 57 Varieties, jigsaw puzzle, 1932, EX, $75.00. (Photo courtesy Donald Friedman)

Heinz, truck, Metalcraft, wht w/various product decals, electric headlights, spare tire mounted on side, 12", NM, A..$650.00

Hood's Sarsaparilla, jigsaw puzzle, 2-sided, Rainy Day/Hood's Balloon Puzzle, 10x15", NM+, A $70.00

Hot Tamales Candies, doll, Tamale Kid, 1967-75, stuffed cloth, 18", NM, minimum value..$35.00

Hushpuppies, bank, dog on rnd base, 1970, vinyl, 8", NM, minimum value..$20.00

Icee, ring, Icee Bear, M, C10 ....$10.00

Jell-O, hand puppet, Mr Wiggle, 1966, red rubber, 6", M..$175.00

Jell-O, hand puppet, Sweet Tooth Sam, General Mills, 1960s, gr vinyl head w/1 long fang & blk top hat, EX+, J5 ....$85.00

Jell-O, kite, 1950s, yel paper w/red lettering, M...............$35.00

Jordache Jeans, doll, cheerleader, Mego, 1981, 12", NRFB ..$30.00

Keebler, bank, Keebler Elf figure, ceramic, lg, NM, S21 ...$60.00

Keebler, bank, Keebler Elf figure, ceramic, sm, NM, S21 .$25.00

Keebler, truck, Nylint, 1986, MIB, P12............................$85.00

Kellogg's, dolls, Bo Peep, Red Riding Hood, Mary Had a Little Lamb, or To Market To Buy a Fat Pig, cloth, 14", VG, A, ea...$50.00

Kellogg's Pop Tarts, bank, Milton the Toaster, 1970s, vinyl, rare, MIB, from $75 to $145.00

Kellogg's Pop Tarts, stencil plates, 1970s, w/Snap! Crackle! & Pop!, Cowboy & Indian, Tony, Toucan Sam & Caveman, EX, H4..$5.00

Kleenex, figures, Kleenex bears, mail-in premium, set of 3, NM, B5 ....$50.00

Kool-Aid, doll, Kool-Aid Kid, 1989, w/pigtails & freckles, 14", VG, from $15 to $25.00

Kool-Aid, doll, Kool-Aid Kid, 1989, w/pigtails & freckles, 9", MIB, from $25 to $35.00

Kool-Aid, snow-cone machine, 1984, plastic, w/packet of Kool-Aid, unused, MIB (sealed), J5 ....$45.00

Lee Jeans, dolls, Buddy Lee, composition with cloth clothes, EX, minimum value, $550.00 each.

Lenox, bank, Lennie Lenox figure, NM, S21..................$400.00

Levi's, rag doll, Knickerbocker, MIB, B5, from $50 to......$75.00

Little Debbie, doll, 1984, vinyl w/cloth dress & straw hat, 11", M, J6..$85.00

Luden's 5th Avenue Candy Bar, pillow, 1970s, stuffed cloth, EX, minimum value...$25.00

Lysol, doll, Lysol Kid, Trudy Corp, 1986, stuffed cloth w/yel hair, NM, minimum value $30.00

M&M, bear, stuffed plush w/cloth M&M shirt, orig tag, M, minimum value $20.00

M&M, dispenser, gr peanut M&M, 3½", M, C11...............$6.00

M&M, dispenser, plain yel M&M holding flowers, 3", M, C11 ....$15.00

M&M, dispenser, present on foot, red, yel or gr plain M&M, 6", M, C11, ea...$35.00

M&M, dispenser, skier, red, yel or gr peanut M&M, 7", M, C11, ea...$35.00

M&M, topper, Olympic soccer, brn peanut, sq base, M, C11..$14.00

M&M, topper, skier, plain or peanut, sq base, M, C11, ea..$8.00

M&M, topper, Valentine, sq base, M, C11 ....$8.00

Michelin, figure, Michelin Man, plastic, 12", NM, J2 ....$100.00

Mobil Gas, truck, Cragstan, ½-cab, red, litho tin, friction, EX+ (VG+ box)..$200.00

Mohawk Carpet, doll, Mohawk Tommy, stuffed cloth, EX, minimum value..$40.00

Morton Salt, doll, Morton Girl, Mattel, 1974, 10", MIB, M15..$40.00

Morton Salt, glider plane, 1930s, EX, C10........................$25.00

Moxie, kite, 1930s, Moxie Flyer, image of Moxie man, EX.$150.00

Mr Softee, flicker ring, EX, from $50 to............................$60.00

Nabisco Pretzels, doll, Mr Salty, 1983, stuffed cloth, NM, minimum value..$25.00

Nestle Quik, doll, Quik Bunny, plush, 1980s mail-in, M, P12..$35.00

Nestle Quik, figure, Quik Bunny, bendable, 6", EX, from $15 to..$20.00

Orange-Crush, truck, London Toy/Canada, diecast, w/up, 6", scarce, VG, A $100.00

Oreo Cookies, figure, Oreo Cookie, bendable, EX, H4 .$5.00

Oscar Mayer, bank, Weinermobile, 1988, plastic, 10", M, J6, $25.00. (Photo courtesy June Moon)

Oscar Mayer, Weinermobile, pedal car, 1994-95, 2 different, P12, ea from $250 to $350.00

Oscar Mayer, Weinermobile, remote control, 1994-95, MIB, P12, from $100 to $200.00

Pepsi-Cola, pull toy, 1945, puppy w/hot dog wagon, wood, 10", EX..$250.00

Pepsi-Cola, Santa doll, Animal Fair Inc, stuffed plush w/fur beard, logo on belt buckle, 20", NM $55.00

Pepsi-Cola, truck, Buddy L, wood, green, 16", NMIB, A, $1,700.00.

Pepsi-Cola, truck, Barclay, 1950s, diecast metal, 2", M..$155.00

Pepsi-Cola, truck, Cragstan, 1950s, litho tin, friction, 11", MIB..$700.00

Pepsi-Cola, truck, Marx, plastic flatbed w/cases of bottles, 7½", NM..$200.00

Pepsi-Cola, truck, Ny-Lint, pressed steel, red & bl w/wht open-sided body, 3 cases of Pepsi, 16", MIB, A................$775.00

Peters Weatherbird Shoes, push toy, pnt wood w/push stick, 11", NM, A..$55.00

Peters Weatherbird Shoes, whistle, yel w/mc graphics, EX, A..$15.00

PF Flyers, Branding Iron Kit, MIP, C10 ....$40.00

PF Flyers, ring, EX, C10..$80.00

Phillips 66, boat, Pier 66 Power Yacht, plastic, red & wht, battery-op, 18", NM..$120.00

Pillsbury, bank, Poppin' Fresh, 1980s mail-in premium, ceramic, M, P12..$35.00

Pillsbury, beanie, Poppin' Fresh, 2 different styles, M, P12, ea from $10 to..$20.00

Pillsbury, doll, Poppin' Fresh, 1972, stuffed cloth, 11", EX...$20.00

Pillsbury, doll, Poppin' Fresh, 1982, stuffed plush, scarce, M, from $30 to..$45.00

Pillsbury, figure, Poppie Fresh, vinyl, M $20.00

Pillsbury, figures, Grandmommer & Grandpopper, vinyl, P12, pr..$195.00

Pillsbury, figures, Poppin' Fresh, coldcast porcelain, various poses, 5", set of 4, MIB, P12 ....$60.00

Pillsbury, finger puppets, Poppin' Fresh & Pals, set of 3, rare, MIB, P12..$235.00

Pillsbury, gumball machine, Poppin' Fresh, w/5-lbs of gum, MIB, P12..$395.00

Pillsbury, jewelry box, Poppin' Fresh, pewter, w/pin, necklace & earrings, EX, P12..$15.00

Pillsbury, key chain, Poppin' Fresh, soft vinyl, MOC, P12 .$6.00

Pillsbury, magnet set, Poppin' Fresh & Poppie, 1970s premium, plastic, scarce, MIP, P12..$35.00

Pillsbury, memo pad, diecut Doughboy in upper left corner, 40 sheets, 7x4", EX, P12 ....$8.00

Pillsbury, playhouse, Poppin' Fresh, vinyl, w/4 finger puppets, NM, from $250 to..$300.00

Pillsbury, stick-on decals, Poppin' Fresh, set of 18, MIP, P12 .$10.00

Planters, dart board, 1980s, wood case w/Planters lettered in yel above Mr Peanut on hinged doors, EX......................$25.00

Planters, doll, Mr Peanut, Chase Bag Co, 1967, stuffed cloth, 21", EX..$30.00

Planters, doll, Mr Peanut, Chase Bag Co, 1970, stuffed cloth, 18", NM $25.00

Planters, puppet, Mr Peanut, 1942, rubber, tan w/blk hat & monocle, 6", EX..$1,000.00

Planters, truck, Mr Peanut's Peanut Wagon, Pyro, yel & red, 5", NM, from $350 to..$450.00

Planters, truck, plastic, red, yel & bl w/enclosed trailer, 6", NM, A..$275.00

Planters, truck, plastic, red, yel & bl w/open stake bed, 6", NM $275.00

Planters, vendor's costume, Mr Peanut, life-size, EX, J6, from $800 to..$900.00

Planters, w/up figure, Mr Peanut, 1950s-60s, gr plastic, 8½", EX..$375.00

Planters, nodder, Mr. Peanut, Lego, papier-mache, NM, $150.00.

Seven-Up, music box, can shape, plays Love Story, NM, J2 ..$50.00
Seven-Up, truck, 1950s, tin, friction, driver moves back & forth in cab with see-through plastic dome, 9", EX+........$335.00
Shell, bank, German, litho tin gas station, door opens & attendant appears when coin is inserted, 5¾", G+, A $165.00
Shell, truck, Metalcraft, red cab w/yel stake bed holding 8 oil drums, blk rubber tires, 12", EX, A..........................$110.00
Shell Fuel Oils, truck, Buddy L, yel & red, handlebars extend from hood, emb spoke wheels, 28½", EX, A $6,000.00
Shell Motor Oil, truck, Metalcraft, red w/yel stake bed, logo on sides, complete w/8 oil cans, 12", NMIB, A $2,500.00
Shoney's, bank, Shoney's bear, vinyl, M, P12...................$20.00
Sinclair, doll, Skippy, 13", NM, A $150.00
Singer Sewing Machines, jigsaw puzzle, Singer Buffalo Puzzle, ca 1890, complete, NM (EX envelope), A..................$350.00

Snuggle Fabric Softener, bear, Lever Bros, 1986, 15", EX, $35.00; Bear, Lever Bros, 1983, 6", EX, $20.00.

Poll Parrot Shoes, bank, cb & metal can shape, yel w/mc bird & red star on wht, 2", EX, A...$35.00
Poll Parrot Shoes, ring, 1950s, brass w/emb parrot, EX, J5 ..$65.00
Popsicle, figure, Popsicle Kids, Matchbox, 1988, 6 different, 6", NRFB, M15, ea $15.00
Popsicle, ring, boot, w/papers, EX, C10............................$65.00
Pure Oil Co, truck, Metalcraft, pressed steel, bl w/wht lettering, electric lights, 15", VG, A $1,200.00
Quake Cereal, Quake Miner's Kit, 1960s mail-in premium, complete, MIB (sealed), H4...$200.00
Quaker Oats, doll, Crackles boy, early 1900s, stuffed cloth, EX, minimum value..$275.00
Raid, doll, Raid Bug, 1980s, plush, 5 different styles, unused, M, P12, ea from $50 to..$125.00
Ralston Purina, doll, scarecrow, 1965, stuffed cloth w/vinyl face, NM, minimum value $40.00
RCA, doll, Radiotron Man, pnt wood, fully jtd, complete w/chest ribbon, 15½", EX, A $1,900.00
RCA Television Service, truck, Marx, plastic, bl w/yel ladder on top, 8½", NM (EX box), A $225.00
Red Goose Shoes, bank, 1920s, red-pnt CI, 9", EX, A ...$135.00
Red Goose Shoes, pull toy, elephant, wht-pnt wood w/red wheels, EX $100.00
Red Goose Shoes, world globe, metal, 9x6" dia, EX, A $55.00
Royal Gelatin, bank, King Royal, 1970s, vinyl, scarce, NM, P12...$225.00
Salamander Shoes, figures, vinyl, set of 6, sm, M, P12 ...$125.00
Sambo's Restaurant, doll, tiger mascot, stuffed plush, 7", NMIB, A $100.00
Sara Lee Bagels, bear, stuffed cloth, NM, minimum value..$20.00
Sealtest Dairy Products, bank, 1950s, gray plastic truck w/blk rubber tires, 7", EX, A...$65.00
Seven-Up, doll, Fresh-Up Freddie, Canadian, stuffed cloth w/rubber head, 15", EX $75.00

Squirt, figure, Squirt Boy, 1961, squeeze vinyl, 6", very rare, M...$450.00
Standard Oil, truck, Japan, litho tin, friction, 8½", EX (VG box), A...$200.00
Star-Kist, bank, Charlie Tuna, 1988, ceramic, 10", M, P12, from $45 to $65.00
Star-Kist, figure, Charlie Tuna, 1970s, vinyl, rare, MIB, P12, from $125 to $150.00
Sun-Maid Raisins, van, gas-powered, early style w/brass grille & headlights, 72", M...$700.00
Sunbeam Bread, doll, Little Miss Sunbeam, stuffed cloth, 17", EX...$30.00
Sunshine Animal Crackers, elephant, 1930s, stuffed cloth, EX, minimum value $85.00
Sunshine Biscuits, truck, Metalcraft, red w/bl stake bed, disk wheels, 12", NM, A $750.00

Swift's Pride Soap & Washing Powder, jigsaw puzzle, 1910, Line Up! Bright & Early..., girl at clothesline, 15x10", EX.**$75.00**

Swiss Miss, doll, Swiss Miss, stuffed cloth w/vinyl face & yel yarn hair, EX, minimum value...**$25.00**

Tagamet, figure, Tagamet Tommy, vinyl, 1988, 5", NM, C17.**$30.00**

Tastee Freeze, doll, Miss Tastee Freeze, 1950s, hard plastic, 7", NM...**$20.00**

Texaco, doll, Texaco Cheerleader, 1973, 11", NRFB, from $100 to...**$125.00**

Texaco, toy tanker, battery-op, MIB, T2, from $150 to .**$200.00**

Texaco, tanker truck, Buddy L, 1950s, 25", NMIB, from $350.00 to $450.00. (Photo courtesy Dunbar Gallery)

Tip Top Bread, punch-out truck, EX, T2 ....**$35.00**

Trix Cereal, doll, Trix rabbit, vinyl, NM, J6.....................**$65.00**

Victrola, jigsaw puzzle, 1922, EX, $75.00.
(Photo courtesy Donald Friedman)

Vlasic Pickles, doll, Stork, Trudy Toys, 1989, fluffy wht fur w/glasses & bow tie, 22", NM.....................................**$40.00**

Walgreens, truck, Marx, metal, wht w/bl detail, blk tires, rear door opens, 20", G, A...**$300.00**

Westinghouse Mazda Lamps, masks, Toonerville Folks, 1920s, cb, Katrinka, Mickey, Skipper & Tomboy, set of 4, EX, A...**$100.00**

Wrangler, doll, Cody or Missy, Ertl, 1982, 11½", MIB, ea.**$55.00**

Advertising Signs, Ads, and Displays

A common advertising ploy used as far back as the late 1900s and still effective today is to catch the eye of the potential consumer with illustrations of well-known celebrities or popular fictional characters. Nowadays, with the intense passion character-collectibles buffs pour into their hobby, searching for these advertising items is a natural extension of their enthusiasm, adding even more diversity to an already multi-faceted collecting field.

Aurora's Godzilla & King Kong Model Kits, poster, 1960s, color glossy, The Invasion Is On!, 11x22", VG+, A.........**$660.00**

Beverly Hillbillies for Kellogg's Corn Flakes, display, Dern Tootin' We Serve Breakfast!, diecut cb, 1964, 10", EX.............**$250.00**

Buck Rogers Onward School Supplies, color weekend newspaper ad, EX, C10..**$35.00**

Bunny Tinker for Easter, flyer, full color, 8x10", EX, from $30 to **$40.00**

Casper & Other Harvey Cartoon Characters, display, ca 1960, cb stand-up, lg diecut Casper over TV screen, 21x16", EX, A3 ....**$500.00**

Chiquita Banded Bananas, poster, United Fruit Co, 1948, paper, image of mascot singing w/banana quartet, 14x14", NM **$100.00**

Family Affair, mobile display, Emenee, 1971, unused, M, A .**$100.00**

Felix Adler for Kellogg's Sugar Smacks, newsprint proof, A Dish You Shouldn't Miss & image, 1953, 14" L, EX **$25.00**

Fonz 'Sit On It' Pin-Back Buttons, display box, Pinning Co, 1970s, box designed like brick wall w/graffiti, VG, J5..**$75.00**

Frosty O's Bear, display, diecut cb, 1959, 39", EX..........**$325.00**

Fun on Wheels Roll a Toys, display, features Disney characters, tin on wood base, electric, 17x12", EX, A, $550.00.

Gene Autry Boots, sign, 1940s, paper, pictures Gene on Champion & head shot w/text in between, 4x13", VG+, A3.........$75.00

Gene Autry Melody Ranch Radio Program, display, 1930s, cb stand-up, Autry on rearing Champion, belt fr, 12x10", EX, A3 ....$175.00

General Mills, Boo Berry ad figure, 1960s, bl & wht vinyl, 8", EX, A $180.00

General Mills, Count Chocula ad figure, 1960s, brn vinyl, 8", EX, A $160.00

General Mills, Frankenberry ad figure, 1960s, pk & orange vinyl, 8", EX, A $190.00

Green Hornet Bike Badge, display, Burry's, 1966, 3-D plastic diecut w/raised images, 48x34", NM, T2, from $3,000 to $4,000.00

Green Hornet Signal Ray, display, Colorforms, 1966, diecut cb, NM, T2 ....$200.00

Hopalong Cassidy for Post Cereals, sign, advertises Hopalong Cassidy trading cards, paper, 1950-51, 30", EX, B10 ....$300.00

Hopalong Cassidy TV Show, flyer, promotion for show on WHNC TV, also advertising Bond & Hoppy Bread labels, EX, V1 ....$48.00

Lone Ranger Toys, Spiegel catalog ad, 1940, full color, EX, from $50 to $75.00

Marvel Comics, store poster, 1980, Marvel Comics On Sale Here, Capt America in corner, red & yel on blk, 15x11", EX, J5 ....$45.00

Mr T, standee, Quaker Cereal, 1980s, cb, Hey Kids...Try My Cereal, life-sz, EX, A $220.00

Post Toasties Rings, ad, 1949, paper, features 16 of 24 premium rings, 8x11", NM, A $150.00

Raggedy Ann & Andy, ad, All 4 Full-Color Art Prints Yours For Only $1, paper, EX $5.00

Raggedy Ann & Andy, ad, Melmac & Stainless by Oneida, shows dolls & dinnerware w/their image, paper, EX ..$12.00

Raggedy Ann and Andy by Knickerbocker, ad, KTC, 1977, Who Will Capture Your Child's Love As They Captured Yours?... and shows dolls, EX, $15.00. (Photo courtesy Kim Avery)

Howdy Doody Fudge Bar, sign, AAA Sign Co., 1980s reproduction, Howdy & product on yellow background, tin, NM, from $20.00 to $35.00. (Photo courtesy Jack Koch)

Junior Tinkertoy, display, motorized, 1935, EX, from $100 to..$125.00

King Features Key Chain Lockets 10¢, display, 1952, cb, featuring comic strips & 12 different characters on lockets, EX, A $165.00

Li'l Abner's Post Cereal Contest, display, Name Honest Abe's Sweetheart, $50,000 in Prizes, diecut cb, 1957, 65", EX $350.00

Lone Ranger Frontier Town, newspaper ad, 1948, full color, EX, from $35 to.........$55.00

Roy Rogers, display, 1950s, cb standup, Roy on Trigger under Double R Ranch gate, signed Happy Trails..., 20x14", EX .$350.00

Roy Rogers Arcade Cards, display sign, ca 1940, features 3 cards w/1¢ symbols & instructions to operate machine, EX, A3 ....$100.00

Roy Rogers for Quaker Oats, display, Roy Rogers Says: I Was Raised on..., diecut cb, 1949-50, 6-ft, NM $1,500.00

Roy Rogers for Quaker Oats, poster, Boys! Girls! Mothers! Get Your Roy Rogers Autographed Cup..., 22", NM......$150.00

Sgt Preston for Quaker Sugar Puffs, newsprint proof, 1957, 21", EX.........$25.00

Sgt Preston's Yukon Trail Cut-Outs, display, Quaker Puffed Wheat, 1940s, cb, Hurry!..., 15x11x4", VG (cb slip case), J5 ....$425.00

Straight Arrow for Nabisco Shredded Wheat, display, National Biscuit Co, 1949-52, diecut cb, 66", NM.............$1,500.00

Straight Arrow Indian & Cowboy Suit, advertisement, EX, C10 ....$80.00
Super Heroes Puffy Stickers, display, Edco, 1977, features Batman characters w/Aquaman & Superman, complete, M, A $85.00
Terrytoon Characters Hankies, display, 1950s, cb gatefold, holds 6 hankies illus w/cartoon characters, scarce, EX+, A3...$275.00
Three Stooges Flasher Rings, display card, 1960s, NM, A ..$40.00
Tinker Toys, ad, Make Young Folks Happy, Keep Happy Folks Young, full color, 1927, EX................................$15.00
Tinker Toys & Christmas, ad, full color, 1927, EX...........$15.00

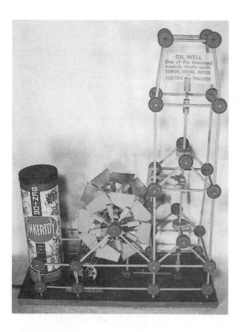

Tinkertoy Oil Well, display, motorized, complete with Senior Tinkertoy container, NM, from $250.00 to $400.00. (Photo courtesy Anne Lewis/Craig Strange)

Tinkertoy Windmill, display, motorized, EX, from $150 to .$200.00
Tom Corbett Space Cadet Rocket-Lite, display, litho cb w/6 plastic pin-on lites, 1950, 13", NM, A.....................$765.00

Woody Woodpecker Time, clock display, Walter Lantz, 1959, Woody pointing to sign on tree, brass hook for clock, easel-back, 20x14", NM, A, $465.00.

Aeronautical

Toy manufacturers seemed to take the cautious approach toward testing the waters with aeronautical toys, and it was well into the second decade of the 20th century before some of the European toy makers took the initiative. The earlier models were bulky and basically inert, but by the '50s, Japanese manufacturers were turning out battery-operated replicas with wonderful details that advanced with whirling motors and flashing lights.

See also Battery Operated; Cast Iron, Airplanes; Model Kits; Windups, Friction, and Other Mechanicals.

Air France Croix De Sud, Joustra, w/up w/battery-op fuselage light, 6-prop, litho tin, 23½" W, rare, NM (NM box), A $2,400.00

Airplane, Girard, clockwork, single-prop, gray-painted tin with yellow prop and disk wheels, 10" wingspan, NMIB, A, $600.00.

Airplane, Tippco, clockwork, single-prop, litho tin w/celluloid tail fin & landing gear, silver & blk, 10" W, NMIB, A...$1,900.00
American Airlines, Japan, battery-op, 4-prop, litho tin w/clear plastic passenger compartment & cockpit, 19" W, EX, A...$250.00
American Airlines DC-7, Linemar, 1950s, battery-op, 4-prop, litho tin, several actions, 19" W, NM.....................$400.00
American Airlines Electra, Linemar, 1950s, battery-op, 4-prop, litho tin, several actions, 19½" W, NM...................$400.00
Amphibian Airplane, Bing, clockwork, 2 overhead engines, pnt tin, silver & brn, 16" W, NM, A $2,000.00
Army Bomber, gear activates when pulled, 3-prop, pressed steel w/paper litho images of pilot & crew, 25" W, G, A.$400.00
Army Helicopter, Japan, friction, litho tin, 6½", MIB, from $75 to $100.00

Army Scout Plane, Steelcraft, single-prop, pressed steel, 22" W, rstr, A..$250.00

Attack Bomber, Hubley #326, 2-prop, red plastic, w/retractable landing gear, 8" W, NM (EX box), A...................$1,650.00

B-5 British Bomber, Arnold, w/up, 2-prop, advances w/sparks, 4½" L, MIB, A..$200.00

BAC Vickers VC-10, mk BOAC, Japan, 1950s, friction, litho tin, 16" W, NMIB, D10..............................$300.00

Beechraft Skyline, TN, battery-op, single-prop, litho tin, 13" W, NM (EX box), A $150.00

Biplane, single-prop, pnt wood, cream w/orange trim, star decals, 11", G, A...$225.00

Black Knight BK-02, friction, litho tin, 13" L, NMIB, A .$225.00

Boeing B-50 Superfortress, Y, battery-operated, four-prop, lithographed tin, advances with spinning props and lights, 19" wingspan, EX (G box), A, $500.00.

Boeing 727, MT, 1960s, 4-prop, battery-op, litho tin, 12½" L, EX $300.00

Bomber D-O LAF, Germany, clockwork, single-prop, litho tin w/compo pilot, 14½" W, EX, A $775.00

Bristol 188 Jet, Marx, 1960s, battery-op, tin & plastic, 9" W, EX $185.00

Comet Jetliner, Japan, friction, litho tin w/red plastic window, inserts for sparking action, 7" W, EX (VG box), A.$200.00

Concorde Super Sonic, battery-op, 21", MIB, L4 ....$225.00

Cragstan Biplane, TN, battery-op, single-prop, litho tin w/plastic prop, 11½" WS, NM (EX box), A.....................$600.00

Cragstan Police Patrol Plane, remote control w/automatic steering & blinking lights, 15½", NMIB, A....................$175.00

Cragstan 7F7 US Navy Biplane, TN, 1950s, battery-op, litho tin, 11½", W, EX...$400.00

Curtiss Jenny Biplane Trainer, S&E, friction, single-prop, 14" W, NM, A..$175.00

Curtiss Jenny Trainer, S&E, friction, single-prop, pnt tin, red, 14" W, MIB, A..$300.00

Dareplane Wingwalker Stunt Set, Mattel, 1978, MIB (sealed), J6..$175.00

Douglas AD-1, Japan, friction, single-prop, litho tin, 7½" W, NM (G box), A...$175.00

Dowae Stunt Plane, Dowae, 1927, wood & cb, complete w/landing gear & application for pilot's certificate, 10" L, NMIB, A..$175.00

EPL-11 Zeppelin, litho tin w/celluloid props, 9½", EX, A $1,100.00

F-101A Voodoo Jet, battery-op, EX, L4........................$250.00

FA-059 Fighter Plane, TN, 1950s, battery-op, litho tin, 13" W, EX $350.00

Fanny Passenger Airliner, France, w/up w/battery-op lights, 4-prop, tin w/cut-out windows, red & silver, 20" W, EX+, A..$525.00

Fighter Plane, Marx, 1960s, remote control, single-prop, litho tin, 7" W, EX...$125.00

Flying Dutchman, Arnold, clockwork, 4-prop, litho tin, 11½" W, EX, A..$150.00

Flying Tiger Line, battery-op, litho tin, NMIB, L4.........$500.00

Flying Wonder, Arnold, litho tin, 10" W, M (worn box) ..$175.00

Fokker Tri-Wing Model, stick & sheet construction w/simulated oil smears, mud on tires, etc, red & wht, 40x48" W, EX, A..$360.00

Grumman Navy Couger Fighter Jet, battery-op, MIB, L4..$450.00

Hi-Wing Monoplane, Wyandotte, pressed steel w/wood wheels, 18" W, NM, A..$400.00

Highway Patrol Helicopter, TN, tin, 16", EX $100.00

Ikarus Airplane, litho tin w/wire supported paper wings, 18" W, NM, A..$3,000.00

Japan Airlines, ATC, friction, 4-prop, litho tin w/rubber wheels, 21½" L, NM, A...$100.00

KLM DC7-C, Raise Up of Rotterdam Holland, travel agency model, solid cast, 28x31 W, EX, A $190.00

Lufthansa Radiant 5600 Passenger Plane, Schuco, 1955, battery-op, 4-prop, tin, see-through cockpit w/crew, 17", EX, A ...$700.00

Martin Bomber, TN, clockwork, litho tin w/chrome-finished tri-motors & propellers, 14" L, NM, A $1,900.00

Military Combat Plane Assembly Kit, Lehmann, w/up, litho tin camoflauge w/iron cross mk, 6" W, NMIB, A..........$300.00

Military Jet Plane, Marx, 1960s, marked US Air Force, battery-operated, lithographed tin, 14½" wingspan, NMIB, $200.00. (Photo courtesy Don Hultzman)

Monocoupe, JDN, friction, single-prop, litho tin, 4" W, EX, A $350.00

Monocoupe, Kingsbury, clockwork, pnt pressed steel, silver w/bl prop & red disk wheels, 10" W, VG, A...................$150.00

Monoplane, Guntherman, clockwork, litho tin, 7½" W, EX,
A $250.00
Navy Helicopter, Japan, friction, litho tin, 11", MIB, from $150
to $200.00

Northwest Airlines, Asahitoy, friction, lithographed tin, 19" wingspan, NMIB, $600.00.

Northwest Airlines, Cragstan, friction, 4-prop, litho tin, side door
opens to reveal flight attendant, 23½" W, EX, A......$175.00
Pan American Vertol Helicopter, battery-op, MIB, L4......$165.00
Pan American World Airways, TN, 1950s, battery-op, 4-prop,
litho tin, 19" W, EX $275.00
Railcar Plane, Marklin, pnt tin, remove wings for transport on
railcar, 8", VG, A..$60.00

Rapid-Fire Tri-Motor, Keystone, gear activates when pulled, three-prop, pressed steel, 24" wingspan, EX, A, $1,700.00.

Right Plane, Schiebles, single-prop, pressed steel w/paper litho
image of pilot & passengers, 27½" W, EX, A $650.00
Sabena Helicopter, Arnold, crank action, litho tin, 9", EX (worn
box), A $125.00

Sea Wolf Atomic Submarine, Sutcliffe, tin, 10", EX (EX box),
A $150.00

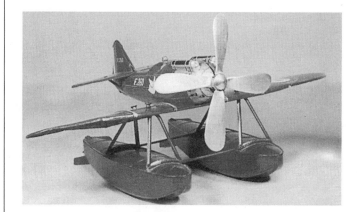

Seaplane with Pontoon, JEP, 1930s, clockwork, single-prop, red with blue and silver striping, 19" wingspan, EX, A, $1,650.00.

Shenandoah Dirigible, litho tin w/celluloid props, 7", VG,
A $650.00
Sky Cruiser Transport Plane, Marx, clockwork, 4-prop, litho tin,
18" W, MIB, A $500.00
Spirit of America Monocoupe, mk PNX 211 on tail, clockwork,
single-prop, litho tin, 6½" W, NM, A.................$1,200.00
Spirit of St Louis, clockwork, single-prop, pnt pressed steel, sil-
ver w/red detail, 13" W, VG, A...............................$275.00
Spirit of St Louis, HTC, mk NX-211 on wing, friction, litho tin,
yel w/blk & red detail, foldable wings, 12" W, EX, A.$350.00
Spirit of St Louis, Metalcraft #800, 1928, metal, gr, assembled,
9x11½" W, EX+, A $50.00
Spirit of St Louis, see also Building Blocks & Construction Toys
Stuka Dive Bomber (WWI Era), rubber band powered, balsa &
silkspan, w/pilot & gunners, 33" W, A $165.00
Top-Wing, Germany, w/up, 3-prop, tin, red & silver, 20" W,
VG, A $425.00
TWA Passenger Jet, TN, battery-op, litho tin & plastic, 14" W,
NM, A $100.00
US Air Force/Navy Helicopter, TN, friction, litho tin, advances
w/spinning props, 10" L, NM (EX box), A $175.00

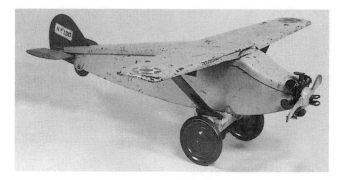

US Mail Plane, Steelcraft, beige fuselage with red wings, prop and tail, 22½" wingspan, EX, A, $400.00.

US Airmail Plane, Keystone, single-prop, pnt pressed steel, olive & red, 24" W, G, A $400.00

US Army Bomber, Marx, w/up, 2-prop, litho tin, 18" W, EX, A..$200.00

US Mail Plane, Steelcraft, mk NY-130 on tail fin, single-prop, gray w/red tail fin & disk wheels, 22½" W, EX, A ..$350.00

USAF F-88 Jet Fighter, friction, litho tin, 9½", scarce, MIB, A $125.00

USAF Grumman F-111 Jet Fighter, TN, battery-op, tin & plastic, advances w/sound, 15½" L, NM (EX box), A ...$125.00

Westland G-AMHK Helicopter, Alps, battery-op, litho tin, w/pilot, 14", EX, A $100.00

XF-160 Mystery Action Plane, battery-op, MIB, L4.......$375.00

Zeppelin w/Airplanes, Akron Toys, pressed steel w/gold crackle finish, 4 tin airplanes hang from side supports, 25", EX $1,300.00

Automobiles and Other Vehicle Replicas

Listed here are the model vehicles (most of which were made in Japan during the 1950s and '60s) that were designed to realistically represent the muscle cars, station wagons, convertibles, budget models, and luxury cars that were actually being shown concurrently on showroom floors and dealers' lots all over the country. Most were made of tin, many were friction powered, some were battery operated. In our descriptions, all are tin unless noted otherwise.

When at all possible, we've listed the toys by the names assigned to them by the manufacturer, just as they appear on the original boxes. Because of this, you'll find some of the same models listed by slightly different names. All vehicles are painted or painted and lithographed tin unless noted.

For more information we recommend *The Golden Age of Automotive Toys, 1925–1941*, by Ken Hutchison and Greg Johnson (Collector Books).

Advisors: Kerry and Judy Irvin (K5).

See also Promotional Cars; specific manufacturers.

Auto-Top Ferrari Convertible, 1960s, Bandai, battery-op, 11", rare, EX $900.00

BMW Convertible, Shuco #2002/Germany, w/up, wht, 5½", EX, A..$65.00

Buick, KO, friction, bl w/chrome detail, 10½", EX (EX box mk New Buick) $250.00

Buick, MSK, friction & battery-op, red w/chrome detail, 6½", NMIB, A $125.00

Buick Riviera Giant Door-Matic Car, Japan, friction, bl w/chrome detail, detachable roof, 11", EX (EX box), A $450.00

Cadallic, 1960, Bandai, friction, bl w/chrome detail, 11½", M, A $265.00

Cadillac, 1950, Bandai, friction, wht w/chrome detail, 11½", NM, A $250.00

Cadillac, 1952, Alps, friction, blk 2-door w/chrome detail, red interior, 11", NMIB.......................$900.00

Cadillac, 1959, Bandai, Model Auto Series, gold w/chrome detail, MIB.......................................$350.00

Cadillac, Marusan, friction, turquoise with chrome detail, rare, MIB, $1,700.00. (Photo courtesy John Turney)

Cadillac, 1962, Yonezawa, friction, lt bl w/gr & wht interior, rare color, 14", NM (EX box)...................$600.00

Cadillac, 1967, Ichiko, friction, red w/chrome & red hubs, w/driver, 28", G+......................................$500.00

Chevrolet Corvair Sedan, NGS, friction, red w/chrome detail, 8", NM (NM box), A $200.00

Chevrolet, Linemar, 1954, friction, tan with black top, chrome detail, 11", NM, A, $1,300.00; Ford Delivery Wagon, Japan, friction, blue with Flowers for Gracious Living decal, 12", MIB, A, $2,100.00.

Chevy Corvette, 1965, Bandai, friction, cream, 8", EX..$150.00

Chevy Corvette, 1968, Taiyo, battery-op, red w/chrome detail, 10", EX..$125.00

Chrysler Airflow X, KT, w/up, red w/chrome detail, advances w/nonfall action, 5", EX+ (VG box), A..................$400.00

Chrysler Imperial Hardtop Sedan, Cragstan, friction, red w/blk top, chrome detail, rear spare, 8", NM (NM box) ...$200.00

Citroen, Bandai, friction, red with cream top, chrome detail, 12", NM, A, $500.00.

Datsun Fair Lady Z, Ichiko, friction, bright yel w/chrome trim, 18", NM (EX box) $250.00

DeSoto, Asahi, friction, red w/chrome detail, 8", EX (EX box mk New DeSoto), A.....................................$175.00

Dodge Sedan, 1959, TN, friction, red w/wht top, chrome detail, fancy hubs, 9", EX.....................................$325.00

Edsel Station Wagon, TN, friction, blk & red w/wht trim, opening rear gate, 10½", NM.....................................$500.00

Elektro Mercedes 230 SL, 1965, Schuco, battery-op, wht w/red interior, chrome detail, 10½", MIB, A $1,500.00

Fiat Convertible, Usagai, friction, lt metallic bl w/chrome detail, 6", NM (EX box), A.....................................$175.00

Fiat Sedan, Usagai, friction, lt bl w/chrome detail, 6", NM (EX box), A.....................................$175.00

Firebird III, Cragstan/Alps, 1950s, 11½", EX.....................$500.00

Ford Ambulance, Bandai, wht w/lg red cross on top, 2 red lights on front fenders, chrome detail, 11¾", EX, A $225.00

Ford Crown Victoria, 1956, Yonezawa, friction, wht over red w/bl roof, chrome detail, 12", MIB $1,500.00

Ford Custom Ranch Wagon, 1955, Bandai, friction, red w/black top, chrome detail, 11½", MIB $375.00

Ford Fairlane, 1956, SAN, friction, scarce chrome version, 13", EX (G box).....................................$750.00

Ford Fairlane 500 Skyliner, Cragstan, remote control, bl & wht w/chrome detail, 11", VG (VG box).......................$350.00

Ford Florist's Van, Bandai, turq w/colorful advertising graphics, opening rear door, 12", VG+, A.............................$135.00

Ford Mustang Coupe, 1965, Bandai, friction, metallic bl w/blk top, chrome detail, 8", NM $200.00

Ford Skyliner, 1958, TN, battery-op, red w/chrome detail, detractable roof, NMIB.....................................$300.00

Ford Station Wagon, 1960, Japan, friction, yel over blk w/Standard Fresh Coffee advertising, 11½", MIB............$2,400.00

Ford Thunderbird Convertible, 1960s, Bandai, battery-op, red w/chrome detail, w/driver & opening door, 11", rare, EX.$200.00

House Trailer & Station Wagon, SSS Toys, friction, red car, wht trailer w/red detail, MIB..................................$225.00

Indianapolis Champion #98 Racer, ET/Japan, litho tin, wht w/red flames, blk rubber tires, w/driver, 18½", VG+, A $1,150.00

Isetta, Bandai, friction, red & cream, 6½", MIB.............$475.00

Jaguar, Distler, battery-op lights, litho tin, bl w/silver trim, blk rubber tires w/silver hubs, 8", EX, A $120.00

Jaguar, 1950s, MT, friction, red w/blk top, chrome detail, 7½", MIB, A.....................................$250.00

Jaguar Coupe, Bandai, friction, red w/chrome detail, blk top, 9", NM (EX box).....................................$675.00

Jaguar Coupe, Japan, friction, cream with black top, chrome detail, 9½", NM (EX box), A, $275.00.

Jaguar E-Type, TT, friction, red w/chrome detail, 11", NM (NM box).....................................$475.00

Lincoln & House Trailer, Miller Ironson, cream diecast car w/bl top, aluminum trailer w/bl trim, 40" overall, NMIB, A.....$3,400.00

Mercedes Benz 300 SE, battery-op, M, L4 ....$150.00

Mercedes 220 S, Schuco, w/up, red w/wht top, chrome detail, 5", EX (VG box), A.....................................$125.00

Ford Two-Door Hardtop, Ichiko, 1957, friction, blue with white top, chrome detail, 9½", VG (VG box), A, $350.00.

Mercedes 230 SL, Alps, battery-operated, red with black top, chrome detail, advances with lights, 10½", M (EX box), A, $400.00.

MG II Convertible, Japan, friction, yel w/chrome detail, mounted rear spare, 8", EX (worn box), A..............$250.00

MG Magnette Mark III Convertible, Japan, friction, 8", EX (EX box), A..$325.00

Oldsmobile Convertible, 1952, Y, friction, red w/chrome detail, 10", EX (EX box)..$500.00

Oldsmobile Toronado, 1966, Bandai, battery-op, red w/blk tires, 11", NM...$200.00

Oldsmobile 98, Ichiko, friction, 2-tone bl w/chrome detail, 8½", NM (EX box), A $300.00

Opal, Y, friction, dark blue with red top, chrome detail, 11½", NM, A, $700.00.

Orion, TM, gr w/chrome detail, blk rubber tires w/chrome hubs, 8¾", MIB, A...$125.00

Packard Hawk Convertible, 1957, Schuco, battery-op, 10½", EX (VG box)..$900.00

Packard Sedan, Alps, friction, red with chrome detail, 16½", NM, A, $3,000.00.

Packard 52, Japan, friction, red w/bright bl tires, chrome detail, 7", EX (EX box), A...................................$150.00

Plymouth Convertible, 1959, friction, red w/wht tail fins, chrome detail, 11", EX...$600.00

Porsche, Bandai, battery-op, cream w/chrome detail, features opening doors, w/driver, 10", NM (EX box)............$200.00

Rambler Sedan, 1950s, Y, friction, brn w/wht top, working wipers, 8", M...$75.00

Renault Floride, Ichiko, friction, red w/blk top, chrome detail, 8", EX (EX box)..$150.00

Rolls Royce Silver Cloud, Bandai, friction, bl w/wht top, chrome detail, 12", scarce, NM (EX box) $350.00

Shasta Travel Trailer, Fleet Line, 1950s, wht & yel w/plastic windows, 11½", scarce, NM (EX box) $400.00

Toyota 2000 GT, Ichiko, friction, red w/chrome detail, 16", NM, A $350.00

Vauxhall Town Coupe, Minic, w/up, gr w/chrome detail, 5", NM (NM box), A...$150.00

Volkswagen Bug, 1963, Bandai, friction, bl w/chrome detail, 8", NM (EX box)...$150.00

Volkswagen Pickup Truck, Bandai, battery-op w/remote control, bl w/VW hubs on blk rubber tires, 8", NMIB, A $300.00

Volvo Amazon Sedan, Bandai, friction, gr w/wht top, chrome detail, 8¼", EX+, A.................................$325.00

Banks

The impact of condition on the value of a bank cannot be overrated. Cast iron banks in near-mint condition with very little paint wear and all original parts are seldom found and might bring twice as much (if the bank is especially rare, up to five times as much) as one in average, very good original condition with no restoration and no repairs. Overpainting and replacement parts (even screws) have a very negative effect on value. Mechanicals dominate the market, and some of the hard-to-find banks in outstanding, near-mint condition may exceed $20,000.00! (Here are a few examples: Girl Skipping Rope, Calamity, and Mikado.) Modern mechanical banks are also emerging on the collectibles market, including Book of Knowledge and James D. Capron, which are reproductions with full inscriptions stating that the piece is a replica of the original. Still banks are widely collected as well, with more than 3,000 varieties having been documented. Beware of unmarked modern reproductions.

For more information we recommend *The Dictionary of Still Banks* by Long and Pitman; *The Penny Bank Book* by Moore; *The Bank Book* by Norman; and *Penny Lane* by Davidson. For information on porcelain and ceramic banks we recommend *Collector's Guide to Banks* by Beverly and Jim Mangus and *Ceramic Coin Banks* by Tom and Loretta Stoddard.

Advisors: Larry Egelhoff (E1) still banks; Dan Iannotti (I3), modern mechanicals; and Diane Patalano (P8).

See also Advertising; Battery-Operated; Character, TV, and Movie Collectibles; Disney; Diecast Collector Banks; Reynolds Banks; Rock 'n Roll; Santa; Western.

MECHANICAL BANKS

Afghanistan Bank, Mechanical Novelty Works, EX, A...$4,950.00

Always Did 'Spise a Mule (Boy on Bench), EX, A......$3,850.00

Always Did 'Spise a Mule (Jockey), Book of Knowledge, NM, I3..$325.00

Always Did 'Spise a Mule (Jockey), J&E Stevens, EX, A..$1,610.00

Artillery Bank, Book of Knowledge, NM, I3 ....$385.00

Artillery Bank, J&E Stevens, G+, A............................$550.00

Auto, John Wright, limited edition of 250, NM, I3 ....$725.00

Bad Accident, J&E Stevens, G $1,400.00

Bad Accident, James Capron, M, I3............................$995.00

Barking Dog, National Co of Boston, wood & tin, EX, A...$1,980.00

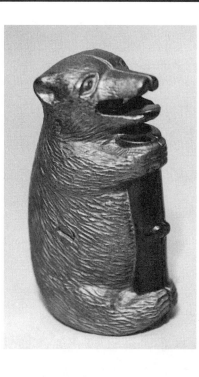

Bear and Tree Stump, gold-painted cast iron, EX, D10, $875.00.
(Photo courtesy Dunbar Gallery)

Cabin Bank, J&E Stevens, NM, A $1,430.00
Calamity Bank, J&E Stevens, Fair, A.......................$12,100.00
Cat & Mouse, Book of Knowledge, M, I3 ....$475.00
Chief Big Moon, J&E Stevens, EX, A $4,400.00
Chief Big Moon, J&E Stevens, G, A $500.00
Clown on Globe, J&E Stevens, VG, A $2,750.00
Clown on Globe, James Capron, M, I3.......................$1,100.00
Columbian Magic Savings, Introduction Co, ca 1892, worn
    pnt..$380.00
Creedmoor Bank, J&E Stevens, w/variations, NM, A...$1,210.00
Dapper Dan, litho tin, EX $240.00
Darktown Battery, J&E Stevens, EX, A $5,000.00
Dentist Bank, Book of Knowledge, NM, I3 ....$275.00
Dog w/Spring Jaw, Germany, pnt wht metal, NM, A .$7,150.00
Eagle & Eaglets, Book of Knowledge, M, I3...................$450.00
Eagle & Eaglets, J&E Stevens, G, from $470 to.............$850.00
Elephant, James Capron, M, I3 ....$285.00
Elephant w/Howdah (Pull Tail), Hubley, VG, from $300
    to...$350.00
Elephant w/Three Stars, unknown mfg, ca 1884, NM, A ..$990.00

Betsy Ross, Davidson/Imswiller, limited edition of 300, bl or red
    dress, M, I3, ea $975.00
Bill E Grin, pnt aluminum, EX....................................$260.00
Bird on Roof, J&E Stevens, EX....................................$1,850.00
Bowler's Strike, Richards/Utexqual, scarce, M, I3 ....$850.00
Boy on Trapeze, Book of Knowledge, NM, I3.................$525.00
Boy on Trapeze, J Barton & Smith, EX $3,080.00
Boy Scout Camp, J&E Stevens, VG, A $1,150.00
Boy Stealing Watermelon, Kyser & Rex, NM, A........$3,520.00
Bull Dog Bank, J&E Stevens, G+, A $850.00
Bull Dog Bank, J&E Stevens, NM, A $2,420.00
Butting Ram (Man Thumbs Nose), EX $5,800.00
Cabin Bank, Book of Knowledge, NM, I3 ....$350.00
Cabin Bank, J&E Stevens, EX, A $575.00

Ferris Wheel, Hubley, EX, A, $5,000.00.

Frog Bank (Two Frogs), J&E Stevens, Fair, A $635.00
Frog Bank (Two Frogs), J&E Stevens, NM, A $5,280.00
Frog Bank (Two Frogs), James Capron, NM, I3 ....$625.00
Frog on Round Base, J&E Stevens, VG $800.00
Girl in Victorian Chair, WS Reed, EX, A....................$6,600.00
Hall's Excelsior, J&E Stevens, VG+, A $385.00
Hall's Liliput, J&E Stevens, NM, A............................$1,320.00
Harold Lloyd, Germany, tin, EX, A $1,100.00
Hen & Chick, J&E Stevens, EX $3,200.00
Horse Race, J&E Stevens, straight base, NM, A.......$11,550.00
Humpty Dumpty, Book of Knowledge, M, I3................$415.00
Humpty Dumpty, Shepard Hardware, G........................$650.00
Independence Hall Tower, Enterprise Mfg, semi-mechanical,
    gold, red & brn, 9½", NM, A $9,900.00
Indian Shooting Bear, Book of Knowledge, M, I3 ....$425.00
Indian Shooting Bear, J&E Stevens, EX, A................$2,600.00

Elephant with Howdah, Hubley, EX, $450.00.
(Photo courtesy Dunbar Gallery)

Jolly N Bank, England, all blk w/wht-accented hair & lips, 6½",
    G, A $145.00
Jolly N Bank, England, red bow tie, 6½", EX, A $450.00
Jolly N Bank, England, yel bow tie, 6½", G, A...............$275.00
Jolly N Bank, Harper, wht collar w/bl bow tie, 4½", G+, A..$95.00
Jonah & the Whale, Shepard Hardware, NM, A $770.00
Jumbo on Wheels, J&E Stevens, EX, A.......................$1,320.00
Leap Frog, Book of Knowledge, MIB, I3 ....$450.00
Leap Frog, Shepard Hardware, NM, A $4,620.00

Leap Frog, Shepard Hardware, VG+, $1,850.00.
(Photo courtesy Dunbar Gallery)

Lion & Monkeys, James Capron, M, I3 ....$1,150.00
Lion & Monkeys, Kyser & Rex, NM, A $3,520.00
Lion & Monkeys, Kyser & Rex, VG...........................$1,100.00
Little Jocko Musical Savings Bank, Strauss, wht-metal figure on
    litho tin base, EX, A $2,640.00
Magic Bank, J&E Stevens, EX, A $3,080.00
Magic Bank, James Capron, M, I3 ....$975.00
Magician Bank, Book of Knowledge, M, I3 ....$425.00
Magician Bank, J&E Stevens, EX, A $5,500.00
Mammy & Child, Kyser & Rex, NM, A $10,450.00

Monkey Bank, Hubley, NM, $2,000.00.
(Photo courtesy Dunbar Gallery)

Mason Bank, Shepard Hardware, EX, A......................$4,800.00
Merry-Go-Round, Kyser & Rex, 4⅝", VG...................$400.00
Milking Cow, Book of Knowledge, NM, I3 ....$350.00
Monkey & Coconut, J&E Stevens, G $700.00
Monkey Bank, James Capron, NM, I3 ....$375.00
Mosque, Judd, EX $2,150.00
Motor Bank, Kyser & Rex, VG.................................$3,450.00
Mule Entering Barn, J&E Stevens, EX $1,900.00
Mule Entering Barn, James Capron, M, I3 ....$825.00
Multiplying Bank, J&E Stevens, NM, A $12,100.00
New Bank, J&E Stevens, EX, A.................................$3,300.00
Novelty Bank, J&E Stevens, G, A $685.00
Novelty Bank, J&E Stevens, NM, A $4,180.00
Organ Bank (Boy & Girl), Kyser & Rex, NM, A........$4,440.00
Organ Bank (Cat & Dog), Kyser & Rex, NM, A........$3,850.00

Owl (Turns Head), J&E Stevens, brown with yellow eyes, EX, $700.00.
(Photo courtesy Dunbar Gallery)

Owl (Turns Head), J&E Stevens, wht, glass eyes, EX, A ..$2,420.00
Paddy & the Pig, Book of Knowledge, M, I3 ....$385.00
Paddy & the Pig, J&E Stevens, EX, A $3,300.00
Penny Pineapple, commemorates Hawaii 50th state, Wilton,
    NM, I3 ....$545.00
Pig in Highchair, J&E Stevens, NM, A.......................$1,540.00
Professor Pug Frog, James Capron, M, I3 ....$1,100.00
Punch & Judy, Book of Knowledge, M, I3 ....$375.00
Punch & Judy, Book of Knowledge, MIB, I3 ....$450.00
Punch & Judy, Shepard Hardware, NM, A $6,050.00
Race Course Runners, James Capron, EX, I3 ....$675.00
Royal Trick Elephant, att to German maker, ca 1900, litho tin,
    NM, A $3,850.00
Santa Claus Bank, Shepard Hardware, EX, A $2,750.00
Speaking Dog, Shepard Hardware, EX, A $3,850.00
Speaking Dog, Shepard Hardware, G, A......................$600.00
Stump Speaker, Shepard Hardware, VG, A $1,150.00
Tammany Bank, J&E Stevens, VG, A $260.00
Teddy & the Bear, Book of Knowledge, NM, I3............$375.00

Teddy & the Bear, J&E Stevens, NM, A $8,250.00
Toad on Stump, J&E Stevens, NM...............................$825.00
Trick Dog, James Capron, NM, I3 ....$625.00
Trick Pony, Book of Knowledge, NM, I3........................$375.00

Trick Pony, Shepard Hardware, EX, $3,100.00.
(Photo courtesy Dunbar Gallery)

Uncle Bugs, Warner Bros, M, I3 ....$215.00
Uncle Remus, Book of Knowledge, M, I3 ....$475.00

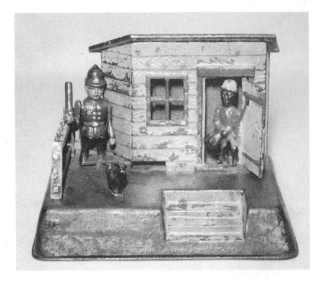

Uncle Remus, Kyser and Rex, NM, $2,000.00.
(Photo courtesy Dunbar Gallery)

Uncle Sam, Book of Knowledge, M, I3...........................$450.00
Uncle Sam, Shepard Hardware, EX, A.........................$1,500.00
US & Spain, Book of Knowledge, M, I3 ....$375.00
US & Spain, J&E Stevens, EX.......................................$550.00
William Tell, J&E Stevens, EX, A $550.00
World's Fair, Book of Knowledge, bronze version, NM, I3 ..$450.00

World's Fair, J&E Stevens, EX, $1,200.00.

Zoo Bank, Kyser & Rex, CI, NM................................$3,520.00

REGISTERING BANKS

Captain Marvel Dime Register, litho tin, EX, C10.........$150.00
Dime Coin Barrel, pnt CI, 4", EX $160.00

Dopey Dime Register, WDE, 1938, lithographed tin, EX, $125.00; Snow White and the Seven Dwarfs Dime Register, WDE, 1938, lithographed tin, EX, $125.00.

Mickey Mouse Dime Register, WDE, 1939, lithographed tin, EX, $300.00.
(Photo courtesy David Longest and Michael Stern)

Jackie Robinson Dime Register, litho tin, 2½" $500.00
Popeye Daily Quarter Bank, litho tin, NM, from $150 to ...$200.00
Popeye Dime Register, metal, M $65.00
Prudential Dime Savings, NP CI, 7¼", EX, A................$150.00
Prudential Nickel Savings, NP CI, 7¼", EX, A..............$150.00
Prudential Quarter Savings, NP CI, 8¼", M, A $220.00
Recording Bank Building w/Dime Register, Pat 1981, NP CI,
    6½", VG, A $275.00
Registering Dime Savings, pnt CI, EX.........................$1,400.00
Superman Dime Register, litho tin, 3", EX, from $215 to..$250.00
Thrifty Elf Dime Register, litho tin, 2½" sq....................$170.00
Uncle Sam Dime Register, litho tin, 2½" sq..................$270.00

STILL BANKS

Airplane (Spirit of Saving), Geo Hunter, cast aluminum, brass
    prop, 7¼", G+, A...$265.00
Airplane (Spirit of Thrift), NP sheet metal, 7½", EX+, A..$550.00
Alamo, Alamo Iron Works, CI, 2¾x3½", VG, A $330.00
Andy Gump Savings, General Thrift Products, lead, 2 figures
    supporting money box, 5¾", EX, A $440.00
Andy Gump Seated on Stump, Arcade, CI, 4½", EX, A.$1,750.00
Apple, pnt CI, 3", EX..$1,975.00
Apple on Leaf, Kyser & Rex, ca 1882, CI, yel & gr, 3", EX+,
    A $1,870.00
Automobile, AC Williams, CI, red 4-door w/NP spoke wheels,
    6", VG, A..$440.00
Baby in Cradle, 1890s, NP CI & steel, 4", EX, A........$1,320.00
Bailey's Centennial Money Bank 1876, JS Semon, CI, NP base,
    4", VG, A..$200.00
Bank Building w/Clock, Hubley, CI, silver w/gold trim, 6", VG,
    A $525.00

Bank Building w/Cupola, J&E Stevens, CI, gr w/red trim, 3¼",
    EX, A $330.00
Bank Building w/Cupola, J&E Stevens, CI, lt brn w/bl roof, red
    trim, 4⅛", VG, A $285.00
Bank Building w/Eagle on Cupola, US, CI, dk gold, 9¾", VG,
    A $1,760.00
Barrel w/Beaky, Metal Moss, wht metal, 4⅛", MIB, A...$265.00
Barrel w/Bugs Bunny, Metal Moss, wht metal, 5½", MIB, A.$385.00
Barrel w/Daffy Duck, Metal Moss, wht metal, 4¼", MIB, A..$330.00
Barrel w/Elmer Fudd, Metal Moss, wht metal, 5½", MIB, A...$330.00
Barrel w/Porky Pig, Metal Moss, wht metal, 4½", MIB, A..$385.00
Barrel w/Sniffles, Metal Moss, wht metal, 5⅛", MIB, A.$265.00
Baseball on Three Bats, Hubley, CI, silver & red, 5½", EX,
    A $1,650.00
Bear (Honey Seated Leaning Forward), CI, gold, 2½", VG,
    A $715.00
Bear (Teddy), Arcade, CI, metallic gold, 2½", NM, A ..$285.00
Bear Standing Begging, pnt CI, 5¼", EX, A $110.00
Bear Stealing Pig, CI, gold, 5½", VG, A $1,430.00
Bear w/Honey Pot, Hubley, CI, brn w/bl & yel pot, 6½", NM,
    A $220.00
Bell, wht metal, emb floral design, bottom unscrews to retreive
    coins, 5½", VG, A...$140.00
Billy Bounce (Give Billy a Penny), Hubley, CI, silver w/red trim,
    4¾", VG, A $385.00
Bird Cage, CI & tin, 3⅞", VG $100.00
Black Man's Head in Hat (Two Faced), AC Williams, CI, 3¼",
    VG, A $65.00
Black Native's Head, CI, gold, ring in nose, mouth open,
    EX...$600.00
Boat (Battleship Maine), Grey Iron, CI, japanned w/gold trim,
    4½", NM, A..$525.00

**Baseball Player, AC
Williams, painted cast
iron, 5¾", EX, $350.00.**
(Photo courtesy Dunbar Gallery)

**Boy Scout, AC Williams,
gold-painted cast iron with
red trim on hat, 6", EX,
$150.00.** (Photo courtesy Dunbar Gallery)

Boat (Battleship Oregon), J&E Stevens, CI, gray w/gold trim, 6", VG, A $330.00

Boat (Battleship Texas), J&E Stevens, CI, wht, 10¼", EX, A..$1,430.00

Boat (Side-wheeler), Arcade, CI, 7½", EX, A................$285.00

Boat (When My Fortune Ship Comes In Sailboat), Brighton, CI, yel, 5½", G, A $525.00

Boston State House, Smith & Egge, CI, gold w/red trim, 5⅛", VG, A..$2,860.00

Boy Scout (w/Belt Buckle & Scarf), Hubley, CI, brn w/gold trim, 7", EX+, A $1,100.00

Boy Standing on Baseball, Hubley, CI, gold w/red trim, 5¾", VG, A..$3,740.00

Boy w/Large Football, pnt CI, 5⅛", EX $1,760.00

Buffalo (Amhurst Stoves), 1930s, CI, 5¼", NM, A $275.00

Building w/Bear Stealing Honey From Beehive, Sydenham & McOustra, ornate detail, CI, gold, 7", VG, A..........$175.00

Buster Brown & Tige, AC Williams, CI, gilt w/red accents, 5¼", VG, A..$115.00

Buster Brown & Tige Good Luck Horseshoe & Horse, Arcade, CI, blk & gold, 4¾", EX, A $300.00

Cadet Officer, Hubley, CI, bl w/gold trim, 5¾", VG, A.$990.00

Camel, AC Williams, CI, gold w/red saddle & blanket, 7¼", VG $220.00

Camel (Oriental), US, CI, blk w/gr rocker base, 3¾", EX, A $935.00

Camel w/Backpack Kneeling, Kyser & Rex, CI, japanned, 2½", EX, A $500.00

Campbell Kids, AC Williams, CI, gold, 3½", EX, A......$300.00

Capitalist, pnt CI, 5", EX $1,350.00

Captain Kidd, US, CI, blk w/mc trim, 5½", VG $300.00

Castle w/Two Towers, Harper, CI, japanned, 7", EX+, A.$1,650.00

Cat on Tub, pnt CI, 4⅛", G..................................$150.00

Cat Seated, pnt lead, glass eyes, 5¼", EX $1,400.00

Cat w/Ball, AC Williams, CI, dk gray & blk cat playing w/gold ball, 5½", EX, A $350.00

Century of Progress (1934), pnt CI, 4½", EX..............$1,350.00

Charley McCarthy Seated on Suitcase, Vanio, wht metal w/wooden jaw, 5½", VG, A $200.00

Church (West Side Presbyterian), CI, silver, 3¾x4", EX, A .$330.00

Church Towers w/Cross (Three), USA, CI, blk, 6¾", VG, A..$1,045.00

Church w/Clock Tower, Germany, litho & pnt tin, wht w/red roof, 11½", VG, A $415.00

City Bank Building w/Director's Room on Top, Harper, CI, japanned, 4⅛", VG, A $240.00

Clock (Grandfather), japanned CI, 5½", EX+, A $130.00

Clock (Time Is Money), HC Hart, tin face w/CI top & base, paper insert & dial, 5", NM, A..................................$220.00

Clock Bank (Street), AC Williams, CI w/steel back, red w/gold face, 6", EX, A $550.00

Clock w/Movable Hands, Judd, CI, blk w/NP dial, 4½", EX, A $200.00

Clown with Pointed Hat, AC Williams, cast iron, 6¼", EX+, $275.00.
(Photo courtesy Dunbar Gallery)

Colonial Gentleman, ceramic, 2¼", EX $200.00

Colorado Savings Bank (Four-Gabled), CI, gr w/brn roof, 10½", EX+, A $3,520.00

Columbia Tower, pnt CI, 6⅞", EX..................................$110.00

County Bank Building, Harper, CI, japanned, 4¼", VG, A ..$265.00

Cow (Holstein), Arcade, CI, blk & wht, 4½" L, NM, A..$715.00

Cow on Case, J&E Stevens, bronze, 4½", NM, A $420.00

Crown Bank, pnt CI, 3⅝", EX $110.00

Crown Bank (Footed), pnt CI, 4½", EX......................$1,150.00

Devil's Head (Two-Faced), AC Williams, CI, red & blk, 4¼", VG, A $600.00

Dirigible, AC Williams, CI, silver, 6½", NM, A $220.00

Dog (Basset Hound), CI, blk, 3", rare color, G, A.......$1,045.00

Dog (Basset Hound), CI, gold, 3", EX..........................$290.00

Dog (Boston Bull Terrier), Vindex, CI, dk brn & wht, 5¼", NM, A $200.00

Dog (Lost), US, CI, 5⅜", VG, A..................................$385.00

Dog (Puppo on Pillow), Hubley, CI, blk & wht, 6", NM, A..$460.00

Dog (Puppo Seated), Hubley, CI, blk & wht, 5", EX, A...$175.00

Dog (Scottie Seated), Hubley, CI, blk w/red collar, 5x6", NM, A $300.00

Dog (Scottie), wht metal, blk, w/locking trap, 5", NMIB, A ..$220.00

Dog (Spitz), Grey Iron, CI, brn, 4¼", VG, A $275.00

Dog on Tub, pnt CI, 4", EX..................................$240.00

Dolphin (Boy in Boat), US, CI, gold, 4½", EX+, A $825.00

Donald Duck, WDE, diecast, early long-billed version holding pile of coins, 6½", G, A.................................$330.00

Donkey, AC Williams, CI, brn w/dk red saddle, 6¾", NM, A $350.00

Donkey w/Hinged Saddle, pnt wht metal, 3½", worn pnt ..$65.00

Double Door, pnt CI, 5½", EX...................................$250.00

Doughboy Soldier, Grey Iron, CI, 7", VG, A...............$330.00

Duck, AC Williams, CI, metallic gold, 5", VG, A $330.00

Duck (Round), CI, yel w/red bill & head, blk eyes looking up, Kenton trap, 4", EX, A...$330.00

Dutch Boy on Barrel, Hubley, CI, red, yel & bl w/tan barrel, 5½", EX+, A..$130.00

Dutch Girl, Grey Iron, CI, gold, 6½", VG, A...............$385.00

Eagle w/Shield, pnt CI, 4", EX................................$600.00

Eggman (Caricature of Wm Howard Taft), Arcade, CI, gold, 4⅛", VG, A..$2,640.00

Egyptian Tomb, pnt CI, 6¼", EX..............................$360.00

Eiffel Tower, Sydenham & McOustra, ca 1908, CI, japanned w/gold highlights, 8¾", scarce, VG, A $1,045.00

Elephant in Circus Clothes, mc pnt CI, 4", NM............$350.00

Elephant on Tub, AC Williams, CI, silver w/red & gold trim, 5½", NM, A..$275.00

Elephant Seated w/Turned Trunk, US, CI, gold, 4¼", EX, A .$880.00

Elephant w/Howdah, Hubley, pnt CI, 4¼", NM+, A.......$75.00

Elephant w/Howdah on Wheels, AC Williams, CI, metallic gold w/red spoke wheels, 4⅛", VG, A $165.00

Empire State Bank New York City, bronzed metal, 8", EX+, A $50.00

English Church, CI, japanned w/colored tin simulating glass windows, 5½", rare, VG, A $430.00

Fidelity Trust Vault (w/Lord Fauntleroy), J Barton Smith, CI, gr, 5", VG, A...$420.00

Flat Iron Bank Building (Triangular), Kenton, CI, 3¼", VG+, A..$385.00

Flat Iron Bank Building (Triangular), Kenton, CI, 5¾", G-, A..$350.00

Football Player, AC Williams, CI, gold, 6", EX, A.........$385.00

Fort (Round), Kenton, CI, blk, 4⅛", EX, A $500.00

Fort Mt Hope, pnt CI, 3", EX....................................$600.00

Foxy Grandpa, Hubley, ca 1920, pnt CI, 5½", VG.........$330.00

Fruit Basket, pnt CI, 2¾", EX...................................$600.00

Gas Pump, Arcade, CI, red w/gold trim, 5¾", NM, A..$1,100.00

Gas Pump, US, CI, red w/gold globe, 5¾", rpl hose, EX, A $275.00

General Sheridan on Horse, Arcade, CI, 6", VG, A $310.00

George V Royal Bank, Chamberlin & Hill/England, CI, japanned, 5¼", NM, A...$310.00

Give Me a Penny Sharecropper, pnt CI, 5½", NM, A ...$880.00

Globe on Arc, Grey Iron, CI, red, 5¼", EX, A...............$155.00

Globe on Pedestal Base w/Eagle Atop, Enterprise, ca 1875, CI, 5¾", EX, A $220.00

Globe Safe on Rectangular Base, CI, red, emb combination door, 3", G, A..$120.00

Globe Safe w/Claw Feet, Kenton, electroplated, blk & copper, hinged door w/combination lock, 5", EX, A............$240.00

Globe Savings Bank Building, Kyser & Rex, ca 1889, CI, japanned w/gold & red trim, 7⅛", VG, A............$1,650.00

Golliwog, Harper, CI, red, wht & blk, 6¼", EX+, A......$825.00

Goose, pnt CI, 3¾", EX..$240.00

Help the Children of Wisconsin, half-figure of boy on lettered base, CI, gold, 7", NM, A $650.00

Hen on Nest, US, CI, gold w/red trim, 3⅜", EX, A $1,540.00

Hippo, pnt CI, 2", NM...$5,400.00

Home Bank Building (Man in Doorway), Judd, CI, japanned, 4", EX+, A..$600.00

Home Savings Bank (Dog's Head Finial), CI, 5¾", EX..$320.00

Horse on Tub w/Blanket, AC Williams, CI, 5¼", VG+, A ..$95.00

Horse Prancing (Beauty), CI, blk w/gold trim, 4¾", EX, A.$350.00

Horse Prancing on Base, AC Williams, CI, glossy blk w/wht hooves, 7½", NM, A $265.00

Horse Prancing w/One Leg Up, CI, metallic gold, w/belly band, 5", VG, A..$220.00

Horse Standing (Beauty), Arcade, CI, blk w/gold trim, 4⅛", NM, A..$240.00

Horse Standing (My Pet), CI, blk, 4", VG, A.................$250.00

Horse Standing (Workhorse), Arcade, CI, gr, 4⅛", EX, A.$470.00

House (Colonial), pnt CI, 4", VG...............................$220.00

House w/Cupola (2-Story), J&E Stevens, pnt CI, 6", VG, A ..$415.00

Ice Box (Kelvinator), Arcade, CI, wht, 4", NMIB, A.$1,980.00

Independence Hall, Enterprise, CI, japanned w/gold highlights, 9½", EX+, A..$3,080.00

Independence Hall, US, CI, gold, 11", VG, A $990.00

Indian Head (Two-Faced), AC Williams, CI, gold, 4½", EX, A $2,640.00

Indian Scout w/Tomahawk, Hubley, CI, brn w/red & gold trim, 6", EX, A..$200.00

Jewel Chest, CI, gold, scroll design, footed, 6⅛", VG, A..$110.00

Junior Cash Register, J&E Stevens, nickel-plated cast iron, 5¼", VG+, $150.00; Beehive, J Harper, cast iron, 4⅛", EX+, $525.00. (Photo courtesy Dunbar Gallery)

Junior National Bank, Logan Specialty Co, tin w/paper cutouts of kids at plastic teller's window, 7", MIB, A...........$150.00

Key, Wm J Somerville, ca 1905, CI, gold, 5½", VG, A.$350.00

King Midas, Hubley, CI, flesh & yel, 4½", NM+, A...$1,650.00

Kodak Bank, J&E Stevens, NP CI, 5", EX, A $175.00

Lamb in Stride, Grey Iron, CI, japanned, 5½", NM, A..$220.00

Lamb Standing, CI, gold, 4¼", EX, A...........................$265.00

Liberty Bell, Arcade, bronzed CI, w/support bar, emb lettering, 4", EX+, A...$65.00

Lichfield Cathedral, Chamberlin & Hill/England, ca 1908, CI, japanned, 6½", EX, A...$300.00

Lion, AC Williams, gold-painted cast iron, 6¼", EX, $65.00.

Lion Upright on Tub, AC Williams, CI, metallic gold w/red & bl trim, 5¼", NM, A...$265.00

Log Cabin (Leftside Chimney), Kyser & Rex, ca 1882, CI, red, 2½x3¼", EX, A...$175.00

Log Cabin Bank, Chein, cabin shape, litho tin, 3", EX, A .$235.00

Mailbox (Postal Savings Bank/US Mail), electroplated steel, glass front, 4-section top, 5½", EX, A.........................$75.00

Mailbox (Sidewalk), Linemar, litho tin, front label lists times & days for pickup, key opens top, 3¼", M, A $25.00

Mailbox (US Mail), CI, gr, coin slot in back, perforated sides & back, 3½", EX, A...$65.00

Mammy w/Spoon, AC Williams, 1920s, pnt CI, 6", EX+, A $235.00

Marietta Silo, CI, wht w/silver dome top, 5½", EX+, A.$440.00

Mermaid (Girl in Boat), US, CI, gold, 4½", VG, A.......$660.00

Mickey Mouse, aluminum, standing w/hands on hips, pointed nose, 8¼", VG, A...$3,300.00

Mickey Mouse, England, silver-plated CI, standing in suit & bow tie, 6¼", M, A..$125.00

Middy, US, ca 1887, CI, 5¼", VG, A $130.00

Money Bag ($100,000), US, CI, chrome-plated, 3½", NM, A...$600.00

Mosque Bank Building, CI, 3¼", EX, A...........................$85.00

Multiplying Bank Building, J&E Stevens, CI, red, wht & bl, 6½", VG, A..$1,760.00

Mutt & Jeff, AC Williams, CI, gold, 4¼", VG, A..........$130.00

North Pole Bank (Ice Cream Freezer), Grey Iron, CI, NP, 4¼", EX, A..$460.00

Old Doc Yak Conversion, Arcade, CI, wht, red & blk, 4½", EX, A..$650.00

Oscar the Goat, CI, blk & wht w/tan horns & hooves, exaggerated cartoon features, 2nd casting, 7¾", EX, A $110.00

Owl, Vindex, CI, gray & wht, 4¼", M, A......................$300.00

Owl on Tree Limb (Be Wise), AC Williams, CI, metallic gold, 5", VG, A..$200.00

Palace, Ives, ca 1885, CI, japanned & hand-pnt, gold highlights, 8", EX, A $2,090.00

Pelican, Hubley, CI, wht w/yel bill & gr base, 4¾", NM, A..$880.00

Piano, Roche Novelty Co, NP CI, w/combination locking trap, 8", VG+, A...$465.00

Pig (A Christmas Roast), CI, blk, 3¼", VG, A $200.00

Pig (I Made Chicago Famous), CI, orange, 5¼", VG, A ..$195.00

Pingree Potato, US, CI, 5¼", G, A.............................$650.00

Policeman on Safe, Harper, CI, blk, 5¼", VG, A $2,640.00

Policeman Standing w/Arms Down, Arcade, CI, bl w/gold trim, 5½", G, A...$200.00

Policeman w/Club in Hand (Mulligan), AC Williams, CI, blk, 5¾", EX, A..$195.00

Porky Pig, Hubley, ca 1930, CI, NM, A.......................$440.00

Possum, Arcade, CI, metallic gold, 4½", G, A..............$500.00

Possum, Arcade, CI, silver, 2½", NM, A.......................$550.00

Possum N Taters (Billy Possum), Harper, CI, gold, 3", EX, A...$3,960.00

Presto Bank Building, AC Williams, CI, silver w/gold top, 3½", EX, A...$65.00

Prosperity Bank, Chein, 1930s, tin, bl, cream & silver pail w/bail hdl, orig key on top, 4", rare, VG+, A.....................$65.00

Punch & Judy Theatre, Germany, litho tin, 3", VG, A..$220.00

Rabbit, dated 1884, wht on gr base, 2¼", VG, A $825.00

Rabbit Lying Down, CI, brn, 2⅛", VG, A....................$220.00

Rabbit Seated (Large Wing-Nut Version), Hubley, pre 1906, CI, gray & wht, 4½", VG...$175.00

Rabbit Standing w/Ears Up, AC Williams, CI, gold, 6¼", VG, A...$310.00

Radio (Crosley), Kenton, CI, gr, 4½", EX, A $250.00

Radio (GE), Arcade, floor type, CI, gr, 4", G, A.............$250.00

Radio (Majestic Floor Model), nickel-plated cast iron, 4½", EX+, $550.00.
(Photo courtesy Dunbar Gallery)

Radio (Radio Bank), Kenton, 1927, pnt CI, w/3 combination knobs, 4½", EX, A...$190.00

Red Goose Shoes, 1920s, CI, red, 9", EX, A...................$135.00

Reindeer, AC Williams, gold-painted cast iron, 9½", NM, $265.00. (Photo courtesy Dunbar Gallery)

Reindeer, AC Williams, CI, gold, 9½", VG, A $65.00
Rhino, Arcade, CI, blk w/gold horn & pnt features, 2½", rpt, A $200.00
Rhino, Arcade, CI, blk, 5", VG, A................................$600.00
Rooster, Hubley, CI, metallic gold w/red comb & waddle, 5", NM, A $350.00
Rooster, Polish, CI, blk & gold, 5½", EX, A $1,045.00
Roy Rogers & Trigger Savings Bank, Ohio Art, litho tin, 6x8", MIP, A $240.00
Rumplestiltskin, CI, gold, 6", VG, A $90.00
Safe, CI, japanned, cutout filigree detail, orig key mk June 1896, 3½", EX+, A $125.00
Safe, CI, red & gray w/blk scroll design, hinged door w/key lock, 4¾", EX, A $300.00
Safe (Arabian), Kyser & Rex, CI, japanned, 4½", VG, A..$150.00
Safe (Bank of Industry), Kenton, NP CI, 5½", VG, A...$500.00
Safe (Daisy), CI & sheet metal, key lock, 3½", VG, A $65.00
Safe (Double-Door), NP CI, 5¾", G, A........................$220.00
Safe (Moon & Star), CI, blk w/gold trim, 5⅛", VG, A..$110.00
Safe (National), CI & sheet metal, red w/NP door, 5", EX, A $110.00
Safe (National), NP CI, 4¾", EX, A..............................$110.00
Safe (Savings Bank), Kenton, CI, silver, emb filigree door, 4½", VG+, A...$125.00
Safe (Savings Deposit), Kenton, electroplated CI, emb filigree door, 4", EX, A $165.00
Safe (State), CI & sheet metal, red w/NP door, 4½", VG, A ...$55.00
Safe (State), NP CI, 4⅛", VG, A....................................$90.00
Safe (Time), EM Rouch, NP CI, emb w/eagle & stars, 7", VG, A $550.00

Safe (Union), NP CI, 3¼", VG, A..................................$90.00
Sailor Saluting, Hubley, CI, silver w/bl scarf, 5¼", rpt, A .$55.00
Santa Holding Tree, Wing, CI, red suit & wht beard w/gold bears, tree & trim, 6", NM, A..............................$2,860.00
Santa Sleeping in Arm Chair, USA, pnt wht metal, red suit, wht trim, metallic gold chair, 8", EX+, A $75.00
Santa Standing Next to Tree, Ives, NP CI, flocked tree, 7¼", NM, A $990.00
Satchel, CI, electroplated bronze, 3½", NM, A.............$200.00
Save & Smile Money Box, England, CI, blk, red & wht, 4¼", NM, A $600.00
Sewing Machine, Germany, tin & iron, 5⅛", EX+, A ...$500.00
Sharecropper, AC Williams, pnt CI, 5½", VG, A..........$190.00
Shell Out, J&E Stevens, ca 1882, CI, wht, 4¾", VG, A .$240.00
Skyscraper, Kenton, CI, silver w/gold tiered roof, 5¾", VG, A $660.00
Skyscraper (Triangular), Hubley, silver w/gold trim, 6", G, A $1,650.00
Soldier Holding Rifle (Doughboy ?), Hubley, CI, bronze-tone w/flesh face, 6", EX, A $550.00
Songbird on Stump, AC Williams, CI, gold, 4¾", EX, A..$240.00
Squirrel w/Nut, CI, gold, 4⅛", VG, A $770.00

St. Bernard with Package, AC Williams, cast iron, 7", EX, D10, $250.00. (Photo courtesy Dunbar Gallery)

State Bank Building, Kenton, CI, japanned w/gold trim, 3", EX+, A...$220.00
State Bank Building, Kenton, CI, japanned w/gold trim, 6", EX, A $200.00
State Bank Building, Kenton, CI, japanned w/gold trim, 9", NM, A $770.00
State Bank Building, US, CI, japanned w/gold trim, 6¾", VG, A $990.00
Statue of Liberty, AC Williams, CI, 9½", EX, A............$265.00
Statue of Liberty, Kenton, CI, gr w/gold highlights, 6½", EX, A $385.00
Stove (Gas Stove Bank), Bernstein Co, CI w/tin sides, blk, 5½", NM, A $220.00
Stove (Heatorola), Kenton, CI, gr, 4½", VG, A $110.00

Stove (Hot Point Electric), Arcade, CI, wht w/gray trim, 6",
    VG, A $525.00
Stove (Mellow Furnace), Liberty Toy, CI, 3½", G, A......$55.00
Stove (Parlor), Schneider & Trenkamp, CI, red inserts simulate
    fire, 6¼", EX, A $265.00
Stove (Roper), Arcade, CI & sheet metal, wht, 4", NM,
    A $745.00
Tabernacle Savings Building, Keyless Lock Co, CI, copper-tone,
    2½x5", EX, A $2,860.00
Tank Savings, Ferrosteel, ca 1919, CI, rear spoke wheels, 9½",
    VG, A $385.00
Telephone (Baby Bell), Kantor, tin, early wall phone, 10", EX+,
    A $330.00
Three Wise Monkeys, AC Williams, CI, metallic gold, 3¼",
    NM, A $350.00
Tower Bank Building, Harper, CI, japanned w/red roof & door,
    gold trim, 9¼", EX, A.....................................$990.00
Tower Bank Building, Kyser & Rex, CI, japanned w/red roof &
    gold highlights, 7", VG, A $265.00
Train Engine & Tender, smiling face on front, copper-plated
    wht metal, 5¼", EX+, A....................................$75.00
Trolley Car, Kenton, CI, silver, 5¼", EX, A..................$825.00
Trolley Car (Main Street), AC Williams, CI, gold, 6¾", VG,
    A $350.00
Trolley Car (Marquee Atop), 1899, CI, japanned, 4½", EX+,
    A $200.00
US Treasury Building, Grey Iron, CI w/sheet-metal base, wht
    w/red roof & trim, 3¾", EX+, A $440.00
Villa, Kyser & Rex, ca 1894, building w/4 corner towers &
    arched windows, finial atop, CI, 5½", EX, A...........$920.00
Washington Monument, AC Williams, CI, gold, 6⅛", VG,
    A $240.00
White City Puzzle Barrel on Wheeled Cart, ca 1984, NP CI, 5",
    EX+, A $420.00
World Time, Arcade, CI w/paper timetables, 4⅛", EX+,
    A $350.00
World's Fair Building, US, CI, wht w/red & gold, 6", VG,
    A $1,210.00
Yellow Cab, Arcade, CI, yel & blk, w/driver, 7¾", EX+,
    A $770.00
Zeppelin (Graf), AC Williams, CI, silver, 6½", EX, A ..$200.00
Zepplin Dock (Duralumin Used in Airship Akron), silver, 7¼",
    EX, A $330.00

Barbie Dolls and Friends

    No one could argue the fact that vintage Barbie dolls are
holding their own as one of the hottest areas of toy collecting on
today's market. Barbie doll was first introduced in 1959, and
since then her face has changed three times. She's been blond
and brunette; her hair has been restyled over and over, and it's
varied in length from above her shoulders to the tips of her toes.
She's worn high-fashion designer clothing and pedal pushers.
She's been everything from an astronaut to a veterinarian, and
no matter what her changing lifestyle required, Mattel (her
'maker') has provided it for her.

    Though even Barbie doll items from recent years are bought
and sold with fervor, those made before 1970 are the most
sought after. You'll need to do a lot of studying and comparisons
to learn to distinguish one Barbie doll from another, but it will
pay off in terms of making wise investments. There are several
books available; we recommend them all: *The Wonder of Barbie*
and *The World of Barbie Dolls* by Paris and Susan Manos; *The
Collector's Encyclopedia of Barbie Dolls and Collectibles* by Sibyl
DeWein and Joan Ashabraner; *The Story of Barbie, First and Second Editions* by Kitturah B. Westenhouser; *Barbie Doll Fashion,
Vol. 1, 1959 – 1967*, and *Barbie Doll Fashion, Vol. II, 1968 –
1974*, by Sarah Sink Eames; *Barbie Exclusives, Books I and II*, by
Margo Rana; *Barbie, The First 30 Years, 1959 Through 1989*, by
Stefanie Deutsch; *A Decade of Barbie Dolls and Collectibles, 1981
– 1991*, by Beth Summers; *The Barbie Doll Boom, 1986 – 1995*,
Collector's Encyclopedia of Barbie Doll Exclusives and More, and
Thirty Years of Mattel Fashion Dolls, all by J. Michael Augusty-
niak; *The Barbie Years, 1959 to 1996, First, Second, and Third
Editions*, by Patrick C. Olds; *Collector's Guide to 1990s Barbie
Dolls* by Maria Martinez-Esguerra; *Skipper, Barbie Doll's Little Sis-
ter*, by Scott Arend, Karla Holzerland, and Trina Kent; *Collec-
tor's Guide to 1990s Barbie Dolls* by Maria Martinez Esguerra;
Collector's Guide to Barbie Doll Vinyl Cases by Connie Craig
Kaplan; and *Collector's Guide to Barbie Doll Paper Dolls* by Lorraine Mieszala (all published by Collector Books).

    Remember that unless the box is mentioned in the line (orig
box, MIB, MIP, NRFB, etc.), values are given for loose items. As
a general rule, a mint-in-the box doll is worth about twice as
much as one mint, no box. The same doll, played with and in
only good condition, is worth half as much (or even less). Never-
removed-from-box examples sell at a premium.

    Advisor: Marl Davidson (D2).

DOLLS

Allan, 1963, pnt red hair, straight legs, MIB, D2............$125.00
Allan, 1963, pnt red hair, straight legs, orig swimsuit & sandals,
    VG, M15 ....$65.00
Allan, 1964, pnt red hair, bendable legs, orig outfit, VG,
    M15 ....$165.00
Barbie, #1, 1958-59, blond hair, MIB, D2 ....$9,950.00
Barbie, #1, 1958-59, brunette hair, MIB, D2, minimum
    value $1,000.00
Barbie, #2, brunette hair, MIB, D2 ....$8,500.00
Barbie, #2, 1959, blond hair, MIB, D2......................$9,000.00
Barbie, #3, 1960, blond hair, MIB, D2......................$2,400.00
Barbie, #3, 1960, blond hair, orig swimsuit, NM, D2 .....$950.00
Barbie, #3, 1960, brunette hair, MIB, D2 ....$2,250.00
Barbie, #4, 1960, blond hair, MIB, D2......................$1,100.00
Barbie, #4, 1960, brunette hair, MIB, D2 ....$1,500.00
Barbie, #5, 1961, blond hair, orig swimsuit, NM, D2 .....$325.00
Barbie, #5, 1961, brunette hair, orig swimsuit, NM, D2 .$400.00
Barbie, #5, 1961, red hair, MIB, D2 ....$1,300.00
Barbie, #6, blond hair, orig swimsuit, NM, D2 ....$325.00
Barbie, #6, brunette hair, orig swimsuit, NM, D2 ....$350.00
Barbie, #6, red hair, replica swimsuit, NM, D2 ....$600.00
Barbie, American Girl, 1964, blond hair, orig swimsuit, NM,
    D2..$550.00

Barbie #3 wearing Solo in the Spotlight, 1960, blond hair, MIB, minimum value $3,500.00.

Barbie, American Girl wearing Fashion Editor outfit, 1964, brunette hair, M, $600.00 (doll only).
(Photo courtesy Cindy Sabulis)

Barbie, Angel Lights, 1993, NRFB, D2 ....$110.00
Barbie, Anniversary Star, 1992, Walmart 30th Anniversary, MIB $45.00
Barbie, Antique Rose, FAO Schwarz, 1996, NRFB, D2 .$300.00
Barbie, Back to School, 1992, MIB $30.00
Barbie, Ballerina on Tour, 1976, MIB, M15 ....$100.00
Barbie, Ballroom Beauty, 1991, NRFB $50.00

Barbie, Benefit Performance, porcelain, 1987, NRFB, D2 ..$600.00
Barbie, Bubble-Cut, 1961, blond or brunette hair, MIB, D2, ea $500.00
Barbie, Bubble-Cut, 1961, brunette hair, orig swimsuit, NM, D2 ....$200.00
Barbie, Bubble-Cut, 1961, jet blk hair, MIB, D2 ....$650.00
Barbie, Bubble-Cut, 1961, red hair, MIB, D2 ....$600.00
Barbie, Bubble-Cut w/side part, 1962-64, blond hair, MIB, D2 ....$2,000.00
Barbie, Bubble-Cut w/side part, 1962-64, blond hair, orig swimsuit, VG, M15 ....$165.00
Barbie, Busy Gal, 1994, NRFB, D2 ....$75.00
Barbie, Canadian, 1987, Dolls of the World, NRFB, D2 ..$75.00
Barbie, Chinese, 1993, Dolls of the World, NRFB, D2 ....$45.00
Barbie, Circus Star, 1994, FAO Schwarz, NRFB, D2 .....$100.00
Barbie, Color Magic, 1966, blond hair, orig swimsuit & hair band, NM, D2 ....$650.00
Barbie, Country Looks, 1992, MIB $30.00
Barbie, Cute 'N Cool, 1991, MIB $30.00
Barbie, Doctor, 1987, NRFB, M15 ....$35.00
Barbie, Dramatic New Living, 1970, blond or red hair, NRFB, D2, ea $350.00
Barbie, Easter Fun, 1993, MIB $35.00
Barbie, Egyptian Queen, 1993, Great Eras, NRFB, D2 ...$175.00
Barbie, Elizabethan, 1994, Great Eras, NRFB, D2 ....$55.00
Barbie, Empress Bride, 1992, Bob Mackie, MIB, D2 ...$1,200.00
Barbie, English, 1991, Dolls of the World, NRFB, D2 ......$75.00
Barbie, Evening Extravaganza, 1993, Classique Collection, NRFB, D2 ....$100.00
Barbie, Evening Pearl, porcelain, 1995, Presidential Series, NRFB, D2 ....$300.00
Barbie, Evening Sparkle, 1990, Hills, MIB.....................$45.00
Barbie, Fashion Photo, 1977, MIB, M15 ....$85.00
Barbie, Fashion Queen, 1963, orig swimsuit & turban, complete w/3 wigs & stand, NM $275.00
Barbie, Feelin' Groovy, 1986, MIB.................................$175.00
Barbie, Flapper Girl, 1993, Great Eras, NRFB, D2 ....$275.00
Barbie, Flight Time, 1989, NRFB, M15 ....$40.00
Barbie, Goddess of the Moon, 1996, Bob Mackie, NRFB, M15..$175.00
Barbie, Gold Jubilee, 1994, NRFB, D2............................$850.00
Barbie, Gold Sensation, 1993, porcelain, MIB, D2 ....$350.00
Barbie, Golden Greetings, 1989, FAO Schwarz, MIB $275.00
Barbie, Greek, 1985, Dolls of the World, NRFB, D2........$70.00
Barbie, Hawaiian, 1975, MIB, M15..................................$85.00
Barbie, Holiday, 1988, NRFB, D2, minimum value $1,000.00
Barbie, Holiday, 1989, NMIB, D2....................................$200.00
Barbie, Holiday, 1989, NRFB, D2 ....$300.00
Barbie, Holiday, 1990, NRFB, D2 ....$300.00
Barbie, Holiday, 1991, NRFB $300.00
Barbie, Holiday, 1992, NRFB, D2 ....$200.00
Barbie, Holiday, 1993, NRFB, D2 ....$200.00
Barbie, Holiday, 1995, NRFB, D2 ....$75.00
Barbie, Holiday, 1996, NRFB, D2 ....$50.00
Barbie, Holiday Jewel, 1995, porcelain, NRFB, D2 ....$250.00
Barbie, Hot Looks, 1991, MIB...$35.00
Barbie, India, 1981, Dolls of the World, NRFB, D2 ....$150.00
Barbie, Japanese, 1984, Dolls of the World, NRFB, D2..$150.00

Barbie, Holiday, 1994, NRFB, $200.00. <small>(Photo courtesy Lee Garmon)</small>

Barbie, Kenyan, 1993, Dolls of the World, NRFB, D2 .....$35.00
Barbie, Lavender Surprise, 1989, MIB.............................$50.00
Barbie, Live Action, 1971, orig outfit, NM, D2.............$150.00
Barbie, Magic Moves (Black), 1985, NRFB, M15 ....$35.00
Barbie, Malibu, 1971, MIP $85.00

Barbie, Neptune Fantasy, Bob Mackie, 1992, NRFB, $1,000.00. <small>(Photo courtesy Lee Garmon)</small>

Barbie, Masquerade Ball, 1993, Bob Mackie, NRFB, D2 .$450.00
Barbie, Midnight Gala, 1994, Classique Collection, NRFB, D2..$95.00
Barbie, Miss, 1964, pnt hair, orig swimsuit & hat, complete w/3 wigs & stand, NM, D2......................................$400.00
Barbie, Moon Goddess, 1996, Bob Mackie, NRFB, D2 ..$165.00
Barbie, Moonlight Rose, 1991, NRFB.............................$40.00
Barbie, Newport, 1973, NRFB, M15 ....$175.00
Barbie, Night Sensation, 1991, FAO Schwarz, MIB.......$150.00
Barbie, Olympic Gymnast, 1995, NRFB, D2 ....$75.00
Barbie, Oriental, 1980, Dolls of the World, NRFB, D2 ....$95.00
Barbie, Parisienne, 1980, Dolls of the World, MIB, M15...$200.00
Barbie, Peach Pretty, 1989, NRFB $50.00

Barbie, Peruvian, 1985, Dolls of the World, NRFB, $85.00.
<small>(Photo courtesy Beth Summers)</small>

Barbie, Picnic Pretty, 1992, Osco, NRFB.........................$30.00
Barbie, Pink Jubilee, 1987, Walmart, MIB.......................$85.00
Barbie, Platinum, 1991, Bob Mackie, MIB, D2 ....$600.00
Barbie, Ponytail, 1961, blond hair, orig swimsuit, VG, M15 ....$285.00
Barbie, Pretty in Purple (Black), 1992, NRFB $50.00
Barbie, Quick Curl Miss America, 1972, MIB...............$125.00
Barbie, Regal Reflections, 1992, Spiegel, NRFB.............$350.00
Barbie, Royal, 1979, Dolls of the World, NRFB, D2 ......$195.00
Barbie, Royal Slendor, porcelain, 1993, Presidential series, NRFB, D2 ....$300.00
Barbie, Satin Nights, 1992, MIB $65.00
Barbie, Savvy Shopper, 1994, Bloomingdales, NMIB, D2 ..$85.00
Barbie, Silver Screen, 1993, FAO Schwarz, NRFB, D2..$295.00
Barbie, Snow Princess, 1994, Seasons Series, NRFB, M15 ....$135.00
Barbie, Sophisticated Lady, 1990, porcelain, NRFB, M15 ..$225.00
Barbie, Standard, 1970, blond hair, MIB, D2 ....$700.00

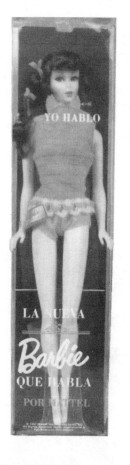

Barbie, Spanish Talking, 1968, brunette hair, NMIB, $300.00.

Barbie, Standard, 1970, red hair, orig swimsuit, NM, D2, minimum value $1,000.00
Barbie, Starlight Waltz, 1995, Ballroom Beauty Series, NRFB, D2..$75.00
Barbie, Sterling Wishes, 1991, Spiegel, NRFB, D2 ....$150.00

Barbie, Swirl Ponytail, 1964, brunette hair, NRFB, minimum value $1,000.00.
(Photo courtesy Paris and Susan Manos)

Barbie, Swirl Ponytail, 1964, blond hair, orig swimsuit, NM, D2/M15...$400.00
Barbie, Swirl Ponytail, 1964, red hair, orig swimsuit, NM, D2...$450.00
Barbie, Talking, 1968, blond or brunette hair, orig swimsuit, NM, D2, ea $175.00
Barbie, Toothfairy, 1993, Walmart, MIB $25.00
Barbie, Trailblazin', 1991, MIB $30.00
Barbie, Truly Scrumptious, 1968, NRFB, D2.................$500.00
Barbie, Twist 'N Turn, 1964, red hair, orig swimsuit & bow, EX, D2 ....$350.00
Barbie, Twist 'N Turn, 1966, blond hair, orig swimsuit & cover-up, NM, D2..$250.00
Barbie, Twist 'N Turn, 1967, blk hair, orig outfit, NM, D2..$325.00
Barbie, Twist 'N Turn, 1967, blond hair, orig swimsuit, NM, D2 ....$265.00
Barbie, Twist 'N Turn, 1968, brunette hair, NRFB, D2 ..$900.00
Barbie, Twist 'N Turn, 1968, red hair, orig swimsuit, NM, D2 ....$250.00
Barbie, Twist 'N Turn, 1969, brunette hair, orig swimsuit, NM, D2...$275.00
Barbie, Twist 'N Turn, 1970, brunette hair, orig swimsuit & bow, NM, D2 ....$300.00
Barbie, Walk Lively, 1972, NRFB, D2 ....$300.00
Barbie, Winter Fantasy, 1990, FAO Schwarz, NRFB, D2..$295.00
Barbie as Belle, 1996, NRFB, D2...................................$100.00
Barbie as Cinderella, 1996, Children's Collector Series, NRFB, D2 ....$35.00
Barbie as Dorothy, 1995, Hollywood Legend Series, NRFB $85.00
Barbie as Little Bo Peep, Children's Classic Series, NRFB, D2 ....$125.00
Barbie as My Fair Lady, Embassy Ball, 1995, Hollywood Legends Series, NRFB, D2...................................$90.00
Barbie as Scarlett, 1994, Hollywood Legends Series, gr velvet dress or gr & wht picnic dress, NRFB, D2, ea $55.00

Fluff, Living, 1971, NRFB, minimum value $175.00.

Barbie as Scarlett, 1994, Hollywood Legends Series, red dress, NRFB, D2 ....$75.00
Barbie as Sleeping Beauty, 1992, NRFB....................$35.00
Brad, Talking, 1971, M, D2 ....$125.00
Brad, 1969, bendable legs, NRFB, M15 ....$175.00
Cara, Deluxe Quick Curl, 1976, MIB.........................$65.00
Chris, 1967, blond hair, orig outfit, NM, D2 ....$125.00
Christie, Sun Lovin', 1978, NRFB, M15 ....$65.00
Christie, Talking, 1968, orig swimsuit, EX, M15 ....$150.00
Christie, Twist 'N Turn, 1968, red hair, MIB, D2 ....$500.00
Francie, Growin' Pretty Hair, 1970, MIB, D2.................$200.00
Francie, Hair Happenin's, 1970, orig outfit, EX, D2.......$150.00
Francie, Twist 'N Turn, 1966, blond hair, NRFB, D2 ....$800.00
Francie, 1966, blond hair, orig swimsuit, bendable legs, NM, D2 ....$200.00
Jamie, New & Wonderful Walking, orig outfit, NM, D2..$300.00
Jamie, Walking, brunette hair, orig outfit, NM, D2 ....$275.00
Kelly, Yellowstone, 1973, NRFB, D2 ....$450.00
Kelly Quick Curl, 1972, NRFB, D2 ....$175.00
Ken, Free Movin', 1975, NRFB, M15 ....$100.00
Ken, Gold Medal Skier, 1975, NRFB, M15 ....$115.00

Ken, 1962, painted hair, straight legs, MIB, $225.00.

Ken, Mod Hair, 1972, MIB, $100.00. (Photo courtesy Stefanie Deutsch)

Ken, Mod Hair, 1972, NRFB, M15 ....$115.00
Ken, Sun Valley, 1973, NRFB, M15 ....$125.00
Ken, Talking, 1969, MIB..$275.00
Ken, 1961, flocked blond or brunette hair, orig outfit, straight legs, VG (VG box), M15, ea.....................$185.00
Ken, 1961, flocked blond or brunette hair, orig outfit, straight legs, NM, D2, ea $165.00
Ken, 1965, pnt brunette hair, orig swimsuit, bendable legs, NM, D2 ....$225.00
Ken as Cowardly Lion, 1996, Hollywood Legend Series, NRFB, D2 ....$200.00

Ken as Prince Charming, 1991, NRFB.............................$35.00
Ken as Prince Phillip, 1992, NRFB $30.00
Ken as Rhett, 1994, Hollywood Legends Series, NRFB, D2..$75.00
Ken as The Beast, 1991, NRFB $35.00
Ken Busy Talking, 1972, orig outfit, VG, M15 ....$85.00

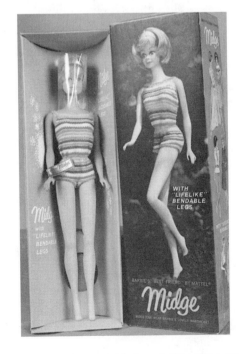

Midge, 1963, bendable legs, MIB, $500.00.

Midge, 1963, blond hair, straight legs, MIB, D2 ....$150.00
Midge, 1963, blond hair, straight legs, nude, EX, D2........$75.00

Midge, 1963, red hair, orig swimsuit & ribbon, bendable legs, M, D2 ....$450.00
Midge, 30th Anniversary, 1992, porcelain, MIB, D2 .....$175.00
PJ, Free Moving, 1975, orig swimsuit, NM.......................$85.00
PJ, Live Action, 1971, orig outfit, VG, M15 ....$125.00
PJ, New & Groovy Talking, 1969, NRFB, M15 ....$275.00
PJ, Sun Lovin', 1978, NRFB, M15 ....$65.00
PJ, Sweet Roses, 1983, NRFB, M15 ....$65.00
PJ, Talking, 1970, orig outfit, NM, D2 ....$165.00

Skipper, 1965, bendable legs, MIB, $150.00.

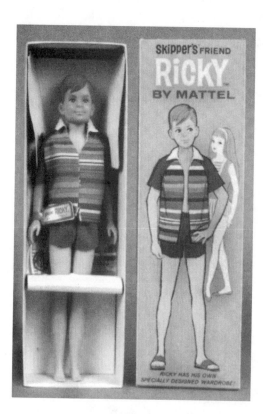

Ricky, 1965, MIB, $175.00.

Skooter, 1965, straight legs, MIB, $150.00.

Skipper, Cool Tops, MIB...$35.00
Skipper, Dramatic New Living, 1970, orig swimsuit, NM, D2..$50.00
Skipper, Growing Up, 1974, NRFB $125.00
Skipper, Living, 1970, MIB $125.00
Skipper, Malibu, 1975, MIB, M15................................$50.00
Skipper, Pose 'N Play, 1973, MIP................................$125.00
Skipper, Quick Curl, 1973-75, MIB $75.00
Skipper, Twist 'N Turn, 1969, red hair, orig outfit & shoes, rpl headband, M, D2 ....$200.00
Skipper, 1964, red hair, orig swimsuit, rpl shoes, bendable legs, M15...$65.00
Skipper, 1965, red hair, orig swimsuit, bendable legs, NM, D2 ....$100.00
Skipper, 1970, brunette hair, straight legs, MIB, D2 ......$225.00
Skooter, Funtime, 1976, NRFB, minimum value............$200.00
Skooter, 1963, brunette hair, orig swimsuit & bows, MIB, D2 ....$175.00
Skooter, 1965, blond hair, bendable legs, MIB, D2 ....$225.00
Stacey, Twist 'N Turn, 1968, blond hair, orig swimsuit, NM, D2...$300.00
Stacey, Twist 'N Turn, 1968, red hair, orig swimsuit, NM, D2...$300.00

Stacey, Twist 'N Turn, 1969, blond hair, orig swimsuit, VG, M15 ....$180.00
Stacie, Toontown, 1993, MIB $40.00
Steffie, Busy Talking, 1972, orig outfit, NM, M15 ....$275.00
Steffie, Walk Lively, 1968, orig outfit, NM, D2 ....$180.00
Tiff, Pose 'N Play, 1972, NRFB, minimum value............$500.00
Todd, 1965, NRFB, D2...$225.00
Tutti, 1966, brunette hair, dressed in Cookin' Goodies, EX, D2...$50.00

Tutti, 1966, brunette hair, orig outfit, NM, D2 ....$85.00
Whitney, Jewel Secrets, 1986, NRFB, D2 ....$95.00
Whitney, Perfume Pretty, 1987, NRFB, M15 ....$85.00
Whitney, Style Magic, 1988, NRFB, M15 ....$65.00

CASES

Barbie, Francie, Casey & Tutti, 1966, hard plastic, NM, minimum value $100.00
Barbie, Francie & Skipper, 1965, blk vinyl w/colorful image, rare, NM, minimum value $75.00
Barbie, 1963, blk background, EX $25.00
Barbie & Ken, 1963, bl, rectangular, complete w/hangers & drawers, VG, M15 ....$40.00
Barbie & Midge Travel Pals, 1963, blk, rnd, NM, D2 ....$150.00
Barbie & Skipper Vanity Trunk, 1965, vinyl, rare, NM, minimum value $250.00
Barbie Goes Travelin', 1965, EX $195.00
Barbie Trousseau Trunk, hard plastic, NM, minimum value ..$95.00
Francie, 1965, pk & wht, hexagon, NM, D2 ....$35.00

Golden Dream Barbie, 1980, $10.00.
(Photo courtesy Beth Summers)

Ken in Rally Days, 1962, teal, EX, D2/M15 ....$20.00
Miss Barbie, 1963, blk patent leather w/zipper closure, EX, D2 ....$100.00
Pink & Pretty Barbie, 1982, vinyl w/metal closure, M......$10.00
Purse-Pal, vinyl, pk or bl background, strap hdl, rare, NM, ea, minimum value $150.00
Skipper, 1964, bl background, rare, NM $150.00

Skipper and Skooter, made in France, blue or yellow background, EX, $100.00 each. (Photo courtesy Stefanie Deutsch)

Skipper & Skooter, 1965, blk vinyl hatbox shape, rare, NM..$75.00
Tutti, #3561, orange w/flowers, EX, P2 ....$20.00
Tutti, #3568, yellow, EX, P2 ....$30.00
Tutti & Chris Patio Picnic Case, NM................................$100.00
Tutti Play Case, various colors, EX, ea $35.00
Tutti's Playhouse, 1965, M, D2 ....$150.00

CLOTHING AND ACCESSORIES

Action Fashion, Skipper & Fluff, MOC, minimum value..$75.00
Altogether Elegant, Francie, #1242-0, complete, NM, D2..$125.00
American Airlines Captain, Ken, #779-1, complete, M, D2 ..$225.00
Arabian Nights, Ken, #774-0, complete, NM, D2 ....$165.00
Baby Doll Pinks, Barbie, #3403-1, complete, M, D2.........$45.00
Barbie & the Rockers, several variations, 1985, NRFB, ea ..$20.00
Barbie Cheerleader Set, #7278, 1990, NRFP $10.00
Barbie in Holland, #823-2, complete, NM, D2...............$125.00
Barbie Pet Show Fashions, several variations, 1986, NRFB, ea $15.00
Barbie's Boudoir Fashion Pak, #1834, MOC...................$165.00
Beachy Peachy, Skipper, #1938, NRFB, minimum value .$175.00
Beauty & the Beast Dinner Fashion, Barbie, #3152, 1992, MIP..$30.00
Best Buy Fashion Pak, Skipper, #7771, NRFP, minimum value $35.00
Birthday Beauty, Tutti, #3617, dress only, EX, P2 ....$20.00
Bloomin' Blue, Tutti, #8593, NRFB.................................$125.00
Bold Gold, Ken, #1436-1, complete, M, D2.......................$35.00
Bride's Dream, Barbie, #947-2, complete, EX, D2 ....$85.00
Busy Morning, Barbie, #956-1, complete, NM, D2 ....$150.00

Ken and Allan, made in France, rare, M, $300.00.
(Photo courtesy Paris and Susan Manos)

Campus Hero, Ken, #770, complete, VG, M15 ....$35.00
Campus Sweetheart, Barbie, #1616-0, complete, M, D2 ..$595.00
Cheerleader, Barbie, #876-1, complete, EX, D2 ....$75.00
Chill Chasers, Skipper, #1926, 1966, complete, M...........$50.00
Cinderella's Ballgown, Barbie, #1275, 1991, NRFB..........$30.00
Confetti Cutie, Skipper, #1700-0, Sears Exclusive, complete,
    NM, D2 ....$250.00
Cookie Time, Skipper, #1912, NRFB, minimum value ..$150.00
Country Clubbin', Ken, #1400, NRFB......................$175.00
Daisy Crazy, Skipper, #1732, 1970, NRFB $75.00
Dancing Doll, Barbie, #1621-1, complete, NM, D2 ....$295.00
Dandy Lines, Ken, Designer Originals #3797, 1981, NRFB ...$20.00
Day-To-Night, Barbie, several variations, 1984, MIP, ea.$15.00
Day-To-Night, Ken, several variations, 1984, MIP, ea.....$15.00
Dr Ken, #793, complete, VG, M15 ....$45.00
Dreamy Blues, Barbie, #1456-0, complete, M, D2 ....$65.00
Drizzle Sizzle, Skipper, #1972, 1969, NRFB...................$125.00
Drum Majorette, Barbie, #875, complete, VG, M15 ....$50.00
Fashion Shiner, Barbie, 1961-3, coat only, NM, D2...........$25.00
First Things First, Francie, #1252-2, complete, NM, D2 ..$55.00
Flower Girl, Tutti, #3615, complete, NM, M15 ....$125.00
Flower Power, Skipper, #3373, 1972, MIP $45.00
Fluff, Dramatic New Living, 1971, MIB.........................$175.00

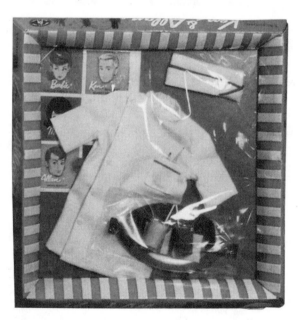

Fountain Boy, Ken, #1407, 1964, NRFB, $150.00.
(Photo courtesy Stefanie Deutsch)

Fraternity Dance, Barbie, #1638-0, complete, EX, D2 ...$225.00
Fun Runners, Skipper, #3372, complete, M $55.00
Gad Abouts, Francie, #1250-0, complete, NM, D2 ....$150.00
Get-Ups 'N Go Weekend Wardrobe, Skipper, #9166, complete,
    M..$50.00
Glimmer Glamour, Barbie, #1547-0, replica hose, VG, D2..$395.00
Going Bowling, Ken, #1403-0, complete, NM, D2..........$25.00
Golden Girl, Barbie, #911-1, complete, NM, D2.............$70.00
Graduation, Ken, #795, NRFB, D21 ....$75.00
Handsome for School, Todd, #7484, NRFB.....................$45.00
Hats 'N Hats, Skipper & Skooter, MOC, minimum value .$50.00

Hearts 'N Flowers, Skipper, #1945, complete, NM........$165.00
Heavenly Holidays, Barbie, #4277, NRFP $55.00
Hiking Holiday, Ken, #1412-3, complete, NM, D2 ....$85.00
Ice Breaker, Barbie, #942-1, complete, EX, D2 ....$40.00
Jeepers Creepers, Skipper, #1966, NRFB, minimum value...$150.00
Jeepers Creepers, Skipper, #1966, 1969, complete, M $85.00
Jump Into Lace, Barbie, #1823-0, complete, M, D2.........$65.00

Ken in Mexico, MIB, $135.00; Time for Tennis, #790, MIB, $125.00. (Photo courtesy June Moon)

Kinderparty, Tutti, #7983, NRFB, minimum value $150.00
King Arthur, Ken, #773, NRFB $325.00
Land & Sea, Skipper, #1917, complete, M $65.00
Learning To Ride, Skipper, #1935, complete, NM.........$175.00
Lights Out, Ricky, #1501, NRFB, D2................................$75.00
Little Red Riding Hood, Barbie, #880, NRFB, D2..........$600.00
Lolapaloozas, Skipper, #1947, complete, M, minimum value....$85.00
Lots of Lace, Skipper, #1730, NRFB, minimum value $50.00
Masquerade, Ken, #794-0, complete, M, D2 ....$65.00
Mini Chex, Francie, #1209-0, complete, NM, D2 ....$75.00
Miss Astronaut, Barbie, #1641, suit only, VG, M15 ....$55.00
Nifty Knickers, Skipper, #3291, NRFB, minimum value..$50.00
Nightly Negligee, Barbie, #965-6, complete, NM, D2......$45.00
Nighty Nice Fashion Pak, Skipper, 1970, MOC..............$35.00
Orange Blossom, Barbie, #987-0, complete, NM, D2 ....$50.00
Oscar de la Renta for Barbie, several variations, 1984, NRFB,
    ea...$35.00
Peachy Fleecy, Barbie, #915-1, complete, NM, D2...........$95.00
Pink Moonbeams, Barbie, #1694-1, complete, NM, D2.$125.00
Pink Princess, Skipper, #1747, complete, M $75.00
Plaid Lad, Todd, #8595, NRFB..................................$75.00
Platter Party, Skipper, #1914-0, complete, M, D2 ....$55.00
Poodle Parade, Barbie, #1643-3, complete, NM, D2 ......$550.00
Popover, Skipper, #1943, 1967, complete, M $70.00
Puddle Jumpers, Skipper, #3601, NRFB, minimum value.$65.00
Real Sporty, Skipper, #1961, 1968, complete, M..............$50.00
Red Sensation, Skipper, #1901, 1964, complete, M $45.00
Registered Nurse, Barbie, #991-0, complete, NM, D2 ......$90.00
Rolla Scoot, Skipper, #1940, 1967, NRFB....................$195.00
Roller Skate Date, Ken, #1405-1, complete, NM, D2 ......$55.00
Roman Holiday, Barbie, #968-3, complete, NM, D2......$695.00

Red, White, and Wild, Ken, #1829, 1972, NRFB, from $60.00 to $80.00. (Photo courtesy Stefanie Deutsch)

Sand Castles, Tutti, #3603, complete, M, P2....................$75.00
Seein' the Sights, Ken, #1421-0, complete, NM, D2......$250.00

Ski Party, Barbie, Designer Collection #7079, 1983, NRFB...$12.00
Skimmer 'N Scarf Fashion Pak, Skipper & Fluff, 1971, MIP.$45.00
Skimmy Stripes, Skipper, #1956, 1968, complete, M $100.00
Skippin' Rope, Tutti, #3604, red top & pants only, EX, P2 ..$20.00
Skippin' Rope, Tutti, #3604, 1966, complete, M..............$50.00
Sleeping Beauty Peasant Dress, Barbie, #4614, 1992, NRFP ..$25.00
Some Shoes Fashion Pak, Skipper & Fluff, 1971, MIP $50.00
Sorority Meeting, Barbie, #937-2, dress only, NM, D2.....$25.00
Springtime Magic, Barbie, #7092, NRFB $50.00
Stormy Weather, Barbie, #949-5, complete, NM, D2 ......$35.00
Stripes Away, Barbie & Francie, #1775, MIB.................$250.00
Suede Scene, Ken, #26, complete, VG, M15 ....$15.00
Sunday Dress, Tutti, #2650, NFRB, minimum value........$55.00
Sunday Suit, Ricky, #1503, complete, NM $35.00
Sunny Pastels, Skipper, #1910, NRFB, minimum value .$125.00
Sweater Girl, Barbie, #976-2, complete, EX, D2...............$55.00
Tea Party, Skipper, #1924, NRFB, minimum value........$250.00
Teeter Timers, Skipper, #3647, NRFB, minimum value...$50.00
Tennis Anyone, Barbie, #941-0, complete, NM, D2 ....$45.00
Tennis Tunic, Francie, #1221-0, complete, NM, D2........$45.00
Tiff, Pose 'N Play, 1972, NRFB..................................$395.00
Touchdown, Ken, #779, MIB $75.00
Town Toggs, Skipper, #1922, 1965, complete, M.............$75.00
Travel Fashion Playset, Barbie, #9264, 1984, NRFB $15.00
Two for the Ball, Francie, #1232, complete, VG, M15 ..$125.00
Underliners, Barbie, #1821-2, complete, NM, D2 ....$65.00
Water Sports Fashion Playset, Barbie, #9263, 1984, NRFB ..$15.00
Way Out West, Ken, #1720, NRFB, D2 ....$75.00

Ship Ahoy, Skipper, #1918, complete, M, minimum value $75.00.

Ship Shape, Tutti, #3602, somplete, NM, P2 ....$15.00
Shoe Parade, Skipper & Skooter, MOC, minimum value .$95.00
Shoe Parade Fashion Pak, Skipper & Skooter, 1965, MOC .$95.00
Silk 'N Fancy, Skipper, #1902, complete, M.....................$50.00
Silken Flame, Barbie, #977-0, complete, NM, D2 ....$75.00
Skater's Waltz, Barbie, #1629-0, complete, NM, D2 ......$175.00
Skating Fun, Skipper, #1908, 1964-66, complete, M........$50.00

Wedding of the Year, Barbie, #5743, 1982, NRFB, $20.00.
(Photo courtesy Beth Summers)

Wedding of the Year, Bridesmaid's Dream, Barbie, #5745, 1982,
NRFB $20.00
Wedding of the Year, Suited for the Groom, Ken, #5744, 1982,
NRFB $15.00

What's New at the Zoo, Skipper, #1925, NRFB, minimum value $125.00
White Delight, Barbie, #3799, Designer Originals, NRFP.$20.00
Winter Holiday, Barbie, #975-2, complete, EX, D2..........$65.00

FURNITURE, ROOMS, HOUSES, AND SHOPS

Barbie & Ken Little Theater, 1964, complete, NMIB, D2..$600.00
Barbie & Skipper Deluxe House, Sears Exclusive, 1965, complete, EX, minimum value $80.00
Barbie & Skipper School, 1965, complete, rare, EX, minimum value...$500.00
Barbie Country Living House, 1973-77, complete, EX.....$75.00
Barbie Dream Bed, 1982, complete, MIB..........................$25.00
Barbie Dream Buffet, 1985, complete, MIB $25.00
Barbie Dream House, 1961, 1st edition, complete, NM, D2.$150.00
Barbie Fashion Living Room, 1985, complete, MIB........$35.00
Barbie Fashion Plaza, 1975, NMIB, M15..........................$100.00
Barbie Housemate, 1966, complete, D2 ....$150.00
Barbie Ice Cream Shoppe, 1987, complete, MIB..............$50.00
Barbie Loves McDonald's, 1983, NRFB $50.00
Barbie Mountain Ski Cabin, Sears Exclusive, complete, EX..$35.00
Barbie Soda Shoppe, 1988, complete, MIB.......................$40.00
Barbie Starlight Bed, 1990, complete, MIB $30.00
Barbie Wash & Watch Dishwasher, 1991, complete, MIB..$20.00
Barbie's Dream Kitchen-Dinette, 1964, complete, EX ...$250.00
Barbie's Room-Fulls Country Kitchen, 1974, NRFB, D2 .$50.00
Barbie's Room-Fulls Firelight Living Room, 1974, NRFB, D2...$125.00
California Dream Barbie Hot Dog Stand, 1988, complete, MIB $50.00
Cinderella Magical Ballroom, 1991, MIB $60.00
Cool Tops Skipper T-Shirt Shop, 1989, complete, MIB ..$20.00
Francie & Casey Housemates, 1966, complete, NM, D2..$200.00

Francie House, 1966, complete, EX, minimum value $75.00.
(Photo courtesy Paris and Susan Manos)

Go-Together Bunk Beds, Skipper 'N Skooter, 1965, NRFB, minimum value $200.00
Go-Together Dining Room, Barbie 'N Skipper, 1965, NRFB, minumum value...$250.00

Go-Together Lawn Swing & Planter, 1964, complete, MIB, D2..$150.00
Go-Together Swing, 1964, complete, M, D2..................$100.00
Magical Mansion, 1990, NRFB, D2 ....$1,000.00
Pink Sparkles Refrigerator/Freezer, 1990, NRFB.............$25.00
Pink Sparkles Washer & Dryer, 1990, NRFB $25.00
Skipper's Dream Room, 1964, complete, M, D2 ....$500.00
Superstar Barbie Piano Set, 1989, complete, MIB $25.00
Suzy Goose, Skipper's Jeweled Bed, 1965, MIB, D2 ....$150.00
Suzy Goose, Skipper's Jeweled Wardrobe, 1965, complete, rare, MIB, minimum value $275.00
Suzy Goose, Tutti & Todd's Dutch Bedroom, rare, complete, M, minimum value...$800.00
Suzy Goose Vanity, 1963, complete, EX, D2 ....$35.00
Sweet Roses Vanity & Nightstand, 1987, NRFB.............$25.00
Tutti & Chris House, 1967, complete, NM, D2 ....$125.00

Tutti Ice Cream Stand, 1965, rare, NM, $295.00.
(Photo courtesy Marl Davidson)

World of Barbie House, 1966, complete, EX, D2............$150.00

GIFT SETS

Barbie, Ken & Midge Pep Rally, 1964, NRFB, from $1,000 to $1,300.00
Barbie, Special Expressions, 1989, Woolworth, MIB........$40.00
Barbie & Kelly Gardening Fun, 1996, NRFB, D2.............$45.00
Barbie Deluxe 100 Piece Gift Set, 1992, complete, MIB..$60.00
Barbie for President, Toys 'R Us, 1991, NRFB.................$75.00
Barbie Loves Elvis, 1996, NRFB, D2 ....$75.00
Barbie Mix 'N Match Set, 1963, NRFB, from $2,000 to..$3,000.00
Beach Fun Barbie & Ken, 1993, complete, MIB.............$35.00
Birthday Beauties, Tutti, #3617, 1968, NRFB $175.00
Cinderella Gift Pack, Disney Classics, 1992, NRFB.......$125.00
Clowning Around, Tutti, #3606, 1967, complete, M $65.00
Color Magic Set, 1965, complete, rare, MIB, D2 ....$4,000.00
Denim Fun Barbie, Ken & Skipper, 1989, NRFB $60.00

Barbie & Ken Campin' Out, 1983, NRFB, $100.00.
(Photo courtesy Beth Summers)

Denim'n Ruffles Barbie & High Stepper Western Gift Set, 1995, NRFB, $100.00. (Photo courtesy J. Michael Augustyniak)

Dressing Fun Barbie, 1993, complete, MIB $55.00
Francie & Her Swingin' Separates, 1966, Sears, MIB, minimum value $1,000.00
Francie Rise & Shine, 1971, NRFB, minimum value..$1,000.00
Happy Birthday Barbie, 1984, NRFB $75.00
Happy Halloween Barbie & Kelly, Target, 1996, NRFB, D2 .$70.00
Island Fun Barbie & Ken, 1993, complete, MIB $35.00
Jamie Strollin' in Style, Sears, 1972, MIB.......................$425.00
Living Barbie Action Accents, Sears Exclusive, 1970, complete, MIB..$450.00
Living Fluff Sunshine Special, Sears Exclusive, 1971, complete, MIB, minimum value $350.00
PJ Swingin' in Silver, Sears, 1970, complete, MIB $800.00
Sharin' Sisters, 1992, NRFB, D2 ....$25.00
Skipper & Her Swing-A-Rounder Gym, 1972, complete, MIB.$300.00
Skipper Bright & Breezy, 1969, Sears Exclusive, complete, MIB, minimum value...$895.00

Skipper on Wheels, 1965, complete, MIB, $600.00.
(Photo courtesy Paris and Susan Manos)

Skooter w/Her Cut 'N Button Costumes, 1965-67, complete, MIB, minimum value $250.00
Sparkle Eyes Barbie Dressing Room & Fashion Set, 1992, complete, MIB $65.00
Swing-A-Ling Tutti, 1967-68, MIB $475.00
Tennis Stars Barbie & Ken, 1986, NRFB.........................$55.00
Twirly Curls Barbie, 1982, NRFB....................................$60.00
Wedding Party Midge, 1990, NRFB, D2 ....$150.00
Western Stampin' Barbie, 1993, 1993, complete, MIB.....$45.00

VEHICLES

Airplane, Irwin, 1963, turquoise and cream, rare, EX, minimum value $500.00.

Allan's New Roadster (known as Skipper's Sports Car), Irwin, 1965, gr, NRFB, minimum value $250.00
Austin Healy, Irwin, 1962, red & wht, very rare, NRFB, D2...$3,500.00
Barbie Goin' Boating, Sears Exclusive, 1973, NM, D2 .....$50.00
Barbie Jeep, 1987, MIB $15.00
Barbie Motor Bike, 1983, MIB $35.00
Beach Buggy for Skipper, Irwin, 1964, rare, MIB, minimum value..$500.00
Cinderella Wedding Carriage & Horse, 1991, MIB..........$55.00
Ferrari, 1987-88, red or wht, MIB, D2, ea $50.00
Ken's Hot Rod, Irwin, 1961, NM, D2 ....$165.00

Porsche, 1991, pk, working headlights, NRFB..................$50.00
Ten Speeder, 1973, MIB, D2......................................$25.00
1957 Belair Chevy, 1989, 1st edition, aqua, MIB...........$150.00
1957 Belair Chevy, 1990, 2nd edition, pk, MIB.............$125.00

MISCELLANEOUS

Barbie & Francie Color Magic Fashion Designer Set, 1966-67, complete, MIB...$450.00

Barbie and the Rockers Dress Up Set, Color-forms, 1986, MIB, $5.00. (Photo courtesy Beth Summers)

Barbie Dress-Up Kit, Colorforms, 1975, MIB..................$35.00
Beauty Bath, Barbie, 1975, MIB, M15...........................$45.00
Binder, Barbie & Skipper in School Days, vinyl, pk background, rare, NM, minimum value.......................................$150.00
Book, Barbie in Dream Vacation, Hasbro Listen 'N Look series, 1984, M...$5.00
Book, Barbie's New York Summer, Random House, 1962, EX, D2..$25.00
Book, Happy-Go-Lucky Skipper, by Carl Memling, Random House, 1965, hardcover, NM, from $65 to.................$75.00
Box, Ken, 1961, EX, D2..$50.00
Box, Ponytail Barbie, 1962, G, D2...............................$65.00
Box, Skipper, 1963, EX+, D2......................................$75.00
Charm Bracelet, Peter Brams Designs, 1989, sterling silver w/8 charms, MIB...$150.00
China Dinner Set, Barbie, Chilton Globe Inc, 1989, 16 pcs, NRFB...$30.00
Colorforms, Malibu Barbie, 1972, NMIB, J2....................$50.00
Comic Book, Barbie, Marvel Comics, 1991, several issues, M, ea...$3.00
Diary, My Very Own Diary By Barbie, Western Publishing, 1985, NM..$5.00
Embroidery Set, Barbie, Ken & Midge, 1963, complete, MIB, from $200 to...$250.00
Embroidery Set, Skipper, Standard Toycraft, 1965, complete, rare, MIB, minimum value....................................$200.00
Game, Barbie Shopping Spree Giant Card Game, Western Publishing, 1991, complete, MIB...........................$5.00
Headphones, Barbie, Nasta/Mattel, 1984, built-in radio w/volume switch, M...$35.00
Paper Dolls, Barbie, Ken & Midge, Whitman #1976, 1963, uncut, M...$80.00
Paper Dolls, New 'N Groovy PJ, Whitman #1981, 1970, uncut, M...$50.00
Paper Dolls, Skooter Fashion-Go-Round, Whitman #4639, 1965, rare, uncut, M, minimum value.....................$200.00
Polly Pocket, Barbie, 1994, M, D2...............................$12.00
Pose Me Pretty Beauty Set, Barbie, 1984, complete w/makeup & hair accessories, MIB...$20.00

Barbie Mattel-A-Phone, M, minimum value $100.00.
(Photo courtesy Paris and Susan Manos)

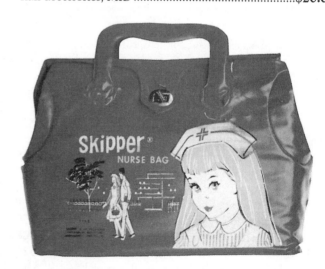

Skipper Nurse Bag, vinyl, complete, rare, minimum value $300.00.

Poster, Dream Room Barbie, 1989, w/space for name, M ...$5.00

Puzzle, fr-tray; Barbie, Western Publishing, 1985, bedroom scene, complete, M $5.00

Puzzle, fr-tray; Skipper, Whitman, 1965, Skipper wearing School Days, complete, rare, M, minimum value...................$60.00

Puzzle, jigsaw; Nostalgic Barbie, American Publishing, 1989, 550 pcs, MIB..$25.00

Puzzle, jigsaw; Skipper & Skooter, Whitman, 1965, picnic scene, complete, MIB $50.00

Quick Curl Boutique, Barbie, 1974, VG, M15................$45.00

Scrapbook, 1964, features Swirl Ponytail Barbie, NM, D2 .$65.00

Sing-A-Long Radio, Barbie, Nasta/Mattel, 1989, pk w/decal, 6x9", M $50.00

Skipper Electric Drawing Set, Lakeside, 1964, complete, MIB..$125.00

Skipper's Spelling Board, Bar Zim, rare, NM, minimum value $300.00

Video, Barbie & the Rockers Out of This World, Hi-Tops Video, 1987, MIB $15.00

Wallet, 1964, Skipper wearing Masquerade, vinyl, bl or yel background, rare, NM, ea from $55 to.............................$65.00

Battery-Operated Toys

From the standpoint of being visually entertaining, nothing can compare with the battery-operated toy. Most (probably as much as 95%) were made in Japan from the '40s through the '60s, though some were distributed by American companies — Marx, Ideal, and Daisy, for instance — who often sold them under their own names. So even if they're marked, sometimes it's just about impossible to identify the actual manufacturer. Though batteries had been used to power trains and provide simple illumination in earlier toys, the Japanese toys could smoke, walk, talk, drink, play instruments, blow soap bubbles, and do just about anything else humanly possible to dream up and engineer. Generally, the more antics the toy performs, the more collectible it is. Rarity is important as well, but first and foremost to consider is condition. Because of their complex mechanisms, many will no longer work. Children often stopped them in mid-cycle, rubber hoses and bellows aged and cracked, and leaking batteries caused them to corrode, so very few have survived to the present intact and in good enough condition to interest a collector. Though it's sometimes possible to have them repaired, unless you can buy them cheap enough to allow for the extra expense involved, it is probably better to wait on a better example. Original boxes are a definite plus in assessing the value of a battery-op and can sometimes be counted on to add from 30% to 50% (and up), depending on the box's condition, of course, as well as the toy's age and rarity.

We have made every attempt to list these toys by the name as it appears on the original box. Some will sound very similar. Many toys were reissued with only minor changes and subsequently renamed. Battery toys in general are down in price — except for the rare ones. Now might be a good time to buy them because they probably will come back in stronger demand as so many other toys have always done. For more information we recommend *Collecting Toys* by Richard O'Brien (Books Americana) and *Collecting Battery Toys* by Don Hultzman (Collector Books).

Advisors: Tom Lastrapes (L4); Judy and Kerry Irvin (K5).

See also Aeronautical; Automobiles and Other Vehicle Replicas; Boats; Marx; Robots and Space Toys.

ABC Fairy Train, MT, children shake as train advances w/lights & sound, litho tin, 14", EX (EX box).......................$175.00

Accordion Bear, Alps, 1950s, several actions, litho tin & plush, remote control, 11", EX (EX box)............................$800.00

Accordion Player Hobo w/Monkey, Alps, seated hobo plays accordion while monkey plays cymbals, MIB, L4 ....$575.00

Accordion Playing Bunny w/Baby Bunny Playing Cymbals, Alps, 1950s, several actions, 12", EX $400.00

Acrobat Clown, YM, 1960s, litho tin, 9", EX (EX box) .$125.00

Airmail Helicopter, KO, advances w/flashing lights & spinning props, mostly tin, 10", EX (EX box) $225.00

Alfa Romeo Magico, Schuco #2010, red w/blk tires, remote control, 9½", NM (EX box), A..................................$850.00

Amazing Spider-Man Diesel Train, NMIB, B5 ....$65.00

Andy Gard Combat Knights No 143, General Molds & Plastic Corp, 1950s, several actions, 10", EX......................$165.00

Animal Helicopter, MT, rare, MIB, L4...........................$575.00

Annie Tugboat, Y, 1950s, mystery action w/lights & sound, 12½", EX...$175.00

Anti-Aircraft Jeep, TN, 1950s, litho tin, several actions, 11", EX..$300.00

Antique Fire Car, TN, 1950s, several actions, litho tin, 10", EX..$300.00

Antique Gooney Car, Alps, 1960s, wht open touring car w/animated driver, 4 actions, 9", MIB $150.00

Arctic Explorer Sled, Sears Exclusive, advances w/flashing lights & revolving props, tin & plastic, 16", NMIB..........$850.00

Arctic Snowmobile, MT, MIB, L4 ....$475.00

Arthur-A-Go-Go Drummer, Alps, 1960s, several actions, 10", MIB, L4...$750.00

Astro Dog (Snoopy look-alike), Y, 1960s, several actions, 11", EX $200.00

Automatic Toll Gate, Sears, 1955, litho tin, 17" base, 8" Valiant car, EX $300.00

B-Z Porter, MT, 1950s, figure on platform truck w/3 pcs of luggage, 7", MIB, L4..$375.00

B-Z Rabbit, MT, 1950s, several actions, litho tin, 7", EX ..$125.00

Baby Bertha the Watering Elephant, Mego, 1960s, 3 actions, 10", rare, MIB, L4..$1,250.00

Ball Blowing Clown, TN, 1950s, several actions, litho tin & celluloid, 11", EX...$275.00

Ball Playing Dog, Linemar, 1950s, 3 actions, tin & plush, 9", M, L4..$175.00

Balloon Blowing Monkey, Alps, 1950s, several actions, 11", MIB, L4...$225.00

Balloon Bunny, Y, remote control, rare, MIB, L4..........$375.00

Bambi, see Walking Bambi

Barber Bear, TN, 1950s, barber clips & combs child's hair w/several other actions, tin & plush, 10", EX (EX box), L4.........$600.00

Barney Bear the Drummer Boy, Alps/Cragstan, 1950s, plush & tin w/cloth clothes, remote control, 11", M, L4 ......$250.00

Bart Simpson on Skateboard, Mattel, remote control, 6", M, K1..$60.00

Bartender, Rosko, several actions, litho tin & vinyl w/cloth clothes, 11½", MIB, L4..................................$85.00

Batman & Robin Batcycle, Hong Kong, plastic, 7", NM (NM box)..$465.00

Batmobile, ASC, 1960s, litho tin, remote control, 9", NMIB....$600.00

Batmobile, Taiwan, 1980s, litho tin, 10", M (NM box), A.$300.00

Bear Chef, see Cuty Cook

Bear the Cashier, MT, 1950s, several actions, 7½", MIB .$425.00

Bear the Magician, MT, 1960s, several actions, 12½", scarce, EX (EX box), minimum value $2,000.00

Bear the Shoemaker, TN, 1950s, hammers shoe & smokes pipe, litho tin & plush, 9", MIB, L4..........................$575.00

Bear Typist, TN, 1950s, several actions, litho tin & plush, 7½", scarce, EX...$800.00

Beauty Parlor Bear w/Lighted Dryer Stand, S&E, 1950s, several actions, litho tin & plush, 9½", rare, EX..............$1,000.00

Begging Puppy, Y, 1960s, several actions, 9", EX............$100.00

Big Dipper, Technofix, 1960s, 3 cars travel track, litho tin, 21", EX $200.00

Big John Indian Chief, TN, 1960s, several actions, litho tin, 12½", MIB...$125.00

Big Wheel Ice Cream Truck, Taiyo, 1970s, several actions, 10", EX $125.00

Billy the Kid Sheriff, Y, 1950s, several actions, 10½", EX..$350.00

Bimbo the Drumming Clown, Alps/Cragstan, 1950s, several actions, litho tin, 9", rare, NM...............................$600.00

Bimbo the Drumming Clown, Alps/Cragstan, 1950s, several actions, lithographed tin with cloth clothes, 9", rare, NMIB, $650.00. (Photo courtesy Don Hultzman)

Bingo the Clown, TN, 1950s, 13", rare, NMIB, L4........$475.00

Black Smithy Bear, TN, 1950s, litho tin & plush, 9", EX, L4 ....$375.00

Blacksmith Bear, A1, 1950s, several actions, tin & plush w/cloth clothes, 10", NMIB...$375.00

Blushing Frankenstein, TN, pants fall down & he blushes, tin & rubber, 12½", NM (EX box), A $385.00

Blushing Gunfighter, Y, 1960s, several actions, litho tin w/cloth shirt, 11", EX (G box) $250.00

Blushing Willie, Y, 1960s, pours drink into glass w/several actions, litho tin w/cloth clothes, vinyl face, 10", NMIB...$150.00

Bob's Farm Tractor, MT, 1950s, detachable driver, several actions, 9", rare, EX..$185.00

Bobby the Drinking Bear, Y, 1950s, several actions, 10", MIB, L4...$675.00

Bongo Monkey, Alps, 1960s, several actions, litho tin & plush w/plastic hat, 9½", EX...$165.00

Bowling Bank, MB Daniel, 1960s, several actions, 10", EX...$185.00

Bruno Accordion Bear, Y, 1950s, several actions, litho tin & plush w/cloth clothes, 10½", EX..............................$285.00

Bubble Blowing Boy, Y, 1950s, several actions, NM $300.00

Bubble Blowing Bunny, Y, 1950s, several actions, litho tin, 7", EX...$200.00

Bubble Blowing Dog, Y, 1950s, litho tin, 8", M, L4........$275.00

Bubble Blowing Kangaroo, MT, 1950s, several actions, litho tin, 9", rare, NM...$400.00

Bubble Blowing Monkey, Alps, 1959, litho tin, 10", EX ..$200.00

Bubble Blowing Popeye, Linemar, 1950s, several actions, litho tin, 12", rare, EX, minimum value $2,000.00

Bubble Blowing Road Roller, MT, MIB, L4....................$250.00

Bubble Blowing Washing Bear, Y, 1950s, several actions, litho tin & plastic, 8", NM...$350.00

Bubbling Bull (Wild West Rodeo), Linemar, 1950s, several actions, litho tin, EX, 8"...$200.00

Bunny the Cashier, MT, 1950s, several actions, litho tin, 7½", EX...$300.00

Bunny the Magician, Alps, 1950s, several actions, litho tin & plush w/cloth clothes, 14½", MIB.........................$450.00

Burger Chef, Y, 1950s, several actions, litho tin & plush, 9", EX...$200.00

Busy Bizzy Friendly Bug, MT, 1950s, 3 actions, litho tin, 6", EX...$125.00

Busy Housekeeper Bear, Alps, 1950s, several actions, 8½", MIB...$325.00

Calypso Joe, Linemar, Black man advances & plays drum, tin w/cloth clothes, remote control, 10", EX................$600.00

Cappy the Happy Baggage Porter, Dog, Alps, 1960s, several actions, litho tin, 12", EX..$100.00

Captain Blushwell, Y, 1960s, several actions, tin & vinyl w/cloth clothes, 11", MIB, L4..$175.00

Captain Hook, Marusan, 1950s, 3 actions, 11", scarce, NM, minimum value..$1,600.00

Captain Kidd Pirate Ship, Yonezawa, 1960s, several actions, litho tin, 13", rare, EX $400.00

Casino King Slot Machine, Waco, EX, L4....................$100.00

Champion Boat 2-J, Bandai, 1950s, litho tin, 12", NM..$250.00

Champion Racer No 301, TN, advances w/sparks, litho tin, 18", NMIB, A...$400.00

Chap the Obedient Dog, Rosko, 1960s, 3 actions, MIB, L4..$175.00

Charley Weaver Bartender, TN, 1962, several actions, litho tin & vinyl w/cloth clothes, 12", EX..............................$125.00

Charlie the Drumming Clown, Alps, 1960s, several actions, 9½", MIB, L4 ....$325.00

Cheerful Dachshund, Y, 1960s, several actions, 8½", EX .$85.00

Chemical Fire Engine, HTC, 1950s, several actions, 10", EX $200.00

Chimp & Pup Rail Car, Cragstan, 1950s, several actions, 9", rare, EX $225.00

Chimp w/Xylophone, Y, 1970s, complete w/4 records & hammer, 8", rare, EX $200.00

Chimpy the Jolly Drummer, Alps, 1950s, several actions, 9", EX $75.00

Chippy the Chipmunk, Alps, 1950s, 4 actions, MIB, L4 ..$225.00

Christmas Lantern, Japan, glass Santa & cb tree, 5", EX (EX box), A $125.00

Chuckling Charlie the Hysterical Laughing Clown, SH, 1960s, several actions, EX $300.00

Cindy the Meowing Cat, Tomiyama, 1950s, several actions, 12", EX $100.00

Circus Elephant, MIB, L4 ....$325.00

Circus Fire Engine, MT, 1960s, several actions, litho tin, 11", EX $265.00

Circus Lion, Rock Valley, tap circus carpet for several actions, lithographed tin and plush, 10", EX (EX box), A, $500.00.

Circus Queen Seal, Playthings, rare, MIB, L4 ....$375.00

Clancy the Great, Ideal, 1960s, 3 actions, EX, L4 ....$150.00

Clancy the Great, Ideal, 1960s, 3 actions, MIB, L4 ....$375.00

Climbing Donald Duck on His Friction Fire Engine, Linemar, 1950s, 18", scarce, EX, minimum value $1,200.00

Clown & Lion, MT, 1960s, several actions, 12", EX $475.00

Clown Magician, Alps, 1950s, several actions, litho tin & vinyl w/cloth clothes, 12", MIB..$475.00

Clown on Unicycle, MT, 1960s, 3 actions, litho tin, 10½", EX $425.00

Clucking Clara, CK, MIB, L4 ....$225.00

Cock-A-Doodle-Doo Rooster, Mikuni, 1950s, several actions, litho tin, 8", EX $165.00

Coffeetime Bear, TN, 1960s, several actions, litho tin & plush, 10", EX..$250.00

College Jalopy, Linemar, advances w/lights & sound, litho tin w/4 figures, remote control, 9½", EX (EX box) $450.00

Comic Choo-Choo, Cragstan, 1960s, 3 actions, 10", EX..$85.00

Comic Road Roller, Bandai, 1960s, several actions, 9", EX..$150.00

Cragstan Crapshooter, Y, 1950s, 4 actions, 9", MIB, L4.$175.00

Cragstan Dilly Dalmatian, MIB, L4 ....$250.00

Cragstan One-Arm Bandit, Y, 1960s, 3 actions, 6", MIB, L4..$250.00

Cragstan Playboy, 1960s, several actions, litho tin, 13", EX $200.00

Cragstan Skin Diver, rare, EX (EX box), L4 ....$475.00

Cragstan Telly Bear, S&E, 1950s, several actions, litho tin & plush w/cloth clothes, 9", MIB $500.00

Cragstan Western Locomotive, 1950s, several actions, 12", EX..$50.00

Cragstan Yo-Yo Clown, 1960s, 3 actions, 9", NM, L4....$375.00

Cuty Cook (Bear Chef), Y, 1960s, several actions, 9½", EX..$495.00

Cuty Cook (Hippo Chef), Y, 1960s, several actions, 10", MIB $650.00

Cycling Daddy, Bandai, 1960s, several actions, 10", EX.$225.00

Cyclist Clown, K, advances w/flashing light, tin w/cloth clothes, remote control, 7", EX (EX box), L4 ....$675.00

Cyclist Penguin, K, 1950s, several actions, litho tin, 6½", EX $425.00

Daisy the Jolly Drumming Duck, Alps, 1950s, drum mk Cragstan Melody Band, litho tin & plush, 9", EX $285.00

Daisymatic Tractor 'N Trailer, Daisy, MIB, L4 ....$150.00

Dancing Dan w/His Mystery Mike, Bell Prod, 1950s, 13½", EX $200.00

Dandy the Happy Drumming Pup, Cragstan/Alps, 1950s, litho tin & plush, EX, L4 ....$200.00

Dennis the Menace Xylophone Player, Rosko, 1950s, plays London Bridge, 9", MIB.....................................$375.00

Dentist Bear, S&E, 1950s, several actions, 9½", EX.......$400.00

Dick Tracy Police Car, Linemar, 1949, litho tin, remote control, 8", EX (EX box), D10 ....$475.00

Dip-ie the Whale, SH, 1950s, 3 actions, litho tin, 13", MIB...$375.00

Drinking Captain, S&E, 1960s, several actions, lithographed tin and vinyl with cloth clothes, 12", MIB, $175.00. (Photo courtesy Martin and Carolyn Berens)

Disney Acrobats, Linemar, Mickey, Donald or Pluto, 9½", NMIB, ea $400.00

Disneyland Fire Engine, Linemar, 1950s, several actions, 18", rare, EX $700.00

Dog Sled, TN, 1950s, several actions, litho tin, 14", NM.$600.00

Dolly Seamstress (Dolly Dressmaker), TN, 1950s, several actions, litho tin & vinyl w/cloth clothes, 7", MIB .$375.00

Donald Duck Locomotive, MT, 1970, several actions, tin & plastic, 9", EX $300.00

Donny the Smiling Bulldog, Tomiyama, 1961, 3 actions, 8½", EX $150.00

Doxie the Dog, Linemar, 1950s, several actions, 9", EX ...$65.00

Dozo the Steaming Clown, Rosko, 1960s, litho tin w/cloth clothes, 10", MIB, L4...$575.00

Drinking Dog, Y, pours milk into cup & drinks, light-up eyes, tin & plush, 9", scarce, NMIB......................$225.00

Drinking Licking Cat, TN, 1950s, pours & drinks from cup, plastic, plush & litho tin, 10", MIB, L4.........................$325.00

Drinking Monkey, Alps, 1950s, several actions, 10", MIB..$175.00

Drumming Mickey Mouse, Linemar, 1950s, several actions, litho tin, 10", rare, NM, minimum value $1,400.00

Drumming Polar Bear, Alps, 1960s, 3 actions, 12", EX ..$200.00

Drumming Target Bear, MT, EX, L4............................$275.00

Dune Buggy, TPS, 1960s, 3 actions, plastic, 11", EX $100.00

Electric Vibraphone, TN, 1950s, 3 actions, litho tin, 5½", NM $150.00

Electro Fire Engine, Linemar, MIB, L4 ....$175.00

Electro Sand Loader w/Conveyor, Linemar, MIB, L4.....$225.00

Electronic Periscope Firing Range, Cragstan, 1950s, 3 actions, litho tin, 11", EX $200.00

Excalibur Car, Bandai, 1960s, 3 actions, litho tin, 10", EX ..$165.00

Expert Motorcyclist, MT, 1950s, rider mounts & dismounts, litho tin, 11½", MIB, L4 ....$1,000.00

Father Bear Reading & Drinking in His Old Rocking Chair, MT, 1950s, tin & plush w/cloth clothes, 9½", rare, EX $350.00

FBI Godfather Car #17, red version, bump-&-go action w/lights & sound, plastic, 10", MIB $150.00

Feeding Baby Bear, Y, EX, L4..$175.00

Feeding Bird Watcher, Linemar, 1950s, several actions, litho tin & plush, 9", MIB $600.00

Fido the Xylophone Player, Alps, 1950s, litho tin & plush, several actions, 9", MIB, L4.....................................$475.00

Fire Chief Emergency Car, Linemar, 1954 Chevy, several actions, litho tin, 9", EX......................................$165.00

Fire Chief Mystery Action Car, TN, 1960s, several actions, litho tin, 10", EX $150.00

Firebird Dashmobile, Remco, 1960s, several actions, litho tin, 13", EX...$225.00

Firefly Bug, TN, 1950s, 3 actions, litho tin, 9", MIB $150.00

Fishing Polar Bear, Alps, bear pulls fish out of pond, throws it in basket & squeals, plush & tin, 10", MIB, L4...........$325.00

Flexie the Pocket Monkey, Alps, 1960s, 3 actions, 12", EX .$150.00

Flintstone Yacht, Remco, 1961, mostly plastic, 17", EX.$200.00

Flintstones Paddy Wagon, Remco, 1961, 18", NM (EX box) $475.00

Flipper the Spouting Dolphin, Bandai, MIB, L4.............$125.00

Flippy the Only Roller Skating Monkey That Skis, Alps, 1950s, 3 actions, 12", rare, EX $275.00

Flutterbirds, Alps, 2 birds fly above birdhouse as 1 chirps in door, mixed materials, 27", rare, NMIB, A $650.00

Flying Circus, Tomiyama, 1960s, 3 actions, 17", rare, EX, minimum value $1,000.00

Ford Mustang Stunt Car, Japan, 1969, NMIB, D10........$175.00

Ford 4000 HD Forklift, Alps, 1950s, several actions, litho tin, 11½", rare, NM...$300.00

Frankenstein, Poynter Prod, 1970s, several actions, mostly plastic w/cloth clothes, 12", EX...........................$125.00

Frankie the Roller Skating Monkey, Alps, 1950s, 3 actions, remote control, 12", MIB, L4 ....$250.00

Fred Flintstone's Bedrock Band, Alps, Fred plays drums & cymbals, litho tin & vinyl w/cloth clothes, 9", NM (NM box), A $675.00

French Cat, Alps, 1950s, several actions, 10", EX $100.00

Fruit Juice Counter, K, 1960s, 3 actions, tin & plastic, 8", NM $250.00

Funland Cup Ride, Sonsco, 1960s, kids spin around in cups, 7", EX $200.00

G-Man Patrol Car, Linemar, advances with lighted guns and sound, remote control, 8½", MIB, $325.00.
(Photo courtesy Harry and Jody Whitworth)

Galloping Horse & Rider w/Hoof Beat Horse, Cragstan, 1960s, 9", VG...$275.00

Gino Neapolitan Balloon Blower, Japan, lifts bubble wand over tank, rings bell & eyes move, tin, 10", EX (EX box), A $175.00

Godzilla, Bullmark, 1960s, several actions, litho tin & plastic, remote control, 10½", EX $600.00

Godzilla, Mattel, 1977, advances on wheels w/flames & several other actions, plastic, 19", NM (NM box)...............$250.00

Gorilla, MT, advances & roars w/several other actions, wht plush over tin, remote control, 10", NMIB, A........$350.00

Grand-Pa Car, Y, 1950s, several actions, litho tin, 9", EX .$100.00

Grand-Pa Panda, MT, sits in rocking chair & eats popcorn, eyes light, 9", MIB..$450.00

Green Hornet Secret Service Action Car, ASC, 1960s, several actions, litho tin, 11", scarce, NM, minimum value ..$800.00

Growling Tiger Trophy Plaque, Cragstan, 1950s, 3 actions, 10", rare, NM $250.00

Happy 'N Sad Magic Face Clown, Y, 1960s, plays cymbals as facial expressions change, 10", MIB........................$300.00

Happy Band Trio, MT, 1970s, dog, rabbit & bear play instruments on litho tin stage, 11", MIB, L4....................$675.00

Happy Fiddler Clown, Alps, 1950s, several actions, litho tin w/cloth clothes, 9½", NM $465.00

Happy Miner, Bandai, 1960s, 3 actions, 11", MIB, L4...$1,100.00

Happy Santa One-Man Band, Alps, 9", MIB, L4 ....$300.00

Happy the Clown Puppet Show, Y, 1960s, three actions, lithographed tin and vinyl with cloth clothes, 10", EX (EX box), $400.00. (Photo courtesy Don Hultzman)

Haunted House Mystery Bank, Disneyland promo/Brumberger, 1960s, several actions, litho tin, 7", MIB $475.00

High Jinks at the Circus, Alps, clown w/performing monkey, several actions, MIB, L4 ....$375.00

Highway Patrol Cycle, MT, 1950s, several actions, litho tin w/full-figure driver, 12", EX.......................................$800.00

Highway Patrol Helicopter, MT, 1960s, several actions, litho tin & plastic, 9½", MIB $150.00

Hoop Zing Girl, Linemar, girl performs hula-hoop, tin & celluloid w/cloth clothes, 12", rare, NMIB, A $500.00

Hoopy the Fishing Duck, Alps, 1950s, several actions, 10", MIB, L4 ....$575.00

Hooty the Happy Owl, Alps, 1960s, several actions, 9", MIB, L4 ....$185.00

Hot Rod 15B, TN, litho tin, w/driver, MIB....................$350.00

Hungry Baby Bear, Y, 1950s, mama bear feeds baby w/several actions, tin & plush w/cloth clothes, 9½", MIB $275.00

Hungry Cat, Linemar, cat reaches in fishbowl w/several actions, tin & plush, 9", MIB, A...$725.00

Hungry Hound Dog, Y, 1950s, several actions, 9½", VG .$375.00

Hy-Que Monkey, TN, 1960s, several actions, litho tin, 17", EX $300.00

Ice Cream Eating Bear, lifts spoon to mouth, tin & plush, 9½", scarce, EX, A $475.00

Ice Cream Vendor, TN, 1950s, advances w/ringing bell & lights, litho tin, 10", rare, EX (EX box) $1,400.00

Indian Joe, Alps, 1960s, several actions, mixed materials, 11", EX (EX box) $165.00

Japanese Bullet Train, MT, litho tin w/plastic track, MIB, L4 ....$175.00

Jo-Jo the Flipping Monkey, TN, 1970s, 10", EX............$100.00

Jocko the Drinking Monkey, Linemar, pours drink & lifts to mouth as eyes light, litho tin w/cloth clothes, 11", NMIB, A $250.00

John's Farm Truck, TN, 1950s, several actions, 9", MIB, L4 ..$325.00

Johnny Speedmobile, Remco, 1960s, 3 actions, mostly plastic, 15", rare, EX..$285.00

Jolly Bambino the Eating Monkey, Alps, 1950s, eats candy w/several actions, tin & plush, 10", MIB, L4 ....$700.00

Jolly Bear the Drummer Boy, K, 1950s, several actions, NM, L4 ....$275.00

Jolly Bear w/Robin, MT, 1950s, 3 actions, 10", rare, MIB...$975.00

Jolly Peanut Vendor, TN, 1950s, bear pushes peanut cart w/several actions, litho tin & plush, 8", EX.....................$425.00

Jolly Penguin, TN, 1950s, several actions, plush over tin, remote control, 7", EX...$200.00

Jolly Popcorn Vendor, TN, bear pushes car w/several actions, litho tin & plastic, 9", VG (VG box) $325.00

Jolly Santa on Snow, Alps, 1950, several actions, MIB, L4 ....$400.00

Josie the Walking Cow, Daiya, 1950s, several actions, plush over tin, EX...$125.00

Jungle Jumbo, BC, 1950s, several actions, tin & plush, 10", scarce, EX..$600.00

Jungle Trio, Linemar, 1950s, monkeys & elephant play instrument on platform, 8", rare, M.................................$650.00

Kissing Couple, Ichida, 1950s, car advances as bird spins & chirps on hood, couple kiss, etc, tin, 10", EX (G box), A $250.00

Lady Pup Tending Her Garden, Cragstan, 1950s, several actions, litho tin w/cloth clothes, 8", EX............................$350.00

Lighthouse, Alps, train travels track & several other actions, litho tin & celluloid, 7", rare, NM (EX box), A...$1,800.00

Lite-O-Wheel Go Kart, Rosko, 1950s, 3 actions, NM, L4 ..$200.00

Lite-O-Wheel Lincoln, Rosko, 1950s, litho tin, 10½", EX .$300.00

Little Indian, TN, 1960s, 3 actions, litho tin, 9", rare, EX ..$165.00

Loop-the-Loop Monkey, TN, 1960s, performs on bar, 10", EX $100.00

Loop-the-Loop Power Plane, MIB, L4 ....$325.00

Lucky Seven Dice Throwing Monkey, Alps, throws dice & chatters, plush, tin & plastic, 12", MIB.....................$185.00

M-4 Combat Tank, Taiyo, several actions, litho tin, 11½", EX $165.00

M-81 Tank, MT, 1960s, several actions, litho tin, 8½", EX ..$200.00

Mac the Turtle, Y, 1960s, rolls over barrel w/several actions, litho tin w/cloth clothes, 8", EX................................$200.00

Magic Man Clown, Marusan, 1950s, several actions, litho tin w/cloth clothes, 11", NM $450.00

Magic Snowman, Santa Creations, 1950s, several actions, complete w/broom, pipe & ball, 11", EX $150.00

Main Street, Linemar, 1950s, cars navigate track w/buildings, litho tin, 19½", scarce, NM, minimum value.......$1,000.00

Major Tooty, Alps, 1960s, drum major plays drum, 14", MIB, L4 ....$275.00

Make-Up Bear, MT, 1960s, sits in chair w/mirror & puts on make-up, tin & plush, 9", scarce, NM, minimum value $1,000.00

Mambo the Jolly Drumming Elephant, Alps, 1950s, plays drum & cymbals, tin & plush, 9½", MIB, L4 ....$375.00

Marshal Wild Bill, Y, advances & fires guns w/lights & sound, litho tin w/cloth clothes, remote control, 11½", MIB, A..$475.00

Marvelous Fire Engine, Y, 1960s, several actions, litho tin, 11", EX $200.00

Marvelous Locomotive, TN, 1950s, mk C7021, several actions, litho tin, 10", rare, EX $165.00

Mary's Little Lamb, Alps, 1950s, 3 actions, 10½", EX....$200.00

Maxwell Coffee-Loving Bear, TN, 1960s, 10", NMIB, L4 ..$250.00

McGregor, TN, Scotsman rises from trunk & smokes cigar w/several actions, litho tin w/cloth clothes, 12", NM, A..$165.00

Melody Camping Car, Y, 1970s, 3 actions, 10", EX........$125.00

Merry Rabbit, K, 1950s, several actions, litho tin, 11", rare, EX..$200.00

Merry-Go-Round Truck, TN, 1957, advances as carousel spins in truck bed, litho tin, remote control, MIB, A.......$725.00

Mexicalli Pete, Alps, 1960s, 3 actions, MIB, L4 ....$325.00

Mickey Mouse Flying Saucer, MT, MIB, L4 ....$275.00

Mickey Mouse Loop the Loop, Illco, MIB, D10 ....$175.00

Mickey Mouse Melody Railroad, Frankonia/WDP, 1967, rare, MIB, L4 ....$1,600.00

Mickey Mouse Sand Buggy, MT, 1960s, several actions, litho tin & plastic, 11", EX......................................$300.00

Mickey Mouse Tow Truck, Andy Gard, 1950s, remote control, 7½", EX..$600.00

Mickey Mouse, see also Drumming Mickey Mouse

Mickey the Magician, Linemar, raises wand, lifts hat and chick appears, lithographed tin, 10½", scarce, NM (EX box), A, $2,400.00.

Microphone Dancer, National Co, Black man attached to lamp-post dances wildly, voice activated, 12", EX, A.......$225.00

Mighty Mike the Barbell Lifter Bear, K, 1950s, several actions, tin & plush, 10½", EX..$300.00

Mimi Poodle w/Bone, TN, 1950s, several actions, 11", EX ..$100.00

Mischievous Monkey, MT, monkey scoots up & down tree in front of doghouse, litho tin, EX (EX box)...............$375.00

Mother Bear, MT, sits in rocking chair & knits, head nods & eyes light, tin & plush, 10", MIB, L4 ....$300.00

Mother Goose, Yonezawa, MIB, L4 ....$250.00

Mr Fox the Magician, Cragstan, fox lifts hat to reveal rabbit, litho tin, 9", MIB, L4...$700.00

Mr Fox the Magician Blowing Magical Bubbles, fox lifts hat & bubbles come out, litho tin w/cloth clothes, 9", NMIB, A $550.00

Mr MacPooch, SAN, 1950s, dog advances & lifts lit-up & smoking pipe to mouth, remote control, 8", MIB, L4 ....$350.00

Mr Magoo Car, Hubley, 1961, advances w/crazy action, litho tin w/cloth top, 9", MIB..$375.00

Mr Strong Pup the Mighty Weightlifter, K, 1950s, several actions, 9", EX...$300.00

Mr Traffic Policeman, A1, policeman blows whistle & turns as light changes, 13", MIB, L4....................................$575.00

Mumbo Jumbo Hawaiian Drummer, Alps, 1960s, 3 actions, litho tin & vinyl, 10", EX..$200.00

Musical Bulldog, SAN, 1950s, bulldog plays piano, litho tin & plush w/cloth clothes, 8½", rare, EX, minimum value.........$1,200.00

Musical Cadillac, Irco, 1950s, advances & plays music, tin, 9", VG (VG box) $350.00

Musical Comic Jumping Jeep, Alps, several actions, 12", EX .$125.00

Musical Dancing Sweethearts, KO, 1950s, litho tin, 10", scarce, EX..$400.00

Musical Marching Bear, Alps, 1950s, beats drum & blows horn, tin & plush w/cloth pants, 11", EX $600.00

Musical Show Boat, Gakken, 1960s, litho tin & plastic, 13", EX..$250.00

Musical Train, Japan, plastic, MIB, J6............................$50.00

Musical Vegetable Truck, Bandai, 1960s, several actions, 10½", EX..$275.00

Mystery Mike the Minstrel Man, Bell Products, 1960s, 14", EX..$140.00

Mystery Police Car, TN, bump-&-go action w/figure moving gun side to side, litho tin, 9½", VG (VG box), A..........$175.00

M101 Aston-Martin Secret Ejector Car, Daiya, 1960s, ejects passenger w/several other actions, tin, 11", EX........$400.00

Naughty Dog & Buzzing Bee, MT, several actions, tin & plush, 10", EX..$125.00

Nautilus Periscope, Cragstan, MIB, L4 ....$225.00

New Adventures of Clown, NMIB, L4 ....$675.00

New Flip-Flap Flyer, Taiwan, 1960s, mostly plastic, 14", EX..$100.00

New Service Car (World News), TPS, 3 actions, litho tin, 9½", EX..$400.00

New Silver Mountain Express, MT, 1960s, 3 actions, 16", EX..$85.00

Nutty Mads Car, Linemar, 1960s, 3 actions, MIB, L4 ....$675.00

Nutty Nibs, Linemar, 1950s, several actions, pnt tin w/paper skirt, 12", EX, L4..$875.00

Ol' MacDonald's Farm Truck, Frankonia, 1960s, several actions, complete w/plastic animals, EX................................$100.00

Old Fashioned Fire Engine, MT, 1950s, MIB, L4 ....$300.00

Old Fashioned Hot Rod, Bandai, 1960s, several actions, litho tin, 6½", NM $250.00

Open Sleigh, MT, 1950s, 2 dogs pull sled w/Eskimo, litho tin, 16", rare, M $700.00

Overland Stage Coach, MT, 1950s, several actions, lithographed tin and plastic, 18", NM (NM box), $300.00.
(Photo courtesy Don Hultzman)

Passenger Bus, Y, 1950s, several actions, litho tin, 16", EX ..$465.00

Pat O'Neill the Fun Loving Irishman, TN, several actions, litho tin w/cloth clothes, 11", NM (NM box) $325.00

Pat the Dog, Alps, 1950s, several actions, MIB, L4 ....$175.00

Pat the Roaring Elephant, Y, 1950s, several actions, litho tin, 9", EX $300.00

Pepi the Tumbling Monkey, Yanoman, 1960s, MIB, L4 ..$100.00

Peppermint Twist Doll, Haji, 1950s, litho tin, 12", EX ..$300.00

Performing Circus Lion, MIB, L4 ....$500.00

Perky Pup, Alps, 1960s, 3 actions, 8½", EX $100.00

Pete the Indian, Bandai, MIB, L4 ....$175.00

Pete the Policeman, Bandai, M, L4 ....$125.00

Pete the Talking Parrot, TN, 1950s, several actions, litho tin & plush, 18", EX $400.00

Picnic Bear, Alps, 1950s, pours & drinks w/realistic motion, litho tin & plush, 10", EX (EX box), A $200.00

Picnic Bunny, Alps, 1950s, several actions, plush & tin, 10", MIB, L4..$200.00

Picnic Poodle, TPS, 1950s, several actions, 7", EX...........$85.00

Pierrot-Monkey Cycle, MT, bump-&-go action w/lights & sound, litho tin w/vinyl head, 10", NM (G box), A..............$450.00

Piggy Cook, Y, cooks egg w/several actions, mixed materials, 10", MIB, A $350.00

Pink Panther One Man Band, Illco, 1970s, plays drum & cymbals, 11", EX..$125.00

Pinky the Clown, MIB, L4 ....$500.00

Pinocchio Xylophone Player, TN, 1962, plays 'London Bridge,' tin w/rubber head, 9", MIB, L4 ....$350.00

Pipie the Whale, Alps, 1950s, litho tin, 12", EX $300.00

Playful Pup in Shoe, Y, 1960s, 3 actions, 10", EX...........$100.00

Playing Monkey, S&E, 1950s, several actions, complete w/hat & yo-yo, 10", EX $400.00

Pleasant Kappa, ATD, 1950s, several actions, litho tin, 10", scarce, NM, minimum value $1,000.00

Pluto Lantern, Linemar, tin & glass figure w/rubber ears, tongue & tail, 6½", NM (EX box), A $450.00

Polar Bear, Alps, 1970s, 3 actions, 8", EX......................$150.00

Police Car No 5, TN, 1950s, several actions, litho tin, 9½", NM $200.00

Popcorn Eating Panda, MT, NM, L4 ....$175.00

Popcorn Vendor, S&E/Cragstan, bear pedals cart while umbrella spins & popcorn pops, litho tin & plush, 8", MIB, L4 .$575.00

Popcorn Vendor, TN, duck pushes wagon w/bump-&-go action as popcorn pops, 8", MIB, L4 ....$575.00

Popcorn Vendor Truck, TN, 1960s, 3 actions, litho tin, 9", EX $300.00

Popeye, see also Bubble Blowing Popeye and Smoking Popeye

Popeye in Rowboat, Linemar, remote control, litho tin, 10½", M (torn box), A $6,600.00

Poverty Pup Bank, Poynter/Alabe, 1966, 6", MIB, L4....$100.00

Pretty Peggy Parrot, Rosko, several actions, litho tin & plush, 10", EX (EX box), L4..$425.00

Princess the Begging Poodle, Alps, 1950s, several actions, 9", EX $35.00

Puffy Morris, Y, 1960s, smokes real cigarette, 10", MIB, L4..$375.00

Quacking Duckling, Linemar, 1950s, 3 actions, litho tin, 5½", EX $125.00

Radar Jeep, TN, 1950s, several actions, litho tin, 11", EX .$300.00

Radicon Boat, MT, 1950s, remote control, rare, MIB, L4 .$900.00

Raggedy Ann Vacuum Cleaner Doll, Nasta, 1973, bump-&-go action, plastic, 10", MIB $35.00

Rajah Rey the Indian Prince, TN, 1960s, several actions, 12", rare, EX $675.00

Rambling Ladybug, MT, 1960s, litho tin, 8", EX............$125.00

Randy the Walking Monkey, A1, NMIB, L4..................$175.00

Reading Bear, Alps, 1950s, several actions, 9", M, L4 ....$525.00

Root Beer Counter, K, 1960s, three actions, lithographed tin and plastic, 8", EX, $200.00. (Photo courtesy Don Hultzman)

Reading Bear, Alps, 1950s, 5 actions, 9", M, L4 ....$525.00

Ricki the Begging Poodle, Rock Valley, 1950s, several actions, 9", EX $65.00

Roaring Gorilla Shooting Gallery, MT, 1950s, litho tin, complete w/gun & darts, EX $400.00

Roaring Lion, Rosko, 1950s, several actions, plush over tin, 11", NMIB...$200.00

Rock 'N Roll Monkey, Rosko, 1950s, monkey plays guitar & sways, 13", MIB, L4 ....$350.00

Rocky (Fred Flintstone look-alike), Linemar, 1960s, litho tin & vinyl, 3" dia, EX...................................$200.00

Rocky the Beer Man, Hong Kong, 1970s, several actions, mostly plastic, 10", EX $85.00

Roll-Over Rover, Mego, 1970s, 3 actions, plastic, 9", EX.$35.00

Rover the Poodle Bell Ringer, Alps, 1960s, 3 actions, 10½", EX $125.00

Royal Cub in Buggy, S&E, 1950s, several actions, 8", EX..$300.00

Sam the Shaving Man, Plaything Toy, 1960s, several actions, MIB, L4...$450.00

Sam the Shaving Man, Plaything Toy, 1960s, several actions, 11½", EX...$300.00

Sammy Wong the Tea Totaler, TN, 1950s, several actions, 10", EX $325.00

Santa Claus on Reindeer Sleigh, MT, 1950s, several actions, litho tin & plastic, 17", rare, EX $575.00

Santa Claus Phone Bank, S&E, 1950s several actions, remote pay phone, litho tin, 8", scarce, EX........................$800.00

Santa Copter, MT, 1950s, 3 actions, 8½", MIB.............$225.00

Santa on Rotating Globe, HTC, 1950s, several actions, litho tin w/cloth outfit, 14", EX (EX box)......................$700.00

School Bus, Cragstan, 1950s, litho tin, 20½", NM.........$150.00

Searchlight Truck, MT, 1950s, 3 actions, litho tin, 11", EX $325.00

Shaggy the Friendly Pup, Alps, 1950s, 3 actions, 8", EX ..$35.00

Shark U-Control Racing Car, Remco, 1961, plastic, 19", EX.$165.00

Shoe-Shaking Dog, MT, 1950s, several actions, litho tin, 8", EX $125.00

Shooting Bear, SAN, advances, lifts gun & fires, light-up eyes, litho tin, remote control, 10", EX, A $325.00

Shooting Cowboys in Barrel, EX, L4............................$575.00

Shutter-Bug Photographer, TN, 1950s, several actions, litho tin, rare, EX $800.00

Shuttling Freight Train, Cragstan, 1950s, several actions, litho tin, complete w/track, MIB $225.00

Sikorsky Rescue Army Helicopter, Alps, 1950s, several actions, litho tin, 11", EX $185.00

Skating Circus Clown, TPS, 1950s, litho tin, 6", scarce, NM, minimum value $1,000.00

Skiing Santa, MT, 1960s, several actions, litho tin, 12", EX ..$300.00

Skipping Monkey, TN, 1960s, 9½", EX $85.00

Skyliner Sports Car, TN, 1950s, several actions, litho tin, 9", EX...$225.00

Sleeping Baby Bear, Linemar, 1950s, several actions, litho tin, detachable alarm clock, 9", MIB $475.00

Slurpy Pup, TN, 1960s, several actions, litho tin & plush, 6½", MIB...$100.00

Smokey Bear Jeep, MT, 1950s, advances w/lights & sound, litho tin, 10", rare, EX, L4...$675.00

Sleepy Pup, Alps, 1960s, several actions, plush, 12", EX (EX box), $85.00. (Photo courtesy Don Hultzman)

Smoking Bulldozer, Daiya, 1960s, 3 actions, 9½", EX $225.00

Smoking Bunny, SAN, 1950s, several actions, litho tin, 10½", EX...$200.00

Smoking Elephant, Marusan, 1950s, several actions, litho tin, 9", EX...$265.00

Smoking Grandpa, SAN, 1950s, eyes closed, 9", rare, MIB, L4..$475.00

Smoking Grandpa, SAN, 1950s, eyes open, 9", MIB, L4..$300.00

Smoking Jet Plane, TN, 1950s, several actions, litho tin, 12", EX...$300.00

Smoking Popeye, Linemar, 1950s, several actions, lithographed tin, 9½", rare, NM (EX box), A, $1,900.00.

Smoking Volkswagen, Aoshin, 1960s, litho tin, NM, J6..$175.00

Smoky Bill in His Old Fashioned Car, TN, 1960s, several actions, litho tin, 9", NM $250.00

Snake Charmer & Casey the Trained Cobra, Linemar, 1950s, several actions, litho tin & plastic, 8", NM $500.00

Snappy the Happy Bubble Blowing Dragon, TN, 1960s, several actions, litho tin, 30", scarce, NM $4,000.00

Sneezing Bear, Linemar, 1950s, raises tissue & sneezes, light-up eyes, litho tin, 9½", MIB, L4..................................$475.00

Sneezing Bear, Linemar, 1950s, several actions, litho tin, 9", EX..$275.00

Snoopie the Non-Fall Dog, Amico, 1960s, 3 actions, litho tin, 8", EX..$100.00

Spanking Bear, Linemar, 1950s, mama bear spanks baby w/several other actions, litho tin & plush, 9", EX, L4......$275.00

Sparky the Seal, MT, 1950s, several actions, litho tin w/celluloid ball, 7", EX...$165.00

Spin-A-Disk Monkey, S&E, 1950s, several actions, complete w/hat & disk, 10", EX $300.00

Spirit of 1776 Locomotive, MT, 1976, several actions, 16", EX $35.00

Strange Explorer, DSK, advances as gorilla tries to turn tank over, litho tin, 8", EX (G box), A $250.00

Stunt Car, MT, 1960s, litho tin, 10½", EX.....................$100.00

Stunt Plane, TPS, 1960s, 3 actions, litho tin, 10½" W, EX ..$200.00

Super News Copter, SH, 1960s, several actions, litho tin, 16", EX $200.00

Super Susie, Linemar, 1950s, bear pushes groceries on conveyor belt w/several other actions, tin & plush, 8", EX.....$800.00

Superior Ambulance, Asakusa Toy, 1960s, 3 actions, litho tin, 12", EX..$300.00

Superman Tank, Linemar, 1958, figure stops tank, pushes it backwards & lifts it up, litho tin, 10", NM (NM box), A $3,500.00

Suzette the Eating Monkey, Linemar, 1950s, several actions, litho tin, 9", rare, EX $600.00

Suzy-Q Automatic Ironer, GW, 1950s, several actions, litho tin, 7", EX..$185.00

Swimming Duck, Bandai, 1950s, several actions, litho tin, 8", rare, MIB..$185.00

Switchboard Operator, Linemar, 1950s, several actions, litho tin & vinyl, 7½", EX $700.00

Teddy Go-Kart, Alps, 1960s, several actions, lithographed tin and plush, 10½", EX (EX box), $200.00.
(Photo courtesy Don Hultzman)

Talking Batmobile, Hong Kong, 1977, press button to talk, plastic, 9½", rare, MIB, A...$300.00

Talking Police Car, Y, 1960s, mystery action, litho tin, 14", NM $150.00

Tarzan, Marusan, 1966, several actions, litho tin, 13", scarce, NM, minimum value..$1,000.00

Taxi Cab, Y, 1960s, mk ¼ Mile 65¢ on door, litho tin, several actions, 9", VG...$185.00

Teddy Bear Circus Acrobat, Tomiyama, 1950s, 3 actions, 15", rare, EX...$1,000.00

Teddy Bear Swing, Yonezawa, performs flips on bar, litho tin & plush, 13", MIB, L4..$575.00

Teddy the Artist, Yonezawa, 1950s, simulates drawing, complete w/9 templates, MIB, L4 ....$500.00

Teddy the Champ Boxer, Y, 1950s, several actions, 9", EX..$300.00

Teddy the Manager, S&E, 1950s, several actions, litho tin, 8", rare, EX..$600.00

Teddy the Rhythmical Drummer, Alps, 1960s, 3 actions, 11", EX $200.00

Telephone Bear, Linemar, 1950s, 7½", MIB, L4 ....$450.00

Telephone Rabbit, MT, rocks & talks on phone w/moving mouth, litho tin & plush, 10", scarce, NM, A $165.00

Thunderbird Speedster w/Automatic Action, TN, 1950s, several actions, litho tin, 11", rare, EX.................................$625.00

Tinkling Locomotive, MT, 1960s, several actions, 9½", EX ..$85.00

Tinkling Trolley, MT, 1950s, several actions, litho tin, 10½", MIB $225.00

Titan the Tumbler, Cragstan, MIB, L4 ....$500.00

Tom & Jerry Formula Racing Car, MT, 1960s, 3 actions, litho tin, EX..$175.00

Tom & Jerry Helicopter, MT, 1960s, 3 actions, tin & plastic, 9½", EX..$225.00

Tom & Jerry Locomotive, MT, bump-&-go action, litho tin & plastic, 9", NM (NM box)..$165.00

Topo Gigio Xylophone Player, TN, 1960s, 3 actions, litho tin, 10½", scarce, NM, minimum value $1,000.00

Traffic Policeman, A1, 1950s, several actions, litho tin, 14", EX $350.00

Traveler Bear, K, 1950s, 3 actions, 8", NM, L4 ....$375.00

Trumpet Playing Bunny, Alps, 1950s, several actions, litho tin, 10", EX..$300.00

Tubby the Turtle, Y, 1950s, 3 actions, litho tin, 7", EX .$100.00

Tumbles the Bear, Yanoman, 1960s, litho tin, 8½", MIB..$165.00

Turn-O-Matic Gun Jeep, TN, 1960s, several actions, litho tin, 10", EX..$200.00

Twin Racing Cars, Alps, 1950s, 3 actions, MIB, L4 ....$675.00

Tyrannosaurus, Toytown, 1970s, several actions, mostly plastic, 9", EX..$165.00

U-Control Racer #4, Cragstan, w/driver, MIB................$550.00

U-Turn Cadillac, KO, advances as figure raises his arm for turn signal, litho tin, 8½", NM (EX box), A $300.00

Union Mountain Monorail, MIB, L4 ....$225.00

VIP Busy Boss Bear, S&E, 1950s, several actions, 8", EX, L4 ....$350.00

Walking Bambi, Linemar, 1950s, several actions, litho tin, 9", scarce, NM..$400.00

Walking Bear w/Xylophone, Linemar, 1950s, several actions, litho tin, 10", scarce, EX..$600.00

Walking Cat, Linemar, 1950s, 3 actions, litho tin, 6", EX..$85.00
Walking Donkey, Linemar, 1950s, 9", EX......................$175.00
Walking Elephant, Linemar, 1950s, 3 actions, litho tin, 8½", EX..$185.00
Walking Knight in Armour, MT, 1950s, several actions, rare, NMIB, L4 ....$3,000.00
Waltzing Matilda, TN, rare, MIB, L4............................$900.00
Warpath Indian, Alps, 3 actions, litho tin, 12", EX $165.00
Wee Little Baby Bear, see Reading Bear
Whirlybird Helicopter, Remco, 1960s, 3 actions, 25", EX ..$160.00
Wild West Rodeo, see Bubbling Bull
Willie the Walking Car, Y, 1960s, several actions, 8½", EX...$225.00
Windy the Juggling Elephant, TN, 1950s, 10½", MIB, L4..$325.00
Winston the Barking Bulldog, Tomiyama, 1950s, 3 actions, 10", EX $150.00
Worried Mother Duck & Baby, TN, 1950s, 3 actions, 11", MIB, L4..$225.00
Xylophone Bear, Linemar, non-walking version, rare, NM, L4..$675.00
Xylophone Bear, Linemar, walking version, rare, MIB, L4 .$575.00

Beanie Babies

Who can account for this latest flash in collecting that some liken to the rush for Cabbage Patch dolls we saw many years ago! The appeal of these stuffed creatures is disarming to both children and adults, and excited collectors are eager to scoop up each new-found treasure. There is much to be learned about Beanie Babies. For instance, there are different tag styles and these indicate date of issue:

#1, Swing tag: single heart-shaped tag

#2, Swing tag: heart-shaped; folded, with information inside; narrow lettering

#3, Swing tag: heart-shaped; folded, with information inside; wider lettering

#4, Swing tag: heart-shaped; folded, with information inside; wider lettering with no gold outline around the 'ty'; yellow star on front; first tag to include a poem and birth date

#1 Swing tag

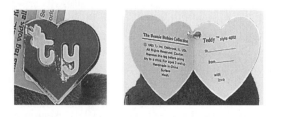

#2 Swing tag

#3 Swing tag

#4 Swing tag

#5 Swing tag

#5, Swing tag: heart-shaped; folded with information inside; different font on front and inside; birth month spelled out; no style numbers listed, web site listed

(Note: for current Beanies with a #1, #2, or #3 tag, add at least $30.00 to $50.00 to the prices suggested below.)

Unless information is given to the contrary, the following listings are for current issues in mint condition; discontinued (retired) items will be noted. We have tried to indicate all the issues that have been discontinued/retired in our descriptions, but by the time this publication is actually in print, there will no doubt be others; the market is just that volatile, as are the prices/values.

Advisor: Amy Hopper.

See also Fast Food Collectibles.

Almond the Bear, #4246, beige, from $6 to $10.00
Amber the Cat, #4243, gold tabby, from $6 to $10.00
Ants the Anteater, #4195, retired, from $10 to $15.00
Baldy the Eagle, #4074, retired...$20.00
Batty the Bat, #4035, retired, from $10 to.........................$15.00
Batty the Bat, #4035, tie-dyed, retired, from $15 to $20.00
Beak the Kiwi, #4211, from $6 to $10.00
Bernie the St Bernard, #4109, retired, from $10 to...........$15.00
Bessie the Cow, #4009, brn, retired...................................$60.00
Blackie the Bear, #4011, retired, from $10 to $20.00
Blizzard the Tiger, #4163, wht, retired $20.00
Bones the Dog, #4001, brn, retired...................................$20.00
Bongo the Monkey, #4067, brn, w/matching body & tail color, retired, from $40 to..$65.00
Bongo the Monkey, #4067, brn, w/matching paws & face, retired, from $10 to..$20.00

Ally the Alligator, #4032, retired, $50.00.
(Photo courtesy Robin Hicks)

Brittania the Bear, #4601, Ty UK exclusive, from $250 to .**$300.00**

Bronty the Brontosaurus, #4085, bl, retired, minimum value **$800.00**

Brownie the Bear, #4010, retired, minimum value **$3,000.00**

Bruno the Terrier, #4183, retired, from $10 to **$15.00**

Bubbles the Fish, #4078, yel & blk, retired **$155.00**

Bucky the Beaver, #4016, retired **$35.00**

Butch the Bull Terrier, #4227, from $6 to **$10.00**

Canyon the Cougar, #4212, from $6 to **$10.00**

Caw the Crow, #4071, retired, minimum value **$600.00**

Cheeks the Baboon, #4250, from $6 to **$10.00**

Chilly the Polar Bear, #4012, retired, minimum value ..**$1,000.00**

Chip the Cat, #4121, calico, retired, from $10 to **$15.00**

Chocolate the Moose, #4015, retired, from $10 to **$15.00**

Chops the Lamb, #4019, wht w/blk face, retired **$175.00**

Claude the Crab, #4083, tie-dyed, retired, from $10 to **$15.00**

Clubby the Bear, Beanie Babies Official Club exclusive (mail order only), from $40 to **$65.00**

Clubby the Bear II, 1999 Official Club exclusive available w/Platinum club kit, from $20 to................................**$30.00**

Congo the Gorilla, #4160, retired, from $10 to **$15.00**

Coral the Fish, #4079, tie-dyed, retired, minimum value ...**$150.00**

Crunch the Shark, #4130, retired, from $10 to **$15.00**

Cubbie the Bear, #4010, brn, retired **$40.00**

Curly the Bear, #4052, brn, retired, from $15 to **$25.00**

Daisy the Cow, #4006, blk & wht, retired, from $10 to **$15.00**

Derby the Horse, #4008, 1st issue, brn, fine mane & tail, retired..**$2,800.00**

Derby the Horse, #4008, 2nd issue, coarse mane & tail, retired, from $20 to..**$25.00**

Derby the Horse, #4008, 3rd issue, brn, wht star on forehead, retired, from $15 to..................................**$25.00**

Derby the Horse, #4008, 4th issue, fine hair mane & tail w/wht star on forehead, retired, from $10 to........................**$15.00**

Digger the Orange Crab, #4027, retired, minimum value **$500.00**

Digger the Red Crab, #4027, retired, minimum value **$100.00**

Doby the Doberman, #4100, retired, from $10 to **$15.00**

Doodle the Rooster, #4171, tie-dyed, retired **$45.00**

Dotty the Dalmatian, #4100, retired, from $10 to **$15.00**

Early the Robin, #4190, from $6 to **$10.00**

Ears the Rabbit, #4018, brn, retired **$20.00**

Echo the Dolphin, #4180, retired....................................**$20.00**

Eggbert the Baby Chick, #4232, from $6 to **$10.00**

Erin the Irish Bear, #4186, retired, from $15 to **$30.00**

Eucalyptus the Koala, #4240, from $6 to **$10.00**

Ewey the Lamb, #4219, from $6 to **$10.00**

Fetch the Golden Retriever, #4189, retired, from $10 to .**$15.00**

Flash the Dolphin, #4021, retired **$115.00**

Fleece the Lamb, #4125, retired, from $10 to **$15.00**

Flip the Cat, #4012, retired **$35.00**

Floppity the Bunny, #4118, lilac, retired..........................**$25.00**

Flutter the Butterfly, #4043, tie-dyed, retired, minimum value **$900.00**

Fortune the Panda Bear, #4196, from $6 to **$10.00**

Freckles the Leopard, #4066, retired, from $10 to............**$15.00**

Fuzz the Bear, #4237, from $10 to **$15.00**

Garcia the Bear, #4041, tie-dyed, retired, from $150 to .**$225.00**

Germania the Bear, #4236, Ty UK exclusive, from $300 to..**$450.00**

Gigi the Poodle, #4191, from $6 to **$10.00**

Glory the Bear, #4188, retired, from $25 to **$45.00**

Goatee the Mountain Goat, #4235, from $6 to **$10.00**

Gobbles the Turkey, #4034, retired, from $10 to..............**$15.00**

Goldie the Goldfish, #4023, retired..................................**$40.00**

Goochy the Jellyfish, #4230, from $6 to **$10.00**

Gracie the Swan, #4126, retired, from $10 to **$20.00**

Grunt the Razorback Pig, #4092, retired..........................**$125.00**

Halo the Angel Bear, #4208, from $10 to **$15.00**

Happy the Hippo, #4061, 1st issue, gray, retired, minimum value **$400.00**

Hippity the Rabbit, #4119, retired, $25.00.
(Photo courtesy Robin Hicks)

Happy the Hippo, #4061, 2nd isssue, lavender, retired .$25.00
Hippie the Bunny, tie-dyed, #4218, from $6 to.................$10.00
Hissy the Snake, #4185, retired, from $10 to $15.00
Holiday Teddy (1997), #4200, retired, from $50 to..........$80.00
Holiday Teddy (1998), #4204, retired, from $40 to..........$70.00
Hoot the Owl, #4073, retired....................................$40.00
Hope the Praying Bear, #4213, from $10 to $15.00
Hoppity the Bunny, #4117, pk, retired.............................$25.00
Humphrey the Camel, #4060, retired, minimum value .$1,500.00
Iggy the Iguana, #4038, retired, from $10 to $15.00
Inch the Worm, #4044, mc, yarn antennae, retired..........$25.00
Inky the Octopus, #4028, 1st issue, tan, retired, minimum
    value $550.00
Inky the Octopus, #4028, 2nd issue, tan, w/mouth, retired,
    minimum value $500.00
Inky the Octopus, #4028, 3rd issue, retired, from $15 to ..$30.00
Jabber the Parrot, #4197, from $6 to $10.00
Jake the Mallard Duck, #4199, from $6 to $10.00
Jolly the Walrus, #4082, retired..................................$25.00
Kicks the Soccer Bear,#4229, from $10 to $15.00
Kiwi the Toucan, #4070, retired, minimum value..........$150.00
Knuckles the Pig, #4247, from $6 to $10.00
Kuku the Cockatoo, #4192, from $6 to $10.00
Lefty the Donkey, #4057, w/American Flag, retired, minimum
    value...$200.00
Legs the Frog, #4020, retired $35.00
Libearty the Bear, #4057, w/American flag, retired, minimum
    value...$300.00
Lizzy the Lizard, #4033, tie-dyed, retired, minimum value....$800.00
Loosy the Goose, #4206, from $6 to...............................$10.00
Lucky the Ladybug, #4040, 7 glued-on felt spots, retired ..$150.00
Lucky the Ladybug, #4040, 11 spots, retired, from $15 to...$25.00
Lucky the Ladybug, #4040, 21 spots, retired $400.00
Luke the Lab, #4214, from $6 to $10.00
Mac the Cardinal, #4225, from $6 to $10.00
Magic the Dragon, #4088, retired, from $35 to.................$50.00
Manny the Manatee, #4081, retired...............................$125.00
Maple the Bear, #4600, Canadian exclusive, minimum value.$175.00
Mel the Koala Bear, #4162, retired, from $10 to..............$15.00
Millennium the Bear, #4226, from $10 to.........................$15.00
Mooch the Spider Monkey, #4224, from $6 to $10.00
Mystic the Unicorn, #4007, 1st issue, retired, minimum
    value $225.00
Mystic the Unicorn, #4007, 2nd issue, coarse mane, brn horn,
    retired, from $25 to...$35.00
Mystic the Unicorn, #4007, 3rd issue, coarse mane, iridescent
    horn, retired, from $20 to $30.00
Mystic the Unicorn, #4007, 4th issue, rainbow mane, retired,
    from $10 to...$15.00
Nana the Monkey, #4067, 1st issue of Bongo, retired, minimum
    value $3,700.00
Nanook the Husky, #4104, retired, from $10 to $15.00
Neon the Seahorse, #4239, tie-dyed, from $6 to..............$10.00
Nibbler the Rabbit, #4216, from $6 to $10.00
Nibbly the Rabbit, #4217, from $6 to $10.00
Nip the Cat, #4003, 2nd issue, gold, retired, minimum value.$700.00
Nip the Cat, #4003, 3rd issue, gold w/wht paws, retired, from
    $25 to $30.00

Nuts the Squirrel, #4114, retired, from $10 to $15.00
Osito the Mexican Bear, sold in US, from $10 to............$20.00
Patti the Platypus, #4025, purple, from $20 to.................$25.00
Patti the Platypus, #4025, maroon, retired, minimum value .$450.00
Paul the Walrus, #4248, from $6 to $10.00

Peace the Bear, #4053, tie-dyed with embroidered peace sign, $10.00. (Photo courtesy Robin Hicks)

Peanut the Elephant, #4062, lt bl, retired $25.00
Peanut the Elephant, #4062, royal bl, retired, minimum
    value $4,200.00
Pecan the Bear, gold, from $6 to $10.00
Peking the Panda Bear, #4013, retired, minimum value ..$1,000.00
Pinchers the Lobster, #4026, retired, from $15 to.............$25.00
Pinky the Flamingo, #4072, retired, from $10 to $15.00
Pouch the Kangaroo, #4161, retired, from $10 to.............$15.00
Pounce the Cat, #4122, brn, retired, from $10 to $15.00
Prance the Cat, #4123, gray, retired, from $10 to.............$15.00
Prickles the Hedgehog, #4215, from $6 to $10.00
Princess the Bear, #4300, retired, from $20 to $30.00
Puffer the Puffin, #4181, retired, from $10 to $15.00
Pugsly the Dog, #4105, retired, from $10 to.....................$15.00
Pumkin' the Pumpkin, #4205, retired, from $25 to..........$45.00
Quackers the Duck, #4024, no wings, retired, minimum
    value $1,300.00
Quackers the Duck, #4024, w/wings, retired, from $20 to ..$25.00
Radar the Bat, #4091, retired, minimum value..............$130.00
Rainbow the Chameleon, #4037, retired, from $10 to $15.00
Rex the Tyrannosaurus, #4086, retired, minimum value .$700.00
Righty the Elephant, #4086, w/American flag, retired, minimum
    value...$200.00
Ringo the Racoon, #4014, retired, from $10 to................$15.00
Roam the Buffalo, #4209, from $6 to $10.00
Roary the Lion, #4069, retired, from $10 to....................$15.00

Rocket the Bluejay, #4202, from $6 to $10.00
Rover the Dog, #4101, red, retired $25.00
Sammy the Bear, tie-dyed, #4215, from $10 to $15.00
Santa, #4203, retired, from $25 to $45.00
Scat the Cat, #4231, from $6 to $10.00
Schweetheart the Orangutan, #4252, from $6 to..............$10.00
Scoop the Pelican, #4107, retired, from $10 to.................$15.00
Scorch the Dragon, #4210, from $6 to $10.00
Scottie the Terrier, #4102, retired, from $15 to...............$25.00
Seamore the Seal, #4029, wht, retired $150.00
Seaweed the Otter, #4080, retired, from $10 to $30.00
Signature Bear (1999), #4228, from $10 to......................$15.00
Silver the Cat, #4242, gray tabby, from $6 to $10.00
Slippery the Seal, #4222, from $6 to $10.00
Slither the Snake, #4031, retired, minimum value......$1,000.00
Sly the Fox, #4115, 1st issue, all brn, retired..................$135.00
Sly the Fox, #4115, 2nd issue, brn w/wht belly, retired, from $10
    to $15.00
Smoochy the Frog, #4039, retired, from $10 to...............$15.00
Snip the Siamese Cat, #4120, retired, from $10 to $15.00
Snort the Bull, #4002, red w/beige feet, retired, from $10
    to $15.00
Snowball the Snowman, #4201, retired, from $30 to $50.00
Spangle the American Bear, from $10 to $20.00
Sparky the Dalmatian, #4100, retired $125.00
Speedy the Turtle, #4030, retired, from $30 to $35.00
Spike the Rhinoceros, #4060, retired, from $10 to $15.00
Spinner the Spider, #4036, retired, from $10 to $20.00
Splash the Whale, #4022, retired......................................$115.00
Spooky the Ghost, #4090, retired..$40.00
Spot the Dog, #4000, 1st issue, no spot on back,
    retired..$1,300.00
Spot the Dog, #4000, 2nd issue, spot on back, retired.........$50.00
Spunky the Cocker Spaniel, #4184, retired, from $10 to..$15.00
Squealer the Pig, #4005, retired...$30.00
Steg the Stegosaurus, #4087, tie-dyed, retired, minimum
    value $850.00
Stilts the Stork, #4221, retired, from $10 to $15.00
Sting the Mantaray, #4007, tie-dyed, retired, minimum
    value $150.00
Stinger the Scorpion, #4193, retired, from $10 to $15.00
Stinky the Skunk, #4017, retired, from $10 to..................$15.00
Stretch the Ostrich, #4182, retired, from $10 to...............$15.00
Stripes the Tiger, #4065, 1st issue, retired $300.00
Stripes the Tiger, #4065, 2nd issue, retired, from $15 to ..$25.00
Strut the Rooster, #4171, retired, from $10 to $15.00
Swirly the Snail, #4249, from $6 to $10.00
Tabasco the Bull, #4002, red, retired, minimum value ...$150.00
Tank the Armadillo, #4031, 2nd issue, retired, minimum
    value $150.00
Teddy Bear, #4050, brn, new face, retired, from $75 to..$130.00
Teddy Bear, #4050, brn, old face, retired....................$2,300.00
Teddy Bear, #4051, teal, new face, retired..................$1,700.00
Teddy Bear, #4051, teal, old face, retired $1,500.00
Teddy Bear, #4052, cranberry, new face, retired $1,700.00
Teddy Bear, #4052, cranberry, old face, retired...........$1,500.00
Teddy Bear, #4055, violet, new face, retired $1,700.00
Teddy Bear, #4055, violet, old face, retired.................$1,500.00

Teddy Bear, #4056, magenta, new face, retired...........$1,700.00
Teddy Bear, #4056, magenta, old face, retired.............$1,500.00
Teddy Bear, #4057, jade, new face, retired..................$1,700.00
Teddy Bear, #4057, jade, old face, retired...................$1,500.00
Tiny the Chihuahua, #4234, from $6 to $10.00
Tiptoe the Mouse, #4241 from $6 to $10.00
Tracker the Basset Hound, #4198 $6 to $10.00
Trap the Mouse, #4042, retired, minimum value $1,000.00
Tuffy the Terrier, #4108, retired, from $10 to..................$15.00
Tusk the Walrus, #4076, retired, minimum value $115.00

Twigs the Giraffe, #4068, retired, $25.00.
(Photo courtesy Robin Hicks)

Ty Employee Billionaire Bear (1998), brn, new face, dollar sign
    on chest, minimum value.....................................$1,500.00
Ty Employee Christmas Bear (1997), violet, new face, minimum
    value $2,800.00
Ty Rep #1 Bear (Dec 1998), red, new face, #1 on chest, only 253
    made & issued to sales reps, minimum value........$8,500.00
Valentina the Bear, #4233, from $6 to $10.00
Valentino the Bear, #4058, wht w/red heart, retired $20.00
Velvet the Panther, #4064, retired....................................$35.00
Waddle the Penguin, #4075, retired..................................$30.00
Waves the Whale, #4084, retired, from $15 to $25.00
Web the Spider, #4041, retired, minimum value............$700.00
Weenie the Dachsund, #4013, retired................................$30.00
Whisper the Deer, #4187, from $6 to $10.00
Wise the Owl, #4194, retired, from $15 to........................$30.00
Wiser the Owl, 1999 graduation owl, from $6 to.............$10.00
Wrinkles the Bulldog, #4103, retired, from $10 to $15.00
Zero the Penguin, #4207, retired, from $25 to $45.00
Ziggy the Zebra, #4063, retired...$25.00
Zip the Cat, #4004, all blk, retired, minimum value......$800.00
Zip the Cat, #4004, blk w/wht paws, retired $35.00
Zip the Cat, #4004, blk w/wht tummy, retired, minimum
    value $275.00

BEANIE BUDDIES

Ty produces several different extensive lines of animals, all of which are highly collectible now. The Beanie Buddies line in particular is of special interest to Beanie Babies collectors, since these animals are a larger version of Beanie Babies.

Beak the Kiwi, retired, from $25 to $40.00
Bongo the Monkey, from $10 to...$20.00
Bubbles the Fish, from $10 to $30.00
Chilly the Bear, from $10 to $30.00
Chip the Cat, from $10 to $20.00
Erin the Irish Bear, from $20 to $40.00
Fuzz the Bear, from $20 to $40.00
Hippity the Bunny, from $10 to $15.00
Hope the Praying Bear, from $20 to $40.00
Humphrey the Camel, from $10 to $30.00
Jabber the Parrot, from $10 to $15.00
Jake the Mallard Duck, from $10 to $15.00
Millennium the Bear, from $20 to $40.00
Patti the Platypus, from $10 to $30.00
Peanut the Elephant, royal bl, from $10 to $15.00
Peking the Panda, from $10 to $30.00
Pinky the Flamingo, from $10 to $15.00
Princess the Bear, from $20 to $40.00
Quackers the Duck, from $10 to $15.00
Rover the Dog, from $10 to $15.00
Smoochy the Frog, from $10 to $15.00
Snort the Bull, from $10 to $15.00
Squealer the Pig, from $10 to $15.00
Stretch the Ostrich, from $10 to $15.00
Teddy the Bear, cranberry, from $20 to $40.00
Tracker the Basset Hound, from $10 to $15.00
Twigs the Giraffe, retired, from $85 to $125.00
Waddle the Penguin, from $10 to $15.00

Bicycles, Motorbikes, and Tricycles

The most interesting of the vintage bicycles are those made from the 1920s into the '60s, though a few even later models are collectible as well. Some from the '50s were very futuristic and styled with sweeping Art Deco lines; others had wonderful features such as built-in radios and brake lights, and some were decked out with saddlebags and holsters to appeal to fans of Hoppy, Gene, and many other western heroes. Watch for reproductions.

Condition is everything when evaluating bicycles, and one worth $2,500.00 in excellent or better condition might be worth as little as $50.00 in unrestored, poor condition. But here are a few values to suggest a range.

Advisor: Richard Trautwein (T3).

Barnes White Flyer Tandem, wht w/red seats, rear steering, rstr, from $1,200 to $1,500.00
Bowden, boy's, red futuristic design w/chrome trim & wht-wall tires, chrome rear carrier, wht grips, M, from $3,400 to $3,700.00

Bowden Space Lander, limited reissue of the 1950 issue, EX, from $700 to $900.00
Columbia Century, girl's, late 1800s, pneumatic safety complete w/rear brakes & fenders, rpl seat, G, from $1,000 to...$1,200.00
Columbia Chainless, boy's, blk, rstr, from $1,200 to ...$1,600.00
Columbia Chainless 2-Speed Safety, boy's, 1903, cushion fr, pneumatic tires, EX, from $2,000 to $2,700.00

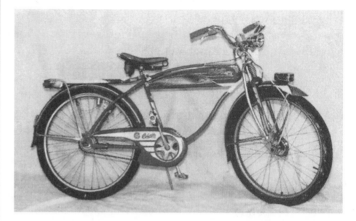

Columbia Five Star, boy's, 1952, two-tone cream and maroon, three-speed, VG, from $1,100.00 to $1,200.00.

Columbia RX5, boy's, 50th Anniversary replica, gr & wht, EX, from $200 to $400.00
Elgin Blackhawk, boy's, 1934, rstr...............................$2,000.00
Elgin Deluxe, girl's, 1940, w/horn tank, headlight, illuminated rear rack & skirt guards, G, from $350 to.................$550.00
Evinrude Imperial Steam Flow, 1937, red-pnt aluminum w/blk seat, w/speedometer, horn & lock, rare, EX, from $9,500 to...$11,000.00
Hawthorne Comet, boy's, Montgomery Ward, 1938, fender light, rear carrier & rear-wheel kickstand, EX $500.00
Hawthorne 2-Speed, boy's, Montgomery Ward, 1937, red & wht w/wht-wall tires, EX $450.00
Huffy BMX, boy's, 1970s, red w/blk accents, VG, from $100 to..$150.00

Indian, boy's, 1920, red with black seat, high pressure pneumatic safety, EX, from $1,200.00 to $1,800.00.

JC Higgins, boy's, Sears, maroon w/gold tank, shock-absorber springs, rstr, EX $600.00

JC Higgins, boy's, 1957, red w/wht-wall tires, rstr, from $800 to $900.00

JC Higgins Color-Flo, boy's, gray & wht w/wht-wall tires, jeweled tank, bat wing head lamp, rstr, from $1,200 to $1,500.00

JC Higgins Color-Flo, girl's, gray & wht w/wht-wall tires, jeweled tank, bat wing head lamp, rstr, from $800 to $1,000.00

Monarch Silver King 26-X, boy's, 1939, silver, w/streamlined horn light & electric taillight, rare, EX, from $2,000 to $3,000.00

Monark Silver King, girl's, 1936, silver, open lug fr w/streamlined seat & stainless fenders, VG, from $350 to.....$500.00

Raleigh Chopper, boy's, 1970s, purple w/red accents, EX, from $150 to $250.00

Roadmaster Luxury Liner, girl's, metallic gr w/chrome fenders, 26", EX, from $500 to $700.00

Rouse-Hazard Overland, girl's, late 1800s, pneumatic safety, all orig, from $900 to...$1,000.00

Schwinn Autocycle, tan & cream w/luggage rack, rstr ..$1,500.00

Schwinn Black Phantom, complete w/accessories, EX ..$1,650.00

Schwinn Collegiate Sport, boy's, 1970, bright yel, 5-speed, EX, from $150 to $250.00

Schwinn Corvette, boy's, 1960s, gr & wht, 3-speed, middle weight, G, from $150 to $200.00

Schwinn D97XE, boy's, 1939, cream & red w/Goodyear All Weather wht-wall tires, EX, from $1,000 to.........$1,500.00

Schwinn Fair Lady, 1960s, yel, VG, from $150 to $250.00

Schwinn Fiesta, girl's, 1960, pk & wht, middle weight, VG, from $100 to $150.00

Schwinn Fleet, boy's, 1970s, red & wht, VG, from $100 to...$150.00

Schwinn Green Phantom, boy's, 1951, 26", EX..............$700.00

Schwinn Jaguar Mark 2, boy's, 1955, red w/Westwind wht-wall tires, 3-speed, EX, from $700 to $800.00

Schwinn Panther, boy's, 1960, bl & wht, G, from $350 to...$500.00

Schwinn Scrambler, boy's, 1975, red w/wht accents, EX, from $100 to $200.00

Schwinn Speedster, boy's, 1970s, bl w/chrome accents, 6-speed, EX, from $200 to $250.00

Schwinn Speedster, boy's, 1970s, red, EX, from $100 to...$150.00

Schwinn Starlet, girl's, 1955, gr & cream, VG $175.00

Schwinn Sting Ray Tornado, boy's, 1970s, red and yellow, NM, from $150.00 to $250.00.

Schwinn Sting Ray Lil Chik, girl's, 1970s, pk & wht, NM, from $150 to...$250.00

Schwinn Town & Country, 1952 dealer demo, gr w/child's carrier, middle weight tandem, EX, from $400 to.........$500.00

Schwinn Victory Sports Tourist, girl's, 1947, red, VG, from $250 to $350.00

Sears Free Spirit, boy's, 1960s, red, w/tank, EX, from $100 to $150.00

Shelby Western Flyer Speedline Airflow, boy's, 1937, rstr ...$3,800.00

Silver King Racer, boy's, 1935, silver w/Gillette Road Racer tires, rstr, from $1,000 to......................................$1,500.00

Silver King Wingbar, girl's, 1939, tool-box seat, jeweled light on front fender, butterfly kickstand, EX.......................$600.00

Swiss Alenax, boy's, lt bl, lever action, EX, from $200 to...$300.00

Motorbikes

Indian Motorcycle, Citan, 1940s-50s, blk & cream w/Indian Motorcycle logo, rstr...$4,200.00

Monarch Super-Twin, 1949, blk w/red-orange trim, chrome fender headlight, rear wheel kickstand, EX $3,200.00

Spaceliner, girl's, Sears, bl-gr w/chrome fenders, wht seat & grips, electric light & horn, 67", EX........................$200.00

Speed Bike, Metal Specialties, 1930, red, pneumatic tires w/red spokes, G $850.00

Whizzer Sportsman, w/windshield & spring seat, rear carrier, 20", rstr $3,200.00

Tricycles

Clock Chain Drive, all metal w/rubber-tired spoke wheels, wooden hand grips, 24x31", VG, minimum value...$700.00

Colson Adult Tricycle, 1900, 2-wheel drive w/rear differential, EX, from $525 to $750.00

Donaldson Jockey Cycle, scooter-type handlebars, rubber tires, 24½x37", rpt...$850.00

Early American, wood, metal tires w/wooden spoke rims, straight handlebars, orig cloth-coverd seat, 30x49", EX, A ...$1,980.00

Gendron Pioneer, red, wide-spoked front wheel, 19½", G..$375.00

Good Humor Trike, 1955, chain drive, opening door in rear compartment, 36", EX, from $1,000 to.................$1,400.00

Horse, pnt carved wood horse on 3 wooden disk wheels, center grip hdl, leatherette saddle, 29x26", VG, A.............$385.00

Murray Airflow Jr, pnt pressed steel, 17½", G $200.00

Velocipede, 1970, gr, 16", rstr $600.00

Black Americana

Black subjects were commonly depicted in children's toys as long ago as the late 1870s. Among the most widely collected today are the fine windup toys made both here and in Germany. Early cloth and later composition and vinyl dolls are favorites of many; others enjoy ceramic figurines. Many factors enter into evaluating Black Americana, especially in regard to the handmade dolls and toys, since quality is subjective to individual standards. Because of this you may find wide ranges in dealers' asking prices. In order to better understand this field of collecting, we recommend *Black Collectibles Sold in America* by P.J. Gibbs; and *Black Dolls: 1820 – 1991* and *Black Dolls, Book II*, both by Myla Perkins.

Advisor: Judy Posner (P6).

See also Banks; Battery-Operated Toys; Schoenhut; Windups, Friction, and Other Mechanicals.

Banjo, Swanee River, USA, plastic w/image of boy playing banjo by riverboat, 15", MIB, A $100.00
Bank, baby nodder w/alligator, Kenmar/Japan, 1950s, pnt bsk, 6x7", EX, P6.........................$125.00
Book, Charlotte Steiner's Story-Book Theatre, 1944, Little Black Sambo w/5 other story books, EX, P6 ....$225.00
Book, Daily Express Children's Manual, 1933, 6 pop-ups, hardcover, rare, EX, A $400.00
Book, Golly's Surprise Book For Boys & Girls, Robertsons/England, 8 pgs of games, tricks, cutouts, puppet, A $150.00
Book, Kentucky Twins, Raphael Tuck & Sons Ltd, 1910, hardcover, EX $475.00
Book, Little Black Sambo, Donahue, early 1900s, hardcover, 62 pgs, EX+, A.........................$125.00
Book, Little Black Sambo, Macmillan, 1933, illus by Frank Dobias, hardcover, 45 pgs, rare, EX, P6 ....$135.00
Book, Little Black Sambo, Saalfield, 1942, illus by Ethel Hays, cloth-type cover, EX, P6.........................$110.00
Book, Little Black Sambo, Whitman Tell-A-Tale, 1959, illus by Violet La Mont, EX, P6.........................$90.00
Book, Little Black Sambo, Whitman Top-Top Tales, 1961, illus by Bonnie & Bill Rutherford, 28 pgs, EX, P6.............$90.00
Book, Little Brown Koko, by Blanche Seale Hunt, Am Colortype, 1940, illus by Dorothy Wagstaff, hardcover, EX.............$95.00
Book, Magic Drawing Book, 1930s, 2 pgs of the alphabet w/images for tracing, 7½x4½", unused, M, P6...........$45.00
Book, My Favorite Story Book, Saalfield, illus by Ethel Hays, hardcover, 16 pgs, EX, P6 ....$95.00
Book, Polly & Her Dollys, by Ajo, Blackie & Son Ltd, 1933, hardcover, 20 pgs, EX, P6.........................$125.00

Book, Turkey Trott, by Kate Gambold Dyer, 1942, Janet Robsun illus, Platt & Munk, hardcover, EX.........................$95.00
Book, Uncle Remus & His Friends, by Joel Chandler Harris, 1920, illus by AB Frost, hardcover, 357 pgs, EX, P6 ..$80.00
Book, Watermelon Pete & Other Stories, Rand McNally, 1927, hardcover, EX $85.00
Coloring Book, Little Brown Koko, 1941, illus by Dorothy Wadstaff, 22 pgs, unused, EX, P6 ....$125.00
Dexterity Puzzle, Sambo, Fun Inc, 1950s, bl plastic head figure w/exaggerated features, MIP, P6.........................$65.00
Dice Toy, Alco/Britain/HK, spring-activated plunger spins Black man's head & pr of dice, 2" dia, NM, A...................$100.00

Doll, Beloved Belindy, Georgene Novelties, stuffed cloth, replaced clothes, 13½", NM, minimum value, $1,200.00.
(Photo courtesy Myla Perkins)

Book, *Pop-Up Little Black Sambo*, Blue Ribbon, 1934, one pop-up, NM, $275.00.
(Photo courtesy Larry Jacobs)

Dolls, unmarked, 1940s – 50s, stuffed cloth with yarn hair, original clothing, 12", EX, $225.00 for the pair.
(Photo courtesy PJ Gibbs)

Doll, golliwog, stuffed cloth w/glued-on oilcloth features, red striped pants, bl jacket, yel shirt, 16", EX, P6 ....$95.00

Doll, golliwog, stuffed cloth w/orange shirt & red pants, plush hair, 12", EX, P6 ....$65.00

Doll, pickaninny, 1950s, inflatable plastic w/flasher eyes, yel skirt & hair bow, 10", EX, P6 ....$35.00

Doll, topsy-turvy, Topsy & Little Eva, 1920s, stuffed cotton w/embroidered features, 11½", VG, P6...................$125.00

Doll, topsy-turvy, 1930s, stockinette-type, cotton w/embroidered features, different print on ea side of dress, 17", P6....$95.00

Doll Kit, Sambo, Bucilla Needlework, 1950s, complete, P6..$95.00

Figure, baby doll, Japan, 1920s, bsk w/pnt features, 3 tufts of hair w/red bows, 4", EX, P6................................$65.00

Figure, boy riding alligator, Germany, 1920s, bsk, 3" L, NM $125.00

Figure, Dancing Sambo, cb, pull string & he dances, 12", MIP, A...$55.00

Figure, little girl holding doll, Germany, 1920s, bsk, 8½", NM $175.00

Figure, Mammy Tinker, Toy Tinkers, 1920, wood with original decal, 7½", NM, $125.00. (Photo courtesy Craig Strange)

Figure, minstrel on platform, 1900s, jtd wood, mechanical, 16" oblong platform, NM, A $175.00

Figure Set, wedding party, SK, prewar, celluloid, set of 6, 2¾", EX (EX box), A $350.00

Game, Alabama Coon, Germany, complete, rare, NMIB, from $400 to..$500.00

Game, Amos 'N Andy Card Party, AM Davis, 1930, cb, 6 tally & 2 score cards, VG (VG box), A $95.00

Game, Arch-Pool Bowling, 1927, MIB, A.....................$100.00

Game, Bean-Em, All-Fair, 1931, complete, NMIB, from $300 to $350.00

Game, Cake Walk, Parker Bros, 1920, complete, NMIB, from $350 to...$400.00

Game, Coon Hunt, Parker Bros, 1920, complete, NMIB .$400.00

Game, Darkey Ten Pins, Milton Bradley, complete, rare, NMIB, from $600 to $700.00

Game, Hit Me Hard, Klesfeld Works, 1920, complete, NM..$175.00

Game, Little Black Sambo, Cadaco-Ellis, EX (EX box), $100.00. (Photo courtesy David Longest)

Game, Little Black Sambo, Einson-Freeman, 1934, NMIB, A...$250.00

Game, Old Barn Door Target, Parker Bros, 1920-30, complete, NMIB..$450.00

Game, Piccaninny Bowling, Spears, 1928, complete, NMIB..$425.00

Game, roulette wheel, pnt wood, numbers around 4 cut-out heads, 3½" dia, scarce, EX, A.........................$500.00

Game, Sambo Target, tin over cb, mc graphics, no easel, 21x13½", G, A $150.00

Game, Skillets & Cakes, Milton Bradley, 1946, complete, EX (EX box), from $150 to $200.00

Game, target, wood, black man's face drops & asks Who Said Chicken?, 12", EX, A $365.00

Game, Watch on de Rind, All-Fair, 1931, complete, NMIB $350.00

Game, Zoo Hoo, Lubbers & Bell, 1924, complete, NM (EX box) $165.00

Jack-in-the-Box, Germany, 1950s, golliwog jumps out, 7", EX+, A..$250.00

Mask, Al Jolson, papier-mache, w/mouth wide open, 11½", G, A..$200.00

Noisemaker, unmarked, 1920 – 40, painted tin, 4" dia, EX, $65.00. (Photo courtesy PJ Gibbs)

Paper Dolls, Betty & Billy, Whitman, 1955, uncut, NM, P6 ...**$125.00**

Pull Toy, Little Jasper, Wood Commodities, 1944, 10", NM (EX box)..**$300.00**

Puppet, marionette, boy, wood w/tan cloth overalls, red & wht checked shirt & straw hat, 15", VG, A **$85.00**

Puppet, marionette, Pelham, minstrel strumming banjo, wood w/cloth clothes, mouth moves, 13", MIB, A...........**$200.00**

Puzzle, fr-tray, Little Black Sambo, New Play Craft for Nursery Centers, Auckland, 1930s, wood, 11x9", EX, P6 .....**$125.00**

Puzzle, fr-tray, Little Black Sambo, USA, 1945, pictures Jumbo w/umbrella & Mumbo putting on Sambo's jacket, M, A..**$100.00**

Puzzle, fr-tray, Tea for Two, 1920s, image of cook being scared by bears, 8x10", complete, NMIB, P6 ....**$145.00**

Puzzle, jigsaw, cabin scene w/pickaninnies eating watermelon & dancing, 10", complete, EX, A **$155.00**

Puzzle, jigsaw, Dark Town Fancy Ball, 1880s, very rare, EX+, A **$275.00**

Ramp Walker, Mammy, 1920s, wood in cloth print dress, 4½", scarce, M, A **$75.00**

Record, Little Brave Sambo, Peter Pan, 1950, EX (EX sleeve), A..**$65.00**

Record, Tales of Uncle Remus, Capitol, 1947, 78 rpm, 3-record set, EX (EX cover), P6 ....**$90.00**

Record & Book Set, Little Black Sambo, Music You Enjoy Inc, 1941, EX, P6 ....**$125.00**

Stacking Blocks, 1940s, set of 5 storybook blocks featuring Sambo & Tiger, EX, P6 ....**$125.00**

Transfers, Aunt Martha's Hot Iron Transfers, 1930s, pickaninnies doing various chores, unused, M, P6 ....**$70.00**

Boats

Though some commercially made boats date as far back as the late 1800s, they were produced on a much larger scale during WWI and the decade that followed and again during the years that spanned WWII. Some were scaled-down models of battleships measuring nearly three feet in length. While a few were actually seaworthy, many were designed with small wheels to be pulled along the carpet or out of doors on dry land. Others were motor-driven windups, and later a few were even battery operated. Some of the larger manufacturers were Bing (Germany), Dent (Pennsylvania), Orkin Craft (California), Liberty Playthings (New York), and Arnold (West Germany).

Advisor: Richard Trautwein (T3).

See also Cast Iron, Boats; Battery-Operated Toys; Tootsietoys; Windups, Friction, and Other Mechanicals; and other specific manufacturers.

Aircraft Carrier, Japan, friction, litho tin, complete w/jet plane, 15", EX (EX box), A..**$235.00**

Aircraft Carrier, Japan, friction, litho tin, complete w/Navy plane, 7", EX (EX box), A **$150.00**

Aircraft Carrier, Y, friction, litho tin, 5 jets attached to deck, 4 deck guns & 2 side guns, 11", NM (EX box), A **$275.00**

Battleship, Bing, clockwork, pnt tin, 2-tone gray, 12", EX, A...**$1,000.00**

Battleship, Orkin, clockwork, wht, cream-& red-pnt pressed steel w/several brass fixtures, 32", EX, A **$3,600.00**

Battleship, Orobr, clockwork, litho tin w/paper flag, 2 stacks & lifeboats, pilot house on top deck, 11", EX, A **$700.00**

Battleship HMS Albion, Marklin, 1902-04, pressed steel, railed deck, wheeled carriage, 22", EX.........................**$13,700.00**

Battleship Inflexible, 1895, steam-powered, tinplate and copper, 40", NM, A, $11,000.00.

Battleship Maine, Bliss, paper lithograph on wood, rare, EX, $1,600.00. (Photo courtesy David Longest)

Battleship Texas, litho tin & wood, NM **$950.00**

Cabin Cruiser, Linemar, 1950s, mk Vacationer 22, battery-op, litho tin, 12", EX, from $200 to.............................**$275.00**

Cabin Cruiser, Orkin, clockwork, pnt steel w/glassine windows, detailed cockpit w/enunciator, 30", EX, A **$1,400.00**

Cabin Cruiser, T Cohn, 1950s, w/up, litho tin, advances w/spinning prop, 14½", NM (EX box), from $100 to **$150.00**

Dreadnought Flotilla, Hess, clockwork, litho tin, w/5 sm boats on wire armature, 6", EX, from $700 to **$900.00**

Ferryboat Union, Bing, clockwork, red-& bl-pnt tin w/yel detail, 2 paddles wheels & ventilators, 16", VG **$700.00**

Gunboat, Bing, clockwork, pnt tin, GBN Bavaria plaque on deck, 21½", G, A...**$825.00**

Gunboat, Germany, flywheel mechanism, litho tin w/center stack & railed sides, 9", EX...................................**$150.00**

King Vessel, Ives, clockwork, hand-pnt tin, w/pilot house & lifeboat, 1 mast & funnel, 10½", EX, from $600 to .$800.00

Lackawanna Railroad Ferryboat, CK, clockwork mechanism, litho tin, rnd pilot house, 1 stack, 10", NM, A $275.00

Launch, mk Clyde Model Dockyard & Engine Depot — Glasgow; Made in Saxony..., pressed steel, steam-powered, 43", EX, A $650.00

Luxury Liner, Wolverine, w/up, litho tin, 14", EX (EX box), A $200.00

Luxury Liner, Wolverine, w/up, red w/lithoed swimming pool, lifeboats & shuffleboard, 14½", NM (NM box) $250.00

Mayflower, Reed, paper lithograph on wood with cardboard sails and rigging, decks lift for storage, 32", EX, from $825.00 to $1,000.00.

Mighty Aircraft Carrier, Cragstan, friction, litho tin, 9½", EX (EX box), A $200.00

Motorboat, Orkin, clockwork, maroon- & wht-pnt pressed steel w/red hull, 30", EX $3,500.00

Motorboat, wood w/battery-op IMP outboard motor, 24", EX, A...$450.00

Ocean Liner, Arnold, w/up, red- & bl-pnt tin w/wht upper deck, 2 masts & stacks, 2 tiers of lifeboats, 13½", EX....$1,000.00

Ocean Liner, Bing, clockwork, hand-pnt tin, w/pilot house, 2 stacks & masts, bow & stern flags, 12½", EX, A ..$1,000.00

Ocean Liner, Bing, clockwork, red, wht- & bl-pnt pressed steel, 3 stacks & 2 masts, 2 railed passenger decks, 16", EX $1,900.00

Ocean Liner, Bing, clockwork, red- & wht-pnt tin, single stack, 6", VG, A $175.00

Ocean Liner, Fleischmann, clockwork, red-, wht- & bl-pnt tin, railed stern & bow, 2 stacks & masts, 16", NM, A ..$1,400.00

Ocean Liner, Fleischmann, clockwork, wht-pnt tin w/bl hull stripe, brn deck, 2 stacks & masts, 16", NM, A $1,400.00

Ocean Liner, Germany, friction, litho tin, 3 stacks, 7¼", EX, A $750.00

Ocean Liner, Marklin, red-, blk- & wht-pnt tin, 2 stacks & flags, 6 lifeboats, 28", EX, A..$8,400.00

Pacific Star Yacht, pnt wood w/3 cloth sails, 21", NMIB..$200.00

Pond Yacht, wood hull w/weighted keel, functional rigging & sails, 30", EX, A $550.00

Pond Yacht, 1890s, wood hull w/early sloop in natural varnish, leaded keel, cloth sails, 33", EX, from $1,000 to ..$1,200.00

Racing Scull, Bing, w/up, litho tin, single rower, 8", EX, A .$1,375.00

River Launch, Germany, clockwork, pnt tin, single stack w/billowing smoke, 8½", VG+, A................................$525.00

River Yacht, Germany, clockwork, red- & cream-pnt tin, flat figures under rear canopy, 17½", rstr, A $1,850.00

Riverboat, Carette, wht w/red striping & brn hull, brass boiler, railed sides, 18", rpt, EX................................$665.00

Riverboat Liberty, Liberty Playthings, 1920, w/up, wood & brass, complete w/3 litho tin figures, 17", rare, EX, A $850.00

Riverboat Queen Mary, Marusan, battery-op, litho tin, advances w/sound & smoke, 14", EX (EX box) $275.00

Runabout Motorboat, wood hull w/canopy, steel cover on deck, w/up outboard motor, 17", G+, A $175.00

Sea Babe Speed Boat, battery-op, pnt tin & wood, 13", EX (EX box), from $125 to.....................................$150.00

Sea Comber, Fleet Line, 1960s, battery-op, mostly plastic, 18½", EX $200.00

Sea Wolf, Fleet Line, 1950s, battery-op, mostly wood, 18", NM, from $150 to $200.00

Seagull Motorboat, w/up, wood hull w/canopy, steel cover on front deck, 17", EX, A $225.00

Side-Wheeler, Orobr, w/up, red & wht litho tin, single stack, 8½", VG, A $350.00

Side-Wheeler Atlantic, Althof Bergmann, pnt tin, NM, D10 ....$4,500.00

Speedboat, ca 1920, steam-powered, gray-pnt pressed steel w/brn deck, 26", EX, from $1,000 to $1,400.00

Speedboat, Kellermann, clockwork, pnt & stained wood, driver w/bsk head, 24", EX..$1,200.00

Speedboat, Orkin, clockwork, pnt steel, working compass, opening hatch, w/driver, 27", G+, from $400 to............$600.00

Speedboat, Orkin, clockwork, pnt wood w/diecast fittings, working compass, w/driver, 26", VG+, minimum value ..$650.00

Speedboat Sea-Fury, 1948, red & blk plastic w/metal motor, 16", EX, A $150.00

Speedboat Viking with Johnson outboard motor, Fleet Line, 1960s, battery-operated, mostly plastic, 11", EX (EX box), $225.00.
(Photo courtesy Don Hultzman)

SS America, Wyandotte, w/up, litho tin, w/shuffleboard, lifeboats, US mail plane, etc, 12", EX, A $150.00

Steamboat, Weeban, gray-pnt tin w/exposed brass boiler, 16", G $500.00

Steamboat George Washington, Marklin, steam-powered, pressed steel, 9½", EX, A $1,100.00

Submarine, Marklin, w/up, gray-pnt tin w/blk stripe, lg side flippers, deck railing, 23", EX $3,000.00

Torpedo Boat, Bing, steam-powered, gray-pnt tin w/red hull, 4 masts, 3 cannons, railed battle station, 27½", NM, A $3,100.00

Torpedo Boat, Bing, 2-tone gray-pnt tin w/blk trim, 2 torpedo chutes, guns & lifeboats, 16", VG $550.00

Tugboat, Buddy L, driven by compressed air motor below deck, pressed steel, 28", EX, A, $8,500.00.

Tugboat Neptune, TM, battery-op, litho tin, several actions, 15", EX (worn box), from $85 to..............................$125.00

US Merchant Marine Steamship, Ives, w/up, movable rudder, NM $2,000.00

Books

Books have always captured and fired the imagination of children, and today books from every era are being collected. No longer is it just the beautifully illustrated Victorian examples or first editions of books written by well-known children's authors, but more modern books as well.

One of the first classics to achieve unprecedented success was *The Wizard of Oz* by author L. Frank of Baum — such success, in fact, that far from his original intentions, it became a series. Even after Baum's death, other authors wrote Oz books until the decade of the 1960s, for a total of more than forty different titles. Other early authors were Beatrix Potter, Kate Greenaway, Palmer Cox (who invented the Brownies), and Johnny Gruelle (creator of Raggedy Ann and Andy). All were accomplished illustrators as well.

Everyone remembers a special series of books they grew up with, the Hardy Boys, Nancy Drew Mysteries, Tarzan — there were countless others. And though these are becoming very collectible today, there were many editions of each, and most are very easy to find. Generally the last few in any series will be most difficult to locate, since fewer were printed than the earlier stories which were likely to have been reprinted many times. As is true of any type of book, first editions or the earliest printing will have more collector value. For more information on series

books as well as others, we recommend *Collector's Guide to Children's Books, 1850 – 1950, Volume I* and *II*, by Diane McClure Jones and Rosemary Jones (Collector Books).

Big Little Books came along in 1933 and until edged out by the comic-book format in the mid-1950s sold in huge volumes, first for a dime and never more than 20¢ a copy. They were printed by Whitman, Saalfield, Goldsmith, Van Wiseman, Lynn, and World Syndicate, and all stuck to Whitman's original layout — thick hand-sized sagas of adventure, the right-hand page with an exciting cartoon, well illustrated and contrived so as to bring the text on the left alive. The first hero to be immortalized in this arena was Dick Tracy, but many more were to follow. Some of the more collectible today feature well-known characters like G-Men, Tarzan, Flash Gordon, Little Orphan Annie, Mickey Mouse, and Western heroes by the dozens. (Note: At the present time, the market for these books is fairly stable — values for common titles are actually dropping. Only the rare, character-related titles are increasing.) For more information we recommend *Big Little Books*, by Larry Jacobs (Collector Books).

Little Golden Books were first published in 1942 by Western Publishing Co. Inc. The earliest had spines of blue paper that were later replaced with gold foil. Until the 1970s the books were numbered from 1 to 600, while later books had no numerical order. The most valuable are those with dust jackets from the early '40s or books with paper dolls and activities. The three primary series of books are Regular (1-600), Disney (1-140), and Activity (1-52). Books with the blue or gold paper spine (not foil) often sell at $8.00 to $15.00. Dust jackets alone are worth $20.00 and up in good condition. Paper doll books are generally valued at about $30.00 to $35.00, and stories about TV Western heroes at $12.00 to $18.00. First editions of the 25¢ and 29¢ cover-price books can be identified by a code (either on the title page or the last page); '1/A' indicates a first edition while a 'number /Z' will refer to the twenty-sixth printing. Condition is important but subjective to personal standards. For more information we recommend *Collecting Little Golden Books, Volumes I* and *II*, by Steve Santi. The second edition also includes information on Wonder and Elf books. For further study we recommend *Whitman Juvenile Books* by David and Virginia Brown (Collector Books).

Advisors: Ron and Donna Donnelly (D7), Big Little Books; Joel Cohen (C12), Disney Pop-Up Books; Ilene Kayne (K3), Big Golden Books, Little Golden Books, Tell-a-Tale, and Wonder Books.

See also Black Americana; Coloring, Activity, and Paint Books; Rock 'n Roll.

BIG LITTLE BOOKS

Adventures of Huckleberry Finn, Whitman #1422, 1939, NM $45.00

Adventures of Popeye, Saalfield #1051, 1934, scarce, EX, M14..$150.00

Alice in Wonderland, Whitman #759, EX $55.00

Andy Panda & Tiny Tom, Whitman #1425, 1944, EX, M14..$40.00

Big Chief Wahoo & the Lost Pioneers, Whitman #1432, EX...$40.00

Blondie in Hot Water, Whitman #1410, NM $45.00

Buccaneers, Whitman #1646, 1958, VG, M14 ....$15.00

Buck Jones & the Two-Gun Kid, Whitman #1404, 1937, EX, M14...$35.00

Buck Rogers & the Depth Men of Jupiter, Whitman #1169, EX+, M14 ....$75.00

Bugs Bunny & His Pals, Whitman #1496, EX $50.00

Bugs Bunny & the Pirate Loot, Whitman #1403, 1947, EX, M14 ....$40.00

Bullet Benton, Whitman #1169, 1939, EX, M14.............$35.00

Buz Sawyer & Bomber 13, Whitman #1415, 1946, VG, M14...$35.00

Captain Easy Behind Enemy Lines, Whitman #1474, 1943, EX $45.00

Chester Gump in the City of Gold, Whitman #1146, EX ..$40.00

Convoy Patrol, Whitman #1469, 1942, NM $40.00

Cowboy Stories, Whitman #724, NM.............................$60.00

Dan Dunn on the Trail of Wu Fang, Whitman #1454, VG..$35.00

Detective Dick Tracy & the Spider Gang, Whitman #1446, EX..$75.00

Dick Tracy Out West, Whitman #723, VG, M14 ....$95.00

Dick Tracy Returns, Whitman #1495, 1939, NM $75.00

Dick Tracy Solves the Penfield Mystery, Whitman #1137, VG, $55.00.

Donald Duck Headed for Trouble, Whitman #1430, VG, M14...$35.00

Donald Duck Up in the Air, Whitman #1486, NM, M14..$55.00

Ella Cinders & the Mysterious House, Whitman #1106, EX, M14...$45.00

Flash Gordon in the Jungles of Mongo, Whitman #1424, EX, M14...$60.00

Flint Roper & the Six Gun Showdown, Whitman #1467, EX $30.00

G-Man & the Gun Runners, Whitman #1469, EX+ $50.00

G-Man & the Radio Bank Robberies, Whitman #1434, 1937, EX $50.00

G-Man in Action, Saalfield #1173, 1940, VG, M14 ....$30.00

G-Man Breaking the Gambling Ring, Whitman #1493, 1938, NM, $75.00. (Photo courtesy Harry and Jody Whitworth)

G-Man on the Crime Trail, Whitman #1118, 1936, EX ..$50.00

G-Men on the Job, Whitman #1168, 1935, EX $50.00

Gang Busters in Action, Whitman #1451, 1938, VG, M14...$35.00

Gene Autry Cowboy Detective, Whitman #1494, 1940, EX .$60.00

Gene Autry Special Ranger, Whitman #1428, 1941, NM, M14..$75.00

George O'Brien & the Hooded Riders, Whitman #1457, EX..$25.00

Green Hornet Returns, Whitman #1496, 1941, NM, M14...$145.00

Hal Hardy in the Lost Land of Giants, Whitman #1413, EX....$40.00

Invisible Scarlet O'Neil Versus the King of the Slums, Whitman #1406, EX...$45.00

Jane Withers in Keep Smiling, Whitman #1463, EX........$50.00

Joe Palooka's Great Adventure, Whitman #1168, VG, M14 ..$35.00

Jungle Jim, Whitman #1138, 1936, NM, M14 ....$75.00

Little Orphan Annie and the Mysterious Shoemaker, Whitman #1449, NM, $65.00.
(Photo courtesy Larry Jacobs)

Katzenjammer Kids in the Mountains, Saalfield #1305, 1934, scarce, NM..$100.00

Ken Maynard in Western Justice, Whitman #1430, EX ...$35.00

King of the Royal Mounted Gets His Man, Whitman #1452, EX+ $60.00

Laughing Dragon of Oz, Whitman #1126, rare, NM $225.00

Little Orphan Annie & Chizzler, Whitman #748, 1933, VG, M14..$55.00

Lone Ranger & the Menace of Murder Valley, Whitman #1465, EX...$40.00

Lone Ranger & the Silver Bullets, Whitman #1498, EX+..$60.00

Lone Ranger on the Barbary Coast, Whitman #1421, 1944, VG, M14..$30.00

Mandrake the Magician & the Midnight Monster, Whitman #1431, NM $55.00

Mickey Mouse & the Stolen Jewels, Whitman #1464, NM..$75.00

Mickey Mouse in the Foreign Legion, Whitman #1428, 1940, EX, M14..$65.00

Moon Mullins & the Plushbottom Twins, Whitman #1134, VG, M14...$35.00

Nancy & Sluggo, Whitman #1400, EX $75.00

Oswald the Lucky Rabbit, Whitman #1109, EX..............$60.00

Our Gang on the March, Whitman #1451, 1942, NM.....$65.00

Perry Winkle & the Rinkeydinks, Whitman #1199, EX ..$40.00

Robinson Crusoe, Whitman #719, EX $45.00

Roy Rogers King of the Cowboys, Whitman #1476, NM .$60.00

Shadow & the Living Death, Whitman #1430, NM $200.00

Silver Streak, Whitman #1155, 1935, VG, M14 ....$40.00

Skeezix Goes to War, Whitman #1414, EX+ $45.00

Smilin' Jack & the Speed Pilot, Whitman #1473, VG, M14...$30.00

Snow White & the Seven Dwarfs, Whitman #1460, 1938, VG, M14..$60.00

Spike Kelly of the Commandos, Whitman #1467, NM, M14 ..$45.00

Tailspin Tommy — Hooded Flyer, Whitman #1423, 1937, NM, M14..$50.00

Tarzan & the Ant Men, Whitman #1444, NM $75.00

Tarzan the Untamed, Whitman #1452, NM $85.00

Terry & the Pirates Shipwrecked on Desert Island, Whitman #1412, EX, M14 ....$50.00

Texas Kid, Whitman #1429, 1937, EX, M14 ....$35.00

Thumper & the Seven Dwarfs, Whitman #1409, EX $75.00

Tim McCoy on Tomahawk Trail, Whitman #1436, EX, M14..$35.00

Tiny Tim in the Big Big World, 1945, EX+ $50.00

Tom Mix Plays Lone Hand, Whitman #1173, 1935, VG+, M14..$45.00

Two-Gun Montana, Whitman #1104, VG, M14 ....$25.00

Uncle Wiggily's Adventures, Whitman #1405, EX $40.00

Wash Tubbs in Pandemonia, Whitman #751, EX $45.00

Wimpy the Hamburger Eater, Whitman #1458, 1938, VG, M14..$45.00

Wings of the USA, Whitman #1401, EX+ $30.00

Zane Grey's Tex Thorne Comes Out of the West, Whitman #1440, EX..$30.00

DELL FAST ACTION BOOKS BY WHITMAN

Adventures of Charlie McCarthy & Edgar Bergen, NM ..$85.00

Bugs Bunny & the Secret of Storm Island, NM $75.00

Perry Winkle and the Rinkeydinks Get a Horse,
Whitman #1487, NM, $45.00. (Photo courtesy Larry Jacobs)

Phantom & the Girl of Mystery, Whitman #1416, NM ...$70.00

Popeye & Queen Olive Oyl, Whitman #1458, EX $45.00

Popeye — Deep Sea Mystery, Whitman #1499, EX, M14..$50.00

Radio Patrol Outwitting Gang Chief, Whitman #1496, EX, M14..$35.00

Red Ryder — Code of the West, Whitman #1427, NM...$60.00

Return of Tarzan, Whitman #1102, 1936, EX+, M14 ......$75.00

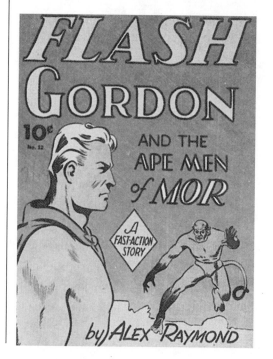

Flash Gordon and the Ape Men of Mor, NM, $125.00. (Photo courtesy Larry Jacobs)

Dan Dunn Secret Operative 48 & the Zeppelin of Doom, NM......$120.00

Dick Tracy & the Chain of Evidence, NM......$125.00

Dick Tracy Detective & Federal Agent, NM......$150.00

Donald Duck Out of Luck, NM......$200.00

Dumbo the Flying Elephant, NM......$125.00

G-Man on Lightning Island, NM......$85.00

Gene Autry in Gun Smoke, NM......$120.00

Katzenjammer Kids, NM......$90.00

Little Orphan Annie Under the Big Top, NM......$140.00

Mickey Mouse & Pluto, NM......$90.00

Mickey Mouse the Sheriff of Nugget Gulch, NM......$175.00

Pinocchio & Jiminy Cricket, NM......$100.00

Red Ryder Brings Law to Devil's Hole, NM......$80.00

Tailspin Tommy & the Airliner Mystery, NM......$100.00

Tarzan the Avenger, rare, NM......$200.00

Tom Mix in the Riding Avenger, NM......$90.00

LITTLE GOLDEN BOOKS

Aladdin & His Magic Lamp, #371, A edition, EX, K3......$14.00

Animal Counting Book, #584, E edition, EX, K3......$5.00

Baby Dear, #466, C edition, EX, K3......$12.00

Baby's Day Out, #113-01, A edition, EX, K3......$15.00

Baby's Mother Goose, #422, J edition, EX, K3......$6.00

Bambi, #106-60, F edition, EX, K3......$2.00

Beauty & the Beast — Teapot's Tale, #104-70, A edition, EX, K3......$5.00

Ben & Me, #D37, A edition, EX, K3......$22.00

Big Bird's Day on the Farm, #200-50, C edition, EX, K3......$4.00

Bobby the Dog, #440, A edition, EX, K3......$28.00

Book of God's Gifts, #112, F edition, EX, K3......$5.00

Bugs Bunny Carrot Machine, #127, B edition, EX, K3......$5.00

Bugs Bunny Pioneer, #111-66, A edition, EX, K3......$6.00

Bullwinkle, #462, A edition, EX, K3......$20.00

Buster Cat Goes Out, #302-57, D edition, EX, K3......$2.00

Captain Kangaroo & the Beaver, #427, A edition, EX, K3..$12.00

Cave Kids, #539, A edition, EX, K3......$25.00

Chicken Little, #413, F edition, EX, K3......$2.00

Christmas Tree That Grew, #458-1, A edition, EX, K3......$6.00

Cinderella's Friends, #D17, A edition, EX, K3......$15.00

Cindy Bear, #442, C edition, EX, K3......$6.00

Color Kittens, #86, A edition, EX, K3......$22.00

Come Play House, #44, D edition, EX, K3......$40.00

Cookie Monster & the Cookie Tree, #159, C edition, EX, K3......$6.00

Dale Evans & the Coyote, #253, A edition, EX, K3......$22.00

Dale Evans & the Lost Gold Mine, #213, A edition, EX, K3..$12.00

Doctor Dan Circus, #399, A edition, no band-aids, EX, K3.$14.00

Donald Duck & Santa Claus, #D27, E edition, EX, K3....$12.00

Donald Duck & the Witch, #D34, A edition, EX, K3......$15.00

Donald Duck Instant Millionaire, #102-44, H edition, EX, K3......$4.00

Donnie & Marie, #160, A edition, EX, K3......$10.00

Dumbo, #D3, H edition, K3......$22.00

Exploring Space, #342, A edition, EX, K3......$14.00

First Bible Stories, #198, A edition, EX, K3......$22.00

Fozzie's Funnies, #111-87, A edition, EX, K3......$5.00

Friendly Book, #199, A edition, EX, K3......$12.00

Fuzzy Duckling, #78, C edition, EX, K3......$10.00

Goodbye Tonsils, #327, D edition, EX, K3......$4.00

Hansel & Gretel, #17, D edition, EX, K3......$15.00

Happy Little Whale, #393, F edition, EX, K3......$6.00

How To Tell Time, #285, C edition, EX, K3......$14.00

Howdy Doody & Santa Claus, #237, A edition, EX, K3..$30.00

Huckleberry Hound Builds a House, A edition, NM......$15.00

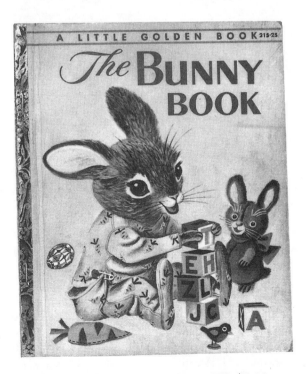

Bunny Book, #215, A edition, EX, $6.00.

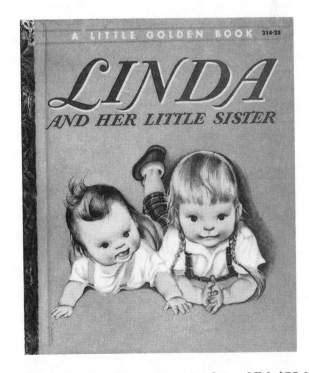

Linda and Her Little Sister, #214, A edition, NM, $75.00.

Inspector Gadget in Africa, #107-49, A edition, EX, K3 ....$5.00

Jingle Bells, #553, A edition, EX, K3 ....$10.00

Kitty on the Farm, #200-57, B edition, EX, K3 ....$3.00

Large & Growly Bear, #510, C edition, EX, K3 ....$6.00

Lassie Finds a Way, #456, A edition, EX, K3 ....$18.00

Let's Go Shopping, #208-58, C edition, EX, K3 ....$3.00

Little Fat Policeman, #91, A edition, EX, K3 ....$15.00

Little Mommy, #569, B edition, EX, K3 ....$25.00

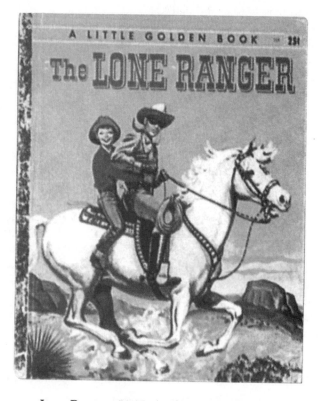

Lone Ranger, #263, A edition, EX, $25.00.

Loopy De Loop Goes West, #417, A edition, EX, K3 ....$8.00

Magilla Gorilla, #547, A edition, EX, K3 ....$12.00

Mary Poppins, #D113, B edition, EX, K3 ....$10.00

Mickey Mouse Picnic, #D15, D edition, EX, K3 ....$25.00

My Little Golden Book of Jokes, #424, A edition, EX, K3 .$15.00

My Little Golden Picture Dictionary, #90, A edition, EX, K3 ....$15.00

National Velvet, #431, A edition, EX, K3 ....$12.00

Naughty Bunny, #377, A edition, EX, K3 ....$25.00

Night Before Christmas, #20, D edition, EX, K3 ....$10.00

Nursery Tales, #14, C edition, EX, K3 ....$18.00

Old Mother Hubbard, #591, B edition, EX, K3 ....$5.00

Oscar's New Neighbor, #109-67, A edition, EX, K3 ....$5.00

Our Flag, #388, A edition, EX, K3 ....$8.00

Party in Shariland, #360, A edition, EX, K3 ....$18.00

Pebbles Flintstone, #531, A edition, EX, K3 ....$25.00

Pepper Plays Nurse, #555, A edition, EX $10.00

Peter & the Wolf, #D5, C edition, EX, K3 ....$10.00

Peter Rabbit, #313, A edition, EX, K3 ....$18.00

Pinocchio, D edition, #D8, EX, K3 ....$18.00

Pixie & Dixie & Mr Jinks, A edition, EX $15.00

Poky Little Puppy's Special Day, #371, EX, K3 ....$4.00

Raggedy Ann & Andy Help Santa Claus, #156, B edition, EX, K3 ....$5.00

Raggedy Ann & Fido, A edition, EX............................$15.00

Rin Tin Tin & Rusty, #246, B edition, EX, K3 ....$12.00

Road Runner, #122, F edition, EX, K3 ....$3.00

Robin Hood, #D48, A edition, EX, K3 ....$10.00

Robotman & Friends at School, #110-58, A edition, EX, K3...$6.00

Rootie Kazootie Baseball Star, #190, A edition, EX, K3...$20.00

Roy Rogers & Cowboy Toby, #195, A edition, EX, K3 ....$15.00

Rupert the Rhinoceros, #201-57, E edition, EX, K3 ....$4.00

Saggy Baggy Elephant, #36, C edition, EX, K3 ....$8.00

Santa's Toy Shop, #D16, A edition, EX, K3 ....$12.00

Savage Sam, #10359, A edition, EX, K3 ....$12.00

Seven Dwarfs Finds a House, #D35, B edition, EX, K3 ....$15.00

Shaggy Dog, #D82, B edition, EX, K3 ....$12.00

Shazam, #110-36, B edition, EX, K3............................$5.00

Shy Little Kitten, #23, F edition, EX, K3 ....$15.00

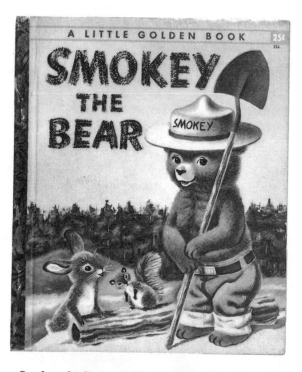

Smokey the Bear, #224, A edition, EX, $20.00.

Smokey Bear & the Campers, #423, B edition, EX, K3 ....$10.00

Supercar, #492, B edition, EX, K3 ....$35.00

This Is My Family, #312-22, A edition, EX, K3 ....$10.00

Three Billy Goat's Gruff, #173, A edition, EX, K3 ....$16.00

Tom & Jerry Meet Little Quack, A edition, EX, from $15 to..$20.00

Tom & Jerry's Party, #235, E edition, EX, K3 ....$8.00

Tommy's Wonderful Ride, #63, F edition, EX, K3 ....$8.00

Two Little Gardeners, #308-58, D edition, EX, K3............$3.00

Two Little Miners, #66, A edition, EX, K3 ....$15.00

Uncle Wiggily, #148, A edition, EX, K3 ....$15.00

Wally Gator, #502, A edition, EX, K3 ....$20.00

Waltons, #134, B edition, EX, K3 ....$10.00

We Help Mommy, #352, C edition, EX, K3 ....$20.00

Wild Kingdom, #151, A edition, EX, K3.........................$8.00

Willie Found a Wallet, #309-58, B edition, EX, K3...........$6.00

Winnie the Pooh & the Honey Patch, #101-24, B edition, EX, K3 ....$3.00

Yogi Bear, A edition, EX $15.00

Zorro, #D68, B edition, EX, K3 ....$14.00

POP-UP & MOVABLE BOOKS

Alice in Wonderland, Modern Publishers, 4 pop-ups, 8 pgs, EX, K3 ....$12.00

Anne of Green Gables — A Big Imagination, 1993, 12 pop-ups, 6 movable, EX, K3 ....$10.00

Anne of Green Gables — Adventures at School, 1993, 12 pop-ups, 6 movable, EX, K3 ....$10.00

Barbie Rockin' Rappin' Dancin' World Tour, Western, 1992, 1st edition, 5 pop-ups, 4 movable, 12 pgs, EX, K3 ....$20.00

Buck Rogers in a Dangerous Mission, Blue Ribbon, 1934, 1 pop-up, NM $450.00

Buck Rogers Strange Adventures in the Spider-Ship, Blue Ribbon, 1935, 3 pop-ups, M.........................$450.00

Christmas on Stage, by Charlotte Byj, 1950, 5 pop-ups, spiral-bound, EX (orig brn box), K3 ....$40.00

Cinderella, Blue Ribbon, 1933, 4 pop-ups, NM.............$425.00

Dick Tracy Capture of Boris Arson, Blue Ribbon, 1935, 3 pop-ups, NM $375.00

Dino & the Mouse Who Had Hiccups, 1974, 4 pop-ups, 8 pgs, EX, K3 ....$25.00

Flying Nun, 1982, 5 pop-ups, 10 pgs, EX, K3 ....$6.00

Jack & the Beanstalk, 1944, 5 pop-ups, w/dust jacket, EX, K3 ..$50.00

Jolly Old St Nicholas, 1992, musical, 1 pop-up, 2 movables, 12 pgs, EX, K3 ....$15.00

King Neptune Babes in the Woods, Blue Ribbon, 1930s, four pop-ups, NM, C12, $1,500.00. (Photo courtesy Joel Cohen)

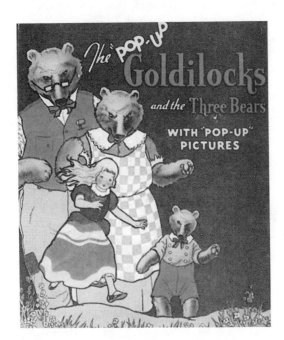

Goldilocks and the Three Bears, Blue Ribbon, 1934, three pop-ups, NM, $200.00. (Photo courtesy Larry Jacobs)

Hocus Pocus, 1991, 1 pop-up, 11 movable, 14 pgs, EX, K3 ..$15.00

Hopalong Cassidy at the Double Ranch, Garden City, 1950, EX, A $100.00

Hopalong Cassidy Lends a Helping Hand, Bonnie Books, 1950, 2 pop-ups, EX, A.......................$65.00

Jack & the Beanstalk, Blue Ribbon, 1933, 1 pop-up, M.$150.00

Mickey Hop-La! Une Partie de Polo, Hachette, 1930s, three pop-ups, NM, C12, $1,500.00. (Photo courtesy Joel Cohen)

Little Red Riding Hood, Blue Ribbon, 1933, 1 pop-up, NM ..$150.00

Mickey Mouse in King Arthur's Court, M, C12..........$1,500.00

Mickey Mouse in Ye Olden Days, Blue Ribbon, 1934, 1 pop-up, NM..$475.00

Mickey Mouse Waddle Book, Blue Ribbon, 1934, M, C12 ...$3,500.00

Minnie Mouse, WDE, 1930s, 3 pop-ups, M $400.00

Mother Goose, Blue Ribbon, 1934, 3 pop-ups, NM $250.00

My Pop-Up Book of Sleeping Beauty, 4 pop-ups, 10 pgs, EX, K3 ....$10.00

New Adventures of Tarzan, Pleasure Books, 1935, 3 pop-ups, scarce, NM, A..$450.00

New at the Zoo, Random House, 5 pop-ups, 10 pgs, EX, K3 ....$10.00

Night Before Christmas, 1993, 3 pop-ups, 1 movable, 8 pgs, EX, K3 ....$10.00

Peter Rabbit, Blue Ribbon, 1934, 1 pop-up, NM............$350.00

Popeye Among the White Savages, Blue Ribbon, 1934, 1 pop-up, NM..$325.00

Popeye w/the Hag of the Seven Seas, 1935, 3 pop-ups, EX ...$450.00

Puss In-Boots, Blue Ribbon, 3 pop-ups, NM..................$250.00

Raggedy Ann & Andy, Saalfield, 1944, animated by Julian Wehr, all pgs movable, EX $65.00

Raggedy Ann & Raggedy Andy on the Farm — A Pop-Up Book About Animals, Derrydale/Macmillan, 1992, EX, from $8 to $12.00

Raggedy Ann & the Daffy Taffy Pull, Hallmark/Bobbs-Merrill, 1972, EX..$30.00

Rainbow Round-A-Bout, 1992, 2 pop-ups, 2 revolving pictures, 10 pgs, EX, K3 ....$15.00

Seven Natural Wonders of the World, 1991, 7 pop-ups, 30 pgs, EX, K3 ....$15.00

Sleeping Beauty, Blue Ribbon, 1934, 1 pop-up, NM......$150.00

Tale of Two Bad Mice, 1990, 5 pop-ups, 10 pgs, EX, K3 ..$15.00

Tim Tyler in the Jungle, Blue Ribbon, 1935, 3 pop-ups, NM $325.00

Tom & Jerry Book of Numbers, 11 lift-up flaps, 28 pgs, EX, K3 ....$15.00

Wings — A Pop-Up Book of Things That Fly, Random House, 1991, 1st edition, 6 pop-ups, 6 movable, 16 pgs, EX, K3..$25.00

Wizard of Oz Waddle Book, Blue Ribbon, 1934, scarce, NM $250.00

101 Dalmatians, Belgium, 1972, 6 pop-ups, scarce, NM, M8 ....$70.00

Tell-a-Tale by Whitman

Bedknobs & Broomsticks, #2541, 1971, EX, K3 ....$5.00

Bible Stories, #828, 1947, EX, K3................................$8.00

Big Red Pajama Wagon, Top Top Tale #2479, 1949, EX, K3 .$10.00

Child's Garden of Verses, #2497, 1964, EX, K3 ....$5.00

Cinderella, #2552, 1954, EX, K3 ....$8.00

Cinnamon Bear, #2674, 1961, fuzzy pgs, EX, K3..............$15.00

Daniel's New Friend, #2560, 1968, EX, K3 ....$5.00

Donald Duck & the New Birdhouse, #2520, 1956, EX, K3 ..$8.00

Donald Duck Full Speed Ahead, #2552, 1953, EX, K3......$5.00

Fawn Baby, Big Tell-a-Tale #2428, 1966, EX, K3 ....$6.00

Flintstones & Dino, Top Top Tale #2460, 1961, EX, K3 ...$8.00

Flying Sunbeam, #849, 1950, EX, K3 ....$10.00

Frisker, #2426, 1956, EX, K3 ....$5.00

Howdy Doody's Clarabelle Clown & the Merry-Go-Round, 1955, EX..$20.00

Johnny Appleseed, #808, 1949, EX, K3 ....$20.00

Lady, #2552, 1954, EX, K3..$8.00

Lassie the Busy Morning, #2484, 1973, EX, K3................$5.00

Little Miss Muffet, #2464-33, 1958, EX, K3 ....$5.00

Little Red Riding Hood, #2651, 1953, EX, K3................$8.00

Mickey Mouse & the Mouseketeers, #2454-35, 1977, EX, K3 ....$5.00

Mother Goose, #2638, 1958, EX, K3 ....$6.00

Mr Grabbit, #2526, 1952, EX, K3 ....$8.00

Mr Moggs' Dogs, #2652, 1954, fuzzy pgs, EX, K3 ....$15.00

Patrick & the Duckling, Top Top Tale #2456, 1963, fuzzy, EX, K3 ....$10.00

Patrick the Fuzziest Bunny, Top Top Tale #5071, 1946, fuzzy, w/dust jacket, EX, K3..$35.00

Pete's Dragon, #2428-3, 1977, EX, K3..........................$4.00

Pinocchio, #26, 1961, EX, K3......................................$4.00

Princess Who Never Laughed, #2610, 1961, EX, K3 ....$5.00

Raggedy Ann & Andy on the Farm, 1975, EX..................$8.00

Road Runner & the Birdwatchers, #2509, 1968, EX, K3 ....$5.00

Roy Rogers' Surprise for Donnie, #943, 1954, EX, K3 ......$20.00

Slowpoke at the Circus, #2457, 1973, EX, K3..................$8.00

Sneezer, #854, 1954, w/dust jacket, EX, K3 ....$30.00

Story About Me, Big Tell-a-Tale #2427, 1966, EX, K3 ......$6.00

Surprise for Howdy Doody, #2573, 1950, EX, K3 ....$30.00

Three Little Pigs, #921, 1958, EX, K3 ....$5.00

Tommy & Timmy, #2656, 1951, fuzzy pgs, EX, K3..........$12.00

Tortoise & the Hare, Top Top Tale #2455, 1963, fuzzy, EX, K3 ....$15.00

Tweety, #2481, 1953, EX, K3......................................$10.00

Uncle Scrooge Rainbow Runaway, Big Tell-a-Tale #2422, 1965, EX, K3 ....$10.00

Walt Disney Bear Country, #2612, 1954, EX, K3 ....$8.00

Whitman Miscellaneous

Annie Oakley in Danger at Diablo, 1955, hardcover, EX, $20.00.
(Photo courtesy David and Virginia Brown)

Annette & the Mystery at Moonstone Bay, 1962, hardcover, EX..$10.00
Bedknobs & Broomsticks, 1971, hardcover, EX................$12.00
Betty Grable & the House of Cobwebs, 1947, hardcover, w/dust jacket, EX................................$25.00
Black Beauty, 1955, hardcover, EX................$8.00
Donald Duck, 1st edition, hardcover, rare, EX, C12...$1,200.00
Dr Kildare Assigned to Trouble, 1963, hardcover, EX......$12.00
Eight Cousins, 1955, hardcover, EX................$5.00
Flipper — Mystery of the Black Schooner, 1966, hardcover, EX................................$12.00
Gene Autry & the Big Valley Grab, 1954, hardcover, EX.$25.00
Gilligan's Island, 1966, hardcover, EX................$20.00
Green Hornet — Case of the Disappearing Doctor, 1966, hardcover, VG, J5................$25.00
Howdy Doody & the Magic Lamp, 1954, EX................$20.00
Howdy Doody's Island Adventure, Cozy Corner series, 1955, EX................$20.00
Huckleberry Finn, 1955, hardcover, EX................$8.00
Lassie & the Mystery at Blackberry Bog, 1956, hardcover, EX................$15.00

Oscar the Trained Seal, by Mabel Neikirk, 1948, EX.......$35.00
Pinocchio, 1939, softcover, EX, C1................$35.00
Pinocchio — Tale of a Puppet, 1967, hardcover, EX.........$5.00
Red Ryder & the Thunder Trail, 1956, hardcover, EX.......$15.00
Rin Tin Tin & the Ghost Wagon Train, 1958, hardcover, EX................$18.00
Roy Rogers & the Enchanted Canyon, 1954, hardcover, EX................$25.00
Snow White & the Seven Dwarfs, 1938, softcover, 96 pgs, EX+, A3................$50.00
Story of Clarabelle Cow, 1938, hardcover, EX................$40.00
Story of Minnie Mouse, WDE, 1938, 94 pgs, EX, K3.......$85.00
Tammy — Adventure in Hollywood, 1964, hardcover, EX..$20.00

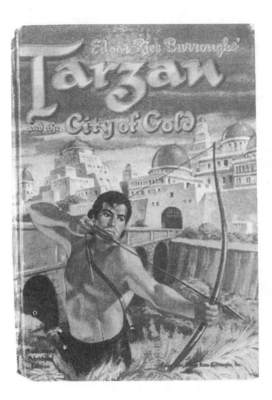

Tarzan and the City of Gold, 1954, hardcover, VG, $15.00. (Photo courtesy David and Virginia Brown)

Lassie and the Secret of the Summer, 1958, hardcover, VG, $12.00. (Photo courtesy David and Virginia Brown)

Lone Ranger & the War Horse, Cozy Corner, 1951, EX, A3................$25.00
Lucy & the Madcap Mystery, 1963, hardcover, EX.........$30.00
Mickey Mouse & Pluto the Pup, 1936, hardcover, NM .$125.00
Mickey Mouse ABC Story, 1937, hardcover, NM.........$150.00
Mickey Mouse Annual, 1937, hardcover, w/dust jacket, EX+, A................$350.00
Mickey Mouse in Pigmyland, 1936, softcover, EX, M8 ....$75.00
Mickey Mouse Mother Goose, 1937, hardcover, NM $150.00
Mighty Mouse & the Scarecrow, 1954, hardcover, EX, J5..$15.00

Walt Disney's Famous Seven Dwarfs, 1938, EX, M8........$45.00
Walton Boys in Rapids Ahead, 1958, hardcover, EX..........$5.00
Wise Little Hen, 1935, hardcover, w/dust jacket, NM, A .$150.00
Wonderful Wizard of Oz, 1970, hardcover, EX $5.00
Woody Woodpecker Shoots the Works, hardcover, EX, from $15 to................$20.00

WONDER BOOKS

A Puzzle for Raggedy Ann & Andy, 1957, EX.................$20.00
A Surprise for Mrs Bunny, #601, EX, K3.........$5.00
Bedtime Stories, #507, 1946, illus by Masha, EX, K3.......$15.00
Billy & His Steam Roller, #537, 1951, EX, K3....................$5.00
Boy Who Couldn't Eat His Breakfast, #815, 1963, EX, K3.$6.00
Casper & Wendy Adventures, #855, 1969, EX, K3..........$10.00
Cinderella, #640, 1954, EX, K3................$10.00
Counting Book, #692, 1957, EX, K3................$8.00

Deputy Dawg & the Space Man, 1961, hardcover, NM, A .$25.00
Do You Know the Magic Word, #578, 1952, EX, K3..........$5.00
Favorite Nursery Tales, #1504, 1953, EX, K3 ....$10.00
Felix the Cat, #665, 1953, NM, C1.....................................$40.00
Five Little Finger Playmates, #522, 1949, EX, K3 ....$15.00

Flash Gordon and the Baby Animals, 1956, EX, $30.00.
(Photo courtesy Marvelous Books)

Gandy Goose, #695, 1957, EX, K3 ....$10.00
Giraffe Who Went to School, #551, 1951, EX, K3.............$8.00
Hans Christian Andersen's Fairy Tales, #599, 1952, EX, K3...$8.00
Hector Heathcote & the Knights, 1965, hardcover, NM, A.$25.00
Heidi, #532, 1950, EX, K3...$10.00
How the Clown Got His Smile, #566, 1951, EX, K3........$12.00
It's a Lovely Day, #632, 1956, EX, K3 ....$5.00
It's a Secret, #540, 1950, EX, K3 ....$10.00
Let's Go to School, #691, 1954, EX, K3..........................$10.00
Little Audrey & the Moon Lady, #759, 1977, EX, K3 ....$8.00

Little John Little, #558, 1951, EX, K3................................$5.00
Little Lost Puppy, #528, 1976, EX, K3................................$6.00
Little Peter Cottontail, #641, 1956, EX, K3........................$8.00
Make-Believe Parade, #520, 1949, EX, K3........................$15.00
My First Book of Riddles, #745, 1960, EX, K3 ....$5.00
Night Before Christmas, #858, 1974, EX, K3 ....$5.00
Pecos Bill, #767, 1961, EX, K3 ....$12.00
Puppy Who Found a Boy, #561, 1951, EX, K3....................$8.00
Raggedy Andy's Surprise, #604, 1953, EX, K3 ....$10.00
Shy Little Horse, #1509, 1947, sculptured cover, EX, K3 .$15.00
Sleeping Beauty, #635, 1956, EX, K3 ....$5.00
Surprise Doll, #519, 1949, EX, K3 ....$30.00
Too Little Fire Engine, #526, 1950, EX, K3 ....$5.00
Twelve Days of Christmas, #651, 1956, EX, K3 ....$8.00
Who Lives Here, #669, 1958, EX, K3.................................$8.00
Why the Bear Has a Short Tail, #508, 1946, EX, K3........$10.00
Wonder Book of Cowboys, #640, 1956, EX, K3.................$8.00

MISCELLANEOUS

ABC Book, Jr Elf/Rand McNally, 1955, EX, K3 ....$5.00
ABC Nursery Rhymes, McLoughlin Bros, ca 1900, hardcover,
    EX $225.00
Addams Family Strikes Back, Pyramid, 1965, paperback, NM,
    C1..$45.00
Adventures of Mickey Mouse, McKay, 1931, 1st edition, hard-
    cover, NM...$350.00
Adventures of Superman, 1942, hardcover, w/dust jacket, EX,
    A $200.00
Aladdin & the Wonderful Lamp, McLoughlin Bros Little Color
    Classics, 1940, EX, K3 ....$20.00
Amos Learns To Talk, Elf/Rand McNally, 1950, EX, K3 ...$5.00

Mr. Bear Squash-You-All-Flat, 1950, extremely rare, EX, $145.00.
(Photo courtesy Marvelous Books)

Animal Fun ABC, Hayes Litho Co, ca 1900, illustrated by Harry Roundtree, softcover, rare, EX, $55.00.
(Photo courtesy Marvelous Books)

Animal Stories, Pied Piper, 1946, hardcover, w/dust jacket, EX, K3...$30.00

Bat Masterson, Bantam, 1958, paperback, NM, C1..........$18.00

Black Beauty, by Anna Sewell, Winston publisher, 1927, cloth cover, EX..$60.00

Blondie's Family, Treasure Books, 1954, EX, K3...............$25.00

Bobby's Diary, 1944, hardcover, w/dust jacket, EX, K3....$35.00

Bouncing Bear, Jr Elf/Rand McNally, 1945, EX, K3...........$8.00

Brady Bunch Adventure on the High Seas, Tiger Beat, 1973, paperback, NM, C1.....................................$35.00

Brave Little Tailor, WD, 1938, hardcover, EX.................$35.00

Brownie the Little Bear Who Liked People, McLoughlin Bros Little Color Classics, 1939, EX, K3.....................$20.00

Bunny Twins, Elf/Rand McNally, 1964, EX, K3.................$5.00

Campbell Kids at Home, Elf/Rand McNally, 1964, EX, K3.$35.00

Chester the Little Pony, Elf/Rand McNally, 1951, EX, K3.$8.00

Child's Visit to the Zoo, USA, 1905, hardcover, EX+, A..$100.00

Choo-Choo Train, Bonnie Books, 1946, hardcover, w/dust jacket, EX, K3...$35.00

Christmas Treasure Book, Simon & Schuster, 1950, 38 pgs, EX, K3...$40.00

Cinderella, Treasure Book, 1954, illus by Ruth Ives, EX, K3...$10.00

Cinderella & the Sleeping Beauty, USA, 1905, hardcover, EX+, A...$100.00

Cowboy Eddie, Elf/Rand McNally, 1951, EX, K3...............$8.00

Cup of Sun, by Joan Walsh Anglund, 1967, hardcover, w/dust jacket, EX, K3..................................$10.00

Ferdinand the Bull, Dell, 1936, softcover, scarce, EX, M8..$75.00

Fox Grows Old, Samuel Lowe, 1946, EX, K3...................$10.00

Friendly Fairies, by Johnny Gruelle, Donohue, 1919, hardcover, EX..$85.00

Funny Stories About Mickey Mouse & Donald Duck, 1945, hardcover, EX, J2....................................$65.00

G-Men Trap the Spy Ring, by Laurence Dwight Smith, 1939, hardcover, w/dust jacket, EX..........................$75.00

Gene Autry & the Red Shirt, Sandpiper, 1951, 78 pgs, EX, K3..$30.00

Gene Autry & the Red Wood Pirates, hardcover, w/dust jacket, EX, S18...$30.00

Gingerbread Man, McLoughlin Bros Little Color Classics, 1939, EX, K3...$20.00

Goody Two Shoes, Samuel Lowe, 1944, softcover, EX, K3.$10.00

Grimm's Fairytales, USA, 1905, hardcover, EX, A........$100.00

Happy Time w/the Lollipop Dragon, Happy Day, 1982, EX, K3...$8.00

Honey Bear, by Dixie Wilson, 1923, hardcover, EX........$55.00

Hopalong Cassidy, Dell, 1950s, paperback, photo cover, VG+, A3..$95.00

Hopalong Cassidy & His Young Friend Danny, Bonnie Books, 1950, w/dial built into cover, EX, A....................$50.00

Huckleberry Hound Giant Story Book, Hanna-Barbera, 1960s, hardcover, EX, from $20 to......................$25.00

Land of the Giants, Pyramid, 1968, softcover, EX, J5.......$15.00

Lassie in the Forbidden Valley, 1960, hardcover, VG, H4.$5.00

Little Bear's Adventures, by Frances Margaret Fox, 1937, hardcover, EX, G16.......................................$50.00

Dilly Dally Sally, Saalfield, 1940, softcover, rare, VG, $45.00. (Photo courtesy Marvelous Books)

Little Brown Bear, by Elizabeth Upham, Platt & Munk, 1942, hardcover with worn dust jacket, VG, $45.00; *Peek-A-Boo Pam,* McLoughlin Bros, 1927, hardcover, G, $25.00. (Photo courtesy June Moon)

Dippy the Goof, WD, 1938, hardcover, EX.....................$35.00

Donald Duck & the Boys, WD, 1948, hardcover, M........$75.00

Duck of Dingle Dell & Other Stories, McLoughlin Bros Little Color Classics, 1941, EX, K3......................$15.00

Elmer the Elephant, WDE, linen-like cover, EX..............$85.00

Farmer in the Dell, Elf/Rand McNally, 1967, EX, K3.........$6.00

Little Orphan Annie — A Willing Helper, Cupples & Leon, hardcover, EX...$60.00

Little Penguin, Jr Elf/Rand McNally, 1960, EX, K3...........$5.00

Little Red Riding Hood & the Big Bad Wolf, McKay, 1934, hardcover, NM...$65.00

Little Swiss Guard, Bruce, 1955, EX, K3 ....$15.00

Lone Ranger on Gunsight Mesa, by Fran Striker, Grosset & Dunlap, hardcover, w/dust jacket, EX $40.00

Lone Ranger's New Deputy, Sandpiper, 1951, hardcover, EX, K3 ....$30.00

Marcella — A Raggedy Ann Story, by Johnny Gruelle, Donohue, 1929, hardcover, EX $85.00

Mickey Mouse Adventures, by David McKay, 1932, hardcover, VG, M8...$75.00

Mickey Mouse in Giantland, David McKay, 1930s, hardcover, EX $100.00

Mickey Sees the USA, Heath, 1944, hardcover, EX, M8 .$55.00

Mother Goose, Elf/Rand McNally, 1955, EX, K3 ....$10.00

Mr Jinks & Pixie & Dixie, Comic Book series, 1960s, hardcover, EX, from $20 to..$30.00

Mr Snitzel's Cookies, Jr Elf/Rand McNally, 1950, EX, K3 ..$10.00

My Favorite Story Book, Saalfield, 1942, illus by Ethel Hays, hardcover, 16 pgs, EX, P6 ....$150.00

New Neighborhood, Bonnie Books, 1954, EX, K3 ....$10.00

Night Before Christmas, USA, 1905, hardcover, very rare, EX, A $125.00

Noddy & the Magic Eraser, by Enid Blyton, Saalfield, 1954, softcover, EX, K3 ....$15.00

Pebbles Flintstone, Big Golden Book, 1960s, EX, C17 .....$25.00

Pee Wee & the Sneezing Elephant, 1944, hardcover, w/dust jacket, EX, K3 ....$35.00

Peter Pig & His Airplane Trip, McLoughlin Bros Little Color Classics, 1943, EX, K3 ....$18.00

Peter Potamus & the Pirates, Whitman Tiny-Tot Tales, 1968, hardcover, VG, M17...$15.00

Pinocchio, Grosset & Dunlap, 1939, hardcover, VG, M14 .$35.00

Please Come to My Party, Jolly Book, 1952, EX, K3 ....$15.00

Pluto & the Puppy, Grosset & Dunlap, 1937, hardcover, w/dust jacket, NM..$250.00

Porky Pig's Duck Hunt, Saalfield, 1938, features 1st appearance of Daffy Duck, heavy linen stock, full color, EX, A3 .....$350.00

Practical Pig, WD, 1938, hardcover, EX $45.00

Prayers for Little Children, Jr Elf/Rand McNally, 1944, EX, K3 ....$10.00

Prince Valiant Companions in Adventure, Nostalgia Press, 1974, comic reprints by Harold Foster, hardcover, NM, A..$25.00

Puss in Boots, McLoughlin Bros Little Color Classics, 1941, EX, K3 ....$15.00

Raggedy Andy Stories, by Johnny Gruelle, Donohue, 1920, hardcover, VG $35.00

Raggedy Ann & Andy's Animal Friends, by Johnny Gruelle, 1974, hardcover, EX $25.00

Raggedy Ann & the Hoppy Toad, McLoughlin Bros, 1940, Johnny Gruelle artwork, hardcover, VG+, A $50.00

Raggedy Ann Picture Book, by Johnny Gruelle, Saalfield Artcraft, 1947, cloth, EX $55.00

Raggedy Ann Stories, by Johnny Gruelle, PF Volland, 1918, hardcover, EX $85.00

Red Ryder Secret of Wolf Canyon, hardcover, w/dust jacket, EX, S18 ....$35.00

Roy Rogers on the Double R Ranch, Sandpiper, 1951, 78 pgs, EX, K3 ....$30.00

Roy Rogers Raiders of Sawtooth Ridge, hardcover, w/dust jacket, EX, S18 ....$30.00

Rumpy, 1945, hardcover, w/dust jacket, EX, K3 .:...........$35.00

School Days in Disneyville, Heath, 1939, NM, M8.........$35.00

Seven Wonderful Cats, Elf/Rand McNally, 1956, EX, K3 ..$12.00

Shari Lewis Bedtime Stories, 1961, paperback, EX, H4 ......$5.00

Snow White & the Seven Dwarfs, Grosset & Dunlap, 1938, hardcover, EX $95.00

***Stories from Uncle Remus**, Saalfield, 1934, illustrated by A.B. Frost, EX, $125.00.* (Photo courtesy Marvelous Books)

Story of Santa Claus, Bruce, 1959, EX, K3.......................$10.00

Sunny Tales, McLoughlin Bros Little Color Classics, 1942, EX, K3 ....$15.00

Tarzan, Grosset & Dunlop, hardcover, EX, C10...............$25.00

Teddy Bear Tales, by Joan Walsh Anglund, 1985, 1st edition, EX, K3 ....$20.00

Teddy the Terrier, Elf/Rand McNally, 1962, EX, K3........$15.00

Terry & the Pirates, Random House, 1946, hardcover, rare, VG, M14..$30.00

Things To Make & Do for Christmas, Treasure Book, 1953, EX, K3 ....$30.00

Timothy the Little Brown Bear, Jr Elf/Rand McNally, 1949, EX, K3 ....$10.00

Tom Thumb, Elf/Rand McNally, 1959, EX, K3 ....$8.00

Topo Gigio in Little Country Cottage, Bonanza, 1965, EX, A.$15.00

Voyage to the Bottom of the Sea, 1966, hardcover, VG, A..$40.00

Walt Disney's Pinocchio, Random House, 1939, hardcover, VG $95.00

Water Babies & Other Stories, Heath, 1940, EX, M8 ......$35.00

Water Babies Circus, Heath, 1940, illus by WD Studio, 78 pgs, EX, K3 ....$25.00

Wizard of Oz, Grosset & Dunlap, 1939, by L Frank Baum, illus by Oskar Lebeck, hardcover, EX, A $125.00

Wonderful Plane Ride, Elf/Rand McNally, 1949, EX, K3...$15.00
Yogi Bear, Comic Book series, 1960s, hardcover, EX, from $20
    to $30.00

Breyer

Breyer collecting seems to be growing in popularity, and
though the horses dominate the market, the company also made
dogs, cats, farm animals, wildlife figures, dolls, and tack and
accessories such as barns for their models. They've been in con-
tinuous production since the '50s, all strikingly beautiful and
lifelike in both modeling and color. Earlier models were glossy,
but since 1968 a matt finish has been used, though glossy and
semiglossy colors are now being re-introduced, especially in special runs. (A special run of Family Arabians was done in the
glossy finish in 1988.)

One of the hardest things for any model collector is to
determine the value of his or her collection. The values listed
below are for models in excellent to near mint condition. This
means no rubs, no scratches, no chipped paint, and no breaks —
nothing that cannot be cleaned off with a rag and little effort. A
model which has been altered in any way, including having the
paint touched up, is considered a customized model and has an
altogether different set of values than one in the original finish.
The models listed herein are completely original. For more information, refer to *Breyer Animal Collector's Guide, Second Edition*,
by Felicia Browell (Collector Books).

    Advisor: Carol Karbowiak Gilbert (G6).

CLASSIC SCALE MODELS

Andalusian Foal (Hanoverian Family), matt bay, 1992-93, G6..$15.00
Andalusian Foal (Sears Classic Andalusian Family), matt bay,
    1984, G6 ....$15.00
Andalusian Mare (Sears Classic Andalusian Family), alabaster,
    1984, G6 ....$20.00
Andalusian Stallion (Sears Classic Andalusian Family), dapple
    gray, 1984, G6...$20.00
Arabian Foal, matt blk, 1973-82, G6 ....$25.00
Arabian Foal, matt chestnut, 1973-82, G6 ....$25.00
Arabian Foal (Desert Arabian Family), matt bay, 1992-94, G6.$10.00
Arabian Mare (Bedouin Family Gift Set), 1995-96, G6...$10.00
Arabian Mare (Desert Arabian Family), matt red bay, 1992-94,
    G6 ....$15.00
Arabian Stallion (Sears Classic Arabian Family), matt bay,
    1984-85, G6...$30.00
Black Beauty, 1980-93, G6...$15.00
Black Stallion (Black Stallion Returns Set), 1983-93, G6 .$15.00
Black Stallion Sham (King of the Wind Set), blood bay, 1990-
    93, G6 ....$15.00
Bucking Bronco, matt bay, 1967-70, G6.........................$100.00
Duchess (Black Beauty Family Set), matt bay, 1980-93, G6.$15.00
Ginger (Hanoverian Family), lt bay, 1992-93, G6............$15.00
Ginger (Pony for Keeps Set), matt alabaster, 1990-91, G6 ..$15.00
Jet Run (Sears US Olympic Team), matt chestnut, 1987,
    G6 ....$30.00

Jet Run (US Equestrian Team Gift Set), matt bay, 1980-93,
    G6 ....$15.00
Johar (Black Stallion Returns Set), matt alabaster, 1980-
    93, G6 ....$15.00
Johar (Eagle & Pow Wow Set), blk pinto, 1995, G6........$35.00
Keen (US Equestrian Team Gift Set), matt chestnut, 1980-93,
    G6 ....$15.00
Kelso (Fine Horse Family), matt roan, 1994-96, G6.........$15.00

Kelso, 1975 – 90, dark bay, $20.00.
(Photo courtesy Carol Karbowiak Gilbert)

Lady Roxana (King of the Wind Set), matt alabaster, 1990-93,
    G6 ....$15.00
Lipizzan Stallion, matt alabaster, 1975-80, G6 ....$40.00
Man O' War, matt red chestnut, 1975-90, G6..................$25.00
Merrylegs (Black Beauty Family), dapple gray, 1980-93,
    G6 ....$15.00

**Might Tango (US Equestrian Team Set), 1980 – 91,
dapple gray, $15.00.** (Photo courtesy Carol Karbowiak Gilbert)

Might Tango (Pony for Keeps Set), lt dapple gray, 1990-91, G6..$15.00

Mustang Foal (Fine Horse Family), matt roan, 1994-96, G6 ....$15.00

Mustang Foal (Trakehner Family), matt bay, 1992-94, G6..$12.00

Mustang Mare (Mustang Family Gift Set), blk blanket appaloosa, 1995-96, G6 ....$15.00

Mustang Stallion (Pony for Keeps Set), chestnut w/gray legs, 1990-91, G6..$15.00

Polo Pony, matt bay, 1976-82, G6.............................$60.00

Quarter Horse Foal, palomino, 1975-82, G6....................$20.00

Quarter Horse Mare (JC Penney Quarter Horse Family Set), dk chestnut, 1991, G6 ....$25.00

Quarter Horse Mare (Sears Collector's Edition Appaloosa Family), chestnut blanket, 1986, G6.........................$30.00

Quarter Horse Stallion (Montgomery Ward Appaloosa Family), blk blanket, 1984, G6 ....$30.00

Rearing Stallion, matt alabaster, 1965-76 & 1978-85, G6..$25.00

Rearing Stallion, matt bay, 1965-80, G6........................$30.00

Ruffian, matt bay, 1977-90, G6.................................$35.00

Sagr (Black Stallion Returns Set), matt sorrel, 1983-93, G6 ....$15.00

Silky Sullivan, matt brn, 1975-90, G6 ....$25.00

Silky Sullivan (Fine Horse Family), dk chestnut, 1994-96, G6 ....$15.00

Terrang, buckskin, 1995, G6 ....$15.00

TRADITIONAL SCALE

Action Appaloosa Foal, 1989-93, G6...........................$20.00

Action Foal (from JC Penney Pinto Mare & Foal Set), 1984-85, G6 ....$35.00

Action Stock Horse Foal, matt chestnut, 1984-86, G6 ....$20.00

Adios Famous Standardbred, 1969-80, G6......................$40.00

American Indian Pony, 1988-91, G6.............................$35.00

Appaloosa Foal (JC Penney Breyer Collector's Family Set), matt bay peppercorn, 1986, G6...............................$25.00

Brahma Bull, 1958 – 93, $50.00.
(Photo courtesy Carol Karbowiak Gilbert)

Appaloosa Performance Horse (Brenda Breyer Gift Set), dk chestnut blanket, 1980-85, w/doll & tack, G6...........$50.00

Appaloosa Stallion (Horses International), alabaster & sorrel w/blk blanket & red roan, 1989, G6 ....$60.00

Balking Mule, matt bay chestnut, 1968-73, G6.............$150.00

Bear Cub, brn-faced version, 1967-73 ....$25.00

Belgian, chestnut w/red & yel ribbon, 1965-80, G6 ....$100.00

Belgian, glossy dapple gray or blk, 1964-67, G6, ea $650.00

Belgian, woodgrain, 1964-65, G6.............................$1,000.00

Belgian (Montgomery Wards), semi-gloss blk w/yel & red ribbon, 1982-83, G6 ....$50.00

Bison...$50.00

Black Beauty, 1979-88, G6.................................$30.00

Boxer, 1954-73...$30.00

Calf...$30.00

Cantering Welsh Pony, matt bay w/yel ribbons, 1971-73, G6 ....$100.00

Cantering Welsh Pony, matt chestnut w/no ribbons, 1979-81, G6 ....$50.00

Cantering Welsh Pony, matt chestnut w/red ribbons, 1971-76, G6 ....$55.00

Cantering Welsh Pony (Horses Great & Small Set), blk w/no ribbons, 1992, G6 ....$40.00

Cantering Welsh Pony (Small World), matt liver chestnut w/gr ribbons, 1988, G6 ....$100.00

Cantering Welsh Pony (Small World), matt red dun w/bl ribbons, 1988, G6..$100.00

Clydesdale Foal, lt bay, 1990-91, G6..........................$25.00

Clydesdale Mare, matt chestnut, 1969-89, G6.................$25.00

Clydesdale Stallion, glossy bay w/gold ribbons, 1958-63 (possibly earlier), G6 ....$200.00

Clydesdale Stallion, matt bay w/gold bobs & tail ribbon, 1964-72, G6 ....$70.00

Clydesdale Stallion, woodgrain, 1960-65, G6.................$250.00

Clydesdale Stallion (Sears Horses Great & Small Set), 1992, G6 ....$40.00

Clydsdale Foal, lt bay, 1990 – 91, G6..........................$25.00

Clydsdale Foal (Horses International), blk, gray or dapple gray, 1988, G6, ea..$50.00

Cow $35.00

Donkey, w/red baskets, 1958-60, G6 ....$75.00

Donkey, 1958-74, G6......................................$25.00

Family Arabian Foal, glossy alabaster, 1961-66, G6.........$15.00

Family Arabian Foal, glossy charcoal, 1961-67, G6 ....$25.00

Family Arabian Foal, glossy palomino, 1961-66, G6 ....$15.00

Family Arabian Foal, matt bay w/hind socks, 1989-90, G6..$20.00

Family Arabian Foal (JC Penney), lt chestnut, 1983, G6 ....$40.00

Family Arabian Mare, glossy gray blanket appaloosa, 1961-67, G6 ....$35.00

Family Arabian Mare, glossy palomino, 1961-66, G6.......$30.00

Family Arabian Mare, matt liver chestnut, 1988, G6.......$40.00

Family Arabian Mare, 1967-87................................$20.00

Family Arabian Mare (JC Penney), lt or dk chestnut, 1982-83, G6, ea..$60.00

Family Arabian Stallion, glossy alabaster, 1959-66, G6....$30.00

Family Arabian Stallion, matt bay w/hind socks, 1989-90, G6...$35.00

Family Arabian Stallion, woodgrain, 1963-67, G6.........$100.00

Family Arabian Stallion (JC Penney), matt liver chestnut or matt chestnut, 1982-83, G6, ea..................................$55.00

Fighting Stallion, glossy alabaster, 1961-64, G6.............$125.00

Fighting Stallion, glossy Copenhagen, 1963-65, G6...$1,000.00

Fighting Stallion, glossy palomino, 1961-67, G6............$100.00

Fighting Stallion, Wedgewood, 1963-65, G6..............$1,000.00

Five-Gaiter Commander, glossy florentine w/blk & gold ribbons, 1964-65, G6..$1,500.00

Five-Gaiter Commander, glossy gold charm w/blk & gold ribbon, 1964-65, G6...$1,500.00

Five-Gaitor Commander, sorrel w/red & wht ribbons, 1963-85, G6..$40.00

Friesian (Action Drafters Set), dk bay, 1994-96, G6........$20.00

Fury Prancer, glossy blk pinto, 1954-63, G6..................$100.00

Fury Prancer, woodgrain, 1958-62, G6..........................$350.00

Goliath the American Cream Draft Horse, 1995-present, G6..$75.00

Grazing Foal Bows, blk, 1964-70, G6...............................$50.00

Grazing Mare Buttons, palomino, 1964-81, G6...............$40.00

Lying Foal, 1969 – 84, black blanket appaloosa, $30.00.
(Photo courtesy Carol Karbowiak Gilbert)

Grazing Mare (JC Penney Serenity Set), 1995, buckskin, $25.00. (Photo courtesy Carol Karbowiak Gilbert)

Mego (Breyerfest Dinner Model), 1995, signed, $100.00.
(Photo courtesy Carol Karbowiak Gilbert)

Halla Famous Jumper, matt bay, 1977-85, G6 ....$60.00

Hanoverian (Horses International), dapple gray, 1986, G6 .$200.00

Hyskos the Egyptian Arabian, 1991 Commemorative Edition, G6 ....$75.00

Indian Pony, buckskin, 1970-72, G6................................$250.00

Jumping Horse Stonewall, 1965-88, G6...........................$60.00

King the Fighting Stallion, palomino, 1968-73, G6 ....$75.00

Lady Phase (JC Penney Traditional Horse Set), dapple gray, 1990, G6 ....$75.00

Legionario (Breyerfest Raffle Model), glossy florentine, 1991, only 21 made, G6 ....$1,750.00

Legionario (JC Penney), flocked wht, 1985, G6.............$125.00

Lying Foal, blk blanket appaloosa, 1969-84, G6 ....$30.00

Lying Foal, buckskin, 1969-73 & 1975-76, G6.................$50.00

Misty (Breyerfest Raffle Model), glossy florentine, 1990, only 21 made, G6 ....$1,700.00

Morgan, woodgrain, 1963-85, G6 ....$750.00

Morganglanz, 1980-87, G6 ....$60.00

Mother Bear, brn-faced version, 1967-73.........................$35.00

Mustang, glossy florentine, semi-rearing, 1963-65, G6..$1,500.00

Mustang, glossy gray blanket appaloosa, semi-rearing, 1961-66, G6..$150.00

Mustang, Wedgewood, semi-rearing, 1963-65, G6......$1,500.00

Old Timer, matt alabaster, 1966-76, G6 ....$50.00

Pacer (Brenda Breyer & Sulky Set), 1982-87, complete, G6 ....$100.00

Palomino (Breyer Rider Gift Set), 1976, w/doll & tack, only 5 made, G6 ....$250.00

Pony of the Americas, bay blanket appaloosa, 1979-84, G6...$40.00

Prancing Arabian Stallion, flea bit gray, 1988-89, G6......$40.00

Proud Arabian Foal, mahogany bay, 1973-80, G6 ....$20.00

Proud Arabian Foal Shah, glossy bay, 1956-60, G6 ....$60.00

Proud Arabian Mare, red chestnut, 1991-92, G6.............$40.00

Proud Arabian Mare Sheba, glossy bay, 1956-60, G6.....$125.00

Proud Arabian Stallion, alabaster, 1971-76 & 1978-81, G6...$45.00
Quarter Horse Gelding, glossy bay, 1959-66, G6...........$150.00
Quarter Horse Yearling, liver chestnut, 1970-80, G6.......$40.00
Racehorse, woodgrain, 1958-66, G6 ....$250.00
Rearing Stallion, 1965-76 & 1978-86, ea....................$25.00
Roy Belgian Drafter, matt sorrel, 1989-90, G6.................$45.00
Running Foal, chestnut pinto, 1991-93, G6 ....$20.00
Running Foal, glossy Copenhagen, 1963-65, G6............$800.00
Running Mare, glossy florentine, 1963-64, G6............$1,500.00
Running Mare Sugar, dapple gray, 1963-73, G6..............$75.00

Running Mare, 1971 – 73, red roan, $100.00.
(Photo courtesy Carol Karbowiak Gilbert)

Running Stallion, charcoal, 1968-71, G6......................$250.00
San Domingo (Marguerite Henry), chestnut pinto, 1977-87,
    G6...$40.00

Sham, 1984 – 88, red bay, $45.00.
(Photo courtesy Carol Karbowiak Gilbert)

Scratching Foal, red roan, 1970-73, G6 ....$100.00
Sea Star (Marguerite Henry), dk chestnut, 1980-87, G6..$20.00
Secretariat (Racehorse Set), glossy chestnut, 1990, G6....$45.00
Shetland Pony, glossy lt chestnut pinto, 1960-73, G6......$40.00
Shetland Pony, matt bay, 1973-88, G6 ....$25.00
Spanish Barb, porcelain, 1994, limited edition, G6........$250.00
Spanish Barb, 1988-89, G6....................................$40.00
Stallion (JC Penney English Horse Collector Set), sandy bay,
    1988, G6...$35.00
Stock Horse Foal, pinto, smooth coat, 1983-88, G6........$25.00
Stock Horse Mare, blk blanket appaloosa, 1983-88, G6...$35.00
Stock Horse Mare, matt sorrel, leg up, 1982, G6.............$40.00
Stormy (Marguerite Henry), 1977-present, G6................$15.00
Suckling Foal (Thoroughbred Mare & Foal Gift Set), lt chest-
    nut, 1973-84, G6 ....$30.00

Thoroughbred Mare, 1973 – 84, dark chestnut bay, $50.00.
(Photo courtesy Carol Karbowiak Gilbert)

Tobe Rocky Mountain Horse, 1995-96, G6......................$20.00
Touch of Class, matt bay, 1986-88, G6............................$40.00
Trakehner, semi-gloss & matt bay, 1979-84, G6 ....$30.00
True Bay Stallion (JC Penney Clydesdale Family Set), 1982-84,
    G6 ....$75.00
Western Horse, glossy blk pinto, 1954-76, G6..................$50.00
Western Horse, glossy wht, 1951-63, G6 ....$60.00
Western Pony, dk brn, 1955-57, G6 ....$150.00
Western Prancer, glossy blk pinto, 1961-66, G6............$100.00
Winchester (Breyerfest Raffle Model), 1994, G6........$1,700.00

Bubble Bath Containers

Since back in the 1960s when the Colgate-Palmolive Company produced the first Soaky, hundreds of different characters and variations have been marketed, bought on demand of the kids who saw these characters day to day on TV by parents willing to try anything that might make bathtime more appealing.

Purex made their Bubble Club characters, and Avon and others followed suit. Most Soaky bottles came with detachable heads made of brittle plastic which cracked easily. Purex bottles were made of a softer plastic but tended to loose their paint.

Rising interest in US bubble bath containers has created a collector market for those made in foreign countries, i.e, UK, Canada, Italy, Germany, and Japan. Licensing in other countries creates completely different designs and many characters that are never issued here. Foreign containers are generally larger and are modeled in great detail, reminiscent of the bottles that were made in the US in the '60s. Prices may seem high, considering that some of these are of fairly recent manufacture, but this is due to their limited availability and the costs associated with obtaining them in the United States. We believe these prices are realistic, though many have been reported much higher. Rule of thumb: pay what you feel comfortable with — after all, it's meant to be fun. And remember, value is affected to a great extent by condition. Unless noted otherwise, our values are for examples in near-mint condition. Bottles in very good condition are worth only about 60% to 65% of these prices. For slip-over styles, add 100% if the bottle is present. For more information we recommend *Collector's Guide to Bubble Bath Containers* by Greg Moore and Joe Pizzo (Collector Books).

Advisors: Matt and Lisa Adams (A7).

Alvin (Chipmunks), Colgate-Palmolive, red sweater w/wht A, w/contents, neck tag & puppet, M, A7......................$50.00
Alvin (Chipmunks), Colgate-Palmolive, yel sweater w/red A or red sweater w/yel A, EX+, A7 ....$30.00

Alvin (Chipmunks), Soaky, Reckards, 6x6", M, A7.........$30.00
Aristocats, Avon, 1971, NM, from $5 to....................$8.00
Atom Ant, Purex, 1965, rare, EX+, A7 ....$40.00
Auggie Doggie, Purex, 1967, rare, EX+, A7.................$45.00
Baba Looey, Purex, 1960s, brn w/bl neckerchief or orange w/blk neckerchief, NM, A7, ea $35.00
Baloo Bear, Colgate-Palmolive, 1966, slipover only, NM, A7...$20.00
Bambi, Colgate-Palmolive, 1960s, NM, from $20 to $25.00
Bamm-Bamm, Purex, 1960s, NM, A7 ....$35.00
Barney & Baby Bop, Kid Care, M, ea from $5 to $8.00
Barney Rubble, Milvern (Purex), 1960s, bl outfit w/yel accents, NM+, A7 ....$35.00
Batman, Colgate-Palmolive, 1966, NM, from $50 to $60.00
Batmobile, Avon, 1979, EX+, A7 ....$20.00
Bert (Sesame Street), Minnetonka, holding boat, orig tag, M, A7...$8.00
Betty Bubbles, Lander, 1950s, several variations, NM, A7, ea..$35.00
Big Bad Wolf, Tubby Time, 1960s, rare, NM, A7 ....$40.00
Big Bird, Minnetonka, holding scrub brush & soap, w/tag, NM, A7..$8.00
Blabber Mouse, Purex, 1960s, rare, NM, from $100 to...$125.00
Bozo the Clown, Colgate-Palmolive, 1960s, NM, A7 ......$30.00
Breezly the Bear, Purex, 1960s, rare, NM, from $125 to.$150.00
Brontosaurus, Avon, 1970s, MIB, A7 ....$15.00
Broom Hilda, Lander, 1977, rare, EX, A7 ....$30.00
Brutus (Popeye), Colgate-Palmolive, 1965, red shorts w/red & wht striped shirt, EX, A7 ....$40.00
Bugs Bunny, Colgate-Palmolive, 1960s, NM, A7 ....$30.00

Beatles, Paul McCartney, Colgate-Palmolive, EX, from $100.00 to $125.00.
(Photo courtesy Greg Moore and Joe Pizzo)

Casper the Friendly Ghost, Colgate-Palmolive, 1960s, EX+, $30.00.
(Photo courtesy Greg Moore and Joe Pizzo)

Bugs Bunny, Colgate-Palmolive, 1960s, slipover only, NM, from $10 to $15.00

Bugs Bunny, DuCair Bioescence, 1989, 50th Anniversary, M, A7..$8.00

Bullwinkle, Colgate-Palmolive, 1964-66, several color variations, NM+, A7, ea...............................$40.00

Bullwinkle, Fuller Brush, 1970s, rare, NM, from $50 to ...$60.00

California Dream Barbie, DuCair Bioescence, 1987, NM, from $10 to $15.00

Care Bears, AGC, 1984, several variations, NM, ea from $5 to $10.00

Cecil Sea Serpent, Purex, 1960s, M, A7 ....$75.00

Checks the Chipmunk, Benjamin Ansehl, 1990s, NM, A7..$10.00

Cinderella, Colgate-Palmolive, 1960s, movable arms, NM+, A7...$30.00

Clown, Jergans, 1960s, NM, from $10 to $15.00

Concertina, Avon, 1970, yel, MIB, A7...............................$15.00

Cookie Monster, Minnetonka, holding sailboat, w/tag, M, A7 ....$8.00

Creature From the Black Lagoon, Colgate-Palmolive, 1963, NM+, A7...$125.00

Deputy Dawg, Colgate-Palmolive, 1960s, gray, yel & bl, cap hat, NM, A7......................................$30.00

Deputy Dawg, Colgate-Palmolive, 1960s, yel & blk, VG+, A7 ....$30.00

Dick Tracy, Colgate-Palmolive, 1965, NM, A7...............$50.00

Dino, Purex, 1960s, rare, NM+, A7 ....$85.00

Donald Duck, Colgate-Palmolive, 1960s, wht & bl, EX+, A7...$20.00

Dopey, Colgate-Palmolive, 1960s, bank, purple & yel, NM, A7...$30.00

Droop-A-Long Coyote, Purex, 1960s, rare, EX+, A7 ....$35.00

Dum Dum, Purex, 1964, rare, EX+, A7 ....$100.00

El Cabong, Knickerbocker, 1960s, blk, yel & wht, rare, NM, A7..$75.00

Elmer Fudd, Colgate-Palmolive, 1960s, hunting outfit, NM, A7..$30.00

Elmo, Softsoap, 1992, NM, from $5 to.............................$10.00

Esmeralda (Hunchback of Notre Dame), Kid Care, 1996, NM, from $5 to..$10.00

ET, Avon, 1983, wearing bathrobe, NM+, A7 ....$10.00

Felix the Cat, Colgate-Palmolive, 1960s, bl, blk or red, EX+, A7..$30.00

Fire Truck, Colgate-Palmolive, 1960s, red w/ladder & movable wheels, NM, A7......................................$35.00

Flintstones Fun Bath, Roclar (Purex), 1970s, MIB (sealed), A7..$75.00

Flipper Riding a Wave, Kid Care, M, A7 ....$8.00

Fozzie Bear, Calgon, Treasure Island outfit, M, A7.............$8.00

Frankenstein, Colgate-Palmolive, 1963, EX, A7 ....$90.00

Fred Flintstone, Purex, 1960s, blk & red, NM, A7 ....$30.00

GI Joe, DuCair Bioescence, 1980s, several variations, NM, A7, ea..$10.00

Goofy, Colgate-Palmolive, 1960s, red, wht & blk w/cap head, M, A7..$25.00

Gravel Truck, Colgate-Palmolive, 1960s, orange & gray w/movable wheels, NM, A7......................$40.00

Holly Hobbie, Benjamin Ansehl, 1980s, several variations, M, A7, ea..$15.00

Hot Wheels Race Car, Cosrich, 1993, NM, from $10 to..$15.00

Huckleberry Hound, Knickerbocker, bank, red & blk, w/contents & orig neck card, M, A7................$60.00

Huckleberry Hound, Milvern, 1960s, 15", M, A7.............$40.00

Huckleberry Hound, Selcol, 1960s, bank, bl w/yel bow tie, rare, EX+, A7..$100.00

Felix the Cat, Colgate-Palmolive, 1960s, blue variation, $30.00.
(Photo courtesy Greg Moore and Joe Pizzo)

Lippy the Lion, Purex, 1962, rare, $35.00.
(Photo courtesy Greg Moore and Joe Pizzo)

Humpty Dumpty, Avon, 1960s, NM, from $5 to $10.00
Incredible Hulk, Benjamin Ansehl, 1990, NM, from $20 to..$25.00
Irwin Troll, Lander, 1970s, w/contents, M, A7................$25.00
Jiminy Cricket, Colgate-Palmolive, 1960s, gr, blk & red, NM, A7 ....$25.00
Jinx w/Pixie & Dixie, Purex, 1960s, NM, from $25 to......$30.00
Jurassic Park Dinosaur, Cosrich, 1992, NM, from $5 to ...$10.00
King Louie, Colgate-Palmolive, 1960s, slipover only, NM+, A7..$40.00
Lamb, Tubby Time, 1960s, rare, NM, from $40 to $45.00
Little Mermaid, Kid Care, 1991, M, A7 ....$5.00
Little Orphan Annie, Lander, 1977, NM, from $25 to.....$30.00
Lucy (Peanuts), Avon, 1970, red dress, MIB, A7 ....$20.00
Magilla Gorilla, Purex, 1960s, movable or non-movable arms, NM, A7, ea..$35.00
Mickey Mouse, Colgate-Palmolive, 1960s, dressed as band leader, NM, A7..$30.00
Mighty Mouse, Colgate-Palmolive, 1960s, EX, A7..........$25.00
Mighty Mouse, Lander, 1978, rare, VG+, A7 ....$20.00
Miss Piggy, Calgon, Treasure Island outfit, M, A7.............$8.00
Morocco Mole, Purex, 1966, rare, EX, A7 ....$100.00
Mousketeer Girl, Colgate-Palmolive, 1960s, red or bl skirt, NM, A7, ea..$30.00
Mr Do Bee, Manon Freres, 1960s, rare, NM+, A7 ....$75.00
Mr Magoo, Colgate-Palmolive, 1960s, EX+, A7...............$25.00
Mr Wise, Wise Snack Foods, rare, NM, from $45 to $50.00
Mummy, Colgate-Palmolive, 1960s, NM.......................$100.00
Mush Mouse, Purex, 1960s, rare, EX, A7 ....$30.00
Muskie, Colgate-Palmolive, 1960s, NM+, A7 ....$40.00
My Little Pony, Benjamin Ansehl, 1990, any character, NM, ea from $15 to..$20.00
Oscar the Grouch, Minnetonka, holding trash can lid, M, A7..$8.00
Panda Bear, Tubby Time, 1960s, wht & blk w/cap head, EX, A7 ....$20.00
Pebbles Flintstone, Purex, 1960s, gr shirt w/yel shorts or purple shirt w/bl shorts, EX, A7, ea $35.00
Percy the Penguin, Cleftwood, 1960s, NM, from $25 to ..$30.00
Peter Potamus, Purex, 1960s, M, A7 ....$25.00
Pinocchio, Colgate-Palmolive, 1960s, red & wht or solid brn or red, M, A7, ea..$25.00
Pluto, Avon, 1970, NM, from $5 to $8.00
Pluto, Colgate-Palmolive, 1960s, orange w/cap head, NM, A7 ....$25.00
Pokey, Novelty Packaging, 1987, NM, from $35 to..........$40.00
Popeye, Colgate-Palmolive, 1965, NM+, A7....................$50.00
Popeye, Colgate-Palmolive, 1977, rare, NM, A7 ....$35.00
Popples, DuCair Bioescence, 1988, NM, from $5 to.........$10.00
Porky Pig, Colgate-Palmolive, 1960s, bl or red tuxedo, EX+, A7..$25.00
Power Rangers, Kid Care, 1994, any character, M, A7, ea .$8.00
Punkin' Puss, Purex, 1966, rare, VG, A7 ....$30.00
Quick Draw McGraw, Purex, 1960s, several variations, NM, A7, ea..$30.00
Raggedy Ann, Lander, 1960s, rare, NM, from $55 to $65.00
Robin, Colgate-Palmolive, 1966, NM, A7.......................$75.00
RoboCop, Cosway, 1990, M, A7 ....$10.00
Rocky the Flying Squirrel, Colgate-Palmolive, 1962, NM, from $20 to $25.00

Ricochet Rabbit, Purex, 1960s, $50.00.
(Photo courtesy Greg Moore and Joe Pizzo)

Santa, Colgate-Palmolive, NM, A7 ....$25.00
Schroeder (Peanuts), Avon, 1970, MIB, A7.....................$25.00
Scooby Doo, Colgate-Palmolive, 1977, NM, from $40 to .$45.00
Scoots the Squirrel, Benjamin Ansehl, 1990s, NM, A7 ...$10.00
Secret Squirrel, Purex, 1966, rare, VG+, A7 ....$45.00
Simon (Chipmunks), Colgate-Palmolive, 1960s, 3 color variations, w/contents, tag & puppet, M, A7, ea $50.00
Simon (Chipmunks), Colgate-Palmolive, 1960s, 3 color variations, EX, ea $25.00
Simpsons, Cosrich, 1980s, any character, NM, ea from $15 to $20.00

Superman, Avon, 1978, MIB, $40.00.
(Photo courtesy Martin and Carolyn Berens)

Skeletor (Masters of the Universe), Ducair Bio, NM+, A7 .$15.00
Sky Dancer, Cosrich, 1995, M, A7..................................$5.00
Smokey Bear, Colgate-Palmolive, 1960s, NM, A7 ....$25.00
Smokey the Bear, Lander, 1970s, NM, A7......................$25.00
Snaggle Puss, Purex, 1960s, pk w/gr hat, NM, A7, from $45
    to $50.00
Sneezly, Purex, 1960s, rare, NM, from $150 to..............$175.00
Snoopy as Flying Ace, Avon, 1969, MIB, A7..................$20.00
Snoopy on Snow Flyer, Avon, 1973, MIB, A7 ....$20.00
Snow White, Colgate-Palmolive, 1960s, bank, bl & yel, NM,
    A7 ....$30.00
Snow White, Kid Care, 1993, M, A7..............................$5.00
Speedy Gonzales, Colgate-Palmolive, 1960s, EX, A7.......$30.00
Spider-Man, Benjamin Ansehl, 1990, M, A7..................$25.00
Spider-Man, Kid Care, M, A7..$8.00
Spouty Whale, Roclar/Purex, M, A7..............................$25.00
Squiddly Diddly, Purex, 1960s, rare, NM, A7..................$75.00
Superman, Colgate-Palmolive, 1965, EX+, A7................$50.00

Sylvester and Tweety, Ducair Bioescence, 1988, from $10.00 to $15.00.
(Photo courtesy Greg Moore and Joe Pizzo)

Sylvester the Cat w/Microphone, Colgate-Palmolive, 1960s,
    EX+, A7...$30.00
Tasmanian Devil, Kid Care, 1992, EX, A7 ....$8.00
Teenage Mutant Ninja Turtles, Kid Care, 1990, any character,
    M, A7, ea $8.00
Tennessee Tuxedo, Colgate-Palmolive, 1965, NM, A7 ...$30.00
Theodore (Chipmunks), Soaky, wht w/bl T, w/contents, neck
    tag & puppet, M, A7 ....$50.00
Three Little Pigs, Tubby Time, 1960s, any character, rare, M,
    A7, ea...$40.00
Thumper, Colgate-Palmolive, 1960s, EX, A7..................$25.00
Tidy Toy Race Car, red or bl w/movable wheels, NM, A7,
    ea $50.00

Top Cat, Colgate-Palmolive, 1963, bl or red shirt, EX+,
    A7 ....$30.00
Touche Turtle, Purex, 1964, standing, NM+, A7............$40.00
Tweety Bird on Cage, Colgate-Palmolive, NM+, A7.......$30.00
Tweety Bird on Stump, Colgate-Palmolive, 1960s, slipover only,
    from $15 to..$20.00
Wally Gator, Purex, 1963, rare, M, A7 ....$50.00
Wendy the Witch, Colgate-Palmolive, 1960s, NM, A7...$30.00
Where's Waldo, Cosrich, 1989, M, A7 ....$5.00
Winsome Witch, Purex, 1965, rare, NM+, A7................$30.00
Wolfman, Colgate-Palmolive, 1963, bl or red pants, NM+,
    A7 ....$100.00
Woodstock as Flying Ace, Avon, 1969, NM, from $15 to..$20.00
Woodsy Owl, Lander, 1970s, complete w/stickers, NM,
    A7...$50.00
Woody Woodpecker, Colgate-Palmolive, 1977, rare, NM, from
    $40 to $45.00
Yakky Doodle Duck, Roclar (Purex), w/contents & neck card,
    M, A7...$25.00
Yogi Bear, Purex, 1960s, several variations, NM, A7, ea..$40.00

FOREIGN

Action Man (Battle Force), Rosedew Ltd/UK, kneeling
    w/machine gun, camo outfit, M, A7 ....$35.00
Aladdin, Damascar/Italy, standing w/arms crossed, M, A7 ..$35.00
Aladdin, Prelude/UK, holding lamp, comes apart at waist, M,
    A7 ....$20.00
Alf, PE/Germany, 1980s, NM, A7..................................$40.00
Alice in Wonderland, Aidee International Ltd/UK, 1993, stand-
    ing in grass w/rabbit, NM, A7 ....$35.00
Aliens, Grosvenor/UK, topper, M, A7 ....$25.00
Angus the Panda (Creature Comforts), Rosedew Ltd/UK, blk &
    wht w/tan glasses, hand outstretched, M, A7.............$30.00
Ariel (Little Mermaid), Damascar/Italy, 1995, sitting on purple
    rock, NM, A7 ....$35.00
Baloo (Jungle Book), Boots/England, 1965, NM, from $60 to..$70.00
Barbie, Grosvenor/UK, 1995, pk & wht wedding dress w/heart
    tag, M, A7 ....$30.00
Barney Rubble, Damascar/Italy, 1995, wearing Water Buffalo hat
    w/bowling ball, M, A7 ....$35.00
Barney Rubble, Rosedew/UK, leaning on club, M, A7.....$35.00
Bart Simpson, Grosvenor/UK, 1995, EX, A7...................$35.00
Batman, Grosvenor/UK, 1992, c DC Comics, gray suit & blk
    cape, NM, A7 ....$35.00
Batman (Animated), Damascar/Italy, 1994, NM, from $30
    to..$35.00
Batman (Batman Forever), Prelude/England, 1995, NM,
    A7 ....$35.00
Batmobile (Batman Forever), Prelude/UK, 1995, body lifts for
    bottle, M, A7 ....$35.00
Beast (Beauty & the Beast), Prelude/UK, 1994, movable arms,
    comes apart at waist, lg, NM, A7 ....$35.00
Belle (Beauty & the Beast), Centura/Canada, 1994, yel gown &
    gloves, NM, A7..$25.00
Big Bird, Grosvenor/UK, 1995, w/wht towel, M, A7.......$30.00
Boo Boo Bear, Damascar/Italy, sitting on 3 picnic baskets eating
    an apple, M, A7 ....$35.00

Brutus, Damascar/Italy, 1990s, NM, from $40 to $45.00

Bubbasaurus, Belvedere/Canada, 1995, bank, NM, A7 ....$15.00

Budgie Helicopter, Euromark/UK, bl w/yel hat, M, A7 ....$35.00

Bugs Bunny, Centura/Canada, 1994, purple robe, holds carrot, NM, A7 ....$30.00

Bugs Bunny, Prelude/UK, gr trunks & red shoes, arms posed, M, A7 ....$35.00

Bump (Elephant), Rosedew/UK, bl w/yel overalls, bandage on head, M, A7 ....$20.00

Buzz Lightyear, Centura/Canada, comes apart at waist, M, A7 ....$30.00

Captain Scarlet, Euromark/UK, 1993, NM, A7 ....$35.00

Casper the Friendly Ghost, Damascar/Italy, 1995, sitting on a pumpkin, glow-in-the-dark, NM, A7 ....$35.00

Casper the Friendly Ghost, Euromark/UK, 1995, NM, A7 ..$35.00

Casper's Uncles, Damascar/Italy, 1996, NM $35.00

Cinderella, Damascar/Italy, 1994, gray & wht gown, NM, A7 ....$35.00

Cindy Bear, Damascar/Italy, sitting on purple rock, M, A7 .$35.00

Cookie Monster, Grosvenor/UK, 1995, EX, A7 ....$15.00

Daffy Duck, Prelude/UK, 1994, wearing shark suit, NM, A7 .$35.00

Dino (Flintstones), Damascar/Italy, 1995, standing on food dish w/giant bone, M, A7 ....$35.00

Dino (Flintstones), Rosedew/UK, 1990s, NM, A7 ....$35.00

Donald Duck, Mann & Schroder/German, 1970s, standing w/arms on hips, M, A7 ....$45.00

Donald Duck, Rosedew/UK, 1990s, bl boat, MIB, A5 ......$35.00

Donald Duck (Mickey & Pals), Centura/Canada, 1995, driving yel boat, NM, A7 ....$25.00

Dopey & Sneezy, Grosvenor/UK, 1995, NM, A7 ....$35.00

Dracula Horror Bubbles, Jackel/UK, 1994, NM, A7 ....$35.00

Edd the Duck, Euromark/UK, 1990, NM, A7 ....$30.00

Eeyore, Grosvenor/UK, 1997, NM, from $25 to $30.00

Fireman Sam, Rosedew/UK, 1993, NM, A7 ....$35.00

Flipper, Euromark/UK, 1996, riding a wave, M..............$35.00

Frankenstein Horror Bubbles, Jackel/UK, 1994, NM $35.00

Fred Flintstone, Damascar/Italy, 1994, standing w/golf club, M, A7 ....$35.00

Fred Flintstone, Rosedew/UK, standing at attention, M, A7 ....$35.00

Garfield, Grosvenor/UK, 1981, NM...............................$35.00

Genie (Aladdin), Prelude/UK, sitting w/arms crossed, NM, A7 ....$35.00

Huckleberry Hound, John H Gould Ltd/UK, 1960s, NM, A7 ....$50.00

Hulk Hogan, Fulford/Canada, 1986, NM, from $15 to $20.00

Hunchback of Notre Dame, Grosvenor/UK, 1996, NM ...$35.00

Jafar (Aladdin), Grosvenor/UK, standing w/scepter & bird on shoulder, M, A7 ....$35.00

James Bond, BRB/UK, 1970s, rare, NM, from $100 to...$120.00

Jasmin (Aladdin), Prelude/UK, 1994, gr outfit, holds bird in hand, NM, A7 ....$35.00

Jemima Puddleduck (Beatrix Potter), Grosvenor/UK, 1990, M, A7 ....$30.00

Jerry & Tuffy, Damascar/Italy, 1990s, NM $35.00

Leo Lion, Belvedere/Canada, 1990s, bank, NM, A7 ....$15.00

Little Mermaid, Grosvenor/UK, 1991, sitting in clam shell, A7..$30.00

Louie Duck, Rosedew/UK, gr outfit & hat, M, A7 ....$35.00

Magic Princess, Boots/UK, 1996, NM, A7.....................$30.00

Matchbox Dump Truck, Grosvenor/UK, 1994, M, A7.....$35.00

Matchbox Road Grader, Grosvenor/UK, 1994, NM, from $30 to $35.00

Mickey Mouse, Centura/Canada, 1994, red shirt w/bl pants & yel shoes, M, A7 ....$30.00

Mickey Mouse (Fantasia), Centura/Canada, 1994, red robe, bl star & moon hat, NM, A7..$30.00

Minnie Mouse, Centura/Canada, 1994, in pk gown, A7 ..$30.00

Mowgli & Kaa (Jungle Book), Prelude/UK, 1994, snake wrapped around boy, NM, A7..$35.00

Nala (Lion King), Centura/Canada, sitting on pk base, M, A7 ....$30.00

Noddy, Grosvenor/UK, red shirt & bl shorts, w/dog, M, A7 ....$25.00

Olive Oyl, Damascar/Italy, 1995, sitting w/hands clasped, M, A7 ....$35.00

Oscar the Grouch, Grosvenor/UK, 1995, NM, A7..........$35.00

Paddington Bear, Cottsmore/UK, 1992, NM, A7 ....$35.00

Pebbles & Bamm-Bamm, Damascar/Italy, sitting on sabertooth tiger, M, A7 ....$35.00

Percy (Thomas the Tank), Grosvenor/UK, 1994, on blk tracks & gray bricks, NM, A7 ....$15.00

Peter Rabbit, Grosvenor/UK, 1995, bl coat, NM, A7......$30.00

Pingu Penguin, Grosvenor/UK, standing on igloo, M, A7.$30.00

Pink Panther, Segura/Spain, 1995, NM, from $35 to $40.00

Pink Panther, UK, 1972, standing at attention, M, A7....$75.00

Pinocchio, Holland, 1970s, NM, from $40 to...................$45.00

Pocahontas, Centura/Canada, 1995, sitting on rock in grass, NM, A7 ....$25.00

Polly Pocket Castle, Centura/Canada, 1995, NM, A7 .....$30.00

Popeye, Damascar/Italy, standing on spinach crate, M, A7 .$35.00

Popeye, Rosedew Ltd/UK, 1987, holding spinach can, blk base, NM, A7 ....$40.00

Power Rangers, Centura/Canada, 1994, any character, NM, A7, ea $30.00

Pumba & Timon (Lion King), Grosvenor/UK, Timon on Pumba's back, M, A7 ....$35.00

RoboCop, Euromark/UK, 1990, standing on gray bricks, NM, A7 ....$35.00

Rupert Bear, Euromark/UK, w/backpack, NM, A7...........$40.00

Scooby Doo, Damascar/Italy, 1995, sitting, NM, A7........$40.00

Scrappy Doo, Damascar/Italy, 1995, coming out of well w/water creature, NM, A7 ....$35.00

Sleeping Beauty, Damascar/Italy, 1994, standing w/rose, NM, A7, from $30 to $35.00

Smurf (Cook), IMPS/Belgium, 1991, NM, A7 ....$40.00

Smurf (Papa), IMPS Brussels/Germany, 1991, NM, A7 ...$40.00

Snow White, Centura/Canada, 1994, standing, NM, A7.$25.00

Snow White, Grosvenor/UK, sitting on grass w/bunny & deer, M, A7 ....$30.00

Snowman, Grosvenor/UK, 1990s, NM, A7 ....$30.00

Sonic Hedgehog, Matey/UK, 1991, standing on red & bl game button, NM, A7 ....$35.00

Spider-Man, Euromark/UK, 1995, walking over trash can & tire, rare, NM, A7 ....$35.00

Superman, Damascar/Italy, 1995, flying pose, M, A7, from $35 to $40.00

Superman, Euromark/UK, 1994, NM, A7.......................$30.00

Sylvester & Tweety, Warner Bros/UK, Tweety sitting on Sylvester's head, M, A7 ....$35.00
Tasmanian Devil, Centura/Canada, 1994, NM, A7 ....$30.00
Thomas the Tank, Bandai/Japan, 1992, NM, A7 ....$30.00
Thunderbird, ITC Ent/UK, gr or yel, M, A7, ea $35.00
Tigger, Grosvenor/UK, 1997, NM................................$30.00
Tinkerbell, Tom Fields Ltd/UK, NM $35.00
Troll, Euromark/UK, 1990s, several variations, NM, ea ...$30.00
Ultimate Warrior, Grosvenor/UK, 1991, NM, A7 ....$35.00
Wallace & Gromit, Euromark/UK, 1996, NM..................$30.00
Wile E Coyote, Prelude Ltd/UK, w/rocket backpack, M, A7....$20.00
Wilma Flintstone, Damascar/Italy, 1995, washing clothes in pelican's bill, NM, A7 ....$35.00
Wilma Flintstone, Rosedew Ltd/UK, 1993, topper, cartoon outfit, NM, A7 ....$20.00
Winnie the Pooh, Grosvenor/UK, 1997, NM..................$30.00
Woodstock (Peanuts), unknown maker/UK, flying red plane, yel w/blk heart-shaped glasses, M, A7.............................$35.00

Yogi Bear, Cindy Bear, and Boo Boo Bear, Damascar/Italy, M, A7, $35.00 each. (Photo courtesy Matt and Lisa Adams)

Zebedee the Magic Roundabout, Grosvenor/UK, 1992, NM, from $20 to..$25.00
101 Dalmatians, Grosvenor/UK, 1995, mama w/pup on head & 1 in front of her, NM, from $25 to $30.00

Buddy L

First produced in 1921, Buddy L toys have escalated in value over the past few years until now early models in good original condition (or restored, for that matter) often bring prices well into the four figures when they hit the auction block. The business was started by Fred Lundahl, founder of Moline Pressed Steel Co., who at first designed toys for his young son, Buddy. They were advertised as being 'Guaranteed Indestructible,' and indeed they were so sturdy and well built that they just about were. Until wartime caused a shortage, they were made of heavy-gauge pressed steel. Many were based on actual truck models; some were ride-ons, capable of supporting a grownup's weight. Fire trucks with hydraulically activated water towers and hoisting towers

that actually worked kept little boys entertained for hours. After the war, the quality of Buddy Ls began to decline, and wood was used to some extent. Condition is everything. Remember that unless the work is done by a professional restorer, overpainting and amateur repairs do nothing to enhance the value of a toy in poor condition. Professional restorations may be expensive, but they may be viable alternatives when compared to the extremely high prices we're seeing today. In the listings that follow, toys are all pressed steel unless noted.

Advisors: Kerry and Judy Irvin (K5).
See also Advertising; Boats.

CARS AND BUSSES

Buick, plastic, 5", EX, from $10 to....................................$20.00
Flivver Coupe, blk w/red spoke wheels, slant-back rear, 11", EX, A...$850.00
Flivver Roadster, blk w/red spoke wheels, simulated soft top, 11", NM, A...$1,500.00
Ford Model T, #210B, EX..$500.00

Greyhound Bus, #755, blue and white with decals, clockwork mechanism, 16", NMIB, A, $825.00.

Greyhound Bus, wood w/decals, internal bell activates from knob in rear, destination boards on roof, 18", VG, A $600.00
Passenger Bus, 30", scarce, EX, from $3,500 to............$4,000.00
Scarab, red w/chrome detail, blk rubber tires, 10", VG, from $250 to..$350.00
Town & Country Car, wood, woodie model w/gray roof, metal window frames, 18½", EX, A $800.00
Woodie Station Wagon, maroon-pnt wood w/simulated woodgrain finish, celluloid windows, 19", EX, A $700.00

CONSTRUCTION

Cement Mixer, gr w/drum & chute mounted on wheeled base, lever action, 11", NM, A...$450.00
Cement Mixer, gray w/boiler, drum, hopper & tow bar mounted to base, red water tank & wheels, rpt, 15", A $350.00
Dredge, #270, 20", rstr, A $650.00
Hoisting Tower, #350, EX, from $700 to $900.00
Mobile Power Digger, orange & yel w/red chassis, gr crane, 20", EX $250.00

Derrick, red, 21½", NM, A, $400.00; Sand Loader, blue with red decals, 18", NM, A, $1,000.00; Railway Steam Shovel, black with red corrugated roof, decal on side, 22½", EX, A, $700.00.

Pile Driver, #260, 23", EX, A $2,500.00

Road Roller, green with red detail, VG, A, $3,200.00.

Sand Screener, #300, NM, from $1,200 to $1,500.00
Steam Shovel, #220, 24", VG, A $275.00

FIREFIGHTING

Fire Station, wood and fiberboard, 9x15½", EX, from $1,200.00 to $1,500.00.

Aerial Ladder Truck, red & yel enclosed cab w/NP ladder on hand-op turntable, 38", EX, A $3,400.00
Aerial Ladder Truck, red w/wht extension ladder on swivel base & 1 on ea side, 27", MIB, A $250.00
Fire Chief Car, red-pnt wood w/chrome bell on hood, 18½", NM, A $750.00
Hook & Ladder Truck, #205, EX, from $1,400 to $1,500.00
Hook & Ladder Truck, #859, wood, 21½", EX $450.00
Insurance Patrol Truck, #205C, NM $2,200.00
Ladder Truck, red-pnt wood w/open bench seat, unpnt ladders, 19½", NM, A $300.00

Pumper Truck, open bench seat, red with nickel-plated boiler and railed rear platform, 23", VG, A, $1,700.00; Ladder Truck, open bench seat, red, 26", NM, A, $1,700.00.

Pumper Truck, rider, #29, 26", rstr $1,200.00

OUTDOOR TRAINS

Caboose, red, platforms at each end, cupola on top, 20", NM, A $1,200.00
Coal Car (Gondola), blk w/red decals, retains orig Boston Dept storage tag, 21", EX $1,000.00
Locomotive & Tender, steam, blk, loco features handrails, bell & fire box, 72-oz water tank in tender, 26", EX, A $1,700.00
Tank Car, red w/blk frame & straps, ladder on sides, filler caps on top, 15½", NM, A $1,900.00
Tank Car, yel w/blk frame & trucks, center ladder, 19½", EX $1,500.00

TRUCKS AND VANS

Army Transport w/Cannon, spoke wheels, 27", EX, from $250 to $350.00
Army Truck, #506, 20½", NM, from $250 to $300.00
Big Show Circus Truck, #484, wood, 25½", EX $900.00

Baggage Truck, black enclosed cab with yellow stake bed, with hand truck and barrel skid, 26½", EX, A, $6,600.00.

Buddy L Van Lines Long Distance Moving Truck, orange- & blk-pnt wood w/decals on sides, yel hubs, 27", VG, A $450.00
Coal Truck, #202, 24", NM, from $3,000 to $4,000.00
Dump Truck, #434, 1936, yel & red, electric headlights, 19½", G $300.00

Dump Truck, black cab with red dump, electric lights, 20½", NM, A, $1,200.00.

Dump Truck, rider, gray and blue, 26", NM, A, $1,200.00.

Emergency Auto Wrecker, #3317, NM, from $200 to....$250.00
Excavator Truck w/Steam Shovel, 2-tone gray & bl w/orange & bl steam shovel, 21", EX, A $900.00
Express Line Truck, blk w/gr screen body, hinged rear door, 26", EX, A $2,000.00
Federal Van Lines Moving Truck, bl- & red-pnt wood w/wht lettering, blk wheels w/NP hubs, 21", VG, A $875.00
Flivver Huckster Delivery Truck, blk w/enclosed blk cab, red spoke wheels, 14", NM, A......................................$4,600.00

Ford Dump Truck, #211A, 1926-30, bl w/open driver's seat, red spoke wheels, 11", NM, from $1,700 to $2,000.00
Huckster Truck, blk w/canopied bed, red spoke wheels, 14", NM, from $4,500 to $5,000.00
Hy-Way Maintenance Truck w/Cement Mixer, yel & bl enclosed cab, yel & red mixer in flat bed, w/ramp, 10½", EX, A $600.00
Hydraulic Dump Truck, #201A, 24½", G $1,000.00
Hydraulic Missile Launcher, MIB $700.00

Ice Delivery Truck, doorless cab, black and yellow, 25½", EX, A, $2,000.00.

International Dump Truck, rider, 25", NM $600.00
Lumber Truck, #203A, 24", rstr, A $1,100.00
Maintenance Truck w/Cement Mixer, yel & red enclosed cab w/mixer in open bed, w/ramp, 20", EX, A................$650.00
Milk Truck, wht-pnt wood w/blk top, Buddy L Milk Farms decal on side, complete w/milk carton & bottles, 13", EX, A......$650.00
Mister Buddy Ice Cream Van, EX, from $150 to $200.00
Oil Truck, #206A, 24", rstr, A $1,300.00

Parcel Delivery Truck, beige and brown with decals, 24", G, A, $275.00.

Railway Express Truck, #204A, mesh panels & hinged solid rear doors on removable van body, 25", G, A $525.00
Repair-It Truck, 24", VG, from $150 to $200.00
Robotoy Truck, red w/gr dump & blk chassis, moves forward & reverse w/transformer, 21", VG............................$1,000.00
Sand & Gravel Truck, #202A, 26", rstr, A..................$1,350.00
Stake Truck, #203, 25", rstr, A $800.00
Tank Line Truck, enclosed blk cab w/gr tank, 24½", NM, A..$1,700.00

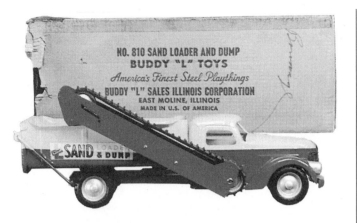

Sand Loader and Dump Truck, yellow and blue with red sand loader, 23", NM, A, $550.00.

Telephone Maintenance Repair Truck & Trailer, #450, complete w/ladder & rope, 16", EX (EX box)................$500.00
Timber Truck, yel- & blk-pnt wood w/pegs along bed, 25", VG, A $150.00
US Mail Truck, brn w/wht roof, decals on sides, 20½", NM, A $350.00
Victory Jeep & Cannon, wood, EX, from $150 to..........$200.00
Wrecker, rider, red & wht w/emb spoke wheels, child's seat & hand-op crank in back, 32", NM, A $3,500.00
Zoo-A-Rama Truck & Cage, complete w/plastic monkeys & polar bears, 20", NMIB, A..$250.00

Building Blocks and Construction Toys

Toy building sets were popular with children well before television worked its mesmerizing influence on young minds; in fact, some were made as early as the end of the 18th century. Important manufacturers include Milton Bradley, Joel Ellis, Charles M. Crandall, William S. Tower, W.S. Read, Ives Manufacturing Corporation, S.L. Hill, Frank Hornby (Meccano), A.C. Gilbert Brothers, The Toy Tinkers, Gebruder Bing, R. Bliss, S.F. Fischer, Carl Brandt Jr., and F. Ad. Richter (see Richter Anchor Stone Building Sets). Whether made of wood, paper, metal, glass, or 'stone,' these toys are highly prized today for their profusion of historical, educational, artistic, and creative features. For further information on Tinkertoys, read *Collector's Guide to Tinkertoys* by Craig Strange (Collector Books).

Richter's Anchor (Union) Stone Building Blocks were the most popular building toy at the beginning of the 20th century. As early as 1880, they were patented in both Germany and the USA. Though the company produced more than six hundred different sets, only their New Series is commonly found today (these are listed below). Their blocks remained popular until WWI, and Anchor sets were one of the first toys to achieve international 'brand name' acceptance. They were produced both as basic sets and supplement sets (identified by letters A, B, C, or D) which increased a basic set to a higher level. There were dozens of stone block competitors, though none were very successful. During WWI the trade name Anchor was lost to

A.C. Gilbert (Connecticut) who produced Anchor blocks for a short time. Richter responded by using the new trade name 'Union' or 'Stone Building Blocks,' sets considered today to be Anchor blocks despite the lack of the Richter's Anchor trademark. The A.C. Gilbert Company also produced the famous Erector sets which were made from about 1913 through the late 1950s.

Note: Values for Richter's blocks are for sets in very good condition; (+) at the end of the line indicates these sets are being reproduced today.

Advisor: George Hardy (H3), Richter's Building Blocks.

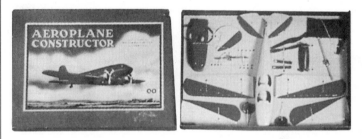

Aeroplane Constructor, Meccano, complete, NMIB, A, $700.00.

American Logs, Halsam, complete, EX (EX box) $40.00
American Plastic Bricks, Halsam, 1950s, EX (EX container), M17..$35.00
American Skyline, Elgo, 1950s, complete, NM (VG box), T2..$35.00
Big Boy Tinkertoy, Spalding/Toy Tinkers, 1950s-60s, complete, EX (G container) $45.00

Electric Motor Tinkertoy Set, Spalding, 1954 – 57, complete, EX (EX container), $75.00.
(Photo courtesy Craig Strange)

Big Tinkertoy for Little Hands, Questor, 1976, complete, EX (VG container)..$25.00

Building Bricks, Auburn Rubber, 1950s, complete, EX (EX canister), T2..$40.00

Double Tinkertoy, Toy Tinkers, 1927, complete, EX (EX container) $40.00

Erector Set, Gilbert #5½, MIB..........................$175.00

Erector Set, Gilbert #6½, MIB..........................$165.00

Erector Set, Gilbert #7, EX (EX wooden box) $250.00

Erector Set, Gilbert #7½, complete w/catalog, EX (EX wooden box)..$350.00

Erector Set, Gilbert #8, EX (EX wooden box)...............$850.00

Fiddlesticks Giant Toy Builder Set, Knickerbocker, 1979, features Marvel Super Heroes, missing few pcs, NMIB, M17..$80.00

Follo-Me-Tinker, Toy Tinkers, 1921-28, complete, EX (EX box)..$85.00

Giant Tinker, Toy Tinkers, 1926, complete, EX (EX box)..$225.00

Girder & Panel Build-A-Home, Kenner, 1962, complete, EX (EX canister), T2 ....$35.00

Girder & Panel Build-A-Home, Kenner, complete, NM (VG box), $50.00. (Photo courtesy June Moon)

Lincoln Logs, paper label marked Original Lincoln Logs the All American Toy, complete, EX (G box), A, $50.00.

Girder & Panel International Airport, Kenner, 1977, complete, EX (EX box), from $30 to.............................$40.00

Junior Tinkertoy, Toy Tinkers, 1933, complete, EX (EX container) $25.00

Microrail City, Mego, 1978, complete, EX (EX box)........$50.00

Mold Master Road Builder, Kenner, 1964, unused, NMIB, J2 ....$125.00

Old Hickory Building Blocks, Newton & Thompson Mfg, early, complete, EX (worn box) $300.00

Rowly-Boat Tinker, Toy Tinkers, 1924 – 27, complete, EX (EX box), $185.00. (Photo courtesy Craig Strange)

Senior Tinkertoy the Ten Thousand Wonder Builder, Toy Tinkers, 1933, complete, EX (EX container)...................$40.00

Spirit of St Louis, Metalcraft, builds over 250 airplanes, complete, VG (VG box), A $300.00

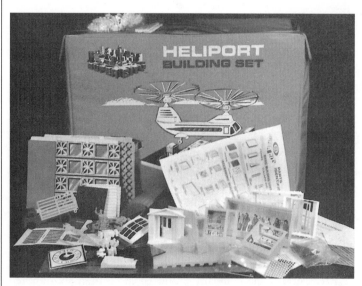

Super City Heliport Building Set, Ideal, 1968, complete, EX (EX vinyl case), from $40.00 to $50.00. (Photo courtesy Linda Baker)

Tinker Fun Forms, Spalding, 1966, complete, EX (EX box)..$25.00

Tinker Go-Round, Toy Tinkers, 1929, complete, NMIB ..$150.00

Tinker Jack & Jill, Toy Tinkers, 1930-35, complete, EX (VG container) $65.00

Tinker Zoo No 737, Spalding, 1962-70, complete, EX (EX container) $25.00

Tinker Zoo No 747, Spalding, 1962-70, complete, EX (EX container) $30.00

Tinkercraft Kit No 1, Toy Tinkers, 1939, complete, EX (VG box) **$65.00**

Tinkertoy Panel Builder #600, Toy Tinkers/Spalding, 1958, complete, EX (EX container) $30.00

Tinkertoy Panel Builder #800, Toy Tinkers/Spalding, 1958, complete, EX (EX container) **$40.00**

Tinkertoy Wonder Builder, Toy Tinkers, complete, EX (EX container), $35.00. (Photo courtesy Craig Strange)

Wood Airplane Kit, Fisher-Price Arts & Crafts, 1982 – 85, complete, MIB, C13, $35.00. (Photo courtesy Brad Cassity)

Tog'l Toy Chest, Mattel, 1969, complete, EX (G box) $25.00

Tumble Tinker, Toy Tinkers, 1920-21, complete, EX (EX box) **$175.00**

Wood Sailboat Kit, Fisher-Price Arts & Crafts, 1982-85, complete, MIB, C13 ....$30.00

ANCHOR STONE BUILDING SETS BY RICHTER

American House & Country Set #206, VG, H3.............$600.00
American House & Country Set #208, VG, H3.............$600.00
American House & Country Set #210, VG, H3.............$700.00
DS Set #E3, w/metal parts & roof stones, VG, H3 ....$60.00
DS Set #3A, w/metal parts & roof stones, VG, H3...........$60.00
DS Set #5, w/metal parts & roof stones, VG, H3 ....$120.00
DS Set #5A, w/metal parts & roof stones, VG, H3 ....$150.00
DS Set #7, w/metal parts & roof stones, VG, H3 ....$270.00
DS Set #7A, w/metal parts & roof stones, VG, H3 ....$200.00
DS Set #9A, w/metal parts & roof stones, VG, H3 ....$250.00
DS Set #11, w/metal parts & roof stones, VG, H3 ....$675.00
DS Set #11A, w/metal parts & roof stones, VG, H3 ......$300.00
DS Set #13A, w/metal parts & roof stones, VG, H3 ......$325.00
DS Set #15, w/metal parts & roof stones, VG, H3 ......$1,500.00
DS Set #15A, w/metal parts & roof stones, VG, H3 .....$475.00
DS Set #19A, w/metal parts & roof stones, VG, H3 .....$475.00
DS Set #21A, w/metal parts & roof stones, VG, H3 .....$975.00
DS Set #23A, w/metal parts & roof stones, VG, H3 .....$750.00
DS Set #25A, w/metal parts & roof stones, VG, H3 ...$1,500.00
DS Set #27, w/metal parts & roof stones, VG, H3 ......$6,000.00
Fortress Set #402, VG, H3...$100.00
Fortress Set #402A, VG, H3 ....$130.00
Fortress Set #404, VG, H3..$250.00
Fortress Set #404A, VG, H3 ....$275.00
Fortress Set #406, VG, H3..$500.00
Fortress Set #406A, VG, H3 ....$400.00
Fortress Set #408, VG, H3...$1,000.00
Fortress Set #408A, VG, H3 ....$800.00
Fortress Set #410, VG, H3...$1,800.00
Fortress Set #410A, VG, H3 ....$1,000.00
Fortress Set #412A, VG, H3 ....$1,500.00
Fortress Set #414, VG, H3...$5,000.00
German House & Country Set #301, VG, H3...............$500.00
German House & Country Set #301A, VG, H3 ....$500.00
German House & Country Set #303, VG, H3 ....$1,000.00
German House & Country Set #303A, VG, H3 ....$2,000.00
German House & Country Set #305, VG, H3 ....$3,000.00
GK-BK Great-Castle Set, VG, H3................................$9,950.00
GK-NF Set #6, VG, H3 (+) $140.00
GK-NF Set #6A, VG, H3 (+) $160.00
GK-NF Set #8, VG, H3...$300.00
GK-NF Set #10, VG, H3...$480.00
GK-NF Set #10A, VG, H3 (+) $200.00
GK-NF Set #12, VG, H3...$680.00
GK-NF Set #12A, VG, H3 (+) $250.00
GK-NF Set #14A, VG, H3..$250.00
GK-NF Set #16, VG, H3 ....$1,180.00
GK-NF Set #16A, VG, H3..$300.00
GK-NF Set #18A, VG, H3..$400.00
GK-NF Set #20, VG, H3 ....$2,000.00

GK-NF Set #20A, VG, H3..............................$500.00
GK-NF Set #22A, VG, H3..............................$500.00
GK-NF Set #24A, VG, H3..............................$600.00
GK-NF Set #28, VG, H3 ....$4,000.00
GK-NF Set #28A, VG, H3..............................$1,200.00
GK-NF Set #30A, VG, H3..............................$1,200.00
GK-NF Set #32B, VG, H3..............................$1,600.00
GK-NF Set #34, VG, H3 ....$7,000.00
KK-NF Set #5, VG, H3..................................$90.00
KK-NF Set #5A, VG, H3.................................$90.00
KK-NF Set #7, VG, H3.................................$180.00
KK-NF Set #7A, VG, H3...............................$115.00
GK-NF Set #8A, VG, H3 (+)...........................$180.00
KK-NF Set #9A, VG, H3...............................$120.00
KK-NF Set #11, VG, H3...............................$315.00
KK-NF Set #11A, VG, H3..............................$275.00
KK-NF Set #13A, VG, H3..............................$300.00
KK-NF Set #15A, VG, H3..............................$450.00
KK-NF Set #17A, VG, H3..............................$750.00
KK-NF Set #19A, VG, H3..............................$1,500.00
KK-NF Set #21, VG, H3...............................$4,500.00
Neue Reihe Set #102, VG, H3.........................$100.00
Neue Reihe Set #104, VG, H3.........................$150.00
Neue Reihe Set #106, VG, H3.........................$200.00
Neue Reihe Set #108, VG, H3.........................$300.00
Neue Reihe Set #110, VG, H3.........................$600.00
Neue Reihe Set #112, VG, H3 ....$1,000.00
Neue Reihe Set #114, VG, H3 ....$1,500.00
Neue Reihe Set #116, VG, H3 ....$2,000.00

California Raisins

The California Raisins made their first TV commercials in the fall of 1986. The first four PVC figures were introduced in 1987, the same year Hardee's issued similar but smaller figures, and three 5½" Bendees became available on the retail market. In 1988 twenty-one more Raisins were made for retail as well as promotional efforts in grocery stores. Four were graduates identical to the original four characters except standing on yellow pedestals and wearing blue graduation caps with yellow tassels. Hardee's increased their line by six.

In 1989 they starred in two movies: *Meet the Raisins* and *The California Raisins — Sold Out*, and eight additional characters were joined in figurine production by five of their fruit and vegetable friends from the movies. Hardee's latest release was in 1991, when they added still four more. All Raisins issued for retail sales and promotions in 1987 and 1988 (including Hardee's) are dated with the year of production (usually on the bottom of one foot). Of those released for retail sales in 1989, only the Beach Scene characters are dated, and these are actually dated 1988. Hardee's 1991 series are also undated.

Advisors: Ken Clee (C3) and Larry DeAngelo (D3).
Other Sources: C11, W6.

Applause, Captain Toonz, w/bl boom box, yel glasses & sneakers, Hardee's Second Promotion, 1988, sm, M.............$3.00

Applause, FF Strings, w/bl guitar & orange sneakers, Hardee's Second Promotion, 1988, sm, M $3.00
Applause, Michael Raisin, Special Edition, 1989, M........$15.00
Applause, Rollin' Rollo, w/roller skates, yel sneakers & hat mk H, Hardee's Second Promotion, 1988, sm, M $3.00
Applause, SB Stuntz, w/yel skateboard & bl sneakers, Hardee's Second Promotion, 1988, sm, M $3.00
Applause, Trumpy Trunote, w/trumpet & bl sneakers, Hardee's Second Promotion, 1988, sm, M $3.00
Applause, Waves Weaver I, w/yel surfboard connected to foot, Hardee's Second Promotion, 1988, sm, from $3 to $6.00
Applause, Waves Weaver II, w/yel surfboard not connected to foot, Hardee's Second Promotion, 1988, sm, M...........$4.00
Applause-Claymation, Banana White, yel dress, Meet the Raisins First Edition, 1989, M $20.00
Applause-Claymation, Lick Broccoli, gr & blk w/red & orange guitar, Meet the Raisins First Edition, 1989, M $20.00
Applause-Claymation, Rudy Bagaman, w/cigar, purple shirt & flipflops, Meet the Raisins First Edition, 1989, M......$20.00
CALRAB, Blue Surfboard, board connected to foot, Unknown Promotion, 1988, M..............................$35.00

CALRAB, Blue Surfboard, Unknown Promotion, 1987, M, $50.00. (Photo courtesy Larry DeAngelo)

CALRAB, Christmas Issue, 1988, w/candy cane, M.........$12.00
CALRAB, Christmas Issue, 1988, w/red hat, M $12.00
CALRAB, Hands, left hand points up, right hand points down, Post Raisin Bran Issue, 1987, M $4.00
CALRAB, Hands, pointing up w/thumbs touching head, First Key Chains, 1987, M $5.00
CALRAB, Hands, pointing up w/thumbs touching head, Hardee's First Promotion, 1987, sm, M $3.00
CALRAB, Microphone, right hand in fist w/microphone in left, Post Raisin Bran Issue, 1987, M $6.00
CALRAB, Microphone, right hand points up w/microphone in left, Hardee's First Promotion, 1987, M $3.00
CALRAB, Microphone, right hand points up w/microphone in left, First Key Chains, 1987, M..............................$5.00

CALRAB, Guitar, First Commercial Issue, 1988, M, $8.00. (Photo courtesy Larry DeAngelo)

CALRAB, Saxophone, gold sax, no hat, First Key Chains, 1987, M $5.00

CALRAB, Saxophone, gold sax, no hat, Hardee's First Promotion, 1987, sm, M $3.00

CALRAB, Saxophone, inside of sax pnt red, Post Raisin Bran Issue, 1987, M $4.00

CALRAB, Singer, microphone in left hand not connected to face, First Commercial Issue, 1988, M $6.00

CALRAB, Sunglasses, index finger touching face, First Key Chains, 1987, M..$5.00

CALRAB, Sunglasses, index finger touching face, orange glasses, Hardee's First Promotion, 1987, M $3.00

CALRAB, Sunglasses, right hand points up, left hand points down, orange glasses, Post Raisin Bran Issue, 1987, M...$4.00

CALRAB-Applause, Bass Player, Second Commercial Issue, 1988, M, $8.00.

CALRAB, Sunglasses II, eyes not visible, aqua glasses & sneakers, First Commercial Issue, 1988, M............................$6.00

CALRAB, Sunglasses II, eyes visible, aqua glasses & sneakers, First Commercial Issue, 1988, M $25.00

CALRAB, Winky, hitchhiking pose & winking, First Commercial Issue, 1988, M...$6.00

CALRAB-Applause, AC, 'Gimme-5' pose, Meet the Raisins Second Edition, 1989, M..$175.00

CALRAB-Applause, Alotta Stile, purple boom box, Hardee's Fourth Promotion, 1991, sm, MIP (w/collector's card).$15.00

CALRAB-Applause, Anita Break, shopping w/Hardee's bags, Hardee's Fourth Promotion, 1991, sm, MIP (w/collector's card) $15.00

CALRAB-Applause, Benny, w/bowling ball & bag, Hardee's Fourth Promotion, 1991, sm, MIP (w/collector's card).$12.00

CALRAB-Applause, Boy in Beach Chair, Beach Theme Edition, 1988, M, $15.00. (Photo courtesy Larry DeAngelo)

CALRAB-Applause, Boy w/surfboard, purple board, brn base, Beach Theme Edition, 1988, M $15.00

CALRAB-Applause, Cecil Tyme (Carrot), Meet the Raisins Second Promotion, 1989, M $225.00

CALRAB-Applause, Girl with Tambourine, Raisin Club Issue, 1988, M, $15.00. (Photo courtesy Larry DeAngelo)

CALRAB-Applause, Drummer, Second Commercial Issue, 1988, M $8.00

CALRAB-Applause, Girl w/Boom Box, purple glasses, gr shoes, brn base, Beach Theme Edition, 1988, M..................$15.00

CALRAB-Applause, Girl w/Tambourine (Ms Delicious), yel shoes, Second Commercial Issue, 1988, M $15.00

CALRAB-Applause, Hands, Graduate w/both hands pointing up & thumbs touching head, Graduate Key Chains, 1988, M..$85.00

CALRAB-Applause, Hip Band Guitarist (Hendrix), w/headband & yel guitar, Third Commercial Issue, 1988, M..$25.00

CALRAB-Applause, Hip Band Guitarist (Hendrix), Second Key Chains, 1988, small, M, $65.00.
(Photo courtesy Larry DeAngelo)

CALRAB-Applause, Hula Girl, yel shoes & bracelet, gr skirt, Beach Theme Edition, 1988, M $15.00

CALRAB-Applause, Lenny Lima Bean, purple suit, Meet the Raisins Second Promotion, 1989, M......................$150.00

CALRAB-Applause, Microphone (female), yel shoes & bracelet, Third Commercial Issue, 1988, M..............$12.00

CALRAB-Applause, Microphone (female), yel shoes & bracelet, Second Key Chains, 1988, sm, M................$45.00

CALRAB-Applause, Microphone (male), left hand extended w/open palm, Second Key Chains, 1988, sm, M........$45.00

CALRAB-Applause, Mom, yel hair, pk apron, Meet the Raisins Second Promotion, 1989, M, from $150 to $175.00

CALRAB-Applause, Piano, bl piano, red hair, gr sneakers, Meet the Raisins First Edition, 1989, M..............................$35.00

CALRAB-Applause, Saxophone, blk beret, bl eyelids, Third Commercial Issue, 1988, M $15.00

CALRAB-Applause, Saxophone, Graduate w/gold sax, no hat, Graduate Key Chains, 1988, M $85.00

CALRAB-Applause, Singer (female), reddish purple shoes & bracelet, Second Commercial Issue, 1988, M $12.00

CALRAB-Applause, Sunglasses, Graduate w/index fingers touching face, orange glasses, Graduate Key Chains, 1988, M $85.00

CALRAB-Applause, Valentine, boy holding heart, Special Lover's Edition, 1988, M...$8.00

CALRAB-Applause, Valentine, girl holding heart, Special Lover's Edition, 1988, M...$8.00

CALRAB-Claymation, Sunglasses, Singer, Hands, Saxophone, Graduate on yel base, Post Raisin Bran, 1988, ea, from $45 to $65.00

MISCELLANEOUS

Backpack, maroon & yel w/3 figures, 1987, EX, W6........$35.00

Balloon, lead singer, CTI Industries, 1988, EX, W6 ....$8.00

Bank, cereal box with lid, plastic, EX, from $10.00 to $15.00. (Photo courtesy June Moon)

Baseball Cap, 1988, EX, W6 ....$5.00

Beach Towel, CALRAB, M $50.00

Belly Bag, bl or yel nylon fabric w/Conga Line, 1988, EX, W6, ea...$25.00

Book, Birthday Boo Boo, 1988, EX, W6 ....$12.00

Book, Raisin the Roof, 1988, EX, W6 ....$12.00

Bookmark, various images, D3, ea $3.00

Bulletin Board, Singer & Conga Line or Beach Scene, Rose Art, 1988, MIP, W6, ea...$35.00

Chalkboard, Singer & Conga Line, Rose Art, 1988, MIP, W6..$35.00

Clay Factory, Rose Art, 1988, complete, MIB $40.00

Colorforms, MIB (sealed), P12 ....$35.00

Coloring Book, California Raisins on Tour, Marvel, 1988, unused, EX $12.00

Crayon-By-Number Set, Rose Art, 1988, complete, MIB...$40.00

Cross-Stitch Pattern, Leaflet #1, #3, #4 or #6, 1988, M, W6, ea...$12.00

Doll, vinyl w/suction cups, 1987, lg version, EX, W6 ....$5.00

Doll, vinyl w/suction cups, 1987, sm version, EX, W6......$10.00

Door Knob Hanger, various images, 9x4", D3, ea $5.00

Figure, Imperial Toy, 1987, inflatable vinyl, 42", MIB, W6, from $40 to $50.00

Figure, w/bl tennis shoes, cloth, 1987, EX, W6 ....$5.00

Game, California Raisin board game, Decipher Inc, 1987, MIB, from $15 to...$20.00

Key Chain, glasses & orange tennis shoes, metal, 1988, MOC, W6..$3.00

Official Fan Club Watch Set, MIP, P12, from $35 to.......$50.00

Patch, Ice Capades w/Raisin Singer, felt, 1988, EX, W6 ....$8.00

Picture Album, 1988, EX, W6...$25.00

Poster, Join the California Raisin Club, 1990, EX, W6 ....$12.00

Puffy Stick-On, 1987, EX, W6...$10.00

Punching Bag, Imperial Toys, 1987, inflatable, 36", MIB, W6 ....$60.00

Puppet, female figure w/yel or gr shoes, Bendy/Sutton Happenings, 1988, MIB, W6, ea $30.00

Puppet, male w/yel shoes & glasses, Bendy/Sutton Happenings, 1988, MIB, W6 ....$35.00

Puzzle, American Publishing, 1988, 500 pcs, MIB, W6 ....$20.00

Record, California Raisins Sing the Hit Songs, 78 rpm, Priority Records, 1987, EX (EX sleeve), W6 ....$20.00

Record, Rudolph the Red-Nosed Reindeer, 45 rpm, 1988, EX (EX sleeve), W6...$30.00

Refrigerator Magnets, Hands, Orange Sunglasses, Microphone, Saxophone, 1988, ea from $45 to............................$50.00

School Kit, w/promotion ideas, activities, recipes, etc, 1988, M, W6...$30.00

School Kit, w/ruler, pencil sharpener, eraser & pencil holder, 1988, MOC, W6..$40.00

Shoulder Bag, bl & orange w/dancing raisins, 1988, MOC, W6...$25.00

Sleeping Bag, purple, 1988, EX, W6.................................$40.00

Sticker Album, w/slide-o-scope, Diamond Publishing, 1988, M, W6 ....$15.00

Suspenders, I Heard It Through the Grapevine, yel, 1987, EX, W6 ....$35.00

Tambourine, raisins on stage, 1987, EX, W6 ....$15.00

Tambourine & Kazoo, Imperial Toy Corporation, 1987, MOC, P12/W6, from $35 to $45.00

Target Game, 1988, foam rubber, 12", EX $15.00

Tote Bag, yel w/Conga Line, 1987, EX, W6......................$20.00

Umbrella, lady raisins on the beach, 1988, EX, W6 ....$45.00

Video, Meet the Raisins, 1988, MIP, W6 ....$25.00

Video, Raisins Sold Out, 1990, MIP, W6 ....$25.00

Watercolor-By-Number Set, Rose Art, complete, 1988, EX, W6 ....$30.00

Wind-up Toy, figure w/hands up & gr bracelet, 1987, EX, W6 ....$12.00

Wind-up Toy, figure w/right hand up & orange glasses, 1987, MOC, W6, from $5 to...$10.00

Candy Containers

As early as 1876, candy manufacturers used figural glass containers to package their candy. They found the idea so successful that they continued to use them until the 1960s. The major producers of these glass containers were Westmoreland, West Bros., Victory Glass, J.H. Millstein, J.C. Crosetti, L.E. Smith, and Jack and T.H. Stough. Some of the most collectible and sought after today are the character-related figurals such as Amos 'N Andy, Barney Google, Santa Claus, and Jackie Coogan, but there are other rare examples that have been known to command prices of $1,000.00 and more. Some of these are Black Cat for Luck (that books for $1,800.00, even in worn paint); Cat Winking, Stretched Neck ($3,800.00 – 4,200.00); Irish Hat ($3,500.00 – 4,000.00); and Car, Black and White Taxi ($1,000.00 – 1,200.00). There are many reproductions; know your dealer. For a listing of these reproductions, refer to *Schroeder's Antiques Price Guide*.

For more information we recommend *The Collector's Guide to Candy Containers*, written by Doug Dezso, our advisor for this category, and Leon and Rose Poirier (Collector Books). The plate numbers in the following listings refer to this book.

For other types of candy containers, see Halloween; Pez Dispensers; Santa Claus.

Airplane, plate #81, from $110 to $135.00
Baby Chick, plate #7, from $100 to................................$125.00

Barney Google by Barrel, plate #188, from $1,200.00 to $1,500.00. (Photo courtesy Doug Dezso and Leon and Rose Poirier)

Barney Google on Pedestal, plate #189, from $250 to....$350.00
Baseball Player by Barrel, plate #190, from $700 to.......$850.00

Winross Truck, New America Highway Series, 1989, red Ford long-nose tandem axle with dual stacks, features Champion Raisins, M, $125.00. (Photo courtesy Larry DeAngelo)

Bear on Circus Tub, plate #2, from $400 to $600.00
Binoculars (Victor), plate #98, from $150 to $250.00
Black Cat for Luck, plate #5, from $1,800 to...............$2,200.00
Boob McNutt, plate #193, from $6,500 to....................$8,000.00
Bulldog on Oblong Base, plate #17, from $40 to...............$50.00
Cannon, plate #386, from $800 to $1,000.00
Cash Register, plate #420, from $500 to $600.00
Charlie Chaplin by Barrel, plate #196, from $450 to $600.00
Electric Runabout, plate #163, from $85 to $100.00
Felix the Cat by Barrel, plate #250, from $550 to..........$700.00
Felix the Cat on Tub, plate #201, from $3,000 to.......$3,500.00
Fire Ladder Truck, plate #254, from $200 to $275.00
Gun, hook grip, plate #396, from $25 to $35.00
Gun (Kolt), plate #393, from $150 to $200.00
Gun (VG Co Revolver), plate #404, from $25 to............$35.00

Hot Doggie, plate #23, from $1,000.00 to $1,200.00.
(Photo courtesy Doug Dezso and Leon and Rose Poirier)

Hound Dog w/Hat, plate #28, from $35 to.......................$50.00
Indian Motorcycle w/Driver, plate #446, from $500 to ..$600.00
Kiddie Kar, plate #430, from $225 to $275.00
Lawn Swing, plate #314, from $700 to............................$900.00

Nurser (Lynne Doll), plate #122, from $25.00 to $35.00.
(Photo courtesy Doug Dezso and Leon and Rose Poirier)

Liberty Bell, plate #93, from $175 to.............................$225.00
Limousine, plate #169, from $65 to................................$100.00
Locomotive (Mapother's), plate #499, from $275 to......$325.00
Milk Bottle (Dolly's Milk), plate #109, from $50 to.........$75.00
Piano, plate #460, from $200 to $250.00
Powder Horn, plate #411, from $65 to $95.00

Queen Mary, plate #103, from $350.00 to $450.00.
(Photo courtesy Doug Dezso and Leon and Rose Poirier)

Rabbit Crouching, plate #54, from $100 to $125.00
Rabbit on Dome, plate #65, from $450 to......................$525.00
Rabbit Pushing Chick in Eggshell Cart, plate #61, from $250
    to $350.00
Racer (Stough's), plate #473, from $60 to.......................$75.00
Rocking Horse, plate #46, from $275 to $325.00
Rocking Horse w/Rider, plate #47, from $175 to............$225.00
Santa Claus (Uruguay), plate #286, from $350 to $425.00
Santa Claus in Long Coat, plate #279, from $350 to......$400.00
Skookum by Tree Stump Barrel, plate #207, clear or pnt, from
    $150 to $225.00
Station Wagon, plate #178, from $35 to $50.00
Telephone, plate #222, from $1,000 to.......................$1,250.00
Telephone (Millstein Tele-Bank), Variation A, plate #233, from
    $50 to $75.00
Telephone (Millstein Tot), plate #234, from $30 to $40.00
Toonerville Trolley, plate #214, from $750 to $1,000.00

Cast Iron

Realistically modeled and carefully detailed cast-iron toys enjoyed their heyday from about the turn of the century (some companies began production a little earlier) until about the 1940s when they were gradually edged out by lighter-weight toys that were less costly to produce and to ship. (Some of the cast irons were more than 20" in length and very heavy.) Many were vehicles faithfully patterned after actual models seen on city streets at the time. Horse-drawn carriages were phased out when motorized vehicles came into use.

Some of the larger manufacturers were Arcade (Illinois), who by the 1920s was recognized as a leader in the industry; Dent (Pennsylvania); Hubley (Pennsylvania); and Kenton (Ohio). In the 1940s Kenton came out with a few horse-drawn toys which are collectible in their own right but naturally much less valuable than the older ones. In addition to those already noted, there were many minor makers; you will see them mentioned in the listings.

For more detailed information on these companies, we recommend *Collecting Toys* by Richard O'Brien (Books Americana). Note: World record prices continue to climb for mint and mint-in-box examples which are generally found at most larger toy shows. Prices for rare toys can be absolutely breathtaking. However, prices for common toys are generally stable and have not changed much.

Advisor: John McKenna (M2).

See also Banks; Pull and Push Toys.

AIRPLANES

America Airplane, gray with red detail, three-prop, with pull string, 17" wingspan, NM, A, $6,000.00.

Bremen Airplane, Hubley, gr, 6½", VG, A $525.00
Fokker Airplane, Vindex, red-orange w/gr undercarriage & bl motor, NP prop, 8" W, NM, A $6,000.00
Fokker Airplane, Vindex, silver w/NP prop & disk wheels, 10" W, scarce, EX, A $5,000.00

Friendship Airplane, Hubley, yellow with nickel-plated props, 11" L, repaint, A, $5,000.00.

Lindy Airplane, Hubley, gray w/emb red letters, NP prop & disk wheels, 10" W, EX, A..............................$1,300.00
Lindy Glider, Hubley, red & yel w/NP disk wheels, integral pilot, 6" W, rpt, EX, A..............................$500.00
Lucky Boy Airplane, Dent, gr w/NP prop & disk wheels, 9½" W, rpt, VG, A $450.00
Lucky Boy Tri-Motor, Dent, orange w/NP props & disk wheels, 7" W, rpt, EX, A $850.00
Monocoupe, Arcade, orange & blk w/NP prop, rubber tires, w/pilot, 11" W, NM, A $2,700.00
Question Mark Airplane, Dent, gr w/NP props & disk wheels, 12½" W, rpt, EX, A..............................$1,200.00
TAT Airplane, Kilgore, red & yel w/NP prop, 13½" W, NM, A.......................................$4,100.00

BOATS

Adirondack Paddle-Wheeler, Dent, wht w/yel details, 15", EX, A.......................................$900.00
City of New York Paddle-Wheeler, Wilkins, wht w/blk stacks & red trim, 15", EX, A $1,250.00
City of New York Riverboat, mc, 15", VG+, A............$1,550.00
Racing Skull, Wilkins, w/8 oarsmen, 14", VG+, A $2,600.00
Riverboat, Harris, mc, 7½", EX, A..............................$550.00
Showboat, Arcade, 1929, red, wht & gr, 10½", EX, A..$1,650.00
Static Speedboat w/Johnson Seahorse Motor, Hubley, 9½", EX, A.......................................$4,500.00
Steamboat, Arcade, gold w/red detail, 7½", EX, A.........$285.00

CHARACTER

Alphonse on Mule Cart, Kenton, nodding head figure on 2-wheeled cart, mc, 6½", VG, A.......................................$325.00
Andy Gump Car, Arcade, red & gr w/wht rubber tires, figure in blk suit, 7¼", EX, A $2,700.00
Chester Gump Cart, Arcade, figure in yel cart w/red spoke wheels, wht horse, 7½", G, A $275.00
Popeye, Olive Oyl & Wimpy, Hubley, 3", EX, A $850.00
Popeye Spinach Wagon, Hubley, red w/blk rubber tires, mc figure, 6", M, A.......................................$1,400.00
Popeye Spinach Wagon, Hubley, red w/blk rubber tires, mc figure, 6", G, A $250.00

CIRCUS ANIMALS AND ACCESSORIES

Overland Circus Band Wagon, Kenton, red w/yel spoke wheels, 6 musicians, driver & 2 wht horses w/riders, 15", EX, A.......................................$800.00
Overland Circus Cage Wagon, Kenton, red w/gold trim, disk wheels, w/bear & driver, 9", rpt, EX, A....................$950.00
Overland Circus Cage Wagon, Kenton, yel w/wht disk wheels, w/driver & bear, 9", EX, A $1,650.00
Overland Circus Calliope Wagon, Kenton, red w/yel spoke wheels, w/2 wht horses & 4 figures, 14", EX.........$1,650.00
Royal Circus Cage Wagon, Hubley, bl w/gold trim, yel spoke wheels, w/driver, 2 gray horses & lion, 9½", VG.....$925.00
Royal Circus Cage Wagon, Hubley, gr w/yel spoke wheels, w/driver, bear & 2 blk horses, 15½", EX, A $1,200.00

Overland Circus Band Wagon, Kenton, red with yellow spoke wheels, six musicians, driver, and two white horses with riders, 15", MIB, A, $1,500.00.

CONSTRUCTION

See Also Boxed Sets.

Austin Autocrat Worm Drive Roller, Arcade, gray w/gr spoke wheels, NP driver, 7½", G, A $475.00
Austin Roll-A-Plane Road Roller, Arcade, 1928 model, gray w/red spoke wheels, NP driver, 7½", NM, A $3,100.00
Buckeye Ditch Digger, Kenton, red & gr w/NP chain drive, cast wheels w/chain treads, 9", EX, A $1,000.00
Caterpiller Tractor, Arcade, 1929 model, gr w/red spoke wheels, NP driver & chain treads, 6½", VG, A $700.00
Cement Mixer Truck, Kenton, red & gr w/NP drum & dump, wht rubber tires, w/driver, 8½", EX, A $1,400.00
Hercules Road Roller, Hubley, gr w/blk wooden wheels, w/driver, orig showroom tag, 5", M, A.....................$600.00

Huber Road Roller, Hubley, green with ornate nickel-plated wheels, original nickel-plated driver, EX, $450.00.
(Photo courtesy Dunbar Gallery)

Huber Road Roller, Hubley, gr w/ornate NP wheels, rpl NP figure, 8", EX, A...$350.00

Huber Steam Roller, Hubley, orange w/NP roller & ornate tires, 8", EX, A...$500.00
Jaeger Cement Mixer, Kenton, red w/NP mixer on flat body, rubber tires, 7", NMIB, A.....................................$3,300.00

Jaeger Cement Mixer, Kenton, red with nickel-plated operating pieces, spoke wheels, 6", G, A, $300.00; Jaeger Cement Mixer, Kenton, silver with red and green frame, nickel-plated drum and scoop, white rubber tires, 8", VG, A, $600.00.

John Deere Crawler Tractor, gr & yel w/blk rubber treads, 7", EX (EX box), A...$385.00
Lansing Cement Bucket, Vindex, gr w/red spoked wheels, w/salesman's sample tag & decal, 6½", M, A $5,500.00
Panama Steam Shovel, Hubley, red & gr w/NP shovel, wht rubber tires, cast figures on trailer, 12", VG, A..........$1,000.00
Road Roller, Kenton, red w/NP spoke wheels, red-pnt wood front roller, w/driver, 7", M, A $475.00
Steam Shovel, Arcade, red & gr w/chain treads & spoke wheels, pressed steel hoist & bucket, 10", rare, NM, A ..$11,000.00
Steam Shovel Truck, Hubley, red & gr w/wht rubber tires, NP shovel, integral figure at side, 10", NM, A...............$550.00

FARM TOYS

See Also Horse-Drawn and Boxed Sets.

Allis-Chalmers Model WC Tractor, Arcade #3740, orange w/blk rubber tires, NP driver, 7¼", NMIB, A $1,900.00
Allis-Chalmers Tractor, Arcade, orange w/blk rubber tires, NP driver & extended steering post, 7", EX, A $1,000.00
Allis-Chalmers Tractor & Dump Trailer, Arcade, orange w/blk rubber tires, w/driver, 13", NMIB, A $2,200.00
Allis-Chalmers Tractor & Dump Trailer, Arcade, red & gr w/wht rubber tires, integral driver, 13", NM, A.......$450.00
Case Combine, Vindex, silver w/red spoke wheels & trim, 12", EX, A...$2,450.00
Case Hay Loader, Vindex, red w/yel spoke wheels, 9", EX, A.$2,450.00
Case Model L Tractor, Vindex, gray w/red spoke wheels, w/driver, 7", NM, A $2,400.00
Case 3-Bottom Plow, Vindex, red w/yel spoke wheels, 10", rpt, EX, A...$1,500.00
Caterpiller Tractor, Arcade #270 Y, yel w/steel treads, exposed engine, NP driver, 8", NMIB, A $4,500.00
Corn Harvester, Arcade #702, red & yel w/blk rubber tires, 5½", MIB, A...$950.00

Farmall Model A Tractor, Arcade, red w/gold trim, blk rubber tires, NP driver, 7½", MIB, A..................$2,500.00

Farmall Model M Tractor, Arcade, gr w/blk & wht wooden wheels, w/driver, 5½", NM, A $650.00

Farmall Model M Tractor, Arcade, red w/blk rubber tires, NP driver, 7½", NMIB, A..................$1,650.00

Farmall Tractor, Arcade, red w/wht rubber tires, integral driver, 6", NM, A..................$1,500.00

Ford Tractor w/Earth Hauler, Arcade, red & wht w/blk rubber tires, integral driver, 14", VG, A $1,100.00

Fordson Model 9N Tractor and Plow, Arcade, 1939, salesman's sample, gray and red with driver, 9", MIB, A, $4,400.00; Whitehead and Kales Wagon, Arcade, red with removable stake sides, disk wheels, 7", NM, A, $1,300.00.

Fordson Tractor, Arcade, gray w/gold trim, red spoke wheels, copper-finished driver, 6", MIB, A..........................$850.00

Fordson Tractor w/Scoop, gr w/red spoke wheels, NP driver & scoop, 9", EX, A $1,650.00

Hay Cart, Vindex, gr w/red spoke wheels & hitch bar, 7½", VG, A...$4,100.00

Hay Rake, Arcade, red & yel w/gr seat, NP spoke wheels, 7", MIB, A $1,500.00

International Harvester Tractor, Arcade, red w/blk rubber treads, NP driver, 7½", NMIB, A..........................$2,850.00

John Deere Model D Tractor, Vindex, gr w/yel spoke wheels, NP driver & pulleys, 6", EX, A...................................$2,475.00

John Deere Farm Wagon, Vindex, gr w/red spoke wheels, removable bed, 8", G, A $1,750.00

John Deere Gas Engine, Vindex, gr w/silver trim, w/operative pulley & flywheel, 5", EX, A....................................$935.00

John Deere Harvester, Vindex, silver w/yel spoke wheels, 13½", EX, A..$4,100.00

John Deere Manure Spreader, Vindex, red w/gr seat, yel spoke wheels, 14", M, A...................................$2,750.00

John Deere Model A Tractor, Arcade, gr w/blk rubber tires & yel hubs, NP driver, 7", MIB, A..........................$2,100.00

John Deere Thresher, Vindex, silver & gr w/yel spoke wheels, 15", NM, A..$4,125.00

John Deere Van Brunt Drill, Vindex, red w/yel disk wheels, NP drill disks, 9¾", EX, A....................................$2,750.00

McCormick-Deering Spreader, Arcade, red w/yel hitch, NP spoke wheels, 14½", MIB, A..........................$1,300.00

McCormick-Deering Thresher, Arcade, gr w/red trim, NP spoke wheels, 9½", VG, A $550.00

McCormick-Deering Thresher, Arcade, gray w/red trim, yel spoke wheels, NP shoot & pulleys, 10", MIB, A ..$2,500.00

McCormick-Deering Thresher, Arcade, salesman's sample, yel w/red trim, NP grain pipe & spoke wheels, 9½", NM, A..$1,300.00

McCormick-Deering Wagon, Arcade, gr w/red hitch & spoke wheels, removable open bench, 12", MIB, A $1,650.00

McCormick-Deering 10-20 Tractor, Arcade, gray w/gold trim & red treads, NP driver, 7½", EX, A..........................$400.00

McCormick-Deering 2-Bottom Plow, Arcade, red w/bl & silver blades, spoke wheels, 7", NMIB, A......................$1,650.00

Oliver Orchard Tractor, Hubley, gr w/blk rubber tires, red driver, 5", NM, A $450.00

Oliver Row-Crop 70 Tractor, Arcade, gr or red w/blk rubber tires, NP driver, 7", NMIB, ea..............................$1,750.00

Oliver Superior Spreader, Arcade, yel w/blk trim, NP rotor axle, rubber tires, 9½", MIB, A $2,300.00

Tandem Disk Harrow, Arcade, red & bl, 5½", MIB, A ..$1,500.00

Tractor, Arcade, red w/gold trim, blk wooden wheels, w/driver, 6", EX, A..$350.00

Tractor w/Front High-Lift Scoop Bucket, gr w/red spoke wheels, NP driver, lever action, 9", VG, A $1,200.00

Whitehead & Kales Tractor, Arcade #2, gray w/gold trim, blk rubber tires, copper-finished driver, 6", NMIB, A ...$950.00

FIREFIGHTING

Only motor vehicles are listed here; **see also Horse-Drawn and Boxed Sets.**

Fire Chief Car, Arcade, red w/name stenciled on roof, blk rubber tires, 5½", G, A $165.00

Fire Chief Car, Kenton, red with nickel-plated disk wheels, integral driver, 5½", NM, $1,400.00.
(Photo courtesy Dunbar Gallery)

Ford Pumper Truck, Arcade, 1941 model, red w/blk rubber tires, 6 firemen, 13", VG, A $450.00

Ladder Truck, Arcade, red w/yel ladders, wht rubber tires, 3 cast figures, 16", EX, A....................................$1,700.00

Ladder Truck, Kenton, red w/NP extension ladder, disk wheels w/yel hubs, 9", NM, A....................................$1,750.00

Ladder Truck, Kenton, red w/NP extension ladder, yel spoke wheels, 12", NM, A..$2,850.00

Ladder Truck, Skoglund & Olsen, red w/NP supports, tin ladder, wht rubber tires, w/driver, 16", rpt, A $700.00

Ladder Truck, Kenton, red with nickel-plated extension ladder, yellow spoke wheels, integral driver, 14", NM, A, $3,300.00.

Mack Ladder Truck, Arcade, red w/yel ladders, NP spoke wheels, 10", NM, A..............................$1,700.00
Mack Ladder Truck, red w/yel ladders, NP spoke wheels & driver, 18", rpt, A.............................$500.00
Pontiac Fire Truck, Arcade, red w/NP grille, wht rubber tires, integral firemen, 8⅝", EX, A..............$300.00
Pumper Truck, Arcade, red w/NP trim, 6 bl-pnt figures w/red & wht hats, 13", MIB, A.....................$2,800.00

Pumper Truck, Hubley, red with black rubber tires and spoke wheels, with driver, 11", NM, D10, $750.00.
(Photo courtesy Dunbar Gallery)

Pumper Truck, Hubley, red w/NP grille & boiler, wht rubber tires, 2 firemen, 6½", EX, A...............$250.00
Pumper Truck, Kenton, early model w/spoke wheels, w/driver & rear fireman, 11", VG, A.................$400.00
Water Tower Truck, Kenton, red w/gr extension crane, NP disk wheels, 12", NM, A......................$1,750.00

HORSE-DRAWN AND OTHER ANIMALS

Bakery Wagon, Kenton, wht w/red spoke wheels, w/driver & single blk horse, 13", VG, A.................$250.00
Cement Mixer, Kenton, orange & gr w/NP drum & scoop, w/driver & single blk horse, 14", NM, A..........$1,650.00
Coal & Wood Wagon, Wilkins, gr w/yel spoke wheels, w/driver & single blk horse, 12", EX, A.............$775.00
Coal Wagon, Hubley, red w/yel spoke wheels, w/driver & single blk horse, 15", rpr shaft, A.............$250.00
Contractor's Dump Wagon, Arcade, gr w/emb gold lettering, blk rubber tires, 1 wht & 1 blk horse, 13", NM, A........$825.00

Covered Wagon, Kenton, gr w/gold trim & red spoke wheels, cloth cover, w/driver, 1 blk horse & 1 wht, 15½", M, A.......$600.00
Dray Wagon, Kenton, gr w/red spoke wheels, w/driver, 1 blk horse & 1 wht, 14", EX, A.................$175.00
Dray Wagon, Pratt & Letchworth, w/decorated foot board, 2 blk horses w/red trim, 17", VG, A..........$1,150.00
Farm Wagon, Arcade, red box-type w/driver & 2 gray horses, 11", EX, A................................$600.00
Farm Wagon, Arcade, red w/gr detail & blk rubber tires, w/driver & 2 dapple gray horses, 11", NM, D10, from $750 to.........$1,250.00
Farm Wagon, Kenton, gr w/red spoke wheels, w/driver & 2 wht horses, 14½", EX, A......................$150.00
Farm Wagon, Wilkins, red w/yel spoke wheels, w/driver & 2 blk horses, 14", VG, A.....................$1,200.00
Farm Wagon w/Side Dump, Arcade, red & gr w/NP spoke wheels, 2 blk horses w/gold trim, 13½", NM, A.$11,000.00
Fire Chief Wagon, Pratt & Letchworth, red w/NP detail, w/driver & wht horse, 14", VG, A.............$2,300.00
Fire Ladder Wagon, Ives, w/driver, rear fireman & 2 blk horses, 21", EX, A..........................$2,300.00
Fire Ladder Wagon, Ives, w/driver & rear fireman, 1 wht horse & 1 blk, 25", VG, A...................$1,375.00
Fire Ladder Wagon, Kenton, red w/2 yel ladders, spoke wheels, w/driver, 2 blk horses & 1 wht on wheeled fr, 16", NM, A.$250.00
Fire Ladder Wagon, Pratt & Letchworth, w/bell ringing mechanism, w/driver, rear fireman & 2 wht horses, 24", EX, A........$4,100.00
Fire Patrol Wagon, Kenton, red w/yel spoke wheels, 4 integral firemen & 3 horses, 12", EX, A..........$650.00

Fire Pumper and Engine House, Ives, EX, D10, $11,000.00.
(Photo courtesy Dunbar Gallery)

Fire Pumper, Kenton, red w/gold highlights, yel spoke wheels, 3 horses on wheeled fr, 17", G, A.........$400.00
Fire Pumper, Pratt & Letchworth, w/bell ringer, w/driver, rear fireman & 2 horses, 18", EX, A..........$5,700.00
Fire Pumper, Wilkins, brass-look boiler w/silver trim, spoke wheels, 3 horses, 19", G, A..............$500.00
Hansom Cab, Arcade, blk w/gold trim, spoke wheels, single gray horse w/wht mane & tail, 10½", EX, A...$2,100.00
Hansom Cab, blk w/yel spoke wheels, w/driver & single gray horse, 8", EX, A.........................$400.00
Hansom Cab, Kenton, bl w/yel spoke wheels, w/driver & single wht horse, 11½", NM, A.................$350.00

Hansom Cab, Kenton, blk w/yel spoke wheels, w/driver, passenger & single wht horse, 16", EX, A $350.00

Hay Mower, Wilkins, red w/yel spoke wheels, w/driver & 2 blk horses, 10", EX, A.....................................$3,300.00

Ice Wagon, blk w/red spoke wheels, w/driver & 2 blk horses, 14", G+, A...$300.00

Ice Wagon, Hubley, red w/yel top, yel spoke wheels, w/driver & 2 blk horses, 15½", VG, A $800.00

Log Cart, Kenton, yel w/red spoke wheels, driver atop tree trunk, 2 blk oxen, 14", EX, A.....................................$825.00

Milk Wagon, Kenton, wht w/red spoke wheels, w/driver & single blk horse, 12½", MIB, A $825.00

Phaeton, Hubley, red 2-wheeled cart w/spoke wheels, w/driver, passenger & single blk horse, 12½", G, A $450.00

Phoenix Fire Pumper, Ives, 2 sm wheels on boiler simulates pumping action, w/driver & 2 horses, 19", VG, A...........$1,375.00

Plantation Cart, Kenton, red w/yel spoke wheels, w/driver & oxen, 11", EX, A..$350.00

Police Patrol Wagon, Kenton, w/driver & 3 policemen, 1 blk horse & 1 silver, 16", VG, A $900.00

Pony Cart, Dent, blk w/yel spoke wheels, lady driver, 9½", VG, A $350.00

Sand and Gravel Wagon, Kenton, green with embossed gold lettering, red spoke wheels, one white and one black horse, 15", MIB, A, $600.00; Surrey, Kenton, blue with yellow spoke wheels, red canopy with gold fringe, with driver, passenger and two white horses, 13", M, A, $475.00.

Sand & Gravel Wagon, Kenton, red w/gr spoke wheels, NP driver & single blk horse, 10", MIB, A $400.00

Santa in Sleigh, Hubley, gr w/gold highlights, 2 reindeer on red spoke wheels, 17", EX, A $1,100.00

Santa in Sleigh, white with gold detail, two reindeer on red spoke wheels, 16", EX, D10, from $1,000.00 to $2,000.00.
(Photo courtesy Dunbar Gallery)

Stake Wagon, Kenton, gr w/red spoke wheels, w/driver, 1 blk horse & 1 wht, 14", NM, A..................................$300.00

Sulky, Kenton, yel w/NP spoke wheels, w/driver & blk horse, 7¼", MIB, A $350.00

MOTOR VEHICLES

Note: Description lines for generic vehicles may simply begin with 'Bus,' 'Coupe,' or 'Motorcycle,' for example. But more busses will be listed as 'Coach Bus,' 'Coast-To-Coast,' 'Greyhound,' 'Interurban,' 'Mack,' or 'Public Service' (and there are other instances); coupes may be listed under 'Ford,' 'Packard,' or some other specific car company; and lines describing motorcycles might also start 'Armored,' 'Excelsior-Henderson,' 'Delivery,' 'Policeman,' 'Harley-Davidson,' and so on. Look under 'Yellow Cab' or 'Checker Cab' and other cab companies for additional 'Taxi Cab' descriptions. We often gave any lettering or logo on the vehicle priority when we entered descriptions, so with this in mind, you should have a good idea where to look for your particular toy. Body styles (Double-Decker Bus, Cape-Top Roadster, etc.) were also given priority.

See Also Boxed Sets.

American Oil Co Truck, Dent, dk bl w/gold trim, NP wheels, w/driver, 10½", EX, A..$2,300.00

Arctic Ice Cream Truck, Kilgore, bl & red w/NP disk wheels, emb wht lettering, 8", rpt, VG, A $250.00

Army Tank, Arcade #400, gr camoflage w/blk rubber treads, top opens, 8", NM, A $1,000.00

Auto Express Truck, Kenton, red w/yel spoke wheels, 6½", VG, A $300.00

Bell Telephone Truck, Hubley, gr w/NP disk wheels, 3½", EX, A $350.00

Bell Telephone Truck, Hubley, gr w/NP spoke wheels, w/driver, 7", NM, A $600.00

Bell Telephone Truck, Hubley, gr w/wht rubber tires, complete w/driver & tools, 9¼", EX, A $750.00

Bell Telephone Truck, Hubley, gr w/wht rubber tires, red hubs, w/pole trailer, drill, ladder & tools, 9", EX, A..........$900.00

Borden's Milk Truck, Hubley #110, white with red lettering, white rubber tires, 6", VG, $850.00. (Photo courtesy Dunbar Gallery)

Bell Telephone Truck, Hubley, gr w/wht rubber tires, w/driver, 8", EX, A...$275.00

Bell Telephone Truck, Hubley, gr w/wht rubber tires, 4", EX, A...$350.00

Borden's Milk Truck, Arcade, silver milk-bottle shape w/wht rubber tires, red hubs, 6", VG, A $1,000.00

Borden's Milk Truck, Hubley, wht w/NP spoke wheels, 7½", NM, A...$6,500.00

Buick Coupe, Arcade, 1927 model, bl-gr & blk w/wht rubber tires & blk spokes, NP trim & driver, 8½", NM, A...$13,750.00

Bus, Pickwick Nite Coach, bl w/orange stripe, NP disk wheels, 14", VG, A...$2,750.00

Bus, Pickwick Nite Coach, Kenton, gr w/orange stripe, NP disk wheels, 9½", VG, A..$1,500.00

Bus, Pickwick Nite Coach, red w/gr stripe, NP disk wheels, 11", EX, A...$3,000.00

Bus, Seto, Skoglund & Olsen, red w/wht rubber tires & bl hubs, NP grille, 11", VG+, A..$350.00

Car Carrier, AC Williams, red with nickel-plated spoke wheels, green carrier with three Austin sedans, 12", EX, A, $850.00.

Car Carrier, AC Williams, red w/NP spoke wheels, gr carrier w/3 Austin sedans, 12", NMIB, A $2,200.00

Car Carrier, Arcade, gr Ford model A w/red trailer, NP spoke wheels, w/3 cars, 19", EX, A..................................$3,100.00

Car Carrier, Arcade, gr w/rubber tires, red flat-bed trailer, no cars, 19½", VG, A..$800.00

Car Carrier, Arcade, gr w/wht rubber tires, gr flat-bed trailer w/3 Austin sedans, 14", NM, A $1,000.00

Car Carrier, Arcade, gr w/wht rubber tires, red trailer w/3 sedans, 14¼", NM, A..$3,300.00

Car Carrier, Arcade, red w/wht rubber tires, flat-bed trailer w/3 cars, 14", NM, A...$2,750.00

Car Carrier, Hubley, red w/NP disk wheels, bl trailer w/3 bl integral Buick coupes, 10", NM, A $1,400.00

Car Carrier, Hubley, red w/wht rubber tires, red 2-tiered trailer w/4 vehicles, 10¼", NM, A.................................$750.00

Car Carrier, Kenton, red w/wht rubber tires, blk trailer w/1 red & 3 yel open roadsters, 18", EX, A $2,400.00

Chevrolet Coupe, Arcade, 1928 model, blk & gray w/NP spoke wheels & rear spare, 8¼", NM, A.....................$2,300.00

Chevrolet Stake Truck, Arcade, 1938 model, gr w/red fenders, wht rubber tires, 4¼", NM, A..........................$825.00

Chevrolet Superior Roadster, Arcade, 1925 model, blk w/blk-pnt spoke wheels, w/driver, 7", G, A....................$550.00

Chevrolet Utility Stake Truck, Arcade, 1925 model, blk & wht w/spoke wheels, NP driver, 9", EX, A $950.00

Chrysler Airflow, mk Century of Progress, Arcade, silver w/wht rubber tires & red hubs, NP grille, 4", EX, A.....$600.00

City Ambulance, Arcade, 1932 model, bl w/emb lettering, wht rubber tires w/red hubs, 5½", VG, A......................$525.00

Coupe, Arcade, gray w/wht rubber tires & red hubs, NP grille & bumper, 5", VG, A...$700.00

Coupe, Arcade, lt bl w/wht rubber tires & red hubs, NP trim, opening rumble seat, 6½", rpt, A...........................$225.00

Coupe, Hubley take-apart model, bl & wht w/gr top, wht rubber tires, 2 side spares, 6½", NM, A............................$850.00

Coupe, Kenton, red & blk w/wht-pnt disk wheels & red hubs, rear spare, 8", VG, A..$1,700.00

Coupe, Kenton, saleman's sample, red w/silver disk wheels & red hubs, tag, 5⅛", NM, A..................................$1,000.00

Delivery Cycle, mk Flowers, Hubley, bl w/wht rubber tires, 5¼", EX, A...$700.00

Delivery Van, AC Williams, 1936 model, bl w/wht rubber tires & red hubs, 4½", VG, A $550.00

Delivery Van, Arcade, 1925 model, deep bl w/wht stripe, NP disk wheels, side spare, sq rear opening, 8¼", rpt, A...$935.00

DeSoto Sedan, Arcade, red w/wht rubber tires & bl hubs, NP trim, decal on door, 6", EX, A.............................$275.00

Dodge Airflow, Hubley, brn w/wht rubber tires, NP trim, 8", NM, A...$1,600.00

Dodge Coupe, Arcade, 1922, blk w/NP spoke wheels, removable rear spare, cast driver, 9", EX, A............................$950.00

Double-Decker Bus, Arcade, 1929 model, gr w/gold trim, wht rubber tires w/red hubs, 8", EX, A.....................$600.00

Double-Decker Bus, Arcade #3180-X, gr w/gold trim, 3 passengers on upper deck, 8", MIB, A...........................$1,200.00

Double-Decker Bus, Kenton, gr & red w/gold trim, wht rubber tires, 11½", EX, A...$1,300.00

Double-Decker Bus, Kenton, lt bl w/orange stripe, disk wheels, rear steps, 6¼", VG, A..$400.00

Double-Decker Bus, Kenton, red & gr w/gold trim, wht rubber tires, 10", NM, A...$700.00

Double-Decker Bus, Yellow Coach, Arcade, gr w/blk rubber tires, 13½", VG, A...$1,650.00

Double-Decker Bus, Yellow Coach, Arcade, red w/blk rubber tires, 13", EX, A..$2,300.00

Dump Truck, Kenton, enclosed bl cab w/lt bl dump, gold trim, NP disk wheels & winch, 9", NM, A...................$4,600.00

Dump Truck, Kilgore, bl w/rust-colored dump, NP disk wheels, lever action dump, 8½", VG, A..........................$225.00

Ford Aviation Gasoline Tanker Truck, Kilgore, 1931 model, bl w/cream running boards, 12¼", NM, A $3,500.00

Ford Coupe, Arcade, bl w/NP spoke wheels & driver, 6½", VG, A...$275.00

Ford Lowboy Machinery Hauler, Kilgore, 1931 model, bl w/cream running boards, NP spoke wheels & winch, 12¼", NM, A...$2,750.00

Ford Model A Coupe, Arcade, bl w/NP spoke wheels, w/driver, 6½", NM, A...$2,400.00

Ford Model A Dump Truck, Arcade, gr & red w/ NP spoke wheels, side dump, 13½", VG, A................................$2,200.00

Ford Model A Coupe, Arcade, blue with nickel-plated spoke wheels, no driver, 5", EX, $300.00. (Photo courtesy Dunbar Gallery)

Ford Model A Dump Truck, Arcade, red w/gr dump, NP spoke wheels, orig decal, 7", EX, A $550.00

Ford Model A Stake Truck, Arcade, bl w/NP spoke wheels, orig decal, 7½", VG+, A $650.00

Ford Model A Stake Truck, Arcade, blue with nickel-plated spoke wheels, with driver and original decal, 7½", VG, $750.00. (Photo courtesy Dunbar Gallery)

Ford Model T Anthony Dump Truck, Arcade, 1927 model, blk open cab w/gray dump, NP spoke wheels, 8⅛", NM, A $1,200.00

Ford Model T Coupe, Arcade, blk w/wht spoke wheels, w/driver, 6½", EX, A $385.00

Ford Model T Pickup Truck, Arcade, red w/NP spoke wheels & driver, 8½", NM, A.....................................$2,750.00

Ford Model T Stake Truck, Arcade, blk & red w/wht rubber tires & red spokes, NP driver, 9", A $385.00

Ford Model T Touring Car, Arcade, blk w/spoke wheels, 6¼", VG, A.....................................$185.00

Ford Sedan, Arcade, red w/NP spoke wheels & driver, 6½", NM, A.....................................$1,650.00

Ford Stake Truck, Arcade, gr w/NP trim, wht rubber tires w/red hubs, 5", VG, A $1,000.00

Ford Superior Touring Car, Arcade, blk w/wht rubber tires & spoke wheels, NP driver, 6", EX, A.....................$1,000.00

Ford Tudor, Arcade, lt bl w/NP spoke wheels, 5", M, A.$750.00

Ford Tudor, Arcade, red w/gold trim, NP spoke wheels & driver, 6½", VG, A.....................................$1,000.00

Ford Wrecker, Arcade, red w/gr Weaver crane, NP spoke wheels & driver, 8½", NM, A.....................................$825.00

Gasoline Tanker, Hubley, 1938 model, yel diamond-T w/wht rubber tires & red hubs, NP grille, 6½", M, A......$1,200.00

Gasoline Truck, Hubley, red w/wht stamped lettering, spoke wheels, w/driver, 9", VG, A $1,900.00

Greyhound Bus, Century of Progress, Arcade, bl & wht trailer-type w/wht rubber tires, 7½", NMIB, A $1,300.00

Greyhound Bus, Century of Progress, Arcade, bl & wht w/wht rubber tires, 10", NM, A.....................................$450.00

Greyhound Bus, Century of Progress, Arcade, blue and white with white rubber tires, 12", EX, $350.00.
(Photo courtesy Dunbar Gallery)

Greyhound Bus, Century of Progress, Arcade, bl & wht w/wht rubber tires, 12, NMIB, A $825.00

Greyhound Bus, Century of Progress, Arcade, bl & wht w/wht rubber tires, 14", NMIB, A.....................................$3,000.00

Greyhound Bus, Great Lakes 1936 Exposition, Arcade, bl & wht w/wht rubber tires, 11", EX, A $935.00

Greyhound Bus, Greyhound Lines, Arcade, bl & wht w/wht rubber tires, 7½", EX, A $450.00

Greyhound Bus, Greyhound Lines, Arcade, bl & wht w/wht rubber tires, 11", MIB, A.....................................$1,300.00

Greyhound Bus, 1933 Chicago World's Fair, Arcade, bl & wht w/wht rubber tires, G+, A $200.00

Harley-Davidson Civilian Motorcycle, Hubley, lt bl w/gold trim, spoke wheels, 6", EX, A.....................................$350.00

Harley-Davidson Civilian Motorcycle, Hubley, orange w/gold trim, blk rubber tires w/spoke wheels, w/driver, 8", EX, A.....................................$2,400.00

Harley-Davidson Civilian Motorcycle, Hubley, orange w/wht rubber tires & spoke wheels, w/driver, 6", VG, A....$300.00

Harley-Davidson Civilian Motorcycle w/Sidecar, Hubley, olive-gr w/gold trim, spoke wheels, w/driver, 6¼", EX, A..$550.00

Harley-Davidson Hill Climber, Hubley, olive gr w/gold trim, blk rubber tires w/spoke wheels, w/driver, 8½", EX, A ..$2,800.00

Harley-Davidson Police Motorcycle, bl w/NP spoke wheels, w/driver, 7", VG, A $600.00

Harley-Davidson Police Motorcycle, Hubley, orange w/blk rubber tires & spoke wheels, w/driver, 9", EX, A $875.00

Harley-Davidson Police Motorcycle, Hubley, red w/wht rubber tires & spoke wheels, w/driver, 5½", VG, A............$300.00

Harley-Davidson Police Motorcycle w/Sidecar, Hubley, bl w/gold trim, wht rubber tires, w/driver, 5¼", VG+, A............$400.00

Harley-Davidson Police Motorcycle w/Sidecar, Hubley, olive w/rubber tires & spoke wheels, w/driver & passenger, 9", G, A $700.00

Harley-Davidson Police Motorcycle with Sidecar, Hubley, olive with rubber tires and nickel-plated spokes, with driver and passenger, 9", NM, D10, $1,600.00. (Photo courtesy Dunbar Gallery)

Hathaway's Bread Van, Arcade, blk & wht w/yel trim, wht rubber tires w/yel hubs, w/driver, International decals, VG, A..$935.00
Hill Climber Motorcycle #2, Hubley, lt bl w/blk trim, wht rubber tires w/spoke wheels, 6", EX, A.........................$700.00
Ice Truck, Kenton, red w/NP disk wheels & driver, 6", NM, A..$500.00
Indian Crash Car, Hubley, gr w/wht rubber tires & spoke wheels, 7", VG, A...$450.00
Indian Crash Car, Hubley, red w/blk rubber tires & spoke wheels, w/driver, 11½", EX, A..............................$2,000.00

Indian Crash Car, Hubley, red with replaced white rubber tires, integral driver, 5", EX, $400.00.

Indian Motorcycle, Hubley, yel w/NP 4-cylinder engine, blk rubber tires w/spoke wheels, 9", EX, A.........................$700.00
Indian Parcel Post Motorcycle, Hubley, red w/blk rubber tires & spoke wheels, w/driver, 8½", VG+, A $825.00
Indian Police Motorcycle, Hubley, gr w/NP 4-cylinder engine, blk rubber tires w/spoke wheels, 9", EX, A $950.00
Indian Police Motorcycle, Hubley, red w/NP 4-cylinder engine, blk rubber tires w/spoke wheels, 9", VG, A $750.00

Indian Police Motorcycle w/Sidecar, Hubley, red & gold w/blk rubber tires & spoke wheels, w/passenger, 8½", EX, A.......$850.00
International Baby Dump Truck, Arcade, red w/wht rubber tires, NP winch & driver, 10½", VG, A $550.00
International Baby Dump Truck, Arcade, yel w/wht rubber tires, NP winch & driver, 10½", VG, A $600.00
International Baby Pickup Truck, Arcade, red w/wht rubber tires & red disk wheels, 10", VG, A $600.00
International Baby Wrecker, Arcade, red w/gr Weaver crane, wht rubber tires w/red hubs, w/driver, 12", EX, A.........$1,000.00

International Baby Wrecker, Arcade, red with nickel-plated disk wheels, 11½", EX, D10, from $1,100.00 to $1,200.00. (Photo courtesy Dunbar Gallery)

International Delivery Van, Arcade, 1932 model, bl w/yel stipes, wht rubber tires w/yel hubs, w/driver, 9½", VG, A .$935.00
International Dump Truck, Arcade, gr & red w/NP trim, wht rubber tires w/red hubs, 10", EX, A.....................$2,200.00
International Dump Truck, Arcade, gr & yel w/blk rubber tires, 11", NM, A...$550.00
International Stake Truck, Arcade, gr w/wht rubber tires & red hubs, 11½", MIB, A $7,700.00
International Stake Truck, Arcade, red w/blk rubber tires & NP hubs, 11½", MIB, A $1,900.00

Interurban Bus, Dent, green with white rubber tires, 9", NM, D10, from $1,800.00 to $1,900.00.
(Photo courtesy Dunbar Gallery)

Lincoln Sedan, Hubley, lt bl w/NP grille & bumpers, wht rubber tires w/red hubs, 7", EX+, A $685.00

Lincoln Touring Car, AC Williams, bl-gr w/gold trim, NP spoke wheels & rear spare, 9¼", NM, A..........................$1,500.00

Lincoln Touring Car, AC Williams, gray w/gold trim, NP spoke wheels & rear spare, 7", NM, A $825.00

Livestock Truck, Kilgore, bl w/red stake bed, NP disk wheels, 8⅛", EX, A $700.00

Machinery Transport, AC Williams, red w/gr dual trailers, wht rubber tires, w/driver & bl road scraper, 21½", EX, A....$3,100.00

Mack American Gasoline Tanker Truck, Arcade, red w/wht rubber tires, red hubs, w/driver, 12¾", NM, A $2,000.00

Mack Coal Dump Truck, Arcade, red w/wht stenciled lettering, wht rubber tires w/red hubs, 10", EX, A $1,100.00

Mack Dump Truck, Arcade, bl w/NP spoke wheels & winch, w/driver, 12", NM, A $4,400.00

Mack Dump Truck, Arcade, bl w/NP spoke wheels & winch, w/driver, 12", G, A $550.00

Mack Dump Truck, Arcade, turq w/NP spoke wheels, w/driver, 8¼", VG, A $825.00

Mack Gasoline Truck, Arcade, red w/gold trim, NP spoke wheels & driver, 4½", rstr, A $800.00

Mack Gasoline Truck, Arcade, red w/wht rubber tires, NP driver, 13", G, A...$1,000.00

Mack Gasoline Truck (Lubrite), Arcade, gray w/gold trim, wht rubber tires w/gray hubs, w/driver, 12¾", NM, A.$4,100.00

Mack Ice Truck, Arcade, bl w/NP spoke wheels, w/driver, 7", EX, A...$1,100.00

Mack Lubrite Gasoline Truck, Arcade, w/driver, 13", EX, A $2,300.00

Mack Milk Truck, Arcade, gr & red w/NP spoke wheels & driver, w/2 milk cans, 11½", G, A $1,200.00

Mack Stake Truck, AC Williams, bl w/NP spoke wheels, 5", NM, A...$400.00

Mack Wrecker, Arcade, red w/gr crane, red spoke wheels, w/driver, 12½", VG, A..$1,200.00

Midget Line Sedan & Trailer, Hubley, gr w/wht rubber tires, 6½", VG, A $225.00

Motor Express Truck, Hubley, red & gr w/wht rubber tires, 9", NM, A $550.00

Motorcycle, Vindex, gr w/NP 4-cylinder engine, blk rubber tires w/spoke wheels, 8½", G, A $400.00

Moving & Storage Van, AC Williams, red w/NP disk wheels, 4", NM, A $600.00

Mullins Red Cap Trailer & Sedan, Arcade, lt bl w/wht rubber tires, red hubs, 8¾", NM, A $385.00

Oldsmobile Coupe, Vindex, bl w/NP spoke wheels, w/rumble seat & cast rear spare, 6", M, A.............................$3,300.00

Oldsmobile Coupe, Vindex, gr w/NP spoke wheels, opening rumble seat & rare spare, 8", NM, A $4,900.00

PDQ Delivery Cycle, Vindex, red w/blk rubber tires & spoke wheels, w/driver, 8½", VG, A $935.00

Plymouth Coupe, Arcade, yel w/NP trim, wht rubber tires, open rumble seat, 5", VG, A $250.00

Plymouth Stake Truck, Arcade, 1934 model, red w/NP trim, wht rubber tires, 4¾", NM, A $385.00

Police Motorcycle, AC Williams, dk bl w/wht rubber tires & wooden disk wheels, w/driver, 7", EX, A $400.00

Police Motorcycle, Champion, bl w/NP spoke wheels, 5", VG, A $200.00

Police Motorcycle, Champion, bl w/NP spoke wheels, 7", VG, A $175.00

Police Motorcycle w/Armored Shield, Hubley, red w/blk rubber tires & red spokes, w/driver, 8½", EX, A $1,600.00

Police Motorcycle w/Electric Headlight, Hubley, red w/wht rubber tires & wooden disk wheels, 6", VG, A $475.00

Police Motorcycle w/Sidecar, Champion, bl & red w/wht rubber tires, w/driver, 6¼", VG, A $300.00

Police Motorcycle with Sidecar, Hubley, red with black rubber tires and nickel-plated spokes, with driver, 8½", VG, $400.00. (Photo courtesy Dunbar Gallery)

Police Motorcycle w/Sidecar, Hubley, red w/blk rubber tires & spoke wheels, w/driver & passenger, 8½", VG, A ...$450.00

Pontiac Coach, Vindex, 1929 model, gr w/NP spoke wheels, 5½", VG, A $1,700.00

Pontiac Roadster, Vindex, lt bl w/NP spoke wheels & rear spare, 7¼", M, A...$8,800.00

Pontiac Sedan, Vindex, orange w/NP spoke wheels & rear spare, 5½", M, A $3,850.00

Pontiac Stake Truck, Arcade, gr w/wht rubber tires & red hubs, 6", NM, A $700.00

Racer #3, Champion, red Deco style w/wht rubber tires, w/driver, 8", EX, A $200.00

Racer #5, Hubley, yel w/wht rubber tires & red hubs, integral driver, 9½", EX, A..$2,100.00

Racer, Hubley, orange boat-tail with white rubber tires, 7", EX, D10, $450.00. (Photo courtesy Dunbar Gallery)

Racer #8, Hubley, silver w/red trim, wht rubber tires, integral driver, 5½", NM, A $175.00

Racer #9, Arcade, red boat-tail w/wht rubber tires & spoke wheels, w/driver & passenger, 8", G, A $1,100.00

Racer w/Moving Pistons, Hubley, silver w/red tailfin & trim, blk rubber tires w/spokes, 10", NM, A $5,700.00

Railway Express Truck, Hubley, gr w/wht rubber tires & red hubs, 5", VG, A $150.00

Red Top Cab, Arcade, red, wht & blk w/disk wheels & rear spare, w/driver, 8", EX, A.......................................$2,400.00

REO Coupe, Arcade, red w/wht rubber tires, opening rumble seat, 7", rpt, A $1,000.00

REO Coupe, Arcade, yel w/blk & red trim, NP spoke wheels & rear spare, opening rumble seat, 9½", VG, A.......$1,700.00

Roadster, AC Williams, 1936 model, bl w/NP windshield & bumper, wht rubber tires w/red hubs, 4¼", EX, A ...$450.00

Roadster, Kenton, 1922 model, red w/gray disk wheels, 5", NM, A...$700.00

Roadster, Vindex, gr w/NP spoke wheels & rear spare, 5½", M, A...$2,700.00

Sedan, Arcade, lt bl w/wht rubber tires & red hubs, NP grille, headlights & bumper, 4½", EX, A.......................$1,100.00

Sedan, Vindex, red-orange w/NP spoke wheels & rear spare, 7¼", NM, A $5,500.00

Stake Truck, Arcade, bl w/wht rubber tires & red hubs, 7", EX, A..$600.00

Stake Truck, Arcade, orange w/NP spoke wheels, 7½", G+, A..$350.00

Stake Truck, Arcade, 1929 model, gr w/NP spoke wheels & driver, 8½", EX, A $2,600.00

Stake Truck, Arcade, 1931 model, gr w/wht rubber tires & red spokes, NP driver, 11½", VG, A.........................$1,000.00

Taxi Cab, Arcade, lt bl w/wht rubber tires, NP grille, 6½", VG, A...$400.00

Taxi Cab, mk Century of Progress, Arcade, orange & blk w/wht rubber tires, NP grille, 6½", VG, A.................$600.00

Taxi Cab, mk Century of Progress, Arcade, orange w/blk trim, wht rubber tires, NP grille, 4½", G-, A...............$275.00

Traffic Car, Hubley, red & bl w/blk rubber tires & spoke wheels, w/driver, 11½", G, A.....................................$1,100.00

Transport Service Truck, Arcade, red cab & trailer w/wht rubber tires, 7⅛", G, A $175.00

Trolley, New York World's Fair, Arcade, bl w/wht top, 10½", EX, A...$825.00

Trolley, New York World's Fair, Arcade, bl w/wht top, 7", EX, A..$275.00

White Delivery Van, Arcade, lt bl w/NP disk wheels & driver, opening rear door, 8½", NM, A.........................$7,700.00

White Moving Van, Arcade, bl w/NP disk wheels, opening rear door, 13½", EX, A $7,700.00

Wrecker, Arcade, gr w/silver trim, blk rubber tires, wire toe crane, 5½", NM, A...$385.00

Wrecker, Arcade, orange w/blk rubber tires, NP crane, 5½", EX, A..$275.00

Wrecker, Arcade, red w/gr winch, NP spoke wheels, w/driver, 12", EX, A..$935.00

Wrecker, Arcade, red w/wht rubber tires, NP grille & crank, 6½", EX+, A $900.00

Wrecker, Champion, red C-style cab w/NP trim, wht rubber tires, 8¼", NMIB, A...$1,540.00

Wrecker, Kenton, green with white rubber tires, 7", D10, $275.00. (Photo courtesy Dunbar Gallery)

Stake Truck, Champion, green with white rubber tires, 7½", EX, D10, $450.00. (Photo courtesy Dunbar Gallery)

Stake Truck, Vindex, bl w/NP disk wheels, 9½", MIB, A..$9,900.00

Stake Truck, Vindex, red-orange w/NP disk wheels, 6", NM, A...$4,900.00

Standard Oil Gasoline Tanker, Kenton, red w/wht rubber tires, 12½", VG, A...$1,100.00

Studebaker Ice Truck, red w/wht rubber tires, 7", MIB, A ..$2,200.00

Taxi Cab, Arcade, blk & wht w/disk wheels & rear spare, 5", G-, A...$225.00

Wrecker, Kilgore, bl w/cream running boards & red crane, NP spoke wheels, 9", NM, A......................................$3,300.00

Wrecker, Vindex, bl w/red crane, NP disk wheels, w/orig saleman's sample tag & decal, 7", M, A......................$1,100.00

Yellow Cab, Arcade, orange & blk w/wht-pnt disk wheels & orange hubs, w/driver, 8", NM, A $1,200.00

Yellow Cab, Arcade, 1927 model, orange & blk w/NP disk wheels & orange hubs, 5½", EX, A $550.00

Yellow Cab, Arcade, 1932, orange & blk w/gold trim, wht disk wheels w/orange hubs, w/driver, 9", NM, A $1,540.00

Yellow Cab, Arcade, 1941 model, yel w/blk & silver trim, blk rubber tires, w/driver & passenger, 8¼", NMIB, A $2,400.00

Yellow Cab (Parmalee), Arcade, yel & blk w/wht rubber tires, 8¼", EX, A $5,500.00
10-Ton Stake Truck, Hubley, red w/wht rubber tires, NP grille & headlights, 8½", M, A............................$825.00

TRAINS

Freight Car No 4, Wilkins, orange w/gold stenciling, conductor on top, NM, A.....................................$900.00
Locomotive & Tender, mk Big Six, Welker & Crosby, mc, 11", G+, A...$200.00
Locomotive & Tender w/Open Car, Pat May 25 1880, red, 14½", VG+, A..$400.00
Pullman Deluxe Express, Arcade, lt bl w/silver roof, rubber tires, 16½", EX, A..............................$1,650.00
Pullman Railplane, Arcade, red, rubber tires, 8¾", EX, A...$350.00

Set, Hubley, EX, D10, $650.00.
(Photo courtesy Dunbar Gallery)

BOXED SETS

AC Williams, 2 fire trucks, coupe, roadster, sedan & stake truck w/interchangable bodies, MIB, A $1,100.00

Arcade, Farm Set (Montgomery Ward), complete, NMIB, A, $600.00.

Arcade, Fire Set, 2 pumper trucks, ladder truck, fire chief's car & ambulance, red w/wht rubber tires, MIB, A $2,200.00
Arcade, Fordson Tractors, various colors, set of 12, 3½", NMIB, A..$1,550.00
Arcade, racer, airplane, 2 fire trucks, wrecker, dump truck, stake truck, coupe, sedan & panel truck, MIB, A..........$4,900.00

Arcade, racer, wrecker, fire engine, coupe & sedan, MIB, A...$2,100.00
Arcade, Road Construction Set, 14 pcs, NMIB (no graphics on insert), A......................................$2,100.00
Arcade, Road Construction Set, 6 pcs, NMIB (graphics on insert), A...$1,300.00
Arcade, Road Construction Set, 6 pcs, NMIB (no graphics on insert), A...$825.00
Arcade, stake truck, dump truck, coupe & wrecker, mc w/NP spoke wheels, MIB, A...........................$350.00
Arcade, Transportation Set, Motor Express tractor & trailer, sedan w/trailer, bus & racer, silver & red, MIB, A .$2,100.00
Dent, Toyland's Treasure Chest, gasoline truck, stake truck & 2 coupes, various colors, EX (EX box), A $800.00

MISCELLANEOUS

Arcadia Airport, Arcade, wht-pnt wood w/bl stenciling & red roof finials, 2 airplanes, 12x7½", EX, A...................$550.00
Cream Separator w/Bucket, Arcade, blk w/NP trim, 5", MIB, A...$2,200.00
Fire House, Arcade, Engine Co No 99, 1941, wht-pnt wood w/red stenciled lettering, EX, A $600.00
Garage, Arcade, 2-car, wht-pnt wood w/gr stenciled windows, gr roof, 13x10", EX, A...............................$1,000.00
Gas Pump, Arcade, orange w/rope hose, NP crank turns & raises meter, 6½", EX, A..................................$850.00

Gas Station, Arcade, marked Gasoline-Motor Oils, 14x9", VG, A, $950.00.

Lily Dale Sled, J&E Stevens, gr w/yel trim & bl runners, emb lettering, 5", EX, A.................................$900.00
Polar Bear, Hubley, 1920s, 3", EX, A $175.00
Scales, Arcade, #4044, red & silver, w/weights, 4", MIB, A ...$550.00

Catalogs

In any area of collecting, old catalogs are a wonderful source for information. Toy collectors value buyers' catalogs, those from toy fairs, and Christmas 'wish books.' Montgomery Ward issued their first Christmas catalog in 1932, and Sears followed a year later. When they can be found, these 'first editions' in excellent condition are valued at a minimum of $200.00 each. Even later issues may sell for upwards of $75.00, since it's those from the '50s and '60s that contain the toys that are now so collectible.

Advisor: Bill Mekalian (M4).

American Flyer, 1949, G, G1 ....$25.00
American Miniature Railway Co, 1909, 24 pgs, EX, A ..$450.00
Aurora, 1970, M $120.00
Avalon Crafts & Activities, 1971, EX, M4 ....$10.00
Breyer Animal Creations, 1976, EX, M4 ....$20.00
Buddy L Train Sets, 1976, EX, M4 ....$50.00
Coleco Toys, 1972, EX, M4 ....$20.00
Colorforms, 1973, EX, M4 ....$10.00
Columbia Bicycles, 1920, EX, from $50 to $75.00
Corgi Toys, 1969, M $10.00
Fisher-Price Toys, 1950, EX $135.00
Furga Dolls, 1970, EX, M4 ....$50.00
Galoob, 1973, EX, M4 ....$30.00
Gilbert Toys/American Flyer Trains, 1950, 56 pgs, EX $50.00
Hasbro Romper Room, 1972, EX, M4 ....$50.00
Janex Toy Corp, 1973, EX, M4 ....$10.00
Marx Toys, 1972, EX, M4....................................$100.00
Marx 1965 Toy Line, NM $145.00
Movin' w/Mattel, 1976, EX, M4..........................$100.00
Ohio Art, 1974, Woody Woodpecker on cover, EX $50.00
Parker Bros Games & Toys, 1976, EX, M4 ....$80.00
Revell Toys, 1953, EX...$35.00

Schoenhut Toy and Doll Catalogue 1928 and Schoenhut's Marvelous Toys, The Humpty Dumpty Circus, VG, $100.00 each.

Strombecker Tootsietoy, 100th Anniversary, 1976, EX, M4 ..$100.00

Tinkertoys for 1924, EX, from $40.00 to $50.00.

(Photo courtesy Craig Strange)

Tinkertoys, 1926, EX, from $40 to $50.00
Tinkertoys, 1932, EX, from $40 to $50.00
Tonka, 1963, NM $100.00
Tootsietoy, 1968, NM $75.00
Tyco, 1975, EX, M4 ....$25.00
Vogue Dolls, 1978, EX..$40.00
William's Toys That are Out of This World, 1958, 435 pgs, EX, A $275.00

Cereal Boxes and Premiums

This is an area of collecting that attracts crossover interest from fans of advertising as well as character-related toys. What makes a cereal box interesting? Look for Batman, Huckleberry Hound, or a well-known sports figure like Larry Bird or Roger Maris on the front or back. Boxes don't have to be old to be collectible, but the basic law of supply and demand dictates that the older ones are going to be expensive! After all, who saved cereal boxes from 1910? By chance if Grandma did, the 1910 Corn Flakes box with a printed-on baseball game could get her $750.00. Unless you're not concerned with bugs, it will probably be best to empty the box and very carefully pull apart the glued flaps. Then you can store it flat. Be sure to save any prize that might have been packed inside. For more information we recommend *Cereal Box Bonanza, The 1950s, ID and Values* (Collector Books), and *Sixties Cereal Boxes and Premiums* by Scott Bruce.

Advisor: Scott Bruce (B14); Larry Blodget (B2), Post Cereal cars.

Other Sources: T2.

General Mills Cheerios, 1954, w/Lone Ranger comic book, EX...$300.00

General Mills Cheerios, 1957, Disneyland Adventure story & picture to color on back, EX.................................$100.00

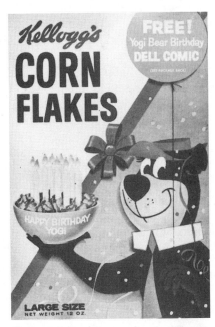

Kellogg's Corn Flakes, 1962, with Yogi Bear Birthday Dell Comic, EX, $300.00.
(Photo courtesy Scott Bruce)

General Mills Cheerios, 1958, Annette doll and outfits on back, EX, $300.00.
(Photo courtesy Scott Bruce)

General Mills Cocoa Puffs, 1959, conductor hat cutout on back, EX $50.00

General Mills Sir Grapefellow, biplane glider offer, NM, from $125 to...$200.00

General Mills Sugar Smiles, 1953, cut-out lips on back, EX ..$100.00

General Mills Trix, 1955, Tonto belt offer, EX $350.00

General Mills Trix, 1960, Corvair sweepstakes on back, EX ..$125.00

General Mills Wheaties, 1956, blackboard on back, EX ..$75.00

General Mills Wheaties, 1956, Mousketeer record offer, EX...$100.00

General Mills Wheaties, 1957, Lone Ranger or Tonto poster offer on back, EX $300.00

General Mills Wheaties, 1995, Larry Bird Commemorative, NM $15.00

Kellogg's All Stars, 1960, Huckleberry Hound cartoon cutouts on back, EX $125.00

Kellogg's Corn Flakes, 1955, Norman Rockwell girl on front, Tony Tiger dingle-dangle on back, EX $100.00

Kellogg's Corn Flakes, 1955, Superman belt & buckle offer, EX...$250.00

Kellogg's Corn Flakes, 1957-58, electric train offer, EX .$100.00

Kellogg's Fruity Pebbles, 1972, Flintmobile, NM..............$95.00

Kellogg's OKs, 1959-60, Big Otis Catapult game, EX.....$100.00

Kellogg's Pep, 1952, Tom Corbett, EX..........................$450.00

Kellogg's Pep Whole Wheat Flakes, Canadian, 1957, w/prop top, football player on front, EX..............................$50.00

Kellogg's Raisin Bran, 1950, Disney Joinies, EX.............$150.00

Kellogg's Rice Krispies, 1953, Howdy Doody doll offer, EX....$300.00

Kellogg's Rice Krispies, 1954, Howdy Doody & friends cut-out masks on back, EX...$350.00

Kellogg's Rice Krispies, 1955, w/Lady & the Tramp figures, EX.$125.00

Kellogg's Rice Krispies, 1958, Woody Woodpecker kazoo offer, EX $125.00

Kellogg's Rice Krispies, 1960, Woody Woodpecker bike contest, VG $45.00

Kellogg's Rice Krispies, 1973, Snap! Crackle! & Pop! towel & washcloth offer, VG...$25.00

Kellogg's Sugar Corn Pops, 1952, features Wild Bill Hickok w/cut-out derringer & badge on back, EX...............$150.00

Kellogg's Sugar Frosted Flakes, 1955, Mary Hartline magic doll offer, EX...$225.00

Kellogg's Sugar Pops, 1950s, Andy Devine as Jingles on front w/Make 'Em Ourself Moccasins on back, EX, A........$75.00

Kellogg's Sugar Pops, 1958, Wild Bill Hickok & Colt Six-Shooter offer, EX $225.00

Kellogg's Sugar Smacks, 1957, features Smaxey the Seal, chance to win Admiral TV on back, EX, $150.00.
(Photo courtesy Scott Bruce)

Kellogg's Sugar Smacks, 1953, features Paul Jung, EX $300.00

Kellogg's Sugar Smacks, 1956, w/Guy 'N Andy badge, EX .$175.00

Kellogg's Sugar Smacks, 1959, Smaxey the Seal cutouts on back, EX $100.00

Kellogg's Sugar Smacks, 1964, Quick Draw McGraw w/road race game on back, NM $350.00

Nabisco Rice Honeys, 1967, Bambi puppet show kit, EX.$175.00

Nabisco Shredded Wheat, 1956, Rin-Tin-Tin insignia patch, NM...$95.00

Nabisco Shredded Wheat Juniors, 1959, Tobor robot offer, EX $100.00

Nabisco Wheat Honeys, 1956, Buffalo Bee hummer toy on back, EX $100.00

Nabisco Wheat Honeys, 1957, w/plastic dinosaur, EX ...$100.00

Nabisco Wheat Honeys, 1964, w/Bert the Chimney Sweep pop-up toy, EX $150.00

Post Alpha Bits, 1960, Fury Adventure Kit offer, EX $150.00

Post Cornfetti, 1954, w/Captain Jolly comic book, EX ..$150.00

Post Crispy Critters, 1962, football trading cards on back, EX.$225.00

Post Grape-Nut Flakes, 1950, features Hopalong Cassidy, EX.$200.00

Post Grape-Nuts, 1967, Dr Dolittle's carnival, NM..........$75.00

Post Raisin Bran, 1950-51, w/Hopalong Cassidy badge, EX ..$400.00

Post Raisin Bran, 1953, w/Captain Video figure, EX......$350.00

Post Raisin Bran, 1988, California Raisins cassette offer, EX, W6 ....$15.00

Quaker Muffets Shredded Wheat, 1956, Sgt Preston 10-in-1 kit offer, EX $125.00

Quaker Puffed Rice, 1950, Sgt Preston Yukon Adventure cards, EX $150.00

Quaker Puffed Wheat, 1937, EX, $1,250.00 for sign and cereal box. (Photo courtesy Scott Bruce)

Quaker Puffed Wheat, 1951, features Gabby Hayes western gun collection, EX $200.00

Quaker Quisp, bank offer, M, from $600 to $750.00

PREMIUMS

Sure, the kids liked the taste of the cereal too, but in families with more than one child there was more clamoring over the prize inside than there was over the last bowlfull! In addition to the 'freebies' included in the boxes, many other items were made available — rings, decoders, watches, games, books, etc. — often for just mailing in boxtops or coupons. If these premiums weren't free, their prices were minimal. Most of them were easily broken, and children had no qualms about throwing them away, so few survive to the present. Who would have ever thought those kids would be trying again in the '90s to get their hands on those very same prizes, and at considerable more trouble and expense. Note: Only premiums that specifically relate to cereal companies or their character logos are listed here. Other character-related premiums are listed in the Premiums category.

Apple Jack, mug w/hat lid, 1967, plastic, VG $50.00

Boo Berry, figure, vinyl, 8", EX, from $200 to................$300.00

Buffalo Bee, bowl rider, 1960s, plastic, NM $10.00

Cap'n Crunch, binoculars, 1975, bl plastic, MIP $15.00

Cap'n Crunch, Bo'Sun whistle, 1964, plastic, 3", EX $10.00

Post's Sugar Crisp, 1954, Roy Rogers paint set offer, EX, $200.00.
(Photo courtesy Scott Bruce)

Post Sugar Crisp, 1955, Ted Williams patch offer, EX ...$350.00

Post Sugar Crisp, 1958, Mighty Mouse TV game, EX.......$95.00

Post Sugar Crisp, 1961, Looney Tunes character mask cutouts on back, EX...$100.00

Post Toasties, 1951, punch-out canoes on back, EX $50.00

Post Toasties, 1952-53, Roy Rogers pop-out card on back, EX.$300.00

Post Toasties, 1958, w/Li'l Abner cutout, VG $95.00

Post Toasties Corn Flakes, 1959, Linda Williams doll offer, EX..$85.00

Cap'n Crunch, coloring book, EX, T2.................$25.00
Cap'n Crunch, compass, 1966, 8", EX.................$45.00
Cap'n Crunch, hand puppet, 1966, any character, paper, 9", EX,
    ea.................$20.00
Cap'n Crunch, imprint set, EX, J2.................$45.00
Cap'n Crunch, ring, plastic figure, scarce, M, V1.........$300.00
Cap'n Crunch, Sea Cycle, MIB, V1.................$25.00
Cap'n Crunch, treasure chest bank, 1966, 6" L, EX.........$45.00

Cap'n Crunch, wiggle figures, 1969, EX, $50.00 each.
(Photo courtesy Scott Bruce)

Champy & Mr Fox, hand puppets, 1957, cloth & vinyl, 7½",
    EX, ea.................$50.00
Chex, secret agent ring, NM, C10.................$50.00
Cornelius C Sugarcoat, walking toy, 1959, plastic, 6", EX..$200.00
Count Chocula, figure, vinyl, 8", EX, from $200 to.......$300.00
Dig-'em, iron-on patch, 1974, glow-in-the-dark, MIP......$12.00
Dig-'em, secret decoder, MIP, V1.................$15.00
Frankenberry, figure, vinyl, 8", EX, from $200 to.........$300.00
Fruit Brute, figure, vinyl, 8", EX, from $200 to.............$300.00
Great Honey Crunchers, magnifying lens/blowpipe, moon
    orbiter, 1972, bl plastic, MIP.................$35.00
Honeycomb Kid, ring, 1966, 24-karat gold, EX.............$75.00
Huckleberry Hound, figure, 1959, plastic, several different, 1½"
    to 2", EX, ea.................$25.00
Huckleberry Hound, fun cards, 1959, several different, 3½", EX,
    ea.................$10.00
Kix Characters, trading cards, 1966, 3", EX, ea.................$5.00
Lucky Charms, bicycle propeller, plastic figure, EX, V1...$15.00
Marky Maypo, bank, 1960s, EX.................$100.00
Post Alpha Bits, bike streamers, 1970s, plastic, MIP.........$5.00
Post Alpha Bits, pocket printer, 1970s, plastic, MIP.........$5.00
Post Honeycomb, monster mitt, 1974, w/red eyeball, plastic, M.$15.00
Post Honeycomb, yo-yo, 1970s, glow-in-the-dark, MIP......$5.00
Post Raisin Bran, rings, Andy Gump, Perry Winkle, Smilin'
    Jack, etc, MIP, C10, ea.................$35.00

Post Vehicle, Ford, bl, F&F Mold, EX.................$40.00
Post Vehicle, Ford Custom Fordor, Magno Power, red, F&F
    Mold, M (orig mailer).................$50.00
Post Vehicle, 1954 Club Coupe, Sierra brn, F&F Mold, M.$30.00
Post Vehicle, 1954 Mercury 2-door, yel w/silver-pnt bumpers,
    F&F mold, EX.................$30.00
Post Vehicle, 1954 Mercury 4-door, yel, F&F Mold, rpl posts o/w
    EX.................$20.00
Post Vehicle, 1954 Rancho Wagon, Bloomfield, F&F Mold,
    EX.................$30.00
Post Vehicle, 1954 Sunliner, Torch red, F&F mold, EX...$30.00
Post Vehicle, 1955 Crown Victoria, Sea Sprite, F&F Mold, EX.$15.00
Post Vehicle, 1956 Ford/Fruehauf gasoline transport, aluminum,
    F&F Mold, EX.................$20.00
Post Vehicle, 1956 Greyhound Highway Traveler, bl, F&F
    Mold, rare, EX.................$35.00
Post Vehicle, 1956 Greyhound Super Sceni-cruiser, bl, F&F
    Mold, rare, EX.................$35.00
Post Vehicle, 1957 Custom 4-door, Inca gold, F&F Mold, M.$25.00
Post Vehicle, 1960 Plymouth Hardtop, Twilight bl, F&F Mold,
    EX.................$15.00
Quake, cavern helmet, 1967, plastic, 10", EX.............$225.00
Quake, doll, 1968, stuffed cloth, 11", EX.........................$75.00

Quake, ring, friendship, 1966, blue plastic, EX, $300.00.
(Photo courtesy Scott Bruce)

Quake, ring, leaping lava, 1966, gr & clear plastic, EX..$250.00
Quake, ring, world globe, 1966, red plastic, EX.............$400.00
Quisp, doll, 1968, stuffed cloth, 11", EX.........................$75.00
Quisp, laser light, 1969, plastic, 7", EX.........................$175.00
Quisp, propeller beanie, 1966, M, from $500 to.............$600.00
Quisp, ring, friendship, 1966, bl plastic, EX.................$600.00
Quisp, ring, meteorite, 1966, red & clear plastic, EX.....$200.00
Quisp, ring, space disk whistle, 1966, gr plastic, EX.......$200.00
Quisp, ring, space gun, 1966, red plastic, EX.................$200.00
Sgt Preston, Yukon Adventure cards, 1950, EX, B10, ea..$15.00
Sherman & Peabody, wiggle picture, 1960, 1", EX..........$10.00
Smaxey the Seal, pin-back button, 1957, 1" dia, EX........$10.00
Snap! Crackle! & Pop, Magic Color Cards, 1933, cb, NM (NM
    envelope).................$75.00

Snap! Crackle! & Pop!, hand puppets, 1950, cloth & vinyl, 8", EX, ea $40.00

Snap! Crackle! & Pop!, ring, 1950s, rubber face w/brass band, changes expressions when you spin dial, EX, J5.......$175.00

Tony the Tiger, doll, 1954, inflatable vinyl, 45", EX......$300.00

Tony the Tiger, iron-on patch, 1974, glow-in-the-dark, cloth, 2", MIP $12.00

Toucan Sam, bicycle license plate, 1973, bl plastic, 3x6", EX...$10.00

Toucan Sam, decoder, M (sealed), V1 ....$20.00

Toucan Sam, doll, 1964, stuffed cloth, 8", EX $30.00

Trix, rocket, 1969, plastic, spring-fired, 3", EX $25.00

Trix, wallet, w/flasher image of Trix rabbit & cereal box, M (sealed), V1 ....$15.00

Twinkles the Elephant, bank, 1960, red, 9", EX.............$350.00

Twinkles the Elephant, sponge, 1960-61, 4", EX..............$25.00

Woody Woodpecker, kazoo, 1958, red plastic, 6½", EX...$35.00

Character and Promotional Drinking Glasses

Once given away by fast-food chains and gas stations, a few years ago you could find these at garage sales everywhere for a dime or even less. Then, when it became obvious to collectors that these glass giveaways were being replaced by plastic, as is always the case when we realize no more (of anything) will be forthcoming, we all decided we wanted them. Since many were character-related and part of a series, we felt the need to begin to organize these garage-sale castaways, building sets and completing series. Out of the thousands available, the better ones are those with super heroes, sports stars, old movie stars, Star Trek, and Disney and Walter Lantz cartoon characters. Pass up those whose colors are worn and faded. Unless another condition or material is indicated in the description, values are for glass tumblers in mint condition. Cups are plastic unless noted otherwise.

There are some terms used in our listings that may be confusing if you're not familiar with this collecting field. 'Brockway' style tumblers are thick and heavy, and they taper at the bottom. 'Federal' is thinner, and top and diameters are equal. For more information we recommend *Collectible Drinking Glasses, Identification and Values*, by Mark E. Chase and Michael J. Kelly (Collector Books); and *The Collector's Guide to Cartoon and Promotional Drinking Glasses* by John Hervey. See also Clubs, Newsletters, and Other Publications.

Advisor: Mark E. Chase (C2).

Other Sources: B3, C1, C10, C11, D9, D11, J2, H11, I2, J7, M8, M16, P3, P6, P10, R2, S20, T2.

Abbott & Costello, see Arby's Actor Series

Al Capp, Brockway, 1975, 16-oz, flat bottom, Joe Btsptflk, from $60 to $80.00

Al Capp, Brockway, 1975, 16-oz, flat bottom, Mammy, Pappy, Sadie, Lil' Abner, Daisy Mae, ea, from $50 to $70.00

Animal Crackers, Chicago Tribune/NY News Syndicate, 1978, Louis, scarce, from $25 to $35.00

Animal Crackers, Chicago Tribune/NY News Syndicate, 1978, Lyle Dodo, Gnu, Lana, Eugene, ea, from $7 to $10.00

Annie Oakley, see Western Heroes

Apollo Series, Marathon Oil, Apollo 11, Apollo 12, Apollo 13, Apollo 14, ea, from $2 to $4.00

Apollo Series, Marathon Oil, carafe, from $6 to $10.00

Aquaman, see Super Heroes

Arby's, Actor Series, 1979, 6 different, smoke-colored glass w/blk & wht images, silver trim, numbered, ea, from $7 to $10.00

Arby's, Bicentennial Cartoon Character Series, 1976, 10 different, 5", ea, from $18 to $25.00

Arby's, Bicentennial Cartoon Character Series, 1976, 10 different, 6", ea, from $20 to $30.00

Arby's, see also specific name or series

Archies, Welch's, 1971, 6 different w/many variations, ea .$3.00

Archies, Welch's, 1973, 6 different w/many variations, ea .$3.00

Avon, Christmas Issues, 1969-72, 4 different, ea, from $2 to....$5.00

Baby Huey & Related Characters, see Harvey Cartoon Characters

Batman & Related Characters, see Super Heroes

Battlestar Galactica, Universal Studios, 1979, 4 different, ea, from $7 to $10.00

BC Ice Age, Arby's, 1981, 6 different, ea, from $3 to $5.00

Beatles, Dairy Queen, group photo & signatures in wht starburst, gold trim, Canadian, from $95 to $125.00

Beverly Hillbillies, CBS promotion, 1963, rare, NM, A.$200.00

Buffalo Bill, see Western Heroes or Wild West Series

Bugs Bunny & Related Characters, see Warner Bros

Bullwinkle, Rocky & Related Characters, see Warner Bros or PAT Ward

Burger Chef, Burger Chef & Jeff, Now We're Glassified!, from $15 to $25.00

Burger Chef, Endangered Species Collector's Series, 1978, Tiger, Orang-Utan, Panda, Bald Eagle, ea, from $5 to $7.00

Burger Chef, Friendly Monsters Series, 1977, 6 different, ea, from $20 to $35.00

Burger Chef, Presidents & Patriots, 1975, 6 different, ea, from $7 to $10.00

Burger King, Collector Series, 1979, 5 different Burger King characters featuring Burger Thing, etc, ea, from $4 to.$6.00

Burger King, Dallas Cowboys, Dr Pepper, 6 different, ea, from $7 to $15.00

Burger King, Have It Your Way 1776-1979 Series, 1976, 4 different, ea, from $4 to $6.00

Burger King, see also specific name or series

Calamity Jane, see Wild West Series

Captain America, see Super Heroes

Casper the Friendly Ghost & Related Characters, see Arby's Bicentennial or Harvey Cartoon Characters

Charlie McCarthy & Edgar Bergen, Libbey, 1930s, set of 8, M (EX illus display box), A $600.00

Chilly Willy, see Water Lantz

Cinderella, Disney/Libbey, 1950s-1960s, set of 8............$120.00

Cinderella, see also Disney Collector's Series or Disney Film Classics

Clarabell, see Howdy Doody

Currier & Ives, Arby's, 1975-76, 4 different, titled, ea, from $3 to $5.00

Currier & Ives, Arby's, 1976, 4 different, numbered, ea, from $3 to $5.00

Daffy Duck, see Warner Bros

Daisy Mae, see Al Capp

Dick Tracy, 1940s, frosted, 8 different characters, 3" or 5", ea, from $50 to $75.00

Dilly Dally, see Howdy Doody

Dinosaur Series, see Welch's

Disney Characters, 1936, Mickey, Minnie, Donald, Pluto, Clarabelle, Horace, F Bunny, 4¼" or 4¾", ea, from $30 to.$50.00

Disney Characters, 1989, frosted juice, Mickey, Minnie, Donald, Daisy, Goofy or Scrooge face, ea, from $5 to...............$8.00

Disney Characters, 1990, frosted tumblers, Mickey, Minnie, Donald, Daisy, Goofy, or Scrooge face images, ea, from $5 to $8.00

Disney Collector Series, Burger King, 1994, mc images on clear plastic, 8 different, MIB, ea..$3.00

Disney Film Classics, McDonald's/Coca-Cola/Canada, Peter Pan, Cinderella, Fantasia or Snow White & the Seven Dwarfs, ea..$15.00

Disney's All-Star Parade, 1939, 10 different, ea, from $40 to .$75.00

Disney, see also Wonderful World of Disney or specific character

Domino's Pizza, Avoid the Noid, 1988, 4 different, ea $7.00

Donald Duck, Donald Duck Cola, 1960s-70s, from $15 to..$20.00

Donald Duck or Daisy, see also Disney or Mickey Mouse (Happy Birthday)

Dudley Do-Right, see Arby's Bicentennial or PAT Ward

Dynomutt, see Hanna-Barbera

Elmer Fudd, see Warner Bros

Elsie the Cow, Borden, Elsie & Family in 1976 Bicentennial parade, red, wht & bl graphics, from $5 to...................$7.00

Elsie the Cow, Borden, 1950s, wht head image on waisted style, from $15 to $20.00

Elsie the Cow, Borden, 1960s, yel daisy image, from $10 to..$12.00

Empire Strikes Back, see Star Wars Trilogy

ET, Army & Air Force Exchange Service, 1982, 4 different mc images, rnd bottom, ea, from $5 to...........................$10.00

ET, Pepsi/MCA Home Video, 1988, 6 different, ea, from $15 to..$25.00

ET, Pizza Hut, 1982, 4 different, ftd, from $2 to..................$4.00

Fantasia, see Disney Film Classics or Mickey Mouse (Through the Years)

Flintstone Kids, Pizza Hut, 1986, 4 different, ea, from $2 to...$4.00

Flintstones, Welch's, 1962 (6 different), 1963 (2 different), 1964 (6 different), ea, from $8 to $12.00

Flintstone Kids, Pizza Hut, 1986, Betty, from $2.00 to $4.00.

Flintstones, see also Hanna-Barbera

Foghorn Leghorn, see Warner Bros

Ghostbusters II, Sunoco/Canada, 1989, 6 different, ea, from $5 to $8.00

Goonies, Godfather's Pizza/Warner Bros, 1985, 4 different, from $4 to $8.00

Great Muppet Caper, McDonald's, 1981, 4 different, 6", ea ..$2.00

Green Arrow, see Super Heroes

Green Lantern, see Super Heroes

Hanna-Barbera, Pepsi, 1977, Brockway, Yogi/Huck, Josie/Pussycats, Mumbly, Scooby, Flintstones, Dynomutt, ea, from $20 to $35.00

Hanna-Barbera, 1960s, jam glasses featuring Flintstones, Yogi Bear, Quick Draw, Cindy Bear, Huck, rare, ea, from $75 to $110.00

Harvey Cartoon Characters, Pepsi, 1970s, Richie Rich, static pose, from $15.00 to $25.00.

Happy Days, Dr Pepper, 1977, Fonzie or Richie, ea, from $8 to $12.00

Happy Days, Dr Pepper, 1977, Ralph, Joanie, Potsie, ea, from $8 to $12.00

Happy Days, Dr Pepper/Pizza Hut, 1977, Fonzie or Richie, ea, from $10 to.......................................$15.00

Happy Days, Dr Pepper/Pizza Hut, 1977, Ralph, Joanie, Potsie, ea, from $8 to.......................................$12.00

Harvey Cartoon Characters, Pepsi, 1970s, action pose, Casper, Baby Huey, Wendy, Hot Stuff, ea, from $8 to $15.00

Harvey Cartoon Characters, Pepsi, 1970s, static pose, Casper, Baby Huey, Wendy, Hot Stuff, ea, from $12 to $20.00

Harvey Cartoon Characters, Pepsi, 1970s, static pose, Sad Sack, scarce, from $25 to.....................................$35.00

Harvey Cartoon Characters, see also Arby's Bicentennial Series

He-Man & Related Characters, see Masters of the Universe

Hopalong Cassidy's Western Series, ea, from $25 to $30.00

Hot Dog Castle, Collector Series, 1977, Abilene Past, Abilene Present, Abilene Future, ea, from $6 to.......................$8.00

Hot Stuff, see Harvey Cartoon Characters or Arby's Bicentennial

Howard the Duck, see Super Heroes

Howdy Doody, Welch's/Kagran, 1950s, 6 different, emb bottom, ea, from $15 to..$20.00

Huckleberry Hound, see Hanna-Barbera

Incredible Hulk, see Super Heroes

Indiana Jones & the Temple of Doom, 7-Up (w/4 different sponsers), 1984, set of 4, ea, from $8 to $15.00

Indiana Jones: The Last Crusade, wht plastic, 4 different, ea, from $2 to..$4.00

James Bond 007, 1985, 4 different, ea, from $10 to $15.00

Joe Btsptflk, see Al Capp

Joker, see Super Heroes

Josie & the Pussycats, see Hanna-Barbera

Jungle Book, Disney/Canada, 1966, 6 different, numbered, 4⅞", ea, from $40 to..$75.00

Jungle Book, Disney/Canada, 1966, 6 different, numbered, 6½", ea, from $30 to..$60.00

Jungle Book, Disney/Pepsi, 1970s, Bagheera or Shere Kahn, unmk, ea, from $60 to.......................................$90.00

Jungle Book, Disney/Pepsi, 1970s, Mowgli, unmk, from $40 to $50.00

Jungle Book, Disney/Pepsi, 1970s, Rama, unmk, from $50 to $60.00

Keebler, Soft Batch Cookies, 1984, 4 different, ea, from $7 to $10.00

Kellogg's, 1977, 6 different, Tony, Toucan Sam, Big Yella, Snap! Crackle! & Pop!, Dig 'Em, Tony Jr, ea, from $7 to....$10.00

King Kong, Coca-Cola/Dino De Laurentis Corp, 1976, from $5 to $8.00

Laurel & Hardy, see Arby's Actor Series

Leonardo TTV Collector Series, Pepsi, Underdog, Go-Go Gophers, Sweet Polly, Simon Bar Sinister, 6", ea, from $15 to $25.00

Leonardo TTV Collector Series, Pepsi, Underdog, Sweet Polly, Simon Bar Sinister, 5", ea, from $8 to $15.00

Leonardo TTV, see also Arby's Bicentennial Series

Li'l Abner & Related Characters, see Al Capp

Little Rascals, see Arby's Actor Series

Lone Ranger, see Western Heroes

Mae West, see Arby's Actor Series

Mark Twain Country Series, Burger King, 1985, 4 different, ea, from $8 to...$10.00

Masters of the Universe, Mattel, 1983, Teels, He-Man, Skeletor, Man-at-Arms, ea, from $5 to.................................$10.00

Masters of the Universe, Mattel, 1986, Orko, He-Man/Battle Cat, Skeletor/Panthor, Man-at-Arms, ea, from $3 to ..$5.00

McDonald's, All-Time Greatest Steelers Team, 1982, 5 different, ea, from $5 to...$8.00

McDonald's, McDonaldland Action Series, 1977, 6 different, ea $5.00

McDonald's, McDonaldland Collector Series, 1970s, 6 different, ea $4.00

McDonald's, McVote, 1986, 3 different, ea, from $4 to......$6.00

MGM Collector Series, Pepsi, 1975, Tom, Jerry, Tuffy, Barney, Droopy or Spike, ea, from $10 to.............................$15.00

Mickey Mouse, Happy Birthday, Pepsi, 1978, Daisy & Donald, from $12 to...$15.00

Mickey Mouse, Happy Birthday, Pepsi, 1978, Horace & Clarabelle, from $15 to...$20.00

Mickey Mouse, Happy Birthday, Pepsi, 1978, Mickey, Minnie, Donald, Goofy, Pluto, Uncle Scrooge, ea, from $6 to..$10.00

Mickey Mouse, Mickey's Christmas Carol, Coca-Cola, 1982, 3 different, ea $10.00

Mickey Mouse, Through the Years, K-Mart, glass mugs w/4 different images (1928, 1937, 1940, 1955), ea, from $3 to $5.00

Mickey Mouse, Through the Years, Sunoco/Canada, 1988, 6 different (1928, 1938, 1940, 1955, 1983 & 1988), ea, from $6 to $10.00

Mickey Mouse, see also Disney Characters

Mister Magoo, Polomer Jelly, many different variations & styles, ea, from $25 to...$35.00

NFL, Mobil Oil, helmets on wht bands, Redskins, Bills, Steelers, Eagles, Buccaneers, low, flat bottom, ea, from $3 to $5.00

NFL, Mobil Oil, helmets on colored bands, Colts, Oilers, Steelers, Cowboys, low, ftd, ea, from $2 to..........................$4.00

Nightmare Before Christmas, plastic, M, H9 ....$45.00

Norman Rockwell, Saturday Evening Post Series, Arby's, early 1980s, 6 different, numbered, ea, from $2 to...............$4.00

Norman Rockwell, Saturday Evening Post Series, Country Time Lemonade, 4 different, w/authorized logo, ea, from $3 to..$5.00

Norman Rockwell, Saturday Evening Post Series, Country Time Lemonade, 4 different, no logo, ea, from $3 to $5.00

Norman Rockwell, Summer Series, Arby's, 1987, 4 different, tall, ea, from $3 to...$5.00

Norman Rockwell, Winter Series, Arby's/Pepsi, 1979, 4 different, short, ea, from $3 to.......................................$5.00

PAT Ward, Pepsi, late 1970s, action pose, Dudley in canoe, Rocky in circus, Bullwinkle w/balloons, 5", ea, from $8 to...$10.00

PAT Ward, Pepsi, late 1970s, static pose, Boris, Natasha, Mr Peabody, 5", ea, from $10 to...................................$15.00

PAT Ward, Pepsi, late 1970s, static pose, Boris & Natasha, 6", from $20 to...$25.00

PAT Ward, Pepsi, late 1970s, static pose, Bullwinkle, brn lettering, no Pepsi logo, 6", from $20 to $25.00

PAT Ward, Pepsi, late 1970s, static pose, Bullwinkle, wht or blk lettering, 6", from $15 to $20.00

PAT Ward, Pepsi, late 1970s, static pose, Bullwinkle, 5", from $25 to $30.00

PAT Ward, Pepsi, late 1970s, static pose, Dudley Do-Right, blk lettering, 6", from $15 to $20.00

PAT Ward, Pepsi, late 1970s, static pose, Dudley Do-Right, red lettering, no Pepsi logo, 6", from $15 to $20.00

PAT Ward, Pepsi, late 1970s, static pose, Dudley Do-Right, 5", from $15 to $20.00

PAT Ward, Pepsi, late 1970s, static pose, Rocky, brn lettering, no Pepsi logo, 6", from $20 to $25.00

PAT Ward, Pepsi, late 1970s, static pose, Rocky, wht or blk lettering, 6", from $15 to $20.00

PAT Ward, Pepsi, late 1970s, static pose, Rocky, 5", from $20 to $25.00

PAT Ward, Pepsi, late 1970s, static pose, Snidley Whiplash, wht or blk lettering, 6", from $15 to $20.00

PAT Ward, Pepsi, late 1970s, static pose, Snidley Whiplash, 5", from $10 to $15.00

PAT Ward Collector Series, Holly Farms Restaurants, 1975, Bullwinkle, Rocky, Natasha, Boris, ea, from $30 to ...$50.00

PAT Ward, see also Arby's Bicentennial Series

Peanuts Characters, Camp Snoopy, McDonald's, 1983, wht plastic, Lucy or Snoopy, ea, from $5 to $8.00

Peanuts Characters, I Have a Strange Team, Let's Break for Lunch!, I Got It! I Got It!, plastic, ea, from $5 to $8.00

Peanuts Characters, Kraft, 1988, Snoopy in pool, Lucy on swing, Snoopy on surfboard, Charlie Brown flying kite, ea.....$2.00

Peanuts Characters, Snoopy for President, Dolly Madison Bakery, 4 different, ea, from $4 to $6.00

Peanuts Characters, Snoopy sitting on lemon or Snoopy sitting by lg red apple, pedestal bottom, ea, from $2 to $3.00

Peanuts Characters, Snoopy Sport Series, Dolly Madison Bakeriy, 4 different, ea, from $4 to $6.00

Penguin, see Super Heroes

Pepsi, Historical Advertising Posters, 1979, 4 different, blk & wht, ea, from $8 to $10.00

Pepsi, Night Before Christmas, 1982-83, 4 different, ea, from $4 to $6.00

Pepsi, Twelve Days of Christmas, 1976, ea, from $1 to $3.00

Pepsi, see also specific names or series

Peter Pan, see Disney Film Classics

Pinocchio, Dairy Promo/Libbey, 1938-40, 12 different, ea, from $15 to $25.00

Pinocchio, see also Disney Collector's Series or Wonderful World of Disney

Pluto, see Disney Characters

Pocahontas, Burger King, 1995, 4 different, MIB, ea $3.00

Popeye, Kollect-A-Set, Coca-Cola, 1975, Popeye, from $7 to ...$10.00

Popeye, Kollect-A-Set, Coca-Cola, 1975, 6 different, any except Popeye, ea, from $5 to $7.00

Popeye, Pals, Popeye's Famous Fried Chicken, 1979, 4 different, ea, from $10 to $20.00

Popeye, 10th Anniversary Series, Popeye's Famous Fried Chicken/Pepsi, 1982, 4 different, ea, from $10 to $15.00

Porky Pig, see Looney Tunes/Warner Bros

Quick Draw McGraw, see Hanna-Barbera

Rescuers, Pepsi, 1977, Brockway tumbler, Brutus & Nero, Evinrude, Orville, Bernard, Bianca, Penny, ea, from $8 to..$15.00

Rescuers, Pepsi, 1977, Brockway tumblers, Madame Medusa, from $25 to $30.00

Return of the Jedi, see Star Wars Trilogy

Richie Rich, see Harvey Cartoon Characters

Riddler, see Super Heroes

Ringling Bros Circus Clowns Series, Pepsi, 1980s, 8 different, ea $12.00

Ringling Bros Circus Poster Series, Pepsi, 1980s, 6 different, ea $20.00

Road Runner & Related Characters, see Warner Bros

Robin, see Super Heroes

Rocky & Bullwinkle, see Arby's Bicentennial or PAT Ward

Roy Rogers Restaurant, 1883-1983 logo, from $5 to $7.00

Sad Sack, see Harvey Cartoon Characters

Sadie Hawkins, see Al Capp

Scooby Doo, see Hanna-Barbera

Sleeping Beauty, American, late 1950s, 6 different, ea, from $15 to $20.00

Sleeping Beauty, Canadian, late 1950s, 12 different, ea, from, $20 to $25.00

Smurf's, Hardee's, 1982, 8 different, ea, from $1 to $3.00

Smurf's, Hardee's, 1983, 6 different, ea, from $1 to $3.00

Snidley Whiplash, see PAT Ward

Snoopy & Related Characters, see Peanuts Characters

Snow White & the Seven Dwarfs, Bosco, 1938, ea, from $25 to $45.00

Snow White & the Seven Dwarfs, Libbey, 1937-38, ea, from $15 to $24.00

Snow White & the Seven Dwarfs, Libbey, 1937-38, verses on back, various colors, 8 different, ea, from $60 to $80.00

Snow White & the Seven Dwarfs, see also Disney Collector's Series or Disney Film Classics

Spider-Man or Spider-Woman, see Super Heroes

Star Trek, Dr Pepper, 1976, 4 different, ea, from $20 to...$25.00

Star Trek, Dr Pepper, 1978, 4 different, ea, from $30 to...$40.00

Star Wars Trilogy: Empire Strikes Back, Burger King/Coca-Cola, 1980, Luke Skywalker, from $7.00 to $10.00.

Star Trek II: The Search for Spock, Taco Bell, 1984, 4 different, ea, from $3 to $5.00

Star Trek: The Motion Picture, Coca-Cola, 1980, 3 different, ea, from $10 to...$15.00

Star Wars Trilogy: Empire Strikes Back, Burger King/Coca-Cola, 1980, 4 different, ea, from $7 to $10.00

Star Wars Trilogy: Return of the Jedi, Burger King/Coca-Cola, 1983, 4 different, ea, from $6 to $8.00

Star Wars Trilogy: Star Wars, Burger King/Coca-Cola, 1977, 4 different, ea, from $12 to $15.00

Sunday Funnies, 1976, Broom Hilda, from $100 to........$150.00

Sunday Funnies, 1976, Orphan Annie, Smilin' Jack, Moon Mullins, Gasoline Alley, Terry & Pirates, Brenda Starr, ea, from $8 to $15.00

Super Heroes, Marvel, 1978, Federal tumbler, Captain America, Hulk, Spider-Man, Thor, ea, from $100 to $150.00

Super Heroes, Marvel, 1978, Federal tumbler, Spider-Woman, from $100 to $250.00

Super Heroes, Marvel/7-Eleven, 1977, Captain America, Fantastic Four, Howard the Duck, Thor, ea, from $20 to $35.00

Super Heroes, Marvel/7-Eleven, 1977, Federal tumbler, Amazing Spider-Man, from $30 to $45.00

Super Heroes, Marvel/7-Eleven, 1977, Incredible Hulk, from $25 to $35.00

Super Heroes, Pepsi Super (Moon) Series/DC Comics, 1976, Green Arrow, from $20 to $30.00

Super Heroes, Pepsi Super (Moon) Series/DC Comics, 1976, Riddler, Green Lantern, Joker, Penguin, ea, from $40 to..$60.00

Super Heroes, Pepsi Super (Moon) Series/DC Comics or NPP, 1976, Batman, Batgirl, Robin, Shazam!, ea, from $10 to $15.00

Super Heroes, Pepsi Super (Moon) Series/NPP, 1976, Riddler, Green Lantern, Joker, Penguin, ea, from $20 to $40.00

Superman, NPP/M Polanar & Son, 1964, 6 different, various colors, 4¼" or 5¾", ea, from $20 to............................$35.00

Superman, see also Super Heroes, Pepsi Super (Moon) Series

Sylvester the Cat, see Warner Bros

Tasmanian Devil, see Warner Bros

Tom & Jerry & Related Characters, see MGM Collector Series

Tweety Bird, see Looney Tunes or Warner Bros

Underdog & Related Characters, see Arby's Bicentennial or Leonardo TTV

Universal Monsters, Universal Studio, 1980, ftd, Frankenstein, Mummy, Mutant, Wolfman, Dracula, Creature, ea, from $75 ....$125.00

Urchins, Coca-Cola/American Greetings, 1976-78, swimming, baseball, skating, tennis, golf, bicycling, ea, from $3 to .$5.00

Walter Lantz, Pepsi, 1970s, Chilly Willy or Wally Walrus, ea, from $35 to...$55.00

Walter Lantz, Pepsi, 1970s, Cuddles, from $60 to.............$80.00

Walter Lantz, Pepsi, 1970s, Space Mouse, from $150 to..$250.00

Walter Lantz, Pepsi, 1970s, Woody Woodpecker, from $10 to $20.00

Walter Lantz, Pepsi, 1970s-80s, Anty/Miranda, Chilly/Smedley, Wally/Homer, Cuddles/Oswald, ea, from $20 to........$30.00

Walter Lantz, Pepsi, 1970s-80s, Buzz Buzzard/Space Mouse, from $20 to $30.00

Walter Lantz, Pepsi, 1970s-80s, Woody Woodpecker/Knothead & Splinter, ea, from $15 to...$20.00

Walter Lantz, see also Arby's Bicentennial Series

Warner Bros, Arby's, 1988, Adventures Series, ftd, 4 different, Bugs, Daffy, Porky, Sylvester & Tweety, ea, from $35 to.........$45.00

Warner Bros, Marriott's Great America, 1989, 4 different, Porky, Bugs, Taz, Sylvester, ea, from $5 to.................$10.00

Warner Bros, Marriott's Great America, 1975, 12-oz, 6 different, Bugs & related characters, ea, from $25 to.................$30.00

Warner Bros, Pepsi, 1973, Brockway 12-oz tumbler, Daffy, Bugs, Tweety, Porky, Sylvester, Road Runner, ea, from $10 to..$15.00

Warner Bros, Pepsi, 1973, Federal 16-oz tumbler, Bugs Bunny, wht lettering, from $8 to...$12.00

Warner Bros, Pepsi, 1973, Federal 16-oz tumbler, Cool Cat, blk lettering, from $10 to..$15.00

Warner Bros, Pepsi, 1973, Federal 16-oz tumbler, Elmer Fudd, wht lettering, from $5 to...$8.00

Universal Monsters, Universal Studios, Frankenstein, from $50.00 to $75.00.

Warner Bros, Pepsi, 1976, Sylvester and Tweety, Interaction series, from $5.00 to $10.00.

Warner Bros, Pepsi, 1973, Federal 16-oz tumbler, Henry Hawk, blk lettering, from $25 to..$40.00

Warner Bros, Pepsi, 1973, Federal 16-oz tumbler, Speedy Gonzales, blk lettering, from $6 to $10.00

Warner Bros, Pepsi, 1973, wht plastic, 6 different, Bugs, Daffy, Porky, Sylvester, Tweety, Road Runner, ea, from $3 to.$5.00

Warner Bros, Pepsi, 1976, Interaction, Beaky Buzzard & Cool Cat w/kite, or Taz & Porky w/fishing pole, from $8 to........$10.00

Warner Bros, Pepsi, 1976, Interaction, Bugs & Yosemite w/cannon, Yosemite & Speedy Gonzales panning gold, ea, from $10 to $15.00

Warner Bros, Pepsi, 1976, Interaction, others from $5 to.$10.00

Warner Bros, Pepsi, 1979, Collector's Series, rnd bottom, Bugs, Daffy, Porky, Sylvester, Tweety, Road Runner, ea, $7 to .$10.00

Warner Bros, Welch's, 1974, action poses, 8 different, sayings around top, ea, from $2 to...$4.00

Warner Bros, Welch's, 1976-77, 8 different, names around bottom, ea, from $5 to $7.00

WC Fields, see Arby's Actor Series

Welch's, Dinosaur Series, 1989, 4 different, ea $2.00

Welch's, see also Archies, Howdy Doody or Warner Bros

Wendy's, Clara Peller (Where's the Beef?) or Clara Peller (no phrase), ea, from $4 to $6.00

Wendy's, Cleveland Browns, Dr Pepper, 1981, 4 different, ea, from $5 to...$8.00

Western Heroes, Annie Oakley, Buffalo Bill, Wild Bill Hickok, Wyatt Earp, ea, from $8 to $12.00

Western Heroes, Lone Ranger, from $10 to......................$15.00

Wild Bill Hickok, see Western Heroes

Wild West Series, Coca-Cola, Buffalo Bill, Calamity Jane, ea, from $10 to...$15.00

Wile E Coyote, see Warner Bros

Winnie the Pooh, Sears/WDP, 1970s, 4 different, ea, from $15 to $25.00

Wizard of Oz, Coca-Cola/Krystal, 1989, 50th Anniversary Series, 6 different, ea, from $10 to...........................$15.00

Wizard of Oz, Swift's, 1950s-60s, fluted bottom, Flying Monkeys or Emerald City, ea, from $15 to $20.00

Wizard of Oz, Swift's, 1950s-60s, fluted bottom, Glinda, from $15 to $25.00

Wizard of Oz, Swift's, 1950s-60s, fluted bottom, Wicked Witch, from $35 to..$50.00

Wonder Woman, see Super Heroes

Wonderful World of Disney, Pepsi, 1980s, Snow White, Pinocchio, Alice, Lady & the Tramp, Bambi, 101 Dalmatians, ea $25.00

Woody Woodpecker & Related Characters, see Arby's Bicentennial or Walter Lantz

Wyatt Earp, see Western Heroes

Yogi Bear, see Hanna-Barbera

Yosemite Sam, see Warner Bros

Ziggy, 7-Up Collector Series, 4 different, ea, from $4 to.....$7.00

Character Bobbin' Heads

Frequently referred to as nodders, these papier-mache dolls reflect accurate likenesses of the characters they portray and have become popular collectibles. Made in Japan throughout the 1960s, they were sold as souvenirs at Disney, Universal Studios, and Six Flags amusement parks, and they were often available at roadside concessions as well. Papier-mache was was used until the mid-'70s when ceramic composition came into use. They were very susceptible to cracking and breaking, and it's difficult to find mint specimens — little wonder, since these nodders were commonly displayed on car dashboards!

Our values are for nodders in near-mint condition. To calculate values for examples in very good condition, reduce our prices by 25% to 40%.

Advisors: Matt and Lisa Adams (A7).

Andy Griffith, 1992, ceramic, NM, J6 ....$75.00
Barney Fife, 1992, ceramic, NM, J6................................$75.00
Beetle Bailey, NM, A7, from $100 to............................$150.00
Bugs Bunny, NM, A7, from $100 to..............................$175.00
Charlie Brown, Japan, ceramic w/gr baseball cap & mitt, NM, A7 ....$60.00
Charlie Brown, sq blk base, NM......................................$95.00
Charlie Brown, 1970s, no base, sm, NM, A7 ....$45.00
Colonel Sanders, 2 different styles, NM, A7, ea from $100 to $125.00
Danny Kaye, kissing, NM, A7..$100.00
Danny Kaye & Girl, kissing, NM, A7, pr.......................$150.00
Dobie Gillis, NM, A7, from $250 to $300.00
Donald Duck, Walt Disney World, sq wht base, NM, A7 ..$75.00
Donald Duck, 1970s, rnd gr base, NM, A7 ....$75.00
Donny Osmond, wht jumpsuit w/microphone, NM, A7, from $100 to...$150.00
Dr Ben Casey, NM, A7, from $100 to............................$125.00
Dr Kildare, A7, from $100 to $125.00
Dumbo, rnd red base, NM, A7 ....$100.00
Elmer Fudd, NM, A7, from $100 to $175.00
Foghorn Leghorn, NM, A7, from $100 to.......................$175.00
Goofy, Disneyland, arms at side, sq wht base, NM, A7 ....$75.00
Goofy, Walt Disney World, arms folded, sq wht base, NM, A7 ....$75.00

Hobo and China Man, Japan, 1960s, composition, NM, $65.00 each. (Photo courtesy June Moon)

Linus, Japan, ceramic, baseball catcher w/gr cap, NM, A7 ..$60.00
Linus, Lego, sq blk base, NM, A7.....................................$95.00
Little Audrey, NM, A7, from $100 to............................$150.00
Lt Fuzz (Beetle Bailey), NM, A7, from $100 to.............$150.00
Lucy (Peanuts), Japan, ceramic, gr baseball cap & bat, NM,
    A7 ....$60.00

Phantom of the Opera and Wolfman, square base, rare, NM, $500.00 each. (Photo courtesy Matt and Lisa Adams)

Lucy (Peanuts), Lego, square black base, NM, $95.00.
(Photo courtesy June Moon)

Schroeder (Peanuts), Lego, lg, NM $95.00
Sgt Snorkel (Beetle Bailey), NM, A7, from $100 to $150.00
Smokey the Bear, w/shovel, rnd base, NM, A7, from $125 to...$200.00
Smokey the Bear, w/shovel, sq base, NM, A7, from $125 to $200.00
Snoopy, as Flying Ace, 1970s, no base, NM, A7 ....$45.00
Snoopy, as Joe Cool, 1970s, no base, sm, NM, A7............$45.00
Snoopy, in Christmas outfit, 1970s, no base, sm, NM, A7 .$45.00
Snoopy, Japan, ceramic, gr baseball cap & mitt, NM, A7 ..$60.00

Lucy (Peanuts), 1970s, no base, sm, NM, A7 ....$45.00
Mammy (Dogpatch USA), NM, A7 ....$75.00
Mary Poppins, Disneyland, 1960s, wood, w/umbrella & satchel,
    5¾", M..$95.00
Maynard Krebs (Dobie Gillis), holds bongos, NM, A7, from
    $250 to...$350.00
Mickey Mouse, Disneyland, red, wht & bl outfit, sq wht base,
    NM, A7 ....$100.00
Mickey Mouse, Walt Disney World, bl shirt & red pants, NM,
    A7 ....$75.00
Mickey Mouse, yel shirt & red pants, rnd gr base, NM, A7....$75.00
Mr Peanut, moves at waist, w/cane, NM, A7, from $150 to.$200.00
New York World's Fair Boy & Girl, kissing, NM, A7 ....$125.00
Oodles the Duck (Bozo the Clown), NM, A7, from $150 to .$200.00
Pappy (Dogpatch USA), NM, A7...................................$75.00
Peppermint Patti, Japan, ceramic, gr baseball cap & bat, NM,
    A7 ....$60.00
Phantom of the Opera, Universal Studios of California, gr face,
    NM, A7 ....$150.00
Pig Pen (Peanuts), Lego, NM..$95.00
Pluto, 1970s, rnd gr base, NM, A7 ....$75.00
Porky Pig, NM, A7, from $100 to $175.00
Raggedy Andy, bank, mk A Penny Earned, NM, A7 ....$75.00
Raggedy Ann, bank, mk A Penny Saved, NM, A7 ....$75.00
Roy Rogers, Japan, 1962, compo, sq gr base, 6½", M, from $150
    to..$200.00
Roy Rogers, NM, A7, from $150 to $200.00

Snoopy, Lego, square black base, NM, $95.00.
(Photo courtesy June Moon)

Space Boy, blk space suit & helmet, NM, A7.................$75.00
Speedy Gonzales, NM, A7, from $100 to.......................$175.00
Three Little Pigs, bl overalls & yel cap, rnd red base, NM, A7,
    ea..$100.00
Topo Gigio, standing w/apple, orange or pineapple, NM, A7,
    ea $75.00
Topo Gigio, standing w/out fruit, NM, A7 ....$75.00
Tweety Bird, NM, A7, from $100 to...............................$175.00
Wile E Coyote, NM, A7, from $100 to...........................$175.00
Winnie the Pooh, 1970s, rnd gr base, NM, A7, from $100 to...$150.00
Woodstock, Japan, ceramic, w/bat, NM, A7....................$60.00
Woodstock, 1970s, no base, sm, NM, A7.........................$45.00
Yosemite Sam, NM, A7, from $100 to............................$175.00
Zero (Beetle Bailey), NM, A7, from $100 to $150.00

Character Clocks and Watches

Clocks and watches whose dials depict favorite sports and TV stars have been manufactured with the kids in mind since the 1930s, when Ingersoll made a clock, a wristwatch, and a pocket watch featuring Mickey Mouse. The #1 Mickey wristwatch came in the now-famous orange box commonly known as the 'critter box,' illustrated with a variety of Disney characters. There is also a blue display box from the same time period. The watch itself featured a second hand with three revolving Mickey figures. It was available with either a metal or leather band. Babe Ruth stared on an Exacta Time watch in 1949, and the original box contained not only the watch but a baseball with a facsimile signature.

Collectors prize the boxes about as highly as they do the watches. Many were well illustrated and colorful, but most were promptly thrown away, so they're hard to find today. Be sure you buy only watches in very good condition. Rust, fading, scratches, or other signs of wear sharply devaluate a clock or a watch. Hundreds have been produced, and if you're going to collect them, you'll need to study *Comic Character Clocks and Watches* by Howard S. Brenner (Books Americana) for more information.

Note: Our values are typical of high retail. A watch in exceptional condition, especially an earlier model, may bring even more. Dealers (who will generally pay about half of book when they buy for resale) many times offer discounts on the more pricey items, and package deals involving more than one watch may sometimes be made at as much as a 15% discount.

Advisor: Bill Campbell (C10).

See also Advertising; California Raisins.

CLOCKS

Bambi Wall Clock, 1970s, yel plastic w/image of Bambi & friends in forest, battery-op, 11x11", NM, J5 ....$65.00
Barbie Talking Alarm Clock, Quartz, 1983, Barbie & Ken posing in front of clock face, pk plastic case, M $20.00
Bart Simpson Talking Alarm Clock, Wesco/English, 9" 3-D figure w/skateboard under arm, MIB, K1 ....$35.00
Batman & Robin Talking Alarm Clock, Janex, 1974, 3-D image of Batman running behind car beside round clock, EX $50.00

Betty Boop Pendulum Clock, Poppo, pnt wood figure w/dial in middle, eyes move, 14½", EX...................................$500.00
Big Bad Wolf Alarm Clock, Ingersoll, wolf w/nodding head surrounded by pigs, rnd red case, 4½", EX, from $600 to..$800.00
Bozo Alarm Clock, Larry Harmon/French, 1960s, Bozo on face, rnd, rare, EX, A $150.00

Bugs Bunny Alarm Clock, Ingraham, Bugs laying down with carrot, 4", EX, from $150.00 to $200.00. (Photo courtesy Dunbar Gallery)

Bugs Bunny Travel Alarm Clock, Seth Thomas, 1970, image of Bugs w/glow-in-the-dark hands, bl case, M, J5...........$65.00
Bugs Bunny Wall Clock, Seth Thomas, 1970, bl plastic case w/image of Bugs holding carrot, electric, 10" dia, NM, J5...............$85.00
Cinderella Alarm Clock, Bradley/Japan, image of Cinderella leaving slipper on steps, 3" dia, scarce, MIB $125.00
Cinderella Wall Clock, Phinney Walker, 1970s, red metal w/image of Cinderella trying on slipper, 8" dia, NM, J5 ....$65.00
David Cassidy Wall Clock, 1972, NM $100.00
Davy Crockett Animated Clock, Haddon, 1950s, log cabin w/silkscreened image at right of clock face, 4x12", EX, from $500 to...$800.00
Disneyland Alarm Clock, Bradley, musical analog, image of Mickey as band leader w/parade of characters, EX, P6 ....$125.00
Donald Duck Alarm Clock, Bayard, 1930s, Donald's hands keep time, bl-pnt metal case & base, 5" dia, NM, A........$250.00
Flintstones Alarm Clock, Sheffield, 1960s, ceramic figure of Fred w/dial in center, 8½", EX $185.00
Fred Flintstone, glazed ceramic figure w/clock inserted in stomach, 12", M, from $150 to.......................................$200.00
Fred Flintstone Alarm Clock, 1973, full-figure image & Yabba Dabba Doo, arms keep time, yel case w/red bells, M..$55.00
Goofy Wall Clock, Welby by Elgin, 1970s, bl plastic w/full-color image of Goofy pointing time, 8" dia, NM, J5 ....$65.00
Howdy Doody & Clarabelle Alarm Clock, Janex, 1974, Howdy & Clarabelle figures at right & bottom, EX $85.00
Howdy Doody Alarm Clock, Leadworks, 1988, Howdy on bronco, 10", EX...$65.00

Howdy Doody Alarm Clock, Western Clock, 1954, mk Copyright 1954 Kagran Corp w/Howdy's image on face, metal case, 5", EX $450.00

Lone Ranger, Bradley/Elgin, 1981, Lone Ranger riding Silver on face, silver case, MIB, from $100 to $125.00

Maggie Simpson Alarm Clock, MIB, from $100 to $125.00

Max Headroom Wall Clock, shaped like a wristwatch, NMIB, B5 ....$65.00

Mickey Mouse Alarm Clock, House Martin, Mickey playing piano while Minnie dances, red case w/yel bells, NMIB $175.00

Mickey Mouse Alarm Clock, Ingersoll, 1930s, electric, lg rotating Mickey, gr case, 4x4", NMIB $2,200.00

Mickey Mouse Alarm Clock, Ingersoll, 1940s, Mickey's hands point time, tan case, 5" dia, VG (box mk Luminous Hands), A $325.00

Mickey Mouse Alarm Clock, Ingersoll, 1948, full-figure Mickey on face, wht plastic case, w/orig guarantee, MIB, A $1,300.00

Mickey Mouse Alarm Clock, Phinney-Walker, 1960s, analog movement, dbl bell, 4", EX, P6 ....$75.00

Mickey Mouse Clock Radio, WDP/Bradley, full-color image of Mickey pointing, red case, plastic, 4x4", M $50.00

Mickey Mouse Wall Clock, Hamilton, 1970s, gr metal alarm clock shape w/Mickey's face, red hands, 10" dia, EX, J5 ....$75.00

Mighty Mouse Alarm Clock, 1960s, Mighty Mouse points time, orange case w/yel bells, NM, J5 ....$85.00

Minnie Mouse Alarm Clock, Bradley, 1976, Minnie in purple polka-dot dress, dbl bell, purple-pnt metal case, M, P4 ....$100.00

Mr Peanut Alarm Clock, Lux, Mr Peanut's arm points time, 3" dia, NM, A $125.00

Peanuts Alarm Clock, Janex, 1974, Charlie Brown & Snoopy sleeping next to rnd dial, EX, from $30 to $45.00

Pinocchio Alarm Clock, Bayard/France, 1967, various characters beside numbers surround Pinocchio, EX...................$250.00

Pinocchio Alarm Clock, Bayard, 1939, Pinocchio w/animated Jiminy Cricket on his head, rnd, EX+, A.................$250.00

Planters, 1980, plaque style w/image of Mr Peanut & It's Always Time for Planters...1906, battery-op, 17x13", MIB, P4.$100.00

Popeye Alarm Clock, KFS, Popeye's hands keep time, EX, $500.00. (Photo courtesy David Longest)

Popeye Alarm Clock, Smith Alarm/Great Britain, Popeye & Swea Pea at play, rnd wht case, EX (EX box)..........$385.00

Raggedy Ann and Andy Alarm Clock, Bobbs-Merrill/West Germany, 1971, full-color image, red case, 5½" dia, M, $95.00.
(Photo courtesy Kim Avery)

Pluto Alarm Clock, Bayard, 1964, NM, $250.00; Mickey Mouse Alarm Clock, Bayard, 1964, NM, $300.00.

Pluto Wall Clock, Allied, plastic figure w/clock attached to his chest, hands shaped as dog bones, 8", EX (EX box).$450.00

Popeye Alarm Clock, New Haven, litho tin w/colorful image on face, case & base, 4", EX, A $850.00

Raggedy Ann & Andy Talking Alarm Clock, Equity, rnd dial above raised image of Raggedy Ann & Andy, NM....$35.00

Roy Rogers & Trigger Alarm Clock, Ingraham, desert scene, Roy on Trigger gallops & ticks off seconds, 4x4", NMIB, A $450.00

Sesame Street Talking Alarm Clock, rnd dial in building w/Big Bird reading to Ernie & Oscar the Grouch, 11", EX..$35.00

Shmoo Pendulette Alarm Clock, Lux, 1950, figural w/dial in middle, 8", EX (EX box)..$200.00

Smokey the Bear Alarm Clock, Bradley, 1950s, image & Prevent Forest Fires on face, wht case w/bl bells, 7", NMIB, A $150.00

Snoopy Alarm Clock, Equity, 1965, Live It Up a Little, EX, J2 ....$45.00

Snow White and the Seven Dwarfs Alarm Clock, Bayard, 1960, Snow White surrounded by dwarfs at each number, 4½" dia, NM, $300.00. (Photo courtesy Michael Stern)

Tweety Bird Talking Alarm Clock, Janex, 1978, battery-op, EX, J2 ....$75.00
Underdog Alarm Clock, Germany, 1970s, Underdog's hands keep time, yel plastic octagonal case, 3", NM, J5 ....$195.00
Winnie the Pooh Alarm Clock, Sunbeam, 1980s, MIB ...$75.00
Woody Woodpecker Alarm Clock, Columbia Time, image of Woody w/spatula in Woody's Cafe, rnd silver case, 4", EX, A $155.00
Woody Woodpecker Alarm Clock, Westclox, image of nodding Woody w/spatula at Cafe tree, rnd wht case, 5½", EX, A .$175.00

POCKET WATCHES

Buster Brown & Tige, Ingersoll, 1908, Buster & Tige surrounded by lettering, rnd chrome case, EX, A $475.00

Captain Marvel, Fawcett, 1948, full figure, rnd chrome case, gr plastic strap, EX, A $250.00
Dan Dare, Ingersoll/Great Britain, 1950s, image of space scene w/spaceship & gun ticking off seconds, MIB $800.00
Donald Duck, Ingersoll, Donald w/hands on hips, emb Mickey on back, rnd silver case, G, A $275.00
James Bond 007 Spy Watch, Gilbert, w/secret lenses, EX (EX box)...$300.00
Jeff Arnold, Ingersoll, England's cowboy mounted on horse w/animated pistol arm, rnd chrome case, EX, A......$350.00
Lone Ranger, 1970, Lone Ranger & Silver on face, bl strap, silver chain, NM, from $75 to................................$95.00
Mary Marvel, Fawcett, 1948, full figure, rnd chrome case, red plastic strap, VG, A $125.00
Mickey Mouse, Bradley, 1960s, full-figure Mickey on face, tin case, 2" dia, MIB, A..$155.00
Mickey Mouse, Bradley, 1970s, full-figure Mickey on face, plastic, 2" dia, EX, M8...$50.00
Mickey Mouse, Ingersoll, 1934, Mickey in red shorts, NM, A $785.00
Mickey Mouse, Ingersoll, 1934, Mickey in yel shorts, rare, NM, A..$2,000.00
Popeye, Ingersoll, 1935, Popeye in center w/various characters between numbers, 2" dia, EX, A............................$650.00
Roy Rogers, Bradley, 1959, lg image of Roy w/sm image of Roy on Trigger in background, w/stopwatch feature, EX $450.00
Superman, New Haven, 3-quarter figure, rectangular chrome case, w/stopwatch feature, EX, A $600.00
Three Little Pigs, Ingersoll/WD, 1935, pigs & wolf on red face, rnd chrome case, VG, A $1,000.00
Three Stooges, mk FTTC, Moe pulling Curly's tooth out w/pliers, NP case, 2" dia, EX............................$100.00
Tom Mix, Ingersoll, ca 1933, Tom on rearing horse, bk emb w/phrase, rnd chrome case, EX $3,500.00

WRISTWATCHES

Alice in Wonderland, Ingersoll, image of Alice, pk fabric strap, EX (EX rnd pk box w/clear plastic teacup) $250.00
Annie Oakley, New Haven, 1951, Annie w/animated 6-shooter, blk leather strap w/stamped pattern, EX $200.00

Amazing Spider-Man, Dabs, 1981, blue plastic band, NM (NM red plastic case), T2, $75.00. (Photo courtesy Bill Bruegman)

Archie, Rouan, 1960s, Archie's head revolves as it ticks, red band, NM, A $100.00

Babe Ruth, Exacta Time, Swiss, rnd chrome case, chrome stretch band, EX (baseball-shaped box), A..............$500.00

Batman, Fossil, 1990 limited edition, complete w/pin, M (M litho tin box), J5 ....$125.00

Batman, Marcel, 1966, batwings keep time on rnd face encased in blk plastic wings, no band, EX, J5 ....$200.00

Beatles, 1960s, silver & gray face w/line drawing of ea member at 12, 3, 6 & 9, blk vinyl band, EX, A $350.00

Big Jim, Bradley, 1973, figure in red shorts w/arms as hands, Big Jim in bl & red lettering, blk vinyl band, NM, J5 ....$150.00

Bozo the Clown, Bradley, 1960s, Bozo on face, rpl red band, EX, J5 ....$75.00

Bozo the Clown, 1960s, image & Bozo the Clown in red letters on face, rpl red vinyl band, EX, J5 ....$50.00

Bugs Bunny, Richie, 1951, Bugs w/carrot, rnd chrome case, red leather strap, EX, A $165.00

Buzz Lightyear, Fossil, 1996, limited edition of 7,500, complete w/certificate & plaque, M (M tin container), M8 ...$125.00

Captain Marvel, Fawcett, 1948, Captain Marvel holding airplane, rnd chrome case, vinyl strap, MIB, from $500 to $600.00

Casper the Ghost, Bradley, 1960s, Casper flies over mountains on bl dial, wht vinyl band, NM, J5 ....$150.00

Cat in the Hat, 1972, NM $250.00

Cinderella, Bradley, Cinderella's arms keep time, complete w/3 interchangeable bands, EX (EX case), from $100 to..$150.00

Cinderella, Timex, 1958, Cinderella on face, pk band, complete w/plastic Cinderella figure, EX (EX box), A............$150.00

Cinderella, Timex/WDP, Cinderella's face covers dial, complete w/plastic slipper & storybook box, NMIB, A...........$475.00

Cool Cat, Sheffield, 1960s, full-figure image, rpl band, VG, J5...$50.00

Dale Evans, Bradley, 1950s, rnd horseshoe image, rectangular gold-tone case, tan leather strap, EX (EX box)........$275.00

Davy Crockett, Bradley, 1956, rnd face, tan leather band w/silver engraving, unused but nonworking, NM (pop-up box), A $350.00

Dennis the Menace, 1960s, bl-trimmed face w/image of Dennis & Ruff, rpl band, EX, J5..$75.00

Dick Tracy, New Haven/New Syndicate, 1948, Tracy pointing gun on face, orig beige band, EX (EX box), A.........$300.00

Dizzy Dean, US, full-figure hurling baseball, rectangular gold-tone case, gold-tone stretch band, VG, A................$450.00

Donald Duck, Bradley, 1985, 50th Anniversary Registered Edition, battery-op, complete w/paperwork, MIB, P6...$150.00

Donald Duck, Ingersoll/US Time, image of Donald w/lg arm hands, chrome case, bl strap, EX (EX box) $635.00

Dopey Dwarf, Dopey's hands keep time, chrome case, yel plastic strap w/blk stitching, EX, A $200.00

Dukes of Hazzard, LCD Quartz, Unisonic, 1981, stainless steel band, NRFB, H4 ....$40.00

Elmer Fudd, Sheffield, 1960s, Elmer in hunting outfit, wht vinyl band, NMIB, J5 ....$150.00

Flintstones, Bradley, 1960s, close-up image of Fred & Pebbles, rpl red band, NM, J5..$65.00

Flipper, 1960s, gr image of Flipper jumping on blk face, rpl band, EX, J5 ....$65.00

Fonzie, Time Trends, 1976, blk leather band, NM, from $65 to $75.00

Gene Autry, New Haven, 1951, Gene w/animated 6-shooter, rnd chrome case, blk leather strap w/silver stenciling, EX, A $220.00

Gerber Baby, 1970s, Gerber Baby's face covers face, brn vinyl band, EX...$35.00

Girl From UNCLE, 1960s, pk face w/blk line drawing & numbers, rpl band, EX, J5 ....$65.00

Goofy, Helbros, 1971, Goofy & numbers run backwards, rare, NM (NM plastic box) $1,000.00

Hazel, 1971, bust image, red band, NM, A $65.00

Hopalong Cassidy, US Time, 1950, bust-portrait on face, western motif on blk band, complete w/saddle display, MIB, A $625.00

Howdy Doody, Ideal Watch Co, complete w/Howdy figure, MIB..$500.00

Howdy Doody, Quartz/Concepts Plus Inc, 1987, Howdy on face, red band, MOC..$50.00

Jerry Lewis, Helbros, 1960s, MIB, A $300.00

Joe Palooka, New Haven, 1947, Joe wearing boxing gloves, rectangular chrome case, brn leather strap, VG, A........$200.00

Josie & the Pussycats, Bradley, 1971, complete w/3 bands, MIB, from $300 to $350.00

Lassie, 1960s, image of Lassie sitting, wht w/name in bl, NM..$75.00

Li'l Abner, New Haven, saluting animated Am flag, rnd chrome case, brn leather strap, VG, A $220.00

Lone Ranger, 1950s, flasher image of Roy on rearing Trigger & waving hat, Many Happy Trails..., leather band, EX.$200.00

Madonna, Quartz, plastic, neon, 3 styles, MOC, ea..........$35.00

Mary Marvel, Marvel Importing Corp, 1948, Mary in flying pose on face, MIB, T2, from $800 to $1,100.00

Mickey Mouse, Bradley, 1977, Mickey Mouse 50th Birthday, red band, MIP, M8...$125.00

Mickey Mouse, Bradley, 50th Anniversary, image w/lg dial arms, rnd chrome base, blk lizard strap, NMIB...................$85.00

Mickey Mouse, Ingersoll/Mickey Mouse Electric, image w/lg dial arms, blk vinyl strap, NMIB $200.00

Dick Tracy, New Haven, 1930s, original band, NMIB, A, $400.00.

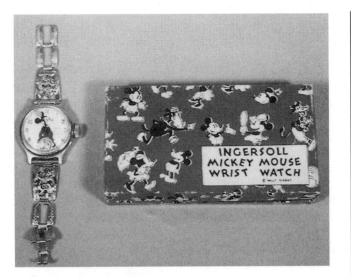

Mickey Mouse, Ingersoll, 1933, Mickey with large dial hands and seconds dial, chrome case and bracelet strap, NMIB, $900.00. (Photo courtesy David Longest and Michael Stern)

Mickey Mouse, Ingersoll/US Time, 1947, Mickey on rectangular face, red vinyl band, NM (EX box), A.......................$350.00

Mickey Mouse, Kelton/WDP, 1946, sq gold-tone case, brn leather band, EX, A...$450.00

Mickey Mouse, US Time, 1958, Mickey on face, red band, complete w/plastic Mickey figure, EX (EX box), A........$200.00

Minnie Mouse, Bradley, 1970s, Minnie's hands point time, rpl band, EX, J5..$35.00

Minnie Mouse, Timex, 1958, red band, complete w/figure, NM...$225.00

Miss Piggy, Timex, 1982, image of Miss Piggy w/animated hearts, digital, MIB...$65.00

Nightmare Before Christmas, Timex, digital, Jack's face on dial, MIP, H9..$40.00

Nightmare Before Christmas, Timex, features Lock, Shock & Barrel, MIB..$175.00

Partridge Family, 1970s, family photo on face, NM, from $150 to...$200.00

Pluto, Ingersoll, 1948, head shot on blk face, bl hands, rnd chrome case, blk plastic strap, VG, A.......................$165.00

Popeye, New Haven, 1935, Popeye & sm images of various characters, rectangular chrome case, blk leather strap, VG, from $550 to...$700.00

Porky Pig, Sheffield, 1960s, Porky tipping his hat, bl band, NM (NM box), J5 ....$150.00

Raggedy Ann, Bradley/Bobbs-Merrill, 1971, full-figure image on face, red band, M (M case), from $65 to $75.00

Ricochet Rabbit, 1960s, full-figure image & Ricochet Rabbit in blk & wht letters, wht band, NM, A........................$500.00

Rocketeer, Hope, 1991, digital, metal w/plastic band, NMOC, M8..$35.00

Roy Rogers, Ingraham, Roy & Trigger on rectangular face, silver expansion band, NM (NM box), A.........................$500.00

Roy Rogers, Ingraham, 1951, Roy & Trigger on rectangular face, brn strap, NM (NM box) $400.00

Rudolph the Red-Nosed Reindeer, USA, rectangular chrome case, red vinyl strap, EX..$75.00

Shadow, Hope/Universal Studios, 1994, unused, NM, C10.$250.00

Shirley Temple, Shirley saluting on bl & wht face, rnd chrome case, red plastic strap, EX, A $125.00

Shirley Temple, Swiss made, signature on face, rnd chrome case w/3 interchangable colored straps, EX (EX box), A ..$350.00

Smitty, New Haven, 1935, full-figure image, rectangular chrome case, blk leather strap, EX, A $225.00

Smokey Bear, Hamilton, 1960s, Smokey points time w/shovels, orig band, MIB, J5..$150.00

Snow White, USA/WDP, image of Snow White, rnd plastic case, yel strap, complete w/wall hanging, EX (EX box)........$175.00

Space Mouse, Webster, 1960s, blk & wht image on face, red band, MIB, J5...$65.00

Spider-Man, Hope, 1990, flip-top cover designed as Spider-Man's head, red vinyl strap, MOC, T2.......................$25.00

Superman, Bradley, Superman image, rnd gold-tone case, gold-tone stretch band, EX (EX lt bl cylindrical box) $175.00

Superman, Superman image, brn leather band, EX, A $85.00

Tom Corbett Space Cadet, Ingraham, 1951, image of Tom w/lightning bolt hands, chrome case, metal stretch band, NM, P4...$165.00

Tweety Bird, Topolino/Swiss, image w/lg dial arms, rnd chrome case, red leather strap, EX (EX box)..........................$50.00

Woody (Toy Story), Fossil, limited edition of 7,500, complete w/certificate, plaque & rnd tin case, M, M8 ....$125.00

Woody Woodpecker, Ingraham, image of Woody, chrome case, red strap, EX $325.00

Zorro, US Time, name in script, chrome case, blk leather strap w/silver-stamped designs, w/display hat, EX (EX box).........$400.00

Character, TV, and Movie Collectibles

To the baby boomers who grew up glued to the TV set and addicted to Saturday matinees, the faces they saw on the screen were as familiar to them as family. Just about any character you could name has been promoted through retail merchandising to some extent; depending on the popularity they attain, exposure may continue for weeks, months, even years. It's no wonder, then, that the secondary market abounds with these items or that there is such wide-spread collector interest. For more information, we recommend *Collector's Guide to TV Memorabilia, 1960s & 1970s, 1st and 2nd edition*, by Greg Davis and Bill Morgan; *Howdy Doody* by Jack Koch; *Character Toys and Collectibles, Vols I and II*, and *Cartoon Toys and Collectibles Identification and Value Guide* by David Longest; *The World of Raggedy Ann Collectibles* by Kim Avery; and *Cartoon Friends of the Baby Boom Era* by Bill Bruegman.

Note: Though most characters are listed by their own names, some will be found under the title of the group, movie, comic strip, or dominant character they're commonly identified with. The Joker, for instance, will be found in the Batman listings.

Advisors: Lisa Adams (A7), Dr. Dolittle; Jerry and Ellen Harnish (H4); Larry Doucet (D11), Dick Tracy; Ed Janey (J2); Trina and Randy Kubeck (K1), The Simpsons; Norm Vigue (V1); TV Collector (T6); Casey's Collectible Corner (C1); Bill Stillman (S6), Wizard of Oz; Bill Bruegman (T2).

See also Action Figures; Battery-Operated; Books; Chein; Character Clocks and Watches; Coloring, Activity, and Paint Books; Dakins; Disney; Dolls, Celebrity; Fisher-Price; Games; Guns; Halloween Costumes; Lunch Boxes; Marx; Model Kits; Paper Dolls; Pin-Back Buttons; Plastic Figures; Playsets; Puppets; Puzzles; Records; Toothbrush Holders; View-Master; Western; Windups, Friction, and Other Mechanicals.

A-Team, Colorforms, 1983, MIB (sealed), V1 ....$25.00
A-Team, Grenade Toss, Placo, 1983, MIB (sealed), M17 ..$75.00
A-Team, Mr T's Water War, Lakeside, 1983, attach to hose & it sprays water, MIB, C1 ....$50.00
Addams Family, gumball machine, w/1" plastic figures & 4 blk & wht photos, rare, M, H4 ....$25.00
Addams Family, key chain, Thing, MOC, F1 ....$6.00
Addams Family, paint book set, Wet the Brush & Bring Out the Colors, Saalfield, 1965, rare, NMIB, from $350 to ..$400.00
Alice in Wonderland, tea set, Plasco, 12 pcs, NMIB $65.00
Alvin & the Chipmunks, bank, Alvin, plastic, NM, S21 .$12.00
Alvin & the Chipmunks, doll, Alvin, Theodore or Simon, Ideal, 1983, talker, plush, 18", NM, ea $40.00
Alvin & the Chipmunks, doll, Alvin, Theodore or Simon, Knickerbocker, 1963, plush, 14", NM, ea $50.00
Alvin & the Chipmunks, harmonica, Plastic Inject Co, 1959, MOC $85.00
Alvin & the Chipmunks, kite, Roalex, 1960s, MIP $65.00
Alvin & the Chipmunks, slide-tile puzzle, Roalex, 1959, MIP $65.00
Alvin & the Chipmunks, Stuff & Lace Set, Hasbro, 1959, complete, MIB $75.00
Andy Panda, bank, book shape, litho tin, EX, from $75 to ..$100.00
Annie, doll, Knickerbocker, 1977, stuffed cloth w/Sandy in dress pocket, 15", MIB, M17 ....$40.00
Annie, Sing-a-Long Radio, LJN, bl plastic w/picture of Annie & Sandy, 8", M $50.00
Archies, Jughead Ring Toss Game, 1987, MOC, H4 ....$15.00
Archies, Loonies, Jaru, 1986, MOC $10.00
Archies, pencil-by-number set, Art Award, 1987, complete, MIB $15.00
Archies, Pick-Up Sticks, Ja-Ru, 1986, MOC, H4 ....$10.00
Archies, pocket puzzle, Jaymar, 1960s, MOC $25.00
Archies, ring, sterling silver, MIB (w/certificate), C10 ..$185.00
Atom Ant, magic slate, Watkins-Strathmore, 1967, cb w/lift-up erasable film sheet, NM, T2 ....$40.00
Back to the Future, Action Hoverport & Action Hovercars, Texaco premium, 1989, MOC, H4, ea $6.00
Banana Splits, Big Blow Whistles, Laramie, 1970s, set of 3, 5", MOC, M17 ....$35.00
Banana Splits, doll, Hasbro, 1969, any character, rubber, 4", MIB, ea $100.00
Banana Splits, doll, Hasbro, 1969, any character, stuffed cloth, EX, ea $150.00
Banana Splits, flute set, Larami, 1973, plastic, set of 3, MOC, C1 ....$55.00
Banana Splits, harmonica, Larami, 1973, MOC $45.00
Banana Splits, Kut-Up Kit, Larami, 1973, MOC $30.00
Banana Splits, Paint-by-Number set, Hasbro, 1969, MIB .$125.00
Banana Splits, slide-tile puzzle, Roalex, MIP $100.00

Banana Splits, Stitch-A-Story, Hasbro, 1969, MIB $85.00
Banana Splits, Talking Telephone, Hasbro, 1969, MIB .$175.00
Banana Splits, tambourine, Larami, 1973, MIP $40.00
Barney Google & Spark Plug, figure, mk Germany/DeBeck on base, bsk, 3", EX $200.00
Barney Google & Spark Plug, figures, Schoenhut, jtd wood w/cloth costumes, 8½" to 9", EX, A $650.00
Batman, Activity Box, Whitman, 1966, complete, rare, MIB, J5 ....$65.00
Batman, bank, NPPI, 1966, ceramic figure, hands on hips, NM, C1 ....$90.00
Batman, bank, Transogram, 1966, vinyl figure, 20", VG, J5 .$45.00
Batman, banner, Batman Vs the Riddler, 1966, wht cloth w/colorful image, 27", EX, J5 ....$100.00
Batman, Batmobile riding toy, 1966, blk plastic w/decals, silver bats on wheels, 22", VG, J5 ....$150.00
Batman, Batphone, Marx, 1966, red plastic, says 10 different phrases, 8", MIB, T2, from $300 to $400.00
Batman, Batplane w/Launcher, AHI, 1975, styrofoam plane launches from plastic gun, MOC, J5 ....$45.00
Batman, belt, Morris Belt, 1966, plain blk vinyl belt w/brass buckle, MOC, J5 ....$50.00
Batman, bicycle ornament, Empire, 1966, plastic figure w/spring clamp, 8", MOC, T2 ....$50.00
Batman, Cast 'N Paint, 1976, unused, MIB, J5 ....$45.00
Batman, charm bracelet, 1966, complete w/6 pnt brass charms, EX (EX card), J5 ....$75.00
Batman, Colorforms, 1966, complete, NMIB, ...$55.00
Batman, doll, Commonwealth Toy & Novelty, 1966, stuffed cloth, 17", NM, A $125.00
Batman, doll, 1966, stuffed cloth w/molded plastic face, felt cape, 27", NM, T2, from $100 to $200.00
Batman, Electronic Project-A-Light, AHI/Canadian, 1978, blk plastic, battery-op, MIB, J5 ....$55.00
Batman, Fiddlesticks, Knickerbocker, 1979, complete, EX (EX box), J5 ....$45.00
Batman, figure, Batman, Fun Things/NPPI, 1966, rubber w/elastic string, 5", NM (EX card) $125.00
Batman, figure, Robin, Fun Things/NPPI, 1966, rubber w/elastic string, 5", NM (EX card) $65.00
Batman, figure set, Batman, Robin & Joker, Ideal, 1966, hard plastic, 3", NMIP $125.00
Batman, film, Adventures of Batman, Doom of the Rising Sun, Columbia, 1950s, 8mm, NMIB, T2, from $40 to $50.00
Batman, flashlight, Nasta, 1981, plastic figure, 4", MOC, J5 ..$15.00
Batman, Flying Batplane, Remco, 1966, bl vacuform plastic w/attached remote control guide cable, MIB, from $200 to $300.00
Batman, Flying Batscout, Tarco, 1966, figure in center of flying disk, MOC, J5 ....$50.00
Batman, flying toy, Ideal, 1966, figure flies across string, inflatable vinyl, EX (EX card), J5 ....$100.00
Batman, Follow the Color Magic Rub-Off Set, Whitman, 1966, complete, EX (EX box), J5 ....$55.00
Batman, Fun Poncho, 1976, w/mask & hood, MIP (sealed), V1 ....$40.00
Batman, helmet & cape, Ideal, 1966, bl plastic cowl-shaped helmet & bl vinyl cape w/drawstring, MIB, T2, from $200 to $300.00

Batman, kite, Sky, 1974, inflatable vinyl, 45", MIP, J5 ....$45.00

Batman, Latch Hook Kit, 1970s, makes 12x12" rug, MIB, J5..$25.00

Batman, Magic Eyes Story Set, Sawyers, 1966, complete, MIP, T2..$50.00

Batman, Magnetic Maze Chase Game, Nasta, 1980, NMOC, J5..$25.00

Batman, pencil sharpener, 1975, plastic figure, 3", EX, J5 ..$15.00

Batman, Picture Gun, Marx, 1966, bl plastic, complete w/3 rolls of filmstrips, MIB, from $100 to......................$200.00

Batman, pin, 1966, Zonk!, purple border, MOC, J5........$45.00

Batman, Pix-A-Go-Go, Joker, Embree, 1966, complete w/8 Magic Picture Episodes, MOC, J5......................$65.00

Batman, pocket puppet, Durham, 1970s, flat figure w/jtd arms & legs, 10", MOC, J5................................$35.00

Batman, poster, Ciro Art Corp, 1966, glow-in-the-dark, Batman & Robin swinging on ropes, 18x14", MIP, T2..........$50.00

Batman, Print Putty, Colorforms, 1966, MOC, J5............$45.00

Batman, roller skates, Larami, 1970s, plastic w/Batman figures at toe of ea, 8", EX, J5....................................$35.00

Batman, Sky Hero, Marx, 1977, plastic figure shoots across yard w/rubber-band launcher, 10", NMOC, J5..................$45.00

Batman, slide-tile puzzle, American Publishing, 1977, red plastic, MOC, J5..$25.00

Batman, Sparkle Paints, Kenner, 1966, complete, EX (EX box), T2..$75.00

Batman, squirt gun, Durham, 1970s, plastic figure, 4", MOC, J5..$35.00

Batman, String Art Kit, Smith House, 1976, complete, EX (EX box)..$25.00

Batman, sunglasses, 1966, blk plastic bat design w/red & gr sticker on side, EX..$25.00

Batman, Supersonic bicycle siren, Empire, 1978, plastic, battery-op, MOC, J5..$35.00

Batman, toy watch, Marx, 1978, MOC............................$20.00

Batman, Trace-A-Graph, Emenee, 1966, complete, MIB, from $100 to..$125.00

Batman, Tru-Dimension Picture Kit, Colorforms, 1976, complete, MIB..$20.00

Batman, wallet, Standard Plastics, 1966, yel vinyl w/full-color image, NM, T2, from $40 to........................$50.00

Batman, Whirl-O-Tron, Durham, 1977, magnetic Batman top runs back & forth over hand control, MOC, J5.........$45.00

Batman, wrist compass, 1966, MOC, J5..........................$65.00

Batman, wrist radio, Remco, 1960s, MIB......................$100.00

Batman & Robin, bop bag, Arco, 1981, inflatable vinyl, 48", MIB..$25.00

Batman & Robin, Coloring Set, Hasbro, 1966, complete, EX (EX box), T2..$75.00

Batman & Robin, figure set, 1960s-70s, hard rubber figures on bat-shaped bases, 4", EX, J5........................$45.00

Batman & Robin, pinball machine, Marx, 1966, 22x10", EX, J2..$100.00

Batman & Robin, sticker sheet, 1966, Batman & Robin Charter Member...Society, 3½" dia, set of 4, EX, J5..............$35.00

Batman & Superman, Code Flasher, Gordy Int, 1973, bl plastic communicators catch light & send signals, MOC, J5..$35.00

Batman Puppet Theatre, Ideal/Sears Exclusive, 1966, w/Batman, Robin & Joker hand puppets, MIB, T2, minimum value............$1,000.00

Batman Returns, Colorforms, EX (EX box), B10............$10.00

Battlestar Galactica, wallet, Larami, 1978, silver vinyl w/mc space vehicle, MOC, M17..$20.00

Beany & Cecil, Beany-Copter, Mattel, 1950, unused, MOC, J2..$150.00

Beany & Cecil, Cartoon Kit, Colorforms, 1960s, complete, EX (worn box), from $100 to........................$125.00

Betty Boop, Big Dress-Up Set, Colorforms, 1970s, complete, MIB, from $35 to..$45.00

Betty Boop, doll, Cameo/Fleischer Studios, pnt compo head & body w/jtd wood arms & legs, red dress, 13½", VG, A.......$1,200.00

Betty Boop, doll, Play by Play Toys, 1992, stuffed cloth w/vinyl head, 14", EX, H4..$15.00

Betty Boop, figure, chalkware, 14", NM....................$275.00

Betty Boop, figure, Japan, prewar, celluloid, 8", NM, A ...$85.00

Betty Boop, figure, Jaymar, 1930s, jtd wood, 4", M.........$100.00

Betty Boop, figure set, Bimbo Orchestra, Fleischer Studios, set of 3 in different poses, MIB........................$500.00

Betty Boop, ukelele, wood w/silkscreened image of Betty, Bimbo & Koko, 21", NM......................................$250.00

Beverly Hillbillies, Cartoon Kit, Colorforms, 1963, MIB .$75.00

Beverly Hills 90210, hand-held video game, Micro Games of America, 1993, NM, F1..$20.00

Beverly Hills 90210, license plate, Fantasy Plates, 1991, any character, M, F1, ea..$5.00

Bionic Woman, bank, Animals Plus, 1970, Bionic Woman posed on pile of rocks, plastic, NM, C1....................$45.00

Bionic Woman, Beauty Salon, 1970s, MIB, B5 ....$50.00

Bionic Woman, Dip Dots Painting Design Book, Kenner, 1977, unused, EX $20.00

Bionic Woman, Play-Doh Action Playset, Kenner, 1977, NMIB $25.00

Bionic Woman, Styling Boutique, Kenner, 1977, NMIB .$45.00

Bionic Woman, tattoos & stickers, Kenner, 1976, complete w/8 stickers & 28 tattoos, MIP, M17 ....$20.00

Blabbermouse, doll, Knickerbocker, EX, C17 ....$60.00

Black Hole, Golden Book of Things To Do, 1979, complete, unused, NM, C1...$20.00

Blippy, jack-in-the-box, Mattel, M, from $100 to $150.00

Blondie & Dagwood, blocks, Gaston, 1950s, paper litho on wood, change positions for various expressions, VG (G box), J5...$25.00

Blondie & Dagwood, Blondie's Peg Set, KFS, 1930s, complete, NMIB, minimum value $100.00

Blondie & Dagwood, dexterity puzzle, 1940s, paper litho under glass w/red metal case, 5x3", EX, J5.............................$25.00

Boob McNutt, doll, Star Co, 1927, stuffed oilcloth w/felt pants & hat, 34", rare, EX, A $300.00

Bozo the Clown, bank, 1972, plastic, lg, NM, S21 ....$35.00

Bozo the Clown, Decal Decorator Kit, Meyercord, 1950s, unused, EX (EX box), M17...$40.00

Bozo the Clown, doll, talker, M, $65.00.
(Photo courtesy Cindy Sabulis)

Bozo the Clown, Stitch-a-Story, Hasbro, 1967, MOC, J2 ..$50.00

Bozo the Clown, talking book, MIP (sealed), J2 ....$55.00

Bozo the Clown, toy pocket watch, Japan/Larry Harmon, 1960s, plastic, tin & paper, MIP, P4.....................................$15.00

Brady Bunch, Brain Twisters, Larami, 1973, MOC $25.00

Brady Bunch, Dominoes, Larami, 1973, MOC $25.00

Brady Bunch, Fan Club Kit, Tiger Beat, 1972, complete, MIB, from $150 to $200.00

Brady Bunch, Hex-A-Game, Larami, 1973, MOC, C1 ....$45.00

Brady Bunch, tambourine, Larami, 1973, MOC $25.00

Brady Bunch, tea set, Larami, 1973, plastic, MOC...........$25.00

Brothers Grimm, school kit, Hasbro, 1962, NMOC, J2....$50.00

Buck Rogers, Colorforms Adventure Set, 1979, MIB, C1...$30.00

Buck Rogers, Cosmic Conquests Printing Set, Stamperkraft/Dille, missing few stamps, VG (VG box) $225.00

Buck Rogers, helmet, 1935, brn canvas-lined velour w/chromed ear ornaments & celluloid eye shield, VG, A $550.00

Buck Rogers, Midget Caster Set, 1934, extremely rare, VG (VG box), J2 ....$750.00

Buck Rogers, Official Utility Belt, Remco, 1979, plastic, complete, NMIB, P4...$55.00

Buck Rogers, Shaker Maker, Ideal, 1980, MIB (sealed), C1..$35.00

Bugs Bunny, bank, pnt metal, Bugs w/carrot leaning on tree trunk, 6", EX $135.00

Bugs Bunny, bank, Warner Bros, 1981, ceramic figure w/present, EX, S21 ....$50.00

Bugs Bunny, Cartoon Kit, Colorforms, early, complete, NMIB $75.00

Bugs Bunny, Chatterchum, Mattel, 1976, 7", VG, M15...$30.00

Bugs Bunny, doll, Warner Bros, 1950s, stuffed cloth w/plastic face, NM, from $75 to $125.00

Bugs Bunny, doll, 1950s, dressed as Davy Crockett, stuffed felt with cloth clothing and coonskin cap, EX, $325.00.
(Photo courtesy David Longest)

Bugs Bunny, Magic Rub-Off Pictures, Whitman, complete, EX (EX box), from $75 to $100.00

Bugs Bunny, magic slate, Golden, 1987, MIP (sealed), P3 .$5.00

Bugs Bunny, poster, I Want You, Bugs as Uncle Sam w/pals, 22x16", EX, H4 ....$5.00

Bugs Bunny, pull toy, Bugs on tricycle, paper litho on wood w/bells on back wheels, NM $350.00

Bugs Bunny, ring toss, Larami, 1981, MOC, F1 ....$15.00

Bugs Bunny, Silly Putty, Ja-Ru, 1980, MOC, H4...............$5.00

Bugs Bunny, Toot-A-Tune, Warner Bros, plastic figure, NM (NM box), from $100 to...$150.00

Bullwinkle, see Rocky & Bullwinkle

Cabbage Patch Kids, Colorforms, 1983, complete, EX (EX box)..$10.00

Captain America, bath puppet, MIP.........................$40.00

Captain America, bicycle license plate, Marx, 1967, litho tin w/raised image, NM, T2.............................$50.00

Captain America, blk-light poster, Third Eye, 1971, 21x33", NM, T2...$30.00

Captain America, doll, Amsco, 1970s, Super Baby series, stuffed cloth w/vinyl head, 8", NM (VG box), J5.................$45.00

Captain America, figure, Transogram, 1966, vacuform plastic w/glider wings, 12", MOC, T2.......................$50.00

Captain America, flashlight, Gordy International, 1980, plastic w/paper decal, 3½", MIP, T2.........................$30.00

Captain America, kite, Pressman, 1966, full-color image, MIP, T2..$65.00

Captain America, ring, from bubble gum machine, 1966, yel rubber w/figure, NM, T2...............................$50.00

Captain Kangaroo, Fun-Damental Activity Set, Lowe, 1977, NM (sealed), T2...$20.00

Captain Kangaroo, TV Eras-O-Board Set, Hasbro, 1956, complete, M (VG box), T2..$30.00

Captain Marvel, key chain, 1940s, plastic w/Capt Marvel & Jr on front, ...Capt Marvel Club on back, EX, J5...........$75.00

Captain Marvel, Magic Flute, MOC, C10................$125.00

Captain Planet & the Planeteers, Deluxe Ecology Test Kit, MIP, F1...$25.00

Care Bears, bank, Wish Bear on star, compo, NM, S21 ...$20.00

Care Bears, figure, 10 different characters, Kenner, 1984, 3", MOC, B5, ea...$15.00

Care Bears, phonograph, 1983, MIB (sealed), B5...........$125.00

Casper the Ghost, bank, ceramic figure, NM, T2..........$200.00

Casper the Ghost, doll, Mattel, 1971, talker, NM, J2.....$115.00

Casper the Ghost, jewelry set, AAI Inc, 1995, 10 pcs, MOC, F1...$15.00

Casper the Ghost, music box, Mattel, 1960, litho tin w/crank hdl, plays theme song, EX, from $55 to.....................$65.00

Casper the Ghost, Stitch-a-Story, Hasbro, 1967, MOC (sealed), J2..$50.00

Casper the Ghost, toss-up balloon, Pioneer Rubber, 1950s, floats through air & lands on feet, inflates to 3-ft, MOC, M17...$70.00

Centurians, Magnetix Playset, Am Publishing, 1986, MIP (sealed), M17...$25.00

Charlie Brown, see Peanuts

Charlie Chaplin, doll, unknown maker, 1970s, cloth w/china face, 15", MIB, M17..$100.00

Charlie Chaplin, figure, Germany, celluloid, 3", VG, A ..$65.00

Charlie McCarthy, doll, 1930s, compo, movable mouth, 13", EX, J2...$250.00

Charlie McCarthy, figure, Chase & Sanborn premium, litho cb w/movable arms & mouth, NM (EX mailer), A $100.00

Charlie McCarthy, figure, Jaymar, 1939, jtd wood, 5½", rare, NM, A $675.00

Charlie's Angels, backpack, Travel Toys, 1977, vinyl w/group photo on top flap, M, from $65 to.....................$75.00

Charlie's Angels, Beauty Kit, Fleetwood, 1977, plastic comb & mirror, any character, MOC, ea.............................$15.00

Charlie's Angels, Fashion Dress-Up Set, HG Toys, 1977, complete w/shoes, purse, watch & sunglasses, MIB, from $75 to..$100.00

Charlie's Angels, Hide-A-Way House, Hasbro, 1978, MIB, from $75 to...$100.00

Charlie's Angels, magic slate, Whitman, 1977, cb w/lift-up erasable film sheet, M, from $25 to.....................$30.00

Charlie's Angels, Paint-by-Number Deluxe Set, Hasbro, 1978, MIB, from $35 to..$45.00

Charlie's Angels, Poster Art Kit, HG Toys, 1977, MIP, from $25 to..$35.00

Charlie's Angels, poster put-ons, Kelly, Sabrina or Kris, 1970s, NM, F1, ea...$6.00

Charlie's Angels, record player, 1970s, NM...................$75.00

Charlie's Angels, toy watch, GLJ Toys, 1977, MOC, from $35 to..$45.00

Charlie's Angels, walkie-talkies, LJN, 1970s, MIB, from $100 to...$125.00

Child's Play, doll, Chucky, Play by Play, 1992, stuffed cloth w/real hair, 24", MIB, F1.................................$65.00

Child's Play, doll, Chucky, Play by Play, 1992, stuffed cloth w/real hair, 12", MIB, F1.................................$25.00

CHiPs, bicycle siren, 1970s, EX.................................$20.00

CHiPs, sunglasses, Fleetwood, 1977, MOC...................$15.00

CHiPs, wallet, Imperial, 1981, vinyl w/badge & logo on front, MIP...$12.00

Chitty-Chitty Bang-Bang, doll, Mr Potts, Mattel, 1969, talker, stuffed plush w/corduroy jacket, 24", MIB.............$150.00

Chitty-Chitty Bang-Bang, Paste & Stick Set, Whitman, 1968, scarce, EX (EX box), M17..................................$65.00

Chitty-Chitty Bang-Bang, wrist flashlight, Bantamlite, 1968, MOC, M17..$45.00

Chucky, See Child's Play

Cookie Monster, see Sesame Street

Daffy Duck, doll, Mighty Star, 1971, stuffed plush, 19", NM, F8...$25.00

Daffy Duck, Silly Putty, Ja-Ru, 1980, MOC, H4.............$5.00

Dennis the Menace, Colorforms, 1961, complete, NMIB...$50.00

Dennis the Menace, Paint-by-Number-Set, Determined, 1971, MIB (sealed), M17...$40.00

Dennis the Menace, phonograph, Hank Ketcham, 1960s, NM, from $100 to...$150.00

Dick Tracy, Crimestopper Play Set, Hubley, MIB, $200.00. (Photo courtesy Larry Doucet)

Dennis the Menace, Play Dentist, Pressman, 1954, few pcs missing, EX, scarce, from $150 to.....................................$200.00

Deputy Dawg, doll, Ideal, 1960s, stuffed cloth w/vinyl head, red vest & blk plastic hat, EX, from $75 to.....................$100.00

Dick Tracy, Black Light Magic Kit for Amateur Detectives, Chester Gould, complete, MIB, from $150 to $200.00

Dick Tracy, camera, Seymour, 1950s, 127mm, scarce, NMIB, D11..$100.00

Dick Tracy, Cartoon Kit, Colorforms, 1962, complete, EX (EX box) $75.00

Dick Tracy, doll, Bonnie Braids, Ideal, 1951-53, jtd rubber w/vinyl head, 14", NM, minimum value.................$150.00

Dick Tracy, doll, Bonny Braids Walker, Ideal, 1953, plastic w/vinyl head, 13½", NM, minimum value...............$125.00

Dick Tracy, doll, Dick Tracy, pnt compo w/cloth clothes, movable mouth, 14½", EX, A $250.00

Dick Tracy, doll, Honey Moon, Ideal, 16", MIB............$250.00

Dick Tracy, doll, Sparkle Plenty, Ideal, 1947 – 50, rubber with plastic head, yarn hair, 14", NM, minimum value, $200.00.
(Photo courtesy Judith Izen)

Dick Tracy, figure, Bonnie Braids, Charmore, 1951, plastic, 1¼", MOC, D11 ....$50.00

Dick Tracy, figure, Dick Tracy, Rubb'r Niks, complete, NMOC, D11 ....$45.00

Dick Tracy, figure, Dick Tracy, 1930s, pnt lead, EX, D11 ..$30.00

Dick Tracy, flashlight, 1950s, bl & red w/etched image of Tracy on side, pocket sz, NMIB, D11 ....$75.00

Dick Tracy, Junior Detective Kit, Golden Press, 1962, complete, NMIB, T2 ....$40.00

Dick Tracy, magnifying glass, Larami, 1979, MOC, C1 ...$20.00

Dick Tracy, Mini Color Televiewer, Larami, 1972, NMIP, D11...$25.00

Dick Tracy, Secret Service Phone, Lan-Dee, 1930s, paddle shape, 7½", VG, A $100.00

Dick Tracy, Sparkle Paints, Kenner, 1963, unused, complete, MIB, T2 ....$50.00

Dick Tracy, Special Agent Set, Larami, 1972, complete, NMIP, D11..$40.00

Dick Tracy, TV Watch, Ja-Ru, NMOC, D11 ....$20.00

Dick Tracy, washing machine, Sparkle Plenty, Kalon Radio Corp, 1940s, litho tin, 12x8" dia, VG, J5...............$100.00

Dick Tracy, 2-Way Wrist Radio, Remco, MIB $100.00

Ding Dong School, Mr Bumps Set, U-Products, 1950s, unused, NMIB, A...$100.00

Ding Dong School, record player, RCA, 1950s, EX+, A ..$200.00

Ding Dong School, scrapbook, Whitman, 1950s, VG, A .$40.00

Donkey Kong, figure, Donkey Kong Ape, Donkey Kong Jr, Mario or Pauline, Coleco, 1981, PVC, 2½", MOC, H4, ea $8.00

Dr Dolittle, Animal Fist Faces, EX (EX box), J2............$40.00

Dr Dolittle, jack-in-the-box, Giraffe, 1967, plays 'The Bear Went Over the Mountain,' NM..............................$40.00

Dr Dolittle, medical playset, Hasbro, NM, A7.................$75.00

Dr Dolittle, Mystery Chamber Magic Set, Remco, 1939, NMIB, A7 ....$30.00

Dr Dolittle, periscope, Bar-Zim, NMIP, A7 ....$30.00

Dr Dolittle, Ride-Em Rocker, Pushmi-Pullyu, AJ Renzi, 1974, NM, A7...$50.00

Dr Dolittle, Stitch-a-Story, Hasbro, NMIP, A7...............$25.00

Dr Kildare, scrapbook, 1962, 14x11", unused, NM, J2......$65.00

Dr Seuss, doll, Cat in the Hat, Coleco, 1983, stuffed plush, MIB, from $75 to..$90.00

Dr Seuss, doll, Horton the Elephant, Coleco, 1983, stuffed plush, EX, C17 ....$50.00

Dr Seuss, doll, Sam I Am, Eden, 1970s, stuffed plush, NM, H4..$185.00

Dr Seuss, doll, Thidwick the Big Hearted Moose, Coleco, 1983, plush, 16", NM, F8..$75.00

Dr. Seuss, riding toy, Cat in the Hat, Coleco, 1983, NM, B5, $75.00. (Photo courtesy Martin and Carolyn Berens)

Dr Seuss, ring, Cat in the Hat, gold-colored metal w/head view, NM, P4...$5.00

Dr Seuss, See 'N Say Talking Storybook, Friends of Dr Seuss, Mattel, 1970, NM, B5...$200.00

Dracula, doll, Commonwealth Toy & Novelty Co, talker, stuffed cloth, NMIB, H4 ....$95.00

Dukes of Hazzard, backpack, Remco, 1981, denim-type material w/image of General Lee, NM, C1...............................$40.00

Dukes of Hazzard, Colorforms, 1981, NM (NM box), C1...$30.00

Dukes of Hazzard, guitar, plastic, w/orig decals, VG, H4 ..$35.00

Dungeons & Dragons, Colorforms, 1983, EX (EX box), B10....$10.00

Ella Cinders, doll, Horsman, 1925, molded compo w/cloth dress, 18", EX, A..$300.00

Elmer Fudd, bank, Metal Moss Mfg, Elmer beside tree stump, 6", NM (NM box)..$250.00

Elmer Fudd, mask, Warner Bros, cb, NM, from $60 to.....$90.00

Elmer Fudd, pull toy, Elmer in fire chief car, paper litho on wood, EX...$300.00

Emmett Kelly, doll, 1960s, vinyl w/cloth outfit, 13", EX, M17..$50.00

Emmett Kelly Circus, Colorforms, 1960, complete, NMIB..$40.00

ET, figure, 1982, talker, 7", MIB, C1..................................$60.00

ET, photo album, M (sealed), V1...$12.00

ET, Presto Magix Rub-Down Transfer Game, 'Halloween,' MIP H4 ....$10.00

ET, ring, face, MOC, C10..$20.00

ET, Spaceship Launcher, LJN, 1982, push button & ET pops out, MOC, C1...$35.00

Family Affair, Buffy Make-Up & Hairstyling Set, Amsco, 1971, MIB $50.00

Family Affair, Cartoon Kit, Colorforms, 1970, MIB........$35.00

Family Affair, doll, Buffy, Mattel, 1967, bendable, w/Mrs Beasley doll, EX, A...$165.00

Family Affair, doll, Buffy, Mattel, 1967, talker, w/Mrs Beasley doll (nontalker), VG+, A...$55.00

Family Affair, figure, Buffy & Mrs Beasley, 6", no glasses, EX, H4...$50.00

Family Affair, rag doll, Mrs Beasley, Mattel, 1968, red or bl dress, 10", EX, ea...$15.00

Family Matters, doll, Steve Urkel, Hasbro, 1991, MIB, from $30 to $40.00

Fantasic Four, blk-light poster, Wonderful World of the Fantastic Four, Third Eye, 1971, 21x33", NM, T2 ....$30.00

Fanny Brice, doll, Ideal, 12½", redressed, EX, A, $150.00.

Fat Albert & the Cosby Kids, figure, Rudy, Bill or Bucky, Tedro Enterprises, 1982, MOC, H4, ea $30.00

Fearless Fly, kite, Roalex, 1967, plastic w/full-color image, MIP, T2...$200.00

Felix the Cat, doll, unmk, velour w/yel neck ribbon, button eyes, 9½", rare, NM, A...$400.00

Felix the Cat, figure, celluloid, Japan, 1920s, jtd arms, 5", EX, A..$300.00

Felix the Cat, figure, Pat Sullivan, 1922, jtd wood, w/decal, 8", NM, A..$475.00

Felix the Cat, figure, Schoenhut, jtd wood, orig decals on chest & foot, 5½", rare, EX..$1,200.00

Felix the Cat, Magna-Slide Cartoon Drawing Kit, Multiple Toys, 1960s, EX $75.00

Felix the Cat, pull toy, Nifty, 1920s, Felix in red roadster mk Speedy Felix, 12", EX, A...$300.00

Felix the Cat, tea set, Germany, 1920s, iridescent lusterware, service for 6, M...$900.00

Felix the Cat, TV Color Set, Lido, 1950s, complete, NMIB.$175.00

Flash Gordon, Colorforms Adventure Set, 1980, MIB, C1/M17, from $30 to...$35.00

Flash Gordon, slide-tile puzzle, Defenders of the Earth, Ja-Ru, 1985, MOC, C1...$18.00

Flash Gordon, space outfit, Esquire Novelty, 1950s, complete, EX (EX box) $425.00

Flintstones, Baby Pebbles Cave House, Ideal, 1964, M, M15 ....$175.00

Flintstones, bank, Barney & Bamm-Bamm, Homecraft, hard plastic, 13", M, B5...$75.00

Flintstones, bank, Dino & Pebbles, hard plastic, 14", M, B5.....$40.00

Flintstones, bank, Fred, Homecraft, hard plastic, 14", M, B5....$75.00

Flintstones, bank, Kanley, 1988, tin can shape w/image of Fred, Pebbles & Bamm-Bamm, NM, C1 ....$30.00

Flintstones, bank, Pebbles, Transogram, 1960s, plastic, EX, A..$45.00

Flintstones, bank, Wilma w/Pebbles, plastic, NM, S21 ....$30.00
Flintstones, bubble pipe, Bamm-Bamm, 1960s, 8", EX, J2 ..$20.00

Flintstones, Building Boulders, Kenner, MIB, T2, from $75.00 to $100.00. (Photo courtesy Bill Bruegman)

Flintstones, doll, Barney, Hanna-Barbera, 1960s, stuffed plush, NM..$55.00
Flintstones, doll, Fred or Barney, Knickerbocker, 1960s, plush & vinyl, 12", NM, ea from $75 to................................$85.00
Flintstones, doll, Pebbles, Ideal, 1950s, movable arms & legs, orig outfit, 12", NM, C1...$120.00
Flintstones, doll, Pebbles, Kenner, 1970s, EX, C17 ....$20.00
Flintstones, figure, Wilma, Giant Plastics, 1968, bendable rubber, w/red dress, 4", EX (EX card) $60.00
Flintstones, figure set, Flintstone Circus, Kohner, 1960s, complete w/7 figures & 8 pcs of circus equipment, NMIB..........$85.00
Flintstones, gumball machine, Fred, Hasbro, 1968, plastic head figure, 8", EX..$50.00
Flintstones, Paint'em Pals, Craftmaster, 1978, MIB (sealed), C1...$25.00
Flintstones, Play Fun Set, Whitman, 1965, complete, EX (EX box)..$65.00
Flintstones, Rotodraw, England, 1969, missing board, NM (EX box)..$60.00
Flip the Frog, figure, 1930s, celluloid, 7", NM, from $300 to ..$400.00
Flipper, bank, 1960s, plastic figure, 17½", NM.................$50.00
Flipper, jack-in-the-box, Mattel, 1966, litho tin, NM....$150.00
Flipper, squirt gun, 1960s, plastic figure, MOC................$40.00
Flipper, sticker set (similar to Colorforms), 1965, MIB (sealed), V1..$50.00
Flipper, ukelele, Mattel, 1968, MIP..........................$100.00
Flub-A-Dub, see Howdy Doody
Freddy Kreuger, see Nightmare on Elm Street
Free Willy, figure, Applause, PVC, 3", M, F1......................$5.00
G-Man, Police Set, Pressman, complete, rare, EX (EX box)...$250.00
G-Man, Signal Lite, litho metal, 7", EX.........................$175.00
G-Men, DeLuxe Training Outfit, New York Toy & Game, 1937, complete, extremely rare, EX (EX box) $450.00
G-Men, Laboratory Outfit, New York Toy & Game, 1936, complete, rare, MIB...$375.00
G-Men, Secret Communication Set, New York Toy & Game, 1936, complete, rare, EX (EX box) $375.00

G-Man, siren, Walt Reach Toy by Courtland, litho tin, 2x3½", M, $95.00. (Photo courtesy Harry and Jody Whitworth)

Garfield, bank, Enesco, Garfield bowling, NM, S21, from $35 to...$45.00
Garfield, bank, Enesco, Garfield w/knife & fork, NM, from $35 to...$45.00
Garfield, bank, Enesco, 1978, Garfield in rabbit suit sitting on egg, NM, S21 ....$40.00
Garfield, Colorforms, 1980s, complete, MIB, from $25 to ..$35.00
Garfield, doll, Dakin, 1982, stuffed plush, 24", NM.........$45.00
Garfield, doll, Mattel, 1983, talker, 10", VG, from $40 to ..$50.00
Garfield, figure, Garfield as Santa, vinyl, 6", B5 ....$25.00
Garfield, figure, Garfield on roller skates, ceramic, 2", EX, W2...$10.00
Garfield, jack-in-the-box, Pop Goes the Odie, MIB, W2.$30.00
Garfield, play money, MIP, W2................................$3.00
Garfield & Odie, figure, 1984, ceramic, NM, W2............$25.00
Garfield & Odie, figures, Bully/Germany, PVC, 2", NM, W2, ea...$10.00
Garrison's Gorillas, Garrison's Gorillas' Gear, Auburn Rubber/ABC, 1968, complete, EX (EX box) $100.00
Gilligan's Island, baseball cap, Am Needle, 1994, stitched logo, EX, F1..$10.00
Gilligan's Island, figure, Gilligan, Turner, vinyl w/molded clothes, 9", M..$20.00
Gilligan's Island, note pad, 1960s, Gilligan & Skipper on cover, glossy, unused, M, C1 ....$75.00
Goldilocks & the Three Bears, doll, Storybook Small-Talk by Mattel, 1976, MIB $60.00
Gomer Pyle, baseball cap, Am Needle, 1994, stitched graphics, NM, F1..$10.00
Goose Bumps, rings, set of 4, MOC, C10........................$35.00
Green Hornet, Black Beauty balloon, 1966, MIP, T2 ....$100.00
Green Hornet, Electric Drawing Set, Lakeside, 1966, complete, MIB, T2 ....$225.00
Green Hornet, flasher ring, Vari-Vue, 1960s, silver plastic, changes from Green Hornet to Kato, NM, C1 ....$70.00
Green Hornet, kite, Roalex, 1967, MIP, T2 ....$200.00
Green Hornet, Magic Rub-Off, Whitman, 1966, complete, MIB $200.00
Green Hornet, Print Putty, Colorforms, 1966, MOC, T2..$50.00
Green Hornet, Stardust Touch of Velvet Art, Hasbro, 1966, complete, NMIB, T2 ....$200.00

Green Hornet, Oil Painting by Numbers Set, Hasbro, MIB, T2, from $300.00 to $500.00. (Photo courtesy Bill Bruegman)

Green Hornet, Thingmaker Mold, Mattel, 1966, complete, MOC...$225.00

Green Hornet, walkie-talkies, Remco, 1966, gr plastic, 2 way electromagnetic, 9", MIB, T2...................................$400.00

Green Hornet, wrist radios, Remco, 1966, gr plastic, 4", NMIB, T2...$200.00

Gremlins, Colorforms Deluxe Set, MIB, P12....................$65.00

Gremlins, doll, Gizmo, Quiron, 1984, plush, 14", rare, MIB, F1 ....$150.00

Gremlins, Rub 'N Play Transfers, Colorforms, complete, MIP, F1..$10.00

Gremlins II, magic slate, Golden, 1990, cb w/lift-up erasable film sheet, EX, F1 ....$8.00

Grim Reaper, Monster Cycle, Ideal, 1978, NM, H4, from $40 to..$50.00

Gulliver's Travels, doll, King Little, Ideal, wood & compo, orig decal, 12", EX $575.00

Gulliver's Travels, doll, Prince David, Ideal, 1939, compo w/cloth cape & tights, 11", EX...................................$350.00

Gumby & Pokey, Adventure Costumes, Lakeside, 1965, Cowboy, Astronaut or Fireman, MOC, H4, ea $20.00

Gumby & Pokey, Colorforms, 1988, MIB.........................$10.00

Gumby & Pokey, figure, Gumby or Pokey, Jesco, 1980s, bendable, MOC, H4/M17, ea from $10 to $15.00

Gumby & Pokey, Lolly Pop-Up Puppet, 1967, unused, MIB, J2 ....$65.00

Gunsmoke, see Western category

Hair Bear Bunch, doll, Bubi Bear, Sutton, 1971, stuffed, rare, NM, H4...$50.00

Happy Days, Colorforms, Fonzie, unused, EX (EX box), J2..$30.00

Happy Days, doll, Fonzie, 1976, stuffed cloth, 16", NM ...$25.00

Happy Days, guitar, Fonzie, 1976, MIB (sealed), J2 ....$75.00

Hardy Boys, poster put-ons, Shawn Cassidy or Parker Stevenson, 1970, NM, F1, ea $6.00

Hogan's Heroes, writing tablet, 1965, unused, NM, A $30.00

Homey the Clown, see In Living Color

Howdy Doody, Bee-Nee Kit, 1950s, NMIB, J5 ....$65.00

Howdy Doody, Circus Wagon, 1950s, plastic, bops up & down when pushed, 5", EX, A...$300.00

Howdy Doody, coloring set, Kagran, complete w/cards, colored pencils, etc, EX (EX box), A $150.00

Howdy Doody, doctor kit, Ja-Ru, 1987, MOC, H4/J5 ......$15.00

Howdy Doody, doll, Applause, 1988, stuffed cloth, 11", EX..$15.00

Howdy Doody, doll, Applause, 1988, stuffed cloth, 18", EX..$30.00

Howdy Doody, doll, beanbag body, EX $25.00

Howdy Doody, doll, Effanbee, 1947, cloth w/compo head, hands & feet, sleep eyes, 20", EX, minimum value $425.00

Howdy Doody, doll, Beehler, plastic w/cloth clothes, jaws move, 7", NM (NM box) $250.00

Howdy Doody, doll, Ideal, 1950s, movable eyes & mouth, EX $175.00

Howdy Doody, doll, Princess, Beehler, plastic w/cloth clothes, eyes open & close, 7", NM (EX box) $225.00

Howdy Doody, figure, Flub-A-Dub, Tee-Vee Toys/Kagran, plastic, push lever & his mouth moves, 3", VG (G box) $150.00

Howdy Doody, film, A Trip to Fun Land, Castle Films, 1950s, 8mm, NMIB, $65.00. (Photo courtesy Jack Koch)

Howdy Doody, Flip-A-Ring, Flub-A-Dub, Flip-A-Ring Inc, 1950, MIP, J5 ....$45.00

Howdy Doody, Magic Piano, Kagran, yel w/colorful image of Howdy & friends, 15x10", EX (EX box) $575.00

Howdy Doody, paint set, Milton Bradley, complete, NM (NM box)..$200.00

Howdy Doody, Paint-by-Number-set, Art Award, 1976, EX (EX box)..$30.00

Howdy Doody, pinball game, Ja-Ru, 1987, MOC.............$15.00

Howdy Doody, pull toy, France, Howdy on tricycle, wood & plastic, 9x8", EX+, A...$300.00

Howdy Doody, Sand Forms, Ideal, 1952, MOC..............$125.00

Howdy Doody, sewing cards, Princess Summerfall-Winterspring, Milton Bradley, 1950s, EX (EX box) $100.00

Howdy Doody, slide-tile puzzle, Howdy Doody & His Famous TV Friends, Roalex, 1950s, EX $125.00

Howdy Doody, Sparkle Gun, Ja-Ru, 1987, MOC $10.00

Howdy Doody, sparkler, Ja-Ru, 1987, lever action, MOC, H4 ..$10.00

Howdy Doody, spurs, Ja-Ru, 1987, MOC.........................$15.00

Howdy Doody, target set, Ja-Ru, 1987, MOC....................$10.00

Howdy Doody, Time Teacher, AH Schwab, late 1960s, plastic board w/image of Howdy above clock, unused, MIP..$95.00

Howdy Doody, top, LBZ/West Germany, litho tin, NM ..$125.00

HR Pufnstuf, bop bag, Coleco, 1970, MIP $50.00

HR Pufnstuf, doll, Pufnstuf or Witchiepoo, My Toy, 1973, stuffed cloth, 16", MIB, ea from $300 to $400.00

HR Pufnstuf, pillow doll, 1970s, M, from $65 to...............$75.00

Huckleberry Hound, Cartoon Kit, Colorforms, 1962, complete, NMIB $65.00

Huckleberry Hound, chalkboard, Pressman, 1960s, diecut image above board, EX, from $40 to $50.00

Huckleberry Hound, doll, Boo-Boo, Knickerbocker, 1960s, gr cloth body w/pk bow tie, vinyl face, rare, EX.............$75.00

Huckleberry Hound, doll, Knickerbocker, plush & vinyl, 20", EX, J2 ....$55.00

Huckleberry Hound, Flip Show, 1961, EX (EX box), J2...$40.00

Huckleberry Hound, ring, plastic, EX, C10......................$50.00

I Dream of Jeannie, magic slate, Rand McNally, 1975, cb w/lift-up erasable film sheet, NM $65.00

I Love Lucy, Packaway Cut-Out Doll Kit, Whitman, 1953, NMIB, A..$150.00

Impossibles, magic slate, Watkins-Strathmore, 1969, cb w/lift-up erasable film sheet, NM $55.00

In Living Color, doll, Homey the Clown, Acme, 1992, stuffed cloth, 24", NM, H4..$35.00

Incredible Hulk, bank, Renzi, 1979, plastic bust figure, 15", NM, T2 ....$25.00

Incredible Hulk, Hide-A-Way Play Case, Sears Exclusive, 1978, MIB $75.00

Incredible Hulk, Paint-by-Number set, Hasbro, 1982, unused, MIB, T2 ....$30.00

Incredible Hulk, push toy, 1979, plastic, 7", EX, J8 ....$25.00

Incredible Hulk, Rub 'N Play, Colorforms, 1979, complete, MIB, C1..$30.00

Inspector Gadget, Shrinky Dinks, Colorforms, 1983, MIB, C1 ....$30.00

Iron Man, Marvel Flyer, Topps, 1966, stiff paper, 9", EX (EX envelope), T2...$50.00

Jackie Coogan, figure, Japan, prewar, celluloid, 5", NM, A.$100.00

James Bond, Thunderball Paint Set, British, 1965, EX, A ..$175.00

Jetsons, doll, George, Nanco, 1989, stuffed cloth, 13", EX, H4..$10.00

Jetsons, Flip Disc Shooting Game, MOC, H4....................$8.00

Joan Palooka, doll, Ideal, 1953, jtd latex w/vinyl head, 14", NM, minimum value...$85.00

Josie & the Pussycats, jewelry set, Larami, 1973, MOC....$30.00

Julia, Dress-Up Kit, Colorforms, 1969, MIB....................$45.00

Junior G-Man, cap, felt beanie-type w/image of Junior G-Man holding machine gun, rare, EX.................................$475.00

Junior G-Men, Fingerprint Set, Hale-Nass Corp, early 1940s, complete, EX (G box) $200.00

Justice League of America, Paint-by-Number-set, Hasbro, 1967, complete, EX (EX box), T2.....................................$150.00

Katzenjammer Kids, figures, Hans & Franz, 1930s, celluloid, rare, EX, pr $375.00

King Kong, bank, plastic figure, 17", NM, J2 ....$35.00

King Kong, bank, Universal Statuary, 1952, pnt plaster, 11", M $100.00

King Kong, Panoramic Play Set, Colorforms, 1976, complete, EX (EX box), M17...$25.00

King Kong, ring, MIP, C10...$10.00

Knight Rider, Colorforms Adventure Set, 1982, MIB, C1 .$35.00

Knight Rider, Self-Inking Stamp Set, Larami, 1982, complete, MOC, C1 ....$30.00

Kojak, Harbor Patrol Set, Continental Plastics, 1978, MOC, M17 ....$30.00

Krazy Kat, doll, Averill, stuffed felt w/applied face, orig orange neck ribbon, 18", VG, A $500.00

Krazy Kat, pull toy, Chein, litho tin w/wood & paper bellows, 7", EX $700.00

Lady Lovelylocks & the Pixitails, Colorforms, 1986, EX (EX box), B10..$10.00

Land of the Lost, Cosmic Signal, Larami, 1975, MOC.....$20.00

Land of the Lost, doll, Stink, Tiger, pull-string talker, MIB, J6..$85.00

Land of the Lost, Safari Shooter, Larami, 1975, MOC.....$25.00

Lassie, A Day in the Life of Lassie Play Kit, Plas-Trix, 1956, unused, NMIB, A...$200.00

Lassie, doll, Knickerbocker, 1960s, plush w/vinyl face, glass eyes, 12", VG, T2...$15.00

Lassie, ring, gold version, M, C10 ....$225.00

Lassie, ring, Good Luck, EX, C10...................................$165.00

Laugh-In, Electric Drawing Set, Lakeside, 1969, EX (VG box), J2, from $75 to..$100.00

Laugh-In, flicker rings, set of 5, NM, H4 ....$20.00

Laurel & Hardy, bank, Laurel, Play Pal, 1972, plastic, 14", NM, M17 ....$65.00

Laurel & Hardy, carriage, Spanish, folding litho tin chair on 4 wheels, EX, A $300.00

Laurel and Hardy, figures, vinyl with cloth clothes, 13", NM, $150.00 for the pair. (Photo courtesy Martin and Carolyn Berens)

Laurel & Hardy, Fuzzy Felt Playset, Standard Toykraft, 1962, complete, NMIB..$75.00

Laurel & Hardy, w/up figures, 1970s, hand-pnt plastic, 5" & 6", NM, J6, pr...$125.00

Laverne & Shirley, Secretary Set, Harmony, 1977, MOC..$35.00

Leave It To Beaver, baseball cap, Beaver, Am Needle, 1994, stitched graphics, EX, F1 ....$10.00

Leave It To Beaver, Eras-O-Picture Book, Hasbro, 1959, EX, A $85.00

Li'l Abner, Magic Picture Charm Bracelet & Ring, Pal Plastics, NM (EX card)..$85.00

Liddle Kiddles, Dress-Up Kit, Colorforms, 1968, complete, MIB $35.00

Liddle Kiddles, Electric Drawing Set, Lakeside, 1968, complete, MIB $50.00

Linus, see Peanuts

Little Bo Peep, oven & sink, Wolverine, litho metal, EX...$40.00

Little House on the Prairie, Colorforms, 1978, MIB.........$35.00

Little Lulu, bank, Play Pal Plastics, 7½", NM, J6.............$50.00

Little Lulu, crossword puzzle book, Whitman, 1974, unused, M, C1 ....$45.00

Little Lulu, doll, 1944, stuffed cloth w/red dress & yarn hair, 15", scarce, EX, M17 ....$200.00

Little Lulu, dusting powder, House of Tre-Jur, 1958, complete, EX (EX box), J5 ....$65.00

Little Lulu, perfume set, NMOC, T2 ....$60.00

Little Orphan Annie, doll, Japan, prewar, celluloid, 7½", M, A $300.00

Little Orphan Annie, figure, Harold Gray, pnt celluloid, jtd arms, name on paper belt, 7½", NM, A...................$500.00

Little Orphan Annie, toy stove, 1930s, metal with upper deck baking oven and electric warmer, NM, $200.00.

Little Orphan Annie & Sandy, figures, Jaymar, jtd wood, 5", EX, pr..$165.00

Little Orphan Annie & Sandy, figures, 1950s, pnt plastic, Annie in red dress, 1½" & 1", EX...............................$65.00

Little Red Riding Hood, bank, Napco, NM.................$125.00

Little Red Riding Hood, doll, Deluxe Reading, 1955, rubber w/washable synthetic hair, 23", MIB......................$125.00

Little Red Riding Hood, tea set, early 1900s, shows various scenes from the story, lithographed tin, eight pieces, EX, $375.00. (Photo courtesy David Longest)

Looney Tunes, Cartoon-O-Craft Molding & Coloring Set, Warner Bros, complete, EX (EX box), from $100 to .$150.00

Looney Tunes, Cartoon-O-Graph Sketch Board, Warner Bros, 1950s, complete, EX (EX box) $125.00

Lucy, see Peanuts

M*A*S*H, helicopter, Durham, 1975, unused, EX (EX box), A $100.00

Maggie & Jiggs, comb, Maggie figure, celluloid, push her hair & comb appears, M, A.......................................$150.00

Maggie & Jiggs, figures, celluloid, standing hand-in-hand, 6½", EX, A $385.00

Maggie & Jiggs, figures, Schoenhut, jtd wood w/cloth clothes, complete w/rolling pin & pail, 8" & 6", EX, pr $1,200.00

Magilla Gorilla, doll, Ideal, 1960s, bendable felt body w/vinyl head, complete w/felt accessories, 8", EX, A.............$85.00

Magilla Gorilla, squeeze toy, Screen Gems/Spain, 1967, vinyl w/hand-pnt features, 8", VG $125.00

Mama Katzenjammer w/Hans & Fritz, figure set, bsk, German, 1920s, 3", NM, A...$465.00

Man From Atlantis, Dip Dot Painting Kit, Kenner, 1977, NRFB, H4 ....$130.00

Man From UNCLE, Secret Print Putty, Colorforms, 1965, complete, NMOC...$80.00

Mandrake the Magician, Magic Kit, Transogram, 1949, complete, EX (EX suitcase style case), T2 ....$300.00

Marilyn Monroe, bank, China, 1960s, vinyl figure on base mk Funtime Savings, Seven Year Itch dress, 12", MIB, A $175.00

Marvel Super Heroes, checkers set, Hasbro, 1976, MIP (sealed), J5 ....$45.00

Marvel Super Heroes, Colorforms, 1983, complete, MIB, T2..$20.00

Marvel Super Heroes, Deluxe Sparkle Paints, Kenner, 1967, unused, MIB, T2...$150.00

Marvel Super Heroes, Fiddlesticks Giant Toy Builder Set, Knickerbocker, 1979, missing few pcs, NMIB, M17 ..$80.00

Marvel Super Heroes, Intercom Set, Vanity Fair, 1978, wht plastic w/decal of Batman & Superman, battery-op, MIB, C1 ....$75.00

Marvel Super Heroes, light-up drawing desk, Lakeside, 1977, complete, EX (EX box), T2 ....$40.00

Marvel Super Heroes, New Super Heroes Sparkle Paints, Kenner, 1967, unused, MIB, T2 ....$75.00

Marvel Super Heroes, record case, 1977, 18x15", EX, T2.$25.00

Masters of the Universe, bank, Skeletor, HG Toys, 1984, plastic, 6", MOC, M17 ....$30.00

Masters of the Universe, Colorforms, EX (EX box), B10 ..$15.00

Masters of the Universe, He-Man Superblobo, Unique, 1984, inflatable vinyl, expands to 7-ft, MIP, M17 ....$20.00

Masters of the Universe, Magnetix Playset, Am Publishing, 1985, MIP (sealed), M17 ....$25.00

Max Headroom, Fingertronic Puppet, Bendy Toys, 1987, finger holes in bk of head for action, 6", MIB, M17 ....$20.00

Mighty Mouse, charm bracelet, House of Charms, 1950s, 6 pnt charms w/Mighty Mouse & other Terry Toon characters, EX, A $50.00

Mighty Mouse, Launcher Pistol, Ja-Ru, 1981, MOC, H4 .$15.00

Mighty Mouse, magic slate, Lowe, 1950s, cb w/lift-up erasable film sheet, NM, T2 ....$50.00

Mighty Mouse, squeeze toy, Terrytoon, 1950s, pnt vinyl w/red felt cape, 10", EX $75.00

Moon Mullins, ventriloquist doll, Pure Oil Co premium, 1938, heavy stock paper, unpunched, 20x11", EX, A $65.00

Moon Mullins & Kayo, figures, Jaymar, jtd wood, 5½" & 4", EX, pr $200.00

Mork & Mindy, gumball machine, Mork, Hasbro, 1980, Mork figure sits on top, EX $25.00

Mork & Mindy, Magic Show Playset, Colorforms, 1980, MIB $30.00

Mork & Mindy, Mork From Ork Dress-Up Set, Colorforms, 1979, MIB $15.00

Mork & Mindy, Shrinky Dinks, Colorforms, 1979, MIB (sealed), C1 ....$25.00

Mother Goose, dishes, Ideal, 1940s, plastic, 26 pcs, MIB $150.00

Mr. Magoo, doll, Ideal, 1964, stuffed cloth with vinyl head, felt jacket with knitted scarf, 15", EX, minimum value, $75.00.
(Photo courtesy Judith Izen)

Mother Goose, jack-in-the-box, plays 'Mother Goose' song, NM $25.00

Mother Goose, Nursery Pianette, Schoenhut, 1940s, VG (VG box) $125.00

Mr Fantastic, flashlight, 1978, miniature, NMOC, J2 ......$45.00

Muppet Babies, doll, Kermit or Miss Piggy, Hasbro, 1985, 12", MIB, H4, ea $35.00

Muppets, bank, Miss Piggy, Sigma, NM, S21 ....$50.00

Muppets, Colorforms, 1984, EX (EX box), B10 ....$10.00

Muppets, doll, Kermit the Frog, Fisher-Price, 1976, foam-stuffed body w/vinyl head, 18", VG, H4 ....$25.00

Muppets, doll, Miss Piggy, Fisher-Price, 1980, foam-stuffed body w/vinyl head, rooted hair, purple dress, 14", EX $20.00

Muppets, stick puppet, Kermit the Frog, Fisher-Price, 1979, plastic, 3½", MOC, H4 ....$5.00

Mushmouth, doll, Ideal, 1960s, bendable felt body w/vinyl head, red felt vest, orig tag, 8", EX, A............................$120.00

Mutt & Jeff, drum, Converse, 1930, litho tin, 8" dia, EX, A..$200.00

Mutt & Jeff, figures, HC Fischer/US-Stasco, pnt celluloid, 4" & 5", EX, A $275.00

My Favorite Martian, Magic Trick Set, Gilbert, 1964, EX (EX box), A..$200.00

New Zoo Revue, doll, Charlie Owl, Rushton Co, 1971, w/tag, EX, C17 ....$75.00

New Zoo Revue, doll, Freddie, Kamar, 1977, stuffed plush, EX $30.00

Nightmare on Elm Street, doll, Freddy Kreuger, Matchbox, talker, 18", NRFB, H4 ....$50.00

Nightmare on Elm Street, make-up kit, Freddy Krueger, Collegeville, 1988, MIB, F1 ....$10.00

Nightmare on Elm Street, sticker album, 1991, M (M coffin-shaped box), F1 ....$30.00

Olive Oyl, see Popeye

Oswald Rabbit, magic slate, Saalfield, 1962, EX $35.00

Pacman, bank, EX, S21 ....$20.00

Partridge Family, bulletin board, 1970s, red cork w/music staff logo in wht, 18x24", EX, from $75 to......................$100.00

Partridge Family, doll, Patti Partridge, Ideal, 1971, MIB, from $125 to...$150.00

Patty Duke, Charm Jewelry Set, Standard Toykraft, 1963, complete w/jewelry box & charms, NMIB, from $65 to...$75.00

Patty Duke, Glamour Set, Standard Toykraft, 1963, complete w/comb, brush & mirror, NMIB, from $65 to $75.00

Peanuts, bank, Lucy at desk, ceramic, NM, S21 ....$30.00

Peanuts, bank, Snoopy, Lego, 1950s, chalkware, 8", VG, M17 ....$45.00

Peanuts, bank, Snoopy on rainbow, compo, NM, S21......$25.00

Peanuts, Colorforms, How's the Weather Lucy, EX (EX box), H11 ....$30.00

Peanuts, Colorforms, Peanuts Preschool, VG (VG box), H11..$25.00

Peanuts, Colorforms, Snoopy & Woodstock, EX (EX box), H11..$25.00

Peanuts, doll, Charlie Brown, 1950s, vinyl, 9", VG, J2.....$75.00

Peanuts, doll, Charlie Brown, 1963, pillow-type, stuffed printed cloth, EX, C17 ....$40.00

Peanuts, doll, Linus, Hungerford, in red shirt w/hand out, 8", MIP, H11 ....$75.00

Peanuts, doll, Lucy, rag-type, red dress, 14", VG, H11 .....$20.00

Peanuts, doll, Lucy, 1963, pillow-type, stuffed printed cloth, NM, C17...$40.00

Peanuts, doll, Peppermint Pattie, Determined Toys, 1970s, rag-type, 14", MIB...$30.00

Peanuts, doll, Snoopy, 1963, pillow-type, stuffed printed cloth, VG, C17 ....$35.00

Peanuts, doll, Snoopy as Santa, Applause, 1992, plush, 15", MIP, H11 ....$35.00

Peanuts, doll, Woodstock as Santa, Applause, plush, 9", MIP, H11 ....$20.00

Peanuts, drum, Chein, 1960s, litho tin w/image of all characters, 9" dia, scarce, EX (VG box), M17 ....$100.00

Peanuts, figure, Lucy in hula skirt, 1989, 3", M, H11.........$6.00

Peanuts, figure, Lucy Skiddler, Mattel, complete, NM, C17..$75.00

Peanuts, figure, Snoopy as Joe Cool, 3", M, H11 ....$8.00

Peanuts, figure, Snoopy in rowboat, 4", M, H11 ....$10.00

Peanuts, guitar, Snoopy, Mattel, crank action, NM $50.00

Peanuts, jack-in-the-box, Snoopy, Mattel, 1960s, litho tin, NM, from $75 to $85.00

Peanuts, megaphone, Charlie Brown, Chein, 1970, rare, EX, H11 ....$25.00

Peanuts, See & Say, Snoopy Says, Mattel, VG, H11........$50.00

Peanuts, Sing-Along Radio, Snoopy, Determined, EX, H11..$80.00

Peanuts, Snoopy Sign-Mobile Coloring Set, Avalon, 1977, MIB, H11 ....$70.00

Peanuts, tea set, Chein, complete, MIB, H11 ....$50.00

Peanuts, windup figures, M, from $5.00 to $10.00 each.
(Photo courtesy Martin and Carolyn Berens)

Pee Wee's Playhouse, Colorforms, 1988, MIB, B10/D9 ....$20.00
Peppermint Pattie, see Peanuts

Pee Wee's Playhouse, doll, Vance the Talking Pig, Matchbox, 1988, MIB, B5, $55.00. (Photo courtesy Martin and Carolyn Berens)

Phantom of the Opera, Rub-Ons Magic Picture Transfers, Hasbro, 1966, complete, NMIB, T2 ....$75.00

Phantom of the Opera, slide-tile puzzle, Defenders of the Earth, Ja-Ru, 1985, MOC, J5 ....$25.00

Pink Panther, Silly Putty, Ja-Ru, 1980, MOC, H4 ....$10.00

Pinky Lee, doll, Lose Your Head, rubber, squeeze body & head pops off, 9", NM, H4....................................$95.00

Pinky Lee, paint set, Gabriel, 1950s, complete, NMIB, J5..$75.00

Pinky Lee, party packet, 1950s, complete, M (NM mailer), J5 ....$100.00

Planet of the Apes, bank, General Ursus, Apac Prod, 1967, plastic, 18", NM, J6................................$30.00

Planet of the Apes, Colorforms Adventure Set, 1967, EX (EX box) $30.00

Planet of the Apes, doll, Cornelius, 1973, rubber, 6", EX+, H4......$40.00

Pokey, see Gumby and Pokey

Popeye, bank, Popeye, plastic figure, NM, S21 ....$30.00

Popeye, bank, Sweet Pea, Vandor, NM, S21 ....$175.00

Popeye, Barber Set, Larami, 1980, complete w/scissors, comb & razor, MOC, F1 ....$12.00

Popeye, Bifbat paddle, 1929, wood, no ball, 11", EX $15.00

Popeye, Bubble Set, Transogram, 1935, complete, MIB, A $125.00

Popeye, Cartoon Kit, Colorforms, 1957, few pcs missing, G (G box), P4.....................................$55.00

Popeye, colored chalk, Am Crayon, complete, EX (VG box), from $100 to $125.00

Popeye, doll, Jeep, King Features, 1935, jtd wood, decal on chest, 8¼", EX, A $500.00

Popeye, doll, Jeep, King Features, 1935, jtd wood w/decal on chest, 13", EX, A $950.00

Popeye, doll, Olive Oyl, Effanbee, stuffed cloth w/rubber head & compo feet, orig heart-shaped tag, 16", EX, A $325.00

Popeye, doll, Popeye, King Features, 1935, jtd wood, w/pipe in mouth, 14", EX, A.................................$1,800.00

Popeye, doll, Popeye, Play by Play, stuffed cloth w/vinyl head, M, H4..................................$20.00

Popeye, doll, Popeye, stuffed oilcloth, 11½", EX $75.00

Popeye, figure, Bluto, Italy/KFS, 1940s-50s, rubber w/hand-pnt details, 8", NMIP $125.00

Popeye, figure, Olive Oyl, mk Olive Oyl by KFS & Made in USA, jtd wood, 5", EX.................................$85.00

Popeye, figure, Popeye, Chein, 1931, jtd wood & compo w/plastic hat brim, orig decal on foot, 8", EX $400.00

Popeye, figure, Popeye, 1930s, celluloid, 4", NM, D10...$275.00

Popeye, figure, Popeye, 1930s, chalkware, 12", EX, D10, from $400 to...$500.00

Popeye, film, Fancy Skater, 1960s, 8mm, EX (EX box), J5 .$15.00

Popeye, flasher ring, Vari-Vue, 1960s, silver plastic, switches from Popeye to his buck-toothed nephew, NM, C1 ..$30.00

Popeye, floating toy, 1950s-60s, vinyl boat w/Popeye figure on top, 6", NMIP, J5 ....$45.00

Popeye, harmonica, metal w/full-color decal, 4", EX (EX box)...$165.00

Popeye, jack-in-the-box, Popeye in the Music Box, Mattel, litho tin w/various characters on all sides, NM, from $150 to....$200.00

Popeye, lantern, Linemar, tin & glass w/rubber pipe, battery-op, 7½", NM (EX box), A....................................$675.00

Popeye, Magic Play Around, Amsco, complete, NM (NM box)..$300.00

Popeye, Metal Tapping Set, Dank, 1957, complete, unused, MIB, A..$325.00

Popeye, Paint-o-graf, Milton Bradley, 1935, complete, EX (EX box)..$350.00

Popeye, Pencil-by-Number Set, 1959, unused, MIB, V1 ..$35.00

Popeye, pogs, various characters, set of 20 in bag, EX, F1 ...$6.00

Popeye, Popeye the Printer Stamp Set, Stamper Kraft, EX (EX box)..$175.00

Popeye, sparkler, Chein, lithographed tin, lever action, NMIB, A, $385.00.

Popeye, squeaker, Olive Oyl, rubber, 8½", VG, A............$85.00

Popeye, Stitch-A-Story, Hasbro, 1967, MOC, J2 ....$55.00

Popeye, Stow-A-Way Slate, Lowe, 1957, 12x8", unused, NM, T2..$30.00

Popeye, Strength Tester Muscle Builder, Wedled Plastics, 1940, pull on hdl to measure strength, EX, A....................$150.00

Popeye, xylophone pull toy, Metal Masters, wood & metal, 10½", EX...$125.00

Popeye & Olive Oyl, figures, Japan, prewar, jtd wood w/heads mounted on springs, rnd bases, 9", EX, A $600.00

Popeye & Olive Oyl, Slinky pull toy, Linemar, litho tin heads w/Slinky bodies on 4-wheeled platform, 6½", EX, A...$800.00

Popeye & Sweet Pea, pull toy, 1930s, paper litho on wood, NM, from $150 to $200.00

Porky Pig, bubble gum machine, Banko Matic, 1970s, plastic figure, 9½", EX (EX box), J5 ....$25.00

Porky Pig, figure, 1930s, chalkware, 7", EX $75.00

Porky Pig, jack-in-the-box, Mattel, 1960s, litho tin, NM $150.00

Prince Valiant, figure, 1942, pressed wood figure on base, 6", NM, T2..$200.00

Princess of Power, Butterflyer, Mattel, MIB, B5 ....$40.00

Punky Brewster, doll, Galoob, 1984, 18", NRFB, M15 .....$40.00

Raggedy Andy, bulletin board, Manton Cork Corp, diecut, 23", MIP $30.00

Raggedy Andy, doll, Applause, stuffed cloth w/yarn hair, several facial variations, 8", EX, ea.............................$12.00

Raggedy Andy, doll, Applause, 1986, stuffed cloth w/yarn hair, 25", EX...$50.00

Raggedy Andy, doll, Georgene, 1938-40, stuffed cloth w/yarn hair, 19", EX, from $375 to...............................$400.00

Raggedy Andy, doll, Little Raggedy, Direct Connect International, 1990, cloth w/rubber head, 6½", MIB $12.00

Raggedy Andy, doll, Reliable/Canada, stuffed cloth w/yarn hair, 19", EX, from $175 to...............................$200.00

Raggedy Andy, Sew & Love, Colorforms, 1975, complete, MIB...$25.00

Raggedy Ann, bank, Pussy Willow Creations/Bobbs-Merrill, 1981, seated w/puppy, ceramic w/yarn hair, 6", M.....$25.00

Raggedy Ann, Busy Apron, Whitman/Bobbs-Merrill, 1969, MIB...$35.00

Raggedy Ann, doll, Applause, 1986, stuffed cloth w/yarn hair, 36", EX...$80.00

Raggedy Ann, doll, Georgene, 1940-45, cloth w/yarn hair, awake on 1 side, asleep on the other, 12½", EX, from $275 to...$325.00

Raggedy Ann, doll, Georgene, 1946-63, stuffed cloth w/yarn hair, 22", EX, from $125 to...............................$145.00

Raggedy Ann, doll, Heart-to-Heart Raggedy Ann, Playskool, 1992, press hand on heart to hear heartbeat, 17", MIB..........$45.00

Raggedy Ann, doll, Knickerbocker, musical, stuffed cloth w/yarn hair, 15", MIB $95.00

Raggedy Ann, doll, Little Raggedy, Direct Connect International, 1990, cloth w/rubber head, 6½", MIB $12.00

Raggedy Ann, doll, Nasco, 1975, plastic w/cloth clothes, yarn hair, fully jtd, 9", EX...$20.00

Raggedy Ann, iron, Gabriel/Bobbs-Merrill, 1970, metal w/plastic hdl, 6½", EX, from $25 to....................................$30.00

Raggedy Ann, jewelry box, Durham/Bobbs-Merrill, 1972, plays Raindrops Keep Falling on My Head, M, from $25 to .$30.00

Raggedy Ann, jump rope, Hallmark/Bobbs-Merrill, plastic hdls, MIP $22.00

Raggedy Ann, Krazy Ikes, Western Pub/Bobbs-Merrill, 1968, MOC..$25.00

Raggedy Ann, Learn-To-Dress Doll, Miner Industries/Bobbs-Merrill, 1972, 14½", MOC......................................$35.00

Raggedy Ann, pajama bag doll, Knickerbocker, 1960s, several dress styles, 27", M, ea $35.00

Raggedy Ann, Pop-Up Tea Party, Colorforms, complete, MIB $30.00

Raggedy Ann, sewing kit, Pussy Willow Creations/Bobbs-Merrill, 1981, Raggedy Ann & hearts on front, metal closure, M $20.00

Raggedy Ann, sink, Hasbro/Bobbs Merrill, 1978, plastic, 20", MIB $50.00

Raggedy Ann & Andy, bank, Determined/Bobbs-Merrill, 1971, seated, papier-mache, 6", M $25.00

Raggedy Ann & Andy, bank, Lefton, NM, ea $25.00

Raggedy Ann & Andy, beach ball, Ideal, 1974, vinyl, inflates to 20", MIP..$35.00

Raggedy Ann & Andy, beanbag chair, Bobbs-Merrill, 1975, full-color image on wht, rare, M $50.00

Raggedy Ann & Andy, camper, Buddy L/Bobbs Merrill, metal & plastic, complete w/figures, EX $45.00

Raggedy Ann & Andy, dolls, inflatable vinyl, Raggedy Ann: 14½", Andy: 12", M, ea...$35.00

Raggedy Ann & Andy, Fun-Filled Playtime Box, Whitman, 1976, complete w/coloring books, paper dolls, puzzles, etc, MIB $30.00

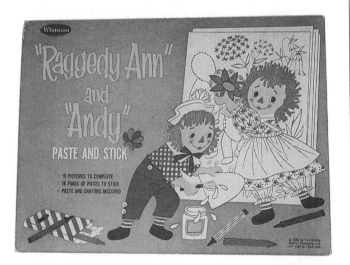

Raggedy Ann and Andy, Paste and Stick, Whitman, 1968, MIB, $30.00.

Raggedy Ann & Andy, Play-Pak, Colorforms, 1988, complete, MIB...$15.00

Raggedy Ann & Andy, tambourine, Kingsway/Bobbs-Merrill, 1977, plastic, 6" dia, MOC....................................$20.00

Raggedy Ann & Andy, tea set, Wolverine/Bobbs-Merrill, 1978, plastic & metal, 26 pcs, MIB......................................$50.00

Rambo, knife & sheath, Largo, 1986, plastic, MIP, F1 .....$12.00

Rambo, walkie-talkies, Largo, 1985, complete w/headband, MOC, M17 ....$30.00

Ranger Rick, see Yogi Bear

Reg'lar Fellas, doll, Aggie, Jimmie or Puddin' Head, Bucherer, jtd metal & compo w/cloth clothes, 8", EX, ea from $350 to $450.00

Reg'lar Fellers, Microscope Set, complete, EX (EX box) ..$275.00

Ricochet Rabbit, doll, Ideal, 1960s, bendable felt body w/vinyl head, w/felt accessories, orig tag on leg, 8", EX, A...$125.00

Ripcord, magic slate, Lowe, 1963, cb w/lift-up erasable film sheet, unused, NM, A..$40.00

Robin, see Batman

Robin Hood, hat, Official Films, 1950s, gr & brn felt w/image & lg feather, scarce, NM, M17 ....$45.00

Robin Hood, iron-on patch, Johnson & Johnson, 1956, Bondex fabric, 3x3", MOC, M17..$25.00

Rocky & Bullwinkle, blackboard, Frolic Toys, 1970s, diecut figure at top, 12x16", scarce, VG, A.................................$50.00

Rocky & Bullwinkle, Bullwinkle Electric Quiz Game, 1971, MOC (sealed), J2..$40.00

Rocky & Bullwinkle, Castanets, Larami, 1972, MOC, C1 .$20.00

Rocky & Bullwinkle, dish set, Melmac, Bullwinkle graphics, EX, C10..$65.00

Rocky & Bullwinkle, doll, Bullwinkle, Mattel, 1971, pull-string talker, 11", EX, B5 ....$125.00

Rocky & Bullwinkle, doll, Bullwinkle, Wallace Berrie, 1982, plush, 10", EX, C17..$30.00

Rocky & Bullwinkle, figure, any character, Wham-O, MOC, ea $25.00

Rocky & Bullwinkle, figure set, Rocky, Natasha & Boris, 1991, bendable, MOC, V1 ....$20.00

Rocky & Bullwinkle, spelling & counting board, Larami, 1969, MOC, C1 ....$28.00

Rocky & Bullwinkle, telescope, Larami, 1970s, features Bullwinkle, MOC, H4...$10.00

Roger Ramjet, figure, Magic Triangle Toys, 1966, rubber, 6", MOC, T2 ....$200.00

Scrappy, xylophone pull toy, paper lithograph on wood, EX, $375.00. (Photo courtesy David Longest)

Saturday Night Live, figure, Wayne or Garth, PVC, 4", M, F1, ea $6.00

Scooby Doo, doll, Sutton, 1970s, stuffed plush, EX, H4 ...$40.00

Scooby Doo, gumball machine, Hasbro, 1968, clear plastic head w/yel base, EX, J5 ....$25.00

Scooby Doo, necklace, Kings Island, MOC, C17 ....$30.00

Scrappy, paint set, New Jersey Crayon Co, 1930s, complete, NM (EX box) $100.00

Sesame Street, bank, Big Bird on toy box, ceramic, NM, S21 .$20.00

Sesame Street, bank, Big Bird w/egg, compo, NM, S21 ....$20.00

Sesame Street, bank, Ernie on train, ceramic, NM, S21 ...$20.00

Sesame Street, doll, Big Bird, Ideal, talks w/tape player, 25", VG, M15 ....$55.00

Sesame Street, doll, Big Bird, Playskool, 1970s, pull-string talker, 22", VG, M15 ....$25.00

Sesame Street, doll, Cookie Monster, Hasbro, 1970s, stuffed plush w/ping-pong ball eyes, 12", VG $15.00

Sesame Street, piano, Cookie Monster, Gabriel, 1976, plastic, Cookie Monster's eyes twirl when played, 9½", EX...$15.00

Sesame Street, snack set, Chilton Globe, 1988, complete, MIB, M17 ....$20.00

Silverhawks, Colorforms, 1986, EX (EX box), B10...........$15.00

Simpsons, air mattress, Mattel, inflatable vinyl, 72x30", MIP, K1 ....$30.00

Simpsons, Airwalker, Bart, Anagram International, Mylar, MIP, K1 ....$15.00

Simpsons, chalk, Bart, Noteworthy, 3-D sculptured & colored, MOC, K1 ....$10.00

Simpsons, doll, Bubble Blowin' Lisa, Mattel, complete w/4-oz bottle of bubble solution, 10½", MIB, K1 ....$50.00

Simpsons, doll, Really Rude Bart, Mattel, w/2 noisemakers, 18", MIB, K1 ....$50.00

Simpsons, doll, Sweet Suckin' Maggie, Mattel, sucks pacifier, 18", MIB, K1 ....$60.00

Simpsons, Double Stamp Set, Lisa, Jaru, MIP, K1 ....$15.00

Simpsons, figure, any character, Mattel, PVC, ea w/5 inter-changeable balloons, MOC, K1, ea from $20 to $25.00

Simpsons, figure, Bart w/slingshot, Presents, bendable, 9", MIP, K1 ....$16.00

Simpsons, figure, Homer, Jesco, bendable, 6", MOC, K1 .$15.00

Simpsons, figure, Lisa, Jesco, bendable, 3½", MOC, K1 ...$15.00

Simpsons, figure, Maggie, Presents, bendable, 6", M, K1 ..$16.00

Simpsons, figure, Marge, Presents, bendable, 9½", M, K1 .$15.00

Simpsons, flashlight, Bart, Happiness Express, 3-D figure in gr shirt on side of red flashlight, MOC, K1 ....$12.00

Simpsons, Flip Face, Bart, Jaru, MOC, K1 ....$10.00

Simpsons, frisbee, Bart, Betras Plastics, wht w/image & Radical Dude!, M, K1 ....$5.00

Simpsons, hand-held video game, Bart Vs Homersaurus, Tiger, MIP, K1..$35.00

Simpsons, hand-held video game, Cupcake Crisis, Acclaiment, MIP, K1..$25.00

Simpsons, pinball game, Jaru, plastic, MIP, K1 ....$10.00

Simpsons, Pop Gun Target, Homer, Jaru, MIP, K1..........$10.00

Simpsons, poster book, Button-Up, complete w/8 tear-out posters, NM, K1 ....$8.00

Simpsons, Rad Rollers, Spectra Star, set of 6 marbles, MOC, K1 ....$15.00

Simpsons, rag doll, Bart, Dandee, stuffed cloth, 11", MOC, K1 ....$20.00

Simpsons, rag doll, Lisa, Dandee, stuffed cloth, 11", MOC, K1 ....$20.00

Simpsons, slide-tile puzzle, Bart, Jaru, set of 4, NM, K1....$15.00

Simpsons, Sofa & Boob Tube, Mattel, MIB, K1 ....$60.00

Simpsons, stick-on doll, Bart, Dandee, rag-type w/suction cups on hands & feet, several variations, 8", MIB, K1, ea .$16.00

Simpsons, Time & Money, Marge, Jaru, MIP, K1............$10.00

Sinbad Jr, Magic Belt, Voplex, 1965, red plastic w/bl & wht plastic diamond-shaped buckle, battery-op, NMIB, T2 ..$160.00

Six Million Dollar Man, fan club kit, 1970s, NM, A........$85.00

Skeezix, doll, Live Long Toys, 1924, stuffed printed cloth, 14", EX, A $85.00

Skippy, paint & coloring set, ATW, 1935, complete, NMIB, A...$135.00

Smokey the Bear, doll, 1967, 15", MIB, M15 ....$125.00

Smokey the Bear, magic slate, Watkins-Strathmore, 1969, EX, A $85.00

Smurfs, clip-on figure, Papa Smurf, Applause, 1991, set of 4, MOC, F1 ....$10.00

Smurfs, Colorforms, complete, EX (EX box), B5 ....$35.00

Smurfs, doll, Papa Smurf, stuffed cloth, press tummy & it plays Smurfy Melody, 13", MIB, F1 ....$25.00

Smurfs, Fun Club Packet, w/newsletters & stickers, EX, B5.$45.00

Smurfs, Magic Talk Papa Smurf's Lab, Mattel Preschool, complete, MIB, from $40 to $50.00

Smurfs, Musical Tree-Go-Round, Irwin, complete, MIB, F1..$30.00

Smurfs, punching balloon, set of 6 w/various characters, NM, F1 ....$15.00

Smurfs, sewing cards, MIB (sealed), B5 ....$25.00

Snoopy, see Peanuts

Snydley Whiplash, figure, Wham-O, 1971, bendable, MOC, H4 ....$15.00

Soupy Sales, doll, Sunshine Dolls, 1956, 6", MIB, J2 .....$235.00

Spark Plug, see Barney Google

Sparkle Plenty, see Dick Tracy

Spider-Man, bank, Renzi, 1979, plastic bust figure, 15", EX, T2 ....$25.00

Spider-Man, bicycle license plate, Marx, 1967, litho tin w/raised image, 2x4", NM, T2 ....$50.00

Spider-Man, Buddy L Set, 1980, complete w/4 vehicles, MIB, T2 ....$200.00

Spider-Man, Code Breaker, Gordy, 1980, MOC, C1........$30.00

Spider-Man, Color 'N Recolor Action Pictures, Avalon, 1977, unused, MIB, T2 ....$50.00

Spider-Man, Colorforms Adventure Set, 1974, complete, MIB, from $20 to..$25.00

Spider-Man, Communication & Code Set, HG Toys, 1978, complete, MIB, T2 ....$100.00

Spider-Man, doll, Energized Spider-Man, Remco, 11", EX (G box), H4 ....$40.00

Spider-Man, Fly 'Em High Parachutist & Launcher, AHI, 1979, M (VG card), C1 ....$30.00

Spider-Man, poster, Hudson Pharmaceutical Corp, 1975, glossy, 30x20", EX $50.00

Spider-Man, Reading Motivation Kit, McGraw-Hill Films, 1975, complete in suitcase-style box, NM, T2 ....$300.00

Spider-Man, Sharp Shooter, Larami, 1978, MOC, T2 .....$40.00

Spider-Man, Spider-Man & the Marvel Heroes Rub 'N Play Magic Transfer Set, Colorforms, 1978, complete, MIB, T2 ....$50.00

Spider-Man, TV chair, Carlin Playthings, 1978, inflatable vinyl, MIB, T2 ....$50.00

Spider-Man, walkie-talkies, Nasta, 1984, plastic, battery-op, MIB, T2 ....$50.00

Spider-Man, wallet, 1978, brn plastic w/image of Spider-Man on yel circle, NM, C1 ....$18.00

Spider-Man, Web Maker, Chemtoys, 1977, complete, MOC, T2 ....$100.00

Starsky & Hutch, handcuffs & wallet, Fleetwood, 1976, MOC...$25.00

Starsky & Hutch, walkie-talkies, Mettoy, 1970s, MIB, from $65 to $75.00

Steve Canyon, Jet Helmet, Ideal, 1959, wht plastic w/gr shades, visors & decals, MIB, T2 ....$100.00

Superman, balloon, 1960s, flying pose, NM, J5 ....$15.00

Superman, bank, Enesco, 1987, compo, MIB, S21 ....$85.00

Superman, bank, NPPI, 1974, plastic, NM, S21 ....$55.00

Superman, Cartoonist Stamp Set, 1966, complete, MOC..$75.00

Superman, Crazy Foam, American Aerosol, 1974, metal canister w/full-color image, plastic cap, NM, T2....................$50.00

Superman, doll, Ideal, 1939, jointed wood with red cloth cape, 12", EX, from $800.00 to $1,000.00.

Superman, doll, Mego, 1970s, talker, stuffed cloth, 24", EX, J5 .$45.00

Superman, figure, Ben Cooper, 1970s, rubber, 5", M, J5...$15.00

Superman, Flip Flashlight, Bantamlite, 1966, bl plastic w/decal, complete w/key chain, MOC $150.00

Superman, gym bag, DC Comics, 1971, yel & bl vinyl w/image & logo, 9x12", NM, T2 ....$50.00

Superman, Horseshoe Set, Superswim Inc, 1950s, complete, EX (EX box), T2..$65.00

Superman, Kiddie Paddlers, Superswim Inc, 1956, bl rubber swimming fins, NMIB, T2 ....$100.00

Superman, Movie Viewer, Acme, 1940, complete w/5 boxes of film, NMIB, T2, from $300 to..................................$400.00

Superman, Muscle Building Set, Peter Puppet Playthings, 1954, complete, NMIB, T2, from $400 to $500.00

Superman, Oil Painting-by-Numbers Set, Hasbro, 1968, unused, complete, NMIB, T2 ....$50.00

Superman, playsuit, Funtime Playwear, 1954, complete w/Superman's Buddy comic book, rare, EX (EX box), from $400 to $500.00

Superman, scrapbook, Saalfield, 1940, 50 pgs, NM, T2 .$200.00

Superman, slide-tile puzzle, Roalex, 1966, 4x5", MIP, T2, from $65 to $75.00

Superman, Thingmaker Accessory Kit, Mattel, 1960s, complete, MOC, J5..$85.00

Superman, wallet, 1966, yel vinyl w/colorful graphics, w/magic pad & pencil, etc, NM, J5 ....$85.00

Tales of Wells Fargo, jail key & agent badge set, 1950s, scarce, MOC, M17 ....$85.00

Tarzan, Jungle Animals Set, Salco/Banner, 1966, complete, unused, NM (EX box) $200.00

Tarzan, Magic Rub-Off Picture Set, Whitman, 1966, complete, VG (VG box), A $25.00

Tarzan, Weebles Jungle Hut, Romper Room/ Hasbro, 1976, MIB, $85.00. (Photo courtesy June Moon)

Tasmanian Devil, doll, Mighty Star, 1970s, stuffed cloth, EX, C17..$40.00

Tasmanian Devil, doll, 1980, stuffed plush, 13", EX.........$15.00

Teenage Mutant Ninja Turtles, bank, Leonardo, made in Taiwan, NM, S21 ....$25.00

Teenage Mutant Ninja Turtles, Colorforms, 1989, EX (EX box), B10..$10.00

Teenage Mutant Ninja Turtles, tote bag, Mirage Studio, 1989, repeated design, 14x8", NM, M17............................$20.00

Teenage Mutant Ninja Turtles, water bopper, 1990, inflatable, 3-ft, MIP, M17..$25.00

Terminator, video & doll, pulled from market, rare, MIB, P12..$95.00

Thief of Bagdad, doll, Sabu, jtd compo w/cloth costume, 16", EX+, A..$650.00

Thor, pillow, Marvel Comics, 1968, inflatable plastic w/colorful image, 12x12", MIP, T2 ....$100.00

Three Stooges, dolls, Exclusive Premier/Target, 10", set of 3, F1 ....$150.00

Three Stooges, dolls, One Stop Toy, 1996, plush w/vinyl heads, wearing football uniforms, 13", set of 3, M, F1.........:$40.00

Three Stooges, figures, Applause, 1988, orig tags & stands, set of 3, 14", M, H14 ....$140.00

Three Stooges, Slap-Stick-On, Colorforms, 1959, scarce, MIB, M17..$300.00

Tom & Jerry, Checkers Game, Ja-Ru, 1990, MOC, H4 ...$10.00

Tom & Jerry, guitar, Mattel, 1960s, plastic, NM, from $125 to..$175.00

Tom & Jerry, Music Maker, Mattel, 1960s, litho tin, plays theme song, NM, from $65 to..............................$75.00

Tom Corbett Space Cadet, Model-Craft Molding & Coloring Set, complete, rare, MIB, A $165.00

Toonerville Trolley, figure set, bsk, Japan, w/Katrinka, Skipper, Mickey McGuire & Trolley, approx 2" to 3", NM, A.$300.00

Tweety Bird, doll, Chatter Chum, Mattel, 1976, MIB, P12 ....$45.00

Tweety Bird, lantern, Amico, 1950s, tin & glass, battery-op, 5½", EX...$85.00

Uncle Wiggily, bank, Chein, insert penny & he raises carrot to mouth, litho tin, 5", NM, A $350.00

Uncle Wiggily, doll, Georgene, stuffed cloth, orig clothes, 20", NM..$550.00

Underdog, harmonica, 1957, yel & gr plastic w/raised image of Underdog & Simon Bar Sinister, 7", NM, C1 ....$70.00

Underdog, harmonica, 1975, yel plastic w/figure at both ends, 8", EX, T2 ....$20.00

Universal Monsters, iron-on transfers, 1964, set of 6, M (NM T-shirt-shaped card), H4 ....$185.00

Universal Monsters, Monster Balls, Illco, 1980s, any character, NMOC, ea $25.00

Universal Monsters, pencil sharpener, Mummy, Universal Pictures, 1960s, plastic figure, 3", EX, V1........................$40.00

Universal Monsters, Stick 'N Lift Monsters Kit, Am Publishing, 1980s, MIB (sealed), M17 ....$65.00

Welcome Back Kotter, beanbag chair, Barbarino, 1970s, yel w/photo image, EX, from $50 to...............................$60.00

Welcome Back Kotter, chalkboard, Board King, 1976, M..$45.00

Welcome Back Kotter, Colorforms, 1970s, complete, EX (EX box), B10 ....$35.00

Welcome Back Kotter, jump rope, MSS, 1977, MIP, A ...$35.00

Welcome Back Kotter, record case, Komack/Walper, 1976, color photos on both sides, EX, M17...................................$90.00

Welcome Back Kotter, slide-tile puzzle, 1976, MOC........$15.00

Where's Waldo, doll, Waldo, Mattel, MIB, B5................$60.00

Where's Waldo, figure set, Applause, PVC, set of 5, M, F1 ..$12.00

Wizard of Oz, bank, Dorothy, Arnart Imports, 1960s, hand-pnt, orig paper tag, 7", NMIB, S6 ....$825.00

Wizard of Oz, bank, Scarecrow, Arnart Imports, 1960s, hand-pnt, orig paper tag, 7", NMIB, S6........................$100.00

Wizard of Oz, bank, Tin Woodsman, Arnart Imports, 1960s, hand-pnt, orig paper tag, 7", MIB, S6 ....$135.00

Wizard of Oz, doll, Dorothy, Ideal, 1939-40, jtd compo w/red-checked rayon dress, 15½", M, minimum value...$1,000.00

Wizard of Oz, doll, Scarecrow, Ideal, 1939, stuffed cloth with painted mask face and yarn hair, 17", NM, $800.00.
(Photo courtesy Judith Izen)

Wizard of Oz, figure, Cowardly Lion or Tin Woodsman, Multiple, 1960s, rubber, 6", EX, ea..................................$55.00

Wizard of Oz, jack-in-the-box, Scarecrow, 1967, plays 'Hail Hail the Gang's All Here,' NM $50.00

Wizard of Oz, Magic Kit, Fun Inc, 1960s, complete w/10 tricks, NMIB..$50.00

Wizard of Oz, toy watch, Scarecrow & Tin Woodsman, Occupied Japan, 1940s, red fabric band, M, S6 ....$50.00

Wolfman, flashlight keychain, Basic Fun, 1995, MOC, M17.$12.00

Wonder Woman, Colorforms Adventure Set, 1976, EX (EX box), J2..$30.00

Wonder Woman, Magnetic Maze Chase Game, Nasta, 1980, plastic, MOC, J5 ....$35.00

Wonder Woman, slide-tile puzzle, 1978, EX, M17 ....$30.00

Woodstock, see Peanuts

Woody Woodpecker, harmonica, early, plastic figure, 6", EX, J2..$30.00

Woody Woodpecker, kazoo, Linden, 1960s, red plastic figure, 7", EX...$25.00

Woody Woodpecker, Music Maker, Mattel, 1960s, litho tin w/hand crank, plays theme song, EX, from $55 to.....$65.00

Yogi Bear, bop toy, 1960s, plastic roly poly figure w/weighted bottom, 7", EX, J5 ....$45.00

Yogi Bear, bubble pipe, Hanna-Barbera, 1960s, red plastic figure, NM, from $20 to..$25.00

Yogi Bear, Cartoonist Stamp Set, Lido, 1960s, MOC, M17..$45.00

Yogi Bear, doll, Ranger Rick, Giacotelli, stuffed cloth, 10", rare, NM..$65.00

Yogi Bear, doll, Yogi, Knickerbocker, EX, C17...............$50.00

Yogi Bear, camera, 1960s, MIB, $65.00.
(Photo courtesy June Moon)

Yogi Bear, doll, Yogi, Playtime, 1960s, plush w/felt hat, collar & tie, 17", EX..$50.00
Yogi Bear, doll, Yogi, 1977, pillow-type w/bells inside, 15", NM..$25.00
Yogi Bear, pencil box, Kanley/Australia, 1980s, silver metal w/colorful image, unused, NM, C1.............................$25.00
Yogi Bear, Wipe-Off Coloring Cloth, Hanna-Barbera, 1960s, MIP, from $25 to $35.00
Yogi Bear & Huckleberry Hound, slide-tile puzzle, Roalex, 1960, plastic, MOC, C1...$45.00

Chein

Though the company was founded shortly after the turn of the century, this New Jersey-based manufacturer is probably best known for the toys it made during the '30s and '40s. Wind-up merry-go-rounds and Ferris wheels as well as many other carnival-type rides were made of beautifully lithographed tin even into the '50s, some in several variations. The company also made banks, a few of which were mechanical and some that were character-related. Mechanical, sea-worthy cabin cruisers, space guns, sand toys, and some Disney toys as well were made by this giant company; they continued in production until 1979.

Advisor: Scott Smiles (S10).

See also Banks; Disney; Sand Toys.

WINDUPS, FRICTIONS, AND OTHER MECHANICALS

Aquaplane, 1939, advances w/spinning prop, 8½", EX (EX box) $500.00
Barnacle Bill Floor Puncher, 1930s, figure punches bag on rectangular base, litho tin & celluloid, 7", EX, A $700.00
Barnacle Bill in Barrel, 1930s, waddles back & forth in barrel, 7", NM, A..$400.00
Big Top Tent, 1961, spins & opens to reveal clown, tin w/plastic dome, 10", EX (EX box) $200.00
Clown Floor Puncher, clown hits punching bag, 8½", EX, A ..$750.00
Dan-Dee Oil Truck, litho tin w/balloon tires, NM.........$475.00
Disneyland Ferris Wheel, spins w/bell sound, litho tin, 17", NM, A $600.00
Fancy Groceries Truck, 6", EX, A $350.00
Felix the Cat on Scooter, 7", EX, A $650.00
Hand-Standing Clown, 5", EX, from $125 to $150.00

Barnacle Bill, advances in waddling motion, 6½", NM, $300.00.
(Photo courtesy Dunbar Gallery)

Drummer Boy, 1930s, NM, $300.00.
(Photo courtesy Scott Smiles)

Happy Hooligan, 1932, advances in waddling motion, 6", NM, from $1,400 to $1,500.00
Hercules Coal Truck, blk Mack cab w/gr body, yel & red side plates, 19½", EX, A...$1,700.00
Hercules Ferris Wheel, spins w/ringing bell, 17", NM, from $350 to...$450.00
Hercules Roadster, red w/blk top & running boards, 17½", G, A .$350.00
Indian in Headdress, 1930s, EX, from $150 to................$175.00
Junior Truck, mk 420 on doors, gr w/red tires, half-figure driver, 8", EX..$350.00
Marine, EX, from $200 to...$250.00
Musical Aero Swing, 4 gondolas spin around w/music, litho tin, 11", VG (VG box), A...$750.00

Native on Turtle, 1930s, advances w/moving head, 8", NM (EX box)..$450.00

Penguin, advances in waddling motion, 4", EX $125.00

Playland Merry-Go-Round, horses & swans circle w/bell sound, 10", EX (EX box) $650.00

Playland Whip, 4 kids in cars fly around base w/bobbing heads, 20" base, EX (EX box) $800.00

Popeye Drummer, advances & plays parade drum, 7", NM, A $2,700.00

Popeye Floor Puncher, litho tin figure hits celluloid bag on rectangular base, 7", EX, from $1,200 to.....................$1,300.00

Popeye Heavy Hitter, 1932, figure rings strength meter bell, litho tin, 12", rare, EX, A.....................................$3,500.00

Popeye in Barrel, 1932, waddles back & forth in barrel, litho tin, 7", G, A...$475.00

Popeye in Barrel, 1932, waddles back & forth in barrel, litho tin, 7", EX, A..$600.00

Popeye on Roof, 1930s, Popeye dances atop roof, litho tin, NM, from $800 to $1,000.00

Popeye Overhead Puncher, 1932, 9½", rare, NM $2,500.00

Popeye Shadow Boxer, advances in vibrating motion w/swinging arms, litho tin, 7", rare, VG, A $1,700.00

Popeye Waddler, 1932, 6½", G, A.................................$500.00

Popeye Waddler, 1932, 6½", NM, $1,300.00.

Seaplane, 1930s, 9", EX, $250.00.
(Photo courtesy Dunbar Gallery)

Racer #52, tin w/wooden wheels, EX $200.00

Ride-A-Rocket Carousel, 4 rockets w/figures circle tower, litho tin w/celluloid props, 18", NM.........................$900.00

Roller Coaster, 1930s, w/2 cars & bell, 19", NM (NM box)..$450.00

Roller Coaster, 1950s, 19", EX $300.00

Santa Claus (Walking Dwarf), early, waddles around w/present, litho tin, 6", NMIB, A...$800.00

Ski Boy, advances on snow skiis, 8", NM, A..................$275.00

Ski Ride, kids travel to top of ride, 19½", EX (EX box)..$1,100.00

Toyville Dump Truck, red, gr & yel, 9", NM, A.............$350.00

Yellow Taxi, early, mk Yellow Taxi Main 7570, 6", EX .$200.00

MISCELLANEOUS

Cathedral Organ, turn crank & music plays, litho tin, 9½", NMIB, from $175 to...$225.00

Junior Bus, litho tin, 9", G, A......................................$200.00

Popeye Sparkler, 1959, sparks fly behind clear red window inserts, plunger action, EX (EX box) $275.00

Pull Toy, cat on 3-wheeled platform, litho tin, 7½", EX, A.$500.00

Pull Toy, Krazy Kat Express, 1932, pnt wood w/litho tin lion on front, 12", scarce, EX...$1,600.00

Top, 1930s, litho tin w/various images of children's toys, NM $100.00

Top, 1970s, features Disney characters, litho tin w/plastic knob, 6½" dia, EX...$35.00

Chinese Tin Toys

China has produced toys for export since the 1920s, but most of their tin toys were made from the 1970s to the present. Collectors are buying them with an eye to the future, since right now, at least, they are relatively inexpensive.

Government-operated factories are located in various parts of China. They use various numbering systems to identify types of toys, for instance, ME (metal-electric — battery operated), MS (metal-spring — windup), MF (metal friction), and others. Most toys and boxes are marked, but some aren't; and since many of the toys are reproductions of earlier Japanese models, it is often difficult to tell the difference if no numbers can be found.

Prices vary greatly depending on age, condition, availability, and dealer knowledge of origin. Toys currently in production may be discontinued at any time and may often be as hard to find as the earlier toys. Records are so scarce that it is difficult to pinpoint the start of production, but at least some manufacture began in the 1970s and 1980s. If you have additional information (toy name and number; description as to size, color variations, actions, type, etc.; and current market), please contact our advisor. In the listings below, values are for new-in-the-box items. Advisor: Steve Fisch (F7).

#ME021, police car, current, 16½x5x5", F7, from $55 to..$125.00

#ME060, tank, remote control, 1970s, 7x4x4", F7, from $35 to...$75.00

#ME084, jet plane, current, 12½x13x5", F7, from $35 to..$75.00

#ME086, Shanghai bus, F7, from $85 to $150.00

#ME087, jetliner, 1980s, 19x18x3", F7, from $55 to **$125.00**

#ME089, Universe car, 1970s, F7, from $85 to..............**$150.00**

#ME093, open-door trolley, discontinued, 10x5x4", F7, from $25 to...**$35.00**

#ME095, fire chief car, current, 12½x5x5", F7, from $35 to ..**$75.00**

#ME097, police car, 13x5x5", F7, from $35 to.................**$75.00**

#ME099, UFO spaceship, current, 8x8x5", F7, from $35 to..**$75.00**

#ME100, robot (resembles 1980s Star Strider robot), current, 12x4x6", F7, from $35 to..**$125.00**

#ME102, spaceship, blows air, current, 13x5x4", F7, from $35 to...**$75.00**

#ME104, locomotive, 15½x4x7", F7, from $35 to...........**$75.00**

#ME105, locomotive, 9½x5½x5½", F7, from $35 to.......**$75.00**

#ME379, dump truck, discontinued, 13x4x3", F7, from $25 to...**$35.00**

#ME603, hens & chickens, F7, from $35 to......................**$50.00**

#ME610, hen laying eggs, current, 7x4x6", F7, from $25 to.**$50.00**

#ME611, News car or World Cap car, 5x16½x5", F7, ea, from $55 to...**$125.00**

#ME614, automatic rifle, current, 23x2x8", F7, from $25 to ..**$35.00**

#ME630, Photo car, older version, 12½x5x5", from $35 to..**$125.00**

#ME677, Shanghai convertible, 1970s, 12x5x3", F7, from $60 to...**$100.00**

#ME679, dump truck, discontinued, 13x4x3", F7, from $25 to..**$50.00**

#ME699, fire chief car, current, 10x5x2", from $25 to **$50.00**

#ME756, anti-aircraft armoured tank, F7, from $35 to.....**$75.00**

#ME767, Universe boat, current, 10x5x6", F7, from $35 to...**$75.00**

#ME767, Universe boat, 1970s, 10x5x6", F7, from $75 to...**$150.00**

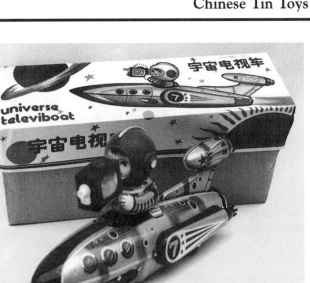

#ME777, Universe Televiboat, 1970s, 15x4x7", from $75.00 to $100.00. (Photo courtesy Steve Fisch)

#ME782, locomotive, 1970s-80s, battery-op, 10x4x7", from $35 to **$75.00**

#ME801, Lunar Explorer, 1970s, 12x6x4", F7, from $75 to..**$125.00**

#ME809, anti-aircraft armoured car, 1970s, 12x6x6", F7, from $75 to...**$100.00**

#ME821, Cicada, 1970s, 10x4x4", F7, from $50 to.........**$125.00**

#ME824, patrol car, 1970s, 11x4x3½", F7, from $35 to ...**$75.00**

#ME842, camel, discontinued, 10x4x7", F7, from $35 to .**$50.00**

#ME884, police car, VW bus style, current, 11½x5x5", F7, from $35 to...**$75.00**

#ME895, fire engine, 1970x, 10x4x4", F7, from $50 to **$85.00**

#ME972, open-door police car, 9½x4x4", F7, from $35 to...**$100.00**

#ME984, jet plane, 13x14x4½", F7, from $35 to **$75.00**

#MF032, Eastwind Sedan, current, 6x2x2", F7, from $8 to..**$15.00**

#MF033, pickup truck, current, 6x2x2", F7, from $8 to....**$15.00**

#MF044, sedan, Nissan style, 9x3½x3", F7, from $10 to ..**$25.00**

#MF046, sparking carbine, 18x5x1", F7, from $20 to **$35.00**

#MF052, sedan, 8x3x2", F7, from $15 to.........................**$25.00**

#MF083, sedan, current, 6x2x2", F7, from $8 to..............**$15.00**

#MF107, airplane, 6x6x2", F7, from $20 to......................**$35.00**

#MF111, ambulance, current, 8x3x3", F7, from $15 to **$20.00**

#MF127, Highway patrol car, 9½x4x3", F7, from $20 to..**$50.00**

#MF132, ambulance, 1980s, 10x4x4", F7, from $15 to.....**$35.00**

#MF134, tourist bus, current, 6x2x3", F7, from $15 to **$25.00**

#MF135, red flag convertible, current, F7, from $35 to **$75.00**

#MF136, double-decker train, current, 8x2x3", F7, from $15 to **$20.00**

#MF146, Volkswagen, 5x2x2", F7, from $10 to **$20.00**

#MF151, Shanghai pickup, 1970s, 12x4x4", F7, from $50 to..**$100.00**

#MF154, tractor, 1970s, 5x3x4", F7, from $25 to.............**$50.00**

#MF162, motorcycle, 6x2x4", F7, from $15 to..................**$35.00**

#MF163, fire truck, current, 6x2x3", F7, from $35 to **$75.00**

#MF164, construction truck, 1970s, 7x3x5", F7, from $35 to.**$75.00**

#MF164, Volkswagen, current, 4x2x3", F7, from $10 to ..**$15.00**

#MF170, train, current, 10x2x4", F7, from $15 to **$25.00**

#MF171, convertible, current, 5x2x2", F7, from $8 to......**$15.00**

#MF184, coach bus, 12½x4x4", F7, from $15 to...............**$30.00**

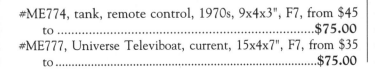

#ME770, Mr. Duck, current, 9x7x5", from $25.00 to $50.00. (Photo courtesy Steve Fisch)

#ME774, tank, remote control, 1970s, 9x4x3", F7, from $45 to **$75.00**

#ME777, Universe Televiboat, current, 15x4x7", F7, from $35 to **$75.00**

#MF185, dbl-decker bus, current, 11x5x3", F7, from $15 to .**$25.00**
#MF193, soft-cover truck, 1970s, 11x3x4", F7, from $50 to...**$75.00**
#MF201, oil tanker, 1970s, 14x4x4", F7, from $15 to.......**$25.00**
#MF203, sedan, 10½x4x2½", F7, from $25 to...................**$50.00**
#MF206, panda truck, current, 6x3x2", F7, from $10 to...**$20.00**
#MF216, airplane, discontinued, 9x9x3", F7, from $15 to.**$35.00**
#MF234, sedan, 6x2x2", F7, from $15 to...........................**$25.00**
#MF239, tiger truck, 10x3x4", F7, from $15 to.................**$30.00**
#MF240, passenger jet, 13x11x4", F7, from $30 to...........**$35.00**
#MF249, flying boat, 1970s, 6x6x2", F7, from $35 to.......**$75.00**
#MF254, Mercedes Sedan, current, 8x4x3", F7, from $15 to...**$25.00**
#MF274, tank, 1970s, 3x2x2", F7, from $8 to...................**$15.00**

#MF294, Mercedes Sedan, friction, 7x3x2", from $12.00 to $20.00. (Photo courtesy Steve Fisch)

#MF298, traveling car, 8½x4x3½", F7, from $15 to.........**$25.00**
#MF304, race car, discontinued, 10x4x3", F7, from $15 to.**$35.00**
#MF309, sedan, 9x2x3½", F7, from $20 to **$35.00**
#MF310, Corvette, 3x2x3", F7, from $10 to **$15.00**
#MF316, 1953 Corvette, current, F7, from $20 to............**$50.00**
#MF317, Corvette convertible, current, 10x4x3", F7, from $20 to...**$50.00**
#MF320, Mercedes sedan, current, 7x3x2", F7, from $10 to .**$20.00**
#MF321, Buick convertible, current, 11x4x3", F7, from $20 to...**$50.00**
#MF322, Buick sedan, current, 11x4x3", F7, from $20 to .**$50.00**
#MF329, 1956 Corvette convertible, current, 10x4x4", F7, from $20 to...**$50.00**

#MF326, Mercedes gull-wing sedan, current, 9x3x2", from $15.00 to $25.00. (Photo courtesy Steve Fisch)

#MF330, Cadillac Sedan, current, 11x4x3", F7, from $15 to .**$35.00**
#MF339, 1956 Corvette, current, 10x4x4", F7, from $20 to...**$50.00**
#MF340, Cadillac convertible, current, 11x4x3", F7, from $20 to **$50.00**
#MF341, convertible, 12x4x3", F7, from $20 to **$50.00**
#MF342, sedan, 12x4x3", F7, from $20 to........................**$50.00**
#MF712, locomotive, current, 7x2x3", F7, from $10 to....**$15.00**
#MF713, taxi, current, 5x2x2", F7, from $8 to.................**$15.00**
#MF714, fire chief car, current, 5x2x2", F7, from $8 to....**$15.00**
#MF714, fire chief car, current, 5x2x2", F7, from $8 to....**$15.00**
#MF716, ambulance, 1970s, 8x3x3", F7, from $15 to.......**$30.00**
#MF717, dump truck, discontinued, 10x3x5", F7, from $15 to **$35.00**

#MF718, ladder truck, 10x3x4", from $15.00 to $35.00. (Photo courtesy Steve Fisch)

#MF721, light tank, current, 6x3x3", F7, from $15 to **$20.00**
#MF722, jeep, current, 6x3x3", F7, from $15 to **$20.00**
#MF731, station wagon, current, 5x2x2", F7, from $8 to .**$15.00**
#MF735, rocket racer, current, 7x3x3", F7, from $15 to...**$35.00**
#MF742, flying boat, current, 13x4x4", F7, from $15 to...**$35.00**
#MF743, Karmann Ghia sedan, current, 10x3x4", F7, from $15 to **$45.00**
#MF753, sports car, current, 8x3x2", F7, from $15 to.......**$25.00**
#MF782, circus truck, current, 9x3x4", F7, from $15 to...**$25.00**
#MF787, Lucky open car, current, 8x3x2", F7, from $15 to ..**$25.00**
#MF798, patrol car, current, 8x3x3", F7, from $15 to.......**$25.00**
#MF800, race car #5, current, 6x2x2", F7, from $10 to **$20.00**
#MF804, locomotive, current, 16x3x5", F7, from $15 to..**$25.00**
#MF832, ambulance, current, 5x2x2", F7, from $8 to **$15.00**
#MF844, double-decker bus, current, 8x4x3", F7, from $15 to...**$20.00**
#MF861, space gun, 1970s, 10x2x6", F7, from $45 to.......**$75.00**
#MF893, animal van, current, 6x2x3", from $15 to..........**$20.00**
#MF900, police car, current, 6x3x2", F7, from $8 to **$15.00**
#MF910, airport limo bus, current, 15x4x5", F7, from $20 to ...**$35.00**
#MF923, torpedo boat, 8x3x3", F7, from $15 to **$25.00**
#MF951, fighter jet, 1970s, 5x4x2", F7, from $15 to........**$20.00**
#MF956, sparking tank, current, 8x4x3", F7, from $15 to ..**$20.00**
#MF957, ambulance helicopter, 7½x2x4", F7, from $15 to....**$35.00**
#MF958, poultry truck, current, F7, from $15 to **$20.00**

#MF959, jeep, discontinued, 9x4x4", F7, from $15 to $20.00

#MF974, circus truck, 6x2x4", F7, from $15 to $20.00

#MF985, fowl transporter, current, 12x3x4", F7, from $25 to ...$50.00

#MF989, noisy locomotive, 1970s, 12x3x4", F7, from $25 to ..$50.00

#MF993, mini car, current, 5x2x2", F7, from $8 to...........$15.00

#MF998, sedan, current, 5x2x2", F7, from $8 to $15.00

#MS002, jumping frog, current, 2x2x2", F7, from $8 to ...$15.00

#MS006, pecking chicken, 1970s, 2x1x1", F7, from $8 to.$15.00

#MS011, roll-over plane, current, 3x4x2", F7, from $10 to..$20.00

#MS014, single-bar exerciser, 1970s, 7x6x6", F7, from $25 to..$50.00

#MS057, horse & rider, 1970s, 6x2x5", F7, from $20 to...$35.00

#MS058, old-fashion car, current, 3x3x4", F7, from $15 to...$20.00

#MS082, jumping frog, current, 2x2x2", F7, from $8 to ...$15.00

#MS083, jumping rabbit, current, 3x3x2", F7, from $8 to ..$15.00

#MS085, xylophone girl, current, 7x3x9", F7, from $20 to ...$35.00

#MS107, jumping Bambi, current, 5½x6", F7, from $15 to...$20.00

#MS134, sparking jet, current, F7, from $15 to $30.00

#MS166, crawling baby, vinyl head, current, 5x4x5", F7, from $15 to $20.00

#MS405, ice-cream vendor, current, F7, from $10 to $20.00

#MS405, jumping zebra, current, 5x2x4", F7, from $10 to..$20.00

#MS565, drumming panda/wheel, current, 5x3x5", F7, from $10 to..$20.00

#MS568, sparrow, current, 5x2x2", F7, from $10 to $15.00

#MS569, oriole, current, 5x2x2", F7, from $10 to $15.00

#MS575, bear w/flash camera, current, 6x3x4", F7, from $15 to..$35.00

#MS702, motorcycle, current, 7x4x5", F7, from $15 to....$35.00

#MS704, bird music cart, 1970s, 3x2x5", F7, from $15 to...$25.00

#MS709, motorcycle w/sidecar, current, 7x4x5", F7, from $15 to..$35.00

#MS710, tricycle, current, 5x3x5", F7, from $15 to..........$20.00

#MS713, washing machine, 3x3x5", F7, from $15 to $20.00

#MS765, drummer, 5x3x6", F7, from $15 to....................$25.00

#MS827, sedan, steering, 1970s, 9x3x3", F7, from $50 to..$75.00

#MS858, girl on goose, current, 5x3x3", F7, from $15 to .$25.00

#PMS102, rolling cart, current, 3x2x1", F7, from $15 to..$20.00

#PMS105, jumping dog, current, 3x2x6", F7, from $15 to.$25.00

#PMS106, jumping parrot, current, 3x2x6", F7, from $15 to..$25.00

#PMS108, duck family, current, 10x2x3", F7, from $15 to ...$25.00

#PMS113, Fu dog, current, 4x2x3", F7, from $15 to.........$25.00

#PMS119, woodpecker, current, 3x2x6", F7, from $15 to .$25.00

#PMS210, clown riding bike, current, 4x2x5", F7, from $15 to $25.00

#PMS212, elephant on bike, current, 6x3x8", F7, from $15 to $35.00

#PMS213, duck on bike, current, 6x3x8", F7, from $15 to.$35.00

#PMS214, lady bug family, current, 13x3x1", F7, from $15 to $25.00

#PMS215, crocodile, current, 9x3x1", F7, from $15 to.....$20.00

#PMS217, jumping rabbit, current, 3x2x6", F7, from $15 to.$25.00

#PMS218, penguin, current, 3x2x6", F7, from $15 to $30.00

#PS013, boy on tricycle, current, 2x4x4", F7, from $12 to .$25.00

Coloring, Activity, and Paint Books

Coloring and activity books from the early years of the twentieth century are scarce indeed and when found can be expensive if they are tied into another collectibles field such as Black Americana or advertising; but the ones most in demand are those that represent familiar movie and TV stars of the 1950s and 1960s. Condition plays a very important part in assessing worth, and though hard to find, unused examples are the ones that bring top dollar — in fact, as much as 50% to 75% more than one even partially used.

Advisor: Diane Albert (T6).

See also Advertising.

Addams Family, paint book, Saalfield, 1965, unused, EX $100.00

Adventures of Batman, coloring book, Whitman, 1966, few pgs colored, NM, C1......................................$30.00

Aladdin & His Magic Lamp, coloring book, Saalfield, 1970, unused, EX, T2...$20.00

Alice in Wonderland, sticker book, Whitman, 1951, some stickers applied, VG, M8.............................$25.00

Alvin & the Chipmunks, coloring book, Saalfield, 1960, unused, NM..$45.00

Amazing Spider-Man, coloring book, Marvel Books, 1983, unused, EX...$15.00

Amazing Spider-Man, sticker book, Whitman, 1976, unused, EX, T2...$20.00

Andy Panda, coloring book, Whitman, 1944, unused, EX .$30.00

Atom Ant, coloring book, Watkins-Strathmore, 1965, unused, EX, T2...$25.00

Bambi, paint book, WDP, 1941, unused, EX $65.00

Banana Splits, coloring book, Whitman, 1969, several pgs colored, EX, J5...$25.00

Barney Google & Snuffy Smith, Lowe, 1963, few pgs colored, EX, T2...$20.00

Batman, color-by-number book, Whitman, 1966, oversized, unused, M, J5/C17 ....$35.00

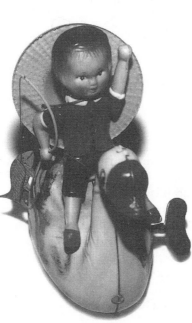

#MS858, girl on goose, older style, 5x3x3", from $25.00 to $50.00.
(Photo courtesy of Steve Fisch)

Batman, Robin & Penguin Giant Comics To Color, Whitman, 1976, unused, NM, A $15.00

Batman, sticker book, Whitman, 1966, unused, EX, J5 ....$45.00

Batman w/Robin the Boy Wonder, dot-to-dot & coloring book, Vasquez Bros, 1967, unused, NM $50.00

Beatles, coloring book, Saalfield, 1964, unused, EX, R2.$100.00

Beverly Hillbillies, coloring book, Whitman, 1964, unused, EX..$30.00

Beverly Hillbillies, punch-out book, Whitman, 1960s, unused, EX, J5 ....$85.00

Bewitched, activity book, Treasure, 1965, unused, EX $20.00

Bionic Woman, coloring book, Treasure Books, 1976, unused, NM, M17 ....$30.00

Black Hole, coloring book, Whitman, 1979, unused, NM, P4..$10.00

Black Hole, punch-out book, Whitman, 1979, unpunched, NM, M17 ....$30.00

Blondie, coloring book, Artcraft, 1967, unused, NM, C1.$40.00

Blondie, paint book, Whitman, 1947, unused, EX............$40.00

Bobby Sherman Paint & Color Album, Artcraft, 1971, unused, EX..$35.00

Bonanza, coloring book, Artcraft, 1960, unused, M..........$50.00

Brady Bunch, coloring book, Whitman, 1974, unused, EX.$45.00

Brenda Starr, coloring book, Saalfield, 1964, unused, M, A..$30.00

Buffalo Bill & Calamity, coloring book, Whitman, 1957, unused, EX $30.00

Bugs Bunny and Porky Pig, paint book, Whitman, 1946, unused, EX, $50.00. (Photo courtesy David Longest)

Bugs Bunny Private Eye, coloring book, Whitman, 1957, unused, VG, T2 ....$15.00

Bullwinkle, coloring book, General Mills premium, 1963, unused, EX $30.00

Bullwinkle, coloring book, 1969, unused, NM, V1 ....$25.00

Candid Camera, coloring book, 1963, unused, EX, A $35.00

Captain America, coloring book, Whitman, 1966, unused, NM, from $40 to..$50.00

Captain Gallant, coloring book, 1956, unused, NM, C1 .$45.00

Captain Kangaroo, dot-to-dot book, 1977, unused, NM, C1 .$20.00

Captain Kangaroo's Treasure House, punch-out book, Whitman, 1959, unpunched, NM, J5 ....$65.00

Captain Marvel, paint book, 1942, unused, NM, T2 ....$75.00

Centurians, coloring book, Golden, 1986, unused, M, M17...$10.00

CHiPs, coloring book, 1983, unused, NM, C1 ....$15.00

Choo Choo Charlie, coloring book, Whitman, 1970, rare, unused, EX $50.00

Cisco Kid, Saalfield, 1954, photo cover, oversized, unused, NM, A3 ....$60.00

Curiosity Shop, punch-out book, Artcraft, 1971, unpunched, EX, J5 ....$35.00

Dale Evans, coloring book, Whitman, 1957, oversized, few pgs colored, EX, A3 ....$50.00

Davy Crockett, punch-out book, 1955, NM, A $100.00

Davy Crockett, story & coloring book, Topline/England, 1950s, scarce, unused, EX $100.00

Dennis the Menace, coloring book, Whitman, 1961, few pgs colored, NM, C1 ....$40.00

Dick Tracy, coloring book, Saalfield, 1946, unused, EX, D11 ...$45.00

Dick Tracy Junior Detective Kit, punch-out book, 1962, unused, M, D11 ....$25.00

Disneyland, sticker book, Whitman, 1967, unused, NM ..$45.00

Donald Duck, coloring book, Watkins-Strathmore, 1963, unused, EX, J5 ....$25.00

Donald Duck & His Friends, A Great Big Punchout, Whitman, 1961, unused, NM, A $100.00

Donny & Marie, coloring book, Whitman, 1977, unused, EX..$10.00

Donny & Marie, sticker book, Whitman, 1977, unused, EX.....$15.00

Donny Osmond, Keepsake photo/activity book, Artcraft, 1973, unused, NM, C1..$30.00

Doris Day, coloring book, Whitman, 1954, unused, NM .$35.00

Dr Dolittle & His Animals, coloring book, 1967, few pgs colored, EX $10.00

Dudley Do-Right, coloring book, Whitman, 1972, few pgs colored, EX, H4 ....$15.00

Dudley Do-Right Comes to the Rescue, coloring book, Saalfield, 1969, unused, M, J5 ....$35.00

Dukes of Hazzard, coloring book, 1981, few pgs colored, EX....$25.00

Dune, activity book, Grosset & Dunlop, 1984, unused, M .$8.00

Elizabeth Taylor, coloring book, Whitman, 1952, few pgs colored, EX, J5 ....$35.00

Elvis, coloring book, 1984, unused, EX $40.00

F-Troop, coloring book, Saalfield, 1967, unused, NM, A.$55.00

Family Affair, coloring book, Whitman, 1968, unused, EX $25.00

Fantasia, paint book, Whitman, 1940, rare, unused, EX, A..$300.00

Felix the Cat, coloring book, 1957, unused, M, V1 ....$50.00

Flash Gordon, paint book, Whitman, 1936, unused, EX ..$55.00

Flintstones, coloring book, 1971, unused, EX, C1 ....$20.00

Flintstones, sticker book, Whitman, 1966, unused, NM ..$35.00

Flipper, coloring book, Whitman, 1965, unused, NM, M17 .$30.00

Flying Clippers, coloring book, Saalfield, 1950s, few pgs colored, EX, M17 ....$30.00

Flying Nun, coloring book, Saalfield, 1968, unused, EX...$35.00

Fonzie, coloring book, Treasure Books, 1976, unused, M .$25.00

Fun w/Elmer Fudd, coloring book, Watkins-Strathmore, 1963, unused, NM $35.00

Garrison's Gorillas, coloring book, Whitman, 1968, unused, EX $45.00

Gene Autry Cowboy Adventures, coloring book, Merrill, 1941, unused, EX $85.00

Grace Kelly, coloring book, Whitman, 1956, few pgs colored, EX, J5 ....$45.00

Green Acres, coloring book, Whitman, 1967, few pgs colored, EX $25.00

Green Acres, coloring book, Whitman, 1967, unused, EX ..$35.00

Green Hornet, coloring book, Whitman, 1966, unused, NM, T2 ....$75.00

Green Hornet, Danger! or Kato's Revenge, coloring book, Watkins-Strathmore, 1966, used, M, J5, ea $65.00

Gumby & Pokey, coloring book, Western Publishing, 1966, unused, NM, T2 ....$30.00

Hayley Mills in Search of the Castaways, coloring book, Whitman, 1962, unused, NM, from $20 to $25.00

Hopalong Cassidy, coloring book, Lowe, 1950, unused, EX, from $55 to $75.00

Hot Wheels, sticker book, 1985, unused, EX, S13 ....$8.00

Howdy Doody & Clarabelle, coloring book, Whitman, 1955, unused, EX $20.00

Howdy Doody Follow the Dots, Whitman, 1955, unused, EX...$30.00

Humpty Dumpty, coloring book, Lowe, 1950s, unused, NM, T2 ....$10.00

Incredible Hulk, sticker book, Whitman, 1979, unused, M, C1 ....$25.00

Iroquois Trail, coloring book, Saalfield, 1950, photo cover, unused, EX, A3 ....$75.00

Jabberjaw & the Neptunes, coloring book, Rand McNally, 1976, unused, NM, C1 ....$35.00

Jetsons, color-by-number book, Whitman, 1963, unused, VG $25.00

Johnny Lightning, sticker book, Whitman, 1970, unused, NM $25.00

Julia, coloring book, Saalfield, 1968, unused, EX.............$25.00

Korg, coloring book, Artcraft, 1975, unused, EX, H4, from $10 to $15.00

Land of the Giants, coloring book, Whitman, 1969, unused, NM $45.00

Land of the Lost, coloring book, Whitman, 1975, unused, NM, C1 ....$35.00

Last Starfighter, activity book, unused, NM, B10 ....$5.00

Laurel & Hardy, coloring book, Whitman, 1968, unused, M, A $25.00

Laverne & Shirley, activity book, Playmore, 1983, unused, NM, C1 ....$20.00

Liddle Kiddles, coloring book, Whitman, 1966, unused, EX.$30.00

Liddle Kiddles, sticker book, Whitman, 1966, unused, M ..$55.00

Lieutenant, coloring book, Saalfield, 1964, unused, NM, A...$40.00

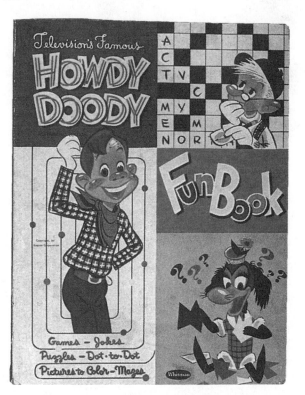

Howdy Doody Fun Book, Whitman, 1953, unused, EX, $45.00. (Photo courtesy Jack Koch)

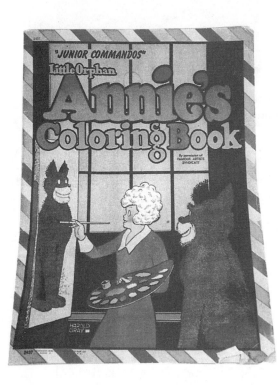

Little Orphan Annie's Coloring Book, 1943, unused, NM, $75.00. (Photo courtesy David Longest)

Huckleberry Hound, coloring book, Whitman #1134, 1963, few pgs colored, EX, B10...$10.00

Little Orphan Annie, coloring book, Artcraft, 1974, unused, M, J5 ....$25.00

Lone Ranger, coloring book, Whitman, 1946, unused, EX ..$85.00

Lone Ranger, coloring book, Whitman, 1959, several pgs colored, EX, C1...$35.00

Magic Land of Allakazam, coloring book, 1962, unused, EX..$45.00

Magilla Gorilla Vs Yogi Bear for President, coloring book, Whitman, 1964, unused, EX, from $20 to $30.00

Man From UNCLE, coloring book, Watkins-Strathmore, 1965, unused, EX, A...$55.00

Mickey Mouse Book for Coloring, Saalfield, 1936, several pgs colored, scarce, EX, M8 ....$70.00

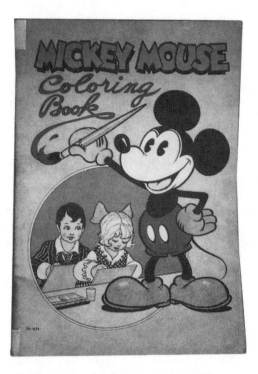

Mickey Mouse, coloring book, Saalfield, 1930s, unused, EX, $125.00. (Photo courtesy David Longest and Michael Stern)

Mighty Mouse, sticker book, Whitman, 1967, unused, NM, T2...$50.00

Mork Book of Orkian Fun, activity book, Wonder, 1979, unused, EX, M17...$20.00

Mother Goose, paint book, Saalfield, 1908, unused, EX...$40.00

Mr Peabody, coloring book, Whitman, 1977, unused, NM, J5...$15.00

Mr Rogers Neighborhood Festival, activity book, Whitman, 1974, unused, NM $10.00

Mrs Beasley, coloring book, Whitman, 1972, unused, NM, C1...$45.00

Munsters, sticker book, Whitman, 1965, unused, M $75.00

My Three Sons, coloring book, Whitman, 1967, unused, NM, C1...$45.00

Nanny & the Professor, coloring book, Saalfield, 1971, unused, EX...$25.00

New Kids on the Block, coloring book, Golden, 1990, unused, EX...$5.00

New Zoo Revue, coloring book, Artcraft, 1973, unused, EX.$10.00

Northwest Passage, coloring book, Lowe, 1959, unused, EX, A...$35.00

Oswald the Rabbit, cut-out coloring book, Funtime, 1953, unused, NM, C1...$25.00

Parade of Comics, sticker book, Saalfield, 1968, unused, EX, T2...$50.00

Partridge Family, coloring book, Saalfield, 1971, unused, EX.$25.00

Patty Duke, coloring book, Whitman, 1964, unused, VG, A.$25.00

Pebbles & Bamm-Bamm, coloring book, Whitman, 1964, unused, NM, J2...$25.00

Pinocchio, paint book, Whitman/WDE, 1939, few pgs pnt, EX, M8...$35.00

Pinocchio, paint book, Whitman/WDE, 1939, unused, EX, from $75 to...$100.00

Planet of the Apes, coloring book, Artcraft, 1975, unused, EX, B10...$16.00

Popeye, A Great Big Punchout, Whitman, 1961, unused, NM, A...$125.00

Porky Pig, coloring book, Leon Schlesinger, 1930s, unused, EX, from $125 to...$175.00

Raggedy Ann, coloring book, Saalfield, 1951, unused, EX, $20.00.

(Photo courtesy Kim Avery)

Raggedy Ann, sticker book, Whitman, 1962, unused, EX ..$15.00

Raggedy Ann & Andy, activity book, Whitman, 1982, unused, EX...$5.00

Raggedy Ann & Andy, coloring book, Saalfield, 1944, unused, EX...$25.00

Raggedy Ann & Andy, dot-to-dot book, Whitman, 1978, unused, EX $10.00

Raggedy Ann & Andy See-A-Word, puzzle book, Whitman, 1981, unused, EX $5.00

Raggedy Ann's Trace 'N Rub, Random House, 1987, unused, EX...$5.00

Reg'lar Fellers, paint book, Whitman, unused, EX, T2.....$30.00

Rin-Tin-Tin, coloring book, Whitman, 1955, EX, C10...$30.00

Robot Man & Friends, coloring book, 1986, EX, B10.........$6.00

Rocketeer, sticker book, Western Pub, 1991, unused, M....$5.00

Roger Ramjet, coloring book, Whitman, 1966, unused, NM, T2...$50.00

Roy Rogers & Dale Evans Ranch Tales, coloring book, Whitman, 1953, several pgs colored, EX $35.00

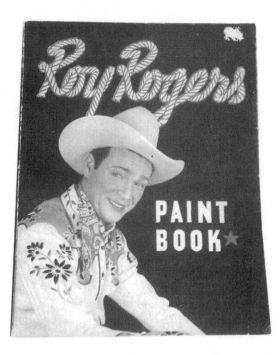

Roy Rogers, paint book, Whitman, 1944, unused, NM, $50.00. (Photo courtesy David Longest)

Rudolph the Red-Nosed Reindeer, coloring book, Lowe, 1963, unused, EX, T2..$15.00

Sabrina, coloring book, Whitman, 1971, few pgs colored, VG, from $10 to...$20.00

Shadow, coloring book, Artcraft, 1974, unused, M, A $20.00

Sigmund & the Sea Monsters, coloring book, Saalfield, 1975, unused, scarce, M, M17 ....$65.00

Six Million Dollar Man, activity book, Saalfield, 1975, unused, M...$25.00

Sky Rocket, coloring book, Lowe, 1959, unused, NM, T2..$15.00

Smilin' Jack, coloring book, Saalfield, 1946, unused, EX, T2 ....$30.00

Smokey the Bear, coloring book, Whitman, 1969, unused, M, J5...$45.00

Snow White & the Seven Dwarfs, paint book, WDE, 1938, unused, EX $75.00

Soupy Sales, activity book, EX, B10 ....$8.00

Space Ghost, coloring book, Whitman, 1965, unused, NM, T2...$30.00

Spider-Man, see also Amazing Spider-Man

Spider-Man & the Oyster Mystery, coloring book, Whitman, 1976, unused, NM $10.00

Star Trek, coloring book, Saalfield, 1968, unused, NM, A ..$35.00

Steve Canyon, coloring book, Saalfield, 1952, few pgs colored, EX, T2 ....$30.00

Steve Canyon's Interceptor Station, punch-out book, Golden, 1959, unused, NM, J5 ....$45.00

Strange World of Mr Mom, coloring book, 1962, unused, M, V1...$30.00

Super Heroes, How To Draw, sketch & coloring book, Golden, 1983, unused, EX $15.00

Superboy, coloring book, Whitman, 1967, unused, NM, T2..$50.00

Superman, coloring book, Saalfield, 1947, oversized, unused, NM, T2, from $150 to..............................$200.00

Superman, coloring book, Whitman, 1960s, several variations, unused, M, ea from $40 to $50.00

Tales of the Texas Rangers, coloring book, Saalfield, 1958, NM..$30.00

Tarzan, punch-out book, Whitman, 1967, unpunched, NM, J5/V1, from $35 to $45.00

That Girl, coloring book, Saalfield, 1967, unused, EX, A...$25.00

Thief of Bagdad, coloring book, Saalfield, 1940, unused, EX, A...$65.00

Three Stooges, coloring & activity book, Playmore, 1983, few pgs colored, NM, H4...............................$12.00

Three Stooges, coloring book, Lowe, 1959, unused, EX, A ...$75.00

Tinker Toy, paint book, Whitman, 1939, unused, EX......$40.00

Tom & Jerry, coloring book, Whitman, 1952, few pgs colored, EX..$20.00

Tom Corbett Space Cadet, punch-out book, Saalfield, 1952, unpunched, NM, J5 ....$65.00

Tweety Bird, coloring book, Whitman, 1955, few pgs colored, EX, T2 ....$20.00

Universal Monsters, Mark & See Book, w/4 monster cards, NM, B10...$5.00

V, coloring book, Cliveden Press/England, 1985, unused, NM, C1...$45.00

Walt Disney's Fairy Tales, coloring book, Whitman, 1960s, EX...$35.00

Walt Disney's Magic Forest, coloring book, Watkins-Strathmore, 1959, few pgs colored, EX, T2 ....$15.00

Walt Disney Paint Book, Whitman, 1937, VG, $50.00.

Walt Disney's Swim Fun, coloring book, Whitman, 1957, unused, VG $12.00

Waltons, color & activity book, Whitman, 1975, unused, EX $15.00

Waltons, sticker book, Whitman, 1975, unused, EX $25.00

Whirlybirds, coloring book, Whitman, 1959, unused, EX, A ..$25.00

Winnie the Pooh & Friends, punch-out book, Golden, 1983, unpunched, NM..$15.00
Wonderbug Down Mexico Way, coloring book, Whitman, 1978, unused, EX $15.00
Yogi Bear & His Friends, A Great Big Punchout, Whitman, 1961, unused, NM, A $100.00
Zorro, coloring book, Whitman, 1958, few pgs colored, EX, C1 ...$40.00
Zorro, coloring book, Whitman, 1958, VG+, A $30.00
101 Dalmatians, coloring book, Whitman, 1960, unused, EX ..$25.00

Comic Books

For more than a half a century, kids of America raced to the bookstand as soon as the new comics came in for the month and for 10¢ an issue kept up on the adventures of their favorite super heroes, cowboys, space explorers, and cartoon characters. By far most were eventually discarded — after they were traded one friend to another, stacked on closet shelves, and finally confiscated by Mom. Discount the survivors that were torn or otherwise damaged over the years and those about the mundane, and of those remaining, some could be quite valuable. In fact, first editions of high-grade comics books or those showcasing the first appearance of a major character often bring $500.00 and more. Rarity, age, and quality of the artwork are prime factors in determining value, and condition is critical. If you want to seriously collect comic books, you'll need to refer to a good comic book price guide such as Overstreet's.

Advisor: Ken Mitchell (M14).

Other Sources: A3, P3, K1 (for Simpson's Comics).

Adventures of Jerry Lewis, #21, G+ $10.00
Adventures of Mighty Mouse, St John #2, 1952, EX+......$55.00
Adventures of Pinky Lee, #3, VG, from $20 to.................$25.00
Adventures of the Fly, Dell #20, NM, M14 ....$30.00

Amazing Spider-Man and Dr. Doom, Marvel Comics #5, EX, $150.00.

Al Capp's Wolf Gal, Dell #2, 1952, VG+, M14 ....$40.00
Andy Griffith, Dell #1252, EX $75.00
Annie Oakley & Tagg, Dell #575, EX, M14 ....$25.00
Aquaman, Dell #1, 1962, EX, M14 ....$175.00
Atomic Mouse, #1, VG+, A3 ....$75.00
Avengers, Marvel #1, 1963, EX.....................................$500.00
Bambi's Children, Dell Four-Color #30, VG, A3 ....$145.00
Banana Splits, #3, VG+, A3 ....$10.00
Bat Masterson, Dell #4, 1960, VG, C1 ....$35.00
Batman, DC Comics #4, 1940, EX, M14 ....$900.00
Beany & Cecil, Dell #2, 1962, scarce, EX, M17.................$25.00
Ben Casey, #5, VG, A3..$10.00
Best of Donald Duck & Scrooge, Dell #2, 1967, EX+, M14..$30.00
Beverly Hillbillies, #7, VG+, A3 ....$18.00
Bill Boyd Western, #9, VG, A3......................................$25.00
Black Rider, Marvel #8, photo cover, VG+, A3 ....$95.00
Blaze Carson, #2, VG, A3..$30.00
Bonanza, Dell #210, 1962, EX, M14 ....$125.00
Brady Bunch, Dell #2, 1970, EX, from $30 to $40.00
Brave & the Bold, Dell #43, EX+, M14 ....$225.00
Brer Rabbit's Sunken Treasure, Wheaties premium, 1951, NM, M8...$15.00
Bugs Bunny, Dell Four-Color #164, VG, M14 ....$30.00
Bugs Bunny Halloween Parade, Dell Giant #1, EX, M14 ..$100.00
Calling All Kids, Dell #11, 1947, VG, M14 ....$6.00
Captain Marvel Adventures, Dell #24, 1943, EX, M14..$175.00
Captain Midnight, Dell #37, EX+, M14 ....$85.00
Casper the Friendly Ghost, Dell #15, EX, M14.................$20.00
Chilling Tales of Terror, Dell #4, 1970, NM, M14 ....$8.00
Chip 'n Dale, Dell Four-Color #581, VG, A3 ....$10.00
Christmas in Bedrock, Gold Key #31, 1965, EX, M17......$20.00
Cisco Kid, Dell #17, VG+, A3 ....$20.00
Conqueror, Dell Four-Color #690, VG+, A3....................$40.00
Daktari, #1, VG+, A3 ....$12.00
Dale Evans, DC Comics #6, VG+, A3 ....$95.00
Dale Evans Queen of the West, Dell #479, EX, M14 .....$100.00
Dark Shadows, #9, VG+, A3 ....$20.00
Davy Crockett Frontier Fighter, Dell #3, 1955, EX, M14.$15.00
Dennis the Menace, Standard #13, 1955, EX, M17..........$25.00
Donald Duck & the Inca Gold, Wheaties premium, 1951, NM, M8..$15.00
Donald Duck in Mathmagicland, Dell #1198, EX, M14...$45.00
Earth Man on Venus, Avon, 1951, EX, J5 ....$325.00
Elmer Fudd, Dell #689, NM, M14 ....$25.00
Felix the Cat, Dell #61, 1946, VG, M14 ....$35.00
Flash Gordon, Dell #5, 1967, EX, M14 ....$10.00
Flash Gordon, Dell Four-Color #10, 1943, scarce, EX, M14 .$350.00
Flintstones, March of Comics #317, EX, M14 ....$15.00
Flipper, Gold Key #2, 1966, photo cover, EX+, M17........$35.00
Gidget, Dell #1, 1966, EX...$35.00
Grandma Duck's Farm Friends, Dell #873, NM, M14 ......$40.00
Green Hornet, #1, VG, A3..$40.00
Gunsmoke, Dell #844, EX+, M14 ....$25.00
Gunsmoke, Dell Four-Color #0844, EX $45.00
Hercules Unchained, Dell Four-Color #1121, VG+, A3..$25.00
Horse Soldiers, Dell, 1959, G+, A....................................$20.00
Hunchback of Notre Dame, Dell #854, 1957, EX, M17 ...$40.00
I Dream of Jeannie, Dell #1, 1966, NM, from $40 to........$50.00

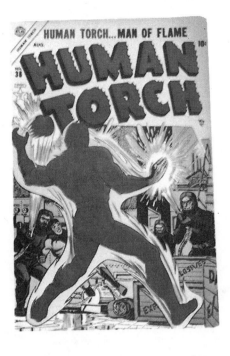

Human Torch, 1954, EX, $125.00.

I Love Lucy, #3, G+, A3 ....$30.00
Incredible Hulk, Dell #108, EX, M14.........................$15.00
Iron Man, Dell #10, NM, M14 ....$25.00
Jack Pearson's Tales of the Texas Rangers, Dell Four-Color
        #648, G, A3 ....$6.00
Jesse James, Dell Four-Color #757, G+, A3 ....$15.00
Jetsons, Gold Key #35, EX, M14 ....$15.00

John Carter of Mars, Gold Key #1, 1964, VG, M14 ....$20.00
John Wayne, Toby Press #4, 1950, photo cover, EX.........$55.00
Journey to the Center of the Earth, Dell Four-Color #1060, G,
        A3 ....$10.00
Jungle Jim, Dell #12, 1949, G, M14 ....$10.00
Justice League of America, Dell #6, VG, M14 ....$50.00
Katzenjammer Kids, Dell #32, 1946, VG, M14.................$35.00
Kid Montana, Dell #10, NM, M14.................................$15.00
Lady & the Tramp, Dell #1, 1955, VG, M14..................$30.00
Lassie, Dell #27, NM, M14 ....$15.00
Legends of Daniel Boone, #3, G, A3 ....$30.00
Lil' Abner, Dell #61, 1947, NM, M14..........................$190.00
Little Lulu, Dell #207, NM, M14................................$6.00
Littlest Outlaw, Dell Four-Color #609, VG+, A3.............$15.00
Lone Ranger, Dell #37, EX+, M14 ....$45.00
Lone Ranger, March of Comics #310, photo cover, EX+,
        M14...$45.00
Lone Ranger Movie, Dell Giant, 1956, EX+, A...............$50.00
Looney Tunes Merrie Melodies, Dell, 1940s, EX, from $50 to...$70.00
Man From UNCLE, #8, VG+, A3.................................$15.00
Man in Space, Dell Four-Color #716, VG, A3 ....$20.00
Mandrake the Magician, Dell #5, NM, M14....................$12.00
Marge's Little Lulu, Dell #74, NM, M14........................$60.00
Marge's Tubby, Dell #461, 1953, G, M14.......................$10.00
Marvel Tales, Dell #121, 1954, VG, M14........................$35.00
Maverick, Dell #980, EX+, M14..................................$40.00
MGM'S Mouse Musketeers, Dell #728, NM, M14 ....$15.00
Mickey Mouse, Dell Four-Color #27, 1943, VG, M14 ...$160.00
Mickey Mouse & the Mystery Sea Monster, Wheaties premium,
        1950, NM, M8..$15.00
Minnie Mouse Girl Explorer, Wheaties Premium, 1951, NM,
        M8...$15.00
Monkees, Dell #1, 1967-68, NM $40.00
Munsters, Dell #4, EX, M14 ....$15.00
Mutt & Jeff, Dell #24, VG+, M14................................$30.00

Phantom, Gold Key, 1964, EX, $25.00.

My Favorite Martian, Dell #3, EX, M14..........................$30.00
Mysterious Adventures, Dell #8, 1952, VG, M14.............$50.00
Mystery in Space, Dell #12, NM, M14..........................$175.00
Nancy & Sluggo, Dell #145, EX, M14 ....$15.00
Nanny & the Professor, Dell #2, EX, M14 ....$25.00
Oswald the Rabbit, Dell #102, EX, M14.........................$30.00
Outlaws of the West, Dell #15, VG+, M14......................$15.00
Parent Trap, Dell #1210, VG+, M14 ....$20.00
Partridge Family, Charlton #19, 1973, EX $15.00
Peter Pan, Dell #926, 1958, VG, M14.............................$20.00
Peter Panda, Dell #31, 1958, EX, M14............................$20.00
Playful Little Audrey, Dell #1, EX, M14........................$110.00
Pogo Possum, Dell #1, 1949, G, M14..............................$75.00
Raggedy Ann & Andy, Dell #2, 1946, VG $35.00
Raggedy Ann & the Camel w/the Wrinkled Knees, Dell Junior
     Treasury #8, 1957, G+..$30.00
Rawhide Kid, Dell #12, EX, M14 ....$35.00
Red Ryder, #105, VG, A3 ....$25.00
Restless Gun, Dell Four-Color #1146, VG+, A3 ....$25.00
Richie Rich, Dell #23, VG+, M14 ....$15.00
Rin-Tin-Tin, Dell #476, VG+, M14 ....$15.00
Robin Hood, Dell #413, 1952, EX, M14..........................$30.00
Rocky Lane, #5, VG, A3..$50.00
Roy Rogers, #10, VG+, A...$45.00
Savage Tales, Dell #1, EX, M14.......................................$50.00
Sgt Fury, Dell #15, VG, M14...$12.00

Shadow, DC #1, 1973, EX, $15.00.

Sheena, Queen of the Jungle, Dell #16, EX, M14.............$35.00
Smilin' Jack, Dell #149, 1947, NM, J5 ....$75.00
Snow White & the Seven Dwarfs, Dell #382, VG, M14..$25.00
Space Family Robinson, Dell #16, EX, M14 ....$20.00
Space Ghost, Dell #1, NM, M14...................................$250.00
Spin & Marty, Dell #5, 1958, EX+, M14 ....$45.00

Star Trek, Dell #3, 1967, EX+, M14 ....$135.00
Steve Canyon, Dell #939, EX, M14 ....$30.00
Straight Arrow, #1, G+, A3 ....$55.00
Strange Adventures, Dell #17, VG, M14.........................$85.00
Superboy, Dell #89, VG+, M14..$60.00
Superman, Dell #25, 1941, VG, M14.............................$225.00
Superman's Girlfriend Lois Lane, Dell #13, NM, M14...$100.00
Tales From the Crypt, Dell #28, VG, M14 ....$90.00
Tales To Astonish, Dell #40, NM, M14 ....$245.00
Tarzan, DC Comics #207, NM, M14 ....$10.00
Tarzan, Dell #27, 1951, EX, M14 ....$35.00

Tarzan's Jungle Annual, Dell #2, 1953, EX, $40.00.

Tex Ritter, Dell #35, EX, M14 ....$25.00
That Darn Cat, Gold Key, 1965, photo cover, EX, M17 ..$20.00
This Is Your Life Donald Duck, Dell #1109, NM, M14..$125.00
Three Stooges, Dell #1170, 1961, VG, M17 ....$30.00
Tom & Jerry, Dell #115, EX, M14...................................$20.00
Tom & Jerry Summer Fun, Dell Giant #1, VG+, A3 ....$35.00
Tom Mix, Fawcett #2, VG, A3 ....$110.00
Top Cat, Dell #3, 1962, VG, M17...................................$12.00
Top Cat, Gold Key #5, 1963, NM, M14 ....$30.00
True FBI Adventures, True Comics #68, 1948, EX $65.00
Two-Gun Kid, Dell #40, EX, M14...................................$35.00
Underworld Crime, Dell #3, 1952, EX+, M14 ....$60.00
Vacation in Disneyland, Dell #1025, NM, M14.............$140.00
Voyage to the Deep, Dell #1, 1962, EX, M14 ....$10.00
Walt Disney's Uncle Scrooge, Dell #211, NM, M14 ....$10.00
Weird Fantasy, Dell #11, VG+, M14 ....$45.00
Western Tales, Dell #32, 1956, EX+, M14 ....$80.00
Wild Bill Elliot, Dell #9, EX+, M14 ....$45.00
Wild Wild West, Dell #2, 1966, VG, M14 ....$12.00
Wonder Woman, Dell #34, G, M14.................................$30.00
Woody Woodpecker, Dell #350, 1947, EX, M14.............$25.00
Wyatt Earp, Dell #860, NM, M14 ....$75.00
Zane Grey's Stories of the West, Dell #270, VG+, M14...$15.00

X-Men, Marvel Comics, EX, $100.00.

Corgi

Corgi vehicles are among the favorites of the diecast collectors; they've been made in Great Britain since 1956, and they're still in production today. They were well detailed and ruggedly built to last. Some of the most expensive Corgi's on today's collector market are the character-related vehicles, for instance, James Bond (there are several variations), Batman, and Man From U.N.C.L.E.

Values are for mint-in-the-box or mint-in-package examples. Other Sources: G2, L1, N3, W1.

#50, Massey-Ferguson 50B Tractor	$50.00
#50, Massey-Ferguson 65 Tractor	$110.00
#51, Massey-Ferguson Tipper Trailer	$25.00
#53, Massey-Ferguson Tractor Shovel	$100.00
#54, Fordson Half-Track Tractor	$160.00
#54, Massey-Ferguson Tractor Shovel	$50.00
#55, David Brown Tractor	$50.00
#55, Fordson Major Tractor	$100.00
#56, Plough	$25.00
#57, Massey-Ferguson Tractor & Fork	$110.00
#58, Beast Carrier	$40.00
#60, Fordson Power Major Tractor	$100.00
#61, Four-Furrow Plough	$20.00
#62, Ford Tipper Trailer	$20.00
#64, Conveyor on Jeep	$75.00
#66, Massey-Ferguson Tractor	$85.00
#67, Ford Super Major Tractor	$90.00
#69, Massey-Ferguson Tractor Shovel	$100.00
#71, Fordson Disc Harrow	$20.00
#72, Ford 5000 Tractor & Trencher	$130.00
#73, Massey-Ferguson Tractor & Saw	$125.00
#74, Ford 5000 Tractor & Scoop	$100.00
#100, Dropside Trailer	$20.00

#101, Platform Tractor	$20.00
#102, Pony Trailer	$25.00
#104, Dolphin Cabin Cruiser	$30.00
#107, Batboat & Trailer	$125.00
#109, Penny Burn Trailer	$50.00
#112, Rice Horse Box	$45.00
#150, Surtees TS9	$40.00
#150, Vanwall, regular	$70.00
#151, Lotus XI, regular	$80.00
#151, McLaren Yardley M19A	$30.00
#152, BRM Racer	$80.00
#152, Ferrari 312 B2	$35.00
#153, Bluebird Record Car	$125.00
#153, Team Surtees	$35.00
#154, Ferrari Formula I	$50.00
#154, Lotus John Player	$45.00
#154, Lotus Texaco Special	$45.00
#155, Shadow FI Racer	$40.00
#156, Shadow FI, Graham Hill	$40.00
#158, Lotus Climax	$50.00
#158, Tyrrell-Ford Elf	$40.00
#159, Cooper Maserati	$50.00
#159, Indianapolis Racer	$45.00
#160, Hesketh Racer	$45.00
#161, Elf-Tyrrell Project 34	$50.00
#161, Santa Pod Commuter	$45.00
#162, Quartermaster Dragster	$40.00
#162, Tyrell P34 Racer	$40.00
#163, Santa Pod Dragster	$50.00
#164, Wild Honey Dragster	$50.00
#165, Adams Bros Dragster	$40.00
#166, Ford Mustang	$45.00
#167, USA Racing Buggy	$35.00
#169, Starfighter Jet Dragster	$40.00
#170, John Wolfe's Dragster	$40.00
#190, Lotus John Player Special	$60.00
#191, McLaren Texaco-Marlboro	$65.00
#200, BMC Mini 1000	$50.00
#200, Ford Consul, dual colors	$200.00
#200, Ford Consul, solid colors	$175.00
#200m, Ford Consul, w/motor	$200.00
#201, Austin Cambridge	$160.00
#201, Saint's Volvo	$150.00

#201m, Austin Cambridge, $200.00.
(From the collection of Al Rapp)

#202, Morris Cowley..$150.00
#202, Renault R16 ....$40.00
#202m, Morris Cowley, w/motor.........................$175.00
#203, Detomaso Mangust $40.00
#203, Vauxhall Velox, dual colors $200.00
#203, Vauxhall Velox, solid colors....................$175.00
#203, Vauxhall Velox, w/motor, dual colors.................$300.00
#203, Vauxhall Velox, w/motor, red or yel $200.00
#204, Morris Mini-Minor, bl $200.00
#204, Rover 90, other colors $175.00
#204, Rover 90, wht & red, 2-tone $300.00
#204m, Rover 90, w/motor $200.00
#205, Riley Pathfinder, bl....................................$175.00
#205, Riley Pathfinder, red $130.00
#205m, Riley Pathfinder, w/motor, bl $175.00
#205m, Riley Pathfinder, w/motor, red $225.00
#206, Hillman Husky, metallic bl & silver $175.00
#206, Hillman Husky Estate, metallic bl & silver, 2-tone..$175.00
#206, Hillman Husky Estate, solid colors.........$130.00
#206m, Hillman Husky Estate, w/motor $175.00
#207, Standard Vanguard $125.00
#207m, Standard Vanguard, w/motor $175.00
#208, Jaguar 2.4 Saloon $140.00
#208m, Jaguar 2.4 Saloon, w/motor $180.00
#208s, Jaguar 2.4 Saloon, w/suspension............$135.00
#209, Riley Police Car $120.00
#210, Citroen DS19...$90.00
#210s, Citroen DS19, w/suspension $100.00
#211, Studebaker Golden Hawk $125.00
#211m, Studebaker Golden Hawk, w/motor........$175.00
#211s, Studebaker Golden Hawk, plated, w/suspension.$125.00
#213, Jaguar Fire Chief $150.00
#213s, Jaguar Fire Chief, w/suspension..............$200.00
#214, Ford Thunderbird $125.00
#214m, Ford Thunderbird, w/motor.....................$300.00
#214s, Ford Thunderbird, w/suspension $100.00
#215, Ford Thunderbird Sport...............................$125.00
#215s, Ford Thunderbird Sport, w/suspension $100.00
#216, Austin A-40, red & blk $175.00
#216, Austin A-40, 2-tone bl $100.00
#216m, Austin A-40, w/motor $300.00
#217, Fiat 1800 ....$80.00

#218, Austin Martin DB4......................................$110.00
#219, Plymouth Suburban $95.00
#221, Chevrolet Impala Cab $110.00
#222, Renault Floride $90.00
#223, Chevrolet Police $110.00
#224, Bentley Continental $100.00
#225, Austin 7, red $100.00
#225, Austin 7, yel..$300.00
#226, Morris Mini-Minor $100.00
#227, Mini-Cooper Rally.......................................$275.00
#228, Volvo P-1800 ....$80.00
#229, Chevrolet Corvair..$70.00
#230, Mercedes Benz 222, red $75.00
#231, Triumph Herald..$100.00
#232, Fiat 2100 ....$75.00
#233, Heinkel Trojan $90.00

#234, Ford Consul Classic, $85.00.
(From the collection of Al Rapp)

#235, Oldsmobile Super 88....................................$75.00
#236, Motor School, right-hand drive.............$90.00
#237, Oldsmobile Sheriff's Car........................$100.00
#238, Jaguar MK10, metallic gr or silver $190.00
#238, Jaguar MK10, metallic red or bl.........................$125.00

#220, Chevrolet Impala, $80.00.
(From the collection of Al Rapp)

#246, Chrysler Imperial, metallic turquoise, $250.00.
(From the collection of Al Rapp)

#239, VW Karman Ghia	$90.00
#240, Fiat 500 Jolly	$145.00
#241, Chrysler Ghia	$80.00
#242, Fiat 600 Jolly	$175.00
#245, Buick Riviera	$95.00
#246, Chrysler Imperial, red	$110.00
#247, Mercedes Benz 600 Pullman	$75.00
#248, Chevrolet Impala	$80.00
#249, Morris Mini-Cooper, wicker	$130.00
#251, Hillman Imp	$100.00
#252, Rover 2000, metallic bl	$80.00
#252, Rover 2000, metallic maroon	$165.00
#253, Mercedes Benz 220SE	$90.00
#255, Motor School, left-hand drive	$225.00
#256, VW 1200 East Africa Safari	$200.00
#258, Saint's Volvo P1800	$165.00
#259, Citroen Le Dandy, bl	$180.00
#259, Citroen Le Dandy, maroon	$120.00
#259, Penguin Mobile	$50.00
#260, Renault R16	$45.00
#261, James Bond's Aston Martin DB5	$235.00
#261, Spiderbuggy	$100.00
#262, Capt Marvel's Porsche	$65.00
#262, Lincoln Continental Limo, bl	$180.00
#262, Lincoln Continental Limo, gold	$100.00

#273, Rolls Royce Silver Shadow	$100.00
#274, Bentley Mulliner	$80.00
#275, Mini Metro, colors other than gold	$25.00
#275, Mini Metro, gold	$75.00
#275, Rover 2000 TC, gr	$75.00
#275, Rover 2000 TC, wht	$160.00
#275, Royal Wedding Mini Metro	$25.00
#276, Oldsmobile Toronado, metallic red	$70.00
#276, Triumph Acclaim	$20.00
#277, Monkeemobile	$300.00
#277, Triumph Driving School	$25.00
#279, Rolls Royce Corniche	$30.00
#280, Rolls Royce Silver Shadow, other colors	$50.00
#280, Rolls Royce Silver Shadow, silver	$80.00
#281, Metro Datapost	$20.00
#281, Rover 2000 TC	$150.00
#282, Mini Cooper Rally Car	$90.00
#283, DAF City Car	$40.00
#284, Citroen SM	$45.00
#285, Mercedes Benz 240D	$25.00
#286, Jaguar XJ12C	$45.00
#287, Citroen Dyane	$25.00
#288, Minissima	$20.00
#289, VW Polo	$25.00
#290, Kojak's Buick, no hat	$125.00
#290, Kojak's Buick, w/hat	$75.00
#291, AMC Pacer	$20.00
#291, Mercedes Benz 240 Rally	$35.00

#263, Rambler Marlin, $75.00.
(From the collection of Al Rapp)

#264, Incredible Hulk	$75.00
#264, Oldsmobile Toronado	$85.00
#265, Supermobile	$65.00
#266, Chitty-Chitty Bang-Bang, orig	$350.00
#266, Chitty-Chitty Bang-Bang, replica	$125.00
#266, Superbike	$60.00
#267, Batmobile, red 'Bat'-hubs	$400.00
#267, Batmobile, w/red whizzwheels	$500.00
#267, Batmobile, w/whizzwheels	$140.00
#268, Batman's Bat Bike	$70.00
#269, James Bond's Lotus	$100.00
#270, James Bond's Aston Martin, w/tire slashers, 1/43 scale	$250.00
#270, James Bond's Aston Martin, w/whizzwheels, 1/43 scale	$120.00
#271, Ghia Mangusta De Tomaso	$65.00
#271, James Bond's Aston Martin	$90.00
#272, James Bond's Citroen 2CV	$60.00
#273, Honda Driving School	$40.00

#292, Starsky and Hutch Ford Torino, $85.00.
(From the collection of Al Rapp)

#293, Renault 5TS	$20.00
#294, Renault Alpine	$20.00
#298, Magnum PI's Ferrari	$50.00
#299, Ford Sierra 2.3 Ghia	$20.00
#300, Austin Healey, red or cream	$150.00
#300, Austin Healey Sports Car, bl	$300.00
#300, Chevrolet Corvette	$100.00

#300, Ferrari Daytona $25.00	#316, Ford GT 70..............................$50.00
#301, Iso Grifo 7 Litre.........................$60.00	#316, NSU Sports Prinz $90.00
#301, Lotus Elite $25.00	#317, Mini Cooper Monte Carlo $200.00
#301, Triumph TR2 Sports Car $150.00	#318, Jaguar XJS $25.00
#302, Hillman Hunter Rally, kangaroo........$130.00	#318, Lotus Elan, copper $300.00
#302, MGA Sports Car $140.00	#318, Lotus Elan, metallic bl...............$110.00
#302, VW Polo $20.00	#318, Lotus Elan, wht........................$250.00
#303, Mercedes Benz 300SL $100.00	#319, Jaguar XJS $35.00
#303, Porsche 924 ....$20.00	#319, Lamborghini P400 GT Miura $35.00
#303, Roger Clark's Ford Capri $75.00	#319, Lotus Elan, gr or yel $140.00
#303s, Mercedes Benz 300SL, w/suspension...$100.00	#319, Lotus Elan, red $100.00
#304, Chevrolet SS350 Camaro $65.00	#319, Lotus Elan, bl $100.00
#304, Mercedes Benz 300SL, yel & red $100.00	#320, Saint's Jaguar XJS.....................$85.00
#304s, Mercedes Benz 300SL, w/suspension ...$100.00	#321, Monte Carlo Mini Cooper, 1965 .....$300.00
#305, Mini Marcos GT 850 ....$65.00	#321, Monte Carlo Mini Cooper, 1966, w/autographs ...$600.00
#305, Triumph TR3............................$145.00	#321, Porsche 924, metallic gr $70.00
#306, Fiat X1/9 ....$30.00	#321, Porsche 924, red $25.00
#306, Morris Marina $65.00	#322, Rover Monte Carlo $180.00
#307, Jaguar E-Type $125.00	#323, Citroen DS19 Monte Carlo.............$180.00
#307, Renault $20.00	#323, Ferrari Daytona 365 GTB4 ....$25.00
#308, BMW M1 Racer, gold plated...........$110.00	#324, Marcos Volvo 1800 GT $70.00
#308, BMW M1 Racer, yel $25.00	#325, Chevrolet Caprice......................$65.00
#308, Monte Carlo Mini $100.00	#325, Ford Mustang Competition $80.00
#309, Aston Martin DB4 ....$125.00	#326, Chevrolet Police Car $40.00
#309, Aston Martin DB4, w/spoked hubs $175.00	#327, Chevrolet Caprice Cab $40.00
#309, VW Turbo $20.00	#327, MGB GT................................$130.00
#310, Chevrolet Corvette, bronze $165.00	#328, Hillman Imp Monte Carlo $125.00
#310, Chevrolet Corvette, red or silver.......$65.00	#329, Ford Mustang Rally....................$50.00
#310, Porsche 924 ....$20.00	#329, Opel Senator, bl or bronze $40.00
#311, Ford Capri, orange $125.00	#329, Opel Senator, silver $50.00
#311, Ford Capri, red $80.00	#330, Porsche Carrera 6, wht & bl $120.00
#311, Ford Capri, w/gold hubs................$150.00	#330, Porsche Carrera 6, wht & red $60.00
#312, Ford Capri S $35.00	#331, Ford Capri Rally.......................$90.00
#312, Jaguar E-Type............................$100.00	#332, Lancia Fulvia Sport, red or bl $60.00
#312, Marcos Mantis..........................$50.00	#332, Lancia Fulvia Sport, yel & blk.........$125.00
#313, Ford Cortina, bronze or bl $100.00	#332, Opel, Doctor's Car $50.00
#313, Ford Cortina, yel.......................$300.00	#334, Ford Escort $20.00
#314, Ferrari Berlinetta Le Mans.............$65.00	#334, Mini Magnifique $90.00
#314, Supercat Jaguar $30.00	#335, Jaguar 4.2 Litre E Type $125.00
#315, Lotus Elite $35.00	#336, James Bond's Toyota 2000GT $365.00
#315, Simca Sports Car, metallic bl...........$190.00	#337, Chevrolet Stingray.....................$65.00
	#338, Chevrolet SS350 Camaro $75.00
	#338, Rover 3500 ....$30.00
	#339, Rover 3500 Police Car.................$30.00
	#339, 1967 Mini Cooper Monte Carlo, w/roof rack $300.00
	#340, Rover Triplex.........................$25.00
	#340, 1967 Sunbeam IMP Monte Carlo $135.00
	#341, Chevrolet Caprice Racer $25.00
	#341, Mini Marcos GT850 ....$60.00
	#342, Lamborghini P400 GT Miura $60.00
	#342, Professionals Ford Capri...............$80.00
	#342, Professionals Ford Capri, w/chrome bumpers........$100.00
	#343, Pontiac Firebird.......................$55.00
	#344, Ferrari 206 Dino Sport................$70.00
	#345, Honda Prelude $25.00
	#345, MGC GT, orange $300.00
	#345, MGC GT, yel $125.00
	#346, Citroen 2 CV $20.00

#315, Simca Sports Car, silver, $65.00.
(From the collection of Al Rapp)

#347, Chevrolet Astro 1 ....$50.00

#348, Flower Power Mustang Stock Car, $140.00.
(From the collection of Al Rapp)

#348, Vegas Ford Thunderbird $85.00
#349, Pop Art Morris Mini, minimum value $1,500.00
#350, Thunderbird Guided Missile $125.00
#351, RAF Land Rover $80.00
#352, RAF Vanguard Staff Car $100.00
#353, Road Scanner $60.00
#354, Commer Military Ambulance $110.00
#355, Commer Military Police $135.00
#356, VW Personnel Carrier $135.00
#357, Land Rover Weapons Carrier $180.00
#358, Oldsmobile Staff Car $125.00
#359, Commer Army Field Kitchen $165.00
#370, Ford Cobra Mustang $25.00
#371, Porsche Carrera $40.00
#373, Peugeot 505 ....$25.00
#373, VW Police Car, Polizei $150.00
#374, Jaguar 4.2 Litre E Type $90.00
#374, Jaguar 5.3 Litre $70.00
#375, Toyota 2000 GT $75.00
#376, Chevrolet Stingray Stock Car $50.00
#377, Marcos 3 Litre, wht & gray $100.00
#377, Marcos 3 Litre, yel or bl $60.00
#378, Ferrari 308 GT $25.00
#378, MGC GT $140.00
#380, Alfa Romeo P33 ....$45.00
#380, Beach Buggy $40.00
#381, Renault Turbo $20.00
#382, Lotus Elite $25.00
#382, Porsche Targa 911S $50.00
#383, VW 1200, red or orange $70.00
#383, VW 1200, Swiss PTT $130.00
#383, VW 1200, yel ADAC $200.00
#384, Adams Bros Probe 15 ....$50.00
#384, Renault 11 GTL, cream $20.00
#384, Renault 11 GTL, maroon $40.00
#384, VW 1200 Rally $70.00
#385, Porsche 917 ....$40.00
#386, Bertone Runabout $50.00
#387, Chevrolet Corvette Stingray $100.00
#388, Mercedes Benz C111 ....$40.00
#389, Reliant Bond Bug 700, gr $100.00

#389, Reliant Bond Bug 700 ES, orange $60.00
#391, James Bond 007 Ford Mustang $250.00
#392, Bertone Shake Buggy $40.00
#393, Mercedes Benz 350 SL, metallic gr....$100.00
#393, Mercedes Benz 350 SL, wht or bl $65.00
#394, Datsun 240Z, East African Safari $45.00
#396, Datsun 240Z, US Rally $45.00
#397, Can Am Porsche Audi $35.00
#400, VW Driving School, bl $65.00
#400, VW Driving School, red $140.00
#401, VW 1200 ....$60.00
#402, Ford Cortina GXL, wht w/red stripe ...$80.00
#402, Ford Cortina GXL Police, wht $50.00
#402, Ford Cortina GXL Polizei $150.00
#403, Bedford Daily Express $150.00
#403, Thwaites Dumper $45.00
#403m, Bedford KLG Plugs, w/motor $230.00
#404, Bedford Dormobile, cream, maroon & turq ...$110.00
#404, Bedford Dormobile, yel & 2-tone bl ..$200.00
#404, Bedford Dormobile, yel w/bl roof $125.00
#404m, Bedford Dormobile, w/motor $160.00
#405, Bedford Utilicon Fire Department, gr .$160.00
#405, Bedford Utilicon Fire Department, red ...$200.00
#405, Chevrolet Superior Ambulance $40.00
#405, Ford Milk Float $25.00
#405m, Bedford Utilicon Fire Tender, w/motor ...$225.00
#406, Land Rover $80.00
#406, Mercedes Ambulance $35.00
#406, Mercedes Benz Unimog $50.00
#407, Karrier Mobile Grocers $150.00
#408, Bedford AA Road Service $150.00
#409, Allis Chalmers Fork Lift $30.00
#409, Forward Control Jeep $50.00
#409, Mercedes Dumper $50.00
#411, Karrier Lucozade Van $160.00
#411, Mercedes 240D, orange $80.00
#411, Mercedes 240D Taxi, cream or blk $65.00
#411, Mercedes 240D Taxi, orange w/blk roof ...$35.00
#412, Bedford Ambulance, split windscreen ...$130.00
#412, Bedford Ambulance, 1-pc windscreen ...$250.00
#412, Mercedes Police Car, Police $50.00
#412, Mercedes Police Car, Polizei $40.00
#413, Karrier Bantam Butcher Shop $150.00
#413, Mazda Maintenence Truck $50.00
#413s, Karrier Bantam Butcher Shop, w/suspension ...$200.00
#414, Bedford Military Ambulance $120.00
#414, Coastguard Jaguar $45.00
#415, Mazda Camper $50.00
#416, Buick Police Car $40.00
#416, Radio Rescue Rover, bl $125.00
#416, Radio Rescue Rover, yel $400.00
#416s, Radio Rescue Rover, w/suspension, bl ...$100.00
#416s, Radio Rescue Rover, w/suspension, yel ...$425.00
#417, Land Rover Breakdown $110.00
#417s, Land Rover Breakdown, w/suspension $85.00
#418, Austin Taxi, w/whizzwheels $50.00
#419, Ford Zephyr, Rijks Politie $350.00
#419, Ford Zephyr Politie $300.00

#419, Jeep......$30.00
#420, Airbourne Caravan......$100.00
#421, Bedford Evening Standard......$200.00
#422, Bedford Van, Corgi Toys, bl w/yel roof......$500.00
#422, Bedford Van, Corgi Toys, yel w/bl roof......$200.00
#422, Riot Police Wagon......$45.00
#423, Rough Rider Van......$45.00

#424, Ford Zephyr Estate Car, $85.00.
(From the collection of Al Rapp)

#424, Security Van......$30.00
#425, London Taxi......$25.00
#426, Chipperfield's Circus Booking Office......$300.00
#426, Pinder's Circus Booking Office......$50.00
#428, Mister Softee's Ice Cream Van......$200.00
#428, Renault Police Car......$25.00
#429, Jaguar Police Car......$40.00
#430, Bermuda Taxi, metallic bl & red......$400.00
#430, Bermuda Taxi, wht......$125.00
#430, Porsche 924 Polizei......$30.00
#431, VW Pickup, metallic gold......$300.00
#431, VW Pickup, yel......$100.00
#432, Vanatic Van......$30.00
#433, VW Delivery Van......$100.00
#434, Charlie's Angels Van......$50.00
#434, VW Kombi......$100.00
#435, Karrier Dairy Van......$125.00
#435, Superman Van......$50.00
#436, Citroen Safari......$100.00
#436, Spider Van......$50.00
#437, Cadillac Ambulance......$100.00
#437, Coca-Cola Van......$50.00
#438, Land Rover, gr......$60.00
#438, Land Rover, Lepra......$400.00
#439, Chevrolet Fire Chief......$100.00
#440, Mazda Pickup......$30.00
#441, Jeep......$25.00
#441, VW Toblerone Van......$135.00
#443, Plymouth US Mail......$110.00

#440, Ford Consul Cortina Super Estate Car, with golfer and caddy, $160.00. (From the Collection of Al Rapp)

#445, Plymouth Suburban......$90.00
#447, Walls Ice Cream Van......$275.00
#448, Police Mini Van, w/dog & handler......$200.00
#448, Renegade Jeep......$20.00
#450, Austin Mini Van......$100.00
#450, Austin Mini Van, w/pnt grille......$160.00
#450, Peugeot Taxi......$25.00
#452, Commer Lorry......$130.00
#453, Commer Walls Van......$200.00
#454, Commer Platform Lorry......$130.00
#455, Karrier Bantam 2-Ton......$120.00
#456, ERF Dropside Lorry......$110.00
#457, ERF Platform Lorry......$100.00
#457, Talbot Matra Rancho, gr or red......$25.00
#457, Talbot Matra Rancho, wht or orange......$45.00
#458, ERF Tipper Dumper......$85.00
#459, ERF Moorhouse Van......$375.00
#459, Raygo Road Roller......$40.00
#460, ERF Cement Tipper......$90.00
#461, Police Vigilant Range Rover, Police......$35.00
#461, Police Viligant Range Rover, Politie......$80.00
#462, Commer Van, Co-op......$125.00
#462, Commer Van, Hammonds......$170.00
#463, Commer Ambulance......$100.00
#464, Commer Police Van, City Police, minimum value..$300.00
#464, Commer Police Van, County Police, bl......$110.00
#464, Commer Police Van, Police, bl......$100.00
#464, Commer Police Van, Police, gr......$750.00
#464, Commer Police Van, Rijks Politie, bl, minimum value...$300.00
#465, Commer Pickup Truck......$65.00
#466, Commer Milk Float, Co-op......$170.00
#466, Commer Milk Float, wht......$70.00
#467, London Routemaster Bus......$75.00
#468, London Transport Routemaster, Church's Shoes, red.$200.00
#468, London Transport Routemaster, Design Centre, red...$250.00
#468, London Transport Routemaster, Gamages, red.....$200.00

#468, London Transport Routemaster Bus, Corgi Toys, brn, gr or cream $1,000.00
#468, London Transport Routemaster Bus, Corgi Toys, red..$100.00
#468, London Transport Routemaster Bus, Madame Tussand's, red $200.00
#468, London Transport Routemaster Bus, Outspan, red.$60.00
#470, Disneyland Bus...$40.00
#470, Forward Control Jeep...$60.00
#470, Greenline Bus $20.00
#471, Silver Jubilee Bus $40.00

#471, Smith's-Karrier Mobile Canteen, $140.00.
(From the Collection of Al Rapp)

#471, Woolworth Silver Jubilee Bus $40.00
#472, Public Address Land Rover $150.00
#474, Ford Musical Walls Ice Cream Van $250.00
#475, Citroen Ski Safari $150.00
#477, Land Rover Breakdown, w/whizzwheels.................$60.00
#478, Forward Control Jeep, Tower Wagon $75.00
#479, Mobile Camera Van $150.00
#480, Chevrolet Impala Cab $80.00
#480, Chevrolet Police Car $80.00
#481, Chevrolet Police Patrol Car $125.00

#482, Chevrolet Fire Chief Car, $100.00.
(From the Collection of Al Rapp)

#482, Range Rover Ambulance.......................................$50.00
#483, Dodge Tipper $50.00
#483, Police Range Rover, Belgian $75.00
#484, AMC Pacer Rescue $30.00
#484, AMC Pacer Secours...$50.00
#484, Livestock Transporter $60.00
#484, Mini Countryman Surfer, w/silver grille $175.00

#485, Mini Countrynman Surfer, w/unpnt grille $225.00
#486, Chevrolet Kennel Service $100.00
#487, Chipperfield's Circus Parade $200.00
#489, VW Police Car..$30.00
#490, Touring Caravan $25.00
#490, VW Breakdown Truck...$95.00
#491, Ford Escort Estate $100.00
#492, VW Police Car, Politie $275.00
#492, VW Police Car, Polizei $80.00
#492, VW Police Car, w/gr mudguards $300.00
#493, Mazda Pickup...$35.00
#494, Bedford Tipper, red & silver $175.00
#494, Bedford Tipper, red & yel $80.00
#495, Opel Open Truck..$20.00

#497, Man From UNCLE Gun Firing Thrush-Buster, $300.00. (From the collection of Al Rapp)

#497, Man From UNCLE, wht, minimum value $600.00
#499, Citroen, 1968 Olympics $175.00
#500, US Army Rover $400.00
#503, Chipperfield's Circus Giraffe Transporter $125.00
#506, Sunbeam Imp Police $125.00
#508, Holiday Minibus $110.00
#509, Porsche Police Car, Polizei $80.00
#509, Porsche Police Car, Ritjks Politie........................$150.00
#510, Citroen Tour De France $125.00
#511, Chipperfield's Circus Poodle Pickup $600.00
#513, Alpine Rescue Car $350.00
#647, Buck Rogers' Starfighter $75.00
#648, Space Shuttle $50.00
#649, James Bond's Space Shuttle.................................$80.00
#650, BOAC Concorde, all others (no gold logo on tail)...$30.00
#650, BOAC Concorde, gold logo on tail......................$100.00
#651, Air France Concorde, all others (no gold tail design)...$50.00
#651, Air France Concorde, gold tail design..................$140.00
#651, Japan Air Line Concorde $400.00
#653, Air Canada Concorde $325.00
#681, Stunt Bike $250.00
#700, Motorway Ambulance $20.00
#701, Intercity Minibus $20.00
#703, Breakdown Truck...$20.00
#703, Hi Speed Fire Engine $20.00
#801, Ford Thunderbird...$25.00

#801, Noddy's Car, $450.00.
(From the collection of Al Rapp)

#802, Mercedes Benz 300 Sl	$25.00
#802, Popeye's Paddle Wagon	$550.00
#803, Beatle's Yellow Submarine	$550.00
#803, Jaguar XK120	$20.00
#804, Jaguar XK120 Rally	$20.00
#804, Jaguar XK120 Rally, w/spats	$50.00
#804, Noddy's Car, Noddy only	$275.00
#804, Noddy's Car, w/Mr Tubby	$350.00
#805, Hardy Boy's Rolls Royce	$300.00
#805, Mercedes Benz 300 SC	$20.00
#806, Lunar Bug	$150.00
#806, Mercedes Benz 300 SC	$20.00
#807, Dougal's Car	$300.00
#808, Basil Brush's Car	$225.00
#809, Dick Dastardly's Racer	$150.00
#810, Ford Thunderbird	$25.00
#811, James Bond's Moon Buggy	$500.00
#831, Mercedes Benz 300 SL	$25.00
#851, Magic Roundabout Train	$350.00
#852, Magic Roundabout Carousel	$800.00
#853, Magic Roundabout Playground	$1,500.00
#859, Mr McHenry's Trike	$250.00
#900, German Tank	$50.00
#901, British Centurion	$50.00
#902, American Tank	$50.00
#903, British Chieftain Tank	$50.00
#904, King Tiger Tank	$50.00
#905, SU100 Tank Destroyer	$50.00
#906, Saladin Armoured Car	$50.00
#907, German Rocket Launcher	$75.00
#908, French Recovery Tank	$75.00
#909, Quad Gun Tank, Trailer & Field Gun	$60.00
#920, Bell Helicopter	$30.00
#921, Hughes Helicopter	$30.00
#922, Sikorsky Helicopter	$30.00
#923, Sikorsky Helicopter Military	$30.00

#925, Batcopter	$75.00
#926, Stromberg Helicopter	$75.00
#927, Chopper Squad Helicopter	$60.00
#928, Spidercopter	$90.00
#929, Daily Planet Helicopter	$65.00
#930, DAAX Helicopter	$60.00
#931, Jet Police Helicopter	$50.00

CORGITRONICS

#1001, Corgitronics Firestreak	$80.00
#1002, Corgitronics Landtrain	$50.00
#1003, Ford Torino	$30.00
#1004, Corgitronics Beep Beep Bus	$40.00
#1005, Police Land Rover	$30.00
#1006, Roadshow, Radio	$50.00
#1007, Land Rover & Compressor	$50.00
#1008, Chevrolet Fire Chief	$40.00
#1009, Maestro MG1600	$50.00
#1011, Firestreak	$40.00

EXPLORATION MODELS

#2022, Scanotron	$60.00
#2023, Rocketron	$60.00
#2024, Lasertron	$60.00
#2025, Magnetron	$60.00

GIFT SETS

#1, Car Transporter Set	$850.00
#1, Ford Sierra & Caravan	$40.00
#1, Ford 500 Tractor & Beast Trailer	$160.00
#2, Land Rover & Pony Trailer	$180.00
#2, Unimog Dumper	$150.00
#3, Batmobile & Batboat, w/'Bat'-hubs	$400.00
#3, Batmobile & Batboat, w/whizzwheels	$210.00
#3, RAF Land Rover & Missile	$250.00
#4, Country Farm Set	$75.00
#4, RAF Land Rover & Missile	$500.00
#5, Agricultural Set	$300.00
#5, Country Farm Set, w/no hay	$90.00
#5, Racing Car Set	$300.00
#6, Rocket Age Set	$1,000.00
#6, VW Transporter & Cooper Maserati	$175.00

#7, Daktari Set, $150.00.
(From the collection of Al Rapp)

#7, Tractor & Trailer Set $130.00
#8, Combine Harvester Set $400.00
#8, Lions of Longleat $200.00
#9, Corporal Missile & Launcher $600.00
#9, Tractor w/Shovel & Trailer $200.00
#10, Centurion Tank & Transporter $140.00
#10, Jeep & Motorcycle Trailer $40.00
#10, Rambler Marlin, w/kayaks $210.00
#11, ERF Truck & Trailer $200.00
#11, London Set, no Policeman $135.00
#11, London Set, w/Policeman $600.00
#12, Chipperfield's Circus Crane Truck & Cage $300.00
#12, Glider Set $80.00
#12, Grand Prix Set $450.00
#13, Fordson Tractor & Plough $150.00
#13, Peugeot Tour De France $90.00
#13, Renault Tour De France $150.00
#14, Giant Daktari Set $500.00
#14, Tower Wagon $100.00
#15, Land Rover & Horsebox..................................$100.00

#24, Constructor Set, $150.00.
(From the collection of Al Rapp)

#15, Silvertone Set...$1,800.00
#16, Ecurie Ecosse Set $500.00
#17, Land Rover & Ferrari $200.00
#17, Military Set $85.00
#18, Emergency Set $80.00
#18, Fordson Tractor & Plough..............................$125.00
#19, Chipperfield's Circus Rover & Elephant Trailer $325.00
#19, Emergency Set $80.00
#19, Flying Club Set $85.00
#20, Car Transporter Set, minimum value $900.00

#20, Emergency Set..$70.00
#20, Golden Guinea Set $300.00
#21, Chipperfield's Circus Crane & Trailer, minimum value ..$1,600.00
#21, ERF Milk Truck & Trailer..............................$350.00
#21, Superman Set $250.00
#22, James Bond Set $265.00
#23, Chipperfield's Circus Set, w/Booking Office $1,000.00
#23, Spiderman Set $200.00
#24, Mercedes & Caravan $50.00
#25, Mantra Rancho & Trailer..................................$50.00
#25, Shell or BP Garage Set, minimum value $1,600.00
#25, VW Transporter & Cooper Masarati $160.00
#26, Beach Bug Set $50.00
#26, Matra Rancho & Racer.......................................$75.00
#27, Priestman Shovel Set..$195.00
#28, Mazda Pickup & Dinghy, w/trailer $60.00
#28, Transporter Set $800.00
#29, Ferrari Racing Set $80.00
#29, Jeep & Horsebox $40.00
#29, Tractor & Trailer...$140.00
#30, Grand Prix Set...$285.00
#30, Pinder's Circus Rover & Trailer.....................$135.00
#31, Buick Riviera & Boat $225.00
#31, Safari Set $100.00
#32, Lotus Racing Set..$110.00
#32, Tractor & Trailer...$170.00
#33, Fordson Tractor & Carrier $150.00
#35, Chopper Squad $60.00
#35, London Set $175.00
#36, Tarzan Set $250.00
#36, Tornado Set $250.00
#37, Fiat & Boat..$60.00
#37, Lotus Racing Team $500.00
#38, Jaguar & Powerboat $75.00
#38, Mini Camping Set $100.00
#38, Monte Carlo Set $600.00
#40, Batman Set $275.00
#41, Ford Transporter Set.......................................$850.00
#41, Silver Jubilee State Landau.............................$40.00

#40, Avengers, red and white vehicles, $650.00.
(From the collection of Al Rapp)

#42, Agricultural Set..$80.00
#43, Silo & Conveyor...$65.00
#44, Police Rover Set...$65.00
#45, All Winners Set..$800.00
#45, Royal Canadian Mounted Police....................$85.00
#46, All Winners Set..$600.00
#46, Super Karts..$30.00
#47, Ford Tractor & Conveyor...............................$195.00
#47, Pony Club Set..$50.00
#48, Ford Transporter Set......................................$600.00
#48, Jean Richards' Circus Set..............................$200.00
#48, Scammell Transport Set.................................$900.00
#49, Flying Club Set..$50.00

HUSKIES

Huskies were marketed exclusively through the Woolworth stores from 1965 to 1969. In 1970, Corgi Juniors were introduced. Both lines were sold in blister packs. Models produced up to 1975 (as dated on the package) are valued from $15.00 to $30.00 (MIP), except for the character-related examples listed below.

#1001A, James Bond's Aston Martin, Husky on base $200.00
#1001B, James Bond Aston Martin, Junior on base........$175.00
#1002A, Batmobile, Husky on base..............................$200.00
#1003A, Bat Boat, Husky on base................................$125.00
#1003B, Bat Boat, Junior on base................................$85.00
#1004A, Monkeemobile, Husky on base.......................$200.00
#1004B, Monkeemobile, Junior on base.......................$175.00
#1005A, UNCLE Car, Husky on base...........................$175.00
#1005B, UNCLE Car, Junior on base...........................$1,500.00
#1006A, Chitty-Chitty Bang-Bang, Husky on base........$200.00
#1006B, Chitty-Chitty Bang-Bang, Junior on base $175.00
#1007, Ironside Police Van...$140.00
#1008, Popeye Paddle Wagon......................................$200.00
#1011, James Bond Bobsleigh......................................$300.00
#1012, Spectre Bobsleigh...$300.00
#1013, Tom's Go-Kart...$75.00
#1014, Jerry's Banger..$75.00
#1017, Ford Holmes Wrecker.......................................$175.00

MAJOR PACKS

#1100, Carrimore Low Loader, red cab $140.00
#1100, Carrimore Low Loader, yel cab..........................$225.00
#1100, Mack Truck..$900.01
#1101, Carrimore Car Transporter, bl cab.....................$250.00
#1101, Carrimore Car Transporter, red cab...................$135.00
#1101, Hydrolic Crane...$50.00
#1102, Crane Fruehauf Dumper...................................$65.00
#1102, Euclid Tractor, gr...$150.00
#1102, Euclid Tractor, yel..$200.00
#1103, Airport Crash Truck...$85.00
#1103, Euclid Crawler Tractor......................................$125.00
#1104, Machinery Carrier..$150.00
#1104, Racehorse Transporter......................................$125.00
#1105, Berliet Racehorse Transporter...........................$60.00
#1106, Decca Mobile Radar Van $170.00

#1107, Berliet Container Truck $60.00
#1107, Euclid Tractor & Dozer, red $375.00
#1107, Euclid Tractor & Dozer, orange $300.00
#1108, Bristol Bloodhound & Launching Ramp............$125.00
#1108, Michelin Container Truck.................................$50.00
#1109, Bristol Bloodhound & Loading Trolley..............$130.00
#1109, Michelin Truck..$50.00
#1110, JCB Crawler Loader...$60.00
#1110, Mobilgas Tanker..$300.00
#1110, Shell Tanker..$3,000.00
#1111, Massey-Ferguson Harvester $150.00
#1112, Corporal Missile on Launching Ramp...............$160.00
#1112, David Brown Combine......................................$120.00
#1113, Corporal Erector & Missile................................$375.00
#1113, Hyster...$50.00
#1113, Hyster Sealink...$135.00
#1115, Bloodhound Missile $110.00
#1116, Bloodhound Missile Platform $100.00
#1116, Refuse Lorry $30.00
#1117, Bloodhound Missile Trolley...............................$65.00
#1117, Faun Street Sweeper $30.00
#1118, Airport Emergency Tender................................$70.00
#1118, International Truck, Dutch Army.......................$300.00
#1118, International Truck, gr.......................................$150.00
#1118, International Truck, US Army $275.00
#1119, HDL Hovercraft...$100.00
#1120, Midland Coach..$220.00
#1121, Chipperfield's Circus Crane $250.00
#1121, Corgimatic Ford Tipper $50.00
#1123, Chipperfield's Circus Animal Cage.....................$140.00
#1124, Corporal Missile Launching Ramp.....................$80.00
#1126, Ecurie Ecosse Transporter.................................$200.00
#1126, Simon Snorkel Dennis Fire Engine $60.00
#1127, Simon Snorkel Bedford Fire Engine...................$110.00
#1128, Priestman Cub Shovel......................................$75.00
#1129, Mercedes Truck...$25.00
#1129, Milk Tanker..$275.00
#1130, Chipperfield's Circus Horse Transporter............$275.00
#1130, Mercedes Tanker, Corgi $25.00
#1131, Carrimore Machinery Carrier............................$135.00
#1131, Mercedes Refrigerated Van...............................$20.00
#1132, Carrimore Low Loader......................................$250.00
#1132, Scania Truck...$20.00
#1133, Troop Transporter $250.00
#1134, Army Fuel Tanker..$400.00
#1135, Heavy Equipment Transporter $435.00
#1137, Ford Tilt Cab w/Trailer $125.00
#1138, Carrimore Car Transporter, Corgi.....................$150.00
#1140, Bedford Mobilgas Tanker $300.00
#1140, Ford Transit Wrecker.......................................$25.00
#1141, Milk Tanker..$300.00
#1142, Holmes Wrecker..$150.00
#1143, American LaFrance Rescue Truck $125.00
#1144, Berliet Wrecker..$80.00
#1144, Chipperfield's Circus Crane Truck....................$600.00
#1145, Mercedes Unimog Dumper...............................$50.00
#1146, Tri-Deck Transporter $185.00
#1147, Ferrymaster Truck..$130.00

#1148, Carrimore Car Transporter	$160.00
#1150, Mercedes Unimog Snowplough	$60.00
#1151, Scammell Co-op Set	$350.00
#1151, Scammell Co-op Truck	$250.00
#1152, Mack Truck, Esso Tanker	$85.00
#1152, Mack Truck, Exxon Tanker	$140.00
#1153, Priestman Boom Crane	$80.00
#1154, Priestman Crane	$100.00
#1154, Tower Crane	$75.00
#1155, Skyscraper Tower Crane	$60.00
#1156, Volvo Cement Mixer	$60.00
#1157, Ford Esso Tanker	$50.00
#1158, Ford Exxon Tanker	$75.00
#1159, Ford Car Transporter	$85.00
#1160, Ford Gulf Tanker	$55.00
#1161, Ford Aral Tanker	$85.00
#1163, Circus Cannon Truck	$70.00
#1164, Dolphinarium	$145.00
#1169, Ford Guiness Tanker	$85.00
#1170, Ford Car Transporter	$70.00

Dakins

Dakin has been an importer of stuffed toys as far back as 1955, but it wasn't until 1959 that the name of this San Francisco-based company actually appeared on the toy labels. They produced three distinct lines: Dream Pets (1960 – early 1970s), Dream Dolls (1965 – mid-1970s), and licensed characters and advertising figures, starting in 1968. Of them all, the latter series was the most popular and the one that holds most interest for collectors. Originally there were seven Warner Brothers characters. Each was made with a hard plastic body and a soft vinyl head, and all were under 10" tall. All in all, more than fifty cartoon characters were produced, some with several variations. Advertising figures were made as well. Some were extensions of the three already existing lines; others were completely original.

Goofy Grams was a series featuring many of their character figures mounted on a base lettered with a 'goofy' message. They also utilized some of their large stock characters as banks in a series called Cash Catchers. A second bank series consisted of Warner Brothers characters molded in a squatting position and therefore smaller. Other figures made by Dakin include squeeze toys, PVCs and water squirters.

Advisor: Jim Rash (R3).

Alice in Wonderland, set of 3 w/Alice, Mad Hatter & White Rabbit, artist Faith Wick, 18", MIB	$300.00
Baby Puss, Hanna-Barbera, 1971, EX+, R3	$100.00
Bambi, Disney, 1960s, MIP, R3	$35.00
Bamm-Bamm, Hanna-Barbera, w/club, 1970, EX, R3	$35.00
Barney Rubble, Hanna-Barbera,1970, EX, R3/B10	$40.00
Benji, 1978, cloth, VG	$20.00
Bozo the Clown, Larry Hagman, 1974, EX, R3	$35.00
Bugs Bunny, Warner Bros, 1971, MIP, R3	$30.00
Bugs Bunny, Warner Bros, 1976, MIB (TV Cartoon Theater box)	$40.00

Bugs Bunny, Warner Bros, 1978, MIP (Fun Farm bag)	$20.00
Bullwinkle, Jay Ward, 1976, MIB (TV Cartoon Theater box), R3	$60.00
Cool Cat, Warner Bros, w/beret, 1970, EX+, R3	$30.00
Daffy Duck, Warner Bros, 1968, EX, R3	$30.00
Daffy Duck, Warner Bros, 1976, MIB (TV Cartoon Theater box)	$40.00
Deputy Dawg, Terrytoons, 1977, EX, R3	$50.00
Dewey Duck, Disney, straight or bent legs, EX, R3	$40.00
Dino Dinosaur, Hanna-Barbera, 1970, EX, R3	$40.00
Donald Duck, Disney, 1960s, straight or bent legs, EX, R3	$20.00
Donald Duck, Disney, 1960s, straight or bent legs, NMIP	$30.00
Dream Pets, Bull Dog, cloth, EX	$15.00
Dream Pets, Hawaiian Hound, cloth, w/surfboard & orig tag, EX	$15.00
Dream Pets, Kangaroo, cloth w/camera, wearing beret, EX	$15.00
Dream Pets, Midnight Mouse, cloth, w/orig tags, EX	$15.00
Dudley Do-Right, Jay Ward, 1976, MIB (TV Cartoon Theater box), R3	$75.00
Dumbo Disney, 1960s, cloth collar, MIB, R3	$25.00
Elmer Fudd, Warner Bros, 1968, hunting outfit w/rifle, EX, R3	$125.00

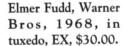

Elmer Fudd, Warner Bros, 1968, in tuxedo, EX, $30.00.

Elmer Fudd, Warner Bros, 1978, MIP (Fun Farm Bag), R3	$75.00
Fred Flintstone, Hanna-Barbera, 1970, EX, R3/B10, from $35 to	$40.00
Goofy, Disney, cloth clothes, EX	$20.00
Goofy Gram, Bull, I'm Mad About You, EX, R3	$25.00
Goofy Gram, Dog, Congratulations Dumm-Dumm, EX, R3	$25.00
Goofy Gram, Frog, Happy Birthday, EX, R3	$25.00
Goofy Gram, Kangaroo, World's Greatest Mom, EX, R3	$25.00

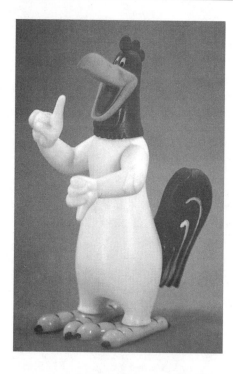

Foghorn Leghorn,
Warner Bros, 1970,
EX+, $75.00.

Hokey Wolf,
Hanna-Barbera,
1971, EX+,
$100.00.
(Photo courtesy Jim Rash)

Goofy, Disney, cloth
clothes, original tag,
NM, $25.00.

Goofy Gram, Pepe Le Peu, You're a Real Stinker, 1971,
   EX $55.00
Goofy Gram, Tiger, To A Great Guy, EX, R3 ....$25.00
Hoppy Hopperroo, Hanna-Barbera, 1971, EX+, R3 ....$100.00
Huckleberry Hound, Hanna-Barbera, 1970, EX+, R3 ......$60.00
Huey Duck, Disney, straight or bent legs, EX, R3............$30.00
Jack-in-the Box, bank, 1971, EX, R3 ....$25.00
Lion in Cage, bank, 1971, EX, R3 ....$25.00
Louie Duck, Disney, straight or bent legs, EX, R3 ....$30.00
Merlin the Magic Mouse, Warner Bros, 1970, EX+..........$25.00
Mickey Mouse, Disney, 1960s, cloth clothes, EX, R3 ....$20.00
Mighty Mouse, Terrytoons, 1978, EX, R3......................$100.00
Minnie Mouse, Disney, 1960s, cloth clothes, EX, R3 ....$20.00
Monkey on a Barrel, bank, 1971, EX, R3........................$25.00

Olive Oyl, King Features, 1974, cloth clothes, MIP, R3...$50.00
Olive Oyl, King Features, 1976, MIB (TV Cartoon Theater
   box), R3 ....$40.00
Oliver Hardy, Larry Harmon, 1974, EX+, R3 ....$30.00
Opus, 1982, cloth, w/tag, 12", EX, B10 ....$15.00
Pebbles Flinstone, Hanna-Barbera, 1970, EX, R3 ....$35.00
Pepe Le Peu, Warner Bros, 1971, EX $55.00
Pink Panther, Mirisch-Freleng, 1971, EX+, R3 ....$50.00
Pink Panther, Mirisch-Freleng, 1976, MIB (TV Cartoon The-
   ater box), R3 ....$50.00
Pinocchio, Disney, 1960s, EX.......................................$20.00
Popeye, King Features, 1974, cloth clothes, MIP, R3 ....$50.00
Popeye, King Features, 1976, MIB (TV Cartoon Theater box),
   R3...$50.00
Porky Pig, Warner Bros, 1968, EX, R3 ....$30.00
Porky Pig, Warner Bros, 1976, MIB (TV Cartoon Theater box),
   R3...$40.00
Practical Pig, EX $45.00
Ren & Stimpy, water squirters, Nickelodeon, 1993, EX, R3 ..$10.00
Road Runner, Warner Bros, 1968, EX, R3 ....$30.00
Road Runner, Warner Bros, 1976, MIB $45.00
Scooby Doo, Hanna-Barbera, 1980, EX, R3....................$75.00
Scooby Doo, Hanna-Barbera, 1982, EX+, R3 ....$75.00
Seal on Box, bank, 1971, EX, R3...................................$25.00
Second Banana, Warner Bros, 1970, EX, R3 ....$35.00
Snagglepuss, 1971, EX $100.00
Speedy Gonzales, Warner Bros, MIB (TV Cartoon Theater
   box), R3 ....$50.00
Stan Laurel, Larry Harmon, 1974, EX+, R3 ....$30.00
Swee' Pea, beanbag doll, King Features, 1974, VG, R3 ....$40.00
Sylvester, Warner Bros, 1968, EX, R3 ....$20.00
Sylvester, Warner Bros, 1976, MIB (TV Cartoon Theater box),
   R3...$40.00

Rocky Squirrel, Jay Ward, 1976, MIB (TV Cartoon Theater box), $60.00.

Speedy Gonzales, Warner Bros, M, $35.00.

Sylvester, Warner Bros, 1978, MIP (Fun Farm bag), R3...$20.00
Tasmanian Devil, Warner Bros, 1978, rare, EX (Fun Farm bag) $400.00
Tiger in Cage, bank, 1971, EX, R3 ....$25.00
Top Banana, Warner Bros, NM, C17 ....$25.00
Tweety Bird, Warner Bros, 1976, MIB (TV Cartoon Theater box), R3 ....$40.00
Tweety Bird, 1969, EX $20.00
Underdog, Jay Ward, 1976, MIB (TV Cartoon Theater box), R3 ....$150.00
Wile E Coyote, Warner Bros, 1968, MIB, R3 ....$30.00
Wile E Coyote, Warner Bros, 1976, MIB (TV Cartoon Theater box), R3 ....$40.00
Yogi Bear, Hanna-Barbera, 1970, EX, R3......................$60.00

Yosemite Sam, Warner Bros, 1968, MIB..........................$40.00
Yosemite Sam, Warner Bros, 1976, MIP (Fun Farm bag), R3 .$40.00

ADVERTISING

Bay View Bank, 1976, EX+, R3......................................$30.00
Bob's Big Boy, 1974, w/hamburger, EX+, R3 ....$150.00
Budding Meats, Buddie Bull, 1970s, cloth, EX................$30.00
Christian Bros Brandy, St Bernard, 1982, cloth, VG........$30.00
Crocker National Bank, Cocker Spaniel, 1979, cloth, 12", VG..$20.00
Diaperene Baby, Sterling Drug Co, 1980, EX, R3.............$40.00
Freddie Fast, 1976, M, P12 ....$100.00
Glamour Kitty, 1977, EX, R3 ....$200.00
Hobo Joe's Restaurant, bank, Hobo Joe figure, EX, P12 ...$95.00
Kernal Renk, American Seeds, 1970, rare, EX+, R3 ......$300.00
Li'l Miss Just Rite, 1965, EX+, R3 ....$75.00
Miss Liberty Bell, 1975, MIP, R3....................................$75.00
Quasar Robot, bank, 1975, NM, R3..................................$125.00
Sambo's Boy, 1974, EX+, R3 ....$75.00
Sambo's Tiger, 1974, EX+, R3 ....$125.00

Smokey the Bear, 1976, M, $25.00.
(Photo courtesy Martin and Carolyn Berens)

Woodsy Owl, 1974, MIP, R3..$60.00

Diecast

Diecast replicas of cars, trucks, planes, trains, etc., represent a huge corner of today's collector market, and their manufacturers see to it that there is no shortage. Back in the 1920s, Tootsietoy had the market virtually by themselves, but one by one other companies had a go at it, some with more success than others. Among them were the American companies of Barclay, Hubley, and Manoil, all of whom are much better known for other types of toys. After the war, Metal Masters, Smith-Miller, and Doepke Ohlsson-Rice (among others) tried the market with varying degrees of success. Some companies were phased out over the years, while many more entered the market with fervor. Today it's those fondly remembered models from the '50s and '60s that many collectors yearn to own. Solido produced well-modeled, detailed little cars; some had dome lights that actually came on when the doors were opened. Politoy's were cleanly molded with good detailing and finishes. Mebetoys, an Italian company that has been bought out by Mattel, produced several; and some of the finest come from Brooklyn, whose Shelby (signed) GT-350H Mustang can easily cost you from $900.00 to $1,000.00 when you can find one.

In 1968 the Topper Toy Company introduced its line of low-friction, high-speed Johnny Lightning cars to be in direct competition with Mattel's Hot Wheels. To gain attention, Topper sponsored Al Unser's winning race car, the 'Johnny Lightning,' in the 1970 Indianapolis 500. Despite the popularity of their cars, the Topper Toy Company went out of business in 1971. Today the Johnny Lightnings are highly sought after, and a new company, Playing Mantis, is reproducing many of the original designs as well as several models that never made it into regular production.

If you're interested in Majorette Toys, we recommend *Collecting Majorette Toys* by Dana Johnson; ordering information is given with Dana's listing under Diecast, in the section called Categories of Special Interest in the back of the book. Dana is also the author of *Collector's Guide to Diecast Toys & Scale Models* and *Matchbox Toys, 1947 – 1998, Third Edition*, both published by Collector Books.

Advisor: Dan Wells (W1).

Other Sources: P3, N3, S5.

See also Corgi; Dinky; Diecast Collector Banks; Farm Toys; Tootsietoys; Hot Wheels; Matchbox; Tekno.

Ahi, Alfa Romeo Giuletta Sprint, M $16.00
Ahi, Dodge Military Ambulance, M $12.00
Ahi, Dodge Military Crane Truck, M $12.00
Ahi, Dodge Military Tank Carrier, M.......................$12.00
Ahi, Jaguar Mk IX, M..$16.00
Ahi, Mercedes-Benz 220SE, M...............................$16.00

Ahi, Volvo PV 544, M...$16.00
Ahi, 1903 Rambler, M..$12.00
Ahi, 1915 Ford Model T, M......................................$12.00
Aurora Cigar Box, Ford J Car, yel, MIB $35.00
Aurora Cigar Box, Mako Shark, bl, MIB $35.00
Aurora Cigar Box, Mercury Cougar, MIB..................$35.00
Aurora Cigar Box, Porsche 904, red, MIB................$35.00
Aurora Cigar Box, Thunderbird, yel, MIB................$35.00
Bandii, Mazda RX7 25i, M.......................................$5.00
Bandii, Nisson JAL Vacuum Car, M $5.00
Bandii, Porsche 903, silver, M...............................$16.00
Barlux, Fiat Ambulance, #101, M $30.00
Barlux, Road Roller, M...$16.00
Barlux, Tyrell-Ford, M..$10.00
BBR, Ferrari 308GTB Coupe, red, M.......................$178.00
BBR, 1939 Alfa Romeo 6C 2500, M........................$160.00
BBR, 1959 Ferrari 250 GTE, M...............................$160.00
Bburago, Chevrolet Corvette, 1957, M.....................$20.00
Bburago, Ferrari 512 BB, M $20.00
Bburago, Jaguar SS 100, 1937, M $30.00
Bburago, Porsche 911S, M....................................$20.00
Bburago, Renault RE20 Formula One, 1980, M.........$40.00
Bburago, Tyrell P34/2 Formula One, 1976, M $40.00
Benbros, Army Land Rover, M.................................$25.00
Benbros, Bedford Articulated Low Loader, M.............$25.00
Best Toys of Kansas, Coupe #98, M........................$30.00
Best Toys of Kansas, Sedan #87, M $30.00
Buby, Ford Mustang II Cobra, M $5.00
Buby, VW Buggy, M $5.00
CD, Delage Limousine, M $100.00
CD, MG Record Car, M $100.00
Chad Valley, Ambulance, M $35.00
Chad Valley, Commer Milk Truck, w/8 milk cans, M....$175.00
Charbens, Fire Engine, #OC25, M $25.00
Charbens, Tanker, M...$65.00
Charbens, 1905 Packard Runabout, M.....................$20.00
CIJ, Cattle Trailer, #3/28, 1962, M $55.00
CIJ, Fire Engine, #3/30, 1959, M...........................$110.00
CIJ, Renault Floride, #3/58, 1960, M......................$55.00

Ashton, New Orleans Ahrens-Fox Piston Fire Pumper, 1:43 scale, NM, $110.00. (Photo courtesy Dana Johnson)

Clover, Melroe (Bobcat) M-200 Loader, 1959 – 62, replica of first machine built by the Melroe Co., 1:25 scale, $20.00. (Photo courtesy Dana Johnson)

Conrad, Volkswagen Polo C, M $9.00
Conrad, Volvo Titan L395 Flatbed Truck, M $48.00
Dalia, Go-Kart, red & bl, M $90.00
Dalia, Vesper Scooter, gr, M $75.00
Dalia-Solido, Fiat Abrath Record, orange, red, or wht, M .$100.00
Dalia-Solido, Jaguar D Le Mans, red, gr, or bl, M $100.00
Danbury Mint, 1959 Cadillac Series 62 Convertible, red, M .$125.00
Danbury Mint, 1965 Pontiac GTO, lavender & wht, M ..$125.00
Diapet, Datsun Tow Truck, #272, M $18.00
Diapet, Datsun 280Z Police Car, #P53, M $18.00
Diapet, Mitsubishi GTO, #SV27, M $21.00
Dugu, 1893 Benz Victoria, 1964, M $40.00
Dugu, 1925 Lancia Lambda Sedan, 1962, M $50.00
Dugu, 1936 Fiat 500A Coupe, 1966, M $60.00
Durham Classics, 1938 Lincoln Zephyr Coupe, blk, M ..$100.00
Durham Classics, 1941 Chevrolet Suburban 'Niagara Falls,'
   M $110.00
Eligor, 1932 Ford Roadster Fire Chief, M $25.00
Eligor, 1958 Chrysler New Yorker Convertible, M $25.00
Enchanted, 1937 Packard Victoria, M $85.00
Enchanted, 1949 Buick Riveria, M $115.00
Enchanted, 1957 Chevrolet Nomad, M $85.00
Enchantment Land Coach Builders, 1931 Cadillac Indy 500
   Pace Car, wht, M $140.00
Enchantment Land Coach Builders, 1957 Chevrolet Nomad,
   M $110.00
Enchantment Land Coach Builders, 1968 Pontiac Convertible,
   M $100.00
Ertl, 1969 Plymouth Hemi Roadrunner, yel, M $30.00
Ertl, 1971 Buick GSX, blk & gold, M $30.00
Ertl, 1995 Dodge Ram Truck, red or blk, M $25.00

Ertl, Corvette Stingray, 1:18 scale, NM, $30.00.
(Photo courtesy Dana Johnson)

First Gear, Morton Salt Stake Bed Truck, M $30.00
First Gear, Royal Crown Cola Beverage Truck, M $40.00
Franklin Mint, 1913 Ford Model T, M, from $115 to $135.00
Franklin Mint, 1953 Cadillac Eldorado, wht & red, M, from $85
   to $125.00
Franklin Mint, 1953 Chevrolet Corvette, cream & red, M, from
   $85 to $125.00
Goldvarg, 1946 Ford Deluxe Sedan, M, from $62 to $89.00
Goldvarg, 1954 Chevrolet Bel-Air 4-door Sedan, M $89.00
Goodee, 1953 GMC Pickup Truck, 6", M $25.00

Goodee, 1955 Ford Fuel Truck, 3", M $15.00
Guiloy, Harley-Davidson Custom Sport Motorcycle, M ..$18.00
Guiloy, 1948 Indian Chief Motorcycle, M $30.00
Guisval, 1928 Lincoln 4-Door Sedan, M $15.00
Guisval, 1979 Chevy Camaro, M $15.00
Hubley, Auto Transport, red w/silver detail, complete w/4 plas-
   tic sedans, 14", MIB, A $250.00
Hubley, Dump Truck, gr & red w/silver detail, 14 blk rubber
   tires, 16", MIB, A $400.00
Hubley, Farm Tractor, red w/blk rubber tires & red spokes, 9",
   MIB, A $225.00
Hubley, Farm Tractor & Wagon, red w/blk rubber tires, 9½",
   MIB, A $125.00
Hubley, Farm Truck & Tractor, yel w/blk rubber tires, gr plastic
   tractor on truck bed, 10", MIB, A $275.00
Hubley, Poultry Truck, red & wht w/crates, complete w/plastic
   chickens, 10", MIB, A $275.00
Hubley, Power Shovel & Front End Loader, Mighty Metal series,
   yel & red w/blk rubber treads, 16", MIB, A $600.00
Hubley, Road Scraper, yel w/silver scraper, blk rubber tires, 10",
   MIB, A $165.00
Hubley, Sports Car, yel w/blk convertible top, 13", rare, MIB,
   A $935.00

Hubley, Stockyard Truck, red with yellow stake van body, complete with animals, 10", MIB, A, $200.00.

Hubley, Tractor, orange w/blk rubber tires, 7", MIB, A .$165.00
Hubley, Tractor, red w/blk rubber tires & yel hubs, 7", MIB,
   A $125.00
Hubley, Tractor Loader, orange w/silver scoop, blk rubber tires,
   12", MIB, A $165.00
Hubley Kiddie Toys, Dump Truck, #510, MIB $250.00
Hubley Kiddie Toys, Sedan, #452, 7", MIB..................$30.00
Hubley Kiddie Toys, 10-pc set w/sedans, fire trucks, Texaco Oil
   trucks & airplanes, MIB, A $1,200.00
Hubley Kiddie Toys, 4-pc set w/dump truck, sports car, airplane
   & log truck, MIB, A $350.00

Hubley, US Fish Hatchery Truck, red with plastic aquarium, 10", MIB, A, $450.00.

Hubley Kiddie Toys, Custom Sports Car, yellow, 13", rare, MIB, A, $850.00.

Hubley Kiddie Toys, Midget Racers, MIB, A, $1,000.00.

Hubley Kiddie Toys, 4-pc set w/sports car, airplane, tractor & stake truck, MIB, A $385.00
Joal, Adams Probe 16, M $25.00
Joal, Chrysler 150, M $25.00
Joal, Jaguar E-Type Roadster, M $30.00
Johnny Lightning, Condor, 1970, MOC $120.00

Johnny Lightning, 101 Custom El Camino, 1994, metallic blue, NM, $5.00 ($12.00 for FAO Schwarz version). (Photo courtesy Dana Johnson)

Johnny Lightning, Custom Eldorado, 1969, MOC $125.00
Johnny Lightning, Custom GTO, 1969, MOC $250.00
Johnny Lightning, Custom Pipe Dream, 1971, MOC $90.00
Johnny Lightning, Custom Spoiler, 1995, MOC $5.00
Johnny Lightning, Custom Twin Blaster, 1971, MOC $90.00

Johnny Lightning, Indy 500 Racing Set, NRFB, J6, $450.00. (Photo courtesy June Moon)

Johnny Lightning, Ramchargers, 1997, M $5.00
Johnny Lightning, Sand Stormer, 1970, MOC $30.00
Johnny Lightning, White Lightning Funny Car, 1969, M. $12.00

Kansas Toy & Novelty Co, Army Truck, #74, 2¼", M $50.00
Kansas Toy & Novelty Co, Chevrolet Sedan, 2¼", M.....$40.00
Kansas Toy & Novelty Co, Truck, #20, 3⅛", M.............$30.00
Lansing Slik Toys, Fastback Sedan, #9600, 7", M...........$40.00
Lansing Slik Toys, Tanker Truck, #9705, 4", M $30.00
Lledo, Delivery Va, 1983, M...$10.00
Lledo, Ford Model T Tanker, 1983, M................................$10.00
Lledo, Greyhound Scenicruiser Bus, 1987, M $20.00
Lledo, Lond Distance Coach, 1985, M................................$10.00
Londontoy, Auto Transport, lg, M....................................$100.00
Londontoy, Beverage Truck, 6", M....................................$30.00
Londontoy, City Bus, 4", M..$30.00
Londontoy, Panel Delivery Truck, 6", M $40.00
Londontoy, 1941 Ford Pickup, 4" $25.00
Lone Star, Chevy Corvair, coral, M $65.00
Lone Star, Chevy Corvair, wht, M.....................................$90.00
Lone Star, Dodge Dart Phoenix, metallic bl, M................$95.00
Maisto, 1992 Bugatti EB110, red or bl, M $30.00
Maisto, 1996 Ferrari F355 Coupe, red or yel, M..............$12.00
Majorette, Chrysler 180, metallic gr, M $10.00
Majorette, Dodge Safari Truck, yel w/pnt streaks off hood,
    M..$10.00
Majorette, VW Golf, red, M..$4.00

**Majorette, Volkswagen 1302 Beetle, lime green, NM,
$5.00.** (Photo courtesy Dana Johnson)

Majorette, 4x4 Country Pickup w/Fifth-Wheel Camper Trailer,
    #313-B v.3, red & wht, M...$5.00
Majorette Club/Super Club, Ford GT 40, lt bl or wht, 1997,
    M..$8.00
Majorette Crazy Roadsters, Ford Mustang Dunkin Orange,
    M..$3.00
Majorette Sonic Flashers, Ambulance, M.........................$10.00
Majorette Special Forces 220, Military Police, #230-5, M..$3.00
Majorette Super Series, Mustang Convertible, #204-S, red,
    M..$3.00
Mebetoys, Fiat 850, 1966, M $30.00
Mebetoys, Maserati Bora, 1973, M....................................$40.00
Mebetoys, Porsche 912 Rally, 1974, M $40.00
Mebetoys, Volkswagen 1303, 1974, M..............................$30.00
Mercury, Caravan Trailer, 1946, M....................................$50.00
Mercury, Fiat 131 Fire Chief, 1971, M $25.00
Mercury, Fiat 131 Rally, 1974, M $25.00
Mercury, Mercedes Grand Prix, 1947, M..........................$95.00

Mercury, Michigan 310 Road Scraper, 1958, M $55.00
Mercury, Osi Silver Fox, 1969, M $55.00
Mercury, Sigma Grand Prix, 1969, M $35.00
Mercury, Stagecoach, 1969, M...$75.00
Mercury, Studebaker Golden Hawk, 1957, M $200.00
Mira, 1953 Chevy Pickup, M..$25.00
Mira, 1955 Buick Century Convertible, 2-tone, M $25.00
Nostalgic, 1934 LaSalle Roadster, M.................................$65.00
Nostalgic, 1936 Ford Van, maroon, M...............................$65.00
Racing Champions, 1969 Dodge Ram, #12, bl, M $6.00
Racing Champions, 1969 Pontiac GTO 'Judge' #52, blk, M $6.00
Ralstoy, North American Van Lines Tractor-Trailer, M..$30.00
Ralstoy, Safety-Kleen Van, M, from $30 to $45.00
Road Champs, Greyhound Eagle Coach, M........................$5.00
Road Champs, 1993 Chevy Caprice State Police Car (various
    states), 1995, M...$5.00
Road Champs, 1994 Ford Crown Victoria State Police Car (var-
    ious states, 1996, M, ea..$5.00
Schabak, 1992 Audi 80 Sedan, M......................................$17.00
Schabak, Ford Fiesta, 1989, M...$20.00
Schabak, VW Jetta, 1984, M...$20.00
Schuco, Audi 80 LS, 1972, M...$25.00
Schuco, BMW 535 Doctor's Car, 1976, M.........................$25.00
Schuco, Ford Capri RS, 1974, 2½", M...............................$10.00
Schuco, Krupp Cement Mixer, 3⅝", M $60.00
Schuco, Linoff Road Paver, 5", M $60.00
Schuco, Porsche 917, 1972, 2½", M...................................$15.00
Schuco, Volkswagen Polo, 1975, M...................................$25.00
Scottoys, Fiat 1100 Saloon, M...$40.00
Scottoys, Fiat 600 Saloon, M...$28.00
Siku, BMW Police Car, M, from $5 to...............................$10.00
Siku, Mercedes ADAC, 1975-81, M...................................$18.00
Siku, Police Bat Transporter, 1989, M..............................$25.00
Siku, Volkswagen 181 Military, 1976-79, M.....................$20.00
Solido, Kaiser Jeep M 34, M $20.00

Solido, Peugeot 205 GTI, 1984, red, NM, $15.00.
(Photo courtesy Jeff Koch and Dana Johnson)

Solido, 1936 Ford Tanker, 1994, M....................................$30.00
Solido, 1940 Dodge Fire Dept Recovery Truck, M $20.00
Solido, 1962 Ferrai 2.5 L, 1995 reissue, M $20.00
Solido, 1978 Jaguar XJ 12, M...$10.00
Tomica, Cadillac Ambulance, #F-2, M..............................$12.00
Tomica, Canter Garbage Truck, M $4.00

Tomica, Toyota 2000-GT, #22-05, ca 1974, M $10.00
Tomica Dandy, Mini Cooper, #DJ015, M.....................$22.00
Tomica Dandy, Nissan Skyline, M...............................$18.00

Tri-ang Minic, Ships, M892, 1960, features SS United States, complete with booklet, NMIB, $325.00.
(Photo courtesy Eddy Kao)

Diecast Collector Banks

Thousands of banks have been produced since Ertl made its first model in 1981, the 1913 Model T Parcel Post Mail Service #9647. The Ertl company was founded by Fred Ertl, Sr., in Dubuque, Iowa, back in the mid-1940s. Until they made their first diecast banks, most of what they made were farm tractors. Today they specialize in vehicles made to specification and carrying logos of companies as large as Texaco and as small as your hometown bank. The size of each 'run' is dictated by the client and can vary from a few hundred up to several thousand. Some clients will later add a serial number to the vehicle; this is not done by Ertl. Other numbers that appear on the base of each bank are a four-number dating code (the first three indicate the day of the year up to 365 and the fourth number is the last digit of the year, '5' for 1995, for instance). The stock number is shown only on the box, never on the bank, so it is extremely important that you keep them in their original boxes.

Other producers of these banks are Scale Models, incorporated in 1991, First Gear Inc., and Spec-Cast, whose founders at one time all worked for the Ertl company.

In the listings that follow, unless another condition is given, all values are for banks mint and in their original boxes. (#d) indicates a bank that was numbered by the client, not Ertl.

Advisors: Art and Judy Turner (H8), who provided us with all listings that do not include the codes of other dealers.

Other Sources: S5.

Key: JLE — Joseph L. Ertl

ERTL

A&W Root Beer, #3, 1918 Ford, #2972............................$39.00
A&W Root Beer, #5, 1923 Chevy, #B544.......................$33.00
A-Treat Beverages, Air Express Plane, #B765 ....$42.00
A-Treat Beverages, 1956 Ford Pickup, #F548.................$26.00
Aberpoyle Antique Market, 1938 Chevy, #4868............$35.00
ABF Freight System, 1917 Ford, #F795 ....$30.00
AC Spark Plugs, 1950 Chevy, #2901 ....$34.00
Ace Hardware, #3, 1932, Ford, #9459 ....$28.00
Ace Hardware, #7, 1925 Kenworth, #F397 ....$20.00
Adidas, 1938 Chevy, #B634 ....$38.00
Affiliated Foods, 1932 Ford, #9830 ....$195.00
Agway, #2, 1918 Ford, #9195 ....$75.00
Agway, #7, 1912 Ford, #7615 ....$25.00
Alka-Seltzer, 1918 Ford, #9155 ....$95.00
All-Star Game, 1923 Chevy, #3269 ....$35.00
Allegheny Airlines, DC-3 Plane, #H153 ....$65.00
Allen Organ Company, 1931 Hawkeye, #9892 ....$45.00
Almond Joy Candy Bar, 1923 Chevy, #7653 ....$23.00
American Red Cross, #1, 1913 Ford, #9294 ....$75.00
Amoco, 1905 Ford, #1333 ....$69.00
Amoco, 1935 Mack, JLE, #8013....................................$22.00
Amoco Motor Club, #4, 1920 International, JLE, #3102 .$25.00
Amoco Red Crown, 1923 Chevy, #1320 ....$20.00
Amoco Standard Oil, 1935 Mack Tanker, #3006............$20.00
Amoco Stanolind Polarine, #4, 1932 Ford, #7657........$125.00
Amoco Torch Classic, 1905 Ford, #7635 ....$21.00
Anheuser-Busch, #12, Trolley Car, #B601.....................$22.00
Anheuser-Busch, #16, 1951 GMC, #F-274 ....$22.00
Anheuser-Busch, #4, 1932 Ford, #9498 ....$45.00
Anheuser-Busch, #8, 1932 Ford, #9552 ....$22.00
Ar-Jay Sales, 1923 Chevy, #9799 ....$19.00
Arm & Hammer, 1923 Chevy, #2096 ....$75.00
Arm & Hammer, 1950 Chevy, #9859............................$179.00
Armstrong Tires, 1913 Ford, #9975 ....$34.00
Atlanta Falcons, 1913 Ford, #1248 ....$35.00
Atlantic Refining, #2, 1931 Hawkeye Wrecker, #7623 ....$27.00
Atlas Van Lines, #3, 1913 Ford, #9577 ....$29.00
Atlas Van Lines, 1931 Hawkeye, #F884..........................$26.00

Baby Ruth, 1926 Mack Bulldog, #9096, M, $45.00.

Baltimore Gas & Electric, 1950 Chevy, #9752 ....$65.00
Barq's Root Beer, 1932 Ford, #9072 ....$45.00
Barrick Farms, 1913 Ford, #9271 ....$18.00
Baseball, Atlanta Braves, 1917 Ford, #B357 ....$25.00
Baseball, Chicago Cubs, 1905 Ford, #3249 ....$25.00
Baseball, LA Dodgers, 1905 Ford, #3247 ....$9.00
Baseball II, Houston Astros, 1917 Ford, #B364 ....$18.00
Baseball II, Kansas City Royals, 1917 Ford, #B375 ....$18.00
Baseball III, Florida Marlins, 1938 Chevy, #F722 ....$20.00
Baseball III, New York Yankees, 1938 Chevy, #F725 ....$25.00
Basketball, Boston Celtics, 1918 Ford, #B473 ....$22.00
Basketball, Chicago Bulls, 1918 Ford, #B475 ....$14.00
Basketball II, Indiana Pacers, 1956 Ford Pickup, #B891 ...$20.00
Basketball II, New York Knicks, 1956 Ford Pickup, #B896..$20.00
Bassett Furniture, 1931 Hawkeye, #B812 ....$39.00
Bell Telephone, 1932 Ford, #9803 ....$35.00
Ben Franklin, 1938 Chevy, #B289 ....$23.00
Bethlehem Steel, #2, Step Van, #3946 ....$65.00
Bethlehem Steel, #4, 1931 Hawkeye, #F489 ....$49.00
Bi-County Ambulance, 1923 Chevy, #9093 ....$27.00
Big A Auto Parts, #6, 1931 Hawkeye, #9949 ....$25.00
Big Bear Family Center, 1905 Ford, #9006 ....$25.00
Black & Decker, #2, 1940 Ford, #H060 ....$45.00
Boulder Beer, 1918 Ford, #9623 ....$28.00
Brach's Candy, 1923 Chevy, #7675........................$35.00
Breyer's Ice Cream, 1905 Ford, #9028 ....$65.00
Brickyard 400 ('95), P-51 Mustang Plane, #0518 ....$45.00
Brinks Security, Armored Truck, #F116 ....$19.00
British American Oil, #2, 1932 Ford, #9509 ....$35.00
British American Oil, #3, 1931 Hawkeye Wrecker, #3808..$32.00
Budweiser, #1, Stearman Plane, #37535...................$27.00
Budweiser, Blimp, #36001 ....$19.00
Budweiser, Staggerwing Plane, #48007 ....$32.00
Budweiser/Bill Elliot #11, Vega Plane, #0374 ....$14.00
Buffalo Oil Co, 1931 Hawkeye Tanker, #9578 ....$25.00
Bumper to Bumper Auto Parts, 1950 Chevy, #9877 ....$35.00
Bush's Pork & Beans, 1905 Ford, #1357....................$25.00
Campbell's Soup, Trolley Car, #B621 ....$19.00
Campbell's Soup, 1957 Chevy Stake Truck, #F603 ....$29.00
Campbell's Soup (Season's Greetings), 1923, Chevy, #F500 .$22.00
Canada Dry, 1913 Ford, #2133............................$125.00
Carl Buddig, 1913 Ford, #2106...........................$55.00
Carl's Chicken, Step Van, #9089 ....$25.00
Carlisle Productions, 1951 Ford Pickup, #F971 ....$19.00
Carlisle Thundering Herd, 1913 Ford, #9682 ....$19.00
Carnation, 1913 Ford, #9178.............................$34.00
Cars & Parts Magazine, 1932 Ford, #1322 ....$12.00
Case Cutlery, 1932 Ford, #F223 ....$75.00
Castrol Oil, #2, 1926 Mack Tanker, gr wheels, #9464......$49.00
Castrol Oil GTX, 1913 Ford, #9701.......................$28.00
Caterpiller, 1931 Hawkeye, #2353 ....$25.00
Caterpiller, 1932 Ford, #2432 ....$30.00
Central Tractor Farm & Family, Stearman Plane, #37517 .$47.00
Central Tractor Farm & Family, 1938 Chevy, #3836.......$20.00
Champion Spark Plug, #1, 1918 Ford, #9067...............$39.00
Champlin Refining, 1931 International, JLE, #4088........$19.00
Check the Oil, #3, 19312 Hawkeye Wrecker, #9599 ....$19.00
Cheetos, Step Van, #9023 ....$30.00

Chemical Bank, 1905 Ford, #1662 ....$30.00
Cherry Smash, #3, 1918, Ford, #2869 ....$39.00
Cherry Smash, #5, 1913 Ford, #F083 ....$40.00
Chevrolet, #1, Vega Plane, #35011 ....$55.00
Chevrolet Heartbeat, 1950 Chevy, #9761 ....$28.00
Chevrolet OK Used Cars, 1923 Chevy, #9317 ....$18.00
Chevron Gasoline, Vintage Plane, #40010...............$39.00
Chevron Gasoline, 1931 Hawkeye Wrecker, #2962........$32.00
Chiquita Bananas, 1913 Ford, #9662 ....$65.00
Christmas, #1, 1913 Ford, #9584 ....$85.00
Citgo Gas, #6, 1936 Dodge Panel Truck, #74029 ....$18.00
Citgo Lubricants, #2, 1918 Ford, #9456 ....$75.00
Citgo Lubricants, #3, 1905 Ford, #9854 ....$55.00
Citgo Lubricants, #5, 1925 Kenworth, #3779 ....$45.00
Citizens Bank, Armored Truck, #B856 ....$25.00
Clark Oil & Refining, 1925 Kenworth Tanker, #B457 ....$32.00
Classic Motor Books, 1932 Ford, #9883 ....$30.00
Coast to Coast Hardware, Air Express Plane, #F204 ....$38.00
Coast to Coast Hardware, 1925 Kenworth, #B037 ....$25.00
Coastal Refining, 1931 Hawkeye Tanker, #B393 ....$22.00
Coca-Cola, Trolley Car, #B902 ....$30.00
Coca-Cola, 1920 International, JLE, #3015 ....$75.00
Coca-Cola, 1929, International Tanker, JLE, #4075 ....$34.00
Coca-Cola, 1936 Chevy, #B901 ....$30.00
Coca-Cola, 1937 Ford Semi, #F610 ....$22.00
Coca-Cola (Santa), 1931 Hawkeye, #B225 ....$35.00
Coca-Cola 600, Vintage Plane, #0225 ....$39.00
Coke/Charlotte Speedway, 1929 Ford, #1013 ....$49.00
Coker Tire, 1931 Hawkeye, #F424 ....$29.00
Conoco Oil, Vega Plane, #35030 ....$55.00
Conoco Oil, 1929 International, JLE, #4003 ....$28.00
Continental Airlines, DC-3 Plane, #F154 ....$42.00
Continental Insurance, 1932 Ford, #9665 ....$29.00
Coors Beer, Stearman Plane, #F583 ....$25.00
Corona Beer, 1925 Kenworth, #F399 ....$19.00
Country Fresh, 1923 Chevy, #2944 ....$23.00
Cowtown Rodeo, 1931 Hawkeye, #B454 ....$19.00
CR Friendly Stores, 1931 Hawkeye, #F597 ....$15.00
Cub Foods, 1931 Hawkeye, #9042........................$29.00
Cycle AM Motorcross, 1913 Ford, #9204 ....$75.00
Dairy Queen, #03, 1918 Ford, #9033....................$95.00
Dairy Queen, #14, 1951 GMC, #B661 ....$30.00
Dairy Queen, #16, 1925 Kenworth, #F524 ....$32.00
Dairy Queen, #7, 1950 Chevy, #9178 ....$135.00
Dallas Fire Dept, 1926 Fire Truck, #2911 ....$95.00
Daytona Bike Week, 1920 International, JLE, #3111......$95.00
DeLavel, Step Van, #9681 ....$95.00
Delco Batteries, 1938 Chevy, #F781 ....$65.00
Delco Radio, 1950 Chevy, #9082 ....$95.00
Diamond Motor Oil, 1931 International, JLE, #4079.......$19.00
Diamond Walnuts, 1955 Cameo Pickup, #4952 ....$29.00
Dixie Brewing Co, 1937 Ford Semi, #9728 ....$59.00
Doumax Marshmallows, 1925 Kenworth, #F026 ....$34.00
Dr Pepper, DC-3 Plane, #F482 ....$32.00
Dr Pepper, 1905 Ford, #9739 ....$59.00
Dr Pepper, 1918 Ford, #9841 ....$39.00
Dr Pepper, 1926 Mack, #9235 ....$65.00
Drake Hotel, 1913 Ford, #2113 ....$125.00

DuPont, 1923 Chevy, #1353 ....$75.00
DuPont/Jeff Gordon #24, Vintage Plane, #0426 ....$44.00
Dutch Girl Ice Cream, 1931 Hawkeye, #9049 ....$29.00
Eastman Chemical I, #3, 1918 Ford Tanker, #B024 ....$50.00
Eastman Chemical II, #1, 1955 Cameo Pickup, #B262 ....$85.00
Eastview Pharmacy, 1950 Chevy, #1317....................$125.00
Eastwood Co, #3, 1931 Hawkeye, #2985....................$75.00
Eastwood Co, 1926 Fire Truck, #1666 ....$59.00
Eastwood Co II, #1, 1951 GMC, #B274....................$14.00
Elmer's Glue, 1918 Ford, #F608....................$20.00
Emergency Medical Services, 1923 Chevy, #F140............$29.00
Ephrata Fair, #2, 1950 Chevy, #7541 ....$40.00
Ephrata Fair, #6, 1955 Cameo Pickup, #B742 ....$9.00
Erickson Oil Products, 1937 Ford Semi, #F107..............$36.00
Ertl Air Express, Air Express Plane, #B270 ....$32.00
Ertl Toys, 1918 Ford, #9831....................$24.00
Eskimo Pie, 1931 Hawkeye, #H120....................$22.00
Esso, Orion Plane, #42509 ....$34.00
Esso, 1939 Dodge Airflow, #B285 ....$35.00
Exxon, #2, Stearman Plane, #37534....................$19.00
Exxon, P-51 Mustang Plane, #47004....................$45.00
Exxon, 1931 International Tanker, JLE, #4076 ....$75.00
Exxon, 1991 Ford F700 Tanker, #F924 ....$27.00
Exxon Stanavo Eagle, Vega Plane, #35050 ....$39.00
Fannie Farmer Candies, 1913 Ford, #2104 ....$29.00
Farm & Dairy, 1931 Hawkeye, #B075 ....$26.00
Farm & Fleet (Mills), 1916 Ford, #H156 ....$22.00
Farm & Fleet (Quality), 1925 Kenworth, #B552 ....$19.00
Farm Bureau Co-Op, 1918 Ford, #9220 ....$25.00
Farm Toy Capitol, #4, 1932 Ford, #9779 ....$35.00
Farmers' Almanac, 1913 Ford, #1359 ....$24.00
Federal Express, Step Van, #9334 ....$45.00
Fina Oil, 1905 Ford, #9043 ....$29.00
Fina Oil, 1932 Ford, #9285 ....$25.00
Firehouse Films, 1926 Fire Truck, #9465 ....$39.00
Food City 500, 1923 Chevy, #B019 ....$39.00
Football, Detroit Lions, Stearman Plane, #F711 ....$24.00
Football, Pittsburgh Steelers, Stearman Plane, #F687 ......$29.00
Football I, Chicago Bears, 1931 Hawkeye, #3574..............$29.00
Football I, Denver Broncos, 1931 Hawkeye, #B170..........$49.00
Football II, Dallas Cowboys, 1955 Cameo Pickup, #B327 ..$29.00
Football II, Indianapolis Colts, 1955 Cameo Pickup, #B345.$15.00
Football III, Arizona Cardinals, 1951 GMC, #B828.........$20.00
Football III, Cleveland Browns, 1951 GMC, #B842.........$29.00
Football IV, Buffalo Bills, 1857 Chevy, #F625..................$24.00
Football IV, New Orleans Saints, 1957 Chevy, #F649 .....$21.00
Forbes Magazine, 1950 Chevy, #9978 ....$34.00
Ford, 1905 Ford, #0865....................$23.00
Ford Motor Company, 1912 Ford, #9348 ....$39.00
Ford Motorsports, 1913 Ford, #1658 ....$35.00
Ford Motorsports, 1932 Ford, #9693 ....$45.00
Ford New Holland, 1917 Ford, #0374 ....$20.00
Fordson, #2, 1912 Ford, #0306 ....$20.00
Fram Filters, 1925 Kenworth, #B722 ....$75.00
Frame Mica, 1923 Chevy, #F835....................$30.00
Gilmore Oil Co, 1925 Kenworth, #9244....................$24.00
Gilmore Oil Co, 1931 International Tanker, JLE Sampler, #4009 ....$59.00

Global Van Lines, 1913 Ford, #1655....................$45.00
Golden Flakes, Step Van, #9118 ....$65.00
Goodwrench/Dale Earnhardt #3, F16 Plane, #0471.........$59.00
Goody's Headache, 1920 International, JLE, #5037-38, matched set....................$29.00
Goodyear, 1931 Hawkeye Wrecker, #3614 ....$29.00
Goodyear Racing, Vega Plane, #0326 ....$24.00
Graffiti USA, 1950 Chevy, #7694....................$25.00
Granny Goose Chips, 1913 Ford, #9979 ....$49.00
Grapette Soda, 1932 Ford, #9885 ....$65.00
Grapette Soda, 1950 Chevy, #2779....................$39.00
Great Train Store, 1950 Chevy, #7536 ....$37.00
GTE, 1950 Chevy, #9661 ....$34.00
Gulf Oil, Vintage Plane, #35006 ....$48.00
Gulf Oil, 1918 Ford Tanker, #1368 ....$28.00
Gulf Oil, 1926 Mack, #9158....................$49.00
Gulf Oil, 1926 Mack Tanker, #7652 ....$45.00
Gulf Oil, 1931 Hawkeye, #B277....................$26.00
Gulf Oil, 1956 Ford Pickup, #H017 ....$32.00
Gulf Power Co, Bucket Truck, #F335 ....$35.00
Gulfpride, 1951 GMC, #B450 ....$27.00
Hamm's Beer, Ford Semi, #T542 ....$23.00
Hamm's Beer, 1913 Ford, #2145 ....$75.00
Hamm's Beer, 1926 Mack, #7619....................$65.00
Hancock Oil Co, 1930 DTT, #2795....................$32.00
Harget & Sons, 1932 Ford, #7661 ....$29.00
Harley-Davidson, F-16 Plane, #99213....................$59.00
Harley-Davidson, VR1000 Superbike, #98209 ....$125.00
Harley-Davidson (Wilwerts), #1, 1920 International, JLE, #3031 ....$349.00
Hart-Parr Tractors, 1913 Ford, #2296 ....$20.00
Hawkeye Tech, 1913 Ford, #9533 ....$25.00
Heartland Popcorn, 1905 Ford, #9250 ....$24.00
Heatcraft (Lennox), 1926 Mack, #7562....................$50.00
Heineken Beer, #1, 1918 Ford, #9570 ....$125.00
Henny Penny, 1931 Hawkeye, #9691 ....$25.00
Henny Penny, 1932 Ford, #9946 ....$25.00
Hershey Antique Auto Club, 1932 Ford, #B741..............$24.00
Hershey Chocolate, 1931 Hawkeye, #9349....................$30.00
Hershey Chocolate Almonds, 1912 Ford, #1351 ....$23.00
Hershey Cocoa, 1905 Ford, #9665....................$55.00
Hershey Milk Chocolate, 1912 Ford, #1350 ....$29.00
Hershey Syrup, 1931 Hawkeye Tanker, #F014 ....$16.00
Hershey Trolley Car, #B310 ....$18.00
Hershey Ice Cream (100th Anniversary), 1931 Hawkeye, #B735 ....$69.00
Hills Dept Store, 1913 Ford, #9768....................$23.00
Holiday Wholesale, Step Van, #9470 ....$36.00
Hollycliff Farms, 1926 Mack, #9972....................$25.00
Home Hardware, 1917 Ford, #9011....................$28.00
Home Savings & Loan, 1932 Ford, #9309 ....$34.00
Hormel Foods, 1917 Ford, #9451....................$49.00
Hostess Cup Cakes, 1913 Ford, #9422 ....$30.00
House of Books, 1913 Ford, #9246 ....$40.00
Humble Oil Co, #3, 1935 Kenworth Tanker, #3839 ....$29.00
Humble Oil Co, DC-3 Plane, #45003....................$55.00
Humble Oil Co, 1950 Chevy Pickup, #F855....................$35.00
Husker Harvest, 1925 Mack, JLE, #3012....................$15.00

HWI Hardware, 1923 Chevy, #1365 ....$17.00
IGA, 1917 Ford Pickup, #F951 ....$20.00
IGA, 1955 Cameo Pickup, #3830 ....$19.00
Imperial Oil, #1, 1931 Hawkeye Tanker, #9455 ....$49.00
Indian Motorcycle, Vintage Plane, #40017.....................$55.00
Indian Motorcycle, 1920 International, JLE, #3070 ....$24.00
Ingersoll Rand, 1938 Chevy, #B446 ....$39.00
International Harvester, 1959 Chevy El Camino, #4450 .$28.00
Iowa Gas, 1931 Hawkeye, #9589 ....$49.00
Jacuzzi Whirlpool Bath, 1923 Chevy, #B868 ....$25.00
JC Penney, 1918 Ford, #1328 ....$39.00
JC Penney, 1923 Chevy, #9447 ....$25.00
JC Penney, 1931 Hawkeye, #9444 ....$20.00
JC Penney, 1950 Chevy, #9640 ....$25.00
JC Penney, 1951 GMC, #H860 ....$35.00
JC Whitney, 1925 Kenworth, #B496 ....$30.00
JF Good Co, 1931 Hawkeye, #9720 ....$27.00
JI Case, 1913 Ford, #0668 ....$19.00
JI Case, 1923 Chevy, #0255......................................$24.00
JI Case, 1931 International, JLE, #0734 ....$19.00
Jiffy Lube, #3, 1955 Cameo Pickup, #B997 ....$25.00
Jim Beam, 1948 Peterbilt Semi, #F957 ....$22.00
Jim Beam Distribution 5 - 1990, #5, 1918 Ford, #2964.....$35.00
Jim Beam Distribution 9 - 1989, 1917 Ford, #9647..........$25.00
John Deere, #002, Vega Plane, #35024 ....$55.00
John Deere, #003, Vintage Plane, #40019 ....$45.00
John Deere, #102, 1926 Mack, #5534 ....$115.00
John Deere, #105, 1955 Cameo Pickup, #5614..............$22.00
John Deere, #108, 1925 Kenworth, #5689 ....$18.00
Jolly Roger Motorcycle Club, 1925 Kenworth, #B034......$49.00
Jolt Cola, 1913 Ford, #9232 ....$38.00
K-Mart, 1931 International, JLE, #5043 ....$32.00
Kauffman's Fruit Farm, 1918 Ford, #7560 ....$25.00
Kawasaki Motorcycles, Vega Plane, #35031 ....$14.00
Kerr-McGee, #2, 1913 Ford, #9130 ....$55.00
Kerr-McGee, #5, 1937 Ford Semi, #9983 ....$35.00
Kerr-McGee, DC-3 Plane, #B538................................$75.00
Key Aid Distributors, 1931 Hawkeye, #9648 ....$25.00
Key Aid Distributors, 1932 Ford, #9944 ....$29.00
King Edward Cigars, 1913 Ford, #9854 ....$29.00
Kingsport Press, 1923 Chevy, #2933 ....$49.00
Kiwanis International, #1, 1905 Ford, #9882 ....$26.00
Kiwi Shoe Polish, 1925 Kenworth Stake Truck, #F870....$39.00
Kodak, #1, 1905 Ford, gold spokes, #9985 ....$225.00
Kraft Dairy Group, 1917 Ford, #9675 ....$35.00
Kraft Foods, 1905 Ford, #B203 ....$45.00
Kroger Foods, 1925 Kenworth, #3757 ....$16.00
Kwik Shop, 1918 Ford, #B226 ....$22.00
Lakeside Speedway, 1950 Chevy, #7522 ....$25.00
Lawson Products, #2, 1931 Hawkeye, #9261.................$35.00
Lawson Products, #6, 1905 Ford, #B036......................$22.00
Lennox, #5, 1926 Mack, #7561 ....$35.00
Lennox, #7, 1950 Chevy, #9590.................................$28.00
Lion Coffee, 1913 Ford, #9306 ....$49.00
Lion Oil Co, #3, 1938 Chevy, #3203 ....$27.00
Lion Oil Co, 1931 Hawkeye, #7617 ....$24.00
Lionel Trains, Stearman Plane, #37525 ....$55.00
Lipton Tea Co, 1932 Ford, #9087 ....$35.00

Loftland Co, #2, 1955 Cameo Pickup, #B995 ....$25.00
Lone Star Beer, 1926 Mack, #9167 ....$42.00
Loon Mountain, 1940 Ford, JLE, #6044........................$40.00
Luden's Candies, 1923 Chevy, #F105 ....$35.00
Madison Electric, 1913 Ford, #9589 ....$75.00
Magnolia Oil, 1931 Sterling, JLE, #4022 ....$29.00
Marathon Oil, 1929 International Tanker, JLE, #4044 ....$29.00
Marland Oil Co, 1920 International, JLE, #3079 ....$27.00
Marsh Supermarket, #2, 1912 Ford, #B015 ....$25.00
Marshall Fields, 1913 Ford, #1650................................$39.00
Massey-Ferguson, 1913 Ford, #1348 ....$22.00
Massey-Harris, 1955 Cameo Pickup, #1868 ....$22.00
Mayfield's Creamery, 1923 Chevy, #F509 ....$32.00
Maytag, #3, 1948 Dia Rio Semi, #F196 ....$45.00
McCormick-Deering Farmall, 1925 Kenworth, #0440 .....$24.00
McDonald's, Step Van, #H300......................................$24.00
McDonald's, 1953 Ford, #H301....................................$22.00
McDonald's Racing/Bill Elliot #27, F-16 Plane, #0523.....$39.00
Medicine Shoppe, #6, 1932 Ford, #F575 ....$28.00
Mellow Bank, #1, 1913 Ford, #9318 ....$25.00
Merit Oil Co, 1926 Mack Tankard, #9980 ....$75.00
Merita Bread, 1913 Ford, #9316 ....$22.00
Michelin Tires, 1931 International, JLE, #5046 ....$28.00
Miller Beer, 1905 Ford, #2116 ....$39.00
Miller Beer, 1936 Fire Truck, #9268 ....$25.00
Miller Genuine Draft, Vintage Plane, #40042................$37.00
Miller High Life Beer, 1950 Chevy, #9269 ....$29.00
Miller Lite, Vega Plane, #35060...................................$38.00
Minnesota Industrial Tools, Step Van, #9308 ....$25.00
Mobil Oil, 1913 Ford, #9743 ....$55.00
Mobil Oil, 1926 Mack, #9760 ....$65.00
Mobil Oil, 1931 Hawkeye, #9742..................................$59.00
Mobil Oil, 1937 Ford Semi, #9971 ....$75.00
Mobil Oil (Aero), DC-3 Plane, #B626............................$95.00
Mobil Oil (Gargoyle), #2, 1931 Hawkeye, #9717............$35.00
Monroe Shocks, 1931 Hawkeye, #9350 ....$22.00
Montgomery Ward, #2, 1917 Ford, #9052 ....$59.00
Moormans MFG Co, #2, 1913 Ford, #9472 ....$50.00
Moormans Mfg Co, #6, 1932 Ford, #F418......................$45.00
Mounds Candy Bar, 1923 Chevy, #8652........................$24.00
Mountain Dew, Vega Plane, #35040 ....$29.00
Myers Food Rite, 1938 Chevy, #4896 ....$23.00
Nabisco Almost Home Cookies, 1913 Ford, #1653 ....$48.00
NASCAR Racing, Vega Plane, #00312............................$39.00
National City Bank, 1918 Ford, H027 ....$19.00
National Van Lines, 1913 Ford, #9505 ....$59.00
Nestle's Crunch, 1931 Hawkeye, #1316.........................$32.00
Nestle's Quik Chocolate, 1913 Ford, #9347....................$35.00
Oklahoma Oil Marketers, 1931 Hawkeye Tanker, #9592...$49.00
Old El Paso, 1905 Ford, #7636 ....$45.00
Old Milwaukee Beer, 1918 Ford, #9173 ....$35.00
Old Style Beer, 1913 Ford, #F359.................................$19.00
Old Style Beer, 1951 GMC, #F358 ....$21.00
Oliver Tractors, Orion Plane, #42501............................$32.00
Olympia Beer, Vega Plane, #35022 ....$29.00
Pabst Beer, 1918 Ford, #B984......................................$19.00
Pabst Beer, 1938 Chevy, #F587....................................$20.00
Pan American, 1931 International, #4081.......................$29.00

Pennzoil, 1918 Ford, #7676 ....$29.00
Pennzoil, 1925 Kenworth Tanker, #9246......................$24.00
Pennzoil, 1932 Ford, #9018 ....$13.00
Pennzoil, 1939 Dodge Airflow, #4871 ....$29.00
Pep Boys, 1923 Chevy $24.00
Pepsi-Cola, Trolley Car, B655 ....$24.00
Pepsi-Cola, 1910 Mack Tanker, #H147 ....$38.00
Pepsi-Cola, 1923 Chevy, #7502 ....$28.00
Pepsi-Cola, 1931 International, JLE, #5025 ....$75.00
Pepsi-Cola, 1940 Ford Pickup, #F-912 ....$32.00
Pepsi-Cola, 1953 Ford Bottle, #F913 ....$23.00
Pet Milk, 1913 Ford, red wheels, #1652 ....$45.00
Philadelphia Cream Cheese, 1913 Ford, #9835 ....$38.00
Philgas, 1938 Chevy, #B039 ....$125.00
Phillips 66, #2, 1932 Ford, #9121 ....$35.00
Phillips 66, Vega Plane, #35028 ....$75.00
Phillips 66, 1926 Mack, #9231 ....$250.00
Prairie Farms Milk, 1923 Chevy, #3958 ....$19.00
Price Waterhouse, 1925 Kenworth Barrel, #H216............$30.00
PSI Energy, Bucket Truck, #3593..........................$32.00
Publix, 1926 Mack, #9693 ....$24.00
Publix (Bakery), 1951 GMC, #B504 ....$18.00
Publix (Deli), 1905 Ford, #7689 ....$25.00
Publix (Floral), 1912 Ford, #F993 ....$22.00
Publix (Food & Pharmacy), 1918 Ford, #F256 ....$22.00
Publix (Produce), 1932 Ford, #9696.......................$29.00
Purina Mills Inc, 1913 Ford, #9103 ....$35.00
Quaker Oats, 1925 Kenworth, #B268 ....$125.00
Quaker Oats, 1955 Cameo Pickup, #H359 ....$35.00
Quaker State Oil, 1913 Ford, #9195 ....$95.00
Quaker State Oil, 1926 Mack, #9196.......................$32.00
Quality Farm & Fleet, 1925 Kenworth, #B552 ....$19.00
Radio Flyer, 1931 Hawkeye, #3549 ....$55.00
Radio Shack, 1931 Hawkeye, #9646 ....$38.00
Rajah Temple, 1931 Hawkeye Wrecker, #2999................$34.00
RC Cola, 1917 Ford, #9827 ....$35.00
RCA, #3, 1926 Mack, #9275 ....$45.00
RCA, #6, 1932 Ford, #9621 ....$35.00
Red Crown Gasoline, Orion Plane, #42504..................$34.00
Red Crown Gasoline, 1918 Ford, #1367 ....$24.00
Red Rose Tea, 1913 Ford, #2130 ....$34.00
Red Wolf Beer, P-51 Plane, #47017 ....$50.00
Reese's Peanut Butter Cups, 1923 Chevy, #9808............$28.00
Reese's Pieces, 1950 Chevy, #9809 ....$28.00
Remington, Vega Plane, #35059 ....$29.00
Remington Arms, 1925 Kenworth, #B607 ....$15.00
Richard Petty, 1950 Chevy, #2168.........................$35.00
Ringling Bros Circus, 1913 Ford, #9027..................$145.00
Robinson Brick Co, 1931 Hawkeye, #F974...................$32.00
Roush Gourmet Foods, 1931 Hawkeye, #F093.................$26.00
Route 66, #3, 1938 Chevy, #3529 ....$29.00
Royalite Oil Co, #1, 1931 Hawkeye, #9568 ....$29.00
Ryder Truck Rental, 1931 International, JLE, #5054 ....$28.00
Safeguard Soap, 1950 Chevy, #7508 ....$35.00
Safety Kleen, Step Van, #9289 ....$45.00
Samuel Adams Beer, 1918 Ford, #B421 ....$32.00
Sara Lee, 1950 Chevy, #9941 ....$65.00
Schwan's Ice Cream, #1, 1950 Chevy, #9210 ....$95.00

Scott Paper, 1931 Hawkeye, #9453 ....$27.00
Scott Tissue, 1917 Ford, #9652 ....$29.00
Seagrams Ginger Ale, 1931 Hawkeye, #F964 ....$45.00
Sealed Power/Speed-Pro, 1905 Ford, #1663 ....$19.00
Sears, 1913 Ford, #2129 ....$45.00
Seven-Eleven, 1926 Mack, #9155 ....$39.00
Seven-Up, 1913 Ford, #1662 ....$125.00
Shamrock Oil Co, 1931 Hawkeye Tanker, #9676 ....$32.00
Shell Oil Co, #5, DC-3 Plane, #45005 ....$36.00
Shell Oil Co, Trimotor Plane, #F927 ....$44.00
Shell Oil Co, 1935 Mack, JLE, #3011 ....$39.00
Shell Oil Co, 1939 Dodge Airflow, #4866 ....$35.00
Sico Independent Oil Co, 1925 Kenworth Stake Truck, #9224 ....$25.00
Signal Motor Oil, 1931 Hawkeye, #2164 ....$26.00
Signal Oil Co, 1931 Hawkeye, #1321 ....$25.00
Signal Oil Co, 1931 International, JLE $29.00
Sinclair, #2, 1926 Mack, #2120 ....$65.00
Sinclair, #6, 1939 Dodge Airflow, #B522 ....$35.00
Skelly Oil Co, 1931 International Tanker, JLE, #3035 ....$28.00
Slice, Step Van, #9709 ....$25.00
Smith & Wesson, 1951 GMC, #B410..........................$17.00
Smith Corona, 1931 Ford, #1355 ....$25.00
Smithsonian Institution, 1912 Ford, #3616 ....$50.00
Smokecraft, 1918 Ford, #9493 ....$30.00
Smokey Bear, 1913 Ford, #9124 ....$85.00
Snap-on Tools, 1951 GMC, #F209 ....$39.00
Sora 'N Strip, 1950 Chevy, #9658.........................$19.00
Southern States Oil, #1, 1926 Mack, #9199 ....$195.00
Southern States Oil, #2, 1926 Mack, #9797 ....$42.00
Southwest Airlines, 1950 Chevy, #9976 ....$50.00
Sparklettes Water, 1926 Mack, #9741 ....$24.00
Sparton Food Stores, 1913 Ford, #9247 ....$21.00
Spur Gasoline, 1937 Ford Semi, #3901 ....$24.00
Star Tribune Newspaper, Step Van, #H223..................$29.00
State Farm Insurance, 1931 Hawkeye Wrecker, #B002....$75.00
Steel City Beer, 1931 International, #5049 ....$27.00
Steelcase, #3, 1932 Ford, #9604 ....$22.00
Strohs Beer, 1918 Ford, #7679............................$45.00
Sun Oil Co, 1931 International, JLE, #4037...............$28.00
Sunbeam Bread, 1913 Ford, #9631 ....$34.00
Sunmaid Raisins, 1905 Ford, #9575 ....$35.00
Sunoco, #1, Vintage Plane, #40011 ....$45.00
Sunoco, 1931 Hawkeye Tanker, #3791 ....$35.00
Sunray Oil Co, 1930 DTT, #2969 ....$27.00
Super Valu, #4, 1951 GMC, #B420..........................$21.00
Super Valu, Air Express Plane, #B419 ....$30.00
Supertest Petroleum, #2, 1931 Hawkeye Wrecker, #2782 ..$29.00
Sweet & Low, 1950 Chevy, #9466 ....$52.00
Swiss Farm Stores, 1931 Hawkeye, #B114 ....$27.00
Tabasco Sauce, 1905 Ford, #9878 ....$25.00
Terminex Pest Control, 1932 Ford, #9346 ....$29.00
Texaco, #03, Stearman Plane, #F121 ....$29.00
Texaco, #06, 1926 Mack, #9040............................$75.00
Texaco, #09, 1925 Kenworth State Truck, #9385 ....$35.00
Texaco, #12, 1910 Mack, #F122 ....$29.00
Texaco Lubricants, 1929 International, JLE, #4028 ....$95.00
Thomas English Muffins, 1932 Ford, #9129.................$50.00

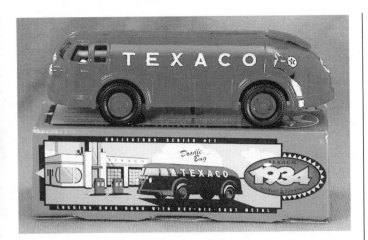

Texaco Doodle Bug, 1934 Diamond T Tanker, MIB, $30.00.

Tide Laundry Detergent, 1913 Ford, #7509	$45.00
Titlist Golf Balls, 1913 Ford, #9489	$55.00
Tom's Snack Foods, Step Van, #1337	$25.00
Tonka, 1913 Ford, #9739	$35.00

Total Hardware Coast to Coast, Semi, M, $30.00.

Total Petroleum, 1931 Hawkeye Tanker, #2967	$17.00
Toy Farmer Country Store, 1913 Ford, #1664	$22.00
Toys R Us, 1918 Ford, #4587	$27.00
Tractor Supply, #01, 1913 Ford, #1349	$35.00
Tractor Supply, #07, 1917 Ford, #9356	$25.00
Tractor Supply, #10, 1926 Mack, #9133	$35.00
Tropicana Orange Juice, 1932 Ford, #9798	$35.00
True Value Hardware, #02, 1926 Mack, #1362	$110.00
True Value Hardware, #14, 1951 GMC, #F266	$25.00
True Value Hardware, Air Express Plane, #F265	$49.00
True Value Hardware, 1918 Ford, #9623	$25.00
Trustworthy Hardware, #2, 1905 Ford, #9395	$95.00
Trustworthy Hardware, #7, 1918 Ford, #9377	$25.00
TRW, #2, 1923 Chevy, #3921	$65.00
Turkey Hill Markets, #1, 1913 Ford, #9614	$21.00
Tydol Flying A, 1931 Hawkeye Tanker, #9123	$29.00
Unical 76 (Molo Oil Co), 1935 Mack, #3005	$25.00
Unique Garden Center, 1913 Ford, #9202	$39.00
United Airlines, 1926 Mack, #9152	$35.00

United Hardware Hank, 1917 Ford, #7635	$15.00
United Hardware Hank, 1940 Ford, JLE, #6074	$19.00
United Parcel Service, 1912 Ford, #9704	$35.00
United Van Lines, 1917 Ford, #9715	$26.00
US Army Air Corps, Vega Plane, #12700	$19.00
US Mail, 1905 Ford, #7641	$27.00
US Mail, 1918 Ford, #9843	$45.00
US Navy, Air Express Plane, #F017	$25.00
USAF Thunderbirds, F-16 Plane, #46002	$19.00
UTZ Potato Chips, Step Van, #9542	$29.00
V&S Variety Store, #1, 1905 Ford, #9622	$45.00
Valvoline, 1937 Ford Semi, #9260	$30.00
Vickers Oil, 1931 Hawkeye Tanker, #9942	$22.00
Vitalizer, 1932 Ford, #9602	$22.00
Walgreen Drug Store, 1913 Ford, #9531	$29.00
Walnut Brewing, 1931 Hawkeye, #9695	$27.00
Washington Apples, 1931 Hawkeye, #9559	$38.00
Watkins Inc, #1, 1913 Ford, #F435	$45.00
West Bend, 1913 Ford, #9237	$34.00
Wheelers, 1993 Ford, #1358	$35.00
White Castle, #1, 1931 International, JLE, #5045	$29.00
White Rose Gasoline, 1931 Hawkeye Tanker, #1657	$29.00
Winchester, Stearman Plane, #37540	$39.00
Winn Dixie, 1917 Ford, #9911	$19.00
Winn Dixie, 1926 Mack, #9014	$25.00
Winn Dixie, 1931 Hawkeye, #7693	$20.00
Winston Racing Series, 1940 Ford, JLE, #6053	$18.00
Wireless, 1950 Chevy, #2953	$20.00
Wix Filters, 1932 Ford, #9810	$125.00
Wix Filters, 1955 Cameo Pickup, #9756	$65.00
Wolfgang Candy, 1913 Ford, #9440	$35.00
Wonder Bread, 1913 Ford, #9161	$48.00

FIRST GEAR

AC Gilbert Erector, 1957 International Van, #19-0111	$29.00
Akers Motor Lines, Mack B-61 Semi, #19-1468	$58.00
All American Plaza, 1957 International Wrecker, #19-1467	$40.00
American Flyer, 1951 Ford Stake Truck, #19-0118	$49.00
Anheuser-Busch Eagle Snacks, #2, 1952 GMC Van, #19-1140	$25.00
Anheuser-Busch Eagle Snacks, #3, 1951 Ford Stake Truck, #19-1191	$65.00
Anheuser-Busch Eagle Snacks, #4, Mack B-61 Semi, #19-1394	$39.00
Anheuser-Busch Eagle Snacks, 1951 Ford Van, #19-1121	$75.00
Armstrong Tires, Mack B-61 Semi, #19-1465	$74.00
Atlantic Refining, 1951 Ford Tanker, #10-1290	$27.00
Bare Truck Center, 1957 International Wrecker, #19-1457	$39.00
BASF Corp Glasurit Paint, #2, 1951, Ford Van, #29-1042	$95.00
BASF Corp R-M Diamond, #3, 1951 Ford Stake Truck, #19-1126	$175.00
Blue Diamond Co, Mack B-61 Dump Truck, #19-1934	$150.00
BP Gasoline, Mack B-61 Semi, #19-2006	$65.00
Budweiser, Mack B-61 Semi, #19-1912	$66.00
Burlington Truck Lines, 1956 White Semi, #18-1545	$65.00
Busch Light Beer, 1952 GMC Van, #19-1622	$37.00
Campbell's Soup, Mack B-61 Semi, #19-1314	$65.00

Cape Cod Potato Chips, Mack B-61 Semi, #19-1279.......$58.00

Cape Cod Potato Chips, 1957 International Van, #19-1193 .$32.00

Carlisle Collector Events, Mack B-61 Semi, #19-1781.....$49.00

Carlisle Collector Events, 1957 International Wrecker, #19-1732 ....$38.00

Chevrolet (See the USA), 1949 Chevy Van, #19-1410...$28.00

Chevrolet Motor Co, 1949 Chevy, #10-1328 ....$32.00

Chevron Gasoline, 1952 Ford Tanker, #19-1021 ....$40.00

Citgo, 1957 International Tanker, #29-1248 ....$59.00

Civil Defense, 1949 Chevy, #19-1355.................................$29.00

Coker Tire, 1951 Ford Stake Truck, #19-1249 ....$45.00

Cole's Express, Mack B-61 Semi, #19-1826 ....$85.00

Conrock Corp, Mack B-61 Dump Truck, #19-1956 ....$49.00

CP Ward Construction, Mack B-61 Dump Truck, #19-1827.$75.00

Custom Chrome, 1951 Ford Stake Truck, #18-1161 ....$54.00

Daisy Air Rifles, Mack B-61 Semi, #10-0123 ....$74.00

Daisy Air Rifles, 1951 Ford Box, #10-0124 ....$38.00

Daisy Air Rifles, 1952 GMC Van, #10-0126 ....$30.00

Daisy Red Rider, 1957 International, #10-0125.................$30.00

Eastern Express, 1953 Ford Box, #19-1481 ....$32.00

Eastwood Club, #6, 1955 DT Wrecker, #19-1918 ....$48.00

Eastwood Co, 1952 GMC Wrecker, #19-0109....................$79.00

Eastwood Museum, 1951 Ford Van, #19-1010................$115.00

Exxon, Mack B-61 Semi, #19-1708.....................................$44.00

Exxon Aviation, 1957 International Tanker, #19-1800 ....$35.00

Falstaff Brewing, #2, 1949, Chevy Panel, #19-1546.........$27.00

First Gear Inc, 1951 Ford Stake Truck, #19-0120.............$40.00

First Gear Inc, 1953 White Semi, #19-0010 ....$150.00

First Gear Inc, 1955 Dia-T Tow Truck, #19-0009 ....$75.00

Ford Motorcraft, 1951 Ford Tanker, #20-1124 ....$25.00

Ford Quality Parts, 1951 Ford Box, #20-1123 ....$25.00

Frank Dibella Moving, 1957 International Moving Van, #19-1450 ....$45.00

Global Van Lines, Mack B-61 Semi, #19-1810.................$69.00

Global Van Lines, 1957 International Moving Van, #19-1801 ....$50.00

GMC Truck & Coach Division, 1952 GMC Stake Truck, #10-1253 ....$29.00

Graham Trucking Co, 1952 GMC Box, #19-1066 ....$35.00

Graham Trucking Co, 1956 White Semi, #18-1844........$62.00

Grapette Soda, Mack B-61 Semi, #19-1619 ....$75.00

Great Northern Railway, 1957 International Box, #19-1175.$32.00

Gulf Oil, #1, 1957 International Wrecker, #19-1336 ....$79.00

Gulf Oil, 1953 Ford Pickup, #19-1618 ....$35.00

Gulf Oil, 1953 Kenworth Bull Nose, #19-1727................$69.00

Gulf Oil, 1953 White 3000 Tanker, #19-1913 ....$65.00

Hamm's Beer, 1953 Ford, #29-1480 ....$35.00

Hershey Cocoa, 1952 GMC Sack, #19-1273 ....$38.00

Hershey Milk Chocolate, 1952 GMC Box, #19-1765 ......$29.00

Hooker Headers, 1957 International Van, #10-1284........$39.00

Hostess Cup Cakes, Mack B-61 Semi, #19-1530 ....$58.00

Hostess Cup Cakes, 1949 Chevy, #19-1494.....................$25.00

Howard Johnson's, Mack B-61 Semi, #18-1796...............$65.00

Howard Johnson's, 1952 GMC Van, #18-1795 ....$29.00

Humble Oil Co, Mack B-61 Semi, #19-1395...................$175.00

Humble Travel (Exxon), 1957 International Wrecker, #18-1677 ....$45.00

Iowa Hawkeyes, 1952 GMC Van, #29-1268 ....$42.00

JC Whitney, 1952 GMC Tanker, #10-1215 ....$35.00

JC Whitney, 1957 International Wrecker, #10-1207 ....$45.00

Kazan Temple Shrine Circus, 1947 Chevy Panel Truck, #29-1413 ....$35.00

Lanser's Garage, 1952 GMC Wrecker, #19-1049 ....$39.00

Lone Star Beer, 1952 GMC Van, #10-1258.......................$32.00

Marathon Oil, 1953 Ford Tanker, #9361 ....$24.00

Mayflower Transit Co, 1953 Kenworth Semi, #19-1803 ..$79.00

Mercury Marine, Mack B-61 Tanker, #19-1266 ....$75.00

Michelin Tires, Mack B-61 Semi, #19-1502 ....$65.00

Michelin Tires, 1957 International Van, #29-1621 ....$29.00

Mobil Oil, Mack B-61 Semi, #19-1556 ....$65.00

Mobil Oil, 1949 Chevy, #19-1500......................................$34.00

Mobil Oil, 1952 GMC Tanker, #29-1231 ....$45.00

Mobil Oil, 1953 Ford Tanker, #29-1501 ....$28.00

Mobil Oil, 1957 International Tanker, #19-1405 ....$25.00

Mobilgas, 1957 International Tanker, #20-1678 ....$29.00

Mobilgas, 1957 International Wrecker, #18-1381 ....$95.00

Moon Pie (Banana), 1951 Ford Box, #19-1627 ....$28.00

Moon Pie (Chocolate), 1951 Ford Box, #19-1626............$28.00

Morton Salt, 1952 GMC Sack, #19-1130 ....$32.00

Motor City Ford, 1953 Ford Pickup, #307000.................$39.00

Mountain Dew, 1952 GMC Bottle, #19-1730 ....$28.00

Moxie Cola, 1952 GMC Bottle, #19-0119.........................$55.00

Mushroom Transportation, 1956 White Semi, #19-1854.$60.00

National Motorcycle Museum, 1951 Ford Van, #29-1274.$48.00

New York Fire Dept, 1957 International Wrecker, #19-1401..$55.00

Northern Pacific Railroad, Mack B-61 Semi, #19-1560 ...$58.00

Northern Pacific Railroad, 1953 Ford Pickup, #19-1559 ..$17.00

Olympia Beer, 1952 GMC, #29-1482 ....$25.00

Pennsylvania Raildroad, Mack B-61 Semi, #19-1435.......$44.00

Pennzoil, 1952 GMC Wrecker, #19-1062..........................$49.00

Pepsi-Cola, 1951 Ford F-6 Bottler's Truck, MIB, $50.00.

Pepsi-Cola (Santa), 1951 Ford Bottle, #19-1092 ....$95.00

Pez Candy, #2, 1957 International Box, #29-1714 ....$49.00

Phillips 55, 1951 Ford Tanker, #19-1034........................$49.00

Phillips 66, 1957 International, #19-1337.........................$85.00

Phillips 66 Pipeline, #1, 1951 Ford Flatbed, #19-1427 .....$49.00

Phillips 66 Pipeline, #2, 1949 Chevy Panel, #19-1831 .....$39.00
PIE Trucking, 1952 GMC Van, #10-1043 ....$50.00
PIE Trucking, 1953 Kenworth Bullnose Semi, #18-1477 .$73.00
Police Dept, 1957 International Wrecker, #19-1264 ....$35.00
Quaker Oats, Buckboard & Horses, #0004 ....$65.00
Railway Express, Mack B-61 Semi, #19-1654 ....$65.00
RC Cola, 1951 Ford Bottle, #19-1131 ....$45.00
RC Cola, 1952 GMC Bottle, #19-1739 ....$24.00
Red Crown Gasoline, 1951 Ford, #19-1631 ....$35.00
Red Star Express, Mack B-61 Semi, #19-1312 ....$205.00
Remington, Mack B-61 Semi, #10-1292 ....$74.00
Remington I-Goose, 1952 GMC Van, #10-1134 ....$35.00
Remington II-Elk, 1953 Ford Van, #10-1573 ....$35.00
Roadrunner Express, 1951 Ford Van, #19-1108 ....$45.00
Roadway Express, 1953 Ford, #10-1379 ....$38.00
Rolling Thunder Cycles, #1951 Ford Box, #28-1141 ....$29.00
Schultz Co Grand Pianos, 1957 International Box, #19-
1332 ....$42.00

Shell Aviation Fuel, 1957 International R-190 with Fuel Tanker, MIB, $40.00.

Shell Oil Co, 1952 GMC Tanker, #28-0105 ....$49.00
Shell Oil Co, 1957 International Stake Truck, #19-1565 .$29.00
Shell Oil Co, 1957 International Tanker, #29-1270 ....$34.00
Smith & Wesson, 1952 GMC Stake Truck, #10-1326 .....$29.00
Special Export, 1951 Ford Stake Truck, #10-1259 ....$32.00
Spra 'N Strip, 1952 GMC Wrecker, #19-1769 ....$38.00
State Highway Dept, Mack B-61 Dump Truck, #19-1813 .$75.00
Storey Wrecker, 1957 International Wrecker, #19-1665 .$38.00
Strohs Beer, 1952 GMC Van, #10-1353 ....$39.00
Sunshine Biscuits, Mack B-61 Semi, #10-1472 ....$56.00
Sunshine Biscuits, 1957 International, #10-1473 ....$32.00
Texaco Pipeline, #2, 1953 Ford Pickup, #19-1688 ....$96.00
Texaco Pipeline, 1949 Chevy Panel Truck, #19-1391 ...$175.00
TNT Trucking, Mack B-61 Semi, #10-1598 ....$49.00
Tollway & Tunnel, 1957 International Wrecker, #19-1439 .$55.00
True Value Hardware, Mack B-61 Semi, #10-1486 ....$55.00
True Value Hardware, 1953 Ford Van, #19-1490 ....$34.00
US Army, 1957 International, #19-1389 ....$28.00

US Mail, Mack B-61 Semi, #19-1302 ....$65.00
US Mail, 1953 Ford Van, #19-1441 ....$40.00
Utica Club Beer, Mack B-61 Semi, #18-1697 ....$69.00
Valley Asphalt Co, Mack B-61 Dump Truck, #19-1958 ..$65.00
West Coast Freight, 1952 GMC Box, #19-1007 ....$32.00
Winchester, 1957 International Box, #18-1319 ....$22.00
Wonder Bread, Mack B-61 Semi, #19-1529 ....$58.00
Wonder Bread, 1949 Chevy, #19-1493 ....$19.00

RACING CHAMPIONS

AC Delco, Kenworth Semi, #250 ....$35.00
Alliance Racing/Seltzer #59, 1934 Biplane, #386 ....$40.00
Army Desert Storm/Allan Kulwicki #7, T-Bird, #478 ......$55.00
Atlanta Speedway/Hooters 500, 1934 Biplane, #253 ....$75.00
Brickyard 400, Chevy Lumina, #457 ....$40.00
Chevy Thunder, 1931 Travel Air, #0656 ....$40.00
Curt Turner, Vega Airplane, #320 ....$75.00
Darlington Speedway, Model A Panel, #201 ....$70.00
Daytona International Speedway, Model A Pickup, #255 .$30.00
DuPont Racing/Jeff Gordon #24, Kenworth Semi, #367 ..$40.00
First Union 400 (4/18/93), Model A Panel, #218 ....$25.00
Ford Motorsports, 1934 Biplane, #460 ....$60.00
French's Mustard/Black Flag #43, Pontiac, #462 ....$35.00
Goodwrench/Dale Earnhardt, 1955 Panel, #467 ....$50.00
Hardees/Mello Yello/Ward Burton, Chevy Lumina, #413 .$40.00
Havoline/Davy Allison #28, T-Bird, #446 ....$75.00
Interstate Batteries/Dale Jarret, 1955 Chevy, #474 ....$30.00
Kleenex/Jerry Spencer #10, Chevy Lumina, #407 ....$65.00
Kodak Racing/Ernie Irvan #4, Chevy Lumina, #344 ....$40.00
Kyle Petty, 1955 Convertible, #473 ....$25.00
LA Raiders, T-Bird, #552 ....$25.00
Leo Jackson/Harry Gant, Chevy Lumina, #2284 ....$30.00
Manheim Auction, Harry Gant #7, Chevy Lumina, #2270 ..$40.00
Mello Yello, Kyle Petty, Pontiac, #356 ....$55.00
Motorcraft/Geoff Bodine #15, T-Bird, #338 ....$25.00
NASCAR Racing #93/Kenworth Semi, #313 ....$35.00
New Hampshire, Model A Panel Truck, #233 ....$35.00
Petty Enterprises/Petty #42, 1934 Biplane, #449 ....$90.00
Polaroid/S Robinson #35, Chevy Lumina, #2803 ....$35.00
Pontiac/Rusty Wallace #2, Pontiac, #428 ....$160.00
Quaker State, B Bodine #26, T-Bird, #339 ....$25.00
Racing Champs Club #93/Chevy Lumina, #371 ....$100.00
Raybestos/Sterling Marlin #8, T-Bird, #337 ....$30.00
Slim Jim/D Green #44, Chevy Lumina, #463 ....$40.00
STP/Richard Petty #43, Pontiac, #360 ....$40.00
Tide/Darrel Waltrip #17, Chevy Lumina, #405, orange ...$65.00
US Air/Greg Sacks #77 Winston Cup, T-Bird, #2248 ......$40.00
Valvoline/Mark Martin #6, T-Bird, #334 ....$50.00

SPEC-CAST

A&W Root Beer, 1932 Ford, #1553 ....$29.00
AACA (Michigan Region), 1936 Dodge, #700010 ....$20.00
Agway, #11, 1936 Dodge Pickup, #72030 ....$25.00
Alabama, 1955 Chevy, #50029 ....$23.00
Allied Van Lines, 1929 Ford, #2551 ....$20.00
Allis Chalmers, 1929 Ford, #2028 ....$25.00

American Airlines, 1929 Ford Fire Pumper, #02053 ....$22.00
Bell System, 1931 Ford, #1004 ....$24.00
Big A Auto Parts, #09, 1929 Ford Wrecker, #1075 ....$19.00
Big A Auto Parts, #13, 1948, Ford Pickup, #68506 ....$28.00
Big A Auto Parts #11, 1936 Dodge Panel Truck, #74028...$22.00
Brickyard 400, 1955 Chevy Convertible, #0459 ....$59.00
Campbell's Soup, 1955 Chevy, #50013 ....$28.00
Campbell's Soup, 1957 Ford Sedan, #58006 ....$23.00
Canada Tire, 1940 Ford Pickup, #3888 ....$28.00
Cheerios, 1942 Chevy, #75005 ....$28.00
Chevrolet Motor Co, 1937 Chevy Convertible, #0489....$22.00
Chrome Specialties, 1955 Chevy, #50045 ....$45.00
Citgo, 1929 Ford, #2514 ....$29.00
Citgo, 1940 Ford Tanker, #65501 ....$25.00
Clark Oil & Refining, #4, 1929 Ford Pickup, #1082 ....$24.00
Classic Auto Series, 1955 Chevy Convertible, #55002 ....$22.00
Classic Motorbooks, 1929 Ford, #1562 ....$28.00
Classic Motorbooks, 1955 Chevy, #50032 ....$28.00
Classic Street Rods, 1929 Ford, #2578 ....$25.00
Coca-Cola 600, Kenworth Semi, #30001 ....$48.00
Coca-Cola 600, 1929 Ford, #2711 ....$55.00
Conoco Oil, 1929 Ford, #2002 ....$29.00
Conoco Oil, 1937 Chevy Tanker, #17506 ....$22.00
Cooper Tire, #3, 1929 Ford, #2518 ....$45.00
Cooper Tire, #5, 1940 Ford, #67508 ....$35.00
Coors Field, 1942 Chevy, #75025 ....$38.00
Country Music, Billy Ray Cyrus, 1929 Ford, #2588.........$23.00
Country Music, Randy Travis, 1937 Chevy, #15019........$12.00
Crown Petroleum, #5, 1929, Ford Tanker, #2043............$29.00
Darlington 500, 1929 Ford, #2706.............................$65.00
Daytona 500 STP, 1929 Ford, #0231 ....$22.00
Diamond Rio, 1940 Ford, #67503 ....$23.00
Drag Specialties, #2, 1931 Ford, #2524 ....$95.00
Ducks Unlimited, 1929 Ford, #1028 ....$45.00
Ducks Unlimited, 1937 Chevy, #15014 ....$45.00
Eastwood Club, #2, 1931 Ford Wrecker, #1303 ....$15.00
Eastwood Co, #4, Orion Plane, #42503 ....$44.00
Eastwood Co II, #3, 1957 Ford Ranchero, #2635............$29.00
Eatons of Canada, 1929 Ford, #0178..........................$28.00
Essolube Motor Oil, 1936 Dodge, #74003 ....$32.00
Fina Oil, 1929 Ford, #2004 ....$28.00
Ford, 1929 Ford Fire Truck, #2025 ....$20.00
Ford Sales & Service, 1940 Ford, #67502 ....$22.00
Frito Lay, 1936 Dodge Pickup, #72041........................$28.00
Gilmore Oil Co, 1940 Ford Tanker, #65504 ....$25.00
Gold Metal Flour, 1916 Studebaker, #25025 ....$22.00
Golden Rule Lumber, 1940 Ford Pickup, #62518............$22.00
Goodyear, 1937 Chevy, #15001 ....$19.00
Goodyear Tire Co, 1955 Chevy Convertible, #5006 ....$20.00
Gulf Oil, 1929 Ford, #1558.....................................$27.00
Gulf Oil, 1940 Ford Tanker, #65505 ....$25.00
Hamm's Beer, 1929 Ford, #1014 ....$29.00
Hamm's Beer, 1936 Dodge Panel Truck, #74032............$22.00
Harley-Davidson, Vega Plane, #99203 ....$49.00
Harley-Davidson, 1916 Studebaker, #99215 ....$52.00
Heinz (HJ) Co, 1929 Ford, #1018 ....$19.00
Heinz 57, 1916 Studebaker, #22502 ....$22.00

Hemmings Motor News, 1936 Dodge Panel Truck, #74000 .$29.00
Hemmings Motor News, 1957, Ford Ranchero, #57008...$29.00
Hershey Chocolate Milk, 1916 Studebaker, #27503 ....$32.00
Hershey Milk Chocolate, 1936 Dodge, #74012 ....$23.00
Holman Moody Performance, 1929 Ford, #0315 ....$15.00
Hooters Atlanta 500, 1929 Ford, #2709......................$75.00
Hot Wheels, 1929 Ford Panel Truck, #316500 ....$49.00
House of Kolor, 1937 Chevy, #15013..........................$24.00
Humble Oil Co, 1936 Dodge Tanker, #72032 ....$27.00
Indian Motorcycle, 1948 Ford Panel Truck, #68012 ....$29.00
Indian Motorcycle, 1955 Chevy Convertible, #55014 .....$22.00
Iola Old Car Show, 1929 Ford, #2535.........................$27.00
Iowa Hawkeyes, 1955 Chevy Convertible, #55012 ....$25.00
JC Penney, 1929 Ford, #4885 ....$28.00
JC Penney, 1940 Ford Pickup, #4737 ....$28.00
JC Whitney, 1916 Studebaker, #22520........................$29.00
Jewel Tea, 1931 Ford, #2584 ....$65.00
John Deere, 1936 Dodge Panel Truck, #74042 ....$24.00
Kentucky Fried Chicken, 1940 Ford Panel Truck, #67519 ..$22.00
Lennox (100th Anniversary), #2, 1940, Ford, #62525 .....$55.00
Lionel Trains, 1955 Chevy, #303500 ....$32.00
Little Debbie Snack Cakes, 1929 Ford, #2503 ....$28.00
Louisville Slugger, 1931 Ford, #1036..........................$25.00
Mailboxes Etc, #1, 1950 Chevy, #9215 ....$79.00
Mobil Oil, 1940 Ford Tanker, #65506 ....$35.00
Mobilgas, 1936 Dodge Tanker, #72007........................$28.00
Mooseheart Farms, 1916 Studebaker, #22511 ....$25.00
Motorcraft Racing #15, 1929 Ford, #0307 ....$19.00
Nabisco, 1929 Ford, #2508 ....$28.00
Olympia Beer, 1929 Ford, #2528 ....$15.00
Oreo Cookies, 1916 Studebaker, #25013 ....$22.00
Pabst Beer, 1929 Ford, #1512 ....$29.00
Pepsi-Cola, 1936 Dodge Fire Truck, #72034.................$34.00
Planters Peanuts, 1957 Ford Sedan, #58008..................$22.00

Quaker State Racing, 1929 Ford, M, $25.00.

Red Crown Gasoline, 1929 Ford Wrecker, #2036 ....$17.00
Red Crown Gasoline, 1940 Ford Tanker, #65502.............$25.00
Remington, 1929 Ford, #2617 ....$28.00
Richmond Pontiac 400, 1929 Ford, #0212 ....$32.00
Rockingham A/C Delco, 1955 Chevy, #0249..................$22.00
Rockingham Raceway, 1929 Ford, #0210 ....$65.00

Sears, 1929 Ford, #1201 ....$79.00
Sentry Hardware, #1, 1957 Chevy, #55017......................$28.00
Sentry Hardware, #5, 1955 Chevy, #50030......................$19.00
Sentry Hardware, 1936 Dodge Convertible, #70006 ....$22.00
Shell Oil Co, 1929 Ford, #02039....................................$17.00
Shell Oil Co, 1936 Dodge Tanker, #72008.....................$32.00
State Highway Patrol, 1937 Chevy, #15007 ....$14.00
State Highway Patrol, 1940 Ford Convertible, #60004 ....$23.00
Sturges 53rd Annual Rally, 1937 Chevy, #15004...........$125.00
Sunsweet, 1916 Studebaker, #20001 ....$22.00

Sunsweet, 1929 Ford, 75th Anniversary, #1012, M, $35.00.

Sunsweet, 1929 Ford, #1508..$35.00
Sunsweet, 1955 Chevy Convertible, #55001 ....$22.00

Texaco Petroleum Products, Ford Model A Truck, Liberty Classics, MIB, J6, $55.00. (Photo courtesy June Moon)

Tractor Supply Company, 1916 Studebaker, #22527 ....$28.00
True Value Hardware (Tru-Test), 1937 Chevy, #15026T.$18.00
Trustworthy Hardware, #11, 1957 Ford Ranchero, #57001 ..$18.00
Trustworthy Hardware, #9, 1916 Studebaker, #22500......$18.00
Trustworthy Hardware, 1929 Ford, #1013.........................$25.00
US Army Ambulance, 1937 Chevy, #15018 ....$19.00
US Mail, 1916 Studebaker, #25019.................................$26.00
V&S Renniger TV Hardware, 1929 Ford, #2554..............$17.00

Wheaties, 1940 Ford, #67518...$23.00
Wheaties, 1955 Chevy, #50044.......................................$19.00
Winchester, Peterbilt Semi, #32509................................$32.00
Winchester, 1929 Ford, #02601 ....$29.00
Wire Works, 1957 Ford Ranchero, #324500....................$32.00

Dinky

Dinky diecasts were made by Meccano (Britain) as early as 1933, but high on the list of many of today's collectors are those from the decades of the '50s and '60s. They made commercial vehicles, firefighting equipment, farm toys, and heavy equipment as well as classic cars that were the epitome of high style, such as the #157 Jaguar XK120, produced from the mid-'50s through the early '60s. Some Dinkys were made in France; since 1979 no toys have been produced in Great Britain. Values are for examples mint and in the original packaging unless noted otherwise.

See also Soldiers.

#100, Lady Penelope's Fab 1, luminous pk $400.00
#100, Lady Penelope's Fab 1, pk.....................................$250.00
#101, Sunbeam Alpine $175.00
#101, Thunderbird II & IV, gr $300.00
#101, Thunderbird II & IV, metallic gr $400.00
#102, Joe' Car $135.00
#102, MG Midget $250.00

#104, Spectrum Pursuit Vehicle, $200.00.

#105, Triumph TR2...$200.00
#106, Austin Atlantic, bl or blk $150.00
#106, Austin Atlantic, pk...$350.00
#106, Prisoner Mini Moke...$260.00
#106, Thunderbird II & IV..$120.00

#107, Sunbeam Alpine	$150.00
#108, MG Midget	$200.00
#108, Sam's Car, gold, red or bl	$160.00
#108, Sam's Car, silver	$120.00
#109, Aston Healey 100	$160.00
#109, Gabriel Model T Ford	$150.00
#110, Aston Martin DB5	$110.00
#111, Cinderella's Coach	$50.00
#111, Triumph TR2	$160.00
#112, Austin Healey Sprite	$125.00
#112, Purdey's Triumph TR7	$75.00
#113, MGB	$110.00
#114, Triumph Spitfire, gray, gold or red	$125.00
#114, Triumph Spitfire, purple	$170.00
#114, Triumph Spitfire, red	$125.00
#115, Plymouth Fury	$125.00
#116, Volvo 1800S	$100.00
#117, Four Berth Caravan	$60.00
#120, Happy Cab	$60.00
#120, Jaguar E-Type	$110.00
#121, Goodwood Racing Gift Set	$2,000.00
#122, Touring Gift Set	$2,000.00
#122, Volvo 265 Estate Car	$50.00
#123, Mayfair Gift Set	$3,000.00
#123, Princess 2200 HL	$60.00
#124, Rolls Royce Phantom V	$80.00
#125, Fun A'Hoy Set	$250.00
#128, Mercedes Benz 600	$80.00
#129, MG Midget	$400.00
#129, VW 1200 Sedan	$80.00
#130, Ford Consul Corsair	$85.00
#131, Cadillac El Dorado	$150.00
#131, Jaguar E-Type, 2+2	$150.00
#132, Ford 40-RV	$60.00
#132, Packard Convertible	$165.00
#133, Cunningham C-5R	$130.00
#134, Triumph Vitesse	$100.00
#135, Triumph 2000	$100.00
#136, Vauxhall Viva	$80.00
#137, Plymouth Fury	$130.00
#138, Hillman Imp	$100.00
#139, Ford Cortina	$115.00
#139a, Hudson Commodore Sedan, dual colors	$350.00
#139a, Hudson Commodore Sedan, solid colors	$225.00
#139a, US Army Staff Car	$350.00
#140, Morris 1100	$80.00
#141, Vauxhall Victor	$80.00
#142, Jaguar Mark 10	$100.00
#143, Ford Capri	$100.00
#144, VW 1500	$100.00
#145, Singer Vogue	$100.00
#146, Daimler V8	$100.00
#147, Cadillac 62	$100.00
#148, Ford Fairlane, gr	$125.00
#148, Ford Fairlane, metallic gr	$225.00
#149, Citroen Dyane	$50.00
#149, Sports Car Gift Set	$1,800.00
#150, Rolls Royce Silver Wraith	$100.00
#151, Triumph 1800 Saloon	$150.00
#151, Vauxhall Victor 101	$100.00
#152, Rolls Royce Phantom V	$85.00
#153, Aston Martin	$100.00
#153, Standard Vanguard-Spats	$145.00
#154, Ford Taunus 17M	$85.00
#155, Ford Anglia	$120.00
#156, Mechanized Army Set	$5,000.00
#156, Rover 75, dual colors	$300.00
#156, Rover 75, solid colors	$150.00
#156, Saab 96	$100.00
#157, BMW 2000 Tilux	$100.00
#158, Riley	$140.00
#158, Rolls Royce Silver Shadow	$100.00
#159, Ford Cortina MKII	$100.00
#159, Morris Oxford, dual colors	$300.00
#159, Morris Oxford, solid colors	$140.00
#160, Austin A30	$125.00
#160, Mercedes Benz 250 SE	$90.00
#161, Austin Somerset, dual colors	$300.00
#161, Austin Somerset, solid colors	$150.00
#161, Ford Mustang	$100.00
#162, Ford Zephyr	$135.00
#162, Triumph 1300	$85.00
#163, Bristol 450 Coupe	$100.00
#163, VW 1600 TL, metallic bl	$150.00
#163, VW 1600 TL, red	$75.00
#164, Ford Zodiac MKIV, bronze	$200.00
#164, Ford Zodiac MKIV, silver	$100.00
#164, Vauxhall Cresta	$125.00
#165, Ford Capri	$90.00
#165, Humber Hawk	$150.00
#166, Renault R16	$60.00
#166, Sunbeam Rapier	$135.00
#167, AC Acceca, all cream	$300.00
#167, AC Acceca, dual colors	$140.00
#168, Ford Escort	$100.00
#168, Singer Gazelle	$140.00
#169, Fire Corsair	$100.00
#169, Studebaker Golden Hawk	$160.00
#170, Ford Fordor, dual colors	$300.00
#170, Ford Fordor, solid colors	$125.00
#170, Lincoln Continental	$120.00
#170m, Ford Fordor US Army Staff Car	$350.00
#171, Austin 1800	$100.00
#171, Hudson Commodore, dual colors	$350.00
#172, Fiat 2300 Station Wagon	$75.00
#172, Studebaker Land Cruiser, dual colors	$300.00
#172, Studebaker Land Cruiser, solid colors	$165.00
#173, Nash Rambler	$110.00
#173, Pontiac Parisienne	$85.00
#174, Mercury Cougar	$85.00
#175, Cadillac El Dorado	$100.00
#175, Hillman Minx	$140.00
#176, Austin A105, cream or gray	$150.00
#176, Austin A105, cream w/bl roof, or gray w/red roof	$250.00
#176, Austin A105, gray	$150.00
#176, NSU R80, metallic bl	$180.00

#176, NSU R80, metallic red	$80.00	#202, Customized Land Rover	$50.00
#177, Opel Kapitan	$100.00	#202, Fiat Abarth 2000	$50.00
#178, Mini Clubman	$60.00	#203, Customized Range Rover	$50.00

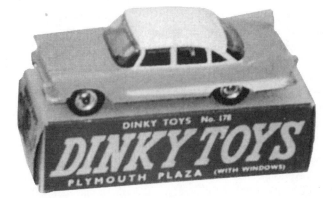

#178, Plymouth Plaza, blue with white roof, $400.00.

#178, Plymouth Plaza, pk, gr or 2-tone bl	$150.00	#204, Ferrari	$55.00
#179, Opel Commodore	$70.00	#205, Talbot Labo, in bubble pkg	$325.00
#179, Studebaker President	$170.00	#206, Customized Corvette Stingray	$70.00
#180, Rover 3500 Sedan	$40.00	#207, Triumph TR7	$50.00
#181, VW	$100.00	#208, VW Porsche 914	$65.00
#182, Porsche 356A Coupe, cream, red or bl	$130.00	#210, Alfa Romeo 33	$65.00
#182, Porsche 356A Coupe, dual colors	$325.00	#210, Vanwall, in bubble pkg	$200.00
#183, Fiat 600	$100.00	#211, Triumph TR7	$80.00
#183, Morris Mini Minor	$100.00	#213, Ford Capri	$75.00
#184, Volvo 122S, red	$130.00	#214, Hillman Imp Rally	$100.00
#184, Volvo 122S, wht	$375.00	#215, Ford GT Racing Car	$70.00
#185, Alpha Romeo 1900	$125.00	#216, Ferrari Dino	$70.00
#186, Mercedes Benz 200	$100.00	#217, Alfa Romeo Scarabo	$50.00
#187, De Tomaso Mangusta 5000	$75.00	#218, Lotus Europa	$65.00
#187, Volkswagen	$100.00	#219, Jaguar XJS Coupe	$65.00
#187, Volkswagen Karmann Ghia Coupe	$135.00	#220, Ferrari P5	$55.00
#188, Ford Berth Caravan	$60.00	#221, Corvette Stingray	$60.00
#188, Jensen FF	$75.00	#222, Hesketh Racing Car, dk bl	$60.00
#189, Lamborghini Marzal	$65.00	#222, Hesketh Racing Car, Olympus Camera	$100.00
#189, Triumph Herald	$120.00	#223, McLaren M8A Can-Am	$50.00
#191, Dodge Royal Sedan, cream w/bl flash	$300.00	#224, Mercedes Benz C111	$55.00
#191, Dodge Royal Sedan, cream w/brn flash, or gr w/blk flash	$170.00	#225, Lotus Formula 1 Racer	$55.00
		#226, Ferrari 312/B2	$50.00
#192, Desoto Fireflite	$165.00	#227, Beach Bunny	$55.00
#192, Range Rover	$50.00	#228, Super Sprinter	$60.00
#193, Rambler Station Wagon	$115.00	#236, Connaught Racer	$125.00
#194, Bentley S Coupe	$130.00	#237, Mercedes Benz Racer	$125.00
#195, Range Rover Fire Chief	$60.00	#238, Jaguar Type-D Racer	$140.00
#196, Holden Special Sedan	$75.00	#239, Vanwall Racer	$125.00
#197, Austin Countryman, orange	$325.00	#240, Cooper Racer	$70.00
#197, Morris Mini Traveller	$100.00	#240, Dinky Way Gift Set	$130.00
#197, Morris Mini Traveller, dk gr & brn	$400.00	#241, Lotus Racer	$80.00
#197, Morris Mini Traveller, lime gr	$300.00	#241, Silver Jubilee Taxi	$50.00
#198, Rolls Royce Phantom V	$115.00	#242, Ferrari Racer	$85.00
#199, Austin Countryman, bl	$115.00	#243, BRM Racer	$80.00
#200, Matra 630	$75.00	#243, Volvo Police Racer	$50.00
#201, Plymouth Stock Car	$75.00	#244, Plymouth Police Racer	$50.00
#201, Racing Car Set	$750.00	#245, Superfast Gift Set	$225.00
		#246, International Car Gift Set	$235.00
		#249, Racing Car Gift Set	$1,500.00
		#249, Racing Car Gift Set, in bubble pkg	$1,800.00
		#250, Mini Cooper Police Car	$75.00
		#251, USA Police Car, Pontiac	$80.00
		#252, RCMP Car, Pontiac	$100.00
		#254, Austin Taxi, yel	$120.00
		#254, Police Range Rover	$65.00
		#255, Ford Zodiac Police Car	$80.00
		#255, Mersey Tunnel Police Van	$100.00
		#255, Police Mini Clubman	$50.00
		#256, Humber Hawk Police Car	$140.00
		#257, Nash Rambler Canadian Fire Chief Car	$100.00
		#258, USA Police Car, Cadillac, Desoto, Dodge or Ford	$150.00
		#259, Bedford Fire Engine	$130.00
		#260, Royal Mail Van	$160.00
		#260, VW Deutsch Bundepost	$185.00

#261, Ford Taunus Polizei $275.00
#261, Telephone Service Van $150.00
#262, VW Swiss Post PTT Car, casting #129 ....$250.00
#262, VW Swiss Post PTT Car, casting #181, minimum
    value $600.00
#263, Airport Fire Rescue Tender $70.00
#263, Superior Criterion Ambulance........................$115.00
#264, RCMP Patrol Car, Cadillac $175.00
#264, RCMP Patrol Car, Fairlane $135.00
#265, Plymouth Taxi $170.00
#266, ERF Fire Tender...$75.00
#266, ERF Fire Tender, Falck $100.00
#266, Plymouth Taxi, Metro Cab $150.00
#267, Paramedic Truck $75.00
#267, Superior Cadillac Ambulance $100.00
#268, Range Rover Ambulance $60.00
#268, Renault Dauphine Mini Cab............................$135.00

#269, Ford Transit Police Accident Unit, $60.00.

#269, Jaguar Motorway Police Car $140.00
#270, AA Motorcycle Patrol $75.00
#270, Ford Panda Police Car $70.00
#271, Ford Transit Fire, Appliance $75.00
#271, Ford Transit Fire, Falck $150.00
#271, TS Motorcycle Patrol $265.00
#272, ANNB Motorcycle Patrol $300.00
#272, Police Accident Unit..$60.00
#273, RAC Patrol Mini Van $165.00
#274, Ford Transit Ambulance $50.00
#275, Brink's Armoured Car, no bullion $75.00
#275, Brink's Armoured Car, w/gold bullion $200.00
#275, Brink's Armoured Car, w/Mexican bullion........$1,000.00
#276, Airport Fire Tender $100.00
#276, Ford Transit Ambulance $60.00
#277, Police Range Rover $60.00
#277, Superior Criterion Ambulance........................$115.00
#278, Plymouth Yellow Cab $50.00
#278, Vauxhall Victor Ambulance $100.00
#279, Aveling Barford Diesel Roller $80.00
#280, Midland Mobile Bank.......................................$140.00
#281, Fiat 2300 Pathe News Camera Car $175.00
#281, Military Hovercraft $65.00
#282, Austin 1800 Taxi...$85.00

#282, Land Rover Fire, Appliance.............................$60.00
#282, Land Rover Fire, Falck $80.00
#283, BOAC Coach $130.00
#283, Single-Decker Bus $80.00
#284, London Austin Taxi $70.00
#285, Merryweather Fire Engine $80.00
#285, Merryweather Fire Engine, Falck....................$150.00
#286, Ford Transit Fire, Falck $160.00
#288, Superior Cadillac Ambulance $85.00
#288, Superior Cadillac Ambulance, Falck................$150.00
#289, Routemaster Bus, Esso, purple $750.00
#289, Routemaster Bus, Esso, red $100.00
#289, Routemaster Bus, Festival of London Stores.........$200.00
#289, Routemaster Bus, Madame Tussaud's.................$150.00
#289, Routemaster Bus, Silver Jubilee......................$40.00
#289, Routemaster Bus, Tern Shirts or Schwepps $150.00
#290, Double-Decker Bus $150.00
#290, SRN-6 Hovercraft $60.00
#291, Atlantean City Bus $70.00
#292, Atlantean City Bus, Regent or Ribble $150.00
#293, Swiss Postal Bus $60.00
#295, Atlantean City Bus, Yellow Pages $70.00
#296, Duple Luxury Coach $50.00
#296, Police Accident Unit..$100.00
#297, Silver Jubilee Bus, National or Woolworth.............$60.00
#298, Emergency Services Gift Set, minimum value...$8,000.00
#299, Crash Squad Gift Set $80.00
#299, Motorway Services Gift Set, minimum value $700.00
#299, Post Office Services Gift Set, minimum value......$650.00
#300, London Scene Gift Set $85.00
#302, Emergency Squad Gift Set................................$100.00
#303, Commando Gift Set $120.00
#304, Fire Rescue Gift Set $120.00
#305, David Brown Tractor $85.00
#308, Leyland 384 Tractor..$75.00
#309, Star Trek Gift Set...$150.00
#319, Week's Tipping Farm Trailer............................$40.00
#320, Halesowen Harvest Trailer $60.00
#321, Massey-Harris Manure Spreader $60.00
#322, Disc Harrow $50.00
#323, Triple Gang Mower $50.00
#324, Hay Rake $50.00
#325, David Brown Tractor & Harrow $135.00
#340, Land Rover...$85.00
#341, Land Rover Trailer...$40.00
#342, Austin Mini Moke $70.00
#342, Moto-Cart $75.00
#344, Estate Car $95.00
#344, Land Rover Pickup...$50.00
#350, Tony's Mini Moke $150.00
#351, UFO Interceptor $80.00
#352, Ed Straker's Car, red $100.00
#352, Ed Straker's Car, yel or gold-plated.....................$140.00
#353, Shado 2 Mobile $85.00
#354, Pink Panther $60.00
#355, Lunar Roving Vehicle.......................................$60.00
#357, Klingon Battle Cruiser $80.00
#358, USS Enterprise...$80.00

#359, Eagle Transporter $75.00
#360, Eagle Freighter $75.00
#361, Galactic War Chariot $75.00
#362, Trident Star Fighter $75.00
#363, Cosmic Zygon Patroller, for Marks & Spencer........$70.00
#364, NASA Space Shuttle, w/booster......................$100.00
#366, NASA Space Shuttle, w/no booster.......................$60.00
#367, Space Battle Cruiser....................................$80.00
#368, Zygon Marauder $80.00
#370, Dragster Set...$70.00
#371, USS Enterprise, sm version $60.00
#372, Klingon Battle Cruiser, sm version $60.00
#380, Convoy Skip Truck.....................................$30.00
#381, Convoy Farm Truck.....................................$30.00
#382, Wheelbarrow...$25.00
#382 Convoy Dumper...$30.00
#383, Convoy NCL Truck......................................$40.00
#384, Convoy Fire Rescue Truck $35.00
#384, Grass Cutter $25.00
#384, Sack Truck...$25.00
#385, Convoy Royal Mail Truck $40.00
#386, Lawn Mower $100.00
#389, Med Artillery Tractor..................................$100.00
#390, Customized Transit Van $50.00
#398, Farm Equipment Gift Set $2,000.00
#399, Farm Tractor & Trailer Set $200.00
#400, BEV Electric Truck......................................$70.00
#401, Coventry-Climax Fork Lift, orange $70.00
#401, Coventry-Climax Fork Lift, red.....................$500.00
#402, Bedford Coca-Cola Truck.............................$230.00
#404, Conveyancer Fork Lift $50.00
#405, Universal Jeep..$50.00
#406, Commer Articulated Truck............................$165.00
#407, Ford Transit..$60.00
#408, Big Ben Lorry, bl & yel, or bl & orange $350.00
#408, Big Ben Lorry, maroon & fawn $200.00
#408, Big Ben Lorry, pk & cream.......................$2,000.00
#409, Bedford Articulated Lorry $175.00
#410, Bedford Van, Danish Post or Simpsons.............$125.00
#410, Bedford Van, MJ Hire, Marley or Collectors' Gazette .$60.00
#410, Bedford Van, Royal Mail $40.00
#411, Bedford Truck...$140.00
#412, Bedford Van AA $60.00
#413, Austin Covered Wagon, lt & dk bl, or red & tan.$650.00
#413, Austin Covered Wagon, maroon & cream, or med & lt
     bl $200.00
#413, Austin Covered Wagon, red & gray, or bl or cream.$450.00
#414, Dodge Tipper, all colors other than Royal bl........$100.00
#414, Dodge Tipper, Royal bl.................................$175.00
#416, Ford Transit Van..$50.00
#416, Ford Transit Van, 1,000,000 Transits $200.00
#417, Ford Transit Van..$50.00
#417, Leyland Comet Lorry....................................$175.00
#418, Leyland Comet Lorry....................................$175.00
#419, Leyland Comet Cement Lorry........................$250.00
#420, Leyland Forward Control Lorry $125.00
#421, Hindle-Smart Electric Lorry $100.00
#422, Thames Flat Truck, bright gr.........................$200.00

#422, Thames Flat Truck, dk gr or red.....................$100.00
#425, Bedford TK Coal Lorry.................................$160.00
#428, Trailer, lg...$50.00
#429, Trailer..$45.00
#430, Breakdown Lorry, all colors other than tan & gr ..$1,000.00

#430, Breakdown Lorry, red and green, $1,000.00.

#430, Breakdown Lorry, tan & gr............................$175.00
#430, Johnson Dumper $60.00
#432, Foden Tipper $60.00
#432, Guy Warrior Flat Truck................................$400.00
#433, Guy Flat Truck w/Tailboard $350.00
#434, Bedford Crash Truck $125.00
#435, Bedford TK Tipper, gray or yel cab $100.00
#435, Bedford TK Tipper, wht, silver & bl $250.00
#436, Atlas COPCO Compressor Lorry....................$100.00
#437, Muir Hill Loader $50.00
#438, Ford D 800 Tipper, opening doors.................$50.00
#439, Ford D 800 Snow Plough & Tipper................$85.00
#440, Mobilgas Tanker $175.00
#441, Petrol Tanker, Castrol $175.00
#442, Land Rover Breakdown Crane $50.00
#442, Land Rover Breakdown Crane, Falck..............$70.00
#442, Petrol Tanker, Esso......................................$175.00
#443, Petrol Tanker, National Benzole.....................$175.00
#449, Chevrolet El Camino Pickup $120.00
#449, Johnson Road Sweeper $70.00
#450, Bedford TK Box Van, Castrol $150.00
#451, Johnston Road Sweeper, opening doors $70.00
#451, Trojan Van, Dunlop......................................$175.00
#452, Trojan Van, Chivers.....................................$175.00
#454, Trojan Van Cydrax $175.00
#455, Trojan Van, Brooke Bond Tea $175.00
#470, Austin Van, Shell-BP $175.00
#475, Ford Model T $100.00
#476, Morris Oxford $100.00
#477, Parsley's Car $100.00
#480, Bedford Van, Kodak $160.00
#481, Bedford Van, Ovaltine $160.00
#482, Bedford Van, Dinky Toys $175.00

#485, Ford Model T w/Santa Claus..................\$150.00
#486, Morris Oxford, Dinky Beats.....................\$150.00
#490, Electric Dairy Van, Express Dairy \$100.00
#491, Electric Dairy Van, NCB or Job Dairies.....\$150.00
#492, Election Mini Van.....................................\$350.00
#492, Loudspeaker Van \$125.00
#500, Citroen 2-CV...\$65.00
#501, Citroen Police, DS-19 ....\$100.00
#501, Foden Diesel 8-Wheel, 2nd cab \$600.00

#502, Foden Flat Truck, \$1,000.00.

#503, Foden Flat Truck, 1st cab.................\$1,200.00
#503, Foden Flat Truck, 2nd cab, bl & orange \$400.00
#503, Foden Flat Truck, 2nd cab, bl & yel \$1,200.00
#503, Foden Flat Truck, 2nd cab, 2-tone gr........\$3,000.00
#504, Foden Tanker, red.................................\$800.00
#504, Foden Tanker, 1st cab, 2-tone bl.........\$500.00
#504, Foden Tanker, 2nd cab, red.................\$600.00
#504, Foden Tanker, 2nd cab, 2-tone bl.........\$3,500.00
#505, Foden Flat Truck w/Chains, 1st cab.....\$3,000.00
#505, Foden Flat Truck w/Chains, 2nd cab \$450.00
#505, Maserati 2000 ....\$135.00
#506, Aston Martin \$125.00
#509, Fiat 850 ....\$55.00
#510, Peugeot 204..\$60.00
#511, Guy 4-Ton Lorry, red, gr or brn..........\$900.00
#511, Guy 4-Ton Lorry, 2-tone bl..................\$350.00
#512, Guy Flat Truck, all colors other than bl or red \$750.00
#512, Guy Flat Truck, bl or red......................\$400.00
#512, Lesko Kart \$125.00
#513, Guy Flat Truck w/Tailboard..................\$400.00
#514, Alfa Romeo Giulia...................................\$85.00
#514, Guy Van, Lyons...................................\$2,000.00
#514, Guy Van, Slumberland..........................\$600.00
#514, Guy Van, Spratt's...................................\$600.00
#514, Guy Van, Weetabix............................\$3,500.00
#515, Ferrari 250 GT \$135.00
#517, Renault R8...\$95.00
#518, Renault 4L..\$50.00
#519, Simca 100...\$50.00
#520, Chrysler New Yorker \$225.00

#521, Bedford Articulated Lorry \$175.00
#522, Big Bedford Lorry, bl & yel..................\$350.00
#522, Big Bedford Lorry, maroon & fawn \$200.00
#522, Citroen DS-19 ....\$225.00
#523, Simca 1500..\$60.00
#524, Panhard 24-CT..\$75.00
#524, Renault Dauphine.................................\$145.00
#525, Peugeot 403-U...\$90.00
#526, Mercedes-Benz 190-SL........................\$180.00
#527, Alfa Romeo 1900....................................\$110.00
#529, Vespa 2-CV...\$125.00
#530, Citroen DS-23..\$60.00
#531, Leyland Comet Lorry, all colors other than bl or brn .\$250.00
#531, Leyland Comet Lorry, bl or brn...........\$500.00
#531, Leyland Comet Lorry, orange & bl \$250.00
#532, Bedford Comet Lorry w/Tailboard \$250.00
#532, Lincoln Premiere....................................\$225.00
#533, Leyland Cement Wagon........................\$200.00
#533, Peugeot...\$100.00
#534, BMW 1500...\$90.00
#535, Citroen 2-CV..\$60.00
#538, Buick Roadmaster \$300.00
#538, Renault 16-TX..\$45.00
#539, Citroen ID-19..\$110.00
#540, Opel Kadett..\$65.00
#541, Simca Versailles.....................................\$130.00
#542, Simca Taxi..\$125.00
#543, Renault Floride.......................................\$125.00
#545, De Soto Diplomat...................................\$150.00
#546, Austin-Healey..\$200.00
#548, Fiat 1800 Familiare \$100.00
#550, Chrysler Saratoga..................................\$275.00
#551, Ford Taunus, Polizei \$175.00
#551, Rolls Royce \$285.00
#551, Trailer...\$60.00
#552, Chevrolet Corvair...................................\$120.00
#555, Fire Engine, w/extension ladder \$135.00
#555, Ford Thunderbird \$200.00
#556, Citroen Ambulance................................\$150.00
#558, Citroen..\$95.00
#559, Ford Taunus...\$95.00
#561, Blaw-Knox Bulldozer.............................\$100.00
#561, Blaw-Knox Bulldozer, plastic...............\$500.00
#561, Citroen Van, Gervais \$225.00
#561, Renault Mail Car.....................................\$65.00
#562, Muir-Hill Dumper....................................\$80.00
#563, Blaw-Knox Heavy Tractor.....................\$100.00
#563, Estafette Pickup......................................\$90.00
#564, Armagnac Caravan \$70.00
#564, Elevator Loader......................................\$100.00
#566, Citroen Police Van.................................\$130.00
#568, Ladder Truck...\$150.00
#569, Dump Truck...\$165.00
#570, Peugeot Van...\$75.00
#571, Coles Mobile Crane................................\$140.00
#572, Dump Truck, Berliet...............................\$140.00
#576, Panhard Tanker, Esso \$350.00
#577, Simca Van, Bailly \$200.00

#578, Simca Dump Truck..$165.00
#580, Dump Truck...$135.00
#581, Container Truck, Bailly....................................$200.00
#581, Horse Box, British Railway..............................$200.00
#581, Horse Box, Express Horse Van..........................$800.00
#582, Pullman Car Transporter..................................$160.00
#584, Covered Truck...$135.00
#585, Dumper..$135.00
#587, Citroen Van, Philips...$110.00
#589, Berliet Wrecker...$135.00
#590, City Road Signs Set..$70.00
#591, AEC Tanker, Shell...$225.00
#591, Country Road Signs Set.......................................$70.00
#592, Gas Pumps, Esso..$80.00
#593, Road Signs Set..$45.00
#595, Crane..$265.00
#595, Traffic Signs Set...$45.00
#597, Fork Lift...$80.00
#601, Austin Para Moke...$85.00
#602, Armoured Command Car.....................................$50.00
#603, Army Personnel, box of 12................................$125.00
#604, Land Rover Bomb Disposal Unit........................$70.00
#609, 105mm Howitzer & Gun Crew............................$50.00
#612, Commando Jeep...$50.00
#615, US Jeep & 105mm Howitzer...............................$60.00
#616, AEC Articulated Transporter & Tank...............$110.00
#617, VW KDF w/Antitank Gun....................................$75.00
#618, AEC Articulated Transporter & Helicopter........$100.00
#619, Bren Gun Carrier & Antitank Gun.....................$65.00
#620, Berliet Missile Launcher..................................$140.00
#621, 3-Ton Army Wagon...$100.00
#622, Bren Gun Carrier..$50.00
#622, 10-Ton Army Truck...$140.00
#623, Army Covered Wagon..$80.00
#625, 6-Pounder Antitank Gun.....................................$40.00
#626, Military Ambulance...$100.00
#640, Bedford Military Truck......................................$300.00
#641, Army 1-Ton Cargo Truck.....................................$75.00
#642, RAF Pressure Refueller.....................................$130.00
#643, Army Water Carrier...$110.00
#650, Light Tank...$160.00
#651, Centurion Tank...$120.00
#654, Mobile Gun..$50.00
#656, 88mm Gun...$50.00
#660, Tank Transporter...$130.00
#661, Recovery Tractor...$150.00
#662, Static 88mm Gun & Crew.....................................$60.00
#665, Honest John Missile Erector.............................$175.00
#666, Missile Erector Vehicle w/Corporal Missile & Launching
    Platform..$350.00
#667, Armoured Patrol Car...$50.00
#667, Missile Servicing Platform Vehicle...................$250.00
#668, Foden Army Truck...$50.00
#670, Armoured Car..$65.00
#671, MKI Corvette (boat)..$40.00
#671, Reconnaissance Car..$165.00
#672, OSA Missile Boat...$40.00
#673, Scout Car..$50.00

#674, Austin Champ, olive drab....................................$60.00
#674, Austin Champ, wht, UN version.........................$500.00
#674, Coast Guard Missile Launch................................$45.00
#675, Motor Patrol Boat..$45.00
#676, Armoured Personnel Carrier...............................$80.00
#676, Daimler Armoured Car, w/speedwheels...............$60.00
#677, Armoured Command Vehicle..............................$110.00
#677, Task Force Set..$100.00
#678, Air Sea Rescue..$60.00
#680, Ferret Armoured Car...$60.00
#681, DUKW..$60.00
#682, Stalwart Load Carrier..$60.00
#683, Chieftain Tank..$55.00
#686, 25-Pounder Field Gun..$40.00
#687, Convoy Army Truck...$25.00
#687, Trailer...$35.00
#688, Field Artillery Tractor...$60.00
#690, Mobile Antiaircraft Gun....................................$100.00
#690, Scorpion Tank...$50.00
#691, Striker Antitank Vehicle.....................................$60.00
#692, Leopard Tank...$60.00
#692, 5.5 Med Gun...$60.00
#693, 7.2 Howitzer...$60.00
#694, Hanomag Tank Destroyer.....................................$60.00
#695, Howitzer & Tractor..$250.00
#696, Leopard Antiaircraft Tank...................................$60.00
#697, 25-Pounder Field Gun Set...................................$150.00
#698, Tank Transporter & Tank...................................$230.00
#699, Leopard Recovery Tank..$70.00
#699, Military Gift Set...$400.00
#700, Spitfire MKII RAF Jubilee..................................$150.00
#701, Shetland Flying Boat..$650.00
#702, DH Comet Jet Airliner.......................................$200.00
#704, Avro York Airliner...$175.00
#705, Viking Airliner..$100.00
#706, Vickers Viscount Airliner, Air France.................$150.00
#708, Vickers Viscount Airliner, BEA..........................$150.00
#710, Beechcraft S35 Bonanza......................................$85.00
#712, US Army T-42A..$85.00
#715, Beechcraft C-55 Baron...$60.00
#715, Bristol 173 Helicopter...$85.00
#716, Westland Sikorsky Helicopter..............................$90.00
#717, Boeing 737...$85.00
#718, Hawker Hurricane..$85.00
#719, Spitfire MKII..$85.00
#721, Junkers Stuka..$80.00
#722, Hawker Harrier..$80.00
#723, Hawker Executive Jet...$60.00
#724, Sea King Helicopter...$75.00
#725, Phantom II...$100.00
#726, Messerschmitt, desert camouflage.....................$100.00
#726, Messerschmitt, gray & gr...................................$200.00
#727, US Air Force F-4 Phantom II..............................$300.00
#728, RAF Dominie..$80.00
#729, Multi-Role Combat Aircraft.................................$75.00
#730, US Navy Phantom...$100.00
#731, SEPECAT Jaguar..$80.00
#731, Twin-Engine Fighter..$60.00

#732, Bell Police Helicopter, M*A*S*H........................$100.00
#732, Bell Police Helicopter, wht & bl $60.00
#733, German Phantom II...$200.00
#733, Lockhead Shooting Star Fighter.........................$50.00
#734, Submarine Swift...$60.00
#735, Glouster Javelin $60.00
#736, Bundesmarine Sea King..................................$90.00
#736, Hawker Hunter $60.00
#737, P1B Lightning Fighter $90.00
#738, DH110 Sea Vixen Fighter $70.00
#739, Zero-Sen...$100.00
#741, Spitfire MKII...$100.00
#749, RAF Avro Vulcan Bomber $3,500.00
#750, Call Telephone Box..$50.00
#751, Lawn Mower $100.00
#752, Goods Yard Crane..$70.00
#752, Police Box $50.00
#755, Standard Lamp, single arm $30.00
#756, Standard Lamp, dbl arm..................................$30.00
#760, Pillar Box...$40.00
#766, British Road Signs, Country Set A $100.00
#767, British Road Signs, Country Set B $100.00
#768, British Road Signs, Town Set A $100.00
#769, British Road Signs, Town Set B $100.00
#770, Road Signs, set of 12 ....$150.00
#771, International Road Signs, set of 12 ....$160.00
#772, British Road Signs, set of 24 ....$200.00
#773, Traffic Signal..$30.00
#777, Belisha Beacon $30.00
#781, Petrol Pumping Station, Esso $100.00
#782, Petrol Pumping Station, Shell $80.00
#784, Dinky Goods Train Set....................................$80.00
#785, Service Station $200.00
#786, Tire Rack..$50.00
#787, Lighting Kit...$40.00
#796, Healey Sports Boat...$65.00
#798, Express Passenger Train..................................$170.00
#801, Mini USS Enterprise.......................................$60.00
#802, Mini Klingon Cruiser......................................$60.00
#815, Panhard Armoured Tank..................................$150.00
#817, AMX 13-Ton Tank $125.00
#822, M3 Half-Track...$150.00
#893, UNIC Pipe-Line Transporter............................$275.00
#894, UNIC Boilot Car Transporter...........................$275.00
#900, Building Site Gift Set......................................$1,500.00
#901, Guy 4-Ton Lorry, see #501
#902, Foden Flat Truck, see #502
#903, Foden Flat Truck w/Tailboard, see #503
#905, Foden Flat Truck w/Chains $450.00
#911, Guy 4-Ton Lorry, see #511
#912, Guy Flat Truck, see #512
#913, Guy Flat Truck w/Tailboard, see #513
#914, AEC Articulated Lorry.....................................$150.00
#915, AEC Flat Trailer..$100.00
#917, Guy Van, Spratts $350.00
#917, Mercedes Benz Truck & Trailer $120.00
#917, Mercedes Benz Truck & Trailer, Munsterland $300.00
#918, Guy Van, Ever Ready $500.00

#919, Guy Van, Golden Shred...................................$1,000.00
#920, Guy Warrior Van, Heinz $3,000.00
#921, Bedford Articulated Lorry $175.00
#922, Big Bedford Lorry..$175.00

#923, Big Bedford Van, Heinz Baked Beans can, $600.00.

#923, Big Bedford Van, Heinz Ketchup bottle $2,000.00
#924, Aveling-Barford Dumper..................................$110.00
#925, Leyland Dump Truck.......................................$235.00
#930, Bedford Pallet-Jekta Van, Dinky Toys $250.00
#931, Leyland Comet Lorry, all colors other than bl & brn .$200.00
#931, Leyland Comet Lorry, bl & brn.........................$500.00
#932, Leyland Comet Wagon w/Tailboard $200.00
#933, Leyland Comet Wagon.....................................$200.00
#934, Leyland Octopus Wagon, all colors other than bl &
        brn $300.00
#934, Leyland Octopus Wagon, bl & yel.....................$2,000.00
#936, Leyland 8-Wheel Test Chassis $150.00
#940, Mercedes Benz Truck $85.00
#943, Leyland Octopus Tanker, Esso $300.00
#944, Shell-BP Fuel Tanker $300.00
#944, Shell-BP Fuel Tanker, red wheels $500.00
#945, AEC Fuel Tanker, Esso....................................$150.00
#945, AEC Fuel Tanker, Lucas $150.00
#948, Tractor-Trailer, McLean $365.00
#949, Wayne School Bus..$350.00
#950, Foden S20 Fuel Tanker, Burmah.......................$100.00
#950, Foden S20 Fuel Tanker, Shell $100.00
#951, Trailer...$50.00
#952, Vega Major Luxury Coach $140.00
#953, Continental Touring Coach..............................$400.00
#954, Fire Station $300.00
#954, Vega Major Luxury Coach, no lights $130.00
#955, Fire Engine $140.00
#956, Turntable Fire Escape, Bedford $125.00
#956, Turntable Fire Escape, Berliet $225.00
#957, Fire Services Gift Set......................................$600.00
#958, Snow Plough...$260.00
#959, Foden Dump Truck...$175.00

#960, Lorry-Mounted Concrete Mixer...........................$125.00
#961, Blaw-Knox Bulldozer, see #561
#961, Vega Major Luxury Coach $250.00
#962, Muir-Hill Dumper...$80.00
#963, Blaw-Knox Heavy Tractor....................................$100.00
#963, Road Grader $75.00
#964, Elevator Loader $100.00
#965, Euclid Rear Dump Truck $80.00
#965, Terex Dump Truck $275.00
#966, Marrel Multi-Bucket Unit.....................................$130.00
#967, BBC TV Mobile Control Room $250.00
#967, Muir-Hill Loader & Trencher $80.00
#968, BBC TV Roving Eye Vehicle................................$260.00
#969, BBC TV Extending Mast Vehicle.........................$275.00
#970, Jones Cantilever Crane $100.00
#971, Coles Mobile Crane..$145.00
#972, Coles 20-Ton Lorry, mounted crane, yel & blk $200.00
#972, Coles 20-Ton Lorry, mounted crane, yel & orange..$130.00
#973, Eaton Yale Tractor Shovel $80.00
#973, Goods Yard Crane $90.00
#974, AEC Hoyner Transporter......................................$110.00
#975, Ruston Bucyrus Excavator....................................$375.00
#976, Michigan Tractor Dozer...$75.00
#977, Commercial Servicing Platform Vehicle $250.00
#977, Shovel Dozer...$75.00
#978, Refuse Wagon..$100.00
#979, Racehorse Transporter...$400.00
#980, Coles Hydra Truck...$85.00
#980, Horse Box, British Railways $200.00
#980, Horse Box Express $800.00
#984, Atlas Digger $85.00
#984, Car Carrier..$225.00
#985, Trailer for Car Carrier $125.00
#986, Mighty Antar Low Loader w/Propeller $400.00
#987, ABC TV Control Room..$375.00
#988, ABC TV Transmitter Van $375.00

#989, Car Carrier, Auto Transporters, $2,000.00.

#990, Pullman Car Transporter w/4 Cars $2,500.00
#991, AEC Tanker, Shell Chemicals............................$225.00
#992, Avro Vulcan Delta Wing Bomber $3,000.00
#994, Loading Ramp for #992 ....$30.00
#997, Caravelle, Air France $300.00
#998, Bristol Britannia Canadian Pacific.......................$300.00
#999, DH Comet Jet..$225.00

Disney

Through the magic of the silver screen, Walt Disney's characters have come to life, and it is virtually impossible to imagine a child growing up without the influence of his genius. As each classic film was introduced, toy manufacturers scurried to fill department store shelves with the dolls, games, battery-ops, and windups that carried the likeness of every member of its cast. Though today it is the toys of the 1930s and 1940s that are bringing exorbitant prices, later toys are certainly collectible as well, as you'll see in our listings. Even characters as recently introduced as Roger Rabbit already have their own cult following.

For more information we recommend *Character Toys and Collectibles, First and Second Series*, and *Antique & Collectible Toys, 1870–1950*, by David Longest; *Stern's Guide to Disney Collectibles* by Michael Stern (there are three in the series); *The Collector's Encyclopedia of Disneyana* by Michael Stern and David Longest; *Disneyana* by Cecil Munsey (Hawthorne Books, 1974); *Disneyana* by Robert Heide and John Gilman; *Walt Disney's Mickey Mouse Memorabilia* by Hillier and Shine (Abrams Inc., 1986); *Tomart's Disneyana Update Magazine*; and *Elmer's Price Guide to Toys* by Elmer Duellman (L-W Books).

Advisors: Joel J. Cohen (C12); Don Hamm (H10), Rocketeer.

See also Battery-Operated; Books; Bubble Bath Containers; Character and Promotional Drinking Glasses; Character Clocks and Watches; Chein; Coloring, Activity, and Paint Books; Dakins; Fisher-Price; Games; Lunch Boxes; Marx; Paper Dolls; Pez Dispensers; Pin-Back Buttons; Plastic Figures; Pin-Back Buttons; Puppets; Puzzles; Ramp Walkers; Records; Sand Toy; Toothbrush Holders; View-Master; Western; Windups, Friction, and Other Mechanicals.

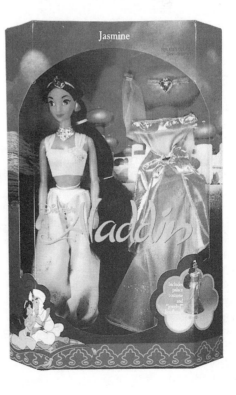

Aladdin, doll, Jasmine, Mattel, 1992, 8", MIB, $25.00.

Aladdin, doll, Arabian Lights Jasmine, Mattel, 1993, MIB .$30.00

Aladdin, doll, Genie, Mattel, 1992, stuffed cloth w/vinyl head, 11", MIB..$25.00

Aladdin, doll, Genie or Prince Ali, Applause, vinyl w/cloth clothes, 10", MIB, F1, ea.....................................$15.00

Aladdin, doll, Jasmine, Mattel, 1993, stuffed plush w/vinyl head, 14", MIB..$20.00

Aladdin, doll, Prince Ali, Mattel, 1992, 8", MIB.............$25.00

Aladdin, figure, any character, Mattel, 5", MOC, F1, ea..$10.00

Aladdin, Jasmine Gift Pack, Mattel, 1993, MIB.............$125.00

Aladdin, Water Jewel Magic Gift Set, Mattel, 1994, MIB..$65.00

Alice in Wonderland, bank, Leeds, NM, S21.................$175.00

Alice in Wonderland, figure, March Hare, Marx, 1960s, plastic w/bendable arms & legs, cloth clothes, 6", scarce, EX, M8..$75.00

Alice in Wonderland, Stitch-A-Story, Hasbro, 1969, complete, NMIB...$25.00

Alice in Wonderland, tea set, Plasco, emb plastic, 11 pcs, M (EX box mk Tea Time Dishes), A......................$75.00

Alice in Wonderland, tea set, WDP, 1960s, china, various images, 11 pcs, MIB, P6.....................................$150.00

Aristocats, doll, Duchess, 1970, stuffed plush, 15", NM ...$50.00

Babes in Toyland, doll, Toyland Soldier, Gundikins, 1961, plush w/rubber head, 9½", scarce, EX, M8 ....$40.00

Bambi, Colorforms, 1966, complete, NMIB.....................$20.00

Bambi, doll, Steiff, velvet w/blk glass eyes, 5½", M........$150.00

Bambi, doll, Steiff, velvet w/blk glass eyes, 9", M $225.00

Bambi, figure, Bambi & Thumper, Leonardi/England, 1940s, chalkware, 9x6", EX, A $200.00

Bambi, figure, Thumper, Am Pottery, 1930s, ceramic, 4", NM, M8...$75.00

Beauty & the Beast, doll, Beast, Mattel, 1993, plush w/cloth clothes, NMIB $30.00

Big Bad Wolf, see Three Little Pigs

Cinderella, bank, Leeds, NM, S21....................................$85.00

Cinderella, doll, WDP, 1950, stuffed cloth w/yarn hair, NM .$350.00

Cinderella, dolls, Cinderella & Prince Charming, Effanbee, hard plastic, orig wrist tags, 14", EX, pr...........................$350.00

Cinderella, wastebasket, 1950s, metal, tells story w/graphics, 19x10" dia, EX, A..$50.00

Disney, embroidery set, features Snow White, Donald, Mickey, Ferdinand, etc, complete, EX (EX box), M8.............$85.00

Disney, Ex-Pan-Dees, 1960s, sponge toy featuring Mickey, Minnie, Pluto, Goofy, Donald & Daisy, MIB (sealed), M17 ....$50.00

Disney, Film Strip Lantern, Johnson of Hendon, mk WD — Mickey Mouse Ltd, EX (EX box) $225.00

Disney, Movie Studio To Color & Erect, WDE, 1939, complete, EX (EX box) $200.00

Disney, tea set, Beswick of England, 1940s, features Pluto, Figaro, Bambi & Thumper, 4 pcs, M, M8 ....$155.00

Disney, top, Chein, 1973, various characters on blue and white striped top, tin, 6" dia, NM, $50.00. (Photo courtesy Linda Baker)

Disney, top, 1934, Disney characters playing instruments, litho tin, 10" dia, VG, A...$450.00

Disneyland, Character Play World, fold-away, unused, MIB, J2...$125.00

Disneyland, Safety Blocks, Halsam, wood, EX (EX box)..$200.00

Disneyland, scrapbook, Whitman, 1955, softcover, unused, scarce, EX, M17 ....$50.00

Disneyland, tea set, 1950s, litho tin, features several characters, 14 pcs, MIB, D10...$250.00

Disneyland, xylophone, Original Concert Grand, w/music stand, MIB, P6...$135.00

Donald Duck, bank, Donald & Nephews on TV, Brechner, NM, S21...$85.00

Donald Duck, bank, Donald holding life bouy w/rope, WDE, 1938, compo, 6½", VG, A $150.00

Donald Duck, bank, Donald in Santa suit, Leeds, NM...$300.00

Donald Duck, bank, Donald waving, Japan, 1960s, ceramic, 6", M, J6...$50.00

Donald Duck, crib toy, compo w/wire arms & legs, EX ..$225.00

Donald Duck, doctor kit, WDP, 1940s, EX (EX box).....$125.00

Donald Duck, doll, Dancing Donald, Hasbro, 1977, stuffed cloth w/vinyl head, squeeze hands for action, 18", EX $35.00

Disney, Magic Erasable Pictures, 1950s, Transogram, 1950s, unused, MIB, $50.00. (Photo courtesy David Longest and Michael Stern)

Donald Duck, doll, Knickerbocker, 1930s, dressed as drum major, stuffed felt, 9", rare, NM $1,400.00

Donald Duck, doll, Knickerbocker, 1936, stuffed cloth, EX, D10, from $650 to $850.00

Donald Duck, figure, Borgfeldt, 1935, celluloid, 5", EX, J2..$1,000.00

Donald Duck, figure, Fun-E-Flex, wood, sledding, M..$1,500.00

Donald Duck, figure, Japan, 1930s, bsk, bugler, 3", NM, M8..$125.00

Donald Duck, figure, Japan, 1930s, bsk, Donald on scooter, EX $250.00

Donald Duck, figure, Japan, 1930s, bsk, hands on hips, long bill, 4½", rare, NM, M8..$450.00

Donald Duck, figure, Japan, 1930s, bsk, head turned right, long bill, 2", EX, M8 ....$65.00

Donald Duck, figure, Japan, 1930s, bsk, movable arms, 6", EX, A..$475.00

Donald Duck, figure, Japan, 1930s, bsk, walking w/bill up, 3", NM, M8 ....$85.00

Donald Duck, figure, Japan, 1930s, bsk, 2", NM, M8 ....$75.00

Donald Duck, figure, Jumpkins, Kohner, 1960s, plastic figure on string, 5", MOC, H4 ....$70.00

Donald Duck, hat, mesh w/vinyl beak, rolls eyes & quacks when squeezed, 10", rare, EX, A..$125.00

Donald Duck, jack-in-the-box, early, celluloid, NM $850.00

Donald Duck, magic slate, Whitman, 1970s, NM, J6 ....$25.00

Donald Duck, paint box, Transogram, 1948, Donald painting on cover, litho tin, EX, M8..$50.00

Donald Duck, jack-in-the-box, Spear, composition figure with felt clothes, EX, $275.00. (Photo courtesy Michael Stern)

Donald Duck, pencil sharpener, Japan, prewar, celluloid figure, 3", NM, A $350.00

Donald Duck, pull toy, Chad Valley, 1930s, Donald in rowboat, paper litho on wood, 12", NM, A $575.00

Donald Duck, pull toy, Donald Duck Ice Cream Wagon, Marjay, litho wood, 9", scarce, NM (NM box), A................$400.00

Donald Duck, roly poly, jtd celluloid figure sitting atop, 4", EX $325.00

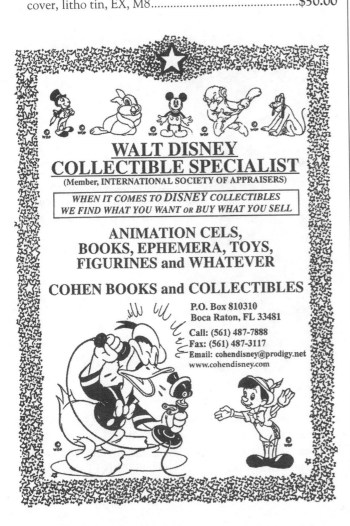

Donald Duck, tea set, lithographed tin, six pieces, NMIB, D10, from $250.00 to $350.00. (Photo courtesy Dunbar Gallery)

Donald Duck, sweeper, Ohio Art/WDE, litho wood, EX..$125.00
Donald Duck, telephone/bank, NN Hill Brass/WDE, 1930s, red-pnt metal w/Mickey figure behind dial, EX $500.00

Donald Duck, watering can, Ohio Art, WDE, 1938, lithographed tin, 3", NM, $350.00. (Photo courtesy David Longest and Michael Stern)

Donald Duck, Weebles figure, 1973, EX, J6......................$15.00
Donald Duck, Whirl-A-Tune Music Maker, Ideal, 1965, NMIB, M17..$80.00
Donald Duck & Minnie Mouse, sweeper, Ohio Art/WDE, 1930s, litho tin w/wood hdl, EX............................$225.00
Donald Duck & Pluto, figure, celluloid, Pluto pulling Donald on sled, 4", EX, A $475.00
Ducktales, Colorforms, 1986, NMIB, B10 ....$15.00

Ferdinand the Bull, figure, 1930s, chalkware, EX, minimum value $100.00. (Photo courtesy David Longest and Michael Stern)

Dumbo, bank, Leeds, NM, S21...$85.00
Dumbo, doll, Cameo Doll Prod, 1941, compo w/cloth ears, 8", EX, A...$300.00
Dumbo, doll, compo w/felt ears & celluloid eyes, orig decal, 8", EX..$275.00
Dumbo, doll, 1940s, stuffed plush w/celluloid eyes, EX ..$125.00
Elmer the Elephant, bank, Japan/WDP, 1930s, bsk figure, rare, NM, from $300 to...$400.00
Fantasia, figure, Centaurette, Vernon Kilns, 1940, ceramic, blond version, 5", M, A...$800.00
Fantasia, figure, Pegasus, Vernon Kilns, 1940, ceramic, 4¾", M, A...$350.00
Fantasia, figure, Unicorn, Vernon Kilns, 1940, ceramic, 5½", M, A...$525.00
Ferdinand the Bull, doll, Knickerbocker, compo, 10", NM.$575.00
Ferdinand the Bull, figure, Japan, 1930s, bsk, 3", VG, M8..$45.00
Ferdinand the Bull, Put the Tail on Ferdinand the Bull Party Game, Whitman/WDE, 1938, complete, EX (EX box) .$85.00
Figaro, see Pinocchio
Goofy, bank, Goofy Gone Fishing, WDP/Japan, compo, NM, S21 ....$25.00
Goofy, doll, Merry Thoughts/England, stuffed cloth, 12", EX $75.00
Goofy, figure, Japan, 1930s, bsk, 2", EX, M8.....................$75.00
Goofy, figure, Jumpkins, Kohner, 1960s, plastic figure on string, 5", MOC, H4 ....$70.00
Goofy, Weebles figure, 1973, EX, J6.................................$15.00

Horace Horsecollar, figure, Fun-E-Flex, wood with rope tail, rare, EX, $1,000.00.
(Photo courtesy David Longest and Michael Stern)

Horace Horsecollar, figure, Japan, 1930s, bsk, 3½", VG, M8..$110.00
Hunchback of Notre Dame, Colorforms, MIB (sealed), B10 ....$10.00
Hunchback of Notre Dame, doll, Quasimodo, Phoebus, Frollo or Esmarelda, Applause, 1996, vinyl, 9", MIB, F1, ea $12.00
Hunchback of Notre Dame, figure set, Applause, 1996, PVC, set of 6, 3", M, F1 ....$20.00

Jiminy Cricket, see Pinocchio

Jungle Book, doll, Baloo, Japan, stuffed velvet & felt, 6", NM, G16 ....$50.00

Jungle Book, Ex-Pan-Dees Instant Sponge Toy, James Industries, 1966, unused, MIB, H4 ....$30.00

Lady & the Tramp, Colorforms Cartoon Kit, 1962, complete, NMIB $35.00

Lady & the Tramp, figure, Peg, Hagen-Renaker, 1950s, 2", NM, M8 ....$165.00

Lady & the Tramp, figures, Lady & Tramp, Schuco, Noah's Ark, 1950s, 2½" & 3", NM (NM separate boxes), G16...$450.00

Lady & the Tramp, pull toy, Tramp, 1950s, hard plastic figure on platform, NM, from $200 to $300.00

Lady & the Tramp, wallet, WDP, 1950s, red vinyl, NM, from $30 to $40.00

Lion King, Colorforms, 1994, NMIB, B10 ....$8.00

Mary Poppins, tea set, 1964, plastic, MIB, P6 ....$100.00

Mickey Mouse, banjo, Noble & Cooley, EX $400.00

Mickey Mouse, bank, Mickey standing next to treasure chest, Crown/WD, 1938, compo, trap door on base, 6", EX, A.$650.00

Mickey Mouse, bank, Mickey waving, Japan, 1960s, ceramic, 6", M, J6 ....$50.00

Mickey Mouse, bank, Zell Products, 1934, leatherette book shape, 4x3", EX, M8 ....$175.00

Mickey Mouse, Big Little Set, WDE, 1930s, complete, EX (EX box), from $75 to $100.00

Mickey Mouse, camera, Ensign, 1930s, box type, VG (G box) $325.00

Mickey Mouse, camera, Mick-A-Matic, plastic head figure w/flash cube on top, MIB $50.00

Mickey Mouse, Candy Factory, Remco, 1973, NMIB, F8.$75.00

Mickey Mouse, cane, WDE, 1933, wood w/compo Mickey figure on hdl, 32", scarce, EX, A $400.00

Mickey Mouse, Colorforms, box lid pictures Pluto licking Mickey's face, MIB, A $45.00

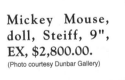

Mickey Mouse, doll, Steiff, 9", EX, $2,800.00.
(Photo courtesy Dunbar Gallery)

Mickey Mouse, crib toy, wood figure w/bells as hands, EX..$175.00

Mickey Mouse, doll, Dean's Rag, 5", EX $700.00

Mickey Mouse, doll, Hasbro, 1975, squeeze hands & he walks, 20", VG, M15 ....$25.00

Mickey Mouse, doll, Horsman, 1980s, 50 Year Anniversary, talker, stuffed cloth, MIB $65.00

Mickey Mouse, doll, Knickerbocker, 1930s, Mickey as band leader, EX $2,000.00

Mickey Mouse, doll, Knickerbocker, 1930s, no tail version, stuffed cloth w/felt ears, compo shoes, 12", EX, A...$500.00

Mickey Mouse, doll, Knickerbocker, 1936, cloth & compo, 12", EX, D10, from $500 to $700.00

Mickey Mouse, doll, Sun Rubber, 1950s, 10", VG, M15 ..$65.00

Mickey Mouse, doll, 1930s, stuffed printed fabric, standing w/hands on hips, 6", NM+, A $100.00

Mickey Mouse, doll, 1930s, stuffed sateen w/felt ears & gloves, velveteen head & boots, leatherette eyes, 19", EX, A $250.00

Mickey Mouse, dominoes, Halsam/WDE, 1935, complete, EX (EX box), from $275 to $375.00

Mickey Mouse, drum, Noble & Cooley/WDE, metal, image of Mickey playing drum, EX $175.00

Mickey Mouse, drum, Ohio Art, 1930s, tin & paper, 6" dia, scarce, NM, M8 ....$450.00

Mickey Mouse, figure, Germany, lead, w/umbrella, 5", EX, A.$1,400.00

Mickey Mouse, figure, Japan, prewar, celluloid, jtd, 5", EX, A.$200.00

Mickey Mouse, figure, Japan, 1930s, bsk, in nightshirt, 4", EX, M8 ....$135.00

Mickey Mouse, figure, Japan, 1930s, bsk, Mickey in canoe, 5", NM $2,000.00

Mickey Mouse, figure, Japan, 1930s, bsk, movable arms, 8½", NM $3,500.00

Mickey Mouse, figure, Japan, 1930s, bsk, playing drum, 3", EX, M8 ....$175.00

Mickey Mouse, figure, jtd wood w/compo head, lollipop hands, gr shorts & shoes, decal on chest, 9", VG, A $775.00

Mickey Mouse, figure, wood, Fun-E-Flex, w/decal, 5", scarce, NM, A $525.00

Mickey Mouse, figure, 1970s, bsk, Mickey on sled, 4", M, M8.$20.00

Mickey Mouse, figure, 1970s, bsk, Mickey w/kite, 4", M, M8 ..$20.00

Mickey Mouse, figure set, Japan, 1930s, bsk, Mickey as pitcher, catcher & batter, 3½", EX, A $550.00

Mickey Mouse, figure set, Japan, 1930s, bsk, Mickey w/sword, rifle & flag, 3" to 4", M, A $475.00

Mickey Mouse, flashlight, USA Lite, litho tin, EX (EX box) $1,500.00

Mickey Mouse, Funny Facts Electric Quiz Game, WDE, 1930s, complete, rare, EX, from $700 to $1,000.00

Mickey Mouse, gumball machine, Hasbro, 1968, head form on red base, NM $50.00

Mickey Mouse, Kodak Theatre, MIB, B5 ....$35.00

Mickey Mouse, mask, 1930s, blk litho on wht formed mesh canvas, EX, minimum value $125.00

Mickey Mouse, Movie Projector, Keystone, complete, EX (EX box) $650.00

Mickey Mouse, music box, Schmidt, 50th Birthday, Mickey as Magician, plays It's a Small World, M, P6 ....$75.00

Mickey Mouse, nodder, 1930s, ceramic, standing on base w/hands on hips, EX+, A $450.00

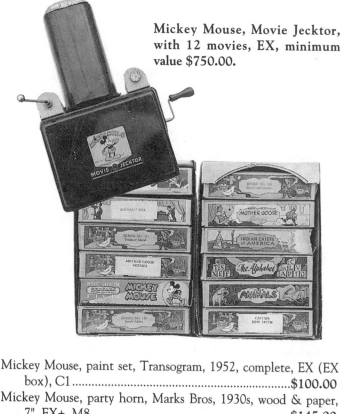

Mickey Mouse, Movie Jecktor, with 12 movies, EX, minimum value $750.00.

Mickey Mouse, paint set, Transogram, 1952, complete, EX (EX box), C1...$100.00

Mickey Mouse, party horn, Marks Bros, 1930s, wood & paper, 7", EX+, M8..$145.00

Mickey Mouse, piano, Marks Bros/WDE, 1930s, wood, 8 keys, EX, from $2,000 to...$3,000.00

Mickey Mouse, picture card album, 1930s, holds 1st 48 cards in the series, 10x6", VG, J5.................................$45.00

Mickey Mouse, Picture Printing Set, Fulton Specialty/WDE, 1935, complete, NMIB, from $300 to..................$400.00

Mickey Mouse, Pin the Tail on Mickey Party Game, Marks Bros, complete, EX (EX box) $125.00

Mickey Mouse, Posie doll, Ideal, 1950s, EX (EX box), J2.$50.00

Mickey Mouse, pull toy, Toy Kraft/WDE, 1935, dog pulling sleigh-type wagon w/image of Mickey, 15", EX $250.00

Mickey Mouse, pull toy, 1930s, wood wagon w/decal on 1 side, orig pull string & knob, 9", EX, A..........................$350.00

Mickey Mouse, rattle, Japan, 1930s, celluloid, 3 images of Mickey playing different instruments, 8", EX, A $125.00

Mickey Mouse, riding toy, Mengel/WDE, 1930s, wood, 16", rare, EX, A $650.00

Mickey Mouse, riding toy, Mickey Mouse Bus Lines, Gong Bell, 1955, litho tin & wood, 20", rare, EX (EX box), A..$1,400.00

Mickey Mouse, Rolatoy, WD, 1930s, celluloid w/rattle inside, NM, from $200 to...$300.00

Mickey Mouse, Rub 'N Play Magic Transfer Set, Colorforms, 1978, unused, MIB, C1 ....$30.00

Mickey Mouse, Safety Blocks, Halsam/WDE, 1930s, 20 pcs, EX (EX box), from $150 to $250.00

Mickey Mouse, saxophone, WDE, 1930s, NM, from $450 to...$650.00

Mickey Mouse, slot machine, Belgium, wood cabinet w/rnd glass dial front, Mickey Mouse pointer, 28", EX, A......$2,200.00

Mickey Mouse, Slugaroo, Gardner/WDP, complete & unused w/cb display sign, NMIB.................................$75.00

Mickey Mouse, sparkler, WD, Mickey's face w/name on bow tie, 5½", EX, A $450.00

Mickey Mouse, stove, Empire, metal, electric, EX.........$650.00

Mickey Mouse, sweeper, Ohio Art, 1930s, litho tin & wood, EX...$225.00

Mickey Mouse, Talkie Jecktor, Movie Jecktor Co, 1935, complete w/films, record & speaker horn, EX (EX box)..........$1,350.00

Mickey Mouse, tea set, Borgfeldt, head figure on teapot, 10 pcs, EX+, A...$450.00

Mickey Mouse, telephone, NN Hill Brass Co, marked Walt Disney, metal and wood with cardboard figure, 8", EX, $175.00.
(Photo courtesy Michael Stern)

Mickey Mouse, Tinkersand Pictures, Toy Tinkers Inc, complete, EX (EX box) $150.00

Mickey Mouse, tool chest, 1930s, lithographed metal, EX, $275.00. (Photo courtesy John Turney)

Mickey Mouse, top, WDE, 1935, litho tin w/image of various characters playing instruments, 9½" dia, VG $175.00

Mickey Mouse, Toy Lantern Outfit, England, 1930s, complete w/battery-op lantern & slides, EX (EX box), from $550 to $750.00

Mickey Mouse, wash tub, Chein, 1930s, image of Mickey & Minnie doing laundry & going on a picnic, tin, 5" dia, rare, NM..$225.00

Mickey Mouse, washing machine, Ohio Art, litho tin, rare, NM $750.00

Mickey Mouse, watering can, Ohio Art, 1930s, litho tin w/image of Mickey watering flowers, 5", EX $200.00

Mickey Mouse, Weebles figure, 1973, EX, J6 ....$15.00

Mickey Mouse, Weebles Magic Kingdom, Hasbro/Romper Room, 1974, MIB, J6......................................$125.00

Mickey Mouse, Yarn Sewing Set, Marks Bros, 1930s, complete, rare, EX (EX box), from $500 to $650.00

Mickey Mouse & Donald Duck, drum, WDE, 1930s, tin & paper, EX $350.00

Mickey Mouse & Donald Duck, figure, celluloid, arms wrapped in dancing pose, 3½", EX, A...............................$1,200.00

Mickey Mouse & Donald Duck, figure, Windsor/Canada, 1930s, bsk, Mickey & Donald in canoe, rare, EX, M8.....$1,350.00

Mickey Mouse & Donald Duck, magic slate, 1951, EX, J2 ..$25.00

Mickey Mouse & Donald Duck, pull toy, Chad Valley, Donald & Mickey in boat, wood, EX.....................................$425.00

Mickey Mouse & Donald Duck, telephone, WDE, 1938, litho tin w/cb diecut of Mickey & Donald, EX+, A $525.00

Mickey Mouse & Donald Duck, Weather Forecaster, hard plastic child's barometer, EX (EX box), from $175 to ...$275.00

Mickey Mouse & Minnie, figures, Japan, 1930s, bsk, sitting in chairs, Minnie in cloth dress, 3", pr, EX, A $225.00

Mickey Mouse & Minnie, figures, wood, Fun-E-Flex, w/decals, 3¾", EX, pr $85.00

Mickey Mouse & Minnie, party horn, Granger/Canada, litho cb, 7½", EX, A $100.00

Mickey Mouse & Minnie, party horn, Marks Bros/WDE, 1935, litho cb, 7", EX, A $165.00

Mickey Mouse & Minnie, playhouse, Andrews, 1934, litho cb w/pie-eyed Mickey & Minnie peering out windows, EX, A.....$225.00

Mickey Mouse & Minnie, scrapbook, 1930s, cover shows Minnie pasting Mickey's nose, 11x15", EX, J5 ....$145.00

Mickey Mouse & Minnie, tambourine, Noble Cooley/WDE, image of Minnie watching Mickey juggle, NM $300.00

Mickey Mouse & Minnie, tea set, mk WD Japan, 1936, lustreware w/caramel trim, service for 6, EX $335.00

Mickey Mouse & Pluto, night light/music box, classic 1950s TV screen design, NM, J8....................................$150.00

Mickey Mouse Club, Build-Up Blocks, Eldon, 1950s, complete, M (NM tower-like box), C1..............................$45.00

Mickey Mouse Club, card games, Jiminy Cricket & 2 Mickey Mouse Clubs, Russel Mfg, complete, EX (EX display box)..$100.00

Mickey Mouse Club, CB Radio, Durham Industries, 1977, MIB, J6..$25.00

Mickey Mouse Club, Clubhouse, Hasbro/Romper Room, 1970s, MIB, J6..$125.00

Mickey Mouse Club, Dance-A-Tune, Jaymar, complete, MIB.$125.00

Mickey Mouse Club, Loony-Kins, complete, NMIB, A .$150.00

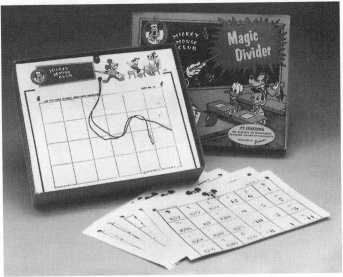

Mickey Mouse Club, Magic Divider, Jaymar, complete, NMIB, minimum value $35.00. (Photo courtesy Michael Stern)

Mickey Mouse and Minnie, tea set, Ohio Art, 1930s, marked Walt Disney, lithographed tin, complete, NMIB, $500.00. (Photo courtesy David Longest and Michael Stern)

Mickey Mouse Club, Mousegetar Jr, Mattel, 1950s, plastic 4-string w/crank, EX, M8...............................$200.00

Mickey Mouse Club, Mousekartooner, Mattel, 1950s, EX (EX box), J2..$65.00

Mickey Mouse Club, projector, Stephens, 1950s, plastic, complete w/4 films, MIB $125.00

Mickey Mouse Club, stamp book, by Kathleen N Daly, Golden Press, 1956, EX.......................................$40.00

Minnie Mouse, bank, Minnie in house, WDE/Japan, compo, NM, S21..$20.00

Minnie Mouse, doll, Gund, 1940s, stuffed cloth w/leather-type shoes, 18", scarce, VG, M17.....................................$275.00

Minnie Mouse, doll, Knickerbocker, 1930s, Minnie as cowgirl, EX...$3,000.00

Minnie Mouse, doll, Sun Rubber, 1950s, 10", VG, M15 ..$65.00

Minnie Mouse, doll, 1930s, stuffed printed cloth w/embroidered trim, standing w/hands on hips, 5", M, A $75.00

Minnie Mouse, figure, celluloid, jtd arms & neck, Japan, prewar, 5", EX, A...$125.00

Minnie Mouse, figure, Fun-E-Flex, wood, 7", EX............$450.00

Minnie Mouse, figure, Japan, 1930s, bsk, hands on hips looking up, 3½", M...$175.00

Minnie Mouse, figure, Japan, 1930s, bsk, in nightshirt, 4", EX..$150.00

Minnie Mouse, figure, Japan, 1930s, bsk, w/umbrella & purse, 4", EX, M8...$75.00

Minnie Mouse, Minnie Picture Toast, Hoan Products, 1988, M (EX card), M17...$25.00

Minnie Mouse, roly poly, Minnie sitting atop ball, celluloid, EX..$900.00

Mouseketeers, television, 1950s, lithographed tin with paper scroll, VG, $150.00. (Photo courtesy David Longest and Michael Stern)

Nightmare Before Christmas, doll, Jack, Applause, MIB.$175.00

Nightmare Before Christmas, doll, Sally, Applause, MIB .$300.00

Nightmare Before Christmas, figure, Evil Scientist, Hasbro, 1993, MOC, H4...$130.00

Nightmare Before Christmas, figure, Lock, Shock & Barrel in bathtub on wheels, Applause, PVC, M, H4..............$10.00

Nightmare Before Christmas, figure, Mayor, Hasbro, 1993, MOC, H4...$100.00

Nightmare Before Christmas, figure, Sally, Hasbro, 1993, MOC, H4...$100.00

Nightmare Before Christmas, figure set, Lock, Shock & Barrel, Hasbro, 1993, w/3 masks, MIB, J6.......................$125.00

Pagemaster, doll, Richard, Applause, 1994, plush, 11", M, F1 .$15.00

Pagemaster, key chains, Applause, 1994, PVC, set of 5, MOC, F1 ....$10.00

Peter Pan, figure, Tinkerbell, 1980s, porcelain, w/gold string for hanging, 6", M, P6...$75.00

Nightmare Before Christmas, figure, Jack as Santa, Hasbro, 1993, MOC, $75.00. (Photo courtesy June Moon)

Peter Pan, hatbox, Ne Evel/WDP, 1950s, faux gr leather on cb w/flocked image of Peter Pan & Tinkerbelle, NM, P4.$175.00

Peter Pan, Television Studio, Admiral TV premium, 1952, cb, M..$165.00

Peter Pan, Tinker Bells, Peter Puppet, move handle & Tinkerbell plays bells, tin & plastic, 16", rare, NMIB $500.00

Pinocchio, clicker, Jiminy Cricket, 1950s, yel plastic head figure, NM, M8...$20.00

Pinocchio, Color Box, Transogram/WDP, 1948, litho tin, EX, A...$75.00

Pinocchio, doll, Figaro, jtd compo, 7", EX $375.00

Pinocchio, doll, Geppetto, Chad Valley, wood w/cloth clothes, orig tag, EX...$1,100.00

Pinocchio, doll, Jiminy Cricket, Ideal, 1930s, jtd wood, orig felt hat brim & collar, 8", EX..............................$425.00

Pinocchio, doll, Jiminy Cricket, Knickerbocker, 1939, compo w/felt clothes & hat, 10", NM, A.........................$900.00

Pinocchio, doll, Pinocchio, Ideal, 1939, wood & compo, 20", NM, from $800 to...$900.00

Pinocchio, doll, Pinocchio, Ideal, 1940s, jtd wood & compo, 11", NM (NM rare box) $550.00

Pinocchio, doll, Pinocchio, Knickerbocker, 1939, celluloid w/cloth clothes, NM, from $500 to........................$700.00

Pinocchio, doll, Pinocchio, Knickerbocker, 1939, compo w/cloth clothes, 30", NM, from $2,000 to...........$3,000.00

Pinocchio, figure, Geppetto, Multi-Products, 1940s, bsk, 2", NM, M8...$100.00

Pinocchio, figure, Gideon, Multi-Products, 1940s, 2¼", EX+, M8..$75.00

Pinocchio, figure, Honest John, Multi-Products, 1940s, bsk, 2", EX, M8..$75.00

Pinocchio, doll, Ideal, 1940s, jointed wood and composition, 11", NM (NM rare box), $550.00. (Photo courtesy David Longest and Michael Stern)

Pinocchio, figure, Jiminy Cricket, Multi-Products, 1940s, bsk, 5", NM, M8..$100.00
Pinocchio, figure, Pinocchio, Fun-E-Flex, wood, 5", scarce, VG, M8...$200.00
Pinocchio, figure, Pinocchio, Multi-Products, 1940s, bsk, 2", NM, M8............................$100.00
Pinocchio, figure, Pinocchio, Multi-Products, 1940s, bsk, 5", NM, M8..........................$125.00
Pinocchio, jack-in-the-box, Marx, compo figure w/cloth clothes, paper litho box, 6x6", EX $250.00
Pinocchio, mask, Einson-Freeman/WDP, Gillette Razor Blades premium, 1939, paper, EX $25.00
Pinocchio, mask, Figaro, Gillette premium, 1939, paper, EX, C1 ....$35.00

Pinocchio, tea set, Ohio Art, 1930s, lithographed tin, 18 pieces, rare, EX, minimum value $150.00. (Photo courtesy David Longest and Michael Stern)

Pinocchio, Pin the Nose on Pinocchio Party Game, Parker Bros, 1939, EX (EX box) $135.00
Pinocchio, Pinocchio Circus, 1939 premium, punch-out set w/standup accessories, EX................$75.00
Pinocchio, Puppet Show, Whitman, complete w/stage & 8 characters, EX (EX box) $125.00
Pinocchio, roly poly, celluloid, 5", EX....................$175.00
Pinocchio, tea set, ceramic w/red trim, 8 pcs, EX $250.00
Pluto, bank, Pluto, WDP/Japan, compo, NM, S21 ....$20.00

Pluto, doll, Schuco, 1950s, 13" long, EX, minimum value $350.00. (Photo courtesy Dunbar Gallery)

Pluto, figure, Fun-E-Flex, Ideal, wood w/felt ears & rope tail, EX $350.00
Pluto, figure, 1930s, bsk, Pluto sitting, 2½", EX, M8........$85.00
Pluto, lantern, Linemar, tin & glass figure w/rubber ears, tongue & tail, battery-op, 6½", NM (EX box), A $450.00
Pluto, Peppy Puppet, Kohner, miniature plastic marionette, MOC...........................$55.00
Pluto, pull toy, Playful Pluto, Jaymar, 1950s, Pluto moves back & forth as cage spins in middle, wood, 8", EX, A $300.00
Pluto, pull toy, unmk, 1940s, litho wood w/fabric ears & rope tail, orig pull-string w/ball end, 12", NM $135.00
Pluto, rocking chair, 1950s, stuffed vinyl w/wooden rockers, Pluto & pups on chair back, 32", EX, J5 ....$150.00
Pluto the Pup, figure, Borgfeldt/WDE, jtd wood w/cloth ears, 6", NM (EX box mk Mickey Mouse's Dog) $600.00
Rocketeer, backpack, promo for AMC Theatres, leather-like, H10, from $75 to $125.00
Rocketeer, beach towel, promo for AMC Theatres, 2 designs, NM, H10, ea $30.00
Rocketeer, figure, Applause, vinyl, 9", MOC, H10...........$20.00
Rocketeer, Gee Bee plane, Spectra Star, MIB, H10 ....$45.00
Rocketeer, poster, features Disney Channel, M, H10.......$50.00
Rocketeer, Poster Pen Set, Rose Art #1921, 1991, complete, MOC, from $20 to $30.00
Rocketeer, roll-along figures, Applause, 1990, PVC, set of 3, M, F1 ....$15.00
Rocketeer, umbrella, Pyramid Handbag Co, EX, H10, from $75 to...........................$100.00
Rocketeer, wallet, Pyramid Handbag Co, M, H10...........$40.00

Roger Rabbit, see Who Framed Roger Rabbit

Sleeping Beauty, Dress Designer Kit, Colorforms, 1959, complete, MIB, P6...$65.00

Sleeping Beauty, figure, Flora, Hagen-Renaker, 1950s, 2", NM, M8...$150.00

Sleeping Beauty, figure, Merryweather, Hagen-Renaker, 1950s, 2", scarce, EX+, M8...$165.00

Sleeping Beauty, Magic Bubble Wand, 1950s, MIP.........$40.00

Sleeping Beauty, Paint-by-Number set, Transogram, 1959, complete, MIB, from $85 to $95.00

Sleeping Beauty, ring, 1950s, silver plastic w/bl plastic shield, removable sword, EX, J5...$45.00

Sleeping Beauty, sewing set, Transogram, 1959, unused, scarce, EX, M8...$65.00

Snow White & the Seven Dwarfs, bank, Snow White, Leeds, NM $125.00

Snow White & the Seven Dwarfs, bank, Snow White beside wishing well, NM, S21 ....$100.00

Snow White and the Seven Dwarfs, doll, Happy, Chad Valley, 1930s, stuffed cloth with felt clothes, 12", EX, minimum value $300.00.
(Photo courtesy David Longest and Michael Stern)

Snow White and the Seven Dwarfs, card game, Castell Bros., 1930s, complete, EX (EX box), minimum value $75.00.

Snow White & the Seven Dwarfs, coloring set, Whitman/WDE, 1930s, complete, EX (EX box), from $150 to $200.00

Snow White & the Seven Dwarfs, Dance 'N Play Deluxe Gift Set, Mattel, 1993, MIB...$45.00

Snow White & the Seven Dwarfs, doll, Bashful, Ideal, stuffed cloth w/molded oilcloth face mask, 12", EX $225.00

Snow White & the Seven Dwarfs, doll, Dopey, Ideal, 1937, stuffed cloth, 12", NM, from $250 to $450.00

Snow White & the Seven Dwarfs, doll, Dopey, Madame Alexander, 1930s, compo w/cloth clothes, NMIB...$325.00

Snow White & the Seven Dwarfs, doll, Grumpy, Knickerbocker, 8", scarce, EX, M8...$250.00

Snow White & the Seven Dwarfs, doll, Snow White, Knickerbocker, 1938, compo w/cloth clothes, MIB, from $750 to $1,000.00

Snow White & the Seven Dwarfs, doll, Snow White, Storybook Small-Talk by Mattel, 1970, MIB.........................$125.00

Snow White & the Seven Dwarfs, dolls, dwarfs, Knickerbocker, 1938, compo w/cloth clothes, NM, ea from $300 to.$500.00

Snow White and the Seven Dwarfs, doll, Snow White, Storybook Small-Talk by Mattel, 1970, MIB, $125.00.
(Photo courtesy J. Michael Augustyniak)

Snow White & the Seven Dwarfs, figure, Bashful, Japan, 1930s, bsk, 3", NM, M8 ....$50.00

Snow White & the Seven Dwarfs, figure, Doc, Japan, 1930s, bsk, 3", NM, M8...$50.00

Snow White & the Seven Dwarfs, figure, Dopey, Japan, 1930s, bsk, 3", EX+, M8...$40.00

Snow White & the Seven Dwarfs, figure, Grumpy, Japan, 1930s, bsk, 3", NM, M8 ....$50.00

Snow White & the Seven Dwarfs, figure, Happy, Japan, 1930s, bsk, 3", NM, M8 ....$50.00

Snow White & the Seven Dwarfs, figure, Sleepy, Am Pottery, ceramic, 5½", NM, M8..............................$175.00

Snow White & the Seven Dwarfs, figure, Sleepy, Japan, 1930s, bsk, 3", NM, M8 ....$50.00

Snow White & the Seven Dwarfs, figure, Sleepy, Seiberling Rubber, 1930s, 5", EX, M8 ....$45.00

Snow White & the Seven Dwarfs, figure, Sneezy, Japan, 1930s, bsk, 3", NM, M8..............................$50.00

Snow White & the Seven Dwarfs, figure, Snow White, Am Pottery, ceramic, 1930s, 6", NM, M8 ....$295.00

Snow White & the Seven Dwarfs, figure, Snow White, Japan, 1930s, bsk, 4", NM, M8..............................$60.00

Snow White & the Seven Dwarfs, ironing board, Wolverine, litho metal, EX..............................$40.00

Snow White & the Seven Dwarfs, rattle, WDE, 1930s, celluloid, EX, from $150 to..............................$200.00

Snow White & the Seven Dwarfs, Talking Telephone, Hasbro, 1967, complete w/8 records, MIB, J6..............................$225.00

Snow White & the Seven Dwarfs, tea set, Aluminum Goods Mfg, 1937, 10 pcs, MIB..............................$300.00

Snow White & the Seven Dwarfs, tea set, Marx, WDP, china, 23 pcs, EX (EX box)..............................$375.00

Snow White & the Seven Dwarfs, Tinkersand Pictures, Toy Tinkers Inc, WDE, 1937, complete, EX (EX box)...$125.00

Snow White & the Seven Dwarfs, watering can, Ohio Art, 1930s, litho tin, 8", EX..............................$200.00

Space Jam, figure set, Playmates, 1996, set of 3, MIB, F1 .$30.00

Sword in the Stone, ring, 1970s premium, bl or pk plastic, EX, M8, ea..............................$12.00

Three Little Pigs, doll, Big Bad Wolf, Gund, stuffed plush w/vinyl face & hands, EX..............................$95.00

Three Little Pigs, dolls, Lars/Italy, playing instruments, stuffed felt, set of 3, 13", EX..............................$1,100.00

Three Little Pigs, figure, Big Bad Wolf, Japan, 1930s, bsk, 3½", NM, M8..............................$100.00

Three Little Pigs, figure set, Fun-E-Flex, Ideal, wood, EX.$400.00

Three Little Pigs, figures, Borgfeldt, bsk, playing instruments, 3", NM (EX box mk Who's Afraid of the Big Bad Wolf).$600.00

Three Little Pigs, tea set, Ohio Art/WDE, 1935, gr litho tin, complete, NM..............................$350.00

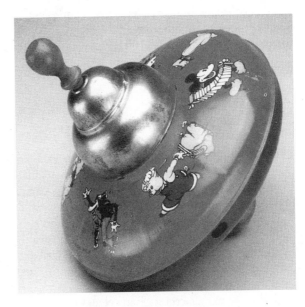

Three Little Pigs, top, lithographed metal, NM, minimum value $200.00. (Photo courtesy Michael Stern)

Three Little Pigs, washing machine, Chein, litho tin, complete w/wringer & pedestal base, 8", A..............................$355.00

Thumper, see Bambi

Toy Story, Colorforms, 1993, complete, MIB, F1/M17 ....$15.00

Toy Story, figure, any character, Thinkway Toys, 6", MOC, F1, ea..............................$15.00

Toy Story, figure, Mr Potato Head, Hasbro/Playskool, MIB, F1..............................$25.00

Toy Story, figure, Woody or Buzz Lightyear, PVC, 3", MOC, F1, ea..............................$6.00

Toy Story, pull toy, Slinky Dog, MIB, F1..............................$20.00

Who Framed Roger Rabbit, doll, Roger Rabbit, LJN, 1987, inflatable vinyl, 3-ft, NM, F1..............................$12.00

Who Framed Roger Rabbit, doll, Roger Rabbit, stuffed plush, 24", M..............................$75.00

Who Framed Roger Rabbit, figure, Jessica, Applause, 1987, PVC, 3", M, F1..............................$10.00

Who Framed Roger Rabbit, stick doll, Roger Rabbit, Applause, figure on 8" stick, EX, F1..............................$15.00

Who Framed Roger Rabbit, Wacky Heads (hand puppet), Roger Rabbit, Applause, NM, F1..............................$12.00

Winnie the Pooh, doll, Piglet, Gund, 1960s, stuffed cloth, 12", NM..............................$50.00

Winnie the Pooh, doll, Pooh, Gund, 1960s, stuffed cloth w/name on sweater, 9", EX..............................$225.00

Three Little Pigs, doll, Big Bad Wolf, Ross, 1934, original tag, NM, from $1,500.00 to $2,500.00. (Photo courtesy Dunbar Gallery)

Winnie the Pooh, doll, Pooh, Knickerbocker, 1963, bl shirt, 13",
  EX, J2 ....**$75.00**

Winnie the Pooh, doll, Pooh, 1979, wearing red velvet shirt
  w/Disneyland Grad Night ribbon, 12", VG, M15 ......**$55.00**

Winnie the Pooh, doll, Tigger, Sears, 1970s, stuffed plush, EX,
  C17...**$35.00**

Winnie the Pooh, doll set, Pooh, Tigger, Eeyore, Roo & Piglet,
  Sears, squeeze vinyl, EX, C17 ....**$50.00**

Winnie the Pooh, figure, Pooh, Kanga, Piglet or Tigger,
  Beswick, ceramic, M, P6, ea **$75.00**

Winnie the Pooh, top, Ohio Art, 1960s, clear plastic cone-shaped
  dome w/wooden hdl & lithoed graphics, EX, P6..........**$75.00**

101 Dalmatians, Colorforms, 1961, complete w/booklet,
  NMIB **$40.00**

Dollhouse Furniture

    Back in the '40s and '50s, little girls often spent hour after
hour with their dollhouses, keeping house for their imaginary
families, cooking on tiny stoves (that sometimes came with
scaled-to-fit pots and pans), serving meals in lovely dining
rooms, making beds, and rearranging furniture, most of which
was plastic, much of which was made by Renwal, Ideal, Marx,
Irwin, and Plasco. Jaydon made plastic furniture as well but sadly
never marked it. Tootsietoy produced metal items, many in
boxed sets.

    Of all of these manufacturers, Renwal and Ideal are consid-
ered the most collectible. Renwal's furniture was usually
detailed; some pieces had moving parts. Many were made in
more than one color, often brightened with decals. Besides the
furniture, they made accessory items as well as 'dollhouse' dolls
of the whole family. Ideal's Petite Princess line was packaged in
sets with wonderful detail, accessorized down to the perfume
bottles on the top of the vanity. Ideal furniture and parts are
numbered, always with an 'I' prexif. Most Renwal pieces are also
numbered.

    Advisor: Judith Mosholder (M7).

Acme, see-saw, red w/yel hdls, M7 ....$10.00
Acme, shoofly, gr w/wht seat, M7 ....$10.00
Acme, stroller, pk w/bl or wht wheels, M7, ea $6.00
Acme, swing, red, gr & yel, M7 ....$20.00
Acme, tommy horse, red w/yel seat, M7............................$18.00
Allied, chair, dining; red, M7 ....$2.00
Allied, hutch, red, M7 ....$4.00
Allied, vanity, pk, M7 ....$3.00
Arcade, bathroom set, wht-pnt CI, 5 pcs, EX, A $300.00
Arcade, bedroom set, gr-pnt CI, 5 pcs, EX, A $1,300.00
Arcade, Boone kitchen cabinet, wht-pnt CI w/silver trim, 8",
  NMIB, A...$935.00
Arcade, Crane kitchen sink, wht-pnt CI w/NP faucet, 5",
  NMIB, A...$450.00
Arcade, dining room set, brn-pnt CI w/gold highlights, 9 pcs,
  EX, A...$1,300.00
Arcade, dining room set, red-pnt CI w/gold highlights, 9 pcs,
  EX, A...$1,600.00
Arcade, GE refrigerator, red-pnt CI w/decal on door, 7", NM,
  A..$700.00
Arcade, Gurney refrigerator, wht-pnt CI w/silver trim, 5½",
  NMIB, A $1,000.00
Arcade, laundry set, yel-pnt CI, 4 pcs, EX, A $800.00
Arcade, piano & stool, bl-pnt CI, 4½x5", EX, A $385.00
Arcade, Roper gas stove, wht-pnt CI w/silver trim, 6", NMIB,
  A..$700.00
Arcade, sofa & lounge chair, rose-pnt CI w/maroon trim, NM,
  A..$850.00
Best, bed, pk, M7..$5.00
Best, doll, baby; M7..$4.00
Best, rocking horse, pk, M7 ....$12.00
Block House Inc, table, coffee; Swedish blond maple, M7..$18.00
Block House Inc, table, end; Swedish blond maple, 3-legged,
  M7 ....$2.00
Blue Box, chair, kitchen; avocado, M7...............................$2.00
Blue Box, sink, bathroom; w/shelf unit, M7 ....$4.00
Blue Box, table, dressing; wht w/pk, M7............................$4.00
Blue Box, vanity, tan w/heart-shaped mirror, M7 ....$3.00
Donna Lee, chair, kitchen; wht, M7...................................$5.00
Donna Lee, sink, kitchen; wht, M7 ....$6.00

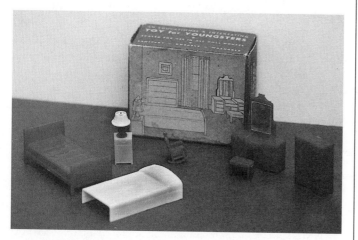

Allied, bedroom set, eight pieces, MIB, T5, $80.00.
(Photo courtesy Marcie Tubbs)

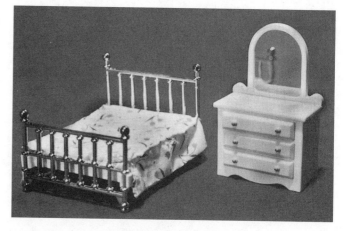

**Fisher-Price, bedroom set, #255, brass bed with white
dresser and mirror, M, C13, $6.00.** (Photo courtesy Brad Cassity)

Donna Lee, stove, wht, M7 ....$6.00

Donna Lee, table, kitchen; wht, M7 ....$6.00

Endeavor, armoire, wht w/red, M7 ....$5.00

Endeavor, hutch, wht w/red, M7 ....$5.00

Endeavor, refrigerator, ivory, opening door, M7 ....$5.00

Endeavor, stove, ivory, M7 ....$5.00

Fisher-Price, bathroom, #253, w/sink, toilet & shower, gr, M, C13 ....$6.00

Fisher-Price, chair & rug set, #268, w/wingback chair, footstool, oriental rug & potted plant, M, C13 ....$8.00

Fisher-Price, desk set, #261, w/roll-top desk, swivel chair & spinning globe, M, C13 ....$6.00

Fisher-Price, dinette, #251, complete, M, C13.................$5.00

Fisher-Price, dollhouse family, #265, w/mom, dad & 2 daughters, M, C13 ....$10.00

Fisher-Price, kitchen set, #252, w/oven, refrigerator & sink, M, C13 ....$8.00

Fisher-Price, music room, #258, w/piano, stool & stereo, M, C13 ....$8.00

Fisher-Price, nursery, #257, w/crib, armoire & rocking horse, M, C13 ....$10.00

Fisher-Price, patio set, #260, w/chair, chaise lounge, grill & collie dog, M, C13 ....$8.00

Grand Rapids, chest of drawers, wood w/stained finish, M7.$20.00

Grand Rapids, dresser w/mirror, wood w/stained finish, M7 .$20.00

Grand Rapids, hutch, wood w/stained finish, M7 ....$20.00

Grand Rapids, rocker, wood w/stained finish, M7 ....$18.00

Ideal, living room chairs, $15.00 each; tilt-top table, $45.00; floor lamp, $25.00; fireplace, $35.00; floor radio, $10.00; sofa, $20.00; coffee table, $10.00; table lamp, $20.00; end table, $6.00. (Photo courtesy Judith Mosholder)

Ideal, buffet, dk brn or marbleized maroon, M7, ea $10.00

Ideal, chair, dining room; marbleized maroon w/bl, red or yel seat, M7, ea $10.00

Ideal, china closet, marbleized maroon or dk brn swirl, M7, ea $15.00

Ideal, doll, baby; w/diaper, M7 ....$10.00

Ideal, end table/night stand, ivory w/bl, M7................$8.00

Ideal, hamper, bl, M7 ....$6.00

Ideal, highboy, ivory w/bl, M7 ....$18.00

Ideal, highboy, marbleized maroon, M7 ....$15.00

Ideal, lamp, table; dk brn w/rose swirl shade, M7.............$20.00

Ideal, potty chair, bl, M7 ....$15.00

Ideal, sewing machine, marbleized maroon or brn, M7, ea..$20.00

Ideal, shopping cart, wht w/red basket, M7 ....$40.00

Ideal, table, dining; dk marbleized maroon, M7 ....$20.00

Ideal, table, picnic; wht, M7 ....$20.00

Ideal, tub, corner; bl w/yel, M7 ....$18.00

Ideal, tub, ivory w/blk, M7 ....$10.00

Ideal, vanity, ivory w/bl, M7..........................$18.00

Ideal, vanity, marbleized maroon, M7 ....$15.00

Ideal Petite Princess, boudoir chaise lounge, bl, M7 ....$25.00

Ideal Petite Princess, buffet, complete, M7 ....$25.00

Ideal Petite Princess, dressing table set, complete, M7 .....$28.00

Ideal Petite Princess, Fantasy family, M7 ....$75.00

Ideal Petite Princess, Fantasy telephone set, M7............$22.00

Ideal Petite Princess, kitchen sink/dishwasher, M7 ....$100.00

Ideal Petite Princess, Little Princess bed, bl, M7.............$40.00

Ideal Petite Princess, Lyre table set, complete, M7 ....$20.00

Ideal Petite Princess, refrigerator/freezer, complete, M7.$190.00

Ideal Petite Princess, Regency hearthplace, w/accesories, M7 .$25.00

Ideal Petite Princess, rolling tea cart, complete, M7.........$25.00

Ideal Petite Princess, Royal grand piano, complete, M7 ...$30.00

Ideal Petite Princess, sofa, brocade, M7.....................$25.00

Ideal Petite Princess, table, dining room; M7................$15.00

Ideal Petite Princess, vanity, M7 ....$50.00

Ideal Young Decorator, bed, rose-colored spread, M7.......$35.00

Ideal Young Decorator, buffet, marbleized maroon, M7 ...$20.00

Ideal Young Decorator, chair, dining room; marbleized maroon w/yel seat, M7 ....$10.00

Ideal Young Decorator, diaper pail, yel w/bl, M7 ....$25.00

Ideal Young Decorator, hutch, dining room; marbleized maroon, M7 ....$25.00

Ideal Young Decorator, sink, bathroom; yel w/bl, M7 ......$40.00

Irwin, accessory, dustpan, bl, orange or yel, M7, ea.............$4.00

Irwin, accessory, pail, dk bl, M7.........................$6.00

Irwin, accessory, tray, lt bl, M7 ....$3.00

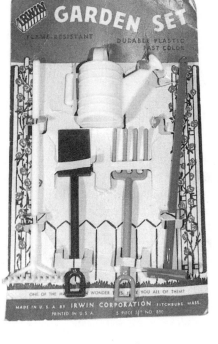

Irwin, garden set, MOC, T5, $75.00.
(Photo courtesy Marcie Tubbs)

Jaydon, bed, reddish brn swirl, w/spread, M7 ....$18.00

Jaydon, buffet, reddish brn, M7...$4.00

Jaydon, chair, dining; reddish brn swirl, M7 ....$2.00

Jaydon, chair, living room; reddish brn swirl, M7 ....$15.00

Jaydon, chest of drawers, reddish brn swirl, M7.................$6.00

Jaydon, piano w/bench, reddish brn swirl, M7 ....$12.00

Kilgore, baby carriage, bl-pnt CI w/NP cover & spoke wheels, 4", EX, A...$75.00

Kilgore, bed, gr-pnt CI, M7 ....$60.00

Kilgore, buffet, bl-pnt CI, M7..$50.00

Kilgore, chair, bedroom; gr-pnt CI, M7.............................$40.00

Kilgore, chair, living room; red-pnt CI, rpt, M7 ....$45.00

Kilgore, icebox, ivory-pnt CI, M7.....................................$50.00

Kilgore, playground set, bl-pnt CI, 3 pcs, NM, A $75.00

Kilgore, potty chair, bl-pnt CI, M7 ....$60.00

Kilgore, Sally Ann Household Toy Set, complete nursery set, painted cast iron, NMIB, A, $700.00.

Kilgore, sink, bathroom; bl-pnt CI, M7.............................$50.00

Kilgore, sink, kitchen; tan-pnt CI, M7...............................$75.00

Kilgore, table, dressing; gr-pnt CI, M7 ....$60.00

Marx, Babyland Nursery Set, complete, unused, NMIB.$465.00

Marx, bathroom set, dk ivory, hard plastic, 4 pcs, M7 ......$20.00

Marx, bedroom set, dk ivory, hard plastic, 8 pcs, M7........$40.00

Marx, buffet, maroon or brn swirl, hard plastic, M7, ea $3.00

Marx, buffet, tan w/molded fruit, hard plastic, M7.............$3.00

Marx, chair, living room; red, hard plastic, M7 ....$3.00

Marx, chair, living room; yel or red, tufted seat, hard plastic, M7, ea $5.00

Marx, chest of drawers, pk, hard plastic, M7 ....$5.00

Marx, crib, gr w/molded bottle & rattle, hard plastic, M7 ..$5.00

Marx, dining room set, brn, soft plastic, 7 pcs, M7 ....$20.00

Marx, dining room set, brn swirl, hard plastic, 7 pcs, M7 .$30.00

Marx, dresser w/mirror, tan, hard plastic, M7.....................$3.00

Marx, hamper, ivory, hard plastic, M7 ....$3.00

Marx, hamper, pk, peach, bl or ivory, hard plastic, M7, ea.$5.00

Marx, highboy, yel, hard plastic, M7 ....$5.00

Marx, hutch, brn, soft plastic, M7 ....$3.00

Marx, hutch, maroon swirl, hard plastic, M7 ....$5.00

Marx, laundry basket, chartreuse, soft plastic, M7 ....$3.00

Marx, nightstand, yel, hard plastic, M7...............................$5.00

Marx, piano, red or yel, hard plastic, M7, ea.....................$15.00

Marx, playpen, pk, soft plastic, M7......................................$3.00

Marx, playpen, pk w/emb Donald Duck, hard plastic, M7 ..$8.00

Marx, refrigerator, wht, hard plastic, M7.............................$3.00

Marx, refrigerator, yel, soft plastic, M7...............................$3.00

Marx, sink, kitchen; yel or ivory, soft plastic, M7, ea.........$3.00

Marx, sofa, lt gr or bright yel, hard plastic, M7, ea............$3.00

Marx, sofa, red or yel, soft plastic, M7, ea..........................$3.00

Marx, sofa, yel or red, hard plastic, M7, ea.........................$5.00

Marx, stove, ivory or wht, hard plastic, M7, ea $5.00

Marx, stove, yel or ivory, soft plastic, M7, ea $3.00

Marx, table, coffee; lt gr, hard plastic, M7.........................$10.00

Marx, table, dining room; dk maroon swirl, hard plastic, M7.$3.00

Marx, toilet, ivory, hard plastic, M7 ....$3.00

Marx, toilet, pk, peach, bl or ivory, hard plastic, M7, ea $5.00

Marx, TV/phono, red, soft plastic, M7 ....$3.00

Marx, vanity, yel, hard plastic, M7 ....$5.00

Marx Little Hostess, chaise lounge, ivory w/pk, M7 ....$10.00

Marx Little Hostess, chest of drawers, rust, block front, M7..$10.00

Marx Little Hostess, piano & bench, MIB, M7.................$35.00

Marx Little Hostess, table, tilt-top; blk w/gold stenciling, M7.$10.00

Marx Little Hostess, vanity, ivory, M7...............................$10.00

Mattel Littles, armoire, M7..$8.00

Mattel Littles, bed, w/cover & pillow, MIB, M7 ....$15.00

Mattel Littles, chair, living room; M7 ....$4.00

Mattel Littles, doll, Belinda; w/chairs & pop-up room setting, MIB, M7..$25.00

Mattel Littles, doll, Hedy; w/sofa & pop-up room setting, MIB, M7...$25.00

Mattel Littles, dresser & lamp, MIB, M7 ....$12.00

Mattel Littles, sink/icebox, MIB, M7 ....$12.00

Mattel Littles, sofa, M7..$8.00

Mattel Littles, stove, w/kettle & coffeepot, MIB, M7.......$15.00

Mattel Littles, table, drop-leaf; w/plates & cups, MIB, M7 .$15.00

Plasco, bathroom set, 5 pcs & floor plan, MIB, M7 ....$65.00

Plasco, buffet, brn, tan or marbleized reddish brn, M7, ea ..$4.00

Plasco, chair, dining room; brn, M7 ....$3.00

Plasco, chair, dining room; brn w/striped paper seat cover, M7 ....$4.00

Plasco, dining room set, 8 pcs, MIB, M7 ....$55.00

Plasco, doll, baby; pk, M7 ....$25.00

Plasco, dresser, tan w/yel detail, 3 drawers, M7................$15.00

Plasco, highboy, brn, tan, maroon or brn swirl, M7, ea.......$8.00

Plasco, kitchen counter, pk, no-base style, M7 ....$3.00

Plasco, kitchen counter, wht w/bl base, M7 ....$6.00

Plasco, nightstand, brn, tan or mauve, M7, ea $3.00

Plasco, nightstand, ivory, stenciled, M7 ....$5.00

Plasco, refrigerator, pk or wht, no-base style, M7, ea..........$3.00

Plasco, refrigerator, wht w/bl base, M7 ....$5.00

Plasco, sink, bathroom; pk or turq, M7, ea $4.00

Plasco, sofa, lt bl w/brn base, M7 ....$8.00

Plasco, sofa, teal or turq, no-base style, M7, ea...................$3.00

Plasco, stove, pk, no-base style, M7 ....$3.00

Plasco, stove, wht w/bl base, M7...$5.00

Plasco, table, coffee; brn or marbleized brn, M7, ea $3.00

Plasco, table, kitchen; lt bl, M7 ....$5.00

Plasco, table, patio; bl w/ivory legs, M7.............................$4.00

Plasco, toilet, turq w/wht seat, M7......................................$8.00

Plasco, vanity, marbleized brn, no mirror-style, M7...........$5.00

Plasco, vanity, pk, w/mirror, M7...$5.00

Plasco, vanity & bench, pk, no-mirror style, M7 ....$8.00
Renwal, bathinette, bl, no decal, M7 ....$8.00

Renwal, bathinette, pink with decal, $15.00; carriage, with insert, blue with pink wheels, $30.00; highchair, pink with decal, $25.00; baby, $10.00; cradle, pink with decal, $35.00; potty chair, blue with decal, $12.00. (Photo courtesy Judith Mosholder)

Renwal, bed, brn w/ivory spread, M7 ....$8.00
Renwal, buffet, brn, opening drawer, M7 ....$8.00
Renwal, Busy Little Mother Set, MIB..........................$350.00
Renwal, carpet sweeper, M7 ....$85.00
Renwal, carriage, pk w/bl wheels, spread insert, M7 ....$30.00
Renwal, chair, barrel; bl w/brn base, stenciled, M7 ....$10.00
Renwal, chair, barrel; dk red w/brn base, M7 ....$12.00
Renwal, chair, club; bl w/brn base, M7............................$8.00
Renwal, chair, club; ivory w/brn base, stenciled, M7........$10.00
Renwal, chair, teacher's; bl, M7 ....$18.00
Renwal, china closet, blk, stenciled, non-opening door, M7..$25.00
Renwal, china closet, brn, stenciled, M7 ....$15.00
Renwal, clock, kitchen; ivory or red, M7, ea $20.00
Renwal, clock, mantle; ivory or red, M7,ea......................$10.00
Renwal, cradle, pk or bl w/doll insert, M7, ea.................$30.00
Renwal, desk, student's; red, brn or yel, M7, ea $12.00
Renwal, doll, baby; M7 ....$10.00
Renwal, doll, brother; metal rivets, M7.........................$30.00
Renwal, doll, brother; plastic rivets, M7 ....$25.00
Renwal, doll, father; bl suit, metal rivets, M7 ....$30.00
Renwal, doll, mechanic; no cap, M7.............................$100.00
Renwal, doll, mechanic; w/cap, M7 ....$150.00
Renwal, doll, mother; pk, plastic rivets, M7 ....$25.00
Renwal, doll, nurse; M7 ....$40.00
Renwal, doll, sister; yel dress, metal rivets, M7 ....$25.00
Renwal, fireplace, brn or ivory w/insert, brn logs & andirons, M7, ea $35.00
Renwal, hamper, ivory, M7..$3.00
Renwal, hamper, lime gr, opening lid & cb backing, M7 .$10.00
Renwal, highboy, brn, opening drawers, M7 ....$8.00
Renwal, highboy, pk or bl, M7, ea..................................$15.00
Renwal, ironing board, pk or bl, w/iron, M7, ea $22.00
Renwal, lamp, floor; red w/ivory shade, M7 ....$15.00
Renwal, lamp, floor; yel w/ivory shade, M7 ....$20.00

Renwal, lamp, table; yel w/ivory or wht shade, M7, ea $10.00
Renwal, Little Red Schoolhouse & Furniture, MIB, from $300 to $325.00
Renwal, mop, M7...$45.00
Renwal, piano, marbleized brn, M7 ....$30.00
Renwal, playground slide, bl w/red, M7 ....$22.00
Renwal, playpen, bl w/pk bottom or pk w/bl bottom, M7, ea.$15.00
Renwal, refrigerator, turq, w/opening door & 2 shelves, M7 ..$15.00
Renwal, scales, red, M7..$10.00
Renwal, sink, ivory w/blk, opening door, M7...................$15.00
Renwal, sink, pk w/lt bl, M7 ....$5.00
Renwal, sink, turq w/blk, M7 ....$8.00
Renwal, sofa, ivory w/brn base, M7 ....$18.00
Renwal, sofa, pale pk w/brn base, M7...........................$15.00
Renwal, stove, ivory w/blk or red, opening door, M7, ea..$15.00
Renwal, stove, lt turq, non-opening door, M7 ....$12.00
Renwal, table, cocktail; brn, M7 ....$10.00
Renwal, table, cocktail; metallic red, M7 ....$15.00
Renwal, table, dining; brn, stenciled, M7 ....$20.00
Renwal, table, folding; copper, M7...............................$18.00
Renwal, table, folding; gold, M7..................................$15.00
Renwal, telephone, yel w/red, M7 ....$22.00
Renwal, toilet, turq or ivory w/blk, M7, ea......................$9.00
Renwal, toydee, bl or pk, M7, ea $6.00
Renwal, toydee, bl w/Little Boy Blue decal, M7 ....$12.00
Renwal, vacuum cleaner, M7......................................$25.00
Renwal, vanity, brn, stenciled, simplified style, M7..........$10.00
Renwal, washing machine, bl or pk w/bear decal, M7, ea.$30.00
Sonia Messer, sofa, lt gr fabric, M7 ....$80.00
Sonia Messer, table, walnut stain w/lighter wood inlaid design, M7...$60.00
Strombecker, baby grand piano, walnut, M7....................$20.00
Strombecker, bathroom set, complete w/sandpaper & instructions, MIB, M7..$90.00
Strombecker, bedroom set, complete w/sandpaper & instructions, MIB, M7..$75.00
Strombecker, chair, living room; aqua, M7....................$10.00
Strombecker, living room set, complete w/sandpaper & instructions, MIB, M7..$75.00
Strombecker, radio, floor; walnut w/etched detail, M7.....$12.00
Strombecker, sink, ivory or aqua, M7, ea $8.00

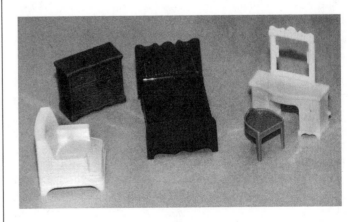

Superior, bedroom set, $30.00.
(Photo courtesy Marcie Tubbs)

Strombecker, sofa, red, M7 ....$10.00
Strombecker, toilet, yel, ivory or aqua, M7, ea $10.00
Strombecker, tub, ivory or aqua, M7, ea $10.00
Superior, bed, bright yel, M7 ....$5.00
Superior, chair, dining room; yel, M7 ....$3.00
Superior, chair, kitchen; olive gr, M7 ....$3.00
Superior, chair, living room; M7 ....$5.00
Superior, chest of drawers, bl, gr, yel, turq or plum, M7, ea ..$5.00
Superior, hutch, pk or red, M7, ea $5.00
Superior, refrigerator, wht, M7 ....$5.00
Superior, sofa, brn, M7 ....$5.00
Superior, table, coffee; bright yel, M7 ....$8.00
Superior, tub, yel or red, M7, ea $5.00
Superior, vanity & bench, yel, M7 ....$10.00
Superior, vanity w/mirror, bl, M7 ....$5.00
Superior, washing machine, wht, M7 ....$5.00

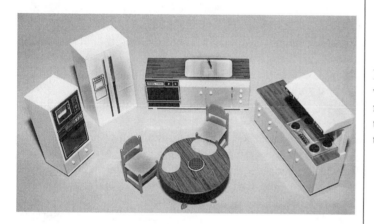

Tomy Smaller Homes, oven with microwave and cherry pie, $55.00; refrigerator, $15.00; sink/dishwasher with two racks, $15.00; stove with hood, $15.00; kitchen table, $8.00; kitchen chairs, $3.00 each. (Photo courtesy Judith Mosholder)

Tomy Smaller Homes, armoire, M7 ....$10.00
Tomy Smaller Homes, bar, kitchen; M7 ....$12.00
Tomy Smaller Homes, bentwood rocker, M7 ....$8.00
Tomy Smaller Homes, refrigerator, M7............................$15.00
Tomy Smaller Homes, sofa, 2-pc, M7 ....$12.00
Tomy Smaller Homes, sofa, 3-pc, M7 ....$15.00
Tomy Smaller Homes, table, coffee; M7 ....$10.00
Tomy Smaller Homes, table, end; M7...............................$8.00
Tootsietoy, bed, bl or pk w/slotted headboard & footboard, M7, ea..$18.00
Tootsietoy, bedroom set, girl's; complete, MIB..............$125.00
Tootsietoy, chair, dining room; brn or ivory, M7, ea $7.00
Tootsietoy, chair, living room; gold wicker-style w/cushion, M7 ....$18.00
Tootsietoy, living room furniture set, complete, MIB..$225.00
Tootsietoy, rocker, gold or ivory wicker-style w/cushion, M7, ea $22.00
Tootsietoy, sofa, gold or ivory wicker-style w/cushion, M7, ea $25.00
Tootsietoy, table, living room; gold, M7 ....$20.00
Tootsietoy, vanity bench, pk w/bl speckled seat, M7........$15.00

Tootsietoy, dining room furniture set, MIB, $225.00.

Wolverine, bed w/headboard, M7 ....$12.00
Wolverine, dresser w/mirror, M7....................................$10.00
Wolverine, playpen, M7 ....$8.00

Dollhouses

Dollhouses were first made commercially in America in the late 1700s. A century later, Bliss and Schoenhut were making wonderful dollhouses that even yet occasionally turn up on the market, and many were being imported from Germany. During the '40s and '50s, American toy makers made a variety of cottages; today they're all collectible.

Advisor: Bob and Marcie Tubbs (T5).
Other Sources: M15.

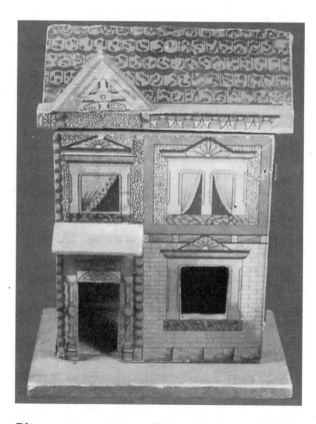

Bliss, two-story, paper lithograph on wood, blue roof, arched glassine windows with lace curtains, 14", EX, $650.00. (Photo courtesy David Longest)

Bliss, 2-story Colonial mansion, paper litho on wood, hinged dbl front doors, 2 columns & 4 front steps, 18x16", VG..**$325.00**

Bliss, 2-story w/2 rooms, paper litho on wood, yel siding, red roof, 2 upper windows, 16½", VG, A......................**$250.00**

Fisher-Price, #250, 3-story w/5 rooms, spiral staircase, w/2 figures, 1978-80, M, C13 ....**$40.00**

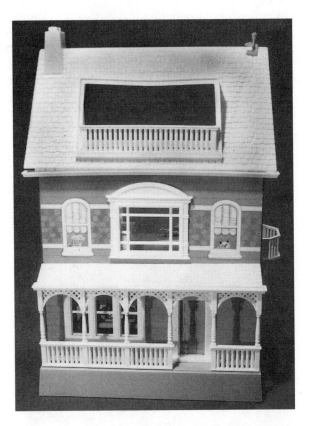

Fisher-Price, #280, three-story light-up with five rooms, battery-operated, seven outlets, 1981 – 84, M, C13, $30.00. (Photo courtesy Brad Cassity)

Germany, stable, 2-story, 3 stalls w/2 rooms & porch above, paper litho & pnt wood, dk bl roof, w/3 horses, 16", VG, A...**$550.00**

Germany, 2-story, red brick w/red gabled roof, wht lattice on 2nd-story porch, 2 chimneys, 1900, 19x13", EX......**$900.00**

Germany, 2-story w/2 rooms, paper litho on wood, red siding & bl roof, lithoed windows, 11", EX, A.........................**$250.00**

Germany, 3-story w/8 rooms, cream-pnt wood w/red gabled roof & dormers, 2 balconies, lattice trim, 1920, 23x38", EX..**$850.00**

Hand-Made, 2-story w/3 rooms & opening front, gr clapboard siding, simulated brick chimney, furnished, 22x19", EX.**$355.00**

Hand-Made, 4-room townhouse w/front opening, faux red brick w/gray roof, front stoop, 20½", EX, A......................**$200.00**

Jayline, 2-story w/5 rooms, litho tin, gr siding over wht w/red bricks, purple roof, 1949, 14½x18½", VG, T5 ....**$50.00**

Keystone, 2-story w/fold-in wings, fiberboard, w/staircase, built-in fireplace, etc, 60 pcs of furniture, 1950s, EX........**$400.00**

Marx, split-level, gray siding & yel brick, wht roof, w/fireplace, set of steps & breakfast bar, EX, M7..........................**$80.00**

Marx, split-level, gray siding & yel brick, wht roof, w/pool, doorbell, light fixture & 60 pcs of furniture, EX, M7......**$125.00**

Marx, split-level, red siding, gray roof, patio above garage, VG, M7...**$65.00**

Marx, 2-story Colonial w/breezeway, clapboard over brick, w/54 pcs of furniture, 1960s, missing chimney & weathervane **$80.00**

Marx, 2-story w/7 rooms, litho tin, wht clapboard over mc stone, red roof, ¾" scale, VG, T5 ....**$100.00**

McLoughlin Bros, Dolly's Playhouse, folding 2-story, paper litho on wood, printed furniture, 1890s, 18½", NMIB, A..**$375.00**

Rich, bungalow, Arts and Crafts style, lithographed cardboard, white with red roof, 1930s, 32x21", VG, T5, $200.00. (Photo courtesy Marcie Tubbs)

Rich, litho fiberboard w/red roof, bl shutters, front porch w/benches, 1940s, 16x24", VG, T5.........................**$135.00**

Unknown maker, two-story, simulated brick on wood with brown and white trim, two bay windows with railed entry, 34", EX, A, $1,700.00.

Schoenhut, 2-room bungalow, wood w/emb cb roof, front porch w/steps, litho walls & floor, electrified, 17x17x15", EX, A..$600.00

Schoenhut, 2-story, brick & stone w/red roof, porch w/turned columns, glass windows, removable roof & side, 23x23", VG $1,100.00

T Cohn, 2-story w/single patio, 4-color litho w/red tiled roof, w/50 pcs of furniture, 1948, ¾" scale, EX................$335.00

Tomy Smaller Homes, split-level, fiberboard w/brn plastic roof, furnished, 1970s, ¾" scale, EX $200.00

Tootsietoy, 2-story Victorian cottage w/3 rooms, pressed board, yel w/red trim, gr shingled roof, 1900s, 23", EX.......$475.00

Unknown maker, bungalow w/5 rooms, pnt wood w/glass windows, front & side porches, lift-off roof, 27x24", EX, A.........$900.00

Unknown maker, Mansford, 3-story w/2 rooms on ea floor, front opening w/lift-off roof, orig wallpaper, late 1800s, 29x26", VG...$2,200.00

Wolverine, Colonial Mansion, no garage, ½" scale, EX, M7..$50.00

Wolverine, Country Cottage #800, 1986, ½" scale, EX, M7.$50.00

SHOPS AND SINGLE ROOMS

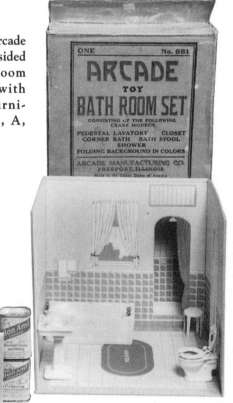

Bathroom, Arcade #681, three-sided cardboard room complete with cast-iron furniture, NMIB, A, $2,200.00.

Grocery Store, Germany, pnt wood, hinged sides open to reveal drawers, shelves & accessories, 21x16", EX, A $475.00

Grocery Store, Wolverine, litho tin, separate counter, 1930s, missing some accessories, 12x15½", G, A................$150.00

Hometown Meat Market, Marx, litho tin w/3 walls, 1930, complete w/accessories, NMIB.......................................$450.00

Kitchen, bl-pnt & stenciled tin walls w/red stove, working water pump & various accessories, 11" W, VG, A $400.00

Kitchen, bl-pnt tin walls w/litho tin stove, w/various litho tin accessories, 18½" W, VG, A $300.00

Kitchen, Germany, wood w/center stove alcove, wallpapered, w/wood table, assorted tinware & accessories, 12x22", VG..$700.00

Kitchen, yel-pnt & stenciled tin walls w/red stove, working water pump & various accessories, 19" W, G, A $350.00

Modern Kitchen Set, Marx, litho tin, complete, NMIB.$250.00

Newlyweds Bathroom #192, 3-sided litho tin room complete w/furniture, 1925, 3x5x3", MIB $250.00

Newlyweds Dining Room, Marx #194, 3-sided litho tin room complete w/furniture, 1925, 3x5x3", MIB...............$250.00

Laundry Room, Arcade #716, three-sided cardboard room complete with cast-iron accessories, NMIB, A, $2,500.00.

Newlyweds Kitchen, Marx #190, 3-sided litho tin room complete w/furniture, 1925, 3x5x3", MIB $250.00

Newlyweds Parlor, Marx #193, 3-sided litho tin room complete w/furniture, 1925, 3x5x3", MIB $250.00

Rockaway Stable, Bliss, wood & cb, w/2 horses, sled & jockey, 11½x9½", EX, A $800.00

Stable, Germany, pnt wood w/paper litho roof, w/gates & accessories, 32x47", EX, A..$550.00

Victorian Room, 3-sided room w/bl, red & gold walls & floors, ca 1900, 7x12x7½", EX, A......................................$275.00

Dolls and Accessories

Obviously the field of dolls cannot be covered in a price guide such as this, but we wanted to touch on some of the later plastic dolls from the '50s and '60s, since so much of the collector interest today is centered on those decades. For in-depth information on dolls of all types, we recommend these lovely doll books, all of which are available from Collector Books: *Doll Values, Antique to Modern*, Vols, I, II, and III and *Modern Collectible Dolls* by Patsy Moyer; *Madame Alexander Collector's Dolls Price Guide #22* by Linda Crowsey; *The World of Raggedy Ann Collectibles* by Kim Avery; *Collector's Guide to Ideal Dolls*, Vols I and II, by Judith Izen; *Talking Toys of the 20th Century* by Kathy and Don Lewis; *Collector's Encyclopedia of American Composition Dolls, 1900 – 1950*, by Ursula R. Mertz; and *Effanbee Dolls* and *Collector's Encyclopedia of Madame Alexander Dolls, 1965 – 1990*, by Patricia Smith. Other books are referenced in specific subcategories.

See also Action Figures; Barbie and Friends; Character, TV, and Movie Collectibles; GI Joe; and other specific categories.

BABY DOLLS

Remnants of baby dolls have been found in the artifacts of most primitive digs. Some are just sticks or stuffed leather or animal skins.

Baby dolls teach our young nurturing and caring. Mothering instincts stay with us, and aren't we lucky as doll collectors that we can keep 'mothering' even after the young have 'flown the nest.'

Baby dolls come in all sizes and mediums: vinyl, plastic, rubber, porcelain, cloth, etc. Almost everyone remembers some baby doll they had as a child. The return to childhood is such a great trip. Keep looking and you will find yours.

Advisor: Marcia Fanta (M15).

Baby Brother Tender Love, Mattel, NRFB, B5 ....$75.00
Baby Cheerful Tearful, Mattel, 1966, 6½", MIB...............$75.00
Baby Cuddles, Ideal, 1930-40, rubber w/compo head, re-dressed, 22", EX...$150.00
Baby Dreams, Ideal, 1975-76, soft cloth w/vinyl head, 17", MIB, minimum value $50.00
Baby Ducky, Ideal, 1932-39, rubber w/compo head, orig outfit, 11", EX...$65.00
Baby Giggles, Ideal, 1967, 15", MIB..............................$95.00
Baby Kissy, Ideal, 1962, 23", NRFB, M15 ....$325.00
Baby Love Light, Mattel, 1971, stuffed cloth w/vinyl head & hands, NMIB $30.00
Baby Luv 'N Care, Topper, vinyl, rooted hair, orig yel & wht polka-dot outfit, 19", MIB...$40.00
Baby Pat-A-Burp, Mattel, 1963, orig outfit, 17", VG, M15...$70.00

Baby Small-Walk, Mattel, 1968, MIB, $55.00.
(Photo courtesy J. Michael Augustyniak)

Baby Tender Love, Mattel, 1971, orig outfit, 16", VG, M15.$25.00
Baby This 'N That, Remco, 1976, orig outfit, EX $40.00
Baby Tippee Toes, Mattel, 1967, 16", MIB, M15 ....$95.00
Belly Button Baby, Ideal, 1971, vinyl, several variations, 9½", MIB, ea...$65.00
Betsy Wetsy, Ideal, 1937-38, orig dress, EX (EX box) $300.00
Betsy Wetsy, Ideal, 1954-56, 16", MIB, minimum value ..$125.00
Black Butterball, Effanbee, 1969, vinyl, sleep eyes, orig wht lacy outfit & bonnet, EX, minimum value $75.00
Bye-Bye Baby, Ideal, 1960, vinyl, re-dressed, 25", NM.....$75.00
Cabbage Patch Baseball All-Star, Coleco, 1986, several different, M, ea from $55 to $75.00

Cabbage Patch Preemie, Coleco, w/pacifier & orig pk sleeper, VG, M15 ....$35.00

Cabbage Patch Talking Kid, Coleco, 1987, several different, M, ea, minimum value $225.00

Cabbage Patch Teenie Tiny Preemie Twins, Oriental or Hispanic, M, ea $50.00

Cabbage Patch Twins, Coleco, 1985-86, M, from $75 to .$125.00

Cabbage Patch World Traveler, Coleco, 1985, several different, M, ea from $55 to $75.00

Dancerella, Mattel, 1976, 15", MIB $75.00

Dancerina, Mattel, 1972, plastic & vinyl, blond hair, orig tutu, 17", M $100.00

Drinkee Walker, Horsman, 1988, plastic & vinyl, rooted hair, orig outfit, NM, minimum value $35.00

Dy-Dee Baby, Effanbee, 1935, complete w/wardrobe, 11", MIB $425.00

Gabbigale, Kenner, 1972, 19", MIB, M15 ....$65.00

Goody Two Shoes, Ideal, 1965, vinyl, orig bl dress, 19", NMIB, minimum value...$125.00

Heartbeat Baby, Effanbee, 1942, compo w/cloth dress, clockwork mechanism, EX, 17", minimum value $200.00

I Love You Dolly, Uneeda, 1989, cloth w/vinyl head, orig outfit, 14", EX $20.00

Johnny Playpal, Ideal, 1959, re-dressed, 24", NM..........$225.00

Little Betsy Wetsy, Ideal, 1957, complete w/diaper & bottle (12 outfits sold separately), MIB, minimum value...........$75.00

Little Lost Baby, Ideal, 1968, soft body w/vinyl head, 22", MIB, minimum value...$85.00

Little Miss Echo, American Character, 1964, 28", MIB, M15 ....$225.00

Magic Baby Tender Love, Mattel, 1978, 14", MIB, M15..$30.00

My Bottle Baby, Ideal, 1979-80, stuffed cloth w/vinyl head, 14", MIB, minimum value...$40.00

Patty Playpal, Ideal, 1959, in print dress w/pinafore, 35", NM .$375.00

Patty Playpal, Ideal, 1960s, in nurse's uniform, 36", M, M15...$325.00

Patty Playpal, Ideal, 1980s, reissue, 36", MIB, M15........$375.00

Plassie, Ideal, 1942, stuffed cloth w/hard plastic head, orig dress, 19", EX, minimum value $150.00

Posie, Ideal, 1954-56, plastic & vinyl, rooted saran hair, 23", NMIB, minimum value $150.00

Posie Baby, Lucky Bell, 1992, foam-stuffed body w/vinyl head, arms & legs, orig yel & wht outfit, 13½", EX.............$20.00

Pretty Curls, Ideal, 1981-82, orig outfit, EX $40.00

Rub-A-Dub Dolly, Black, Ideal, 1979-80, 16", NRFB, M15 .$50.00

Rub-A-Dub Dolly in Tugboat Shower, Ideal, 1974-78, 17", MIB..$65.00

Saucy Walker, Ideal, 1960-61, orig red print dress & pinafore, 28", MIB, minimum value $200.00

Suzy Playpal, Ideal, 1959-60, orig purple dotted dress, 28", NM, minimum value..$300.00

Talking Patty Playpal, Ideal, 1986, 27", MIB, M15 ....$225.00

Tearful Tender Love, Mattel, 1971, 16", VG, M15 ....$45.00

Tearie Dearie, Ideal, 1963-67, vinyl, orig outfit, 9", EX....$40.00

Tearie Dearie Twins, Ideal, 1963, vinyl, orig outfits, 9", EX .$65.00

Teeny Tiny Tears, American Character, 1960s, vinyl, re-dressed, 12", EX...$45.00

Tender Love & Kisses, Mattel, 1976, 14", MIB, M15......$25.00

Tiny Baby Tender Love, Mattel, 1971, orig outfit, 11½", VG, M15...$35.00

Tiny Kissy, Ideal, 1963-66, vinyl, orig red outfit w/wht pinafore, 16", MIB, minimum value $95.00

Tiny Tears, American Character, 1950s, orig outfit, 12", VG, M15..$125.00

Poor Pitiful Pearl, Tristar, 16", MIB, $95.00.
(Photo courtesy Marcia Fanta)

Tiny Thumbelina, Ideal, 1962 – 68, 14", MIB, $185.00.
(Photo courtesy Judith Izen)

Tiny Tubber, Effanbee, 1976, orig print dress, 11", rare, MIB, M17..$75.00

Upsy Dazy, Ideal, 1973, soft foam w/vinyl head, flat spindle hands, 15", EX...$40.00

BETSY MCCALL

The tiny 8" Betsy McCall doll was manufactured by the American Character Doll Co. from 1957 through 1963. She was made from high-quality hard plastic with a bisque-like finish and hand-painted features. Betsy came in four hair colors — tosca, red, blond, and brunette. She had blue sleep eyes, molded lashes, a winsome smile, and a fully jointed body with bendable knees. On her back there is an identification circle which reads McCall Corp. The basic doll wore a sheer chemise, white taffeta panties, nylon socks, and Maryjane-style shoes, and could be purchased for $2.25.

There were two different materials used for tiny Betsy's hair. The first was a soft mohair sewn into fine mesh. Later the rubber scullcap was rooted with saran which was more suitable for washing and combing.

Betsy McCall had an extensive wardrobe with nearly one hundred outfits, each of which could be purchased separately. They were made from wonderful fabrics such as velvet, taffeta, felt, and even real mink. Each ensemble came with the appropriate footwear and was priced under $3.00. Since none of Betsy's clothing was tagged, it is often difficult to identify other than by its square snap closures (although these were used by other companies as well).

Betsy McCall is a highly collectible doll today but is still fairly easy to find at doll shows. Prices remain reasonable for this beautiful clothes horse and her many accessories. For further information we recommend *Betsy McCall, A Collector's Guide*, by Marci Van Ausdall.

Advisor: Marci Van Ausdall (V2).

See also Clubs and Newsletters.

Doll, American Character, orig outfit, multi-jtd, 29", MIB, V2 ....$250.00
Doll, Ideal, all orig, M, V2......................................$225.00
Doll, orig outfit w/pk tissue & booklet, 8", MIB, V2 ......$225.00
Doll, starter kit #9300, blond hair w/side part, complete, EX (worn card), V2, minimum value..............................$225.00
Doll, TV Time, #9153, all orig, M, V2 ....$150.00
Doll, Uneeda, all orig, 11½", EX, V2..........................$45.00
Doll, w/trunk & wardrobe, 14", M $500.00
Doll, wearing pk Prom Time formal, 8", EX, V2............$150.00
Doll, wearing 1959 gr ballerina outfit & slippers, EX, V2 ..$175.00

Everyday Calendar, Milton Bradley, EX (worn box), $25.00.
(Photo courtesy Robert Kimble)

Doll, American Character, Playtime outfit, 14", EX, $250.00.
(Photo courtesy Robert Kimble)

Outfit, Bar-B-Q, MOC, $125.00.
(Photo courtesy Marci Van Ausdall)

Outfit, April Showers, complete, EX, V2.........................$45.00
Outfit, fur stole & muff, MIB, V2....................................$150.00
Outfit, Prom Time Formal, bl, EX, V2 ....$50.00
Outfit, Sunday Best, 1957, complete, EX, V2...............$100.00

Doll, American Character, in Town & Country outfit, 8", M $175.00

Outfit, Zoo Time, complete, VG, V2 ....$50.00
Pattern, McCall's #2247, uncut, V2 ....$25.00

BLYTHE BY KENNER

Blythe by Kenner is an 11" doll with a slender body and an extra large head. You can change her eye color by pulling a string in the back of her head. She came with different hair colors and had fashions, cases, and wigs that could be purchased separately. She was produced in the early 1970s which accounts for her 'groovy' wardrobe.

Advisor: Dawn Parrish (P2).

Case, #33241, image of blond-haired doll wearing Pow-Wow Poncho, orange background, vinyl, EX, P2 ....$50.00
Doll, brunette, wearing Medieval Mood, EX, P2 ....$50.00
Doll, lt red hair, wearing Golden Goddess, EX, P2 ....$50.00
Doll, red hair, wearing Love 'N Lace, EX, P2 ....$50.00
Outfit, Aztec Arrival, complete, EX, P2..........................$50.00
Outfit, Golden Goddess, NRFB, P2 ....$75.00
Outfit, Kozy Kape, complete, EX, P2..............................$50.00
Outfit, Lounging Lovely, NRFB, P2.................................$75.00
Outfit, Love 'N Lace, NRFB, P2......................................$75.00
Outfit, Pleasant Peasant, missing shoes, EX, P2 ....$40.00
Outfit, Pow-Wow Poncho, complete, EX, P2 ....$50.00
Outfit, Priceless Parfait, missing 1 boot, EX, P2............$45.00
Wig, Lemon, complete w/instructions, M, P2 ....$75.00

CELEBRITY AND PERSONALITY DOLLS

Celebrity and character dolls have been widely collected for many years, but they've lately shown a significant increase in demand. Except for the rarer examples, most of these dolls are still fairly easy to find at doll shows, toy auctions, and flea markets, and the majority are priced under $100.00. These are the dolls that bring back memories of childhood TV shows, popular songs, favorite movies, and familiar characters. Mego, Mattel, Remco, and Hasbro are among the largest manufacturers.

Condition is a very important worth-assessing factor, and if the doll is still in the original box, so much the better! Should the box be unopened (NRFB), the value is further enhanced. Using mint as a standard, add 50% for the same doll mint in the box and 75% if it has never been taken out. On the other hand, dolls in only good or poorer condition drop at a rapid pace.

Advisor: Henri Yunes (Y1).

Abba, Matchbox, 1978, 4 different, 9", MIB, ea..............$85.00
Abbott & Costello (Who's on First), Ideal, 1984, gift set, 12", MIB, Y1 ....$100.00
Al Lewis (Grandpa Munster), Remco, 1964, 6", MIB $200.00
Alan Alda (Hawkeye from M*A*S*H), Woolworth, 1976, MOC, Y1 ....$30.00
Alexandra Paul (Stephanie from Baywatch), Toy Island, 1997, 11½", NRFB, Y1 ....$35.00
Andy Gibb, Ideal, 1979, 7½", NRFB $50.00
Angie Dickinson (Police Woman), Horsman, 1976, 9", MIB.$60.00
Annissa Jones (Buffy from Family Affair), Mattel, 1967, talker, 10" w/5" Mrs Beasley doll, MIB, Y1 ....$300.00

Annissa Jones (Buffy from Family Affair), Mattel, 1967, 6" w/3" Mrs Beasley doll, MIB $125.00
Barbara Eden (I Dream of Jeannie), Libby Majorette Doll Corp, 1966, 20", rare, NRFB $500.00
Barbara Eden (I Dream of Jeannie), outfit, Remco, 1977, several variations, for 6" dolls, MIP, ea $12.00
Barbara Eden (I Dream of Jeannie), Remco, 1972, 6½", NRFB $100.00
Beatles, Remco, 1964, ea member w/instrument, ea from $150 to $200.00
Beverly Hills 90210, accessory, Peach Pit Snack Shop, Mattel, 1992, complete, MIB $100.00
Beverly Hills 90210, Mattel, 1991, 5 different, 11½", MIB, ea...$65.00
Beverly Hills 90210, outfits, Mattel, 1992, several different, MIP, ea..$20.00
Beverly Johnson, Real Models Collection, Matchbox, 1989, 11½", NRFB $55.00
Bobby Orr, Regal, 1975, 12", rare, MOC $800.00
Boy George, LJN, 1984, 11½", scarce, MIB.................$135.00
Brooke Shields, LJN, 1982, 1st issue, 11½", NRFB $50.00
Brooke Shields, LJN, 1983, 2nd issue, in swimsuit w/suntan body, 11½", rare, NRFB $95.00
Brooke Shields, LJN, 1983, 3rd issue, Prom Party outfit, 11½", rare, NRFB $200.00
Captain & Tenille, Mego, 1970s, 12", MIB, ea................$60.00
Carol Channing (Hello Dolly), Nasco Dolls, 1962, 11½", rare, MIB $350.00
Cher, Mego, 1976, 1st issue, pk dress, 12", NRFB (orange box)..$70.00
Cher, Mego, 1977, 2nd issue, Growing Hair, 12", NRFB (photo on pk box)..$80.00
Cher, Mego, 1981, 3rd issue, red swimsuit, 12", rare, NRFB (photo on box)..$95.00
Cheryl Ladd (Kris from Charlie's Angels), Hasbro, 1977, jumpsuit & scarf, 8½", MOC..............................$40.00
Cheryl Ladd (Kris from Charlie's Angels), Mattel, 1978, 11½", NRFB $80.00
Cheryl Tiegs, Real Models Collection, Matchbox, 1989, 11½", NRFB $55.00
Christy Brinkley, Real Models Collection, Matchbox, 1989, 11½", NRFB $55.00
Clark Gable (Rhett Butler), World Dolls, 1980, 1st edition, 12", NRFB $65.00
Claudia Schiffer, Top Models Collection, Hasbro, 1995, 11½", rare, MIB $100.00
David Hasselhoff (Mitch from Baywatch), Toy Island, 1997, 12", NRFB, Y1 ....$35.00
Debbie Boone, Mattel, 1978, 11", MIB, H4.....................$50.00
Dennis Rodman (Bad As I Wanna Be), Street Players, 1995, 11½", MIB, Y1 ....$55.00
Desi Arnez (Ricky Ricardo), Applause, 1988, 17", MIB...$50.00
Desi Arnez (Ricky Ricardo), Hamilton Presents, 1991, 15½", MIB $40.00
Diahann Carroll (Julia), Mattel, 1969, 1st edition, gold & silver jumpsuit, straight hair, talker, 11½", NRFB $200.00
Diahann Carroll (Julia), Mattel, 1969, 1st edition, 2-pc nurse uniform, 11½", NRFB $200.00
Diahann Carroll (Julia), Mattel, 1970, 2nd edition, 1-pc nurse uniform, 11½", NRFB, Y1 ....$200.00

Diahann Carroll (Julia), Mattel, 1971, 2nd edition, gold & silver jumpsuit, Afro hair style, talker, 11½", NRFB........$200.00

Diahann Carroll (Julia), outfit, Leather Weather, Mattel, 1969, NRFB...$165.00

Diana Ross, Mego, 1977, wht & silver dress, 12", NRFB..$125.00

Diana Ross (of the Supremes), Ideal, 1969, 19", NRFB..$150.00

Dick Clark, Juro, 1958, 24", MIB $250.00

Dolly Parton, Eegee, 1980, 1st edition, red jumpsuit, 12", NRFB $65.00

Dolly Parton, Eegee, 1987, 2nd edition, blk jumpsuit or cowgirl outfit, 11½", NRFB, ea.......................................$50.00

Dolly Parton, Goldberger, 1996, red checked dress or long blk dress, 11½", NRFB, ea $30.00

Dolly Parton, World, 1987, red gown, 18", NRFB, M15 .$100.00

Donna Douglas (Ellie Mae), 1964, jeans w/rope belt or yel dress, MIB, Y1, ea..$65.00

Donny & Marie, outfits, Mattel/Sears Exclusive, 1977, several different, MIP, ea..$50.00

Donny & Marie Osmond, Mattel, 1976, gift set, 11½", NRFB $100.00

Dorothy Hamill, 1977, red olympic outfit w/medal, 11½", NRFB.$75.00

Dr J (Julias Erving), Shindana, Deluxe Set, 1977, w/outfits, 9½", MIB $400.00

Dr J (Julias Erving), Shindana, 1977, w/basketball, 9½", MIB .$100.00

Drew Carey, Creation, 1998, 11½", NRFB, Y1................$30.00

Elizabeth Montgomery (Samantha from Bewitched), Ideal, 1965, 12", rare, MIB $600.00

Elizabeth Taylor (Butterfield 8 or Cat on a Hot Tin Roof), Tristar, 1982, 11½", MIB, ea..................................$125.00

Elizabeth Taylor (Father of the Bride, Butterfield 8 or Cat on a Hot Tin Roof), World Doll, 1989, 11½", MIB, ea $65.00

Elizabeth Taylor (The Bluebird), Horsman, 1976, w/3 outfits, 12", NRFB...$150.00

Elvis, Eugene, 1984, issued in 6 different outfits, 12", MIB, ea.$60.00

Elvis (Aloha Hawaii), World Dolls, 1984, porcelain, wht jumpsuit, MIB $200.00

Elvis (Burning Love), World Doll, 1984, 21", MIB........$110.00

Elvis (Teen Idol, Jailhouse Rock or '68 Special), Hasbro, 1993, numbered edition, 12", MIB, ea $50.00

Farrah Fawcett (Jill from Charlie's Angels), Hasbro, 1977, jumpsuit & scarf, 8½", MOC...................................$40.00

Farrah Fawcett (Jill from Charlie's Angels), Mego, 1976, 1st edition, wht jumpsuit, 12", NRFB (photo on gr box).....$60.00

Farrah Fawcett (Jill from Charlie's Angels), Mego, 1981, lavender swimsuit, 12", rare, NRFB (photo on purple box)........$95.00

Flip Wilson/Geraldine, Shindana, 1970, plush w/vinyl head, 2-sided, 16", MIB, M15 ....$65.00

Flo-Jo, LJN, 1989, pk & bl athletic outfit w/bag, 11½", MIB .$60.00

Fran Dresher (Nanny), Street Players, 1995, 3 different outfits, talker, 11½", MIB...$55.00

Fred Gwynne (Herman Munster), Presents, 1990, plush w/vinyl head, 12", MIB...$35.00

Fred Gwynne (Herman Munster), Remco, 1964, MIB...$150.00

Grace Kelly (The Swan or Mogambo), Tri-Star, 1982, 11½", MIB, ea $125.00

Groucho Marx, Effanbee, 1983, 17", MIB, M15 ....$90.00

Jaclyn Smith (Kelly from Charlie's Angels), Hasbro, 1977, jumpsuit & scarf, 8½", MOC $40.00

Jaclyn Smith (Kelly from Charlie's Angels), Mego, 1978, bl dress, 12", rare, NRFB......................................$125.00

Jaleel White (Steve Urkel), Hasbro, 1991, cloth & vinyl, 17", MIB...$50.00

James Dean, DSI, 1994, Rebel Rouser or City Streets outfit, 12", NRFB, M15, ea $75.00

Jimmy Osmond, Mattel, 1978, 9", MIB.........................$75.00

Jimmy Walker (JJ from Good Times), Shindana, 1975, cloth & vinyl, 15", MIB, Y1 ....$50.00

Joe Namath, Mego, 1970, 11½", rare, MIB....................$400.00

John Stamos (Jesse from Full House), Tiger, 1993, 11½", MIB, Y1 ....$40.00

John Travolta (On Stage...Superstar), Chemtoy, 1977, 12", NRFB...$125.00

John Wayne, Effanbee, 1981, Great Legends series, Spirit of the West outfit, 17", MIB.....................................$125.00

John Wayne, Effanbee, 1982, Great Legends series, Guardian of the West outfit, 18", MIB..................................$125.00

Judy Garland (Wizard of Oz), Effanbee, 1984, Great Legends series, w/Toto & basket, 14½", MIB $100.00

Judy Garland (Wizard of Oz), Multitoys, 1984, 50th Anniversary, rare, MIB $100.00

Julie Andrews (Mary Poppins), Horsman, 1964, 1st edition, 12", MIB, Y1 ....$125.00

Julie Andrews (Mary Poppins), Horsman, 1964, 3-pc gift set, 11" w/5" Michael & Jan dolls, rare, NRFB....................$250.00

Julie Andrews (Mary Poppins), Horsman, 1973, 2nd edition, 11", MIB, Y1 ....$75.00

Karen Mulder, Top Models Collection, Hasbro, 1995, 11½", rare, MIB...$100.00

Kate Jackson (Sabrina from Charlie's Angels), Hasbro, 1977, jumpsuit & scarf, 8½", MOC $40.00

Lucille Ball (as Lucy Ricardo), Mattel, Collector Edition, 1996, NRFB, minimum value $75.00.
(Photo courtesy J. Michael Augustyniak)

Kate Jackson (Sabrina from Charlie's Angels), Mattel, 1978, red & wht dress, 11½", NRFB $60.00

KISS, Ace Frehley, Gene Simmons, Paul Stanley or Peter Criss, Mego, 1978, 12", NRFB, ea......................................$125.00

Kristy McNichol (Buddy from Family), Mattel, 1978, w/extra outfit, 9", MIB..$45.00

Kristy McNichol (Buddy from Family), Mego, 9½", MIB, Y1 ....$40.00

Laurel & Hardy, Knickerbocker, 1960s, cloth bodies w/vinyl heads, 9½", MIB, ea..$65.00

Laverne & Shirley, Mego, 1977, 12", NRFB, pr $125.00

Lenny & Squiggy, Mego, 1977, 12", NRFB, pr $200.00

Linda Carter (Wonder Woman), Mego, 1976, 1st issue, w/military uniform, rare, 12", MIB (photo on box) $85.00

Lucille Ball (I Love Lucy), 1952, cloth, 26", rare, NRFB, Y1..$800.00

Macaully Caulkin (Kevin from Home Alone), THQ Inc, 1989, screams, MIB, Y1 ....$25.00

Madonna (Breathless Mahoney), Applause, 1990, blk evening gown w/gold trim & heels, 10", MIB.........................$40.00

Madonna (Breathless Mahoney), Playmates, 1990, plastic, bl dress, 19", NRFB...$60.00

Mae West, Effanbee, 1982, Great Legends series, 18", MIB .$120.00

Marie Osmond, Mattel, 1976, 11", MIB..........................$50.00

Marie Osmond, Mattel, 1976, 30", MIB $115.00

Marilyn Monroe, DSI, 1993, issued in 6 different outfits, 11½", NRFB, ea...$60.00

Marilyn Monroe, Tristar, 1982, issued in 4 different outfits, 16", NRFB, ea $110.00

Marla Gibbs (Florence from The Jeffersons), 1978, 16", MIB, M15...$100.00

Mary Kate/Ashley Olsen (Michelle from Full House), cloth body w/vinyl head, talker, 15", MIB.................................$40.00

MC Hammer, Mattel, 1991, gold outfit w/boom box, 11½", MIB...$85.00

MC Hammer, Mattel, 1991, purple outfit, 11½", MIB.....$70.00

MC Hammer, outfit, Mattel, 1992, several different, MIP, ea...$15.00

Michael Jackson, LJN, 1984, issued in 4 different outfits, 11½", NRFB $70.00

Michael Jackson (King of Pop Singing Doll), Streetlife, 1995, 11½", rare, MIB, Y1 ....$250.00

Mr T, Galoob, 1983, 1st edition, bib overalls, 12", MIB...$60.00

Mr T, Galoob, 1983, 2nd edition, talker, vest & jeans, 12", MIB...$75.00

Naomi Campbell, Top Models Collection, Hasbro, 1995, 11½", rare, MIB...$100.00

New Kids on the Block, 1990, 1st issue, Hangin' Loose, 5 different dolls, 12", MIB, ea $40.00

New Kids on the Block, 1990, 2nd issue, In Concert, 5 different dolls, 12", MIB, ea..$50.00

OJ Simpson, Shindana, Deluxe Set, 1975, w/several outfits & accessories, 9½", MIB...$450.00

OJ Simpson, Shindana, 1975, 9½", MIB, Y1 ....$250.00

Pam Dawber (Mork & Mindy), Mattel, 1979, 8½", MIB .$50.00

Pamela Anderson Lee (CJ from Baywatch), Toy Island, Deluxe Set, 1998, 11½", NRFB, Y1...............................$50.00

Pamela Anderson Lee (CJ from Baywatch), Toy Island, 1997, 11½", NRFB, Y1 ....$35.00

Parker Stevenson (Frank from the Hardy Boys), Kenner, 1978, 12", NRFB, H4..$50.00

Marilyn Monroe (Seven Year Itch), Tristar, 1982, 11½", NRFB, $100.00. (Photo courtesy Henri Yunes)

Prince Charles and Princess Diana, Goldberger, 1982, wedding outfits, 12", rare, MIB, $550.00.
(Photo courtesy Martin and Carolyn Berens)

Patty Duke (Patty Duke Show), Horsman, 1967, 12½", rare, NRFB $400.00

Prince Charles, Goldberger, 1982, military wedding outfit, 12", NRFB $250.00

Prince Charles, Goldberger, 1982, Palace Guard outfit, 12", rare, NRFB $350.00

Prince Charles, Peggy Nisbet/England, 1984, wedding outfit, 8", MIB $100.00

Prince Charles & Princess Diana, Goldberger, 1982, wedding outfits, gift set, 12", very rare, NRFB $600.00

Princess Diana, Danbury Mint, 1985, pk dress, 15", MIB .$110.00

Princess Diana, Goldberger, 1982, silver dress, 11½", rare, NRFB $350.00

Princess Diana, Goldberger, 1982, wedding gown, 11½", NRFB $450.00

Princess Diana, Peggy Nesbit/England, 1984, wedding gown, 8", M $100.00

Redd Fox, Shindana, 1977, cloth, talker, MIB $45.00

Rex Harrison (Dr Dolittle), accessory, Talking Puddleby Cottage, Mattel, 1968, vinyl, complete, M $130.00

Rex Harrison (Dr Dolittle), Mattel, 1967, w/Polynesia Parrot, 6", NRFB $65.00

Rex Harrison (Dr Dolittle), Mattel, 1967, w/Pushmi-Pullyu & Polynesia, 6", MIB $90.00

Rex Harrison (Dr Dolittle), Mattel, 1969, cloth body w/vinyl head, talker, 24", MIB $130.00

Richard Chamberlain (Dr Kildare), Bing Crosby Productions, 1962, rare, MIB..$350.00

Robin Williams (Mork & Mindy), Mattel, 1979, w/space pak, 9", MIB $45.00

Sally Ann Howes (Truly Scrumptious from Chitty-Chitty Bang-Bang), Mattel, 1969, pk dress, talker, 11½", MIB......$450.00

Sally Ann Howes (Truly Scrumptious from Chitty-Chitty Bang-Bang), Mattel, 1969, wht dress, 11½", MIB $400.00

Sally Field (Flying Nun), Hasbro, 1967, 12", MIB.........$200.00

Sally Field (Flying Nun), Hasbro, 1967, 5", MIB.............$80.00

Sarah Stimson (Little Miss Marker), Ideal, 1980, 12", MIB.$40.00

Saved by the Bell, Tiger, 1992, 6 different, 11½", NRFB, Y1, ea $40.00

Selena, Arm Enterprises, 1996, 11½", MIB $50.00

Shaun Cassidy (Joe from the Hardy Boys), Kenner, 1978, 12", NRFB $50.00

Shirley Temple, Ideal, 1934, Stand Up & Cheer outfit, 15", EX $700.00

Shirley Temple, Ideal, 1957, orig bl & pk flocked dress, 12", VG, M15..$150.00

Shirley Temple, Ideal, 1972, Stand Up & Cheer outfit, 16", MIB, M15 ....$160.00

Shirley Temple, Ideal, 1982, issued in 6 different outfits, 8", MIB, M15, ea $60.00

Shirley Temple, Ideal, 1984, Glad Rags to Riches outfit, 16", rare, MIB, M15 ....$125.00

Sonny Bono, Mego, 1976, 12", NRFB (orange box).......$150.00

Soupy Sales, Sunshine Dolls, 1965, 6", NRFB, J2..........$235.00

Spice Girls (Girl Power), Galoob, 1997, 1st issue, 5 different, 11½", NRFB, Y1 ....$70.00

Spice Girls (On Tour), Galoob, 1997, 2nd issue, 5 different, 11½", NRFB, Y1 ....$60.00

Spice Girls (Superstar Spice Collection Gift Set), Galoob, 1998, 3rd issue, 11½", NRFB, Y1 ....$350.00

Susan Dey (Laurie from Partridge Family), Remco, 1973, 16", rare, MIB...$250.00

Sylvester Stallone (Over the Top), Lewco Toys, 1986, 20", NRFB $35.00

Sylvester Stallone (Rocky), Phoenix Toys, 1983, 8", MOC, H4 ....$45.00

Shirley Temple, Ideal, 20", NMIB, sold at McMasters 1996 auction for $2,000.00.

Suzanne Somers (Chrissy from Three's Company), Mego, 1970s, 12½", MIB, $85.00.
(Photo courtesy Greg Davis and Bill Morgan)

Tatum O'Neal (International Velvet), Kenner, 1979, 11½", MIB $85.00

Three Stooges, Collins, 1982, set of 3, 13", MOC.........$140.00

Twiggy, Mattel, 1967, 11½", rare, MIB $400.00

Twiggy, outfit, #1725, 1968, NRFB, $200.00.
(Photo courtesy J. Michael Augustyniak)

Twiggy, outfit, Twiggy Turnouts, #1726, 1968, NRFP ...$200.00

Vanilla Ice, THQ, 1991, issued in 3 different outfits, 12", NRFB, ea..$50.00

WC Fields, 1980, 16", M, J6, $85.00.
(Photo courtesy June Moon)

Vanna White, Pacific Media/Home Shopping Network, 1990, issued in 20 different outfits, 11½", NRFB, ea...........$50.00

Vanna White, Totsy Toys, 1990, limited edition, wedding dress, rare, MIB...$125.00

Vince Edwards (Ben Casey), Bing Crosby Productions, 1962, 12", rare, MIB $400.00

Vivian Leigh (Scarlett), World Dolls, 1980, 1st issue, 12", NRFB...$65.00

Wayne Gretsky, Mattel, 1982, The Great Gretsky/Le Magnifique, 11½", MIB..$150.00

Wayne Gretsky, outfit, Mattel, 1982, several different, MIP, ea...$100.00

Yvonne De Carlo (Lily Munster), Remco, 1964, MIB ...$150.00

CHATTY CATHY

In their book, *Chatty Cathy Dolls, An Identification & Value Guide*, authorities Kathy and Don Lewis (L6) tell us that Chatty Cathy (made by Mattel) has been the second most popular doll ever made. She was introduced in the 1960s and came as either a blond or a brunette. For five years, she sold very well. Much of her success can be attributed to the fact that Chatty Cathy talked. By pulling the string on her back, she could respond with eleven different phrases. During her five years of fame, Mattel added to the line with Chatty Baby, Tiny Chatty Baby and Tiny Chatty Brother (the twins), Charmin' Chatty, and finally Singing' Chatty. Charmin' Chatty had sixteen interchangeable records. Her voice box was activated in the same manner as the above-mentioned dolls, by means of a pull string located at the base of her neck. The line was brought back in 1969, smaller and with a restyled face, but it was not well received.

Advisors: Kathy and Don Lewis (L6).

See Also Coloring, Activity, and Paint Books; Paper Dolls; Puzzles.

Doll, Charmin' Chatty, MIB, $275.00.
(Photo courtesy Kathy Lewis)

Armoire, Chatty Cathy, L6 ....$175.00
Bedspread, Chatty Baby, twin-sz, L6 ....$400.00
Carrying Case, Chatty Baby, pk or bl, L6, ea $45.00
Carrying Case, Tiny Chatty Baby, pk or bl, L6, ea $35.00
Cover & Pillow Set, Tiny Chatty Cathy, L6 ....$75.00
Crib, Tiny Chatty Baby, MIB, L6 ....$300.00
Doll, Black Chatty Baby, M, L6 ....$650.00
Doll, Black Chatty Baby, w/pigtails, M, L6 ....$1,500.00
Doll, Black Chatty Cathy, 1962, pageboy-style hair, M, L6 ..$1,200.00
Doll, Black Tiny Chatty Baby, M, L6 ....$650.00
Doll, Charmin' Chatty, auburn or blond hair, bl eyes, 1 record,
    M, L6 ....$250.00
Doll, Chatty Baby, brunette hair, red pinafore over wht romper,
    orig tag, MIB, L6 ....$250.00
Doll, Chatty Baby, early, brunette hair, brn eyes, M, L6 .$160.00
Doll, Chatty Baby, early, ring around speaker, blond hair, bl
    eyes, M, L6 ....$250.00
Doll, Chatty Baby, open speaker, blond hair, bl eyes, M, L6 .$250.00
Doll, Chatty Baby, open speaker, brunette hair, bl eyes, M,
    L6 ....$250.00
Doll, Chatty Baby, open speaker, brunette hair, brn eyes, M,
    L6 ....$375.00
Doll, Chatty Cathy, brunette hair, brn eyes, M, L6 ....$375.00
Doll, Chatty Cathy, early, brunette hair, bl eyes, M, L6...$85.00
Doll, Chatty Cathy, later issue, open speaker, blond hair, bl eyes,
    M, L6 ....$750.00
Doll, Chatty Cathy, later issue, open speaker, brunette hair, bl
    eyes, M, L6 ....$750.00
Doll, Chatty Cathy, later issue, open speaker, brunette hair, brn
    eyes, M, L6 ....$850.00
Doll, Chatty Cathy, mid-year or transitional, brunette hair, brn
    eyes, M, L6 ....$650.00
Doll, Chatty Cathy, mid-year or transitional, brunette hair, bl
    eyes, M, L6 ....$650.00
Doll, Chatty Cathy, mid-year or transitional, open speaker,
    blond hair, bl eyes, M, L6 ....$600.00
Doll, Chatty Cathy, patent pending, brunette hair, bl eyes, M,
    L6 ....$750.00
Doll, Chatty Cathy, patent pending, cloth over speaker or ring
    around speaker, blond hair, bl eyes, M, L6 ....$750.00
Doll, Chatty Cathy, porcelain, 1980, MIB, L6 ....$750.00
Doll, Chatty Cathy, reissue, blond hair, bl eyes, MIB, L6...$80.00
Doll, Chatty Cathy, soft face, w/pigtails, blond, brunette or
    auburn hair, M, L6, ea $550.00
Doll, Chatty Cathy, unmk prototype, brunette hair, bl eyes, M,
    L6 ....$900.00
Doll, Chatty Cathy, unmk prototype, brunette hair, brn eyes, M,
    L6 ....$1,000.00
Doll, Chatty Cathy, unmk prototype, cloth speaker, blond hair,
    M, L6 ....$900.00
Doll, Singin' Chatty, blond hair, M, L6 ....$250.00
Doll, Singin' Chatty, brunette hair, M, L6 ....$275.00
Doll, Tiny Chatty Baby, blond hair, bl eyes, M, L6 ....$250.00
Doll, Tiny Chatty Baby, brunette hair, bl eyes, M, L6 ...$275.00
Doll, Tiny Chatty Baby, brunette hair, brn eyes, M, L6 .$300.00
Dolls, Tiny Chatty Twins, M, L6, ea $250.00
Jewelry Set, Chatty Cathy, MIP, L6 ....$150.00
Nursery Set, Chatty Baby, NRFB, L6 ....$200.00

Outfit, Charmin' Chatty, Cinderella, MIP, L6 ....$115.00
Outfit, Charmin' Chatty, Let's Go Shopping, MIP, L6 ....$85.00
Outfit, Charmin' Chatty, Let's Play Birthday Party, MIP, L6 .$100.00
Outfit, Charmin' Chatty, Let's Play Nurse, MIP, L6 ....$90.00
Outfit, Charmin' Chatty, Let's Play Pajama Party, MIP, L6 .$100.00
Outfit, Charmin' Chatty, Let's Play Tea Party, MIP, L6 ....$100.00
Outfit, Charmin' Chatty, Let's Play Together, MIP, L6 ...$75.00
Outfit, Chatty Baby, Leotard set, MIP, L6 ....$75.00
Outfit, Chatty Baby, Outdoors, MIP, L6 ....$75.00
Outfit, Chatty Baby, Overall set, pk or bl, MIP, L6, ea $65.00
Outfit, Chatty Baby, Party Pink, MIP, L6 ....$100.00
Outfit, Chatty Baby, Playsuit, MIP, L6 ....$45.00
Outfit, Chatty Baby, Sleeper set, MIP, L6 ....$55.00
Outfit, Chatty Cathy, Nursery School, MIP, L6 ....$145.00
Outfit, Chatty Cathy, Party Coat, MIP, L6 ....$150.00
Outfit, Chatty Cathy, Party Dress, bl gingham, MIP, L6..$250.00
Outfit, Chatty Cathy, Pink Peppermint Stick, MIP, L6 .$150.00
Outfit, Chatty Cathy, Playtime, MIP, L6 ....$145.00
Outfit, Chatty Cathy, Red Peppermint Stick (Candystripe),
    MIP, L6 ....$400.00
Outfit, Chatty Cathy, Sleepytime, MIP, L6 ....$125.00
Outfit, Chatty Cathy, Sunday Visit, MIP, L6 ....$200.00
Outfit, Chatty Cathy, Sunny Day, MIP, L6 ....$200.00
Outfit, Tiny Chatty Baby, Bye-Bye, MIP, L6 ....$65.00
Outfit, Tiny Chatty Baby, Dashin' Dots, MIP, L6 ....$175.00
Outfit, Tiny Chatty Baby, Fun Time, MIP, L6 ....$140.00
Outfit, Tiny Chatty Baby, Night-Night, MIP, L6 ....$90.00
Outfit, Tiny Chatty Baby, Pink Frill, MIP, L6 ....$125.00
Outfit, Tiny Chatty Baby, Playmate, bl gingham, MIP, L6.$250.00
Pattern, Chatty Baby, uncut, L6 ....$18.50
Pattern, Chatty Cathy, uncut, L6 ....$18.50
Pencil-Point Bed, Chatty Cathy, L6 ....$350.00
Play Hats, Charmin' Chatty, L6 ....$55.00
Play Table, Chatty Baby, L6 ....$175.00
Stroll-a-Buggy, Chatty Baby, 9-way, complete, L6 ....$300.00
Stroller, Chatty Baby, Walkin' Talk, L6 ....$500.00
Stroller, Chatty Cathy, 5-way, complete, L6 ....$225.00
Tea Cart, Chatty Cathy, w/2 trays, L6 ....$100.00
Teeter-Totter, Tiny Chatty Baby Twins, L6 ....$500.00

CRISSY AND HER FAMILY

Ideal's 18" Crissy doll with growing hair was very popular
with little girls of the early 1970s. She was introduced in 1969 and
continued to be sold throughout the 1970s, enjoying a relatively
long market life for a doll. During the 1970s, many different versions of Crissy were made. Numerous friends followed her success,
all with the growing hair feature like Crissy's. The other Ideal
'grow hair' dolls in the line included Velvet, Cinnamon, Tressy,
Dina, Mia, Kerry, Brandi, and Cricket. Crissy is the easiest member in the line to find, followed by her cousin Velvet. The other
members are not as common, but like Crissy and Velvet loose
examples of these dolls frequently make their appearance at doll
shows, flea markets, and even garage sales. Only those examples
that are in excellent or better condition and wearing their original
outfits and shoes should command book value. Values for the rare
black versions of the dolls in the line are currently on the rise, as
demand for them increases while the supply decreases.

Advisor: Cindy Sabulis (S14).

Baby Crissy, 1973-76, pk dress, EX $45.00
Baby Crissy, 1973-76, pk dress, MIB, M15 ....$125.00
Baby Crissy (Black); 1973-76, pk dress, EX $80.00
Brandi (Black); 1972-73, orange swimsuit, EX $75.00
Cinnamon, Curly Ribbons (Black); 1974, EX $70.00
Cinnamon, Curly Ribbons; 1974, EX $45.00
Cinnamon, Hairdoodler (Black); 1973, EX $70.00
Cinnamon, Hairdoodler; 1973, EX $40.00
Cinnamon, 1972-74, EX $40.00
Crissy, Beautiful; 1969, orange lace dress, EX $40.00
Crissy, Country Fashion; 1982-83, EX $20.00
Crissy, Country Fashion; 1982-83, MIB, M15 ....$45.00
Crissy, Look Around; 1972, EX $40.00
Crissy, Magic Hair (Black); 1977, EX $75.00
Crissy, Magic Hair; 1977, EX $30.00
Crissy, Magic Hair; 1977, NRFB $100.00
Crissy, Movin' Groovin' (Black); 1971, EX $80.00
Crissy, Movin' Groovin'; 1971, EX $35.00
Crissy, Swirla Curler (Black); 1973, EX $80.00
Crissy, Swirla Curler; 1973, EX $35.00
Crissy, Twirly Beads; 1974, MIB, M15 ....$65.00

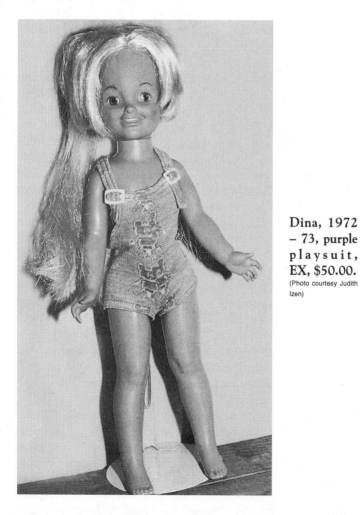

Dina, 1972 – 73, purple playsuit, EX, $50.00.
(Photo courtesy Judith Izen)

Kerry, 1971, gr romper, EX $55.00
Mia, 1971, turq romper, EX $50.00

Tara (Black); 1976, yel gingham outfit, EX $75.00
Velvet, Beauty Braider; 1973, EX $35.00
Velvet, Look Around (Black); 1972, EX $75.00
Velvet, Look Around; 1972, EX $35.00
Velvet, Movin' Groovin'; 1971, EX $35.00
Velvet, Swirly Daisies, 1974, EX $35.00

Velvet, Swirly Daisies, 1974, MIB, $65.00.
(Photo courtesy Judith Izen)

Velvet, Swirly Daisies (Black); 1974, EX $75.00
Velvet, 1970, 1st issue, purple dress, EX $55.00
Velvet, 1982 reissue, EX $30.00

DAWN

Dawn and her friends were made by Deluxe Topper, ca 1970s. They're becoming highly collectible, especially when mint in the box. Dawn was a 6" fashion doll, part of a series sold as the Dawn Model Agency. They were issued in boxes already dressed in clothes of the highest style, or you could buy additional outfits, many complete with matching shoes and accessories.

Advisor: Dawn Parrish (P2).

Dawn's Apartment, complete w/furniture $50.00
Doll, Dancing Angie, NRFB $30.00
Doll, Dancing Dale, NRFB $50.00
Doll, Dancing Dawn, NRFB $30.00
Doll, Dancing Gary, NRFB $40.00
Doll, Dancing Glory, NRFB $30.00
Doll, Dancing Jessica, NRFB $30.00
Doll, Dancing Ron, NRFB $40.00
Doll, Dancing Van, NRFB $50.00

Doll, Daphne, Dawn Model Agency, gr & silver dress, NRFB $75.00

Doll, Dawn Head to Toe, pk & silver dress, NRFB..........$90.00

Doll, Dawn Majorette, NRFB...$75.00

Doll, Kip Majorette, NRFB..$45.00

Doll, Longlocks, NRFB...$30.00

Doll, Maureen, Dawn Model Agency, red & gold dress, NRFB $75.00

Doll, Denise, NRFB, $75.00.
(Photo courtesy Pat Smith)

Outfit, Bell Bottom Flounce, #0717, NRFB, $25.00.
(Photo courtesy Pat Smith)

Outfit, Black Tie 'N Tux, #8393, NRFB, P2 ....$50.00

Outfit, Bluebelle, #0722, dress & shawl, NM, P2 ....$10.00

Outfit, Down the Aisle, #0816, dress & veil, NM, P2 ......$10.00

Outfit, Fuchsia Flash, #0612, NRFB, P2.............................$35.00

Outfit, Green Fling, #8113, MIB...$25.00

Outfit, Long 'N Leather, #8125, wht version, NRFB, P2..$40.00

Outfit, Sheer Delight, #8110, MIB......................................$25.00

Outfit, Singing in the Rain, #0724, MIB $25.00

Outfit, Skinny Minny, #0611, NRFB, P2 ....$30.00

Outfit, What a Racket, #8116, MIB.....................................$25.00

DOLLY DARLINGS BY HASBRO

    Dolly Darlings by Hasbro are approximately 4" tall and have molded or rooted hair. The molded-hair dolls were sold in themed hatboxes with small accessories to match. The rooted-hair dolls were sold separately and came with a small brush and comb. There were four plastic playrooms that featured the rooted-hair dolls. Hasbro also produced the Flower Darling series which were 2" dolls in flower corsages. The Dolly Darlings and Flower Darlings were available in the mid to late 1960s.

    Advisor: Dawn Parrish (P2).

Doll, Ron, NRFB, $30.00.
(Photo courtesy Pat Smith)

Beth at the Supermarket, #8500, NRFB, P2 ....$50.00

Daisy Darling, #8572, complete, EX, P2............................$25.00

Honey, #8533, NRFB, P2 ....$50.00

Rose Darling, #8575, NRFB, P2 ....$50.00

Shary Takes a Vacation, #8504, doll only, EX, P2............$10.00

Slick Set, #8541, doll only, EX, P2....................................$25.00

Slumber Party, #8512, doll only, EX, P2 ....$25.00

Tea Time, #8510, NRFB, P2 ....$50.00

Violet Darling, #8571, doll only, EX, P2...........................$15.00

Doll, Dinah, NRFB..$75.00

Doll, Gary, NRFB..$30.00

Doll, Jessica, NRFB..$30.00

FISHER-PRICE

Though this company is more famous for their ruggedly durable, lithographed wooden toys, they made dolls as well. Many of the earlier dolls (circa mid-70s) had stuffed cloth bodies and vinyl heads, hands, and feet. Some had battery-operated voice boxes. In 1981 they introduced Kermit the Frog and Miss Piggy and a line of clothing for both. For company history, see the Fisher-Price category. For more information, we recommend *Fisher-Price Toys* by our advisor for this category.

Advisor: Brad Cassity.

Audrey, #203, 1974-76, cloth & vinyl w/removable jeans, MIB, C13..$50.00
Baby Ann, #204, 1974-76, cloth & vinyl w/removable nightgown & diaper, M, C13 ....$25.00
Bobbie, #243, 1979-80, M, C13.................................$10.00
Bundle Up Baby, #244, 1980-82, M, C13 ....$10.00
Elizabeth (Black), #205, 1974-76, cloth & vinyl w/removable skirt, M, C13..$25.00
Honey, #208, 1977-80, yel & wht print dress, MIB, C13....$50.00
Jenny, #201, 1974-76, cloth & vinyl w/removable skirt, MIB, C13..$50.00
Joey, #206, 1975, cloth & vinyl w/removable jacket & sneakers, MIB, C13 ....$50.00
Mary, #200, 1974-77, cloth & vinyl w/removable skirt & apron, MIB, C13 ....$50.00
Muffy, #241, 1979-80, M, C13 ....$20.00
Musical Baby Ann, #204, 1975-76, MIB, C13...............$250.00
My Friend Jenny, #209, 1984-85, M, C13.....................$20.00
My Friend Jenny, #212, 1979-81, M, C13......................$20.00
My Friend Karen, #8121, 1990, only 200 made, M, C13 ..$125.00
My Friend Mandy, #210, 1977-78, M, C13 ....$20.00
My Friend Mikey, #205, 1982-84, MIB, C13 ....$30.00
Natalie, #202, 1974-76, cloth & vinyl w/removable skirt & bonnet, M, C13..$25.00
Special Birthday Mandy, #4009, 1985, MIB, C13 ....$50.00

FLATSYS

Flatsy dolls were a product of the Ideal Novelty and Toy Company. They were produced from 1968 until 1970 in 2", 5", and 8" sizes. There was only one boy in the 5" line; all were dressed in '70s fashions, and not only clothing but accessory items such as bicycles were made as well.

In 1994 Justoys reissued Mini Flatsys. They were sold alone or with accessories such as bikes, rollerblades, and jet skis.

Advisor: Dawn Parrish (P2).

Baby Flatsy, EX, P2 ....$10.00
Bonnie Flatsy, sailing, NRFB, P2.................................$55.00
Candy, Happy Birthday, complete, EX, P2 ....$35.00
Candy Mountain Flatsy, lavender ice-cream truck w/pk wheels, EX, P2 ....$15.00
Casey Engineer, complete, EX, P2................................$35.00
Cookie Flatsy, w/bl & red stove, EX, P2........................$15.00
Cory Flatsy, print mini-dress, NRFB, P2 ....$60.00
Cory Flatsy, silver pantsuit, complete, EX, P2................$40.00
Dale Fashion Flatsy, hot pk maxi, NRFB, P2 ....$60.00
Dale Fashion Flatsy, 2-pc wet-look outfit, NRFB, P2 ....$60.00
Dewie Flatsy, complete, EX, P2 ....$30.00

My Friend Becky, #218, 1982 – 84, M, C13, $20.00.
(Photo courtesy Brad Cassity)

Dewie Flatsy, NRFB, $60.00.
(Photo courtesy Martin and Carolyn Berens)

Fall Mini Flatsy Collection, NRFB, P2............................$65.00
Filly Flatsy, complete, EX, P2 ....$15.00
Flatsy Casey, NRFB..$65.00

Flatsy in Locket/Frame, MIP...$50.00
Flatsy's Townhouse, complete, EX $75.00
Flatsy's Townhouse, house only, EX, P2.........................$50.00
Flower Time Mini Flatsy, complete, EX $40.00
Gwen Fashion Flatsy, gr hair, peach poncho & boots, NRFB,
    P2...$65.00
Munch-Time Flatsy, Lemonade boy or girl, EX, ea..........$15.00
Munch-Time Flatsy Clock, NRFB, P2 ....$75.00
Nancy Flatsy, nurse w/baby carriage, EX, P2 ....$25.00
Play Time Flatsy, NRFB...$75.00
Rally Flatsy, complete, NM $40.00
Sandy Flatsy, beach outfit, NRFB, P2 ....$50.00
Spinderella Flatsy, complete, M $50.00
Summer Mini Flatsy Collection, NRFB, P2 ....$65.00
Susie Flatsy, complete, EX, P2 ....$15.00

GALOOB'S BABY FACE DOLLS

Galoob's Baby Face dolls were first available on the toy market in 1991. By the end of 1992 the short-lived dolls were already being discounted by toy stores. Although they were targeted as play dolls for children, it didn't take long for these adorable dolls to find their way into adult collectors' hearts. The most endearing quality of Baby Face dolls are their expressive faces. Sporting big eyes with long soft eyelashes, cute pug noses, and mouths that are puckered, pouting, smiling, or laughing, these dolls are delightful and fun. The 13" heavy vinyl Baby Face dolls are jointed at the shoulders, elbows, knees, and hips. Their jointed limbs allow for posing them in more positions than the average doll and adds to the fun of displaying or playing with them. Old store stock of Baby Face dolls was plentiful for several years, and since these dolls are still relatively new as collectibles, it isn't difficult to find never-removed-from-box examples.

Advisor: Cindy Sabulis (S14).

Activity Stroller, MIB, S14 ....$25.00
Asian Versions, NRFB, S14, from $65 to $80.00
Asian Versions, re-dressed, S14, from $20 to $25.00
Bathtub Babies, NRFB, from $40 to $50.00
Bathtub Babies, re-dressed, S14, from $15 to $20.00
Black Versions, NRFB, S14, from $60 to $75.00
Black Versions, re-dressed, S14, from $20 to $25.00
Hispanic Versions, NRFB, S14, from $65 to $85.00
Hispanic Versions, re-dressed, S14, from $20 to $25.00
Outfits, NRFB, S14, from $20 to $25.00
White Version, So Silly Sally, NRFB, S16, minimum value .$200.00
White Versions, any other than So Silly Sally, NRFB, S16, from
    $40 to $50.00
White Versions, re-dressed, S14, from $15 to $20.00

GERBER BABIES

The first Gerber Baby dolls were manufactured in 1936. These dolls were made of cloth and produced by an unknown manufacturer. Since that time, six different companies working with leading artists, craftsmen, and designers have attempted to capture the charm of the winsome baby in Dorothy Hope Smith's charcoal drawing of her friend's baby, Ann Turner (Cook). This drawing became known as the Gerber Baby and was adopted as the trademark of the Gerber Products Company, located in Fremont, Michigan. For further information see *Gerber Baby Dolls and Advertising Collectibles* by Joan S. Grubaugh.

Advisor: Joan S. Grubaugh (G8).

Amsco, 1972-73, baby & feeding set, vinyl, complete, 14",
    NMIB, G8 ....$85.00
Amsco, 1972-73, pk & wht rosebud sleeper, vinyl, 10", NM, G8,
    from $45 to...$55.00
Amsco, 1972-73 (Black), pk & wht rosebud sleeper, vinyl, 10",
    NM, G8, from $60 to...$100.00

So Sad Brooke, original outfit, from $40.00 to $50.00.
(Photo courtesy Pat Smith)

Atlanta Novelty, Baby Drink and Wet (Black), 1979 – 81, 12", complete with trunk and accessories, M, $100.00. (Photo courtesy Joan S. Grubaugh)

Arrow Rubber & Plastic Corp, 1965-67, pk & wht bib & diaper, 14", MIB, G8, from $45 to...$60.00

Atlanta Novelty, 1978, 50th Anniversary, eyelet skirt & bib, stuffed cloth & vinyl, 17", NRFB, G8, from $75 to ...$95.00

Atlanta Novelty, 1979, flowered bed jacket w/matching pillow & coverlet, 17", NRFB, G8, from $75 to $95.00

Atlanta Novelty, 1979, snowsuit w/matching hood, 17", NRFB, G8, from $75 to $95.00

Atlanta Novelty, 1979-81, Baby Drink & Wet, 17", complete in trunk, M, G8, from $75 to $85.00

Atlanta Novelty, 1979-81, bl or rose velour dress w/wht blouse, Black, 17", M, ea, from $75 to $85.00

Atlanta Novelty, 1979-81, snowsuit w/matching hood, Black, 17", NRFB, G8, from $75 to.....................................$85.00

Atlanta Novelty, 1979-81, w/'mama' voice, Black, 17", NRFB, from $75 to..$85.00

Atlanta Novelty, 1979-81, w/'mama' voice, several different outfits, 17", NRFB, G8, ea, from $75 to $85.00

Atlanta Novelty, 1981, collector's edition, vinyl w/eyelet lace christening gown in wicker basket, 12", NRFB, G8, from $75 to $85.00

Atlanta Novelty, 1981 limited edition, wht eyelet christening gown, porcelain w/soft body, 14", NRFB, G8, from $275 to $350.00

Atlanta Novelty, 1985, Bathtub Baby, vinyl, 12", MIB, G8, from $70 to $85.00

Lucky Ltd, 1989, Birthday Party Twins, 6", NRFB, G8 ....$40.00

Lucky Ltd, 1989, wht christening gown, cloth & vinyl, 16", EX, G8 ....$40.00

Toy Biz, 1994-95, Potty Time Baby, vinyl, 15", NRFB, G8 ....$25.00

Toy Biz, 1995, Lullaby Baby, plays Brahms' Lullaby, cloth & vinyl, 11", NRFB, G8 ....$25.00

Toy Biz, 1996, Baby Care Set, MIB, G8.........................$25.00

HOLLY HOBBIE

Sometime around 1970 a young homemaker and mother, Holly Hobbie, approached the American Greeting Company with some charming country-styled drawings of children. Her concepts were well received by the company, and since that time over four hundred Holly Hobbie items have been produced, nearly all marked HH, H. Hobbie, or Holly Hobbie.

Advisor: Helen McCale (M12).

Creative Craft Plaque Set, 1972, MIB (sealed), B10 ....$20.00

Doll, Country Fun Holly Hobbie, 1989, 16", NRFB.........$25.00

Doll, Grandma Holly, Knickerbocker, cloth, 14", MIB $20.00

Doll, Grandma Holly, Knickerbocker, cloth, 24", MIB $30.00

Doll, Holly Hobbie, Heather, Amy or Carrie, Knickerbocker, cloth, 6", MIB, ea...$10.00

Doll, Holly Hobbie, Heather, Amy or Carrie, Knickerbocker, cloth, 9", MIB, ea...$15.00

Doll, Holly Hobbie, Heather, Amy or Carrie, Knickerbocker, cloth, 16", MIB, ea...$25.00

Doll, Holly Hobbie, Heather, Amy or Carrie, Knickerbocker, cloth, 27", MIB, ea...$35.00

Doll, Holly Hobbie, Heather, Amy or Carrie, Knickerbocker, cloth, 33", MIB, ea...$45.00

Doll, Holly Hobbie, 1988, scented, clear ornament around neck, 18", NRFB...$40.00

Doll, Holly Hobbie Bicentennial, Knickerbocker, cloth, 12", MIB $30.00

Doll, Holly Hobbie Day 'N Night, Knickerbocker, cloth, 14", MIB $20.00

Sun Rubber, 1955 – 58, original nightgown, M, $175.00.
(Photo courtesy Joan S. Grubaugh)

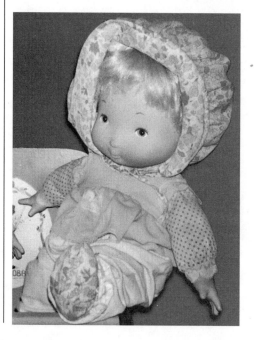

Doll, Holly Hobbie, stuffed cloth with vinyl head and hands, original outfit, VG, $10.00.
(Photo courtesy Helen McCale)

Sun Rubber, 1955-58, re-dressed, 12", VG, G8, from $50 to..$75.00

Doll, Holly Hobbie Dream Along, Holly, Carrie or Amy, Knickerbocker, cloth, 9", MIB, ea..............................$15.00

Doll, Holly Hobbie Dream Along, Holly, Carrie or Amy, Knickerbocker, cloth, 12", MIB, ea...........................$20.00

Doll, Holly Hobbie Talker, cloth, 4 sayings, 16", MIB $30.00

Doll, Little Girl Holly, Knickerbocker, 1980, cloth, 15", MIB..$30.00

Doll, Robby, Knickerbocker, cloth, 9", MIB.....................$20.00

Doll, Robby, Knickerbocker, 1981, cloth, 16", MIB.........$30.00

Dollhouse, M $300.00

Heather Doll Making Kit, complete, EX, B10 ....$25.00

Sewing Machine, Durham, 1975, plastic & metal, battery-op, 5x9", EX, M17..$40.00

Sing-A-Long Electric Parlor Player, Vanity Fair, 1970s, complete w/booklet, scarce, NMIB, M17...........................$45.00

JEM

The glamorous life of Jem mesmerized little girls who watched her Saturday morning cartoons, and she was a natural as a fashion doll. Hasbro saw the potential in 1985 when they introduced the Jem line of 12" dolls representing her, the rock stars from Jem's musical group, the Holograms, and other members of the cast, including the only boy, Rio, Jem's road manager and Jerrica's boyfriend. Each doll was posable, jointed at the waist, head, and wrists, so that they could be positioned at will with their musical instruments and other accessory items. Their clothing, their makeup, and their hairdos were wonderfully exotic, and their faces were beautifully modeled. The Jem line was discontinued in 1987 after being on the market for only two years. Our values are given for mint-in-box dolls. All loose dolls are valued at about $8.00 each.

Clash, complete, MIB (not shown), $40.00.
(Photo courtesy Lee Garmon)

Accessory, Jem Roadster, AM/FM radio in trunk, scarce, EX $150.00

Accessory, Jem Soundstage, Starlight House #14, EX, from $40 to $50.00

Accessory, Jem Speaker & Dressing Room, complete, NM.$100.00

Doll, Aja, complete, MIB $40.00

Doll, Ashley, curly blond hair, complete, MIB $25.00

Doll, Banee, waist-length blk hair, complete, MIB...........$25.00

Doll, Danse, pk & blond hair, complete, MIB $40.00

Doll, Jem/Jerrica, Glitter & Gold, complete, MIB............$50.00

Doll, Jetta, blk hair w/silver streaks, complete, MIB.........$40.00

Doll, Kimber, red hair, complete, MIB............................$40.00

Doll, Krissie, dk skin w/brn curly hair, complete, MIB $25.00

Doll, Pizzaz (Misfits), chartreuse hair, complete, MIB $40.00

Doll, Raya, complete, MIB $40.00

Doll, Rio, Glitter & Gold, complete, MIB.......................$50.00

Doll, Roxy, blond hair, complete, MIB $40.00

Doll, Shana (Holograms Band), purple hair, complete, MIB .$40.00

Doll, Stormer, bl hair, complete, MIB..............................$40.00

Doll, Video, complete, MIB..$40.00

Outfit, City Lights, MIP, $15.00.
(Photo courtesy Pat Smith)

Outfit, Midnight Magic, MIP $20.00

Outfit, Purple Haze, MIP $15.00

Outfit, Up 'N Rockin', MIP..$15.00

LIDDLE KIDDLES

From 1966 to 1971, Mattel produced Liddle Kiddle dolls and accessories, typical of the 'little kid next door.' They were made in sizes ranging from a tiny ¾" up to 4". They were all posable and had rooted hair that could be restyled. Eventually there were Animiddles and Zoolery Jewelry Kiddles, which were of course animals, and two other series that represented storybook and nursery-rhyme characters. There was a set of extraterrestrials, and lastly in 1979, Sweet Treets dolls were added to the assortment.

In the mid-1970s Mattel reissued Lucky Locket Kiddles. The dolls had names identical to the earlier lockets but were not of the same high quality.

In 1994–95 Tyco reissued Liddle Kiddles in strap-on, clip-on, Lovely Locket, Pretty Perfume, and baby bottle collections.

Loose dolls, if complete and with all their original accessories, are worth about 50% less than the same mint in the box. Dressed, loose dolls with no accessories are worth 75% less. For more information, refer to *Little Kiddles, Identification and Value Guide*, by Paris Langford (Collector Books).

Advisor: Dawn Parrish (P2).

Other Sources: S14.

Alice in Wonderliddle, missing story book, NM $150.00
Apple Blossom Kologne, #3707, MIP, P2 ....$60.00
Aqua Funny Bunny, #3532, complete, EX, P2 ....$35.00
Aqua Funny Bunny, #3532, MIP, P2 ....$100.00
Babe Biddle, #3505, complete, M, P2.........................$50.00
Baby Din-Din, #3820, complete, M, P2 ....$75.00
Baby Rockaway, #3819, MIP, P2................................$150.00
Beach Buggy, #5003, NM, P2 ....$50.00
Beat-a-Diddle, #3510, MIP, P2 ....$500.00
Blue Funny Bunny, #3532, MIP, P2 ....$100.00
Bunson Burnie, #3501, complete, M, P2......................$75.00
Calamity Jiddle, #3506, complete w/high-saddle horse, M,
     P2 ....$75.00
Chitty-Chitty Bang-Bang Kiddles, #3597, MOC $250.00
ChocoLottie's House, #2501, MIP, P2 ....$40.00
Cinderiddle's Palace, #5068, plastic window version, M, P2.$85.00
Cookin' Kiddle, #3846, complete, M, P2 ....$150.00
Florence Niddle, #3507, complete, M, P2....................$75.00
Flower Charm Bracelet, #3747, MIP, P2......................$25.00
Flower Pin Kiddle, #3741, MIP, P2 ....$50.00
Freezy Sliddle, #3516, complete, M, P2.......................$65.00
Frosty Mint Kone, #3653, complete, M, P2 ....$75.00
Greta Grape, #3728, complete, M, P2.........................$50.00
Greta Griddle, #3508, complete, M, P2 ....$85.00
Heart Charm Bracelet Kiddle, #3747, MIP, P2..............$25.00
Heart Ring Kiddle, #3744, MIP, P2............................$50.00
Henrietta Horseless Carriage, #3641, complete, M, P2 ....$75.00
Honeysuckle Kologne, #3704, MIP, P2 ....$60.00
Hot Dog Stand, #5002, M $60.00
Howard Biff Boodle, #3502, complete, M, P2 ....$75.00
Jewelry Kiddles Treasure Box, #3735 & #5166, M...........$40.00
Kampy Kiddle, #3753, complete, M, P2.......................$150.00
Kiddle Kolognes Sweet Three Boutique, #3708, NRFB .$150.00
Kiddle Komedy Theatre, #3592, EX $50.00
Kiddles Sweet Shoppe, #3807, NRFB $200.00
Kiddles 'N Kars Antique Fair Set, #3806, NRFB............$200.00
King & Queen of Hearts, #3784, MIP, P2 ....$200.00
Kleo Kola, #3729, complete, M, P2 ....$50.00
Kola Kiddles Three-Pak, #3734, 1967, NRFB................$175.00
Lady Lace, #A3840, MIP, P2....................................$85.00
Laffy Lemon, #3732, MIP, P2...................................$85.00
Larky Locket, #3539, complete, EX, P2 ....$25.00
Lenore Limousine, #3643, complete, M, P2.................$85.00
Liddle Biddle Peep, #3544, complete, M, P2 ....$125.00

Liddle Diddle, #3503, complete, M, $75.00.
(Photo courtesy Cindy Sabulis)

Liddle Kiddle Kolony, #3571, M $35.00
Liddle Kiddle Kottage, #3534, EX $40.00
Liddle Kiddles Kabin, #3591, EX, P2 ....$25.00
Liddle Kiddles Kastle, #3522, M $55.00
Liddle Kiddles Klub, #3521, M $30.00
Liddle Kiddles Open House, #5167, MIB, P2................$40.00
Liddle Kiddles Pop-Up Boutique, #5170, M..................$30.00
Liddle Kiddles Pop-Up Playhouse, #3574, M $30.00
Liddle Kiddles Ranch House, #3524, M $30.00

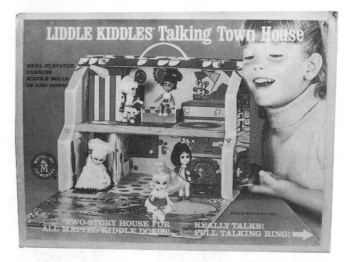

Liddle Kiddles Talking Townhouse, #5154, MIB, $75.00.
(Photo courtesy Martin and Carolyn Berens)

Liddle Kiddles 3-Story House, M..............................$75.00
Liddle Lion Zoolery, #3661, complete, M, P2.................$200.00

Lilac Locket, #3540, MIP, P2 ....$75.00
Limey Lou Spoonfuls, #2815, MIP, P2 ....$25.00

Lola Liddle, #3504, MIP, $50.00.
(Photo courtesy Paris Langford)

Lolli-Grape, #3656, complete, M, P2 ....$60.00
Lolli-Lemon, #3657, MIP, P2.............................$175.00
Lolli-Mint, #3658, MIP, P2 ....$75.00
Lorelei Locket, #3717, MIP, P2 ....$75.00
Lorelei Locket, #3717, 1976 version, MIP, P2 .....$25.00
Lottie Locket, #3679, complete, M, P2 ....$35.00
Lottie Locket, #3719, 1976 version, MIP, P2 ....$25.00
Lou Locket, #3537, MIP, P2 ....$75.00
Luana Locket, #3680, complete, M, P2 ....$35.00
Luana Locket, #3680, Gold Rush version, MIP, P2 ....$85.00
Lucky Locket Kiddles Jewel Case, #3542, M $65.00
Luscious Lime, #3733, complete, M, P2 ....$55.00
Luvvy Duvvy Kiddle, #3596, MIP, P2 ....$100.00
Millie Middle, #3509, complete, M, P2 ....$125.00
Miss Mouse, #3638, MIP, P2 ....$95.00
Nappytime Baby, #3818, complete, M, P2 ....$75.00
Olivia Orange Kola Kiddle, #3730, MIP, P2 ....$80.00
Orange Merigue Skediddle Play Clothes, #3585, MIP, P2 ..$35.00
Peter Paniddle, #3547, NRFP, P2..........................$350.00
Pink Funny Bunny, #3532, MIP, P2 ....$100.00
Pretty Priddle, #3549, complete, M, P2 ....$75.00
Rapunzel & the Prince, #3783, MIP, P2 ....$200.00
Robin Hood & Maid Marion, #3785, MIP $200.00
Romeo & Juliet, #3782, MIP, P2...........................$200.00
Rosemary Roadster, #3642, complete, M, P2 ....$75.00
Santa Kiddle, #3595, MIP, P2 ....$60.00
Shirley Skediddle, #3766, MIP, P2.......................$75.00
Shirley Strawberry, #3727, complete, M, P2 ....$50.00
Sizzly Friddle, #3513, complete, M, P2 ....$75.00
Sleep 'N Totsy Outfit, #LK5, MIP, P2 ....$25.00
Slipsy Siddle, #3754, complete, M, P2 ....$125.00
Snap-Happy Bedroom, #5172, complete, M $15.00

Snap-Happy Living Room, #5173, NMIP, P2 ....$20.00
Snap-Happy Patio Furniture, #5171, MIP, P2 ....$30.00
Snoopy Skediddler & His Sopwith Camel, M $150.00
Suki Skediddle, #3767, complete, M, P2 ....$25.00
Suki Skediddle, #3767, MIP, P2 ....$75.00

Surfy Skediddle, #3517, complete, M, $75.00.
(Photo courtesy Cindy Sabulis)

Sweet Pea Kologne, #3705, MIP, P2 ....$60.00
Swingy Skediddle, #3789, MIP, P2 ....$200.00
Teeter Time Baby, #3817, complete, P2 ....$75.00
Teresa Touring Car, #3644, complete, M, P2 ....$75.00
Tiny Tiger, #3636, MIP, P2..................................$100.00
Trikey Triddle, #3515, complete, M, P2 ....$75.00
Vanilly Lilly, #2819, MIP, P2 ....$25.00
Violet Kologne, #3703, MIP, P2...........................$60.00
Windy Fliddle, #3514, complete, M, P2 ....$85.00
World of Kiddles Beauty Bazaar, #3586, NRFB $300.00

LITTLECHAPS

In 1964 Remco Industries created a family of four fashion dolls that represented an upper-middle class American family. The Littlechaps family consisted of the father, Dr. John Littlechap, his wife, Lisa, and their two children, Judy and Libby. Their clothing and fashion accessories were made in Japan and are of the finest quality. Because these dolls are not as pretty as other fashion dolls of the era and their size and placement of arms and legs made them awkward to dress, children had little interest in them at the time. This lack of interest during the 1960s has created shortages of them for collectors of today. Mint and complete outfits or outfits never-removed-from-box are especially desirable to Littlechap collectors. Values listed for loose clothing ensembles complete with all their small accessories. If only the main pieces of the outfit are available, then the value could go down significantly.

Advisor: Cindy Sabulis (S14).

Carrying Case, EX, S14..$25.00
Doll, Doctor John, MIB, S14....................................$60.00
Doll, Judy, MIB, S14...$65.00
Doll, Libby, MIB, S14...$45.00
Doll, Lisa, MIB, S14..$60.00
Family Room, Bedroom, or Doctor John's Office, EX, S14,
    ea $125.00
Outfit, Doctor John, complete, EX, S14, from $15 to.......$30.00
Outfit, Doctor John, NRFB, S14, from $30 to $50.00
Outfit, Judy, complete, EX, S14, from $25 to...................$40.00
Outfit, Judy, NRFB, S14, from $35 to $75.00
Outfit, Libby, complete, EX, S14, from $20 to.................$35.00
Outfit, Libby, NRFB, S14, from $35 to $50.00
Outfit, Lisa, complete, EX, S14, from $35 to $75.00
Outfit, Lisa, NRFB, S14, from $35 to.............................$75.00

MATTEL TALKING DOLLS

For more information refer to *Talking Toys of the 20th Century* by Kathy and Don Lewis (Collector Books).
    Advisor: Kathy Lewis (L6).
    See also Disney; Character, TV, and Movie Memorabilia.

Baby Beans, EX, S14 ....$25.00
Baby Drowsey, Black, 1968, 15", MIB..........................$125.00
Baby First Step, 1967, MIB, L6 ....$150.00
Baby Secret, 1966, red hair, 18", EX.........................$75.00
Baby See 'N Say, 1964, MIB, L6 ....$150.00
Baby Small Talk, outfit, 1968, several different, MIP, ea from
    $40 to $45.00
Baby Small Talk, 1968, MIB, L6 ....$75.00
Baby Teenietalk, 1966, orig dress, 17", VG, M15 ....$75.00
Cynthia, M, S14...$45.00
Hi Dottie, complete w/telephone, 17", EX, S14...............$50.00
Matty the Talking Boy, 1961, MIB $300.00
Sister Small Talk, 1968, blond hair, EX $55.00

Sister Belle, 1961, MIB (not shown), $300.00.
(Photo courtesy Kathy Lewis)

Tatters, M...$85.00
Teachy Keen, 1966, MIB, L6 ....$125.00
Timey Tell, MIB, L6 ....$110.00

NANCY ANN STORYBOOK

Nancy Ann Storybook Dolls were introduced in 1936, in San Francisco, California, by Rowena Haskin (Nancy Ann Abbott). They were made of painted bisque with jointed arms and legs, mohair wigs, and painted eyes. There were also hard plastic dolls such as Muffie, Miss Nancy Ann Style Show, Debbie, etc., all in a variety of sizes. In the 1950s and '60s a 10½" Miss Nancy Ann and Little Miss Nancy Ann were featured, both vinyl fashion-type dolls with high-heeled shoes.

Boy Blue, pnt bsk, all orig w/gold foil tag & brochure, 8", NM
    (NM blue-dot box), minimum value.........................$35.00

Debut, Commencement Series, hard plastic, sleep eyes, all original with gold wrist tag, 5", NM (NM box), minimum value, $75.00.

Lassie Fair, pnt bsk, all orig w/gold foil tag, 5", NM (NM fuchsia-
    dot box), minimum value $50.00
Lucy Locket, pnt bsk, all orig, 5", NM, minimum value.$275.00
Miss Nancy Ann, vinyl, mk Nancy Ann on head, all orig, 10½",
    NM, minimum value $85.00
Muffie, hard plastic, non-walker, several variations, 8", NM, ea,
    minimum value $175.00
Muffie, hard plastic, walker, several variations, 8", NM, ea, mini-
    mum value $150.00
Muffie, vinyl, walker, several variations, 8", NM, ea, minimum
    value..$175.00
New Moon, Operette Series, hard plastic, all orig w/tag, 5", min-
    imum value $125.00
Portuguese, pnt bsk, jtd legs, all orig w/wrist tag, 5", NM, mini-
    mum value $325.00
Thursdays Child Has Far To Go, pnt bsk, all orig w/silver tag, 5",
    NM (NM pk-dot box), minimum value $75.00

To Market To Market, pnt bsk, all orig w/silver tag, 5", NM (NM bl-dot box), minimum value $75.00

ROCKFLOWERS BY MATTEL

Rockflowers were introduced in the early 1970s as Mattel's answer to Topper's Dawn Dolls. Rockflowers are 6½" tall and have wire articulated bodies that came with mod sunglasses attached to their heads. There were four girls and one boy in the series with eighteen groovy outfits that could be purchased separately. Each doll came with their own 45 rpm record, and the clothing packages were also in the shape of a 45 rpm record.

Advisor: Dawn Parrish (P2)

Case, Rock Flowers on Stage, vinyl, 3 compartments, NM..$30.00
Doll, Doug, #1177, NRFB, P2 ....$45.00

Doll, Heather, NRFB, $35.00.
(Photo courtesy J. Michael Augustniak)

Doll, Iris, #1176, NRFB $40.00
Doll, Lilac, #1167, NRFB, P2 ....$35.00
Doll, Rosemary, #1168, NRFB, P2 ....$45.00
Gift Set, Rockflowers in Concert, w/Heather, Lilac & Rosemary, NRFB...$100.00
Outfit, Flares 'N Lace, #4057, NRFP................................$15.00
Outfit, Frontier Gingham, #4069, NRFP $20.00
Outfit, Long in Fringe, #4050, NRFP.........................$15.00
Outfit, Overall Green, #4067, NRFP, P2 ....$10.00
Outfit, Tie Dye Maxi, #4053, NRFP $15.00
Outfit, Topped in Lace, #4058, NRFP, P2 ....$15.00

STRAWBERRY SHORTCAKE

It was around 1980 when Strawberry Shortcake came on the market with a bang. The line included everything to attract small girls — swimsuits, bed linens, blankets, anklets, underclothing, coats, shoes, sleeping bags, dolls and accessories, games, and many other delightful items. Strawberry Shortcake and her friends were short lived, lasting only until the middle of the decade.

Advisor: Geneva Addy (A5).

Big Berry Trolley, 1982, EX..$40.00
Doll, Almond Tea, 6", MIB...$25.00
Doll, Angel Cake, 6", MIB $25.00
Doll, Apple Dumpling, 6", MIB....................................$25.00
Doll, Apricot, 15", NM..$35.00
Doll, Baby Needs a Name, 15", NM..............................$35.00
Doll, Berry Baby Orange Blossom, 6", MIB $35.00
Doll, Butter Cookie, 6", MIB.......................................$25.00
Doll, Cafe Olé, 6", MIB $35.00
Doll, Cherry Cuddler, 6", MIB $25.00
Doll, Lime Chiffon, 6", MIB..$25.00
Doll, Mint Tulip, 6", MIB...$25.00
Doll, Raspberry Tart, 6", MIB......................................$25.00
Doll, Strawberry Shortcake, 12", NRFB........................$45.00
Doll, Strawberry Shortcake, 15", NM $35.00
Dollhouse, M..$150.00
Dollhouse Furniture, attic, 6-pc, rare, M......................$140.00
Dollhouse Furniture, bathroom, 5-pc, rare, M $65.00
Dollhouse Furniture, bedroom, 7-pc, rare, M.................$90.00
Dollhouse Furniture, kitchen, 11-pc, rare, M.................$100.00
Dollhouse Furniture, living room, 6-pc, rare, M $85.00
Figure, Almond Tea w/Marza Panda, PVC, 1", MOC, B5 .$10.00

Figure, Cherry Cuddler with Gooseberry, Strawberryland Miniatures, MIP, from $15.00 to $20.00.
(Photo courtesy Martin and Carolyn Berens)

Figure, Lemon Meringue w/Frappo, PVC, 1", MOC, B5 ..$10.00
Figure, Lime Chiffon w/balloons, PVC, 1", MOC $10.00

Figure, Merry Berry Worm, MIB $25.00
Figure, Mint Tulip w/March Mallard, PVC, MOC, B5 ....$10.00
Figure, Purple Pieman w/Berry Bird, poseable, MIB.........$35.00
Figure, Raspberry Tart w/bowl of berries, MOC................$10.00
Figure, Raspberry Tart w/Rhubarb, PVC, 1", MOC, B5 ...$10.00
Figure, Sour Grape w/Dregs, Strawberryland Miniatures, MIP, B5, from $15 to $20.00
Storybook Play Case, M, B5 ....$35.00
Stroller, Coleco, 1981, M, J6..$85.00
Telephone, Strawberry Shortcake figure, battery-op, EX .$85.00

SUNSHINE FAMILY BY MATTEL

The Sunshine Family was produced and sold from 1974 to 1982. The first family consisted of the father, Steve, his wife, Stephie, and their daughter, Baby Sweets. In 1976 Mattel added The Happy Family (an African-American family consisting of mom, dad, and their two children). The line also included grandparents, playsets, vehicles, and a lot of other accessories that made them so much fun to play with. For more information we recommend *Thirty Years of Mattel Fashion Dolls* by J. Michael Augustyniak (Collector Books).

Camping Craft Kit, 1974, complete, MIP, minimum value .$35.00
Craft Store, 1976, complete, MIB, minimum value..........$70.00
Doll, Little Hon (Black), 1977, complete w/nursery set, MIB, minimum value...$65.00

Doll, Little Sweets, 1975, complete with nursery set, MIB, minimum value $35.00. (Photo courtesy J. Michael Augustyniak)

Doll & Craft Case, Sears Exclusive, 1977, vinyl, EX, minimum value...$25.00

Doll Set, Grandparents, 1976, MIB, minimum value $60.00
Doll Set, Happy Family (Black), 1975, MIB, minimum value...$60.00
Doll Set, Watch 'em Grow Greenhouse, 1977, limited edition, complete w/3 dolls, craft kit & seeds, MIB, minimum value $100.00
Doll Set, 1976, Steve, Stephie & Baby Sweets, MIB, minimum value..$65.00
Family Farm, 1977, rare, complete, MIB, minimum value ..$140.00
Kitchen Craft Kit, 1974, complete, MIP, minimum value.$35.00
Nursery Craft Kit, 1976, complete, MIP $25.00
Outfit, 1975, several variations, MIP, minimum value, ea..$15.00
Outfit, 1976, several variations, MIP, minimum value, ea..$15.00
Outfit, 1978, several variations, MIP, minimum value, ea..$30.00
Sunshine Family Home, 1974, 4 rooms, complete w/furniture, EX, minimum value $65.00
Surrey Cycle, 1975, MIB, minimum value $35.00
Van w/Piggyback Shack, 1975, complete, MIB, minimum value...$50.00

TAMMY

In 1962 the Ideal Novelty and Toy Company introduced their teenage Tammy doll. Slightly pudgy and not quite as sophisticated-looking as some of the teen fashion dolls on the market at the time, Tammy's innocent charm captivated consumers. Her extensive wardrobe and numerous accessories added to her popularity with children. Tammy had a car, a house, and her own catamaran. In addition, a large number of companies obtained licenses to issue products using the 'Tammy' name. Everything from paper dolls to nurse's kits were made with Tammy's image on them. Her success was not confined to the United States; she was also successful in Canada and several other European countries.

Interest in Tammy has risen quite a bit in the past year according to Cindy Sabulis, co-author of *Tammy, the Ideal Teen* (Collector Books). Values have gone up and supply for quality mint-in-box items is going down. Loose, played-with dolls are still readily available and can be found for as low as $10.00 at doll shows. Values are given for mint-in-box dolls.

Advisor: Cindy Sabulis (S14).

Accessory Pak, #9181-80, w/curlers, comb, brush, mirror & hair spray, MIP, S14 ....$20.00
Accessory Pak, #9184-80, w/telephone, telephone directory, pizza & sandals, MIP, S14.....................................$20.00
Accessory Pak, #9220-5, w/skirt, belt, handkerchief, date book, & hanger, NRFP, S14...................................$30.00
Accessory Pak, #9233-8, w/jumper, purse, shoes & hanger, NRFP, S14 ....$25.00
Accessory Pak, #9241-1, w/shirtwaist dress, belt & hanger, NRFP, S14 ....$35.00
Accessory Pak, unknown #, w/broom, mop, dustpan, soap, wax & cloth, MIP, minimum value $50.00
Accessory Pak, unknown #, w/tape recorder, 2 detachable reels, microphone & speaker, MIP $40.00
Case, Dodi, gr background, EX, S14................................$30.00
Case, Misty, Dutch door-type, blk background, EX, S14 ..$30.00

Case, Misty, pk & wht background, EX, S14 ....$25.00
Case, Misty & Tammy, hatbox style, EX, S14 ....$40.00
Case, Pepper, hatbox style, turq background, EX, S14 .....$40.00
Case, Pepper & Patti, Montgomery Ward's Exclusive, red background, EX $50.00

Case, Tammy and Her Friends, green background, M, $30.00. (Photo courtesy Cindy Sabulis)

Case, Tammy & Her Friends, pk or gr background, EX, S14, ea $25.00
Case, Tammy Evening in Paris, bl, blk or red background, EX, S14, ea...$20.00
Case, Tammy Model Miss, red or blk background, EX, S14, ea $25.00
Case, Tammy Traveler, red or gr background, EX, S14, ea ..$45.00
Doll, Bud, MIB, S14, minimum value............................$500.00
Doll, Dodi, MIB, S14 ....$75.00
Doll, Glamour Misty the Miss Clairol Doll, MIB, S14 ...$150.00
Doll, Grown Up Tammy, MIB, S14 ....$75.00
Doll, Grown Up Tammy (Black), MIB, S14, minimum value..$300.00
Doll, Misty, MIB, S14..$100.00
Doll, Misty (Black), MIB, S14, minimum value.............$500.00
Doll, Patti, MIB, S14...$200.00
Doll, Pepper, MIB, S14...$65.00
Doll, Pepper (Canadian version), MIB, S14 ....$75.00
Doll, Pepper (trimmer body & smaller face), MIB, S14....$75.00
Doll, Pepper w/'carrot'-colored hair, MIB, S14 ....$75.00
Doll, Pos'n Dodi, M (decorated box), S14 ....$150.00
Doll, Pos'n Dodi, M (plain box), S14...............................$75.00
Doll, Pos'n Misty & Her Telephone Booth, MIB, S14...$125.00
Doll, Pos'n Pepper, MIB, S14...$75.00
Doll, Pos'n Pete, MIB, S14..$125.00
Doll, Pos'n Salty, MIB, S14...$125.00
Doll, Pos'n Tammy, MIB, S14.......................................$100.00
Doll, Pos'n Tammy & Her Telephone Booth, MIB, S14..$100.00

Doll, Pos'n Ted, MIB, S14...$100.00
Doll, Tammy, MIB, S14...$75.00
Doll, Tammy's Dad, MIB, S14...$65.00
Doll, Tammy's Mom, MIB, S14..$70.00
Doll, Ted, MIB, S14...$65.00
Outfit, Dad & Ted, pajamas & slippers, #9456-5, MIP, S14 .$20.00
Outfit, Dad & Ted, sweater, shorts & socks, #9476-3, MIP, S14 ....$25.00
Outfit, Pepper, Birthday Party, #9326-0, complete, M, S14..$45.00
Outfit, Pepper, Snowflake, #9339-3, complete, M, S14....$50.00
Outfit, Pepper & Dodi, Hyland Fling, #9336-9, MIP, S14..$75.00
Outfit, Tammy, Beauty Queen, #9769-4 or #9947-3, MIP, S14 ....$80.00
Outfit, Tammy, Miss Ballerina, #9136-3 or 9936-6, complete, M, S14, ea..$35.00
Outfit, Tammy, Nurse's Aide, #9120-7 or #9928-3, MIP, S14, ea $80.00
Outfit, Tammy, Wedding Belle, #9212-0 or #9958-0, complete, rare, M, S14, minimum value ea $100.00
Outfit, Tammy's Mom, Hidden Glamour, #9417-7, MIP, S14 ....$40.00
Outfit, Tammy's Mom, Nighty Nite, #9415-1, MIP, S14 .$30.00
Pepper's Juke Box, M, S14..$65.00
Pepper's Treehouse, MIB, S14.......................................$150.00
Tammy & Ted Catamaran, MIB, S14..............................$200.00
Tammy Bubble Bath Set, NRFB, S14...............................$75.00
Tammy's Bed, Dresser & Chair, MIB, S14........................$85.00

Tammy's Car, MIB, S14, $75.00.
(Photo courtesy Cindy Sabulis)

Tammy's Ideal House, M, S14, minimum value $100.00
Tammy's Juke Box, M, S14...$50.00

TRESSY

American Character's Tressy doll was produced in this country from 1963 to 1967. The unique feature of this 11½" fashion doll was that her hair 'grew' by pushing a button on her stomach. Tressy also had a little (9") sister named Cricket. Numerous fashions and accessories were produced for these two dolls. Never-removed-from-box Tressy and Cricket items are rare, so unless indicated, values listed are for loose, mint items. A never-removed-from-box item's worth is at least double its loose value.

Advisor: Cindy Sabulis (S14).

Apartment, M, S14	$150.00
Beauty Salon, M, S14	$125.00
Case, Cricket, M, S14	$30.00
Case, Tressy, M, S14	$25.00
Doll, Pre-Teen Tressy, M, S14	$75.00

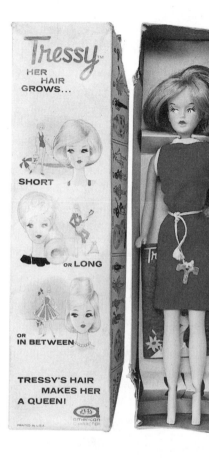

Doll, Tressy, MIB, S14, $90.00.
(Photo courtesy Cindy Sabulis)

Doll, Tressy in Miss America Character outfit, NM, S14	$65.00
Doll, Tressy w/Magic Makeup Face, M, S14	$25.00
Doll Clothes Pattern, M, S14	$10.00
Gift Paks w/Doll & Clothing, NRFB, S14, minimum value ea	$100.00
Hair Accessory Paks, NRFB, S14, ea	$20.00
Hair Dryer, M, S14	$40.00
Hair or Cosmetic Accessory Kits, M, S14, minimum value, ea	$50.00
Millinery, M, S14	$150.00
Outfits, MOC, S14, ea	$30.00
Outfits, NRFB, S14, minimum value ea	$65.00

UPSY DOWNSYS BY MATTEL

The Upsy Downsy dolls were made by Mattel during the late 1960s. They were small, 2½" to 3½", made of vinyl and plastic. Some of the group were 'Upsies' that walked on their feet, while others were 'Downsies' that walked or rode fantasy animals while upsidedown.

Advisor: Dawn Parrish (P2).

Baby So-High, #3828, complete, M	$75.00
Downy Dilly, #3832, complete, P2	$75.00
Downy Dilly, #3832, NRFB, P2	$150.00
Flossy Glossy, #3827, doll & playland, EX, P2	$25.00
Funny Feeder, #3834, Gooey Chooey only, P2	$25.00
Hairy Hurry Downsy Wizzer, #3838, complete, P2	$150.00
Miss Information, #3831, NRFB, P2	$150.00
Mother What Now, #3829, complete, P2	$75.00
Pocus Hocus, #3820, complete, M	$75.00
Pudgy Fudgy, #3826, NRFB, P2	$150.00

Farm Toys

It's entirely probable that more toy tractors have been sold than real ones. They've been made to represent all makes and models, of plastic, cast iron, diecast metal, and even wood. They've been made in at least 1/16th scale, 1/32nd, 1/43rd, and 1/64th. If you buy a 1/16th-scale replica, that small piece of equipment would have to be sixteen times larger to equal the size of the real item. Limited editions (meaning that a specific number will be made and no more) and commemorative editions (made for special events) are usually very popular with collectors. Many models on the market today are being made by the Ertl company.

Advisor: John Rammacher (S5).
See also Cast Iron, Farm.

Agco Allis 6690 Tractor w/Duals, Ertl, 1/64th scale, #1286, MIB, S5	$5.00
Agco R-52 Combine, Ertl, 1/64th scale, #1282, MIB, S5	$10.00
Agco 6680 w/Front Wheel Assist, Ertl, 1/64th scale, #1245, MIB, S5	$4.00
Allis Chalmers Tractor, Ertl, 1/16th scale, MIB	$30.00
Allis Chalmers 220, Ertl, 1/43rd scale, #2336, MIB, S5	$6.00
Allis-Chalmers WD Tractor, Product Miniature Co, 1947-50, 1/16 scale, NMIB, A	$200.00
Brent Dual-Wheel Grain Cart, Ertl, 1996 Farm Show, red or gr, 1/64th scale, MIB, S5, ea	$20.00
Case IH Combine, Ertl, 1/64th scale, #655, MIB, S5	$10.00
Case IH Gravity Wagon, Ertl, 1/64th scale, #1864, MIB, S5	$3.00
Case IH Hay Rake, Ertl, 164th scale, #210, MIB, S5	$3.00
Case IH Mixer Mill, 1/64th scale, #480, MIB, S5	$3.00
Case IH Planter, Ertl, 1/64th scale, #478, MIB, S5	$3.00
Case IH Self-Prop Windrower, Ertl, 1/64th scale, #4405, MIB, S5	$8.00
Case IH 1586 w/Loader, Ertl, 1/16th scale, #416, MIB, S5	$25.00
Case IH 2188 Combine, Ertl, 1995 Farm Show Edition, 1/64th scale, #4607, MIB, S5	$15.00
Case IH 4-Wheel Drive, Ertl, 1993 Farm Show, 1/64th scale, MIB, S5	$6.00
Case IH 5130 Row Crop, Ertl, 1/64th scale, #229, MIB, S5	$4.00

Case IH 5130 Row Crop, 1991 Farm Show, 1/64th scale, #229, MIB, S5 ....$10.00

Case IH 5131 Row Crop, Ertl, 1/64th scale, #229, MIB, S5 .$3.00

Case IH 7140 Mechanical Front-Drive Tractor, Ertl, 1/64th scale, #616, MIB, S5 ....$4.00

Case IH 7220 w/Loader, Ertl, 1/64th scale, #460, MIB, S5 .$5.00

Case L Tractor, Ertl, 150 Year Collector's Edition, 1/16th scale, #252, MIB, S5 ....$35.00

Case 800, Ertl, Collector's Edition, 1/16th scale, #693, MIB, S5 ....$40.00

Caterpillar 32 Ford Panel Truck, Ertl, 1/43rd scale, #7707, MIB, S5 ....$6.00

CIH Maxxum 5120 w/Duals, Ertl, 1/64th scale, #241, MIB, S5 ....$4.00

CIH 7150 Front Wheel Assist, Ertl, 1992 Farm Show, 1/64th scale, #285, MIB, S5 ....$10.00

Deluxe Farm Set, Slik Toy, complete w/tractor, harrow, raker & grader, NM (EX box) $135.00

Deutz Allis Barge Wagon, Ertl, 1/64th scale, #2241, MIB, S5.$3.00

Deutz Allis 6260 Tractor, Ertl, 1/64th scale, #1241, MIB, S5..$3.00

Deutz Allis 9150 Orlando Show Tractor, Ertl, 1/16th scale, #1280, MIB, S5 ....$200.00

Farmall Cub, Ertl, 1/16th scale, #235, MIB, S5 ....$20.00

Farmall Super M-T-A Tractor, Ertl, 1/16th scale, #445, MIB, S5 ....$20.00

Farmall 140 Tractor, Ertl, 1995 Farm Show, 1/16th scale, MIB, S5 ....$35.00

Ford Precision Classic 2N, Ertl, 1/16th scale, #354, MIB, S5 ....$95.00

Ford Precision Classic 8N, Ertl, 1/16th scale, #352, MIB, S5 ....$95.00

Ford Tractor, Aluminum Model Toys, silver & red plastic w/blk rubber tires, 9", NMIB $175.00

Ford Tractor w/Loader, Ertl, 1/64th scale, #897, MIB, S5 ..$5.00

Ford 7740 w/Loader, Ertl, 1/64th scale, #387, MIB, S5 ....$5.00

Ford 8340 w/4-Wheel Drive, Ertl, 1/16th scale, #877, MIB, S5 ....$50.00

Ford 901 Power Master Tractor, Ertl, 1/64th scale, #927, MIB, S5 ....$4.00

Fordson Model F Tractor, Ertl, 1/64th scale, #301, MIB, S5 .$18.00

Fordson Super Major Tractor, Ertl, 1/16th scale, MIB......$30.00

Genesis 8870 w/4-Wheel Drive, Ertl, 1/64th scale, #392, MIB, S5 ....$4.00

Hesston Round Baler, Ertl, 1/64th scale, #2263, MIB, S5 ..$4.00

Hesston SL-30 Skidsteer Loader, Ertl, 1/64th scale, #2267, MIB, S5 ....$5.00

IH Anhydrous Ammonia Tank, Ertl, 1/64th scale, #1550, MIB, S5 ....$3.00

IH Farmall Cub, Ertl, 1/16th scale, #653, MIB, S5 ....$18.00

IH 1586 Tractor, Ertl, 1/16th scale, #463, MIB, S5 ....$18.00

IH 1586 Tractor w/Loader, Ertl, 1/16th scale, #416, MIB, S5..$25.00

International Farmall Tractor, 1947-50, Product Miniature Co, plastic, 8", EX (EX box), A $150.00

Farmall 350 Tractor, Ertl, 1/16th scale, MIB, $55.00.

International 1066 5,000,000th Tractor, Ertl, 1/16th scale, MIB, $175.00.

Farmall 706 Diesel Tractor, Ertl, 1/16th scale, #2307, MIB, S5 ....$25.00

Ford F Tractor, Ertl, Collector's Edition, 1/16th scale, #872, MIB, S5 ....$45.00

Ford F-250 Pickup w/Livestock, Ertl, 1/64th scale, #311, MIB, S5 ....$5.00

Ford New Holland Combine, Ertl, 1/64th scale, #815, MIB, S5 ....$10.00

Ford Powermaster Tractor, Hubley, #961, 11", NM (EX box) $185.00

International 600 Diesel Tractor, Ertl, 1/16th scale, #282, MIB, S5 ....$20.00

John Deere Bale Throw Wagon, Ertl, 1/64th scale, #5755, MIB, S5 ....$4.00

John Deere Combine, Ertl, 1/64th scale, #5604, MIB, S5...$10.00

John Deere Compact Utility Tractor, Ertl, 1/16th scale, MIB, S5 .$16.00

John Deere Cotton Picker, Ertl, 1/80th scale, #1000, MIB, S5 ....$6.00

John Deere Fertilizer Spreader, Ertl, 1/64th scale, #5558, MIB, S5 ....$3.00

John Deere Excavator, Ertl, 1/64th scale, MIB, $10.00.

John Deere Forage Harvester, Ertl, 1/64th scale, #566, MIB, S5 ....$3.00

John Deere GP Standard, Ertl, Collector's Edition, 1/16th scale, #5767, MIB, S5 ....$35.00

John Deere GP Tractor, Ertl, 1/16th scale, #5801, MIB, S5..$25.00

John Deere Gravity Wagon, Ertl, 1/64th scale, #5552, MIB, S5 ....$3.00

John Deere Historical Set, Ertl, 1/64th scale, #5523, 4 pcs, MIB, S5 ....$10.00

John Deere Model A Tractor, Ertl, 1/16th scale, #539, MIB, S5 ....$18.00

John Deere Mower Conditioner, Ertl, 1/64th scale, #5657, MIB, S5 ....$3.00

John Deere Overtime Tractor, Ertl, 1/16th scale, #5811, MIB, S5 ....$25.00

John Deere Rotary Cutter, Ertl, 1/64th scale, #5600, MIB, S5 ....$4.00

John Deere Skid Loader, Ertl, 1/64th scale, #5536, MIB, S5 ....$5.00

John Deere Skid Steer Loader, Ertl, 1/64th scale, #5622, MIB, S5 ....$5.00

John Deere Utility Tractor, Ertl, 1/16th scale, #516, MIB, S5 ....$15.00

John Deere w/Duals, Ertl, 1/64th scale, #5734, MIB, S5.....$4.00

John Deere Waterloo Engine, Ertl, 1/16th scale, #5645, MIB, S5 ....$20.00

John Deere 12-A Combine, Ertl, 1/16th scale, #5601, MIB, S5 ....$45.00

John Deere 12-Row Planter, Ertl, 1/64th scale, #576, MIB, S5 ....$5.00

John Deere 3010, Ertl, Collector's Edition, 1/16th scale, #5635, MIB, S5 ....$38.00

John Deere 3010 Tractor, Ertl, 1/16th scale, #5635, MIB, S5 ....$20.00

John Deere 4020 Precision #3, Ertl, 1/16th scale, #5638, MIB, S5 ....$95.00

John Deere 494-A 4-Row Planter Precision Classic, Ertl, 1/16th scale, #5838, MIB, S5 ....$125.00

John Deere 5020 Tractor, Ertl, 1/64th scale, #5776, MIB, S5 ....$4.00

John Deere 630 LP Tractor, Ertl, 1/43rd scale, #5599, MIB, S5 ....$5.00

John Deere 70 Tractor, Ertl, 1/16th scale, #5611, MIB, S5...$22.00

John Deere 7800 w/Loader, Ertl, 1/64th scale, #5652, MIB, S5 ....$5.00

John Deere 8870 4-Wheel Drive Tractor, Ertl, 1/64th scale, #5791, MIB, S5 ....$5.00

John Deere 95 Combine, Ertl, 1/64th scale, #5819, MIB, S5 .$10.00

Knudson 4400 4-Wheel Drive Tractor w/Duals, Ertl, 1/64th scale, #TF4400, MIB, S5 ....$20.00

Massey-Ferguson 3070 w/Loader, Ertl, 1/64th scale, #1176, MIB, S5 ....$5.00

Massey-Ferguson Bale Processor, Ertl, 1/64th scale, #1093, MIB, S5 ....$3.00

Massey-Ferguson Challenger, Ertl, 1/16th scale, #1103, MIB, S5 ....$25.00

Massey-Ferguson 3120 Tractor, Ertl, 1/64th scale, #1177, MIB, S5 ....$4.00

Massey-Ferguson 555 Tractor, Ertl, 1/16th scale, #1105, MIB, S5 ....$22.00

Massey-Ferguson 699 Tractor w/Loader, Ertl, 1/64th scale, #1125, MIB, S5 ....$5.00

Massey-Harris 44 Special Tractor, Ertl, 1/16th scale, #1115, MIB, S5 ....$18.00

Massey-Harris 55 Wide-Front, Ertl, 1/16th scale, #1292, MIB, S5 ....$20.00

McCormick Farmall 130 Tractor, Ertl, 1993 Lafayette Farm Toy Show Edition, 1/16th scale, MIB..................$45.00

McCormick-Deering Farmall, 1992 Lafayette Farm Toy Show Edition, MIB $45.00

McCormick-Deering WD-40 Tractor, Wheat Belt Works, 1/16th scale, MIB $265.00

Minneapolis Moline G750, Ertl, 1/16th scale, #4375, MIB, S5 ....$25.00

Minneapolis Moline G750, Ertl, 1994 National Tractor Show, 1/16th scale, #4375, MIB, S5 ....$80.00

Tractor, Hubley Kiddie Toy, 7", MIB, A, $125.00.

New Holland Baler, Ertl, 1/64th scale, #337, MIB, S5........$3.00

New Holland Forage Harvester, Ertl, 1/64th scale, #372, MIB, S5 ....$4.00

New Holland Mower Conditioner, Ertl, 1/64th scale, #322, MIB, S5........$4.00

Oliver 1555 Diesel Tractor, Ertl, 1/16th scale, #2223, MIB, S5 ....$22.00

Oliver 1655 w/Wide Front, Ertl, 1/16th scale, #4472, MIB, S5 ....$20.00

Tru Scale Wagon, red-pnt tin, 7½", EX $20.00

Fast-Food Collectibles

Fast-food collectibles are attracting a lot of attention right now — the hobby is fun and inexpensive (so far), and the little toys, games, buttons, and dolls originally meant for the kids are now being snatched up by adults who are much more likely to appreciate them. They were first included in kiddie meals in the late 1970s. They're often issued in series of up to eight or ten characters; the ones you'll want to watch for are Disney characters, popular kids' icons like Barbie dolls, Cabbage Patch Kids, My Little Pony, Star Trek, etc. But it's not just the toys that are collectible. So are the boxes, store signs and displays, and promotional items (like the Christmas ornaments they once sold for 99¢). Supply dictates price. For instance, a test market box might be worth $20.00, a box from a regional promotion might be $10.00, while one from a national promotion could be virtually worthless.

Toys don't have to be old to be collectible, but if you can find them still in their original package, so much the better. Though there are exceptions, a loose toy is worth one half to two thirds the value of one mint in package. (The values given here are for MIP items unless noted otherwise.) For more information we recommend *McDonald's® Happy Meal® Toys — In the USA* and *McDonald's® Happy Meal® Toys — Around the World,* by Joyce and Terry Losonsky; and *Tomart's Price Guide to Kid's Meal Collectibles (Non-McDonald's)* and *Kid's Meal Collectibles Update '94 – '95* by Ken Clee. Both authors are listed under Fast-Food Collectibles in the Categories of Special Interest section of this book. We also recommend *McDonald's® Collectibles* by Gary Henriques and Audre DuVall (Collector Books).

Advisors: Bill and Pat Poe (P10); Scott Smiles (S10), Foreign.
Other Sources: C3, C11, I2, K1 (Simpsons), M8, P3.

ARBY'S

Babar's World Tour, finger puppets, 1990, ea..............$3.00
Babar's World Tour, pull-back racers, 1992, ea..................$3.00
Babar's World Tour, squirters, 1992, ea.....................$2.00
Babar's World Tour, stampers, 1991, ea $3.00
Babar's World Tour, storybooks, 1991, ea.....................$3.00
Babar's World Tour, vehicle, 1990, ea...................$3.00
Little Miss, 1981, ea $4.00
Looney Tunes Car Tunes, 1989, ea $3.00
Looney Tunes Characters, 1987, oval base, ea...................$5.00
Looney Tunes Characters, 1988, standing, ea....................$5.00

Looney Tunes Fun Fingers, 1989, ea....................$5.00
Mr Men, 4 different, ea $5.00
Snow Domes, 1995, Yogi or Snagglepuss, ea $5.00
Winter Wonderland Crazy Cruisers, 1995, ea...................$4.00
Yogi Bear Fun Squirters, 1994, ea....................$4.00

BURGER KING

Action Figures, 1991, ea $3.00
Aladdin, 1992, ea...................$3.00
Aladdin Hidden Treasures, 1994, ea $2.00
Archies, 1991, 4 different, ea....................$4.00
Beauty & the Beast, 1991, 4 different, ea $4.00
Beetlejuice, 1990, 6 different, ea....................$2.00
Bone Age, 1989, 4 different, ea $5.00
Bonkers, 1993, 6 different, ea $3.00
Capitol Critters, 1992, 4 different, ea...................$2.00
Captain Planet Flipover Star Cruisers, 1991, 4 different, ea .$2.00
Cool Stuff, 1995, 5 different, ea....................$3.00
Crayola Christmas Bears, 1986, plush, 4 different colors, ea.$5.00
Dino Crawlers, 1994, 5 different, ea...................$2.00
Gargoyles, 1995, 1st or 2nd set, ea...................$3.00
Glo Force, 1996, 5 different, ea $3.00

Glow-in-the-Dark Troll Patrol, 1993, four different, $3.00 each.

Go-Go Gadgets, 1991, 4 different, ea...................$3.00
Good Goblin', 1989, 3 different, ea...................$3.00
Goofy & Max Adventures, 1995, any except yel runaway car, ea...................$3.00
Goofy & Max Adventures, 1995, yel runaway car $4.00
Hunchback of Notre Dame, 1995, hand puppets, 4 different, ea...................$10.00
Hunchback of Notre Dame, 1996, 8 different, ea $4.00
It's Magic, 1992, 4 different, ea...................$2.00
Kid Transporters, 1990, 6 different, ea $2.00
Life Savers Freaky Fellas, 1992, 4 different colors, ea..........$2.00
Lion King, 1994, 7 different, ea $3.00
Lion King, 1995, finger puppets, 6 different, ea $3.00

Little Mermaid, 1993, Urchin squirt gun, Flounder squirter, or Sebastian w/up, ea..$3.00

McGruff Cares for You, 1991, 4 different songbook & tape sets, ea...$6.00

Mini Record Breakers, 1989, 6 different, ea $2.00

Mini Sports Games, 1993, 4 different, ea $3.00

Minnie Mouse, 1992 ....$6.00

Miss Daisy's Trolley w/Chip & Dale, 1993 ....$6.00

Nerfuls, 1989, 3 different, ea..$4.00

Nightmare Before Christmas, watches, set of 4, EX, H9...$40.00

Oliver & Co, 1996, 5 different, ea...................................$3.00

Pinocchio Summer Infatables, 1992, 5 different, ea..........$4.00

Pocahontas, 1995, 8 different, ea....................................$3.00

Pocahontas, 1996, finger puppets, 6 different, ea $3.00

Pranksters, 1994, 5 different, ea.....................................$3.00

Purrtenders, 1988, Free Wheeling Cheese Rider or Flip Top Car, ea $2.00

Purrtenders Sock-Ems, Christmas 1987, stuffed plush animals, 4 different, ea..$5.00

Rodney Reindeer & Friends, 1986, 4 different, ea $5.00

Silverhawks, 1987, pencil topper.....................................$5.00

Simpsons, 1990, 5 different, ea.......................................$2.00

Spacebase Racers, 1989, 4 different, ea $3.00

Sports All-Stars, 1994, 5 different, ea.............................$4.00

Super Powers, door shield $8.00

Super Powers, 1987, Aquaman tub toy.............................$6.00

Surprise Celebration Parade, 1992, 4 different, w/track, ea..$6.00

Teenage Mutant Ninja Turtles Bike Gear, 1993, ea $3.00

Top Kids Wild Spinning Tops, 1994, 4 different, ea..........$2.00

Toy Story, 1995, Action Wing Buzz $6.00

Toy Story, 1995, Rex Dinosaur, RC Racer, Mr Potato Head, or Army Recon Squadron, ea.......................................$3.00

Toy Story, 1995, Woody $8.00

Trak-Pak Golden Jr Classic Books, 1988, 4 different, ea $4.00

Water-Mates, 1991, any except Snaps/rowboat w/pk shirt or Wheels/hovercraft w/bl control panel, ea..................$3.00

Water-Mates, 1991, Snaps/rowboat w/pk shirt or Wheels/hovercraft w/bl control panel, ea $6.00

World Travel Adventure Kit, 1991, 4 different, ea.............$5.00

Z-Bots w/Pogs, 1994, 5 different, ea................................$2.00

DAIRY QUEEN

Alvin & the Chipmunks Music Makers, 1994, 4 different, ea.$5.00

Baby's Day Out Books, 1994, 4 different, ea $12.00

Bobby's World, 1994, 4 different, ea................................$5.00

Dennis the Menace, 1994, 4 different, ea.........................$6.00

Radio Flyer, 1991, miniature wagon $5.00

Rock-A-Doodle, 1991, 6 different, ea...............................$7.00

Space Shuttle, 6 different, ea..$3.00

Tom & Jerry, 1993, 4 different, ea...................................$6.00

DENNY'S

Adventure Seekers Activity Packet, 1993, ea $2.00

Dino-Makers, 5 different, ea..$3.00

Flinstones Rock 'N Rollers, 1991, Fred w/guitar or Barney w/saxophone, ea..$4.00

Flintstones, 1989, Fred & Wilma or Barney & Betty, plush, ea...$8.00

Flintstones, 1989, Pebbles & Bamm-Bamm, plush, pr $12.00

Flintstones, 1990, vehicles, 3 different, ea......................$4.00

Flintstones Dino Racers, 1991, 3 different, ea..................$4.00

Flintstones Fun Squirters, 1991, 5 different, ea $4.00

Flintstones Glacier Gliders, 1990, Barnery playing hockey, Bamm-Bamm on sled or Dino, ea..............................$3.00

Jetson's Go Back to School, 1992, 4 different, ea.............$3.00

Jetson's Space Cards, 1992, 6 different, ea $4.00

Jetson's Space Travel Fun Books, 1992, 6 different, ea $3.00

Jetson's Space-Age Puzzle Ornaments, 1992, ea.............$3.00

DOMINOS PIZZA

Avoid the Noid, 1988, 3 different, ea................................$5.00

Donnie Domino, 1989, 4"..$6.00

Keep the Noid Out, 1987, 3 different, ea.........................$5.00

Noid, 1989, bookmark $10.00

HARDEE'S

Apollo Spaceship, 1995, 3-pc set.....................................$12.00

Balto, 1995, 6 different, ea...$3.00

Beach Bunnies, 1989, 4 different, ea $2.00

Bobby's World (At the Circus), 1996, 5 different, ea....$3.00

Breakman's World, 1995, 4 different, ea $3.00

Camp California, 1994, 4 different, ea $3.00

Dinobend Buddies, 1994, 4 different, ea..........................$3.00

Dinosaur in My Pocket, 1993, 4 different, ea...................$3.00

Eek! the Cat, 1995, 6 different, ea...................................$3.00

Eureka Castle Stampers, 1994, 4 different, ea $3.00

Fender-Bender 500 Racers, 1990, 5 different, ea $3.00

Flintstones First 30 Years, 4 different, ea........................$3.00

Gremlin Adventures Read-Along Book & Record, 1984, 5 different, ea..$6.00

Halloween Hideaway, 1989, 4 different, ea......................$2.00

Homeward Bound II, 1996, 5 different, ea........................$3.00

Kazoo Crew Sailors, 1991, 4 different, ea $3.00

Marvel Super Heroes in Vehicles, 1990, 4 different, ea......$3.00

Mickey's Christmas Carol, 1984, plush figures, 4 different, ea..$6.00

Micro Super Soakers, 1994, 4 different, ea.......................$3.00

Mouth Figurines, 1989, 4 different, ea.............................$3.00

Muppets Christmas Carol, 1993, finger puppets, 4 different, ea.$4.00

Nickelodeon School Tools, 1995, 6 different, ea $3.00

Nicktoons Cruisers, 1994, 8 different, ea.........................$3.00

Pound Puppies, 1986, plush, 4 different, ea $5.00

Pound Puppies & Pur-R-Ries, 1987, plush, 5 different, ea..$5.00

Shirt Tales, 1990, plush figures, 5 different, ea...................$5.00

Smurfs Funmeal Pack, 1990, 6 different, ea......................$3.00

Speed Bunnies, 1994, 4 different, ea................................$3.00

Swan Princess, 1994, 5 different, ea................................$4.00

Tattoads, 1995, 4 different, ea $3.00

Tune-A-Fish, 1994, 4 different, ea $3.00

Waldo & Friends Holiday Ornaments, 1991, 3 different, ea ..$4.00

Waldo & Friends Straw Buddies, 1990, 4 different, ea........$3.00

Walt Disney Animated Film Classic, 1985, plush, 5 different, ea $6.00

X-Men, 1995, 6 different, ea $3.00

JACK-IN-THE-BOX

Bendable Buddies, 1975, 4 different, ea.............................$10.00
Bendable Buddies, 1991, 5 different, ea.............................$3.00
Finger Puppets, 1994, 5 different, ea $10.00
Garden Fun Seed Packages, 1994, 3 different, ea................$5.00
Jack Pack Make-A-Scene, 1990, 3 different, ea $4.00
Star Trek the Next Generation, 1994, 6 different, ea.........$5.00

LONG JOHN SILVER'S

Berenstain Bears Books, 1995, 4 different, ea......................$3.00
Fish Car, 1989, 3 different, ea...$3.00
Free Willy II, 1995, 5 different, ea.....................................$4.00
I Love Dinosaurs, 1993, 4 different, ea $4.00
Map Activites, 1991, 3 different, ea $4.00
Once Upon a Forest, 1993, 2 different, ea..........................$4.00
Sea Watchers, 1991, mini kaleidoscopes, 3 different, ea.....$5.00
Treasure Trolls, 1992, pencil toppers, 4 different, ea $3.00
Water Blasters, 1990, 4 different, ea $4.00

McDonald's

Airport, 1986, Fry Guy Flyer, Grimace Ace, or Birdie Bent Wing
    Blazer, ea $4.00
Airport, 1986, Ronald McDonald seaplane.........................$5.00
Airport, 1986, under age 3, Fry Guy Flyer (floater) $5.00
Aladdin & the King of Thieves, 1996, any except under age 3,
    ea $3.00
Amazing Wildlife, 1995, ea...$2.00
Animaniacs, 1995, any except under age 3, ea...................$3.00
Animaniacs, 1995, under age 3, ea $5.00
Babe, 1996, 7 different, ea...$3.00
Bambi, 1988, 4 different, ea $5.00
Barbie/Hot Wheels, 1991, Barbie, any except under age 3, ea..$5.00
Barbie/Hot Wheels, 1991, Barbie, under age 3, Costume Ball or
    Wedding Day Midge, ea...$8.00
Barbie/Hot Wheels, 1991, Hot Wheels, ea $4.00
Barbie/Hot Wheels, 1993, Barbie, any except under age 3, ea.$3.00
Barbie/Hot Wheels, 1993, Barbie, under age 3, Rose Bride .$4.00
Barbie/Hot Wheels, 1993, Hot Wheels, any except under age 3,
    ea $3.00
Barbie/Hot Wheels, 1993, Hot Wheels, under age 3, Hammer,
    or Wrench, ea $4.00
Barbie/Hot Wheels, 1994, Barbie, any except Camp Teresa
    (variation) or under age 3, from $4 to $5.00
Barbie/Hot Wheels, 1994, Barbie, under age 3, Barbie Ball.$5.00
Barbie/Hot Wheels, 1994, Camp Teresa $8.00
Barbie/Hot Wheels, 1995, Barbie, any except Black Lifeguard
    Barbie & under age 3, ea...$3.00
Barbie/Hot Wheels, 1995, Barbie, unger age 3, Lil' Miss Candi
    Stripe..$4.00
Barbie/Hot Wheels, 1995, Hot Wheels, any except age 3, ea..$3.00
Barbie/Hot Wheels, 1995, Hot Wheels, under age 3, Key Force
    truck $4.00
Barbie/Hot Wheels, 1996, Barbie, any except under age 3, ea..$3.00

Barbie/Hot Wheels, 1996, Hot Wheels, under age 3, mini steer-
    ing wheel $4.00
Barbie/Mini Streex, 1991, Barbie, any except under age 3,
    ea..$3.00
Barbie/Mini Streex, 1992, Barbie, under age 3, Sparkle
    Eyes $4.00
Barbie/Mini Streex, 1992, Mini Streex, any except under
    age 3 ....$2.00
Barbie/Mini Streex, 1992, Mini Streex, under age 3, Orange
    Arrow $4.00
Barnyard (Old McDonald's Farm), 1986, 6 different, ea.....$8.00
Batman, 1992, 6 different, ea...$3.00
Batman (Animated), 1993, any except under age 3, ea $3.00
Batman (Animated), 1993, under age 3, Batman $4.00
Beanie Babies, 1996, any except Pinky the Flamingo, ea from $8
    to $15.00
Beanie Babies, 1996, Pinky the Flamingo, from $15 to $25.00
Beanie Babies, 1998, any except Bongo the Monkey, Doby the
    Doberman or Twigs the Giraffe, ea from $5 to.............$8.00
Beanie Babies, 1998, Bongo the Monkey, Doby the Doberman
    or Twigs the Giraffe, ea from $10 to $15.00
Bedtime, 1989, drinking cup, M $3.00
Bedtime, 1989, Ronald, set of 4, ea $3.00
Bedtime, 1989, wash mitt, bl foam $5.00
Berenstain Bears, 1987, any except under age 3, ea $5.00
Berenstain Bears, 1987, under age 3, Mama or Papa w/paper
    punch-outs, ea..$8.00
Boats & Floats, 1987, Fry Kids raft or McNuggets lifeboat, w/sep-
    arate sticker sheet, ea, from $8 to $10.00

Cabbage Patch Kids, Lindsey Elizabeth, 1992, $2.00.

Cabbage Patch Kids/Tonka Trucks, 1992, Cabbage Patch Kids,
    any except under age 3, ea..$2.00

Tonka Trucks, cement mixer, 1992, $2.00.

Cabbage Patch Kids/Tonka Trucks, 1992, Tonka Trucks, under age 3, dump truck $4.00
Changeables, 1987, 6 different, ea $5.00
Chip 'N Dale Rescue Rangers, 1989, 4 different, ea............$4.00
Circus Parade, 1991, ea $5.00
COSMc Crayola, 1988, under age 3, So Big, w/2 crayons & activity sheet $5.00
Crayola Stencils, 1987, any except under age 3, ea.............$2.00
Crayola Stencils, 1987, under age 3, Ronald......................$6.00
Crazy Creatures w/Popoids, 1985, 4 different, ea $5.00
Dink the Little Dinosaur, 1990, Regional, 6 different, M, ea.$5.00
Dinosaur Days, 1981, 6 different, ea $2.00
Disney Favorites, 1987, activity book, Sword & the Stone...$5.00
Disneyland — 40 Years of Adventures, 1995, ea $3.00
Ducktails, 1987, ea from $5 to $6.00
Ducktails II, 1988, launch pad in airport............................$5.00
Ducktails II, 1988, Scrooge McDuck in Car or Huey, Louie & Dewey on surf ski, ea...$7.00
Ducktails II, 1988, Webby on tricycle $8.00
Fast Mac II, 1985, wht squad car, pk cruiser, red sports car, or yel jeep, ea $5.00
Feeling Good, 1985, comb, Captain, red.............................$2.00
Feeling Good, 1985, Fry Guy on duck $4.00
Feeling Good, 1985, mirror, Birdie $3.00

Flintstone Kids, 1988, $8.00 each.
(Photo courtesy Martin and Carolyn Berens)

Feeling Good, 1985, soap dish, Grimace $5.00
Feeling Good, 1985, under age 3, Grimace in tub, H4........$4.00
Flintstone Kids, 1988, under age 3, Dino $12.00
Friendly Skies, 1991, Ronald or Grimmace, ea $8.00
Friendly Skies, 1994, United hanger w/Ronald in plane ..$10.00
Fun w/Food, 1989, ea $10.00
Funny Fry Friends, 1989, under age 3, Little Darling or Lil' Chief, ea $6.00
Ghostbusters, 1987, pencil case, Containment Chamber ...$5.00
Ghostbusters, 1987, pencil sharpener, ghost $3.00
Gravedale High, 1991, regional, 5 different, ea...................$5.00
Halloween (What Am I Going To Be), 1995, any except under age 3, ea...$3.00
Halloween (What Am I Going To Be), 1995, under age 3, Grimace in pumpkin $4.00
Halloween McNuggets, 1993, any except under age 3, ea ..$3.00
Halloween McNuggets, 1993, under age 3, McBoo Mc Nugget $4.00
Happy Birthday 15 Years, 1994, any except Tonka or Muppet Babies, ea from $3 to...$5.00
Happy Birthday 15 Years, 1994, Muppet Babies #11 train pc $8.00
Happy Birthday 15 Years, 1994, Tonka train pc, from $10 to .$15.00
Happy Pail, 1986, 5 different, M, ea $5.00
Hook, 1997, 4 different, ea $3.00
Jungle Book, 1989, set of 4, MIP $15.00
Jungle Book, 1990, under age 3, Junior or Mowgli, ea $9.00
Lego Building Set, 1986, helicopter or airplane, ea.............$3.00
Lego Building Set, 1986, race car or tanker boat, ea $6.00
Lego Motion, 1989, any except under age 3, ea $5.00
Lego Motion, 1989, under age 3, Giddy Gator or Tuttle Turtle, ea $6.00
Little Gardener, 1989, Birdie, shovel, Fry Kids planter, Grimace rake or Ronald water can, ea $2.00
Little Golden Book, 1982, 5 different, M, ea $3.00
Little Mermaid, 1989, 4 different, ea.....................................$5.00
Littlest Pet Shop/Transformers, 1996, any except under age 3, ea.$3.00
Littlest Pet Shop/Transformers, 1996, under age 3, ea........$4.00
Looney Tunes Quack-Up Cars, 1993, 4 different, ea $2.00
Mac Tonight, 1988, under age 3, skateboard $8.00
Mac Tonight, 1988, 4 different, ea $6.00
Marvel Super Heroes, 1996, any except under age 3, ea $3.00
Marvel Super Heroes, 1996, under age 3 ....$4.00
McDino Changeables, 1991, any except under age 3, ea $3.00
McDino Changeables, 1991, under age 3, Bronto Cheesburger or Small Fry Ceratops, ea $4.00
McDonald's Star Trek, 1979, from $5 to $6.00
McDonaldland Band, 1986, Fry Kid Trumpet, Pan Pipes, or Grimace Saxophone, ea $3.00
McDonaldland Band, 1986, Ronald harmonica..................$5.00
McDonaldland Dough, 1990, M, ea $5.00
McNugget Buddies, 1988, any except Corny w/red popcorn belt or Cowpoke w/scarf, ea $2.00
McNugget Buddies, 1988, Corny w/red popcorn belt or Cowpoke w/scarf, ea $4.00
Mickey's Birthdayland, 1988, any except under age 3, ea...$2.00
Mickey's Birthdayland, 1988, under age 3 ....$6.00
Mix 'Em Up Monsters, 1989, Bibble, Corkle, Gropple, or Thugger, ea $3.00

Moveables, 1988, any except Ronald, M, ea $8.00
Moveables, 1988, Ronald, M $9.00
Muppet Treasure Island, 1996, tub toys, any except under age 3,
    ea $3.00
Muppet Treasure Island, 1996, under age 3, book for bath .$4.00
Muppet Workshop, 1995, ea..$2.00
Mystery of the Lost Arches, 1992, Magic Lens Camera
    (recalled) $4.00
Mystery of the Lost Arches, 1992, micro-cassette/magnifyer,
    phone/periscope, or flashlight/telescope, ea $3.00
New Archies, 1988, 6 different, M, ea....................................$6.00
New Food Changeables, 1989, any except under age 3, ea .$2.00
New Food Changeables, 1989, under age 3, Pals Changeables
    Cube $4.00
Oliver & Co, 1988, 4 different, M, ea $2.00
Peanuts, 1990, any except under age 3 ....$3.00
Peanuts, 1990, under age 3, Charlie Brown egg basket or
    Snoopy's potato sack, ea $5.00
Polly Pocket/Attack Pack, 1995, any except under age 3, ea .$2.00
Polly Pocket/Attack Pack, 1995, under age 3, ea $3.00
Potato Heads, 1992, 8 different, ea..$4.00
Power Rangers, 1995, any except under age 3, ea $3.00
Powers Ranger, 1995, under age 3 ....$4.00
Rescuers Down Under, 1990, any except under age 3, ea ...$1.00
Rescuers Down Under, 1990, under age 3, Bernard in cheese ..$3.00
Runaway Robots, 1987, 6 different, M, ea............................$3.00
Safari Adventure, 1980, cookie molds, Ronald or Grimace, red
    or yel, ea $3.00
Safari Adventure, 1980, sponge, Ronald sitting cross-legged, M.$5.00
School Days, 1984, eraser, Birdie or Grimace, M, ea $3.00
School Days, 1984, pencil, Grimace, Ronald, or Hamburglar, M,
    ea $3.00
School Days, 1984, ruler, M...$4.00
Sea World of Texas, 1988, 4 different, M, ea.....................$10.00
Snow White & the Seven Dwarfs, 1993, any except under age 3,
    ea $3.00
Snow White & the Seven Dwarfs, 1993, under age 3, Dopey or
    Sneezy, ea $4.00
Space Rescue, 1995, any except under age 3, ea $3.00
Space Rescue, 1995, under age 3, Astro Viewer.................$4.00
Spider-Man, 1995, any except under age 3, ea....................$3.00
Spider-Man, 1995, under age 3 ....$4.00
Sports Balls, 1990, ea $3.00
Stomper Mini 4x4, 1986, 15 different, M, ea $8.00
Super Looney Tunes, 1991, any except under age 3, ea......$3.00
Super Looney Tunes, 1991, under age 3, Daffy Duck as Bat
    Duck, ea $4.00
Super Mario Brothers, 1990, any except under age 3, ea $3.00
Super Mario Brothers, 1990, under age 3, Super Mario $4.00
Tale Spin, 1990, any except under age 3, ea $3.00
Tale Spin, 1990, under age 3, Baloo's Seaplane or Wildcat's Fly-
    ing Machine, ea..$4.00
Totally Toy Holiday, 1995, any except under age 3, ea from $3
    to $4.00
Totally Toy Holiday, 1995, under age 3, ea from $4 to.......$5.00
Totally Toys, 1993, any except Magic Nursery (boy) or under
    age 3, ea..$2.00
Totally Toys, 1993, under age 3, Key Force car...................$3.00

Totally Toys, 1993, under age 3, Magic Nursery (boy or girl), ea
    from $5 to..$6.00
Turbo Macs, 1988, any except under age 3, M, ea $4.00
Turbo Macs, 1988, under age 3, Ronald in soft rubber car, M.$6.00
VR Troopers, 1996, any except under age 3, ea $3.00
VR Troopers, 1996, under age 3 ....$4.00
Water Games, 1992, ea...$4.00
Wild Friends, 1992, regional, any except under age 3, ea ...$4.00
Winter Worlds, 1983, ornament, Birdie or Mayor McCheese, M,
    ea $8.00
Winter Worlds, 1983, ornament, Grimace or Hamburgler, M,
    ea $6.00
Winter Worlds, 1983, ornament, Ronald McDonald, M $3.00
Young Astronauts, 1992, any except under age 3, ea $2.00
Young Astronauts, 1992, under age 3, Ronald in lunar rover..$4.00
Zoo Face, 1988, 4 different, ea...$4.00

101 Dalmatians, 1991, $4.00 each.

PIZZA HUT

Air Garfield, kite, 1993..$6.00
Air Garfield, parachute, 1993 ....$8.00
Beauty & the Beast, 1992, hand puppets, 4 different, ea $4.00
Brain Thaws, 4 different, 1995, ea..$4.00
Eureeka's Castle, 1990, hand puppets, 3 different, ea..........$5.00
Land Before Time, 1988, hand puppet, Sharptooth............$8.00
Land Before Tome, 1988, hand puppet, Cara, Littlefoot, Spike,
    or Duckie, ea $5.00
Marvel Comics, 4 different, 1994, ea....................................$4.00
Mascot Misfits, 4 different, 1995, ea.....................................$4.00
Pagemaster, 4 different, 1994, ea $4.00
Rocketeer, punch-out paper figural airplane-like flyer, unused,
    EX+, H4 ....$8.00
Squirt Toons, 5 different, 1995, ea $5.00
Universal Monsters, 1991, hologram cards, 3 different, ea .$5.00

SONIC

Airtoads, 6 different, ea...$4.00
All-Star Mini Baseballs, 1995, 5 different, ea.....................$4.00

Animal Straws, 1995, 4 different, ea $3.00
Bone-A-Fide Friends, 1994, 4 different, ea......................$3.00
Brown Bag Bowlers, 1994, 4 different, ea $5.00
Brown Bag Buddies, 1993, 3 different, ea $4.00
Brown Bag Juniors, 1989, 4 different, ea $5.00
Creepy Strawlers, 1995, 4 different, ea $5.00
Flippin' Food, 1995, 3 different, ea $3.00
Food Train, 1995, set of 7 cars w/engine $22.00
Go Wild Bills, 1995, 4 different, ea $3.00
Holiday Kids, 1994, 4 different, ea..................................$4.00
Monster Peepers, 1994, 4 different, ea $3.00
Shoe Biters, 1995, 4 different, ea $5.00
Squishers, 1995, 4 different, ea $5.00
Super Sonic Racers, 1995, 4 different, ea $3.00
Totem Pal Squirters, 1995, 4 different, ea $5.00
Very Best Food, 1996, 4 different, ea...............................$4.00
Wacky Sackers, 1994, set of 6..$20.00

SUBWAY

Battle Balls, 1995-96, 4 different, ea................................$3.00
Bobby's World, 1995, 4 different, ea.................................$4.00
Bump in the Night, 1995, 4 different, ea $5.00
Cone Heads, 1993, 4 different, ea.....................................$4.00
Explore Space, 1994, 4 different, ea..................................$4.00
Hackeysack Balls, 1991, 5 different, ea............................$4.00
Hurricanes, 1994, 4 different, ea.......................................$4.00
Inspector Gadget, 1994, 4 different, ea.............................$4.00
Monkey Trouble, 1994, 5 different, ea $3.00
Santa Claus, 1994, under age 3, Comet the Reindeer........$5.00
Save the Wildlife, 1995, 4 different, ea $3.00
Tale Tale, 1995, any except under age 3, ea......................$4.00
Tale Tale, 1995, under age 3, Bunyan & Babe the Blue Ox .$5.00
Tom & Jerry, 1995, 4 different, ea.....................................$3.00

TACO BELL

Congo, 1995, watches, 3 different, ea.................................$5.00
Happy Talk Sprites, Spark, Twinkle, or Romeo, 1983, plush, ea..$6.00
Hugga Bunch, Fluffer, Gigglet or Tuggins, 1984, plush, ea.$8.00
Mask, 1995, It's Party Time switchplate or Milo w/mask, ea..$4.00
Pebble & the Penguin, 1995, 3 different, ea.......................$5.00
The Tick, 1995, finger puppet, Arthur Wall Climber or
   Thrakkorzog, ea...$4.00
The Tick, 1996, Arthur w/wings or Sewer Urchin, ea........$4.00

TARGET MARKETS

Adventure Team Window Walkers, 1994-95, 4 different, ea..$4.00
Muppet Twisters, 1994, 3 different, ea $4.00
Olympic Sports Weiner Pack, 1996, figures, 4 different, ea.$4.00
Roll-O-Fun Coloring Kit, 1995, 3 different, ea $4.00
Targeteers, 1992, 5 different, ea...$5.00
Targeteers, 1994, 5 different, rooted hair, ea......................$4.00

WENDY'S

Alf Tales, 1990, 6 different, ea..$2.00

All Dogs Go To Heaven, 1989, 6 different, M, ea $2.00
Animalinks, 1995, 6 different, ea $2.00
Ballsasaurus, 1992, 4 different, ea......................................$4.00
Cybercycles, 1994, 4 different, ea.......................................$3.00
Definitely Dinosaurs, 1988, 4 different, ea........................$4.00
Definitely Dinosaurs, 1989, 5 different, ea........................$4.00
Dino Games, 1993, 3 different, ea.......................................$3.00
Endangered Animal Games, 1993, any except under age 3, ea..$2.00
Endangered Animal Games, 1993, under age 3, elephant
   puzzle $3.00
Fast Food Racers, 1990, 6 different, ea $3.00
Felix the Cat, 1990, plush figure..$2.00
Felix the Cat, 1990, Story Board, Zeotrope, Milk Cap set, or Ask
   Felix toy, ea...$3.00
Felix the Cat, 1990, under age 3, rub-on set......................$4.00
Furskins Bears, 1986, 4 different, plush, M, ea $6.00
Gear Up, 1992, handlebar streamers or back-off license plate,
   ea $2.00
Glo-Ahead, 1993, any except under age 3, ea....................$2.00
Glo-Ahead, 1993, under age 3, finger puppet $3.00
Glofriends, 1989, 9 different, M, ea...................................$2.00
Gobots, 1986, Odd Ball/Monster, M $8.00
Jetsons Space Vehicles, 1989, 6 different, ea......................$5.00
Jetsons: The Movie, 1990, 5 different, ea $3.00
Mega Wheels, any except uner age 3, 1995, M, ea............$2.00
Mega Wheels, under age 3, circus wagon, 1995, M............$3.00
Mighty Mouse, 1989, 6 different, ea...................................$4.00
Potato Head II, 1988, 5 different, M, ea $4.00
Rocket Writers, 1992, 4 different, ea...................................$2.00
Speed Bumpers, 1992, any except under age 3, ea $2.00
Speed Bumpers, 1992, under age 3, Truck Speed Roller.....$3.00
Speed Writers, 1991, any except under age 3, ea $3.00
Speed Writers, 1991, under age 3, paint w/water book $4.00
Tecno Cows, 1995, any except under age 3, ea...................$2.00
Tecno Cows, 1995, under age 3, Diamond tow truck $3.00
Too Cool! For School, 1992, pencil bat or gr pickle pen, ea.$3.00
Wacky Windups, 1991, 5 different, ea.................................$4.00
Weird Writers, 1991, 3 different, M, ea...............................$2.00
World of Teddy Ruxpin, 1987, 5 different, ea from $3 to...$4.00
World Wild Life, 1988, books, 4 different, ea $4.00
World Wild Life, 1988, plush figures, 4 different, ea...........$5.00
Write & Sniff, 1994, any except under age 3, ea.................$2.00
Write & Sniff, 1994, under age 3, stencil set $3.00
Yogi Bear & Friends, 1990, 6 different, ea.........................$3.00

WHITE CASTLE

Bow Biters, 1989, Blue Meany $5.00
Camp White Castle, 1990, fork & spoon, ea......................$4.00
Castle Dude Squirters, 1994, 3 different, ea $3.00
Castle Meal Friends, 1991, Wendell, Princess, or Woofleas,
   ea $9.00
Castleburger Dudes, 1991, 4 different, ea $6.00
Castleburger Friends, 1989, 6 different, ea $5.00
Fat Albert & the Cosby Kids, 1990, 4 different, ea..........$10.00
Glow-in-the Dark Monsters, 1992, 3 different, ea $4.00
Holiday Huggables, 1990, 3 different, ea $6.00
Super Balls, 1994, 3 different, ea $5.00

BOXES AND BAGS

Burger King, Trak-Pak, 1988, ea $8.00

Burger King, 1989, Bone Age, Fairy Tales Cassette or Tricky Treaters, ea from $6 to......................................$7.00

Burger King, 1989, Critter Carton/Punch-Out Paper Masks, ea .$18.00

Hardee's, 1987, Little Golden Books, ea $4.00

Hardee's, 1990, Days of Thunder, Fender Bender 500 Racers, Marvel Super Heroes or Squirters, ea $2.00

Hardee's, 1993, Cruisin' Back to School or Muppets Christmas Carol, ea $2.00

McDonald's, 1987, Good Friends or Real Ghostbusters, ea ..$5.00

McDonald's, 1988, Ducktails II, Fraggle Rock, Mac Tonight, McNugget Buddies, Oliver & Co or Zoo Face, ea from $4 to...$5.00

McDonald's, 1989, Chip 'N Dale Rescue Rangers, Garfield, Little Mermaid or Mickey's Birthdayland, ea from $3 to..$4.00

McDonald's, 1989, Raggedy Ann Schoolhouse...................$5.00

McDonald's, 1989, Rain or Shine (no toys produced to match boxes), ea $5.00

McDonald's, 1990, Beach Toy, Jungle Book, Peanuts, Rescuers Down Under, Super Mario, Tale Spin or Valentine, ea from $2..$3.00

McDonald's, 1990, Dink the Dinosaur.............................$10.00

McDonald's, 1990, Fry Benders or Sportsballs, ea...............$5.00

McDonald's, 1991, Barbie/Hot Wheels, Gravedale High, Hook, Muppet Babies, Tiny Toons or 101 Dalmatians, ea from $2 to $3.00

McDonald's, 1992, Back to the Future, Crayon Squeeze Bottle, Wild Friends or Yo-Yogi, ea from $2 to........................$3.00

McDonald's, 1992, Barbie/Mini Streex, Batman or Tiny Toon Adventures, ea from $1 to $2.00

McDonald's, 1993, Batman, Dino Dinosaurs, Field Trip, Halloween McNugget Buddies or Looney Tunes Quack-Up Cars, ea..$1.00

McDonald's, 1993, Snow White & the Seven Dwarfs........$3.00

Wendy's, 1989, Wendy & the Good Stuff Gang, ea $3.00

Wendy's, 1990, Fast Food Racers, Jetsons The Movie, Micro Machines Super Sky Carrier or Yogi Bear, ea...............$4.00

Wendy's, 1991, Rhyme Time, Weather Watch or Wizard of Wonders, ea $2.00

Wendy's, 1994, Carmen Sandiego Code Cracker, ea..........$2.00

FOREIGN

Burger King, Beauty & the Beast, 1992, set of 4, from $45 to.$55.00

Burger King, Cinderella, 1994, set of 3.............................$45.00

Burger King, Flintstones, 1994, set of 4.............................$40.00

Burger King, Snow White, 1995, set of 4 ....$25.00

Burger King, X-Men, 1996, set of 4 ....$30.00

Burger King (England), Peter Pan, set of 5.......................$35.00

Burger King (England), Robin Hood, 1993, set of 5 ....$25.00

Burger King (England), Taz-Mania Crazies, 1994, set of 4..$20.00

Burger King (England), Tiny Toon Adventures, 1995, set of 4 ....$25.00

Burger King (England), Tom & Jerry, 1995, set of 4........$25.00

Kentucky Fried Chicken (Australia), Simpsons cups, plastic w/figural lids, set of 4, M, K1 ....$30.00

Kentucky Fried Chicken (Australia), Simpsons water squirters, set of 4, M, K1..$15.00

McDonald's, Aristocrats, 1993, set of 4.............................$20.00

McDonald's, Dinosaurs, 1995, set of 4..............................$25.00

McDonald's, Disneyland Paris, 1996, set of 4, MIP, C11..$20.00

McDonald's, Hunchback of Notre Dame, 1994, set of 4 w/boxes...$25.00

McDonald's, Island Getaway, 1966, set of 4 w/boxes........$25.00

McDonald's, McFarm, 1995, set of 4 w/boxes $30.00

McDonald's, McRodeo, 1995, set of 4 w/boxes.................$25.00

McDonald's, Pocahontas, 1996, set of 4 w/boxes..............$25.00

McDonald's, Toy Story, 1996, set of 4 w/boxes.................$35.00

McDonald's, Winter Sports, 1995, set of 4........................$25.00

McDonald's (Australia), Aladdin, set of 4, C11 ....$20.00

McDonald's (Australia), Aladdin Straw Grippers, 1994, set of 4..$15.00

McDonald's (Australia), Bambi, set of 4, C11 ....$25.00

McDonald's (Australia), Dark Wing Duck, 1994, set of 4 ..$20.00

McDonald's (Australia), Flintstone Stationary Series, 1994, set of 4 ....$20.00

McDonald's (Australia), Lion King stampers, 1995, set of 4 ....$15.00

McDonald's (Australia), McDonaldland Sky Spinners, set of 4, C11..$15.00

McDonald's (Australia), McSports, 1995, set of 4 ....$25.00

McDonald's (Australia), Pocahontas finger puppets, 1995, set of 4 ....$25.00

McDonald's (Australia), Summer Fun Toys, 1995, set of 4..$15.00

McDonald's (Australia), Winnie the Pooh cups, 1995, set of 4 ....$25.00

McDonald's (Australia), World Cup, 1994, set of 4 ....$20.00

McDonald's (Australia), Zoomballs, 1995, set of 4...........$15.00

McDonald's (Australia), 101 Dalmatians, 1995, set of 4 ..$25.00

McDonald's (England), Flubber, 1998, set of 4, MIP, C11...$15.00

McDonald's (England), Smurfs, set of 10, MIP.................$75.00

McDonald's (European), Airport, 1995, set of 4 w/boxes .$25.00

McDonald's (European), Aladdin, 1994, set of 4..............$25.00

McDonald's (European), Barbie, 1995, set of 4 w/boxes...$30.00

McDonald's (European), Connect-A-Car, 1991, set of 4.$20.00

McDonald's (European), Disneyland Paris, 1996, set of 4 ..$30.00

McDonald's (European), Euro Disney, 1992, set of 4 ....$35.00

McDonald's (European), Flintstones, 1994, set of 4 w/boxes .$25.00

McDonald's (European), Fly & Drive, 1995, set of 4........$20.00

McDonald's (European), I Like Bikes, 1994, set of 4 ....$20.00

McDonald's (European), Kapt'n Baloo, 1993, set of 4......$20.00

McDonald's (European), Lion King puzzles, 1994, set of 4 .$20.00

McDonald's (European), McDonald's Band w/up figures, 1993, set of 4 w/boxes...$25.00

McDonald's (Germany), Flintstones, 1994, set of 4, MIP, C11 ....$20.00

McDonald's (Germany), Smurfs, set of 10, MIP, C11 ......$75.00

McDonald's (Germany), Smurfs, set of 8, MIP $65.00

McDonald's (Japan), Snoopy, 1996, set of 4 ....$45.00

McDonald's (New Zealand), Batman Forever 3-D pop-up cards, 1995, set of 4 ....$20.00

McDonald's (New Zealand), Disney Fun Riders, 1994, set of 4 ....$25.00

McDonald's (New Zealand), Mystery Riders, 1993, set of 4..$20.00

MISCELLANEOUS

This section lists items other than those that are free with kids' meals, for instance, store displays and memorabilia such as Christmas ornaments and plush dolls that can be purchased at the counter.

Burger King, bear, 1986, Crayola Christmas, plush, 4 different, EX, ea from $8 to $10.00

Burger King, cassette tape, 1989, Christmas Sing-A-Long, several different, MIB, ea from $5 to $8.00

Burger King, doll, Burger King, 1980, stuffed cloth, 18", EX .$20.00

Burger King, doll, Magic King, Knickerbocker, 1980, 20", MIB, M17..$65.00

Burger King, puppets, Toy Story, set of 4, MIP, J8............$40.00

Burger King, Red Skelton record, 45 rpm, 1969, unused, M, A...$30.00

Burger King, Star Wars card set, 1980, unused, NM, A....$25.00

Chuck E Cheese, doll, plush, 13", EX, from $15 to...........$20.00

Chuck E Cheese, yo-yo, EX $5.00

Dairy Queen, doll, Dairy Queen Kid, 1974, stuffed cloth, EX, minimum value $30.00

Dairy Queen, doll, Sweet Nell, 1974, stuffed cloth, EX, minimum value..$30.00

Dominos Pizza, doll, Noid, 1988, plush, 19", MIP.............$30.00

Hardee's, doll, Gilbert Giddy-Up, 1971, stuffed cloth, EX..$25.00

Hardee's, Pound Puppy, MIB $5.00

Hardee's, rag doll, Gilbert Giddy-Up, 15", EX, H4...........$15.00

Little Caesar's, doll, stuffed cloth, 6", H4.........................$15.00

McDonald's, bank, Grimace, 1985, compo, NM, S21 ......$25.00

McDonald's, bank, Ronald McDonald, plastic, NM, S21.$15.00

McDonald's, bank, Ronald's Singing Wastebasket, 1975, NM, from $10 to...$15.00

McDonald's, Birthday Book, 1983, w/Ronald punch-out, M, C11 ....$12.00

McDonald's, birthday hat, 1978, w/Ronald, M, C11 ....$12.00

McDonald's, bop bag, 1978, Grimace, 8", MIP $5.00

McDonald's, cap, Season's Greetings, 1992, M...................$5.00

McDonald's, coloring board, 1981, w/Ronald, Grimace, Hamburglar & Birdie, M, C11 ....$15.00

McDonald's, coloring book, McDonald's Circus, 1987, unused, EX, C11 ....$5.00

McDonald's, coloring calendar, 1980, EX, from $8 to $12.00

McDonald's, display, Berenstain Bears, 1987, EX, from $65 to $85.00

McDonald's, display, Cabbage Patch/Tonka, 1994, NM, C11 ....$40.00

McDonald's, display, Garfield & Odie, 1988, M, W2.......$35.00

McDonald's, display, Hercules, 1997, NM, C11 ....$45.00

McDonald's, display, Jungle Book, w/plastic dome, M, C11 ....$85.00

McDonald's, display, Littlest Pet Shop/Transformer, NM, C11 ....$30.00

McDonald's, display, Mickey's Birthdayland, 1988, plastic dome, NM, C11...$250.00

McDonald's, display, Oliver & Co, 1988, EX, from $50 to.$70.00

McDonald's, display, Sleeping Beauty, 1997, NM, C11 ...$40.00

McDonald's, display, Spider-Man, M, V1 ....$45.00

McDonald's, display, Tiny Toon Flip Car, plastic dome, NM, C11 ....$125.00

McDonald's, display, 101 Dalmatians, 1992, w/plastic dome, M, C11 ....$100.00

McDonald's, doll, Big Mac, Remco, 1976, plastic w/cloth clothes, knob in back for head movement, EX, from $25 to..$35.00

McDonald's, doll, Fry Girl, 1987, stuffed cloth, 4", M, from $8 to..$10.00

McDonald's, doll, Grimace, Remco, 1976, plush fleece w/vinyl feet, knob in back for head movement, EX, from $25 to.........$35.00

McDonald's, doll, Hamburglar, 1980s, cloth and vinyl, 11", NM, $25.00.

McDonald's, doll, Mayor, 1970s, stuffed cloth, 15", from $40 to..$50.00

McDonald's, doll, McDonald's Girl, 1970s, stuffed cloth, NM, minimum value...$30.00

McDonald's, doll, Ronald McDonald, 1971, stuffed cloth, 17", EX...$20.00

McDonald's, frisbee, Ronald McDonald Flyer, EX, V1 ....$8.00

McDonald's, game, tic-tac-toe, figural, EX, V1.................$12.00

McDonald's, hand puppets, Grimace, Ronald, or Hamburglar, cloth w/vinyl heads, MIB, ea $15.00

McDonald's, kite, Movin' On-Movin' Up, M, C11 ....$8.00

McDonald's, McDonaldland Picnic Game, 1981, only 500 produced, M, C11 ....$100.00

McDonald's, music box, 1990, plays Silent Night & Jingle Bells, 2½x2½", MIB, from $25 to $30.00

McDonald's, record, Night Before Christmas, 33⅓ rpm, EX (EX cover), C11 ....$5.00

McDonald's, ring, Ronald McDonald, EX, C10................$15.00

McDonald's, ring toss game, 1978, M, C11 ....$8.00

McDonald's, slippers, Ronald McDonald, NM, from $30.00 to $40.00.

McDonald's, stop watch, plastic, EX....................................$2.00
McDonald's, sweater, 1976, embroidered image of Ronald
    McDonald, rare, NM, P12..$125.00
McDonald's, translite, Back to the Future, 14x14", M,
    C11..$10.00
McDonald's, translite, Bambi, 22x22", M, C11 ....$25.00
McDonald's, translite, Blast Back (Mac Tonight), 14x14", M,
    C11..$12.00
McDonald's, translite, Chip & Dale, 22x22", M, C11......$15.00
McDonald's, translite, Disney Masterpiece, 1996, M,
    C11 ....$12.00
McDonald's, translite, Fraggle Rock, 22x22", M, C11......$12.00
McDonald's, translite, Mac Tonight, M, C11 ....$15.00
McDonald's, translite, Rescuers Down Under, 22x22", M,
    C11 ....$12.00
McDonald's, translite, Super Mario Bros 3, 14x14", M,
    C11 ....$10.00
McDonald's, translite, Super Summer w/Water Can, 22x22", M,
    C11..$25.00
McDonald's, translite, Tiny Toons Wacky Rollers, 14x14", M,
    C11..$10.00
McDonald's, video, Charlottes Web, MIP, C11, from $6
    to...$8.00
McDonald's, video, Wayne's World, MIP, C11, from $6
    to...$8.00
Pizza Hut, kite, Garfield, MIP, B5 ....$15.00
Wendy's, puzzle, Where's the Beef, 1984, 551 pcs, EX,
    S13...$20.00

Fisher-Price

Fisher-Price toys are becoming one of the hottest new trends in the collectors' marketplace today. In 1930 Herman Fisher, backed by Irving Price, Elbert Hubbard, and Helen Schelle, formed one of the most successful toy companies ever to exist. Located in East Aurora, New York, the company has seen many changes since then, the most notable being the changes in ownership. From 1930 to 1968, it was owned by the individuals mentioned previously and a few stockholders. In 1969 it became an aquisition of Quaker Oats, and in June of 1991 it became independently owned. In November of 1993, one of the biggest sell-outs in the toy industry took place: Fisher-Price became a subdivision of Mattel.

There are a few things to keep in mind when collecting Fisher-Price toys. You should count on a little edge wear as well as some wear and fading to the paint. Unless noted otherwise, the prices in the listings are for toys in very good condition. Pull toys found in mint condition are truly rare and command a much higher value, especially if you find one with its original box. This also applies to playsets, but to command the higher prices, they must also be complete, with no chew/teeth marks or plastic fading, and with all pieces present. Another very important rule to remember is there are no standard colors for pieces that came with a playset. Fisher-Price often substituted a piece of a different color when they ran short. Please note that dates on the toys indicate their **copyright date and not the date they were manufactured**.

The company put much time and thought into designing their toys. They took care to operate by their five-point creed: to make toys with (1) intrinsic play value (2) ingenuity (3) strong construction (4) good value for the money and (5) action. Some of the most sought-after pull toys are those bearing the Walt Disney logo.

The ToyFest limited editions are a series of toys produced in conjunction with ToyFest, an annual weekend of festivities for young and old alike held in East Aurora, New York. It is sponsored by the 'Toy Town USA Museum' and is held every year in August. Fisher-Price produces a limited-edition toy for this event; these are listed at the end of this category. (For more information on ToyFest and the museum, write to Toy Town Museum, P.O. Box 238, East Aurora, NY 14052; see display ad this section.) For more information on Fisher-Price toys we recommend *Fisher-Price, A Historical Rarity Value Guide*, by John J. Murray and Bruce R. Fox; and *Fisher-Price Toys* by our advisor Brad Cassity.

Additional information may be obtained through the Fisher-Price Collectors' Club who publish a quarterly newsletter; their address may be found in their display ad (this section) and in the Directory under Clubs, Newsletters, and Other Publications.

Note: Collectors should be aware that since our last edition, values for Fisher-Price toys have decreased 15% on the overall average. Prices listed below are for examples that show only a little edge and paint wear and minimal fading (VG).

Advisor: Brad Cassity (C13).
Other Sources: J2, J6, N2, S20.
See also Dollhouse Furniture; Dollhouses; Dolls.

#5 Bunny Cart, 1948, C13..$75.00
#6 Ducky Cart, 1948, C13..$75.00
#7 Looky Fire Truck, 1950-53 & Easter 1954, C13 ....$100.00
#8 Bouncy Racer, 1960-71, C13......................................$40.00

#7 Doggy Racer, 1942, $200.00.
(Photo courtesy Brad Cassity)

#10 Bunny Cart, 1940, C13..$75.00
#11 Ducky Cart, 1940-42, C13...$75.00
#12 Bunny Truck, 1941, C13...$75.00
#14 Ducky Daddles, 1941, C13 ....$85.00
#15 Bunny Cart, 1946, C13...$75.00
#16 Ducky Cart, 1946, C13...$75.00
#20 Animal Cutouts, 1942, duck, elephant, pony or Scotty dog, C13, ea $50.00
#28 Bunny Egg Cart, 1950, C13 ....$75.00
#50 Bunny Chick Tandem Cart, 1953, no number on toy, C13 .$100.00
#51 Ducky Cart, 1950, C13...$75.00
#52 Rabbit Cart, 1950, C13..$75.00
#75 Baby Duck Tandem Cart, 1953, no number on toy, C13..$100.00
#100 Dr Doodle, 1931, C13..$800.00
#100 Dr Doodle, 1995, 1st Fisher-Price limited edition of 5,000, C13 ....$125.00
#100 Musical Sweeper, 1950, plays Whistle While You Work, C13 ....$200.00
#101 Granny Doodle & Family, 1931, C13 ....$800.00
#102 Drumming Bear, 1931, C13....................................$700.00
#102 Drumming Bear, 1932, fatter & taller version, C13 ...$700.00

#103 Barky Puppy, 1931, C13 ....$700.00
#104 Looky Monk, 1931, C13 ....$700.00
#105 Bunny Scoot, 1931, C13..$700.00
#107 Music Box Clock Radio, 1971, plays Hickory Dickory Dock $2.00
#109 Lucky Monk, 1932, C13...$700.00
#110 Chubby Chief, 1932, C13.......................................$700.00
#110 Puppy Playhouse, 1978-80, C13 ....$10.00
#111 Play Family Merry-Go-Round, 1972-77, plays Skater's Waltz, w/4 figures, C13 ....$30.00
#112 Picture Disk Camera, 1968-71, w/5 picture disks, C13 ....$35.00
#114 Sesame Street Music Box TV, 1984-87, plays People in Your Neighborhood, C13 ....$8.00
#117, Play Family Farm Barnyard, 1972-74, C13..............$25.00
#118 Tumble Tower Game, 1972-75, w/10 marbles, C13....$10.00
#120 Cackling Hen, 1958-66, wht, C13.............................$40.00
#120 Gabby Goose, 1936-37 & Easter 1938, C13 ....$350.00
#121 Happy Hopper, 1969-76, C13.................................$15.00
#122 Bouncing Buggy, 1974-79, 6 wheels, C13 ....$5.00
#123 Cackling Hen, 1966-68, red litho, C13....................$40.00
#123 Roller Chime, 1953-60 & Easter 1961, C13 ....$50.00
#124 Roller Chime, 1961-62 & Easter 1963, C13 ....$35.00
#125 Music Box Iron, 1966-69, C13 ....$50.00
#125 Uncle Timmy Turtle, 1956, red shell, C13............$100.00

#130 Wobbles, 1964 – 67, wobbles when pulled, $40.00.
(Photo courtesy Brad Cassity)

#131 Milk Wagon, 1964-72, truck w/bottle carrier, C13 ....$50.00
#131 Toy Wagon, 1951, driver's head pops up & down when pulled by 2 musical horses, C13 ....$225.00
#132 Dr Doodle, 1957, C13..$85.00
#132 Molly Moo Cow, 1972-78, C13 ....$25.00
#135 Play Family Animal Circus, 1974-76, complete, C13....$60.00
#136 Play Family Lacing Shoe, 1965-69, complete, C13....$60.00
#138 Jack-in-the-Box Puppet, 1970-73, C13 ....$30.00
#139 Tuggy Tooter, 1967-73, C13 ....$40.00
#139 Tuggy Turtle, 1959, C13 ....$100.00
#140 Coaster Boy, 1941, C13...$700.00
#140 Katy Kackler, 1954-56 & Easter 1957, C13 ....$85.00

#114 Music Box TV, 1967 – 83, plays London Bridge and Row Row Row Your Boat, $5.00. (Photo courtesy Brad Cassity)

#141 Snap-Quack, 1947-79, C13 ....$225.00

#142 Three Men in a Tub, 1970-73, 1st version, bell atop spring mast, C13 ....$20.00

#142 Three Men in a Tub, 1974-75, 2nd version, C13 ....$10.00

#145 Humpty Dumpty Truck, 1963-64 & Easter 1965, C13 ...$40.00

#145 Husky Dump Truck, 1961-62 & Easter 1963, C13.....$45.00

#145 Musical Elephant, 1948-50, C13 ....$225.00

#146 Play Pull-A-Long Lacing Shoe, 1970-75, w/6 figures, C13 ....$50.00

#148 Ducky Daddles, 1942, C13 ....$225.00

#148 Jack & Jill TV Radio, wood & plastic, C13 ....$75.00

#149 Dog Cart Donald, 1936, C13.................................$700.00

#150 Barky Budd, 1934, C13 ....$600.00

#150 Pop-Up-Pal Chime Phone, 1968-78, C13.................$40.00

#150 Teddy Tooter, 1940, C13 ....$400.00

#150 Timmy Turtle, 1953-55 & Easter 1956, gr shell, C13 ....$100.00

#151 Happy Hippo, 1962-63, C13.................................$85.00

#152 Road Roller, 1934, C13 ....$700.00

#154 Frisky Frog, 1971-83, squeeze plastic bulb & frog jumps, C13..............$25.00

#154 TV-Radio, 1964-67, Pop Goes the Weasel, wood & plastic, C13..............$25.00

#155 Jack & Jill TV Radio, 1968-70, wood & plastic, C13...$40.00

#155 Moo-oo Cow, 1958-61 & Easter 1962, C13 ....$85.00

#155 Skipper Sam, 1934, C13 ....$850.00

#156 Baa-Baa Black Sheep TV-Radio, 1966-67, wood & plastic, C13...............$50.00

#156 Circus Wagon, 1942, band leader in wagon, C13 ....$400.00

#156 Jiffy Dump Truck, 1971-73, squeeze bulb & dump moves, C13...............$25.00

#158 Katie Kangaroo, 1976-77, squeeze bulb & she hops, C13...............$25.00

#158 Little Boy Blue TV-Radio, 1967, wood & plastic, C13 .$50.00

#159 Ten Little Indians TV-Radio, 1961-65 & Easter 1966, wood & plastic, C13 ....$20.00

#160 Donald & Donna Duck, 1937, C13 ....$700.00

#161 Creative Block Wagon, 1961-64, 18 building blocks & 6 wooden dowels fit into pull-along wagon, C13 ....$75.00

#161 Looky Chug-Chug, 1949, C13 ....$250.00

#161 Old Woman Who Lived in a Shoe TV-Radio, 1968-70, wood & plastic w/see-through window on back, C13 ..$30.00

#162 Roly Poly Boats Chime Ball, 1967-69, C13 ....$10.00

#164 Chubby Cub, 1969-72, C13.................................$20.00

#164 Mother Goose, 1964-66, C13.................................$35.00

#165 Roly Poly Chime Ball, 1967-85, C13 ....$5.00

#166 Bucky Burro, 1955, C13 ....$250.00

#166 Farmer in the Dell TV-Radio, 1963-66, C13 ....$35.00

#166 Piggy Bank, 1981-82, pk plastic, C13 ....$15.00

#168 Magnetic Chug-Chug, 1964-69, C13 ....$50.00

#168 Snorky Fire Engine, 1960, gr litho, 4 wooden fireman & dog, C13...............$175.00

#169 Snorky Fire Engine, 1961, red litho, 4 wooden firemen, C13 ....$175.00

#170 American Airlines Flagship, 1941-42, C13............$700.00

#170 Change-A-Tune Carousel, 1981-83, music box w/crank hdl, 3 molded records & 3 figures, C13 ....$30.00

#171 Pull-Along Plane, 1981 – 88, $5.00.
(Photo courtesy Brad Cassity)

#171 Toy Wagon, 1942, ponies move up & down, bells rings, C13 ....$300.00

#172 Roly Raccoon, 1980-82, waddles side to side, tail bobs & weaves, C13 ....$10.00

#175 Gold Star Stagecoach, 1954, w/2 litho wood mail pouches, C13 ....$275.00

#175 Kicking Donkey, 1937, C13 ....$450.00

#175 Winnie the Pooh TV-Radio, 1971-73, Sears distribution only, C13 ....$65.00

#177 Donald Duck Xylophone, 1946, 2nd version w/'Donald Duck' on hat, C13 ....$300.00

#177 Oscar the Grouch, 1977-84, C13 ....$20.00

#178 What's in My Pocket, 1972-74, 10-pg cloth book w/8 pockets & 8 plastic replicas of boy's pocket items, C13 ....$20.00

#180 Snoopy Sniffer, 1938-55, C13 ....$75.00

#183 Play Family Fun Jet, 1970, 1st version, C13.............$25.00

#189 Pull-A-Tune Blue Bird Music Box, 1969-79, plays Children's Prayer, C13 ....$8.00

#190 Gabby Duck, 1939, C13 ....$350.00

#190 Molly Moo-Moo, 1956, C13.......................$225.00

#190 Pull-A-Tune Pony Music Box, 1969-72, plays Shubert's Cradle Song, C13 ....$10.00

#192 Playland Express, 1962, C13.....................$100.00

#192 School Bus, 1965-78, C13 ....$40.00

#194 Push Pullet, 1971-72, C13 ....$20.00

#195 Teddy Bear Parade, 1938, C13 ....$600.00

#198 Band Wagon, 1940-41, C13 ....$350.00

#201 Woodsy-Wee Circus, 1931, complete, C13 ....$700.00

#205 Walt Disney's Parade, WDE, 1936-41, C13, ea $250.00

#205 Woodsy-Wee Zoo, 1931, C13 ....$700.00

#207 Walt Disney's Carnival, 1936-38, Mickey, Donald, Pluto or Elmer, complete, C13, ea......................$225.00

#207 Woodsy-Wee Pets, 1931, complete w/goat, donkey, cow, pig & cart, C13 ....$700.00

#208 Donald Duck, 1936-38, C13................$400.00

#209 Woodsy-Wee Dog Show, 1932, complete w/5 dogs, C13 ....$700.00

#210 Pluto the Pup, 1936-38, C13 ....$400.00

#211 Elmer Elephant, 1936-38, C13 ....$400.00

#215 Fisher-Price Choo-Choo, 1955, engine w/4 cars, C13 ...$85.00

#225 Wheel Horse, 1935-36, C13 ....$600.00

#234 Nifty Station Wagon, 1960, removable roof, 4 wooden figures & dog, C13...$250.00

#237 Riding Horse, 1936, C13 ....$600.00

#242 Billie Doll, 1979-80, C13.........................$20.00

#250 Big Performing Circus, 1932, complete w/figures, animals & accessories, C13...$950.00

#300 Scoop Loader, 1975-77, C13 ....$25.00

#301 Bunny Basket Cart, 1957, C13 ....$40.00

#301 Shovel Digger, 1975-77, C13 ....$25.00

#302 Chick Basket Cart, 1957, C13 ....$40.00

#191 Golden Gulch Express, 1961, $100.00.
(Photo courtesy Linda Baker)

#183 Play Family Fun Jet, 1971-80, 2nd version, red plastic wings w/bl engines, 4 wooden figures, no hole for gas, C13...$15.00

#185 Donald Duck Xylophone, 1938, mk WDE, C13....$800.00

#189 Looky Chug-Chug, C13..............................$85.00

#305 Walking Duck Cart, 1957 – 64, $40.00.
(Photo courtesy Linda Baker)

#302 Husky Dump Truck, 1978-84, C13 ....$20.00

#303 Adventure People Emergency Rescue Truck, 1975-78, complete, C13 ....$15.00

#303 Bunny Push Cart, 1957, C13 ....$75.00

#304 Adventure People Safari Set, 1975-78, complete, C13 ....$40.00

#304 Chick Basket Cart, 1960-64, C13 ....$40.00

#304 Running Bunny Cart, 1957, C13 ....$75.00

#305 Adventure People Air-Sea Rescue Copter, 1975-80, C13 ....$15.00

#306 Adventure People Sport Plane, 1975-80, orange & wht plane w/gold pilot, C13 ....$8.00

#306 Bizzy Bunny Cart, 1957-59, C13 ....$40.00

#307 Adventure People Wilderness Patrol, 1975-79, C13 ....$20.00

#307 Bouncing Bunny Cart, 1961-63 & Easter 1964, C13 ....$40.00

#309 Adventure People TV Action Team, 1977-78, C13 ....$50.00

#310 Adventure People Sea Explorer, 1975-80, C13 ....$20.00

#310 Mickey Mouse Puddle Jumper, 1953-55 & Easter 1956, C13 ....$125.00

#311 Bulldozer, 1976-77, C13 ....$25.00

#312 Adventure People North Woods Trailblazer, 1977-82, C13 ....$25.00

#312 Running Bunny Cart, 1960-64, C13 ....$45.00

#313 Roller Grader, 1977, C13 ....$35.00

#314 Husky Boom Crane, 1978-82, C13 ....$25.00

#314 Queen Buzzy Bee, 1956-58, C13 ....$40.00

#315 Husky Cement Mixer, 1978-82, C13 ....$30.00

#316 Husky Tow Truck, 1978-80, C13 ....$15.00

#318 Adventure People Daredevil Sports Van, 1978-82, complete, C13 ....$25.00

#319 Husky Hook & Ladder Truck, 1979-85, C13 ....$25.00

#320 Husky Race Car Rig, 1979-82, C13 ....$30.00

#322 Adventure People Dune Buster, 1979-82, complete, C13 ....$15.00

#325 Adventure People Alpha Probe, 1980-84, complete, C13 ....$20.00

#325 Buzzy Bee, 1950, 1st version, dk yel & blk litho, wooden wheels & antenna tips, C13 ....$40.00

#327 Husky Load Master Dump, 1984, C13 ....$35.00

#328 Husky Highway Dump Truck, 1980-84, C13 ....$25.00

#329 Husky Dozer Loader, 1980-84, C13 ....$15.00

#331 Husky Farm Set, 1981-83, C13 ....$25.00

#333 Butch the Pup, 1951, C13 ....$75.00

#334 Adventure People Sea Shark, 1981-84, C13 ....$20.00

#337 Husky Rescue Rig, 1982-83, C13 ....$30.00

#338 Husky Power Tow Truck, 1982-84, C13 ....$25.00

#339 Husky Power & Light Service Rig, 1983-84, C13 ....$30.00

#344 Copter Rig, 1981-84, C13 ....$15.00

#345 Boat Rig, 1981-84, C13 ....$15.00

#345 Penelope the Performing Penguin, 1935, w/up, C13 ...$800.00

#350 Adventure People Rescue Team, 1976-79, C13 ......$20.00

#350 Go 'N Back Mule, 1931, w/up, C13 ....$800.00

#351 Adventure People Mountain Climbers, 1976-79, C13 ....$20.00

#352 Adventure People Construction Workers, 1976-79, C13 ....$15.00

#353 Adventure People Scuba Divers, 1976-81, C13 ....$10.00

#355 Adventure People White Water Kayak, 1977-80, C13 ....$15.00

#355 Go 'N Back Bruno, 1931, C13 ....$800.00

#356 Adventure People Cycle Racing Team, 1977-81, C13 ....$10.00

#358 Adventure People Deep Sea Diver, 1980-84, C13...$10.00

#358 Donald Duck Back-Up, 1936, w/up, C13 ....$800.00

#360 Go 'N Back Jumbo, 1931, w/up, C13 ....$800.00

#365 Puppy Back-up, 1932, w/up, C13 ....$800.00

#367 Adventure People Turbo Hawk, 1982-83, C13 ....$15.00

#368 Adventure People Alpha Interceptor, 1982-83, C13 ...$15.00

#375 Adventure People Sky Surfer, 1978, C13..........................$25.00

#375 Bruno Back-Up, 1932, C13 ....$800.00

#377 Adventure People Astro Knight, 1979-80, C13.......$15.00

#400 Donald Duck Drum Major, 1946, C13 ....$275.00

#400 Tailspin Tabby, 1931-38, rnd guitar, C13 ....$85.00

#401 Push Bunny Cart, 1942, C13 ....$225.00

#402 Duck Cart, 1943, C13 ....$200.00

#404 Bunny Egg Cart, 1949, C13 ....$80.00

#405 Lofty Lizzy Pop-Up Kritter, 1931, C13 ....$225.00

#406 Bunny Cart, 1950-53, C13 ....$50.00

#407 Chick Cart, 1950, C13 ....$50.00

#407 Dizzy Dino Pop-Up Kritter, 1931, C13 ....$225.00

#410 Stoopy Stork Pop-Up Kritter, 1931, C13 ....$225.00

#415 Lop-Ear Looie Pop-Up Kritter, 1934, C13 ....$225.00

#415 Super Jet, 1952, C13..........................$225.00

#420 Sunny Fish, 1955, C13 ....$225.00

#422 Jumbo Jitterbug Pop-Up Kritter, 1940, C13..........$225.00

#423 Jumping Jack Scarecrow, 1979, C13..........................$15.00

#425 Donald Duck Pop-Up, 1938, C13 ....$400.00

#432 Mickey Mouse Choo-Choo, mk WDE, 1938, C13 ...$600.00

#433 Dizzy Donkey Pop-Up Kritter, 1939, C13 ....$125.00

#434 Ferdinand the Bull, 1939, C13 ....$600.00

#435 Happy Apple, 1979, short stem, C13..........................$3.00

#440 Goofy Gertie Pop-Up Kritter, 1935, C13..........................$225.00

#440 Pluto Pop-Up, 1936, mk WDP, C13 ....$100.00

#444 Fuzzy Fido, 1941-42, C13..........................$225.00

#444 Puffy Engine, 1951-54, C13 ....$85.00

#444 Queen Buzzy Bee, 1959, red litho, C13 ....$40.00

#445 Hot Dog Wagon, 1940, C13 ....$250.00

#448 Mini Copter, 1971 – 84, blue lithograph, $10.00.
(Photo courtesy Brad Cassity)

#445 Nosey Pup, 1956, C13...................................$75.00
#447 Woofy Wagger, 1947-48, C13 ....$85.00
#450 Donald Duck Choo-Choo, 1941, 8½", C13...........$375.00
#450 Donald Duck Choo-Choo, 1942, bl hat, C13........$200.00
#450 Kiltie Dog, 1936, C13.................................$400.00
#450 Music Box Bear, 1981-83, plays Schubert's Cradle Song, C13...$15.00
#454 Donald Duck Drummer, 1949, C13 ....$300.00
#455 Tailspin Tabby Pop-Up Kritter, 1939-42, C13 ....$75.00
#456 Bunny & Container, 1939-40, C13......................$225.00
#460 Dapper Donald Duck, 1936, no number on toy, 1936, C13 ....$600.00
#460 Movie Viewer, 1973-85, crank hdl, C13 ....$5.00
#460 Suzie Seal, 1961-63 & Easter 1964, C13.................$40.00
#461 Duck Cart, 1938-39, C13...............................$225.00
#462 Busy Bunny, 1937, C13.................................$200.00
#465 Teddy Choo-Choo, 1937, C13.......................$400.00
#466 Busy Bunny Cart, 1941-44, C13.......................$75.00
#469 Donald's Cart, 1940, C13...............................$400.00
#469 Rooster Cart, 1938-40, C13 ....$400.00
#470 Tricky Tommy, 1936, C13 ....$350.00
#472 Jingle Giraffe, 1956, C13...............................$225.00
#472 Peter Bunny Cart, 1939-40, C13....................$225.00
#473 Merry Mutt, 1949-54 & Easter 1955, C13 ....$75.00
#474 Bunny Racer, 1942, C13................................$225.00
#476 Cookie Pig, 1966-70, C13...............................$50.00
#476 Mickey Mouse Drummer, 1941, C13 ....$300.00
#476 Rooster Pop-Up Kritter, 1936, C13.................$350.00
#477 Dr Doodle, 1940, C13...................................$225.00
#478 Pudgy Pig, 1962, C13....................................$50.00
#479 Donald Duck & Nephews, 1941-42, C13 ....$400.00
#479 Peter Pig, 1959-61 & Easter 1962, C13...................$45.00
#480 Leo the Drummer, 1952, C13.........................$225.00
#480 Teddy Station Wagon, 1942, C13....................$225.00
#485 Mickey Mouse Choo-Choo, 1949, new litho version of #432, C13 ....$100.00
#488 Popeye Spinach Eater, 1939, C13..................$600.00
#494 Pinocchio, 1939, C13....................................$600.00
#495 Running Bunny Cart, 1941, C13 ....$225.00
#495 Sleepy Sue Turtle, 1962-64, C13.......................$45.00
#499 Kitty Bell, 1950, C13....................................$125.00
#500 Donald Duck Cart, 1937, no number on toy, 3 colors, C13 ....$700.00
#500 Donald Duck Cart, 1951, no baton, gr litho background, C13 ....$350.00
#500 Donald Duck Cart, 1953, w/baton, new litho w/yel background, C13 ....$350.00
#500 Pick-Up & Peek Puzzle, 1972-86, C13 ....$10.00
#500 Pushy Pig, 1932-35, C13................................$500.00
#502 Action Bunny Cart, 1949, C13.......................$200.00
#505 Bunny Drummer, 1946, C13..........................$225.00
#507 Pushy Poodle, 1933, C13...............................$550.00
#508 Bunny Bell Drummer, 1949-53, C13..................$85.00
#510 Strutter Donald Duck, 1941, C13 ....$300.00
#512 Bunny Drummer, 1942, C13 ....$225.00
#515 Pushy Pat, 1933-35, C13 ....$550.00
#517 Choo-Choo Local, 1936, C13.........................$550.00
#520 Bunny Bell Cart, 1941, C13 ....$225.00

#525 Cotton Tail Cart, 1940, C13...........................$350.00
#525 Pushy Elephant, 1934-35, C13 ....$550.00
#530 Mickey Mouse Band, 1935, C13 ....$900.00
#533 Thumper Bunny, 1942, C13 ....$500.00
#540 Granny Duck, 1939-40, C13 ....$225.00
#544 Donald Duck Cart, 1942, C13.........................$300.00
#549 Toy Lunch Kit, 1962-79, red w/barn litho, w/thermos, C13 ....$25.00
#550 Toy Lunch Kit, 1957, red, wht & gr plastic barn shape, no litho, C13 ....$40.00
#551 Fruit & Shapes Puzzle, 1974-75, C13 ....$15.00
#555 Rabbit & Bunnies Puzzle, 1974-75, C13 ....$15.00
#558 Jack & Jill Puzzle, 1974-75, C13......................$15.00
#600 Tailspin Tabby Pop-Up, 1947, C13 ....$250.00
#604 Bunny Bell Cart, 1954, C13 ....$100.00
#605 Donald Duck Cart, 1954, C13.........................$300.00
#605 Woodsey Major Goodgrub Mole & Book, 1981, 32 pgs, C13...$15.00
#606 Woodsey Bramble Beaver & Book, 1981, 32 pgs, C13....$15.00
#607 Woodsey Blue Bird & Book, 1981, 32 pgs, C13.......$15.00
#615 Tow Truck, 1960, C13....................................$75.00
#616 Chuggy Pop-Up, 1955, C13............................$100.00
#616 Patch Pony, 1963, C13...................................$50.00

#617 Prancy Pony, 1965 – 70, $30.00.
(Photo courtesy Brad Cassity)

#621 Suzie Seal, 1965-66, ball on nose, C13....................$40.00
#623 Suzie Seal, 1964-65, umbrella on nose, C13 ....$55.00
#625 Playful Puppy, 1961, w/shoe, C13............................$50.00
#626 Playful Puppy, 1963, w/shoe, C13............................$50.00
#628 Tug-A-Bug, 1975-77, C13 ....$5.00
#629 Fisher-Price Tractor, 1962-68, C13 ....$30.00
#630 Fire Truck, 1959, C13....................................$50.00
#634 Drummer Boy, 1967-69, C13...........................$50.00
#634 Tiny Teddy, 1955-57, C13 ....$75.00
#637 Milk Carrier, 1966-85, C13...............................$15.00
#640 Wiggily Woofer, 1957-58, C13..........................$85.00

#641 Toot Toot Engine, 1962-63 & Easter 1964, bl litho, C13	$60.00
#642 Bob-Along Bear, 1979-84, C13	$10.00
#642 Dinky Engine, 1959, blk litho, C13	$60.00
#642 Smokie Engine, 1960-61 & Easter 1962, blk litho, C13	$60.00
#643 Toot-Toot Engine, 1964-87, 4th version, C13	$5.00
#649 Stake Truck, 1960, C13	$50.00
#653 Allie Gator, 1960, C13	$100.00
#654 Tawny Tiger, 1962, C13	$125.00
#656 Bossy Bell, 1960, w/bonnet, C13	$60.00
#656 Bossy Bell, 1961, no bonnet, new litho design, C13	$50.00
#657 Crazy Clown Fire Brigade, 1983-84, MIB, C13	$45.00
#658 Lady Bug, 1961-62, C13	$55.00
#659 Puzzle Puppy, 1976-81, C13	$15.00
#662 Merry Mousewife, 1962, C13	$50.00
#674 Sports Car, 1958-60, C13	$85.00
#677 Picnic Basket, 1975-79, C13	$20.00
#678 Kriss Kricket, 1955, C13	$100.00
#684 Little Lamb, 1964-65, C13	$50.00
#685 Car & Boat, 1968-69, wood & plastic, 5 pcs, C13	$65.00
#686 Car & Camper, 1968-70, wood & plastic, 5 pcs, C13	$50.00
#686 Perky Pot, 1958, C13	$75.00
#694 Suzie Seal, 1979-80, C13	$15.00
#695 Lady Bug, 1982-84, C13	$5.00
#695 Pinky Pig, 1956, wooden eyes, C13	$100.00
#695 Pinky Pig, 1958, litho eyes, C13	$100.00
#698 Talky Parrot, 1963, C13	$100.00
#700 Cowboy Chime, 1951, C13	$250.00
#700 Popeye, 1935, C13	$700.00
#700 Woofy Wowser, 1940, C13	$400.00
#703 Bunny Engine, 1954, C13	$100.00
#703 Popeye the Sailor, 1936, C13	$700.00
#705 Mini Snowmobile, 1971-73, C13	$50.00
#705 Popeye Cowboy, 1937, C13	$700.00
#710 Scotty Dog, 1933, C13	$550.00
#711 Cry Baby Bear, 1967-69, C13	$30.00
#711 Huckleberry Hound, 1961, Sears only, C13	$300.00
#711 Raggedy Ann & Andy, 1941, C13	$850.00
#711 Teddy Trucker, 1949-51, C13	$225.00
#712 Fred Flintstone Xylophone, 1962, Sears only, C13	$250.00
#712 Johnny Jumbo, 1933-35, C13	$550.00
#712 Teddy Tooter, 1957, C13	$250.00
#714 Mickey Mouse Xylophone, 1963, Sears only, C13	$275.00
#715 Ducky Flip Flap, 1964-65, C13	$65.00
#717 Ducky Flip Flap, 1937-40, C13	$400.00
#718 Tow Truck & Car, 1969-70, wood & plastic, C13	$30.00
#719 Busy Bunny Cart, 1936-37, C13	$350.00
#719 Cuddly Cub, 1973-77, C13	$5.00
#720 Fire Engine, 1969, C13	$20.00
#720 Pinnochio Express, 1939, C13	$500.00
#721 Peter Bunny Engine, 1949, C13	$200.00
#722 Racing Bunny Cart, 1937, C13	$350.00
#722 Running Bunny, 1938-40, C13	$225.00

#723 Bouncing Bunny Cart, 1936, C13 ....$350.00
#724 Ding Dong Ducky, 1949-50, C13 ....$225.00
#724 Jolly Jalopy, 1965-78, C13 ....$15.00
#725 Musical Mutt, 1935-36, C13 ....$350.00
#725 Play Family Bath/Utility Room Set, 1972, C13 ....$30.00
#726 Play Family Patio Set, 1970-73, C13 ....$30.00
#727 Bouncing Bunny Wheelbarrow, 1939, C13 ....$350.00
#728 Buddy Bullfrog, 1959, yel body w/red litho coat, C13......$75.00
#728 Buddy Bullfrog, 1961, gr coat w/red & wht pants, C13 ...$75.00
#730 Racing Rowboat, 1952, C13 ....$250.00
#732 Happy Hauler, 1968-70, C13 ....$35.00
#733 Mickey Mouse Safety Patrol, 1956, C13 ....$250.00
#734 Teddy Zilo, 1964-66, C13 ....$45.00
#735 Juggling Jumbo, 1958, C13 ....$250.00
#736 Humpty Dumpty, 1972-79, plastic, C13 ....$4.00
#737 Galloping Horse & Wagon, 1948, C13 ....$250.00
#737 Ziggy Zilo, 1958-59, C13 ....$75.00
#738 Dumbo Circus Racer, 1941, rubber arms, C13 ....$700.00
#738 Shaggy Zilo, 1960, C13 ....$75.00
#739 Poodle Zilo, 1962, C13 ....$75.00
#740 Pushcart Pete, 1936-67, C13 ....$85.00

#741 Teddy Zilo, 1967, $45.00.
(Photo courtesy Brad Cassity)

#741 Trotting Donald Duck, 1937, C13 ....$800.00
#742 Dashing Dobbin, 1938-40, C13 ....$350.00
#744 Doughboy Donald, 1942, C13 ....$600.00
#745 Elsie's Dairy Truck, 1948, w/2 bottles, C13 ....$700.00
#746 Pocket Radio, 1977-78, It's a Small World, wood & plastic, C13..$25.00
#747 Chatter Telephone, 1962-87, C13 ....$40.00
#747 Talk Back Telephone, 1961-62, C13 ....$75.00
#749 Egg Truck, 1947, C13 ....$225.00
#750 Hot Dog Wagon, 1938, C13 ....$400.00
#750 Space Blazer, 1953, C13 ....$400.00
#752 Teddy Zilo, 1948, 1st version, clown outfit w/red cheeks, C13...$350.00
#752 Teddy Zilo, 1948, 2nd version, no outfit, C13.......$325.00
#755 Jumbo Rolo, 1951-52, C13 ....$225.00
#756 Pocket Radio, 1973, 12 Days of Christmas, wood & plastic, C13..$25.00

#757 Howdy Bunny, 1939-40, C13 ....$350.00
#757 Humpty Dumpty, 1957, C13 ....$200.00
#757 Snappy-Quacky, 1950, C13 ....$225.00
#758 Pocket Radio, 1970-72, Mulberry Bush, wood & plastic, C13..$20.00
#758 Pony Chime, 1948-50, C13 ....$200.00
#758 Push-Along Clown, 1980-81, C13 ....$20.00
#759 Pocket Radio, 1969-73, Do-Re-Me, wood & plastic, C13..$20.00
#760 Peek-A-Boo Block, 1970-79, C13 ....$15.00
#760 Racing Ponies, 1936, C13 ....$350.00
#761 Play Family Nursery Set, 1973, C13 ....$30.00
#762 Pocket Radio, 1972-77, Raindrops, wood & plastic, C13..$15.00
#763 Music Box, 1962, Farmer in the Dell, yel litho, C13 .$50.00
#763 Pocket Radio, 1978, Whistle a Happy Tune, wood & plastic, C13..$20.00
#764 Music Box, 1960-61 & Easter 1962, Farmer in the Dell, red litho, C13..$50.00
#764 Pocket Radio, 1975-76, My Name Is Michael, C13....$15.00
#765 Dandy Dobbin, 1941-44, C13 ....$200.00
#765 Pocket Radio, 1976, Humpty Dumpty, wood & plastic, C13..$25.00
#765 Talking Donald Duck, 1955, C13 ....$125.00
#766 Pocket Radio, 1968-70, Where Has My Little Dog Gone?, wood & plastic, C13......................................$25.00
#766 Pocket Radio, 1977-78, I'd Like to Teach the World to Sing, C13..$20.00
#767 Pocket Radio, 1977, Twinkle Twinkle Little Star, C13..$20.00
#767 Tiny Ding-Dong, 1940, C13..................................$400.00
#768 Pocket Radio, 1971-76, Happy Birthday, wood & plastic, C13..$15.00
#770 Doc & Dopey Dwarfs, 1938, C13 ....$1,000.00
#772 Pocket Radio, 1974-76, Jack & Jill, C13 ....$15.00
#773 Tip-Toe Turtle, 1962, vinyl tail, C13 ....$15.00
#774 Pocket Radio, 1967-71, Twinkle Twinkle Little Star, wood & plastic, C13......................................$25.00
#775 Gabby Goofies, 1956-59 & Easter 1960, C13 ....$45.00
#775 Pocket Radio, 1967-68, Sing a Song of Six Pence, wood & plastic, C13......................................$25.00
#775 Pocket Radio, 1973-75, Pop Goes the Weasel, wood & plactic, C13......................................$20.00
#775 Teddy Drummer, 1936, C13 ....$675.00
#777 Pushy Bruno, 1933, C13 ....$725.00
#777 Squeaky the Clown, 1958, C13 ....$250.00
#778 Ice Cream Wagon, 1940, C13 ....$350.00
#778 Pocket Radio, 1967-68, Frere Jacques, wood & plastic, C13..$20.00
#779 Pocket Radio, 1976, Yankee Doodle, wood & plastic, C13..$20.00
#780 Jumbo Xylophone, 1937, C13 ....$275.00
#780 Snoopy Sniffer, 1955-57 & Easter 1958, C13 ....$75.00
#784 Mother Goose Music Chart, 1955, C13 ....$100.00
#785 Blackie Drummer, 1939, C13 ....$625.00
#785 Corn Popper, 1957-58, C13..................................$75.00
#786 Perky Penguin, 1973-75, C13 ....$20.00
#788 Rock-A-Bye Bunny Cart, 1940, C13 ....$300.00

#790 Candy Man Tote-A-Tune Radio, 1979, Let's Go Fly a Kite, plastic, C13 ....$10.00

#792 Music Box, 1980-81, Teddy Bear's Picnic, plastic, C13..$10.00

#793 Jolly Jumper, 1963, C13 ....$50.00

#793 Tote-A-Tune Radio, 1981, When You Wish Upon a Star, plastic, C13 ....$10.00

#794 Big Bill Pelican, 1961, w/cb fish, C13 ....$85.00

#794 Tote-A-Tune Radio, 1982-91, Over the Rainbow, plastic, C13 ....$5.00

#795 Micky Mouse Drummer, 1937, C13 ....$700.00

#795 Musical Duck, 1952, C13 ....$100.00

#795 Tote-A-Tune Radio, 1984-91, Toyland, C13 ....$5.00

#798 Chatter Monk, 1957, C13 ....$100.00

#798 Mickey Mouse Xylophone, 1939, 1st version, w/hat, C13...$450.00

#798 Mickey Mouse Xylophone, 1942, 2nd version, no hat, C13...$450.00

#799 Duckie Transport, 1937, C13 ....$400.00

#799 Quacky Family, 1940-42, C13 ....$150.00

#800 Hot Diggety, 1934, w/up, C13 ....$800.00

#808 Pop'n Ring, 1956-58 & Easter 1959, C13 ....$85.00

#810 Hot Mammy, 1934, w/up, C13 ....$800.00

#810 Timber Toter, 1957-58, C13 ....$85.00

#845 Farm Truck, 1954-55, C13 ....$250.00

#870 Pull-A-Tune Xylophone, 1957-69, w/song book, C13....$35.00

#875, Looky Push Car, 1962-65 & Easter 1966, C13........$50.00

#900 Struttin' Donald Duck, 1939 & Easter 1940, C13 ...$650.00

#900 This Little Pig, 1956-58 & Easter 1959, C13 ....$55.00

#902 Junior Circus, 1963-70, C13 ....$225.00

#904 Beginners Circus, 1965-68, C13 ....$60.00

#905 This Little Pig, 1959-62, C13 ....$50.00

#909 Play Family Rooms, 1972, Sears only, C13 ....$200.00

#910 Change-A-Tune Piano, 1969-72, Pop Goes the Weasel, This Old Man & The Muffin Man, C13....................$30.00

#915 Play Family Farm, 1968-79, 1st version w/masonite base, C13...$40.00

#916 Fisher-Price Zoo, 1984-87, C13 ....$35.00

#919 Music Box Movie Camera, 1968-70, plays This Old Man, w/5 picture disks, C13....................................$40.00

#923 Play Family School, 1971-78, 1st version, C13 ....$25.00

#926 Concrete Mixer, 1959, C13...................$275.00

#928 Play Family Fire Station, 1980-82, C13 ....$75.00

#929 Play Family Nursery School, 1978-79, C13.............$60.00

#931 Play Family Hospital, 1976-78, C13.................$125.00

#932 Amusement Park, 1963, C13 ....$325.00

#932 Ferry Boat, 1979-80, C13 ....$45.00

#934 Play Family Western Town, 1982-84, C13 ....$75.00

#937 Play Family Sesame Street Clubhouse, 1977-79, C13....$75.00

#940 Sesame Street Characters, 1977, C13, ea $3.00

#942 Play Family Lift & Load Depot, 1977-79, C13........$50.00

#943 Lift & Load Railroad, 1978-79, C13..................$50.00

#944 Lift & Load Lumber Yard, 1979-81, C13 ....$50.00

#945 Offshore Cargo Base, 1979-80, C13 ....$65.00

#952 Play Family House, 1969-79, 1st version, C13 ....$35.00

#960 Woodsey's Log House, 1979, w/figures, accessories & 32-pg book, C13..$25.00

#961 Woodsey's Store, 1980, hollow tree w/figures, accessories & 32-pg book, C13 ....$35.00

#962 Woodsey's Airport, 1980, C13 ....$20.00

#969 Musical Ferris Wheel, 1966-72, 1st version w/4 wooden straight-body figures, C13....................................$50.00

#972 Fisher-Price Cash Register, 1960-72, C13.................$50.00

#979 Dump Truck Playset, 1965-70, C13 ....$80.00

#982 Hot Rod Roadster, 1983-84, riding toy w/4-pc take-apart engine, C13......................................$45.00

#983 Safety School Bus, 1959, w/6 figures, Fisher-Price Club logo, C13 ....$250.00

#985 Play Family Houseboat, 1972-76, w/2 deck lounges, figures & accessories, C13......................................$45.00

#987 Creative Coaster, 1964-81, MIB, C13....................$50.00

#990 Play Family A-Frame, 1974-76, C13 ....$75.00

#991 Music Box Lacing Shoe, 1964-67, C13 ....$50.00

#991 Play Family Circus Train, 1973-78, 1st version, w/figures, animals & gondola car, C13......................................$25.00

#991 Play Family Circus Train, 1979-86, 2nd version, w/figures & animals, no gondola car, C13......................................$15.00

#992 Play Family Car & Camper, 1980-84, C13 ....$35.00

#993 Play Family Castle, 1974-77, 1st version, C13.......$100.00

#994 Play Family Camper, 1973-76, C13......................$75.00

#996 Play Family Airport, 1972-76, 1st version, bl airport w/clear lookout tower, C13 ....$75.00

#997 Musical Tick-Tock Clock, 1962-67, C13................$40.00

#997 Play Family Village, 1973-77, C13 ....$75.00

#998 Music Box Teaching Clock, 1968 – 83, $40.00.
(Photo courtesy Brad Cassity)

#999 Huffy Puffy Train, 1958-62, C13 ....$80.00

#1005 Push Cone, 1937-38, C13....................................$400.00

#1006 Floor Train, 1934-38, C13....................................$600.00
#2352 Little People Construction Set, 1985, C13 ....$20.00
#2361 Little People Fire Truck, 1989-90, C13...................$10.00
#2453 Little People Beauty Salon, 1990, C13....................$15.00
#2500 Little People Main Street, 1986-90, C13 ....$50.00

#2525 Little People Playground, 1986 – 90, $15.00.
(Photo courtesy Brad Cassity)

#2526 Little People Pool, 1986-88, C13 ....$15.00
#2551 Little People Neighborhood, 1988-90, C13 ....$55.00
#2552 McDonald's Restaurant, 1990, 1st version, C13 ....$75.00
#2552 McDonald's Restaurant, 1991-92, 2nd version, same pcs
    as 1st version but lg-sz figures, C13 ....$50.00
#2580 Little People Little Mart, 1987-89, C13.................$20.00
#4520 Highway Dump Truck, 1985-86, C13 ....$20.00
#4521 Dozer Loader, 1985-86, C13 ....$15.00
#4550 Chevy S-10 4x4, 1985, C13 ....$25.00
#4551 Pontiac Firebird, 1985, C13...................................$25.00
#4552 Jeep CJ-Renegade, 1985, C13 ....$25.00
#4581 Power Dump Truck, 1985-86, C13.........................$20.00
#6145 Jingle Elephant, 1993, ToyFest limited edition of 5,000,
    C13 ....$100.00
#6464 Gran'Pa Frog, 1994 ToyFest limited edition of 5,000,
    C13 ....$60.00
#6550 Buzzy Bee, 1987, ToyFest limited edition of 5,000,
    C13...$120.00
#6558 Snoopy Sniffer, 1988, ToyFest limited edition of 3,000,
    C13 ....$600.00

**#6575 Toot-Toot, 1989, ToyFest limited edition of 5,000,
$100.00.** (Photo courtesy Brad Cassity)

#6588 Snoopy Sniffer, 1990, Fisher-Price Commemorative lim-
    ited edition of 3,500, Ponderosa pine, C13...............$150.00
#6590 Prancing Horses, 1990, ToyFest limited edition of 5,000,
    C13 ....$100.00

**#6592 Teddy Bear Parade, 1991, ToyFest limited edition of
5,000, $70.00.** (Photo courtesy Brad Cassity)

#6593 Squeaky the Clown, 1995, ToyFest limited edition of
    5,000, C13 ....$150.00
#6599 Molly Bell Cow, 1992, ToyFest limited edition of 5,000,
    C13 ....$175.00

Games

Early games (those from 1850 to 1910) are very often appre-
ciated more for their wonderful lithographed boxes than their
'playability,' and you'll find collectors displaying them as they
would any fine artwork. Many boxes and boards were designed
by commercial artists of the day.

Though they were in a decline a few years ago, baby-boomer
game prices have leveled off. Some science fiction and rare TV
games are still in high demand. Games produced in the Art
Deco era between the World Wars have gained in popularity —
especially those with great design. Victorian games have become
harder to find; their prices have also grown steadily. Condition
and rarity are the factors that most influence game prices.

When you buy a game, check to see that all pieces are there.
The games listed below are complete unless noted otherwise. For
further information we recommend *Baby Boomer Games* by Rick
Polizzi (Collector Books) and *Board Games of the '50s, '60s, and
'70s* (L-W Book Sales). Note: In the listings that follow, assume
that all are board games (unless specifically indicated card game,
target game, bagatelle, etc.) and that each is complete as issued,
unless missing components are mentioned.

Advisor: Paul Fink (F3).

See also Advertising; Black Americana; specific categories.

A-Team, Parker Bros, EX (EX box), B10 ....$20.00

Across the Continent, Parker Bros, 1952, NM (EX box) .$50.00

Addams Family, Milton Bradley, 1973, NM (NM box), C1.$65.00

Advance to Boardwalk, Parker Bros, 1985, EX (EX box) .$20.00

Adventures of Popeye, Transogram, 1957, EX (EX box) ..$65.00

Adventures of Robin Hood, Bettye-B, 1956, few pcs missing, EX (VG box), P4 ....$75.00

Adventures of Sir Lancelot, Lisbeth Whiting, 1957, rare, EX (EX box) $75.00

Adventures of the Nebbs, Milton Bradley, 1934, EX (EX box), A $75.00

Aerial Contest, Spear, G (G box), A............................$100.00

Air Raid Defense Target, Wyandotte, NM (G box), A.$225.00

Aladdin, card game, Parker Bros, 1992, MIB, B10 ....$5.00

Alien, Kenner, 1979, complete, rare, EX (EX box), B10..$50.00

All-Star Basketball Bagatelle, Gotham, 1950, EX (EX box) .$55.00

Alvin & the Chipmunks Acorn Hunt, Hasbro, 1960, EX (EX box) $55.00

Alvin & the Chipmunks Cross Country, Hasbro, 1960, MIB........................$70.00

Alvin & the Chipmunks Go Hollywood, Ideal, 1983, MIB.....$25.00

Amazing Spider-Man, Milton Bradley, 1967, EX (EX box)...$100.00

Amazing Spider-Man & the Fantastic Four, Milton Bradley, 1977, MIB, T2 ....$50.00

Amazing Spider-Man Web Spinning Action, Ideal, 1979, MIB, T2..........................$75.00

American Boys, McLoughlin Bros, early 1900s, EX (EX box), F3...............................$200.00

Angela Cartwright's Buttons & Bows, Transogram, 1960, EX (EX box) $50.00

Animal Twister, Milton Bradley, 1967, EX (EX box).......$25.00

Annie Oakley, Game Gems/T Cohn, 1965, EX (EX box)..$50.00

Annie Oakley, Milton Bradley, 1950s, VG (VG box)......$40.00

Aquaman & the Justice League of America, Hasbro, 1967, NM (NM box), T2.....................$200.00

Archie, Whitman, 1969, EX (EX box), from $40 to.........$50.00

Archie Bunker's Card Game, Milton Bradley, 1972, EX (EX box) $15.00

Arnold Palmer's Inside Golf, David Bremson, 1961, EX (EX box).............................$100.00

Around the World in 80 Days, Transogram, 1957, EX (EX box).............................$50.00

Arrest & Trial, Transogram, 1963, EX (EX box), C1.....$100.00

As the World Turns, Parker Bros, 1966, EX (EX box), B10..$45.00

Astro Launch, Ohio Art, 1963, EX (EX box) $75.00

Atom Ant Saves the Day, Transogram, 1966, NMIB, T2 ..$75.00

Babes in Toyland, Parker Bros, 1961, EX (EX box), from $40 to.............................$50.00

Balaroo, Milton Bradley, 1967, EX (EX box).................$35.00

Bamm-Bamm Color Me Happy, Transogram, 1963, EX (EX box)............................$65.00

Bandit Trail Featuring Gene Autry, Kenton Hardware, 1950s, EX (EX box) $150.00

Baseball, Milton Bradley, 1941, EX (EX box) $55.00

Bash, Milton Bradley, 1965, EX (EX box), B10 ....$25.00

Bat Masterson, Lowell, 1958, EX (EX box) $60.00

Batman, card game, Whitman, 1966, NM (NM box) $50.00

Batman, marble game, 1966, rare, VG (VG box), J5........$45.00

Batman (Animated), 3-D, Parker Bros, EX (EX box), B10..$20.00

Batman & Robin, Hasbro, NMIB.................................$60.00

Batman & Robin, Hassenfeld Bros, 1965, EX (EX box), S16.$75.00

Batman & Robin Target, Hasbro, 1966, MIB, T2 ....$200.00

Batman Adventures of the Caped Crusader, Hasbro, 1973, NM (EX box), J5.........................$35.00

Batman Jigsaw Puzzle Game, Milton Bradley, 1966, EX (EX box), J5.............................$65.00

Batman Pinball, Marx, 1966, EX (EX box).....................$100.00

Auto Racing Game, Milton Bradley, 1930s, VG (VG box), F3, $225.00.
(Photo courtesy Paul Fink)

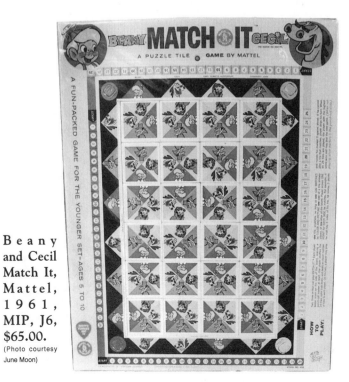

Beany and Cecil Match It, Mattel, 1961, MIP, J6, $65.00.
(Photo courtesy June Moon)

Bats in Your Belfry, Mattel, 1964, EX (EX box) $95.00

Battle-Cry, Milton Bradley, 1961, VG (VG box)............$45.00

Battlestar Galactica, Parker Bros, 1978, EX (EX box), B10 .$20.00

Bazooka Bagatelle, Marx, NM (EX box), A $50.00

Beanbag Buccaneers, Lakeside, 1960s, EX (EX box) $30.00

Beat the Clock, Milton Bradley, 1969, NM (EX box) $40.00

Beetle Bailey the Old Army Game, NMIB $65.00

Ben Casey, Transogram, 1961, EX (EX box), B10 ....$30.00

Ben-Hur, McLoughlin Bros, 1899, VG (VG box), F3.$1,500.00

Benny Goodman Swings Into a Game of Musical Information,
    Toy Creations, 1940s, EX (EX box).........................$100.00

Bermuda Triangle, Milton Bradley, 1976, EX (EX box), J2 .....$35.00

Beverly Hillbillies, Standard Toycraft, 1963, NM (NM box).$75.00

Bewitched, Game Gems, 1965, rare, EX (EX box), B10.$145.00

Bewitched, Stymie card game, Milton Bradley, 1964, EX (EX
    box), J2..$65.00

Bible Game of New Testament Books, David C Cook, 1930s,
    VG (VG box), S16 ....$65.00

Bicycle Race, McLoughlin Bros, EX (EX box), F3..........$925.00

Big Sneeze, Ideal, 1968, EX (EX box) $25.00

Big Town News Reporting, Lowell, 1950s, rare, NMIB, A.$75.00

Bing Crosby's Call Me Lucky, Parker Bros, 1954, EX (EX box),
    from $50 to...$60.00

Blockade, Corey Games, 1941, VG (VG box), S16..........$85.00

Bob Feller's Big League Baseball, Saalfield, 1950s, EX (EX
    box) $125.00

Bobbsey Twins, Milton Bradley, 1957, VG (VG box)......$50.00

Boom or Bust, Parker Bros, 1951, EX (EX box)..............$175.00

Bop the Beetle, Ideal, 1962, MIB $35.00

Bozo the Clown in Circus Land, Lowell, 1965, EX (EX box).$35.00

Brady Bunch, Whitman, 1973, NMIB $85.00

Break-A-Plate Carnival Pitch, Transogram, 1961, EX (EX
    box)..$60.00

Bruce Force Lost in Outer Space, Ideal, 1963, EX (EX box) .$50.00

Buccaneers, Transogram, 1957, EX (EX box), A $45.00

Buckaroo the Cowboy Roundup, Milton Bradley, 1947, NMIB,
    P4 ....$65.00

Bugs Bunny Adventure, Milton Bradley, 1961, EX (EX box) .$40.00

Bullwinkle & Rocky Role Playing Party, TSR, 1988, MIB
    (sealed)..$15.00

Bullwinkle Hide & Seek, Milton Bradley, 1961, NMIB,
    B10/T2..$50.00

Buster Brown & Tige Target, Bliss, early 1900s, VG......$575.00

Calling Superman, A Game of News Reporting, Transogram,
    1954, EX (EX box), T2, from $100 to......................$150.00

Camelot, Parker Bros, 1931, EX (VG box), B10..............$45.00

Camp Granada, Milton Bradley, 1965, EX (EX box) $55.00

Cannonball Run, Cadaco, 1981, EX (EX box), F3 ....$20.00

Captain America, Milton Bradley, 1966, MIB, T2.........$100.00

Captain America w/the Falcon & the Avengers, Milton Bradley,
    1977, MIB, T2 ....$30.00

Captain Kangaroo's Tic Tagaroo, Milton Bradley, 1956, EX (EX
    box)..$35.00

Captain Scarlett & the Mysterons, NMIB, T2 ....$100.00

Captain Video, Milton Bradley, EX (EX box), B10........$125.00

Car 54 Where Are You, Allison, 1963, EX (EX box), A ..$250.00

Carrier Strike Game of Naval Strategy, 1977, NMIB, J2..$40.00

Casper Spooky Marble Maze, 1971, EX (EX box), J2 ....$30.00

Challenge the Yankees, Hasbro, 1964, EX (EX box)......$165.00

Challenge Yahtzee, Lowe, 1972, NM (NM box w/picture of the
    Odd Couple), C1 ....$35.00

Charlie Brown's All-Star, Parker Bros, 1968, VG (VG box),
    S16..$50.00

Charlie's Angels, Milton Bradley, 1977, MIB (sealed), V1..$35.00

Charlie's Angels Target Set, Placo, 1977, MIB.................$50.00

Chester Gump, Milton Bradley, 1930s, scarce, EX (EX box) .$150.00

Cheyenne Target, Mettoy, 1962, EX (EX box) $225.00

Ching Gong, Samuel Gabriel, 1937, EX (EX box), S16...$50.00

Chiromagica, McLoughlin Bros, 1870, EX (EX walnut case),
    A $300.00

Chiromagica, McLoughlin Bros, 1890, VG (VG wood & glass
    box), A..$300.00

Chitty-Chitty Bang-Bang Electric Movie Quiz, Remco, 1968,
    EX (EX box)...$75.00

Choo-Choo Charlie, Milton Bradley, 1969, EX (EX box)..$40.00

Chubby Checker's Limbo, Wham-O, 1961, EX (EX box) ..$65.00

Chuggedy Chug, Milton Bradley, 1955, EX (EX box) $75.00

Cinderella, Parker Bros, 1964, EX (EX box) $50.00

Classic Major League Baseball, Game Time Ltd, 1987, few cards
    missing, EX (EX box), S16 ....$50.00

Clue, Parker Bros, 1949, orig issue, VG (VG box) $50.00

Cobbler & the Elves, Hasbro, 1962, VG (VG box), A.....$75.00

Columbo, Milton Bradley, 1973, EX (EX box), F3 ....$20.00

Concentration, Milton Bradley, 1959, 1st edition, EX (EX box),
    from $40 to..$50.00

Coney Island, Selchow & Righter, 1956, EX (EX box) $40.00

Cowboy Game, Chaffee & Selchow, 1898, EX (EX box), F3.$400.00

Cowboy Roundup, Parker Bros, 1952, VG (VG box), S16 ...$45.00

Crazy Clock, Ideal, 1964, EX (EX box) $50.00

Creature Features, Athol Research, 1975, EX (EX box), S16 ..$125.00

Crow Hunt, Parker Bros, 1930, VG (VG box), S16 ....$65.00

Dark Shadows, Milton Bradley, 1969, NM (NM box) $65.00

Dating Game, Hasbro, 1967, EX (EX box) $50.00

Davy Crockett Indian Scouting, Whitman, NMIB, T2, from $65
    to $85.00

Davy Crockett Radar Action, Ewing, 1955, EX (EX box) ..$85.00

**Buck Rogers Game of the 25th Century AD, Slesinger,
1934, EX (EX box), A, $500.00.**

Davy Crockett Rescue Race, Gabriel, EX (EX box), T2, from $55.00 to $75.00. (Photo courtesy Bill Bruegman)

Detectives, Transogram, 1961, EX (EX box), M17...........$50.00
Dice Ball, Milton Bradley, 1934, VG (VG box), S16.......$60.00
Dick Tracy Crime Stopper, Ideal, 1963, NMIB, T2, from $75 to $100.00
Dick Tracy Detective, Whitman, 1937, EX (G box), J5...$125.00
Dick Tracy Electronic Target, 1961, NMIB, A $100.00
Dick Tracy Marble Maze, Hasbro, 1966, EX (EX box) $75.00

Dick Tracy Target, Marx, 1930s, lithographed tin, NM, $250.00. (Photo courtesy Larry Doucet)

Dick Tracy Target, Marx, 1930s, 17" dia, EX (EX box) .$385.00
Dick Van Dyke, Standard Toycraft, 1964, EX (EX box) ..$75.00
Dino the Dinosaur, Transogram, 1961, MIB, F3...............$75.00
Disneyland Monorail, Parker Bros, 1950s, EX (EX box)...$40.00
Diver Dan, Milton Bradley, 1961, EX (EX box) $50.00
Doctor Dolittle Marble Maze, Hasbro, 1967, EX (EX box)..$40.00
Dollar a Second, Lowell, 1956, scarce, unused, MIB, A ...$75.00
Dolly & Daniel Whale, Milton Bradley, 1963, NMIB, T2 .$50.00
Donald Duck Bean Bag Game, Parker Bros, 1939, EX (EX box)..$150.00
Donny & Marie Osmond TV Show, Mattel, 1976, MIB..$30.00

Dr Kildare, Ideal, 1962, unused, NMIB...........................$65.00
Dragnet, Transogram, 1955, NM (NM box), C1 ....$65.00
Dream House, Milton Bradley, 1968, rare, EX (EX box), S16..$100.00
Drew Pearson's Predict-A-Word, Dee-Jay, 1949, VG (VG box)..$35.00
Dukes of Hazzard, Ideal, 1981, EX (EX box), B10.............$25.00
Duran Duran, Milton Bradley, 1985, MIB $75.00
Eldon Moonsters Target, 1965, scarce, NMIB, M17.........$75.00
Electra Woman & Dyna Girl, Ideal, 1977, MIB $60.00
Electric Hot Potato, Electric Game, 1960, EX (EX box) ..$35.00
Ellery Queen's Case of the Elusive Assassin, Ideal, 1967, EX (EX box) $45.00
Elvis Presley King of Rock, Box Car Int, 1979, NMIB $75.00
Elvis Welcomes You To His World, Duff, 1978, NMIB .$125.00
Enter the Dangerous World of James Bond, Milton Bradley, 1965, EX (EX box), M17 ....$50.00
Espionage, Transogram, 1963, EX (EX box) $50.00
Ethan Allen's All-Star Baseball, Cadaco, 1946, EX (EX box) ..$85.00
Family Ties, Applestreet, 1986, EX (EX box), S16...........$30.00
Fangface, Parker Bros, 1979, EX (EX box), B10................$25.00
Fantastic Four, Milton Bradley, 1978, EX (EX box), B10.$20.00
FBI, Transogram Landmark Game Series, MIB $100.00
FBI Crime Resistance, Milton Bradley, MIB....................$85.00
Fearless Fireman, Hasbro, 1957, EX (EX box) $85.00
Felix the Cat Target, Lido, 1960, EX (EX box) $55.00
Ferdinand's Chinese Checkers w/the Bee, Parker Bros, 1968, EX (EX box) $100.00
Flash & the Justice League of America, Hasbro, 1967, NMIB, T2..$200.00
Flintstones — The Game That Rocked Bedrock, Transogram, 1960s, NMIB, from $75 to..$100.00
Flintstones Big Game Hunt, Whitman, 1962, NM (NM box), C1..$80.00
Flintstones Brake Ball, 1962, EX (EX box), J2................$100.00
Flintstones Cut-Ups, card game, 1960s, EX (EX box), from $75 to $100.00
Flintstones Pitch 'N Bowl, Transogram, 1961, EX (EX box)..$50.00
Flintstones Window Whacker, Transogram, 1962, EX (EX box)..$50.00
Flip It Jackpot, Aurora, 1973, EX (EX box) $45.00
Flip-A-Lid, Hassenfeld Bros, 1950s, VG (VG box), S16..$35.00
Flipper Flips, Mattel, 1965, EX (EX box) $50.00
Flying Nun, Milton Bradley, 1968, MIB, A $150.00
Flying the Beam, Parker Bros, 1941, EX (EX box)............$75.00
Forest Friends, Milton Bradley, 1956, VG (VG box), S16..$35.00
Frankenstein Horror Target, Hasbro, 1965, EX (EX box)..$125.00
Frankenstein Mystery, Hasbro, 1963, NM (NM box) $150.00
Frosty the Snowman, Parker Bros, 1979, VG (VG box), S16..$25.00
Fu Manchu's Hidden Hoard, Ideal, 1967, EX (EX box), from $50 to $60.00
Funky Phantom, Milton Bradley, 1971, EX (EX box), F3.$20.00
G-Men Clue Games, Whitman, scarce, MIB...................$175.00
G-Men Target & Baseball Game, complete w/wooden easel, MIB..$450.00
Gabby Hayes Champion Shooting Target, Haecker Industries, 1950, EX (EX box) $125.00
Game of Authors, Russell Mfg, 1920s, VG (VG box), S16 ....$50.00

Game of Bagatelle, McLoughlin Bros, 1890s, VG (VG box), F3 ....$400.00

Game of Bounce, McLoughlin Bros, late 1800s, EX (EX box), $450.00.
(Photo courtesy David Longest)

Game of Charlie Brown & His Pals, 1959, EX (EX box), V1 ....$55.00

Game of Climbing Monkeys, Spear, VG+ (VG box), A ..$200.00

Game of General Hospital, Cardinal Industries, 1982, VG (VG box), S16, from $40 to............................$50.00

Game of Poor Jenny, All-Fair, 1972, EX (EX box), F3 ...$125.00

Game of Robbing the Miller, McLoughlin Bros, 1888, few pcs missing, VG (VG box) $375.00

Game of Snow White & the Seven Dwarfs, Milton Bradley, 1930s, EX (EX box) $125.00

Game of the District Messenger Boy, McLoughlin Bros, 1886, NM (EX box), A $425.00

Game of the Visit of Santa Claus, McLoughlin Bros, 1890s, VG (VG box), F3........................$1,600.00

Game of Yertle by Dr Seuss, Revell, 1960, EX (EX box) ..$200.00

Game of Yuneek, McLoughlin Bros, late 1800s, EX (EX box)..$700.00

Game of Zulu, McLoughlin Bros, EX (EX box), F3 .....$1,100.00

Gang Busters Official Target, Marx, 1940, EX (EX box), A..$375.00

Gentle Ben RV Quiz, Remco, 1968, NMIB, A $85.00

George of the Jungle, Parker Bros, 1968, EX (EX box) $75.00

Get Smart, card game, Ideal, 1966, unused, NMIB, A $75.00

Get Smart Electronic Question & Answer Machine, Lisbeth Whiting, 1960s, EX, A $225.00

Get the Message, Milton Bradley, 1964, VG (VG box), S16..$40.00

Getaway Chase, DX, 1968, EX (EX box) $60.00

GI Joe Marine Paratroop, Hasbro, 1965, NMIB, T2.........$75.00

Giant Wheel Hot Rod, Remco, 1960, EX (EX box).........$50.00

Giant Wheels Thrills 'N Spills Horse Race, Remco, 1958, EX (EX box), B10..$55.00

Gidget, Standard Toykraft, 1965, NMIB, A $125.00

Gilligan's Island, Game Gems/T Cohn, 1965, EX (EX box) .$225.00

Global Air Race, Replogle Globes, 1952, EX (EX box)....$65.00

Gomer Pyle, Transogram, 1964, EX (EX box) $50.00

Gordo & Pepito, Milton Bradley, 1947, EX (EX box), from $75 to..$100.00

Gracie Allen Murder Case, Milton Bradley, 1939, VG (VG box) $350.00

Gray Ghost, Transogram, 1958, VG (VG box) $60.00

Great American Game of Baseball, Hustler Toys, 1923, lithographed tin, NM, $400.00.

Green Acres, Standard Toykraft, 1965, MIB..................$100.00

Green Ghost, Transogram, 1965, few pcs missing, EX (EX box), J5 ....$65.00

Green Hornet Quick Switch, Milton Bradley, 1966, NMIB, T2 ....$250.00

Groucho's TV Quiz, Pressman, 1954, EX (EX box)..........$75.00

Groucho's You Bet Your Life, Lowell, 1955, rare, EX (EX box), B10 ....$100.00

Gumby & Poky Playful Trails, MIB, T2......................$100.00

Gunsmoke, Lowell, 1959, EX (EX box), M17..................$70.00

Gypsy Fortune Telling Game, McLoughlin Bros, 1890, EX (VG box), A..$800.00

Gypsy Fortune Telling Game, Milton Bradley, 1920, NMIB, F3 ....$150.00

Hair Bear Bunch, Milton Bradley, 1971, EX (EX box), B10 .$30.00

Hands Down, Ideal, 1964, EX (EX box), B10 ....$20.00

Happy Days, Parker Bros, 1976, EX (EX box), B10 ....$20.00

Happy Hooligan, target game, Milton Bradley, 1925, EX (VG box)..$300.00

Hardy Boys Mystery Game: Secret of Thunder Mountain, Parker Bros, 1978, MIB (sealed), V1 ....$50.00

Hardy Boys Treasure, Parker Bros, 1957, EX (EX box).....$65.00

Harlem Globetrotters, Milton Bradley, 1971, contents sealed, MIB, C1 ....$55.00

Have Gun Will Travel, Parker Bros, 1959, EX (EX box) .$75.00

Hawaiian Eye, Lowell, 1963, EX (EX box).........................$80.00

Hector Heathcote's Hasimoto San the Japanese House Mouse, Transogram, 1961, NMIB, C1 ....$55.00

Hee Haw, Dooley Inc, 1975, EX (G box), B10 ....$20.00

Herb Shriner's TV Harmonica Jamboree, 1950s, rare, NMIB, A $200.00

Hi Ho Santa Claus, Whitman, 1962, EX (EX box) $30.00

Hialeah, Milton Bradley, 1930s, VG (VG box)................$75.00

Hocus Pocus, Transogram, 1968, EX (EX box) $65.00

Hogan's Heroes, Transogram, 1965, NMIB, A $125.00

Honey West, Ideal, 1955, unused, NMIB, A $200.00

Hop Off, Parker Bros, 1920, EX (EX box), F3.................$250.00

Hopalong Cassidy Lasso, Transogram, 1950, MIB..........$165.00

Hopalong Cassidy Pony Express Toss, Transogram, 1950, EX (EX box) $100.00

Hopalong Cassidy Shooting Gallery, Automatic Toy, 1950, EX (EX box), A $275.00

Hoppity Hooper, Milton Bradley, 1965, MIB $75.00

How To Succeed, Hasbro, 1950s, EX (EX box) $50.00

Howdy Doody Adventure, Milton Bradley, 1950s, VG (VG box), A..$125.00

Howdy Doody Dominos, Ed-U Cards, 1961, EX (EX box) .$65.00

Howdy Doody TV Game, Milton Bradley, 1950s, EX (EX box), A..$100.00

Howdy Doody's Bowling Game, Parker Bros, 1950, EX (EX box), from $100 to..$125.00

Howdy Doody's 3-Ring Electric Circus, Harret-Gilman, 1950, NMIB..$125.00

Huckleberry Hound Bumps, Transogram, 1960s, EX (EX box), from $150 to $175.00

Huckleberry Hound Western Game, Milton Bradley, 1958, NM (NM box), from $65 to......................................$75.00

Humpty Dumpty, Lowell, 1960, EX (EX box) $50.00

Hurdle Races, Milton Bradley, 1920s, VG (VG box), F3 .$175.00

I Dream of Jeannie, Milton Bradley, 1965, NM (NM box), C1..$100.00

Incredible Hulk w/the Fantastic Four, Milton Bradley, 1978, NMIB, T2...$30.00

Ipcress File, Milton Bradley, 1966, unused, M (EX+ box), A.$40.00

Ironside, Ideal, 1967, EX (EX box) $100.00

It's a Small World, Parker Bros, 1967, EX (EX box), J2 ...$55.00

Jace Pearson's Tales of the Texas Rangers, All-Fair, 1956, EX (EX box) $85.00

Jack & the Beanstalk, National Games, 1941, EX (EX box).$40.00

Jackie Gleason & Away We Go, Transogram, 1955, EX (EX box), A..$150.00

James Bond Message From M, Ideal, 1966, unused, MIB, A..$300.00

James Bond 007 Assault, Victory Games, 1961, EX (EX box), S16 ....$65.00

Jan Murray's Treasure Hunt, Gardner, 1959, EX (EX box).$30.00

Jetsons Fun Pad, Milton Bradley, 1963, EX (EX box), from $75 to..$100.00

Joe Palooka Boxing Game, Lowell, 1952, EX (EX box) .$150.00

John Drake Secret Agent, Milton Bradley, 1966, EX (EX box), B10...$60.00

Journey to the Unknown, Remco, 1968, NMIB, A $200.00

Jumpy Tinker, Toy Tinkers, 1920, VG (worn box) $50.00

Jungle Hunt, Hubley, 1964, EX (EX box) $65.00

Jungle Skittles, American Toy Works, 1950s, EX (EX box)..$50.00

Katzenjammer Kids Hockey, Jaymar, 1950s, missing few minor pcs, EX (EX box), J5 ....$25.00

Ker-Plunk, Ideal, 1967, NMIB, B10 ....$25.00

King Kong, Milton Bradley, 1966, EX (EX box).............$150.00

Knight Rider, Parker Bros, 1983, EX (EX box), B10/S16 .$20.00

Knock Your Block Off, Hasbro, 1964, EX (EX box) $35.00

Knockout, Northwestern, 1950, EX (EX box) $125.00

Kojak Stakeout Detective Game, Milton Bradley, 1975, EX (EX box), B10 ....$25.00

Lai-Shai, Karco, 1943, EX (EX box), S16 ....$50.00

Land of the Giants, Ideal, 1968, EX (EX box) $150.00

Land of the Lost, Milton Bradley, 1975, EX (EX box), B10 ..$25.00

Lassie, T Cohn/Game Gems, 1965, EX (VG box), M17 ..$60.00

Laugh-In's Knock Knock Jokes, Saalfield, 1969, NM (NM box), M17...$50.00

Laugh-In's Squeeze Your Bippy, Hasbro, 1968, scarce, EX (EX box), M17 ....$60.00

Laurel & Hardy Ring Toss, Transogram, 1962, EX (EX box) $25.00

Laverne & Shirley, unused, MIB (sealed), C17 ....$25.00

League Parlor Baseball, Bliss, 1885, paper on wood, EX (VG box), A...$1,200.00

Leave It To Beaver Rocket To the Moon, Hasbro, 1959, EX (EX box)...$50.00

Legend of Jesse James, Milton Bradley, 1966, EX (EX box) ..$55.00

Legend of the Lone Ranger, Milton Bradley, 1981, EX (EX box)...$75.00

Let Them All Come, Spears, 1930s, EX (EX box).........$700.00

Let's Drive, 1969, EX (EX box), B10...............................$25.00

Let's Make a Deal, Ideal, 1964, EX (EX box), B10 ....$22.00

Lie Detector, Mattel, 1960, NM (NM box), J2.................$50.00

Life & Legend of Wyatt Earp, Transogram, 1958, NM (NM box), C1...$100.00

Linus the Lionhearted Uproarious, Transogram, 1965, EX (EX box)...$85.00

Little Cowboy, Parker Bros, late 1800s, EX (EX box), F3.$475.00

Little League Baseball, Standard Toykraft, 1950s, EX (EX box)...$55.00

Little Noddy's Taxi, Parker Bros, 1956, EX (EX box) $100.00

Little Orphan Annie, Milton Bradley, 1927, rare, MIB, T2.$300.00

Little Orphan Annie Pursuit, Selchow & Righter, 1970s, NMIB, T2...$40.00

Little Red School House, Parker Bros, 1952, EX (EX box).$35.00

Lone Ranger, Parker Bros, 1938, VG (VG box), S16.......$95.00

Lone Ranger & the Silver Bullets, Gaffney, 1959, EX (EX box)...$100.00

Lone Ranger & Tonto, Warren, 1978, NM (EX box), C1..$35.00

Lone Ranger Ring-Toss, 1943, NMIB, from $350 to......$450.00

Lone Ranger Target, Marx, 1930s-40s, NM (EX box), from $375 to...$400.00

Looney Tunes, Milton Bradley, 1968, NM (NM box)......$50.00

Lost in Space, Milton Bradley, 1965, EX (EX box) $75.00

Lost in Space 3-D Game, Remco, 1966, EX (EX box) ...$225.00

Love Boat, Ungame, 1980, VG (VG box), S16.................$20.00

Lucy Show, Transogram, 1962, EX (EX box) $175.00

Lucy's Tea Party, Milton Bradley, 1971, VG (VG box), F3 ..$25.00

Ludwig Von Drake Score-A-Matic Ball Toss, Transogram, 1962, EX (EX box)...$50.00

Ludwig Von Drake Tiddly Winks, Whitman, EX (EX box) .$35.00

M*A*S*H Trivia, Golden, 1984, EX (EX box), B10.......$25.00

Mail Express, Milton Bradley, 1920, EX (EX box), F3 ...$250.00

Mammoth Hunt, Cadaco, 1962, EX (EX box).................$40.00

Man From UNCLE, card game, Milton Bradley, 1966, NM (EX box), C1..$30.00

Man From UNCLE, Ideal, 1965, EX (EX box), $50.00.
(Photo courtesy John and Sheri Pavone)

Man From UNCLE Secret Code Wheel Pinball, Marx, 1966, EX (EX box) $325.00

Mandrake the Magician, Transogram, 1966, NMIB, T2 ..$100.00

Mansion of Happiness, Ives, 1864, VG (VG box), A.....$300.00

Marblelite Skee-Ball, Wolverine, litho tin w/battery-op lights, 21½", VG+, A $65.00

Margie, Milton Bradley, 1961, MIB, M17.......................$60.00

Marvel Super Heroes, card game, Milton Bradley, 1978, MIB, T2...$40.00

Marvel Super Heroes Strategy, Milton Bradley, 1980, MIB, T2 ....$25.00

Mary Poppins Carousel, Parker Bros, 1964, MIB (sealed), J2 .$50.00

Masters of the Universe Battle for Eternity, Mattel, 1986, EX (EX box), B10 ....$20.00

McHale's Navy, Transogram, 1962, EX (EX box), B10....$45.00

Melvin Purvis' G-Men Detective Game, Parker Bros, 1930s, NM (NM box) $250.00

Merry Go-Round, Chaffe & Selchow, 1898, EX (EX box), A...$1,700.00

Merry Little Pigs Bagatelle, Durable Toy, prewar, EX (G box), A...$250.00

Merv Griffin's Word for Word, Mattel, 1963, M (EX box), M17...$30.00

Mickey Mantle Big 6 Sports, Gardner, 1950s, VG (VG box), J5 ....$150.00

Mickey Mouse Bagatelle, Chad Valley/Mickey Mouse Ltd, 1930s, EX (EX box), from $800 to........................$1,100.00

Mickey Mouse Circus, Marks Bros/WDE, 1930s, EX (EX box), from $700 to $900.00

Mickey Mouse Club, Parker Bros, 1956, NMIB, A.........$100.00

Mickey Mouse Electric Treasure Hunt, Tudor, 1960, EX (EX box)..$60.00

Mickey Mouse Let Them All Come Ring Toss, Chad Valley/Mickey Mouse Ltd, 1930s, EX (EX box), from $450 to...$650.00

Mickey Mouse Ludo, Chad Valley, 1930s, EX (EX box), from $350 to..$475.00

Mickey Mouse Pop Game, Marks Bros/WDE, 1930s, EX (EX box), from $300 to..$500.00

Mickey Mouse Scatter Ball, Marks Bros, 1935, NM (EX box)...$350.00

Mickey Mouse Soldier Set, bowling game, Marks Bros/WDE, EX (EX box), from $350 to $500.00

Mickey Mouse Tiddly Winks, Chad Valley, rare, EX (EX box), M8..$375.00

Mighty Comics Super Heroes, Transogram, 1966, rare, NMIB, T2..$200.00

Mighty Hercules, Hasbro, 1963, EX (EX box) $250.00

Mighty Mouse, Parker Bros, 1964, NMIB, T2................$75.00

Mighty Mouse Playhouse Rescue, HG Toys, 1956, NMIB, from $85 to $75.00

Mighty Mouse w/His Pals, Milton Bradley, 1957, NMIB, T2 ..$65.00

Milton the Monster, Milton Bradley, 1966, MIB..............$50.00

Miss Popularity the True American Teen, Transogram, 1961, EX (EX box), P4 ....$75.00

Monster Squad, Milton Bradley, 1977, EX (EX box), C1/M17, from $65 to..$75.00

Mork & Mindy, Parker Bros, 1979, MIB (sealed), C1 ......$30.00

Mother's Helper, Milton Bradley, 1969, EX (EX box)......$25.00

Mouse Trap, Ideal, 1963, EX (EX box) $50.00

Mr Ed, Parker Bros, 1960s, NM (NM box), B10..............$75.00

Mr Magoo Visits the Zoo, Lowe, 1961, NMIB.................$75.00

Mr Novak, Transogram, 1963, EX (EX box)....................$50.00

Muppet Game Show, Parker Bros, 1977, EX (EX box), B10.$20.00

Mystery Bank, Milton Bradley, 1965, EX (EX box)........$125.00

Mystery Pistol Target Master, Ohio Art, 1960s, EX (EX box), M17..$95.00

Name That Tune, Milton Bradley, 1959, NMIB, A $50.00

Nancy Drew Mystery, Parker Bros, 1957, EX (EX box)..$100.00

National Velvet, Transogram, 1961, VG (VG box), M17.$35.00

Naval Engagement Civil War, McLoughlin, 1870, EX (EX box), A...$250.00

Nellie Bly, McLoughlin Bros, early 1900s, EX (EX box), F3 .$325.00

New Price Is Right, Milton Bradley, 1973, missing platform, VG (VG box), F3 ....$20.00

New Zoo Revue, Ungame, 1981, EX (EX box), B10.........$30.00

Night Before Christmas, Parker Bros, 1896, EX (EX box), F3 ....$850.00

No Time for Sergeants, Ideal, 1964, EX (EX box), M17 ..$50.00

Nodding Nancy, Parker Bros, 1920s, EX (EX box), F3...$275.00

Off to See the Wizard, Milton Bradley, 1968, NMIB, M17 .$40.00

Old McDonald Little Golden Game, Western, 1977, EX (EX box), B10 ....$15.00

Operation Orbit, Transogram, 1962, EX (EX box).........$125.00

Oscar Robertson's Pro Basketball Strategy, Research Games, 1969, EX (EX box), M17......................................$100.00

Our Gang Tipple-Topple, All-Fair, 1930, EX (EX box), A..$275.00

Outer Limits, Milton Bradley, 1964, MIB, A.................$350.00

Overland Trail, Transogram, 1960, EX (EX box) $65.00

Pacman, card game, Parker Bros, 1982, EX (EX box), B10 ..$10.00

Parlor Croquet, Bliss, 1890, EX (EX box), A.................$125.00

Patty Duke, Milton Bradley, 1963, EX (EX box), M17.....$50.00

Pebbles Flintstone Magnetic Fish Pond, Transogram, 1963, EX (EX box) $55.00

Peeza, Toy Tinkers, 1936, EX (EX box) $60.00

Peg Baseball, Parker Bros, 1930s, EX (EX box), F3, from $65 to $85.00

People Magazine Trivia, Parker Bros, 1984, EX (EX box), B10 ....$20.00

Perils of Pauline, Marx, 1964, EX (EX box) $65.00

Perry Mason Case of the Missing Suspect, Transogram, 1959, EX (EX box), from $50 to...$60.00

Peter Gunn Detective, Lowell, 1960, EX (EX box), M17.$45.00

Peter Pan, Selchow & Righter, 1927, EX (EX box), A ..$100.00

Peter Pan Tiddledy Winks, Whitman, NMIB...................$25.00

Peter Rabbit, Gabriel, 1946, EX (EX box) $75.00

Phantom of the Opera Mystery, Hasbro, 1963, EX (EX box) .$200.00

Phantom Ruler of the Jungle, Transogram, 1966, NMIB, T2.$200.00

Phantom's 3 Game Set for Boys & Girls, Built Rite, 1956, NMIB, T2 ....$100.00

Pie in Your Eye, Ideal, 1966, EX (EX box)......................$30.00

Pigskin, Parker Bros, 1946, EX (EX box) $65.00

Pinocchio Target, American Toy Works, 1940, EX (EX box), from $350 to $450.00

Pinocchio the Merry Puppet, Milton Bradley, 1939, EX (EX box), from $150 to...$250.00

Pirate Plunder, All-Fair, 1950s, VG (VG box), S16.........$50.00

Pirate's Gold, All-Fair, 1946, EX (EX box) $60.00

Planet of the Apes, Milton Bradley, 1967, EX (EX box), C1 .$70.00

Popeye, card game, Whitman, 1934, EX (EX box).........$100.00

Popeye Menu Bagatelle, Durable Toy & Novelty, EX (G box), A, $500.00; Popeye Bubble Target, Durable Toy & Novelty, 1935, VG, A, $325.00.

Popeye Pipe Toss, Rosebud Art, 1930s, EX (EX box), from $100 to..$150.00

Popeye the Sailor Shipwreck, Einson-Freeman, 1933, scarce, EX (EX box), A...$200.00

Popeye's Game, Parker Bros, 1948, EX (EX box), A $250.00

Prediction Rod, Parker Bros, 1970, EX (EX box), B10 .....$35.00

Prince Valiant Crossbow Pistol, Parva Products, 1948, NMIB, T2..$75.00

Prince Valiant Game of Valor, Transogram, 1955, NMIB, T2..$85.00

Quick Draw McGraw, card game, Ed-U, 1961, MIB, from $15 to $20.00

Quick Draw McGraw Private Eye, Milton Bradley, 1960, NMIB, J2/T2...$50.00

Quiz Kids, Parker Bros, 1940, EX (EX box), B10 ....$40.00

Radio Amateur Hour, Milton Bradley, 1930s, VG (VG box), S16 ....$65.00

Raggedy Ann's Magic Pebble, Milton Bradley, 1941, NMIB, T2..$85.00

Raiders of the Lost Ark, Kenner, 1981, NMIB, A $25.00

Pivot Golf, Milton Bradley, MIB, $125.00.
(Photo courtesy Martin and Carolyn Berens)

Raggedy Ann & Andy, Milton Bradley, 1980, MIB, from $15.00 to $20.00. (Photo courtesy Kim Avery)

Ranger Commandos, Parker Bros, 1944, EX (EX box), S16..$70.00

Rat Patrol Desert Combat, Transogram, 1966, NMIB....$135.00

Rat Patrol Spin-To-Win, Pressman, 1967, NMIB..........$100.00

Rebel, Ideal, 1961, VG (VG box), P4.........................$175.00

Red Riding Hood w/Big Bad Wolf & 3 Little Pigs, Parker Bros/WDE, 1930s, EX (EX box).........................$175.00

Red Ryder's 3 Game Set for Boys & Girls, Built Rite, 1956, MIB, A...$165.00

Red Skelton's I Dood It, Zondine, 1947, EX (EX box).....$75.00

Restless Gun, Milton Bradley, 1959, NMIB, M17...........$40.00

Rich Uncle, Parker Bros, 1959, EX (EX box)..................$40.00

Rifleman, Milton Bradley, 1959, EX (EX box)................$65.00

Ripcord, Lowell, 1962, EX (EX box).............................$65.00

Road Runner, Milton Bradley, 1968, NMIB, T2.............$50.00

Robbing the Miller, McLoughlin Bros, 1888, NMIB, F3..$225.00

Rock'Em Sock'Em Robots, Marx, 1966, EX (EX box)....$135.00

Rocket Race to Saturn, Lido, 1950s, NMIB, P4.............$125.00

Rogues, Cardinal, 1963, rare, NMIB, A........................$300.00

Roly Poly Popeye Target, Knickerbocker, 1958, NM (NM box)...$275.00

Rough Riders, Edgar Clark, 1898, EX (EX box), A........$300.00

Ruff & Reddy Spills & Thrills of the Circus, Transogram, 1960s, NM (NM box), from $75 to........................$85.00

Santa's Workshop, Milton Bradley, 1959, EX (EX box)...$50.00

Satellite Space Race, card came, 1957, MIB, A...............$75.00

Scarecrow Target, Ideal, 1965, EX (EX box), H4...........$30.00

Scooby-Doo Where Are You, Milton Bradley, 1973, EX (EX box)...$30.00

Screwball the Mad Mad Mad Game, Transogram, 1960, EX (EX box), B10...$40.00

Sea Hunt Under Water, Lowell, 1960, EX (EX box), A..$100.00

Sea Raiders, Parker Bros, 1945, EX (EX box), F3.............$45.00

Sealab 2020, Milton Bradley, 1973, EX (EX box), B10....$30.00

Sergeant Preston, Milton Bradley, Canadian version, 1956, rare, EX (EX box)...$75.00

Shariland, Transogram, 1959, VG+ (VG box)................$50.00

Shenanigans, Milton Bradley, 1964, EX (EX box), A......$50.00

Shotgun Slade, Milton Bradley, 1960, NMIB, A.............$75.00

Show-Biz, Lowell, 1956, EX (EX box)...........................$60.00

Simpson's Don't Have a Cow, Milton Bradley, MIB (sealed), K1...$30.00

Simpson's Mystery of Life, Cardinal, MIB, K1.................$35.00

Simpsons 3-D Chess Set, MIB, K1...............................$45.00

Sinking of the Titanic, Ideal, 1976, EX (EX box)............$35.00

Siren Sparkle Space Target, Knickerbocker, 1950s, EX (EX box)..$125.00

Six Million Dollar Man, Parker Bros, 1975, EX (EX box), B10...$20.00

Skeezyx, Milton Bradley, 1930, EX (EX box), F3..........$275.00

Skittle Bingo, Aurora, 1973, electric, EX (EX box), B10.$25.00

Sky Lanes, Parker Bros, 1956, EX (EX box)...................$75.00

Slap Stick, Milton Bradley, 1967, MIB, B5....................$40.00

Sleeping Beauty, Parker Bros, 1952, EX (EX box)...........$50.00

Sleeping Beauty, Whitman, 1958, EX (EX box)..............$40.00

Smack-A-Roo, Mattel, 1964, EX (EX box)...................$35.00

Smitty Speed Boat Race, Milton Bradley, 1930s, EX (EX box)...$175.00

Smurf Ahoy, Milton Bradley, 1982, EX (EX box), B10....$20.00

Smurf Game, Milton Bradley, 1981, EX (EX box), B10...$30.00

Snagglepuss, Transogram, 1961, EX (EX box), T2...........$50.00

Snake Eyes, Selchow & Righter, 1940s, EX (EX box)......$75.00

Snoopy & the Red Baron, Milton Bradley, 1970, EX (EX box), B10...$25.00

Snoopy Come Home, Milton Bradley, 1973, EX (EX box), B10...$20.00

Snow White & the Seven Dwarfs, Milton Bradley, 1937, rare, NMIB...$300.00

Snow White & the Seven Dwarfs Target, American Toy Works, 1930s, EX (EX box)...$250.00

Solarquest, Western Publishing, 1986, EX (EX box), S16..$30.00

Soldiers on Guard, McLoughlin Bros, early 1900s, EX (EX box)...$500.00

Sons of Hercules, Milton Bradley, 1966, EX (EX box), A..$75.00

Soupy Sales, Ideal, 1965, EX (EX box).........................$85.00

Space Pilot, Cadaco, 1951, EX (EX box).......................$75.00

Space Shuttle 101, Media/Ungame, 1978, EX (EX box), S16.$25.00

Space: 1999, Milton Bradley, 1976, EX (EX box), B10....$30.00

Speed Buggy, Milton Bradley, 1973, EX (EX box), B10...$30.00

Sprint, Holland Crafts, 1930s, EX (EX box), F3.............$75.00

Spudsie Hot Potato, Ohio Art, NMIB, J2......................$30.00

Spy Detector, Mattel, 1960, EX (EX box), B10...............$30.00

Spy's-A-Poppin, Transogram, 1965, EX (EX box)...........$60.00

Star Trek, Milton Bradley, 1979, EX (EX box)...............$75.00

Star Trek: The Next Generation, Cardinal, 1993, EX (EX box), B10...$20.00

Star Wars: Escape From Death Star, Kenner, 1977, EX (EX box)...$30.00

Starsky & Hutch Official Target Range, EX (VG+ box), H4...$40.00

Steve Allen's Qubila, 1955, scarce, NMIB, A.................$100.00

Steve Canyon, Lowell, 1959, MIB, C1...........................$85.00

Stingray Target, Transogram, 1966, EX (EX box)..........$150.00

Straight Arrow, Selchow & Righter, 1950, EX (EX box).$50.00

Strawberry Shortcake Berry-Go-Round, Parker Bros, 1981, EX (EX box), B10...$15.00

Strawberry Shortcake Housewarming Surprise, Parker Bros, 1983, EX (EX box)...$12.00

Skill-Drive Raceway, Tarco, 1960s, NMIB, J6, $45.00.
(Photo courtesy June Moon)

Super Heroes Bingo, Hasbro, 1978, MIB, J5 ....$35.00
Super Spy, Milton Bradley, 1971, EX (EX box), B10 ....$30.00
Superboy, Hasbro, 1965, rare, EX (EX box)....................$150.00
Supercar to the Rescue, Milton Bradley, 1962, EX (EX box) $125.00
Superman & Superboy, Milton Bradley, 1967, EX (EX box), T2 ....$65.00
Superman Calling, Transogram, 1954, EX (EX box), J2....$200.00
Superman Flying Bingo, Whitman, 1966, EX (EX box), T2.$50.00
Superman II, Milton Bradley, 1981, EX (EX box), B10....$20.00
Superman III, Parker Bros, 1982, EX (EX box), B10 ....$20.00
Superman Radio Quiz Master, 1948, EX (EX box), T2 ....$65.00
Superman Speed, Milton Bradley, 1940, EX (EX box), T2..$200.00
Superman Spin to Win, Pressman, 1957, EX (EX box), T2 .$100.00
Superman Tilt Track Marble Game, Kohner, 1965, EX (EX box), T2 ....$100.00
Swamp Fox, Parker Bros, 1960, EX (EX box) $75.00
Tales of Wells Fargo, Milton Bradley, 1959, NMIB, M17 ..$80.00

Tom & Jerry, Milton Bradley, 1977, EX (EX box), B10 ...$20.00
Tom & Jerry, Transogram, 1965, NMIB, F3, from $75 to .$100.00
Tom Mix Circus, Parker Bros, 1930s, EX (EX box), A...$200.00
Tom Mix in Texas, Klee, scarce, EX (EX box), A $350.00
Toonerville Trolley, Milton Bradley, 1922, NM (NM box), from $200 to $300.00
Top Cop, Cadaco, 1961, EX (EX box) $45.00
Touche Turtle, Transogram, 1962, EX (EX box)............$125.00
Traffic Jam, Harett-Gilmar, 1954, EX (EX box) $50.00
Travel w/Woody Woodpecker, Cadaco, 1956, VG (VG box), T2 ....$75.00
Treasure Island, Harett-Gilmar, 1955, EX (EX box) $55.00
Trip Trap, Remco, 1969, EX (EX box)..............................$45.00
Tru-Action Electric Football, 1954, EX (VG box), S13...$50.00
Truth or Consequences, Gabriel, 1955, EX (EX box).......$50.00
TV Guide's TV Game, Trivia Inc, 1979, EX (EX box), B10..$25.00
Twilight Zone, Ideal, 1964, EX (EX box) $140.00
Twin Target, Milton Bradley, 1920s, VG (VG box), F3 .$225.00
Uncle Scrooge's Gold Rush, Whitman, 1976, EX (EX box), B10..$20.00
Uncle Wiggly, Milton Bradley, 1940s, NMIB...................$50.00
Uranium Rush, Gardner, 1950s, EX (EX box)...............$100.00
Vegetable Nine Pins, pnt papier-mache vegetable people in cabbage container w/tomato ball, 13" cabbage, EX, A..$2,300.00

Talking Football, Mattel, 1971, NMIB, $100.00.
(Photo courtesy Martin and Carolyn Berens)

Talking Monday Night Football, Mattel, 1977, MIB, B5 .$75.00
Tank Battle, Milton Bradley, 1975, EX (EX box), S16 ....$50.00
Teenage Mutant Ninja Turtles Pizza Powers, Random House/Mirage Studios, MIB $20.00
Terry & the Pirates, Whitman, 1937, NMIB, T2 ....$150.00
Terry & the Pirates Sunday Funnies, Ideal, 1972, MIB, C1 ..$45.00
That Girl, Remco, 1969, EX (EX box)..............................$70.00
THE Cat, Ideal, 1966, NMIB, A....................................$200.00
Think-A-Tron, Hasbro, 1961, EX (EX box) $75.00
Three Chipmunks Cross Country, Hassenfeld Bros, 1960, VG (VG box), S16...$40.00
Three Muskateers, Milton Bradley, 1950, NMIB, F3........$60.00
Three Stooges Fun House, Lowell, 1959, EX (EX box) ..$200.00
Thunderbirds, Parker Bros, 1967, NMIB, T2 ....$85.00
Thundercats, Milton Bradley, 1985, EX (EX box), B10 ...$25.00
Tiltin' Milton, Ideal, 1968, EX (EX box).........................$35.00
Time Tunnel, Ideal, 1966, EX (EX box) $125.00
Tin Can Alley, Ideal, 1976, EX (EX box) $50.00
Tiny Tim Game of Beautiful Things, Parker Bros, 1970, EX (EX box) $40.00
Tip-It, Ideal, 1965, MIB, B5 ....$35.00
Today w/Dave Garroway, Athletic Products, 1950s, EX (EX box) $130.00

Wally Gator, Transogram, EX (EX box), T2, from $50.00 to $65.00. (Photo courtesy Bill Bruegman)

Waltons, Milton Bradley, 1975, MIB, $30.00.
(Photo courtesy Greg Davis and Bill Morgan)

Wackiest Ship in the Army, Standard Toykraft, 1965, EX (EX box) $55.00

Walt Disney's Fantasyland, Parker Bros, 1950s, MIB........$40.00

Walt Disney's Three Little Pigs, Einson-Freeman, 1933, scarce, NM (EX box)...$200.00

Walt Disney's Wonderful World of Color, Whitman, 1961, EX (EX box) $50.00

Walter Johnson Baseball Game, early, NM (EX box), A .$400.00

Wanted Dead or Alive, Lowell, 1959, EX (EX box).......$100.00

Wanted Dead or Alive Target, Marx, 1959, EX (EX box).$250.00

Warrey Marble Game, Warrey, early 1900s, folding wood bullet-shaped board w/47 marbles, EX, A......................$250.00

Watermelon Patch, McLoughlin Bros, 1903, VG (VG box), F3...$1,400.00

Welcome Back Kotter, Ideal, 1976, EX (EX box), B10 ....$20.00

Wendy the Good Little Witch, Milton Bradley, 1966, EX (EX box)..$165.00

Western Target, Marx, NM (G box), A $100.00

Wheel of Fortune, Pressman, 2nd edition, 1985, EX (EX box), B10..$15.00

Whirling Jockey Race, McDowell, early 1900s, EX (worn box), A..$325.00

Whirly Bird Play Catch, Innovation, 1950s, endorsed by Warren Spahn, MIB, M17..$60.00

White Shadow, Cadaco, 1970s, rare, EX (EX box), S16 ..$85.00

Who's Afraid of the Big Bad Wolf, board only, Marks Bros, EX..$75.00

Wide World Travel Game, Parker Bros, 1957, EX (EX box), B10..$25.00

Wild Bill Hickok's Cavalry & the Indians, Built-Rite, 1956, EX (EX box) $50.00

Wild Kingdom, Teaching Concepts, 1977, VG (VG box), S16...$20.00

Wild Wild West, Transogram, 1966, MIB, A................$600.00

Winnie the Pooh, Parker Bros, 1954, EX (EX box) $40.00

Wizard of Oz, Cadaco, 1974, EX (EX box), B10..............$35.00

Wonder Woman & the Justice League of America, Hasbro, 1976, MIB, T2 ....$85.00

Wonder Woman Saves the Amazon, Hasbro, 1973, EX (EX box), A...$55.00

Wonderful Game of Oz, Parker Bros, 1922, EX (EX box), A...$450.00

Woody Woodpecker, Milton Bradley, 1959, NM (EX box)......$70.00

Woody Woodpecker Ring Toss, 1958, MIB, V1.............$100.00

Word for Word, Mattel, 1963, VG (VG box), F3............$20.00

World's Fair Panorama, Milton Bradley, 1964, EX (EX box) .$50.00

Wrestle World, Ideal, 1965, EX (EX box), B10 ....$18.00

Yacht Race, Parker Bros, 1961, VG (VG box), S16 ....$85.00

Yankee Trader, Corey Games, 1941, VG (VG box)........$75.00

You Don't Say, Milton Bradley, 1963, EX (EX box), B10...$20.00

Zoo Game, Milton Bradley, 1920s, EX (worn box), F3.....$55.00

Zorro, Whitman, 1965, NMIB, C1...............................$75.00

Zorro Beanbag-Darts, Gardner, 1965, EX (EX box).........$65.00

12 O'Clock High, card game, Milton Bradley, 1965, EX (EX box), A...$40.00

$64,000 Question Jr Edition, Lowell, 1955, EX (EX box), from $40 to...$50.00

77 Sunset Strip, Lowell, 1960, EX (EX box), M17 ....$60.00

12 O'Clock High, Ideal, EX (EX box), T2, from $50.00 to $60.00. (Photo courtesy Bill Bruegman)

Gasoline-Powered Toys

Two of the largest companies to manufacture gas-powered models are Cox and Wen-Mac. Since the late '50s they have been making faithfully detailed models of airplanes as well as some automobiles and boats. Condition of used models will vary greatly because of the nature of the miniature gas engine and damage resulting from the fuel that has been used. Because of this, 'new in box' gas toys command a premium.

Advisor: Richard Trautwein (T3).

Bremer Whirlwind #300, red, Brown Jr engine, 1939, VG, A..$1,250.00

Bremer Whirlwind Racer #8, louvered hood & belly pan, ca 1940, 18", EX, A $2,300.00

Burd Piston Ring Special Racer #4, red, 1940 ignition engine, 20", EX, A $3,400.00

Cessna UC 78 Bobcat (WWII Era Bamboo Bomber), w/pilot, co-pilot & 2 passengers, 42x57½" W, EX, A..........$475.00

Cox AA Fuel Dragster, bl & red, 1968-70, M $125.00

Cox Baja Bug, yel & orange, 1968-73, M.......................$65.00

Cox Delta F-15, Wings Series, gray, 1981-86, M.............$30.00

Cox E-Z Flyer Comanche, wht, NMIB...........................$35.00

Cox Kitty Hawk Spitfire, gr w/yel detail, EX, from $60 to..$80.00

Cox Mercedes Benz W196 Racer, red, 1963-65, EX.........$85.00

Cox P-40 Kitty Hawk, gr w/yel detail, 1964-65, EX, from $65 to...$80.00

Cox Pitts Special Biplane, wht, .20 engine, 1968, EX $50.00

Cox Ryan ST-3, w/pilot & co-pilot, wht & bl, .20 ignition power, M..$65.00

Cox Sandblaster, brn & tan, 1968-72, M........................$65.00

Cox Shrike, red, 1974, M $50.00

Cox Sky Raider, gray, EX (EX box)...............................$85.00

Cox Skymaster, Sure Flyer series, orange w/blk stickers, twin tail, 1976-79, EX $50.00

Cox Snowmobile, silver, 1968, M $100.00

Cox Super Chipmunk, red, wht & bl, 1975-82, M $40.00

Cox Super Sabre F-100, wht or gray, .20 engine, 1958-63, EX, ea from $60 to...$80.00

Cox Thimble Drome Champion Racer, red & bl, no engine, 10", EX $125.00

Cox Thimble Drome Prop Rod, yel plastic w/metal chassis, EX, from $85 to $130.00

Cox Thimble Drome TD-1 Airplane, 1950s, aluminum, MIB .$80.00

Cox Thimble Drome TD-3 Airplane, plastic w/aluminum wings, 1950s, MIB...$60.00

Cox UFO Flying Saucer, Wings Series, wht, 1990-91, M.$25.00

Dooling Bros Arrow Racer #61, mk Yellow Jacket Engineering, 19", EX, A $1,750.00

Dooling Bros F Racer, bl cast magnesium body w/orig upper & lower hammertone finish, 1948, 16", EX, A.........$1,100.00

Dooling Bros F Racer #54, mk Sostilo Offy, blk w/red & gold detail, M, D10 ....$2,100.00

Dooling Bros F Racer #1, red with Knoxville Champ logo, 19", EX, A, $1,000.00; Dooling Bros Frog Cabin Streamliner, cast aluminum, Super Cyclone engine, 1939, EX, $3,200.00.

Dooling Bros Mercury Racer #59, aluminum w/some pnt detail, Hornet engine, ca 1940, 18½", VG, A.................$2,300.00

Dooling Bros Racer #13, series II, maroon & yel, Super Cyclone engine, 1940, EX, A...$2,600.00

Dooling Bros Racer #8, Atwood .60 Champion engine, 1939, 19", EX, A $1,800.00

Dooling Bros Tether Racing Boat, red w/stepped hull design, .61 engine, 1955, 35", EX, A...$500.00

Dreyer Special Racer #2, silver w/red seat, 18", NM, D10, from $2,600 to...$2,800.00

Duesenberg Racer #5, orange w/louvered 3-pc hood & belly pan, Hornet power, 1939, 21½", EX, A.......................$2,600.00

England Special Racer #8, gr-pnt aluminum w/leather seats, centrifical clutch, ca 1948, 16", EX, A $825.00

Fairchild 22 Model Airplane, bl w/wht wings, working shock absorbers & landing gear, 31x47", EX, A.................$225.00

Hiller-Comet #5, red, 1942, 19", EX, D10...................$1,800.00

Hiller-Comet Racer #8, Hiller engine #1082, ca 1940, 18", EX, A...$1,000.00

McCoy Invader #6, yel, McCoy .49 engine, 17", EX, A.$900.00

McCoy Invader Pan #3, bl-pnt wood w/Goldie's graphics, .60 Hornet engine, 1954, 17", VG, A $775.00

McCoy Streamliner, gray, never drilled for engine, 17", NM, A...$475.00

McCoy Streamliner, wht w/red trim, never drilled for engine, ca 1952, 17", EX, A..$300.00

Melcraft Racer, wht w/Champion tires, ignition engine, ca 1948, 16", EX, A...$475.00

Ohlsson & Rice Racer #3, cast aluminum pan, .049 engine, 10", VG+, A...$350.00

Pacgo Racer #8, orange plastic w/yel driver, .09 engine, 11", EX, A...$175.00

Phantom Lady Speedboat, wood, Phantom P-30 engine, 21", EX, A...$650.00

Reuhl Racer #39, Bakelite body, grille & seat, .49 McCoy engine, 1940, 17", EX, A..................................$2,200.00

Speed Demon #18, yel-pnt wood, .60 Bunch engine, 1937-38, 20", EX (EX box), A $5,700.00

Speedboat #37, orange-pnt wood, Apex Skylark engine, ca 1939, 37", EX, A...$1,600.00

Speedway Pacemaker #9, differential & factory gas tank, ca 1954, 18", EX, A...$1,900.00

Spit-Craft Speedboat, plastic, Royal Spitfire engine, 21", NMIB, A..$200.00

Spitfire's Royal Skim'r, wood hull, .065 Spitfire engine, 13", EX, A...$150.00

Testors Cosmic Wind, orange, MIB $50.00

Testors Cosmic Wind, Spirit of '76, M.........................$60.00

Testors Sopwith Camel, Fly 'Em series, NM $35.00

Testors Sprite Indy Car, wht, 1966-68, M.....................$75.00

Tether Boat #223, Hornet engine, 1949-50, EX, A $1,100.00

Wen-Mac '57 Chevy Racer, orange plastic w/decals, 12", VG, A..$225.00

Wen-Mac A-24 Army Attack Bomber, 1962-64, EX $45.00

Wen-Mac Albatross, Flying Wings series, red, wht & bl, EX $40.00

Wen-Mac Cutlass, bl, blk & yel, 1958-60, EX $50.00

Wen-Mac Giant P-40 Flying Tiger, wht, 1959-60, EX.....$45.00

Wen-Mac Mustang Fast-Back, bl, 1968, EX $125.00

Wen-Mac P-63 King Cobra, chrome, 1962-64, EX $50.00

Wen-Mac SBD-5 Navy Dive Bomber, 1962-64, EX.........$50.00

Wen-Mac Turbojet, red & cream w/chrome detail, 1958-64, EX $45.00

GI Joe

GI Joe, the most famous action figure of them all, has been made in hundreds of variations since Hasbro introduced him in 1964. The first of these jointed figures was 12" tall; they can be identified today by the mark each carried on his back: GI Joe T.M. (trademark), Copyright 1964. They came with four different hair colors: blond, auburn, black, and brown, each with a scar on his right cheek. They were sold in four basic packages: Action Soldier, Action Sailor, Action Marine, and Action Pilot. A Black figure was also included in the line, and there were representatives of many nations as well — France, Germany, Japan, Russia, etc. These figures did not have scars and are more valuable. Talking GI Joes were issued in 1967 when the only female (the nurse) was introduced. Besides the figures, uniforms, vehicles, guns, and accessories of many varieties were produced. The Adventure Team series, made from 1970 to 1976, included Black Adventurer, Air Adventurer, Talking

Astronaut, Sea Adventurer, Talking Team Commander, Land Adventurer, and several variations. Joe's hard plastic hands were replaced with kung fu grips, so that he could better grasp his weapons. Assorted playsets allowed young imaginations to run wild, and besides the doll-size items, there were wrist-watches, foot lockers, toys, walkie-talkies, etc., made for the kids themselves. Due to increased production costs, the large GI Joe was discontinued in 1976.

In 1982, Hasbro brought out the 'little' 3¾" GI Joe figures, each with its own descriptive name. Of the first series, some characters were produced with either a swivel or straight arm. Vehicles, weapons, and playsets were available, and some characters could only be had by redeeming flag points from the backs of packages. This small version proved to be the most successful action figure line ever made. Loose items are common; collectors value those still mint in the original packages at two to four times higher.

In 1993 Hasbro reintroduced the 12" line while retaining the 3¾" size. The highlights of the comeback are the 30th anniversary collection of six figures which are already selling in the collector's market at well above retail ($29.00); Soldier, $100.00; Sailor, $140.00; Marine, $90.00; Pilot, $140.00; Black Soldier, $250.00; and Green Beret, $285.00.

Production of the 3¾" figures came to an end in December 1994. For more information we recommend *Collectible Male Action Figures* by Paris and Susan Manos (Collector Books); *Encyclopedia to GI Joe* and *The 30th Anniversary Salute to GI Joe* both by Vincent San Telmo; *Official Collector's Guide to Collecting and Completing*, *Official Guide to Completing 3¾" Series* and *Hall of Fame: Vol II*, and *Official Guide to GI Joe: '64–'78*, all by James DeSimone. There is also a section on GI Joe in *Dolls in Uniform*, a publication by Joseph Bourgeois (Collector Books). Note: All items are American issue unless indicated otherwise. (Action Man was made in England by Hasbro circa 1960 into the 1970s.)

Advisor: Cotswold Collectibles (C6).
Other Sources: D4, D8, M15, P3, T2.
See also Games; Lunch Boxes; Windups, Friction, and Other Mechanicals.

Key: A/M — Action Man

12" GI JOE FIGURES AND FIGURE SETS

Action Marine, complete, EX+, H4..............................$125.00
Action Marine, complete, MIB.......................................$325.00
Action Marine, 30th Anniversary, 1994, NRFB..............$90.00
Action Pilot, complete, EX+, H4.................................$125.00
Action Pilot, NM (EX+ box), H4...................................$400.00
Action Pilot, 30th Anniversary, 1994, NRFB, H4.........$140.00
Action Sailor, complete, EX, H4..................................$125.00
Action Sailor, 30th Anniversary, 1994, NRFB, H4.......$140.00
Action Soldier, complete, EX+, H4.............................$100.00
Action Soldier, NM (EX+ box), H4..............................$300.00
Action Soldier, 30th Anniversary, 1994, NRFB, H4.....$100.00
Adventure Team Adventurer (Black), complete, NM (VG box) $325.00
Adventure Team Air Adventurer, complete, NM, H4 ..$100.00

Action Sailor, complete, EX (EX box), $325.00.
(Photo courtesy Cindy Sabulis)

Adventure Team Air Adventurer, orig outfit, VG, H4 ....$50.00
Adventure Team Land Adventurer, complete, NM.......$125.00
Adventure Team Man of Action, complete, NM (EX+ box), H4 ....$200.00
Adventure Team Man of Action, nude, EX, H4..............$65.00
Adventure Team Sea Adventurer, complete, EX+ (EX+ box), H4 ....$250.00
Adventure Team Talking Astronaut, complete, NM (EX box), H4 ....$375.00

Adventure Team Talking Commander, complete, NM (EX box), $275.00.

Adventure Team Talking Man of Action, complete, EX+, H4 ....$100.00
Air Security, complete, rare, NM, H4 ....$1,000.00
Airborne Military Police, Kay Bee Toys, NRFB, H4 ....$75.00
Airborne Military Police (Black), Kay Bee Toys, rare, NRFB, H4..$100.00
Battle of the Bulge, Toys-R-Us, NRFB, H4 ....$65.00
British Commando w/Chevrons, complete, VG $300.00
Combat Soldier, A/M, complete, MIB...........................$100.00
Crash Crew, few pcs missing, EX, H4............................$150.00
Deep Sea Diver, complete, NM, H4 ....$175.00
Duke, Target limited edition, 1991, NRFB, H4 ....$60.00
Fighter Pilot, complete, NM..$550.00
German Soldier, #8100, complete, MIB.....................$1,750.00
German Stormtrooper, complete, VG $350.00
Green Beret, auburn hair, complete, NM, H4 ....$275.00
Home for the Holiday, Wal-Mart, NRFB, H4 ....$50.00
Home for the Holiday (Black), Wal-Mart, NRFB, H4 .....$70.00
Japanese Imperial Soldier, complete, M $625.00
Joseph Colton Arctic Explorer, 30th Anniversary, mail-order, MIP, H4 ....$150.00

LSO, complete, EX, from $200 to $250.00
Man of Action, Kung Fu hands, complete, MIB.............$325.00
Marine, Toys-R-Us, NRFB, H4.....................................$60.00
Marine Demolition, complete, NM, H4 ....$200.00
Marine Jungle Fighter, complete, NM, H4 ....$850.00
Navy Seal, FAO Schwarz, mail-order, rare, NRFB, H4..$150.00
Nurse, MIB (sealed), H4..$5,000.00
Russian Infantry Man, #8102, complete, M (EX box).$2,700.00
Sea Adventurer, hard hands, complete, EX (EX box) $265.00
Ski Patrol, complete, EX, H4 ....$250.00
Space Ranger Captain, A/M, complete, MIB $100.00
Space Ranger Patroller, A/M, complete, MIB.................$90.00
Special Talking GI Joe Adventure Pack, French Resistance Fighter outfit, MIB $1,350.00
Tank Commander, complete, EX, H4............................$450.00
West Point Cadet, complete, EX, H4 ....$285.00

ACCESSORIES FOR 12" GI JOE

Action Flame Thrower, A/M, gr, w/helmet sticker, MOC .$60.00
Action Rescue Raft Backpack, w/instructions, EX, H4 ....$15.00
Action Soldier Camouflage Netting, MOC, H4..............$45.00
Action Underwater Explorer Backpack, w/instructions, EX, H4 ....$20.00
Action Windboat Backpack, w/instructions, EX, H4 ....$35.00
Adventure Team Danger of the Depths, complete, MIB, H4..$300.00
Adventure Team Flying Rescue Action Pack, MIB..........$65.00
Adventure Team Headquarters, complete, MIB, H4......$250.00
Adventure Team Infiltration Equipment, complete, NMIB..$300.00
Adventure Team Raft, yel, EX $12.00
Adventure Team 1970 Space Walk Mystery Set, complete, MIB, H4 ....$375.00
Air Cadet Hat, EX, H4 ....$25.00
Air Force Air Vest, #7809, MOC (sealed)....................$125.00
Air Force Dress Jacket, MOC.......................................$200.00
Air Force Flag, complete, EX, H4..................................$10.00
Annapolis Cadet Hat, EX, H4..$25.00
Annapolis Cadet Jacket, VG, H4...................................$25.00
Army Communications Radio, gr, EX, H4......................$15.00
Army Helmet, EX, H4...$20.00
Army Poncho, gr, EX $20.00
Army Tent, complete, NM, H4.......................................$35.00
Astro Locker, EX, H4 ....$200.00
Australian Hat, EX, H4...$30.00
Australian Jacket, EX, H4...$35.00
Bivouac Machine Gun Set, #7514, MOC......................$60.00
Bivouac Sleeping Bag, #7515, MOC.............................$55.00
British Commando Equipment, #8304, MOC $250.00
Cadet Pants, wht, EX, H4, from $60 to $70.00
Combat Camouflage Netting Set, #7511, MOC..............$25.00
Combat Mess Kit, #7509, complete, MOC......................$70.00
Communications Field Set, #7703, MOC........................$85.00
Convention Outfit, 1990, complete, rare, M, H4...........$200.00
Crash Crew Extension Ladder Holder, EX, H4................$40.00
Crash Crew Set, #7820, complete, MIB........................$260.00
Danger of the Depths Sea Adventurer Equipment, complete, NMIB...$100.00
Deep Sea Diver Gloves, EX, H4, pr.................................$6.00

Land Adventurer, hard hands, complete, EX (EX box), $265.00.

Deep Sea Diver Sledge Hammer, EX, H4 ....$15.00
Deep Sea Diver Weight Belt, EX, from $20 to................$25.00
Demolition Set, complete, M (EX box) $250.00

Fight for Survival, 1969, complete with Polar Explorer figure, NMIB, $450.00. (Photo courtesy Paris and Susan Manos)

Flying Space Adventure Set, complete, NMIB, H4 ....$595.00
Footlocker, gr, w/tray, EX, H4 ....$20.00
French Greatcoat, French Foreign Legion, A/M, MOC ...$30.00
German Field Pack, EX, H4...$25.00
German Stormtrooper Equipment, #8300, complete, MOC.$265.00
Green Beret Bazooka, EX...$30.00
Green Beret Hat, EX+ $45.00
Green Beret M-16 Rifle, w/strap, EX, H4..........................$40.00
Grenade Launcher, w/lugar, silencer & removable stock, A/M,
   MOC..$30.00
Heavy Weapons Vest, few pcs missing, EX+, H4..............$50.00
Hidden Missile Discovery Set, complete, NM, H4.........$100.00
Indian Brave, A/M, complete, MIB....................................$60.00
Indian Chief, A/M, MIB..$60.00
Japanese Backyard Patrol Uniform, MIP, H4....................$50.00
LSO Coveralls, VG..$40.00
M-1 Rifle, wht, w/strap, EX $25.00
M-60 Machine Gun, complete, EX, H4..............................$60.00
M-60 40-Round Ammo Belt, VG+, H4...............................$30.00
Mae West Life Vest, yel cloth, EX $100.00
Marine Communications Radio, EX, H4 ....$20.00
Marine Flame Thrower, MOC $100.00
Marine Helmet, w/strap, EX+..$45.00
Marine Parachute Set, #7705, complete, M (NM box) ..$225.00
Marine Pup Tent, EX...$35.00
Medic Shoulder Bag, EX...$30.00
Military Police Duffle Bag, #7523, MOC..........................$60.00
Military Police Scarf, red, EX, H4.....................................$25.00
Military Police Set, #7521, complete, M (NM box) ...$1,000.00
Mine Detection Set, A/M, complete, MIB $150.00
Mountain & Artic Set, A/M, complete, MIB $55.00
Mysterious Explosion Set, complete, EX, H4..................$100.00
NATO Night Maneuvers Arsenal, A/M, complete, MOC..$70.00
Navy Attack Helmet, EX+, H4..$30.00
Navy Basics, #7628, MOC $100.00
Parachute Pack, bl pack w/red & wht parachute, EX, H4.$50.00

Parachute Regiments, A/M, complete, MIP....................$75.00
Pilot Survival Set, #7801, complete, MIB........................$950.00
Pursuit Craft Pilot, A/M, complete, MIP $100.00
Ropes of Danger Set, EX+...$100.00
Royal Air Force, A/M, complete, M (EX box)....................$70.00
Russian Belt, EX, H4..$30.00
Russian Soldier Equipment, #8302B, MIP $250.00
SAS Secret Mission, A/M, complete, M (EX box) $85.00
Scramble Pilot Air Vest & Accessories, MOC $100.00
Scramble Pilot Parachute Pack, MOC $90.00
Scuba Bottom, #7604, MOC...$125.00
Scuba Wrist Depth Gauge, decal on face, EX, H4 ....$15.00
Sea Rescue Set, #7601, complete, MIB.............................$650.00
Search for the Abominable Snowman, MIB (sealed) $400.00
Secret Agent Trench Coat, w/disguise mask & bullet-proof vest,
   EX+, H4..$25.00
Secret Mountain Outpost, complete, MIB........................$200.00
Secret of Mummy's Tomb, complete, MIB $250.00
Shark's Surprise w/Sea Adventurer, MIB.........................$275.00
Shore Patrol Billy Club, wht, EX, H4................................$10.00
Shore Patrol Dress Pants, #7641, MOC $65.00
Shore Patrol Helmet, w/strap, EX, H4...............................$25.00
Shore Patrol Jumper, VG..$25.00
Ski Patrol Bear Helmet, w/strap, NM, H4.........................$30.00
Ski Patrol Boots, EX, H4...$15.00
Ski Patrol Gloves, EX, H4...$15.00
Ski Patrol Goggles, w/strap, EX, H4..................................$10.00
Ski Patrol Ice Pick & Rope, VG, H4..................................$15.00
Ski Patrol Jacket & Pants, EX, H4 ....$40.00
Ski Patrol Skis, w/bindings, EX, H4..................................$20.00
Space Booties, silver, EX, H4 ....$15.00
Space Capsule Floatation Collar, Sears, complete, NM, H4 ..$70.00
Space Gloves, silver, EX, H4..$10.00
Space Rifle, A/M, MIP $10.00
Super Joe Helipak, 1977, MIB...$60.00
Super Joe Sonic Scanner, #7538, complete, NMIB, J2.....$50.00
US Air Force Dress Uniform, #7803, complete, M (EX
   box)..$1,450.00
USN Life Ring, w/rope, EX+, H4.......................................$25.00
White Tiger Set, complete, EX $90.00
Workshop Accessories, A/M, M (VG card).......................$20.00
Wrist Camera, EX, H4...$10.00

VEHICLES FOR 12" GI JOE

Action Pack Turbo Copter, MIB (sealed), H4..................$50.00
Action Pilot Space Capsule, complete, MIB $250.00
Adventure Team Avenger Pursuit Craft, complete, MIB, H4.$175.00
Adventure Team Helicopter, yel, VG................................$70.00
Adventure Team Sandstorm Jeep, gr, EX (EX box) $275.00
Adventure Team Skyhawk, MIB (sealed)........................$150.00
Amphibious Duck, complete, EX (EX box), H4.............$750.00
British Armored Car, Irwin, EX, H4 ....$275.00
Crash Crew Truck, VG (VG box), H4...........................$1,300.00
Fire Engine, A/M, MIP $75.00
Iron Knight Tank, #9031, EX (EX box)...........................$250.00
Jet Helicopter, complete, EX (EX box), H4....................$400.00
Motorcycle w/Sidecar, complete, MIB $425.00

Official Jeep Combat Set, complete, EX (EX box) $350.00
Sea Sled & Frogman, EX (EX box), H4 ....$295.00
Sea Wolf Submarine, EX (VG box) $265.00
Space Capsule, Sears Exclusive, MIB $400.00
Team Vehicle, yel ATV, VG (G box) $85.00

1964 – 1969 PAPERWORK

Comic Book from Talking Dolls, EX, H4 ....$30.00
Equipment List, Army, Marine, Pilot or Sailor, fold-out, EX, H4,
 ea $4.00
Instructions, Adventure Team Assembly, EX, H4 ....$5.00
Instructions, Adventures of Rescue Sea Diver, foreign, EX,
 H4 ....$15.00
Instructions, Adventures of the Shark Surprise, foreign, EX,
 H4 ....$15.00
Instructions, Astronaut, EX, H4 ....$10.00
Instructions, Dangers of the Depths, EX $10.00
Instructions, Deep Sea Diver, foreign, EX, H4 ....$15.00
Instructions, Fantastic Freefall, NM, H4 ....$10.00
Instructions, Flying Rescue Action Pack, EX, H4 ....$5.00
Instructions, Sea Sled, VG, H4 ....$12.00
Instructions, Sea Wolf Sub, EX, H4 ....$10.00
Instructions, Sky Dive to Danger, EX $10.00
Instructions, Underwater Explorer Action Pack, EX, H4 ...$5.00
Instructions, White Tiger Hunt, EX, H4 ....$8.00
Instructions, 81-MM Mortar, foreign, EX, H4 ....$10.00
Manual, Action Pilot, narrow, EX $18.00
Manual, Action Pilot, wide, EX $10.00
Manual, Action Soldier, narrow, VG $12.00
Manual, Air Force, foreign, lg, EX, H4 ....$4.00
Manual, Air Force, foreign, sm, VG, H4 ....$4.00
Manual, Air Force, lg, EX, H4 ....$6.00
Manual, Air Force, sm, EX, H4 ....$6.00
Manual, Army, lg, EX, H4 ....$3.00
Manual, Army, sm, EX, H4 ....$4.00
Manual, Counter Intelligence, foreign, EX+, H4 ....$12.00
Manual, Marine, narrow, VG $14.00
Manual, Marine, wide, EX $8.00
Manual, Official Gear & Equipment, EX, H4 ....$15.00
Manual, Official Gear & Equipment, foreign, EX, H4 ....$5.00

3¾" GI JOE FIGURES

Ace, 1983, MIP $25.00
Airborne, 1983, complete, EX, H4 ....$16.00
Airborne, 1983, MIP $50.00
Annihilator, 1989, MOC, H4 ....$15.00
Annihilator, 1989, w/accessories, EX $10.00
Astro Viper, 1988, MIP $12.00
Astro Viper, 1988, w/accessories & ID card, EX, H4 ....$6.00
Barbecue, 1983-85, MOC $35.00
Barbecue Eco Warrior, 1991, MOC, H4 ....$15.00
Baroness, w/accessories, EX, H4 ....$30.00
Bazooka, 1983-85, MOC, H4 ....$35.00
Beachhead, 1983-85, MIP, H4 ....$30.00
Big Boa, 1986, w/accessories, EX, H4 ....$8.00
Big Boa, 1987, MIP $25.00

Blizzard, 1988, w/accessories, EX $8.00
Budo, 1988, w/accessories & ID card, EX $10.00
Buzzer, 1985, MIP $35.00
Captain Grid Iron, 1990, MIP $12.00
Charbroil, 1988, red eyes, MOC $15.00
Chuckles, 1986, w/accessories, EX $8.00
Chuckles, 1987, MOC $26.00
Clutch, 1988, MOC $18.00
Cobra Commander, 1983, MIP $125.00
Cobra HISS Driver, 1983, w/accessories & ID card, EX, H4 ..$12.00
Cobra Soldier, 1983, MIP $60.00
Cobra Stinger Driver, 1982, MIP (factory bag), H4 ....$15.00
Countdown, 1989, MOC $18.00
Cover Girl, 1983, MIP $45.00
Crazylegs, 1986, MOC, H4 ....$15.00
Crimson Master, 1987, MOC $22.00
Crystal Ball, 1986, MOC, H4 ....$15.00
Crystal Ball, 1986, w/accessories & ID card, EX, H4 ....$8.00
Cutter, 1984, MOC $15.00

Darklon, 1989,
EX, $5.00.

Dee-Jay, 1989, MOC $14.00
Deep Six, 1989, MOC $14.00
Deep Six w/Finback, 1992, MOC $15.00
Dial Tone, 1986, w/accessories, NM $10.00
Doc, 1983, w/accessories, EX $8.00
Dojo, 1992, MOC $10.00
Dr Mindbender, 1983-85, MOC, H4 ....$25.00
Dr Mindbender, 1986, w/accessories, EX $10.00
Dreadnok, 1985, MOC $35.00
Duke, 1985, MOC $100.00
Eels, 1985, MOC from $50 to $55.00
Eels, 1992, MOC $10.00
Firefly, 1984, w/accessories, EX, H4 ....$25.00
Flash, 1982, w/accessories, EX, H4 ....$20.00
Flint, 1985, MOC $30.00

Footloose, 1985, MOC..$30.00

Frag Viper, 1989, MOC......................................$15.00

Fridge, 1986, MIP (factory bag)........................$30.00

Fridge, 1987, w/accessories & ID card, EX, H4...............$10.00

Gnawgahyde, 1989, MOC..................................$20.00

Green Beret, limited edition made for NY Convention, 5,000 made, MIB, H4........................$50.00

Grunt, 1982-83, w/accessories, EX, H4...............$20.00

Gyro Viper, 1987, w/accessories, EX, H4...............$10.00

Hardball, 1988, MOC..$18.00

Hardtop, 1987, w/accessories, EX......................$32.00

Hawk, 1987, w/accessories, EX.........................$15.00

Iceberg, 1983-85, MOC.....................................$32.00

Iceberg, 1986, MOC...$32.00

Interrogator, 1991, w/accessories, EX $6.00

Iron Grenadier, 1988, MOC...............................$18.00

Jinx, 1987, w/accessories, NM..........................$10.00

Lady Jaye, 1985, MOC......................................$75.00

Lamphrey, 1985, w/accessories, EX $10.00

Leatherneck, 1983-85, MOC, H4.......................$25.00

Lifeline, 1985, w/accessories, EX, H4................$10.00

Lifeline, 1986, MOC (Chinese) $18.00

Low-Light, 1983-85, MOC, H4..........................$25.00

Mainframe, 1986, MOC.....................................$32.00

Mainframe, 1986, w/accessories, EX, H4...........$10.00

Major Bludd, 1983, w/accessories & ID card, EX...........$15.00

Mega Marine Blast-Off, 1993, MOC...................$12.00

Mega Marine Mega-Viper, 1993, MOC...............$12.00

Mega Marine Mirage, 1993, MOC.......................$12.00

Mega Monster Bio-Viper, 1993, MOC................$15.00

Mercer, 1987, w/accessories, EX $8.00

Metal-Hand, 1990, MOC....................................$15.00

Monkey Wrench, 1983-85, MOC, H4.................$20.00

Motor Viper, 1986, w/accessories, EX, H4...........$8.00

Mutt & Junkyard, 1984, MOC............................$50.00

Night Force Lt Falcon, 1988, w/accessories, EX.............$15.00

Night Force Outback, 1988, w/accessories, EX $15.00

Ninja Force Night Creeper, 1993, MOC..............$8.00

Ninja Force Zartan, 1993, MOC.........................$12.00

Outback, 1987, MOC..$18.00

Ozone, 1993, MOC...$5.00

Payload, 1987, w/accessories, EX $32.00

Psyche-Out, 1987, MOC....................................$22.00

Quick Kick, 1985, MOC....................................$35.00

Ranger-Viper, 1990, MOC.................................$12.00

Raptor, 1987, MOC..$20.00

Recoil, 1989, MOC...$15.00

Recondo, 1984, w/accessories & ID card, EX, H4............$12.00

Recondo, 1989, MOC..$40.00

Red Star Oktober Guard, MOC..........................$15.00

Repeater, 1988, w/accessories, EX......................$10.00

Rip Cord, 1984, MOC..$45.00

Ripper, 1985, w/accessories, EX, H4..................$10.00

Road Pig, 1988, MOC.......................................$20.00

Road Pig, 1988, w/accessories & ID card, EX, H4............$10.00

Roadblock, 1986, MOC......................................$36.00

Rock 'N Roll, 1983, w/accessories, EX $18.00

Scarlett, 1982, w/accessories, EX.......................$32.00

Sci-Fi, 1986, w/accessories, EX $10.00

Sci-Fi, 1991, MOC..$15.00

Scrap Iron, 1984, w/accessories, EX...................$15.00

Sergeant Savage, 1995, MOC............................$6.00

Sergeant Slaughter, 1985 mail-in, w/accessories & ID card, EX........................$25.00

Shipwreck w/Parrot, 1985, MOC $70.00

Shockwave, 1988, MOC....................................$22.00

Short Fuse, 1982, w/accessories, EX, H4............$20.00

Skidmark, 1988, w/accessories & ID card, EX...................$8.00

Slaughter's Renegades Mercer/Taurus/Red Dog, 1987, MOC...$30.00

Slip Stream, 1986, EX, $8.00.

Slip Stream, 1987, w/accessories & ID card, EX $10.00

Snow Job, 1984, w/accessories, EX $15.00

Snow Serpent, 1985, MOC $50.00

Sonic Fighter Dial-Tone, 1990, MOC $18.00

Stalker, 1983, MOC..$65.00

Stalker, 1983, MOC (Japanese) $20.00

Steeler, 1983, MOC...$35.00

Strato Viper, 1982, MOC, H4............................$10.00

Strato Viper, 1986, MIP (factory bag), H4..........$10.00

Street Fighter Blanka, 1993, MOC.....................$10.00

Street Fighter Guile, 1993, MOC.......................$10.00

Street Fighter Ryu, 1993, MOC $10.00

Stretcher, 1990, MOC.......................................$15.00

Sub-Zero, 1990, MOC.......................................$15.00

Super Trooper, 1988 mail-in, w/accessories, EX $22.00

T'Jbang, 1992, MOC...$10.00

Talking Battle Cobra Commander, 1991, MOC $12.00

TARGAT, 1989, MOC..$18.00

Techno-Viper, 1987, w/accessories, EX...............$14.00

Tele-Viper, 1985, MOC.....................................$42.00

Tele-Viper, 1989, MOC.....................................$15.00

Thrasher, 1986, w/accessories, EX $8.00

Tiger Force Roadblock, 1988, w/accessories, EX...............$10.00

Tiger Force Tiger Shark, 1988, MIB................$18.00
Tiger Force Tripwire, 1988, w/accessories, EX.................$10.00
Topside, 1990, MOC, H4 ....$15.00
Torch, 1985, MOC $35.00
Torpedo, 1983, MOC $60.00
Toxo Viper, 1988, MOC $15.00
Toxo-Zombie Eco Warrior, 1991, MOC, H4 ....$15.00
Tunnel Rat, 1987, MOC $25.00
Vapor, 1990, MOC $15.00
Wet Suit, 1986, MOC $45.00
Wild Bill, 1983, w/accessories & ID card, EX, H4 ....$12.00
Wild Bill, 1992, MOC $10.00
Wild Weasel, 1984, w/accessories, EX.................$15.00
Zandar, 1983-85, MOC, H4 ....$25.00
Zandar, 1986, w/accessories, EX..........................$8.00
Zartan, 1984, w/accessories, EX, H4 ....$35.00
Zartan w/Swamp Skier, 1984, MIB $100.00

ACCESSORIES FOR 3¾" GI JOE

Arctic Blast, 1988, complete, MIB, $30.00.
(Photo courtesy Martin and Carolyn Berens)

Armored Missile Vehicle Wolverine w/Covergirl, 1983, MIB.$130.00
Artic Blast, 1988, EX, H4 ....$12.00
Attack Vehicle Vamp w/Clutch, 1982, EX, H4................$40.00
Battle Copter, w/Ace figure, MIB, H4 ....$20.00
Battle Force 2000 Vindicator (Hovercraft), 1987, MIB, H4 ..$25.00
Battle Gear Accessory Pack #1, 1983, MIP.....................$16.00
Battlefield Robot Devastator, 1988, NRFB.............$30.00
Battlefield Robot Radar Rat, 1988, NRFB, H4 ....$30.00
Battlefield Robot Tri-Blaster, 1988, NRFB, H4..............$30.00
Bomb Disposal Unit, 1985, MIP..........................$20.00
Cobra Battle Copter, w/Heli-Viper figure, MIB, H4.........$25.00
Cobra Battle Copter, w/Interrogator figure, MIB, H4.......$25.00
Cobra Condor Z25 Plane, 1988, MIB, H4 ....$80.00
Cobra Emperor w/Air Chariot, 1986, NRFB..............$60.00
Cobra HISS, 1983, w/driver & ID card, EX, H4 ....$35.00
Cobra Overlord's Dictator Vehicle, w/Overlord figure, MIB,
    H4..$25.00

Cobra Wolf w/Ice Viper, 1985, NM $20.00
Crusader Space Shuttle, 1988, NRFB, H4 ....$175.00
Dragonfly Helicopter w/Wild Bill, 1983, complete, EX, H4 .$40.00
Falcon Glider w/Grunt, complete, EX....................$100.00
Forward Observer Unit, 1985, w/accessories, EX $8.00
Hovercraft, 1984 mail-in, MIP.............................$40.00
Jet Pack JUMP & Platform, 1982, MIP (Canadian).........$50.00
LCV Recon Sled, 1983, complete, EX, H4 ....$5.00
Machine Gun, 1983, EX, H4 ....$5.00
Mauler MBT Tank, 1985, NRFB, H4 ....$80.00
Missile Launcher, 1983, EX, H4 ....$5.00
Mobile Missile System, complete, EX $45.00
Motorized Battle Wagon, 1991, MIP....................$35.00
Mountain Climber Motorized Action Pack, 1986, EX, H4.$6.00
P-40 Warhawk w/Pilot Savage, 1995, MIP $35.00
Phantom X-19 Stealth Fighter, 1988, MIB $70.00
Polar Battle Gear, 1983 mail-in, MIP...................$10.00
Q Force Battle Gear, Action Force, MIP................$5.00
SAS Parachutist Attack, Action Force, MIP $35.00
Shark w/Deep Six, complete, EX, H4 ....$25.00
Snow Cat w/Frostbite, 1984, complete, EX, H4.............$25.00
Transportable Tactical Battle Platform, 1985, complete,
    NM...$30.00
Whirlwind Twin Battle Gun, 1983, EX, H4 ....$20.00

MISCELLANEOUS

Adventure Team Colorforms, complete, MIB $75.00
Bop Bag, MIB, minimum value $60.00
Card Game, Whitman, 1965, complete, NM (NM plastic box),
    J5 ....$25.00

Coloring Book, Battle Stations Torpedo, EX, $25.00.

Dog Tag w/Chain, NM, H4 ....$30.00
Magic Slate, Whitman, 1966, cb w/erasable lift-up film sheet,
    EX...$20.00
Mobile Field Walkie Talkie Set, MIB, B5 ....$50.00
Official Fan Club Kit, 1964, complete, MIP, H4 ....$125.00
Official Inter-Com Telephone Set, Hasbro, 1982, NRFB, H4..$30.00

Official Space Capsule & Astronaut Set, made for 1995 convention, w/figure, CD & raft, MIB, H4..........................$175.00

Pencil & Paint Set, 1960s, MIB (sealed), J2 ....$150.00

Poncho & Hood, MIB, minimum value $30.00

Record & Book Set, Secret Spy Mission to Spy Island, EX..$25.00

Rings, Artic Force, Shuttle Crew, Artillery or Tank Corps, EX, H4, ea $2.00

Rub-Ons, Hasbro, 1960s, complete, MIB, J5....................$45.00

Guns

Until WWI, most cap guns were made of cast iron. Some from the 1930s were nickel plated, had fancy plastic grips, and were designed with realistic details like revolving cylinders. After the war, a trend developed toward using cast metal, a less expensive material. These diecast guns were made for two decades, during which time the TV western was born. Kids were offered a dazzling array of weapons, endorsed by stars like the Lone Ranger, Gene, Roy, and Hoppy. Sales of space guns, made popular by Flash Gordon and Tom Corbett, kept pace with the robots coming in from Japan. Some of these early tin lithographed guns were fantastic futuristic styles that spat out rays of sparks when you pulled the trigger. But gradually the space race lost its fervor, westerns were phased out, and guns began to be looked upon with disfavor by the public in general and parents in particular. Since guns were meant to see a lot of action, most will show wear. Learn to be realistic when you assess condition; it's critical when evaluating the value of a gun.

Advisor: Bill Hamburg (H1).

Other Sources: C10, I2, H7, K4, M16.

Alps Cosmic Ray Gun, tin w/attached siren, 5", NM (EX box), A..$125.00

Arliss X-100 Space Gun, 1950, plastic, complete w/darts & powder, 4", EX (EX card), A $50.00

AVC Triple Colt Zumbador Cap Pistol, 1970, diecast w/blk-pnt finish, wht plastic grips, 9", NM (NM box), P4.........$75.00

BCM Space Outlaw Cap Firing Ray Gun, 1969, diecast w/silver finish, red plastic windows, 10", NM, P4 ....$300.00

Buddy L M-99 Paper Cracker Rifle, 1947-49, plastic & aluminum w/purple swirl plastic stock, 26", EX, P4......$125.00

Cossman Spud Gun, 1960, diecast w/silver finish, fires potato plugs, 6", EX..$35.00

Daisy BB Target Pistol, blk-pnt pressed steel w/brn grips, 10", NM (VG box), A..$85.00

Daisy Model 76 Flintlock Rifle, 1970s, brn plastic stock w/gold trim, blk metal barrel, 37", NM, P4............................$50.00

Daisy Rocket Dart Pistol, pressed steel, 8", complete w/darts & target, scarce, NM (NM box), A..............................$200.00

Daisy Targeteer, 1955, blk-pnt pressed steel, 10", NM (G box), A..$125.00

Daisy Zooka Pop Pistol, 1950, red, yel-& bl-pnt pressed steel, 7½", VG, P4 ....$135.00

Dent Mohican Cap Gun, 1930, CI, single shot, 6¼", EX..$100.00

Edison Giocattoli UZ1 Special, 1983, blk plastic w/brn grips, complete w/bullets, NM (NM box)..............................$35.00

Elvin Space Universe Sparking Ray Gun, 1960s, litho tin, 4", NM..$35.00

Empire Plastics Guided Missiles & Launcher, 1950s, 7", NM (NM box) $150.00

Esquire Hide-Away Derringer, 1960, diecast, 3½", EX, P4 ..$30.00

Esquire Lugar Cap Pistol, 1960, diecast w/gold finish, NM, P4..$50.00

Flyrite Products Atom Bubble & Water Gun, 1949, cast aluminum w/red-pnt finish, 7", NM (G box) $200.00

Futuristic Products Strato Gun, 1950s, diecast w/chrome finish, red trim, 9", NM $250.00

Haji Atomic Sparking Ray Gun, 1969, litho tin w/plastic muzzle, 9", NM, P4..$100.00

Hubley Army .45 Cap Pistol, 1950s, diecast w/NP finish, wht plastic grips, 6½", EX, P4....................................$85.00

Hubley Atomic Disintegrator Cap Pistol No 270, 1954, diecast w/zinc finish, red plastic grips, 8", VG, P4 ....$300.00

Hubley Atomic Disintegrator Cap Pistol No 270, 1954, diecast with zinc finish, red plastic grips, 8", NM (VG box), $600.00.

Hubley Colt .38 Gun & Holster, 1958, complete w/2 pistols & brn leather holster mk Colt .38, EX (G box)..........$325.00

Hubley Colt .45 Cap Pistol & Holster, 1958, diecast w/NP finish, wht plastic grips, brn leather holster, NM.........$250.00

Hubley Cowboy Cap Pistol No 275, 1950s, diecast w/NP finish, wht plastic grips w/blk steer, 12", VG, P4................$135.00

Hubley Cowboy Dummy Cap Pistol, 1940, CI w/NP finish, wht plastic grips, 8", NM, P4....................................$175.00

Hubley Cowboy Repeating Cap Pistol, diecast w/steer on wht plastic grips, 12", NM (EX box), A $200.00

Hubley Deputy Cap Pistol, 1957, diecast w/silver finish, 11", VG $75.00

Hubley Electra-Matic .50 Pistol, 1960, bl plastic w/brn grips, battery-op, 7", NM (NM box), P4 ....$150.00

Hubley Flintlock Pistol No 280, 1954, diecast w/NP finish, brn swirl plastic stock, 9", M.....................................$50.00

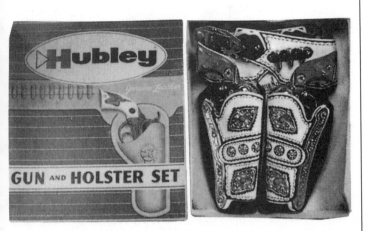

Hubley Gun and Holster Set, diecast pistols with turquoise grips, leather holster with studs and jewels, VG (VG box), A, $175.00.

Hubley Miniature Frontier Colt Cap Pistol No 238, 1960, diecast w/NP finish, w/6 plastic bullets, 4", NM (NM box), P4 ....$65.00
Hubley Model 1860 .44 Cap Pistol, 1959, diecast w/NP finish, wht plastic grips, 13", EX, P4 ....$225.00
Hubley Panther Pistol Derringer & Wrist Holster, 1960, diecast w/NP finish, wht plastic panther grips, 4", NMIB...$150.00
Hubley Pioneer Cap Pistol, 1950s, diecast w/NP finish, translucent brn plastic grips, EX.................................$150.00
Hubley Remington .36 Cap Pistol, 1950s, diecast, 8", NM, P4 ....$125.00
Hubley Ric-O-Shay .45 Cap Pistol, 1959, diecast w/NP finish, blk plastic grips, 13", EX, P4 ....$175.00
Hubley Rodeo Dummy Cap Pistol, 1950s, diecast w/NP finish, wht plastic long horn grips, 8", NM, P4.....................$50.00
Hubley Scout Rifle No 202, 1958, diecast w/NP finish, blk-pnt barrel, brn plastic stocks, 36", EX, P4 ....$125.00

Hubley Secret Rifle Cap Gun, 1960, diecast, steel & plastic, EX, P4 ....$100.00
Hubley Sniper Cap Pistol, 1965, blk plastic w/diecast works, 22", NM..$75.00
Hubley Texan .38 Cap Pistol, 1958, diecast w/NP finish, turq plastic longhorn grips, 10½", EX.............................$150.00
Hubley Texan Cap Pistol, 1940, CI w/NP finish, rearing horse logo, wht plastic steer grips, 9", VG, P4..................$175.00
Hubley Texan Jr Cap Pistol, diecast w/gold-plated finish, blk plastic grips w/red star, 9", MIB..............................$175.00
Hubley Texan Jr Cap Pistol, 1957, diecast w/NP finish, wht plastic grips w/blk steer heads, 9½", EX, P4.............$75.00
Hubley Western Cap Pistol, 1955, diecast w/NP finish, purple swirl plastic longhorn grips, 9", M, P4....................$85.00
Hubley 101 Ranch Cap Gun, 1930, CI, 11½", VG........$245.00
Ideal Pirate Pistol, 1950s, bl & red plastic, friction, 9", EX, P4 .$50.00
Irwin 6-Shooter Cowboy Water Pistol, plastic, MIB $65.00
Ives Chinese Must Go, CI, 1880, 4¾", VG $400.00
Ives Devil's Head Bomb, CI, 1880, 2⅛", EX...............$275.00
Ives Dog Head Bomb, CI, 1880, 2⅛", EX $250.00
Japan Astro Ray Gun, red plastic w/emb image of Saturn, friction, 8½", MIB, A...$100.00
Jyesa Rayo Laser Rifle, 1970s, purple, red & blk plastic w/vibrator & noisemaker action, 21", NMIB, P4..................$50.00
Kenton Lawmaker Cap Pistol, 1941, CI w/silver-pnt finish, wht plastic grips, EX, P4 ....$165.00
Kenton Texas Repeating Cap Pistol, gr-pnt CI w/NP trigger, cylinder & hammer, 5¾", NM (EX box), A...........$250.00
Kilgore American Cap Gun, 1940, CI, revolving cylinder, 9⅜", EX $450.00
Kilgore Big Horn Cap Pistol, 1950s, diecast w/silver finish, 7", NMIB, P4..$100.00
Kilgore Border Patrol Cap Gun, 1935, CI, 4½", VG $85.00
Kilgore Dude Derringer, 1974, diecast w/silver finish, heavy scroll work, blk plastic grips, 4", MOC, P4 ....$25.00
Kilgore Frontier Six-Shooter Cap Pistol, 1960, diecast w/NP finish, blk plastic stag grips, 8½", MOC, P4.................$135.00
Kilgore Mountie Cap Pistol, 1950, diecast w/wht plastic grips, 6", NM (NM box), A $45.00
Kilgore Police Chief Cap Pistol, 1938, CI w/NP finish, 5", EX, P4 ....$75.00
Kilgore Presto Cap Gun, 1940, CI, automatic, 5⅛", VG..$65.00
Kilgore Private Eye Cap Pistol, 1950s, diecast w/silver finish, lift-up cap door, 6½", NMIB, P4 ....$35.00
Kilgore Ra-Ta-Ta-Tat Machine Gun, CI, 5½", NM (EX box), A $350.00
Kilgore Ranger Cap Pistol, 1940, CI w/NP finish, heavy scroll work, red & brn plastic grips, 8½", EX, P4 ....$300.00
Kilgore Trooper Safety Pistol, 1925, CI w/wht enamel finish on grips, 10½", EX, A...$125.00
Knickerbocker 4-Barrel Space Dart Gun, 1960, gray & blk plastic, w/4 rubber-tipped darts, 10", NM, P4 ....$75.00
Langston Super Nu-Matic Jr, 1950, diecast w/red-pnt finish, shoots rolls of paper, EX, P4 ....$55.00
Leslie-Henry Marshal Cap Pistol, 1950s, diecast w/NP finish, wht plastic grips w/blk shamrock, 10", EX, P4.........$125.00
Leslie-Henry Texas Cap Pistol, 1950s, diecast w/NP finish, wht plastic horse head grips, 9", EX, P4 ....$100.00

Leslie-Henry Texas Gold Cap Pistol, 1950s, diecast w/gold finish, blk plastic horse head grips, 9", NM, P4............$135.00

Lone Star Derringer Dueling Set, diecast w/blk-pnt finish, red plastic grips, 3", MIB, P4 ....$65.00

Lone Star Peacemaker 100 Shot Repeater Cap Gun, 1960s, diecast w/silver finish, brn plastic grips, 7", MIB, J5 ..$65.00

Lone Star 9mm Luger Cap Pistol, 1960s, diecast w/blk-pnt finish, brn plastic grips, 8", NM, P4........................$50.00

Long Island Diecasting Inc Texas Cap Pistol, 1960, diecast w/NP finish, wht plastic steer grips, 11", M $150.00

Maco .45 Caliber Automatic Pistol, 1950s, plastic, complete w/target, screwdriver & instructions, 8½", MIB, P4 ..$100.00

Maco 6 in 1 Invader Combination Gun, 1955, plastic tommy style, 28½", rare, NM (NM box) $200.00

Marksman Air Pistol, diecast w/blk-pnt finish, 9", EX (EX box), P4..$50.00

Marubishi Space Gun, 1960s, litho tin w/plastic barrels, friction, 8", EX, P4..$100.00

Marx Blue & Gray Shell Shooting Civil War Cavalry Pistol, 1960-61, bl plastic w/brn grips, 10", VG, P4.............$50.00

Marx Copter Squad Rifle, plastic w/belt feed bullets, removable scope, 27", NM, A $75.00

Marx Siren Signal Pistol, 1950, yel plastic w/siren sound & built-in whistle, 7", NM (NM box), P4.....................$75.00

Marx Siren Sparkling Celebration Pistol, 1940s, red-pnt pressed steel, friction, 7", G, P4 ....$200.00

Marx Space Patrol Atomic Pistol, 1950, plastic, fires w/lights & sound, 8", M (EX box), A.................................$300.00

Marx Sparking Burp Gun, 1950s, 24", EX.......................$85.00

Marx Stag Special Clicker Gun, 1950s, wht plastic w/scroll design, 7", NM, P4 ....$50.00

Marx Thunderguns Rifle, Pistol & Holster Set, 1960, blk vinyl holster, pistol: 12½", rifle: 36", NMIB.....................$350.00

Marx US Army Automatic Rifle, 1960s, plastic BAR-type w/removable bipod, battery-op, 32½", NM, P4 ....$85.00

Mattel Colt Six-Shooter Shootin' Shell Rifle, 1960, plastic w/diecast works, 31", MIB $250.00

Mattel Fanner-50 Cap Pistol, 1965, diecast w/silver finish, plastic stag grips, 11", EX, P4.....................................$125.00

Mattel Fanner-50 Cap Pistol No 543, 1957, first version, diecast w/silver finish, wht plastic grips, MIB $250.00

Mattel Official Winchester Saddle Gun, 1960, plastic & metal, complete, 33", NM (NM box) $250.00

Mattel Rango Fanner-50 Double Holster Set, 1975, 2 diecast guns w/silver finish, blk vinyl holster, 11", MIB, P4 .$225.00

Mattel Shootin' Shell Buffalo Hunter Holster Set, 1960, 9", complete w/6 cartridges, EX $250.00

Mattel Shootin' Shell Fanner Cap Pistol, 1959, diecast w/chrome finish, plastic stag grips, 9", MIB $200.00

Mattel Shootin' Shell Frontier Double Holster Set, 1958, diecast w/chrome finish, brn leather holster, EX $285.00

Mattel Shootin' Shell Frontier Single Holster Set, 1959, 9", complete w/6 2-pc bullets, EX (EX box) $225.00

Mattel Shootin' Shell Snub-Nose .38 Cap Pistol, 1959, diecast w/chrome finish, brn plastic grips, 7", VG, P4 ....$85.00

Mattel Thunder-Burp Machine Gun, 1957, blk plastic, EX, P4...$60.00

Mattel Tommy-Burst Detective Set, 1961, diecast & plastic, complete, EX (EX box) $225.00

Mattel Tommy-Burst Machine Gun, 1963, plastic w/diecast works, camouflage finish, canvas strap, 25", EX, P4...$185.00

McKinnon Gun & Holster Set, girl's, diecast w/wht plastic grips, fancy leather holster, MIB (sealed), A.....................$100.00

Mercury Toy Mfg Planet Clicker Bubble Gun, 1950s, yel plastic w/red trim, 8½", NM (VG box), P4.......................$100.00

Merit Space Pilot Super-Sonic Gun, 1960s, plastic, battery-op, G, P4...$135.00

Mordt Cap Pistol, 1930, CI w/bl-blk lacquered finish, wht celluloid grips, EX...$150.00

National Metal Co Plainsman Cap Gun, diecast w/scroll design on plastic grips, 10½", EX, A.............................$100.00

Nichols Dyna-Mite Derringer, 1950s, diecast w/NP finish, wht plastic grips, 3", MIB, P4 ....$55.00

Nichols Hide-A-Mite Derringer, complete, MOC $50.00

Nichols Mustang 500 Cap Gun, CI w/gold trigger & hammer, MIB..$300.00

Nichols Pasadena Stallion .38 Cap Pistol, 1951, diecast w/NP finish, blk plastic grips, 9½", EX, P4 ....$100.00

Mattel Fanner-50 Deputy Cap Gun, 1957, diecast with plastic grip, leather holster, 11", NM (NM box), A, $300.00; Mattel Fanner-50 Swivelshot Trick Holster Set, 1958, diecast with plastic grip, brn leather holster, MIB, A, $250.00.

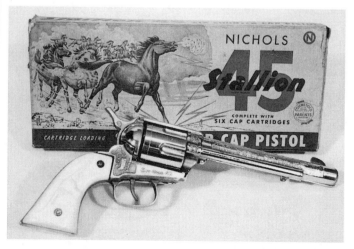

Nichols Stallion .45 Cap Pistol, diecast with white plastic grip, MIB, $450.00. (Photo courtesy John Turney)

Nichols Spitfire Saddle Rifle, 1950s, diecast w/NP finish, 9", MIB, P4 ....$65.00

Nichols Stallion .38 Six-Shooter Cap Pistol, 1955, diecast w/NP finish, wht plastic grips, 9½", MIB $150.00

Nichols Stallion .45 Cap Pistol, 1950, diecast w/NP finish, wht plastic grips w/rearing horse & red jewels, 12", EX ..$225.00

Nichols Stallion .45 Cap Pistol, 1955, diecast w/NP finish, blk plastic stag grips, 12", NM (NM box) $350.00

Nichols Stallion 300 Saddle Rifle, 1958, diecast w/chrome finish, deer & cowboy on fr, blk plastic stock, 27", NMIB, P4 ....$400.00

Nu-Age Products Smoke Ring Gun, 1950s, plastic & metal, 9½", G $175.00

Ohio Art Astro Ray Signal-Dart Gun & Target, 1960s, litho tin & plastic, battery-op, gun: 10", target: 13" dia, EX, P4 ....$100.00

Park Plastics Dee Gee Water Gun, 1950s, blk plastic w/2 brass nozzles, 3", NM, P4 ....$20.00

Park Plastics Sky Lab Manned Spacecraft w/Launcher, 1970s, bl plastic, fires 3" saucers, 5½", MIB, P4 ....$50.00

Park Plastics Squirt Ray Automatic Repeater Water Gun, 1950s, translucent yel plastic w/brass nozzle, NM (NM box), P4 ....$100.00

Pery Super Nova Space Gun, 1980s, wht plastic w/red trim, friction, 17½", MOC, P4 ....$40.00

Plas-Trix Space Water Ray Gun, 1960, translucent orange plastic w/red trigger, 5", EX, P4 ....$45.00

Randall Space Pilot Super-Sonic Gun, 1953, 9", EX $165.00

Ranger Steel Clicka Bubble Shooter, 1950s, bl plastic w/red & yel trim, 8", NM (VG box), P4 ....$100.00

Ranger Steel Cosmic Ray Gun, 1955, pressed steel w/yel plastic barrel, 8½", G, P4 ....$85.00

Ray Line Super Shot Pump Shotgun, 1980, plastic, 30", MOC, P4 ....$55.00

Redondo Galaxia Space Gun, 1980, diecast w/red plastic grips & muzzle, 4", MOC, P4 ....$20.00

Remco Electronic Signal Ray Gun, 1950s, red plastic w/gray trim, internal color wheel, 9", NM (EX box), P4 ....$150.00

Remco US Navy Pom Pom Gun, plastic, battery-op, EX (EX box) $125.00

Renwal Stratoblaster, blk plastic w/missiles & rockets emb on grips, 27", NM (VG box) $150.00

SH Space Ruler Machine Gun, 1950s, litho tin, battery-op, several actions, 22", EX $175.00

Shimmel Super Astro Light Gun, 1970, orange & wht plastic, battery-op, MOC, P4 ....$35.00

Shudo Flash X-1 Space Gun, 1969, litho tin, friction, 5", NM, P4 ....$50.00

Stevens Bang-O Cap Pistol, 1940, CI w/NP finish, wht plastic horse head grips w/gr jewels, 7½", EX, P4 ....$85.00

Stevens Cowboy King 50-Shot Repeater, diecast w/silver finish, faux pearl hdls, 8½", EX (G box), A $125.00

Stevens No 25-50 Shot Pistol, 1930s, CI, EX, J6 ....$75.00

Stevens Western Boy Cap Pistol, 1940, CI w/NP finish, wht plastic grips w/horse, cowboy & red jewels, 8", NM, P4...$100.00

Stevens 49-ER, gold-plated CI w/emb conestoga jewel on wht grips, 9", NM (EX box), A $450.00

Stevens 49-ER, silverplated CI w/emb conestoga & jewel on wht grips, 9", NM (EX box), A $350.00

Thomas Western Water Rifle, 1960s, gray plastic, 27", NM (NM box), P4 ....$50.00

TN Cosmic Gun, bl plastic w/red translucent barrel, battery-op, 10", MIB, P4 ....$55.00

TN Space Control Gun, litho tin, friction, 4", G, P4 ....$30.00

TN Universal Machine Gun, 1950s, litho tin, battery-op, 15", NM $150.00

Topper Sixfinger, 1965, plastic finger shape, fires missiles, complete, 3½", MOC $50.00

Topper/Deluxe Reading Secret Sam Pistol, 1965, plastic, 12", EX, P4 ....$35.00

Unknown Maker, Clicker Ray Gun, 1950s, mottled olive plastic, 5", NM, P4 ....$30.00

Unknown Maker, Potato Gun, 1970, plastic, 6½", MIB, P4.$25.00

Unknown Maker, Space Jet Ray Gun, plastic, friction, 16", unused, MIB, A $75.00

Unknown Maker, Space Patrol Gun, 1960, litho tin, friction, 6", VG, P4 ....$50.00

US Plastic Space Patrol Dart Gun, 1952, blk plastic w/Space Patrol logo, 9½", NM, P4 ....$175.00

USA X-100 Mystery Dart Gun, 1950s, plastic, fires talcum powder filled darts, unused, MOC, A $165.00

Wham-O Air Blaster, 1960, blk plastic, 11", NM, P4.......$85.00

Wyandotte Repeating Cap Pistol, 1935, red-pnt pressed steel, 8½", VG, P4 ....$50.00

CHARACTER

Agent Zero Fanner 50 Cap Pistol, Mattel, 1967, diecast w/blk-pnt finish, plastic woodgrain grips, 11", EX $135.00

Agent Zero-M Night Fighter Tommy Burst Machine Gun, 1964, 27", EX $85.00

Agent Zero-M Shootin' Shell Snub-Nose .38 Cap Pistol, Mattel, 1967, diecast w/chrome finish, blk plastic grips, 7", NM $125.00

Agent Zero-W Rapid Fire Special Rifle, Mattel, 1965, brn & blk plastic, 26", M, P4 ....$125.00

Al Capone Gun Set, Spain, NMOC $50.00

Alan Ladd Cap Gun, Schmidt, diecast w/copper grips, hammer & trigger, 10", rare, NM, A $350.00

Annie Oakley Double Holster Set, Daisy, 1950s, complete w/2 diecast pistols & bullets, M (EX box), A $650.00

Batman & Superman Pop-Pop Pistol, Gordy Int, 1978, clear bl plastic, shoots ping-pong balls, 7", MIP, J5 ....$50.00

Batman Bat Ray Gun, Remco, 1979, blk plastic, battery-op, MIB, J5 ....$55.00

Batman Escape Gun, New Zealand, 1966, plastic, launches spinners & shoots darts, 5", NM $75.00

Batman Rocket Gun, Baravella/Italy, 1960s, red plastic w/gold & silver highlights, 24", NMIB $250.00

Beetle Bailey Cork Gun, Ja-Ru, 1981, plastic, 6", MOC, M17 ....$30.00

Billy the Kid Repeating Cap Pistol, Stevens, diecast metal w/buffalos emb on wht plastic grips, 7½", NM (G box), A $150.00

Buck Rogers Disintegrator Gun & Holster, Daisy, pressed steel w/copper plating, leather holster, 9½", NM $450.00

Buck Rogers Liquid Helium Water Pistol, Daisy, red- & yel-litho metal, 7", EX $200.00

Buck Rogers Sonic Ray Gun, Norton-Honer, 1950, plastic, battery-op, 7", NMIB, A.............$150.00
Buck Rogers XZ-31 Rocket Pistol Pop Gun, Daisy, 1934, bl-pnt pressed steel, 9½", VG.............$150.00
Buck Rogers XZ-31 Rocket Pistol Pop Gun, Daisy, 1934, bl-pnt pressed steel, 9½", EX (EX box).............$400.00
Buffalo Bill Cap Pistol, Kenton, 1931, CI w/lacquered finish, 13½", EX.............$300.00

Buffalo Bill Scout BB Gun, Daisy, 1970, Buffalo Bill medallion on brown stock, 38", NM (G box), A, $185.00.

Captain America Clicker Gun, Larami, 1974, bl plastic, MIP, F8.............$20.00
Captain Meteor Strato Cap Gun, Futuristic, diecast w/chrome finish, red trim, holster fits on belt, 9", EX, A.........$350.00
Cheyenne Cap Pistol, Kilgore, 1959, diecast w/silver finish, brn & wht plastic stag grips, 9", M, P4.............$85.00
Cisco Kid Cap Pistol & Holster, Lone Star, 1960, diecast w/chrome finish, brn plastic horse head grips, 9", M, P4.............$275.00
Cisco Kid 100 Shot Repeater, Lone Star, 1950s, NM (EX+ box), A.............$250.00
Cowpoke Jr Cap Pistol, Lone Star, 1960, diecast w/silver finish, blk-pnt grips, 8", NM, P4.............$65.00
Dan Dare Space Gun, Lone Star, red-pnt metal, 7½", VG..$100.00
Davy Crockett Cap Gun, France/WD, 1950s, plastic & metal w/cb holster, EX.............$50.00
Davy Crockett Clicker Gun, Marx, 1952, litho tin, 10", EX, P4.............$150.00
Davy Crockett Frontierland Flintlock Jr, Hubley, 1950s, w/fringed holster & strap, EX, A.............$150.00
Davy Crockett Pistol & Knife, 1950s, 9" plastic clicker pistol & 12" cutlass-style knife, MOC, P4.............$55.00
Davy Crockett Water Pistol, Knickerbocker, 1950s, blk plastic w/brass nozzle, 9", MOC, P4.............$75.00
Dick Tracy Automatic Repeater Water Gun, Larami, 1971, red tommy-gun shape, NMIP, D11.............$40.00
Dick Tracy Bullet Gun, Ja-Ru, NMOC, D11.............$25.00
Dick Tracy Crimestopper Machine Gun, Larami, 1973, plastic, 14", NMIP, D11.............$40.00
Dick Tracy Machine Pistol, Larami, plastic tommy gun, 9", NMIP, P11.............$40.00
Dick Tracy Power-Jet Squad Gun, Mattel, 1962, plastic & diecast, pump style, 31", M (NM box).............$225.00
Dick Tracy Rapid-Fire Tommy Gun, Parker Johns, 1948, diecast w/gray- & blk-pnt finish, wht canvas sling, 20", VG, P4.$250.00
Dick Tracy Sub-Machine Water Gun, 1950s, red plastic, MIB.............$150.00
FBI in Action Machine Gun, Plastimarx/Mexico, fires w/sound, 19", MOC.............$75.00

Flash Gordon Arresting Ray Gun, Marx, 1930s, litho tin, 10", NM, T2.............$200.00
Flash Gordon Click Ray Pistol, Marx, litho tin, 10", NM (NM box).............$300.00
Flash Gordon Space Set, Ja-Ru, 1981, w/4½" wht plastic gun, laser radio & Flight Plan booklet, MOC, P4.............$30.00
G-Boy Cap Pistol, Acme Novelty Mfg, diecast w/wht plastic grips, 7", MIB.............$100.00
G-Man Automatic, Marx, silver version, litho tin, w/up, 4", EX (EX box), A.............$150.00
G-Man Cap Pistol, Kilgore, CI, 6", EX.............$125.00

G-Man Machine Gun, Marx, lithographed tin with wood stock, fires with sparks and sound, 24", VG, $250.00.
(Photo courtesy Harry and Jody Whitworth)

G-Man Siren Alarm Pistol, Marx, 1936, bl-pnt pressed steel w/G-Man decal, 8½", NM (EX box).............$175.00
G-Man Sparkling Double Action Machine Gun, Marx, litho tin w/wood stock, 24", EX.............$200.00
G-Man Sparkling Pop Pistol, Marx, 1930s, pressed steel, fires sparks, 8", NM (EX box), A.............$175.00
G-Man Sparkling Sub-Machine Gun, Marx, plastic, fires w/sparks & sound, 26", MIB.............$250.00
G-Man Sub-Machine Gun, Marx, plastic, fires w/sparks & sound, 22", MIB.............$275.00
G-Men Machine Gun, litho tin w/detachable wood stock, w/up, 17", EX.............$250.00
G-Men Ray Gun, litho tin, fires w/sparks & sound, 12½", MIB.............$250.00
Gene Autry .44 Cap Pistol, Leslie-Henry, 1950s, diecast w/NP finish, repro wht plastic horse head grips, 11", EX, P4....$185.00
Gene Autry .44 Pistol, Leslie-Henry, 1950s, diecast w/NP finish, emb horse head grips, 11", NM (VG box), A.........$300.00
Gene Autry Cap Gun, Kenton, CI w/orange plastic grips, 6½", EX, A.............$150.00
Gene Autry Cap Pistol, Leslie-Henry, 1950s, diecast w/NP finish, wht plastic horse head grips, 9", EX, P4.............$175.00
Gene Autry Cap Pistol & Holster, Kenton, 1939, CI, plastic grips w/jewels & studs, brn leather holster, 8", NM.$650.00
Gene Autry Flying A Ranch Holster Set, Leslie-Henry, 1950s, diecast w/NP finish, wht plastic horse head grips, 9", MIB.........$700.00
Gene Autry Repeating Cap Pistol, Kenton, CI w/faux pearl grips, 6½", NM (VG box).............$350.00
Gene Autry Repeating Cap Pistol, Leslie-Henry, gold-plated metal w/plastic horse head grips, 9", MIB, A.........$400.00
Gunsmoke Cap Pistol, Leslie-Henry, 1950s, diecast w/NP finish, brn plastic horse head grips, 9", NM, P4.............$150.00

Gunsmoke Holster Set, Halco, complete w/2 Smoky Joe cap guns & blk leather holster mk Matt Dillon, EX (EX box), A $350.00

Have Gun Will Travel Holster Set, Halco, complete w/2 Buffalo Bill cap guns, blk leather holster & bullets, NMIB, A .$400.00

High Chapparral, Redondo, 1960s, diecast w/silver finish, brn eagle grips, 8½", NM, P4...$50.00

Hopalong Cassidy Cap Pistol, Schmidt, 1950, diecast w/gold finish, blk plastic grips w/Hoppy bust, 9", VG.............$400.00

Hopalong Cassidy Gold-Plated Single Shot Cap Pistol, Wyandotte, 1950s, black plastic grips with signature, 7½", NMIB, A, $350.00.

I Spy Gun & Holster Set, Ray Line, 1960s, plastic, w/silencer & shoulder holster, MOC, A.......................................$125.00

James Bond 007 PPK Cap Pistol, Wicke, 1983, blk plastic w/diecast works, 6", MOC, P4 ....$55.00

James Bond 007 Sharpshooter Set, Multiple/Glidrose, 1966, w/plastic pistol, ammo & villain targets, EX (EX card)..........$225.00

Johnny Eagle Lieutenant Automatic, Topper/Deluxe Reading, 1965, bl plastic w/brn grips, 8½", NM, P4 ....$150.00

Johnny Eagle Lieutenant Red River Bullet/Cap Firing Rifle, Topper, 1965, plastic w/diecast works, EX, P4.........$135.00

Kit Carson 50-Shot Repeating Cap Pistol, Kilgore, diecast w/Kit Carson bust emb on plastic grips, 8", EX (EX box), A.$135.00

Lone Ranger Click Pistol, Marx, 1938, pressed steel w/Lone Ranger decal, 8", EX (EX box) $175.00

Lone Ranger Flashlight Pistol, Marx, 1944, battery-op, NMIB...$175.00

Lone Ranger Gun & Holster Set, 1945, complete, NMIB..$350.00

Lone Rider Cap Pistol, Buzz-Henry, 1950, diecast w/NP finish, wht plastic horse head grips, 8", EX, P4 ....$125.00

Man From UNCLE Napoleon Solo Gun Set, Ideal, 1960s, complete, EX (EX box), A $450.00

Pecos Kid Cap Pistol, Lone Star, 1960s, diecast w/red-brn plastic grips, lever release, 8½", MIB, P4........................$50.00

Phantom Water Pistol w/Holster, Nasta, 1975, bl plastic gun & blk plastic holster, MOC, J5 ....$50.00

Planet of the Apes Water Rifle, Knickerbocker, 1968, wht plastic w/gold trim, 15", NM, P4 ....$85.00

Popeye Gun & Holster Set, Halco, 1961, 2 5" diecast pistols & dbl holster, NM (NM diecut card)...........................$150.00

Popeye Pirate Pistol, Marx, 1935, litho tin click gun, 10", NM (EX box), from $300 to $400.00

Popeye Six-Shooter Holster Set, J Halpern, M (M diecut card), A...$200.00

Rangeland Western Holster Set, C Ray Lawyer, 1950s, Hubley Texan Jr cap gun & wht holster w/studs & jewels, MIB $325.00

Ranger Gun, Buzz Henry, diecast w/wht plastic inset grips, 7½", NM (EX box), A $100.00

Ranger Rider Gun & Holster Set, Leslie-Henry, 1950s, complete w/2 diecast pistols & bullets, M (EX box), A $550.00

Red Ranger Dummy Cap Pistol, Wyandotte, 1950s, diecast w/NP finish, wht horse head & horseshoe grips, 9", M........$125.00

Red Ranger Jr Dummy Cap Pistol, Wyandotte, 1955, diecast w/NP finish, wht horse head grips, 8", MIB.............$100.00

Rex Mars Planet Patrol Sparkling Pistol, Marx, 7", EX (EX box) $50.00

Rifleman Flip Special, Hubley, 1959, diecast w/NP finish, brn plastic stock, 32½", EX, P4 ....$225.00

Rin-Tin-Tin Gun & Holster, 1956, VG, A $95.00

Roy Rogers Cap Pistol, Kilgore, 1955, diecast w/NP finish, wht plastic horse head grips, revolving cylinder, M........$400.00

Roy Rogers Cap Pistol, Schmidt, 1950, diecast w/NP finish, crossed-hatched copper-metal grips, 10", EX, P4.....$275.00

Roy Rogers Cowpoke Pistols & Holster, complete w/2 pistols & leather holster, EX $225.00

Roy Rogers Forty Niner Pistol & Spurs, Leslie-Henry, complete, rare, NMIB $1,200.00

Roy Rogers Mini-Cap Gun, w/holster & belt, NM.........$150.00

Roy Rogers Tuck-A-Way Gun, Classy, 1959, diecast w/NP finish, 2", MOC, P4 ....$150.00

Secret Sam Attache Set, Topper/Deluxe Reading, 1965, plastic, NM (EX cb slipcover), P4 ....$250.00

Space Outlaw Cap Firing Ray Gun, BCM, 1960, diecast w/silver finish, red plastic windows, 10", NM (EX box), P4 .$300.00

Space: 1999 Water Gun, 1976, red, wht & bl plastic w/removable tanks, 9", NM, P4...$55.00

Spider-Man Sting Ray Gun, Remco, 1978, plastic, battery-op, MIB, T2 ....$100.00

Texas Ranger Cap Pistol, Leslie-Henry, 1955, diecast w/wht plastic grips, 8½", EX, P4 ....$100.00

Texas Ranger Gun & Holster Set, Leslie-Henry, 1950s, diecast w/amber grips, brn leather holster w/floral design, 9", EX $185.00

Tom Corbett Space Cadet Clicker Gun, Marx, 1952, litho tin, 10", EX, P4..$250.00

Untouchables Machine Gun, Spanish issue, 22", EX (EX box), from $50 to $75.00

Voyage to the Bottom of the Sea Submarine Gun, Remco, 1966, EX, A $125.00

Wagon Train Cap Pistol, Leslie-Henry, 1959, diecast w/antique bronze finish, wht stag grips, 11", NM (G box), P4 .$350.00

Wanted Dead or Alive Mares Laig Cap Pistol, Marx, 1959, plastic w/diecast works, brn plastic stock, 17", EX, P4...**$175.00**
Wells Fargo Pony Express Holster Outfit, Halco, diecast w/4-leaf clover medallions on grips, brn leather holster, NMIB .**$350.00**

Wyatt Earp Buntline Special, Lone Star, diecast w/red plastic grip, 13½", NM (EX box), $300.00.

Wyatt Earp Cap Pistol, Kilgore, 1959, diecast w/NP finish, wht plastic horse head grips, 9", VG, P4 ....**$175.00**
Yellow Submarine Water Pistol, unknown maker, yel plastic, 6", NM, P4 ....**$55.00**
Young Buffalo Bill Cowboy Outfit, Leslie-Henry, complete w/2 8" diecast cap guns & blk leather holster, EX (EX box), A **$225.00**
Zorro Holster Set, Daisy, 1960, Hubley Coyote diecast pistol, blk & gold leather holster, NM (EX box), P4 ....**$275.00**

BB Guns

Values are suggested for BB guns that are in excellent condition.
Advisor: Jim Buskirk.

Daisy (Early), break action, wire stock, B6 ....**$450.00**
Daisy (Early), top lever, wire stock, B6 ....**$600.00**
Daisy '1000' Shot, lever action, wood stock, B6 ....**$250.00**
Daisy '500' Shot, lever action, wood stock, B6 ....**$250.00**
Daisy Model A, break action, wood stock, B6 ....**$200.00**
Daisy Model B, lever action, wood stock, B6 ....**$80.00**
Daisy Model C, break action, wood stock, B6 ....**$200.00**
Daisy Model H, lever action, wood stock, B6 ....**$80.00**
Daisy Model 1938B, Christmas Story/Red Ryder, B6 ....**$65.00**
Daisy Model 21, 1968, dbl barrel, plastic stock, B6 ....**$350.00**
Daisy No 11, lever action, wood stock, B6 ....**$65.00**
Daisy No 12, break action, wood stock, B6 ....**$50.00**
Daisy No 25, pump action, pistol-grip, wood stock, B6 ....**$45.00**
Daisy No 25, pump action, straight wood stock, B6..........**$50.00**
Daisy No 30, lever action, wood stock, B6 ....**$80.00**
Daisy No 40, 'Military,' lever action, wood stock, B6.....**$175.00**
Daisy No 40, 'Military,' w/bayonet, lever action, wood stock, B6 ....**$400.00**

Daisy No 50, copper-plated, lever action, blk wood stock, B6 ....**$80.00**
Daisy No 100, Model 38, break action, wood stock, B6....**$25.00**
Daisy No 101, Model 33, lever action, wood stock, B6 ....**$40.00**
Daisy No 101, Model 36, lever action, wood stock, B6 ....**$35.00**
Daisy No 103, Model 33, Buzz Barton, B6 ....**$200.00**
Daisy No 103, Model 33, lever action, wood stock, B6 ..**$150.00**
Daisy No 104, dbl barrel, wood stock, B6 ....**$550.00**
Daisy No 105, 'Junior Pump Gun,' wood stock, B6 ....**$150.00**
Daisy No 106, break action, wood stock, B6 ....**$25.00**
Daisy No 107, 'Buck Jones Special,' pump action, wood stock, B6 ....**$100.00**
Daisy No 107, pump action, plastic stock, B6 ....**$20.00**
Daisy No 108, Model 39, 'Carbine,' lever action, wood stock, B6 ....**$65.00**
Daisy No 111, Model 40, Red Ryder, aluminum lever, B6..**$50.00**
Daisy No 111, Model 40, Red Ryder, iron lever, B6 ....**$80.00**
Daisy No 111, Model 40, Red Ryder, plastic stock, B6 .....**$30.00**
Daisy No 140, 'Defender,' lever action, wood stock, B6 .**$200.00**
Daisy No 195, Buzz Barton, lever action, wood stock, B6.**$65.00**
Daisy No 195, Model 36, Buzz Barton, lever action, wood stock, B6 ....**$70.00**
King Model 5333, lever action, wood stock, B6...............**$35.00**
King No 1, break action, wood stock, B6 ....**$50.00**
King No 2, break action, wood stock, B6 ....**$50.00**
King No 4, lever action, wood stock, B6..........................**$150.00**
King No 5, 'Pump Gun,' wood stock, B6..........................**$125.00**
King No 5, lever action, wood stock, B6..........................**$150.00**
King No 10, break action, wood stock, B6 ....**$30.00**
King No 17, break action, wood stock, B6 ....**$125.00**
King No 21, lever action, wood stock, B6 ....**$55.00**
King No 22, lever action, wood stock, B6 ....**$55.00**
King No 24, break action, wood stock, B6 ....**$175.00**
King No 24, lever action, wood stock, B6 ....**$65.00**
King No 55, lever action, wood stock, B6 ....**$70.00**
King No 2136, lever action, wood stock, B6 ....**$20.00**
King No 2236, lever action, wood stock, B6 ....**$20.00**
New King, repeater, break action, wood stock, B6 ....**$125.00**
New King, single shot, break action, wood stock, B6 .....**$100.00**

Markham/King 'Chicago,' break action, all wood, B6, $200.00. (Photo courtesy Jim Buskirk)

Related Items and Accessories

Bullets, Mattel Bullet Pak for Winchester Saddle Gun, Bandolier, & Fanner-50 Cap Pistol sets, 1958, MOC, P4.............**$30.00**
Bullets, Mattel Shootin' Shell, 1958, 3 brass cartridges & 35 plastic bullets, MOC, P4..**$35.00**
Bullets, Nichols Stallion, 1950s, 6 bullets on wht plastic strip, M, P4 ....**$30.00**

Bullets, Nichols Stallion, 1960s, 6 bullets on wht plastic strip, M, P4..$20.00

Caps, Buddy-L Paper Refills, 1948, 4 rolls per box, M, P4..$5.00

Caps, Halco Perfo Jet Caps, 1960, 5 rolls per box, M, P4 ...$5.00

Caps, Halco Superb-Loudest-Best Roll Caps, 1950s, 5 rolls per box, M, P4..$5.00

Caps, Kilgore Bang Caps, 10 rolls per box, M, P4 ....$5.00

Caps, Kilgore Mammoth Disc Caps, 20 discs per box, M, P4 ....$5.00

Caps, Kilgore Perforated Roll Caps, 1950s, 5 rolls per box, M, P4 ....$5.00

Caps, Kilgore Round Caps, punchout sheet of 104 caps, M, P4 ....$5.00

Caps, Kilgore Round Caps No 514, 1960, 3 rolls per box, M, P4 ....$4.00

Caps, Kilgore Stick-On Round Caps No 533, 1960, 3 rolls per box, M, P4..$4.00

Caps, Langston Super Nu-Matic Paper Buster Gun Ammunition, 1950, 5 rolls per box, M, P4 ....$5.00

Caps, Mattel Greenie Perforated Roll Caps, 5 rolls per box, M, P4 ....$5.00

Caps, Marx Thundercaps Supersound, 1950s, five rolls per box, M, $5.00. (Photo courtesy Martin and Carolyn Berens)

Caps, Mattel Greenie Stick-M-Caps, 1958, 2 sheets of 60 per box, M, P4..$5.00

Caps, Mattel Greenie Stick-M-Caps, 1958, 8 sheets of 60 per box, M, P4..$10.00

Caps, Nichols Fury 500 Shot Roll Caps, 1 roll per box, M, P4 ....$5.00

Caps, Nichols Stallion Round Caps, 1950s, 100 caps per box, M, P4 ....$5.00

Caps, Nichols Tophand Caps, 1960, 6 boxes in pkg, M, P4..$25.00

Caps, Nichols Tophand 250 Shot Roll Caps, 1 roll per box, M, P4 ....$5.00

Caps, Ohio Art Super Bang Caps, 1970s, 12 strips, MIP, P4 .$3.00

Caps, Star Brand Round Caps, 1960, 100 per box, M, P4...$5.00

Darts, Palmer Space Shooting Darts, 1950s, plastic, MOC, P4 ....$25.00

Gun Rack, 1960, mk Lazy S Ranch, wood & plastic w/longhorn design, horseshoe-shaped hooks, 21", EX.................$75.00

Halloween

Halloween is a uniquely American holiday melded from the traditions of superstitions brought to the new world from Ger-

many and Scotland. St. Matrimony was reportedly the patron saint of this holiday, as it was at this time of the year when the harvest was safely in that betrothals and weddings took place. Most activity for the holiday focused on getting young eligible people married. Trick or Treat was a way of getting rid of bothersome younger siblings. Robert Burns, the poet of Scotland was a major influence on the folklore of the holiday. In this country today, Halloween is a holiday with little or no association with earlier religious rites of any group. It's an evening of fun, frolic, and fantasy filled with a lot of sugar and calories! For further information we recommend *Collectible Halloween* and *More Halloween* both by our advisor Pamela E. Apkarian-Russell. *Halloween III* will be released in the fall.

Advisor: Pamela E. Apkarian-Russell, The Halloween Queen (H9).

See also Halloween Costumes; Candy Containers (for glass examples).

Book, Childrens' Party Book, 1940s, softcover, 23 pgs, EX ..$15.00

Book, Dennison's Bogie Book, 1926, 14th edition, hardcover, EX, A $175.00

Book, Games for Halloween, by Mary E Blain, 1912, hardcover, 60 pgs, w/dust jacket, EX $45.00

Book, Hallowe'en Fun, Willis N Bugbee Co, hardcover, 104 pgs, EX...$45.00

Book, Tip-Top Hallowe'en Book, Willis N Bugbee Co, 1925, hardcover, 87 pgs, EX $45.00

Candy Container, witch, composition with hand-painted face, original clothes and broom, marked Germany, 1910, 14", NM, A, $1,800.00.
(Photo courtesy Dunbar Gallery)

Candy Bag, goblin figure, mesh bag over cotton body w/cb face & feet, German, 1920s, 8", EX..................................$250.00

Candy Container, blk cat w/bulging wiggling eyes, compo, EX, H9...$500.00

Candy Container, devil head, compo, German, 1920s, 3½", EX..$200.00

Candy Container, jack-o'-lantern fisherman, compo, EX, H9...$400.00

Candy Container, jack-o'-lantern, compo, German, 1920s, 3", NM..$200.00

Candy Container, jack-o'-lantern boy riding rooster, compo, German, EX, H9..$1,300.00

Candy Container, jack-o'-lantern on cylinder, cb & pulp, American, 1940s, 10", EX, A..............................$115.00

Candy Container, lemon-head girl, compo, German, EX, H9...$135.00

Candy Container, skull, compo, mk Germany, 1912, 3", EX, A...$250.00

Candy Container, squash man, compo, German, 5", M, A..$200.00

Candy Container, witch on jack-o'-lantern, cb, 6", EX, A .$150.00

Candy Container, witch on shoe, compo, EX, H9..........$400.00

Decoration, blk cat on honeycomb base, cb & crepe paper, 1930s-40s, 10", NM, A $50.00

Decoration, dancing witch, cb & crepe paper, HE Luhrs, 1920s, 18", EX, A...$125.00

Decoration, Halloween a Go-Go Dancers, cb, 1960s, complete w/skeleton & girl, 14", MIP, A...................................$55.00

Diecut, bat, German, 1920s, 8", EX, A.........................$75.00

Diecut, blk cat face, German, 1930s, 8", EX, A $50.00

Diecut, blk cat on jack-o'-lantern, American, 1930s, 12", EX, A...$125.00

Diecut, devil face, German, 16", EX, H9 ....$175.00

Diecut, jack-o'-lantern & quarter moon, German, 1920s, 5" dia, NM...$95.00

Diecut, jack-o'-lantern boy in clown suit, easel-back, 1920s, 15", NM, A $125.00

Diecut, jack-o'-lantern girl in clown suit w/blk cat, easel-back, 1920s, 15", NM, A...$125.00

Diecut, jack-o'-lantern playing drums, German, 1920s, 7½", EX, A...$100.00

Diecut, jack-o'lantern figure w/blk cat, Beistle, 1920s, 16", rare, VG, A $65.00

Diecut, owl & quarter moon, German, 1920s, 5" dia, NM .$100.00

Diecut, witch & quarter moon, German, 1920s, 5" dia, NM, A $125.00

Figure, blk cat on stump, celluloid, 1920s, 3", M, A.......$250.00

Figure, blk cat w/owl face, celluloid, spring tail, 1930s, 4½" L, NM, A..$325.00

Figure, jack-o'-lantern boxer w/top hat, compo, mk Germany, 1920, 4", EX, A..$200.00

Figure, jack-o'-lantern clown, compo, German, 1920s, 4", EX, A...$200.00

Figure, jack-o'-lantern figure w/owl & blk cats, celluloid, 1920s, 4", NM..$200.00

Figure, jack-o'-lantern w/witch & cat face on sides, hard plastic, 1950s, 2½", NM, A...$35.00

Figure, owl on jack-o'-lantern, Viscaloid, 1920s, 3½", EX, A .$250.00

Figure, owl on spooky stump, celluloid, 1930s, 5½", EX.$250.00

Figure, witch holding blk cat w/wobbling head, hard plastic, 7", EX, H9 ....$150.00

Figure, witch on spaceship, hard plastic, EX, H9 ....$200.00

Game, Black Cat Fortune Telling Game, Parker Bros, 1897, complete, EX (G box) $150.00

Game, Cat & Witch, Whitman, 1950s, EX (EX box), A .$50.00

Game, Old Witch Brewsome Stunts, 1920s, NMIB, A $55.00

Game, Ring a Tail, Japan, 1930s, 3½" dia, scarce, EX (G box), A, $195.00. (Photo courtesy Dunbar Gallery)

Game, Zingo Halloween Fortune & Stunt Game, 1930s, EX (EX box), A..$50.00

Horn, litho cb w/blk cats & pumpkins, German, 1920s, 24", VG..$45.00

Horn, litho cb w/pumpkins, bats, owls & blk cats, Marks Bros, 1921, 14½", VG...$35.00

Horn, litho tin w/cats & witches, EX, H9 ....$15.00

Jack-in-the-Box, yel-& red-pnt wood box w/devil head on spring, German, 1920s, EX...................................$500.00

Jack-o'-Lantern, cb, smiling, triangular nose, German, 1920s, 4", NM..$250.00

Jack-o'-Lantern, celluloid, smiling, battery-op, Japan, 1950s, 4", MIB, A...$65.00

Jack-o'-lantern, pulp, frowning, w/stem, American, 1940s, 7", EX..$225.00

Jack-o'-Lantern, pulp, open mouth, American, 1940s, 8", NM..$200.00

Jack-o'-Lantern, pulp, open mouth, double-sided, w/stem, battery-op, American, 1950s, 6½", EX $200.00

Jack-o'-Lantern, pulp, smiling w/eyebrows arched, American, 1940s, 8", EX...$125.00

Jack-o'-Lantern, pulp, smiling w/eyes crossed, pug nose, American, 1940s, 5", NM...$150.00

Lantern, blk cat (full body), pulp, American, 1940s, 7", NM.$300.00

Lantern, blk cat face, cb, German, 1930s, 5", EX $225.00

Lantern, blk cat face, pulp, American, 1940s, 6", EX, A ..$225.00

Lantern, blk cat face on fence, pulp, American, 1940s, 8", EX, A...$200.00

Lantern, blk cat face on pedestal, pulp, American, 1940s, 5", EX...$200.00

Lantern, cat, orange, full figure, EX, H9 ....$300.00

Lantern, cat face, orange, pulp, American, 1940s, 6", NM, A...$200.00

Lantern, devil, cardboard, double-sided, American, 1950s, 7½", EX, A, $125.00.
(Photo courtesy Dunbar Gallery)

Squeaker, jack-o'-lantern clown, hand-painted composition head, jointed arms and feet, original clothes, marked Germany, 1910, 7½", NM, A, $450.00.
(Photo courtesy Dunbar Gallery)

Lantern, jack-o'-lantern man w/protruding tongue, cb & compo, paper insert, 12", EX, H9 ....$2,500.00

Lantern, owl w/wings spread, pressed cb, EX, H9 ....$1,400.00

Lantern, skeleton grinning, pressed cb, w/paper insert, 5", EX, H9 ....$250.00

Mask, Skull, papier-mache, mk Germany, 1920s, 8", EX, A ..$75.00

Mask & Hat, blk cat, paper, 1930s, 11", EX, A................$30.00

Mask & Hat, jack-o'-lantern, paper, 1930s, 11", EX, A....$30.00

Noisemaker, blk cat, cb w/wood hdl, mk Germany, 1920s, 6", EX $150.00

Noisemaker, blk cat, litho tin w/wood hdl, 1950s, 4" dia, EX, A $25.00

Noisemaker, cat face, litho tin, EX, H9............................$15.00

Noisemaker, halloween party scene, litho tin w/wood hdl, Chein, 1910, 3½", VG $25.00

Noisemaker, jack-o'-lantern, litho tin w/plastic horn nose, EX, H9 ....$50.00

Noisemaker, jack-o'-lantern w/top hat, cb w/wood hdl, double-sided, mk Germany, 1920s, 8", EX $200.00

Noisemaker, veggie man, compo w/wood hdl, German, 1920s, 9½", NM, A..$185.00

Noisemaker, witch on broom, litho tin w/wood hdl, 1940s, 5", EX, A $125.00

Pan Knocker, witches, blk cats & jack-o'-lanterns, litho tin, Kirchhof, 1950s, 8½", NM $25.00

Parade Stick, devil head w/rattle, plastic, 1950s-60s, 34", EX, A $75.00

Party Favor, girl in pumpkin patch, celluloid & crepe paper, 1930s, 5", EX, A $150.00

Sparkler, witch face, litho tin, Hale-Ness Corp, 1950s, 6½", NMOC...$50.00

Sparkler, witches, jack-o'-lanterns & blk cats, litho tin, Chein, 1920s, 4½", NMIB...$65.00

Sparkler, witches, jack-o'-lanterns & blk cats, litho tin, Chein, 1940s, 5", EX, A...$50.00

Squeaker, blk cat, mohair, 1930s, 3", NM, A...................$75.00

Stickers, jack-o'-lanterns, 1 sheet, M, H9 ....$12.00

Tambourine, bats & stars on rim, plain cover, litho tin & paper, Ohio Art, 1930s, 6" dia, EX, A.................................$75.00

Tambourine, blk cat face, litho tin, T Cohn, 1940s, 7" dia, EX, A $75.00

Tambourine, children dancing around lg pumpkin, US Metal Toy, 1950s, 6" dia, M...$65.00

Tambourine, children playing w/lg pumpkin, litho tin, Chein, 1930s, 7" dia, NM, A..$85.00

Tambourine, devil's face surrounded by devils w/pitchforks, litho tin, Kirchhof, 1950s, 6½" dia, NM............................$75.00

Tambourine, Mother Goose-type witch, litho tin, EX, H9.$75.00

Tambourine, witch face surrounded by blk cats & bats, litho tin, 1950s, 6" dia, EX..$75.00

Windup Toy, jack-o'-lantern clown, cardboard head with metal legs and feet, original felt outfit, marked Germany, 1920, 10", rare, NM, A, $1,500.00.
(Photo courtesy Dunbar Gallery)

Witch Toy, animated witch tells jokes, battery-op, life-sz, EX, H9 ....$350.00

Halloween Costumes

During the '50s and '60s Ben Cooper and Collegeville made Halloween costumes representing the popular TV and movie characters of the day. If you can find one in excellent to mint condition and still in its original box, some of the better ones can go for over $100.00. MAD's Alfred E. Neuman (Collegeville, 1959–60) usually carries an asking price of $150.00 to $175.00, and The Green Hornet (Ben Cooper, 1966), $200.00. Earlier handmade costumes are especially valuable if they are 'Dennison-Made.'

Advisor: Pamela E. Apkarian-Russell, The Halloween Queen (H9).

Alf, Collegeville, MIB, H9 ....$35.00
Aquaman, Ben Cooper, 1967, complete, NM (EX box), J5 .$125.00
Atom Ant, Ben Cooper, 1965, complete, NMIB, T2 ....$50.00
Baby Kermit, Ben Cooper, 1979, complete, M (EX box), M17 ....$30.00
Barbie Super Star Bride, Collegeville, 1975, MIP $60.00
Bart Simpson, Ben Cooper, 1989, MIB, K1 ....$20.00
Batgirl, Ben Cooper, 1967, MIB, T2 ....$75.00
Batman, Ben Cooper, 1969, complete, NMIB, T2............$95.00
Beatles, any member, Ben Cooper, 1960s, MIB.............$450.00
Bert (Sesame Street), Ben Cooper, 1979, complete, M (EX box), M17..$30.00
Birdman, Ben Cooper, 1967, complete, NMIB, T2 ....$40.00

Charlie's Angels, Sabrina, Collegeville, 1976, MIB, from $65.00 to $75.00.
(Photo courtesy Greg Davis and Bill Morgan)

Blue Meanie (Beatles Yellow Submarine), Collegeville, complete, NMIB..$85.00
Boss Hogg (Dukes of Hazzard), Ben Cooper, 1982, MIB, C1 .$40.00
Brady Bunch, any character, Collegeville, 1970s, MIB, ea from $25 to $35.00
Buffy (Family Affair), Ben Cooper, 1970, MIB, from $55 to $65.00
C-3PO (Star Wars), Ben Cooper, 1977, MIB, C1 ....$45.00
Captain America, Ben Cooper, 1967, complete, NMIB.$125.00
Captain America, Ben Cooper, 1983, complete, EX (VG box), A $35.00
CHiPs, any character, Ben Cooper, 1978, MIB, ea..........$25.00
Clarabelle (Howdy Doody), Collegeville, 1950s, w/metal horn, EX, A $125.00
Cookie Monster, Ben Cooper, 1989, complete, M (EX box), M17...$30.00
Courageous Cat, Halco, 1950s, complete, NMIB, T2.......$75.00
Daredevil, Ben Cooper, 1966, complete, NMIB, T2, from $100 to $125.00
Dick Tracy, Ben Cooper, 1967, complete, EX, T2...........$50.00
Donny Osmond, Collegeville, 1977, MIB.........................$20.00
Dr Doom, Ben Cooper, 1967, complete, rare, NMIB $125.00
Dukes of Hazzard, any character, Ben Cooper, 1982, complete, NMIB, C1, ea from $40 to..$50.00
Electra Woman, Ben Cooper, 1976, MIB $40.00
Fantastic Four, Ben Cooper, 4 on wht circle, complete, NMIB, T2...$200.00
Fantastic Four (Thing), Ben Cooper, 1966, complete, NMIB, T2...$100.00
Farrah Fawcett, Collegeville, 1977, complete, EX (EX box) .$40.00
Flash, Ben Cooper, 1967, complete, NMIB, T2..............$100.00
Flipper, Collegeville, 1964, MIB $80.00
Fonzie, Ben Cooper, 1976, MIB $60.00
Green Hornet, Ben Cooper, 1966, complete, NMIB, T2 .$200.00
Green Hornet & Kato, mask set, MOC, T2 ....$300.00
Green Lantern, Ben Cooper, 1967, MIB, T2 ....$100.00
Green Lantern, Dessart Bros, 1961, complete, NMIB, T2.$400.00
He-Man, mask, Mattel, M, F1 ....$10.00

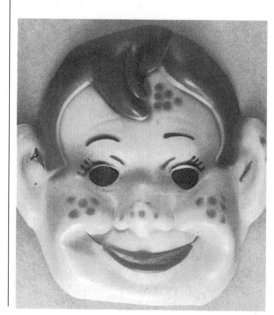

Howdy Doody, mask, 1950s, rubber, movable mouth, EX, $125.00.
(Photo courtesy Jack Koch)

Howdy Doody, mask, 1950-54, cloth, movable mouth, NM.$95.00

HR Pufnstuf, Collegeville, 1970s, MIB $80.00

Hushpuppy, Halco, 1961, complete, EX (EX box), A $65.00

Illya (Man From UNCLE), mask, Halco, 1965, NM, A ...$30.00

Impossibles, Ben Cooper, 1967, complete, NMIB, T2......$50.00

Iron Man, Ben Cooper, 1966, complete, NMIB, T2 ......$200.00

Jed Clampett, 1963, complete, NM..................................$50.00

Jimmy Osmond, Collegeville, 1977, MIB $20.00

King Kong, Ben Cooper, 1976, MIB, H4 ....$75.00

KISS, any member, Collegeville, 1978, MIB, ea.............$125.00

Lampchop, mask, Halco, 1961, NM, A............................$40.00

Laugh-In, Ben Cooper, MIP $40.00

Laura Ingalls, Ben Cooper, 1970, MIB.............................$20.00

Laverne & Shirley, Collegeville, 1977, MIB, ea $25.00

Man From UNCLE, Halco, 1965, Napoleon, mask only, unused, NM, A...$20.00

Mandrake the Magician, Collegeville, 1950s, complete, EX (EX box)..$70.00

Michael Myers (Halloween), mask only, Don Post, latex, M, F1 ....$40.00

Monkees, any member, Bland Charnas, 1967, complete, NMIB, ea...$200.00

Raggedy Ann, mask, Collegeville, 1991, M, $25.00.
(Photo courtesy Kim Avery)

Sigmund & the Sea Monsters, Ben Cooper, 1970s, MIB, from $50 to $60.00

Six Million Dollar Man, Ben Cooper, 1974, complete, EX (EX box), C1 ....$40.00

Space Ghost, Ben Cooper, 1965, MIB, T2, from $75 to.$100.00

Spider-Man, Ben Cooper, 1972, complete, EX (EX box), T2..$50.00

Spider-Woman, Ben Cooper, 1970s, scarce, MIB, T2, from $150 to $200.00

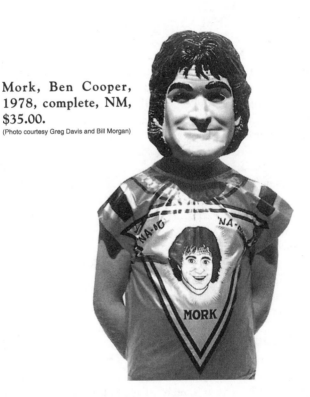

Mork, Ben Cooper, 1978, complete, NM, $35.00.
(Photo courtesy Greg Davis and Bill Morgan)

Mr Fantastic, Ben Cooper, 1967, complete, EX (EX box) ..$50.00

Napoleon (Man From UNCLE), mask only, Halco, 1965, NM, A..$30.00

Phantom, Collegeville, 1956, complete, NMIB, T2.......$150.00

Raggedy Andy, Ben Cooper, 1965, MIB $30.00

Raggedy Andy, mask, Collegeville, 1991, M....................$25.00

Raggedy Ann, Ben Cooper, 1973, MIB............................$25.00

Raggedy Ann, Ben Cooper, 1982, MIB............................$20.00

RoboCop, 1986, mask only, plastic, M, F1 ....$10.00

Shadow, complete, NM, C10 ....$50.00

Shaun Cassidy, 1978, complete, NMIB.............................$30.00

Spock, Ben Cooper, 1970s, complete, EX (EX box), $100.00.

Starsky & Hutch, Ben Cooper, 1976, MIB, ea..................$25.00

Steve Canyon, Halco, 1959, complete, NMIB, T2 ....$50.00

Superman, Ben Cooper, 1950s, complete w/Superman's Buddy comic book, EX (EX box), A $225.00

SWAT, Ben Cooper, 1975, complete, NM (NM box), C1 .$35.00

Tarzan, Ben Cooper, 1975, complete, M (VG box).........$95.00

Tattoo (Fantasy Island), Ben Cooper, 1978, MIB.............$30.00
Thor, Ben Cooper, 1967, mask only, NM $50.00
Top Cat, Ben Cooper, 1965, complete, NMIB $75.00
Welcome Back Kotter, Collegeville, 1976, any character, MIB, ea, $30 to...$40.00
Witchiepoo, Collegeville, 1971, MIB $75.00
Wolfman, 1966, costume only, VG, J2.........................$50.00
Zorro, Ben Cooper, 1955, complete, NM (EX box).........$75.00

Hartland Plastics, Inc.

Originally known as the Electro Forming Co., Hartland Plastics Ind. was founded in 1941 by Ed and Iola Walters. They first produced heels for military shoes, birdhouses, and ornamental wall decor. It wasn't until the late 1940s that Hartland produced their first horse and rider. Figures were hand painted with an eye for detail. The Western and Historic Horsemen, Miniature Western Series, Authentic Scale Model Horses, Famous Gunfighter Series, and the Hartland Sports Series of Famous Baseball Stars were a symbol of the fine workmanship of the '40s, '50s, and '60s. The plastic used was a virgin acetate. Paint was formulated by Bee Chemical Co., Chicago, Illinois, and Wolverine Finishes Corp., Grand Rapids, Michigan. Hartland figures are best known for their uncanny resemblance to the TV Western stars who portrayed characters like the Lone Ranger, Matt Dillon, and Roy Rogers. For more information we recommend *Hartland Horses and Riders* by Gail Fitch. See Also Clubs, Newsletters, and Other Publications.

Advisor: Judy and Kerry Irvin (K5).

Buffalo Bill, NM, $300.00.

See also Sporting Collectibles.

Horses and Riders

Alkine Ike, NM, K5 ....$150.00
Annie Oakley, NM, K5 ....$275.00
Bill Longley, NM, K5 ....$600.00
Brave Eagle, NM, K5 ....$200.00
Brave Eagle, NMIB, K5 ....$300.00
Bret Maverick, miniature series, NM, K5.....................$75.00
Bret Maverick, NMIB, K5 ....$600.00
Bret Maverick, w/coffeedunn horse, NM, K5 ....$500.00
Bret Maverick, w/gray horse, rare, NM, K5..................$600.00
Bullet, NM, K5...$35.00
Bullet, w/tag, NM, K5..$100.00
Cactus Pete, NM, K5 ....$150.00
Champ Cowgirl, NM, K5 ....$150.00
Cheyenne, miniature series, NM, K5 ....$75.00
Cheyenne, w/tag, NM, K5...$190.00
Chief Thunderbird, rare shield, NM, K5........................$150.00
Cochise, NM, K5 ....$150.00
Commanche Kid, NM, K5 ....$150.00
Dale Evans, gr, NM, K5 ....$125.00
Dale Evans, purple, NM, K5 ....$250.00
Dale Evans, rare bl version, NM, K5 ....$500.00
Davy Crockett, NM, K5 ....$500.00
General Custer, NMIB, K5..$250.00
General Custer, repro flag, NM, K5.................................$150.00
General George Washington, NMIB, K5 ....$175.00
General Robert E Lee, NMIB, K5 ....$175.00
Gil Favor, prancing, NM, K5 ....$650.00
Gil Favor, semi-rearing, NM, K5......................................$550.00
Hoby Gillman, NM, K5 ....$250.00
Jim Bowie, w/tag, NM, K5...$250.00
Jim Hardy, NMIB, K5 ....$300.00
Jockey, NM, K5...$150.00
Jockey, repro crop, NM, K5 ....$100.00
Josh Randle, NM, K5..$650.00
Lone Ranger, champ, blk breast collar, NM, K5.............$125.00
Lone Ranger, miniature series, NM, K5 ....$75.00
Lone Ranger, NM, K5 ....$150.00
Lone Ranger, rearing, NMIB, K5 ....$300.00
Matt Dillon, w/tag, NMIB, K5 ....$300.00
Paladin, NMIB, K5..$350.00
Rebel, miniature series, repro hat, NM, K5....................$100.00
Rebel, NMIB, K5...$1,200.00
Rifleman, miniature series, repro rifle, EX, K5 ....$75.00
Rifleman, NMIB $350.00
Ronald MacKenzie, NM, K5 ....$1,200.00
Roy Rogers, semi-rearing, NMIB, K5 ....$600.00
Roy Rogers, walking, NMIB, K5 ....$300.00
Seth Adams, NM, K5 ....$275.00
Sgt Lance O'Rourke, NMIB, K5 ....$300.00
Sgt Preston, repro flag, NM, K5 ....$650.00
Tom Jeffords, NM, K5 ....$175.00
Tonto, miniature series, NM, K5......................................$75.00
Tonto, NM, K5...$150.00
Tonto, rare semi-rearing, NM, K5....................................$650.00

Warpaint Thunderbird, w/shield, NMIB, K5..................$350.00
Wyatt Eart, w/tag, NMIB, K5..............................$250.00

STANDING GUNFIGHTERS

Bat Masterson, NMIB, K5.................................$500.00
Bret Maverick, NM, K5...................................$150.00
Chris Colt, NM, K5.....................................$150.00
Clay Holister, NM, K5..................................$225.00
Dan Troop, NM, K5......................................$500.00
Jim Hardy, NM, K5......................................$150.00
Johnny McKay, NM, K5...................................$800.00
Paladin, NM, K5..$400.00
Vint Bonner, w/tag, NMIB, K5...........................$650.00
Wyatt Earp, NM, K5.....................................$150.00

Horses

Horse riding being the order of the day, many children of the 19th century had their own horses to ride indoors; some were wooden while others were stuffed, and many had glass eyes and real horsehair tails. There were several ways to construct these horses so as to achieve a galloping action. The most common types had rocker bases or were mounted with a spring on each leg.

Davy Crockett Rocking Horse, Rich Toys, 1950s, pressed wood on wood-fr spring base, red, wht & blk, 24", EX, A.$250.00

Gliding Horse, carved and painted wood with hair mane and tail, glass eyes, ears missing otherwise sound, 30x41", A, $700.00.

Gliding Horse, dapple gray w/leather ears, hair tail, celluloid eyes, w/harness & saddle, red base, 32x33", EX, A ..$750.00
Platform Horse, Germany, straw-filled burlap, glass eyes, wood platform w/4 CI spoke wheels, 23x22", EX, A $475.00

Platform Horse, carved wood, black with red saddle and yellow blanket, red platform with cast iron spoke wheels, 30", EX, A, $1,000.00.

Platform Horse, stuffed brn burlap w/hair mane & tail, glass eyes, wood platform w/CI wheels, 25", EX........................$525.00

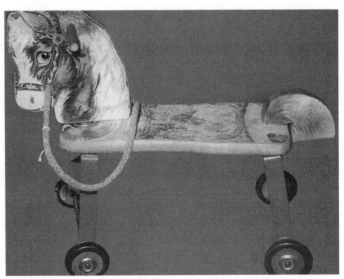

Riding Horse, Gong Bell, 1955, wood with metal legs and rubber wheels, 21½", EX, from $75.00 to $100.00.
(Photo courtesy Linda Baker)

Rocking Horse, convertible, brn & wht hide w/hair mane & tail, glass eyes, red saddle, felt blanket, 35", EX, A $900.00
Rocking Horse, pnt pine w/horse hair mane & tail, leatherette saddle on cloth blanket w/gold fringe, 36" L, G+, A......$1,000.00
Rocking Horse, pnt wood w/glass eyes, leather saddle, remnant of hair mane, scrolled rockers, 26x48", VG, A $475.00
Rocking Horse, wood body w/2-part CI head & neck, metal rockers w/retractable wheels, leather saddle, 26x33", EX, A..$1,265.00

Rocking Horse, wood w/upholstered saddle, metal hand grips, spring-loaded base, 31x34", G, A..............................$400.00

Tricycle Horse, pnt carved wood horse on 3 wooden disk wheels, center handle grip, leatherette saddle, 29x26", VG, A .$385.00

Hot Wheels

When they were introduced in 1968, Hot Wheels were an instant success. Sure, their racy style and flashy custom paint jobs were instant attention-getters, but what the kids loved most was the fact that they were fast! The fastest on the market! It's estimated that more than two billion Hot Wheels have been sold to date — every model with a little variation, keeping up with new trends in the big car industry. The line has included futuristic vehicles, muscle cars, trucks, hot rods, racers, and some military vehicles. A lot of these can still be found for very little, but if you want to buy the older models (collectors call them 'Red Lines' because of their red sidewall tires), it's going to cost you a little more, though many can still be found for under $25.00. By 1971, earlier on some models, black-wall tires had become the standard.

A line of cars with Goodyear tires called Real Riders were made from 1983 until about 1987. (In 1983 the tires had gray hubs with white lettering; in 1984 the hubs were white.) California Customs were made in 1989 and 1990. These had the Real Rider tires, but they were not lettered 'Good Year' (and some had different wheels entirely).

Chopcycles are similar to Sizzlers in that they have rechargable batteries. The first series was issued in 1973 in these models: Mighty Zork, Blown Torch, Speed Steed, and Bruiser Cruiser. Generally speaking, these are valued at $35.00 (loose) to $75.00 (MIB). A second series issued in 1974 was made up of Ghost Rider, Rage Coach, Riptide, Sourkraut, and Triking Viking. This series is considerably harder to find and much more expensive today; expect to pay as much as $250.00 to $350.00 for a mint-in-box example.

Though recent re-releases have dampened the collector market somewhat, cars mint and in the original packages are holding their values and are still moving well. Near mint examples (no package) are worth about 50% to 60% less than those mint and still in their original package, excellent condition about 65% to 75% less.

Advisor: Steve Stephenson.

'31 Doozie, 1977, red line, orange, no tampo, complete, M $40.00

'31 Doozie, 1986, wht walls, maroon w/red-brn fenders, MIP..$12.00

'56 Hi-Tail Hauler, 1977, red line, orange w/yel & bl flame tampo, complete, scarce, M...$65.00

'80s Corvette, 1983, blk walls, gray w/tan & red interior, gold wheels, M...$10.00

Air France Delivery Truck, 1990, blk walls, wht, M (International box) $10.00

Alive '55, 1973, red line, dk bl w/cream interior, VG+ $35.00

Alive '55, 1973, red line, plum w/plum interior, EX+ $120.00

Ambulance, 1970, red line, metallic brn w/cream interior, EX+ $15.00

American Hauler, 1976, red line, dk bl w/red & bl tampo, M.$33.00

American Victory, 1975, red line, lt bl w/red & wht #9 tampo, M (NM rare Japanese box) $75.00

American Victory, 1975, red line, lt bl w/red & wht #9 tampo, M...$30.00

American Victory, 1983, blk walls, lt bl w/dk bl tampo, France, MIP $40.00

AMX/2, 1971, red line, metallic yel w/blk interior, NM ..$40.00

Assault Crawler, 1987, blk walls, olive w/grn, tan & brn camo tampo, M (NM card) $10.00

Auburn 852, 1986, wht walls, gr w/dk gr interior & fenders, M (EX+ card) $8.00

Backwoods Bomb, 1975, red line, lt bl w/yel & lt gr tampo, gray windshield, NM+ $45.00

Baja Bruiser, 1977, red line, dk bl w/plastic chrome base, yel, wht & red tampo, NM+..$50.00

Beach Bomb, 1969, red line, metallic bl w/bl interior, flower decal on roof, complete, EX+ $53.00

Beach Patrol, 1990, blk walls, fluorescent gr w/red interior, magenta, wht & pk tampo, M $10.00

Beatnik Bandit, 1968, red line, metallic aqua, M.............$24.00

Beatnik Bandit, 1968, red line tires, metallic gr, M, $35.00.
(Photo courtesy June Moon)

Bradham Repco F1, 1969, red line, metallic red w/blk interior, M (NM+ Grand Prix Series card) $40.00

Breakaway Bucket, 1974, red line, dk bl w/orange & yel tampo, M..$95.00

Brink's Funny Money, 1977, blk walls, gray, M $35.00

Bronco Four-Wheeler, 1985, blk walls, red, NM+ $6.00

Bugeye, 1971, red line, lt metallic gr w/cream interior, EX+.$24.00

Buzz Off, 1977, red line, gold & chrome w/red & dk red & blk tampo, plastic base, NM $20.00

Bye-Focal, 1971, red line, metallic magenta w/med interior, complete, NM+ $80.00

Captain America, 1979, blk-walls, red, wht & bl, NM.....$20.00

Carabo, 1974, red line, lt gr w/blk interior, orange & bl tampo, M (EX Flying Color card)..$90.00

Cargoyle, 1986, blk walls, orange w/blk eyes & spots, M (International card)..$6.00

Cement Mixer, 1970, red line, metallic olive w/cream interior, complete, EX+ $25.00

Chaparral 2G, 1969, red line, metallic orange w/blk interior, NM $25.00

Chevy Monza 2+2, 1976, red line, Super Chrome, yel & blk tampo, EX+ $15.00

Chief's Special, 1975, red line, red w/yel & wht tampo, M (NM rare Japanese box) $100.00

Classic '31 Woody, 1969, red line, lt metallic magenta w/cream interior, smooth blk roof, NM $50.00

Classic '32 Vicky, 1969, red line, metallic brn w/medium interior, NM+ $34.00

Classic '32 Vicky, 1994, blk walls, metal-flake pk, M (NM card) $7.50

Classic '35 Caddy, 1982, blk walls, tan w/brn interior, M...$4.00

Classic '35 Caddy, 1989, wht walls, silver w/beige interior, pk fenders, NM+ $8.00

Classic '36 Coupe, 1969, red line, metallic yel w/blk interior, smooth blk roof, NM $30.00

Classic '57 T-Bird, 1969, red line, metallic red w/cream interior, EX+ $20.00

Classic Cord, 1971, red line, metallic magenta, complete, M...$225.00

Classic Nomad, 1970, red line, metallic orange w/cream interior, flower decals, NM $50.00

Cockney Cab, 1971, red line, metallic red, complete, NM ..$50.00

Combat Medic, 1988, blk walls, gold & chrome, no horizontal lines, from 20th Anniversary set, M $25.00

Cool One, 1976, red line, plum w/yel & wht tampo, NM+ .$50.00

Custom AMX, 1969, red line, metallic pk w/cream interior, NM $120.00

Custom Baracuda, 1968, red line, metallic aqua, NM $70.00

Custom Camaro, 1968, red line, metallic olive, scarce, NM...$85.00

Custom Continental MK III, 1969, red line, metallic purple w/cream interior, scarce color, EX+ $55.00

Custom Corvette, 1968, red line, metallic magenta w/cream interior, EX $45.00

Custom Cougar, 1968, red line, metallic olive-gold w/cream interior, blk roof, NM..............................$125.00

Custom Cougar, 1968, red line, metallic orange, MIP....$325.00

Custom Dodge Charger, 1969, red line, metallic bl w/cream interior, EX+ $75.00

Custom Eldorado, 1968, red line, metallic olive w/blk roof, MOC...$120.00

Custom Firebird, 1968, red line, metallic gr w/blk roof, cream interior, NM...$60.00

Custom Fleetside, 1968, red line, metallic aqua w/blk interior, NM+ $55.00

Custom Mustang, 1968, red line, metallic bl, rare louvered rear window, EX...$300.00

Custom Mustang, 1968, red line, metallic gold w/cream interior, NM+ $75.00

Custom Mustang, 1968, red line, metallic red w/red interior, rare open scoops, EX $275.00

Custom Mustang, 1994, blk walls, med brn, M (NM card)..$10.00

Custom Police Cruiser, 1969, red line, blk & wht w/cream interior, opaque light, rare prototype w/blk fenders, EX+ $300.00

Custom T-Bird, 1968, red line, lt metallic magenta w/blk roof, NM+ $130.00

Custom VW, 1968, red line, metallic aqua w/cream interior, NM+ $40.00

Demon, 1970, red line, lt metallic gr w/cream interior, NM+ $22.00

Demon, 1994, blk walls, metal-flake bl, Toy Fair limited edition, scarce, M $150.00

Deora, 1968, red line, metallic aqua w/blk interior, M (NM+ card) $220.00

Double Vision, 1973, red line, yel w/cream interior, EX...$60.00

Dump Truck, 1970, red line, metallic bl w/brn bed & yel dump, blk interior, EX+ $25.00

Dune Daddy, 1975, red line, lt gr w/blk interior, orange, yel, bl flower tampo, NM............................$32.00

Dune Daddy, 1975, red line, orange w/blk interior, orange, yel & bl flower tampo, rare, VG........................$100.00

El Rey Special, 1974, red line, dk bl w/yel & orange #1 tampo, rare color, M (NM Flying Colors card) $900.00

El Rey Special, 1974, red line, gr w/yel & orange #1 tampo, NM+ $40.00

Emergency Squad, 1976, red line, red w/gray windshield, M (NM+ bl Flying Colors card)....................$55.00

Emergency Squad, 1977, blk walls, red, M (EX+ card) $8.00

Emergency Squad, 1985, blk walls, yel, M (EX+ International card) $15.00

Evil Weevil, 1971, red line, metallic yel, complete, scarce color, EX+ $50.00

Ferrari 312P, 1974, red line, red w/blk interior, bl & wht tampo, M (M Flying Colors card) $100.00

Ferrari 512S, 1973, red line, fluorescent lime w/blk interior, Shell promotion, MIB $130.00

Fiat Ritmo, France, 1983, blk walls, gray w/brn interior, blk tampo, M (EX+ card) $20.00

Fire Chief Cruiser, 1970, red line, red, no windshield, NM+ .$20.00

Fire Eater, 1977, red line, red w/yel & blk tampo, EX+ $30.00

Fire Engine, 1970, red line, red w/cream interior, complete, EX+ $25.00

Firebird Funny Car, 1989, blk walls, yel w/orange, blk & bl tampo, M (EX card) $4.00

Ford Aerostar, 1991, blk walls, wht, M (NM International box)..$7.00

Ford Escort GT, 1984, blk walls, yel w/red, bl & wht tampo, M (NM International card) $59.00

Ford J-Car, 1968, red line, matallic magenta w/blk interior, NM...$15.00

Ford Mk IV, 1969, red line, metallic bl w/blk interior, NM+ $20.00

Ford Stake Bed Truck, 1983, blk walls, bl, Sunset Trucking logo, M (EX+ Extras card)...........................$7.00

Formula PACK, 1976, blk walls, blk w/orange & yel tampo, rare wheel type, M (EX+ Flying Colors card)....................$85.00

Formula PACK, 1976, red line, blk w/orange & yel tampo, M (NM rare Japanese box) $75.00

Formula 5000, 1976, red line, wht w/bl & red #76 tampo, M (NM Flying Colors card) $45.00

Formula 5000, 1977, blk walls, Super Chrome, bl & red tampo, M $20.00

Funny Money, 1974, red line, plum w/orange & yel tampo, NM+ $60.00

GMC Motor Home, Hong Kong, 1977, blk walls, gold & chrome, no tampo, extremely rare, M $1,000.00

GMC Motor Home, Hong Kong, 1977, red line, orange w/bl, wht & yel tampo, rare, VG+ $300.00

Grass Hopper, 1971, red line, metallic gr w/blk interior, scarce color, NM+ $50.00

Grass Hopper, 1975, red line, lt gr w/blk plastic base, orange & bl tampo, no engine exposed, scarce, NM.................$90.00

Greased Gremlin, 1979, blk walls, red w/bl, yel & wht #5 tampo, M...$10.00

Gremlin Grinder, 1976, red line, Super Chrome, red, gr & blk tampo, M (EX rare Japanese box) $55.00

Gun Bucket, 1976, red line, olive w/wht tampo, VG+ $6.00

Hairy Hauler, 1971, red line, metallic yel w/cream interior, scarce color, NM+ $50.00

Heavy Chevy, 1974, red line, yel w/dk red, lt & dk orange tampo, NM+ $150.00

Heavyweights Cab, red line, metallic gr w/cream interior, no trailer, EX+..$9.00

Hot Bird, 1980, black walls, blue with orange and yellow tampo, scarce color, M, $30.00. (Photo courtesy June Moon)

Hot Heap, 1968, red line, metallic orange w/cream interior, NM+ $30.00

Ice T, 1971, red line, yel w/blk interior, EX+.....................$20.00

Ice T, 1973, red line, dk bl w/blk interior, EX+ $35.00

Ice T, 1974, red line, lt gr w/blk interior, orange & olive tampo, M..$40.00

Indy Eagle, 1969, red line, metallic gr w/blk interior, orig decal, NM..$16.00

Inferno, 1976, red line, yel w/orange, purple & red tampo, NM+ $30.00

Inside Story, 1979, blk walls, gray w/red, yel & bl tampo, NM+ $6.00

Jack Rabbit Special, 1970, red line, wht w/blk interior, M (EX card) $40.00

Jet Threat, 1971, red line, metallic yel, NM $45.00

Jet Threat, 1975, red line, red, Shell promo, M (M card) .$100.00

Khaki Kooler, 1976, red line, olive w/charcoal plastic base, wht tampo, EX..$8.00

King Kuda, 1970, red line, Club Car, chrome, complete, NM..$60.00

Large Charge, 1976, red line, Super Chrome, blk, yel & orange tampo, M..$30.00

Light My Firebird, 1970, red line, metallic bl, complete, NM...$35.00

Lola GT-70, 1969, red line, dk gr w/blk interior, M (NM+ Grand Prix Series card) $50.00

Lola GT-70, 1969, red line, metallic brn, EX.................$25.00

Lotus Turbine, 1969, red line, metallic purple w/blk interior, MIP $30.00

Lowdown, 1976, red line, gold-chrome w/red, wht & bl tampo, M (EX rare Japanese box)..$60.00

Mantis, red line tires, metallic green, 1970, NM, $35.00. (Photo courtesy June Moon)

Mantis, 1970, red line, metallic yel w/cream interior, NM+ .$13.00

Maserati Mistral, 1969, red line, metallic orange w/cream interior, NM $60.00

Maserati Mistral, 1969, red line, metallic purple, M (EX European Series card) $120.00

Maxi Taxi, 1976, red line, yel w/red, wht & blk tampo, M (rare NM red Japanese box) $75.00

Mercedes C-111, 1972, red line, metallic bl w/cream interior, NM+ $120.00

Mercedes SL, 1991, blk walls, M (NM International card) .$10.00

Mercedes 540K, 1988, wht walls, Super Chrome, 20th Anniversary, NM+ $10.00

Mighty Maverick, 1975, red line, lt gr w/bl & wht tampo, scarce color, NM $160.00

Mod Quad, 1970, red line, lt metallic gr w/blk interior, M .$34.00

Mod Quad, 1970, red line, metallic magenta, Howard Reese concept design, NM..$50.00

Mongoose, 1970, red line, red, w/orig cage & prop, NM ..$20.00

Monte Carlo Stocker, 1975, red line, yel w/blk interior, red, wht & bl #38 tampo, M (NM Flying Colors card).........$110.00

Monte Carlo Stocker, 1977, blk walls, yel w/red, wht & bl #38 tampo, NM..$15.00

Moving Van, 1970, red line, metallic gr w/blk interior & gray trailer, NM..$26.00

Mustang Boss, 1971, red line, metallic purple w/cream interior, NM..$150.00

Mustang Stocker, 1976, red line, Super Chrome, orange & magenta tampo, M (NM rare Japanese box)...........$150.00

Mutt Mobile, 1971, red line, metallic aqua, complete, NM ..$40.00

Mutt Mobile, 1994, blk walls, metallic magenta, M (NM card) $8.00

Nitty Gritty Kitty, 1970, red line, metallic bl, complete, EX+ $20.00

Noodlehead, 1971, red line, metallic magenta w/cream interior, scarce color, EX+ $30.00

Olds 442, 1971, red line, metallic bl w/cream interior, complete, NM+ $375.00

Open Fire, 1972, red line, metallic magenta, NM $100.00

P-911, 1976, red line, Super Chrome, red & gr striped tampo, NM $30.00

Paddy Wagon, 1970, red line, dk bl w/gold letters, M (NM card) $30.00

Paramedic, 1977, red line, yel w/red & wht tampo, M (rare NM red Japanese box) $75.00

Peeping Bomb, 1970, red line tires, metallic orange, M, $65.00. (Photo courtesy June Moon)

Peeping Bomb, 1973, red line, red, Shell promotion, MIB .$100.00

Peterbilt Dump Truck, 1983, blk walls, yel, M (EX+ International Extras card)...$6.00

Peterbilt Dump Truck, 1985, blk walls, metal-flake bl, M (NM Workhorses card) $7.00

Peugeot 205 Rallye, 1989, blk walls, wht w/#2 tampo, M (NM International card)..$8.00

Pit Crew, 1971, red line, wht w/cream interior, complete, w/8 stickers, NM..$60.00

Poison Pinto, 1976, red line, lt gr w/yel, blk & wht tampo, NM..$40.00

Police Cruiser, 1973, red line, wht w/blk interior, NM.....$50.00

Porsche Carrera, 1975, red line, yel w/orange & bl tampo, NM $40.00

Porsche Targa Christmas Car, 1996, blk walls, red, w/Santa & passenger, M (NM card) $20.00

Porsche 911, 1976, red line, Super Chrome, orange, red & yel tampo, NM...$20.00

Porsche 917, 1974, red line, orange w/yel, purple & red Porsche tampo, NM..$30.00

Porsche 959, 1989, blk walls, wht w/blk interior, M (VG+ Park 'N Plates card)..$7.00

Porsche 959, 1991, blk walls, yel, Getty promotion, M (M bag)...$5.00

Power Pad, 1970, red line, metallic pk w/blk interior, complete, NM..$50.00

Power Plower Cabover, 1990, blk walls, blk, tandem axle, M ..$4.00

Pro Circuit #2, 1993, blk walls, wht w/Texaco logo, gray Pro Circuit Indy wheels, NM+...$6.00

Pro Circuit #43, 1992, blk walls, bl w/lt bl interior, w/border, STP logo, gray Pro Circuit wheels, M $8.00

Prowler, 1978, blk walls, Super Chrome, NM...................$16.00

Python, 1968, red line, metallic red, EX...........................$8.00

Racer Rig, 1971, red line, wht w/blk interior, complete, NM.$80.00

Ramblin' Wrecker, 1975, red line, wht w/bl windshield, w/phone number, M (NM Flying Colors card) $75.00

Ranger Rig, 1975, red line, gr w/yel tampo, gray windshield, M $50.00

Rapid Transit RTD, 1982, blk walls, wht w/bl tampo on rear window, M (VG+ card)...$5.00

Rapid Transit School Bus, 1984, blk walls, yel, M (NM Team Bus card) $7.00

Rash 1, 1975, red line, gr w/yel, wht & red tampo, M $60.00

Red Baron, 1970, red line, metallic red w/blk interior, sharp point, EX $8.00

Red Baron, 1973, red line, red w/blk interior, dull point, VG+ $4.00

Renault 5 Turbo, 1991, blk walls, bl w/yel, orange & wht tampo, M (NM+ International card)............................$4.00

Road King, 1974, red line, yel, w/orig trailer, rare, EX+ ...$330.00

Road Torch, 1987, blk walls, red w/blk, wht & yel #9 tampo, M (NM International card) $6.00

Rock Buster, 1976, red line, yel w/red, wht & bl #10 tampo, M $30.00

Rock Buster, 1977, blk walls, Super Chrome, NM............$20.00

Rocket Bye Baby, 1973, red line, red, Shell promotion, MIB .$150.00

Rodger Dodger, 1974, red line, plum w/orange & yel flame tampo, EX+ $50.00

RR Silver Shadow, 1969, red line, metallic bl, NM..........$35.00

S'Cool Bus, 1971, red line, yel, NM...............................$120.00

Sand Crab, 1970, red line, metallic pk w/blk interior, EX+...$20.00

Sand Drifter, 1975, red line, yel w/orange & magenta flame tampo, EX+ $35.00

Scooper, 1971, red line, metallic yel, NM+ $80.00

Seasider, 1970, red line, metallic yel w/blk interior, NM+ .$80.00

Second Wind, 1977, red line, wht w/red, yel & purple tampo, NM $30.00

Shelby Turbine, 1969, red line, metallic gr w/blk interior, M (NM Grand Prix Series card) $40.00

Short Order, 1971, red line, gold w/blk interior, M $40.00

Show Hoss II, 1977, red line, yel w/dk red, wht & blk tampo, rare color, M (M rare Japanese box) $600.00

Side Kick, 1972, red line, lt metallic gr, EX $45.00

Side Kick, 1972, red line, metallic gr w/chrome slide-out cockpit, Larry Wood concept design, NM.........................$60.00

Silhouette, 1968, red line, metallic purple, M..................$20.00

Single-Deck Bus, blk walls, red, M (EX+ card) $6.00

Six Shooter, 1971, red line, metallic aqua, M..................$90.00

Sky Show Fleetside, 1970, red line, gold w/blk interior, complete, NM+ $325.00

Snake, 1970, red line, yel, NM+.......................................$30.00

Snake, 1994, blk walls, metal-flake gr, Vintage, M (NM card) $15.00

Snake II, 1971, red line, wht, EX+ $35.00

Snake Rear Engine Dragster, 1972, red line, yel w/clear front wheels, NM...$170.00

Snorkel, 1971, red line, wht w/blk interior, M (NM card)..$200.00

Special Delivery, 1971, red line, metallic bl, complete, NM..$35.00

Splittin' Image, 1973, red line, lt bl, Shell promotion, MIB ..$120.00

Splittin' Image, 1969, red line tires, metallic green, M, $60.00. (Photo courtesy June Moon)

Spoiler Sport, 1977, blk walls, gr w/blk, yel & dk red tampo, 2 rear windows, NM.................................$5.00
Spoiler Sport, 1977, red line, gr w/blk, yel & dk red tampo, scarce, M $50.00
Spoiler Sport, 1980, blk walls, gr w/blk, yel & dk red tampo, 1 lg window, MIP.............................$6.00
Staff Car, 1976, red line, olive w/wht tampo, rare, G $90.00
Steam Roller, 1976, red line, Super Chrome, blk plastic base, yel & bl tampo, M (NM rare Japanese box) $60.00
Steve's Rig Wrecker, 1983, blk walls, wht, M (EX+ Workhorses card) $12.00
Street Eater, 1975, red line, yel w/red & orange flame tampo, M (NM Flying Colors card) $300.00
Street Snorter, 1973, red line, red w/red & orange flame tampo, NM+ $150.00
Strip Teaser, 1973, red line, fluorescent pk, Shell promotion, complete, MIB................................$140.00
Sugar Caddy, 1971, red line, metallic gr, complete, NM ..$35.00
Super Fine Turbine, 1973, red line, red w/blk interior, scarce color, VG...$125.00
Super Van, 1975, red line, plum w/scarce motorcycle tampo, NM...$125.00
SWAT Van Scene, 1979, blk walls, dk bl, VG................$15.00

T-4-2, 1971, red line tires, metallic green, scarce color, M, $35.00. (Photo courtesy June Moon)

Sweet 16, 1973, red line, dk bl w/blk interior, EX+........$110.00
Swingin' Wing, 1973, red line, fluorescent pk, Shell promotion, MIB..............................$130.00
T-Bird Stocker, 1984, blk walls, wht w/dk bl back, red & bl #21 Valvoline tampo, gold wheels, M (NM+ card)..........$30.00
T-Bird Stocker, 1996, blk walls, red & wht, Bill Elliot, Kellogg's promotion, M (EX+ card)............................$7.00
T-4-2, 1971, red line, metallic gr, scarce color, NM.........$30.00
T-4-2, 1971, red line, metallic yel, NM............................$20.00
Team Trailer, 1971, red line, metallic red w/cream interior, NM...$50.00
Thing, 1979, blk walls, dk bl, M............................$15.00
Thor Van, 1979, blk walls, yel, M $10.00
Thunderstreak, 1989, blk walls, bl, Kraco, M (VG+ Park 'N Plates card) $10.00
Thunderstreak, 1994, blk walls, turq, Aquafresh promotion, M (NM+ box) $8.00
TNT Bird, 1970, red line, metallic gr w/blk roof, cream interior, VG+ $15.00
Top Eliminator, 1974, red line, dk bl w/orange, gr & yel tampo, NM+ $60.00
Torero, 1969, red line, metallic aqua w/cream interior, NM .$10.00
Torino Stocker, 1975, red line, red w/yel, bl & wht #23 tampo, NM.....................................$60.00
Torino Stocker, 1979, blk w/yel, orange & wht #3 tampo, NM.....................................$5.00
Tow Truck, 1970, red line, metallic gr w/blk interior, NM..$25.00
Trash Truck, 1985, blk walls, orange w/blk, bl & gr tampo, M (EX Workhorses card) $15.00
Tri Baby, 1970, red line, metallic pk w/cream interior, EX+.......................................$25.00
Turbo Streak, 1996, blk walls, dk bl, Union 76 promotion, M.......................................$4.00
Turbofire, 1970, red line, metallic red w/cream interior, NM.$10.00
Twin Mill, 1973, red line, fluorescent pk, Shell promotion, MIB $135.00
Twin Mill II, 1977, blk walls, Super Chrome, red, wht & bl tampo, NM.....................................$22.00
Vega Bomb, 1975, red line, orange w/red, yel & bl tampo, France, complete, NM.............................$75.00
VW Bug, 1974, red line, orange w/blk, yel & gr tampo, complete, M...$80.00
Warpath, 1975, red line, wht w/red & bl tampo, metal base, M (EX+ Flying Colors card) $120.00
Waste Wagon, 1971, red line, metallic aqua, NM...........$60.00
What 4, 1971, red line, metallic gr w/lt interior, NM.......$40.00
Whip Creamer, 1970, red line, metallic pk w/blk interior, NM $30.00
Whip Creamer, 1994, blk walls, Vintage, metal-flake dk red, M (NM card) $5.00
Winnipeg, 1974, red line, yel w/bl & orange tampo, M .$130.00

RUMBLERS

Bold Eagle, 1972, red line, yel, orig silver driver w/flesh face, silver goggles, training wheels, NM $100.00
Bone Shaker, 1973, red line, wht, orig yel driver w/flesh face, goggles, yel helmet, training wheels, rare, M $300.00

Centurion, 1973, red line, yel-orange w/golden orange lion, orig silver driver w/flesh face, training wheel, M (EX card) $500.00

Choppin' Chariot, 1972, orange, orig bl driver w/full-face mask, wht helmet, missing training wheels, NM $35.00

Devil's Deuce, metallic gr, orig bl driver w/flesh face, blk cowboy hat, training wheels, NM+ $40.00

High Tailer, 1971, orange, orig bl driver w/wht full-face helmet, training wheels, M $40.00

Mean Machine, 1971, dk bl w/red gas tank, training wheels, missing driver, NM+...$35.00

Revolution, 1972, yel, orig bl driver w/flesh face, bl helmet, missing training wheels, NM $45.00

Rip Cord, 1973, bl, orig lime driver w/wht full-face helmet, training wheels, M (EX card) $250.00

Rip Snorter, 1971, orange, orig tan driver w/flesh face, tan helmet, training wheels, NM+ $30.00

Road Hog, 1971, orange, no driver or training wheels, NM..$20.00

Roamin' Candle, 1972, metallic orange-brn, orig brn driver w/wht full-face shield on wht helmet, no training wheels, EX..$15.00

Straight Away, 1972, metallic brn, orig tan driver w/tan full-face shield on wht helmet, training wheels, NM............$25.00

3 Squealer, 1971, orange w/blk tank, orig driver w/helmet & goggles, training wheels, M...$40.00

SIZZLERS

Angeleno M70, 1970, chrome, prof rstr, NM+ $25.00

Anteater, 1971, metallic orange, NM $25.00

Backfire, 1971, lt metallic gr, NM $20.00

Camaro Trans-Am, 1971, wht, scarce color, NM..........$100.00

Co-Motion, 1972, metallic gr, EX+ $30.00

Corvette 4 Rotor, 1976, yel, scarce, NM $80.00

Cuda Trans-Am, 1971, metallic orange, EX $60.00

Dark Shadow, 1976, yel, scarce, NM...............................$50.00

Double Boiler, 1972, metallic yel, scarce, NM $50.00

Ferrari 512S, 1971, red, no stickers, NM..........................$35.00

Firebird Trans-Am, 1970, metallic gr, NM $50.00

Flat Out, 1972, metallic pk, M (NM scarce box)..............$50.00

Hot Head, 1970, metallic gr, M.......................................$40.00

Hot Wings, 1971, metallic olive, EX+ $25.00

Juice Machine, MIB..$25.00

Lamborghini Countach, 1976, metallic orange, scarce, EX+ .$30.00

Law Mill, 1973, metallic bl, scarce, EX+ $30.00

Live Wire, 1971, chrome, M..$35.00

Moon Ghost, 1976, wht, scarce, EX+...............................$55.00

Mustang Boss 302, 1970, M (NM box) $125.00

Short Fuse, 1976, lt gr, scarce, NM $60.00

Sideburn, 1971, blk, EX+...$15.00

Spoil Sport, 1971, metallic red, MIB................................$45.00

Straight Scoop, 1971, metallic lime, MIB $50.00

MISCELLANEOUS

Action City, 1969, yel, EX+ $75.00

Button, Ambulance, metal, NM...$5.00

Button, Bugeye, plastic, M $5.00

Button, Cement Mixer, metal, NM+ $5.00

Button, Beatnik Bandit, metal, NM, $8.00.
(Photo courtesy June Moon)

Button, Classic '31 Ford Woody, metal, NM $5.00

Button, Classic '57 T-Bird, metal, NM..............................$5.00

Button, Classic Cord, plastic, M $5.00

Button, Custom Barracuda, metal, NM $5.00

Button, Evil Weevil, metal, NM+ $8.00

Button, Ice T, plastic, NM+ $5.00

Button, Jet Threat, plastic, M..$10.00

Button, Olds 442, metal, rare, M $25.00

Button, Porsche 917, plastic, rare, M $25.00

Button, Racer Rig, metal, NM+ $10.00

Button, S'Cool Bus, plastic, rare, NM $15.00

Button, Short Order, plastic, M $6.00

Button, Snake II, plastic, NM+ $10.00

Button, Strip Teaser, plastic, NM+ $6.00

Button, Tow Truck, metal, NM+ $5.00

Button, What 4, plastic, NM+..$5.00

Case, 12-car, 1969, yel w/red car on front, NM $30.00

Case, 12-car, 1980, bl, Doozie, Mirada Stocker & CAT vehicles on front, EX $10.00

Case, 12-car pop-up, 1968, orange w/name on front, cars on back, EX $20.00

Case, 24-car, 1969, yel w/wht & bl cars on front, adjustable, EX $20.00

Case, 24-car, 1975, bl w/wht trays, Porsche 917, Super Van & Emergency Squad on front, NM..................................$20.00

Case, 48-car, 1969, yel, adjustable, NM $45.00

Case, 72-car, 1970, blk w/Snake & Mongoose on front, EX..$40.00

Chopcycles, Mighty Zork, metallic gr, M (NM card) $75.00

Chopcycles, Speed Steed, metallic gr, M (NM card)........$75.00

City Machines, 1982, set of 6, MIB.................................$60.00

Collector's Button Book, Rumblers Are Coming, 1970, 3-fold cb, EX+ $70.00

Display Rack, Joiner Pak, 1970, cb counter-top, w/12 unopened Joiner Paks, EX+...$120.00

Dual-Lane Speedometer, 1970, wht & orange, EX+.........$15.00

Game, Hot Wheels Wipe-Out Race, 1969, MIB $40.00

Gran Toro, Chaparral 2G, wht, complete, 1970, NM....$125.00

Gran Toro, Chevy Astro II, 1970, gray, complete, NM....$80.00
Gran Toro, Ford Mark V, metallic bl, 1970, NM $90.00
Gran Toro, T'rantula, metallic gr, complete, 1970, M ...$250.00
Iron-On Patch, 1969, Hot Wheels logo, NM....................$10.00
Lap Counter, 1970, wht & orange, complete, NMIB..........$5.00
Magazine, Hot Wheels Racing World, 1970, 32-pg yearbook,
     VG+ $40.00
Mongoose & Snake Drag Race Set, 1994 reissue, MIB
     (sealed) $40.00
Puzzle, 1970, jigsaw, shows race scene w/Jack Rabbit & 3 other
     cars, M (VG+ box) $20.00
Revvers Haulin' Horses, dk bl, EX.............................$18.00
Revvers Stingin' Thing, lt bl, EX $18.00
Speedometer, 1970, EX...$8.00
Stick-Arounds, MOC $60.00

Super-Charger Sprint Set, complete, EX (EX box), $225.00.

Talking Service Center, 1969, complete, scarce, NM $75.00
Two-Way Super Charger, 1970, EX+...............................$15.00

Housewares

Back in the dark ages before women's lib and career-minded mothers, little girls emulated mommy's lifestyle, not realizing that by the time they grew up, total evolution would have taken place before their very eyes. They'd sew and bake, sweep, do laundry and iron (gasp!), and imagine what fun it would be when *they* were big like mommy. Those little gadgets they played with are precious collectibles today, and any child-size houseware item is treasured, especially those from the '40s and '50s. If you're interested in learning about toy sewing machines, we recommend *Toy and Miniature Sewing Machines* by Glenda Thomas (Collector Books).

Advisor: Lorraine Punchard (P13) author of *Playtime Kitchen Items and Table Accessories*.

CLEANING AND LAUNDRY

Clothes Presser, 1930s, yel & gr tin w/wooden roller, w/up &
     electric, EX..$85.00
Clothes Wringer, stamped Horse Shoe Brand, wood w/rubber
     rollers mounted in basin, CI crank, 10", EX, A $700.00
Iron, Wolverine, 1950s, electric, MIB, H12....................$35.00

Iron, Wolverine, 1960s, litho tin w/red plastic hdl, EX, S13 .$15.00
Laundry Set, Sunny Suzy, 6 pcs, EX................................$100.00
Laundry Set, wood, table marked Peerless, w/2 washtubs, clothes
     wringer, washboard & clothespins, 15½" table, G ..$750.00
Washboard & Tub, 4-legged wooden tub w/metal bands & hdls,
     corrugated tin & wooden scrub board, 8" dia, EX, A.$125.00
Washing Machine, Pretty Maid, Marx, metal & plastic, EX .$150.00
Washing Machine, Wolverine, glass & tin, 10", EX.........$65.00

COOKING

Baking Set, Mother's Little Helper, early, complete w/rolling pin,
     egg beater, bowls, cutter & baking sheets, MIB, H12 .$150.00

Children's Kitchen Set, Krest, 'Beauty Bright' Steel, eight pcs, NMIB, $50.00.

Cooking Set, Mirro, 1940s, 16 pcs, MIB, H12 ....$150.00
Little Mother's Kitchen, Cragstan, 1950s, tin, complete, EX (EX
     box)..$235.00
Stove, Acme, NP CI w/early decorative details, 12", VG+, A.$210.00
Stove, Arcade, Hotpoint Electric Range, #614, wht & gr CI,
     6x5½", MIB, A...$1,980.00
Stove, Blue Bird, bl-pnt CI w/wht trim, overhead spice cabinet,
     6½", EX, A $200.00
Stove, Dainty, CI w/NP door, long chimney pipe, scalloped base,
     22", EX, A...$775.00
Stove, Eagle, bl-pnt CI w/wht trim, curved warmer cabinet
     & opening door, lg grill top w/rail switch panels, 9", EX,
     A...$600.00
Stove, Eagle, NP CI w/ornate design, features dump grate, elevated
     warming oven & 4 removable lids, 12", NM, A...........$550.00
Stove, Eagle, wht-pnt CI w/bl trim, 2 NP pans on range top, 6",
     EX, A $275.00
Stove, Gem, NP CI, Pat 1894, 5x8x4½", NM, A...........$350.00
Stove, Germany, tin w/5 fitted pots, removable burners, blk
     w/NP trim, 10½" W, VG, A $350.00

Stove, Arcade, Daisy, black-painted cast iron with gold trim, 6½x5", MIB, A, $750.00.

Stove, Home, NP CI w/4 removable lids, 4", EX, A $150.00

Stove, Kenton, bl-pnt CI w/Kent emb on NP door, 6", EX, A $450.00

Stove, Lionel, 1930s, gr & cream enameled steel, w/4 operating burners, 37", EX, A..$825.00

Stove, Pet, NP CI w/dump grate, 5 removable lids, 2 pans & a teapot, 11", VG, A $275.00

Stove, Royal, NP CI w/ornate design, removable dump grate, elevated warming oven & 5 removable doors, 11½", NM, A $825.00

Stove, Superior, bl-pnt CI & sheet metal w/NP cook top, 6x5x4", EX, A...$350.00

Stove, Venus, bl-pnt CI & sheet metal w/NP cook top, 5x4½x8½", EX, A..$400.00

Stove, Vindex, gr & wht CI w/NP cook top, overhead cupboard, footed base, 15x13x8", EX, A $1,650.00

Stove, Western Electric Jr, pressed steel, blk w/NP top, 15", EX, A $50.00

Teapot, NP CI w/porcelain knob on lid, spring handle, 6", EX, A $175.00

Waffle Iron, CI, 3 separate pcs w/hdls & emb images of people in various activities, EX, A $100.00

Waffle Iron, Stover Junior, cast iron w/wooden hdls, EX .$175.00

NURSERY

Carriage, wicker, Philadelphia Baby Carriage Factory, metal fr & spoke wheels, parasol holder, wood hdl, 28x33", EX, A $100.00

Carriage, wood, blk oilcloth top w/rear window & landau bars, velvet upholstered interior, spoke wheels, 25x37", EX, A..$450.00

Carriage, wood, diecut horse sides w/stenciling, open seat, spoke wheels, 25x36", VG+, A $475.00

Carriage, wood, Joel Ellis, stenciled w/images of animals & flowers, fringed canopy, oilcloth upholstery, 27x36", EX, A.....$275.00

Carriage, wood, mk Pat Aug 24, 1880, fringed canopy & pillow intact, 22x31", EX, A $315.00

Carriage, wood, 3 wooden spoke wheels, blk oilcloth folding top, litho paper floor covering, w/trim, 23x34", EX, A...$300.00

Grooming Set, 1920s-30s, hand-pnt celluloid brush, comb & rattle w/bl ribbon flowers, M (M floral box), H12 ...$125.00

Stroller, litho tin w/image of puppies & ducks, 1940-50, 6½", NM, G16 ....$110.00

SEWING

Cutting Machine, Singer, wht plastic w/suction-cup foot, EX $50.00

Sewing basket, sq wicker basket on 4 tall legs w/lid & bottom shelf, 17x9", EX..$55.00

Sewing Cabinet, Martha Washington, ca 1930, dk wood w/3 drawers, flip-top side compartments, 18", EX $250.00

Sewing Kit, lid illus w/Victorian girls & Christmas pram, w/mirror, needles, thread, thimble & button, MIB..........$135.00

Sewing Machine, Jaymar, Japan, battery-op w/foot pedal & on-off switch, orange metal w/crinkle finish, EX............$50.00

Sewing Machine, Lindstrom, 1940s, lithographed metal with wood handle, 6x8", EX, $50.00. (Photo courtesy Linda Baker)

Sewing Machine, Little Gem #6103, Western Stamping, hand-op, plastic, EX (EX box) $20.00

Sewing Machine, My Little Pony, Hasbro #5844, 1980s, battery-op w/foot pedal & light, EX $35.00

Sewing Machine, Raggedy Ann, Bobbs-Merrill #5820, Durham Industries/Hong Kong, 1970s, plastic, EX $35.00

Sewing Machine, Romance, Japan, manual or battery-op w/on-off switch, metal w/plastic wheel on wood base, EX ..$65.00

Sewing Machine, Sew Master, KAYanEE Corp of America, hand-op single sheet metal body, black w/flowers, EX $100.00

Sewing Machine, Sew Mate, Hong Kong, 1980s, hand-op, uses yarn & paper, yel & wht plastic, EX...........................$20.00

Sewing Machine, Sew Ette, Japan, 1960s, battery-op w/foot pedal & on-off switch, bl plastic w/crinkle finish, EX..........$50.00

Sewing Machine, Singer Chainstitch, 1980s, battery-op w/foot pedal, plastic, EX $25.00

Sewing Machine, Singer Touch & Sew #67A, battery-op or used w/electric adapter, w/on-off switch, plastic, complete, EX $50.00

Sewing Machine, Universal, Unitoys Inc, manual-op, orange & wht plastic, EX..$30.00

Sewing Machine, Zig Zag, JC Penney Christmas Catalog/Japan, 1973, electric, metal w/metal & nylon gears, EX.......$50.00

MISCELLANEOUS

Boone Kitchen Cabinet, Arcade, mostly CI, wht w/bl-gr trim, 8x5½", M, A..$1,650.00

Garbage Receiver, Sexron Sanitary Ajax, salesman's sample, metal, blk w/gr lid, 4", NM, A..................................$325.00

Ice Cream Freezer, Dana-Peerless, wooden barrel w/CI crank, bail hdl, 7½", EX, A...$125.00

Lawnmower, Pat Oct 1907, salesman's sample, CI w/pressed steel blades & wooden roller, 8½", EX, A $550.00

Scales, Arcade, mk Toledo, red-pnt CI, 5", EX, A $600.00

Scales, Kenton, red-painted cast iron with nickel-plated balance beam and weights, MIB, A, $550.00; Cream Separator, Arcade, black-painted cast iron with nickel-plated bucket and parts, 5", MIB, A, $2,200.00.

Jack-in-the Boxes

Very early jack-in-the-box toys were often made of papier-mache and cloth, fragile material to withstand the everyday wear and tear to which they were subjected, so these vintage German examples are scarce today and very expensive. But even those from the '50s and '60s are collectible, especially when they represent well-known TV or storybook characters. Examples with lithographed space themes are popular as well.

See also Character, TV, and Movie Collectibles; Disney.

Clown, Germany, compo head w/crepe-paper outfit, litho wood box, 3½", EX, A $100.00

Clown, Mattel, 1971, litho tin, EX, J2 ....$50.00

Clown in House, Germany, papier-mache & cloth figure in paper-covered wood box pops out of window, 6½", VG, A $465.00

Devil Head, Germany, 1920s, yel- & red-pnt wood box w/devil on spring, EX, A $875.00

Girl, compo figure w/cloth clothes, paper-covered wooden box, EX $300.00

Jester, Lorraine Novelty Mfg, plays 'Pop Goes the Weasel,' litho metal w/cloth figure, NM $40.00

Jesters, two hand-painted papier-mache heads with fabric hats and fur-lined clothing, paper litho on wood box, 6", G, A, $700.00.

Poodle Wearing Glasses, German, paper label on wood box, papier-mache figure w/wht fur trim, w/squeaker, 4" sq, EX...$300.00

Keystone

Though this Massachusetts company produced a variety of toys during their years of operation (ca 1920–late '50s), their pressed-steel vehicles are the most collectible, and that's what we've listed here. As a rule they were very large, with some of the riders being 30" in length.

Aerial Ladder Truck, 1929, red w/2 ladders, hose reel & bell, wht rubber tires, 28", VG, A $500.00

Airmail Single-Engine Plane #NX-265, 23", VG $550.00

Ambulance, 1929, khaki w/canvas sides & curtains, 28", rstr...$700.00

Coast-to-Coast Bus #84, 32", G, A $1,400.00

Dump Truck, blk w/red chassis & hubs, doorless cab, lever controls, 26", VG...$650.00

Fire Truck, red w/4 ladders, crank-op, 25", EX, A $550.00

Greyhound Bus, bright bl w/silver Greyhound logo, blk rubber tires, 18", G, A...$325.00

Hydraulic Dump Truck, blk w/red frame & hubcaps, brass piston mounted behind cab, 26", VG, A $1,700.00

Moving Van, blk cab w/orange covered bed, blk rubber tires w/orange hubs, G, A $1,000.00

Packard Dump Truck, blk w/red chassis & hubs, crank-op, 26", EX, A..$2,100.00

Packard Sprinkler Tank, blk, yel, gr & red, spigot on rear of tank, 24", rare, VG, A..$2,500.00
Packard US Army Truck, khaki, open bench seat, canvas canopy, 26", VG, A..$550.00

Packard Water Tower Truck, rider, elevating hose tower & hand-op air pressure pump, battery-op light, 29", VG, A, $900.00

Police Patrol Truck, 28", EX..$1,400.00
Railroad Wrecking Car #6600, 20", EX, D10..................$475.00
Railway Express Truck, blk cab w/gr screened-in storage bed, red chassis, blk tires w/red hubs, 26", rstr, A...................$450.00

Steam Roller, blk w/red roof & roller frame, stack on hood, side crank, EX, A, $500.00

Steam Shovel, gray w/red roof & base, blk digging bucket w/hand-crank pulley system, 20", NM, A................$400.00
Truck Loader, khaki w/red base & wheels, grab buckets on chain belt, 20", G, A...$200.00
Truck Loader #44, 18", EX, A..$650.00
US Army Truck, open cab w/cloth-covered back, 26", G, A .$525.00
Wrecker Truck, red w/open bench seat, hand-op crane on body, 27½", EX, A...$900.00

Lehmann

Lehmann toys were made in Germany as early as 1881. Early on they were sometimes animated by means of an inertia-

generated flywheel; later, clockwork mechanisms were used. Some of their best-known turn-of-the-century toys were actually very racist and unflattering to certain ethnic groups. But the wonderful antics they perform and the imagination that went into their conception have made them and all the other Lehmann toys favorites with collectors today. Though the company faltered with the onset of WWI, they were quick to recover and during the war years produced some of their best toys, several of which were copied by their competitors. Business declined after WWI. Lehmann died in 1934, but the company continued for awhile under the direction of Lehmann's partner and cousin, Johannes Richter.

Advisor: Scott Smiles (S10).

AHA Delivery Van, 8", EX, A...$700.00
Ajax Acrobat, litho tin figure w/cloth costume, performs somersaults, 9½", EX, A...$1,400.00

Alabama Coon Jigger, 1910, Black man dances on stage, rare version with checked pants, 10", EX, $700.00.

ALSO Automobile, 1910, yel & red open auto w/driver, 4", VG, A..$400.00
Anxious Bride, pnt & litho tin, 4½", VG+, A...............$500.00
Autin Delivery Cart, 1914-35, boy & pedal car, 4", EX, A.$500.00
Autobus, red & wht dbl-decker bus w/driver, 7", VG, A.$1,300.00
Autohutte (Two Car), Sedan EPL-760 & Gallop parked in wht garage w/red roof, 6", MIB...................................$2,000.00
Baker & Chimney Sweep, 1900-35, baker on front of 3-wheeled cart w/chimney sweep on back, 5½", EX..............$4,500.00
Balky Mule, 1910, clown bounces as cart advances, 8", G, A.$200.00
Berolina Convertible, w/driver, 7", VG, A.................$1,400.00
Bucking Bronco & Cowboy, brn horse, 6½", VG, A......$500.00
Bucking Bronco & Cowboy, wht horse, 6½", VG, A.....$250.00
Buster Brown, seated in open auto, hand-pnt & litho tin, 4", EX..$1,800.00
Captain of Kopenvil, soldier in long brn cloth coat, EX (EX box), A...$4,500.00

Cat & Mouse, blk & wht cat chases mouse, EX, A $1,000.00
Crawling Beetle, Pat 1895, 4½", EX (EX box) $300.00
Dancing Sailor, litho tin w/cloth clothes, cap reads SMS
  Bradenburg, 7", EX (EX box), A $700.00
Dare Devil, man on 3-wheeled cycle, 5", VG+, A..........$400.00
DUO Rooster w/Rabbit on Egg, unmk, 8", EX, A $1,100.00
Echo Motorcycle w/Driver, litho & hand-pnt tin, 8¾", VG,
  A $1,500.00
EHE & Co Vehicle, open bed truck advances in circular motion,
  w/driver, 7", VG, A $500.00
EPL-11 Zeppelin, litho tin w/celluloid prop, 9½", EX, A ..$1,000.00
Express Porter, 1910, porter pulls trunk on 2-wheeled cart, 6",
  EX, from $600 to $700.00
Galop Racer #1, w/driver, yel w/bl stripe, 5½", NM.......$550.00
Going to the Fair, man pushing lady in promenade chair, 6",
  VG, A...$1,700.00
Gustav the Miller, pull string & figure climbs pole to mill, 18",
  EX $350.00
Halloh Rider on Cycle, flywheel mechanism, 8", EX ..$2,100.00
Heavy Swell, litho tin figure w/cloth clothes, 8½", EX, A .$1,800.00
Ikarus Airplane, litho tin w/wire supported paper wings, 18" W,
  NM, A $3,000.00
Kadi, 2 Chinese men carrying tea chest, 7", EX, A $1,200.00
Lehmann Family (Walking Down Broadway), couple w/dog on
  leash, 6½", VG, A $5,000.00
Lila Hansom Cab, w/driver, 2 lady passengers & dog, 5½", VG,
  A...$1,200.00
Lo & Li, seated clown plays accordion for jigger on platform,
  scarce, NM, A $6,000.00
Magic Ball Dancer, ballerina w/arms extended on gyroscope sta-
  bilizer, hand-pnt & litho tin, 6", EX...................$3,300.00
Masuyama Rickshaw, 17", VG, A.............................$1,000.00
Mechanical Flying Bird, pnt tin body w/pasteboard wings, 10"
  W, rpl wings, A..$200.00
Mikado Family, man pulls female passenger in rickshaw, hand-
  pnt & litho tin, 7", EX, A $1,700.00
Miss Blondin, tightrope walker, 10½", NMIB.............$6,000.00
Mixtum, Black driver in 3-wheeled cart, 4½", EX, A .$1,200.00
Naughty Boy, 1903, wht & bl auto w/driver & boy facing ea
  other at center wheel, 5", VG, A $500.00
New Century Cycle, man holding umbrella over driver of 3-
  wheeled vehicle, 5", NMIB.............................$1,500.00
OHO Car, 1903, open auto w/driver, 4", EX, A $400.00
Ostrich Cart (African), 6", VG, A.............................$450.00
Paak-Paak Quack-Quack Duck Cart, Pat 1903, mama duck pulls
  ducklings in 2-wheeled cart, 8", EX, A $450.00
Paddy the Pig, man on pig, 5", G, A $2,000.00
Performing Sea Lion, 7", VG, A................................$200.00
Rad Cycle, uniformed driver on 3-wheeled vehicle, hand-pnt &
  litho tin, 4½", VG, A $575.00
Sedan, 1927, gr w/yel trim, spoke wheels, 6", EX, A.......$225.00
Shenandoah Dirigible, litho tin w/celluloid props, 7", VG,
  A..$650.00
Snik-Snak, man walking 2 dogs, 8", EX.....................$7,500.00
Susi Turtle, advances w/moving head & tail, 5", EX (EX box),
  A..$175.00
Swing Doll, china doll in cloth dress seated in tin swing, 7",
  EX $2,300.00

Tap-Tap Man w/Wheelbarrow, hand-pnt & litho tin, 6½", G,
  A..$175.00

Terra Sedan, solid wheel version, red and black, 10", EX, A, $1,900.00; Titania Sedan, red and blue, electric headlights, 10", VG, A, $600.00; Gala Sedan, blue and white, 12½", rare, VG, A, $850.00.

Terra Towing Co Vehicle, mk EPL-720, 10", NM, A.$1,700.00
Tom the Climbing Monkey, 1903, plain vest, hand-pnt face,
  7½", MIB...$300.00
Tom the Climbing Monkey, 1903, polka-dot vest, litho face,
  7½", rare, MIB..$1,700.00
Tut-Tut, driver in open auto, hand-pnt & litho tin, 6½", EX
  (EX box), A $1,800.00
UHU Amphibious Car, 9", EX, A...............................$650.00
Velleda Touring Car, driver in open touring car w/folding seats,
  10", VG, A $1,200.00

Wild West Bucking Bronco, 7", NMIB, $1,600.00.

Zebra Cart, advances as cowboy bounces up & down in seat,
  7½", VG+, A $300.00
Zig-Zag, 2 men in rocking car w/lg wheels, hand-pnt & litho tin,
  4", VG, A $1,200.00
Zikra Dare Devil, driver on zebra cart, litho tin, 7¼", NM (EX
  box), A $1,300.00
Zulu Ostrich Mail, driver on ostrich-driven cart, 7", EX (EX
  box), A $1,100.00

Lunch Boxes

When the lunch box craze began in the mid-1980s, it was only the metal boxes that so quickly soared to sometimes astronomical prices. But today, even the plastic and vinyl ones are collectible. Though most lunch box dealers agree that with few exceptions, prices have become much more reasonable than they were at first, they're still holding their own and values seem to be stabilizing. So pick a genre and have fun. There are literally hundreds to choose from, and just as is true in other areas of character-related collectibles, the more desirable lunch boxes are those with easily recognized, well-known subjects — western heroes, TV, Disney and other cartoon characters, and famous entertainers. Thermoses are collectible as well. In our listings, values are just for the box unless a thermos is mentioned in the description. If you'd like to learn more about them, we recommend A *Pictorial Price Guide to Metal Lunch Boxes and Thermoses* and a companion book A *Pictorial Price Guide to Vinyl and Plastic Lunch Boxes* by Larry Aikins. For more pricing information, Philip R. Norman (Norman's Olde Store) has prepared a listing of hundreds of boxes, thermoses, and their variations. He is listed in the Categories of Special Interest under Lunch Boxes.

Advisor: Terri Ivers (I2).

Other Sources: C1, C10, G7, J6, J7, M15, T2.

METAL

Adam-12, 1972, VG, I2 ....$50.00
Addams Family, 1974, VG+, N2 ....$75.00

Addams Family, 1974, with thermos, EX, $100.00.

Annie Oakley, 1955, w/thermos, EX, N2 ....$300.00
Archies, 1969, VG+, N2 ....$85.00
Atom Ant, 1966, G, I2 ....$60.00
Batman & Robin, 1966, G, I2 ....$95.00
Battle of the Planets, 1979, w/thermos, M, N2 ....$175.00
Battlestar Galactica, 1978, w/thermos, EX, I2, from $45 to ..$55.00
Beatles, 1965, bl, VG, I2 ....$375.00
Bedknobs & Broomsticks, 1972, VG, I2 ....$30.00

Bee Gees, 1978, EX, I2 ....$40.00
Beverly Hillbillies, 1963, w/thermos, M $500.00

Bionic Woman, 1978, EX, $85.00.

Bobby Sherman, Thermos, 1972, w/thermos, NM $100.00
Bonanza, 1963, gr rim, EX, I2 ....$150.00
Bonanza, 1965, brn rim, VG $65.00
Buck Rogers in the 25th Century, 1979, w/thermos, EX, I2 ..$50.00
Bugaloos, Aladdin, 1971, NM $100.00
Bullwinkle & Rocky, 1962, w/thermos, EX, N2 ....$600.00
Cabbage Patch Kids, 1983, VG, N2 ....$10.00
Care Bear Cousins, 1985, w/thermos, M, N2 ....$45.00
Care Bears, 1983, bl rim, w/thermos, G, I2 ....$20.00
Carnival, 1959, VG, N2 ....$395.00
Cartoon Zoo, 1962, G, I2 ....$80.00
Casey Jones, 1960, dome top, w/thermos, VG, I2 ....$375.00
Central Fire House, dome top, EX, G7 ....$175.00
Chan Clan, 1973, w/thermos, EX, I2 ....$100.00
Charlie's Angels, 1978, w/thermos, M, N2 ....$175.00
Circus Wagon, dome top, EX, G7 ....$135.00
Clash of the Titans, 1980, VG+, N2 ....$20.00
Color Me Happy, 1984, EX, N2 ....$150.00
Cracker Jack, 1979, VG, N2 ....$20.00
Curiosity Shop, 1972, w/thermos, EX, N2 ....$75.00
Dark Crystal, 1982, w/thermos, M, I2 ....$50.00
Davy Crockett at the Alamo, 1955, M, N2 ....$1,000.00
Davy Crockett/Kit Carson, 1955, VG, N2 ....$250.00
Dawn, M, G7 ....$75.00
Dick Tracy, 1967, w/thermos, M $375.00
Disney Express, 1979, w/thermos, M, N2 ....$50.00
Disney Firefighters, 1969, dome top, w/thermos, EX, N2 ..$150.00
Disney on Parade, 1970, VG+, N2 ....$30.00
Disneyland Castle, 1957, w/thermos, M, N2 ....$500.00
Doctor Dolittle, 1967, w/thermos, EX, N2 ....$100.00
Dr Seuss, 1970, w/thermos, M, N2 ....$300.00

Duchess, 1960, w/thermos, VG+, N2..............$135.00
Dukes of Hazzard, 1980, w/thermos, M, N2 ....$50.00

Dukes of Hazzard, 1980, M, $40.00.

Dynomutt, 1976, EX, I2..$50.00
Emergency, 1977, dome top, w/thermos, EX, N2 ....$150.00
Evel Knievel, 1974, w/thermos, VG+, N2 ....$75.00
Fall Guy, 1981, VG+, N2 ....$25.00
Family Affair, 1969, w/thermos, EX, I2..........................$135.00
Fat Albert, EX, C17..$50.00
Fess Parker, 1964, VG, N2 ....$150.00
Flag-O-Rama, 1954, EX, N2..$400.00
Flintstones, 1964, w/thermos, M, N2 ....$400.00
Flintstones, 1971, w/thermos, M, N2 ....$225.00
Flintstones & Dino, 1962, orange, VG, I2.....................$140.00
Flipper, 1967, w/thermos, EX, N2 ....$200.00
Flying Nun, Aladdin, 1968, EX.......................................$125.00
Fox & the Hound, 1982, w/thermos, VG+, N2 ....$25.00
Fraggle Rock, 1984, EX, I2 ....$25.00
Frito's, 1975, VG+, N2 ....$85.00
Gene Autry, 1954, VG+, N2 ....$200.00
Ghostland, 1977, VG...$30.00
Gomer Pyle, 1966, VG $100.00
Goober & the Ghost Chasers, 1974, VG+, N2..............$60.00
Goofy, 1984, VG, N2...$20.00
Gremlins, 1984, w/thermos, VG+, N2 ....$20.00
Gunsmoke, 1959, w/thermos, VG+, N2 ....$250.00
Hair Bear Bunch, 1971, EX, N2 ....$85.00
Happy Days, 1976, VG, I2 ....$30.00
Hardy Boys Mysteries, King Seeley, 1977, w/thermos, NM..$50.00
Heathcliff, 1982, w/thermos, EX, N2 ....$30.00
Hee-Haw, 1970, EX, N2 ....$100.00
Highway Signs, 1968, 1st design, VG+, N2 ....$50.00
Hogan's Heroes, 1966, dome top, EX.............................$300.00
Holly Hobbie, 1979, VG, N2 ....$10.00
Hong Kong Phooey, 1975, w/thermos, EX, N2 ....$75.00

Hopalong Cassidy, 1954, w/thermos, EX, N2, from $300 to..$325.00
Howdy Doody, 1954, EX $300.00
HR Pufnstuf, Aladdin, 1971, EX $75.00
Huckleberry Hound & Quick Draw McGraw, 1961, VG, I2 ..$70.00
Incredible Hulk, 1978, EX, I2...$30.00
Indiana Jones & the Temple of Doom, 1984, w/thermos, VG, I2..$30.00
It's About Time, dome top, NM, G7 ....$400.00
Jet Patrol, 1957, VG $150.00
Jetsons, 1963, dome top, G+, N2 ....$385.00
Jungle Book, 1966, VG+, N2 ....$100.00
Junior Miss, 1963, floral, w/thermos, M $150.00

KISS, 1979, with thermos (not shown), NM, J6, $150.00.
(Photo courtesy June Moon)

Korg 70,000 BC, 1975, G, I2 ....$40.00
Krofft Supershow, 1978, w/thermos, EX+ $100.00
Kung Fu, 1974, EX $50.00
Land of the Lost, 1975, w/thermos, VG, I2...................$75.00
Lidsville, 1971, w/thermos, EX......................................$125.00
Little Dutch Miss, 1959, w/thermos, EX+, N2..............$225.00
Little House on the Prairie, 1978, EX, I2, from $45 to $55.00
Lone Ranger, 1954, EX, N2..$400.00
Lost in Space, 1967, dome top, rare, EX, G7 ....$425.00
Ludwig Von Drake, 1962, w/thermos, EX, N2 ....$200.00
Luggage Plaid, 1955, EX, N2 ....$65.00
Magic of Lassie, 1978, w/thermos, EX, I2 ....$85.00
Major League Baseball, 1968, VG+, N2 ....$35.00
Man From Uncle, 1966, w/thermos, EX, N2 ....$150.00
Marvel Super Heroes, 1976, EX, I2 ....$45.00
Masters of the Universe, 1983, w/thermos, M..............$50.00
Mickey Mouse Club, 1976, yel rim, w/thermos, M, N2 ..$200.00
Monroes, 1967, EX, N2 ....$200.00
Mork & Mindy, 1979, VG, I2 ....$35.00
Mr Merlin, 1981, w/thermos, VG, I2 ....$30.00
Munsters, 1965, G, I2 ....$75.00
Osmonds, 1973, w/thermos, EX, N2...............................$75.00
Pac Man, 1980, w/thermos, NM, N2...............................$60.00

Munsters, 1965, with thermos (not shown), NM, $250.00.
(Photo courtesy June Moon)

Partridge Family, 1971, EX, N2 ....$85.00
Pathfinder, 1959, VG+, N2..$450.00
Peanuts, 1976, red, w/thermos, VG+, N2 ....$30.00

Peanuts, orange rim, with thermos, M, J6, $65.00.
(Photo courtesy June Moon)

Pebbles & Bamm-Bamm, 1971, EX, I2...............................$80.00
Pete's Dragon, 1978, EX, I2 ....$45.00
Pigs in Space, 1977, VG, N2 ....$25.00
Pink Panther, 1984, w/thermos, M, N2...............................$75.00
Pinocchio, 1971, VG, I2 ....$60.00
Pit Stop, 1968, VG+, N2...$200.00
Planet of the Apes, 1974, w/thermos, VG+, N2 ....$100.00
Play Ball, 1969, w/thermos, VG, N2 ....$75.00
Polly Pal, 1974, w/thermos, VG+, N2 ....$25.00
Popeye, 1964, EX..$100.00
Popeye, 1986, w/thermos, VG, I2 ....$40.00
Popples, 1986, w/thermos, M, N2......................................$75.00
Porky's Lunch Wagon, 1959, dome top, EX, I2 ....$400.00
Pro Sports, 1962, EX, N2..$50.00
Racing Wheels, 1977, w/thermos, VG+, N2.....................$35.00

Raggedy Ann & Andy, 1973, VG, I2........................$35.00
Rambo, 1985, w/thermos, M, N2...............................$50.00
Rescuers Down Under, 1977, VG, I2 ....$35.00
Return of the Jedi, 1983, w/thermos, NM $125.00
Rifleman, 1961, w/thermos, EX, N2.........................$400.00
Robin Hood, 1956, VG...$90.00
Ronald McDonald Sheriff of Cactus Canyon, 1982, VG, I2 ..$25.00

Roy Rogers and Dale Evans Double R Bar Ranch, with thermos, EX, $165.00. (Photo courtesy June Moon)

Roy Rogers, 1957, red shirt, G, N2...........................$65.00
Satellite, 1958, w/thermos, VG+, N2 ....$125.00
School Days, 1984, features Mickey & Donald, w/thermos, EX, N2 ....$300.00
Scooby Doo, 1973, yel rim, w/thermos, M, N2 ....$175.00
Secret of Nimh, 1982, w/thermos, M, N2 ....$85.00
Secret Wars, 1984, VG, I2......................................$40.00
Sigmund & the Sea Monsters, Aladdin, 1974, w/thermos, EX $95.00
Six Million Dollar Man, 1978, w/thermos, EX, I2 ....$100.00
Skateboarder, 1977, w/thermos, EX, I2 ....$55.00
Sleeping Beauty, Canadian, 1960, EX, N2.................$700.00
Snoopy's Doghouse, 1968, dome top, w/thermos, M, N2 .$150.00
Snow White & the Seven Dwarfs, 1975, VG, I2 ....$45.00
Space: 1999, 1975, w/thermos, VG, I2 ....$45.00
Sport Goofy, 1983, VG, I2 ....$20.00
Sport Skwirts, 1982, EX, I2 ....$40.00
Star Wars, 1978, w/thermos, EX, N2.........................$65.00
Strawberry Shortcake, 1981, w/thermos, EX, N2.............$25.00
Submarine, 1960, VG+, N2......................................$75.00
Super Powers, 1984, w/thermos, VG, I2 ....$50.00
Supercar, 1962, w/thermos, VG, I2 ....$335.00
Superfriends, 1976, w/thermos, EX, N2......................$50.00
Superman, 1967, VG, I2...$135.00
Tarzan, 1966, w/thermos, EX, N2.............................$125.00
Three Little Pigs, 1982, VG, N2 ....$95.00
Thundercats, 1985, VG, I2......................................$20.00
Tom Corbett Space Cadet, 1954, EX, N2...................$250.00

Traveler, 1962, red rim, VG, N2 ....$45.00
Underdog, 1974, w/thermos, EX, N2 ....$1,000.00
Universal Plaid, 1959, EX, N2.................................$65.00
Voyage to the Bottom of the Sea, 1967, w/thermos, EX, N2 ....$275.00
Wagon Train, 1964, w/thermos, M, N2 ....$500.00
Walt Disney School Bus, 1960s, dome top, EX $50.00
Walt Disney World (Happy 50 Years), 1976, VG, N2 .....$20.00
Waltons, 1973, w/thermos, EX, N2 ....$90.00
Washington Redskins, 1970, VG, N2 ....$200.00
Wee Pals Kid Power, 1973, w/thermos, VG+, N2 ....$50.00
Welcome Back Kotter, 1977, NM, N2 ....$85.00
Wild Wild West, 1969, w/thermos, EX $200.00
Winnie the Pooh, 1976, w/thermos, EX, N2 ....$200.00
Woody Woodpecker, 1972, EX, N2 ....$50.00
Yankee Doodle, 1975, w/thermos, VG, N2 ....$35.00
Yellow Submarine, 1968, EX $275.00
Yogi Bear Memos, NM, from $55 to $65.00
Zorro, 1958, VG, I2 ....$145.00

PLASTIC

A-Team, 1985, red, w/thermos, EX, I2.....................$25.00
Alf, 1987, red, w/thermos, NM, I2 ....$18.00
Barbie, 1990, purple, w/thermos, EX, I2....................$6.00
Batman, 1982, bl, VG, I2...$5.00
Benji, 1974, bl, VG, I2...$8.00
Cabbage Patch Kids, 1983, yel, w/thermos, EX, I2 ....$10.00
California Raisins, 1982, VG, N2.............................$15.00
Chip 'N Dale Rescue Rangers, lt bl, NM, I2 ....$10.00
CHiPs, Thermos, 1977, NM $30.00
Detroit Lions, w/thermos, EX, G7 ....$12.00
Dick Tracy, 1990, w/thermos, NM, N2 ....$10.00
Disney School Bus, 1990, M (sealed), N2 ....$35.00
Flintstones Movie, 1994, rock shape, w/thermos, NM, I2...$15.00
Ghostbusters, 1986, purple, EX, I2 ....$20.00
GI Joe, 1985, w/thermos, EX, G7 ....$10.00
Jem, 1986, purple, w/thermos, EX, I2 ....$14.00
Kermit the Frog, 1981, dome top, EX, N2................$15.00
Little Mermaid, EX, G7 ....$5.00
Looney Tunes, 1988, purple, w/thermos, VG, I2 ....$10.00
Mickey Mouse Head, 1988, w/thermos, M, N2.................$50.00
Mork & Mindy, Thermos, 1978, w/thermos, EX..............$35.00
Mr T, 1984, orange, w/thermos, EX, I2 ....$30.00
My Little Pony, 1989, bl, w/thermos, EX, I2 ....$12.00
Pink Panther, 1984, w/thermos, EX $20.00
Popeye & Son, 1987, yel, 3-D, M, I2.........................$55.00
Pound Puppies, 1986, red, VG, I2 ....$10.00
Robot Man, 1984, EX, N2 ....$20.00
Rugrats, 3-D, EX, G7 ....$10.00
Simpsons, 1990, red, w/thermos, M, I2 ....$15.00
Snoopy, 1981, orange, dome top, w/thermos, EX, N2 ......$35.00
Superman, 1980, dome top, w/thermos, EX, I2.................$40.00
SWAT, 1975, dome top, w/thermos, EX, N2.....................$60.00
Teenage Mutant Ninja Turtles, 1990, purple, w/thermos, M, I2 ....$15.00
Tiny Toon Adventures, 1990, purple, w/thermos, EX, I2.$10.00
Tropicana Orange Juice, 1989, w/thermos, M, N2 ....$65.00

Voltron, 1984, bl, w/thermos, NM, I2............................$15.00
101 Dalmatians, Aladdin, 1990, w/thermos, EX, I2.........$10.00

VINYL

Alvin & the Chipmunks, EX, G7 ....$150.00
Animaniacs, hot pk, EX, I2..$20.00
Annie, 1981, w/thermos, VG, I2.................................$45.00
Barbarino, Aladdin, 1977, brunch bag w/zipper closure, EX, from $65 to $75.00
Betsy Clark, w/thermos, M, I2...................................$90.00
Charlie's Angels, 1977, brunch bag w/zipper closure, NM, from $65 to $75.00
Corsage, 1970, VG, N2...$50.00
Crash Dummies, Tyco, w/thermos, EX, G7.....................$10.00
Dawn, 1970, w/thermos, EX, I2 ....$175.00
Donnie & Marie, 1978, brunch bag, EX, N2 ....$125.00
Dr Seuss, rare, EX, G7 ....$150.00
Girl Scout, 1960, w/thermos, EX, N2.......................$250.00
Go-Go Dancers, 1965-66, red, EX, G7 ....$100.00
Liddle Kiddles, 1968, NM...$150.00
New Zoo Revue, 1975, w/thermos, EX.....................$225.00
Peanuts, 1969, red, w/thermos, M, I2 ....$130.00
Pebbles & Bamm-Bamm, 1971, EX...........................$125.00
Pepsi, 1980, yellow, EX, N2.......................................$50.00
Pussycats, brunch bag, 1968, NM.............................$250.00

Raggedy Ann and Andy, brunch bag, with thermos (not shown), M, $80.00. (Photo courtesy Kim Avery)

Roy Rogers Saddlebag, 1960, EX...............................$225.00
Sesame Street, 1981, yel, w/thermos, M, N2 ....$75.00
Shari Lewis & Her Friends, 1960s, EX, J5 ....$100.00
Shindig, 1960s, NM..$225.00
Snoopy, 1977, brunch bag, w/thermos, EX, N2 ....$95.00
Soupy Sales, 1960s, bl w/red hdl, EX, J5 ....$300.00
Space: 1999, 1974, G, N2 ....$20.00

Swan Lake, 1960, VG+, N2 ....$150.00
Teenage Mutant Ninja Turtles, 1988, bl softee, EX, I2 ......$8.00
Wonder Woman, 1977, w/thermos, VG+, N2.................$150.00
Ziggy, 1979, orange, VG, N2 ....$85.00

THERMOSES

Adam 12, 1972, plastic, EX, I2 ....$25.00
Annie Oakley, 1955, metal w/cork stopper, EX, I2..........$65.00
Archies, 1969, plastic, NM, I2............................$40.00
Atom Ant, 1966, metal, EX $45.00
Banana Splits, 1969, metal, EX $100.00
Barbie, Midge & Skipper, 1965, metal, EX, I2 ....$50.00
Barney & Baby Bop, plastic, EX, G7 ....$5.00
Beverly Hillbillies, 1963, metal, EX, I2 ....$60.00
Bionic Woman, Aladdin, 1977, plastic, EX $15.00
Bobby Sherman, 1972, metal, NM, from $40 to $50.00
Brady Bunch, 1970, metal, VG..........................$50.00
Buck Rogers in the 25th Century, metal, EX, G7 ....$35.00
Bugaloos, Aladdin, 1971, plastic, EX.....................$25.00
Captain Kangaroo, plastic, EX, G7 ....$10.00
Charlie's Angels, 1977, plastic, EX $15.00
CHiPs, 1977, plastic, NM...............................$12.00
Curiosity Shop, 1972, metal, NM, C1 ....$30.00
Davy Crockett, 1955, metal, NM, G7 ....$75.00
Donny & Marie, 1976, plastic, NM........................$15.00
Family Affair, 1969, metal, EX, A $50.00
Flintstones, metal, NM, from $35 to $45.00
Flying Nun, 1968, metal, EX $30.00
Get Smart, 1966, metal, EX, N2..........................$75.00
Green Hornet, 1967, metal, EX, I2 ....$150.00
Guns of Will Sonnett, 1968, metal, EX, N2 ....$75.00
Hee-Haw, metal, EX, G7 ....$25.00
Hopalong Cassidy, 1950, metal, EX $75.00
Hot Wheels, 1969, metal, EX, G7.........................$18.00
Howdy Doody, 1977, plastic, EX, I2 ....$25.00
It's a Small World, metal, EX, I2 ....$90.00
King Kong, 1977, plastic, NM, I2.........................$25.00
Kung Fu, 1974, plastic, EX..............................$15.00
Liddle Kiddles, 1968, metal, NM.........................$35.00
Lidsville, metal, EX, G7 ....$25.00
Little House on the Prairie, 1978, plastic, M $20.00
Man From UNCLE, 1966, metal, EX, A $75.00
Marvel Super Heroes, 1976, plastic, VG, M17 ....$20.00
Mary Poppins, 1964, metal, EX, I2 ....$45.00
Mighty Mouse, 1979, plastic, EX, I2......................$25.00
Mork & Mindy, 1978, plastic, EX, I2 ....$15.00
Muppets, 1979, plastic, EX, G7 ....$10.00
Pac-Man, Aladdin, 1980, plastic, VG, M17.................$12.00
Partridge Family, 1971, metal, EX $40.00
Pinocchio, 1971, plastic, EX, I2..........................$30.00
Precious Moments, 1975, plastic, EX, G7....................$5.00
Pussycats, 1968, metal, NM $55.00
Road Runner, 1970, metal, EX, N2.......................$50.00
Robot Man & Friends, 1984, plastic, EX, I2 ....$12.00
Scooby Doo, metal, EX, G7.............................$25.00
Sigmund & the Sea Monsters, 1974, plastic, EX, I2 ....$40.00
Super Friends, 1976, plastic, EX, M17.....................$30.00

Superman, 1967, metal, EX, I2, from $60 to $70.00
Tarzan, 1966, metal, M.................................$50.00
Tom Corbett Space Cadet, 1952, metal, EX, N2, from $75 to...$85.00
Winnie the Pooh, 1976, plastic, M $70.00
Woody Woodpecker, 1972, plastic, G, I2 ....$30.00

Marbles

Antique marbles are divided into several classifications: 1) Transparent Swirl (Solid Core, Latticinio Core, Divided Core, Ribbon Core, Lobed Core, and Coreless); 2) Lutz or Lutz-type (with bands having copper flecks which alternate with colored or clear bands; 3) Peppermint Swirl (made of red, white, and blue opaque glass); 4) Indian Swirl (black with multicolored surface swirls); 5) Banded Swirl (wide swirling bands on opaque or transparent glass); 6) Onionskin (having an overall mottled appearance due to its spotted, swirling lines or lobes: 7) End-of-Day (single pontil, allover spots, either two-colored or multicolored); 8) Clambroth (evenly spaced, swirled lines on opaque glass); 9) Mica (transparent color with mica flakes added); 10) Sulfide (nearly always clear, colored examples are rare, containing figures). Besides glass marbles, some were made of clay, pottery, china, steel, and even semiprecious stones.

Most machine-made marbles are still very reasonable, but some of the better examples may sell for $50.00 and up, depending on the colors that were used and how they are defined. Guineas (Christensen agates with small multicolored specks instead of swirls) sometimes go for as much as $200.00. Mt. Peltier comic character marbles often bring prices of $100.00 and more with Betty Boop, Moon Mullins, and Kayo being the rarest and most valuable.

From the nature of their use, mint-condition marbles are extremely rare and may be worth as much as three to five times more than one that is near-mint, while chipped and cracked marbles may be worth half or less. The same is true of one that has been polished, regardless of how successful the polishing was. If you'd like to learn more, Everett Grist has written three books on the subject that you will find helpful: *Antique and Collectible Marbles, Machine Made and Contemporary Marbles,* and *Everett Grist's Big Book of Marbles.* Also refer to *MCSA's Marble Identification and Price Guide,* recently re-written by Robert Block (Schiffer Publishing). See Clubs and Newsletters for club information.

Akro Agate, Click Game, 1930, complete with 40 marbles, NMIB, A, $435.00.

Artist-made, angelfish or sea horse, David Salazar, 1⅜", M, B8 ....$100.00
Artist-made, end-of-day or swirl, Jody Fine, 1½", M, B8, ea...$50.00
Artist-made, end-of-day or swirl, Mark Mathews, 1½", M, B8, ea $75.00
Artist-made, end-of-day w/lutz, aventurine or mica, Rolf & Genie Wald, 1½", M, B8, ea $50.00
Artist-made, end-of-day w/lutz or mica, Bill Burchfield, 1½", M, B8, ea $75.00
Artist-made, peppermint w/mica, Mark Mathews, ⅝" to ¾", M, B8 ....$50.00
Artist-made, single flower or 3 flowers, Harry Boyer, 1½", M, B8, ea $50.00
Artist-made, swirl w/lutz, aventurine or mica, Rolf & Genie Wald, 1⅛", M, B8, ea $25.00
Artist-made, swirl w/lutz or mica, Bill Burchfield, 1½", M, B8, ea $75.00
Artist-made, swirls & ribbons, Harry Boyer, 1⅝", M, B8....$50.00
Banded lutz, transparent clear base w/4 lt gr bands, lutz bands edged in white, shooter-sz, NM, A....................$120.00
Clambroth swirl, any color variation, ½" to ⅞", M, B8, ea ..$250.00
Comic, Andy Gump, Peltier Glass, M, B8 ....$125.00
Comic, Annie, Peltier Glass, M, B8....................$150.00
Comic, Betty Boop, Peltier Glass, M, B8 ....$200.00
Comic, Emma, Peltier Glass, M, B8 ....$75.00
Comic, Herbie, Peltier Glass, M, B8 ....$150.00
Comic, Kayo, Peltier Glass, M, B8....................$450.00
Comic, Koko, Peltier Glass, M, B8 ....$125.00
Comic, Moon Mullins, Peltier Glass, M, B8....................$300.00
Comic, Skeezix, Peltier Glass, M, B8 ....$150.00
Comic, Smitty, Peltier Glass, M, B8 ....$125.00

Comic, Tom Mix, Peltier Glass, M, minimum value $500.00. (Photo courtesy Everett Grist)

Divided core swirl, peewee, any variation, ⅜" to ½", M, B8, ea $25.00
Divided core swirl, red cage-type outer bands w/multicolored inner bands, 1⅜", rare, NM, A $250.00
Divided core swirl, 4 yel outer bands w/3 mc inner bands, 1$\frac{1}{16}$", NM, A $100.00
End-of-day, cloud type w/mica, wht w/red & bl blend, 1⅝", NM, B8....................$300.00
End-of-day, onionskin, wht base w/2 transparent pk, 1 bl & 1 gr panel, 1⅝", NM, A....................$350.00
End-of-day, paneled submarine, bright bl, gr & red inner core, outer w/7 wht bands, 1 gr & 1 bl, 1½", rare, G, A...$170.00
End-of-day, peewee, any color, ⅜" to ½", M, B8, ea $50.00
End-of-day, red & wht, 1½", NM, B8 ....$225.00
End-of-day, single pontil cloud w/mica, mc, 1⅝", NM, B8...$550.00
End-of-day, wht w/2 bl & 2 red panels, 1⅞", NM, B8....$250.00
Indian Swirl, any color variation, ½" to ⅞", B8, ea........$125.00
Joseph's coat, transparent bl base w/mc swirl, $\frac{15}{16}$", VG, A .$65.00
Joseph's coat, transparent clear base w/mc swirl, shrunken core w/aventurine, M, A $165.00
Joseph's Coat, 4 layers (extremely rare), mc swirl, 1$\frac{5}{16}$", NM, A $300.00
Latticinio core, lt bl transparent base w/4 mc outer bands, gr core, 1$\frac{9}{16}$", rare, EX, A $125.00

Latticinio Core, red, white, and blue outer bands with yellow core, 1¾", M, $250.00. (Photo courtesy Everett Grist)

Latticinio core, 2 gr on wht & 2 red on wht outer bands, wht core w/2 yel & 1 red bands, 1¼", rare, M, A $185.00
Latticinio swirl, peewee, any color variation, ⅜" to ½", M, B8 ....$25.00
Latticinio swirl, 3 translucent turq & 3 red & wht outer bands, wht core, 1⅞", NM, B8 ....$150.00
Latticinio swirl, 6 red & wht outer bands, yel core, 1⅝", NM, B8 ....$150.00
Lucky Boy Marble Set, set of 28 tiger eye marbles, MIB, A $300.00
Lutz, banded colored glass, any color, ½" to ⅞", M, B8..$200.00
Lutz, banded opaque, any color, ½" to ⅞", M, B8 ....$400.00
Machine-made, Akro Agate, 1930s, boxed set of 100 tri-color agates, M (EX box), A....................$500.00

Machine-made, Akro Agate, 1930s, unopened mesh bag w/27 high-grade marbles, NM, A $85.00
Machine-made, aqua or clear slag, Akro Agate, 9/16" to 11/16", M, B8, ea $8.00
Machine-made, aventurine, Akro Agate, 9/16" to 11/16", M, B8 . $25.00
Machine-made, bl oxblood, Akro Agate, 9/16" to 11/16", M, B8 . $65.00
Machine-made, brn slag, MF Christensen, 1 3/16", NM, B8 .. $75.00
Machine-made, corkscrew, Akro Agate, 4-color, 9/16" to 11/16", M, B8 .... $30.00
Machine-made, corkscrew, Akro Agate, 5-color, 9/16" to 11/16", M, B8 .... $60.00
Machine-made, guinea, Christensen Agate, transparent base w/melted flecks of color, 11/16", M, B8 .... $475.00
Machine-made, lemonade corkscrew or swirl, Akro Agate, 9/16" to 11/16", M, B8, ea $12.50
Machine-made, limeade corkscrew or swirl, Akro Agate, 9/16" to 11/16", M, B8, ea $20.00
Machine-made, limeade oxblood, Akro Agate, 9/16", to 11/16", M, B8 .... $100.00
Machine-made, National Line Rainbo, bumblebee, Peltier Glass, 9/16" to 11/16", M, B8 .... $1,250.00
Machine-made, National Line Rainbo, Liberty, Peltier Glass, 9/16" to 11/16", M, B8 .... $75.00
Machine-made, National Line Rainbo, Superman, Peltier Glass, 9/16" to 11/16", M, B8 .... $125.00
Machine-made, National Line Rainbo, tiger, Peltier Glass, 9/16" to 11/16", M, B8 .... $20.00
Machine-made, National Line Rainbo, zebra, Peltier Glass, 9/16" to 11/16", M, B8 .... $10.00
Machine-made, opaque swirl, Christensen Agate, 2-color, 9/16" to 11/16", M, B8 .... $15.00
Machine-made, opaque swirl, Christensen Agate, 3-color, 9/16" to 11/16", M, B8 .... $35.00
Machine-made, orangeade corkscrew or swirl, Akro Agate, 9/16" to 11/16", M, B8, ea $30.00
Machine-made, oxblood slag, MF Christensen, 9/16" to 11/16", M, B8 .... $110.00
Machine-made, Popeye corkscrew, Akro Agate, purple & yel or red & bl, 9/16" to 11/16", M, B8, ea $65.00
Machine-made, Popeye corkscrew, Akro Agate, red & yel or gr & yel, 9/16" to 11/16", M, B8, ea $12.00
Machine-made, Popeye patch, Akro Agate, red, gr, wht & clear, ¾", rare, NM, B8 .... $150.00
Machine-made, pumpkin oxblood, Akro Agate, ⅝", rare, M, A $155.00
Machine-made, silver oxblood, Akro Agate, 9/16" to 11/16", M, B8 .... $40.00
Machine-made, sunburst, Master Marble, clear, 9/16" to 11/16", M, B8 .... $100.00
Machine-made, swirl, MF Christensen, any color variation, 9/16" to 11/16", M, ea, from $40 to $50.00
Machine-made, swirl, Ravenswood Novelty Works, mc, 9/16" to 11/16", M, B8 .... $10.00
Machine-made, tiger eye, Master Marble, 9/16" to 11/16", M, B8 .... $20.00
Machine-made, yel slag, Akro Agate, 9/16" to 11/16", M, B8 .. $12.00
Machine-made, yel swirl, lt bl base, MF Christensen, 1 9/32", NM, A $25.00
Master Made Marble Set, 1940s, complete w/100 wht, bl & gr solid core marbles, ⅝", EX (EX box), A $150.00
Peppermint swirl, any color variation, ½" to ⅞", M, B8, ea $125.00
Ribbon core swirl, any color variation, ½" to ⅞", M, B8, ea $150.00
Solid core swirl, peewee, any color variation, ⅜" to ½", M, B8, ea $40.00
Solid core swirl, transparent aqua base w/3 sets of opaque wht outer bands, opaque wht core, 9/16", NM, A $65.00
Solid core swirl, 12 yel outer bands w/red, gr & bl middle bands, wht 3-layer solid core 1¼", NM, B8 .... $75.00
Solid core swirl, 8 yel outer bands, red, gr & bl bands on wht core, 1½", NM, B8 .... $125.00
Sulfide, #3, 1 11/16", rare, NM, A $250.00
Sulfide, alligator, 1¾", M $160.00
Sulfide, angel face w/wings, 1¾", M $1,000.00
Sulfide, camel (1 hump) standing on mound of grass, 1½", NM, B8 .... $200.00
Sulfide, child sitting, 1¾", M $600.00
Sulfide, child w/sailboat, 1¾", M $650.00
Sulfide, cow, 1⅞", NM $200.00
Sulfide, crucifix, 1¾", M $600.00

Sulfide, dog with bird in mouth, 1¾", M, $900.00.
(Photo courtesy Everett Grist)

Sulfide, dove, 1⅝", M $165.00
Sulfide, duck seated on mound of grass, 1¼", NM $50.00
Sulfide, elephant standing, sea gr glass, 1¾", NM $400.00
Sulfide, fish, 1½", M $175.00
Sulfide, George Washington bust, 2⅜", NM $650.00
Sulfide, Jenny Lind, 1½", NM $750.00
Sulfide, lamb, 1¾", NM $125.00
Sulfide, lion standing on mound of grass, 2", NM, B8 .... $125.00
Sulfide, Little Boy Blue, 1¾", M $700.00
Sulfide, Nipper dog, 1¾", EX $350.00

Sulfide, papoose, 1¾", M..............................$700.00
Sulfide, parrot, 1½", EX, A............................$100.00
Sulfide, peasant boy on stump w/legs crossed, 1½", NM, B8 .$400.00
Sulfide, rabbit sprinting over grass, 1⅞", NM..............$150.00
Sulfide, ram, 2", very rare, NM, A....................$2,200.00
Sulfide, Santa Claus, 1¾", M.......................$1,200.00
Sulfide, sheep standing on mound of grass, 1¼", NM, B8..$150.00
Sulfide, squirrel w/nut, 2", EX $200.00
Sulfide, woman (Kate Greenaway), 1½", NM, B8 ....$450.00

Marx

Louis Marx founded his company in New York in the 1920s. He was a genius not only at designing toys but also marketing them. His business grew until it became one of the largest toy companies ever to exist, eventually expanding to include several factories in the United States as well as other countries. Marx sold his company in the early 1970s; he died in 1982. Though toys of every description were produced, collectors today admire his mechanical toys above all others.

Advisors: Scott Smiles (S10), windups; Tom Lastrapes (L4), battery-ops.

See also Advertising; Banks; Character, TV, and Movie Collectibles; Dollhouse Furniture; Games; Guns; Plastic Figures; Playsets; and other categories. For toys made by Linemar (Marx's subsidiary in Japan), see Battery-Operated Toys; Windups, Friction, and Other Mechanicals.

BATTERY-OPERATED

Aircraft Carrier, 20", EX, L4 ....$250.00

Alley the Roaring Stalking Alligator, 1960s, several actions, lithographed tin, 17½", MIB, $475.00. (Photo courtesy Don Hultzman)

Barking Boxer Dog, 1950s, litho tin, 7", EX $100.00
Bengali the Exciting New Growling Prowling Tiger, 1961, 3 actions, plush over tin, 18½", EX.............................$200.00
Big Parade, soldiers march together w/drummer in center, plastic, 15" L, VG (VG box) $165.00
Brewster the Rooster, 1950s, several actions, litho tin, 9½", EX...$250.00
Buttons the Puppy w/a Brain, 1960s, several actions, 1960s, tin & plush, 12", EX...$400.00

Colonel Hap Hazard, 1968, several actions, 11", EX $700.00
Electric Convertible, 1950s, forward & reverse action, 20", EX..$300.00

Frankenstein, advances and stops to pick up objects, tin, remote control, 13", M (EX box), A, $3,600.00.

Great Garloo, 1960s, several actions, mostly plastic, complete w/chain & medallion, 23", EX $600.00
Hootin' Hollerin' Haunted House, several actions, litho tin, 11", EX..$1,000.00
Jetspeed Racer #7, advances w/lighted engine & sound, tin w/plastic driver, 17", EX (VG box) $850.00
Land-Sea Air Set, advances w/lights & sound, litho tin, remote control, NM (EX box), A................................$300.00
Marx-A-Copter, 1961, complete, scarce, EX (EX box), M17.$300.00
Marx-A-Serve Table Tennis, rare, MIB, L4 ....$200.00
Mickey the Musician, 1950s, plays xylophone on sq base, plastic & tin, 12", EX...$275.00
Mighty Kong, 1950s, several actions, plush over tin, remote control, 11", EX...$500.00
Nutty Mad Car, advances on rear wheels, stops & shakes w/monster sound, litho tin, 9", EX.........................$200.00
Roarin' Jungle Lion, 1950s, several actions, litho tin, 16", EX...$285.00
Seascape Tugboat, 1950s, 3 actions, litho tin, 6½", EX .$100.00
Teddy Bear Swing, TN, 1950s, 3 actions, NMIB, L4......$425.00
Tricky Tommy the Big Brain Tractor, 1950s, 3 actions, litho tin, 10", EX...$200.00
Whistling Spooky Kooky Tree, 1960s, bump-&-go w/several other actions, litho tin, 14", NM, A $750.00
Yeti the Abominable Snowman, advances w/several actions & grunts, tin, plush & vinyl, 11", NMIB $735.00

PRESSED STEEL

Deluxe Delivery Truck, red & yel w/blk-pnt tires, complete w/cb advertising boxes in back, 11", NM (NM box)........$350.00

Fire Ladder Truck, red w/yel extension ladder on swivel base & 2 supported on sides, 14", EX, A $300.00

Fire Truck, rider, seat mounted on body, hand-crank siren, fire apparatus graphics on side, 31", MIB, A, $225.00.

Heavy Duty Dump Truck, orange and black with high side extension on body, MIB, $300.00. (Photo courtesy John Turney)

Hi-Lift Tractor, orange and black with blue rubber farmer, MIB, $300.00. (Photo courtesy John Turney)

Gasoline Truck, red w/chrome grille, wooden tires, 7", EX, A $150.00

Grocery Truck, red w/bl stake bed, Motor Market decal, complete w/cb product boxes, 14", NMIB, A $500.00

Hi Way Express Truck, mk New York...Chicago...San Francisco, red & yel, 16", NM..................................$350.00

Hook and Ladder Fire Truck No 9, enclosed cab pulls trailer with extension ladder on revolving base, 32½", MIB, A, $350.00.

Lazy Day Farms Stake Truck, bl w/litho tin bed, 18", NMIB, A..$400.00

Marine Corps Truck, canvas top, complete w/2 plastic soldiers, 13", NM (NM box) $250.00

Powerhouse Dump Truck, gr & tan w/blk tires, MIB $300.00

Public Utility Service Truck, orange w/bl trim, canvas top, wooden poles on trailer, 16½", NMIB, A $650.00

Railway Express Truck, features hi-lift tailgate, complete w/advertising boxes & wooden crates, 20", NM (EX box) $700.00

US Mail Truck, red, wht & bl w/blk Lumar tires, dbl opening rear doors, 26", EX $300.00

Wagon, gr w/wooden wheels, complete w/hdl, 8", VG, A ..$85.00

Willy's Jeep w/Lights & Trailer, red w/bl trailer, battery-op headlights, 22", MIB, A..$300.00

WINDUPS, FRICTIONS, AND OTHER MECHANICALS

Aeroplane, litho tin camouflage design, 18" W, NM (EX box), A $500.00

Amos 'N Andy Fresh Air Taxi, 1930, advances, stops & shakes, litho tin, 8", NM (EX box), A $1,600.00

Animal Express, 1930s, 3 litho tin cars mk Bunny Express, complete w/track, scarce, NM (NM box)..............$1,000.00

Archie Jalopy, Mexico, litho tin w/comical sayings in Spanish, 7", EX $300.00

Army Dive Bomber, advances & flips over, litho tin, 8" W, rare, VG (VG box), A $350.00

Astro (Jetsons), 1960s, advances on wheels, plastic, friction, 4", rare, EX, A $375.00

Ballet Dancer, girl dances, pull rod for action, litho tin, 5½", EX (EX box), A $275.00

Barney Rubble's Wreck, 1962, litho tin w/vinyl-headed figure, friction, 7", NM $450.00

Bedrock Express Train, 1962, litho tin, 12", EX $250.00

Blondie's Jalopy, 1935, bump-&-go action, litho tin, 16½", scarce, NM, A $2,600.00

Bluestreak Racer #3, 1930s, litho tin, 3½", EX, from $75 to ...$100.00

Balky Mule, advances with crazy action, lithographed tin, 8½", EX (G box), A, $125.00. (Photo courtesy Scott Smiles)

BO Plenty, advances while holding baby Sparkles, tips hat, 8", NMIB, A...$385.00

Boat-Tail Racer, w/driver, litho tin, 13", EX, A $200.00

Buck Rogers Rocket Police Patrol, 1934, advances w/sparks & sound, litho tin, 11½", NM $1,500.00

Buck Rogers 25th Century Rocket Ship, 1927, advances w/sparks, litho tin, 12", NM (VG box), A.............$2,900.00

Busy Delivery (known as Black Pinocchio Busy Delivery), 1939, pedals cart in all directions, litho tin, scarce, VG....$500.00

Busy Miners, 1930s, coal car travels from station house to mine entrance, litho tin, 17" base, NM (VG box), A $350.00

Butter & Egg Man, 1930s, litho tin, EX, from $800 to...$900.00

Charleston Trio, 1921, jigger dances, boy plays violin & dog w/cane jumps atop cabin, litho tin, 10", EX.............$750.00

Charleston Trio, 1921, litho tin, 10", EX (EX box), A ..$875.00

Charlie Chaplin Walker, litho tin w/CI shoes & cane, 8½", G, A...$825.00

Charlie McCarthy, 1930s, waddles side to side as mouth opens & closes, litho tin, 8½", NM (EX box), A $1,100.00

Charlie McCarthy & Mortimer Snerd Private Car, We'll Mow You Down on side of car, litho tin, 15", G, A......$1,300.00

Charlie McCarthy in His Benzine Buggy, 1938, car advances in erratic pattern as Charlie's head spins, tin, 8", NMIB, A..$2,000.00

Charlie McCarthy the Drummer Boy, Charlie pushes & beats drum, litho tin, 8", NM (EX box), A....................$1,900.00

Chompy Beetle, advances as mouth opens & closes w/clicking noise, litho tin, 6", NM (EX box), A $225.00

Clancy the Cop, advances in waddling motion as facial expressions change, litho tin, 11", EX, A............................$650.00

Climbing Fighting Tank, tin & plastic, 6", NM (EX box), A $175.00

Climbing Fireman, plastic & tin version, fireman climbs ladder, EX (EX box) $250.00

Climbing Fireman, tin version, fireman climbs up ladder, 9", MIB...$300.00

Coast Defense, 1924, plane circles above base w/several actions, litho tin, 9" dia base, NM (G box) $1,000.00

College Jalopy, advances w/crazy action, litho tin, 6", EX...$250.00

Comet Racer #5, 1930s, litho tin, 3½", EX, from $75 to ..$100.00

Coo-Coo Car, 1920s, advances in circular motion as full-figure driver bounces up & down, 7½", EX......................$400.00

Cowboy Rider, 1941, rearing horse vibrates as cowboy spins lariat overhead & aims gun, NMIB.............................$350.00

Crazy Cops Toy Town Police, prototype, figures fight in back seat, litho & hand-pnt pressed steel, 11", G, A $500.00

Dagwood Solo Flight Aeroplane, 1935, forward & reverse action, litho tin, 9", NMIB $1,200.00

Dagwood the Driver, 1935, advances w/crazy action as Dagwood's head spins, litho tin, 8", NM (EX box), A.............$2,400.00

Dan Dipsy Car, advances as figure's head bobs, litho tin & plastic, 6", NM (EX box), A.......................................$500.00

Dapper Dan Coon Jigger, 1910, dances on stage, litho tin, 10", NM (EX box) $1,200.00

Dare Devil Drome, car travels upwards in circles, litho tin & plastic, 9½" dia drome, NM (G box), A.................$300.00

Dare Devil Flyer, 1930, airplane & zeppelin fly around building, litho tin, 13", scarce, EX (G box), A....................$1,900.00

Dick Tracy Police Station, car races out of garage, litho tin w/plastic station doors, station: 9", car: 8", NMIB, A $1,000.00

Dick Tracy Siren Squad Car, advances w/lights & sound, litho tin, 11", scarce, EX (EX box), A $525.00

Dick Tracy Squad Car, lithographed tin with plastic figures, NM, from $300.00 to $400.00. (Photo courtesy Larry Doucet)

Diesel Tractor, litho tin w/rubber treads, full-figure driver, complete w/snowplow attachment, 10", NM, A.............$100.00

Dippy Dumper w/Brutus, advances & throws figure out, litho tin & celluloid, 8½", EX (EX box), A........................$1,300.00

Dipsy-Doodle Bug Dodg'Em, 2 cars travel on base w/non-fall action, litho tin & plastic, 9½" base, NM (EX box), A.............$450.00

Disney Parade Roadster, litho tin w/plastic Mickey, Donald, Huey & Goofy figures, 11", NM (worn box), A $500.00

Disney Turnover Tank, WDP/Mexico, 1950s, Goofy forces tank to turn over, litho tin, 4", rare, EX........................$750.00

Disneyland Jeep, litho tin, friction, 10", EX...................$200.00

Donald Duck Dipsy Car, litho tin w/plastic figure EX (EX box) $500.00

Disneyland Express Train, features Casey Jr and other Disney characters, EX, J6, $165.00. (Photo courtesy June Moon)

Donald Duck Drummer, rocks back & forth while playing drum, litho tin, NMIB...$800.00

Donald Duck Duet, 1946, Goofy dances on platform as Donald plays drum, litho tin, 10½", NM (EX box)..............$950.00

Donald Duck Riding Tractor, plastic, friction, 3½", M (EX box), A..$165.00

Donald Duck Twirly Tail, 1950s, vibrates around w/spinning tail, plastic, 6", NMIB......................................$600.00

Dopey Walker, 1938, advances & vibrates as eyes move up & down, litho tin, 8", VG.................................$275.00

Dora Dipsy Car, advances as figure's head bobs, litho tin & plastic, 6", M (NM box), A................................$575.00

Dottie the Driver, advances as driver's head bobs, litho tin & plastic, 7", NM (EX box), A............................$165.00

Doughboy Tank, advances & soldier pops up from hatch, litho tin, 9½", NM (EX box), A..............................$875.00

Drummer Boy, advances & plays bass drum, litho tin, 8½", NM, A...$450.00

Ferdinand & Matador, WDE, 1939, advances as bull attacks matador's cape, litho tin, 7", EX (EX box)..............$875.00

Ferdinand the Bull, 1938, vibrates around w/spinning tail, litho tin, complete w/cloth flower & bee, 6", MIB..........$475.00

Fighting Tank w/Recoiling Cannon, several actions, litho tin, 10½", scarce, NM (NM box), A............................$675.00

Fire Truck, w/aerial ladders, advances w/lights & siren sound, plastic, 14", EX (EX box), A.............................$185.00

Fire Truck, w/aerial ladders, advances w/siren sound, litho tin, friction, 15", EX (EX box), A...........................$350.00

Flash Gordon Rocket Fighter Ship, 1939, advances w/sparks, litho tin & celluloid, 12", NM (EX box), A.........$2,200.00

Flintstone Tricycle, Fred pedals trike w/bell sound, litho tin & celluloid, 4", NMIB, A...................................$575.00

Flintstone Tricycle, Wilma pedals trike w/bell sound, litho tin & celluloid, 4", NMIB, A.................................$475.00

Flintstones Pals, Barney on Dino or Fred on Dino, litho tin & vinyl, 8½", MIB, ea.....................................$500.00

Flipo the Dog, 1940, jumps & does flips in the air, litho tin, 4", NM (EX box)..$250.00

Funny Fire Fighters, Brutus drives vehicle w/Popeye on top of aerial ladder, litho tin & celluloid, 10", rare, NMIB, A...$4,900.00

Funny Flivver, 1925, advances w/crazy action as driver's head spins, litho tin, 7½", NM (NM box)..................$2,400.00

Funny Tiger, advances & plays drum, litho tin, 7", VG (VG box)...$200.00

Futuristic Car, advances w/sparks & sound, plastic, friction, 10", EX (EX box), A.......................................$125.00

George Jetson, litho tin, 4", NM, A..................$300.00

George the Drummer Boy, 1930s, moving eyes, litho tin, 9", NM...$300.00

George the Drummer Boy, 1930s, stationary eyes, litho tin, 9", NM (EX box)...$300.00

GI Joe & His Jouncing Jeep, litho tin, EX (G box)........$425.00

Golden Goose, 1930s, bobs up & down & lays eggs, litho tin, 9½", NM (NM box), A.................................$375.00

Goofy the Walking Gardener, Goofy pushes cart, litho tin, 9x8", EX..$450.00

Goofy Wheelbarrow, Goofy pushes wheelbarrow, plastic, 5", NM (EX box), A...$225.00

Goofy's Stock Car, litho tin w/image of Donald, Daisy, Pluto & Minnie, friction, 6", NM..............................$250.00

Harold Lloyd Funny Face Walker, 1929, sways as facial expressions change, litho tin, 10½", EX......................$1,000.00

Hey Hey Chicken Snatcher, 1927, Black man carries chicken as dog bites his pants, litho tin, 8½", EX, from $1,100 to.......$1,200.00

Hi-Yo Silver the Lone Ranger, 1939, silver horse version, figure twirls lasso as horse vibrates around, tin, 8", NMIB, A...$925.00

Honeymoon Express, 1927, litho tin, 9½" dia base, EX (EX box)...$225.00

Honeymoon Express, 1940, litho tin, EX (EX box)........$200.00

Honeymoon Express, 1947, litho tin, EX......................$125.00

Hopping Astro, litho tin, 4", NM............................$250.00

Hopping Elroy, 1963, litho tin, 4", MIB..................$1,000.00

Hopping George Jetson, litho tin, 4", NM...............$275.00

Horse & Cart, 2 horses pull driver in farm wagon, litho tin, 11", NMIB, A..$465.00

Huckleberry Hound Car, 1962, litho tin w/vinyl figure, friction, 4", NMIB..$300.00

Huey, Louie & Dewey on Train, plastic, friction, 4", M (EX box), A...$125.00

Jetson Express, litho tin, 13", NM, A.......................$375.00

Joe Penner & His Duck Goo Goo, 1934, advances w/shuffling feet & tips hat, litho tin, 8½", NM......................$475.00

Joy Rider, 1929, advances in erratic motion as driver's head spins, litho tin, 7½", VG...................................$375.00

Jumpin' Jeep, advances in erratic motion, litho tin, 6", NM (NM box), A..$400.00

Jumping Jalopy, 4 figures in car w/allover sayings, litho tin, 7", NM (NM box), A..$700.00

Knockout Champs, boxers on revolving disk in boxing ring, litho tin w/celluloid figures, 7x7" ring, NMIB.........$700.00

Limping Lizzie, 1930s, advances w/undulating motion, litho tin, 7", EX (EX box), A.......................................$500.00

Lincoln Transfer & Storage Co Moving Van, litho tin, 13", EX, A...$450.00

Little Lindy Airplane, advances w/spinning props, tin, friction, 5½", EX (EX box), A.....................................$400.00

Little Orphan Annie Skipping Rope, 1930s, litho tin, 6", EX, from $500 to..$600.00

Little Orphan Annie's Dog Sandy, w/book in mouth, litho tin, 5½", VG...$250.00

Lizzie of the Valley Jalopy, blk w/allover lettering, 7", EX..$300.00

Looping Plane, 1930, advances & flips over, litho tin, 7½" W, EX (EX box)..$300.00

Magic Barn & Tractor, tractor advances, hits barn door & enters, litho tin barn & plastic tractor, 10" barn, MIB, A.....$185.00

Main Street, vehicles navigate track to various shops, litho tin, 24", NM (worn box), A..$575.00

Mary Poppins, 1964, whirls around, plastic, 8", NMIB...$225.00

Mechanical Racer #9, 1930s, 12½", NM, D10, $950.00.
(Photo courtesy Dunbar Gallery)

Mechanical Speed Racer, advances w/sound, litho tin, 6½", NM (EX box), A $450.00

Merry Makers, 1930, 3 mice band members w/band leader atop piano, w/marquee, 9½", NM (NM box), A..........$2,000.00

Mickey Mouse, see also Whirling Tail Mickey Mouse

Mickey Mouse Dipsy Car, 1949, advances w/crazy action as Mickey's head bobs, litho tin & plastic, 6", NM (EX box) $750.00

Mickey Mouse Express, 1950s, Mickey flies above track w/Disneyville station in center, litho tin, 9" dia, NMIB .$1,000.00

Mickey Mouse Go-Mobile, litho tin w/rubber head, friction, 5½", NM (EX box), A.....................................$350.00

Mickey Mouse Scooter, 1959, plastic, friction, 4", NM (NM box)...$250.00

Mickey the Driver, travels to end of table & turns around, litho tin w/plastic figure, 7", NM (NM box), from $750 to $800.00

Midget Special #2, 1930s, lithographed tin, 5", rare, NM, $200.00. (Photo courtesy John Turney)

Mickey the Musician, Mickey plays xylophone while rocking back & forth, tin & plastic, 12", NM (EX box)......$850.00

Midget Racer #5, 1930s, litho tin, w/driver, 5", EX $200.00

Midget Racer #7, 1930s, litho tin, w/driver, 5", EX $200.00

Midget Special #7, 1930s, litho tin, 5", NM $150.00

Mighty Thor Scooter, 1967, plastic, friction, 4", scarce, MIB, A $1,200.00

Milton Berle Car, advances w/crazy action as Milton's head spins, litho tin, 6", NM (EX box), A......................$500.00

Moon Mullins & Kayo Handcar, figures work handlebars, litho tin & steel, 6", complete w/track, EX (EX box), A $1,000.00

Moon Mullins & Kayo Handcar, 6", no track, VG, A....$350.00

Mortimer Snerd, 1939, sways as hat bounces up & down, litho tin, 8½", scarce, VG $300.00

Mortimer Snerd Tricky Auto, 1939, advances w/crazy action as Mortimer's head spins, litho tin, 8", NM (G box), A.........$1,400.00

Mortimer Snerd's Hometown Band, 1930, Mortimer w/lg bass drum, red, wht & bl litho tin, 8½", EX $975.00

Mountain Climber, train travels around oval sloped track, litho tin, 8½" train, NM (G box), A $100.00

Mysterious Pluto, 1939, press tail for action, litho tin, 9", NMIB $650.00

Mystic Motorcycle, 1930s, w/driver, non-fall action, litho tin, 4", EX (G box), A...$200.00

New York Honeymoon Express, 1928, train travels track as plane flies above base with skyscrapers, lithographed tin, 9" dia. base, NMIB, A, $1,000.00.

No 16 Stunt Auto Racers, 1930, release bar for several actions, tin, 11" track, rare, VG (VG box), A $600.00

Old Jalopy, advances w/undulating motion, litho tin, 7", NM (NM box), A $400.00

Old Mother Goose, 1930, litho tin, 9", EX (EX rare box)..$1,900.00

Owl, advances & chirps as eyes & wings move, plush over tin, 7½", NM (G box), A $100.00

Parade Drummer, advances & plays bass drum, litho tin, 8½", VG, A $200.00

Pecos Bill Ridin' Widowmaker, WDP, 1950s, vibrates as cowboy spins lasso, plastic, 10", NMIB $300.00

Peter Rabbit Eccentric Car, advances as figure's head bobs, litho tin & plastic, 5½", NM (NM box), A $500.00

Pikes Peak Mountain Climber, 1930s, trolley car travels track, litho tin, 31" track, EX (EX box), A $600.00

Pinched, 1930, vehicle travels track under bridges w/several actions, litho tin, 10" sq base, EX (EX box), A $1,400.00

Pinocchio, see also Walking Pinocchio

Pinocchio Delivery, 1939, Pinocchio pedals 3-wheeled cart, litho tin, NM..$1,000.00

Pinocchio the Acrobat, 1939, Pinocchio sways back & forth on pole mounted to rocking base, litho tin, G, A.........$300.00

Pluto, see also Roll-Over Pluto and Wise Pluto

Pluto the Drum Major, 1940s, rocks & shakes bell, litho tin w/rubber ears & tail, 6½", EX, A $350.00

Pluto Twirling Tail, 1950s, vibrates around w/spinning tail, plastic, 6", M..$150.00

Police Motorcycle, 1930s, advances w/siren sound, litho tin, 8½", NM (worn box), A $450.00

Police Squad Motorcycle, advances in circular motion w/siren sound, litho tin, 8", NM (NM box), A $575.00

Popeye, see also Walking Popeye

Popeye & Olive Oyl Jiggers, 1934, Olive Oyl plays accordion & sways as Popeye dances on roof, tin, 10", VG, A.....$900.00

Popeye & Olive Oyl Jiggers, 1934, Olive Oyl plays accordion & sways as Popeye dances on roof, tin, 10", NM (NM box), A..$1,900.00

Popeye Express, 1935, train travels under bridges as Popeye circles in plane overhead, litho tin, EX (EX box) $1,500.00

Popeye Express w/Parrot, parrot pops out of crate in wheelbarrow pushed by Popeye, litho tin, 8½", EX, from $650 to..$750.00

Popeye the Champ, Popeye & Bluto in boxing ring, litho tin w/celluloid figures, 7x7" ring, EX, from $1,400 to ..$1,500.00

Popeye the Pilot (Popeye Eccentric Airplane), 1930s, litho tin, 8", NMIB..$2,400.00

Porky Pig, 1939, Porky dressed as cowboy twirls lasso & vibrates around, litho tin, 8½", NMIB, from $700 to $900.00

Porky Pig, 1939, Porky w/umbrella & hat, litho tin, 8½", NM..$400.00

Power Snap Caterpillar Tractor, gold version, w/driver, 10", NM (EX box), A..$200.00

Power Snap Caterpillar Tractor, silver version, w/driver, 10", NM (EX box), A $225.00

Racer #12, 1942, boat-tail style w/driver, litho tin, 16", VG..$200.00

Racer #27, litho tin w/plastic driver, 12", EX (EX box), A $400.00

Rapid Transit Trolley Car, 1929, advances w/lights & sound, litho tin, 9½", NM (G box), A...........................$1,650.00

Red Cap Porter, 1930, Black man w/tooth grin carrying 2 bags, litho tin, EX $650.00

Reversible Climbing 6 Wheel Deluxe Tractor, w/driver, chromed tin w/red tires, wht rubber treads, 11½", NMIB, A..$350.00

Ring-A-Ling Circus, 1925, ringmaster w/elephant, lion & monkey, gr base, several actions, litho tin, 7" dia, EX .$1,250.00

Roll-Over Figaro, 1939, advances & rolls over, litho tin, 9", EX $250.00

Roll-Over Pluto, 1939, advances & rolls over, litho tin, 9", NM (EX box), A..$400.00

Rollover Plane, 1939, advances & rolls onto side, litho tin, 5", EX (EX box), A $350.00

Rookie Cop, 1932, advances, falls over & rights itself, litho tin, 8½", NM (G box), A $500.00

Rookie Pilot, 1938, advances as pilot's head moves back & forth, litho tin, 7", NM (EX box), A..................................$650.00

Roy Rogers Stagecoach Wagon Train, litho tin & plastic, 14", NM (G box), A..$300.00

Royal Coupe, 1920s, litho tin, 9", EX (EX box) $600.00

Sam the City Gardener, figure pushes wheelbarrow, litho tin & plastic, complete w/gardening tools, 8", NMIB, A ..$275.00

Sandy Dog w/Magical Tail, litho tin, MIB, A.................$500.00

Scottie the Guid-A-Dog, 1930, litho tin, 12½", MIB $750.00

Sheriff Sam Whoopee Car, advances w/crazy action as driver's head spins, tin & plastic, 5½", NM (EX box), A $350.00

Siren Police Car, advances w/siren sound, gr-pnt pressed steel w/yel lettering, 15", NM, A..................................$700.00

Skybird Flyer, 1930s, 2 planes circle tower, litho tin, 8", NM.$425.00

Skyhawk Tower Aeroplane, 2 planes circle tower, litho tin w/celluloid props, 8", NM (EX box), A...................$250.00

Smitty Scooter, boy advances on scooter w/realistic action, litho tin, 8", rare, EX, A..$1,400.00

Smokey Joe the Climbing Fireman, 1930s, fireman climbs ladder attached to base, 11½", EX (EX box), from $350 to..$450.00

Snappy Doghouse, 1930, bulldog pops out of house, litho tin, 3½", EX, A $135.00

Snoopy Gus Wild Fireman, 1927, travels in erratic pattern as fireman spins on ladder, tin, 8", rare, EX (EX box)......$1,600.00

Somstepa, 1926, Black man performs jig on stage, litho tin, 8", EX $650.00

Sonic Jet Plane, advances w/sparks & visible engine, plastic, friction, 15", needs new flint, NMIB, A......................$100.00

Sparkling Climbing Tractor Set, litho tin, complete w/plow & cart, 15", MIB, A..$225.00

Sparkling Doughboy Tank, advances w/sparks & sound as soldier pops in & out of hatch, litho tin, 10", EX (EX box), A..$400.00

Sparkling Jet Plane, 1950s, advances w/sound, plastic, friction, 12" L, EX (EX box), A..$65.00

Sparkling Luxury Liner, 1949, litho tin & plastic, friction, 15", NM (NM box)..$200.00

Sparkling Soldier Motorcycle, 1936, advances w/sparking machine gun, litho tin, 8", NM (EX box)...............$600.00

Sparkling Tank, advances w/sparks as soldier pops out of hatch, litho tin, 10", NM (G box), A $400.00

Ring-A-Ling Circus, 1925, ringmaster with elephant, lion, and monkey, green base, several actions, lithographed tin, 7" dia., EX, $1,250.00.

Speed Boy Delivery (Delivery Motorcycle), 1930s, litho tin, 10",
NMIB..$650.00

Speedy Aeroplane, advances w/spinning prop, tin, friction, 6"
W, EX (EX box), A $300.00

Spic & Span, 1925, 2 Black minstrels on stage mk The Hams
What Am, litho tin, 10½", NMIB, A..................$4,500.00

Spic & Span, 1925, 2 Black minstrels on stage mk The Hams
What Am, litho tin, 10½", EX $1,650.00

Spider-Man Tricycle, 1967, litho tin w/vinyl figure, 4", NM,
T2 ....$300.00

Streamline Speedway, 1930s, 2 cars circle track, tin, EX (EX
box), A...$350.00

Subway Express, train travels track enclosed in see-thru tunnel,
litho tin & plastic, 10" dia, NM (G box), A............$150.00

Super Heroe Express Train, 1967, litho tin, 12", NMIB, from
$800 to...$1,000.00

Super Hot Rod 777, advances w/flashing motor block, litho tin
w/plastic driver, friction, 11", MIB........................$400.00

Super Power Combat Tank, 1950s, advances as cannon recoils
& fires, litho tin, 10", NM (EX box), A..................$275.00

Superman Rollover Plane, bl version, Superman rolls plane over,
litho tin, 6½", EX, A.......................................$1,200.00

Superman Rollover Plane, silver version, Superman rolls plane
over, litho tin, 6½", EX, A................................$1,800.00

Taxi Cab, Yellow Cab Co on door, driver & passengers lithoed
in windows, 11", EX (EX box), A $250.00

Thor, 1968, advances in erratic pattern, plastic, 4", MIB, T2.$150.00

Tidy Tim the Clean-Up Man, mk Keep Your City Spic & Span,
litho tin, 8½", EX $500.00

Tom Corbett Sparkling Spaceship, advances w/sparks, litho tin,
12", NM (NM box) $1,500.00

Toyland Milk Wagon, 1929, litho tin w/balloon tires, 10",
MIB...$1,500.00

Tractor & Trailer, 1930s, w/driver, aluminum, 16", NMIB..$275.00

Tricky Fire Chief Car, 1930, travels on base w/non-fall action,
litho tin, 10x6" base, MIB, A $600.00

Tricky Motorcycle, advances w/non-fall action, litho tin, 4¼",
NM (G box), A $200.00

Tricky Taxi on Busy Street, 1930, advances on base w/non-fall
action, litho tin, 10x6" base, NM (NM box), A......$675.00

Tumbling Monkey, circus monkey performs somersaults between
chairs, litho tin, 5", NM (EX box), A $250.00

Turn-Over Tank, 1925, WWII version, flips over, tin, 9½",
scarce, NMIB..$375.00

Twinkle Toes Ballet Dancer, pull rod for action, litho tin, 6", EX
(G box), A..$225.00

Uncle Wiggily Car, 1935, advances as figure's head turns, litho
tin w/Easter motif, 8", EX...................................$1,000.00

Universal Transfer Truck, 1930, litho tin, 12", scarce, EX,
A $1,100.00

US Army Turnover Tank No 3, advances & flips over, litho tin,
8", NM, A...$250.00

Wacky Taxi #77, litho tin w/driver & passengers in windows,
friction, 7", NM $175.00

Walking Popeye, King Features, 1935, carries 2 cages w/lithoed
parrots, 8½", NMIB...$1,100.00

Walt Disney's Television Car, litho tin, friction, 7", M (NM
box), A...$950.00

Walking Pinocchio, 1939, advances in waddling motion as eyes move, lithographed tin, 9", M, D10, from $500.00 to $600.00.
(Photo courtesy Dunbar Gallery)

Walt Disney Train Set, lithographed tin, complete with track, M (worn box), A, $950.00.

Wee Scottie, 1930s, litho tin, 5", NM (NM box), A......$250.00

Whee-Whiz Auto Racer, 1930s, 4 cars race on turning plate,
litho tin, 13" dia plate, rare, NMIB, A $1,000.00

Whirling Tail Mickey Mouse, vibrates around as tail spins, plastic, 7", NMIB, A $350.00

Whoopee Cowboy, 1932, advances w/crazy action, litho tin, 8",
EX $350.00

Whoopee Cowboy, 1932, advances w/crazy action, litho tin, 8",
NM (NM box) $1,500.00

Wise Pluto, advances w/non-fall action & simulates sniffing,
litho tin w/rubber ears & tail, 8", EX (EX box) $375.00

MISCELLANEOUS

Anti-Tank Set, litho tin & cb, complete, rare, EX (EX box), A $1,200.00
Brightlite Filling Station, 1930, complete, tin, 9½" L, NM (EX box) $2,200.00
Circus Truck & Animals, plastic, MIB $325.00
Electric Lighted Railroad Station, 1930s, station mk Glendale Depot, tin & pressed steel, complete, EX (EX box), A $1,000.00
Farm Accessory Set, 1930s, complete w/rake, hoe & hay cutter, EX (EX box), A $125.00
Farm Machinery Set, 1948, complete w/tractor & driver, rake w/driver, trailer, hayer & soil loosener, NMIB $450.00
Freight Depot, mk East-West Coast Fast Freight, complete w/plastic accessories, MIB $300.00
Grocery Truck, red w/bl stake bed, plastic & tin w/Motor Delivery Market decal, complete w/food containers, 14", MIB, A $500.00

Ice Truck, red with yellow stake bed, tin and plastic with Polar Ice Co decal, complete with ice cubes and tongs, 14", MIB, A, $600.00; Milk Truck, cream with white stake bed, tin and plastic with Marcrest Dairy decal, complete with milk glass bottles, 14", MIB, A, $600.00.

Marine Corps Truck, lithographed tin, complete with plastic figures, MIB, $300.00. (Photo courtesy John Turney)

Junior Typewriter, 1957, litho tin w/plastic knobs, 7", EX..$35.00
Marxwriter, plastic w/metal parts, 11", EX $30.00
Military Transport w/Howitzer Cannon, tin w/canvas cover, plastic cannon, 13", MIB, A....................................$250.00
Municipal Aeroplane Hangar, litho tin, complete w/accessories, 3½ x6", NM (G box), A $1,400.00
Pet Shop Delivery Truck, 1950s, plastic, complete w/6 dogs, EX+ (EX box), A...$165.00
Printing Press, litho metal, hand-crank, 10" L, EX $50.00

Roadside Rest Service Station, litho tin, complete, 10x14" base, EX, A $800.00
Sunnyside Service Station, litho tin, complete, EX, A ..$750.00
Tri-City Express Service Truck, litho tin, w/cb advertising boxes in back, 14", NM $285.00
Universal Airport, 1930s, litho tin station mk Weather Bureau-Ticket Office..., w/2 airplanes, 7x12" base, NMIB...$325.00

Matchbox

The Matchbox series of English and American-made autos, trucks, taxis, Pepsi-Cola trucks, steamrollers, Greyhound buses, etc., was very extensive. By the late 1970s, the company was cranking out more than five million cars every week, and while those days may be over, Matchbox still produces about seventy-five million vehicles on a yearly basis.

Introduced in 1953, the Matchbox Miniatures series has always been the mainstay of the company. There were seventy-five models in all but with enough variations to make collecting them a real challenge. Larger, more detailed models were introduced in 1957; this series, called Major Pack, was replaced a few years later by a similar line called King Size. To compete with Hot Wheels, Matchbox converted most models over to a line called SuperFast that sported thinner, low-friction axles and wheels. (These are much more readily available than the original 'regular wheels,' the last of which were made in 1969.) At about the same time, the King Size series became known as Speed Kings; in 1977 the line was reintroduced under the name Super Kings.

In the early '70s, Lesney started to put dates on the baseplates of their toy cars. The name 'Lesney' was coined from the first names of the company's founders. The last Matchboxes that carried the Lesney mark were made in 1982. Today many models can be bought for less than $10.00, though a few are priced much higher.

In 1988, to celebrate the company's 40th anniversary, Matchbox issued a limited set of five models that except for minor variations were exact replicas of the originals. These five were repackaged in 1991 and sold under the name Matchbox Originals. In 1993 a second series expanded the line of reproductions.

Another line that's become very popular is their Models of Yesteryear. These are slightly larger replicas of antique and vintage vehicles. Values of $20.00 to $60.00 for mint-in-box examples are average, though a few sell for even more.

Sky Busters are small-scale aircraft measuring an average of 3½" in length. They were introduced in 1973. Models currently being produced sell for about $4.00 each.

To learn more, we recommend *Matchbox Toys, 1948 to 1993*, and *Matchbox Toys, 1947–1996*, by Dana Johnson; and a series of books by Charlie Mack: *Lesney's Matchbox Toys* (there are two: *Regular Wheel Years* and *Super Fast Years*) and *Universal Years*.

To determine values of examples in conditions other than given in our listings, based on MIB or MOC prices, deduct a minimum of 10% if the original container is missing, 30% if the condition is excellent, and as much as 70% for a toy graded only very good. In the following listings, we have added zeroes ahead of the numbers to avoid the idiosyncrasies of computer sorting.

Advisors: Mark Giles (G2) 1–75 Series; Dan Wells (W1) King Size, Speed Kings, and Super Kings; Matchbox Originals; Models of Yesteryear; Skybusters.

Key:
LW — Laser Wheels (introduced in 1987)
reg — regular wheels (Matchbox Miniatures)
SF — SuperFast

1–75 Series

01-A, Diesel Road Roller, reg, 1953, dk gr, NM, W1 ....$43.00

01-D, Aveling Barford Road Roller, reg, 1962, NM+, W1 ....$18.00

01-E, Mercedes Truck, reg, 1968, orange canopy, blk wheels, MIB, W1 ....$16.00

01-F, Mercedes Transcontinental Haulage Truck, SF, 1970, red w/yel top, spoke wheels, M, W1 ....$5.00

01-G, Mod Rod, SF, 1971, yel, spotted cat label, blk wheels, M (EX+ box), W1 ....$10.00

01-G, Mod Rod, SF, 1971, yel, wildcat head label (scarce), red wheels, M, W1 ....$20.00

01-H, Dodge Challenger, SF, 1976, red w/silver interior, clear windshield, 5-arch wheels, NM+, W1 ....$8.00

02-B, Dumper, reg, 1957, #2 cast, metal wheels, w/driver, NM+, W1 ....$45.00

02-C, Muir Hill Dumper, reg, 1961, Laing decal, blk wheels, M.................$21.00

02-D, Mercedes Trailer, reg, 1968, orig canopy, blk wheels, M, W1 ....$10.00

02-E, Mercedes Trailer, SF, 1969, gold, no labels, 4-spoke wheels, NM, W1 ....$15.00

02-G, Hovercraft, SF, 1976, Rescue, med lt gr w/tan hull, silver scoop, amber windshield, M (NM card), W1.............$11.00

03-A, Cement Mixer, reg, 1953, orig metal wheels, NM+, W1 ....$35.00

03-C, Mercedes Ambulance, reg, 1968, blk wheels, w/orig patient, M (EX box) $14.00

03-D, Mercedes Ambulance, SF, 1970, cream w/bl windshield, 5-spoke fat wheels, opening rear door, w/patient, M, W1 ....$20.00

03-E, Monteverdi Hai, SF, 1973, orange w/ivory interior, bl windshield, M (NM box), W1.................$11.00

04-B, Massey Harris Tractor, reg, 1957, no-fenders version, metal wheels, w/driver, W1 ....$80.00

04-D, Dodge Stake Truck, reg, 1967, gr stakes, blk wheels, MIB, W1 ....$10.00

04-F, Gruesome Twosome, SF, 1971, gold w/cream interior, purple windshield, M (NM box), W1.................$15.00

04-H, '57 Chevy, SF, 1979, Cherry Bomb tampo, red, MIB, W1 ....$5.00

05-C, London Bus, reg, 1961, Visco Static, blk wheels, EX+ .$24.00

05-E, Lotus Europa, SF, 1969, pk w/ivory interior, 5-spoke fat wheels, M (NM box), W1 ....$19.00

06-A, Quarry Truck, reg, 1954, metal wheels, W1 ....$50.00

06-B, Quarry Truck, reg, 1957, blk wheels, NM+, W1 .....$40.00

06-C, Euclid Quary Truck, reg, 1964, blk solid tires, MIB, W1 ....$18.00

06-D, Ford Pickup, reg, 1968, wht grille, orig top, blk wheels, MIB, W1 ....$16.00

06-E, Ford Pickup, SF, 1970, red w/wht top, gr base, silver grille, M, W1 ....$20.00

06-F, Mercedes 350SL, SF, 1973, yel, M (G+ box), W1 ..$11.00

07-A, Milk Float, reg, 1954, gray wheels, scarce, MIB, W1 ....$100.00

07-B, Ford Anglia, reg, 1961, blk wheels, MIB, W1 ....$25.00

07-C, Ford Refuse Truck, red, 1966, blk wheels, scalloped side plates, M, W1 ....$15.00

07-C, Ford Refuse Truck, reg, 1966, blk wheels, scalloped side plates, MIB, W1 ....$17.00

07-C, Ford Refuse Truck, reg, 1966, blk wheels, straight sides, MIB, W1 ....$18.00

07-E, Hairy Hustler, SF, 1971, wht w/checks & stripes, blk base, amber windshield, M (EX box), W1 ....$15.00

07-F, VW Golf, SF, 1976, med lime gr w/yel interior, blk base, amber windshield, w/rack, no labels, M (EX box), W1 ....$9.00

08-D, Caterpiller Tractor, reg, 1964, blk wheels, new treads, M, W1 ....$22.00

08-F, Ford Mustang, SF, 1970, red-orange w/ivory interior, M, W1 ....$35.00

08-H, DeTomasso Pantera, SF, 1975, bl w/blk & wht #17 & striped tampo, blk base, M (NM box), W1 ....$18.00

09-B, Dennis Fire Engine, reg, 1957, #9 cast, blk wheels, EX+, W1 ....$42.00

09-C, Merryweather Marquis Fire Engine, reg, 1959, blk wheels, gold ladder, NM, W1 ....$22.00

09-E, AMX Javelin, SF, 1972, med lime gr w/orange interior, unpnt base, 5-spoke wheels, opening doors, M (NM card), W1 ....$10.00

10-D, Pipe Truck, reg, 1966, blk wheels, silver grille, MIB, W1 ....$15.00

10-E, Pipe Truck, SF, 1970, orange w/silver base, gray pipes, thin wheels, M, W1 ....$24.00

11-A, Esso Road Tanker, reg, 1955, red, metal wheels, decal 85%, NM+, W1 ....$50.00

11-C, Jumbo Crane, reg, 1965, blk wheels, red weight box, MIB, W1 ....$16.00

11-D, Scaffolding Truck, reg, 1969, blk wheels, complete, MIB, W1 ....$17.00

11-E, Scaffolding Truck, SF, 1970, silver, thin wheels, complete, M, W1 ....$24.00

12-A, Land Rover, reg, 1955, metal wheels, complete, MIB, W1.................$40.00

12-C, Safari Land Rover, reg, 1965, bl, tan luggage, blk wheels, MIB, W1 ....$19.00

12-C, Safari Land Rover, reg, 1965, gr, brn luggage, blk wheels, MIB, W1 ....$21.00

12-E, Setra Coach, SF, 1970, gold w/wht roof, clear windshield, skinny wheels, M (EX box), W1 ....$12.00

12-F, Big Bull, SF, 1975, orange w/gr blade, orange rollers, M (NM card), W1.................$12.00

12-G, Citroen CX, SF, 1979, med lt bl w/lt yel interior, silver-gray base, no tampo, M (NM box), W1 ....$5.00

13-A, Bedford Wrecker Truck, reg, 1955, metal wheels, complete, NM+, W1 ....$50.00

13-C, Thames Wrecker Truck, reg, 1961, blk wheels, gray plastic hook, complete, EX+, W1 ....$25.00

13-D, Dodge Wrecker Truck, reg, 1965, yel cab w/gr bed, red hook, blk wheels, NM, W1..$19.00

13-F, Baja Buggy, SF, 1971, med lime gr w/orange interior, red exhaust & flower label, M (NM box), W1................$15.00

14-C, Bedford Ambulance, reg, 1962, blk wheels, MIB, W1 ....$33.00

14-D, Iso Grifo, reg, 1968, blk wheels, NM+ $16.00

14-F, Mini Ha Ha, SF, 1975, red, flesh driver w/brn helmet, mc front wheels, 4-color labels, M (NM box), W1..........$17.00

14-G, Rallye Royale, SF, 1981, wht w/blk base, bl & orange tampo, M (NM box), W1 ....$5.00

14-H, Leyland Gas Tanker, SF, 1982, blk w/gray base, M, W1 ....$5.00

15-A, Prime Mover, reg, 1956, metal wheels, MIB, W1 ...$50.00

15-B, Atlantic Prime Mover, reg, 1959, blk wheels, NM+, W1 ....$39.00

15-D, VW 1500 Saloon, reg, 1968, blk wheels, MIB, W1 ..$23.00

15-E, VW 1500, SF, 1969, med red, front bumper decal, 137 labels, thin wheels, NM+, W1.................................$20.00

15-F, Fork Lift Truck, SF, 1972, red w/blk steering wheel, yel hoist, gray fork, dot-dash wheels, M, W1 ....$11.00

15-G, Hi-Ho Silver, SF, 1981, pearl gray w/red interior, blk base, MIB, W1 ....$10.00

16-D, Case Bulldozer, reg, 1969, orig treads, complete, MIB, W1 ....$25.00

17-A, Bedford Removals Van, reg, 1956, maroon w/gold trim (rare), metal wheels, EX+, W1................................$125.00

17-B, Bedford Removals Van, reg, 1958, gr w/solid letters, metal wheels, NM, W1 ....$45.00

17-D, Hoveringham Tipper, reg, 1963, red base, blk wheels, MIB, W1 ....$16.00

17-E, Horse Box, SF, 1970, red-orange w/gr box, thin wheels, no horses, M, W1 ....$15.00

17-F, Londoner Silver Jubilee Bus, SF, 1972, silver w/charcoal base, dot-dash wheels, MOC, W1 ....$12.50

18-B, Caterpiller Bulldozer, reg, 1958, orig treads, complete, NM+, W1 ....$60.00

18-D, Caterpiller D8 Bulldozer, reg, 1964, orig treads, blk plastic rollers, complete, MIB, A $17.50

18-E, Field Car, reg, 1969, unpnt base, orig top, blk wheels w/red hubs, MIB, W1..$17.00

18-F, Field Car, SF, 1970, yel w/red-brn top, wht interior, unpnt base, no labels, 5-spoke fat wheels, M (EX box), W1 ..$15.00

18-F, Field Car, SF, 1970, yel w/red-brn top, wht interior, unpnt base, 4-spoke fat wheels, M, W1 ....$15.00

19-D, Lotus Racing Car, reg, 1966, gr, blk wheels, MIB, W1 ..$17.00

19-D, Lotus Racing Car, reg, 1966, orange (scarce), blk wheels, NM+, W1 ....$30.00

19-F, Road Dragster, SF, 1970, red w/ivory interior, unpnt base, 8 labels, M (NM+ box), W1.................................$15.00

20-A, Stake Truck, reg, 1956, silver grille, metal wheels, M ..$45.00

20-B, ERF 686 Truck, reg, 1959, blk wheels, EX, W1 ......$35.00

20-C, Chevrolet Impala Taxi, reg, 1965, yel w/red interior, unpnt base, blk wheels, MIB, W1 ....$25.00

20-D, Lamborghini Marzal, SF, 1969, med red, unpnt base, no labels, thin wheels, M (NM+ box), W1.....................$15.00

20-E, Police Patrol, SF, 1975, wht w/orange spinner, unpnt base, frosted windshield, w/labels, NM+, W1 ....$5.00

21-A, Long Distance Coach, reg, 1956, M, W1...............$60.00

21-C, Commer Milk Float, reg, 1961, gr windows, bottle decals, silver wheels, cream load, rare, NM+, W1..............$120.00

21-C, Commer Milk Truck, reg, 1961, gr windows, blk wheels, cow decals, MIB, W1 ....$25.00

21-D, Foden Concrete Truck, 1968, blk wheels, NM, W1 .$6.00

21-F, Rod Roller, SF, 1973, yel w/gr base, w/label, blk rear wheels, M (NM box), W1 ....$13.00

22-C, Pontiac Grand Prix Sports Coupe, reg, 1964, blk wheels, MIB, W1 ....$20.00

22-F, Blaze Buster, SF, 1975, red w/wht interior, blk base, yel ladder, Fire Labels, M (NM card), W1 ....$4.00

23-B, Berkely Cavalier Trailer, reg, 1958, #23 cast, lt bl, metal wheels, EX, W1 ....$23.00

23-D, House Trailer Caravan, reg, 1965, pk, blk wheels, M (NM box), W1 ....$16.00

23-D, VW Camper, SF, 1970, orange w/wht interior, unpnt base, clear windshield, 5-spoke thin wheels, M (NM box), W1 ....$22.00

23-D, Volkswagen Camper, 1970, turquoise with opening roof, M, $12.00. (Photo courtesy Dana Johnson)

23-E, Atlas Truck, SF, 1975, bl w/orange dump, gray interior, unpnt base, amber windshield, dot-dash wheels, MIB, W1 ....$11.00

23-E, Atlas Truck, SF, 1975, bl w/orange dump, silver interior, unpnt base, amber windshield, dot-dash wheels, MOC, W1 ....$11.00

24-A, Weatherall Hydraulic Excavator, reg, 1956, metal wheels, MIB, W1 ....$40.00

24-D, RR Silver Shadow, SF, 1970, med-dk red w/ivory interior, charcoal base, fat wheels, M, W1 ....$17.00

24-F, Shunter Rail Freight, SF, 1979, med gr w/tan panel, red base & undercarriage, M (NM card), W1 ....$8.00

24-G, Datsun 280ZX, SF, 1981, blk w/red interior, hood tampo, 5-spoke wheels, M (NM box), W1 ....$5.00

25-C, BP Petrol Tanker, reg, 1964, yel & gr, blk wheels, MIB, W1 ....$28.00

25-D, Ford Cortina, reg, 1968, w/roof rack (scarce), blk wheels, M, W1 ....$12.00

26-A, Concrete Truck, reg, 1956, silver grille, metal wheels, NM+, W1 ....$45.00

26-C, GMC Tipper Truck, reg, 1968, blk wheels, MIB, W1 ..$10.00

26-E, Big Banger, SF, 1972, red, unpnt base, amber windshield, NM+, W1 ....$13.00

26-F, Site Dumper, SF, 1976, yel w/red dump, blk interior & base, 5-spoke front & 5-crown rear wheels, M (NM box), W1..$5.00

27-A, Bedford Lowloader, reg, 1956, gr & tan, metal wheels, EX+, W1 ....$50.00

27-F, Lamborghini Countach, SF, 1973, red w/silver interior, blk base, amber windshield, #8 tampo, M (EX card), W1 .$13.00

28-A, Bedford Compressor Truck, reg, 1956, metal wheels, NM+, W1 ....$40.00

28-C, Jaguar MK 10, reg, 1964, unpnt motor, blk wheels, MIB, W1 ....$20.00

28-D, Mack Dump Truck, reg, 1968, blk wheels w/red hubs, MIB, W1 ....$14.00

28-E, Mack Dump Truck, SF, 1970, pea gr w/blk axle cover, unpnt base, spiro wheels, M, W1......................$19.00

28-F, Stoat Armored Vehicle, SF, 1974, gold w/blk base, silver hubs, M (EX+ box), W1............................$15.00

28-G, Lincoln Continental MK V, SF, 1979, red w/wht top, tan interior, unpnt base, M (EX+ box), W1....................$10.00

29-B, Austin A55 Cambridge Sedan, reg, 1961, silver wheels, MIB, W1 ....$38.00

29-C, Fire Pumper, reg, 1966, plain sides, blk wheels, MIB, W1 ....$12.00

30-A, Ford Prefect, reg, 1956, olive gr, gray wheels, MIB, W1 ....$50.00

30-C, 8-Wheel Crane Truck, reg, 1965, blk wheels, MIB, W1 ....$16.00

30-E, Beach Buggy, SF, 1970, med pk w/yel interior, unpnt base, M (NM+ box), W1..................................$15.00

30-F, Swamp Rat, SF, 1976, olive w/tan hull, w/labels, M (NM box), W1 ....$5.00

30-I, Mercedes G Wagon, SF, 1985, olive w/tan top, blk base, bl windshield, red cross tampo, M, W1 ....$5.00

31-C, Lincoln Continental, reg, 1964, aqua, blk wheels, MIB, W1 ....$20.00

31-E, Volksdragon, SF, 1971, red w/yel interior, unpnt base, purple windshield, no labels, M, W1 ....$12.00

31-F, Caravan, SF, 1977, wht w/orange door, lt yel interior, unpnt base, M (NM box), W1............................$6.00

32-A, Jaguar XK140, reg, 1957, red (rare), gray wheels, NM+, W1 ....$100.00

32-B, E-Type Jaguar, reg, 1962, clear windows, blk wire wheels, MIB, W1 ....$33.00

32-C, Leyland Petrol Tanker, reg, 1968, gr w/silver grille, blk wheels, MIB, W1 ....$20.00

32-C, Leyland Petrol Tanker, reg, 1968, gr w/wht grille (scarce), MIB, W1 ....$22.00

33-A, Ford Zodiac MK II Sedan, reg, 1957, tan & orange w/gr windshield, gray wheels, MIB, W1 ....$50.00

33-A, Ford Zodiak MK II Sedan, reg, 1957, dk aqua, no-windshield version, metal wheels, NM+, W1 ....$41.00

33-B, Ford Zephyr 6 MK III, reg, 1963, aqua, blk wheels, MIB, W1 ....$42.00

33-D, Lamborghini Miura, SF, 1969, gold w/ivory interior, unpnt base, thin wheels, M (EX+ box), W1 ....$19.00

34-A, VW Microvan, reg, 1957, gray wheels, NM+, W1 .$53.00

34-C, VW Camper, reg, 1967, silver, raised roof, blk interior, NM+, W1 ....$25.00

34-D, VW Camper, reg, 1968, silver, short raised roof, blk wheels, M, W1 ....$10.00

34-E, Formula 1, SF, 1971, yel, 16 bl labels, 4-spoke front & 5-spoke rear wheels, M, W1......................................$10.00

35-A, Marshall Horse Box, reg, 1957, metal wheels, NM+, W1 ....$40.00

35-B, Snowtrac Tractor, reg, 1964, cast sides, orig treads, NM+, W1 ....$25.00

35-C, Merryweather Fire Engine, SF, 1969, med red w/lt gray base, 2 clips, 5-spoke thin wheels, M (NM+ box), W1..........$15.00

35-D, Fandango, SF, 1975, wht w/red interior, red base, clear windshield, silver prop, M (NM card), W1...............$13.00

36-A, Austin A50, reg, 1957, metal wheels, M, W1.........$50.00

36-C, Opel Diplomat, reg, 1966, gold w/silver motor, blk wheels, MIB, W1 ....$13.00

36-F, Formula 5000, SF, 1975, orange w/bl driver, w/labels, Maltese crosss rear wheels, M, W1............................$12.00

36-G, Refuse Truck, SF, 1980, red w/orange-yel dump & hatch, silver-gray base, red tab, no labels, M (NM+ box), W1......$5.00

37-B, Dodge Cattle truck, reg, 1966, metal base, blk wheels, orig cattle still on tree, MIB, W1....................................$12.00

37-A, Coca-Cola Lorry, reg, 1956, no base, lg letters, uneven load (scarce), metal wheels, MIB, W1 ....$125.00

37-B, Coca-Cola Lorry, reg, 1960, w/base, sm letters, even load, blk wheels, M, W1 ....$68.00

37-E, Cattle Truck, SF, 1970, yel & gray, orig cattle on tree, M (NM box), W1 ....$15.00

37-F, Soopa Coopa, SF, 1972, med bl w/unpnt base, Maltese cross wheels, M, W1 ....$15.00

37-G, Skip Truck, SF, 1976, red w/gray interior, blk base, yel skip, clear windshield, M (NM box), W1..................$5.00

38-A, Karrier Refuse Collector, reg, 1957, gray, gray wheels, MIB, W1 ....$43.00

38-C, Honda Motorcycle & Trailer, reg, 1967, plain sides, blk wheels, NM+, W1 ....$19.00

38-D, Honda Motorcycle & Trailer, SF, 1970, pk & yel, w/labels, 5-spoke wheels, M, W1............................$14.00

38-G, Ford Camper, SF, 1980, red cab w/beige camper, gr windshield, no camper windshield, M (VG+ box), W1.......$5.00

39-A, Ford Zodiac Convertible, reg, 1957, turq interior, gray wheels, orig driver, NM+, W1 ....$65.00

39-B, Pontiac Convertible, reg, 1962, yel w/ivory interior, blk base, blk wheels, MIB, W1 ....$70.00

39-C, Ford Tractor, reg, 1967, bl & wht, blk wheels, NM, W1 ....$5.00

39-D, Clipper, SF, 1973, med magenta w/yel interior, gr base, amber windshield, silver pipes, M, W1 ....$13.00

40-A, Bedford, Tipper Truck, reg, 1957, gray wheels, NM+, W1 ....$39.00

40-B, Leyland Royal Tiger Coach, reg, 1961, blk wheels, EX+, W1 ....$20.00

40-C, Hay Trailer, reg, 1967, orig rails, blk wheels, MIB, W1 .$10.00

40-E, Horse Box, SF, 1977, med gr & beige, unpnt base, gr windshield, M (EX+ box), W1 ....$6.00

41-A, D-Type Jaguar, reg, 1957, metal wheels, NM+, W1 ..$66.00

41-D, Ford GT, SF, 1970, wht w/lt gr base, 6 labels, 5-spoke thin wheels, M (EX card), W1 ....$15.00

41-F, Ambulance, SF, 1978, wht w/gray interior, unpnt base, w/labels, M (NM+ box), W1 ....$5.00

42-A, Bedford Evening News Van, reg, 1957, gray wheels, M, W1 ....$47.00

42-B, Studebaker Lark Wagonaire, reg, 1965, lt bl sliding roof, blk wheels, complete, MIB, W1 ....$19.00

42-D, Iron Fairy Crane, SF, 1970, orange w/med lime-gr boom, fat wheels, M, W1 ....$45.00

43-A, Hillman Minx, reg, 1958, bl-gray w/gray roof, metal wheels, NM, W1 ....$35.00

43-B, Aveling Barford Tractor Shovel, reg, 1962, yel & red, blk wheels, MIB, W1 ....$31.00

43-C, Pony Trailer, reg, 1968, tan base, blk wheels, complete, MIB, W1 ....$14.00

43-E, Dragon Wheels, SF, 1972, gr w/blk base, dash-dot wheels, EX+, W1 ....$10.00

44-A, Rolls Royce Silver Cloud, reg, 1958, gray wheels, MIB, W1 ....$46.00

44-B, Rolls Royce Phantom V, reg, 1964, med silver-gray (scarce), blk wheels, MIB, W1 ....$40.00

44-D, GMC Refrigerator Truck, SF, 1970, yel & red w/red axle covers, M (EX+ box), W1 ....$25.00

45-A, Vauxhall Victor, reg, 1958, yel, gr window version, gray wheels, NM+, W1 ....$35.00

45-A, Vauxhall Victor, reg, 1958, yel, no window, gray wheels, NM+, W1 ....$35.00

45-B, Ford Corsair, reg, 1965, unpnt base, blk wheels, boat rack on tree, complete, MIB, W1 ....$18.00

45-C, Ford Group 6, SF, 1970, med gr, unpnt base, silver motor, clear windshield, rnd 7 label, M (NM box), W1 ....$12.00

45-D, BMW 3.0 CSL, 1976, red, M, $10.00.
(Photo courtesy Dana Johnson)

46-B, Pickford's Removal Van, reg, 1960, gr, 3-line decals, blk wheels, MIB, W1 ....$40.00

46-C, Mercedes Benz 300 SE, reg, 1968, metallic bl, blk wheels, MIB, W1 ....$13.00

46-D, Mercedes 300 SE, SF, 1970, cast doors, gold, unpnt base, no labels, 5-spoke thin wheels, M (EX card), W1 ..$20.00

46-E, Stretcha Fetcha Ambulance, SF, 1972, wht w/lt yel interior, red base, bl windshield, MOC, W1 ....$14.00

46-F, Ford Tractor, SF, 1978, bl w/lt yel interior, unpnt base, no harrow, blk hubs, EX+, W1 ....$3.00

47-A, 1-Ton Trojan Van, reg, 1958, gray wheels, NM, W1 ....$50.00

47-B, Commer Ice Cream Canteen, reg, 1963, oval roof, cream, plain side decals, blk wheels, MIB, W1 ....$50.00

47-C, DAF Tipper Truck, reg, 1968, silver & yel w/gray top, blk wheels, MIB, W1 ....$10.00

47-E, Beach Hopper, SF, 1974, plastic windshield, dk bl w/orange interior, pk base, tan driver, M, W1 ....$13.00

48-B, Sport Boat & Trailer, reg, 1961, wht & red w/gold motor, bl trailer, blk wheels, NM, W1 ....$37.00

48-E, Pi-Eyed Piper, SF, 1972, med bl w/amber winshield, 8-stacks engine, 8 roof label, NM+, W1 ....$10.00

49-A, M3 Personnel Carrier, reg, 1958, metal roller w/gray treads, metal wheels, MIB, W1 ....$45.00

49-B, Unimog, reg, 1967, tan & aqua, blk wheels, MIB, W1 ....$20.00

49-C, Unimog, SF, 1970, silver grille, bl w/red base, spiro fat wheels, no labels, NM, W1 ....$16.00

49-D, Chop Suey, SF, 1973, med magenta w/red handlebars, NM, W1 ....$10.00

50-A, Commer Pickup Truck, reg, 1958, tan, gray wheels, NM+, W1 ....$39.00

50-B, John Deere Tractor, reg, 1964, blk wheels, M, W1 .$27.00

50-B, John Deere Tractor, reg, 1964, gray wheels, MIB, W1 ....$31.00

50-C, Kennel Truck, reg, 1969, silver grille (scarce), blk wheels, complete, MIB, W1 ....$15.00

50-D, Kennel Truck, SF, 1970, med gr w/blk base, silver grille, thin wheels, complete, M, W1 ....$28.00

50-E, Articulated Truck, SF, 1973, yel & bl w/purple windshield, w/labels, no tow hook, MOC, W1 ....$4.00

51-A, Albion Chiefton, reg, 1958, Blue Circle Portland Cement decals, gray wheels, NM+, W1 ....$32.00

51-B, John Deere Trailer, reg, 1964, blk wheels, barrels on tree, complete, MIB, W1 ....$29.00

51-C, 8-Wheel Tipper Truck, reg, 1969, Douglas, orange & silver, blk wheels, M, W1 ....$14.00

51-C, 8-Wheel Tipper Truck, reg, 1969, Pointer, yel & silver, blk wheels, NM, W1 ....$9.00

52-B, BRM Racing Car, reg, 1965, bl, blk wheels, M, W1 ..$15.00

52-C, Dodge Charger, SF, 1970, med lime w/red base, no labels, M (NM box), W1 ....$15.00

52-D, Police Launch, SF, 1976, wht & bl w/dk bl windshield, lt bl flags, cast horns, M (EX+ box), W1 ....$6.00

53-A, Aston Martin, reg, 1958, med red (scarce), blk wheels, NM, W1 ....$90.00

53-B, Mercedes Benz 220 SE, reg, 1963, red, blk wheels, NM+, W1 ....$23.00

53-C, Ford Zodiac MK IV, reg, 1968, silver-bl, blk wheels, NM+, W1 ....$16.00

53-D, Ford Zodiac, SF, 1970, med emerald gr, unpnt base, skinny wheels, M, W1 ....$20.00

54-A, Saracen Personnel Carrier, reg, 1958, blk wheels, MIB, W1 ....$34.00

54-B, S&S Cadillac Ambulance, reg, 1965, blk wheels, EX, W1 ....$16.00

54-C, Cadillac Ambulance, SF, 1970, wht w/blk base, silver grille, EX+, W1 ....$18.00

54-E, Personnel Carrier, SF, 1976, olive w/tan seats, gr windshield, dot-dash wheels, M (NM box), W1 ....$6.00

54-F, Mobile Home, SF, 1980, cream w/lt brn door, charcoal base, M (NM box), W1 ....$6.00

54-H, Command Vehicle, SF, 1984, olive, 9 tampo, 8-dot blk wheels, M, W1 ....$5.00

55-A, DUKW, reg, 1958, metal wheels, MIB, W1 ....$46.00

55-B, Ford Fairlane Police Car, reg, 1963, metallic bl, blk wheels, NM+, W1 ....$63.00

55-C, Ford Galaxie Police Car, reg, 1966, blk wheels, MIB, W1 ....$35.00

55-F, Mercury Police Station Wagon, SF, 1971, wht w/red lights, red & yel Police label, M, W1 ....$15.00

55-G, Hellraiser, SF, 1975, wht w/red interior, unpnt base, clear windshield, stars & stripes label, NM, W1 ....$11.00

56-A, London Trolley Bus, reg, 1958, red poles, metal wheels, MIB, W1 ....$51.00

56-B, Fiat 1500 Sedan, reg, 1965, red (scarce), tan luggage, blk wheels, NM, W1 ....$80.00

56-C, BMC 1800 Pininfarina, SF, 1969, gold w/unpnt base, no labels, thin wheels, M (EX+ scarce card), W1 ....$20.00

56-D, Hi-Tailer, SF, 1974, wht w/unpnt base, bl driver, MB5 labels, 5-spoke front wheels, NM, W1 ....$10.00

56-F, Peterbilt Gas Tanker, SF, 1982, olive w/blk base & exhaust, clear windshield, w/Gas tampo, M, W1 ....$5.00

57-A, Wolseley 1500, reg, 1958, lt olive gr w/silver trim, gray wheels, M (EX+ box), W1 ....$41.00

57-C, Land Rover Fire Truck, reg, 1966, complete, M (NM box), W1 ....$12.00

57-E, Eccles Caravan, SF, 1970, cream w/orange top, gr interior, blk axle cover, stripe label, 5-spoke wheels, M, W1 ..$13.00

57-F, Wildlife Truck, SF, 1973, yel w/clear top, unpnt base, red windshield, w/label, orig lion, M (EX card), W1 ....$11.00

58-B, Drott Excavator, reg, 1962, silver motor base, blk plastic rollers, orig treads, M (NM box), W1 ....$44.00

58-E, Woosh-N-Push, SF, 1972, yel w/red interior, 2 labels, Maltese cross front wheels, M, W1 ....$18.00

58-F, Faun Dump Truck, SF, 1976, yel, no tampo, M (EX box), W1 ....$4.00

59-B, Ford Thames Singer Van, reg, 1958, blk wheels, NM, W1 ....$35.00

59-F, Planet Scout, SF, 1975, med gr w/lime gr base, amber windshield, M (EX+ box), W1 ....$20.00

60-A, Morris J-2 Pickup, reg, 1958, red & blk decal, w/window, M (EX box), A.....................$49.00

60-B, Site Hut Truck, reg, 1966, M (NM box), W1 ....$18.00

60-C, Site Hut Truck, SF, 1970, bl, skinny wheels, M (EX+ box), W1 ....$32.00

60-D, Lotus Super Seven, SF, 1971, yel, w/tampo, MOC, W1 .$30.00

61-A, Ferret Scout Car, reg, 1959, no driver, NM, W1 ......$5.00

61-C, Blue Shark, SF, 1971, dk bl w/unpnt base, clear windshield, w/labels, NM, W1 ....$14.00

61-D, Wrecker Truck, SF, 1978, red w/blk base, wht booms & red hooks, amber windshield, no tampo, MIB, W1......$9.00

61-E, Peterbilt Wrecker, SF, 1982, bl w/blk base & exhaust, clear windshield, 8 tampo, M, W1.....................$5.00

62-F, Mercury Cougar Rat Rod Dragster, SF, 1970, lime gr w/unpnt base, 4-spoke rear wheels, w/labels, NM, W1 .$14.00

62-F, Renault 17TL, SF, 1974, red, 9 hood label, 5-spoke wheels, M, W1 ....$11.00

63-A, Ford Service Van, reg, 1959, blk wheels, M, W1....$44.00

63-B, Foamite Airport Crash Tender, reg, 1964, gold nozzle, blk wheels, complete, M (NM box), W1 ....$29.00

63-C, Dodge Crane Truck, 1968, yellow, M, $25.00.
(Photo courtesy Dana Johnson)

63-D, Dodge Crane Truck, SF, 1970, yel w/blk axle covers, fat wheels, M, W1 ....$25.00

63-E, Freeway Gas Tanker, 1973, bl w/blk base, bl trailer base, purple windshield, Aral label (scarce), no hook, MOC, W1 ....$21.00

64-C, MG 1100, SF, 1970, gr (rare) w/unpnt base, thin wheel, W1 ....$175.00

64-D, Slingshot Dragster, SF, 1971, bl w/blk base, red pipes, 9 & flame labels, thin front wheels, MIB, W1 ....$17.00

64-E, Fire Chief Car, SF, 1976, red w/shield label, 5-arch front & 5-crown rear wheels, MOC, W1 ....$13.00

65-A, Jaguar 3.4 Litre Saloon, reg, 1959, bl, gray wheels, EX+, W1 ....$27.00

65-D, Saab Sonnet, SF, 1973, med bl w/yel interior, unpnt base, MIB, W1 ....$12.00

65-E, TWA Airport Coach, SF, 1977, bl w/lt yel interior, unpnt base, amber windshield, MIB, W1.....................$13.00

66-A, Citroen DS19, reg, 1959, gray wheels, NM, W1 ....$39.00

66-B, Harley-Davidson Motorcycle & Sidecar, reg, 1962, blk wheels, NM, W1 ....$79.00

66-D, Greyhound Bus, SF, 1970, silver-gray w/blk base & axle cover, thin wheels, NM, W1 ....$25.00

66-E, Mazda RX500, SF, 1971, orange w/silver interior, wht base, purple windshield, MIB, W1 ....$13.00

67-A, Saladin Armoured Car, reg, 1959, blk wheels, M (EX box), W1 ....$36.00

67-C, VW 1600TL, SF, 1970, purple w/unpnt base, thin wheels, M (EX box), W1 ....$21.00

67-D, Hot Rocker, SF, 1973, med lime gr w/unpnt base, 5-spoke wheels, M, W1 ....$13.00

68-A, Austin MKII Radio Truck, reg, 1959, blk wheels, EX+, W1 ....$28.00

68-B, Mercedes Coach, reg, 1965, aqua (scarce), blk wheels, NM+, W1 ....$82.00

68-C, Porsche 910, SF, 1969, med red w/amber windshield, 68 hood label only, thin wheels, M (NM box), W1 ....$12.00

68-C, Porsche 910, SF, 1969, med red w/amber windshield, 68 hood label only, fat wheels, M (NM box), W1 ....$14.00

68-D, Cosmobile, SF, 1975, med bl w/silver interior, yel base, amber windshield, MOC, W1 ....$29.00

69-A, Commer 30 CWT Nestle's Van, reg, 1959, gray wheels, NM, W1 ....$36.00

69-B, Hatra Tractor Shovel, reg, 1965, orange (scarce), blk wheels w/yel hubs, M, W1 ....$25.00

69-C, RR Silver Shadow, SF, 1969, med bl w/orange-brn interior, blk base, tan tonneau, thin wheels, M (NM+ box), W1 ....$20.00

69-D, Turbo Fury, SF, 1973, med red w/blk base, clear windshield, 69 label, 5-spoke wheels, M (EX+ box), W1 ..$15.00

70-A, Ford Thames Estate Car, reg, 1959, gr windshield, blk wheels, M (EX+ box), W1.............................$38.00

70-B, Ford Grit Spreader, reg, 1966, gray pull, blk wheels, M (EX+ box), W1 ....$15.00

70-C, Ford Grit Spreader, SF, 1970, red & yel, 5-spoke thin wheels, M (NM box), W1 ....$19.00

70-D, Dodge Dragster, SF, 1971, pk w/blk base, lt gr snake label, 4-spoke rear wheels, M (EX box), W1 ....$18.00

70-E, Self-Propelled Gun, SF, 1976, olive w/tan treads, M (EX box), W1 ....$9.00

71-A, Austin 200 Gallon Water Truck, reg, 1959, M (EX box), W1 ....$41.00

71-B, Jeep Gladiator Pickup, reg, 1964, wht interior, blk wheels, M (NM+ box), W1 ....$30.00

71-C, Ford Heavy Wrecker Truck, reg, 1968, red & wht w/gr windshield, red hook, blk wheels, M (NM box), W1 ..$18.00

71-F, Cattle Truck, SF, 1976, red w/orange-yel stakes, silver base, red windshield, blk cattle, no hook, rare, MIB, W1 ....$8.00

72-A, Fordson Tractor, reg, 1959, blk wheels, M (NM+ box), W1 ....$50.00

72-D, Hovercraft, SF, 1972, wht w/blk base, bl windshield, w/labels, M, W1 ....$4.00

72-F, Maxi Taxi, SF, 1973, yel w/blk base, M (on card or in box), W1 ....$9.00

72-G, Dodge Pepsi Delivery Truck, SF, 1982, red & wht w/silver hubs, MIB, W1...$13.00

73-A, 10-Ton Pressure Refueller, reg, 1959, gray wheels, NM+, W1 ....$25.00

73-B, Ferrari F1 Racer, reg, 1962, blk wheels, w/driver, M, W1 ....$33.00

73-C, Mercury Station Wagon, reg, 1968, blk wheels, M (NM+ box), W1 ....$14.00

73-D, Mercury Commuter, 1970, red w/cow label, MIB, W1 ....$17.00

73-F, Model A Ford, SF, 1979, med gr w/dk gr fenders, gr windshield, no spare, MOC, W1 ....$8.00

74-A, Mobile Refreshment Canteen, reg, 1959, silver w/lt bl interior & base, gray wheels, NM+, W1 ....$40.00

74-B, Daimler Bus, reg, 1966, gr, M (NM box), W1.........$20.00

74-C, Daimler Bus, SF, 1970, Esso Extra Petrol, red w/red-pk base, thin wheels, M, W1 ....$20.00

74-F, Orange Peel, SF, 1982, wht w/blk base, dk orange tampo, NM+, W1 ....$5.00

75-B, Ferrari Berlinetta, reg, 1965, gr, unpnt base, blk disk wheels (scarce), M (EX+ box), W1.............................$17.00

75-C, Ferrari Berlinetta, SF, 1970, red w/unpnt base, plain grille, thin wheels, M, W1 ....$25.00

75-D, Alfa Carabo, 1971, M, $10.00.
(Photo courtesy Dana Johnson)

KING SIZE, SPEED KINGS, AND SUPER KINGS

K-01B, Hoveringham Tipper Truck, 1964, w/labels (scarce), M (NM box), W1...$39.00

K-02C, Scammel Heavy Wrecker Truck, 1969, wht w/gr windshield, blk wheels, M (NM box), W1.........................$49.00

K-02D, Car Recovery Vehicle, 1977, med bl w/wht interior, red ramps, clear windshield, w/beige K59 Capri, M (NM box), W1 ....$23.00

K-04A, International Tractor, 1960, w/decals, blk wheels w/gr metal hubs, M (NM box), W1 ....$79.00

K-04C, Leyland Tipper, 1969, dk red w/silver dump, LE labels, blk wheels, M (EX+ box), W1 ....$29.00

K-04D, Big Tipper, 1974, metallic red w/yel dump, 3-stripe labels, M (EX+ box), W1..$8.00

K-05A, Foden Tipper Truck, 1961, blk wheels w/red hubs, M (EX+ box), W1 ....$59.00

K-06D, Motorcycle Transporter, 1976, med dk bl, Team Honda labels, M (NM box), W1.....................................$19.00

K-07B, Refuse Truck, 1967, blk wheels, M (NM box), W1 ..$34.00

K-08B, Guy Warrior Car Transporter, 1967, yel, blk wheels w/red hubs, M (EX box), W1 ....$35.00

K-09A, Diesel Road Roller, 1962, w/red driver, M (NM box), W1 ....$54.00

K-10A, Aveling-Barford Tractor Shovel, 1963, bl-gr, w/air cleaner, blk wheels w/silver metal hubs, NM+, W1...$49.00

K-10B, Pipe Truck, 1967, w/4 orig pipes, EX, W1 ....$24.00

K-11A, Fordson Tractor & Farm Trailer, 1963, bl steering wheel, blk wheels w/red hubs, M (NM box), W1 ......$39.00

K-11B, DAF Car Transporter, 1969, med bl & gold, blk wheel blocks, M (EX+ box), W1 ....$79.00

K-13A, Readymix Concrete Truck, 1963, silver metal wheels, NM, W1 ....$29.00

K-13B, Building Transporter, 1971, med lime w/red base, clear windshield, M (VG+ box), W1 ....$16.00

K-14A, Taylor Jumbo Crane, 1964, yel weight box (scarce), NM+ (NM box), W1...$35.00

K-15B, Londoner Bus, The Royal Wedding 1981, M, $20.00. (Photo courtesy Dana Johnson)

K-15B, Londoner, 1973, Enter a Different World — Harrod's, red w/yel interior, M (EX+ box), W1.........................$19.00

K-16A, Dodge Tractor w/Twin Tippers, 1966, labels, NM+, W1 ....$79.00

K-16B, Petrol Tanker, 1974, Total label, M (NM box), W1..$31.00

K-17A, Lowloader w/Bulldozer, 1967, Laing decals, complete, NM, W1 ....$37.00

K-18A, Articulated Horse Box, 1967, complete, NM+, W1.$44.00

K-19A, Scammell Tipper Truck, 1967, M (NM box), W1 ...$38.00

K-20A, Tractor Transporter, 1968, red tanks, complete, M (EX box), W1..$116.00

K-20C, Peterbilt Wrecker, 1979, dk gr w/charcoal base, unpnt roof mount, red lights, M (NM box), W1 ....$19.00

K-21A, Mercury Cougar, 1968, red interior, M (NM box), W1...$39.00

K-21C, Tractor Transporter, 1974, med bl, complete, M (NM box), W1..$26.00

K-22C, Seaspeed SRN6 Hovercraft, 1974, bl & wht, NM, W1 ....$3.00

K-23B, Lowloader & Bulldozer, 1974, med bl cab w/yel interior, silver-gray base, red & yel dozer, NM+, W1 ....$35.00

K-24A, Lamborghini Miura, 1969, bronze, mag wheels, NM+, W1...$9.00

K-26B, McAlpine Cement Truck, 1979, yel w/blk base, gray barrel, red stripes, clear windshield, M (NM base), W1....$9.00

K-27A, 1971, Camping Cruiser, yel w/orange top, amber windshields, dots labels, M (NM box), W1 ....$10.00

K-29B, Mr Softy Ford Delivery Truck, 1978, wht & lime, M (NM box), W1..$15.00

K-31A, Bertone Runabout, 1971, gr windshield, M (EX box), W1...$4.00

K-31B, Peterbilt Refrigerator Truck, 1978, Christian-Salvesen, M (NM box), W1 ....$31.00

K-33A, Citroen SM, 1972, med magenta, w/tow hook, M (NM box), W $9.00

K-33B, US Steel Cargo Hauler, 1979, bl & wht w/blk crane, M (NM box), W1...$26.00

K-34B, Pallet Truck & Forklift, 1979, wht w/dk bl base, bl K tarp, M (NM box), W1...$23.00

K-35A, Lightning, 1972, red w/Team Matchbox hood & Firestone spoiler, 35 side labels, M (NM box), W1...........$6.00

K-37A, Sand Cat, 1973, orange w/gr spatter, blk top & interior, M (NM box), W1 ....$9.00

K-38A, Gus' Gulper, 1973, pk w/yel interior & roll bar, M (NM box), W1 ....$11.00

K-39A, Mulligan's Mill, 1973, lt gr w/orange interior & roll bar, flames roof label, Firestone spoiler, M (NM box), W1..$15.00

K-40A, Blaze Trailer, 1973, red w/orange interior & antenna, yel base, amber windshield, bl lights, M (NM box), W1....$13.00

K-41B, Brabham F1, 1977, red, Martini & #7 tampo w/Goodyear, M (NM box), W1 ....$8.00

K-45A, Marauder, 1973, burgundy w/yel interior, gr base, clear windshield, wht driver, 7 labels, M (EX+ box), W1 ....$8.00

K-48A, Mercedes 350SLC, 1973, bronze w/yel interior, silver-gray base, amber windshield, M (NM box), W1 ....$10.00

K-62A, Doctor's Emergency Car, 1977, wht w/silver-gray base, amber windshield, Red Cross labels, M (NM box), W1.$13.00

K-67A, Dodge Monaco Fire Chief Car, 1978, yel w/red interior, blk base, amber windshield, M (VG+ box), W1........$12.00

K-98-B, Porsche 944, 1983, red with white lettering, M, $8.00. (Photo courtesy Dana Johnson)

MODELS OF YESTERYEAR MATCHBOX

Y-01B, 1911 Ford Model T, 1964, cream w/maroon top, red base & seats, blk plastic steering wheel, M (EX+ box), W1 ....$22.00

Y-01C, 1936 Jaguar SS, 1977, dk yel w/blk seats, M (NM box), W1 ....$10.00

Y-02A, 1911 B-Type London Bus, 1956, red w/bl driver, unpnt wheels, 8-over-4 windows, NM+, W1.......................$55.00

Y-02B, 1911 Renault 2-Seater, 1963, gr, gr metal steering wheel, brass dash, type-2 radiator, 3-prong spare, MIB, W1 .$15.00

Y-02B, 1911 Renault 2-Seater, 1963, gr, gr metal steering wheel, brass dash, type-1 radiator, rare, MIB, W1 ....$89.00

Y-02D, 1930 Bentley 2½ Litre, 1985, purple w/blk fenders, brn interior, blk rubber tires w/charcoal wheels, MIB, W1 .$15.00

Y-03A, 1907 London E Class Tramcar, 1956, wht roof, News decals, MIB, W1 ....$100.00

Y-03C, 1934 Riley MPH, 1974, bl w/wht seats & radiator, 24-spoke silver wheels, blk rubber tires, 6 labels, MIB, W1 ....$13.00

Y02-C, 1914 Prince Henry Vauxhall, 1970, red and silver with white seats, 26-spoke wire wheels, MOC, $50.00.
(Photo courtesy Dana Johnson)

Y-03D, 1912 Model T Ford Tanker, 1981, Express Dairy tampo, bl & blk w/wht top, red 12-spoke wheels (scarce), MIB, W1..$19.00

Y-04C, 1909 Opel Coupe, 1967, orange & blk w/maroon seats, wht grille, 12-spoke wheels, M (NM box), W1 ....$17.00

Y-05A, 1929 LeMans Bentley, 1958, gold radiator, gr grille & tonneau, silver steering wheel, NM, W1....................$35.00

Y-05C, 1907 Peigeot, 1969, yel & blk w/red seats & grille, amber windows, M (NM box), W1 ....$15.00

Y-05D, 1927 Talbot Van, 1978, Lipton's w/crest labels, gr & blk, 12-spoke wheels, M (NM+ box), W1 ....$16.00

Y-06B, 1926, Type-35 Bugatti, 1961, bl w/red dash, #6 decal, M (NM box), W1..$50.00

Y-06D, 1920 Rolls Royce Fire Engine, 1977, red w/blk seat, orange-brn ladder, 12-spoke gold wheels, M (NM+ box), W1 ....$15.00

Y-07A, 1918, 4-Ton Leyland Van, 1957, red-brn w/cream top, metal wheels, NM+, W1 ....$62.00

Y-07C, 1912 Rolls Royce, 1968, gold w/red ribbed top, base, seats & grille, 12-spoke brass wheels, M (EX box), W1........$13.00

Y-08B, 1914 Sunbeam Motorcycle & Sidecar, 1962, dk gr seat, M (NM+ box), W1..$70.00

Y-08C, 1914 Stutz Roadster, 1969, red w/smooth tan top, copper gas tank, M (EX+ box), W1 ....$15.00

Y-08D, 1945 MG TD, 1978, bl w/tan top, blk interior, 24-spoke chrome wheels, blk rubber tires, M (NM box), W1...$15.00

Y-09A, 1924 Fowler Big Lion Showman Engine, 1958, red w/wht top, gold boiler, 1 silver/1 gold support (rare), NM, W1 ....$59.00

Y-10A, 1908 GP Mercedes, 1958, cream w/lt gr seats, gold trim, blk wheels, NM+, W1 ....$44.00

Y-10C, 1906 Rolls Royce Silver Cloud, 1969, silver w/blk grille, yel seats, wht-walls w/red wheels, MIB, W1..............$22.00

Y-12B, 1909 Thomas Flyabout, 1967, bl w/smooth tan top, dk red grille & seats, body pins, M (EX box), W1 ....$15.00

Y-13A, 1868 Santa Fe Locomotive, 1959, gr, w/decals, NM+, W1 ....$55.00

Y-15B, 1930 Packard Victoria, 1969, tan w/maroon top & seats, red grille, brn base, blk reg tires, MIB, W1.................$15.00

Y-18A, 1927 Cord 812, 1979, plum w/wht top & interior, wht-walls w/silver disk wheels, M (EX+ box), W1............$19.00

Y-19A, 1935 Auburn 851, 1980, khaki & beige w/brn base, orange seats, wht-walls w/red disk wheels, M (NM box), W1...$13.00

Y-20A, 1937 Mercedes 540K, 1981, blk w/maroon seats, wht-walls w/24-spoke chrome wheels, M (NM box), W1.$13.00

Y-21A, 1930 Model A Ford Woody Station Wagon, 1981, bl w/cream rear, blk base, brn interior, M (NM box), W1 ....$15.00

Y-22A, 1930 Model A Ford Van, 1982, beige w/red top, brn base, wht-walls w/24-spoke chrome wheels, M (NM box), W1 ....$13.00

Y-23A, 1922 AEC S-Type Bus, 1982, Schweppes Tonic Water, red w/tan interior, red wheels, blk rubber tires, MIB, W1 ....$13.00

Y-26A, 1913 Crossley Beer Lorry, 1983, Gonzales Byass tampo, wht w/maroon top & grille, red base, M (NM box), W1..$15.00

Y-26A, 1918 Crossley Beer Lorry, 1984, Lowenbrau tampo, M, $20.00. (Photo courtesy Dana Johnson)

Y-29A, Walker Electric Van, 1985, gr w/tan interior, red wheels, M (NM box), W1 ....$12.00

Y-30A, 1920 Model AC Mack Truck, 1985, Acorn Storage, lt bl w/dk bl fenders, dk gray top, brn wheels, M (NM box), W1 ....$13.00

Y-47A, 1929 Morris Van, 1991, blk w/yel top, brn interior, chrome wheels, Lindt labels, M(NM box), W1 ....$15.00

Y-62A, 1932 Ford AA Pickup, 1992, lime gr w/gray top, blk base, brn load, red wheels, blk rubber tires, M (NM box), W1 ....$25.00

Y-63A, 1939 Bedford Truck, 1992, Farrar tampo, red & brn w/blk interior & base, real stone load, chrome wheels, MIB, W1 ....$25.00

SKYBUSTERS

SB-01A, Lear Jet, 1973, Federal Express, purple w/silver base, M (NM+ box), W1 ....$10.00

SB-02A, Corsair A7D, silver-bl w/wht base, clear windshield, tall label, thick axle, MIB, W1 ....$10.00

SB-03A, A300 Air France Airbus, 1973, wht w/silver-gray base, tall tampo, thick axles, MOC, W1 ....$10.00

SB-03B, NASA Space Shuttle, 1980, wht w/gray base, w/labels, MIB, W1 ....$10.00

SB-04A, Mirage F1, 1973, metallic red w/red base, smoke windshield, thick axles, bull's-eye on wings, MOC, W1 ...$12.00

SB-07A, Junkers 87B, 1973, blk w/silver-gray base, cross on wings, swastika on tail, thin axle, rare, NM+, W1.....$90.00

SB-09A, Cessna 402, 1973, med gr w/wht wings & base, clear windshield, w/labels, M, W1...$6.00

SB-10A, Pan Am Boeing 747, 1973, wht w/pearl-gray base, MOC, W1..$17.00

SB-11A, Alpha AT39 Jet, 1973, wht w/red base, bl windshield, MIB, W1...$10.00

SB-12A, Marine Skyhawk A-4F, 1973, dk bl w/wht base, clear windshield, thick axles, MOC, W1............................$10.00

SB-13A, Aero Mexico DC-10, 1973, silver & red w/pearl silver base, MOC, W1...$10.00

SB-15A, Marine Phantom F4E, 1975, gray w/clear windshield, MOC, W1..$6.00

SB-17A, Ram Rod, 1976, red w/wht wings & base, clear windshield, MOC, W1...$10.00

SB-19A, Piper Commanche N246P, 1977, red w/yel wings & base, clear windshield, MIB, W1..............................$10.00

SB-20A, Police Helicopter, 1977, wht w/red base, MIB, W1.$12.00

SB-22A, Tornado F-132, 1978, gray w/wht base, MIB, W1..$5.00

SB-23A, Super Sonic Airlines SST, 1979, wht, MIB, W1 .$7.00

SB-24A, F16 Fighter Jet, 1979, wht w/red wings & base, star labels, MIB, W1..$10.00

SB-26A, Cessna N264H Float Plane, 1981, red w/wht wings & base, blk skis, clear windshield, MIB, W1.................$10.00

SB27A, Marine Harrier Jet, 1981, wht w/red base, clear windshield, MIB, W1...$10.00

Model Kits

While values for military kits seem to have leveled off and others may have actually gone down, this is certainly not the case with the Aurora monster and character kits which, with only a few exceptions, are continuing to increase in value.

Though model kits were popular with kids of the '50s who enjoyed the challenge of assembling a classic car or two or a Musketeer figure now and then, when the monster series hit in the early 1960s, sales shot through the ceiling. Made popular by all the monster movies of that decade, ghouls like Vampirella, Frankenstein, and the Wolfman were eagerly built up by kids everywhere. They could (if their parents didn't object too strongly) even construct an actual working guillotine. Aurora had other successful series of figure kits, too, based on characters from comic strips and TV shows as well as a line of sports stars.

But the vast majority of model kits were vehicles. They varied in complexity, some requiring much more dexterity on the part of the model builder than others, and they came in several scales, from 1/8 (which might be as large as 20" to 24") down to 1/43 (generally about 3" to 4"), but the most popular scale was 1/25 (usually between 6" to 8"). Some of the largest producers of vehicle kits were AMT, MPC, and IMC. Though production obviously waned during the late 1970s and early '80s, with the

intensity of today's collector market, companies like Ertl (who now is producing 1/25 scale vehicles using some of the old AMT dies) are proving that model kits still sell very well.

As a rule of thumb, assembled kits (built-ups) are priced at about 25% to 50% of the price range for a boxed kit, but this is not always true on the higher-priced kits. One mint in the box with the factory seal intact will often sell for up to 15% more than if the seal were broken, though depending on the kit, a sealed perfect box may add as much $100.00. Condition of the box is crucial. For more information, we recommend *Classic Plastic Model Kits* by Rick Polizzi (Collector Books); *Aurora History and Price Guide* by Bill Bruegman; and *Collectible Figure Kits of the '50s, '60s & '70s*, by Gordy Dutt.

Advisors: Mike and Kurt Fredericks (F4); John and Sheri Pavone (P3).

Other Sources: B10, J2, J7, M17, P4.

See also Plasticville.

Adams, Around the World in 80 Days Balloon, 1960, MIB..$325.00

Adams, Chuck Wagon, 1958, MIB $35.00

Adams, Hawk Missile Battery, 1958, MIB $70.00

Addar, Evel Knievel's Ramp Jump, 1974, assembled, EX .$50.00

Addar, Evel Knievel's Wheelie, 1974, MIB $125.00

Addar, Planet of the Apes, Caesar, Dr Zira, Dr Zaius, General Aldo, or General Ursus, 1973-74, MIB, ea $50.00

Addar, Planet of the Apes, Cornelius, 1973, MIB (sealed) ..$90.00

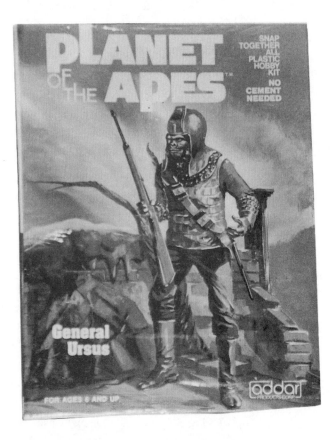

Addar, Planet of the Apes, General Ursus, 1973 – 74, MIB, $50.00. (Photo John and Sheri Pavone)

Addar, Planet of the Apes, Stallion & Soldier, 1974, MIB..$85.00

Addar, Rendezvous in Space, 1975, MIB $40.00

Addar, Super Scenes, Jaws, 1975, NM (VG+ box)...........$30.00

Addar, World Wildlife, Blue Jays, 1975, MIB.................$30.00

Addar, World Wildlife, Outlaw Mustang, 1975, MIB $35.00

AEF, Aliens, Bishop, 1980, MIB $35.00

AEF, Aliens, Frost, 1980s, MIB $25.00

AEF, Aliens, Warrior Alien, 1980s, MIB.........................$40.00

Airfix, Apollo Saturn V, MIB (sealed)..............................$30.00

Airfix, Corythosaurus, 1970, MIB (sealed) $30.00

Airfix, James Bond 007 (You Only Live Twice), Little Nellie
    Autogyro, 1996, MIB, G5...$25.00

Airfix, Mounted Bengal Lancer, 1991, MIB (sealed)........$40.00

Airfix, Skeleton, 1970, MIB $20.00

Airfix, Wildlife Series, Robin, 1979, MIB (sealed)...........$30.00

Alternative Images, Dracula Prince of Darkness, 1992, NMIB .$145.00

AMT, Denny McLain's Horse Hide Hauler, 1970, MIB...$45.00

AMT, Farrah's Foxy Vet, 1970s, MIB (sealed) $35.00

AMT, Flintstone's Family Sedan, 1974, MIB $90.00

AMT, Fred Flintstone's Rock Cruncher or Sports Car, 1974,
    MIB, ea...$50.00

AMT, Girl From UNCLE Car, 1967, MIB $250.00

AMT, Graveyard Ghoul Duo, 1970, MIB.......................$125.00

AMT, Hang-Outs, Cliff Hanger, 1970s, MIB $30.00

AMT, KISS Custom Chevy Van, 1977, MIB $70.00

AMT, Laurel & Hardy '25 T Roadster, 1976, MIB...........$45.00

AMT, Man From UNCLE Car, 1967, MIB $220.00

AMT, Munster Koach, 1964, MIB.................................$150.00

AMT, My Mother the Car, 1965, MIB $75.00

AMT, Sonny & Cher Mustang, 1960s, MIB $225.00

AMT, Star Trek, Exploration, Galileo 7 Shuttlecraft or Romu-
    lan Bird of Prey, 1974-75, MIB, ea...........................$100.00

AMT, Star Trek, Klingon Battle Cruiser, 1968, MIB.....$190.00

AMT, Star Trek, Mr Spock, 1967, MIB $150.00

AMT, Star Trek, USS Enterprise, 1967, orig issue, MIB
    (sealed)..$190.00

AMT, Star Trek: The Motion Picture, USS Enterprise, 1979,
    MIB $70.00

AMT, Surf Woody, 1960s, MIB $65.00

AMT, Wackie Woodie Krazy Kar, 1960s, M (VG sealed
    box) $85.00

AMT/Ertl, A-Team Van, 1983, MIB $30.00

AMT/Ertl, Airwolf Helicopter, 1984, M (EX sealed box) ..$25.00

AMT/Ertl, Back to the Future, Delorian, 1991, MIB (sealed) .$35.00

AMT/Ertl, Batman (movie), Batmobile, 1989, MIB (sealed)..$15.00

AMT/Ertl, Batman (movie), Batmobile, 1990, motorized, MIB
    (sealed)..$20.00

AMT/Ertl, Batman (movie), Batwing, 1990, MIB (sealed) .$30.00

AMT/Ertl, Batman (movie), Joker Goon Car, 1989, MIB
    (sealed)..$16.00

AMT/Ertl, Gigantics, Colossal Mantis, 1996, MIB (sealed) ..$15.00

AMT/Ertl, Munsters Koach & Dragula Cars, 1991, MIB .$100.00

AMT/Ertl, Rescue 911 Police Car or Rescue Helicopter, 1993,
    MIB (sealed), ea...$15.00

AMT/Ertl, Riptide, 1960 Corvette, 1984, MIB (sealed)...$25.00

AMT/Ertl, Star Trek (TV), Kirk, 1994, 12", MIB (sealed)..$25.00

AMT/Ertl, Star Trek (TV), USS Enterprise, 1983, MIB
    (sealed) $20.00

AMT/Ertl, Star Trek III: The Search for Spock, USS Enterprise,
    1984, MIB $35.00

AMT/Ertl, Star Trek V: The Final Frontier, Enterprise/Shuttle-
    craft, 1989, MIB...$25.00

AMT/Ertl, Star Trek VI: Undiscovered Country, Klingon
    Cruiser, 1991, MIB $10.00

AMT/Ertl, Star Trek: Generations, Klingon Bird of Prey, 1995,
    MIB $25.00

AMT/Ertl, Star Trek: The Motion Picture, Klingon Cruiser,
    1984, MIB (sealed) $16.00

AMT/Ertl, Star Trek: The Motion Picture, Vulcan Shuttle,
    1984, MIB (sealed) $70.00

AMT/Ertl, Star Wars, Cut-away Millenium Falcon, 1996, MIB
    (sealed)...$25.00

AMT/Ertl, Star Wars, Han Solo, 1995, MIB (sealed) $30.00

AMT/Ertl, Star Wars, TIE Fighter Flight Display, 1996, MIB.$20.00

Anubis, Jonny Quest, Robot Spy, 1992, MIB $60.00

Anubis, Jonny Quest, Turu the Terrible, 1992, 8½", MIB..$60.00

Anubis, Star Trek: The Next Generation, Borg Ship, 1992, 5¼",
    MIB $70.00

Aoshima, Back to the Future, Delorian, 1989, MIB $40.00

Aoshima, Batman (movie), Batmobile, 1989, MIB $40.00

Apex, Russian Carrier Rocket Vostak, 1990s, MIB $20.00

Arii, Macross, Quiltra-Queleual Ship, MIB $30.00

Arii, Macross, SDF-1 Cruiser Fortress, MIB $20.00

Arii, Regult Missile Carrier, MIB $25.00

Arii, Southern Cross, ATAC-Bowie Emerson, MIB.........$25.00

Atlantic, Goldrake-Toei Animation, Golgoth-Robot of Vega,
    1978, MIB $15.00

Atlantic, Mao/Chinese Revolution, 1975, MIB................$20.00

Aurora, Adventure Series, D'Artagnan the Musketeer, 1966, MIB, H4...$100.00
Aurora, Adventure Series, Spartacus, 1964, MIB..........$275.00
Aurora, Alfred E Neuman, 1969, assembled, EX.............$125.00
Aurora, American Astronaut, 1967, MIB.......................$65.00
Aurora, American Buffalo, 1964, MIB...........................$35.00
Aurora, Archie's Car, 1969, MIB.................................$85.00
Aurora, Aston Martin Spy Car, partially assembled.......$100.00
Aurora, Astronaut, 1967, MIB (yel logo).....................$100.00
Aurora, Banana Splits Banana Buggy, 1969, MIB..........$300.00
Aurora, Batcycle, 1968, MIB......................................$350.00
Aurora, Batman, 1964, MIB.......................................$225.00
Aurora, Batmobile, 1966, MIB....................................$500.00
Aurora, Black Falcon Pirate Ship, MIB..........................$50.00
Aurora, Bloodthirsty Pirates, Blackbeard, 1965, MIB.....$350.00

Aurora, Comic Scenes, Captain America, 1974, MIB ...$100.00
Aurora, Comic Scenes, Lone Ranger, 1974, MIB.............$50.00
Aurora, Comic Scenes, Robin the Teen Wonder, 1974, MIB ..$75.00
Aurora, Comic Scenes, Superman, 1974, MIB.................$50.00
Aurora, Comic Scenes, Tarzan, NRFB (sealed), H4.........$50.00
Aurora, Comic Scenes, Tonto, EX (VG box), H4............$30.00
Aurora, Cougar, 1962, MIB..$65.00
Aurora, Creature From the Black Lagoon, 1969, glow-in-the-dark, MIB..$150.00
Aurora, Creature From the Black Lagoon, 1972, glow-in-the-dark, MIB..$100.00
Aurora, Customizing Monster Kit, MIB, H4..................$120.00
Aurora, Dick Tracy, 1968, MIB..................................$150.00
Aurora, Dick Tracy Space Coupe, 1967, MIB, T2..........$100.00
Aurora, Dr Dolittle & Pushmi-Pullyu, 1968, MIB............$75.00
Aurora, Dr Jekyll as Mr Hyde, 1964, MIB.....................$250.00
Aurora, Dr Jekyll as Mr Hyde, 1969, glow-in-the-dark, MIB...$100.00
Aurora, Dr Jekyll as Mr Hyde, 1972, glow-in-the-dark, MIB...$65.00
Aurora, Dracula, 1969, glow-in-the-dark, MIB.............$100.00
Aurora, Dracula, 1972, MIB (sealed)...........................$200.00
Aurora, Dracula's Dragster, 1964, MIB........................$325.00
Aurora, Famous Fighters, Apache Warrior, 1961, MIB..$325.00

Aurora, Bride of Frankenstein, 1965, MIB, $650.00.
(Photo courtesy Rick Polizzi)

Aurora, Famous Fighters, Roman Gladiator, MIB, $200.00.
(Photo courtesy June Moon)

Aurora, Captain Action, 1966, MIB (sealed), A............$250.00
Aurora, Captain America, 1966, orig issue, MIB...........$400.00
Aurora, Castle Creatures, Frog, 1966, MIB...................$250.00
Aurora, Castle Creatures, Vampire, 1966, MIB..............$175.00
Aurora, Chitty-Chitty Bang-Bang, 1965, assembled, EX .$40.00
Aurora, Comic Scenes, Batman, 1974, MIB...................$65.00

Aurora, Famous Fighters, Confederate Raider, 1959, MIB......$375.00
Aurora, Famous Fighters, Gold Knight of Nice, 1957, MIB....$225.00
Aurora, Famous Fighters, Nike Hercules Missile, 1958, MIB..$300.00
Aurora, Famous Fighters, Red Knight of Vienna, 1957, MIB....$65.00
Aurora, Famous Fighters, Steve Canyon, 1958, MIB $175.00
Aurora, Famous Fighters, The Three Musketeers (Aramis, Athos, or Porthos), 1958, MIB, ea $75.00
Aurora, Famous Fighters, US Air Force Pilot, 1958, MIB.$300.00
Aurora, Famous Fighters, US Marshal, 1958, MIB $85.00
Aurora, Famous Fighters, Viking, 1958, MIB $340.00
Aurora, Forged Foil Buffalo, 1969, MIB $40.00
Aurora, Forged Foil Cougar, 1969, MIB...........................$65.00
Aurora, Forgotten Prisoner of Castlemare, 1966, MIB ...$400.00
Aurora, Forgotten Prisoner of Castlemare, 1969 (Frightening Lightning), MIB $365.00
Aurora, Forgotten Prisoner of Castlemare, 1972, glow-in-the-dark, MIB (sealed) $210.00
Aurora, Frankenstein, 1961, MIB $400.00
Aurora, Frankenstein, 1969, glow-in-the-dark, MIB $75.00
Aurora, Frankenstein's Flivver, 1964, assembled, EX $150.00
Aurora, Frightening Lightning Strikes, Dracula, 1969, MIB $350.00
Aurora, Frightening Lightning Strikes, Frankenstein, 1969, MIB...$400.00
Aurora, Frightening Lightning Strikes, Mummy, 1969, MIB $325.00
Aurora, Frightening Lightning Strikes, Phantom of the Opera, 1969, MIB $325.00
Aurora, Frightening Lightning Strikes, Wolfman, 1969, MIB ..$400.00
Aurora, Godzilla, 1969, glow-in-the-dark, MIB..............$200.00

Aurora, Godzilla, 1972, glow-in-the-dark, MIB..............$150.00
Aurora, Godzilla's Go-Cart, 1966, assembled, EX $675.00
Aurora, Godzilla's Go-Cart, 1966, MIB......................$2,700.00
Aurora, Great American Presidents, George Washington, 1967, MIB...$100.00
Aurora, Great American Presidents, John F Kennedy, 1965, MIB...$200.00
Aurora, Great Moments in Sports, Babe Ruth, assembled, EX, H4..$70.00
Aurora, Great Moments in Sports, Dempsey Vs Firpo, 1965, MIB...$100.00
Aurora, Great Moments in Sports, Jerry West, 1965, MIB.$200.00
Aurora, Great Moments in Sports, Johnny Unitas, 1965, MIB...$150.00
Aurora, Great Moments in Sports, Willie Mays, 1965, MIB..$225.00
Aurora, Green Beret, 1966, MIB.................................$150.00
Aurora, Green Hornet's Black Beauty Car, 1967, MIB..$350.00
Aurora, Guillotine, 1964, orig issue, MIB.....................$650.00
Aurora, Guys & Gals, Dutch Boy & Dutch Girl, 1959, MIB.$200.00
Aurora, Guys & Gals, Indian Chief & Squaw, 1959, MIB......$150.00
Aurora, Guys & Gals, Scotch Lad & Lassie, 1959, MIB..$100.00
Aurora, Hercules & the Lion, 1965, MIB $250.00
Aurora, Hunchback of Notre Dame, 1964, partially assembled..$160.00
Aurora, Hunchback of Notre Dame, 1969, glow-in-the-dark, MIB...$100.00
Aurora, Hunchback of Notre Dame, 1972, glow-in-the-dark, MIB...$65.00
Aurora, Incredible Hulk, 1966, MIB............................$250.00
Aurora, Invaders UFO, 1968, orig issue, MIB...............$210.00
Aurora, James Bond 007, 1966, assembled, EX..............$150.00
Aurora, Jesse James, 1966, MIB..................................$150.00
Aurora, King Kong, 1964, assembled, EX.......................$75.00
Aurora, King Kong, 1964, MIB $400.00
Aurora, King Kong, 1969, glow-in-the-dark, MIB..........$200.00
Aurora, King Kong, 1972, glow-in-the-dark, MIB..........$150.00
Aurora, King Kong's Thronester, 1966, MIB.................$160.00
Aurora, Knights in Shining Armour, King Arthur, 1973, assembled, EX..$75.00
Aurora, Knights in Shining Armour, Richard I, 1973, assembled, EX..$40.00
Aurora, Land of the Giants, Snake Scene, 1968, rare, MIB.$400.00
Aurora, Land of the Giants, Spaceship, 1968, MIB........$325.00
Aurora, Lone Ranger, 1967, MIB................................$250.00
Aurora, Lost in Space, Cyclops only, 1966, MIB...........$900.00
Aurora, Lost in Space, Cyclops w/Chariot, 1966, MIB.$1,500.00
Aurora, Lunar Probe, 1960s, MIB $175.00
Aurora, Mad Dentist, 1972, MIB $375.00
Aurora, Madame Tussaud's Chamber of Horrors Guillotine, 1964, assembled, EX..$175.00
Aurora, Man From UNCLE, Illya Kuryakin, 1966, MIB.$200.00
Aurora, Man From UNCLE, Napoleon Solo, MIB (sealed), H4..$350.00
Aurora, Mod Squad Station Wagon, 1969, MIB............$125.00
Aurora, Monster Scenes, Dr Deadly's Daughter, 1971, MIB..$65.00
Aurora, Monster Scenes, Gruesome Goodies, 1971, MIB...$75.00
Aurora, Monster Scenes, Pain Parlor, 1971, MIB..........$65.00
Aurora, Monster Scenes, Pendulum, 1971, MIB $140.00

Aurora, Guys and Gals, Caballero, 1959, MIB, $100.00.

Aurora, Monster Scenes, Dr. Deadly, 1971, MIB, $65.00.

Aurora, Monster Scenes, Vampirella, 1971, MIB..........$100.00
Aurora, Monsters of the Movies, Creature From the Black Lagoon, 1975, MIB..$150.00
Aurora, Monsters of the Movies, Dracula, 1975, MIB....$250.00
Aurora, Monsters of the Movies, Ghidrah, 1975, MIB...$275.00
Aurora, Monsters of the Movies, Mr Hyde, 1975, MIB $65.00
Aurora, Monsters of the Movies, Rodan, 1975, MIB......$450.00
Aurora, Mummy, 1963, MIB..$250.00
Aurora, Mummy, 1969, glow-in-the-dark, MIB..............$100.00
Aurora, Mummy, 1974, Canadian Issue, glow-in-the-dark, NRFB, H4...$75.00
Aurora, Mummy's Chariot, 1965, assembled, EX $200.00
Aurora, Munsters Living Room, 1964, assembled, EX....$400.00
Aurora, Pan Am Space Clipper: 2001, 1968, MIB $100.00
Aurora, Phantom of the Opera, 1963, MIB $275.00
Aurora, Phantom of the Opera, 1969, glow-in-the-dark, MIB...$125.00
Aurora, Phantom of the Opera, 1972, glow-in-the-dark, MIB...$75.00
Aurora, Prehistoric Scenes, Allosaurus, 1971, MIB........$125.00
Aurora, Prehistoric Scenes, Cave, 1971, MIB $100.00
Aurora, Prehistoric Scenes, Cave Bear, 1971, assembled, EX...$25.00
Aurora, Prehistoric Scenes, Cro-Magnon Man, 1971, MIB $100.00
Aurora, Prehistoric Scenes, Cro-Magnon Woman, assembled, (VG+ box), H4..$40.00
Aurora, Prehistoric Scenes, Cro-Magnon Woman, 1971, MIB $100.00
Aurora, Prehistoric Scenes, Flying Reptile, 1971, MIB $65.00
Aurora, Prehistoric Scenes, Giant Bird, EX (EX box), H4 .$50.00
Aurora, Prehistoric Scenes, Jungle Swamp, 1971, MIB..$100.00
Aurora, Prehistoric Scenes, Neanderthal Man, 1971, MIB...$75.00

Aurora, Prehistoric Scenes, Sabertooth Tiger, partially assembled, NMIB, H4...$60.00
Aurora, Prehistoric Scenes, Sail Back Reptile, 1975, MIB..$55.00
Aurora, Prehistoric Scenes, Spiked Dinosaur, 1971, MIB...$65.00
Aurora, Prehistoric Scenes, Three Horned Dinosaur, 1971, MIB...$65.00
Aurora, Prehistoric Scenes, Tyrannosaurus Rex, 1975, MIB ..$225.00
Aurora, Prehistoric Scenes, Woolly Mammoth, 1971, MIB ...$100.00
Aurora, Rat Patrol, Battle Diorama, 1967, MIB $120.00
Aurora, Robin the Boy Wonder, 1966, MIB (sealed).....$100.00
Aurora, Sir Galahad of Camelot, 1968, MIB $75.00
Aurora, Sir Lancelot of Camelot, 1968, MIB.................$75.00
Aurora, Spider-Man, 1966, MIB $250.00
Aurora, Spider-Man, 1974, MIB (sealed) $160.00
Aurora, Superboy, 1963, MIB $225.00
Aurora, Superman, 1963, MIB $225.00
Aurora, Tarzan, 1967, MIB $165.00
Aurora, Tonto, 1967, MIB $200.00
Aurora, US Army Infantryman, 1959, MIB.....................$75.00
Aurora, Viking Ship, 1962, MIB $60.00
Aurora, Voyage to the Bottom of the Sea, Seaview, 1966, MIB $300.00
Aurora, Wacky Back-Whacker, 1965, MIB.....................$185.00
Aurora, White-Tail Deer, 1962, orig issue, MIB..............$75.00
Aurora, Whoozis?, Alfalfa, 1968, MIB $65.00
Aurora, Whoozis?, Kitty, 1968, MIB $65.00
Aurora, Whoozis?, Snuffy, 1968, MIB $65.00

Aurora, Witch, 1965, built-up, $125.00 – 150.00 (MIB $250.00). (Photo courtesy Rick Polizzi)

Aurora, Witch, 1969, glow-in-the-dark, MIB................$125.00
Aurora, Witch, 1972, glow-in-the-dark, MIB................$100.00
Aurora, Wolfman, 1962, MIB $300.00
Aurora, Wolfman, 1969, MIB $135.00
Aurora, Wolfman, 1972, MIB $120.00
Aurora, Wolfman, 1974, Canadian issue, glow-in-the-dark, NRFB, H4...$85.00

Aurora, Wolfman's Wagon, 1965, MIB $400.00

Aurora, Wonder Woman, 1965, EX (EX box), A $200.00

Aurora, X-15 Rocket-Powered Plane, 1962, MIB (sealed)..$150.00

Aurora, Zorro, 1965, assembled, EX $125.00

Aurora, Zorro, 1965, MIB $400.00

Aurora, 12 O'Clock High, British Spitfire, 1965, MIB...$125.00

Aurora, 12 O'Clock High, B17 Bomber Formation, 1965, MIB $250.00

Aurora, 12 O'Clock High, Focke-Wulf 190, 1965, MIB...$175.00

Aurora, 12 O'Clock High, P51 Mustang, 1965, MIB $150.00

Aurora, 2001: A Space Odyssey, Pan Am Space Clipper, 1968, orig issue, MIB $220.00

Aurora, 2001: A Space Odyssey, Space Shuttle Orion, 1975, MIB (sealed) $170.00

Bachmann, Animals of the World, Alaskan Timber Wolf, 1960s, MIB $40.00

Bachmann, Animals of the World, Cow & Calf, 1959, MIB...$60.00

Bachmann, Animals of the World, Kodiak Bear, 1960s, MIB $40.00

Bachmann, Animals of the World, White-Tail Deer, 1960s, assembled, EX $20.00

Bachmann, Birds of the World, Barn Swallow, 1950s, MIB..$30.00

Bachmann, Birds of the World, Blue Bird, 1960s, MIB (sealed) $35.00

Bachmann, Birds of the World, Bohemian Waxwing, 1950s, MIB $35.00

Bachmann, Birds of the World, Meadowlark, 1950s, MIB..$30.00

Bachmann, Birds of the World, Rose-Breasted Grosbeak, 1950s, MIB...$40.00

Bachmann, Birds of the World, Screech Owl, 1950s, MIB..$45.00

Bachmann, Dogs of the World, Basset Hound, 1960s, MIB.$30.00

Bachmann, Dogs of the World, Dalmatian, 1960s, MIB ..$30.00

Bachmann, Dogs of the World, German Shepard, 1960s, MIB (sealed)...$35.00

Bachmann, Dogs of the World, Poodle, 1960s, MIB $30.00

Bachmann, Fisher Boy, 1962, MIB......................$80.00

Bachmann, Storytown USA, any of 6 Mother Goose tales, 1950s, MIB, ea $50.00

Bandai, Captain Harlock, Queen Esmerelda's Ship, 1980s, MIB $30.00

Bandai, Godzilla, 1984, MIB $50.00

Bandai, Gundam, Mobile Suit Tallgeese, 1995, MIB $30.00

Bandai, Kinggidrah, 1984, MIB.........................$50.00

Bandai, Kinggidrah, 1990, MIB $40.00

Bandai, Prehistoric Animal Series, Stegosaurus, 1973, MIB.$65.00

Bandai, Silly Dracula, 1985, MIB $20.00

Bandai, Star-Blazers, Desslock's Command Cruiser, 1989, MIB $25.00

Bandai, Thunderbird, 1984, MIB $40.00

Bandai, UFO, SHADO Intercepter, MIB $80.00

Best Plastics, Winchester 94, 1950, MIB................$60.00

Billiken, Batman (Type A or Type B), vinyl, MIB, ea ...$200.00

Billiken, Dracula, 1989, vinyl, MIB $275.00

Billiken, Frankenstein, 1988, vinyl, NRFB, H4.............$100.00

Billiken, Gorilla II (King Kong vs Godzilla), 1987, vinyl, NM (NM box) $100.00

Billiken, Laser Blast Alien, 1988, vinyl, MIB $100.00

Billiken, Mummy, vinyl, MIB $220.00

Billiken, Preditor, 1991, vinyl, MIB...................$110.00

Billiken, Saucer Man, MIB, H4 ....$70.00

Billiken, She-Creature, 1989, vinyl, NM (EX+ box) $220.00

Billiken, Ultra Zone, Peguila, 1989, vinyl, MIB..............$90.00

Dark Horse, Frankenstein, 1991, MIB $130.00

Dark Horse, Mummy, 1995, MIB $150.00

Dark Horse, Predator II, Predator, 1994, MIB $175.00

Dimensional Designs, Mad Doctor, 1992, NM (EX (box) ..$75.00

Dimensional Designs, Outer Limits, Man Never Born (Andro), resin, MIB $100.00

Eldon, Moon Survey, 1966, MIB $50.00

Eldon, Pink Panther, 1970s, MIB $75.00

Entex, 1st Dune Buggy, M (EX box) $35.00

Fujimi Mokei, Mad Police, Destroyer Car #1 or Falcon Car #4, 1980s, MIB, ea $50.00

Fundimensions, Space: 1999, Alien, 1976, MIB $40.00

Fundimensions/MPC, Haunted Glo-Head, Ape Man, 1975, M (G box) $35.00

FX, Tales From the Darkside, Gargoyle, resin, 17", MIB .$120.00

Garage Resin Kit, Star Trek: The Next Generation, Duralyne Hypo Spray, MIB $25.00

Geometric Designs, Alien, Alien Warrior, 1996, resin, MIB...$80.00

Geometric Designs, I Was a Teenage Werewolf, 1985, NM (EX+ box) $300.00

Geometric Designs, I Was a Teenage Werewolf, 1990, vinyl or resin, MIB $150.00

Geometric Designs, Star Trek: The Next Generation, Captain Picard or Lieutenant Worf, 1992, vinyl or resin, MIB, ea $35.00

Gerba, US Navy Vanguard Missile, 1950s, MIB.............$200.00

Hawk, Bobcat Roadster, 1962, MIB $30.00

Hawk, Cherokee Sports Roadster, 1962, MIB..............$30.00

Hawk, Cobra II, 1950s, MIB............................$80.00

Hawk, Convair Manned Satellite, 1960, MIB $100.00

Hawk, Explorer 18 Satellite, 1968, MIB $70.00

Hawk, Fox Go-Boy Cart, 1960, MIB.....................$40.00

Hawk, Frantics, Steel Pluckers Havin' a Bash or Totally Fab, 1964, MIB, ea $85.00

Hawk, Jupitor C/Explorer, 1966, MIB...................$50.00

Hawk, Project Vanguard Satellite, 1958, MIB.................$65.00

Hawk, Rocket Power Guided Missiles, 1960s, MIB........$135.00

Hawk, Silly Surfers, Beach Bunny Catchin' Rays or Hodad Makin' the Scene w/Six-Pack, 1964, MIB, ea...........$75.00

Hawk, Weird-Ohs, Daddy the Way Out Suburbanite, 1963, MIB, $100.00. (Photo courtesy John and Sheri Pavone)

Hawk, Silly Surfers, Woodie on a Surfari, 1964, MIB $100.00

Hawk, Weird-Ohs, Daddy the Way Out Suburbanite or Digger the Way Out Dragster, 1963, MIB $100.00

Hawk, Weird-Ohs, Endsville Eddie the Short Stop Stupe, 1963, MIB $75.00

Hawk, Weird-Ohs, Freddy Flameout the Way Out Jockey, 1963, MIB $75.00

Hawk, Weird-Ohs, Huey's Hut Rod, 1969, MIB.............$50.00

Hawk, Weird-Ohs, Leaky Boat Louie the Vulgar Boatman, 1963, MIB $125.00

Hawk, Weird-Ohs, Sling Rave Curvette, MIB $40.00

Hawk, Wild Woodie (Surfer Car), 1965, MIB..................$30.00

Horizon, Batman, 1989, MIB..$80.00

Horizon, Bride of Frankenstein, 1988, assembled $25.00

Horizon, DC Comics, Joker, 1993, partially assembled.....$30.00

Horizon, Dinosaur Series, Apatosaurus, 1993, MIB..........$25.00

Horizon, Dracula, 1988, MIB.......................................$50.00

Horizon, Indiana Jones, Dr Jones, 1993, MIB $20.00

Horizon, Indiana Jones, Indiana, 1993, MIB...................$60.00

Horizon, Jurassic Park, Spitter Dilophosaur, 1993, MIB...$90.00

Horizon, Marvel Universe, Cable, 1994, MIB $40.00

Horizon, Marvel Universe, Cyclops, 1993, MIB $45.00

Horizon, Marvel Universe, Dr Doom, 1991, MIB.............$40.00

Horizon, Marvel Universe, Spider-Man, 1988, MIB........$40.00

Horizon, Marvel Universe, Thor, 1993, MIB...................$50.00

Horizon, Mole People, Mole Man #2, 1988, MIB.............$70.00

Horizon, Mummy, 1993, MIB..$60.00

Horizon, Robocop, ED-209, 1989, MIB $70.00

Horizon, Robocop, Robocop #10, 1989, MIB $60.00

Horizon, Robocop, Robocop #30, 1992, MIB $70.00

Horizon, Terminator 2, T-1000 Terminator #22, 1991, MIB..$20.00

Ideal, Jaguar XK-120 Fix-It Car, NM (NM box) $115.00

Ideal, XP-600 Fix It Car of Tomorrow, 1953-55, partially assembled, M (NM box) $285.00

Imai, Armored Knights, Archduke II, 1984, MIB.............$10.00

Imai, Captain Blue, 1982, MIB.....................................$10.00

Imai, Orguss, Cable, 1994, MIB....................................$40.00

Imai, Orguss, Dr Doom, 1991, MIB...............................$40.00

Imai, Orguss, Spider-Man, 1994, new pose, MIB.............$30.00

Imai, Orguss, Thor, 1993, MIB.....................................$50.00

ITC, Brontosaurus Skeleton, 1962, MIB.......................$100.00

ITC, Bumble Bee, 1950s, MIB......................................$65.00

ITC, Dog Champions, French Poodle, 1959, MIB............$30.00

ITC, Dog Champions, German Shepard, 1959, MIB $30.00

ITC, Explorer Satellite I, 1959, MIB............................$250.00

ITC, Marvel Metal Cocker Spaniel, Elephant, Rhinoceros, or Tiger, MIB, ea..$35.00

ITC, Marvel Metal English Bulldog or Gorilla, 1960, assembled, EX, ea $15.00

ITC, Midget Models, Covered Wagon & Stagecoach, 1962, 3½", MIB $30.00

ITC, Precious Miniatures, Hansom Cab & Coronation Coach, 1960, 3½", MIB $30.00

ITC, Stegosaurus Skeleton, 1950s, MIB.......................$100.00

ITC, Tyrannosaurus Rex Skeleton, 1950s, MIB $100.00

ITC, US Air Drop Paratrooper, 1950s, MIB $60.00

ITC, US Navy Blimp, 1958, MIB..................................$35.00

ITC, Wire Haired Terrier, 1959, MIB...........................$30.00

Kaiyodo, Angurus, 1990s, NM (EX+ box), A $50.00

Kaiyodo, Nelonga, 1990s, M (EX box), A.......................$50.00

KGB, Batman (1960s TV), Batgirl on Cycle, MIB $50.00

Life-Like, Aerial Missiles on Helicopter, 1970s, MIB.......$50.00

Life-Like, Ankylosaurus, 1968, MIB.............................$30.00

Life-Like, Cro-Magnon Man, 1973, MIB $40.00

Life-Like, Neanderthal Man, 1973, MIB.......................$40.00

Life-Like, Protoceratops, 1973, MIB $30.00

Life-Like, World of Stegosaurus, 1970s, MIB.................$30.00

Lindberg, Bad Wheels (Lindy Loonies), Sick Cycle (Big Wheeler), 1971, MIB $160.00

Lindberg, Baywatch, Beach Patrol Pickup, 1995, MIB (sealed) $20.00

Lindberg, Brain Buster, 1965, assembled, EX................$125.00

Lindberg, Brontosaurus, 1979, assembled, EX $12.00

Lindberg, Coo Coo Clock, 1965, MIB $40.00

Lindberg, Dimetrodon, 1979, MIB...............................$20.00

Lindberg, Flying Saucer, 1952, MIB.............................$200.00

Lindberg, Goofy Clock, 1965, assembled, EX $65.00

Lindberg, Green Ghoul, 1965, MIB $50.00

Lindberg, Krimson Monster, 1974, MIB........................$50.00

Lindberg, Lindy Loonys, Big Wheeler or Road Hog, 1965, MIB, ea...$75.00

Lindberg, Lindy Loonys, Scuttle Bucket, 1965, MIB......$100.00

Lindberg, Mad Maestro, 1965, MIB $225.00

Lindberg, Mad Mangler, MIB, $75.00.
(Photo courtesy Rick Polizzi)

Lindberg, Monsters, Krimson Terror, 1965, 5", MIB $130.00
Lindberg, SST Continental, 1958, MIB.....................$175.00
Lindberg, Star Probe, Space Base, 1976, MIB $50.00
Lindberg, US Moon Ship, 1958, MIB $200.00
Lindberg, US Space Station, 1958, MIB.......................$200.00
Lindberg, Wells Fargo Overland Stagecoach, 1960s, MIB..$50.00
Lunar Models, Giant Behemoth, MIB $160.00
Lunar Models, Lost in Space, Chariot, MIB $120.00
Lunar Models, Penny Robinson & Monster #FG47, MIB $130.00
Lunar Models, Pumpkinhead (movie), 1989, MIB $145.00
Max Factory, Guyver Bio Fighter Collection, Gastar, 1990s, MIB...$25.00
Max Factory, Guyver Bio Fighter Collection, Ramoth, 1990s, MIB...$25.00
Monogram, Airacobra P-39, 1973, MIB (sealed)............$25.00
Monogram, Backdraft (movie), Fire Chief Car, 1991, MIB $20.00
Monogram, Bad Medicine, 1970s, assembled, EX............$25.00

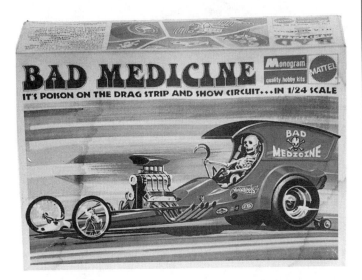

Monogram, Bad Medicine, 1970s, MIB, $60.00.

Monogram, Baja Bandito or Baja Beast, 1969-70, MIB, ea..$55.00
Monogram, Bathtub Buggy, 1960s, MIB $90.00
Monogram, Battlestar Galactica, Cylon Raider, 1979, MIB (sealed) $90.00
Monogram, Beach Boys Lil' Deuce Coupe, 1989, MIB.....$15.00
Monogram, Blue Thunder Helicopter, 1984, MIB............$30.00
Monogram, Boss A Bone, 1969, assembled, EX $25.00
Monogram, Buck Rogers, Starfighter, 1979, MIB.............$70.00
Monogram, Dracula, 1983, MIB.....................................$70.00
Monogram, Flip Out! the Beachcomber, 1965, assembled, EX.$50.00
Monogram, Frankenstein, 1983, MIB $70.00
Monogram, Ghost of the Red Baron, 1969, MIB...........$200.00
Monogram, Giraffes, 1961, MIB.....................................$50.00
Monogram, Go Bots, Cy-Kill, 1984, MIB $40.00
Monogram, Godzilla, 1978, glow-in-the-dark, NMIB.......$85.00
Monogram, Green Hornet Dragster, 1960s, MIB.............$55.00
Monogram, Heritage Edition, Apollo-Saturn V Rocket, 1983, MIB..$25.00

Monogram, Heritage Edition, Apollo Spacecraft, 1984, MIB...$30.00
Monogram, Missile Arsenal, 1959, MIB $200.00
Monogram, Mummy, 1983, MIB....................................$25.00
Monogram, Paddy Wagon, 1968, assembled, EX $25.00
Monogram, Rambo, Combat Chopper, 1985, MIB (sealed)..$40.00
Monogram, Rascal Missile, 1958, MIB..........................$400.00
Monogram, S'cool Bus, 1970, assembled, EX $40.00
Monogram, Sand Crab, 1969, MIB $50.00
Monogram, Shogun Warriors of Dragon, Gaiking, Mazinga, or Raider, 1977, MIB, ea..$35.00

Monogram, Snoopy and His Bugatti Race Car, 1971, MIB, $30.00. (Photo courtesy Rick Polizzi)

Monogram, Snoopy & His Sopwith Camel, 1970, MIB ...$40.00
Monogram, Snoopy on the Highwire, 1972, MIB.............$30.00
Monogram, Space Buggy, 1969, MIB............................$100.00
Monogram, Space Taxi, 1959, MIB $200.00

Monogram, Speed Shift!, 1965, MIB, $300.00.
(Photo courtesy June Moon)

Monogram, Superman, 1974, assembled, EX $25.00
Monogram, Tijuana Taxi, 1960s, MIB............................$85.00
Monogram, TV Orbiter, 1959, MIB $150.00
Monogram, US Missile Arsenal, 1958, MIB...................$210.00
Monogram, Voyage to the Bottom of the Sea Flying Sub, 1968, MIB..$175.00
Monogram, Wolfman, 1983, MIB (sealed) $60.00

Monogram, Young Astronauts, Space Shuttle w/Booster, 1988,
   MIB (sealed) $110.00
Monstrology Models, Mad Monster, 1992, NMIB............$75.00
MPC, Alien, 1979, MIB $70.00

MPC, Barnabas, 1969, MIB, $250.00.
(Photo courtesy Rick Polizzi)

MPC, Barnabas Vampire Van, 1975, MIB......................$200.00
MPC, Batman, 1984, MIB (sealed) $50.00
MPC, Bearcat, 1971, MIB $65.00
MPC, Beatles Yellow Submarine, 1968, MIB (sealed) ...$300.00
MPC, Bed Buggy, 1960s, MIB.......................................$55.00
MPC, Beverly Hillbillies Television Truck, 1968, MIB .$150.00
MPC, Black Hole, Cygnus Spaceship, 1979, MIB (sealed).$130.00
MPC, Black Hole, Maximilian, 1979, assembled, EX.......$20.00
MPC, Black Hole, VINCent, 1979, assembled, EX $20.00
MPC, Boss Bike, 1970s, MIB...$50.00
MPC, Cannonball Run, Emergency Van or Lamborghini Coun-
   tach, 1981, MIB (sealed), ea.....................................$35.00
MPC, CB Freak, 1975, MIB $50.00
MPC, Digger Trike, 1970s, MIB.....................................$45.00
MPC, Disney's Haunted Mansion, Grave Robber's Reward,
   1974, MIB $85.00
MPC, Disney's Haunted Mansion, Play It Again Sam, 1974,
   MIB..$100.00
MPC, Disney's Pirates of the Caribbean, Dead Man's Raft, 1972,
   MIB..$210.00
MPC, Dukes of Hazzard, Daisy's Jeep, 1980, MIB............$50.00

MPC, Dukes of Hazzard, General Lee, 1981, MIB
   (sealed) $120.00
MPC, Fonz & His Bike, 1976, MIB..................................$35.00
MPC, Fonz Dream Rod, 1976, MIB..................................$35.00
MPC, Glo Heads, Ape Man, 1975, MIB.............................$60.00
MPC, Hardcastle's GMC Truck, 1984, MIB (sealed).......$50.00
MPC, Hogan's Heroes Jeep, 1968, MIB $80.00
MPC, Incredible Hulk, 1979, MIB..................................$35.00
MPC, Ironside's Van, 1970, MIB $80.00
MPC, Ma Barker's Getaway Special, 1970s, MIB $40.00
MPC, Mannix Roadster, 1968, MIB $150.00
MPC, Mummy Machine, 1970s, MIB $50.00
MPC, Night Crawler, 1975, assembled, EX $50.00
MPC, Paddy Wagon, 1970s, MIB....................................$60.00

MPC, Pirates of the Caribbean, Condemned to Chains Forever, 1972, MIB, $60.00. (Photo courtesy Rick Polizzi)

MPC, Pirates of the Caribbean, Dead Men Tell No Tales or Fate
   of the Mutineers, 1972, MIB, ea...............................$55.00
MPC, Pirates of the Caribbean, Freed in the Nick of Time,
   1973, MIB..$100.00
MPC, Pirates of the Caribbean, Hoist High the Jolly Roger,
   1972, MIB..$50.00
MPC, Raider's Coach, 1969, MIB.................................$150.00
MPC, Road Runner & the the Beep-Beep T, 1972, MIB.$65.00
MPC, Russian Vostok RD-107, 1975, MIB....................$90.00
MPC, Six Million Dollar, Man Evil Rider or Jaws of Doom,
   1975, MIB, ea..$35.00
MPC, Six Million Dollar Man, 1975, MIB $50.00
MPC, Space: 1999, Eagle I Transporter, 1975, MIB.......$170.00
MPC, Spider-Man, 1978, MIB (sealed) $60.00
MPC, Star Wars, C-3PO, 1977, MIB (sealed) $35.00
MPC, Star Wars, Darth Vader TIE Fighter, 1978, MIB ...$35.00
MPC, Star Wars, Darth Vader Van, 1979, assembled, EX..$20.00
MPC, Star Wars, Imperial Star Destroyer, 1978, assembled,
   EX $30.00
MPC, Star Wars, R2-D2, 1978, MIB...............................$50.00
MPC, Star Wars, X-Wing Fighter, 1978, MIB................$40.00

MPC, Star Wars, Y-Wing Fighter, 1984, MIB $60.00
MPC, Stoker McGurk & His Surf Rod, assembled, EX $50.00
MPC, Strange Changing Mummy, 1974, MIB (sealed)..$100.00
MPC, Strange Changing Time Machine, 1974, MIB.......$75.00
MPC, Strange Changing Vampire, 1974, MIB $55.00
MPC, Superman, 1984, MIB (sealed) $60.00
MPC, Sweat Hogs Dream Machine, 1976, assembled, EX..$30.00
MPC, TJ Hooker, Police Car, 1982, MIB $30.00
MPC, Wacky Races Mean Machine, 1969, MIB...........$100.00
MPC, Wacky Races Pussycat, 1969, MIB $125.00
MPC, Wile E Coyote & the Wile E Willys, 1972, MIB ..$65.00
Multiple, Ripley's Believe It or Not, Iron Maiden, 1966, assem-
    bled, EX...$75.00
Multiple, Ripley's Believe It or Not, Torture Chair or Torture
    Wheel, 1966, MIB, ea $150.00
Nitto, Crusher Joe, Benz 600 SAE Car or BMW-A795 Air Car,
    MIB, ea..$15.00
Palmer, African Tribal Mask, 1950s, MIB....................$70.00
Palmer, American Mastodon Skeleton, 1950s, MIB.........$60.00
Palmer, Brontosaurus Skeleton, 1950s, MIB $60.00
Palmer, Spirit of '76 Diorama, 1950s, MIB $100.00
Palmer, US Navy Vanguard Missile, 1958, MIB.............$230.00
Precision, American Bald Eagle, 1957, assembled, EX $25.00

Precision, Cap'n Kidd Pirate, 1959, MIB, $75.00.
(Photo courtesy Rick Polizzi)

Precision, Royal Bengal Tiger Head, 1957, MIB...............$40.00
Precision, US Navy Frogman, 1959, MIB $40.00
Pyro, Curler, 1970, assembled, EX................................$25.00
Pyro, Der-Baron, 1970, MIB...$75.00
Pyro, Ghost Rider, 1970, MIB $50.00

Pyro, Indian Chief, 1960s, MIB.....................................$60.00
Pyro, Mark Trail's Bald Eagle or Mallard Duck, 1958, MIB,
    ea..$35.00
Pyro, Peacemaker 45, 1960, MIB (sealed).....................$100.00
Pyro, Prehistoric Monsters Dimetrodon, Protoceratops, or
    Stegosaurus, 1968, MIB, ea....................................$30.00
Pyro, Prehistoric Monsters Gift Set, 1950s, MIB...........$125.00
Pyro, Rawhide Cowpuncher, 1958, MIB.........................$60.00
Pyro, Restless Gun Deputy Sheriff, 1958, MIB $60.00
Pyro, Texas Cowboy, 1960s, MIB...................................$60.00
Pyro, Western Figures, Deputy Sheriff, 1961, MIB $35.00
Pyro, Western Figures, Indian Chief, assembled, 1961, EX..$25.00
Pyro, Western Figures, Indian Warrior, 1961, MIB $55.00
Pyro, Wyatt Earp, 1958, MIB $100.00
Remco, Flintstone's Motorized Paddy Wagon, 1961, MIB $200.00
Remco, Flintstone's Motorized Yacht, 1961, assembled, EX .$100.00
Renwal, Vanguard w/Satellite, 1950s, MIB $200.00
Renwal, Visible Pigeon, 1950s, MIB $75.00
Revell, '31 Ford Woody, 1964, MIB...............................$85.00
Revell, Amazing Moon Mixer, 1970, MIB......................$35.00
Revell, Apollo Astronaut on Moon, 1970, MIB.............$100.00
Revell, Apollo Lunar Spacecraft, 1969, MIB (sealed) $175.00
Revell, Astronaut in Space, 1968, MIB $100.00
Revell, Baja Humbug, 1971, MIB..................................$85.00
Revell, Beatles, George Harrison or Paul McCartney, 1964,
    MIB, ea $200.00
Revell, Beatles, John Lennon, 1964, MIB.......................$225.00

Revell, Beatles, Paul McCartney, 1964, MIB, $200.00.
(Photo courtesy Rick Polizzi)

Revell, Beatles, Ringo Starr, 1964, MIB $150.00
Revell, Bonanza, Ben, Hoss & Little Joe, 1966, MIB $160.00
Revell, Charlie's Angels Van, 1977, assembled, EX $15.00

Revell, CHiPs, Ponch's Firebird, 1981, MIB (sealed) $30.00

Revell, Code Red, Emergency Van, 1981, MIB (sealed) ..$20.00

Revell, Corporal Missile, 1958, MIB.................................$100.00

Revell, Disney's Love Bug Rides Again, 1974, MIB $100.00

Revell, Disney's Robin Hood Set #1, 1974, MIB (sealed)..$100.00

Revell, Dr Seuss Zoo, Busby the Tasselated Afgan Yak, 1959, MIB...$95.00

Revell, Dr Seuss Zoo, Gowdy the Dowdy Grackle, 1958, MIB...$85.00

Revell, Dr Seuss Zoo, Grickily, Busby & Roscoe, 1960, MIB...$325.00

Revell, Dr Seuss Zoo, Grickily the Gractus, 1959, MIB ...$85.00

Revell, Dr Seuss Zoo, Horton the Elephant, 1960, rare, MIB...$400.00

Revell, Dr Seuss Zoo, Norval the Bashful Blinket, 1952, MIB...$85.00

Revell, Dr Seuss Zoo, Roscoe the Many Footed Lion, 1959, MIB...$85.00

Revell, Dr Seuss Zoo, Tingo the Noodle Stroodle, 1958, MIB...$85.00

Revell, Dune, Ornithopter, 1985, MIB (sealed) $60.00

Revell, Ed 'Big Daddy' Roth, Angel Fink, 1965, MIB $200.00

Revell, Ed 'Big Daddy' Roth, Brother Ratfink on a Bike, 1964, MIB...$100.00

Revell, Ed 'Big Daddy' Roth, Fink Eliminator, 1990, MIB (sealed)..$60.00

Revell, Ed 'Big Daddy' Roth, Mother's Worry, 1963, MIB .$75.00

Revell, Ed 'Big Daddy' Roth, Mr Gasser, 1963, MIB $150.00

Revell, Ed 'Big Daddy' Roth, Rat Fink, 1990, MIB (sealed) .$55.00

Revell, Ed 'Big Daddy' Roth, Superfink, 1964, MIB.......$300.00

Revell, Ed 'Big Daddy' Roth, Surfink, Revell, 1965, MIB .$150.00

Revell, Endangered Black Panther, California Condor, Mountain Gorilla or Rhino, 1974, MIB, ea $35.00

Revell, Flash Gordon & the Martian, 1965, MIB...........$170.00

Revell, Flipper, 1965, assembled, EX................................$65.00

Revell, Freaky Riders, Korporal Amerika or Shift Kicker, 1971, MIB, ea..$65.00

Revell, Friskie the Beagle Puppy, 1958, MIB $55.00

Revell, Gemini Astronaut, 1967, MIB................................$55.00

Revell, Gemini Capsule, 1967, MIB...................................$75.00

Revell, Happy Days '29 Model Pickup, 1982, MIB...........$30.00

Revell, Hardy Boys Van, 1977, MIB (sealed)....................$40.00

Revell, History Makers, Apollo Saturn-5 Rocket, 1982, MIB...$150.00

Revell, History Makers, Terracruzer & Mace Missile, 1982, MIB...$60.00

Revell, Hunt for Red October, F/A-18 Hornet, 1990, MIB (sealed)..$15.00

Revell, James Bond 007, Moonraker Space Shuttle, 1979, MIB...$25.00

Revell, Jupiter Missile w/Truck & Trailer, 1958, MIB ...$175.00

Revell, Li'l Herbie, 1970s, MIB..$40.00

Revell, Los Angeles Dodgers Electra, 1962, MIB...........$240.00

Revell, Love Bug, 1970s, MIB $50.00

Revell, Lucky Pierre & Nieuport, 1972, MIB....................$45.00

Revell, Lunar Spacecraft, 1970, MIB $125.00

Revell, Magnum PI, 308 GTS Ferrari, 1982, MIB (sealed)..$20.00

Revell, McHale's Navy PT-73, 1965, MIB.........................$75.00

Revell, Mercury/Gemini, 1964, MIB..................................$70.00

Revell, Moon Ship, 1957, MIB $225.00

Revell, Peter Pan Pirate Ship, 1960s, MIB.....................$125.00

Revell, Phantom & the Voodoo Witch Doctor, 1965, MIB .$200.00

Revell, Rif Raf & His Spitfire, 1971, MIB...........................$45.00

Revell, Robocop, Axoid, 1984, MIB....................................$50.00

Revell, Robotech, Nebo, 1984, MIB...................................$20.00

Revell, Robotech, Trigon or VF-1S Battloid, 1985, MIB, ea.$30.00

Revell, Saint's Jaguar XJS, 1979, MIB...............................$25.00

Revell, Sand Crawler, 1985, MIB (sealed)..........................$50.00

Revell, Sassy the Kitten, 1958, MIB...................................$50.00

Revell, Space Pursuit, 1969, MIB.....................................$240.00

Revell, Space Shuttle Challenger, 1982, MIB $20.00

Revell, Space Shuttlecraft, 1959, assembled, EX...........$100.00

Revell, Stink Ray, 1971, assembled, EX.............................$15.00

Revell, Terrier Missile, 1958, MIB...................................$200.00

Revell, X-17 Research Missile, 1957, MIB.........................$65.00

Revell, XSL091 Manned Spaceship, 1957, partially assembled..$400.00

Revell, 1932 V8 Hot Rod, 1954, MIB..................................$65.00

Revell, 1941 (movie), P-40 Flying Tiger, 1979, MIB (sealed)..$40.00

Screamin', Air Assault Martian, 1995, MIB $50.00

Screamin', Bettie Page-Jungle Fever, 1994, MIB $85.00

Screamin', Halloween, Michael Myers, 1996, assembled..$30.00

Screamin', Hellraiser (movie), Chatter Cenobite, 1991, MIB...$50.00

Screamin', Hellraiser (movie), Pinhead Cenobite, 1989, MIB...$80.00

Screamin', Mars Attacks, No Place To Hide, assembled ..$50.00

Screamin', Mary Shelley's Frankenstein, 1994, assembled..$30.00

Screamin', Rocketeer, 1991, MIB.....................................$140.00

Screamin', Star Wars, Boba Fett, 1994, MIB $50.00

Screamin', Suburban Commando, General Suitor Mutant, 1991, MIB...$55.00

Strombecker, Bell XIB Supersonic Rocket, 1950s, MIB.$150.00

Strombecker, Convair Manned Lunar Reconnaissance Vehicle, 1950s, MIB...$250.00

Strombecker, Interplanetary Vehicle, 1959, MIB..........$175.00

Strombecker, Walt Disney's Rocket to the Moon, 1956, MIB...$225.00

Strombecker, Walt Disney's Satellite Launcher, 1958, MIB...$175.00

Strombecker, Walt Disney's Spaceship, 1958, MIB........$300.00

Superior, Beating Heart, 1959, MIB...................................$35.00

Superior, Seeing Eye, 1959, MIB.......................................$35.00

Takara, Crusher Joe, Hunter Diskhound, MIB $20.00

Testors, Davey the Cyclist, 1993, MIB (sealed)...............$15.00

Testors, Grodies!, Steel Pluckers, 1983, MIB...................$50.00

Testors, Top Gun, A-4 Aggressor, 1987, MIB $10.00

Testors, Weird-Ohs, Daddy the Suburbanite, 1993, MIB (sealed)..$20.00

Tomy, Lensman, Boskine Fighter Goblin, 1984, MIB $40.00

Tomy, Lensman, Grappler & Shuttle Truck, 1984, MIB..$40.00

Toy Biz, Ghost Rider, 1996, MIB..$30.00

Toy Biz, Incredible Hulk, 1996, MIB (sealed) $25.00

Toy Biz, Silly Surfer, 1996, MIB (sealed) $30.00

Toy Biz, Storm, 1996, MIB (sealed) $30.00

Toy Biz, Thing, 1996, MIB.................................$20.00
Toy Biz, Wolverine, 1996, MIB (sealed)........................$30.00
Wave, Gargantuas Sandra vs Gaira, NMIB $110.00
Whiting, Space: 1999, Mammoth Model, 1976, MIB $50.00

Movie Posters and Lobby Cards

This field is a natural extension of the interest in character collectibles, and one where there is a great deal of activity. There are tradepapers that deal exclusively with movie memorabilia, and some of the larger auction galleries hold cataloged sales on a regular basis. The hottest genre right now is the monster movies, but westerns and Disney films are close behind.

Advisors: John and Sheri Pavone (P3).

A Man Called Flintstone, insert, 1966, 36x14", rolled, NM, P3 ....$50.00
Abbott & Costello Meet Dr. Jeckyl & Mr Hyde, 1953, 27x22", VG+, A...$300.00
Addams Family, 1991, 41x27, rolled, NM, P3 ....$15.00

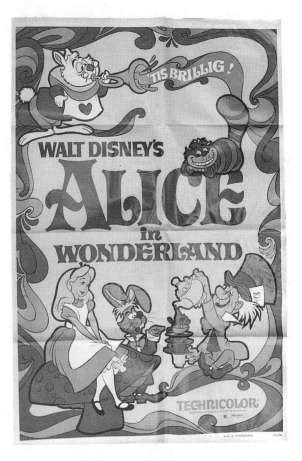

Alice in Wonderland, Walt Disney, 1970s, NM, $45.00.
(Photo courtesy Joel Cohen)

Babes in Toyland, 1961, 41x27", rolled, EX, P3 ....$35.00
Bambi, lobby card, 1948 re-release, shows 2 skunks conversing, 11x14", EX, A...$50.00

Batman, Spanish, 1979, 40x22", EX, J5 ....$65.00
Batman, 1980s, advertises Batman movie on video, 34x22", M, J5 ....$45.00
Beast From Haunted Cave, lobby card, 1959, NM, P3 .....$15.00
Beatles Yellow Submarine, lobby card, rare British version, EX $300.00
Beverly Hillbillies, 1993, 41x27", rolled, NM, P3.............$12.00
Blackbeard's Ghost, 1968, 41x27", EX, M17....................$35.00
Chitty-Chitty Bang-Bang, 1968, 41x27", EX, P3..............$35.00
Cinderella, 1965 re-release, 60x40", rolled, EX $100.00
Cyclone Ranger, lobby card, 1930s, shows Bill Cody in brawl, EX, ...$35.00
Dick Tracy Vs Phantom Empire, 1952, 1-sheet, NM, D11 .$100.00
Dick Tracy's Dilemma, lobby card, 1947, 14x11", EX, from $75 to $100.00
Fantasia, 1963 re-release, 60x40", rolled, EX $65.00
Flipper, 1963, 41x27", EX, P3.................................$30.00
Frankenstein — Asylum of Horrors, 1950s, 27x17", EX, J5 .$300.00
G-Men Never Forget, Chapter 1 — Death Rides the Torrent, lobby card, 11x14", EX $65.00
G-Men Vs Phantom, lobby card, 11x14", NM, A.............$75.00
G-Men Vs The Black Dragon, Chapter 5 — Chestial Murder, lobby card, 1941, scarce, NM, A $50.00
Green Hornet, 1977, 41x27", NM, J5 ....$100.00
Halloween II, 1981, 41x27", EX, P3 ....$45.00
Hi-Yo Silver The Lone Ranger, 1956, 22x28", NM, from $200 to $250.00
Hopalong Cassidy in Colt Comrades, lobby card, 1950s, 11x14", EX, A $50.00

House of Dracula, lobby cards, Universal, 1948, set of eight (two pictured), M, from $1,200.00 to $1,600.00.

I Was a Teenage Werewolf, 1957, 14x36", EX, A $250.00

King Kong, 1976, 41x27", NM, P3.................................$40.00

King Kong Escapes, 1968, 41x27", NM, P3 ....$110.00

Lion King, 41x27", rolled, M, P3...................................$45.00

Little Rascals in Two Too Young, lobby card, ca 1940, 14x11", EX, P6 ....$65.00

Lone Ranger, Episode II — The Silver Bullet, 1938, 1-sheet, NM, from $650 to $1,200.00

Lone Ranger & the Lost City of Gold, lobby card, 1958, NM, from $150 to $175.00

Lone Ranger & the Lost City of Gold, 1958, 1-sheet, NM, from $450 to $650.00

Lone Ranger & Tonto Too!, lobby card, 1956, NM, from $150 to..$175.00

Lone Ranger Rides Again, lobby card, 1939, NM, from $250 to..$300.00

McHale's Navy, 1964, 41x27", EX, P3 ....$55.00

Monster & the Ape, 1956 reissue, 41x27", EX, J5..........$185.00

Monster of the Campus, 1958, Test Tube Terror...Beast Amok on the College Campus!, 27x22", EX, A $100.00

New Adventures of Batman, Columbia Pictures, 1949, 3-sheet, 81x41", NM, from $2,000 to...............................$3,000.00

Night of Dark Shadows, 1971, NM, A...........................$175.00

Phantom of the Opera, Belgian, 1960s, 22x14", EX, J5 ...$65.00

Pinocchio, lobby card, 1954 re-release, 11x14", EX, A.....$85.00

Pocahontas, 41x27", NM, P3.......................................$45.00

Return of Captain America, The Scarab Strikes, lobby card, 1944, 11x14", NM, T2...$50.00

Return of Captain Marvel, 1966, 39x26", EX, T2 ....$100.00

Revenge of Frankenstein, Belgian, 1960s, 20x14", EX, J5...$65.00

Roy Rogers Far Frontier, lobby card, Mexican, 1950s, 12x16", EX, J5 ....$35.00

Sabrina, 1962 reissue, 40x30", rolled, from $75 to..........$100.00

Smoking Guns, lobby card, 1934, features Ken Maynard, VG, A3 ....$50.00

Snow White & the Three Stooges, insert, 1961, 36x14", EX, P3 ....$55.00

Song of Nevada, lobby card, 1944, features Roy Rogers & Dale Evans w/lineup of cowgirls, EX, A3....................$75.00

Song of the South, 1956 re-release, 22x14", EX, A $85.00

Spider-Man, Dragon's Challenge, lobby cards, 1980, set of 8, NM, T2 ....$75.00

Spider-Man, For the First Time on the Screen..., 1977, 40x26", NM, T2 ....$50.00

Springtime in the Rockies, 1937, lobby card, Gene Autry serenading girl w/guitar under tree, NM, A3 ....$125.00

Star Wars, lobby cards, 1977, set of eight (two pictured), 11x14", EX, from $100.00 to $200.00.

Superman Comes to Earth, lobby card, 1948, Jonathan & Martha Kent discovering baby Superman in rocket ship, 11x13", EX $75.00

Superman Comes to Earth, lobby card, 1948, railroad flagman stopping a train, 11x13", EX, T2 ....$50.00

Three Worlds of Gulliver, 1960, 41x27", EX, J5...............$65.00

Tillie the Toiler, 1941, 41x27", EX, M17 ....$150.00

Who Slew Auntie Roo?, 1971, 41x27", EX, P3.................$30.00

Young Frankenstein, 1974, 41x27", EX, P3.....................$55.00

Zorro Rides Again, 1959, 41x27", EX, J5 ....$75.00

5,000 Fingers of Dr T, 1954, silkscreened, 84x24", rolled, EX, J5 ....$175.00

Snow White and the Seven Dwarfs, lobby card, Walt Disney, 1950s, EX, $75.00. (Photo courtesy David Longest and Michael Stern)

Musical Toys

Whether meant to soothe, entertain, or inspire, musical toys were part of our growing-up years. Some were as simple as a windup music box, others as elaborate as a lacquered French baby grand piano.

See also Disney; Character, TV, and Movie Collectibles.

Accordion, Japan, prewar, pictures Japanese children in various costumes, litho cb, 4½", EX, A $75.00

Chime Toy, Chein, 1920s – 30s, lithographed tin, EX, $100.00. (Photo courtesy David Longest)

Cowboy Ge-Tar & Music Box, Mattel, 1952, plays Red River Valley, blk plastic w/decals, rope strap, 14", EX.........$35.00

Harmonica, Strauss, 1925, detachable horn, EX (EX box), A, $150.00.

Drum, emb tin w/litho paper inserts depicting scenes of the Am Revolution including Putnam's Leap, etc, 12" dia, G, A $350.00
Drum, litho tin w/wood rims, Uncle Sam motif, 9" dia, VG, A $150.00
Drum, stamped tin sides w/stars & stripes shield & colored stars, wood rims w/repeated design, 9" dia, VG, A $500.00
Drum, tin w/wood rims, litho paper insert of Washington Crossing the Delaware, 13" dia, VG $900.00
Drum, tin w/wood rims, Union Soldiers in battle, 13" dia, VG $500.00
Drum, wood w/image of children on parade, 10" dia, EX, A..$575.00
Merry-Go-Round Music Box, Ohio Art, litho tin, turn crank for action, 6", NM (worn box), A $185.00

Music Box, 1948, plays four notes when handle is turned, lithographed metal, EX, $50.00. (Photo courtesy Linda Baker)

Piano, unknown maker, wood w/stenciled children's items on front, 7 keys, EX $100.00
Razz-Ma-Tazz Player Piano, Hubley, complete w/disks, MIB, A $75.00
Toyland Band, Ohio Art, 1950s, tin drum set, 8", EX (EX box)...$55.00
Tuneyville Player Piano, Tomy, 1978, plastic, battery-op, complete w/4 plastic records, 8½", EX....................$30.00
Twirl-A-Tune, Mattel, 1951, litho tin w/wood handle, 8", EX..$45.00
Victrola, Atlas, w/2 dbl-sided picture disks, EX, B5........$125.00

Piano, Schoenhut, wood with classical cherubs and dancing children motif, gold-painted trim, eight keys, EX, $200.00.
(Photo courtesy David Longest)

Nodders

Nodders representing comic characters of the day were made in Germany in the 1930s. These were small doll-like figures approximately 3" to 4" tall, and the popular ones often came in boxed sets. But the lesser-known characters were sold separately, making them rarer and harder to find today. While the more common nodders go for $125.00 and under, The Old Timer, Widow Zander, and Ma and Pa Winkle often bring about $350.00 to $400.00 — Happy Hooligan even more, about $625.00. (We've listed the more valuable ones here; any German bisque nodder not listed is worth $125.00 or under.)

Advisor: Doug Dezso (D6).

See also Character Bobbin' Heads; Sports Collectibles.

Auntie Blossom, NM $150.00
Auntie Mamie, NM $250.00
Avery, NM..$200.00
Bill, NM..$200.00
Buttercup, NM $250.00
Chubby Chaney, NM $250.00
Corky, NM...$475.00
Dock, NM $200.00
Fanny Nebbs, NM...$250.00
Ferina, NM...$350.00
Grandpa Teen, NM $350.00
Happy Hooligan, NM $625.00
Harold Teen, NM $150.00
Josie, NM..$425.00

Ambrose Potts, NM, $350.00; Old Timer, NM, $350.00; Ma Winkle, NM, $350.00; Mr. Bailey, NM, $150.00.

Junior Nebbs, NM..$625.00
Lilacs, NM $425.00
Lillums, NM..$150.00
Little Annie Roonie, movable arms, NM $300.00
Little Egypt, NM...$350.00
Lord Plushbottom, NM..$150.00
Ma & Pa Winkle, NM, ea $350.00
Marjorie, NM..$425.00
Mary Ann Jackson, NM $250.00
Max, NM $200.00
Min Gump, NM $150.00
Mr Bibb, NM $400.00
Mr Wicker, NM $250.00
Mushmouth, NM...$175.00
Mutt or Jeff, med or lg, NM, ea $250.00
Mutt or Jeff, sm, NM, ea...$175.00
Nicodemus, NM..$350.00
Our Gang, 6-pc set, MIB $1,200.00
Pat Finnegan, NM $400.00
Patsy, NM $425.00
Pete the Dog, NM $250.00
Pop Jenks, NM $200.00
Rudy Nebbs, NM...$250.00
Scraps, NM $250.00
Uncle Willie, NM..$250.00
Widow Zander, NM...$400.00
Winnie Winkle, NM $150.00

Optical Toys

Compared to the bulky viewers of years ago, contrary to the usual course of advancement, optical toys of more recent years have tended to become more simplified in concept.

See also View-Master and Tru-View.

Cartoon Viewer, Fisher-Price, 1986, yel plastic w/bl litho, several cartridges available, M, C13 ....$15.00

Easy-Show Movie Projector, Kenner, 1966, features Marvel
  Super Heroes, complete, MIB, T2............................$175.00
Flintstones Magic Movies, Embree, 1965, complete, scarce,
  NMIB..$250.00
Give-A-Show Projector, Kenner, 1960s, features Hanna-Barbera
  characters, complete, MIB, from $100 to................$125.00
Give-A-Show Projector, Kenner, 1970s-present, red & bl plas-
  tic, battery-op, 9½", EX...................................$30.00
Hanna-Barbera Television Viewer, Lido, 1960, plastic viewer
  w/paper rolls featuring several characters, VG, P4.....$55.00

Magic Mirror, McLoughlin Bros, paper lithograph image
appears on mercury glass tube, EX (EX wooden box), A,
$1,500.00.

Jolly Theatre, 16mm projector with built-in screen, features
Krazy Cat, Our Gang, Three Stooges, etc, NMIB, A,
$150.00.

Pathe Camera, Marx, 1930s, litho tin camera on adjustable tripod, 6", EX, A...$500.00

Kaleidoscope, Bush, cb tube w/brass element housing
  w/impressed logo, 4-footed wood base, 14", EX, A ..$500.00
Kaleidoscope, Bush, w/patent reissue date of Nov 11 1873, cb,
  wood & glass w/brass turning ring, 10½", EX, A $850.00
Kiddie Kamera, Allied Mfg, 1930s, plain blk metal film
  viewer, sm version, shows, Tracy, Annie, Kayo, etc, EXIB,
  J5 ....$100.00
Komic Kamera, Allied Mfg, 1934, litho tin & wood, complete
  w/filmstrips of various characters, NM.....................$100.00
Komic Kamera Film Viewer Set, features several characters,
  complete w/films, EX (EX box), minimum value $150.00
Magic Lantern, Ernst Plank, CI base, intricate shutter mecha-
  nism, w/18 colored 35mm filmstrips in 7 boxes, 18", EX,
  A..$250.00
Magic Lantern, Germany, pnt tin w/burner & glass chimney on
  wooden base, 9 glass slides in wooden containers, 14", VG,
  A..$150.00
Magic Lantern, GVF, wood w/tin roof, stack & lenses, ornate CI
  feet, EX (G wood box) $350.00
Magic Lantern, JS, red-pnt tin w/kerosene lamp base, extended lens
  & rnd colored glass slide, EX (VG wooden box) $275.00
Magic Lantern, Schoenner, w/3 circular, 7 strip slides & 1 kalei-
  doscopic slide, 12", VG+ (VG+ box), A $200.00
Magic Lantern & Slides, Ernst Plank, blk-pnt steel & brass
  lantern complete w/burner & lens, 11", EX (EX wooden
  box), A $350.00
Movie Viewer Theater, Fisher-Price, 1977-86, plastic, several
  cartridges available, M, C13 ....$25.00

Play N' Show Phono Projector, Kenner, 1969, complete,
MIB, $35.00. (Photo courtesy Martin and Carolyn Berens)

Praxinoscope Theater, early, w/20 image strips & 10 scenic panels, VG (VG wooden box), A $850.00

Projector, Irwin, 1930s, steel with baked-on black enamel, celluloid filmstrip features several characters, 5", NMIB, $175.00.

PXL 2000 Camcorder, Fisher-Price, 1988-89, battery-op, complete, MIB, C13 ....$325.00
See-A-Show Stereo Viewer Set, Kenner, 1966, features Marvel Super Heroes, complete, MIB, T2............................$125.00
Superman Movie Viewer, Chemtoy, 1965, MOC, H4 .....$50.00
Three Stooges Jolly Theatre, Excel, 1947, complete w/projector, film & uncut figures, EX (EX box)...........................$200.00
Top Cat Viewer, Marx, 1962, look through windows of house for colorful actions scenes, plastic, EX (EX box)...........$100.00
Wheel of Life Zoetrope, London Stereoscopic & Photographic Co, w/28 mc strips & 9 geometric paper disks, EX, A.......$350.00

Paper Dolls

Turn-of-the-century paper dolls are seldom found today and when they are, they're very expensive. Advertising companies used them to promote their products, and some were printed on the pages of leading ladies' magazines. By the late 1920s most paper dolls were being made in book form — the doll on the cover, the clothes on the inside pages. Because they were so inexpensive, paper dolls survived the Depression and went on to peak in the 1940s. Though the advent of television caused sales to decline, paper doll companies were able to hang on by making paper dolls representing Hollywood celebrities and TV stars. These are some of the most collectible today. Even celebrity dolls from more recent years like the Brady Bunch or the Waltons are popular. Remember, condition is very important; if they've been cut out, even when they're still in fine condition and have all their original accessories, they're worth only about half as much as an uncut book or box set. Our values are for mint and uncut dolls unless noted otherwise.

For more information, refer to *Price Guide to Lowe and Whitman Paper Dolls* by Mary Young, *Collecting Toys* by Richard O'Brien, and *Toys, Antique and Collectible*, by David Longest.

Advisor: Mary Young (Y2).

Alice in Wonderland, Whitman #928, 1930, stand-ups...$75.00
Alvin & the Chipmunks, Whitman #1927, 1966, stand-ups...$35.00
Baby Beans & Pets, Whitman #1950, 1978 ....$12.00
Baby First Step, Whitman #1997, 1965 ....$35.00
Baby Nancy, Whitman #1060, 1935 ....$75.00

Annette, Whitman #1971, uncut, NM, $50.00.

Baby Sue, Lowe #2786, 1969 ....$15.00
Betty, Jane & Dick, Lowe #130, 1943 ....$22.00
Beverly Hillbillies, Whitman #1955, 1964, NM $75.00
Blondie, Whitman #967, 1948 ....$125.00
Bob Hope & Dorothy Lamour, Whitman #976, 1942 ....$250.00
Brady Bunch, Whitman #1997, 1973, EX $55.00
Bridal Doll Book, Whitman #1986, 1978..........................$16.00
Buffy & Jody, Whitman #1640, 1969, paper doll/coloring book..$25.00
Buffy & Mrs Beasley, Whitman #1995, 1968, NM, C1 ....$60.00
Busy Teens, Lowe #2797, 1959...$15.00
Career Girls, Lowe #1045, 1942 ....$75.00
Cathy Goes to Camp, Merrill #1562, 1954 ....$35.00
Charlie's Angels, Toy Factory, 1977, Sabrina, Jill or Kelly, boxed, ea $35.00
Cheerleaders, Lowe #2741, 1962 ....$15.00
Chitty-Chitty Bang-Bang, Whitman #1982, 1968 ....$40.00
Cinderella Steps Out, Lowe #1242, 1948.........................$60.00
Clara West, McLoughlin #1864-70, doll w/5 outfits, 6", EX, A..$65.00
Claudette Colbert, Saalfield #322, 1943 ....$75.00
Clothes Crazy, Lowe #1046, 1945 ....$35.00
Coke Crowd, Merrill #3445, 1946.....................................$100.00
Cowboys & Indians, Lowe #2105, 1961, stand-ups...........$15.00
Debbie Reynolds, Whitman #1955, 1955 ....$100.00
Dodi, Whitman #1965, 1966, uncut, M $35.00
Donny & Marie, Whitman #1991, 1977, EX $25.00
Double Date, Saalfield #1723, 1957 ....$20.00
Dr Kildare & Nurse Susan, Lowe #2740, M.....................$65.00
Dy-Dee Baby Doll, Whitman #969, 1938 ....$125.00

Fanny Gray, Crosby, Nichols & Co, head figure w/5 outfits, History book & picture of Fanny's cottage, 6½", VG, A .$150.00
Farmyard, Lowe #1254, 1943, stand-ups $10.00
Flossy Fair & Peter Fair, Whitman #981, 1933 ....$75.00
Flying Nun, Saalfield #1317, 1969, EX $45.00

Green Acres, Whitman #1979, 1967, uncut, NM, from $35.00 to $45.00. (Photo courtesy Greg Davis and Bill Morgan)

Flying Nun, Saalfield #6069, 1969, MIB, from $50.00 to $60.00. (Photo courtesy Greg Davis and Bill Morgan)

Frances Brundage, doll w/3 outfits & hats, EX, A $40.00
Gene Autry, Merrill #3482, 1940, stand-ups $85.00
Gene Tierney, Whitman #992, 1947 ....$175.00
Glamour Girl, Whitman #973, 1942 ....$50.00
Glenn Miller & Marion Hutton, Lowe #1041, 1942 ......$300.00
Golden Girl, Merrill #1543, 1953 ....$75.00
Goldilocks, Whitman #1962, 1972 ....$14.00
Growing Up Skipper, Whitman #1013-1, 1978, paper doll/coloring book $20.00
Gulliver's Travels, Saalfield #1261, 1939 ....$125.00
Haley Mills in Moon-Spinners, Whitman, 1964, EX, A ..$40.00
Hart Family, Golden #1526, 1985 ....$5.00
Hedy Lamar, Saalfield #1538, 1951 ....$100.00
Hello Patti, Lowe #1877, 1964 ....$12.00
Indian Stand-Ups, Lowe #1253, 1943 ....$18.00
It's a Date, Whitman 1976, 1956 ....$40.00
Jack & Jill, Lowe #9800, 1963 ....$45.00
Janet Leigh, Lowe #2733, 1958 ....$80.00
Joan's Wedding, Whitman #990, 1942 ....$75.00

I Love Lucy Packaway Kit, Whitman, 1953, EX, $125.00.
(Photo courtesy Bill Bruegman)

Josie & the Pussycats, Whitman #1982, 1971, EX $30.00
Julia, Saalfield #6055, 1970 ....$50.00
Kiddle Kolognes, Whitman #1992-59, 1969 ....$40.00
Lace & Dress Puppy, Lowe #8902, 1975 ....$16.00
Lana Turner, Whitman #964, 1947 ....$200.00
Lennon Sisters, Whitman #1979, 1958 ....$60.00
Let's Play House, Lowe #2708, 1957 ....$20.00

Liddle Kiddles Play Fun, Whitman #4716, 1968..............$45.00
Linda Darnell, Saalfield #1584, 1953......................$100.00
Little Ballerina, Whitman #1963, 1961 ....$20.00
Little Brothers & Sisters, Whitman #971, 1953 ....$25.00
Little Girls, Lowe #2784, 1969.............................$10.00
Little Orphan Annie, Saalfield #299, 1943 ....$100.00
Little Women, Saalfield #1316, 1963........................$30.00
Magic Mindy, Whitman #1991, 1970 ....$14.00
Margaret O'Brien, Whitman #970, 1944 ....$150.00
Mary Martin, Saalfield #287, 1943.........................$125.00
Me & Mimi, Lowe #L144, 1942 ....$40.00
Molly Dolly, Lowe #2757, 1965.............................$16.00
Mopsy & Popsy, Lowe #730, 1972, boxed $8.00
Mother & Daughter, Lowe #1860, 1963 ....$18.00
Mouseketeers, Whitman #1974, 1963, NM $75.00
Movie Starlets, Whitman #960, 1946.......................$100.00
Mrs Beasley, Whitman #1993, 1972, EX......................$25.00
My Baby Book, Whitman #1011, 1942 ....$50.00
My Buddy, Golden #1535, 1986...............................$6.00
Nanny & the Professor, Artcraft #4283, 1971, EX $35.00
Nora Drake, Lowe #989, 1952...............................$45.00
Nurses, Whitman #1975, 1963 ....$50.00
Our Gang, Whitman #900, 1931 ....$200.00
Partridge Family, Saalfield #5137, 1971-72, boxed $50.00
Patty & Pete, Lowe #525, 1941 ....$35.00
Patty Duke, Whitman #1991, 1964, EX.......................$40.00

Pepper & Dodi Garden of Fashion Wardrobe, Whitman #4721, 1965, boxed...........................$45.00
Peter Rabbit, Saalfield #963, 1934, stand-ups $40.00
Petticoat Junction, Whitman #1954, 1964, EX, A $75.00
Play Dollies, Whitman #1025, 1920s $90.00
Playmates, Lowe #1829, 1961 ....$10.00
Portrait Girls, Whitman #966, 1947 ....$75.00
Prom Time, Whitman #2084, 1962............................$35.00
Raggedy Ann, Whitman #1650, 1971..........................$20.00
Raggedy Ann & Andy, Whitman #4319, 1973, boxed.....$20.00
Raggedy Ann & Andy Circus Play Day, Whitman #1838-31, 1980 ....$18.00
Rock Hudson, Whitman #2087, 1957.........................$65.00
Rock Stars, Golden #1682, 1992 ....$5.00
Roy Rogers & Dale Evans, Whitman #998, 1950..........$140.00
School Pals, Whitman #2075, 1964 ....$25.00
Sky Babies, Merrill #1551, 1959 ....$65.00
Sonja Henie, Merrill #3418, 1941.........................$200.00
Sonny & Sue, Lowe #522, 1940.............................$35.00
Sparkle Plenty, Saalfield, 1948, J5......................$65.00
Square Dance, Lowe #2707, 1957 ....$20.00
Starr, Whitman #1982-31, 1980............................$12.00
Strawberry Sue, Whitman #1976-2, 1979 ....$10.00
Sunshine Family, Whitman #1980, 1977......................$12.00

Raggedy Ann and Andy, Saalfield #2754, 1957, EX, $45.00. (Photo courtesy Kim Avery)

Sunshine Fun Family, Whitman #1995, uncut, NM, $15.00. (Photo courtesy Cindy Sabulis)

Susan Dey as Laurie, Artcraft #4218, 1971 ....$35.00
Sweet-Treat Kiddles, Whitman #1993-59, 1969..............$55.00
Sweetie Pie, Lowe #2482, 1958 ....$25.00

Tammy & Pepper, Whitman #1997, 1965 ....$45.00

Tammy School & Sports Clothes, Whitman #4620, 1964, boxed...$45.00

Teddy Bear, J Ottmann, doll w/5 outfits, EX (EX envelope), A $200.00

Teen Queens, Lowe #2710, 1957 ....$20.00

Teen Town, Merrill #3443, 1946 ....$100.00

That Girl, Saalfield #4479, 1967, NM, A $75.00

Three Little Sisters, Whitman #996, 1943 ....$75.00

Tina & Tony, Lowe #1022, 1940 ....$50.00

Tiny Rescue Patrol, Whitman #1916-1, 1978, stand-ups....$8.00

Tom the Aviator, Lowe #1074, 1941 ....$75.00

Toni Hair-Do Cut-Out Dolls, Lowe #960, 1950 ....$50.00

Trixie, Lowe #3920, 1961 ....$35.00

Twiggy, Whitman #1999, M.......................................$50.00

Walt Disney's Fantasia, Whitman #950, 1940, stand-ups.$200.00

Waltons, Whitman #1995, 1975 ....$45.00

Paper-Lithographed Toys

Following the development of color lithography, early toy makers soon recognized the possibility of using this technology in their own field. Both here and abroad, by the 1880s toys ranging from soldiers to involved dioramas of entire villages were being produced of wood with colorful and well-detailed paper lithographed surfaces. Some of the best known manufacturers were Crandall, Bliss, Reed, and McLoughlin. This style of toy remained popular until well after the turn of the century.

Advisors: Mark and Lynda Suozzi (S24).

See Also Black Americana; Boats; Circus Toys; Doll-houses; Games; Musical Toys; Pull Toys; Schoenhut.

ABC Building Blocks, McLoughlin, 1889, shows Barnum's Museum, firehouse, circus interior & train station, rare, NMIB, A $4,950.00

ABC Cut-Out Blocks, Reed, 1890, complete, EX (G box), A $1,500.00

Apple Tree Target Game, crossbow shoots apples out of litho tree w/Harlequin figure atop, EX (VG box), A $200.00

Ark w/Animals, Germany, litho-paper-on-wood ark w/14 pnt wood animals (Nuremburg style), 11", G, A............$250.00

Ark w/Animals, Germany, litho-paper-on-wood ark w/26 pnt-wood animals & 2 people (Nuremburg style), 16", G, A........$415.00

Brownie Artillery, complete w/cannon & 10 figures, 8x12", G (G box), A...$1,500.00

Brownie Blocks, McLoughlin/Palmer Cox, 1891, shows Brownies in various activities, set of 20, 11x13", EX $1,250.00

Brownie Blocks, w/orig booklet showing 6 images made w/20 blocks, 11x14", VG+ (VG+ wooden box), A..........$775.00

Brownie Knockdown Set, figures in various costumes on stands, set of 7, 10", EX, A $225.00

Brownie Nine Pins Game, McLoughlin, complete, EX (EX box), A..$2,700.00

Castle Fort, European, designed to use w/lead soldiers, 13x10" base, G+, A...$250.00

Cinderella Coach, Bliss, 26", EX, A...........................$1,150.00

Cob House Blocks, McLoughlin, architectural set combines the alphabet, pictures, spelling & building blocks, VG (VG box) $1,150.00

Converse Carousel, 5 horse seats hang from wooden rods, clockwork w/internal musical movement, 28" dia, G+, A $1,300.00

Crandall's of Montrose Building Block Set #3, few pcs missing, EX (EX wooden box), A......................................$200.00

Fort Sumpter, Reed, 1890, paper litho on wood, 17½x18", complete, rare, EX, A $950.00

Happiwork Fire Department, Gibson Art, 1924, complete, NM (NM box), A $300.00

Jackson Parke Horse-Drawn Trolley, Bliss, w/orig driver & conductor, 27", EX, A $4,950.00

Jolly Marble Game, 1892, wood, marble travels from cup to cup and onto board which contains numbered holes at one end, EX, A, $450.00.

League Parlor Baseball, Bliss, 1885, paper on wood, EX (VG box), A $1,200.00

Little Playette Theater, w/booklet of productions, unused, A $200.00

Model Village, Spears, complete w/figures & buildings, EX (EX box), A $150.00

Mother Goose Blocks, McLoughlin Bros, 1894, complete, EX (EX box) $475.00

Mother Hubbard's Party, Forbes, knobs on base cause pictures to pop up when pulled, 11", EX, A, $900.00.

Mother Goose Ladder, complete w/children & Brownie figures, 33", EX..$725.00
Mother Goose Target, Reed, complete, 11x18", VG, A.$550.00
Musical Cats, Ives, 1870, 2 cats w/cello & violin, heavy paper, w/up mechanism, 7", EX (worn box), A $550.00
Nesting Blocks, ABCs & children at play, set of 9, 32", VG, A $275.00
Nesting Blocks, ABCs & Three Bears, set of 6, 31", VG, A..$150.00
Nesting Blocks, Cock Robin, set of 10, 41", G, A $125.00
Nesting Blocks, Germany, early automotive, zeppelin, train & trolley, 26", VG+, A...$385.00
Old Guard Target Set, cannon shoots ball at guards on wood bases, ball missing, EX, A $650.00
Pretty Village Boathouse Set, McLoughlin, ca 1898, EX (EX box)...$150.00
Pretty Village Church Set, McLoughlin, 1898, EX (EX box).$150.00
Pretty Village Colonial Park, McLoughlin, 1897 & 1900, EX (EX box) $275.00
Pretty Village Small Set No 2, McLoughlin, 1890, EX (EX box) $250.00
Pussy Cat 5 Pins, litho paper on cb, VG (VG box), A...$450.00

Puzzle Blocks, Germany, set of 30 with image on all sides to make different Santa pictures, complete, VG (VG box), A, $1,500.00.

Puzzle Blocks, boys & girls playing w/animals, w/5 guide sheets, VG (VG box w/slide top), A.....................................$100.00
Puzzle Blocks, Germany, images of boys & girls at play, w/5 guide sheets, VG (VG wood box w/hinged lid), A $150.00
Puzzle Blocks, Germany, 48 blocks w/5 guide sheets, VG+ (VG+ wood box w/hinged lid), A.......................................$475.00
Puzzle Blocks, 72 blocks w/3 scenes, EX (EX wood box w/hinged lid), A $850.00
Rockaway Stable, Bliss, w/2 horses, sled & jockey, 11½x9½", VG+, A $800.00
Santa Claus Travels Cube Puzzle, McLoughlin, 1897, set of 6, 13x10", NMIB, A..$2,500.00
Seneca Spelling Blocks, 1890s, complete, EX (EX box).$300.00
Tir de la Mere Michel Target Game, paper litho on cb, 14x16", EXIB, A $165.00

Train, Reed, marked Duke and Princess, 33", EX, A, $850.00.

Train Set, Bliss, engine w/Lincoln Park RR mail car & Columbian coach, 3-pc, 17", EX...........................$4,200.00

Pedal Cars and Other Wheeled Goods

Just like Daddy, all little boys (and girls as well) are thrilled and happy to drive a brand new shiny car. Today both generations search through flea markets and auto swap meets for cars, boats, fire engines, tractors, and trains that run not on gas but pedal power. Some of the largest manufacturers of wheeled goods were AMF (American Machine and Foundry Company), Murray, and Garton. Values depend to a very large extent on condi-

Air Pilot, American National, orange with green wing and tail, 50", restored, A, $2,300.00.

tion, and those that have been restored may sell for upwards of $1000.00, depending on year and model.

Advisor: Nate Stoller (S7).

Bel Air Chevy Convertible, 1955 model, 1930s, red & cream, 38", rstr, A $2,400.00

Bugatti, Eureka, bright bl w/wht upholstered seat, chrome trim, lg disk wheels, front & rear bumpers, 46", rstr, A.$2,200.00

Bugatti Type 35 Grand Prix Racer, bl w/chrome trim, blk upholstered seat, pneumatic tires, electric power, NM, A.$8,000.00

Caterpillar Diesel Tractor, New London Metal Products, 1950s, yel w/blk detail, rubber treads, rstr, S7, from $3,000 to $6,000.00

Chrysler, Steelcraft, 1941, deep bl w/wht radiator grille & hubs, chrome steering wheel, windshield & trim, S7 ....$2,500.00

Chrysler Roadster, Steelcraft, red & cream w/blk fenders, side spare, disk wheels, 52", NM, A $5,200.00

Chrysler Roadster, Steelcraft, yel w/chrome trim & blk fenders, disk wheels w/yel hubs, 57", VG+, A $2,500.00

Earth Mover, Murray, 1961, yel w/blk lettering & detail, Playload Dump, rstr, S7, from $1,000 to $1,500.00

Ford, Garton, 1937, green with cream detail and interior, restored, S7, from $1,500.00 to $1,800.00. (Photo courtesy Nate Stoller)

FBI Radio Cruiser, 1950s, original condition, 37", EX, $700.00. (Photo courtesy Harry and Jody Whitworth)

Graham-Bradley Jr. Tractor, red with disk wheels and black rubber tires, 41", restored, A, $700.00.

Fire Truck, American National, marked AFD, red with white detail, wood ladders, chrome bell and lights, 63", restored, A, $8,000.00.

Fire Truck #B640, Steelcraft, 1941, red w/wht detail, 2 wooden ladders, chrome bell, rstr, S7, from $1,500 to.......$2,500.00

John Deere Tractor, Ertl, solid cast aluminum w/molded blk rubber tires, John Deere colors, 37", rstr, A $450.00

Packard, Am National, dk wine red w/gold pinstriping, chrome trim & hood ornament, working steering, 29", rstr, A........$3,300.00

Racer #8, BMC, 1950s, yel w/wht hubs, chrome steering & pipes, Gilmore Speedway Special & logo on sides, rstr, S7 ....$2,500.00

Roadster, Am National, 1920s, gray & blk w/red striping, rubber tires w/hubs, side spare, 70", rstr, A $8,000.00

Roamer, Am National, w/tonneau, gr w/yel detail, rstr, from $3,000 to...$5,000.00

Rolls Racer Air Mail Plane, pnt & stenciled wood, EX, from $2,000 to...$3,000.00

Spirit of America Airplane, Steelcraft, mk NC 66 on tail, orange w/blk detail, blk rubber tires w/pnt hubs, 53", EX, A ..$1,000.00

Super Sonic Jet, wht w/red detail, 3-wheeled, EX, from $800 to $1,200.00

Tee-Bird, Murray, bl w/wht detail & lettering, red steering wheels, VG, from $300 to $500.00

Torpedo Streamline Convertible, maroon w/chrome trim, rubber tires, 38", EX, A.......................................$700.00

Roadster, American National, marked ACE, maroon-painted wood with spoke wheels, 33", G, A, $750.00.

Torpedo Convertible, Murray, 1949, white with red interior and hubs, chrome trim with four side vents, restored, S7, $3,000.00. (Photo courtesy Nate Stoller)

US Navy Patrol Plane, Steelcraft, silver w/red & bl trim, 3-wheeled, 48", EX, A $3,000.00

SCOOTERS

Buddy L, blk sturdy platform on 3 wheels, blk & red jtd derrick-type hdl w/wood grip, rubber tires w/red hubs, rstr ..$2,300.00
Coaster Craft, orig red pnt w/flared rear fender, red wheels w/yel stripe, rear wheel kickstand, unused, M $200.00
Gong Bell, hinged wooden seat mk Special Delivery, metal handlebars & bell, rubber tires, EX $125.00
Henley, rectangular platform on base w/4 metal spoke wheels, vertical hdl, 33", G $125.00
Skippy, Gendron, ca 1940, red streamlined style w/wht pinstripe, front & rear fenders, wht tires, 43", rstr................$2,750.00

WAGONS

Buckboard, Old West style w/wood body, wood wheels w/steel bands, 48", VG, A $775.00
Georgie, gray-pnt wood w/pnt landscapes on ends, Georgie lettered on sides w/gold trim, wood spoke wheels, 28" bed, EX $650.00
Horse Wagon, natural wood w/blk-pnt trim, red interior, 4 spoke wheels, wooden shaft, no horse, 24", EX, A............$125.00
Overland, wood w/metal pull hdl, rubber tires, VG, A...$150.00
Pioneer, red-pnt tin w/wood bottom & pull hdl, metal spoke wheels, 25", EX $550.00
Sherwood Spring Coasters, pnt wood w/stenciled lettering, sm spoke wheels, spring-loaded, 41", G+, A $400.00
Staley's Special, ca 1905-15, natural wood w/red disk wheels, name stenciled on sides, VG, A $225.00

Penny Toys

Penny toys were around as early as the late 1800s and as late as the 1920s. Many were made in Germany, but some were made in France as well. With few exceptions, they ranged in size from 5" on down; some had moving parts, and a few had clockwork mechanisms. Though many were unmarked, you'll sometimes find them signed 'Kellermann,' 'Meier,' 'Fischer,' or 'Distler,' or carrying an embossed company logo such as the 'dog and cart' emblem. They were made of lithographed tin with exquisite detailing — imagine an entire carousel less than 2½" tall. Because of a recent surge in collector interest, many have been crossing the auction block of some of the country's large galleries. Our values are prices realized at several of these auctions.

Advisor: Kerry and Judy Irvin (K5).

Airplane & Hangar, Distler, 3", EX, A $350.00
Armored Artillery Gun Carrier, Germany, operating gun, 3½", G, A $125.00
Armored Gun Car, Germany, inertia mechanism, 3", EX, A ..$300.00
Baby Carriage, mk Germany, w/folding cloth hood, 3¾", EX, A..$125.00
Baby in Highchair w/Table, Fischer (?), 2¾", EX, A......$250.00
Baby in Rolling Chair w/Nanny, Meier, 3¼", EX, A......$385.00
Battleship, Fischer (?), 3 stacks w/billowing smoke, 4", VG+, A..$550.00
Biplane, Distler, figure seated on wing, NM, A...........$1,500.00
Bird in Cage, Distler, clockwork w/chirping noise, 3½", EX, A..$185.00
Bird in Cage, Meier, 2 side feeders, pull lever for pecking motion, 2", EX, A $175.00
Boar on platform, Germany, 2½", EX, A $325.00
Boat, Gely, sleek, 2 stacks & flag, 10", VG, A................$900.00
Boxers, Germany, hand-op action figures, 6", VG+, A ..$100.00
Boxers, mk Germany, figures on squeeze action wires, 1½", EX, A $125.00
Boy at School Desk, Meier, top slides out, 2½", EX, A ..$800.00
Boys (2) on Flying Hollander, mk Germany, boys in sailor costumes, 4¼", VG+, A $1,100.00

Cat & Dog, Meier, dog springs out of doghouse, lever action, 4",
EX, A $650.00
Cat & Dog Clicker, Germany, 2¾", EX, A.....................$165.00
Chinese Man on Cart w/Parasol, Distler, parasol rotates, 3¾",
EX, A $465.00
Christmas Tree, Distler, 3½", EX, A............................$125.00
Clown & Donkey on Base, Meier, lever action, donkey kicks as
clown jumps back, 3½", EX, A........................$250.00
Clown Hitting Donkey on Platform, Meier, press lever & don-
key kicks, gr rectangular platform, 3½", VG, A $350.00
Clown in Barrel, Stock, 2½", VG+, A.........................$400.00
Cow on Platform, Meier, 3", EX, A............................$325.00

**Delivery Truck #245, Fischer, with driver, 3½", EX, A,
$175.00; Transporter, Germany, with driver, simulated white
canvas canopy, clockwork, EX, A, $250.00.**

Dirigible, Distler, side-mounted propellers & passenger carriage,
w/pull cord, 3", VG, A $450.00
Dirigible in Hangar, Meier, spring-loaded action causes door to
open & dirigible to appear, 2¾", EX, A $2,300.00
Dog on Platform, Meier, 2½", G+, A $150.00
Double-Decker Bus, Distler (?), clockwork, 4", EX, A ...$325.00
Double-Decker Bus, Fischer, mk General, clockwork, 4¾", EX+,
A $550.00
Double-Decker Bus, KICO, yel & red w/spoke wheels, w/driver,
clockwork, 4½", VG+, A $200.00
Double-Decker Bus, Meier, red & yel w/blk roof, passengers on
roof & lithoed in windows, 3¼", EX, A $1,000.00
Dust Pan, pictures children at play, 4", EX, A $150.00
Elephant Cart, Fischer, nodding head, 5", VG+, A........$100.00
Fat Man Tipping Hat, Kellerman, pull-string action, 3½", EX,
A $150.00

**Express Parcel Delivery Truck, Distler, red and black with
nickel-plated spoke wheels, with driver, clockwork, 3¾",
VG+, A, $175.00; Dump Truck, Fischer, yellow with red
striping, enclosed cab with driver, VG, A, $125.00.**

Fire Ladder Truck, Meier, figures seated on open bench seats w/lad-
ders on platform bed, spoke wheels, 3½", EX, A $225.00
Fire Ladder Truck, red w/chrome trim, disk wheels, yel crank
ladder, w/driver & 4 firemen, 4½", EX, A $200.00
Fire Pumper & Ladder Truck, mc w/wht spoke wheels, w/driver,
6", EX, A $350.00
Fire Pumper Truck, Fischer, red & gold w/open cab, disk wheels,
w/driver, 3", EX, A $150.00
Flying Swing Ride, Germany, 4½", EX, A $125.00
Garage w/Saloon Car & Touring Car, Fischer, 5x4", EX, A...$450.00
Garage w/2 Sedans, Germany, 2½", EX, A.....................$225.00
Gas Station w/Car, Distler, 2¾", EX, A........................$400.00
Geese Pecking in Coop, Germany, crank action, 2¼", G, A..$100.00
Girl & Rooster on Platform, Meier, 3½", EX+, A $465.00
Girl Feeding Chicken on Platform, Meier, yel rectangular plat-
form, 4", NM, A $375.00
Girl on Swing, Distler, ornate yel stand & base, 2½", NM,
A $250.00
Gnome Seated on Egg, Meier, rectangular base, EX, A ..$1,200.00
Gnomes Sawing Log on Platform, 3½", EX, A $220.00
Gnomes w/Anvil, beveled base, lever action, 4", EX, A.$325.00
Gondola on Swinging Platform, Meier, 2¾", EX, A......$325.00
Grand Hotel Omnibus, Meier, no-horse variation, 3", EX,
A $450.00
Grand Hotel Omnibus, Meier, w/horse, 6", EX, A $550.00
Gun Truck, Germany, w/driver, 3", EX, A $125.00
Horse & Jockey on Platform, Germany, 3¼", EX, A......$175.00
Horse-Drawn Cab, Fischer, blk w/gold-tone spoked wheels, wht
horse, w/driver, 4½", EX, A $100.00
Horse-Drawn Cab, Meier, bl w/graphics of passengers in window,
red spoked wheels, dapple-gray horse, 4½", EX, A.....$325.00
Horse-Drawn Carriage, Fischer, driver on open bench seat, sin-
gle horse, spoke wheels, EX, A................................$150.00
Horse-Drawn Dray Wagon, Distler, 5¼", EX, A $275.00
Horse-Drawn Hansom Cab, Germany, w/driver, EX, A..$150.00
Horse-Drawn Landau, Meier, w/driver, 4¾", EX, A.......$250.00

**Horse-Drawn Military Wagon, Meier, yellow and black with
red wheels, polychromed horses, 4½", EX, A, $800.00.**

Horse-Drawn Sulky, Distler, w/driver, spoked wheels, NM,
A $600.00
Horse-Drawn Water Wagon, Meier, 5", VG+, A $275.00
Jigger on Horn, Germany, 5", VG, A $300.00
Jigger on Rooftop, Distler, crank action, 3¾", EX, A $575.00
Lady Pushing Sleigh, girl passenger, w/revolving foot action, 3",
VG+, A $1,000.00
Lady Pushing Stroller w/Child, Meier, 3½", VG+, A.....$500.00

Horse-Drawn Omnibus, marked Grand Hotel, Meier, multicolored with gray horse, 5", EX, A, $325.00.

Ladybug, 2½", EX, A $50.00
Launch w/Sailor, Meier, 4½", VG+, A $750.00
Limousine, brn w/bl trim, w/driver, spoke wheels, 4", NM, A $150.00
Limousine, Meier, colorful graphics around windows, spoke wheels, 3", EX, A $300.00
Lorry, Distler, covered A-frame truck bed, red & gray w/gold trim & spoke wheels, 3½", EX, A $325.00
Lorry, gray w/simulated canvas cover arched over truck bed, wht spoke wheels, w/driver, 4½", G+, A $125.00
Lorry, Meier, simulated cloth cover draped over truck bed, inertia drive, w/driver, 4½", EX, A..............................$215.00
Man in Sailboat on Platform, Meier, 4 spoke wheels, 3", VG, A...$1,300.00
Man w/Twirling Umbrella, Germany, 4", EX, A $75.00
Man w/Wheelbarrow, Germany, 3", EX, A......................$50.00
Mercedes Open Touring Car, Fischer, w/driver, 4½", VG+, A $175.00
Merry-Go-Round, Meier, 3 horses w/riders, 3", VG, A ..$650.00
Merry-Go-Round, 3 swings w/riders, 3", EX, A...........$1,200.00
Monkey on Horn, Distler, 4¾", EX, A............................$250.00
Monkey Whistle, blow whistle & monkey lifts noisemaker to his mouth, 3¼", NM, A...$175.00
Motor Coach, Meier, emb upholstered interior, w/driver, inertia wheel, 3½", EX, A...$1,700.00
Motorcycle, Kellerman, w/driver, inertia wheels, 4", VG+, A $1,150.00
Ocean Liner, Fischer, 2 stacks, 4¼", EX, A $275.00
Ocean Liner, Kellerman, 2 stacks, 9", VG+, A...............$350.00
Ocean Liner, Meier, 2 stacks, 4½", VG+, A...................$450.00
Omnibus w/Roof Rack, Fischer, litho passengers in windows, spoke wheels, 3", EX, A.......................................$700.00
Organ Grinder w/Performing Bear, Germany, bear rotates back & forth, 3¼", EX, A..$1,265.00
Panel Truck #298, Fischer, orange w/blk top, spoke wheels, w/driver, 3½", EX, A...$150.00
Parrot on Horn, Germany, parrot twirls, 4¾", EX, A $200.00
Phonograph, crank-op w/plink-plunk music, 3½", VG+, A ..$175.00
Pickup Truck, Fischer, bl w/red spoke wheels, w/driver, 3¾", EX, A $145.00
Pony Cart, 4", G, A...$50.00
Pool Player, Kellerman, 4", EX, A...............................$225.00
Porter w/Trunk, Fischer (?), 3", EX, A $475.00

Post Van, Meier, motorized, 2¼", EX, A $475.00
Punch Theatre, Meier, Punch hitting soldier in theatre, 4", NM, A...$1,700.00
Rabbit Riding Egg on Wheeled Platform, Meier, spoke wheels, 3", NM, A...$1,700.00

Race Car, Fisher, blue with yellow spoke wheels, with driver, EX, A, $225.00; Train Set, CG and Co, complete, EX, A, $225.00.

Race Car, Meier, w/driver, 3½", G+, A $225.00
Race Car #32, Germany, 4½", VG, A $250.00
Racer #14, Distler, wht w/bl trim, wht spoke wheels w/side spare, w/driver, 4¼", VG, A...$325.00
Racer #2, Meier, bl, 3½", EX, A $2,600.00
Racer #4, Germany, detailed radiator & spoke wheels, w/driver, 5¼", EX, A $750.00
Racing Scull w/Single Oarsman, Levy for Universal Theaters Concession Co, 4¾", G, A.....................................$575.00
Racing Scull w/2 Oarsmen, Germany, 6¾", EX, A $1,150.00
Racing Scull w/3 Oarsmen on 4-Wheeled Platform, Meier, 3½", EX, A $1,750.00
Roadster, Fischer, 2-tone brn, NP spoke wheels, 4¼", EX, A.$165.00
Roadster #948, Meier, open, w/driver, 3½", EX, A.........$750.00
Roller Coaster Car, Germany, mc w/disk wheels, 3", EX, A $50.00
Roosters Fighting, Germany, squeeze action, 5", VG+, A .$145.00
Roosters Pecking, Meier, 4", VG+, A $150.00
Roulette Wheel Game, Germany, 2½" dia, EX (EX box mk Souvenir from the Universal Theaters Consession Co), A............$200.00
Saloon Car, Fischer, w/driver, 4", EX, A.......................$125.00
Saloon Car, Kellerman, bl & yel w/orange trim, w/driver, 3½", VG+, A $75.00
Saloon Car, Meier, gr w/NP spoke wheels, w/driver, 4¼", VG+, A $165.00
Saloon Car, Meier, red w/yel top & wht running boards & fenders, NP spoke wheels, w/driver & passengers, 4¼", EX, A $850.00
Scales, insert penny & dial moves, 6½", VG, A............$165.00
Sedan, Fischer, center door, red, NP spoke wheels, 4", EX, A $150.00
Sedan, Meier, red, 3", VG+, A......................................$125.00
Sewing Machine, Meier, treadle w/operating wheel & needle, 3", EX, A $125.00
Sewing Machine, table model w/operating wheel, 3¼", VG+, A $225.00

Skier on Wheeled Platform, Meier, 4 disk wheels, 2½", NM, A $225.00

Squirrel & Rabbit on Platform, Germany, 3", VG+, A ..$350.00

Stake Truck, Fischer, gold w/open cab, gray disk wheels w/red hubs, 5½", VG+, A $125.00

Stake Truck, Meier, open cab, spoked wheels, lt aqua & gold, w/driver, 3¼", EX, A $275.00

Standard Gas Station w/Car, Germany/US Zone, lever action, 3½", EX, A $100.00

Stork, Germany, slide-on platform controls action, 3", VG, A .$355.00

Stork w/Nest on Platform, Fischer, push lever & mother feeds babies, gr rectangular base, 3", VG, A $600.00

Swan on Platform, Meier, gold spoke wheels, M, A $825.00

Touring Car, Fischer, tan w/cream running boards, red trim, wht spoke wheels, w/driver, 5", EX, A $500.00

Touring Car, Meier, w/driver & lady passenger, 3½", EX, A ..$750.00

Town Car, Distler, w/opening door, inertia drive, 3", EX, A ..$200.00

Train, Distler, engine & tender, inertia drive, 6", EX, A..$185.00

Train, engine & tender w/5 boxcars, 16", G+, A............$175.00

Train, engine & tender w/5 passenger cars, 21", G+, A .$200.00

Train, Meier, engine & tender w/passenger car, stack w/billowing smoke, 5¾", VG+, A..$155.00

Train, Meier, engine w/integral car, 4", EX, A $450.00

Trolley, Kellerman, red & blk w/lithoed passengers, 3", EX, A...$300.00

Trolley, Meier, mc w/lithoed passengers, 2¾", EX, A $325.00

Truck, Fischer, gr, gold & brn w/wht spoke wheels, w/driver, 4½", EX, A $275.00

Vis-A-Vis, red & yel w/NP spoke wheels, w/driver, 3", VG+, A...$200.00

Vis-A-Vis w/Driver, Meier, red w/wht spoke wheels, 3", VG, A...$300.00

Woody Panel Truck, Fischer, dk gold w/blk top & running boards, NP spoke wheels, w/driver, VG+, A............$100.00

Zeppelin Whistle Noisemaker, 3", VG, A $325.00

Pez Dispensers

Pez was originally designed as a breath mint for smokers, but by the '50s kids were the target market, and the candies were packaged in the dispensers that we all know and love today. There is already more than three hundred variations to collect, and more arrive on the supermarket shelves every day. Though early on collectors seemed to prefer the dispensers without feet, that attitude has changed, and now it's the character head they concentrate on. Feet were added in 1987, so if you were to limit yourself to only 'feetless' dispensers, your collection would be far from complete. Some dispensers have variations in color and design that can influence their values. Don't buy any that are damaged, incomplete, or that have been tampered with in any way; those are nearly worthless. For more information refer to *A Pictorial Guide to Plastic Candy Dispensers Featuring Pez* by David Welch and *Collecting Toys #6* by Richard O'Brien. Values are for mint-condition dispensers unless noted otherwise.

Advisor: Richard Belyski (B1).

Other Sources: B10, H4, P10.

Angel, no ft $75.00

Arlene, w/ft, pk, from $3 to $5.00

Asterix Line, Asterix, Obelix, Roman or Getafix, ea, from $4 to $6.00

Baloo, w/ft $15.00

Bambi, no ft $65.00

Barney Bear, no ft $35.00

Barney Bear, w/ft $25.00

Baseball Glove, no ft $225.00

Batgirl, no ft, soft head, MIP $185.00

Batman, no ft $15.00

Batman, no ft, w/cape $100.00

Batman, w/ft, bl or blk, ea, from $3 to $5.00

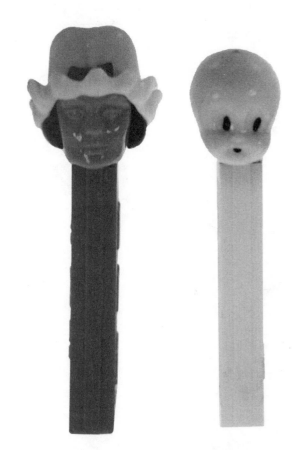

Betsy Ross, no feet, $185.00; Casper, no feet, $225.00.

Bouncer Beagle, w/ft $6.00

Boy, w/ft, brn hair $3.00

Bozo, no ft, diecut $200.00

Bubble Man, w/ft...$20.00

Bubble Man, w/ft, neon hat $6.00

Bugs Bunny, no ft..$20.00

Bugs Bunny, w/ft, from $1 to.................................$3.00

Bullwinkle, no ft $275.00

Candy Shooter, red & wht, w/candy & gun license, unused .$125.00

Captain America, no ft..$100.00

Captain Hook, no ft..$85.00

Charlie Brown, w/ft, from $1 to..............................$3.00

Charlie Brown, w/ft & tongue $20.00

Chick, w/ft, from $1 to...$3.00

Chick in Egg, no ft..$25.00
Chick in Egg, no ft, w/hair $125.00
Chip, w/ft...$100.00
Clown, w/ft, whistle head......................................$10.00
Clown w/Collar, no ft $65.00
Cockatoo, no ft, bl face, red beak $60.00
Cool Cat, w/ft $75.00
Cow (A or B), no ft, bl, ea, from $80 to..............$90.00
Creature From the Black Lagoon, no ft..............$300.00
Crocodile, no ft $95.00
Daffy Duck, no ft...$15.00
Daffy Duck, w/ft, from $1 to....................................$3.00
Dalmatian Pup, w/ft..$50.00
Daniel Boone, no ft $220.00
Dino, w/ft, purple, from $1 to..................................$3.00
Dinosaur, w/ft, 4 different, ea, from $1 to.............$3.00
Doctor, no ft $275.00

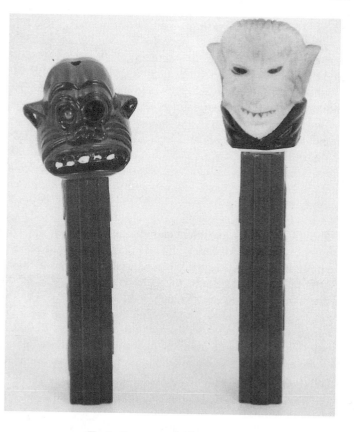

Eerie Spectres, $250.00 each.

Donald Duck and Mickey Mouse, no feet, from $10.00 to $15.00 each. (Photo courtesy Michael Stern)

Donald Duck, no ft, diecut....................................$200.00
Donald Duck's Nephew, no ft..................................$30.00
Donald Duck's Nephew, w/ft, gr, bl or red hat, ea $10.00
Donkey, w/ft, whistle head $10.00
Droopy Dog (A), no ft, plastic swivel ears, MIP $25.00
Droopy Dog (B), w/ft, pnt ears, MIP........................$6.00
Dumbo, w/ft, bl head...$25.00
Elephant, no ft, orange & bl, flat hat $110.00
Fat-Ears Rabbit, no ft, pk head $20.00

Fat-Ears Rabbit, no ft, yel head..............................$15.00
Fireman, no ft...$95.00
Fishman, no ft, gr..$185.00
Foghorn Leghorn, w/ft $95.00
Football Player...$175.00
Fozzie Bear, w/ft, from $1 to....................................$3.00
Frankenstein, no ft...$300.00
Fred Flintstone, w/ft, from $1 to $3.00
Frog, w/ft, whistle head $40.00
Garfield, w/ft, orange w/gr hat, from $1 to...........$3.00
Garfield, w/ft, teeth, from $1 to...............................$3.00
Garfield, w/ft, visor, from $1 to................................$3.00
Gargamel, w/ft...$5.00
Girl, w/ft, yel hair..$3.00
Glowing Ghosts (heads glow in the dark), Polly Pumpkin, Naughty
    Neil, Happy Henry or Slimy Sid, ea, from $4 to $6.00
Gonzo, w/ft, from $1 to...$3.00
Gorilla, no ft, blk head...$95.00
Green Hornet, 1960s, from $200 to $250.00
Gyro Gearloose, w/ft $6.00
Henry Hawk, no ft $65.00
Hulk, no ft, dk gr..$60.00
Hulk, no ft, lt gr, remake...$3.00
Indian, w/ft, whistle head $20.00
Indian Brave, no ft, reddish....................................$175.00
Indian Chief, no ft, yel headdress..........................$125.00
Indian Maiden, no ft..$175.00
Inspector Clouseau, w/ft..$5.00
Jerry Mouse, w/ft, plastic face $15.00
Jerry Mouse, w/ft, pnt face $6.00

Jiminy Cricket, no ft..$275.00
Joker (Batman), no ft, soft head..............................$200.00
Kermit the Frog, w/ft, red, from $1 to.......................$3.00
Knight, no ft..$300.00
Koala, w/ft, whistle head..$40.00
Krazy Animals, Blinky Bill...$6.00
Krazy Animals, Lion, Hippo, Elephant or Gator, ea, from $4 to .$6.00
Lamb, no ft...$15.00
Lamb, w/ft, from $1 to..$3.00
Lamb, w/ft, whistle head..$20.00
Lazy Garfield, w/ft...$5.00
Li'l Bad Wolf, w/ft..$20.00
Lion w/Crown, no ft..$100.00
Lion's Club Lion, minimum value.........................$2,000.00
Lucy, w/ft, from $1 to..$3.00
Make-A-Face, works like Mr Potato Head, minimum value..$2,500.00
Mary Poppins, no ft..$1,300.00
Merlin Mouse, w/ft..$20.00
Mexican, no ft..$250.00
Mickey Mouse, no ft, removable nose or cast nose, ea, from $10
   to..$15.00
Mickey Mouse, w/ft, from $1 to......................................$3.00
Mimic Monkey (monkey w/ball cap), no ft, several colors,
   ea..$40.00
Miss Piggy, w/ft, ea, from $1 to......................................$3.00
Miss Piggy, w/ft, eyelashes...$15.00
Monkey Sailor, no ft, w/wht cap....................................$50.00
Mowgli, w/ft..$15.00

Mr Ugly, no ft..$45.00
Muscle Mouse (gray Jerry), w/ft, plastic nose.................$15.00
Nermal, w/ft, gray..$3.00
Nintendo, Mario, Yoshi, Koopa Trooper or Diddy Dong, ea,
   from $4 to..$6.00
Non-Glowing Ghosts, Polly Pumpkin, Naughty Neil, Happy
   Henry or Slimy Sid...$2.00
Nurse, no ft, brn hair..$175.00
Octopus, no ft, blk..$85.00
Odie, w/ft..$5.00
Olive Oyl, no ft..$200.00
Panda, no ft, diecut eyes..$30.00
Panda, w/ft, remake, from $1 to......................................$3.00
Panda, w/ft, whistle head..$10.00
Papa Smurf, w/ft, red...$6.00
Parrot, w/ft, whistle head..$10.00
Pebbles Flintstone, w/ft, from $1 to................................$3.00
Penguin, w/ft, whistle head...$10.00
Penguin (Batman), no ft, soft head...............................$200.00
Peter Pez (A), no ft...$65.00
Peter Pez (B), w/ft, from $1 to...$3.00
Pilgrim, no ft..$185.00
Pink Panther, w/ft..$5.00
Pinocchio, no ft..$150.00
Pirate, no ft...$45.00
Pluto, no ft, red...$10.00
Pluto, w/ft, from $1 to...$3.00
Policeman, no ft..$65.00
Popeye (B), no ft..$115.00
Popeye (C), no ft, w/removable pipe.............................$110.00
Practical Pig (B), no ft..$30.00

Road Runner, no feet, $20.00; Uncle Sam, no feet, $250.00.

Psychedelic Eye, no ft $700.00
Psychedelic Flower, no ft $750.00
Psychedelic Hand, remake, blk or pk, MOC, ea $20.00
Pumpkin (A), no ft, from $10 to $15.00
Pumpkin (B), w/ft, from $1 to.......................................$3.00
Raven, no ft, yel beak $60.00
Rhino, w/ft, whistle head..$10.00
Ringmaster, no ft $300.00
Road Runner, w/ft...$15.00
Rooster, w/ft, whistle head...$40.00
Rooster, w/ft, wht or yel head, ea $30.00
Rudolph, no ft $60.00
Santa Claus (A), no ft, steel pin $125.00
Santa Claus (B), no ft $125.00
Santa Claus (C), no ft, from $5 to $15.00
Santa Claus (C), w/ft, from $1 to $3.00
Scrooge McDuck (A), no ft $35.00
Scrooge McDuck (B), w/ft $6.00
Sheik, no ft...$30.00
Skull (A), no ft, from $5 to $10.00
Skull (B), w/ft, from $1 to..$3.00
Smurf, w/ft $5.00
Smurfette, w/ft $5.00
Snoopy, w/ft, from $1 to...$3.00
Snow White, no ft $200.00
Snowman (A), no ft..$10.00
Snowman (B), w/ft, from $1 to $5.00
Space Trooper Robot, no ft, full body $325.00
Spaceman, no ft $200.00
Speedy Gonzales (A), w/ft...$15.00
Speedy Gonzales (B), no ft, from $1 to...........................$3.00
Spider-Man, no ft, from $10 to....................................$15.00
Spider-Man, w/ft, from $1 to $3.00
Spike, w/ft, B1 ....$6.00
Star Wars, Darth Vader, C3PO, Storm Trooper or Chewbacca,
    ea, from $1 to $3.00
Star Wars, Princess Leia, Luke Skywalker, Ewok or Boba Fet, ea,
    from $1 to $3.00
Sylvester (A), w/ft, cream or wht whiskers, ea $5.00
Sylvester (B), w/ft, from $1 to.......................................$3.00
Teenage Mutant Ninja Turtles, w/ft, 8 variations, ea, from $1
    to $3.00
Thor, no ft..$300.00
Thumper, w/ft, no copyright..$45.00
Tiger, w/ft, whistle head $10.00
Tinkerbell, no ft...$275.00
Tom, no ft $35.00
Tom, w/ft, plastic face...$15.00
Tom, w/ft, pnt face $6.00
Truck, many variations, ea, minimum value $1.00
Tweety Bird, no ft $10.00
Tweety Bird, w/ft, from $1 to $3.00
Tyke, w/ft...$15.00
Valentine Heart, from $1 to $3.00
Whistle, w/ft, from $1 to...$3.00
Wile E Coyote, w/ft $45.00
Winnie the Pooh, w/ft $75.00
Witch, 3-pc, no ft $10.00

Wolfman, no ft $300.00
Wonder Woman, no ft, soft head.................................$185.00
Wonder Woman, w/ft, from $1 to $3.00
Woodstock, w/ft, from $1 to $3.00
Woodstock, w/ft, pnt feathers......................................$15.00
Yappy Dog, no ft, orange or gr, ea $65.00
Yosemite Sam, w/ft, from $1 to $3.00

MISCELLANEOUS

Bank, truck #1, metal $200.00
Bank, truck #2, metal..$40.00
Body Parts, fit over stem of dispenser & make it look like a per-
    son, many variations, ea..$1.00
Bracelet, pk...$5.00
Bubble Wand...$6.00
Clicker, US Zone Germany, 1950, litho tin, 3½", NM..$300.00
Coin Plate $15.00
Coloring Book, Safety #2, non-English $15.00
Power Pez, rnd mechanical dispenser $5.00
Puzzle, Ceaco, 550 pcs, MIB $30.00
Puzzle, Sprinkbok/Hallmark, 500 pcs $15.00
Refrigerator Magnet Set..$10.00
Tin, Pez Specials, stars & lines on checked background, gold
    colors, 2½x4½", rare, EX $225.00
Toy Car, Johnny Lightning Racing Dreams PEZ racer, from $3
    to $10.00
Watch, pk face w/yel band or yel face w/bl band, ea.........$10.00
Watch, Psychedelic Hand...$10.00

Pin-Back Buttons

Pin-back buttons produced up to the early 1920s were made with a celluloid covering. After that time, a large number of buttons were lithographed on tin; these are referred to as tin 'lithos.'

Character and toy-related buttons represent a popular collecting field. There are countless categories to base a collection on. Buttons were given out at stores and theatres, offered as premiums, attached to dolls or received with a club membership.

In the late '40s and into the '50s, some cereal companies packed one in each box of their product. Quaker Puffed Oats offered a series of movie star pin-backs, but probably the best known are Kellogg's Pep Pins. There were eighty-six in all, so theoretically if you wanted the whole series as Kellogg hoped you would, you'd have to buy at least that many boxes of their cereal. Pep pins came in five sets, the first in 1945, three more in 1946, and the last in 1947. They were printed with full-color lithographs of comic characters licensed by King Features and Famous Artists — Maggie and Jiggs, the Winkles, and Dagwood and Blondie, for instance. Superman, the only D.C. Comics character, was included in each set. Most Pep pins range in value from $10.00 to $15.00 in NM/M condition; any not mentioned in our listings fall into this range. There are exceptions, and we've made sure they're evaluated below.

Nearly all pin-backs are collectible today with these possible exceptions: common buttons picturing flags of various nations, general labor union buttons denoting the payment of dues, and common buttons with clever sayings. Be sure that you buy only buttons with well-centered designs, well-alligned colors, no fading or yellowing, no spots or stains, and no cracks, splits, or dents. In the listings that follow, sizes are approximate.

Advisor: Doug Dezso (D6), Kellogg's Pep Pins only.
Other Sources: C10, D11, S20.
See Also Political; Premiums; Sporting Collectibles.

Ace G-Man, blk lettering on bl, ⅝" dia, rare, EX...........$140.00
Bat Kids Fan Club, 1966, bust portrait on silver, 2½" dia, NM, T2, from $30 to...$40.00
Batman, Creative House, 1966, This Is the Year of the Batman, red & bl on wht, litho tin, 1½", EX, J5.......................$75.00
Batman, I'm a Batman Crimefighter, 1966, red w/bl & wht image of Batman & Robin, 1½" dia, NM, J5.............$15.00
Batman, Join the Secret Society, 1966, colorful image of Batman & Robin, 3½" dia, MIP, J5.....................................$25.00
Batman & Robin Society Charter Member, Button World, 1966, full-color image, 3" dia, EX, from $15 to..........$20.00

Beatles, black and white group photo and red lettering on white background, NM, $25.00.

Beatles, group photo & I've Got My Beatles Movie Tickets Have You? M...$40.00
Beatles, I Love the Beatles, red & bl on wht, NM...........$25.00
Beatles, I'm a Beatle Bug, red, wht & bl, NM...................$25.00
Beatles, I'm a Beatle Fan, In Case of Emergency Call..., red & bl on white, NM...$20.00
Beatles, We All Live in a Yellow Submarine & image on wht background, EX...$15.00
Bill Haley & His Comets Fan Club, blk & wht group photo on wht, 1950s, 2", EX, A...$100.00

Chipmunks, Monarch Music, 1960, photos on yel background, NM, M17...$15.00
Dare Devil Official Member Super Hero Club, Button World, 1966, 3" dia, MIP, T2...$50.00

Donald Duck Jackets, Dry in Any Weather, Norwich Knitting Co Norwich, NY, VG, $350.00.

Elvis, Don't be Cruel, 1950s, red broken heart on wht, 1" dia, EX, J5...$25.00
Flash Gordon, 1974, image of Flash having sword fight w/Ming, 3", NM, C1...$20.00
Fonz Is Cool, Paramount Pictures, 1976, NM.................$10.00
Green Hornet Society Official Member, Button World, 1966, flying insect logo, 3" dia, NM, T2.............................$50.00
Hawkman Super Hero Club Official Member, Button World, 1966, full-color image, 3" dia, EX, T2.......................$25.00
Howdy Doody, I'm For Howdy Doody, lettering around image of Howdy, 1st TV premium, 1¼" dia, NM, A.............$100.00
Howdy Doody, 1976, Howdy Says Howdy & image, 1½" dia, EX...$12.00
Howdy Doody, 1988, Howdy Doody's 40th Birthday, Fries Distribution Co surround image, 3½" dia, EX................$25.00
Howdy Doody, 1988, It's Howdy Doody Time above image, 2¼" dia, EX...$10.00
Incredible Hulk Official Member Super Hero Club, Button World, 1966, 3" dia, NM, T2.......................................$25.00
Iron Man Official Member Super Hero Club, Button World, 1966, 3" dia, MIP, T2...$50.00
Jackie Gleason Fan Club, 1950s, Jackie in checked suit & Awa-a-ay We Go!, 1½" dia, EX, J5...................................$35.00
Joe Hardy (Hardy Boys), 1978, full-color photo, 3" dia, NM, C1...$18.00
Junior G Inspector, red, wht & bl, 1¼" dia, EX................$65.00
Lassie, I Voted for Lassie, 1950s, NM, from $50 to..........$60.00

Mad Magazine, What — Me Worry? I'm Voting Mad — Alfred E Neuman For President, Alfred in center, 1960s, 2½", NM, J5 ....$75.00

Mickey Mouse Club, 1928-30, blk lettering around image of Mickey on orange background, 1¼" dia, NM, A.....$125.00

Mork From Ork, Paramount, 1979, full-color photo, EX $8.00

Raggedy Ann & Andy, Happiness Is Made To Be Shared, Bobbs-Merrill, 1974, Raggedy Ann & Andy in boat, 3½" dia, M $15.00

Red Ryder Pony Contest, EX, C10 ....$20.00

Roy Rogers, Grape Nuts promo, Pat Brady, EX, C10........$20.00

Roy Rogers, Grape Nuts promo, Roy, EX, C10.................$30.00

Roy Rogers, Grape Nuts promo, Sheriff, EX, C10 ....$25.00

Spy Masher, EX, C10..$35.00

Superman, AF/DC Comics Inc, image of Superman lifting up car, 1" dia, NM, A $25.00

Superman Club Official Member, Button World, 1966, full-color image, 3" dia, NM, T2 ....$25.00

Tarzan, 1974, image on bl background, 3" dia, NM, C1...$25.00

Universal Monsters, any character, NM, ea......................$15.00

Welcome Back Kotter, 1970s, several variations w/ea character, NM, ea $8.00

Wonder Woman Sensation Comics, 1940s, full-color portrait w/yel border, 1" dia, NM, T2, from $800 to $1,000.00

KELLOGG'S PEP PINS

BO Plenty, NM..$30.00
Corky, NM...$16.00
Dagwood, NM..$30.00
Dick Tracy, NM..$30.00
Fat Stuff, NM...$15.00
Felix the Cat, NM...$85.00
Flash Gordon, NM..$30.00
Flat Top, NM..$30.00
Goofy, NM...$10.00
Gravel Girtie, NM...$15.00
Harold Teen, NM..$15.00
Inspector, NM..$12.50
Jiggs, NM..$25.00
Judy, NM...$10.00
Kayo, NM...$20.00
Little King, NM $15.00
Little Moose, NM..$15.00
Maggie, NM...$25.00
Mama De Stross, NM..$30.00
Mama Katzenjammer, NM $25.00
Mamie, NM..$15.00
Moon Mullins, NM..$10.00
Olive Oyl, NM..$30.00
Orphan Annie, NM..$25.00
Pat Patton, NM..$10.00
Perry Winkle, NM...$15.00
Phantom, NM...$80.00
Pop Jenks, NM...$15.00
Popeye, NM...$30.00
Rip Winkle, NM..$20.00
Skeezix, NM...$15.00
Superman, NM...$45.00
Toots, NM..$15.00
Uncle Walt, NM..$20.00
Uncle Willie, NM..$12.50
Winkles Twins, NM...$90.00
Winnie Winkle, NM...$15.00

Orphan Annie Likes To Trade at Joseph Spiess Company, 1930s, 1¼" dia, M, A, $200.00.

Spider-Man Official Member Super Hero Club, Button World, 1966, 3" dia, MIP, T2, $50.00.
(Photo courtesy Bill Bruegman)

Plastic Figures

Plastic figures were made by many toy companies. They were first boxed with playsets, but in the early '50s, some became available individually. Marx was the first company to offer single figures (at 10¢ each), and even some cereal companies included one in boxes of their product. (Kellogg offered a series of 16 54mm Historic Warriors, and Nabisco had a line of ten dinosaurs in marbleized, primary colors.) Virtually every type of man and beast has been modeled in plastic; today some have become very collectible and expensive. There are a lot of factors you'll need to be aware of to be a wise buyer. For instance, Marx made cowboys during the mid-'60s in a flat finish, and these are much harder to find and more valuable than the later figures with a waxy finish. Marvel Super Heroes in the fluorescent hues are worth about half as much as the earlier, light gray issue. Because of limited space, it isn't possible to evaluate more than a representative few of these plastic figures in a general price guide, so if you'd like to learn more about them, we recommend *Geppert's Guide* by Tim Geppert. See the Clubs and Newsletters section for information on how to order the *Plastic Figure & Playset Collector* magazine.

Advisors: Mike and Kurt Fredericks (F4); Bob Wilson, Phoenix Toy Soldier Co. (P11).

See also Playsets.

ACTION AND ADVENTURE

Marx, Apollo Astronaut moon walking, 6", wht, NM, F5 ..$12.50
Marx, Apollo Astronaut putting moon rock in bag, 6", wht, EX, F5...$8.50

Marx, Man From Uncle, Napoleon Solo and Illya Kuryakin, 6", NM, $25.00 each.

Marx, Apollo Astronaut w/Am flag, 6", lt bl, NM, F5 ....$24.00
Marx, Apollo Astronaut w/Am flag, 6", wht, NM, F5 ....$18.00
Marx, Apollo Astronaut w/camera at chest, 6", wht, EX, F5 ....$6.50
Marx, Apollo Astronaut walking w/instrument cast, 6", lt bl, NM, F5...$20.00
Marx, Explorers, Apollo Astronauts, 54mm, orange, set of 8 in 7 poses, NM, F5 ....$36.00
Marx, Explorers, Apollo Astronauts, 54mm, wht, set of 14 in 10 poses, NM, F5 ....$60.00
Marx, Explorers, Eskimo spear fishing, 54mm, lt bl, NM, F5...$8.00
Marx, Sports, bowler, 60mm, wht, NM, F5 ....$2.50
Marx, Sports, boxer, 60mm, wht, NM, F5 ....$3.50
Marx, Sports, figure skater, 60mm, wht, NM, F5 ....$2.50
Marx, Sports, golfer, 60mm, wht, NM, F5 ....$3.50
Marx, Sports, hockey player, 60mm, matt lt bl, NM, F5 ..$12.50
Marx, Sports, runner, 60mm, wht, NM, F5 ....$2.50
Marx, Sports, swimmer, 60mm, matt lt bl, NM, F5.............$8.50
Palmer, Creature From the Black Lagoon, 3", bl, G, H4.....$5.00
Palmer, Frankenstein, 3", yel, VG+, H4..........................$18.00
Palmer, King Kong, 3", yel, VG+, H4 ....$19.00
Palmer, Wolfman, 3", yel, VG+, H4 ....$18.00

ANIMALS

Marx, Farm Animals, #PL-0978, red-brn, set of 12 in 11 poses, NM, F5...$48.00
Marx, Farm Animals, mare & foal, red-brn, NM, F5 ....$16.50
Marx, Farm Animals, pig, red-brn, NM, F5.......................$7.50
Marx, Prehistoric Dinosaurs, #PL-0755, lt gr, set of 5 in 3 poses, NM, F5 ....$22.00
Marx, Prehistoric Dinosaurs, #PL-0755, marbled gray, set of 6 in 4 poses, NM, F5 ....$45.00
Marx, Prehistoric Dinosaurs, #PL-0977, gray, set of 8 in different poses, NM, F5 ....$75.00
Marx, Prehistoric Dinosaurs, Allosaurus, gray, NM, F5 ......$3.50
Marx, Prehistoric Dinosaurs, Anklyosaurus, brn, NM, F5...$12.50
Marx, Prehistoric Dinosaurs, Dimetrodon, lt gr, NM, F5....$6.50
Marx, Prehistoric Dinosaurs, Dimetrodon, red-brn, NM, F5 ..$12.50
Marx, Prehistoric Dinosaurs, Kronosaurus, lt gr, NM, F5 .$14.50
Marx, Prehistoric Dinosaurs, Moschops, red-brn, NM, F5.$18.50
Marx, Prehistoric Dinosaurs, Parasaurolophus, gray, NM, F5 ..$18.50
Marx, Prehistoric Dinosaurs, Parasaurolophus, lt gr, NM, F5...$18.50
Marx, Prehistoric Dinosaurs, Plateosaurus, brn, NM, F5 ..$12.50
Marx, Prehistoric Dinosaurs, Plateosaurus, marbled gray, NM, F5 ....$9.50
Marx, Prehistoric Dinosaurs, Stegosaurus, lt gr, NM, F5.....$6.50
Marx, Prehistoric Dinosaurs, Struthiomimus, lt gr, NM, F5 ...$18.50
Marx, Prehistoric Dinosaurs, Styracosaurus, lt gray, NM, F5..$12.50
Marx, Prehistoric Dinosaurs, Triceratops, lt gray, NM, F5 .$7.50
Marx, Prehistoric Dinosaurs, Tyrannosaurus Rex, brn, sleek pose, NM, F5 ....$9.50
Marx, Prize Livestock, Ayrshire cow, cream, NM, F5 ....$8.50
Marx, Prize Livestock, Clydesdale, tan, NM, F5 ....$5.50
Marx, Prize Livestock, Merino ewe, tan, NM, F5 ....$6.50
Marx, Rodeo, horse, rearing, 60mm, cream, NM, F5 ....$20.00
Marx, Rodeo, horse, rearing, 60mm, gray, NM, F5 ....$6.00
Marx, Rodeo, horse, rearing, 60mm, red-brn, NM, F5........$6.00
Marx, Western, bucking bronco, 60mm, cream, NM, F5 .$22.00

Marx, Western, horse, 60mm, red-brn, EX, F5...................$8.50

Marx, Western, longhorn steer, 54mm, red-brn, skinny style, NM, F5..$14.00

Marx, Western, longhorn steer, 60mm, red-brn, chubby style, NM, F5...$8.50

Marx, Wild Animals, alligator, red-brn, NM, F5 ....$3.50

Marx, Wild Animals, bobcat, tan or matt cream, NM, F5, ea..$3.50

Marx, Wild Animals, giraffe, beige, NM, F5....................$14.50

Marx, Wild Animals, grizzly bear, brn, NM, F5 ....$10.00

Marx, Wild Animals, kangaroo, beige, NM, F5...............$16.50

Marx, Wild Animals, ostrich, matt tan, NM, F5 ....$6.50

Marx, Wild Animals, tiger, beige, NM, F5.....................$16.50

Marx, Wildlife, bear, 60mm, brn, NM, F5 ....$6.50

Marx, Wildlife, giraffe, 4", beige, NM, F5 ....$14.50

Marx, Wildlife, lion, 54mm, gray, NM, F5......................$9.50

Marx, Wildlife, tiger, 60mm, red-brn, NM, F5...................$6.50

CAMPUS CUTIES AND AMERICAN BEAUTIES

Marx, Campus Cuties, Lazy Afternoon, Lodge Party, and Stormy Weather, M, $8.00 each.

Marx, Campus Cuties, Dinner for Two, M.........................$8.00

Marx, Campus Cuties, Nighty Night, M $8.00

Marx, Campus Cuties, On the Beach, M $8.00

Marx, Campus Cuties, On the Town, M $8.00

Marx, Campus Cuties, Shoppin Anyone, M $8.00

Marx, Campus Cuties, Shoppin Alone, M $8.00

COMIC, DISNEY, AND NURSERY CHARACTERS

Marx, Disney, Donald Duck, 6", NM, F5 ....$8.00

Marx, Disney, Minnie Mouse, 6", NM, F5 ....$10.00

Marx, Disney, Peter Pan, 6", NM, F5 ....$12.50

Marx, Disney, Snow White, 6", cobalt, NM, F5 ....$5.00

Marx, Disneykins, Alice in Wonderland, NM, F5...........$12.50

Marx, Disneykings, Goofy and Donald, MIB, each from $15.00 to $20.00. (Photo courtesy June Moon)

Marx, Disneykin Play Set, complete, MIB, $150.00.
(Photo courtesy Michael Stern)

Marx, Disneykins, Bambi, NM, F5 ....$10.00

Marx, Disneykins, Brer Rabbit, NM, F5............................$15.00

Marx, Disneykins, Captain Hook, NM, F5 ....$15.00

Marx, Disneykins, Daisy Duck, NM, F5 ....$8.50

Marx, Disneykins, Dewey Duck, NM, F5 ....$8.50

Marx, Disneykins, Donald Duck, NM, F5 ....$8.50

Marx, Disneykins, Dumbo, NM, F5..................................$10.00

Marx, Disneykins, Dumbo Ringmaster, NM, F5 ....$12.50

Marx, Disneykins, Geppetto, NM, F5................................$12.50

Marx, Disneykins, Goofy, NM, F5....................................$8.50

Marx, Disneykins, Grumpy Dwarf, NM, F5 ....$12.50

Marx, Disneykins, Jiminy Cricket, NM, F5.......................$12.50

Marx, Disneykins, Joe Carioca, NM, F5............................$12.50

Marx, Disneykins, Mickey Mouse, NM, F5.......................$10.00

Marx, Disneykins, Minnie Mouse, NM, F5 ....$8.50

Marx, Disneykins, Monty Mouse, NM, F5 ....$8.50

Marx, Disneykins, Panchito, NM, F5 ....$12.50

Marx, Disneykins, Pecos Bill, NM, F5 ....$8.50

Marx, Disneykins, Peter Pan, NM, F5 ....$15.00

Marx, Disneykins, Pinocchio, NM, F5...............................$12.50

Marx, Disneykins, Sleepy Dwarf, NM, F5 ....$8.50

Marx, Disneykins, Snow White, NM, F5...........................$8.50

Marx, Disneykins, Thumper Rabbit, NM, F5....................$10.00

Marx, Disneykins, Timothy Mouse, NM, F5.....................$12.50

Marx, Li'l Abner, 60mm, lt bl, NM, F5.............................$12.50

Marx, Nursery Rhymes, Humpty Dumpty, 60mm, matt gr, NM, F5 ....$12.50

Marx, Nursery Rhymes, Jack & Jill, 60mm, pk, EX, F5 ....$10.00

Marx, Nursery Rhymes, Jack Be Nimble, 60mm, pk, EX, F5.$10.00

Marx, Nursery Rhymes, Little Bo Peep, 60mm, pk, EX, F5 ...$10.00

Marx, Nursery Rhymes, Little Boy Blue, 60mm, pk, EX, F5 .$8.50

Marx, Nursery Rhymes, Little Miss Muffet, pk, NM, F5 .....$12.50

Marx, Nursery Rhymes, Little Red Riding Hood, 60mm, pk, NM, F5..$10.00

Marx, Nursery Rhymes, Mary Had a Little Lamb, 60mm, pk, NM, F5..$10.00

Marx, Tom & Jerry, 4" & 6", NM, F5, pr.........................$55.00

Marx, TV Tinykins, Flintstones, any character, 35mm, hand-pnt, NMIB, ea...$30.00

Marx, TV Tinykins, Flintstones, any character, 35mm, hand-pnt, NM, ea from $15 to..................................$20.00

Marx, TV Tinykins, Huckleberry Hound, Mr Jinx or Dixie, 35mm, hand-pnt, NM, F5, ea from $20 to.................$25.00

Marx, TV Tinykins, Quick Draw McGraw, Augie Doggie or Snooper Cat, 35mm, hand-pnt, NM, F5, ea from $15 to.................$20.00

Marx, TV Tinykins, Yogi Bear, Cindy Bear, Boo Boo or Ranger Smith, 35mm, hand-pnt, NM, F5, ea.........................$14.50

FAMOUS PEOPLE AND CIVILIANS

Marx, Civilians & Workmen, chauffer, 54mm, cream, MIP, F5..$3.00

Marx, Civilians & Workmen, race track pit crewman crouching, 54mm, cream, NM, F5...$10.00

Marx, Civilians & Workmen, race track pit crewman w/binoculars, 54mm, cream, NM, F5 ....$10.00

Marx, Civilians & Workmen, railroad station hobo, 45mm, cream, NM, F5 ....$4.50

Marx, Civilians & Workmen, railroad station people, 45mm, cream, set of 5, NM, F5 ....$20.00

Marx, Civilians & Workmen, railroad station worker w/oil can, 45mm, cream, NM, F5 ....$4.50

Marx, Civilians & Workmen, skin diver & accessories, 54mm, lt bl, NM, F5...$38.00

Marx, International VIPs, Duke of Edinburgh, 60mm, wht, NM, F5 ....$32.00

Marx, International VIPs, Prince Charles, 60mm, wht, NM, F5 ....$20.00

Marx, International VIPs, Princess Anne, 60mm, wht, NM, F5 ....$20.00

Marx, International VIPs, Princess Margaret, 60mm, wht, NM, F5 ....$20.00

Marx, International VIPs, Queen Elizabeth II, 60mm, wht, NM, F5 ....$30.00

Marx, US Presidents, Arthur, 60mm, NM, F5 ....$2.00

Marx, US Presidents, Buchanan, 60mm, NM, F5 ....$3.50

Marx, US Presidents, Johnson, 60mm, NM, F5 ....$4.50

Marx, US Presidents, Lincoln, 60mm, NM, F5 ....$5.50

Marx, US Presidents, Monroe, 60mm, NM, F5...................$3.50

Marx, US Presidents, Wilson, 60mm, NM, F5 ....$3.50

MILITARY AND WARRIORS

Marx, American Heroes, Admiral Dewey, 60mm, wht, NM, F5..$22.00

Marx, American Heroes, Admiral Radford, 60mm, wht, NM, F5 ....$20.00

Marx, American Heroes, Commander Perry, 60mm, wht, NM, F5 ....$38.00

Marx, American Heroes, General Bradley, 60mm, wht, NM, F5 ....$15.00

Marx, American Heroes, General Grant, 60mm, wht, NM, F5 ....$25.00

Marx, American Heroes, General Jackson, 60mm, wht, NM, F5 ....$28.00

Marx, American Heroes, General Lee, 60mm, wht, NM, F5 ....$28.00

Marx, American Heroes, General Patton, 60mm, ivory, NM, F5..$25.00

Marx, American Heroes, General Ridgeway, 60mm, wht, NM, F5 ....$16.00

Marx, American Heroes, General Sheridan, 60mm, wht, NM, F5 ....$35.00

Marx, American Heroes, General Taylor, wht, NM, F5 ...$32.00

Marx, American Revolution, minuteman walking w/musket, 60mm, cream, NM, F5 ....$6.50

Marx, American Revolution, rider on horse, 54mm, lt bl, NM, F5 ....$18.50

Marx, American Revolution, soldiers, 54mm, lt bl, set of 12 in 9 poses, NM, F5 ....$75.00

Marx, Ancient & Medieval Warriors, caveman w/club raised, brn, 6", NM, F5 ....$14.50

Marx, Ancient & Medieval Warriors, knight on guard w/sword & shield, 6", silver, NM, F5 ....$7.50

Marx, Ancient & Medieval Warriors, knight pointing & resting shield, 6", silver, NM, F5 ....$12.50

Marx, Ancient & Medieval Warriors, knight w/axe overhead, 6", silver, NM, F5 ....$8.50

Marx, Ancient & Medieval Warriors, knight w/mace overhead, 6", silver, NM, F5 ....$12.50

Marx, Ancient & Medieval Warriors, knight w/sword overhead, 6", silver, NM, F5 ....$8.50

Marx, Ancient & Medieval Warriors, Viking w/club raised, 6", lt gr, NM, F5 ....$20.00

Marx, Goldmarx Men of Battle, Egyptian w/club & shield raised, 6", NM, F5 ....$34.00

Marx, Goldmarx Men of Battle, knight w/mace & shield, 6", NM, F5 ....$30.00

Marx, Goldmarx Men of Battle, Roman Maximus w/sword & shield, 6", NM, F5 ....$24.00

Marx, Goldmarx Men of Battle, Roman w/sword & shield, 6", NM, F5 ....$26.00

Marx, Goldmarx Men of Battle, Roman w/whip & sword, 6", NM, F5 ....$30.00

Marx, Goldmarx Men of Battle, Viking w/spear & shield, 6", NM, F5 ....$32.00

Marx, Warriors of the World, Cadets; James Henry marching w/rifle, NMIB, F5 ....$22.00

Marx, Warriors of the World, Cadets; Peter Mayes marching w/sword, 60mm, NMIB, F5 ....$22.00

Marx, Warriors of the World, War of 1812; Sailors; aiming rifle, 60mm, NM, F5..$15.00

Marx, Warriors of the World, War of 1812; Sailors; w/cannon swab & cutlass, 60mm, NM, F5 ....$15.00

Marx, Warriors of the World, War of 1812; Sailors; w/telescope, 60mm, NM, F5..$25.00

Marx, Warriors of the World, Confederate Soldiers; Gatt Random loading rifle, 60mm, NM, F5 ....$12.00

Marx, Warriors of the World, Confederate Soldiers; General Longstreet at attention, 60mm, NM, F5 ....$10.00

Marx, Warriors of the World, Confederate Soldiers; Samuel Jackson standing w/cannon swab, 60mm, NM, F5.....$14.00

Marx, Warriors of the World, Korean War Soldiers; J DuBois, 60mm, NMIB, F5 ....$30.00

Marx, Warriors of the World, Korean War Soldiers; W Flanagan, 60mm, NMIB, F5 ....$30.00

Marx, Warriors of the World, Korean War Soldiers; D McKenzie of Canada, 60mm, NM, F5 ....$25.00

Marx, Warriors of the World, Korean War; US Army Soldier-Tom Gabriel, 60mm, NM, F5............................$25.00

Marx, Warriors of the World, Korean War; US Navy Soldier Wally Elson, 60mm, NM, F5 ....$25.00

Marx, Warriors of the World, Mexican War; A Yanez w/pistol, 60mm, NMIB, F5 ....$38.00

Marx, Warriors of the World, Mexican War; F Ruiz marching w/rifle, 60mm, NMIB, F5 ....$32.00

Marx, Warriors of the World, Mexican War; J Abamillo w/rifle, 60mm, NMIB, F5 ....$34.00

Marx, Warriors of the World, Mexican War; US Soldier C Merritt marching w/rifle, 60mm, NMIB, F5 ....$15.00

Marx, Warriors of the World, Mexican War; US Soldier J Costair marching w/rifle, 60mm, NMIB, F5 ....$15.00

Marx, Warriors of the World, Mexican War; US Soldier marching w/rifle, 60mm, NM, F5 ....$10.00

Marx, Warriors of the World, Pirates; Captain Cobham w/hands on belt, 60mm, NMIB, F5 ....$26.00

Marx, Warriors of the World, Pirates; Captain Flood lunging w/cutlass, 60mm, NMIB, F5 ....$26.00

Marx, Warriors of the World, Pirates; Thomas Veale w/shovel, 60mm, NMIB, F5 ....$26.00

Marx, Warriors of the World, Revolutionary War; American fife player J Wilson, 60mm, NMIB, F5 ....$22.00

Marx, Warriors of the World, Revolutionary War; American minuteman R Jayes, 60mm, NMIB, F5 ....$22.00

Marx, Warriors of the World, Revolutionary War; American officer Richard Travis w/sword, 60mm, NMIB, F5 ....$25.00

Marx, Warriors of the World, Revolutionary War; British cannoneer John Brown, 60mm, NMIB, F5 ....$38.00

Marx, Warriors of the World, Revolutionary War; British soldier Horace Swire kneeling w/rifle, 60mm, NMIB, F5......$36.00

Marx, Warriors of the World, Revolutionary War; British soldier Jos Shipman w/sword up, 60mm, NMIB, F5 ....$42.00

Marx, Warriors of the World, Revolutionary War; British solider R Ellis w/rifle at waist, 60mm, NMIB, F5...................$36.00

Marx, Warriors of the World, Romans; Gaius w/sword & shield, 60mm, NMIB, F5 ....$25.00

Marx, Warriors of the World, Romans; Marius w/sword, 60mm, NMIB, F5 ....$25.00

Marx, Warriors of the World, Romans; Maximus w/sword raised, 60mm, NM, F5.......................................$12.00

Marx, Warriors of the World, Romans; Septimus Pius w/spear & shield, 60mm, NMIB, F5 ....$26.00

Marx, Warriors of the World, Romans; Tiberius w/sword & shield, 60mm, NMIB, F5 ....$18.50

Marx, Warriors of the World, Spanish-American Soldiers; L Homer running w/rifle, 60mm, NMIB, F5 ....$18.50

Marx, Warriors of the World, Spanish-American Soldiers; L Manley marching w/rifle, 60mm, NMIB, F5 ....$25.00

Marx, Warriors of the World, Spanish-American Soldiers; Sgt Tad Carter w/sword, 60mm, NMIB, F5 ....$25.00

Marx, Warriors of the World, Union Soldiers; Bill Mason blowing bugle, NM, F5 ....$10.00

Marx, Warriors of the World, Union Soldiers; Harry Dugan kneeling w/pistol, 60mm, NM, F5 ....$10.00

Marx, Warriors of the World, Union Soldiers; Harry Dugan kneeling w/pistol, 60mm, NMIB, F5 ....$20.00

Marx, Warriors of the World, Union Soldiers; Herb Tanner running w/rifle, 60mm, NMIB, F5 ....$16.00

Marx, Warriors of the World, Union Soldiers; Mike Burns aiming rifle, 60mm, NMIB, F5 ....$22.00

Marx, Warriors of the World, US Combat Soldiers; C Hamilton in gas mask, 60mm, NMIB, F5 ....$18.00

Marx, Warriors of the World, US Combat Soldiers; Charley Hamilton in gas mask, 60mm, NM, F5 ....$10.00

Marx, Warriors of the World, US Combat Soldiers; Harry Byrd prone w/rifle, 60mm, NMIB, F5 ....$25.00

Marx, Warriors of the World, US Combat Soldiers; Harry Byrd prone w/rifle, 60mm, NM, F5 ....$12.00

Marx, Warriors of the World, Vikings; Bjorni advancing w/spear raised, 60mm, NM, F5 ....$12.00

Marx, Warriors of the World, Vikings; Eric the Red w/club, 60mm, NMIB, F5..$18.50

Marx, Warriors of the World, Vikings; Gustaf w/spear & shield, 60mm, NMIB, F5 ....$28.00

Marx, Warriors of the World, Vikings; Gustaf w/spear & shield, 60mm, NM, F5..$12.00

Marx, Warriors of the World, Vikings; Haakon aiming bow, 60mm, NMIB, F5 ....$22.50

Marx, Warriors of the World, Vikings; Ketil attacking w/axe & shield, 60mm, NMIB, F5 ....$25.00

Marx, Warriors of the World, Vikings; Leif Ericsson w/sword & winged helmet, 60mm, NMIB, F5 ....$24.00

Marx, Warriors of the World, War of 1812 Sailors; D Pierce aiming rifle, 60mm, NMIB, F5 ....$25.00

Marx, Warriors of the World, War of 1812 Sailors; J St George w/cutlass, 60mm, NMIB, F5 ....$25.00

Marx, Warriors of the World, War of 1812 Sailors; Tom O'Hara aiming rifle, 60mm, NMIB, F5 ....$25.00

Marx, Warriors of the World, War of 1812 Soldiers; Ben Smith w/telescope, 60mm, NMIB, F5 ....$25.00

Marx, Warriors of the World, WWI; E Hoffman throwing grenade, 60mm, NMIB, F5 ....$38.00

Marx, Warriors of the World, WWI; French soldier Andre Tredier w/binoculars, 60mm, NM, F5 ....$10.00

Marx, Warriors of the World, WWI; French soldier Maurice Valery aiming rifle, 60mm, NM, F5 ....$18.00

Marx, Warriors of the World, WWI; German officer Joseph Schnelling w/binoculars, 60mm, NMIB, F5 ....$15.00

Marx, Warriors of the World, WWI; German soldier Friedrich Baden goose-stepping, 60mm, NMIB, F5 ....$38.00

Marx, Warriors of the World, WWI; German soldier H Ehlers charging w/bayonet, 60mm, NMIB, F5 ....$38.00

Marx, Warriors of the World, WWI; German soldier M Hertling kneeling, 60mm, NMIB, F5 ....$38.00

Marx, Warriors of the World, WWII; German soldier Albert Galland advancing w/bayonet, 60mm, NM, F5 ....$18.00

Marx, Warriors of the World, WWII Marines; C Condon at parade rest, 60mm, NMIB, F5 ....$15.00

Marx, Warriors of the World, WWII Marines; S Schultz marching w/rifle, NMIB, F5..$15.00

Marx, Warriors of the World, WWII; British soldier Edward Bartholomew running w/pistol, 60mm, NM, F5 ....$20.00

Marx, Warriors of the World, WWII; British soldier Eugene Black running w/rifle, 60mm, NMIB, F5....................$38.00

Marx, Warriors of the World, WWII; British soldier Eugene Black running w/bayonet, 60mm, NM, F5 ....$20.00

Marx, Warriors of the World, WWII; British soldier Robert Skinner aiming bayonet, 60mm, NM, F5...................$20.00

Marx, Warriors of the World, WWII; British soldier Victor Robertson marching w/rifle, 60mm, NM, F5 ....$20.00

Marx, Warriors of the World, WWII; G Dempsey standing at attention, 60mm, NM, F5 ....$10.00

Marx, Warriors of the World, WWII; German soldier Al Falland advancing w/rifle, 60mm, NMIB, F5 ....$32.00

Marx, Warriors of the World, WWII; German soldier Fritz Kuhn walking w/slung rifle, 60mm, NMIB, F5 ....$30.00

Marx, Warriors of the World, WWII; German soldier Fritz Kuhn walking w/slung rifle, 60mm, NM, F5 ....$18.00

Marx, Warriors of the World, WWII; German soldier Otto Schroeder running w/ammo box, 60mm, NMIB, F5..$30.00

Marx, Warriors of the World, WWII; German soldier Otto Schroeder running w/ammo box, 60mm, NM, F5 .....$18.00

Marx, Warriors of the World, WWII; German soldier Rudolf Ulbricht standing at attention, 60mm, NM, F5.........$16.00

Marx, Warriors of the World, WWII; German soldier Walt Praum standing at attention w/rifle, 60mm, NM, F5 .$16.00

Marx, Warriors of the World, WWII; German soldier Walter Hess throwing grenade, 60mm, NMIB, F5 ....$32.00

Marx, Warriors of the World, WWII; German soldier Walter Hess throwing grenade, 60mm, NM, F5.....................$16.00

Marx, Warriors of the World, WWII; Ken Lane marching w/rifle, 60mm, NM, F5 ....$10.00

Marx, WWII, German soldier crouched w/rifle, 6", gray, EX, F5 ....$7.50

Marx, WWII, German soldier kneeling w/rifle, gray, 6", EX, F5 ....$4.50

Marx, WWII, German soldier standing w/rifle, 6", gray, EX, F5 .$5.50

Marx, WWII, German soldier throwing grenade, 6", gray, NM, F5...$9.50

Marx, WWII, Japanese officer pointing, 6", caramel, EX, F5 ..$6.50

Marx, WWII, Japanese soldier advancing w/bayonet, 6", caramel, EX, F5 ....$6.50

Marx, WWII, Japanese soldier aiming rifle, 6", caramel, NM, F5 ....$12.50

Marx, WWII, Japanese soldier running w/machete, 6", caramel, EX, F5 ....$6.50

Marx, WWII, Marine advancing w/bayonet, 6", waxy gr, EX, F5 ....$2.50

Marx, WWII, Marine running w/carbine rifle, waxy gr, NM, F5 ....$5.50

Marx, WWII, Marine throwing grenade, 6", waxy gr, EX, F5 .$3.50

Marx, WWII, Russian aiming rifle, 6", mint gr, NM, F5 ..$14.50

Marx, WWII, Russian throwing grenade, 6", mint gr, EX, F5 .$7.50

Marx, WWII, Russian w/rifle overhead, 6", mint gr, EX, F5 ......$7.50

Marx, WWII, Russian walking w/bayonet, 6", mint gr, EX, F5..$7.50

Marx, WWII, German soldier running w/rifle slung, 6", gray, EX, F5...$7.50

Tim-Mee, soldier with large weapon, 4½", M, $4.00.

NUTTY MADS

Marx, Lost Teepee, green, NM, $25.00.

Marx, All Heart Hogan, pk w/cream swirl, NM, F5 .... $20.00
Marx, Bullpen Boo Boo, maroon, 1st issue, NM, F5 .... $35.00
Marx, Dippy the Deep Sea Diver, 1st issue, cobalt bl, EX, F5 .. $10.00
Marx, Donald the Demon, gr, NM, C10 .... $15.00
Marx, End Zone Football Player, 1st issue, dk gr, NM, F5 .. $36.00
Marx, Lost Teepee, fluorescent red, NM, F5 .... $25.00
Marx, Rocko the Champ, 1st issue, lime gr, NM, F5 .... $35.00
Marx, Suburban Sidney, dk gr, NM, F5 .... $36.00
Marx, The Thinker, fluorescent red, NM, F5 .... $25.00
Marx, Waldo the Weight Lifter, 1st issue, pk, NM, F5 ..... $25.00

WESTERN AND FRONTIER HEROES

Marx, cavalry bugler w/rifle at side, 6", steel bl, VG, F5 ..... $4.50
Marx, cowboy aiming rifle, 6", rust brn, EX, F5 .... $3.50
Marx, cowboy reaching for pistol, 6", rust brn, NM, F5 ...... $5.50
Marx, cowboy w/2 pistols drawn, 6", rust brn, NM, F5 .... $5.50

Marx, cowboy with rifle and cowboy with lariat, M, ea from $5.00 to $10.00.

Marx, Indian brave throwing spear, 6", light orange, NM, $6.50.

Marx, Famous Americans, Buffalo Bill, 60mm, beige, NM, F5 .... $25.00
Marx, Famous Americans, Davy Crockett, 60mm, gray, scarce, NM, F5 .... $32.00
Marx, Famous Americans, General Custer, 60mm, beige, NM, F5 .... $18.00
Marx, Indian brave aiming bow, 6", rust brn, NM, F5 .... $4.50
Marx, Indian brave attacking w/club & spear, 6", lt orange, NM, F5 .... $5.50
Marx, Indian brave running w/tomahawk & rifle, 6", NM, F5 .. $6.50
Marx, Indian brave w/club & spear, 6", lt orange, EX, F5 ... $3.50
Marx, Indian chief running w/tomahawk & knife, 6", lt orange, EX, F5 .... $3.50
Marx, Indian chief w/spear & shield, 6", lt orange, NM, F5.. $5.50
Marx, Western Characters, Dale Evans, 54mm, cream, NM, F5 .... $5.00
Marx, Western Characters, Lucas McCain, 54mm, cream, NM .$45.00
Marx, Western Characters, Mark McCain, 54mm, cream, NM.. $35.00
Marx, Western Characters, Pat Brady, 54mm, cream, NM, F5 .... $5.00
Marx, Western Characters, Roy Rogers, 54mm, cream, NM, F5 .... $5.00

Plastic Toys

During the 1940s and into the '60s, plastic was often the material of choice for consumer goods ranging from dinnerware and kitchenware items to jewelry and even high-heel shoes. Toy companies used brightly colored plastic to produce cars, dolls, pull toys, banks, games, and thousands of other types of products. Of the more imaginative toys, those that have survived in good collectible condition are beginning to attract a considerable amount of interest, especially items made by major companies.

Chicken on Cart Pull Toy, Ideal, 1950, chicken pecks for food when pulled, 4½", EX, $25.00. (Photo courtesy Linda Basher)

Bowser Wowser Spaniel, Arrow, 1962, fur & satin ears, eyes open & close, w/squeaker, 20", EX $15.00

Delivery Van, Ideal, 1950s, gr, yel & red w/rubber tires, 5", EX $20.00

Fix-It Truck, Ideal, 1951, bl & red, 8", EX $30.00

Kitten, Arrow, 1960, eyes open & close, w/squeaker, 5", EX..$15.00

Li'l Beep Bus, Arrow, 1965, beeps when squeezed, w/pull string, 11", EX $20.00

Motorcycle Cop, Renwal, 1953, red & yel w/bl figure, 9", EX .$125.00

Motorcycle Cop, Renwal, 1953, yel & bl w/red figure, 4", EX ...$75.00

Motorcycle w/Sidecar, Nosco, 1950s, w/policeman figures, red, yel & bl, 5½", EX $125.00

Motorcycle w/Sidecar, Renwal, 1950s, w/passenger, yel, bl & red, 5", EX..$125.00

Roadster, Ideal, 1950, red, 9", EX......................$15.00

Scoop Loader, Ideal, 1950, bl, red & yel w/rubber tires, 8", EX $20.00

Taxi Cab Assortment, Hubley, complete w/3 cars, parking meter & 2 signs, rare, MIB..$575.00

Terrier, Arrow, 1960, eyes open & close, w/squeaker, 9", EX ..$15.00

Truck, Lapin, 1955, yel w/gray wheels, 4½", EX $8.00

Plasticville

From the 1940s through the '60s, Bachmann Brothers produced plastic accessories for train layouts such as buildings, fences, trees, and animals. Buildings often included several smaller pieces — for instance, ladders, railings, windsocks, etc. — everything you could ever need to play out just about any scenario. Beware of reissues.

Advisor: Gary Mosholder, Gary's Trains (G1).

#AD-4 Airport Administration Building, wht sides, bl roof, G1.$55.00

#AP-1 Airport Hangar, EX (EX box), G1.......................$25.00

#BK-1 Bank, EX (EX box), G1...................................$30.00

#BK-1 Bank, gray sides, gr roof, G1............................$30.00

#BN-1 Barn, red roof, EX (EX box), G1 ....$15.00

#BR-2 Trestle Bridge, G1 ....$18.00

#CC-8 Church, EX (EX box), G1 ....$15.00

#CC-9 Church, EX (EX box), G1 ....$15.00

#DE-7 Diner, EX (EX box), G1..................................$20.00

#DH-2 Hardware/Pharmacy, G1................................$18.00

#FB-1 Frosty Bar, yel sides, wht roof, G1...................$15.00

#FG-12 Picket Fence, EX (EX box), G1 ....$15.00

#GO-2 Gas Station (sm), wht sides, red roof, wht insert, G1...$15.00

#GO-3 Gas Station (lg), w/Plasticville logo & pumps, G1...$25.00

#HS-6 Hospital, w/furniture, EX (G box), G1 ....$25.00

#LC-2 Log Cabin, w/chimney & fence, EX (G box), G1 .$22.00

#LH-4 Two-Story Colonial House, wht w/gr roof & trim, EX (G box), G1...$20.00

#LM-3 Freight Station Kit, gr roof, brn platform, EX (G box), G1...$15.00

#MH-2 New England Rancher, wht w/yel trim & brn roof, EX (G box), G1...$18.00

#ON-5 Outdoor Necessities, G1 ....$45.00

#PD-3 Police Station, lt gray, EX (EX box), G1 ....$20.00

#PH-1 Town Hall, EX (EX box), G1 ....$35.00

#PO-1 Post Office, gray front & roof, G1....................$18.00

#RH-1 Ranch House, yel w/wht roof, EX (EX box), G1...$18.00

#SC-4 School, EX (EX box), G1 ....$20.00

#SG-2 Signal Bridge, blk, G1..................................$10.00

#SM-6 Supermarket (sm), EX (EX box), G1 ....$15.00

#SW-2 Switch Tower, brn sides, gray roof, G1 ....$6.00

#WW-3 Wishing Well, brn, G1..................................$3.00

#YW-4 Yard Pump, brn, G1......................................$3.00

#1090 Telephone Booth, EX (EX box), G1 ....$25.00

#1302 Farm Implement Set, yel vehicles w/red trim, G1..$45.00

#1304 Crossing Signal, 2 in blister pack, G1 ....$35.00

#1305 Block Signal, G1...$10.00

#1403 Signal Bridge, EX (EX box), G1 ....$10.00

#1405 Street Signs, EX (EX box), G1 ....$15.00

#1406 Playground Equipment, EX (EX box), G1............$35.00

#1407 Watchman Shanty, brn sides, gray roof, G1.........$12.00

#1408 Windmill, lt gray, EX (EX box), G1 ....$40.00

#1502 Cape Cod House, pk, G1................................$35.00

#1502 Cape Cod House, red & wht, EX (EX box), G1 ....$15.00

#1503 Add-A-Floor, G1..$30.00

#1504 Mobile Home, wht sides, turq roof & trim, G1 ......$55.00

#1600 Church, EX (EX box), G1...............................$15.00

#1606 Animals, set of 18, EX (G box), G1 ....$15.00

#1608 School, EX (EX box), G1 ....$20.00

#1615 Water Tank, brn w/gray base, EX (EX box), G1....$15.00

#1616 Suburban Station, EX (VG box), G1 ....$12.00

#1617 Farm Buildings & Animals, G1 ....$25.00

#1618 TV Station, EX (EX box), G1 ....$40.00

#1621 Motel, w/flowers, EX (G box), G1.....................$15.00

#1622 Dairy Barn, red & gray, EX (EX box), G1 ....$15.00

#1623 Loading Pen, G1 ....$45.00

#1624 House, under construction, lt gray, G1 ....$45.00

#1625 Railroad Work Car, G1..................................$20.00

#1626 Corner Store, G1 ....$45.00

#1627 Hobo Shack, EX (EX box), G1 ....$135.00

#1629 Bungalow, wht sides, gray roof, G1..................$25.00

#1700 Colonial House, EX (EX box), G1 ....$20.00

#1703 Colonial Mansion, wht sides, red roof, G1 ....$30.00

#1803 Colonial Church, G1.....................................$20.00

#1804 Greenhouse, w/flowers, EX (EX box), G1 ....$75.00

#1805 Covered Bridge, G1......................................$25.00

#1806 Roadside Stand, w/pnt, G1.............................$30.00

#1857 Drug Store, G1..$25.00

#1900 Turnpike, G1..$65.00

#1901 Union Station, EX (EX box), G1 ....$25.00

#1904 Cathedral, EX (EX box), G1 ....$30.00

#1906 Factory, tan sides, gray roof, G1......................$35.00

#1907 Apartment House, G1....................................$55.00

#1908 Split-Level House, EX (EX box), G1 ....$25.00

#1911 Suburban Station, brn platform, EX (EX box), G1 ..$12.00

#1912 New England Ranch, G1 ....$28.00

#1918 Park Assortment, G1 ....$35.00

#1922 Two-Story House, red roof w/brn trim, tan sides, EX (orig box), G1..$20.00

#1957 Coaling Station, EX (EX box), G1......................$25.00

Playsets

Louis Marx is given credit for developing the modern-age playset and during the '50s and '60s produced hundreds of boxed sets, each with buildings, figures, and accessories. When combined with a child's imagination, they could bring any scenario alive, from the days of Ben Hur to medieval battles, through the cowboy and Indian era, and on up to Cape Canaveral. Marx's prices were kept low by mass marketing (through retail giants such as Sears and Montgomery Wards) and overseas production. But on today's market, playsets are anything but low priced; some mint-in-box examples sell for upwards of $1,000.00. Just remember that a set that shows wear or has even a few minor pieces missing quickly drops in value. The listings below are complete unless noted otherwise.

Advisors: Bob Wilson, Phoenix Toy Soldier Co. (P11); Mike and Kurt Fredericks (F4).

Adventures of Robin Hood, #4723, Marx, EX (EX box), P11 ....$450.00
Alamo #3546, Marx, 1960, NM (NM box), F5 ....$900.00
Aquaman Justice League of America, Multiple/Canada, 1967, NM (NM box), T2, from $300 to $400.00
Arctic Explorer #3702, Marx, Series 2000, 1958, EX (VG box), F5 ....$750.00

Atomic Cape Canaveral Missile Base #4528, Marx, 1959-60, MIB, F5 ....$165.00
Auto-Laundry, litho tin gas station w/car wash conveyor & 3 cars, 5x18x14", EX (EX box), A...............................$250.00
Babyland Nursery #3379, Marx, 1955, MIB, F5 ....$450.00
Batman Justice League of America, Multiple/Canada, 1967, MIB, T2, from $600 to $700.00
Battle of the Alamo #79-59091C, Marx/Sears Heritage, 1975, MIB, F5 ....$250.00
Battle of the Blue & Gray #2646, Marx, EX (VG box) ..$400.00
Battle of the Blue & Gray #4746, Marx, Series 1000, 1958, EX (EX box) $700.00
Battle of the Blue & Gray #79-59098, Marx/Sears Heritage, 1972, MIB, F5 ....$350.00
Battleground #4749, Marx, 1958, EX (EX box), F5 ....$250.00
Battleground #4752, Marx, Series 2000, 1958, EX (EX box) $350.00
Battleground #4754, Marx, 1962, NM (NM box) $365.00
Battleground #4756, Marx, 1967, NM (EX box), F5 ......$225.00
Ben Hur #4702, Marx, Series 2000, 1959-62, NM (VG box), F5 ....$1,000.00
Boy's Camp #4103, Marx, 1956, MIB, F5 ....$750.00
Cape Canaveral #2656, Marx, MIB, P11 ....$725.00
Cape Canaveral #4528, Marx, 1959-60, EX (EX box) ...$375.00

Cape Canaveral Missile Set #4526, Marx, MIB, $900.00.
(Photo courtesy Bob Wilson)

Captain Gallant of the Foreign Legion #4729, Marx, 1956, NMIB, F5 ....$1,200.00
Cattle Drive, Marx, 1972, NM (NM box), F5 ....$600.00
Civil War Centennial #5929, Marx/Sears Happi-Time, EX (EX box)...$425.00
Comanche Pass #3416, Marx, 1975, MIB, F5 ....$300.00
Cowboy & Indian Camp #3849, Marx, EX (EX box), P11 ..$375.00
Crop Duster Plane Set #0796, Marx, MIB, A.................$200.00
Daktari #3717, Marx, 1967, EX (EX+ cartoon box), F5.$750.00
Davy Crockett at the Alamo #3544, Marx, 1955, VG (VG box), F5 ....$500.00
Day in the Life of Lassie, Plas-Trix, 1956, unused, EX, A..$225.00
Desert Patrol #4174, Marx, 1967, MIB, F5 ....$400.00
Earthquake Tower Rescue, Remco, 1976, complete, rare, VG (VG box), H4 ....$130.00

Farm Irrigated Garden #6021, Marx/Sears Exclusive, 1963, MIB, F5 ....$75.00
Fighting Knights Carry-All Set #4635, Marx, 1968, MIB..$115.00
Flintstones #4672, Marx, 1961, EX (EX box), F5 ....$350.00
Flintstones #5948, Marx, 1962, MIB, F5.......................$450.00
Fort Apache #3680, Marx, 1960, EX+ (EX+ box), F5....$200.00

Fort Apache Carry-All Play Set #4685, Marx, 1968, NM (NM metal case), F5.....................................$100.00
Fort Apache Carry-All Set #4681, 1967, 1st issue, M (M metal case), F5 ....$90.00
Fort Apache Carry-All Set #4685, Marx, 1968, NM (NM metal case) $100.00
Fort Dearborn #3510, Marx, 1952, NM (NM box), F5 ..$400.00
Fort Dearborn #3514, Marx, 1953, MIB, F5 ....$350.00

Fort Apache #3681, Marx, 1973, EX (EX box), $185.00.
(Photo courtesy Bob Wilson)

Fort Apache #3686, Marx/Sears, 1975, EX (EX box), F5 ....$165.00
Fort Apache #5962, Marx/Sears Happi-Time, 1962-63, NM (NM Sears-Allstate box), F5.................................$500.00

Fort Liberty, Hong Kong, 1970, NMIB, J6, $85.00.
(Photo courtesy June Moon)

Fort Mohawk #3752, Marx, Series 1000, 1958, NM (NM box), minimum value...$850.00
Freight Terminal #5420, Marx, MIB, P11 ....$700.00
Giant Battle of the Blue & Gray #4763/4764, Marx, ca 1961, EXIB, F5 ....$1,500.00
Guid-A Traffic PFPC #32, Marx/Sears, EX, P11 ....$100.00

Gun Emplacement Assault Set, Airfix, EX (EX box), $50.00.

Gunsmoke Dodge City #4268, Marx, Series 2000, 1960, rare, MIB $2,500.00
History in the Pacific #4164, Marx, 1972, MIB, F5........$350.00
International Airport Set, Marx, MIB $450.00
Knights & Vikings Castle #4743, Marx, EX (NM box) .$250.00
Lone Ranger Ranch Set, Marx, Series 500, 1940, MIB, from $350 to...$450.00
Lone Ranger Rodeo, Marx, 1940, MIB, from $350 to $450.00
Love Boat, Multi-Toys, 1983, MIB $75.00
Marvel World, Amsco, 1975, complete, NMIB, T2 ....$150.00

Meadow Lane Farms, Ohio Art, 1960s, lithographed tin barn with plastic accessories, complete, EX (EX barn-shaped box), $75.00. (Photo courtesy Linda Baker)

Medieval Castle #4700, Marx, MIB, P11 ....$850.00
Medieval Castle Fort #4709, Marx, EX (EX box)...........$350.00
Modern Farm #3927, Marx/Sears, 1962, MIB, F5..........$275.00
Noah's Ark Miniature Play Set, Marx, NM (NM box) ..$125.00
Pipeline Set #4425, Marx/Canadian Big Inch, 1965, MIB, F5..$500.00

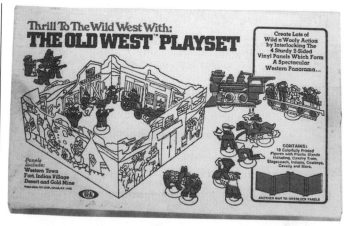

Old West Playset, Ideal, EX (EX box), from $50.00 to $75.00. (Photo courtesy Martin and Carolyn Berens)

Prehistoric Playset #3398, Marx, 1971, MIB...................$125.00
Prehistoric Times #3390, Marx, 1957, EX (G box), F5 ..$225.00
Prince Valiant Castle Fort #4706, Marx, 1954-55, EX (G box), F5 ....$375.00
Project Mercury Cape Canaveral #4524, Marx, 1962, MIB, F5 ....$300.00
Revolutionary War #3401, Marx, Series 500, NMIB, P11...$1,100.00
Rex Mars #7040, Marx, 1952-54, EX (EX box), P11...$1,200.00
Rifleman Ranch #3998, Marx, 1961, Series 1000, EX (EX box), F5 ....$750.00
Rin-Tin-Tin #3627, Marx, EX (EX box) $450.00
Rin-Tin-Tin #3658, Marx, EX (VG box) $325.00
Riverside Construction Set #48-23291, Marx/Montgomery Wards, EX (EX box), F5 ....$300.00
Robin Hood Castle Set #4719, Marx, 1956, MIB...........$450.00
Roy Rogers Fix-It Chuck Wagon & Jeep, Ideal, 1950s, EX (EX box)...$400.00
Roy Rogers Rodeo Ranch #3985, Marx, 1955, MIB, F5 .$550.00
Roy Rogers Rodeo Ranch #3990, Marx, 1950s, NM (EX box), from $200 to $300.00
Roy Rogers Western Town #4528, Marx, 1955, MIB, P11 .$1,200.00

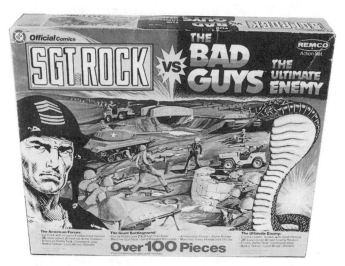

Sgt Rock Vs the Bad Guys, Remco, 1982, NMIB, J6, $85.00. (Photo courtesy June Moon)

Sons of Liberty #79-59147, Marx, 1972-74, EX (EX box), F5 .$400.00
Star Station Seven, Marx #4115, 1978, MIB, J2 ....$125.00

Super Circus #4319, Marx, 1953, EX (EX box), $600.00.

Superior Space Port, T Cohn, 1952, MIB......................$750.00
Superman Justice League of America, Multiple/Canada, 1967,
    EX (EX box), T2, from $300 to................................$400.00
Tricky Action Construction Set, Marx, MIB, P11 ....$150.00

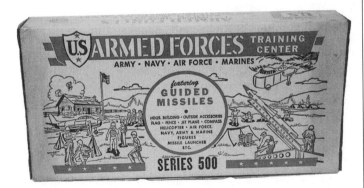

US Armed Forces Training Center, Marx, Series 500, MIB, $450.00. (Photo courtesy John Turney)

Voyage to the Bottom of the Sea Seaview Submarine Set,
    Remco, MIB, T2, from $1,000 to...........................$1,500.00
Wagon Train #4805, Marx/Sears Exclusive, Series 2000, 1960,
    MIB, minimum value $3,000.00
Western Town #4229, Marx, 1952, EX (G box), F5 ......$500.00
Western Town Miniature Town #48-24398, Marx, NM (EX
    box), P4 ....$375.00
Wizard of Oz Munchkinland, Mego, 1976, MIB, J6 ....$450.00
Wonder Woman Justice League of America, Multiple/Canada,
    1967, MIB, T2, from $500 to $700.00
Yogi Bear at Jellystone National Park #4364, Marx, 1962, MIB,
    F5 ....$475.00

Political

As far back as the 19th century, children's toys with a political message were on the market. One of the most familiar was

the 'Tammany Bank' patented by J. & E. Stevens in 1873. The
message was obvious — a coin placed in the man's hand was
deposited in his pocket, representing the kickbacks William
Tweed was suspected of pocketing when he was the head of
Tammany Hall in New York during the 1860s.

Advisors: Michael and Polly McQuillen (M11).

Agnew, Spiro; wristwatch, All American Time Co, caricature
    face, non-working, M11...$30.00
Agnew, Spiro; wristwatch, Swiss made, sq face, expandable
    metal band, non-working, M11 ....$40.00
Bush, George; figure for car window, New Waves, bobbing hand
    under 9" face, NM, M11 ....$10.00
Bush, George; monkey toy, plush monkey w/hat, gripping arms,
    Bush for President '88 on back, 4", NM, M11..............$5.00
Bush, George; squeeze doll, Santa w/Bush's face, rubber, EX,
    M11 ....$20.00
Carter, Jimmy; figure, Amy Peanut, Amy in peanut shell case,
    3", MOC, H4 ....$12.00
Carter, Jimmy; figure, plastic peanut w/Jimmy's face, w/up
    walker, EX, B5 ....$30.00
Carter, Jimmy; radio, Jimmy w/peanut body, vinyl strap, MIB,
    B5 ....$30.00
Carter, Jimmy; wristwatch, 1977, From Peanuts to President,
    caricature face, flexible metal band, M11 ....$35.00
Cleveland/Harrison, wooden block game, VG, M11......$240.00
Clinton, Bill; game, Barrel of Clintons, NM, M11 ....$12.00
Dukakis, Michael; monkey toy, plush monkey w/hat, gripping
    arms, Win in '88 on back, 4", NM, M11 ....$5.00
Eisenhower, Dwight D; harmonica, red, wht & bl plastic w/I
    Like Ike on both sides, 6", VG, M11 ....$25.00
Eisenhower, Dwight D; nodder, 1950s, pnt compo elephant
    w/I'm for Ike, 6½", NM, M11 ....$100.00

Goldwater, Barry; figure, Remco, 1964, NMIB, $35.00.

Eisenhower, Dwight D; Presidential Campaign Car, Lionel, 12", EX, M11 .... $150.00

Eisenhower, Dwight D; walking elephant, plush, battery-op, EX, M11 .... $125.00

Goldwater, Barry; board game, 1964 Presidential Election, MOC, M11 .... $30.00

Hoover, Herbert, hat, gr felt, Hoover for President on band, 5", VG, M11 .... $50.00

Johnson, Lyndon B; figure, Remco, plastic, 5", MIB, M11 .. $35.00

Kennedy, Jackie & John F; nodders, pr $275.00

Kennedy, Jackie; mask, 1960, thin plastic, EX, M11 .... $40.00

Kennedy, John F; board game, The Kennedys, Mt Rushmore caricatures on box, NMIB, M11 .... $55.00

Kennedy, John F; charm bracelet, 1963, MOC $50.00

Kennedy, John F; mask, 1960, thin plastic, EX, M11 .... $40.00

Kennedy, John F; toy boat, Empire, 1960s, soft plastic, 7", EX, M11 .... $75.00

Kennedy, Ted; doll, 1980, cloth caricature, 5½", EX, M11 ... $15.00

Lincoln, Abraham; doll, Effanbee, 1983, 17", MIB, M15 . $70.00

McKinley/Hobart, top, wood w/photos on paper label, G, M11 .... $175.00

Nixon, Richard; clicker, photo & Click w/Dick, NM, M11 .... $10.00

Nixon, Richard; dart board, Stick Dick, 11½" sq, NM, M11 ... $25.00

Nixon, Richard; doll, Tricky Dick, rubber, 5", NMOC, M11 .. $25.00

Nixon, Richard; hand puppet, 1968, plastic head w/cloth body, NM, M11 .... $35.00

Nixon, Richard; music box, 1972, w/up dancer, plays Ta Ra Ra Boom De Yea, NM, M11 .... $175.00

Uncle Sam, nodder, hand-painted composition, NM, $600.00.
(Photo courtesy David Longest)

Reagan, Ronald; voodoo doll, MIP, M11 .... $25.00

Roosevelt, Franklin D; bank, Happy Days, barrel shape, 5", EX, M11 .... $15.00

Roosevelt, Teddy; board game, Rough Riders, Parker Bros, 1900, scarce, EX (VG box), M11 .... $125.00

Roosevelt, Teddy; figure, Schoenhut, wood w/cloth outfit, complete w/rifle, cartridge belt & helmet, 9", EX, A .. $2,850.00

Roosevelt, Teddy; game, German, 1904, drop balls into Teddy's mouth, mirror back w/glass cover, 2¼" dia, VG, M11 .. $850.00

Uncle Sam, bank, ceramic, NM, S21 .... $35.00

Uncle Sam, doll, Dressel/Germany, jtd wood & compo body w/bsk head, cloth outfit w/gray felt top hat, 15", EX, A $1,500.00

Uncle Sam, figure, cloth clothes w/bl rubber hat, 8", rare, MIP, H4 .... $100.00

Washington, George & Martha; dolls, Effanbee, 1935, compo w/cloth clothes, 9", EX, A, pr $250.00

Wilson, Woodrow; puzzle, diecut profile, w/envelope, VG, M11 .... $70.00

Premiums

Those of us from the pre-boomer era remember waiting in anticipation for our silver bullet ring, secret membership kit, decoder pin, coloring book, or whatever other wonderful item we'd seen advertised in our favorite comic book or heard about on the Tom Mix show. Tom wasn't the only one to have these exciting premiums, though, just about any top character-oriented show from the 1930s through the '40s made similar offers, and even through the '50s some were still being distributed. Often they could be had free for a cereal boxtop or an Ovaltine inner seal, and if any money was involved, it was usually only a dime. Not especially durable and often made in somewhat limited amounts, few have survived to the present. Today some of these are bringing fantastic prices, but the market at present is very volatile.

Condition is very important in assessing value; items in pristine condition bring premium prices.

Advisor: Bill Campbell (C10).

Other Sources: J5.

See also Advertising; Cereal Boxes and Premiums; Pinback Buttons.

Annie Oakley, doll, Kellogg's/Canada, 1955, plastic w/cloth & vinyl outfit, 8", EX $25.00

Batman, periscope, Kellogg's, 1966, plastic w/emb logo, 12", MOC, T2, from $65 to $75.00

Batman, ring, Nestle, 1977, M, C10 .... $100.00

Buck Jones, badge, 1930s, enameled brass w/image under horseshoe, NM $125.00

Buck Jones, ring, Club, NM, C10 .... $115.00

Buck Rogers, badge, Chief Explorer, Cream of Wheat, 1935, NM, A $250.00

Buck Rogers, badge, Flight Commander, Cream of Wheat, 1935, NM, A $250.00

Buck Rogers, badge, Solar Scout, 1930s, NM, A $115.00

Buck Rogers, book, Kellogg's, 1932, 34 pgs, NM, A $175.00
Buck Rogers, figure set, Buck, Wilma & Killer Kane, Cocomalt, 1932, lead, 3", VG, A $650.00

Buck Rogers, helmet, Goodyear, 1930s, red rubber, scarce, M, A, $525.00.

Buck Rogers, helmet & rocket pistol set, Cocomalt, 1933, cb & paper, complete w/letter, NM (NM mailer), P4...$1,200.00
Buck Rogers, map of the solar system, Cocomalt, 1933, framed, EX, A $935.00
Buck Rogers, membership card, Rocket Rangers, 1938, w/letter, EX (EX mailer), C10 ....$500.00
Buck Rogers, ring, Repeller Ray, 1930s, gold-tone w/gr stone, VG, from $1,900 to $2,500.00
Buck Rogers, ring, Saturn, Post, 1940s, scarce, NM, A ..$475.00
Buck Rogers, Space Ranger Kit, Sylvania TV, 1952, complete, EX (EX envelope)...$100.00
Buffalo Bill, ring, Nabisco, 1950s, red plastic w/photo in center, EX, J5 ....$25.00
Captain Action, card game, Kool-Pops, 1967, EX (EX box)...$135.00
Captain Marvel, club button, lg, EX, C10 ....$100.00
Captain Marvel, code wheel, EX, C10............................$475.00
Captain Marvel, figure, Reed, 1944, stiff paper, 8", EX (EX envelope), T2 ....$50.00
Captain Marvel, Magic Flute, Lee-Tex, 1946, NMOC, C10..$125.00
Captain Marvel, Magic Membership card, Fawcett, 1940s, EX, T2..$100.00
Captain Marvel, Magic Whistle, 1947, litho cb, NM.....$165.00
Captain Marvel, membership kit, complete, EX, C10....$400.00
Captain Marvel, patch, glow-in-the-dark, rare, M, C10...$500.00
Captain Marvel, ring, Rocket Raider Compass, 1940s, brass w/red & blk enamel lightning design, NM, J5......$1,200.00
Captain Midnight, advertisement for Midnight Secret Squadron ring, EX, C10 ....$95.00
Captain Midnight, Detect-O-Scope (5-Way), 1941, scarce, M (orig mailing tube)...$200.00
Captain Midnight, manual, Secret Squadron, 1957, w/whistle, EX (EX envelope)...$150.00

Captain Midnight, manual, 1940, EX $85.00
Captain Midnight, Mirro-Flash Code-O-Graph, 1946, gold-colored tin & plastic, EX $75.00
Captain Midnight, ring, Flight Commander, NM, C10 .$550.00
Captain Midnight, ring, Marine Corps, 1942, scarce, M, C10..$500.00
Captain Midnight, ring, Seal, M, C10 ....$500.00
Captain Midnight, ring, Secret Compartment, scarce, EX, A $150.00
Captain Midnight, ring, Sun God, 1947, gold-tone w/red plastic stone, EX, A $1,200.00
Captain Midnight, ring, Whirlwind Whistle, 1941, scarce, M, C10 ....$450.00

Captain Midnight, Secret Squadron Manual, 1947, with whistle, EX (original envelope), A, $200.00.

Captain Video, ring, Flying Saucer, 1951, pull string to release saucer, VG, A $450.00
Captain Video, ring, Photo, 1951, gold-tone, G, A........$110.00
Captain Video, ring, Secret Seal, 1951, gold-tone w/emb initials, w/no top, EX, A $55.00
Cicso Kid, mask, Pancho, Tip Top Bread, 1953, VG+, A3..$25.00
Cicso Kid, ring, Club Member, gold-tone w/emb image of Cisco on horse, VG, A $125.00
Cisco Kid, ring, Hat, 1950s, bronze-tone, VG, A $50.00
Davy Crockett, ring, Compass, 1950s, mk Walt Disney/Davy Crockett, gold-tone, VG, A $35.00
Dick Tracy, badge, Secret Service Patrol Inspector General, Quaker, 1930-39, scarce, EX, D11 ....$500.00
Dick Tracy, badge, Secret Service Patrol Lieutenant, 1938, EX, A $85.00
Dick Tracy, badge, Secret Service Patrol Second Year Member, 1939, brass, NM, P4 ....$65.00
Dick Tracy, badge, Secret Service Patrol Sergeant, 1938, NM, J5...$75.00
Dick Tracy, badge, Secret Service Patrol/Member Girl's Division, EX, J5 ....$35.00
Dick Tracy, book, Dick Tracy the Detective & Dick Tracy Jr, Perkins, 1933, softcover, rare, NM, D11 ....$200.00
Dick Tracy, book, Secret Detective Methods & Magic Tricks, Quaker, 64 pgs, NM, D11 ....$65.00
Dick Tracy, button, Secret Service Member, Quaker, 1930-39, bl & gold, EX, D11 ....$30.00

Dick Tracy, charm, 1930s, metal figure, scarce, NM, V1 .$80.00
Dick Tracy, Crimestopper Club Kit, 1961, MIB............$100.00
Dick Tracy, decoder card, Post, 1950s, NM, D11 ....$40.00
Dick Tracy, decoder cards, gr or red, EX, T2, ea..............$15.00
Dick Tracy, hat, Official Club Member, felt, Dick Tracy label
    inside, EX, C10..$100.00
Dick Tracy, ring, Hat, 1940s, EX, J5 ....$250.00
Dick Tracy, ring, Secret Compartment, 1940s, brass, scarce,
    NM, A $200.00
Dick Tracy Jr, Crime Detection Folio, 1942, scarce, MIP
    (unopened), D11 ....$500.00
Dick Tracy Jr, tie clip, 1940, inscr Detective Agency, metal,
    scarce, EX, A..$40.00
Don Winslow, ring, Membership, M, C10 ....$1,275.00

Don Winslow, ring, Squadron of Peace, 1932, gold-tone with embossed serial number, EX, A, $475.00; Superman, ring, Pep Airplane, Kellogg's, 1940s, scarce, NM, A, $185.00.

Dragnet, badge, Dragnet Sergeant 714, brass, NM, J6 ......$25.00
Frank Buck, ring, Adventures, 1938, metal w/emb leopard's
    head, EX, from $1,200 to $1,800.00
Frank Buck, ring, Initial, 1940s, gold-tone metal w/real ivory
    center, EX, A...$385.00
G-Man, manual, Secret Operator, 1936, NM, C10............$65.00
G-Man, Pursuit Ship, 1930s, litho tin w/up, 4", EX, A...$100.00
G-Man, ring, Scarab, NM, C10 ....$1,000.00
G-Man, ring, Secret Operator, 1935, EX, A $100.00
G-Man, see also Junior G-Man
G-Men, Fingerprint Set, New York Toy & Game, 1936, com-
    plete, EX (EX pkg)...$135.00
Gabby Hayes, comic book, Quaker Oats, 1951, EX..........$35.00
Gabby Hayes, ring, Cannon, Quaker Oats, 1951, NM...$185.00
Gene Autry, Adventure Comics & Play-Fun Book, Pillsbury,
    1947, EX, A $100.00
Green Hornet, ring, Seal, 1947, gold-tone w/glow-in-the-dark
    secret compartment, EX, A $950.00
Hopalong Cassidy, ring, Face, EX, C10.............................$55.00
Hopalong Cassidy, ring, Face, rare bronze color, EX, C10 .$125.00
Howdy Doody, cutouts, Blue Bonnet Margarine, 1950s,
    w/Howdy figure & 5 hats, uncut, EX, C1 ....$75.00
Howdy Doody, mask, Howdy, Clarabell or Mr Bluster, Poll Par-
    rot Shoes, 1950s, paper, unpunched, NM, ea $125.00
Howdy Doody, puppet, Mars Candy, 1950s, paper, unpunched,
    15", NM, A...$100.00
Howdy Doody, ring, Clarabell's Horn, 1950s, EX, A......$195.00
Howdy Doody, ring, Flashlight, 1950-54, NM..............$200.00

Howdy Doody, ring, Jack-in-the-Box, 1950s, yel plastic w/red
    center, NM, A...$1,650.00
Howdy Doody, ring, Photo, 1950s, red plastic base, EX .$165.00

Howdy Doody, Snap-A-Wink, Poll Parrot Shoes, 1953, cardboard, EX, $65.00.
(Photo courtesy Jack Koch)

Jack Armstrong, brooch, gardenia, 1939, plastic, NM....$100.00
Jack Armstrong, ring, Centennial Baseball, M, C10...$1,200.00
Jack Armstrong, ring, Dragon-eye Crocodile, EX, C10 ..$800.00
Jack Armstrong, ring, Siren, EX, C10 ....$95.00
Jack Armstrong, Secret Bomb Sight, 1942, 4" wooden sight w/3
    bombs & ships to cut out, MIB, A $475.00
Jack Armstrong, Sound Effect Kit, Wheaties, 1940, complete
    w/siren, whistle, sandpaper, balloon & krinkle paper, MIB,
    A $300.00
Junior G-Man, badge, Chief Operative Melvin Purvis Junior G-
    Man Corps, eagle atop shield, EX $110.00
Junior G-Man, badge, Golden Crust Bread, eagle atop shield,
    EX $125.00
Junior G-Man, badge, Melvin Purvis Girls Division Junior G-
    Man Corps, eagle atop shield w/wings, EX................$85.00
Junior G-Man, badge, World's Fair, eagle atop shield, scarce,
    EX $185.00
Junior G-Man, badge, 6-point star, pot metal, EX $35.00
Junior G-Man, catalog, Jr G-Man Equipment, Post Toasties, EX,
    C10...$55.00
Junior G-Man, prize book, Free Prizes, Jr G-Man Corps, Post
    Toasties, 4-pg color foldout, NM, A $75.00
Junior G-Man, ring, EX, C10 ....$95.00

Little Orphan Annie, see Radio Orphan Annie

Lone Ranger, badge, horseshoe, 1930s, MOC $350.00

Lone Ranger, Bat-O-Ball, Pure Oil Co, 1940, NM, from $75 to $125.00

Lone Ranger, Black-Out Kit, Kix Cereal, 1942, rare, EX (EX envelope), V1 ....$250.00

Lone Ranger, booklet, How To Be a Lone Ranger Health & Safety Scout, Merita Bread, 1954, EX, from $65 to ...$75.00

Lone Ranger, flashlight gun, General Mills, 1952, plastic, 6", rare, EX (EX mailer), A $200.00

Lone Ranger, Lucky Coin, WXYZ Radio Station, 1941, bronze, M (orig mailer), from $250 to $350.00

Lone Ranger, manual, Cramer's Lone Ranger Safety Club, 1940, EX, from $125 to $175.00

Lone Ranger, mask, Buchan's Bread, 1940, cb, NM, from $75 to $150.00

Lone Ranger, pedometer, General Mills, 1948, M, from $75 to $100.00

Lone Ranger, pin-back button, Buchan's Bread, 1938, set of 8 w/various sayings, M, from $250 to $350.00

Lone Ranger, poster, General Mills, 1957, 6", rare, EX (EX mailer), A $200.00

Lone Ranger, ring, Army Air Corps, 1942, gold-tone w/emb emblem, w/no photos, NM, A............................$195.00

Lone Ranger, ring, Atomic Bomb, 1945, EX, C10 ....$160.00

Lone Ranger, ring, Filmstrip Saddle, 1950, w/film, NM, C10.$175.00

Lone Ranger, ring, Flashlight, 1947, complete with instructions, NM (EX mailer), A, $200.00.

Lone Ranger, ring, Marine Corps, 1940s, w/secret compartment & both photos, M, C10 ....$600.00

Lone Ranger, ring, National Defenders Lookaround, EX, C10 ....$110.00

Lone Ranger, ring, 6-Gun, EX, C10 ....$135.00

Lone Ranger, Safety Club Kit, Bond Bread, 1940s, complete, NM (NM mailer), from $175 to...............................$250.00

Lone Ranger, signal siren, Kix Cereal, 1941, complete w/portfolio, rare, M (NM mailer), from $750 to $950.00

Lone Ranger & Tonto, coloring book, Merita Lone Ranger Health & Safety Club, 1950, EX, from $75 to.........$125.00

Major Jet, Film-O-Vision, General Mills, 1954, cb, 8", EX..$20.00

Marvel Super Heroes, Merry Marvel Marching Society Kit, Marvel Comics, 1967, complete, EX (EX envelope), T2 .$200.00

Marvel Super Heroes, Official Swingin' Stationery, Marvel Comics, 1964-68, complete, EX (EX envelope), T2..$100.00

Maverick, coin, Kaiser Foil, 1950s, NM, A $25.00

Pancho, photo, Butter-Nut Bread, 1950s, w/caption, EX, A....$25.00

Radio Orphan Annie, badge, Code Captain, 1939, w/secret compartment, EX (EX mailer), V1 ....$110.00

Radio Orphan Annie, brooch, Girl Alone, M (EX mailer), C10 ....$400.00

Radio Orphan Annie, decoder, Mysto-Magic, 1939, EX ..$50.00

Radio Orphan Annie, decoder, Whirlomatic, 1942, w/instructions, NM..$225.00

Radio Orphan Annie, decoder, 1937, EX, C10...............$50.00

Radio Orphan Annie, decoder, 1940, EX, C10...............$85.00

Radio Orphan Annie, ID bracelet, 1930s, EX, J5 ....$50.00

Radio Orphan Annie, manual, Secret Guard, Quaker, 1941, NM $125.00

Radio Orphan Annie, manual, 1934, EX (EX mailer), C10..$135.00

Radio Orphan Annie, ring, Face, NM, C10 ....$100.00

Radio Orphan Annie, ring, Secret Society, 1936, scarce, EX, A...$200.00

Radio Orphan Annie, whistle, Sandy, 1930s, 3" brass slide w/3-head at top, EX, J5 ....$50.00

Red Ryder, token, 1938, target design on 1 side & Red Ryder emb on the other, 2", EX, J5 ....$25.00

Rin-Tin-Tin, mask, National Biscuit Co, 1956, cb, 8½", EX ..$15.00

Rin-Tin-Tin, ring, Magic Stamp, 1950s, gold-tone metal w/emb head image, VG, A...$245.00

Rin-Tin-Tin, ring, Photo, 4 different, EX, C10, ea...........$20.00

Rin-Tin-Tin, Wonda-Scope, EX, C10 ....$65.00

Roy Rogers, badge, Deputy Sheriff, 1950, w/secret compartment & whistle, NM..$125.00

Roy Rogers, jigsaw puzzle cards, 1956, 4 different, unpunched, NM, ea $25.00

Roy Rogers, ring, Branding Iron, 1950s, M, C10 ....$275.00

Roy Rogers, ring, Hat, 1950s, NM, C10........................$550.00

Roy Rogers, ring, Microscope, 1950s, EX, C10..............$125.00

Roy Rogers, ring, Saddle, 1950s, EX, C10.....................$325.00

Sgt Preston, distance finder, Post Cereal, 1955, complete w/instructions, M (EX mailer), A $125.00

Sgt Preston, Ore Detector, Quaker, w/instructions, MIB, C10 ....$250.00

Sgt Preston, pedometer, M (EX box), C10.....................$95.00

Sgt Preston, trail goggles, Quaker Oats, 1952, cb, EX.......$15.00

Sgt Preston, 10-in-1 Trail Kit, Quaker Oats, 1956, red plastic, complete, 6", EX $800.00

Shadow, ring, Bl Coal, 1941, scarce, NM, from $550 to...$600.00

Sky King, ring, Aztec, EX, from $650 to $800.00

Sky King, ring, Aztec, NMIB (w/papers), C10 ....$1,400.00

Sky King, ring, Magni-Glo, EX $100.00

Sky King, ring, Mystery Picture, EX..............................$900.00

Sky King, ring, TV, 1940s, complete w/4 photos, NM, C10..$250.00

Sky King, Spy Detecto Writer, 1950s, gold version, EX.$135.00

Sky King, Spy Detecto Writer, 1950s, silver version w/brass dial & backing, w/magnifier & rubber stamp, EX, J5........$85.00

Space Patrol, binoculars & magic space pictures, Ralston Purina, 1953, EX $150.00

Space Patrol, cosmic smoke gun, Ralston Purina, 1952-55, red plastic, 4½", EX $300.00

Tom Corbett Space Cadet, Squadron Kit, Kellogg's, 1951 – 52, complete, EX, $200.00. (Photo courtesy Scott Bruce)

Space Patrol, Man From Mars Totem Head, 1950, lithographed cardboard, 15", EX, $100.00. (Photo courtesy Scott Bruce)

Space Patrol, Man From Mars Totem Head, 1950, litho cb, NM (NM envelope), A $150.00
Space Patrol, Project-O-Scope, Ralston Purina, 1953, plastic, NMIB...$250.00
Space Patrol, ring, Hydrogen Ray Gun, 1950s, glow-in-the-dark, VG, A $195.00
Steve Canyon, membership card, 1959, w/place for photo, EX, T2...$25.00
Straight Arrow, bandana, 1949, w/arrow tie ring slide, EX, C10 ....$150.00
Straight Arrow, ring, Arrow, EX, C10 ....$55.00
Straight Arrow, ring, Cave Nugget, no photo, 1951, VG, A..$55.00
Straight Arrow, ring, Face, EX, C10...$95.00
Straight Arrow, target set, EX (EX box), C10 ....$150.00
Superman, comic book, Duel in Space, Kellogg's, 1955, NM, A...$100.00
Superman, Krypton Rocket, Kellogg's, 1950, plastic, complete, MIB...$285.00
Superman, membership kit, 1942, complete, NM, C10 .$400.00
Superman, pin, Junior Defense League, NM, C10.........$215.00
Superman, ring, Crusader, 1940s, silver-tone metal, EX, A $195.00
Terry & the Pirates, ring, Gold Detector, 1940s, NM, A..$100.00
Tom Corbett Space Cadet, ID bracelet, M, C10 ....$135.00
Tom Corbett Space Cadet, membership card, Rocket Light, EX, C10...$50.00
Tom Corbett Space Cadet, patch, rnd, MIP, C10 ....$75.00

Tom Corbett Space Cadett, ring, Face, 1950s, EX, J5 ....$125.00
Tom Mix, arrowhead, glow-in-the-dark, w/orig string, EX, C10...$125.00
Tom Mix, arrowhead & 6-gun, glow-in-the-dark, w/chain, etc, EX, C10 ....$145.00
Tom Mix, badge, Capt Ralston Straight Shooter, 1940s, silver w/belt buckle design & hanging spur, EX+, J5.........$100.00
Tom Mix, badge, Dobie County Sheriff, 1946, w/siren, EX, C10...$75.00
Tom Mix, badge, Ranch Boss, 1938, M $375.00
Tom Mix, badge, Straight Shooters, 1937, NM (EX mailer), C10 ....$200.00
Tom Mix, bird call/telescope, EX, C10 ....$85.00
Tom Mix, compass/magnifyer, 1930s, brass w/fold-out magnifying glass, compass on front, EX, J5 ....$50.00
Tom Mix, compass/magnifyer, 1930s, glow-in-the-dark plastic w/fold-out magnifying glass, compass on front, EX, J5...$50.00
Tom Mix, fob, gold ore, EX, C10 ....$55.00
Tom Mix, manual & 6-gun decoder, Straight Shooters, NM (EX mailer), C10...$300.00
Tom Mix, pocketknife, Straight Shooters, Ralston, NM, C10 ....$60.00
Tom Mix, ring, Circus, EX, C10.................................$65.00
Tom Mix, ring, Magnet, EX, C10 ....$125.00
Tom Mix, ring, Mystery Picture, no photo, C10 ....$125.00
Tom Mix, ring, Siren, EX, C10.................................$115.00
Tom Mix, ring, Sliding Whistle, M, C10.......................$125.00
Tom Mix, ring, Stan Hope Magic Photo, 1930s, NM $400.00
Tom Mix, ring, Straight Shooter, EX, C10....................$100.00
Tom Mix, ring, Tiger Eye, w/TV instructions, NM, C10 .$325.00
Tom Mix, ring, 1930s, advertises Marlin Guns, metal w/target design, NM, A $200.00
Tom Mix, spinner, Gook Luck, EX, C10 ....$75.00
Tom Mix, spurs, Ralston Purina, 1947, metal w/glow-in-the-dark rowels, NM (G mailer), A...$165.00
Tonto, ring, Picture, EX, C10.................................$55.00
Wyatt Earp, ring, 6-Point Star, 1958, sterling silver, EX ..$150.00
Zorro, ring, Logo, EX, C10.................................$75.00

Pressed Steel

Many companies were involved in the manufacture of pressed steel automotive toys which were often faithfully modeled after actual vehicles in production at the time they were made. Because they were so sturdy, some from as early as the 1920s have survived to the present, and those that are still in good condition are bringing very respectable prices at toy auctions around the country. Some of the better-known manufacturers are listed in other sections.

Advisors: Kerry and Judy Irvin (K5).

See also Aeronautical; Buddy L; Keystone; Marx; Pedal Cars and Other Wheeled Goods; Structo; Tonka; Wyandotte.

CARS AND BUSES

Bluebird Racer #335, Kingsbury, dk bl w/blk rubber tires, 19", G+, A $990.00

Bus, Kingsbury, clockwork, bl w/red stripe, wht rubber tires w/red hubs, 16", VG+, A $825.00

Car w/Trailer, Kingsbury, bl car, wht trailer w/bl opening door & wht window blinds, 22½", VG+, A $415.00

Chrysler Airflow, Cor Cor, clockwork w/electric headlights, gr w/NP bumpers & grille, 17", NM, A $2,300.00

Chrysler Airflow, Kingsbury, clockwork w/battery-op lights, gold w/wht rubber tires, 14", VG, A $360.00

Chrysler Airflow Convertible, Kingsbury, w/up, battery-op lights, 14", EX, A...$1,150.00

Citroen Large Rosalie Racer, France, bl w/NP grille, molded driver w/cast metal head, blk rubber tires, 17", G+, A..............$750.00

Citroen Petite Rosalie Racer, red w/NP grille, molded driver w/cast metal head, blk rubber tires, 12", VG+, A....$330.00

Coupe, Girard, battery-op lights, lt gr & orange w/cream top, blk rubber tires, 14", G, A $200.00

Coupe w/Music Box Radio, Kingsbury, clockwork w/electric headlights, beige & brown w/wht rubber tires, 13", VG, A $630.00

Golden Arrow #337, Kingsbury, metallic gold w/blk rubber tires, 21", VG+, A $715.00

Golden Arrow Racer, Kingsbury, clockwork, metallic gold w/blk rubber tires, 21", EX, A $750.00

Hillclimber Closed Touring Car, Dayton, inertia mechanism, red w/thin spoked wheels, 12", VG+, A $330.00

Hillclimber Open Car, Dayton, wood & pressed steel, inertia drive, bl w/spoked wheels, 2 CI figures, 10", G+, A..$210.00

Hillclimber Pickup Truck, Dayton, inertia mechanism, gr w/spoked wheels, w/2 red trunks, orig driver, 13½", G+, A $525.00

Hillclimber Roadster, Dayton, inertia drive mechanism, blk w/gold trim & spoked wheels, 13", G+, A $145.00

Hillclimber Roadster, Dayton, inertia-drive mechanism, dk bl w/blk rubber tires, 13", G, A $220.00

Hillclimber Tonneau, Dayton, inertia mechanism, red w/spoked wheels, 9", G, A..$120.00

Hillclimber Touring Car, Dayton, inertia wheel mechanism, lt gr, 13", VG+, A $300.00

Lincoln Touring Car, Turner, red with gold striping, 26", EX, A, $12,000.00.

Hillclimber Touring Car, Dayton, inertia wheel mechanism, red w/yel trim, 13½", VG, A $275.00

Hillclimber Yellow Cab, Dayton, inertia mechanism, blk & yel w/spoked wheels, tin driver, 10½", G, A $220.00

Junior Sightseeing Bus, friction, Wanamakers Toy Store decal, yel w/blk top, metal wheels, 26", G, A $1,200.00

Motorized Dray, Kingsbury, clockwork, bl w/yel CI spoked wheels, 10", G, A...$250.00

Roadster, Kingsbury, clockwork, lavender, blk rubber tires, electric lights, 12", VG, A $470.00

Roadster, Kingsbury, clockwork, tan & red w/wht rubber tires, 12", VG+, A $550.00

Roadster, Kingsbury, clockwork w/electric headlights, brn & red w/open rumble seat, 12½", EX, A $700.00

Roadster Convertible, Dayton, friction, gr w/blk running boards, metal disk wheels, 2 side spares, 19", G+, A.............$330.00

Rolls Royce, JEP/France, w/up, steering, differential, spring-loaded bumper, electric lights, 2 figures, 20", EX, A.............$4,180.00

Sedan, Kingsbury, clockwork, gr w/chrome detail, wht rubber tires, 14", EX, A $1,000.00

Sedan w/Boat & Trailer, Kingsbury, clockwork, orange car & trailer w/gr boat, 22", EX, A................................$1,400.00

Stutz, Wilkins, spiral spring mechanism, CI driver, 9", G, A......$210.00

Sunbeam Racer #333, Kingsbury, clockwork, red, 19", EX, A $1,700.00

FIREFIGHTING

Aerial Ladder Truck, Doepke, red w/aluminum ladders mounted on turntable, extra ladders housed in fr on body, 33", NM, A $350.00

Auto Aerial Ladder Truck, Kingsbury, red w/yel ladders, wht rubber tires, w/driver, 17", VG, A $130.00

Auto Aerial Ladder Truck, Kingsbury, wht w/red ladders, wht rubber tires, w/driver, 17", EX, A $220.00

Auto Fire Pumper, Kingsbury, clockwork, red w/wht disk wheels, red hubs, brass boiler w/silver trim, w/driver, 11", G, A........$200.00

Auto Fire Pumper, Kingsbury, clockwork, red w/yel spoke wheels, brass-look boiler w/silver trim, 10", VG+, A $300.00

Auto Fire Pumper #726, Kingsbury, clockwork, red w/wht disk wheels, brass-look boiler w/silver trim, w/driver, 9", G, A $50.00

Auto Fire Pumper #770, Kingsbury, clockwork, yel w/red spoke wheels, brass boiler w/silver trim, w/driver, 9½", G+, A..$360.00

Auto Fire Pumper Truck #750, w/CI driver, 9½", G, A $160.00

Auto Ladder Truck #736, Kingsbury, clockwork, red w/yel ladder, disk wheels, w/driver, 9", G, A......................$130.00

Auto Ladder Truck #775, Kingsbury, clockwork, wht w/red ladders & spoke wheels, w/CI driver, w/accessories, 18", G, A..$175.00

Auto Pumper Truck, Kingsbury, clockwork, red w/wht rubber tires, brass-look boiler w/silver trim, w/driver, 11", VG, A..$190.00

Fire Chief Car, Girard, clockwork w/battery-op lights, red & blk w/blk rubber tires, orig decal, 14", rstr, VG, A $220.00

Fire Chief Car, Girard, clockwork w/electric lights, red w/decals on doors, 14½", NM, A.......................................$385.00

Fire Chief Car, Hoge, clockwork w/electric headlights, red w/blk running boards, 14", NM, A......................................$450.00

Fire Chief Siren Coupe, Girard, w/up, red w/decal on door, NM $650.00

Fire House, Kingsbury, clockwork bell-ringing mechanism, red w/gr opening doors, 13x10x9", VG+, A $330.00

Fire Ladder Truck, Kingsbury, w/up, spring-loaded ladder, w/driver, 19", VG+, A...$300.00

Fire Pumper, Kingsbury, w/up, rubber tires, w/driver, 10", EX, A $275.00

Fire Station and Ladder Truck, Kingsbury, clockwork mechanism, 18½" truck, VG, A, $1,000.00.

Fire Water Tower Truck, Sturditoy, w/orig decals, 11", VG, A $1,020.00

Ladder Truck, Kingsbury, simulated upholstered open bench seat, extension ladder & 2 side ladders, 26", VG, A........$1,300.00

Ladder Truck, Victor Bonnet, clockwork, open cab w/extension ladder mounted on turntable, 16", EX, A $250.00

Pumper Truck, Kingsbury, clockwork, red open bench seat w/driver, gold-pnt boiler w/rear platform, 10½", EX, A $250.00

Pumper Truck, Kingsbury, clockwork, red w/wht side hoses, brass boiler, wht rubber tires w/red hubs, 24", G+, A ...$1,075.00

Water Tower Truck, Sturditoy, Am La France decals on sides, open bench seat, elevating water tower, 34", EX, A..$950.00

White Ladder Truck, Kelmet, open bench seat, railed body w/2 wooden ladders, 26", EX, A $1,000.00

Trucks and Vans

Ambulance, Sturditoy, open cab w/bench seat, enclosed van body w/decal, railed rear step, 27", NM, A........$12,000.00

Army Truck, Kingsbury, clockwork, blk rubber tires w/orange hubs, 11", G, A $150.00

Auto Transfer, Kingsbury, red w/yel spoke wheels, w/CI driver, 9¾", G, A $300.00

Dairy Truck, Sturditoy, cream-colored with brass filler caps and rear valves, 34", professionally restored, $4,000.00.

Delivery Truck, Metalcraft, blk w/gr van body, stenciled yel lettering on sides, disk wheels, 12", NM, A $350.00

Dump Truck, Turner, blue, black, and green with red wheels, friction flywheel, 26", EX, A, $1,100.00.

Goodrich Silvertown Tires Winch Truck, Metalcraft, red cab w/cream bed, blk rubber tires, 11½", EX, A.............$385.00

Greyhound Bus, Kingsbury, w/up, lt bl w/wht rubber tires, cut-out windows, 18½", VG, A.....................................$375.00

Heinz Delivery Truck, Metalcraft, electric headlights, wht w/NM decals, blk rubber tires, 12", EX+, A.............$500.00

Mack Dump Truck, Steelcraft, red, 25½", G, A.............$400.00

Mack Jr Army Truck, Little Jim (Steelcraft)/JC Penney, open cab w/arched cloth canopy on bed, tan, red hubs, 23", EX+, A $560.00

Sampson Dump Truck, Gendron, royal bl w/red dump, lever action, 26", EX, A..$5,000.00

Sand & Gravel Truck, Metalcraft, blk w/red dump, stenciled yel lettering on sides, disk wheels, 10½", VG, A $225.00

Shell Motor Oil Stake Truck, Metalcraft, red cab w/yel bed holding 8 oil drums, 12", EX, A...........................$1,100.00

Truck #1718, Kingsbury, clockwork, wht rubber tires, 11", VG+, A $230.00

Truck Wagon, Kingsbury, clockwork, CI spoke wheels, 14½", G, A $150.00

Oil Truck, Sturditoy, black cab with green body, red tank, 26", professionally restored, A, $1,800.00.

US Mail Truck, Sturditoy, 1920s-30s, blk & red, 25½", EX, A...$2,300.00
USA Army Truck, Sturditoy, olive gr, open bench seat, license plate stamped 420, 27", EX, A $475.00
White King Delivery Truck, Metalcraft, red w/yel open bed, disk wheels, 12", G, A...$200.00

MISCELLANEOUS

Auto Field Gun, Kingsbury, clockwork, open 4-wheeled platform w/CI driver at steering wheel, lg rear gun, 11", VG+, A..$155.00
Boy on Sled, Dayton Hillclimber, inertia wheel mechanism, 9", G+, A...$220.00
Cash Register, Buddy L, orange & red w/decals, complete w/play money, M, A...$350.00
Farm Tractor w/2-Wheeled Trailer, clockwork, gr w/blk rubber tires, red hubs, 11", EX, A $185.00
Road Tractor, Wilkins, clockwork, blk w/red canopy & rollers, blk treads, w/driver, 8", G, A...............................$130.00
Train, Hillclimber engine & tender, fly-wheel mechanism, red-orange w/gold trim & spoked wheels, 26", VG+, A...$180.00
Train, Hillclimber engine & tender, mk Double Friction Engine, blk w/gold trim & spoked wheels, 24", G, A...........$275.00
Trolley, Converse, mk City Hall Park, clockwork, orange, w/reversible seats, 16", G, A....................................$190.00

Promotional Vehicles

Miniature Model T Fords were made by Tootsietoy during the 1920s, and though they were not actually licensed by Ford, a few of these were handed out by Ford dealers to promote the new models. In 1932 Tootsietoy was contacted by Graham-Paige to produce a model of their car. These 4" Grahams were sold in boxes as sales promotions by car dealerships, and some were sold through the toy company's catalog. But it wasn't until after WWII that distribution of 1/25 scale promotional models and kits became commonplace. Early models were of cast metal, but during the 1950s, manufacturers turned to plastic. Not only was the material less costly to use, but it could be molded in the color desired, thereby saving the time and expense previously involved in painting the metal. Though the early plastic cars were prone to warp easily when exposed to heat, by the mid-'50s they had become more durable. Some were friction powered, and others held a battery-operated radio. Advertising extolling some of the model's features was often embossed on the underside. Among the toy manufacturers involved in making promotionals were National Products, Product Miniatures, AMT, MPC, and Jo-Han. Interest in '50s and '60s models is intense, and the muscle cars from the '60s and early '70s are especially collectible. The more popularity the life-size model attained, the more popular the promotional is with collectors.

Check the model for damage, warping, and amateur alterations. The original box can increase the value by as much as 30%. Jo-Han has reissued some of their 1950s and 1960s Mopar and Cadillac models as well as Chrysler's Turbine Car. These are usually priced between $20.00 and $30.00.

1953 Chevy Bel Air, bank, brn, plastic, EX+ $95.00
1955 Ford T-Bird red, chrome hubs & wht-wall stickers, EX+ $135.00
1957 Ford T-Bird, red w/blk & wht striped seat, EX.........$75.00
1959 Chrysler New Yorker, gr, EX+ $60.00
1961 Ford Hubley Wagon, wht & yel, NM $65.00
1962 Oldsmobile, MIB...$35.00
1963 Ford Galaxie XL Coupe, tan, NM $95.00
1964 Ford Fairlane, AMT, bl, 8", EX...........................$45.00
1964 Ford Falcon, wht, 2-door hardtop, EX+ $115.00
1964 Ford T-Bird Convertible, AMT, yel, friction, EX $50.00
1965 Chevy Impala, bl, 8½", EX................................$65.00
1965 Ford Mustang Fastback, red, EX $115.00
1966 Buick Riveria, tan, 8½", EX................................$45.00
1966 Ford Mustang, red, 7½", VG $75.00
1966 Pontiac GTO, silver, 2-door hardtop, NM $425.00
1967 Pontiac Firebird, red, 2-door hardtop, M $165.00
1968 Lincoln Continental, red-orange, 4-door sedan, MIB .$65.00
1968 Olds 442, red w/wht interior, MIB $115.00
1969 AMC Javelin, tan, 2-door hardtop, MIB................$95.00
1970 Ford LTD, dk bl, EX+ $85.00
1972 Chevy Flareside Pickup, med bl, MIB...................$165.00
1973 Chevy Camaro, Buccaneer Red, MIB....................$120.00
1974 Olds Cutlass, Colonial Gr, 2-door hardtop, MIB.......$40.00
1976 Dodge Dart, Vintage Red, MIB $50.00
1984 Chevy Corvette, silver, MIB...............................$20.00
1991 Chevy Camaro, blk or teal, MIB, ea......................$15.00
1993 Ford F-150, blk, MIB $20.00
1994 Dodge Viper Coupe, yel, MIB............................$25.00
1996 GMC Jimmy, blk, MIB $25.00

Pull and Push Toys

Pull and push toys from the 1800s often were made of cast iron with bells that were activated as they moved along on wheeled platforms or frames. Hide and cloth animals with glass or shoe-button eyes were also popular, and some were made of wood.
See also specific companies such as Fisher-Price.

Baby Haymaker, Animated Toy Co, litho tin tractor w/various accessories, EXIB, A $220.00

Borden's Dairy Products Horse-Drawn Wagon, Rich Toys, litho tin & wood, 18", VG, A $275.00

Boy on Wheels Pulling Wheeled Bell, pnt tin w/2 CI heart-spoke wheels, 8", G, A $1,100.00

Buffalo Bill on Platform, Fallows, pnt tin w/CI wheels, 2 buffalo rock as toy moves, Bill on horse w/rifle, 9", VG+, A...$3,630.00

Bull on Platform, Shimer, CI w/4 spoke wheels, 7", EX, A...$200.00

Buster Brown & Girl Bell Toy, CI & steel, figures on platform w/3 bells, 4 spoke wheels, 9½", G, A $330.00

Buttercup & Spareribs, Nifty, litho tin, baby & dog on 4-wheeled platform, 7½", VG (rare decorated box), A...........$1,760.00

Cable Car, 1920s, litho tin, red, wht & bl w/emb images of Santa in sleigh w/reindeer, 3½x7¼", EX+, A..........$100.00

Charlie Chaplin Bell Toy, Watrous, NP CI, 2 figures on 4-wheeled platform w/3 bells, EX, A $550.00

Clown & Poodle Bell Toy, Gong Bell, 8", VG, A $600.00

Clown Dog Bell Toy, Gong Bell, 1949, paper litho on wood figure w/4-wheeled metal base, 11", NM, from $75 to.$100.00

Cow on Platform, reddish brn & wht hide-covered w/leather ears, glass eyes, wood base, 4 sm spoke wheels, 7x9", EX, A..$330.00

Ding-Dong Bell Toy, Gong Bell, pnt CI, 9¼", VG, A...$600.00

Dog and Cat Bell Toy, NM, $1,500.00.
(Photo courtesy David Longest)

Dog on Platform Bell Toy, Am Tin, pnt tin w/CI heart-spoke wheels, bell on dog's back, 14", EX, A $825.00

Doggie Handcar Bell Toy, Gong Bell, paper litho on wood figures w/bl-pnt metal base, 14", EX.........................$100.00

Donald Duck in Boat, Chad Valley England, 1930s, paper litho on wood, glides along on 3 wheels, 12", NM, A $575.00

Donkey Bell Toy, Germany (?), cloth-covered donkey in metal harness pulling bell w/2 spoked wheels, 10", G+, A ..$90.00

Duck, Hubley, 1930s, mc CI, when pulled duck waddles & opens mouth, 9½", NM, A.......................................$3,850.00

Elephant Bell Toy, CI w/metal strap, elephant pulling bell w/2 star-spoked wheels, 7", VG, A.................................$175.00

Elephant on Platform, Am, trunk down, pnt tin, gray & blk w/red blanket, gr base, blk spoke wheels, 7x9", VG+, A....$160.00

Elephant on Wheels, Bing, mohair-covered w/shoe button eyes, felt back blanket, tin tag in ear, 9½", G, A $200.00

Felix the Cat & 2 Mice on Platform, Nifty/Pat Sullivan, litho tin, Felix lettered on body, VG, A $550.00

Felix the Cat on Scooter, Nifty/Pat Sullivan, litho tin figure on 3-wheeled scooter, name on tail, 7½", G, A...........$330.00

Fire Hand Pumper (Atlantic), pnt & stenciled tin w/daisy-spoke wheels, bl w/red pump hdl, 10", VG, A $3,850.00

Fisherman on Platform, J&E Stevens, pnt CI w/NP daisy-spoked wheels, Black man reels in fish, 8", EX, A $660.00

Goat on Platform, brn & wht hide-covered papier-mache, gold & red collar, wood base, sm CI spoke wheels, 10½", VG+, A..$415.00

Goat on Platform, dk gray & wht hide-covered wood & compo, gold & red collar, wood base, sm spoke wheels, 11½", EX, A..$635.00

Grasshopper, Hubley, CI w/2 rubber tires, 12", EX, A...$1,100.00

Grasshopper, Hubley, gr-pnt CI, w/articulated legs, 9", EX, A $770.00

Happy Hooligan, 1920s, wood, pnt figure on 4-wheeled platform, 4½x6", EX+, A $120.00

Hoop Toy, Gibbs, litho paper on wood horse in center of 2 lg wooden wheels w/metal pulling harness, 10½" dia, VG, A $415.00

Horse in Stall, papier-mache horse on wheeled platform in wooden stall w/feeding rack, pnt trim, 15½", EX, A..$330.00

Horse on Platform, Am, pnt tin, wind-blown mane & tail, wht w/red saddle, gr base, lg spoke wheels, 6" L, G+, A $550.00

Horse on Platform, Geo Brown (att), pnt & stenciled tin w/CI wheels, dapple gray w/blk mane & tail, 12", VG, A .$770.00

Horse on Platform, hide-covered w/reins, saddle & tattersall blanket, 4 sm spoked wheels, 15", EX, A $385.00

Horse on Platform, Ives, pnt CI, w/jtd legs for walking, 7", wheeled platform missing o/w EX, A $935.00

Horse on Slanted Platform Bell Toy, Gong Bell (att), pnt & stenciled tin w/CI heart-spoke wheels, 9", EX, A $2,420.00

Horse Trotting on Platform, Geo Brown, pnt tin, wht w/orange-pnt saddle, blk hooves, 8", no platform o/w EX, A ..$330.00

Horse w/Jockey on Platform, Fallows (att), pnt tin w/CI wheels, 15", EX, A..$2,090.00

Horse-Drawn Barrel Wagon, papier-mache & wood horse on wheeled platform, wood 13" wagon w/barrel ramp & 9 barrels, EX, A..$240.00

Horse-Drawn Buckboard, Hull & Stafford, pnt tin w/CI spoke wheels, wht horse, w/driver, 16", G, A $3,630.00

Horse-Drawn Buther Wagon, Am Tin, pnt & stenciled tin w/2 CI wheels, single horse, w/driver, 14½", EX, A..........$470.00

Horse-Drawn Cart, wooden horse on platform w/velvet upholstered 2-wheeled cart, 21", VG, A $250.00

Horse-Drawn Covered Wagon, Gibbs, 2 paper litho-on-wood horses pull tin & wood wagon w/CI wheels, 17", VG, A $120.00

Horse-Drawn Dump Cart, Am, pnt & stenciled tin, wht horse, 2 spoke wheels, 15½", G, A $330.00

Horse-Drawn Express Wagon, Geo Brown, pnt & stenciled tin, CI spoke wheels, 2 wht horses w/Am flag, w/driver, 18", EX, A..$1,430.00

Horse-Drawn Fine Groceries Delivery Wagon, Geo Brown, pnt & stenciled tin, CI spoke wheels, 1 horse, 11½", EX, A .$1,050.00

Horse-Drawn Sleigh on Platform, Fallows, pnt tin w/CI wheels, 2 horses rock as toy moves, 9", G+, A $3,850.00

Horse-Drawn Street Car, Am Tin, pnt tin w/CI wheels, red w/bl roof, single horse, 10", G, A $100.00

Horse-Drawn Street Car, Geo Brown, pnt & stenciled tin w/CI wheels, decorated yel w/bl roof, 2 horses, driver, 12", G, A $2,420.00

Horse-Drawn Sulky, Gibbs, paper litho on wood horse pulls metal cart w/CI spoke wheels, 7", EX, A $200.00

Horse-Drawn Surrey, pnt & stenciled tin w/CI spoke wheels, 9", G, A $230.00

Horse-Drawn Trolley, Am, pnt tin, 2 horses, spoke wheels, 9½", G+, A $525.00

Horse-Drawn Trolley, George Brown, trolley marked 8th Ave. & Central Park, red, yellow, and green, white horses, 12", D10, from $2,500.00 to $3,500.00. (Photo courtesy Dunbar Gallery)

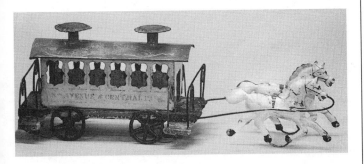

Horse-Drawn US Mail Wagon, lithographed tin, 16½", NM, A, $600.00; Horse-Drawn Milk Wagon, lithographed tin, 16", VG, A, $450.00.

Horse-Drawn Victory Fire Pumper, Fallows, pnt & stenciled tin w/CI wheels, red & blk w/tan horse, 13½", EX, A ..$2,200.00

Horse-Drawn Wagon, mohair-covered horse on platform w/4-wheeled wooden wagon, 26", VG, A $250.00

Horse-Drawn Wm Darker W Philadelphia Trolley, pnt tin, 2 horses, 25", VG+, A..$6,050.00

Horse-Drawn Yankee Notions Wagon, Geo Brown, pnt & stenciled w/CI wheels, red & blk w/2 wht horses, 19½", EX, A...$3,960.00

Horse-Drawn 2-Wheeled Gig, Geo Brown, pnt & stenciled tin, CI spoke wheels, wht horse, w/driver, 13", EX, A ..$1,320.00

Howdy Doody on Tricycle, France, wooden body w/plastic head, 9x8", EX+, A $300.00

Hygeia Ice Wagon, Converse (?), litho tin, w/single horse, 13", VG, A $300.00

Krazy Cat Chasing Mice, Nifty, litho tin figure on 4-wheeled base, 7½", EX, A $660.00

Lady on 4-Wheeled Horse, US Hardware, blk-pnt CI, eccentric front wheels impart rocking action, 6", G, A.............$75.00

Man on Fish Bell Toy, pnt CI, fisherman rocks while fish opens mouth, 5", G+, A $470.00

Mickey McGuire & Mouse on Platform, Performance Toys, pnt wood w/decals, flat jtd figures, 12", VG, A $145.00

Milk Truck, Gong Bell, lithographed tin and wood, MIB, $400.00. (Photo courtesy John Turney)

Motorcycle Rider, European (?), pnt wood articulated figure on 3-wheeled cycle, 9", EX, A..$55.00

Old Woman In Shoe, Ives, pnt CI 2-wheeled shoe w/wood & tin figure in cloth clothing, clothed bsk children, 9", EX, A..$440.00

Old Woman in Shoe, 4-wheeled tin shoe w/clothed figure, 4 clothed china children, 9", scarce version, G, A $2,970.00

Orange County Milk Wagon, Converse (?), litho tin & wood w/CI spoke wheels, 2 horses, bucolic scene atop, 18", EX, A $1,600.00

Rowing Team in Boat, Hustler, 1930s, wood w/metal arms on figures, 14", EX $125.00

Seewsaw Bell Toy, CI & steel, w/2 figures, heart-spoked wheels, 6½", G, A $275.00

Sheep on Platform, German, 1880-1910, papier-mache head, wooden legs, glass eyes, wood platform, metal wheels, 8", EX, A $690.00

Snowflake & Buttercup, litho tin, baby & dog on 4-wheeled platform, 7½", EX, A $600.00

Snowflake & Swipes, litho tin, Black boy walking dog w/toothache on 4-wheeled base, 7½", EX, A $1,100.00

Patriotic Boy Bell Ringer, Althof Bergmann, 1880, hand-painted tin boy mounted on two wheels pulling large bell, 8½", EX, A, $4,950.00.

Springing Dog Bell Toy, Gong Bell, pnt CI, dog springs out of doghouse to attack teasing cat, 8½", EX, A $1,020.00

Sunny Andy Street Railway, litho tin, orange w/lithoed passengers in windows, 21½", G+, A $200.00

Teddy Bear Bell Toy, Watrous, CI & steel, bear in center of platform w/4 spoke wheels, 6½x6", G+, A $470.00

Train, Am, Comet engine w/passenger car, pnt & stenciled tin w/CI spoke wheels, 8½", G, A $415.00

Train (Orion-Baltimore RR), pnt & stenciled tin, CI spoke wheels, engine w/integral tender & 2 coaches, mc, no sz noted, EX, A..$4,070.00

Train (UP RR), pnt & stenciled tin w/CI spoke wheels, engine & tender w/2 cars, mc, 13½", G, A.........................$600.00

Train (Victory), Fallows (?), pnt & stenciled tin w/CI spoke wheels, engine w/integral tender, bell ringer, 13", VG, A......$2,420.00

Train (Victory-Union RR), pnt & stenciled tin w/CI wheels, engine & tender w/Baggage Express & passenger cars, VG, A..$1,760.00

Train Locomotive, Fallows, pnt & stenciled tin w/CI heart-spoke wheels, orange, blk & yel, 8", VG+, A $850.00

Train Locomotive, Geo Brown, pnt & stenciled tin w/wooden base, 3-wheeled, mc, 10", G, A $220.00

Train Locomotive (America), Fallows, pnt & stenciled tin w/CI spoke wheels, cowcatcher, red, blk & bl, no sz noted, EX, A ..$2,200.00

Train Locomotive (Boss), Fallows (?), pnt & stenciled tin w/CI spoke wheels, red & blk w/brass trim, 9", VG+, A ..$630.00

Train Locomotive (Hero), Geo Brown, pnt & stenciled tin w/wood smokestack, boiler front & base, 3-wheeled, 10", VG, A $600.00

Train Locomotive (Leo), Geo Brown, pnt & stenciled tin w/CI wheels & wooden base, blk & yel w/gold trim, 9½", EX, A...$1,265.00

Train Locomotive (New York), Geo Brown, pnt & stenciled tin w/wood stack, boiler front & smokestack, no sz noted, VG, A...$330.00

Train Locomotive (Whistler), Ives, pnt & stenciled tin w/CI fancy-spoke wheels, w/cowcatcher, 12½", VG+, A $4,950.00

Trick Pony Bell Toy, Gong Bell, pnt CI, 8", VG, A.......$580.00

Turtle w/Frog Bell Toy, pnt CI, eccentric wheels impart wobbling motion & activate bell, 4½x6½", EX, A........$525.00

Wild Mule Jack Bell Toy, Gong Bell, pnt CI, 8½", EX, A..$525.00

Puppets

Though many collectible puppets and the smaller scale marionettes were made commercially, others were handmade and are today considered fine examples of folk art which sometimes sell for several hundred dollars. Some of the most collectible today are character-related puppets representing well-known television stars.

Advisor: Bill Bruegman (T2), finger puppets, hand puppets, and push-button puppets; Steven Meltzer (M9), marionettes and ventriloquist dolls.

See also Advertising; Black Americana; Political.

FINGER PUPPETS

Adventure Boy, Remco, 1970, complete w/Skymobile, MIB .$65.00

Crypt Keeper, rubber, set of 3, M, H4 ....$15.00

Fred Flintstone, Knickerbocker, M (VG card), C17........$20.00

Howdy Doody, latex, holes behind mouth, EX, $25.00.
(Photo courtesy Jack Koch)

Howdy Doody, Clarabelle, Dilly & Bluster, rubber, set of 4, 5", EX $100.00

Marvel Super Heroes, Captain America, Hulk, Spider-Man or Thor, Imperial Toy, 1978, vinyl, 3", NM, J5, ea.........$15.00

Monkees, any member, Remco, 1970, EX, ea $35.00

Pebbles & Bamm-Bamm, Knickerbocker, 1972, VG, pr...$10.00

Raggedy Ann and Andy, Hallmark, 1977, vinyl, 3", MOC, ea $30.00. (Photo courtesy Kim Avery)

Raggedy Ann & Andy, Knickerbocker, 1972, vinyl, 3", MOC, ea...$20.00

Ricky Jr (Little Ricky from I Love Lucy), Zany Toys, 1952, vinyl w/cloth outfit, fleece blanket, 8", NMIB, from $400 to .$500.00

Three Stooges, Larry, VG, H4..$75.00

HAND PUPPETS

Alvin (Alvin & the Chipmunks), Knickerbocker, 1963, cloth & vinyl, 12", VG...$40.00

Archie, 1973, plastic & vinyl, EX, C1 ....$45.00

Banana Splits, Bingo, 1968, plastic, EX, J5 ....$45.00

Batman Puppet Theatre, Ideal/Sears Exclusive, 1966, complete w/Batman, Robin & Joker & 20" stage, MIB, T2, minimum value $1,000.00

Beany & Cecil, Cecil & His Disguise Kit, Mattel, 1960, complete, NMIB, from $150 to......................................$200.00

Captain America, Ideal, 1966, plastic & rubber, 11", NM..$100.00

Captain Hook, Gund, cloth & vinyl, EX, T2 ....$30.00

Captain Kangaroo, Rushton, 1960s, cloth & vinyl, EX....$25.00

Cecil (Beany & Cecil), Mattel, 1960s, terrycloth, NM, from $65 to $75.00

Charlie Horse (Shari Lewis), Ideal, 1966, cloth & vinyl, EX, J5 ....$35.00

Dick Tracy, Ideal, 1961, cloth & vinyl, complete w/record, 11", NMIB, T2 ....$125.00

Dilly Dally (Howdy Doody), 1950s, cloth & rubber, EX ..$75.00

Donald Duck, Gund, 1960s, cloth & vinyl, squeaker, MIP $25.00

Addams Family, Fester, Gomez, and Morticia, Ideal, 1964, cloth and vinyl, EX, $75.00 each. (Photo courtesy Judith Izen)

Dopey (Snow White), 1930s, cloth & compo, scarce, EX, M8 .$125.00

Ferdinand the Bull, 1930s, cloth & vinyl, NM $60.00

Flub-A-Dub (Howdy Doody), 1950s, cloth & rubber, EX ..$70.00

Foghorn Leghorn, Warner Bros, 1970s, plush, EX, from $20 to...$30.00

Fox & the Hound, Dial premium, 1981, plush, 9", M, M17, pr...$30.00

Gomez (Addams Family), Ideal, 1964, cloth & vinyl, EX...$75.00

Green Hornet, Ideal, 1966, plastic & vinyl, 10", EX $125.00

Gumby and Pokey, cloth and vinyl, EX, T2, $30.00 each. (Photo courtesy Bill Bruegman)

Hemlock Holmes (Dick Tracy), Ideal, 1961, cloth & vinyl, 11", EX, T2...$75.00

Hopalong Cassidy, 1950s, cloth & vinyl, scarce, NM, J6...$200.00

Hush Puppy (Shari Lewis), Ideal, 1966, cloth & vinyl, EX, J5...$35.00

King Friday (Mr Rogers), Ideal, 1977, cloth & vinyl, 13", EX $20.00

Lady Elaine (Mr Rogers), Ideal, 1977, cloth & vinyl, 13", EX $20.00

Leave It to Beaver, Ward, June & Wally Cleaver, Child Craft, 1968, rubber, scarce, EX $100.00

Linus the Lion-Hearted, Mattel, 1965, talker, NM, from $90 to $100.00

Lone Ranger, 1947, cloth & vinyl, NMIB, from $175 to..$200.00

Mickey Mouse, Gund, 1960s, cloth & vinyl, squeaker, MIP..$65.00

Miss Piggy, Fisher-Price, 1979, foam & vinyl w/silky pk dress, EX $25.00

Morticia (Addams Family), Ideal, 1964, cloth & vinyl, EX ..$75.00

Mr Bluster (Howdy Doody), Zany Toys, cloth & vinyl, 10", EX (EX box) $150.00

Mr Ed, Mattel, 1962, pull-string talker, MIB, T2 ....$200.00

Mr Magoo, 1962, cloth & vinyl, EX, J6 ....$35.00

Muppets, any character, Fisher-Price, 1970s-80s, EX, ea..$10.00

Olive Oyl, Gund, 1950s, cloth & vinyl, 10", EX, T2........$25.00

Ollie (Kukla & Ollie), Davis Toy, 1962, stitch together w/wool, unassembled, MIB, A.....................................$85.00

Owl (Mr Rogers), Ideal, 1977, cloth & vinyl, 13", EX......$20.00

Peter Pan, Gund, cloth & vinyl, EX, T2 ....$35.00

Raggedy Ann, 1960s, cloth w/felt face & hands, yarn hair, 12", EX...$30.00

Raggedy Ann & Andy, Gund, 1965, cloth & rubber, 11", EX, ea..$35.00

Raggedy Ann & Andy, Knickerbocker, 1973, cloth w/yarn hair, 10", MIP, ea $25.00

Road Runner & Wile E Coyote, Warner Bros, 1969, vinyl, NM, pr...$40.00

Robin, Ideal, 1966, cloth & vinyl, NM, P12/T2, from $175 to $200.00

Rootie Kazootie, RK Inc, 1953, cloth & vinyl, 10", EX....$30.00

Roy Rogers, 1950s, cloth & rubber, VG, A $100.00

Smokey the Bear, Ideal, 1960s, plush & vinyl, EX, C17..$50.00

Speedy Gonzales, 1970s, vinyl, EX, C17 ....$15.00

Spider-Man, Ideal, 1966, plastic & soft vinyl, 12", MIP, T2..$200.00

Spider-Man, Imperial, 1979, cloth & vinyl, MIP.............$20.00

Superman/Clark Kent, Peter Puppet, 1954, cloth & vinyl, Superman on 1 side & Clark Kent on the other, 10", NMIB, T2..$300.00

Three Little Pigs, compo & cloth, EX (EX box mk Les 3 Petits Cochons), A $350.00

Three Stooges, Curly, Larry or Moe, 1950s, cloth, EX, ea .$150.00

Tinkerbelle, Gund, talker, cloth & vinyl, EX (EX box) ...$75.00

Tom (Tom & Jerry), Mattel, 1960, talker, cloth & vinyl, NM, from $60 to..$70.00

Topo Gigio, Am Character, 1960s, 12", NRFB, M15...........$125.00

Wonder Woman, Ideal, 1966, cloth & vinyl, 11", MIP, from $200 to...$225.00

Swee' Pea, Gund, 1950s, cloth and vinyl, NM, T2, $50.00.
(Photo courtesy Bill Bruegman)

Wendy (Casper), Gund, 1960s, cloth and plastic, EX, T2, $15.00. (Photo courtesy Bill Bruegman)

MARIONETTES

Alice in Wonderland (unlicensed), Hazelle's, talker, M, M9 .$145.00
Angel, Pelham, MIB, M9 ....$125.00
Bengo the Dog, Pelham, MIB, M9 ....$100.00
Bimbo the Clown, Hazelle's, 800 series, EX, M9 ....$95.00
Buckaroo Bill, Hazelle's, talker, EX, M9 ....$175.00
Captain Hook, Peter Puppet, 1953, 16", rare, NM, M8..$400.00
Clippo the Clown, Curtis Craft, MIB, M9.....................$100.00
Clippo the Clown, Effanbee, WWII, MIB, M9...............$250.00
Clown, Pelham, talker, MIB, M9 ....$125.00
Cop, Pelham, talker, MIB, M9 ....$125.00
Dagwood, Hazelle's, 1950s, MIB, M9 ....$250.00
Donny & Marie Osmond, Madison Ltd, 1978, MIB, pr .$150.00
Emily Ann (Clippo's Girlfriend), Effanbee, M, M9........$160.00
Father, Mother & Son, Effanbee, EX, M9.....................$425.00
Freddy MC, Hazelle's, M, M9....................................$125.00
Gepetto (Pinocchio), Pelham, MIB, M9 ....$160.00
Girl, Pelham, talker, MIB, M9 ....$125.00
Grumpy Dwarf, Alexander, 1938, compo w/cloth clothes, 9",
   NM (G box), A $250.00
Hansel & Gretel, Hazelle's, M, M9, pr..........................$175.00
Heidi (Howdy Doody), Peter Puppet, 1950-54, EX (EX box)..$450.00
Hillbilly, Hazelle's, 800 series, M, M9 ....$95.00
Horse, Pelham, EX (EX box), M9 ....$125.00
Huckleberry Hound, Pelham, 1960s, 9", scarce, NM (NM
   box) $450.00
Jim-Bob & Susy Pigtail, Curtis Craft, 1950, M, M9, pr ..$475.00

Little Boy Blue, Hazelle's, 800 series, compo, M, M9 .....$135.00
Mad Hatter (Alice in Wonderland), Peter Puppet, 1950s, compo
   head & hands w/wooden feet, 14", EX....................$125.00
Marilyn, Hazelle's, talker, EX, M9...............................$225.00
Nurse, Pelham, MIB, M9..$125.00
Old Lady, Pelham, MIB, M9 ....$125.00

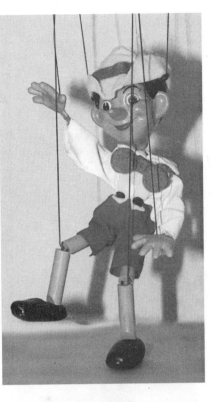

Pinocchio, Pelham, 1960s – 70s, MIB (not shown), $135.00.
(Photo courtesy Steven Meltzer)

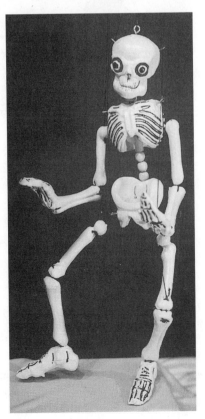

Skeleton, Pelham, 1950s, MIB (not shown), M9, $300.00.
(Photo courtesy Steven Meltzer)

Mr. Bluster, Peter Puppet, 14", MIB, $500.00; Dilly Dally, Peter Puppet, 14", MIB, $550.00.

Peter Pan, Peter Puppet, 1953, 12", rare, M, M8 ....$300.00
Pop Singer, Pelham, any except Hawaiian shirt, M, M9, ea..$300.00
Pop Singer, Pelham, Hawaiian shirt, M, M9 ....$150.00
Prince Charming, Pelham, MIB, M9 ....$125.00
Princess Cindy, Hazelle's, 1952, 14", MIB, M17............$250.00
Sailor, Hazelle's, talker, EX, M9 ....$125.00
Snow White, Madame Alexander, 1938, EX $325.00
Snow White & the Seven Dwarfs, dwarfs, Madame Alexander, any character, EX, ea $250.00
Wolf, Pelham, G, M9 ....$250.00
Wombles (Furry Creatures from English TV show), Pelham, MIB, M9, ea $85.00

PUSH-BUTTON PUPPETS

Atom Ant Tricky Trapeze, Kohner, 1964, EX, T2 ....$25.00
Bambi, Kohner, 1960s, NM, T2 ....$40.00
Bamm-Bamm, Kohner, 1960s, EX $25.00
Batman, Kohner, 1960s, NM $100.00
Bugs Bunny, Kohner, EX $20.00
Candy the Cat, Kohner, 1960s, NM, J6 ....$10.00
Dancer the Dog, Kohner, 1960s, NM, J6 ....$10.00
Davy Crockett, 1950s, rare, NM $195.00

Dino, Kohner, 1960s, M, J6, $65.00.
(Photo courtesy June Moon)

Disney Pop Pals, Kohner, Mickey, Donald, Pluto & Goofy, 3", EX $35.00
Donald Duck Tricky Trapeze, EX $10.00

Flub-A-Dub, Kohner, 1950s, wood w/felt ears, EX $175.00
Fred Flintstone, Kohner, 1960s, M, from $65 to $75.00
Fred Flintstone & Dino, Kohner, 1962, NMIB..............$200.00
Fred Flintstone Tricky Trapeze, Kohner, 1960s, M, from $55 to $75.00
Gabriel the Giraffe, Kohner, 1960s, M, J6 ....$12.00
Hoppy the Hoparoo, M.......................................$65.00
Howdy Doody, Kohner, 1950s, wood w/plastic head, EX, A...$150.00
Lone Ranger, 1960, NM, from $125 to $150.00
Lucky the Lion, Kohner, 1960s, M, J6.........................$12.00
Magilla Gorilla, Kohner, 1960s, M, from $55 to $75.00

Mickey Mouse, Kohner, 1948, wood with plastic base, 6½", NM, $150.00.
(Photo courtesy June Moon)

Pongo (101 Dalmatians), Kohner, 1960s, NM, T2, $45.00.
(Photo courtesy Bill Bruegman)

Olive Oyl, Kohner, NM...$75.00
Paulette the Poodle, Kohner, 1960s, NM, J6 ....$12.00
Pebbles, Kohner, scarce, NMOC, from $35 to $45.00
Pluto, Kohner, wood w/plastic base, 5", EX, A $100.00
Princess Summerfall-Winterspring, Kohner, 1950, NM (EX
    box), A $300.00
Ricochet Rabbit, Kohner, NM $45.00
Secret Squirrel, Kohner, 1960s, EX, J2................................$75.00
Superman & Supergirl, Kohner, 1967, MIB, T2.............$200.00
Superman Tricky Trapeze, Kohner, 1960s, 6", EX, J5.......$65.00
Terry the Tiger, Kohner, 1960s, M, J6 ....$12.00
Wilma Flintstone, Kohner, 1960s, NM, J6 ....$35.00

Charlie McCarthy, Effanbee, tan jacket w/wht shirt & orange print
    bow tie, wht pants & hat, w/monocle, 15½", M $575.00
Dopey (Snow White), Ideal, 1938, compo & cloth, 20", EX..$800.00

Yogi Bear, Kohner, 1960s, M, $65.00.
(Photo courtesy June Moon)

Howdy Doody, Ideal, 1950s, 18", EX, $200.00.
(Photo courtesy Marcia Fanta)

VENTRILOQUIST DOLLS

Ventriloquist dolls have pull-strings from the back of the
neck for mouth movement. Dummies have a hollow body, with
the head mounted on a pole controlled through an opening in
the back of the body. Charlie McCarthy was produced in doll or
hand puppet form by Ideal, Juro, and Goldberger (currently).
Jerry Mahoney was produced by Juro and later by Paul
Winchell's own company. Vinyl-headed ventriloquist dolls are
still being produced by Goldberger and include licensed versions of Charlie McCarthy, Mortimer Snerd, Bozo, Emmet
Kelly, Laurel and Hardy, Howdy Doody, Danny O'Day, WC
Fields, and Groucho.

Charlie McCarthy, Effanbee, blk tux w/wht vest, shirt &
    bow tie, blk top hat, pin-back on lapel, w/monocle, 18",
    EX..$425.00

Howdy Hoody, Ideal, 1950s, stuffed body w/plastic head, cloth
    clothes, 20", EX, A $350.00
Jerry Mahoney, compo head, 24", NM..........................$550.00
Jerry Mahoney, head stick dummy, Juro, 32", MIB........$750.00
Jerry Mahoney, vinyl head (mk Paul Winchell 1966), 22",
    MIB..$350.00
Knucklehead, 1950s, compo head, 24", MIB, M9..........$950.00
Mickey Mouse, Horsman, 1973, hard plastic head w/soft vinyl
    hands, blk tux w/red bow tie, 30", EX $175.00
Monk, Pelham, M, M9..$225.00
Mortimer Snerd, molded plastic body w/orange hair, blk pants &
    vest w/wht shirt, red cummerbund, 26", EX..............$65.00
Pee-Wee Herman, Matchbox, 1988, 25", M (NM box),
    M17...$175.00
Raggedy Ann, 1973, foam body w/plastic head & arms, yarn
    hair, 30", from $85 to $100.00
Rover, Pelham, M, M9..$95.00

Puzzles

Jigsaw puzzles have been around almost as long as games. The first examples were handcrafted from wood, and they are extremely difficult to find. Most of the early examples featured moral subjects and offered insight into the social atmosphere of their time. By the 1890s jigsaw puzzles had become a major form of home entertainment. Cube puzzles or blocks were often made by the same companies as board games. Early examples display lithography of the finest quality. While all subjects are collectible, some (such as Santa blocks) often command prices higher than games of the same period.

Because TV and personality-related puzzles have become so popular, they're now regarded as a field all their own apart from character collectibles in general, and these are listed here as well, under the subtitle 'Character.'

Advisors: Bob Armstrong (A4); Bill Bruegman (T2), Norm Vigue (V1).
See also Advertising.

A Success Story, J Straus, 1950-60, plywood, 100 rnd-knob interlocking pcs, EX (EX box), A4..............................$15.00

Alpine, att Penelope, 1950-60, plywood, 213 1-by-1 rnd-knob interlocking pcs, EX (rpl box), A4 ....$35.00

Approving the Vintage, J Straus, 1930s, plywood, 300 rnd-knob interlocking pcs, EX (EX box), A4..............................$40.00

Artists by the Quayside, Hayter/Victory, 1930-40, plywood, 600 rnd-knob interlocking pcs, EX (rpl box), A4...........$100.00

At Home Abroad, J Straus/Royal, 1940-50, plywood, 1,000 rnd-knob interlocking pcs, EX (EX box), A4 ....$185.00

Autumn, Parker Bros, 1909, plywood, 150 crooked-line 1-way strip pcs, EX (EX box), A4 ....$50.00

Autumn Along the Seine, J Straus, 1940-50, plywood, 310 rnd-knob interlocking pcs, EX (EX box), A4 ....$35.00

Autumn Beauty, Madmar/Blue Ribbon, 1930-40, plywood, 250 long rnd interlocking pcs, EX (EX box), A4..............$50.00

Autumn Glories, Gleason, HA/Cheerio, 1930s, plywood, 318 rnd-knob interlocking pcs, semicolor-line cut, EX (EX box), A4 ....$75.00

Autumn Reflections, early 1900s, wood, 255 push-to-fit pcs, color-line cut, EX (rpl box), A4...............................$100.00

Awaiting Spring's Wispful Breeze, J Straus, 1930s, plywood, 500 rnd-knob interlocking pcs, EX (EX box), A4 ....$65.00

Awaiting the Call, Madmar/Interlox, 1930s, plywood, 1,000 long rnd interlocking pcs, EX (EX box), A4...........$175.00

Bearing the Brunt, FAO Schwarz, 1950s, plywood, 750 random interlocking pcs, EX (EX box), A4 ....$125.00

Beautiful Lake Louise, J Straus, 1950-60, plywood, 1,000 rnd-knob interlocking pcs, EX (EX box), A4 ....$150.00

Beginning of the Hunt, att J Straus, 1930s, plywood, 250 curve-knob interlocking pcs, EX (EX box), A4 ....$30.00

Beyond the Rainbow, Eaton, Scheaffer/Treasure, 1983, cb, 500 diecut rnd-knob interlocking pcs, EX (EX box), A4 .$10.00

Blue Bloods, J Straus, 1960s, plywood, 100 rnd-knob interlocking pcs, EX (EX box), A4 ....$20.00

Bundle of Joy, 1930s, plywood, 380 random interlocking pcs, EX (rpl box), A4...$75.00

Canoeing in the Wilds (Untitled), Parker Bros, 1930s, plywood, 204 interlocking pcs, color-line cut, EX (EX box).....$75.00

Castle in Spain, Milton Bradley/Premier, 1930s, plywood, 300 jagged-knob interlocking pcs, color-line cut, EX (EX box)...$85.00

City of Worchester Picture Puzzle, McLoughlin Bros, 1889, complete, EX (EX box), A, $950.00.

Clipper Red Jacket, J Straus, 1930s, plywood, 300 rnd-knob interlocking pcs, EX (EX box), A4..............................$50.00

Columbus Blocks, McLoughlin Bros, early 1900s, complete, EX (EX box) $700.00

Combat Naval, Schmidt, 1960s, cb, 1,000 diecut rnd-knob interlocking pcs, EX (EX box), A4..............................$20.00

Conference, Hayter/Popular, 1950-60, plywood, 800 rnd-knob interlocking pcs, EX (EX box), A4 ....$125.00

Cottage by the Sea (Untitled), att Tuck/Zag-Zaw, early 1900s, plywood, 305 push-to-fit pcs, EX (rpl box), A4 ....$85.00

Countryside Chat, Tuco-Deluxe, 1940-50, cb, 357 diecut crooked-line pcs, EX (EX box), A4......................................$15.00

Cut Up Birds Scroll Picture Puzzle, Parker Bros, early 1900s, EX (EX box) $250.00

Dessert, Hayes, JM/JMH, 1940s, plywood, 601 1-by-1 rnd-knob interlocking pcs, EX (EX box), A4 ....$125.00

Down from the Mountain Tops, Gleason, HA/Cheerio, 1930s, plywood, 326 rnd-knob interlocking pcs, EX (EX box), A4 ....$75.00

Fire Engine Picture Puzzle, McLoughlin Bros, 1887, complete, EX (EX wooden box), $700.00. (Photo courtesy David Longest)

Eiffel Tower, 1930s, plywood, 300 fantasy-knob interlocking pcs, EX (rpl box), A4 ....$65.00

Eight Bells, Viking, 1932-33, cb, 196 diecut push-to-fit pcs, EX (EX box), A4 ....$15.00

English Country House (Untitled), 1930s, plywood, 400 rnd-knob strip-cut interlocking pcs, EX (rpl box), A4 .....$60.00

Fall Scene (Untitled), 1920s, masonite, 69 push-to-fit pcs, EX (EX box), A4 ....$20.00

Flying Steamship (Untitled), McLoughlin Bros, early 1900s, complete, EX (EX box) $375.00

Four Days Battle, Ravensburger, 1970s, cb, 1,500 diecut rnd-knob interlocking pcs, EX (EX box), A4 ....$20.00

Fox Hunters Meet, Parker Bros, 1930-40, plywood, 308 rnd-knob interlocking pcs, color-line cut, EX (EX box), A4....$125.00

Gang's All Here, Transogram/Gold Medal, 1930s, cb, 200 diecut rnd-knob interlocking pcs, EX (EX box), A4 ....$15.00

General Store (Untitled), early 1900s, pressed board, 106 jagged push-to-fit pcs, color-line cut, EX (rpl box), A4........$40.00

Girl w/Spaniel & Pups (Untitled), Tuco/Deluxe, 1940s, cb, 350 diecut crooked-line pcs, EX (EX box), A4..................$15.00

Glories of Autumn, Galles, 1930s, plywood, 300 sq-knob interlocking pcs, EX (EX box), A4 ....$65.00

Glorious Summer, Western/Whitman, 1930s, cb, 220 diecut crooked-line pcs, EX (EX box), A4 ....$15.00

Grand Canal, Venice, 1930s, plywood, 255 1-by-1 rnd-knob interlocking pcs, EX (EX box), A4 ....$50.00

Grand Canal of Venice, att Brenneman's Pharmacy, 1930-40, plywood, 270 long rnd interlocking pcs, EX (rpl box), A4...$75.00

Grand Canal of Venice, Stoughton/Doubleday-Doran, 1930s, plywood, 400 angular rnd-knob interlocking pcs, EX (EX box), A4...$85.00

Grand Canyon, J Straus, 1950-60, plywood, 500 rnd-knob interlocking pcs, EX (EX box), A4 ....$65.00

Grand Canyon Arizona, J Straus, 1940-50, plywood, 250 rnd-knob interlocking pcs, EX (EX box), A4 ....$35.00

House of Seven Gables, 1930s, cb, 300 diecut sq-knob pcs, EX (rpl box), A4...$15.00

Hunt Is On, J Straus, 1930s, plywood, 300 sq-knob interlocking pcs, EX (EX box), A4 ....$50.00

Hunt Is On, J Straus, 1930s, plywood, 500 rnd-knob interlocking pcs, EX (EX box), A4 ....$65.00

In Full Sail, Chad Valley, 1930s, plywood, 258 rnd-knob interlocking pcs, EX (EX box), A4 ....$65.00

In Search of Adventure, Milton Bradley, 1930s, cb, 200 diecut crooked-line pcs, EX (EX box), A4 ....$15.00

In the Valley, early 1900s, wood, 236 push-to-fit pcs, color-line cut, EX (rpl box), A4...$80.00

Italian Peasants, Parker Bros, 1930s, plywood, 170 jagged-edge interlocking pcs, color-line cut, EX (EX box), A4.....$65.00

Land of the Windmill, 1930s, plywood, 220 long rnd semi-interlocking pcs, EX (EX box), A4 ....$50.00

Lighthouse, J Straus, 1930s, plywood, 500 curve-knob interlocking pcs, EX (EX box), A4 ....$65.00

Lilac Time, J Straus, 1940-50, plywood, 300 rnd-knob interlocking pcs, EX (EX box), A4 ....$50.00

Look 'Em Over, Tuco/Deluxe, 1940s, cb, 350 diecut crooked-line pcs, EX (EX box), A4 ....$20.00

Ludwig's Castle, Austria, 1930s, plywood, 144 curve-knob interlocking pcs, color-line cut, EX (EX box), A4 ....$40.00

Mallards, J Straus, 1930s, plywood, 100 rnd-knob intlocking pcs, EX (EX box), A4 ....$20.00

Mantle Winter, Durrel/Trixy, 1930s, cb, 400 diecut push-to-fit edge-interlocking pcs, EX (EX box), A4....................$15.00

Market Day, Hayes, JM/JMH, 1930s, plywood, 412 rnd-knob semi-interlocking pcs, semicolor-line cut, EX (EX box), A4..$100.00

Mount Holy Cross, Sta-Put, 1930s, plywood, 724 curve-knob interlocking pcs, EX (EX box), A4 ....$125.00

Mount Vesuvius, J Straus, 1930s, plywood, 300 curve-knob interlocking pcs, EX (EX box), A4..........................$50.00

Natures Splendor, Galles, 1930s, plywood, 300 sq-knob interlocking pcs, EX (EX box), A4 ....$75.00

Old Mill in Autumn, J Straus, 1930s, plywood, 200 rnd-knob interlocking pcs, EX (EX box), A4..........................$35.00

Old Tow Path, Tuco/Deluxe, 1940-50, cb, 350 diecut crooked-line pcs, EX (EX box), A4 ....$15.00

On the Shores of Lake Lucerne, C Russell, 1930-40, plywood, 301 rnd-knob interlocking pcs, color-line cut, EX (EX box) $100.00

Over Field & Fence, Leisure Moment, 1930s, masonite, 329 rnd-knob semi-interlocking pcs, EX (EX box), A4...........$50.00

Proposal, Einson-Freeman, 1933, cb, 160 diecut push-to-fit semi-interlocking pcs, EX (EX box), A4....................$15.00

Puppies Playing w/Paint (Untitled), 1930-40, plywood, 205 fantasy-knob interlocking pcs, EX (rpl box), A4 ....$50.00

Quai Vert, Parker Bros, 1920-30, plywood, 350 jagged-edge interlocking pcs, color-line cut, EX (EX box), A4 ..$125.00

Race Between Cutty Sark & Thermopylae, J Straus, 1930s, plywood, 200 curve-knob interlocking pcs, EX (EX box), A4 ....$35.00

Raking the Hay, Parker Bros, early 1900s, plywood, 230 curve-knob semi-interlocking pcs, color-line cut, EX (EX box), A4...$85.00

Rounding the Cape, Glengarry, 1930s, plywood, 300 rnd-knob interlocking pcs, EX (EX box), A4.............................$65.00

Three in One Puzzle Box, Milton Bradley, missing one puzzle, EX (EX box), A, $250.00.

Shepherd w/Flock (Untitled), Parker Bros, 1920s, plywood, 300 earlet-knob interlocking pcs, color-line cut, EX (EX box)..$100.00

Solitude, Byram Specialty Sales, 1930s, plywood, 513 curve-knob interlocking pcs, EX (EX box), A4 ....$85.00

Solitude, Lake Puzzles, 1930s, plywood, 303 long rnd interlocking pcs, color-line cut, EX (EX box), A4 ....$65.00

Summer, J Straus, 1940s, plywood, 300 curve-knob interlocking pcs, EX (EX box), A4 ....$30.00

Times Square, New York, 1940-50, plywood, 185 1-by-1 rnd-knob interlocking pcs, EX (EX box), A4 ....$35.00

Town & Country Picture Puzzles, Parker Bros, 1 town scene & 1 farm scene, complete, NMIB, A..............................$175.00

Tyrolian Waters, Byram Specialty Sales, 1930s, plywood, 319 random-knob interlocking pcs, EX (EX box), A4......$75.00

Unswerving Loyalty, Parker Bros, 1930s, plywood, 65 curl-knob interlocking pcs, color-line cut, EX (EX box), A4.....$35.00

Venice Water Front (Untitled), 1930s, plywood, 278 random-knob interlocking pcs, color-line cut, EX (rpl box), A4 ....$65.00

Washington's First Cabinet, Parker Bros, 1930s, plywood, 85 semi-interlocking pcs, color-line cut, EX (EX box), A4 ....$35.00

Welcome Home, J Straus, 1940-50, plywood, 300 rnd-knob interlocking pcs, EX (EX box), A4..............................$50.00

Western Lake & Hills (Untitled), 1930-40, plywood, 415 fantasy-knob interlocking pcs, EX (rpl box), A4 ....$85.00

Who Killed Cock Robin, England/Dean's Artistic Series, 1890s, complete, EX (EX box) $450.00

Wild Mountain Scenery (Untitled), Parker Bros, 1920-30, plywood, 507 interlocking pcs, color-line cut, EX (rpl box) $175.00

Winter, Parker Bros, 1938, plywood, 509 rnd-knob interlocking pcs, color-line cut, EX (EX box), A4 ....$200.00

Winter in the Country (Untitled), 1930-40, plywood, 410 fantasy-knob interlocking pcs, EX (rpl box), A4.......$85.00

CHARACTER

Alice in Wonderland, jigsaw, Jaymar, complete, EX (EX box), J2..$30.00

Alvin & the Chipmunks, jigsaw, APC, 1984, 125 pcs, MIB..$10.00

Aquaman, jigsaw, Whitman, 1968, 100 pcs, MIB, T2 ......$40.00

Archie, jigsaw, Jaymar, 1969, complete, MIB $40.00

Barney Google & Snuffy Smith, fr-tray, Jaymar, 1940s-50s, complete, NM, C1..$40.00

Batman, fr-tray, Fotorama/Spanish, 1966, Batman & Robin fighting the Eclipso Man, 11x13", NM (sealed), J5 ...$45.00

Batman, fr-tray, Fotorama/Spanish, 1966, 11x13", NM (sealed) $45.00

Batman, jigsaw, APC, 1974, 200 pcs, M (M canister), J5.$20.00

Batman — Crashing the Barrier, jigsaw, Whitman, 1966, 260 pcs, EX (EX box), J5 ....$65.00

Batman at the Docks, fr-tray, Whitman, 1966, complete, EX, J5 ....$35.00

Battlestar Galactica, jigsaw, Parker Bros, 1978, 140 pcs, MIB (sealed), M17..$15.00

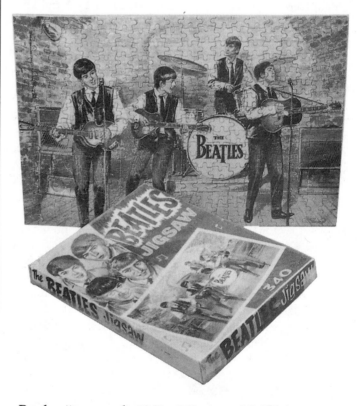

Beatles, jigsaw, early 1960s, 340 pieces, NMIB, $350.00.

Beatles Yellow Submarine, jigsaw, Jaymar, 650 pcs, NMIB..$150.00

Bee Gees, jigsaw, APC, 1979, complete, MIB $35.00

Ben Casey, jigsaw, Milton Bradley, 1962, 600 pcs, MIB (sealed), M17 ....$25.00

Beverly Hillbillies, fr-tray, Jaymar, 1963, complete, NM..$20.00

Beverly Hillbillies, jigsaw, Jaymar, 1963, complete, MIB .$20.00

Untitled (Boy Eating Apples), 1930s, plywood, 135 pieces, EX (replaced box), $25.00. (Photo courtesy Bob Armstrong)

Bonny Braids — Dick Tracy's New Daughter, fr-tray, Saalfield, 1950s, complete, NM..$20.00

Brady Bunch, fr-tray, Whitman, 1972, complete, M $45.00

Buzz Lightyear & Woody, jigsaw, 60 pcs, MIB, F1 ....$8.00

Captain America, fr-tray, Whitman, 1966, complete, 14x11", M, T2..$50.00

Captain Kangaroo, jigsaw, Fairchild, 1950s, complete, EX (EX box), A..$25.00

Captain Kool & the Kongs, fr-tray, Whitman, 1978, complete, EX..$12.00

Captain Marvel Rides the Engine of Doom, jigsaw, 1940s, complete, MIB, T2..$125.00

Charlie's Angels, jigsaw, HG Toys, 1976, 250 pcs, MIB...$30.00

Cinderella, jigsaw, 1950s, complete, EX (EX canister), N2..$30.00

Cisco Kid, fr-tray, Saalfield, complete, 11½x10", NM $40.00

Creature From the Black Lagoon, jigsaw, Golden, 1990, 200 pcs, MIB, B10..$6.00

Dallas, jigsaw, Warren, 1980, features JR, complete, EX (EX box), A..$20.00

Daniel Boone Wilderness Scout, fr-tray, Jaymar, complete, EX, B10..$20.00

Dark Shadows, jigsaw, Milton Bradley, 1969, NMIB........$65.00

David Cassidy, jigsaw, APC, 1972, 500 pcs, MIB $45.00

Davy Crockett, fr-tray, Jaymar, 1950s, 11x14", EX, A......$75.00

Dennis the Mecace, fr-tray, Whitman, 1960, complete, 11x14", NM..$20.00

Dick Tracy, jigsaw, Jaymar, 1961, 60 pcs, MIB, T2...........$50.00

Dilly Dally the Human Bullet, fr-tray, Whitman, 1950s, complete, EX..$40.00

Dimwit, fr-tray, lg or sm, EX, T2, ea..$10.00

Donny & Marie Osmond, fr-tray, Whitman, 1977, complete, M..$20.00

Dr Kildare, jigsaw, Milton Bradley, 1962, complete, EX (EX box), C1..$35.00

Dr Seuss' Cat in the Hat, fr-tray, 1980s, complete, EX, H4..$20.00

Dr Strange, jigsaw, Third Eye, 1971, 500 pcs, MIB, T2..$100.00

Dudley Do-Right, jigsaw, Whitman, 1972, 100 pcs, NM (EX box), C1..$30.00

Dukes of Hazzard, jigsaw, 1981, 200 pcs, EX (EX box), B10..$10.00

Eight Is Enough, jigsaw, APC, 1978, complete, MIB........$15.00

Elvis, jigsaw, 1977, complete, MIB..$35.00

Emergency, jigsaw, Am Publishing, 1975, complete, NM (NM canister), C1..$50.00

Family Affair, jigsaw, Whitman, 1970, 125 pcs, rnd, rare, EX (EX box), M17..$100.00

Fantastic Four, fr-tray, Whitman, 1968, complete, 14x11", scarce, NM..$50.00

Fantastic Four, jigsaw, Third Eye, 1971, 500 pcs, MIB, T2.$100.00

Farrah Fawcett, jigsaw, Am Publishing, 1977, 200 pcs, EX (EX box), M17..$30.00

Flintstones, fr-tray, Whitman, 1964, complete, NM, C1..$45.00

Flipper, fr-tray, 1965, complete, EX, J2..$25.00

Flipper, jigsaw, Whitman Big Little Book series, 1960s, complete, NMIB..$50.00

Fonzie, jigsaw, HG Toys, 1976, complete, EX (EX canister) ..$15.00

Fox & the Hound, fr-tray, Jaymar, complete, EX, B10........$6.00

Frankenstein, fr-tray, Universal, 1991, M (sealed), B10 .....$5.00

Frankenstein, jigsaw, Am Publishing, 1974, complete, EX (EX canister), M17..$15.00

Goldfinger, jigsaw, Milton Bradley, 1965, complete, VG (VG box), A..$35.00

Goofy, fr-tray, Whitman, 1940s, boxed set of 2, NMIB, A ..$85.00

Green Hornet, fr-tray, Whitman, 1966, set of 4, MIB, T2..$75.00

Gulliver's Travels, fr-tray, Saalfield, 1930s, set of 8, complete, EX (EX box), A..$100.00

Gunsmoke, fr-tray, Whitman, 1958, complete, EX, A $30.00

Gunsmoke, jigsaw, Whitman, 1969, 100 pcs, NM (EX box), C1..$45.00

Happy Days, jigsaw, HG Toys, 1976, complete, NMIB, C1.$35.00

Hot Wheels, fr-tray, 1986, EX, B10..$5.00

Howdy Goes West, fr-tray, Whitman, 1953, complete, EX .$40.00

Howdy Doody, frame-tray, Whitman, 1952, complete, EX, $45.00. (Photo courtesy Jack Koch)

Howdy's One-Man Band, fr-tray, Whitman, 1954, complete, EX $50.00

Incredible Hulk, jigsaw, Third Eye, 1971, 500 pcs, MIB, T2...$100.00

Incredible Hulk, jigsaw, Whitman, 1979, 100 pcs, MIB, T2 .....$25.00

Janet Jackson, jigsaw, Milton Bradley, 1991, complete, MIB $10.00

Jetsons, fr-tray, Whitman, 1960s, complete, NM, from $35 to $45.00

Jinks, fr-tray, Whitman, 1960s, complete, NM, from $20 to $30.00

Josie & the Pussycats, jigsaw, Hope, 1972, complete, EX (EX canister) $30.00

Kermit the Frog, fr-tray, Fisher-Price, 1981-82, complete, M, C13..$5.00

King Kong, jigsaw, Chad Valley, 200 3-ply wooden interlocking pcs, scarce, NMIB......................$600.00
Lady & the Tramp, fr-tray, Whitman, 1964, complete, EX, B10......................$10.00
Land of the Giants, jigsaw, Whitman Jr, 1960s, rnd, complete, EX (EX box), J5......................$35.00
Lassie, fr-tray, Whitman, 1966, complete, 14x9", NM, C1 ..$35.00

Lassie, jigsaw, Whitman Big Little Book series, 1960s, complete, NMIB, $50.00. (Photo courtesy Larry Jacobs)

Lone Ranger, fr-tray, Puzzle Craft Industries, 1945, set of 3, complete, NMIB, from $150 to......................$200.00
Lone Ranger, jigsaw, Milton Bradley, 1980, 250 pcs, MIB..$65.00
Love Boat, jigsaw, HG Toys, 1978, 150 pcs, MIB.............$15.00
Madonna, jigsaw, Milton Bradley, 1990, 500 pcs, MIB $10.00
Marvel Super Heroes, jigsaw, Milton Bradley, 1967, 100 pcs, MIB, T2......................$100.00
Masters of the Universe, fr-tray, Golden, 1982, complete, 14x11", NM, M17......................$20.00
MC Hammer, jigsaw, Milton Bradley, 1990, 500 pcs, MIB...$8.00
Michael Jackson, jigsaw, Colorforms, 1984, 500 pcs, MIB..$10.00
Mighty Heroes, fr-tray, Whitman, 1967, complete, 14x11", NM, T2......................$50.00
Mighty Mouse, fr-tray, Jaymar, 1950s, complete, 11x14", NM, T2......................$15.00
Mighty Mouse Playhouse, jigsaw, Fairchild, 1956, complete, MIB, T2......................$20.00
Miss Piggy, fr-tray, Fisher-Price, 1981-82, complete, M, C13 ..$15.00
Mod Squad, jigsaw, Milton Bradley, 1969, complete, MIB......$35.00

Monkees, jigsaw, Fairchild, 1967, complete, MIB.............$45.00
Mr I Magination, jigsaw, Jaymar Television Stars series, 1951, 400 pcs, scarce, NMIB, T2......................$50.00
Muppets, fr-tray, Fisher-Price, 1981-82, complete, M, C13 ..$15.00
New Kids on the Block, jigsaw, Milton Bradley, 1990, 500 pcs, MIB......................$8.00
Patty Duke, jigsaw, Whitman Jr, 1963, 100 pcs, EX (EX box), M17......................$45.00
Paula Abdul, jigsaw, Milton Bradley, 1990, 500 pcs, MIB..$8.00
Peanuts, jigsaw, Charles Schultz, 1960s, complete, EX (worn box), from $50 to......................$75.00
Penelope Pitstop, fr-tray, Whitman, complete, NM, from $20 to.$25.00
Pinky Lee, fr-tray, Gabriel, 1950s, set of 4, EX (VG box), J5......................$85.00
Planet of the Apes, jigsaw, HG Toys, 1967, complete, EX (EX canister), C1......................$40.00
Popeye's Comic Picture Puzzle, jigsaw, Parker Bros, set of 4, EX (EX box)......................$100.00
Quick Draw McGraw, fr-tray, Whitman, 1960, complete, EX, J2......................$25.00

Raggedy Ann and Andy — Do the Raggedy Dance, Playskool, 1987, MIP, $15.00. (Photo courtesy Kim Avery)

Raggedy Ann & Andy, fr-tray, Milton Bradley, 1987, complete, 14½x11", M......................$12.00
Raggedy Ann & Andy Railroad Picture Puzzles, jigsaw, Milton Bradley/Johnny Gruelle, 1944, set of 6, MIB..........$110.00
Raggedy Ann Picture Puzzles, jigsaw, Milton Bradley/Johnny Gruelle, 1940, set of 4, MIB......................$95.00

Road Runner, jigsaw, Whitman, 1980, EX (EX box), J2 ..$20.00

Rod Stewart, jigsaw, 1973, complete, MIB.........................$40.00

Roger Ramjet, fr-tray, Whitman, 1966, complete, 14x11", NM, T2...$75.00

Rookies, jigsaw, Am Publishing, 1975, complete, EX (EX container), M17...$40.00

Shazzam, jigsaw, Whitman Big Little Book series, 1960, complete, NMIB...$50.00

Silver Surfer, jigsaw, Third Eye, 1971, 500 pcs, MIB, T2..$100.00

Simpsons, jigsaw, Milton Bradley, several different, 100 pcs, MIB, K1, ea...$10.00

Simpsons, jigsaw, Milton Bradley, several different, 250 pcs, MIB, K1, ea...$15.00

Six Million Dollar Man, jigsaw, Am Publishing, 1975, 200 pcs, EX (EX container), M17 ....$35.00

Skippy in Jigsaw, complete with three puzzles, EX (EX box), minimum value $65.00. (Photo courtesy David Longest)

Sleeping Beauty, jigsaw, Jaymar, 1960s, complete, NMIB, M8 ....$20.00

Snow White & the Seven Dwarfs, jigsaw, Jaymar, 1940s, 300 pcs, NMIB...$50.00

Space Ghost, fr-tray, Whitman, 1967, complete, 14x11", NM, T2..$50.00

Space Ghost, jigsaw, Whitman, 1967, 100 pcs, MIB, T2 .$25.00

Space Kidettes, fr-tray, Whitman, 1967, complete, M......$40.00

Spider-Man, floor puzzle, Waddington, 1977, 48 pcs, complete, MIB, T2 ....$40.00

Star Trek, fr-tray, Whitman, 1978, complete, 10x8", M, C1 ...$15.00

Story Book Puzzles, USA, 1945, Three Little Pigs, Little Red Riding Hood, Three Bears, Lil' Red Hen, unused, MIB, A..$100.00

Storybook Kiddles, fr-tray, Whitman, 1968, set of 4, complete, MIB..$125.00

Strawberry Shortcake — Life Is the Berries, fr-tray, Craftmaster, 1981, complete, EX...$5.00

Superboy, fr-tray, Whitman, 1968, complete, 14x11", NM, T2..$50.00

Superman, fr-tray, Whitman, 1966, complete, 11x8", NM, T2..$25.00

Superman, jigsaw, Whitman, 1966, 100 pcs, MIB, T2......$25.00

Superman Over the City, jigsaw, Saalfield, 1940, few pcs missing, EX (EX box), M17...$140.00

Sword in the Stone, fr-tray, Whitman, 1963, complete, EX, J2..$20.00

Three Stooges — Hold Your Fire, jigsaw, Colorforms, complete, scarce, EX (EX box), A $475.00

Thunderball, jigsaw, Milton Bradley, 1965, complete, EX (EX box), A...$40.00

Tom & Jerry, fr-tray, Whitman, 1959, complete, NM, C1 ...$25.00

Top Cat, fr-tray, Whitman, 1960s, complete, MIP, from $20 to $25.00

Uncle Wiggily Picture Puzzles, jigsaw, Milton Bradley, 1900, set of 3, NMIB..$200.00

Underdog, fr-tray, Whitman, 1965, complete, 11x14", NM, T2..$20.00

Underdog, jigsaw, Whitman, 1975, 100 pcs, MIB, T2......$25.00

Universal Monsters, fr-tray, Jaymar, 1963, Dracula, Mummy or Frankenstein, complete, NM, H4, ea.......................$150.00

Village People, jigsaw, APC, 1978, complete, MIB..........$20.00

Voyage to the Bottom of the Sea, jigsaw, Milton Bradley, 1966, NMIB...$85.00

Welcome Back Kotter, jigsaw, HG Toys, 1976, 250 pcs, MIB $20.00

Wild Bill Hickok, jigsaw, Built Rite, 1956, 100 pcs, EX (EX box), M17 ....$25.00

Woody Woodpecker, fr-tray, Whitman, 1954, complete, VG, T2..$25.00

Woody Woodpecker, jigsaw, Whitman Big Little Book series, 1960s, complete, NMIB..$50.00

Wyatt Earp, jigsaw, Whitman, 1960s, complete, NM (NM box), C1..$25.00

Yogi Bear, fr-tray, Whitman, 1960s, complete, NM, C1 ..$35.00

Zorro, fr-tray, 1957, complete, EX, J2.............................$35.00

ZZ Top, jigsaw, 1980s, complete, NM (NM canister) $35.00

101 Dalmatians, fr-tray, Jaymar #2720-29, EX, B10 ....$10.00

Radios, Novelty

Many novelty radios are made to resemble a commercial product box or can, and with the crossover interest into the advertising field, some of the more collectible, even though of recent vintage, are often seen carrying very respectible price tags. Likenesses of famous personalities such as Elvis or characters like Charlie Tuna house transistors in cases made of plastic that scarcely hint at their actual function. Others represent items ranging from baseball caps to Cadillacs. To learn more about this subject, we recommend *Collector's Guide to Novelty Radios, Books I* and *II,* by Marty Bunis and Robert F. Breed.

Advisors: Sue and Marty Bunis (B11).

Archie, Vanity Fair/Archie Co, 1977, shaped like a juke box, 6", M..$50.00

Batman, Vanity Fair/DC Comics, 1978, pyramid-shape w/Batman figure in front, 6½", M $150.00

Battlestar Galactica, Universal Studios/Vanity Fair, 1978, 6", EX.$50.00

Bird Cage w/Canary, 8", M..............................$100.00
Blabber Mouse on Cheese, EX, J2....................$35.00
Bubble Yum Bubble Gum, Hong Kong, 3½x5", NM, from $35
    to...$50.00
Bugs Bunny & Elmer Fudd, Warner Bros, NM, from $50 to..$70.00
Bullwinkle, PAT World Productions, plastic 3-D figure, 12",
    M $250.00
Cabbage Patch Kids, Original Appalachian Artworks, 1983,
    purse style, 4½", EX......................................$35.00

Del Monte Pineapple Chunks, M, $75.00.

Firestone Steel Belted Radial Tire, PRI/Hong Kong, 5" dia, NM,
    from $35 to...$50.00
Fleetrite Battery, EX $35.00
Girl w/Dog, Holiday Fair Inc, 1970, 8", M $50.00

**Campbell's Tomato Soup, Hong Kong, EX, from
$35.00 to $50.00.**

Cap'n Crunch, Isis, model #39, NM, from $35 to.............$50.00
Coca-Cola Billboard, Isis, Enjoy Coca-Cola Classic, NM, from
    $75 to...$100.00
Coca-Cola Can, China, 1991, smashed can covered in clear
    plastic, w/carrying strap, NM, from $50 to.................$75.00
Coca-Cola Tote Bag, Randix, 9x15", M $35.00
Coca-Cola Vending Machine, Westinghouse, 1963, 8", M .$150.00
Cookie Crisp Box, Hong Kong, 5", M...........................$75.00
Crayola Rocks, 1994, box shape, NM, from $35 to $50.00
Diet Pepsi Can, M..$30.00
Donald Duck Orange Juice, 3x4½", M............................$50.00
Esso Extra Motor Oil Can, Hitachi, 4", M......................$225.00

**Howdy Doody, cloth and vinyl with controls on front, 14",
NM, from $35.00 to $50.00.**

Hershey's Milk Chocolate, Isis, model #39, NM, from $25 to...**$35.00**

Hi-C, Isis, box shape, 5x3", NM, from $35 to **$50.00**

Hopalong Cassidy, Arvin, 1950, blk or red, 8", NM, ea from $750 to...**$800.00**

Hopalong Cassidy, red, Topper's legs up, NM, C10 ....**$800.00**

Hugga Bunch, Nasta/Hallmark, 1984, wristwatch shape, NM, from $15 to **$25.00**

Incredible Hulk, Marvel Comics, 1978, 7", M **$75.00**

Keebler Animal Crackers, box shape w/braided hdl, NM, from $60 to...**$75.00**

King Kong, Amico, 1986, 13", M.....................................**$35.00**

Kool-Aid Bursts Bottle, Kraft General Foods Inc, 1992, nylon shoulder strap, 8", M...**$35.00**

Little Debbie Swiss Cake Rolls, Isis, model #103, NM, from $25 to **$35.00**

Lunch 'N Tunes Lunch Box, Fun Designs, 1986, 8x8", M**$50.00**

Masters of the Universe, mouth moves w/music, 5½", EX..**$45.00**

Mickey Mouse, Emerson, 1934, Syrocco-type material w/emb images of Mickey playing instruments, 8x8", EX, from $1,500 to **$1,800.00**

Mighty Mouse on Cheese, Vanity Fair/Via Com International, 1978, 5", M, $150.00. (Photo courtesy Marty Bunis and Robert F. Breed)

Mork From Ork Eggship, Concept 2000, 1979, MIB........**$35.00**

Mountain Dew Can, Hong Kong, NM, from $35 to **$50.00**

Mr Pibb Can, M...**$35.00**

Munchie Tunes Lunch Box, Fun Designs, 1986, 8x8", M...**$35.00**

Nabisco Zesty Cheese Nacho Corn Thins, PRI/Hong Kong, 5", M...**$50.00**

Pepsi-Cola Vending Machine, Industrial Contacts Ltd, 6½", M...**$300.00**

Pillsbury Doughboy Clock Radio, Tarcy, 1986, Doughboy standing behind stove, M **$60.00**

Planters Munch 'N Go Backpack, 16x12", M **$75.00**

Polarine Motor Oil Can, Taiwan, scarce, M.................**$100.00**

Polaroid 600 Plus Film Box, China, 5", M **$30.00**

Power Rangers, Micro Games of America, head-shape on rectangular base, NM, from $25 to.....................................**$35.00**

Quick Quaker Oats Container, old style label, NM **$125.00**

Raggedy Ann and Andy, Bobbs-Merrill/Hong Kong, 1975, 8x7", NM, from $35.00 to $50.00. (Photo courtesy Marty Bunis and Robert F. Breed)

Rambo, Talbot Toys, w/headphones, EX **$40.00**

Sears Best Easy Living Paint Can, Hong Kong, NM, from $35 to..**$50.00**

Snow White & the Seven Dwarfs, Emerson, 1938, Syrocco w/cloth speaker, 7x11", NM...............................**$3,000.00**

SOS Box, Miles Inc, 1989, NM, from $35 to...................**$50.00**

Spam, 4x3", M..**$50.00**

Spider-Man, Marvel Comics/Hong Kong, 1979, 5", EX ...**$50.00**

Starforce Robot, Hong Kong, 6", EX................................**$50.00**

Sunshine Cheez-It Snack Crackers, Isis, model #39, NM, from $25 to **$35.00**

Telephone, Hong Kong, red desk-type, 5", M..................**$50.00**

Thunderbirds, ITC Entertainment Group Ltd, 1992, beverage can shape, NM, from $75 to **$100.00**

Yogi Bear, Markson/Hanna Barbera, head figure, NM, from $100 to **$125.00**

1966 Chevy Impala, 8", EX **$75.00**

7-Up Vending Machine, Markatron/Hong Kong, M......**$100.00**

9 Lives Crunchy Meals Cat Food Box, NM, from $50 to .**$75.00**

Ramp Walkers

Ramp walkers date back to at least 1873 when Ives produced two versions of a cast-iron elephant walker. Wood and composition ramp walkers were made in Czechoslovakia and the U.S.A. from the 1930s through the 1950s. The most common were made by John Wilson of Pennsylvania and were sold worldwide. These became known as 'Wilson Walkies.' Most are two-legged and stand approximately 4½" tall. While some of the Wilson Walkies were made of a composite material with wood legs (for instance, Donald, Wimpy, Popeye, and Olive Oyl), most are made with cardboard thread-cone bodies with wood legs and head. The walkers made in Czechoslovakia are similar but they are generally made of wood.

Plastic ramp walkers were primarily manufactured by the Louis Marx Co. and were made from the early 1950s through the mid-1960s. The majority were produced in Hong Kong, but some were made in the United States and sold under the Marx logo or by the Charmore Co., which was a subsidiary of the Marx Co. Some walkers are still being produced today as fast-food premiums.

The three common sizes are (1) small, about 1½" x 2"; (2) medium, about 2¾" x 3"; and (3) large, about 4"x 5". Most of the small walkers are unpainted while the medium or large sizes were either spray painted or painted by hand. Several of the walking toys were sold with wooden plastic or colorful lithographed tin ramps.

Advisor: Randy Welch (W4).

ADVERTISING

Captain Flint, Long John Silvers, 1989, w/plastic coin weight $15.00
Choo-Choo Cherry, Funny Face Kool-Aid, w/plastic coin weight...$60.00
Flash Turtle, Long John Silvers, 1989, w/plastic coin weight .$15.00
Goofy Grape, Funny Face Kool-Aid, w/plastic coin weight....$60.00
Jolly Ollie Orange, Funny Face Kool-Aid, w/plastic coin weight $60.00
Quinn Penguin, Long John Silvers, 1989, w/plastic coin weight $15.00
Root'n Toot'n Raspberry, Funny Face Kool-Aid, w/plastic coin weight...$60.00
Sydney Dinosaur, Long John Silvers, 1989, yel & purple, w/plastic coin weight $15.00
Sylvia Dinosaur, Long John Silvers, 1989, lavender & pk, w/plastic coin weight $15.00

CZECHOSLOVAKIAN

Dog $30.00
Man w/Carved Wood Hat $35.00
Monkey..$35.00
Pig $30.00
Policeman...$60.00

DISNEY CHARACTERS BY MARX

Big Bad Wolf & Mason Pig..$50.00
Big Bad Wolf & Three Little Pigs $150.00
Donald Duck, pulling nephews in wagon............................$35.00
Donald Duck, pushing wheelbarrow, all plastic $25.00

Donald Duck, pushing wheelbarrow, plastic w/metal legs, sm.$25.00
Donald Duck & Goofy, riding go-cart.............................$40.00
Donald's Trio, France, Huey, Louie & Dewey dressed as Indian Chief, cowboy & 1 carrying flowers, NMOC, A $155.00
Fiddler & Fifer Pigs $50.00
Figaro the Cat, w/ball...$30.00
Goofy, riding hippo..$45.00
Jiminy Cricket, w/cello $30.00
Mad Hatter w/March Hare $50.00
Mickey & Donald Riding Alligator...................................$40.00
Mickey Mouse, pushing lawn roller..................................$35.00
Mickey Mouse & Minnie, plastic w/metal legs, sm..........$40.00
Mickey Mouse & Pluto, hunting $40.00
Minnie Mouse, pushing baby stroller $35.00
Pluto, plastic w/metal legs, sm $35.00
Wiggly Walkers, complete set of 4 w/Mickey, Minnie, Pluto & Donald, EX (VG scarce box) $400.00

HANNA-BARBERA, KING FEATURES & OTHER CHARACTERS BY MARX

Astro, Hanna-Barbera $150.00
Astro & George Jetson, Hanna-Barbera.............................$90.00
Astro & Rosey, Hanna-Barbera $95.00

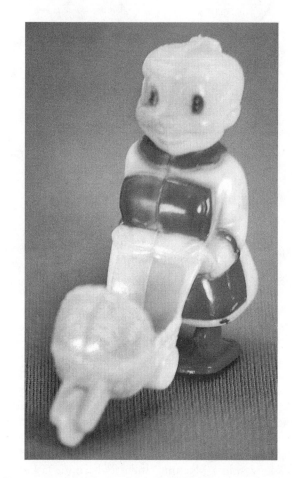

Bonnie Braids' Nursemaid, missing baby, EX, $35.00.

Chilly Willy, penguin on sled pulled by parent, Walter Lantz.$25.00
Fred & Wilma on Dino, Hanna-Barbera...........................$60.00
Fred Flintstone on Dino, Hanna-Barbera..........................$75.00

Hap and Hop Soldiers, $25.00.

Little King & Guards, King Features $70.00
Pebbles on Dino, Hanna-Barbera $75.00
Popeye, Erwin, celluloid, lg $60.00

Popeye and Wimpy, MIB, $85.00.

Popeye Pushing Spinach Can Wheelbarrow $25.00
Santa, w/gold sack $45.00
Santa, w/wht sack $40.00
Santa, w/yel sack $40.00
Santa & Mrs Claus, faces on both sides $50.00
Santa & Snowman, faces on both sides $50.00
Spark Plug $200.00
Top Cat & Benny $65.00
Yogi Bear & Huckleberry Hound, Hanna-Barbera $50.00

MARX ANIMALS WITH RIDERS SERIES

Ankylosaurus w/Clown $40.00

Bison w/Native $40.00
Brontosaurus w/Monkey $40.00
Hippo w/Native $40.00
Lion w/Clown $40.00
Stegosaurus w/Black Caveman $40.00
Triceratops w/Native $40.00
Zebra w/Native $40.00

PLASTIC

Baby Walk-A-Way, lg $40.00
Baseball Player w/Bat & Ball $40.00
Bear $20.00
Boy & Girl Dancing $45.00
Bull $20.00
Bunnies Carrying Carrot $35.00
Bunny Pushing Cart $60.00
Camel w/2 Humps, head bobs $20.00
Chicks Carrying Easter Egg $35.00
Chinese Men w/Duck in Basket $30.00
Chipmunks Carrying Acorns $35.00
Chipmunks Marching Band w/Drum & Horn $35.00
Cow, w/metal legs, sm $20.00
Cowboy on Horse, w/metal legs, sm $30.00
Dachshund $20.00
Dairy Cow $20.00
Dog, Pluto look-alike w/metal legs, sm $20.00
Double Walking Doll, boy behind girl, lg $60.00
Duck $20.00
Dutch Boy & Girl $40.00
Elephant $20.00
Elephant, w/metal legs, sm $30.00
Farmer Pushing Wheelbarrow $30.00

Firemen, $35.00.

Frontiersman w/Dog...$95.00
Goat $20.00
Horse, circus style $20.00
Horse, lg $30.00
Horse, yel w/rubber ears & string tail, lg $30.00
Horse w/English Rider, lg....................................$50.00
Indian Woman Pulling Baby on Travois...........$95.00
Kangaroo w/Baby in Pouch.................................$30.00
Mama Duck w/3 Ducklings.................................$35.00
Marty's Market Lady Pushing Shopping Cart $65.00
Mexican Cowboy on Horse, w/metal legs, sm $30.00
Milking Cow, lg $40.00
Monkeys Carrying Bananas $60.00
Nursemaid Pushing Baby Stroller $20.00
Pig $20.00
Pigs, 2 carrying 1 in basket................................$40.00
Popeye & Wimpy, heads on springs, lg $65.00
Pumpkin Head Man & Woman, faces both sides $100.00
Reindeer...$45.00
Sailors SS Shoreleave $25.00
Sheriff Facing Outlaw $65.00
Teeny Toddler, walking baby girl, Dolls Inc, lg $40.00
Tin Man Robot Pushing Cart...............................$150.00
Walking Baby, in Canadian Mountie uniform, lg...........$50.00
Walking Baby, w/moving eyes & cloth dress, lg...........$40.00
Wiz Walker Milking Cow, Charmore, lg $40.00

WILSON

Black Mammy $40.00
Eskimo...$100.00
Indian Chief...$70.00
Nurse $30.00
Olive Oyl $175.00
Penguin $25.00
Pig...$40.00
Popeye...$200.00
Rabbit...$75.00
Sailor..$30.00

Pinocchio, $200.00; Elephant, $30.00; Donald Duck, $175.00. (Photo courtesy Randy and Adrienne Welch)

Santa Claus $90.00
Soldier..$30.00
Wimpy $175.00

Records

Most of the records listed here are related to TV shows and movies, and all are specifically geared toward children. The more successful the show, the more collectible the record. But condition is critical as well, and unless the record is excellent or better, its value is lowered very dramatically.

Advisor: Peter Muldavin (M21) 45rpm, 78rpm, and Kiddie Picture Disks.

33⅓ RPM RECORDS

Adventures in Toyland, Magic Media, 1976-78, complete w/booklet, EX (EX cover), S13....................................$6.00
Adventures of Mighty Mouse, Rocking Horse, 1957, EX (EX cover), T2 ....$15.00
Aristocats, Stereo, 1970, orig soundtrack, complete w/booklet, EX (EX cover)..$12.00
Around the World With the Chipmunks, Liberty, 1961, VG (VG cover), T2...$15.00
Babes in Toyland, 1961, complete w/booklet, EX (EX cover) .$20.00
Batman & Robin, Tifton, 1966, NM (NM cover), T2, from $40 to $50.00
Candy Man, Disneyland, 1972, G (G cover), S13 ....$6.00
Children's Treasury of Batman Musical Stories, Peter Pan, 1966, EX (EX cover), T2 ....$20.00
Chipmunks Sing the Beatles Hits, Liberty, 1964, scarce, EX (EX cover), M17 ....$85.00
Chitty-Chitty Bang-Bang, Stereo, 1968, orig soundtrack, EX (EX cover) $12.00
Christmas w/Alvin & the Chipmunks, Liberty/Bagdasarian, 1962, VG (VG cover), P4 ....$10.00
Cinderella, A Dream Is a Wish Your Heart Makes, Mickey Mouse Club, 1950s, NM (NM cover), P4..................$15.00
Courageous Cat & Minute Mouse Around the World in a Daze, Simon Says #M-32, 1960s, EX+ (EX+ cover), A.....$100.00
Dark Shadows, Philips, 1969, w/poster, EX (EX cover), M17..$50.00

Gene Autry's Western Classics, Columbia, 1947, set of four, EX (EX cover), A, $65.00; Roy Rogers Souvenir Album, RCA Victor, 1950, set of four, EX (EX cover), A, $85.00; Adventures of the Lone Ranger, Decca, 1957, EX (EX cover), A, $25.00.

Dr Seuss' Horton Hatches the Egg, RCA/Stereo, 1960s-70s, NM (NM cover) $20.00

Fat Albert & the Cosby Kids Halloween, EX (EX cover), F1 ....$12.00

Get Along Gang & the Big Bully, Am Greetings, 1984, complete w/booklet, EX (EX cover) $12.00

Gremlins Read-A-Long Adventure, Vista, 1984, complete w/booklet, EX, M17 ....$20.00

Hey There It's Yogi Bear, Columbia, 1964, EX (EX cover) .$25.00

House at Pooh Corner, Wonderland, 1960s, narrated by Ian Carmichael & Dick Bently, NM (NM cover) $20.00

Huckleberry Hound — The Great Kellogg's TV Show, Colpix, 1960s, EX (EX cover) $20.00

Ichabod & Rip Van Winkle, Decca, 1950s, w/Bing Crosby, EX (EX cover), A $50.00

Jan & Dean Meet Batman, Liberty, 1966, scarce, NM (NM cover), M17 ....$95.00

King Kong, Southern Cross, 1976, orig soundtrack, EX (EX cover), M17 ....$45.00

Linus the Lionhearted, Premier Albums, 1964, VG (VG cover), T2 ....$30.00

Mandrake the Magician, Garabedian, 1973, EX (EX cover), T2 ....$25.00

Merry Christmas From the Brady Bunch, Paramount #PAS-5026, EX (EX cover), J5 ....$65.00

Mickey Mouse Christmas Surprises, Mickey Mouse Club, 1950s-60s, EX (EX cover) $20.00

Peter & the Wolf Narrated by Captain Kangaroo, Everst, 1960, VG (VG cover), T2 ....$10.00

Pink Panther, RCA, 1963, orig soundtrack, NM (EX cover), T2 ....$10.00

Popeye the Sailor Man, 1960s, VG (VG cover) $10.00

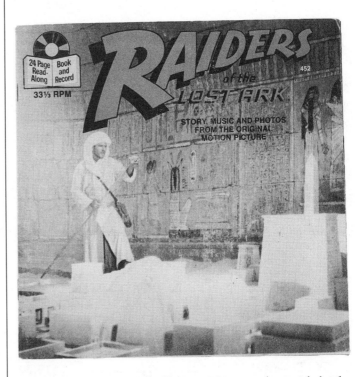

Raiders of the Lost Ark, Vista, 1981, complete with booklet, EX (EX cover), $10.00.

Rin-Tin-Tin, Columbia, 1956, VG (VG cover), A $20.00

Rocky Horror Picture Show, orig soundtrack, 1975, EX (EX cover) $20.00

Scream Along w/Marvel, Marvel Comics, 1967, EX (EX cover), A $50.00

Smurfs All Star Show, Sessions, 1981, VG (VG cover), S13 ..$8.00

Spidey Super Stories, Peter Pan, 1977, EX (EX cover), T2 ..$15.00

Strawberry Shortcake Book of Words, Kid Stuff Records, 1982, VG (VG cover), S13 ....$5.00

Superman, Power Records, 1975, EX (EX cover), T2 ....$25.00

Superman II, Warner Bros, 1980, orig soundtrack, EX (EX cover), M17 ....$30.00

Three Stooges, Peter Pan, 1976, NM (NM cover), C1.....$35.00

Three Stooges Meet Cinderella, Peter Pan, M (sealed), H4 ..$25.00

Voices of Marvel, Marvel Comics, 1964-65, EX (EX cover), T2 ....$50.00

Walt Disney's Story of Alice in Wonderland, Disneyland Records, 1979, complete w/booklet, EX (EX cover) ..$15.00

Wonder Woman, Peter Pan, 1977, complete w/booklet, EX (EX cover), T2 ....$25.00

Wonder Years, Atlantic, 1989, VG+, A $12.00

2001: A Space Odyssey, MGM, EX (EX cover), S13........$10.00

5000 Fingers of Dr T, 1950s, orig soundtrack, lyrics by Dr Seuss, EX (EX cover), M17 ....$45.00

45 RPM RECORDS

Alice in Wonderland, Golden, 1950s, EX (EX sleeve), J5..$25.00

Banana Splits, Doin' the Banana Splits & I Enjoy Being a Boy, Kellogg's premium, 1969, EX (EX sleeve), C1 ....$45.00
Batman, SPC, 1966, EX (EX sleeve), T2, from $20 to $25.00

Batman and Robin, SPC, 1966, EX (EX sleeve), from $20.00 to $25.00 each. (Photo courtesy Bill Bruegman)

Batman & Superman, Wonderland, 1969-71, NM (NM sleeve), T2, from $40 to...$50.00
Bing Crosby Sings Mother Goose, 1957, EX (EX sleeve), M21, from $8 to $15.00
Bozo the Clown, I Like People & Wowee, Little Golden, 1960, EX (EX sleeve), P4 ....$15.00
Captain America & Falcon, Peter Pan, 1974, complete w/20-pg comic book, EX (EX sleeve), F1 ....$10.00
Casper the Friendly Ghost & Little Audrey Says, Little Golden, 1960s, EX (EX sleeve), from $25 to $35.00
Flipper the Fabulous Dolphin, Golden, 1962, EX (EX sleeve), M21, from $10 to.......................................$15.00

Fred and Barney Best Friends, Peter Pan, 1976, first of series, complete with booklet, EX (EX sleeve), $20.00.

Heckle & Jeckle, Little Golden, 1958, EX (EX sleeve), T2 .$25.00
Hopalong Cassidy & the Two-Legged Wolf, Capitol, 1950s, EX (EX sleeve), A......................................$50.00
Hopalong Cassidy in Big Ranch Fire, Capitol, 1950s, EX (EX sleeve), A...$65.00
Howdy Doody & Mother Goose, RCA, 1950s, EX (EX sleeve) $65.00
Howdy Doody & Santa Claus, RCA, 1948-49, EX (EX sleeve) $30.00

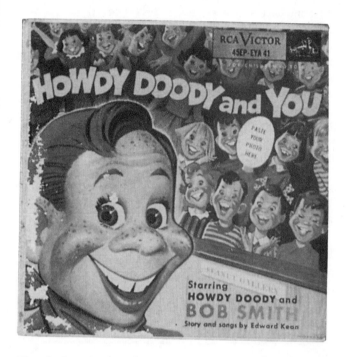

Howdy Doody and You, RCA Victor, 1950 – 54, EX (EX sleeve), $25.00. (Photo courtesy Jack Koch)

Incredible Hulk, Peter Pan, 1981, complete w/20-pg comic book, EX (EX sleeve), F1 ....$10.00
Jiminy Cricket Sings 5 Mickey Mouse Club Songs, WDP, 1955, EX (EX sleeve), P4.................................$25.00
Jungle Book, Colonel Hathi's March & Trust in Me, Disneyland Records, 1967, EX (EX sleeve), M21 ....$20.00
Lady & the Tramp, Golden, Siamese Cat Song & Bella Notte, EX (EX sleeve)..$20.00
Lone Ranger, He Finds Dan Reid, Decca #1-255, 1950s, EX (EX sleeve), A..$50.00
Lone Ranger, He Meets the Stranger From the Past, Decca #1-255, 1950s, EX (EX sleeve), A $50.00
Mighty Mouse Theme Song, Little Golden, EX (EX sleeve), T2...$15.00
Nobody Loves the Hulk, Queen City, 1969, NM (NM sleeve), T2...$100.00
Pinocchio, RCA Victor, 1949, 2-record set w/booklet, VG (VG sleeve), P4...$25.00
Popeye the Sailor Man, Golden, 1957, VG (VG sleeve), T2 ..$12.00
Roy Rogers Had a Ranch, Golden, 1950s, EX (EX sleeve) ..$45.00
Snow White & the Seven Dwarfs, RCA Victor, 1949, 2-record set w/booklet, EX (EX sleeve), P4 ....$30.00

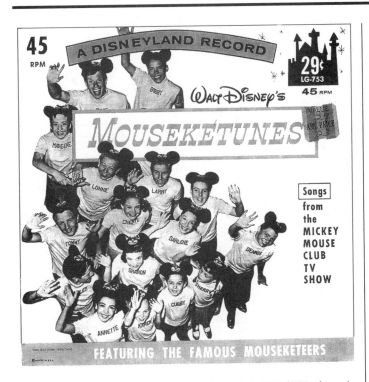

Mouseketunes, Disneyland Record, 1955, EX (EX sleeve), from $25.00 to $35.00. (Photo courtesy Peter Muldavin)

Raggedy Ann and Andy Go To Cookietown, Hallmark, complete with booklet, $35.00. (Photo courtesy Kim Avery)

Spider-Man, Peter Pan, 1981, complete w/20-pg comic book, EX (EX sleeve), F1 ....$10.00

Superman Song & Tarzan Song, Little Golden, 1961, EX (EX sleeve), M21, from $25 to $30.00

Sylvester & Hippety Hopper, Capitol, EX (EX sleeve), from $25 to $35.00

Tom Corbett Space Cadet at the Space Academy, RCA, 1950s, NM (NM sleeve), J5 ....$65.00

Winnie the Pooh & the Heffalumps, 1968, complete w/booklet, EX (EX sleeve) $15.00

Woody Woodpecker & His Talent Show, Capitol, 1949, 2-record set w/booklet, EX (EX sleeve) $20.00

101 Dalmatians, Disneyland Records, 1960s, VG (VG sleeve), M8 ....$20.00

78 RPM PICTURE AND NON-PICTURE RECORDS

Bugs Bunny and the Tortoise, Capitol, 1949, EX (EX cover), from $25.00 to $35.00. (Photo courtesy Peter Muldavin)

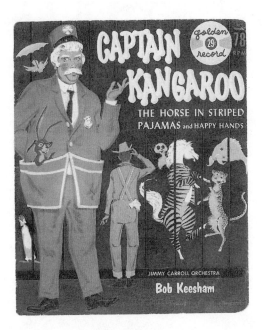

Captain Kangaroo, Horse in the Striped Pajamas and Happy Hands, Golden, 1960, EX (EX cover), from $10.00 to $15.00. (Photo courtesy Peter Muldavin)

Alice in Wonderland, Listen Look Picture Book, 1941, EX (EX cover), from $10 to $15.00

Bozo & His Rocket Ship, Capitol, 1947, EX (EX cover), M21, from $80 to $100.00

Brer Rabbit & the Tar Baby, Capitol CAS-3106, 1940s, EX (EX cover), A $50.00

Bugaloos, Capitol, 1970, EX (EX cover) $30.00

Bugs Bunny, Daffy Duck, Porky Pig & Elmer Fudd in Looney Tunes Merry Melodies, Capitol, complete w/book, EX (EX cover) $45.00

Bugs Bunny & Aladdin's Lamp, Capitol, EX (EX cover), from $35 to $40.00

Churkendoose, Decca, 1946, EX (EX cover), M21, from $10 to $20.00

Cinderella, Listen Look Picture Book, 1941, EX (EX cover)..$10.00

Daffy Duck Meets Yosemite Sam, Capitol CAS-3037, 1940s, features the voice of Mel Blanc, EX (EX cover), J5 ...$45.00

Davy Crockett & the River Pirates, Golden, 1955, EX (EX cover), M21, from $10 to..$15.00

Dennis the Menace Songs, Little Golden, 1960s, NM (NM cover), C1, from $20 to $25.00

Deputy Dawg, 1962, EX (EX cover), C1 ....$20.00

Elmer Elephant, Capitol CAS-3009, 1940s, EX (EX cover), from $25 to $35.00

Genie the Magic Record, Decca, 1946, EX (EX cover), M21, from $15 to..$20.00

Gossamer Wump, Capitol, 1946, EX (EX cover), M21, from $25 to $35.00

Gulliver's Travels, Bluebird, 1939, orig soundtrack, rare, EX (EX cover), from $150 to..$200.00

Hare & the Tortoise, Mercury Childcraft, 1951, EX (EX cover), M21, from $3 to $6.00

Henry Hawk's Chicken Hunt, Capitol, 1940s, features the voice of Mel Blanc, EX (EX cover), from $20 to $30.00

Hey Diddle Diddle, Peter Pan, 1948, EX (EX cover), from $2 to..$3.00

Hopalong Cassidy & the Singing Bandit, 1950s, 2-record set w/booklet, NM (VG cover), J5 ....$45.00

Hopalong Cassidy & the Story of Topper, Capitol, 1952, EX (EX cover), from $50 to..$70.00

Howdy Doody's Laughing Circus, RCA, Little Nipper series, 1950, EX (EX cover)..$50.00

Huckleberry Hound & Yogi Bear, Golden, 1960s, EX (EX cover), from $15 to..$20.00

It's Howdy Doody Time, RCA Victor, 1951, EX (EX cover), M21, from $75 to..$100.00

Little Engine That Could, RCA, 1949, EX (EX cover), M21, from $20 to..$30.00

Little Orley Told by Uncle Lumpy, Decca, 1949, EX (EX cover), M21, from $30 to $35.00

Lone Ranger — He Saves the Booneville Gold, Decca, 1952, No 6 in series, EX (EX cover), M21, from $60 to $80.00

Magic Land of Alla-Kazam, Peter Pan, 1962, NM (EX cover), T2..$10.00

Marge's Little Lulu and Lavender's Blue, Golden Records, 1951, EX (EX cover), from $15.00 to $20.00. (Photo courtesy Peter Muldavin)

Maverick, Golden, 1958, EX (EX cover), M21, from $10 to..$20.00

Mickey & the Beanstalk, Capitol, 1948, complete w/booklet, EX (EX cover), M21, from $75 to $85.00

Mickey Mouse Newsreel Music, Official Mickey Mouse Club Records, 1950s, NM (NM cover), T2 ....$15.00

Mickey Mouse's Christmas Party, Golden, 1950s, 4-record set w/booklet, EX (EX cover), P4 ....$35.00

Mouskethoughts, Official Mickey Mouse Club, 1955, EX (VG cover), M21, from $40 to..$60.00

Mr I Magination, Now We Know, Columbia, 1953, EX (EX cover), M21, from $10 to..$15.00

I'm a Little Teapot, Columbia Playtime, 1950, EX (EX cover), $5.00. (Photo courtesy Peter Muldavin)

Mighty Mouse in Toyland, Peter Pan, 1952, EX (EX cover), from $25.00 to $35.00. (Photo courtesy Peter Muldavin)

Mr Television w/Uncle Milty & Donald Duck, RCA Victor, 1951, scarce, EX (VG cover), M21, from $50 to **$75.00**

Peter & the Wolf, Victor, 1944, EX (EX cover), from $10 to..**$15.00**

Peter Cottontail, Golden, 1950, EX (EX cover), T2...........**$5.00**

Pinocchio, Decca #100, 4-record set, VG (VG cover), A ..**$50.00**

Poky Little Puppy, Little Golden, 1947, EX (EX cover), M21, from $7 to..**$12.00**

Popeye the Sailor Man, Golden, 1957, EX (EX cover), from $10 to **$15.00**

Raggedy Ann's Sunny Songs, RCA, 1933, 3-record set, EX (EX cover), M21, from $125 to **$150.00**

Robin Hood, CRG, 1950, EX (EX cover), M21, from $5 to .**$10.00**

Rootie Kazootie Deetle Dootle, Golden, 1950s, EX (EX cover), A **$25.00**

Roy Rogers in the Television Ambush, RCA Victor, 1951, EX (G cover), M21, from $35 to.......................................**$50.00**

Ruff & Reddy & Professor Gizmo, #558, 1959, EX (EX cover), from $15 to...**$20.00**

Rusty in Orchestraville, Capitol, 1946, EX (EX cover), from $20 to **$35.00**

Scuffy the Tugboat, Golden, 1948, EX (EX cover), M21, from $8 to **$12.00**

Snow White & the Seven Dwarfs, Decca, 1940s, 4-record set, EX (EX cover), A...**$50.00**

Songs by Burr Tillstrom's Kukla, Fran & Ollie, RCA Victor, EX (EX cover), M21, from $50 to **$75.00**

Three Little Pigs, Capitol, 1940s, 2-record set w/booklet, EX (EX cover), A **$50.00**

Thumbelina, Golden, 1951, VG (VG cover), T2 ....**$5.00**

Tom Corbett Space Cadet Song & March, Golden, 1951, M21 ....**$25.00**

Tommy & Jimmy Dorsey Play for Children — My Friend the Ghost, Golden, 1955, EX (VG cover), from $20 to ..**$30.00**

Tweetie Pie, Capitol, EX (EX cover), from $35 to............**$50.00**

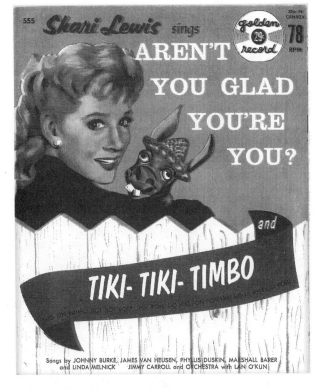

Shari Lewis Sings Aren't You Glad You're You, Golden, 1958, EX (EX cover), from $8.00 to $10.00. (Photo courtesy Peter Muldavin)

Uncle Remus 4 Songs From Song of the South, Mickey Mouse Club/WDP, 1956, EX (EX cover), P4 ....**$35.00**

Walt Disney's Pinocchio, Victor, 1941, orig soundtrack, 3-record set, 1st edition, rare, from $150 to **$250.00**

Walt Disney's Story of Robin Hood, Capitol, 1952, complete w/booklet, EX (EX cover), T2, from $25 to **$35.00**

Western Pony, Star Bright, 1949, complete w/punchouts & cutouts, EX (EX cover), from $10 to.........................**$15.00**

What Is a Boy What Is a Girl by Jackie Gleason, Decca, 1954, EX (G cover), M21, from $10 to...............................**$20.00**

Winnie the Pooh & Eeyore as Told by James Stewart, RCA Victor, 1951, EX (EX cover), from $60 to **$75.00**

Woody Woodpecker & the Scarecrow, Capitol, 1940s, EX (EX cover), A..**$35.00**

KIDDIE PICTURE DISKS

Listed here is a representative sampling of kiddie picture disks that were produced through the 1940s. Most are 6" to 7" in diameter and are made of cardboard with plastic-laminated grooves. They are very colorful and seldom came with original sleeves. Value ranges are for items in very good to near-mint condition. Ultimately, the value of any collectible is what a buyer is willing to pay, and prices tend to fluctuate. Our values are for records only (no sleeves) — note that unlike other records, the value of a picture disk is not diminished if there is no original sleeve.

Alice in Wonderland, Toy Toon Records, 1952, M21, from $10 to **$15.00**

Bicycle Built for Two, Red Raven Movie Records, 1956, NM, M21, from $20 to $30.00

Bunny Easter Party, Voco, 1948, NM, M21, from $40 to .$50.00

Cinderella, Toy Toon Records, 1952, M21, from $10 to ..$15.00

Flash Gordon City of Sea Caves, Record Guild of America, 1948, scarce, NM, M21, from $50 to.........................$75.00

I'm Called Little Buttercup, PicturTone, Gilbert & Sullivan series, 1948, M21, from $15 to $20.00

Jacob's Dream, Bible Storytime, 1948, M21, from $10 to.$15.00

Kitty Cat, Voco, 1948, NM, M21, from $10 to................$20.00

Laugh Laugh Phonograph, Voco, 1948, rare 6" size, from $20 to $25.00

Lionel Train Sound Effects, 1951, NM, M21, from $30 to....$50.00

Little Jack Horner, Pix 104, 1941, 10", from $75 to $90.00

Little Mountain Climber, Voco, 1948, NM, from $10 to.$20.00

Old McDonald Had a Farm, Voco, 1948, rare 6" size, from $20 to $25.00

Old McDonald Had a Farm, Voco, 1948, 7", from $10 to .$15.00

Red Ryder, Record Guild of America, 1948, NM, M21, from $45 to $60.00

Robin Hood, Toy Toon Records, 1952, M21, from $10 to ..$15.00

Elephant Clown, Voco, 1948, NM, from $40.00 to $50.00. (Photo courtesy Peter Muldavin)

The Three Bears with Uncle Henry, Kidisks, KD-77A, 1948, rare, from $15.00 to $25.00. (Photo courtesy Peter Muldavin)

Little White Duck, Red Raven Movie Records M ¾, 1956, rare 6" size, from $30.00 to $40.00. (Photo courtesy Peter Muldavin)

Tom Tom the Piper's Son, Kiddie Rekord, 1925, rare, EX+, from $50.00 to $60.00. (Photo courtesy Peter Muldavin)

'Round & 'Round the Village, Voco, 1948, NM, M21, from $10 to $20.00

Rover the Strong Man, Voco, 1948, NM, M21, from $40 to .$50.00

Singing Mother Goose, Magic Talking Books T-1, 1951, EX (EX cover), M21, from $20 to..$30.00

Swing Your Partner, Record Guild of America, Picture-Play Records PR11A, 1948, M21, from $100 to $150.00

Ten Little Indians, Voco, 1948, from $10 to.....................$20.00

Trial of Bumble the Bee Part II, Vogue, 1947, NM, M21, from $60 to $90.00

Winnie the Pooh & Christopher Robin Songs, RCA Victor, 1933, very rare, NM, M21, from $150 to $250.00

Reynolds Banks

Reynolds Toys began production in 1964, at first making large copies of early tin toys for window displays, though some were sold to collectors as well. These toys included trains, horse-drawn vehicles, boats, a steam toy, and several sizes of Toonerville trolleys. In the early 1970s, they designed and produced six animated cap guns. Finding the market limited, by 1971 they had switched to a line of banks they call 'New Original Limited Numbered Editions (10-50) of Mechanical Penny Banks.' Still banks were added to their line in 1980 and figural bottle openers in 1988. Each bank design is original; no reproductions are produced. Reynolds' banks are in the White House and the Smithsonian as well as many of the country's major private collections. *The Penny Bank Book* by Andy and Susan Moore (Schiffer Publishing, 1984) shows and describes the first twelve still banks Reynolds produced. Values are given for mint-condition banks.

Advisor: Charlie Reynolds (R5).

MECHANICAL BANKS

1M, Train Man Bank, 1971, edition of 30 ....$350.00
2M, Trolley Bank, 1971, edition of 30 ....$450.00
3M, Drive-In, 1971, edition of 10................................$1,000.00
4M, Pirate Bank, 1972, edition of 10 ....$725.00
5M, Blackbeard Bank, 1972, edition of 10......................$650.00
6M, Frog & Fly Bank, 1972, edition of 10 ....$1,200.00
7M, Toy Collector Bank, 1972, unlimited edition $650.00
8M, Balancing Bank, 1972, edition of 10........................$725.00
9M, Save the Girl Bank, 1972, edition of 10..............$2,000.00
10M, Father Christmas Bank, 1972, 1 made ea year at Christmas..$850.00
11M, Gump on a Stump, 1973, edition of 10..............$1,100.00
12M, Trick Bank, 1973, edition of 10..........................$1,000.00
13M, Kid Savings Bank, 1973, edition of 10 ....$1,200.00
14M, Christmas Tree Bank, 1973, edition of 10.............$725.00
15M, Foxy Grandpa Bank, 1974, edition of 10...............$975.00
16M, Happy Hooligan Bank, 1974, edition of 10........$1,075.00
17M, Chester's Fishing Bank, 1974, edition of 10 ....$900.00
18M, Gloomy Gus Bank, 1874, edition of 10..............$2,800.00
19M, Kids' Prank Bank, 1974, edition of 10................$1,100.00
20M, Mary & Her Little Lamb, edition of 20 ....$850.00
21M, Spook Bank, 1974, edition of 10...........................$800.00

22M, Decoy Bank, 1974, edition of 10............................$600.00
23M, Decoy Hen Bank, 1974, edition of 10 ....$600.00
24M, Comedy Bank, 1974, edition of 10.........................$975.00
25M, Bozo Bank, 1974, edition of 10.............................$950.00
26M, Reynolds Foundry Bank, 1974, edition of 15 .....$3,400.00
27M, Toonerville Bank, 1974, edition of 10 ....$1,200.00
28M, Bank of Reynolds Toys, 1974, edition of 10..........$425.00
29M, Simple Simon Bank, 1975, edition of 10...............$925.00
30M, Humpty Dumpty Bank, 1975, edition of 20.......$1,250.00
31M, Three Blind Mice, 1975, edition of 15.................$1,100.00
32M, Clubhouse Bank, 1975, edition of 10.................$1,100.00
33M, Boat Bank, 1975, edition of 10............................$1,500.00
34M, St Nicholas Bank, 1975, edition of 50....................$775.00
35M, Forging America, 1976, edition of 13.................$1,200.00
36M, Suitcase Bank, 1979, edition of 22 ....$825.00
37M, North Wind Bank, 1980, edition of 23 ....$1,100.00
39M, Quarter Century bank, 1982, edition of 25........$4,000.00
40M, Columbia Bank, 1984, edition of 25 ....$1,350.00
41M, Whirligig Bank, edition of 30.............................$1,300.00
42M, Miss Liberty, 1986, edition of 36 ....$1,300.00
42M, Miss Liberty on a Pedestal, 1986, edition of 4....$1,600.00
43M, Auto Giant Bank, 1987, edition of 30 ....$2,250.00
45M, Campaign '88 Bank, 1988, edition of 50............$3,000.00
46M, Hollywood, 1989, edition of 35 ....$750.00
47M, Buffalos Revenge, 1990, edition of 35 ....$900.00
48M, Williamsburg Bank, 1991, edition of 35 ....$725.00
49M, Duel at the Dome, 1992, edition of 50...............$1,000.00

50M, '92 Vote, 1992, edition of 50, $3,000.00.
(Photo courtesy Charlie Reynolds)

51M, Oregon Trail Bank, 1993, edition of 50.................$800.00
52M, Norway Bank (Lillehammer), 1994, edition of 50...$825.00
53M, Shoe House Bank, 1994, edition of 50 ....$950.00

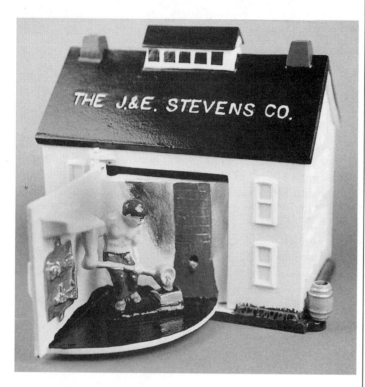

54M, J&E Stevens Co, 1995, edition of 50, $1,850.00.
(Photo courtesy Charlie Reynolds)

55M, Hyakutake Bank (The Comet), 1996, edition of 50..$550.00
56M, '96 Political Wish Bank, 1996, edition of 50.........$900.00

58M, Uncle Louie, 1997, edition of 50, $295.00.
(Photo courtesy Charlie Reynolds)

59M, Friars Favorite Bank, 1997, edition of 50 ....$1,100.00
60M, Wall Street Bank, 1998, edition of 98.................$695.00

STILL BANKS

1S, Amish Man Bank, 1980, edition of 50....................$135.00
2S, Santa, 1980, edition of 50 ....$95.00
3S, Deco Dog, 1981, edition of 50................................$85.00
4S, Jelly Bean King, 1981, edition of 100....................$265.00
5S, Hag Bank, 1981, edition of 50 ....$160.00
6S, Snowman, 1981, edition of 50................................$110.00
7S, Mark Twain, 1982, edition of 50 ....$200.00
8S, Santa, 1982, edition of 50 ....$125.00
10S, Redskins Hog Bank, 1983, edition of 50................$125.00
11S, Lock-Up Savings Bank, 1983, edition of 50 ....$55.00
12S, Miniature Bank Building, 1983, edition of 50........$195.00
13S, Santa in Chimney, 1983, edition of 50 ....$90.00
14S, Santa w/Tree (bank & doorstop), 1983, edition of 25 .$325.00
15S, Redskins NFC Champs, 1983, edition of 35...........$185.00
16S, Chick Bank, 1984, edition of 50 ....$80.00
17S, Ty-Up Bank, 1984, edition of 35 ....$225.00
18S, Tiniest Elephant Bank, 1984, edition of 50...........$110.00
19S, Baltimore Town Crier, 1984, edition of 50..............$75.00
20S, Father Christmas Comes to America, July 4th, 1984, edition of 25 ....$325.00
21S, Campaign '84 Bank, edition of 100......................$250.00
22S, Santa, 1984, edition of 50 ....$100.00
23S, Reagan '85 Bank, 1985, edition of 100 ....$310.00
24S, Columbus Ohio, 1985, edition of 50......................$60.00
25S, Austrian Santa (bank & doorstop), 1985, edition of 25 .$350.00
26S, Halloween Bank, 1985, edition of 50.....................$210.00
27S, 1893 Kriss Kringle Bank (w/tree & candle decorations), 1985, edition of 20 ....$2,400.00
28S, Santa Coming to a Child, 1985, edition of 50........$165.00
29S, Halley's Comet, 1986, edition of 50......................$190.00
30S, 20th Anniversary Bank, 1986, edition of 86...........$165.00
31S, Father Christmas (bank & doorstop), gr, edition of 25 ...$280.00
32S, Santa & the Reindeer, 1986, edition of 50.............$185.00
33S, Charlie O'Conner Bank, 1987, edition of 50............$90.00
34S, Chocolate Rabbit Bank, 1987, edition of 50 ....$110.00
35S, St Louis River Boat, 1987, edition of 60 ....$75.00
36S, German Santa (bank & doorstop), 1987, edition of 25.$275.00
38S, Old Stump Halloween, 1987, edition of 50 ....$95.00
39S, Santa in Race Car, 1987, edition of 100.................$130.00
40S, Technology Education Bank, edition of 88...............$65.00
41S, Super Bowl XXII Redskins, 1988, edition of 50........$90.00
42S, Easter Rabbit Bank, 1988, edition of 50.................$55.00
43S, Florida Souvenir Bank, 1988, edition of 75 ....$90.00
44S, Father Christmas w/Lantern (bank & doorstop), 1988, edition of 35 ....$260.00
45S, Halloween Spook, 1988, edition of 50 ....$90.00
46S, NCRPBC (National Capitol Region Club), 1988, edition of 20 ....$300.00
47S, Santa on Polar Bear, 1988, edition of 75 ....$110.00
49S, Shuffle Off to Buffalo, 1989, edition of 75 ....$70.00
50S, Pocket Pigs, 1989, edition of 75 ....$125.00
51S, Regal Santa (bank & doorstop), 1989, edition of 35 .$275.00
52S, Tiniest Snowman, 1989, edition of 75 ....$60.00

48S, Bush-Quayle, 1989, edition of 100, $260.00.
(Photo courtesy Charlie Reynolds)

53S, Santa on Motorcycle, 1989, edition of 75 ....$105.00
54S, Rabbit w/Mammy, 1990, edition of 75 ....$190.00
55S, Antique Row Sign Post, 1990, edition of 75.............$70.00
56S, Duck w/Puppy & Bee Bank, 1990, edition of 75 ....$110.00
57S, 1895 Santa w/Wreath, 1990, edition of 35 ....$250.00
58S, Santa on a Pig, 1990, edition of 75 ....$140.00

63S, Santa About To Leave, 1992, edition of 25, $290.00.
(Photo courtesy Charlie Reynolds)

64S, Jack-O'-Lantern, 1992, edition of 60 ....$80.00
65S, Santa in Zeppelin, 1992, edition of 100....................$90.00
66S, Clinton Bank, 1993, edition of 100 ....$310.00
67S, Windy City Bank (Chicago Convention), 1993, edition of
    60 ....$85.00
68S, Santa & the Bad Boy (Summer Santa), 1993, edition of
    50 ....$225.00
69S, Arkansas President, 1994, edition of 100................$325.00
70S, Santa & the Good Kids, 1994, edition of 35 ....$260.00
71S, Penny Santa, 1994, edition of 60 ....$125.00
72S, School Days Bank, 1995, edition of 100 ....$95.00
73S, 1880 Snow Santa, 1995, edition of 50 ....$220.00

59S, St. Louis Sally Bank, 1991, edition of 55, $65.00.
(Photo courtesy Charlie Reynolds)

60S, Santa w/Wassail Bowl, 1991, edition of 35.............$250.00
61S, Santa Express Bank, 1991, edition of 55.................$125.00
62S, Pig on Sled Bank, 1992, edition of 55 ....$85.00

**77S, Foxy Grandpa Car and Egelhoff Safe, 1997, edition of
60, $200.00.** (Photo courtesy Charlie Reynolds)

74S, Santa on Donkey, 1995, edition of 50 ....**$110.00**
75S, Clinton/Dole '96 (SBCCA '96), 1996, edition of 100 .**$280.00**
78S, Halloween Witch Bank, 1997, edition of 50 ....**$95.00**
79S, Christmas Time Bank, 1997, edition of 50 ....**$110.00**
80S, Portland Chicks Banks, 1998, edition of 20, pr **$155.00**
81S, Old St Nicholas Bank, 1998, edition of 20 ....**$450.00**

Robots and Space Toys

Space is a genre that anyone who grew up in the '60s can relate to, but whether you're from that generation or not, chances are the fantastic robots, space vehicles, and rocket launchers from that era are fascinating to you as well. Some emitted beams of colored light and eerie sounds and suggested technology the secrets of which were still locked away in the future. To a collector, the stranger, the better. Some were made of lithographed tin, but even plastic toys (Atom Robot, for example) are high on the want list of many serious buyers. Condition is extremely important, both in general appearance and internal workings. Mint-in-box examples may be worth twice as much as one mint-no-box, since the package art was often just as awesome as the toy itself.

Because of the high prices these toys now command, many have been reproduced. Beware!

Advisor: Ed Janey (J2).

See also Marx; Guns, Miscellaneous.

Acrobat, Y, robot does acrobatics, plastic, battery-op, EX, L4 ....**$225.00**
Animal Satellite MS-7, Japan, litho tin, friction, 5", VG, J2 ..**$140.00**
Answer Game Machine Robot, Japan, litho tin, battery-op, 14½", EX (EX box), minimum value **$550.00**
Apollo II American Eagle Lunar Module, DSK, 1950s, litho tin, several actions, battery-op, 10", EX.........................**$300.00**
Apollo Lunar Module, Japan, litho tin & plastic, battery-op, 9", MIB, L4..**$250.00**
Apollo Saturn Two-Stage Moon Rocket, TN, 1960s, several actions, litho tin, battery-op, 24", EX **$225.00**
Apollo Saucer, West Germany, 1950s, litho tin, friction, 4" dia, MIB, A...**$100.00**
Apollo Space Patrol, battery-op, EX (EX box), A **$175.00**
Apollo Spacecraft, MT, 1960s, several actions, w/detachable astronaut, litho tin, battery-op, 10", EX..................**$250.00**
Apollo Z Moon Traveler, TN, 1960s, several actions, litho tin, battery-op, 15", rare, EX **$300.00**
Astrobase, Ideal, 1960s, tin & plastic, battery-op, 11", complete, EX **$365.00**
Astronaut, Daiya, advances, stops & fires machine gun, litho tin, battery-op, 14", NM (EX box) **$1,800.00**
Atlas ICBM Missile Launcher, NMIB, L4 ....**$475.00**
Atom Robot, KO, advances in erratic motion, litho tin, w/up, 6", NM (NM box) **$700.00**
Atom Rocket-15 Interplanetary Spaceship, Y, 1960s, several actions, litho tin, battery-op, 13½", EX...................**$225.00**
Atomic Robot, Japan, advances w/step-over action, litho tin, w/up, 5", NM, A **$750.00**

Big Max Electronic Conveyor Robot, Remco, 1958, complete with truck and metal disks, EX, J6, $265.00. (Photo courtesy June Moon)

Atomic Rocket X-1800, MT, 1960s, several actions, litho tin, battery-op, 9", EX **$300.00**
Billy Blastoff Space Scout, Eldon, 1968, battery-op, 4½", complete, EX **$200.00**
Blue Eagle Space Rocket, battery-op, MIB, L4 ....**$450.00**
Buck Rogers Rocket Police Patrol, Marx, advances w/sparks & sound, litho tin, w/up, 12", NM, A **$950.00**
Captain Robo Space Transporter, Y, 1970s, plastic, battery-op, 13½", EX...**$150.00**
Chief Robot Man, KO, 1950s, several actions, litho tin, battery-op, 12", rare, NM, minimum value **$950.00**
Chief Smoky Advanced Robot Man, KO, 1950s, several actions, litho tin, battery-op, 12", scarce, NM, minimum value **$3,000.00**
Colonel Hap Hazzard, Marx, advances swinging arms, twirling antenna & flashing lights, tin, battery-op, 12", NMIB, A **$1,000.00**
Cragstan Astronaut, Daiya, red or bl version, several actions, litho tin, battery-op, 14", EX, ea **$800.00**
Cragstan Great Astronaut, Alps, 1960s, several actions, litho tin, battery-op, 14", scarce, NM, minimum value **$1,000.00**
Cragstan Ranger Robot, 1960s, several actions, mostly plastic, battery-op, 10½", rare, NM, minimum value **$1,000.00**
Cragstan Satellite, 1950s, litho tin, battery-op, 5½", VG .**$175.00**
Cragstan Talking Robot, NGS, 1960s, 4 phrases, litho tin, battery-op, 11", EX **$800.00**
Cragstan's Mr Robot, Y, 1960s, several actions, litho tin, battery-op, 10½", rare, EX...**$700.00**
Ding-A-Ling Super Return Space Skyway, Topper, 1971, NMIB, J6 (it is important for this to be complete) **$150.00**
Dino Robot, SH, 1960s, several actions, litho tin, battery-op, 11", rare, NM, minimum value **$1,000.00**
Electric Robot, Marx, 1950s, several actions, litho tin, battery-op, 14½", EX...**$200.00**
Electric Robot w/Son, Marx, 1950s, several actions, litho tin, battery-op, 14½", EX **$300.00**
Esso Energy Rocket, battery-op, MIB, L4......................**$375.00**
Excavator Robot, SH, 1960s, several actions, plastic & tin, 10", EX **$200.00**
Fighting Spaceman, SH, 1960s, several actions, battery-op, litho tin, 12", EX **$300.00**

Earth Man, TN, advances and raises rifle with flashing lights and sound, remote control, 9", NMIB, A, $1,200.00; Piston Action Robot, TN, 1950s, advances with lights and sound, tin with rubber hands, remote control, 8", rare, NM, A, $1,100.00.

Flash Space Patrol Z-206, several actions, battery-op, 8", MIB, L4 ....$375.00

Flash Strat-O-Wagon, Wyandotte, rocket-shaped wagon w/wire hdl, litho tin, 6", NMIB, minimum value $225.00

Flashing Rocketship Space Patrol, Irwin, 1950s, several actions, plastic, battery-op, 7½", EX...........................$85.00

Flashy Jim, SNK, advances w/lights & sound, tin, remote control, 8", NM (EX box), A $1,400.00

Flying Saucer Z-101, England, 1950s, litho tin, 7", scarce, EX.$250.00

Gigantor, Yone, advances w/knocking sound, litho tin, w/up, 4", scarce, EX, A $675.00

Hi-Bouncer Moon Scout, Marx, 1968, several actions, battery-op, tin, 11", rare, NMIB $1,700.00

High Wheel Robot, KO, advances w/sparks & spinning gears, litho tin, w/up, 10½", NM (EX box), A $575.00

Interplanetary Rocket, Y, 1960s, several actions, litho tin, battery-op, 15", NM..$175.00

Jupiter Jyro Set, Tomy, 1970s, mostly plastic, battery-op, 13", EX $125.00

Jupiter Robot, Yonezawa, 1950s, several actions, litho tin, battery-op, 13", rare, NMIB $2,000.00

Jupiter Rocket Launching Pad, TN, 1960s, several actions, battery-op, 7", EX $275.00

King Ding Robot, battery-op, litho tin, EX, L4 ....$225.00

King Flying Saucer, KO, 1960s, 3 actions, battery-op, 7½" dia, EX $150.00

Laughing Robot, SH, 1960s, several actions, litho tin, battery-op, 13½", EX $200.00

Laughing Robot, Y, 1970s, 3 actions, mostly plastic, battery-op, 9½", EX...$125.00

Lavender Robot, Modern Toys, rolls forward w/blinking eyes, tin, battery-op, 15", rare, VG (VG box), A..........$4,200.00

Looping Space Tank, Daiya, 1960s, several actions, battery-op, 8", MIB, L4 ....$500.00

Lost in Space Robot, AHI/Azar Hamway, 1977, bump-and-go action with flashing lights, plastic, battery-operated, 10", NMIB, $200.00.

Lost in Space Robot, Remco, 1966, plastic, all red, 12", EX ..$275.00

Lost in Space Robot, Remco, 1966, plastic, all red, 12", EX (EX box)...$500.00

Lost in Space Robot, Remco, 1966, plastic, metallic bl w/red arms, 12", NM (NM box).................................$850.00

Luna Hovercraft, TPS, 1960s, 3 actions, litho tin & plastic, MIB, L4..$325.00

Lunar Captain, TN, 1960s, several actions, battery-op, 13½", EX $225.00

Jet Car Spaceship, Ideal, 1956, 14", EX, J6, $185.00.
(Photo courtesy June Moon)

Lunar Loop, Daiya, 1960s, 3 actions, litho tin, battery-op, 12" dia hoop, EX $200.00

Machine Robot, SH, 1960s, advances w/lights & sound, tin & plastic, battery-op, 12", EX................................$500.00

Man in Space, Alps, 1960s, several actions, litho tin, battery-op, 7", rare, NM..$825.00

Man Made Satellite, Hoku, 1950s, several actions, litho tin, battery-op, 7", scarce, NM (EX box), A $3,000.00

Mando Robot, Brevettato/Italy, tin, controlled w/detachable detachable squeeze pump, 5", rare, EX (EX box), A $2,000.00

Marching Drumming Robot (Babes in Toyland Look-Alike), batter-op, NM..$400.00

Mars Explorer Astronaut, SH, 1960s, advances w/lights & sound, litho tin, battery-op, 10", NM $500.00

Mars King, SH, 1960s, advances w/light-up space scene in chest & sound, litho tin, battery-op, 9½", VG, A $200.00

Mars Rocket, MT, advances w/lights & sound as pilot raises his arm, tin & plastic, battery-op, 15", rare, NMIB, A..$1,600.00

Mars 3 Space Rocket, TN, 1960s, several actions, battery-op, 15", EX..$200.00

Moon Explorer, Bandai, 1960s, several actions, litho tin, battery-op, 17½", rare, EX, minimum value.............$1,200.00

Moon Explorer, KO, advances w/sound & spinning antenna, tin & plastic, crank action, 7", NMIB $850.00

Moon Explorer M-27, Yonezawa, 1960s, several actions, litho tin, battery-op, 7", rare, NM............................$700.00

Moon Express, TPS, 1950s, several actions, litho tin, battery-op, 12", EX..$250.00

Moon Man 001, Hong Kong, 1960s, mostly plastic, battery-op, 6", rare, EX, minimum value $175.00

Moon Orbiter, Yonezawa, advances & spins as astronaut flies above, plastic, w/up, NMIB................................$150.00

Moon Patrol, Gakken, 1960s, several actions, litho tin w/vinyl figure, battery-op, 11½", NM...............................$500.00

Moon Patrol 11, Y, 1960s, several actions, tin & plastic, battery-op, 9" dia, EX..$200.00

Moon Rocket, MT, bump-&-go action w/lights & sound, litho tin, battery-op, 9½", NM (EX box), A $400.00

Moon Rocket, XM-12, Y, 1960s, several actions, litho tin, battery-op, 14½", rare, NM $650.00

Mars 8 Racer, Japan, lithographed tin, friction, NM, $100.00. (Photo courtesy John Turney)

Mercury Space Saucer X-1, Y, 1960s, several actions, battery-op, 8" dia, EX..$150.00

Mighty Robot, MT, advances as sparks shoot from chest, litho tin, w/up, 6", MIB, A...$300.00

Mighty 8 Robot w/Magic Color, MT, 1960s, several actions, battery-op, 12", scarce, NM, minimum value..........$2,400.00

Mond Roboter, Hong Kong, several actions, litho tin, battery-op, 12", rare, EX..$300.00

Monster Robot, SH, 1970s, 3 actions, battery-op, 10", EX .$125.00

Moon Astronaut, Daiya, advances, raises rifle & fires, litho tin, w/up, 9", scarce, NM (EX box), A $2,100.00

Moon City, battery-op, MIB, L4 ....$250.00

Moon Crawler X-12, battery-op, M, L4 ....$100.00

Moon Detector, Y, 1960s, advances w/several actions, litho tin, battery-op, 10½", rare, NM $800.00

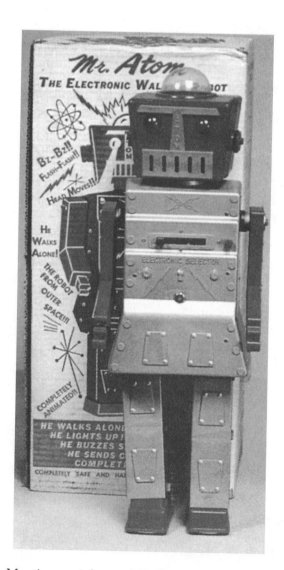

Mr. Atom, Advanced Doll and Toy, 1950s, advances with lights and sound, gray plastic, battery-operated, 18", EX (G box), A, $500.00.

Mr Atomic Robot, Cragstan, 1950s, 3 actions, litho tin, battery-op, 11", scarce, NMIB, minimum value................$5,000.00

Mr Hustler, Taiyo, 1960s, advances & flexes shoulders w/lights & sound, tin, battery-op, 11½", rare, NM (EX box), A...$700.00

Mystery Moon (rare variation of Chief Robot Man), KO, bump-&-go w/lights & sound, battery-op, 12", EX (EX box)..$1,500.00

NASA New Flying Saucer, KO, 1960s, several actions, battery-op, 7½", NM...$250.00

Nike Missile Sam-A7, Daiya, advances w/sparks, litho tin, friction, 18½", NM (EX box) $300.00

Orbit Explorer w/Airborne Satellite, KO, several actions, litho tin & plastic, w/up, 6", VG (G box) $500.00

Pete the Spaceman, Bandai, 1960s, battery-op, MIB, L4..$225.00

Piston Action Robot, TN, 1950s, advances w/lights & sound, tin w/rubber hands, remote control, 8", rare, NM (NM box), A...$1,900.00

Planet Explorer X-80, MT, 1960s, several actions, litho tin, battery-op, 8" dia, EX $185.00

Planet Robot, KO, 1960s, several actions, litho tin, battery-op, 9", rare, EX..$900.00

Radar 'N Scope Space Station, MT, 1960s, several actions, litho tin, battery-op, 6x8", MIB, A.............................$425.00

Radar Robot, SH, advances w/step-over action, plastic, w/up, 7", NM (NM box), A...$125.00

Red Rosko Astronaut, TN, advances w/flashing lights in helmet, battery-op, 13", NM...$1,400.00

Rendezvous 7.8 Space Station, Y, 1960s, several actions, litho tin, battery-op, 15", scarce, NM, minimum value.........$3,000.00

Robby Space Patrol, TN, 1950s, several actions, litho tin, battery-op, 12½", scarce, NM, minimum value.........$4,000.00

Robert the Robot, Ideal, 1940s-50s, red & gray plastic, battery-op, 14", scarce, NMIB, from $250 to.......................$350.00

Robot, Hong Kong, 1970s, advances and stops as gun shoots from chest, lithographed tin, battery-operated, 12", NM, J6, $150.00. (Photo courtesy June Moon)

Radar Robot, TN, 1960s, advances with lights and sound, remote control, 8", scarce, NMIB, A, $1,300.00.

Radar Tank, MT, 1950s, 3 actions, litho tin w/plastic antenna, battery-op, 8", NM $250.00

Radicon Space Pathfinder, battery-op, MIB, L4.........$1,275.00

Robot, Linemar, gold, advances w/swinging arms, lights & sound, tin, remote control, 7", scarce, NM (EX box), A ..$4,800.00

Robot, Y, metallic bl, advances w/lights & sound, tin, battery-op, 11", NM (EX box), A.......................................$1,600.00

Robot Car, Yonezawa, 1950s, several actions, litho tin, battery-op, 9", scarce, NM $2,000.00

Robot Commando, battery-op, MIB, L4 ....$650.00

Robot N, NBK, wooden put-together robot w/meter in chest, battery-op, VG (VG box), A $1,800.00

Robot R-35, MT, 1950s, advances w/swinging arms & light-up eyes, litho tin, remote control, 7", NMIB, A........$1,200.00

Robot Trooper, KO, 1950s, 3 actions, litho tin, battery-op, 7½", scarce, NM, minimum value $1,000.00

Robot w/Smoking & Light-Up Lantern, Linemar, rare red & silver version w/eyebrows, remote control, 8", NM (EX box) $5,800.00

Robot w/Spark, Japan, advances w/sparks in chest, litho tin, w/up, MIB, A..$500.00

Robot YM-3, Masudaya, 1980s, gray plastic, battery-op, 13", MIB, J5..$85.00

Robot YM-3, Masudaya, 1980s, gray plastic, battery-op, 5", MIB, J5 ....$25.00

Robotank TR-2, TN, 1950s, several actions, battery-op, 5", EX $275.00

Robotank-Z, TN, 1960s, several actions, litho tin, battery-op, 10", NM $500.00

Rocket Launching Pad, Y, 1950s, several actions, litho tin, battery-op, 8½", rare, EX..$325.00

Rocket Racer #3, Modern Toys, 1960, advances w/sparks & sound, litho tin, friction, EX (EX box), P4 ....$225.00

Rocket Ranger, Japan, 1950s, guns spin & fire at F-22 jet overhead, litho tin, friction, 6½", NM (EX box), A $650.00

Rocket X-202, Spain, 1950s, litho tin, friction, 10½", VG (G box), A..$100.00

Rocket XB-115, SH, advances w/lights & sound, litho tin & plastic, friction, 12", MIB.................................$175.00

Rocketship XX-2, TN, advances w/spinning tail, litho tin & plastic w/rubber nose, friction, 13", EX, P4.............$300.00

Rotate-O-Matic Super Astronaut, SH, advances w/lights & sound, litho tin, battery-op, 12", MIB.....................$225.00

Rotating Satellite, Gescha, satellite spins around Earth, litho tin, 8", NM (EX box), A $150.00

Roto-Robot, SH, 1960s, several actions, litho tin, battery-op, 8½", EX...$200.00

Rudy the Robot, Remco, 1968, several actions, battery-op, 16", EX $225.00

Satellite in Orbit, SH, 1950s, 3 actions, litho tin w/styrofoam ball, 9", rare, EX...$400.00

Satellite X-107, MT, 1960s, several actions, litho tin, battery-op, 8", rare, NM..$600.00

Saturn V Apollo II Rocket, Hong Kong, plastic & tin, 14", EX (EX box), J2...$200.00

Smoking Engine Robot, SH, 1970s, advances as pistons in chest spin & blow smoke, plastic, battery-op, 10", MIB ...$300.00

Smoking Spaceman, Linemar, 1950s, several actions, litho tin, battery-op, 12", rare, NM....................................$1,800.00

Solar-X Space Rocket, TN, several actions, litho tin & plastic, battery-op, 15", EX (EX box), A $125.00

Sonicon Rocket, Modern Toys, 1960s, litho tin, battery-op, controlled by plastic whistle, 14", NM (NM box), P4...$925.00

Sounding Robot, SH, advances w/sound, plastic, battery-op, 10½", MIB, A..$200.00

Space Bus, Bandai, battery-op, litho tin, NMIB, L4 ....$875.00

Space Capsule #5, MT, 1960s, several actions, litho tin & plastic, battery-op, 10½", EX..................................$300.00

Space Car, Y, 1950s, several actions, litho tin w/styrofoam ball, battery-op, 9½", rare, NM, minimum value $1,000.00

Space Commander, SH, 1960s, several actions, litho tin, battery-op, 10", scarce, NM, minimum value $2,000.00

Space Conquerer, Daiya, 1960s, several actions, litho tin, battery-op, 14", NM...$800.00

Space Dog, Yoshiya, 1950s, advances w/jaw & ear movement, silver-pnt tin w/red detail, clockwork, 7", EX (EX box).$475.00

Space Exploration Train, KO, 1950s, litho tin, 4 pcs, 21", rare, EX $800.00

Space Explorer, SH, silver version, advances & chest opens to reveal Apollo flight, tin, battery-op, 12", NM (NM box)........$350.00

Space Explorer, Yonezawa, 1960s, several actions, litho tin, battery-op, expands to 11½", rare, minimum value ..$1,200.00

Space Explorer S-61, Japan, litho tin, friction, 13", EX, J2 .$65.00

Space Explorer X-7, MT, 1960s, several actions, litho tin, battery-op, 7" dia, EX $185.00

Space Fighter Robot, SH, 1970s, several actions, tin & plastic, 9", NM..$150.00

Space Frontier Saturn 5 Rocket, Japan, 1960s, several actions, litho tin, battery-op, 18", EX.................................$200.00

Space Jet X-001, Bandai, bump-&-go w/flashing lights, sound & smoking engine, litho tin, battery-op, 10", rare, NM..$600.00

Space Orbitestor, Asakusa, 1960s, 3 actions, tin & plastic, battery-op, 8", EX $185.00

Space Patrol Firebird w/Blinking Light, MT, 1950s, 3 actions, litho tin, battery-op, 14", scarce, EX......................$500.00

Space Patrol X-17, MT, 1960s, 3 actions, litho tin w/styrofoam ball, battery-op, 8" dia, EX $185.00

Space Patrol XII Tank, battery-op, VG, L4 ....$185.00

Space Patrol 2019, battery-op, MIB, L4........................$300.00

Space Pioneer Vehicle, MT, 1960s, 3 actions, litho tin, battery-op, 12", EX $300.00

Space Radar Scout Pioneer, MT, advances as rear screen spins w/siren sound, litho tin & plastic, friction, 6", NMIB..$350.00

Space Ranger Flying Saucer No 3, battery-op, MIB, L4 .$175.00

Space Rocket, Japan, advances with lights and sound, lithographed tin, remote control, 14", scarce, NM (EX box), A, $500.00.

Space Rocket Blue Eagle, battery-op, MIB, L4 ....$475.00

Space Scooter, MT, 1960s, astronaut advances on scooter w/lights & sound, litho tin & plastic, battery-op, 8", EX...$200.00

Space Scope, TN, litho cb w/rockets & satellite, complete w/3 interchangeable snap-on heads, 9", EX (EX box), A.$250.00

Space Scout S-17, Y, 1960s, several actions, litho tin & plastic, battery-op, 10", rare, NM $500.00

Space Shuttle Challenger, battery-op, MIB, L4..............$475.00

Space Tank M-41, MT, 1950s, several actions, litho tin w/plastic antenna, battery-op, 9", EX...$200.00

Space Tank X-Y 101, Gama, 1960s, bump-&-go action w/lights, litho tin, battery-op, 8", NM (EX box), A..............$265.00

Space Tank X-4, TN, advances w/sound, litho tin, friction, 7", MIB...$175.00

Space Trip, MT, cars navigate track as space station spins, litho tin, battery-op, 19", EX (EX box)............................$650.00

Space Trooper, Haji, 1950, advances w/sound, litho tin, w/up, 7", NM (EX box)..$2,200.00

Space Whale Ship, Yoshiya, advances w/moving mouth & sparks, litho tin, w/up, 9", EX, A.............................$350.00

Spacecraft Jupiter, K, advances w/sparks, litho tin w/clear plastic dome, w/up, 5" dia, NMIB, A...............................$150.00

Spaceman, N, advances as sparks shoot from chest, litho tin, w/up, 6", NM (EX box), A.......................................$550.00

Spaceman, SH, advances w/sound & spinning antenna, litho tin, w/up, 9", NM (EX box), A...........................$1,100.00

Spaceman Car, Japan, advances w/sound, litho tin, friction, 6", MIB...$1,200.00

Spaceship X-5, MT, 1950s, litho tin, friction, 12", NM (EX box) $1,000.00

Spaceship X-8, Tada, 1960s, several actions, litho tin, battery-op, 8", EX...$200.00

Sparkling Rocket Fighter Ship #5, Marx, advances w/sparks & sound, litho tin, w/up, 12", EX (EX box), A............$650.00

Sparky Robot, KO, 1950s, advances w/sparks & sound, litho tin, w/up, needs new flint, NMIB, A..............................$550.00

Spitz Junior Planetarium, Harmonic Reed Corp, 1956, plastic globe plugs in & shows stars, planets, etc, MIB, M17.$175.00

Star Strider Robot, SH, 1980s, several actions, 12", EX (EX box)..$225.00

Strange Explorer, DSK, 1960s, several actions, battery-op, 7½", EX...$250.00

Super Moon Patroler, Japan, advances w/several actions, litho tin, battery-op, 9", scarce, EX (EX box), A.............$550.00

Super Sonic Space Rocket, KO, 1950s, several actions, litho tin, battery-op, 14", rare, EX......................................$475.00

Super Space Capsule, SH, 1960s, advances, stops & door opens to reveal pilot, tin & plastic, 9", EX......................$200.00

Swinging Baby Robot, Yone, swings back & forth as mouth opens & closes, litho tin, w/up, 6", MIB, A.............$575.00

Swivel-O-Matic Astronaut, SH, 1960s, several actions, litho tin, battery-op, 11½", EX..$165.00

Target Robot, MT, 1950s, several actions, litho tin, battery-op, complete w/gun & darts, 15", scarce, minimum value.......$4,000.00

Thunder Robot, Asakusa, advances w/blinking eyes, tin, battery-op, 11", scarce, NMIB, A.......................................$6,500.00

Turbo Jet Car, Ideal, launches off platform, plastic, w/up, 15", NMIB, A...$200.00

Twikki Robot (Buck Rogers), plastic, w/up, 7", NM.........$75.00

Two-Stage Rocket Launching Pad, TN, 1950s, rocket propels after several actions, litho tin, battery-op, 8", EX (EX box) $500.00

UFO X-05, MT, 1970s, battery-op, MIB, L4 ....$175.00

UFO-X2 Flying Saucer, Daiya, 1960s, mystery action, litho tin & plastic, battery-op, 6" dia, NM (EX box), M17 ...$300.00

USA-NASA Gemini, MT, 1960s, advances w/lights & sound as astronaut circles above, tin, battery-op, 9", EX (VG box), A $300.00

Vanguard Satellite Launcher, Remco, 1960s, battery-op, MIB...$275.00

Video Robot, SH, 1960s, 3 actions, litho tin, battery-op, 10", EX $185.00

Winky Robot, Y, advances w/moving radiation count meter in chest, litho tin, w/up, 9½", scarce, NMIB, A $2,000.00

MISCELLANEOUS

Bank, astronaut, compo, EX, S21 ....$35.00

Bank, Duro Mold, rocket-shape w/emb Mercury, press pilot's head & coin shoots to front, 8", NM (G box), A $150.00

Bank, Hong Kong, 1970s, flying saucer, plastic, saucer revolves & deposits coin, NM (NM box), P4 ....$35.00

Bank, Vacumet Rocketship, 1960s, cast metal w/chrome finish, 13", MIB, P4..$165.00

Bubble Bath Set, Space Mates, Watkins, 1960s, EX (EX box), J2, minimum value..$40.00

Bubble Pipe, Bubble-O-Bill Spaceship, Mattel, 1950s, plastic, 3½", NM (NM box), P4...$65.00

Card Game, Satelite Space Race, 1957, complete, MIB, A.$75.00

Chalk, rocket shape, 1950s, NMIB, J2 ....$20.00

Clock Radio, robot figure, NM, from $50 to....................$75.00

Colorforms, Space Warriors, 1977, MIB (sealed), B10.....$20.00

Dexterity Game, Orbit Yo-Yo, Tom Boy Inc, 1969, Be an Astronaut, It's Fun..., plastic, MOC, P4............................$45.00

Television Spaceman, Alps, 1960s, several actions, lithographed tin, battery-operated, 14½", EX (EX box), minimum value, $800.00. (Photo courtesy Don Hultzman)

Bank, Mr. Robot, Wolverine, 1950s, red, yellow, and clear plastic with gold foil decal, sorts change, 10½", NM, $50.00. (Photo courtesy Plymouth Rock Toy Co)

Game, hand-held, 1950s, plunger activates spinner that points to planets & numbers, 2½" dia, M, A $85.00
Game, Johnny Apollo Moon Landing bagatelle, EX, T2..$25.00
Game, Rockets to the Moon bagatelle, NM, T2...............$25.00
Goggles, Magic Space, 1950s, MOC, J2 ....$50.00
Helmet, Space Patrol, Beemark Plastics, 1950s, complete w/instructions, MIB $700.00
Helmet, USS Space Astronaut, Coleco, VG (VG box), J2 .$125.00
Helmet, Zenith Space Commander, 1950s, EX, J2 ....$100.00
Helmet w/Built-In Walkie-Talkies, Sears, 1970s, wht plastic w/decals to spell names, battery-op, scarce, EX, M17 .$200.00
Kaleidoscope, Space Scope, TN, snap-on heads, MIB, J2.$55.00
Moonmap Puzzle, Rand McNally, 1960s, M (sealed), J2 ..$25.00
Musical Space Scope, TN, 12", EX, J2 ....$50.00
Pocketknife, 1950s, rocket-shape w/built-in siren, yel or red plastic, 3½", EX, J5, ea...$55.00
Poster, Historic Moon Landing, Rand McNally, 24x18", MIP, H4...$5.00
Projector, Zoom Outer Space, M $35.00
Ring, Jupiter, silver, NM, J2 ....$20.00
Space Helmet, Men Into Space, Colonel McCauley, Ideal, 1960, plastic, EX (EX box), A...$100.00
Space Scientist Drafting Set, 1950s, EX (EX box), J2 ......$85.00

Spinner, Space Patrol, M, J2..$25.00
Target Set, Rocket Patrol, 1950s, space scenes, 16x16", MIB, A.$150.00
Walkie-Talkies, Space Patrol, Randall/England, 1955, plastic, 5", MIB $150.00

Rock 'n Roll

From the '50s on, rock 'n roll music has been an enjoyable part of many of our lives, and the performers themselves have often been venerated as icons. Today some of the all-time great artists such as Elvis, the Beatles, KISS, and the Monkees, for instance, have fans that not only continue to appreciate their music but actively search for the ticket stubs, concert posters, photographs, and autographs of their favorites. More easily found, though, are the items that sold through retail stores at the height of their careers — dolls, games, toys, books, magazines, etc. In recent years, some of the larger auction galleries have sold personal items such as guitars, jewelry, costumes, automobiles, contracts, and other one-of-a-kind items that realized astronomical prices. If you're an Elvis or Beatles fan, we recommend *Elvis Collectibles* and *Best of Elvis Collectibles* by Rosalind Cranor (Overmountain Press); and *The Beatles, A Reference and Value Guide*, by Barbara Crawford, Hollis Lamon, and Michael Stern and *Rock-N-Roll Treasures* by Joe Hilton and Greg Moore (both by Collector Books).

Advisors: Bob Gottuso (B3), Beatles, KISS, Monkees; Rosalind Cranor (C15), Elvis.

See also Action Figures; Bubble Bath Containers; Coloring, Activity, and Paint Books; Dolls, Celebrity; Model Kits; Paper Dolls; Pin-Back Buttons; Puppets.

Beatles, ball, blk w/faces & printed signatures on wht oval, The Beatles in red, 9" dia, EX, B3...................................$850.00
Beatles, Beatle Twig, Beatle Twig Inc, complete, NMIP ..$275.00
Beatles, Beatlephones, Koss Electronics, EX (EX box) ..$2,000.00

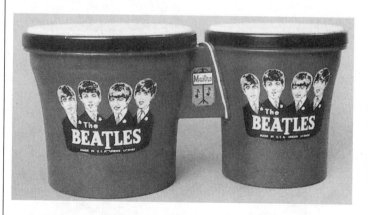

Beatles, bongos, Mastro, red plastic with decals, white top, VG, from $2,500.00 to $3,000.00.

Beatles, book, Out of the Mouths of Beatles, 1964, softcover, VG, R2 ....$15.00
Beatles, book, Yellow Submarine, Signet, paperback, EX.$15.00

Beatles, book, Yellow Submarine Gift Book, hardcover, EX.$90.00

Beatles, brooch, gold-tone banjo w/mop-top figures, movable beaded eyes, pnt hair & strings, EX, B3 ....$65.00

Beatles, brooch, Nems Ent Ltd/Invicta Plastics, guitar w/blk & wht group photo, MOC...$65.00

Beatles, Cartoon Kit, Colorforms, 1966, complete, MIB ..$800.00

Beatles, charm, from gumball machine, record shape w/various images, NM, ea $10.00

Beatles, charm bracelet, Nicky Byrne/Nems Ent Ltd, rnd blk & wht photo of ea member, NMOC...........................$175.00

Beatles, Colouring Set, Kitfix, complete, MIB $1,700.00

Beatles, Dimensionals, Yellow Submarine, Craftmaster, several variations, NMIB, ea $450.00

Beatles, Disk-Go-Case, plastic w/group photo, any color other than brn, ea, from $175 to..............................$225.00

Beatles, Disk-Go-Case, plastic w/group photo, brn, EX..$400.00

Beatles, dolls, Applause, 1988, Sgt Pepper costumes, set of 4 w/stands, 22", M $385.00

Beatles, dolls, Beatles Forever, Applause, Raggedy Ann style, set of 4 w/stands & cb stage, 22", M, B3 ....$450.00

Beatles, dolls, Remco, soft bodies, set of 4, NM, B3 ....$375.00

Beatles, drum, New Beat, blk outline of Ringo's head, hand & signature, complete w/stand, 14" dia, EX, B3...........$675.00

Beatles, guitar, New Sound by Selcol, four-string with faces and autographs, 23", NM, $550.00.

Beatles, figures, cartoon series, 1985, HP resin, set of 4", 6", NM, B3...$150.00

Beatles, figures, Swingers Music Set, NMOC $125.00

Beatles, flasher button, I Like the Beatles surrounded by names, NM..$30.00

Beatles, flasher rings, set of 4, EX, B3.........................$60.00

Beatles, guitar, Beatleist by Mastro, 30", NM $1,000.00

Beatles, guitar, Big Six by Selcol, rare 6-string version, EX ..$650.00

Beatles, guitar, Four Pop by Mastro, 4-string w/faces & autographs, 21", EX $400.00

Beatles, guitar, Junior by Selcol, red plastic w/group photo, paper label, 14", rare, EX, B3 ....$1,500.00

Beatles, guitar, New Beat by Selcol, 4-string, photo & autographs, 32", EX $550.00

Beatles, guitar, Red Jet by Selcol, electric, 31", rare, NM.$1,500.00

Beatles, harmonica, Hohner, 1964, MOC $450.00

Beatles, hummer, Louis F Dow, 1960s, cb w/head shots, NM...$150.00

Beatles, Kaboodle Kit, Standard Plastics, 1960s, photo & facsimile signatures, various colors, NM, ea.....................$900.00

Beatles, key chain, Yellow Submarine, Pride Creations, plastic, EX, B3 ....$60.00

Beatles, megaphone, NEMS, 1964, head shots on wht, orange or yel, EX, ea...$600.00

Beatles, mobile, Sunshine Art Studios, cb pop-outs, unused, MIP, B3...$140.00

Beatles, necklace, Nems Ent Ltd/Randall, heart-shape pennant w/blk & wht group photo, NMOC $175.00

Beatles, nodders, Carmascots, 1964, compo, signatures on gold bases, set of 4, 8", EX (EX box), B3.....................$900.00

Beatles, nodders, plastic, set of 4, 4", M (sealed on Swingers card), B3 ....$100.00

Beatles, Paint Your Own Beatle, Artistic Creations, any member, MIB (sealed), ea $1,500.00

Beatles, pennant, Canadian, Yeh, Yeh, Yeh & faces inside music notes, felt, red, bl & yel on off-wht, 19½", EX, B3 ..$225.00

Beatles, pennant, George & Ringo in red hearts & We Luv You Beatles in red on cream, felt, VG $150.00

Beatles, photo album, Yellow Submarine, A&M Leatherline, 1968, sm...$500.00

Beatles, poster put-ons, Yellow Submarine, unused, MIP ..$225.00

Beatles, punch-out portraits, Whitman, 1964, cb, unpunched, NM..$200.00

Beatles, purse, red vinyl clutch-type w/blk group photo, leather strap, zipper closure, EX, B3 ....$365.00

Beatles, record carrier, Airflite, early 1960s, heavy cb w/group photo & facsimile signatures, for 33 rpm records, NM............$450.00

Beatles, scrapbook, Whitman, color photos on front & back, unused, 11x13", EX, B3 ....$75.00

Beatles, spatter toy, Twirl w/the Beatles, complete w/instructions, NMIP...$375.00

Beatles, stick-ons, Yellow Submarine, Dal Manufacturing Corp, 1968, set of 4, MIP...$75.00

Beatles, sticker, from gumball machine, gold & blk w/faces & names, EX, B3 ....$25.00

Beatles, watercolor set, Yellow Submarine, Craftmaster, complete, MIB $150.00

Beatles, wig, Lowell, MIP, B3.................................$135.00

Bee Gees, transistor radio, Vanity Fair, 1979, 5½", NM, from $10 to **$15.00**

Bobby Sherman, book, Secret of Bobby Sherman, 1971, hardcover, NM **$25.00**

Bobby Sherman, Love Beads, 1971, M, from $40 to **$50.00**

Bobby Sherman, necklace, 1971, blk suede choker w/gold trim, M **$60.00**

Bobby Sherman, ring, Love & Peace, 1971, M **$25.00**

Boy George, doll, cloth, 1984, NM **$100.00**

Boy George & the Culture Club, book, Boy George & the Culture Club, 1984, NM **$25.00**

Boy George & the Culture Club, puffy stickers, 1984, set of 6, M **$15.00**

Chubby Checker, limbo bar, Whamo, 1962, w/record, EX ..**$125.00**

Crosby, Stills & Nash, whistle, ABC Records promo, Whistling Down the Wire, EX, B3 ....**$15.00**

Dave Clark Five, dolls, Remco, NMIB, B3 ....**$500.00**

David Cassidy, book, Young Mr Cassidy, Curtis, 1970s, NM..**$20.00**

David Cassidy, Dress-Up Set, Colorforms, 1972, complete, MIB **$50.00**

David Cassidy, guitar, Carnival Toys, 1970s, plastic, MIB **$100.00**

David Cassidy, slide-tile puzzle, 1970s, M **$35.00**

Dick Clark, diary, 1958, vinyl, 4x4", EX **$125.00**

Dick Clark, doll, Juro, 1958, 24", MIB..............................**$250.00**

Dick Clark, record case, 1958, EX **$75.00**

Donny & Marie Osmond, book, State Fair Mystery, Whitman, 1977, EX..**$15.00**

Donny & Marie Osmond, Colorforms Dress-Up Set, 1976, complete, MIB **$50.00**

Donny & Marie Osmond, Country & Rock Rhythm Set, Gordy, 1976, w/tambourine & microphone, MIP **$20.00**

Donny & Marie Osmond, diary, Continental Plastics, 1977, unused, EX **$15.00**

Donny & Marie Osmond, make-up kit, Mattel, 1976, MIP ..**$25.00**

Donny & Marie Osmond, microphone, LJN, 1977, MIB .**$35.00**

Donny Osmond, nodder, 1970s, 9", M, from $200 to **$250.00**

Elvis, autograph book, Elvis Presley Enterprises, 1956, EX, minimum value **$500.00**

Elvis, balloon toy, California Toytime, image of Elvis as boxer (Kid Galahad) on red balloon w/cb feet, 4", EX **$65.00**

Elvis, bracelet, Elvis Presley Enterprises, 1950s, dog tag, MOC (beware of repros) **$150.00**

Elvis, bracelet, Loving You, Elvis Presley Enterprises, 1956, framed blk & wht photo, MOC (beware of repros), from $100 ....**$150.00**

Elvis, cologne & teddy bear, Be My Teddy Bear, mk Elvis Presley Fragrances, Inc, 7½", EX (EX plastic tube) **$50.00**

Elvis, doll, Hound Dog, Smile Toy Co, stuffed plush w/Elvis lettered on wht neck ribbon, NM, A **$250.00**

Elvis, earrings, Loving You, Elvis Presley Enterprises, 1956, blk & wht photo in 14k gold-plated frames, MOC, from $50 to **$100.00**

Elvis, fan club kit, 1956, w/button, membership card & letter, EX, from $300 to **$400.00**

Elvis, flasher ring, 1957, EX, minimum value **$100.00**

Elvis, guitar, Lapin, 1984, MOC (sealed), B3 ....**$75.00**

Elvis, guitar, Selcol, 1959, UK, 32", rare, EXIB, B3.......**$700.00**

Elvis, figurine, Avon, 1987, from $80.00 to $100.00.

Elvis, necklace, Elvis Presley Enterprises, 1956, Love Me Tender, NMOC, from $175 to.....................................**$225.00**

Elvis, purse, Elvis Presley Enterprises, 1956, bl foldover carryall w/Elvis playing guitar, 5x10", M, from $600 to **$1,000.00**

Elvis, record case, Elvis Presley Enterprises, 1956, NM (cover intact, snap not broken), from $700 to **$800.00**

Elvis, scrapbook, Solid Gold Memories, Ballantine Books, 1977, EX...**$30.00**

Elvis, sideburns sticker from gumball machine, 1950s, EX..**$55.00**

Elvis, Ukette, Selcol, early, turn side knob for music, 14", EX (VG rare box), from $1,000 to **$1,200.00**

Jackson Five, banner, 1960s-70s, blk felt w/I Love Jackson 5 in wht, red trim, 29", NM, J5.................................**$25.00**

John Travolta, poster put-ons, Saturday Night Fever, 1960s, NM, F1...**$6.00**

John Travolta, scrapbook, Sunridge, 1978, EX **$10.00**

KISS, backpack, Thermos, 1979, photo on red canvas, EX..**$95.00**

KISS, belt buckle, 1976, brass w/logo, NM **$35.00**

KISS, Colorforms, 1979, complete, MIB............................**$85.00**

KISS, fan club kit, KISS Army, complete, M.....................**$75.00**

KISS, jacket, colorful flame design w/photos & logo, child-sz, EX, B3 ....**$85.00**

KISS, makeup kit, Remco, 1978, MIB **$90.00**

KISS, pin, Gene Simmons figure w/tongue sticking out, 1995, brass color w/makeup, 3-D, M, H4 ....**$10.00**

KISS, poster, 1979, Honda Kissmobile & group photo, rare, M, P12 ....**$150.00**

KISS, poster put-ons, 1976, 9x10", unused, MOC, J2.......**$20.00**

Mamas and Papas, Show Biz Babies, Remco, MOC, $250.00 each.
(Photo courtesy Bob Gottuso)

KISS, figures, Great Britain, 1980s, hand-painted metal, 2½", MIB, $90.00. (Photo courtesy June Moon)

KISS, guitar, 1977, NM, $150.00.
(Photo courtesy Bob Gottuso)

KISS, Rub 'N Play Magic Transfer Set, Colorforms, 1979, complete, MIB $85.00
KISS, solo picture disks, 12", EX, B3, ea $50.00
Marie Osmond, vanity set, 1970s, MIB $60.00
MC Hammer, backpack, Bustin Products, 1991, vinyl, 2 different styles, 15", M, ea..$20.00
MC Hammer, hand-held video game, Tiger Electronics LCD, 1991, MIP $25.00
MC Hammer, Rap Mike, Impact Toy, 1991, MIB............$25.00
Michael Jackson, bumper sticker, 1984, full-color image, EX, F1 ....$5.00
Michael Jackson, cassette & glove set, Motown, 1984, MIP.....$25.00
Michael Jackson, cassette player, 1984, NM $60.00
Michael Jackson, Colorforms Dress-Up Set, 1984, complete, MIB $25.00
Michael Jackson, key chain, 1988 concert promo, brass, M ..$12.00
Michael Jackson, microphone, LJN, 1984, cordless, MIB.$30.00
Michael Jackson, pin-back button, 1984, Beat-It, photo image, EX, F1 ....$5.00
Michael Jackson, Puzzleforms, Colorforms, 1984, MIP (sealed), C1...$20.00
Michael Jackson, wallet, 1984, nylon, various colors, M, ea .$10.00

Monkees, beach ball, 1980s, Pool It!, inflatable, EX, R2 ..$25.00
Monkees, book, Circus Boy Annual, 1958, hardcover, VG, R2 ..$30.00
Monkees, book, Monkees Go Mod, 1967, paperback, VG, R2 ....$12.00
Monkees, book, Who's Got the Button, Whitman, 1968, hardcover, EX...$25.00
Monkees, fan club kit, 1967, complete, EX (EX mailer)...$200.00
Monkees, flasher ring, flashes from 2 members to the other 2, VG, B3 ....$20.00
Monkees, guitar, Mattel, 1966, 14", NM $150.00

Monkees, tambourine, EX, B3, $85.00.
(Photo courtesy Bob Gottuso)

Monkees, guitar, Mattel, 1966, 20", NM $180.00
Monkees, oil paint set, Monkee Beat, MIB (sealed), B3...$250.00
Monkees, oil paint set, Monkeemania, Art Award, 1967,
     MIB..$200.00
Monkees, picture coin, Kellogg's premium, 1967, any member or
     group photo, EX, ea $15.00
Monkees, playing cards, Raybert, 1967, complete, MIB ...$65.00
Monkees, record case, Mattel, 1966, NM $175.00
Monkees, Show Biz Babies, Remco, set of 4, EX, B3 ......$600.00
Monkees, video, Heart & Soul, Rhino, 1988, M (sealed),
     M17...$20.00
New Kids on the Block, balloons, Unique, 1990, MIP $5.00
New Kids on the Block, Colorforms, 1991, complete, MIB ..$15.00
New Kids on the Block, microphone, Big Step Prod, 1990, MIB .$20.00
New Kids on the Block, yo-yo, Spectra Star, 1990, MOC ..$10.00
Rolling Stones, key chain, Musidor, 1983, MOC $10.00
Rolling Stones, puffy stickers, Musidor, 1983, several variations,
     5½x4", M, ea..$8.00
Rolling Stones, sticker album, Stanley, 1983, NM $15.00
Rolling Stones, 3-D flicker sheet, Vari-Vue, 1960s, image of
     members in surrealistic atmosphere, 7x7", NM, M17 ..$50.00
Shaun Cassidy, guitar, Carnival Toys, 1978, MIP $100.00
Three Dog Night, banner, 1960s-70s, bl felt w/I Love Three Dog
     Night in wht, yel trim, 29", NM, J5 ....$25.00
Van Halen, binoculars, VH logo, EX, B3 ....$18.00
Van Halen, puffy stickers, 1980s, MIP $10.00
Vanilla Ice, Rap Microphone, THQ, 1991, MIB.............$25.00
ZZ Top, mirror, 1980s, 6x6", M $10.00

Russian Toys

Many types of collectible toys continue to be made in Russia. Some are typical novelty windups such as walking turtles and pecking birds, but they have also made robots, wooden puzzles, and trains. In addition they've produced cars, trucks, and military vehicles that are exact copies of those once used in Russia and its Republics, formerly known as the Soviet Union. These replicas were made prior to June 1991 and are marked Made in the USSR/CCCP. They're constructed of metal and are very detailed, often with doors, hoods, and trunks that open.

Because of the terrific rate of inflation in Russia, production costs have risen to the point that some of these toys are no longer being made. Internet exposure has resulted in increasing interest and higher values.

Advisors: Natural Way (N1); David Riddle (R6).

REPLICAS OF CIVILIAN VEHICLES

Aeroflot (Russian Airline) Service Station Wagon, 1/43 scale,
     MIB $22.00
Aeroflot (Russian Airline) Service Station Wagon, 1/43 scale,
     MIB, R6 ....$18.00
Belarus Farm Tractor, 1/43 scale, MIB $20.00
Gorbi Limo, 1/43 scale, metal, MIB, R6..........................$25.00
KamA3 Model #5320 Flat Bed Truck, cab tilts forward, 1/43
     scale, MIB, R6...$35.00

KamA3-53212 Oil Truck, 1/43 scale, MIB, R6, $40.00.
(Photo courtesy David Riddle)

KamA3 Model #53213 Airport Fire Truck, 1/43 scale, MIB,
     R6 ....$40.00
KamA3 Model #5410 Truck Cab, 1/43 scale, MIP, R6 ....$40.00
Lada #212 4x4, trunk, doors & hood open, 1/43 scale, MIB,
     R6..$20.00
Lada #2121 4x4 w/trailer, trunk, doors & hood open, 1/43 scale,
     MIB, R6 ....$20.00
Lada Auto Service Station Wagon, 1/43 scale, MIB $20.00
Lada Sedan, trunk & hood open, 1/43 scale, MIB, R6......$20.00
Lada Station Wagon, trunk & hood open, 1/43 scale, MIB,
     R6 ....$20.00
Moksvitch Medical Services Sedan, 1/43 scale, MIB, R6 .$20.00
Moskvitch Aeroflat (Soviet Airline) Station Wagon, hood
     opens, 1/43 scale, MIB, R6 ....$20.00
Moskvitch Auto Service Station Wagon, hood opens, 1/43
     scale, R6 ....$20.00
Moskvitch Panel Station Wagon, hood opens, 1/43 scale, MIB,
     R6 ....$20.00
Moskvitch Sedan, hood opens, 1/43 scale, MIB, R6........$20.00
Moskvitch Slant-Back Sedan, 1/43 scale, MIB, R6 ....$20.00
Moskvitch Soviet Traffic Sedan, hood opens, 1/43 scale, MIB,
     R6 ....$20.00

Volga Ambulance Station Wagon, 1/43 scale, MIB, R6, $25.00. (Photo courtesy David Riddle)

Moskvitch Station Wagon, hood opens, 1/43 scale, MIB, R6...$20.00
Moskvitch Taxi Sedan, hood opens, 1/43 scale, MIB, R6..$20.00
OMO, 1937 Fire Truck, #1 in series of 6, 1/43 scale, MIB, R6............$40.00
OMO, 1937 Fire Truck, #2 in series of 6, 1/43 scale, MIB, R6............$40.00
RAF Ambulance Van, back & 3 doors open, 1/43 scale, MIB, R6............$25.00
RAF Traffic Police Van, 1/43 scale, MIB, R6 ....$25.00
Volga Sedan, trunk, hood & doors open, 1/43 scale, MIB, R6..$25.00
Volga Taxi Sedan, trunk, hood & doors open, 1/43 scale, MIB, R6............$25.00
Volga Taxi Station Wagon, trunk, hood & doors open, 1/43 scale, MIB, R6............$25.00
Volga Traffic Police Sedan, 1/43 scale, MIB, R6 ....$25.00

REPLICAS OF MILITARY VEHICLES

Armored Car, 1/43 scale, MIB, R6, $15.00.
(Photo courtesy David Riddle)

Armored Personnel Carrier, 1/43 scale, MIB, R6 ....$15.00
Armored Troop Carrier, 1/86 scale, MIB, R6....................$15.00
Cannon, 1/86 scale, MIB, R6 ....$15.00
Cannon (100mm), 1/43 scale, MIB, R6 ....$15.00
Cannon (76mm), 1/43 scale, MIB, R6 ....$15.00
Command Car, 1/86 scale, MIB, R6............................$15.00
N-153 Biplane Fighter, 1/72 scale, MIB, R6 ....$40.00
N-16 Fighter, 1/72 scale, MIB, R6............................$40.00
Rocket Launcher Armored Truck, 1/86 scale, MIB, R6 ...$15.00
Self-Propelled Cannon, 1/86 scale, MIB, R6....................$15.00
SU-100 Self-Propelled Cannon, 1/43 scale, MIB, R6.......$15.00
T-34-85 Tank, metal, rarest from the set of 6, MIB, R6 ...$25.00
Tank, battery-op, 1/72 scale, MIB, R6 ....$45.00
Tank, 1/86 scale, MIB, R6 ....$12.00
Troop Truck, 1/86 scale, MIB, R6 ....$15.00

MISCELLANEOUS

Bird, metal, w/up, MIB, N1...................................$5.00
Car on Garage Lift, MIB, N1................................$8.00
Car Set, metal, 6-pc, MIB, N1..............................$12.00
Car Track, metal, w/up, MIB, N1...........................$30.00

Chicken, metal, MIB, N1 ....$5.00
Chicken Inside Egg, w/up, MIB, N1 ....$5.00
Doll, Maytryoshki, metal, w/up, MIB, N1 ....$18.00
Doll Set, Maytryoshki, wood, Lenin, Stalin, Kruschev, Brezhnez & Gorbechev, made in China, MIB, N1 ....$30.00
Hen, metal, w/up, MIB, N1..................................$8.00
Jet Fighter, plastic, bl, MIB, N1.............................$5.00
Monster Beetle, metal, MIB, N1..............................$8.00
Moon Buggy w/2 Cosmonauts, plastic & metal, w/up, MIB, N1..$15.00
Parking Garage, metal, MIB, N1 ....$30.00
Rooster, metal, w/up, MIB, N1 ....$8.00
Tank, plastic, MIB, N1 ....$5.00
Train Track, metal, w/up, MIB, N1 ....$30.00
WWII Soldiers w/Rifles, cast metal, set of 10, MIB, N1 ...$25.00

Sand Toys and Pails

In the Victorian era a sand toy was a boxed wooden or cardboard scene with a glass front and a mechanism involving a hopper and/or chute leading to a paddle, then to various rods and levers attached to cardboard or tin figures or animals with loosely jointed limbs at the front of the scene. When the sand was poured, the mechanism was activated, and the figures went through a series of movements. These were imported mostly from Germany with a few coming from France and England.

By 1900, having seen the popularity of the European models, American companies were developing all sorts of sand toys, including free-standing models. The Sand Toy Company of Pittsburgh patented and made 'Sandy Andy' from 1909 onward. The company was later bought by the Wolverine Supply & Manufacturing Co. and continued to produce variations of the toy until the 1970s.

Today if you mention sand toys, people think of pails, spades, sifters, and molds, as the boxed scenes have all but disappeared due to their being quite fragile and not surviving use.

We have a rich heritage of lithographed tin pails with such wonderful manufacturers as J. Chein & Co., T. Cohn Inc., Morton Converse, Kirchoff Patent Co., Marx Toy Co., Ohio Art Co., etc., plus the small jobbing companies who neglected to sign their wares. Sand pails have really come into their own and are now recognized for their beautiful graphics and designs. For more information we recommend *Pails by Comparison, Sand Pails and Other Sand Toys, A Study and Price Guide* by Carole and Richard Smythe, our advisors for this category. They are S22 in the Dealer Codes.

Beach Toy Set, Chein, litho tin, complete w/animal molds, sifter & shovel, NMIP, A $225.00
Dutch Mill, Mac Toys, litho tin, 12", NM....................$250.00
Dutch Mill, McDowell Mfg Co, Pittsburg PA, 1927, litho tin, 12", EX, from $250 to....................................$350.00
Funnel Toy, T Cohn, features seesaw w/image of Popeye & Olive Oyl, litho tin, 9", VG, A $250.00
Mill, man w/bucket on ladder at top of slanted conveyor w/sand screen at bottom, pnt tin, 8", G, A $175.00

Mill, Popeye & Olive Oyl, litho tin, 8", EX...................$385.00
Pail, emb tin, boy & girl w/teddy bear & children building sand
    castles, 7", VG...$650.00
Pail, emb tin, boy on horse & girl on goat, wood hdl, 5½",
    VG...$475.00
Pail, emb tin, cats in uniform marching in band, wood hdl, 6",
    VG...$385.00
Pail, emb tin, dog w/puppies, eagle on bottom, wood hdl, 6",
    VG...$350.00
Pail, emb tin, Little Red Riding Hood & the Big Bad Wolf, eagle
    on bottom, wood hdl, 6", VG...............................$475.00

Pail, embossed tin, pre-1900, image on green background, 3", EX, from $250.00 to $400.00. (Photo courtesy Carole and Richard Smythe)

Pail, litho tin, Chein, 1930s, Three Little Pigs, pigs playing
    instruments w/wolf lurking by fence, 6", EX+, A $125.00
Pail, litho tin, Chein, 1940-50, 3 dressed bears, 4", NM, G16 ...$135.00
Pail, litho tin, Chein, 1971, Raggedy Ann & Andy, 8", EX.........$40.00
Pail, litho tin, Happynak, Mickey Mouse Treasure Island, NM $150.00
Pail, litho tin, mk Kewpie Beach, Scootles building sand castle
    w/kewpies, EX...$375.00
Pail, litho tin, no mk, 1925, Scrappy at the Seashore, 8", EX,
    A..$200.00
Pail, litho tin, no mk, 1950s, space scene, 5½", EX, A...$200.00
Pail, litho tin, Ohio Art, frogs dressed in various costumes, artist
    sgn Ruth Horling, 8", NM, A.................................$125.00
Pail, litho tin, Ohio Art, Treasure Island, 4½" dia, VG, A ..$350.00

Pail, lithographed tin, early 1900s, two different scenes surrounded by flowers, 5¼", EX, from $225.00 to $300.00. (Photo courtesy Carole and Richard Smythe)

Pail, litho tin, Ohio Art, 1930s, Donald Duck, EX.........$200.00
Pail, litho tin, Ohio Art, 1930s, Mickey & Minnie in boat, 8",
    EX $325.00
Pail, litho tin, Ohio Art, 1930s, Mickey working in garden, 8",
    EX $300.00
Pail, litho tin, Ohio Art, 1930s, Snow White & the Seven
    Dwarfs, 10", NM $275.00
Pail, litho tin, Ohio Art, 1935, Farm Crest, 4", EX, A ...$500.00
Pail, litho tin, Ohio Art, 1936, Mickey & friends at drink stand,
    NM, from $250 to..$350.00

Sand Ship and Scoop, lithographed tin, with wheels and pull string, 8½" long, EX, minimum value $50.00. (Photo courtesy Linda Baker)

Pail, litho tin, Ohio Art, 1940, Pinocchio, Jiminy & Cleo under the sea, 4¼", rare, EX, A $375.00

Pail, litho tin, T Cohn, 1933, Popeye Under the Sea, 6", EX, A $575.00

Pail & Shovel, litho tin, Ohio Art, 1930s, Pluto pulling Mickey on skates, red shovel, EX $200.00

Pail & Shovel, litho tin, Ohio Art, 1950s, cowboy & Indian, red shovel, EX $50.00

Seesaw, Chein, 1935, sand runs through funnel & creates seesaw action, litho tin, 7", EX $75.00

Shovel, Ohio Art, 1938, Donald Duck & Nephews, litho tin w/wood hdl, EX.....................................$250.00

Sifter, Ohio Art, 1930s, Mickey & Minnie playing in the sand, litho tin w/screen bottom, 6" dia, EX....................$225.00

Sifter, Ohio Art, 1935, Mickey Mouse, litho tin, complete w/3 molds & shovel, NM, A $575.00

Water Pump, mk Germany, early, red w/blk stenciled dogs, EX, from $175 to $250.00

Yankee Sam, jtd wood figure of Uncle Sam on wooden base next to litho tin funnel on base, 18", nonworking o/w VG, A ...$300.00

Santa Claus

Christmas is a magical time for young children; visions of Santa and his sleigh are mirrored in eyes that are wide with the wonder of the Santa fantasy. There are many who collect ornaments, bulbs, trees, etc., but the focus of our listings is Santa himself.

Among the more valuable Santas are the German-made papier-mache figures and candy containers, especially the larger examples and those wearing costumes in colors other than the traditional red.

See also Battery Operated; Books; Reynolds Toys; Windups, Friction, and Other Mechanicals; and other specific categories.

Bank, Santa & Mrs Claus, Norcrest, NM, S21 ....$45.00

Shovel, Ohio Art, 1930s, Mickey and Minnie playing in the sand, lithographed tin, 8", EX, $125.00.
(Photo courtesy David Longest and Michael Stern)

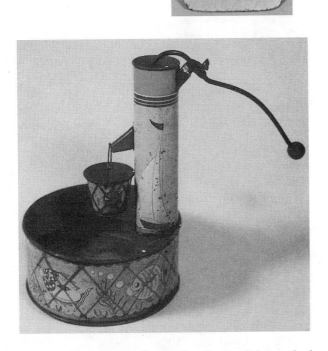

Water Pump, pictures fish and sailboats, lithographed tin, EX, from $175.00 to $225.00. (Photo courtesy David Longest)

Candy Container, 15", papier-mache and cloth, wool beard, flannel clothes, Germany, 15", EX, $1,300.00.

Bank, Santa & Mrs Claus on couch, unmk, NM, S21 ......$45.00

Bank, Santa sleeping in chair, pnt metal, mk USA, 8", EX, A..$75.00

Candy Container, 6", plastic, Santa in Chimney, 1950s, NM, A..$35.00

Candy Container, 8", compo, standing in long robe, blk, pk, brn & wht, EX, A..$125.00

Candy Container, 9", compo & papier-mache, wht beard, red cloth robe w/wht trim & gold belt, w/bag & tree, 1950s, G, A..$50.00

Candy Container, 10", compo & cb, wht fur beard, red felt robe w/wht trim, rope belt, blk boots, G, A.....................$700.00

Candy Container, 11", Belsnickle, molded & pnt figure, purple hooded coat w/bl trim, blk pants, w/tree, EX, A......$400.00

Candy Container, 14", compo, red cloth robe, wht fur beard, w/feather tree & pine cone, 1910, NM, A..............$600.00

Candy Container, 21", Belsnickle, molded and painted figure with arms in front, 1891, VG, A, $4,600.00.

Candy Container, 21", compo, wht fur beard, red felt robe w/bl shoulders, basket on belt, holding feather tree, EX, A $3,850.00

Candy Container, 32", compo & papier-mache, wht beard, red robe w/blk-dotted collar, rope belt, w/twigs, EX, A .$2,750.00

Crib Toy, Santa on swan holding lantern, celluloid, NM..$325.00

Crib Toy, Santa w/bag, celluloid, sm, NM.....................$100.00

Doll, Steiff, 1950s, all orig, w/chest tag, raised script button & stock tag, 12", NM, G16...$350.00

Doll, Steiff, 1970s, orig outfit & glasses, brass button & stock tag, 20½", rare, NM, G16....................................$585.00

Doll, Steiff, 1985, all ID, 12", M, G16 ....$250.00

Lantern, Santa head on base w/hdl, glass & metal, battery-op, 5", MIB, A $100.00

Lantern, Santa w/lantern & sack on rnd base, pnt milk glass, battery-op, 6", MIB, A..$175.00

Mask, German, papier-mache w/crepe hat & cloth beard, 12x8", NM, A $175.00

Mask, Sloan & Woodard, 1904, cb, uncut, 14", rare, M.$100.00

Nodder, Santa w/lantern, celluloid, 7", M, A $425.00

Radio, Tokiwa Electrical Industries Co. Ltd., Santa doll waving, plush and felt with vinyl face, 11", NM, from $100.00 to $125.00. (Photo courtesy Marty Bunis and Robert F. Breed)

Rattle, Santa w/bag & basket of fruit, celluloid, EX $125.00

Roly Poly, papier-mache, 4", VG $250.00

Roly Poly, Schoenhut, hand-pnt compo, 6½", EX, A.$1,500.00

Roly Poly, Schoenhut, hand-pnt compo, 8", EX, A $1,600.00

Santa in Basket, celluloid figure in wire mesh basket, 4", EX, A $100.00

Santa in Truck w/House & Tree in Back, Japan, celluloid, 4", EX, A $75.00

Santa on Sleigh, Germany, wood sleigh w/split log sides, compo figure w/rabbit fur beard & cloth clothes, 12", VG, A $450.00

Santa w/Feather Tree, papier-mache & compo, wht fur beard, gray plush hooded coat w/bl pants, 8", EX, A $950.00

Santa w/Lantern, papier-mache & compo, red cloth robe w/wht trim, 14½", VG, A $1,265.00

Santa w/Toy Bag, bsk, red duster coat w/wht trim, blk belt
    w/buckle & tassels, 4", EX, A $50.00
Santa w/Tree & Basket of Toys, pulp, hand-pnt, 15", EX, A..$325.00

**Squeaker, Rempel, 1950s, Santa waving, latex, 10½", EX
(G box), $30.00.** (Photo courtesy Linda Baker)

Schoenhut

Albert Schoenhut & Co. was located in Philadelphia,
Pennsylvania. From as early as 1872 they produced toys of many
types including dolls, pianos and other musical instruments,
games, and a good assortment of roly polys (which they called
Rolly Dollys). Around the turn of the century, they designed a
line they called the Humpty Dumpty Circus. It was made up of
circus animals, ringmasters, acrobats, lion tamers, and the like,
and the concept proved to be so successful that it continued in
production until the company closed in 1935. During the nearly
thirty-five years they were made, the figures were continually
altered either in size or by construction methods, and these variations can greatly affect their values today. Besides the figures
themselves, many accessories were produced to go along with
the circus theme — tents, cages, tubs, ladders, and wagons, just
to mention a few. Teddy Roosevelt's African hunting adventures
inspired the company to design a line that included not only
Teddy and the animals he was apt to encounter in Africa but
native tribesmen as well. A third line featured comic characters
of the day, all with the same type of jointed wood construction,
many dressed in cotton and felt clothing. There were several,
among them were Felix the Cat, Maggie and Jiggs, Barney
Google and Spark Plug, and Happy Hooligan.

Several factors come into play when evaluating Schoenhut
figures. Foremost is condition. Since most found on the market
today show signs of heavy wear, anything above a very good rat-
ing commands a premium price. Missing parts and retouched

paint sharply reduce a figure's value, though a well-done restoration is usually acceptable. The earlier examples had glass eyes; by
1920 eyes were painted on. Soon after that, the company began
to make their animals in a reduced size. While some of the earlier
figures had bisque heads or carved wooden heads, by the '20s,
pressed wood heads were the norm. Full-size examples with glass
eyes and bisque or carved heads are generally more desirable and
more valuable, though rarity must be considered as well.

During the 1950s, some of the figures and animals were produced by the Delvan Company, who had purchased the manufacturing rights.

Consult the index for Schoenhut toys that may be listed in
other categories.

Advisors: Keith and Donna Kaonis (K6).

HUMPTY DUMPTY CIRCUS ANIMALS

Humpty Dumpty Circus animals with glass eyes, ca.
1903–1914, are more desirable and can demand much higher
prices than the later painted-eye versions. As a general rule, a
glass-eye version is 30% to 40% more than a painted-eye version. (There are exceptions.) The following list suggests values
for both glass eye and painted eye versions and reflects a low
painted eye price to a high glass eye price.

There are other variations and nuances of certain figures:
Bulldog — white with black spots or brindle (brown); open- and
closed-mouth zebras and giraffes; ball necks and hemispherical
necks on some animals such as the pig, leopard, and tiger, to
name a few. These points can affect the price and should be
judged individually.

Key:
GE — glass eyes   PE — painted eyes

Alligator, PE/GE, from $200 to $500.00
Arabian Camel, 1 hump, PE/GE, from $250 to $750.00
Bactrian Camel, 2 humps, PE/GE, from $200 to $1,500.00
Brown Bear, PE/GE, from $200 to...................................$900.00
Buffalo, cloth mane, PE/GE, from $300 to $1,000.00
Buffalo, cvd mane, PE/GE, from $200 to $900.00
Bulldog, PE/GE, from $400 to.....................................$1,600.00
Burro (made to go w/chariot & clown), PE/GE, from $200
    to..$700.00
Cat, PE/GE, rare, from $600 to $2,500.00
Cow, PE/GE, from $250 to $900.00
Deer, PE/GE, from $300 to...$1,000.00
Donkey, PE/GE, from $75 to $200.00
Donkey w/blanket, PE/GE, from $90 to $400.00
Elephant, PE/GE, from $90 to..$300.00
Elephant w/blanket, PE/GE, from $200 to $600.00
Gazelle, PE/GE, rare, from $700 to $3,000.00
Giraffe, PE/GE, from $200 to $800.00
Goat, PE/GE, from $150 to $400.00
Goose, PE only, from $200 to..$600.00
Gorilla, PE only, from $1,200 to $3,000.00
Hippo, PE/GE, from $300 to $900.00
Horse, brn, saddle & stirrups, PE/GE, from $150 to $400.00
Horse, wht, platform, PE/GE, from $125 to $400.00

Rabbit, painted or glass eyes, very rare, from $1,000.00 to $3,000.00; Hyena, painted or glass eyes, very rare, from $1,000.00 to $4,000.00; Wolf, painted or glass eyes, very rare, from $600.00 to $5,000.00.

Kangaroo, PE/GE, from $400 to $1,200.00
Lion, cloth mane, GE only, from $500 to....................$1,200.00
Lion, cvd mane, PE/GE, from $250 to $900.00
Monkey, 1-part head, PE only, from $250 to $450.00
Monkey, 2-part head, wht face, from $300 to $900.00
Ostrich, PE/GE, from $200 to $750.00
Pig, 5 versions, PE/GE, from $200 to $700.00
Polar Bear, PE/GE, from $500 to................................$1,200.00
Poodle, cloth mane, GE only, from $300 to....................$500.00
Poodle, PE/GE, from $125 to..$300.00
Rhino, PE/GE, from $250 to $1,000.00
Sea lion, PE/GE, from $400 to $1,200.00
Sheep (lamb) w/bell, PE/GE, from $200 to....................$700.00
Tiger, PE/GE, from $250 to...$800.00
Zebra, PE/GE, from $250 to..$800.00
Zebu, PE/GE, rare, from $1,000 to $2,500.00

HUMPTY DUMPTY CIRCUS CLOWNS AND OTHER PERSONNEL

Clowns with two-part heads (a cast face applied to a wooden head) were made from 1903 to 1915 and are most desirable — condition is always important. There have been nine distinct styles in fourteen different costumes recorded. Only eight costume styles apply to the two-part headed clowns. The later clowns, ca. 1920, had one-part heads whose features were pressed, and they were no longer tied at the wrists and ankles.

Use the low end of the value range for items in only fair condition. Those in good to very good condition (having very minor scratches and wear, good original finish, no splits or chips, no excessive paint wear or cracked eyes and, of course, complete) may be evaluated by the high end.

Black Dude, reduced size, from $300 to...........................$600.00
Black Dude, 1-part head, purple coat, from $250 to $800.00
Black Dude, 2-part head, blk coat, from $500 to $700.00
Chinese Acrobat, 1-part head, from $200 to $500.00
Chinese Acrobat, 2-part head, rare, from $400 to.......$1,000.00
Clown, early, from $150 to..$500.00
Clown, reduced sz, 1925-53, from $75 to $150.00
Gent Acrobat, bsk head, rare, from $300 to $600.00
Gent Acrobat, 2-part head, very rare, from $600 to....$1,500.00
Hobo, reduced sz, from $300 to $600.00
Hobo, 1-part head, from $200 to $500.00

Hobo, 2-part head, curved-up toes, black coat, from $500 to $1,000.00
Hobo, 2-part head, facet toe ft, from $400 to.................$800.00
Lady Acrobat, bsk head, from $300 to $600.00
Lady Acrobat, 1-part head, from $200 to......................$400.00
Lady Rider, bsk head, from $250 to................................$500.00
Lady Rider, 1-part head, from $200 to $400.00
Lady Rider, 2-part head, very rare, from $600 to........$1,200.00
Lion Tamer, bsk head, rare, from $350 to......................$750.00
Lion Tamer, 1-part head, from $250 to..........................$600.00
Lion Tamer, 2-part head, early, very rare, from $600 to ..$1,200.00
Ring Master, bsk, ca 1912-14, from $400 to $650.00
Ring Master, 2-part head, early, very rare, from $500 to..$1,200.00

Ring Master, one-part head, from $200.00 to $450.00.

HUMPTY DUMPTY CIRCUS ACCESSORIES

There are many accessories: wagons, tents, ladders, chairs, pedestals, tight ropes, weights, and various other items.

Menagerie Tent, later, 1914-20, from $1,200 to $2,000.00
Menagerie Tent, early, ca 1904, from $1,500 to.........$2,500.00
Oval Litho Tent, 1926, from $2,000 to $5,000.00
Sideshow Panels, 1926, pr, from $2,000 to $5,000.00

Schuco

A German company noted for both mechanical toys as well as the teddy bears and stuffed animals we've listed here, Schuco operated from the 1930s well into the '50s. Items were either marked Germany or US Zone, Germany.

Advisor: Candace Gunther, Candelaine (G16).

See also Battery-Operated; Windups, Friction, and Other Mechanicals.

Bears, white and brown, metal eyes, 1950s, EX, minimum value, $275.00 each.

Bear, brn w/cinnamon ears, orig ribbon, 1950, 3½", M, G16..$200.00

Bear, champagne, 1950s, 2½", NM, G16.........................$150.00

Bear, cinammon w/metal eyes, orig ribbon, 1950s, 3½", M, G16..$225.00

Bear, gold w/metal bead eyes, 1950, 2½", NM, G16 .....$165.00

Bear, orange w/metal eyes, shaved muzzle, 1950s, 3½", NM, G16 ....$300.00

Bear, pale gold, orig gr ribbon, 3½", EX, G16................$150.00

Bear, tan, orig red ribbon, 1950s, 3½", NM, G16...........$150.00

Bear Compact, gold mohair over metal, removable head, 1920s, 3½", G $650.00

Bellhop Perfume Monkey, orig bottle & wand, 1930s, 3½", rare, NM, G16 ....$600.00

Berlin Bear, brn w/metal eyes, orig crown, banner & pin, 1950s, 2½", M, G16...$335.00

Bigo-Bello Dog, orig clothes, 14", NM, G16..................$175.00

Bigo-Bello Tiger, cloth label, 1960s, EX, G16 ....$125.00

Bird, Noah's Ark, mc w/orange metal feet, 1950s, 2½", VG, G16 ....$85.00

Black Scottie, Noah's Ark, 1950, 3", MIB, G16.............$225.00

Blackbird, Noah's Ark, 1950, 3", MIB, G16 ....$225.00

Bottle Bear, pk, 3½", rare, NM $1,000.00

Dalmatian, Noah's Ark, 2½", rare, M, G16....................$375.00

Dog Mascot, felt clothes, 1950, 3½", MIB, G16.............$150.00

Duck Mascot, bl & wht striped outfit w/red shoes, 1950, 3½", NMIB, G16..$125.00

Elephant, Noah's Ark, mohair w/felt ears & blanket, fully jtd, 1950, 2½", NM, G16.............................$150.00

Fox, Noah's Ark, 1950, 2½", MIB, G16 ....$285.00

Hedgehog, Noah's Ark, mohair & felt, orig paper label, 2", M..$65.00

Janus Bear, 2 faces (googly & bear), cinnamon, 1950s, 3½", M, G16 ....$850.00

Ladybug, Noah's Ark, 1950, 3", MIB, G16 ....$165.00

Lion, Noah's Ark, 3½", EX, G16...................................$75.00

Monkey, cinnamon w/felt hands & feet, mk Germany, 2½", NM, G16 ....$200.00

Monkey, Noah's Ark, 1950, 3½", M, G16.....................$125.00

Orangutan, Noah's Ark, 1950, 3", very rare, MIB, G16.$325.00

Panda Bear, mohair, blk metal bead eyes, 1950s, 2½", M, G16..$300.00

Penguin, Noah's Ark, 1950, 3", MIB, G16 ....$175.00

Perfume Bear, bright gold, orig bottle, 1920-30, 5", NM, G16..$835.00

Perfume Monkey, cinnamon w/felt hands & ears, 1930, 5", rpl bottle, EX, G16.............................$200.00

Pig, Noah's Ark, wht w/brn spots, 1950, 1¾", NM, G16..$200.00

Raccoon, Noah's Ark, 1950, 3½", M, G16....................$200.00

Siamese Cat, Noah's Ark, orig ribbon, 1950, 3", M, G16.$300.00

Soccer Bear, several outfit variations, 1970, 3½", MIB, G16, ea $325.00

Squirrel, Noah's Ark, 1950, 2½", M, G16 ....$175.00

Tiger, Noah's Ark, 3½", EX $100.00

Tumbling Bear, gold, 1950s, 5", NM, G16....................$850.00

Turtle, Noah's Ark, 1950, 3", NM, G16 ....$175.00

Yes/No Baby Orangutan, orig FAO Schwarz tag, 1948, 8", rare, NMIB, G16...$700.00

Yes/No Bear, blk w/glass eyes, 1950s, 5", rare, EX, G16..$1,100.00

Yes/No Bear, caramel w/glass eyes, 1950, 5", NM, G16..$550.00

Yes/No Bear, chocolate brn w/glass eyes, orig yel ribbon, 1950s, 5", rare, NM, G16...........................$975.00

Yes/No Bear, gold w/jewel faceted eyes, 1920s, 9", EX, G16.$1,950.00

Yes/No Bellhop Monkey, 1920s, 13½", NM, $950.00; Yes/No Monkey, limited edition replica of Tricky Monkey, mohair and felt with glass eyes, 18", NM, $200.00.

Yes/No Cat, 5", M, G16...$650.00

Yes/No Charlie, cream & rust, red felt tongue, 1920-30, 6", rare, NM, G16 ....$550.00

Yes/No Dog, Pekinese-type, glass eyes, 1930s, 6½", G, G16..$200.00

Yes/No Donkey, mohair w/felt ears, orig felt collar & ribbon, 1950, 5", NM, G16 ....$485.00

Yes/No Elephant, mohair w/felt tusks & ears, cloth US Zone tag, 1948, 5", EX, G16...$400.00

Yes/No Gnome, w/glasses, mohair & felt w/velvet pants & felt jacket, 1948, 12", EX, G16..$800.00

Yes/No Monkey, gray w/orig shirt, jacket & handkerchief, 1920s, 12½", rare, NM, G16 ....$750.00

Yes/No Panda, orig pk bow, 1950, 5", MIB, G16.........$1,250.00

Yes/No Rabbit, 5", M, G16...$650.00

Yes/No Terrier, cream w/brn tipping, glass eyes, 1920-30, 6½", rare, NM, G16 ....$800.00

Yes/No Tricky Baby Orangutan, mohair & felt w/glass eyes, 1948, 8", NM, G16...$365.00

Yes/No Tricky Bear, tan, orig red ribbon & US Zone tag, 1948, 13", M, G16...$1,650.00

Yes/No Tricky Elephant, mohair w/felt ears & tusks, glass eyes, 1940-50, NM, G16...$425.00

Yes/No Tricky Monkey, orig ribbon, 1948, 10½", EX, G16........$300.00

Yes/No Tricky Monkey, orig ribbon & tag, 1948, 14", M, G16..$450.00

Yes/No Tricky Orangutan, cinnamon w/glass eyes, 14", NM, G16...$950.00

Yes/No Tricky Panda, orig red ribbon, 1948, 13", rare, NM, G16..$1,850.00

Slot Cars

Slot cars first became popular in the early 1960s. Electric raceways set up in retail storefront windows were commonplace. Huge commercial tracks with eight and ten lanes were located in hobby stores and raceways throughout the United States. Large corporations such as Aurora, Revell, Monogram, and Cox, many of which were already manufacturing toys and hobby items, jumped on the bandwagon to produce slot cars and race sets. By the end of the early 1970s, people were loosing interest in slot racing, and its popularity diminished. Today the same baby boomers that raced slot cars in earlier days are revitalizing the sport. Vintage slot cars are making a comeback as one of the hottest automobile collectibles of the 1990s. Want ads for slot cars appear more and more frequently in newspapers and publications geared toward the collector. As you would expect from their popularity, slot cars were generally well used, so finding vintage cars and race sets in like-new or mint condition is difficult. Slot cars replicating the 'muscle' cars from the '60s and '70s are extremely sought after, and clubs and organizations devoted to these collectibles are becoming more and more commonplace. Large toy companies such as Tomy and Tyco still produce some slots today, but not in the quality, quantity, or variety of years past.

Aurora produced several types of slots: Screachers (5700 and 5800 number series, valued at $5.00 to $20.00); the AC-powered Vibrators (1500 number series, valued at $20.00 to $150.00); DC-powered Thunderjets (1300 and 1400 number

series, valued at $20.00 to $150.00); and the last-made AFX SP1000 (1900 number series, valued at $15.00 to $75.00).

Advisor: Gary Pollastro (P5).

COMPLETE SETS

Atlas, Racing Set #1000, HO scale, G (G box), P5........$100.00

Aurora, Home Raceway by Sears, #79N9513C, VG, P5..$225.00

Aurora, Mario Andretti GP International Challenge, G (G box)..$55.00

Aurora, Stirling Moss #1313 Table Top Racing Set, 1968, NMIB..$125.00

Aurora AFX, Devil's Ditch Set, EX...................................$40.00

Aurora AFX, Revamatic Slot Car Set, EX (EX box)........$75.00

Cox, Ontario 8, #3070, w/Eagle & McLaren, G (G box), P5.$75.00

Eldon, Raceway Set #24, 1/24th scale, VG, P5.............$175.00

Eldon, Sky High Triple Road Race, w/Ferrari, Lotus, Stingray & Porsche, G (G box), P5...$75.00

Ideal, Mini-Motorific Set, #4939-5, EX, P5 ....$85.00

Motorific, GTO Torture Track, lg, EX (EX box) $100.00

Remco, Mighty Mike Action Track, NMIB $100.00

Revell, HiBank Raceway Set #49-9503, w/Cougar GTE & Pontiac Firebird, EX (EX box), P5 ....$150.00

Scalextric, Electric Motor Racing Set, Officially Approved by Jim Clark, made in England, NMIB, P5..........................$400.00

Strombecker, Highway Patrol, VG (VG box) $200.00

Strombecker, Thunderbolt Monza, Montgomery Ward, VG (VG box), P5 ....$150.00

Strombecker, 4 Lane Mark IV Race Set, VG (VG box) $250.00

Tyco, Racing Bandits, EX $30.00

SLOT CARS ONLY

Aurora AFX, '55 Chevy Bel Air, #1913, yel, VG $16.00

Aurora AFX, '57 Chevy Nomad, #1760, EX+ (EX+ box) ..$28.00

Aurora AFX, Autoworld McLaren XIR, #1752, bl & wht, EX ..$14.00

Aurora AFX, Autoworld Porsch #5, wht w/bl stripes, EX.$12.00

Aurora AFX, Blazer, #1917, blk, bl & wht, VG................$12.00

Aurora AFX, Blazer Flamethrower, #1984, wht, red, orange & yel, NM $18.00

Aurora AFX, BMW 3201 Turbo, #1980, yel & orange, EX ..$20.00

Aurora AFX, Camaro Z-28, #1901, red, wht & bl, EX $20.00

Aurora AFX, Capri Trans Am, wht, bl w/lime stripes, EX.$16.00

Aurora AFX, Chevelle Stock Car, #1704, yel, red & blk, EX..$16.00

Aurora AFX, Chevy Nomad, #1760, bl, EX......................$20.00

Aurora AFX, Chevy Nomad, #1760, chrome, EX............$25.00

Aurora AFX, Chevy Nomad, #1760, orange, EX..............$20.00

Aurora AFX, Conventional Cab & Trailer, red & wht, VG..$20.00

Aurora AFX, Corvette #7, #1927, red, wht & bl, VG+....$20.00

Aurora AFX, Corvette Funny Car, orange or purple, G ...$10.00

Aurora AFX, Datsun Baja Pickup, #1745, bl & blk, EX ...$20.00

Aurora AFX, Dodge Charger Stock Car, #1773, bl & blk, VG...$12.00

Aurora AFX, Dodge Charger Stock Car, #1910, wht w/blk hood, EXIB...$25.00

Aurora AFX, Dodge Charger Stock Car #11, wht w/blk hood, EX,..$15.00

Aurora AFX, Dodge Fever Dragster, wht & yel, EX $15.00

Aurora AFX, Dodge Police Van, wht w/blk stripe, VG $15.00

Aurora AFX, Dodge Rescue Van, #1937, red, gr & wht, EX..$15.00

Aurora AFX, Dodge Van, yel w/orange stripe, VG...........$10.00

Aurora AFX, Ferrari, #1763, lt bl & wht, EX.....................$10.00

Aurora AFX, Ferrari #2, #1763, red & wht or wht & bl, EX, ea $10.00

Aurora AFX, Ferrari 512, #1763, wht & bl, EX $12.00

Aurora AFX, Ferrari 512, metallic bl, EX...........................$12.00

Aurora AFX, Ferrari 612, #1751, yel & blk, EX................$10.00

Aurora AFX, Firebird, #1965, blk & gold, EX+ $15.00

Aurora AFX, Firechief Car Overheads, #1986, wht, red & silver, EX..$20.00

Aurora AFX, Ford Baja Bronco, #1901, red, EX $14.00

Aurora AFX, Ford Pickup, #1941, bl w/flames, VG $8.00

Aurora AFX, Ford Street Van, #1943, lt bl & brn, NM ...$14.00

Aurora AFX, Furious Fueler Dragster, #1774, wht & yel, EX.......$15.00

Aurora AFX, Ghostracer Corvette Tomy, bl w/pnt skull, EX......$14.00

Aurora AFX, Grand Am Funny Car, #1702, red, wht & bl, EX..$12.00

Aurora AFX, Jeep CJ-7 Flamethrower, #1987, orange & red, NM...$18.00

Aurora AFX, Lola T-260 Can-Am, wht w/stripes, EX......$14.00

Aurora AFX, Matador Stock Car #5, #1930, orange, blk & red, EX..$18.00

Aurora AFX, Monza GT, #1948, wht & gr, EX $15.00

Aurora AFX, Nissan 300-ZX #33, red, wht & bl, EX........$14.00

Aurora AFX, Peterbilt Lighted Rig, #1156, red & yel, EX..$25.00

Aurora AFX, Peterbilt Shell Rig, #1155, yel, red & wht, EX..$25.00

Aurora AFX, Pinto Funny Car, orange & purple, VG......$10.00

Aurora AFX, Plymouth Roadrunner #43, #1762, bl & wht, EX $20.00

Aurora AFX, Pontiac Grand Am, #10-191, red, wht & bl, EX $15.00

Aurora AFX, Porsche Carrera #3, #1933, wht, red & blk, NM $12.00

Aurora AFX, Porsche 417 Flamethrower #2, #1973, wht & purple, EX..$12.00

Aurora AFX, Porsche 510-K, #1786, gold, chrome & orange stripe, EX..$16.00

Aurora AFX, Porsche 917 #2, #1757, wht & gr, EX $12.00

Aurora AFX, Porsche 917 #2, #1757, wht & purple, EX..$14.00

Aurora AFX, Porsche 917-10, #1747, wht, red & bl, EX..$12.00

Aurora AFX, RC Porsche 917-10 Can Am, red, wht & bl stripe, w/decals, EX..$15.00

Aurora AFX, Roarin' Rolls Golden Ghost, #1781, yel & bl, or wht & blk, EX, ea $18.00

Aurora AFX, Speed Beamer, red, wht & bl stripe, EX......$10.00

Aurora AFX, Turbo Porsche #3, red, wht & bl, no decal, VG $10.00

Aurora AFX, Turbo Turn On, #1755, orange, yel & purple, EX $20.00

Aurora AFX, Twi-Night Beamer, wht, red & bl stripe, VG..$10.00

Aurora AFX, Vega Van Gasser, #1754, yel & red, EX......$15.00

Aurora AFX, VW Baja Bug, #1914, lime, VG $20.00

Aurora Cigarbox, Dino Ferrari, red, EX $20.00

Aurora Cigarbox, Ferrari Berlinetta, red w/wht stripe, NM+...$20.00

Aurora Cigarbox, Ferrari GTO, red w/wht stripe, G.........$10.00

Aurora Cigarbox, Ford GT, wht w/blk stripe, NM+ $20.00

Aurora Cigarbox, Ford J Car, red w/blk stripe, NM+.......$20.00

Aurora Cigarbox, Ford Lola GT, red w/wht stripe, G+ $10.00

Aurora G-Plus, Amrac Can Am, yel & blk w/wht stripe, EX..$15.00

Aurora G-Plus, Camaro (NASCAR) #76, wht, orange & gold, EX..$12.00

Aurora G-Plus, Corvette, #1011, red, orange & wht, EX .$15.00

Aurora G-Plus, Corvette, #1954, orange, red & silver, EX ..$12.00

Aurora G-Plus, Datsun 240-Z, red, wht & bl, EX $14.00

Aurora G-Plus, Ferrari F1, #1734, red & wht, EX.............$25.00

Aurora G-Plus, Indy Special, #1735, blk, red & orange, EX .$17.00

Aurora G-Plus, Indy Valvoline, blk, VG...........................$12.00

Aurora G-Plus, Lotus F1, #1783, blk & gold, EX.............$20.00

Aurora G-Plus, Monza GT #0, wht w/gr stripe, EX $15.00

Aurora G-Plus, Rallye Ford Escort, #1737, gr & bl, EX $15.00

Aurora G-Plus, Shadow Can Am, #1744, wht, red, orange & yel, EX..$15.00

Aurora Thunderjet, '63 Corvette, #1356, yel, EX.............$50.00

Aurora Thunderjet, Chaparral #7, #1377, red & silver, EX....$28.00

Aurora Thunderjet, Chaparral 2F #7, #1410, lime & bl, EX ..$25.00

Aurora Thunderjet, Chaparral 2F Tuff One, wht, EX $25.00

Aurora Thunderjet, Cheetah, #1403, pea gr, EX $40.00

Aurora Thunderjet, Cobra #1375, yel w/blk stripe, VG+ .$30.00

Aurora Thunderjet, Cobra Daytona GT, #1375, metallic bl w/stripes, VG $35.00

Aurora Thunderjet, Cobra GT, #1396, candy bl & silver, EX $60.00

Aurora Thunderjet, Cougar, #1389, wht, EX...................$40.00

Aurora Thunderjet, Dino Ferrari #3 (Tuff One), #1481, red, VG $25.00

Aurora Thunderjet, Dune Buggy Roadster, #1398, bl & blk, EX+ $35.00

Aurora Thunderjet, Ferrari GTO Flamethrower, #1493, lt bl & wht, EX $30.00

Aurora, Snowmobile, #1485-400, yellow with blue figure, MIB, P5, $55.00. (Photo courtesy Gary Pollastro)

Aurora Thunderjet, Ferrari GTO 250, #1368, red w/wht stripes, EX..$25.00

Aurora Thunderjet, Ferrari GTO 250, #1394, Candy Copper, VG $30.00

Aurora Thunderjet, Firebird, bl w/thunderbird on hood, VG..$35.00

Aurora Thunderjet, Ford Car, #1382, wht & bl, VG........$25.00

Aurora Thunderjet, Ford GT 40, #1374, red w/blk stripe, EX..$25.00

Aurora Thunderjet, Ford GT 40, #1395, candy-colored bl, VG .$40.00

Aurora Thunderjet, Ford J Car, #1430, yel & bl, EX $25.00

Aurora Thunderjet, Ford Lola GT, #1378, dk gr w/wht stripe, VG $30.00

Aurora Thunderjet, Ho Dune Buggy, wht w/red & wht stripe top, EX $30.00

Aurora Thunderjet, Hot Rod Coupe, red, VG.................$25.00

Aurora Thunderjet, Indy Racer #11, #1359, red w/blk stripe, EX $30.00

Aurora Thunderjet, International Tow Truck, wht & blk w/red stripe, EX+ $100.00

Aurora Thunderjet, Jaguar XKE, #1358, tan, EX.............$40.00

Aurora Thunderjet, Lola GT, #1378, turq & wht w/bl stripe, VG+ $25.00

Aurora Thunderjet, Lola GT (Tuff Tones) #3, #1471, blk, orange & wht, EX..$45.00

Aurora Thunderjet, Mako Shark Corvette, #1380, wht, EX.$30.00

Aurora Thunderjet, Mangusta Mongoose, #1400, yel cream, EX $45.00

Aurora Thunderjet, McLaren Elva, #1397, wht, red & blk, EX $28.00

Aurora Thunderjet, McLaren Elva Flamethrower, #1431, bl w/wht stripe, VG...$25.00

Aurora Thunderjet, Porsche 904, #1376, bl w/wht stripe, EX $30.00

Aurora Thunderjet, Thunderbird Sports Roadster, #1355, EX.$45.00

Aurora Thunderjet, Wild One Cougar #21, #1419, wht & bl, EX+ $38.00

Aurora Thunderjet, Wild One Mustang 2+2 #7, #1416, wht, red & blk, EX+...$38.00

Aurora Tomy AFX, Speed Beamer #11, #8763, red, wht & bl, EX $15.00

TCR, Blazer, blk, yel w/orange flames, EX $15.00

TCR, Jam Car, yel & blk, EX $15.00

TCR, Mack Truck, wht & red, EX $15.00

TCR, Maintenance Van, wht & red, EX $15.00

TCR, Mercury Stock Car, purple & chrome, VG.............$15.00

Tyco, '40 Ford Coupe, #8534, blk w/flames, EX.............$20.00

Tyco, '57 Chevy, red & orange w/yel stripes, EX.............$20.00

Tyco, A-Team Van, blk w/red stripe, EX.........................$40.00

Tyco, Autoworld Carrera, wht & red w/wht & bl stripe, G ..$10.00

Tyco, Bandit Pickup, blk & yel, EX $12.00

Tyco, Blackbird Firebird, #6914, blk & gold, EX $12.00

Tyco, Blazer, red & blk, VG $10.00

Tyco, Camaro Z-28, bl & wht w/red stripe, EX...............$10.00

Tyco, Camaro Z-28 5.0 Liter #7, red, wht & bl, EX.........$12.00

Tyco, Chaparral 2G #66, #8504, VG $14.00

Tyco, Corvette, fluorescent yel w/blk stripes, EX.............$10.00

Tyco, Corvette #12, wht & red w/bl stripes, EX $12.00

Tyco, Corvette Cliffhanger #2, yel & blk, EX..................$10.00

Tyco, Corvette Curvehanger, silver & chrome w/flames, EX ..$15.00

Tyco, Ferrari F-40, #8967, red, VG $12.00

Tyco, Firebird, #6914, cream & red, VG.........................$12.00

Tyco, Firebird Stockcar #35, EX.....................................$10.00

Tyco, Firebird Turbo #12, blk & gold, EX......................$10.00

Tyco, Funny Mustang, orange w/yel flame, EX $25.00

Tyco, Hardee's Ford #28, red & wht, G $12.00

Tyco, Indy Pennzoil, yel, EX...$15.00

Tyco, Jam Car, yel & blk, EX $10.00

Tyco, Jeep CJ-7, red & lt bl, VG $12.00

Tyco, Lamborghini, red, VG $12.00

Tyco, Lighted Porsche #2, silver w/red nose, EX.............$20.00

Tyco, Lighted Silver Streak Porsche, #918, silver & bl w/gr stripe, EX..$16.00

Tyco, Lighted Silver Streak Porsche #908, silver & red, EX ..$15.00

Tyco, Lighted Super America, #8525, red, wht & bl, EX.$20.00

Tyco, McLaren M-8F, #8505, blk w/red stripe, EX $25.00

Tyco, Mustang #1, orange w/yel flames, VG $20.00

Tyco, Pinto Funny Cargotcha, dk red w/gold stripe, VG..$20.00

Tyco, Porsche Carrera, #8527, yel & blk, EX...................$25.00

Tyco, Porsche 908 #3, gr & silver, EX.............................$16.00

Tyco, Rokar 240-Z #7, blk, EX $10.00

Tyco, Silver Streak Racing Vette, #8556, silver & pk w/orange stripe, VG..$15.00

Tyco, Super America Chaparral 2D, #8525, red, wht & bl, EX $12.00

Tyco, Superbird, #8533, red, wht & bl, VG+ $15.00

Tyco, Thunderbird #15, red & yel, VG............................$10.00

Tyco, Turbo Firebird, blk & gold, EX..............................$12.00

Tyco, Turbo Hopper #27, red, EX...................................$12.00

Tyco, Turbo Porsche #3, yel & orange w/red stripe, EX ...$12.00

Tyco, Van-Tastic, #8539, bl & wht, VG...........................$20.00

ACCESSORIES

Aurora AFX Billboard Retaining Walls, set of 8, EXIB....$15.00

Aurora AFX Carrying Case, blk, 2-level, EX $15.00

Aurora AFX Orange Trigger Style Control, plug-in, EX $6.00

Aurora AFX Terminal Track, plug-in or wire-type, EX, ea....$5.00

Aurora AFX Wall Power Pack, plug-in or wire-type, EX, ea .$8.00

Aurora AFX 45 OHM Hand Controller w/Brakes, EX (EX box)...$15.00

Aurora Model Motoring Hill Track, 9", EX $8.00

Aurora Model Motoring Squiggle Track, 9", EX.................$5.00

Aurora Model Motoring Steering Wheel Controller, EX.$10.00

Aurora Model Motoring Thumb-Style Controller, EX.......$6.00

Aurora Model Motoring Y Turn-Off Track w/Switch, EX..$20.00

Aurora Model Motoring 1968 Thunderjet 500 Manual, EX ..$5.00

Aurora Model Motoring 4-Way Stop Track, 9", EX.........$15.00

Aurora Power Passers Controller, red, EX........................$10.00

Tyco HO Scale 1973-74 Handbook, EX $10.00

Tyco Terminal Pack, EX...$5.00

Tyco Trigger Controller, orange, EX $8.00

Smith-Miller

Smith-Miller (Los Angeles, California) made toy trucks from 1944 until 1955. During that time they used four basic cab designs, and most of their trucks sold for about $15.00 each. Over the past several years, these toys have become very popular, especially the Mack trucks which today sell at premium prices. The company made a few other types of toys as well, such as the train toy box and the 'Long, Long Trailer.'

Advisor: Doug Dezso (D6).

Bekins Van Lines Co. Semi, white with black and red lettering, 34", M, A, $1,000.00.

Bank of America Brinks Truck, 1950s, 14", VG $300.00
Camper, 1950s, aluminum w/steel roof, wood interior, 27", VG $250.00
Fire Ladder Truck, mk St Louis FD, open body w/2 hose reels & ladders on fr support, 24", MIB, A $1,000.00
GMC Materials Truck, w/4 barrels & 3 timbers, EX $300.00

LAFD Aerial Ladder Fire Truck, red with aluminum ladder mounted to turntable, black rubber tires, 25", MIB, A, $750.00.

Mack Custom Union 76 Tanker Truck, NM $600.00
Mack Fire Department Aerial Ladder Truck, 31" L, G...$800.00
Mack Tandem Timber Truck, gr, complete w/lumber, EX .$925.00
MIC Tow Truck, M $1,200.00
Mobiloil Tanker Truck, red w/name & Pegasus logo, 14", VG $450.00
Searchlight Fire Truck, red w/8 battery-op searchlights mounted to railed body frame, 19", MIB, A........................$2,000.00
Searchlight Truck, red Mack cab w/silver body, electric searchlight reads Hollywood Film Ad, 18", NM, A........$2,700.00
Silver Streak Trailer, EX $450.00
SMFD Aerial Ladder Fire Truck, red Mack cab w/separate trailer body, aluminum ladder on revolving base, 36", NM, A..$800.00
West Coast Fast Freight, EX $1,000.00

Snow Domes

Snow domes are water-filled paperweights that come in several different styles. The earliest type was made in two pieces and consisted of a glass globe on a separate base. First made in the middle of the 19th century, they were revived during the '30s and '40s by companies in America, Italy, and Germany. Similar weights are now being imported into the country from the Orient. The most common snow domes on today's market are the plastic half-moon shapes made as souvenirs or Christmas toys, a style that originated in West Germany during the 1950s. Other shapes were made as well, including round and square bottles, short and tall rectangles, cubes, and other simple shapes.

During the 1970s, figural plastic snow domes were especially popular. There are two types — large animate shapes themselves containing the snow scene, or dome shapes that have figures draped over the top. Today's collectors buy them all, old or new. For further information we recommend *Collector's Guide to Snow Domes* by Helene Guarnaccia, published by Collector Books.

Advisor: Nancy McMichael (M18).

ADVERTISING

Air Canada, airplane flying over city in plastic dome, yel ftd base, EX, A...$60.00
American Express Vacations, Collect a World of Memories, graphic of wht plane in bl sky, wht ftd dome, M........$60.00
Coca-Cola, Santa w/bottle, music box base, MIB, A........$75.00
Days Inn, Catch Some Rays at Days, w/2 Flintstone characters, sm oval plastic dome, M18 ....$10.00
Days Inn, The Whole Family Stays at Days, yel & turq, sm oval plastic dome, M18..............................$10.00
Michelin Man, Mr Bib in mountains, European issue, MIB.$30.00
New York Times, 1987, One Constant in an Ever-Changing Market, bear & bull on seesaw in front on paper, M, minimum value $100.00
Newsweek, 1990, No One Covers the World Like Newsweek, name floats around on red bars, globe in background, plastic, M...$70.00
Texaco, tanker truck against cityscape in rnd dome, trapezoid base w/dealer advertising, EX $65.00

CHARACTER

Babar the Elephant, plastic dome on wht ftd base, M.......$15.00
Bugs Bunny, Bugs seated w/globe between legs, w/Elmer Fudd & Sylvester, EX..$90.00
Bugs Bunny, wood w/glass dome, plays Singing in the Rain, MIB $85.00
Charlie Chaplin, Enesco, 1989, MIB $25.00
Creature From the Black Lagoon, figural, MIB................$15.00

Donald Duck, Mickey Mouse, and Pinocchio, Snow Biz/WDP, scarce, M, $100.00 each. (Photo courtesy Nancy McMichael)

Donald Duck, dressed for skiing, glass globe on rnd wooden base, M..$10.00

Donald Duck, Schmid, 1989, Donald w/single-wheeled riding toy on tall dome on rnd bl base w/name in wht, M ...$10.00

Flintstones, Hanna-Barbera, 1975, Fred, Pebbles, Bamm-Bamm & Dino against bl ground, plastic dome on ftd base, NM .$95.00

Garfield, dressed as Uncle Sam, I Want You lettered on base, EX, B5...$30.00

Happy Face, Germany, yel w/legs & arms in tall dome w/glitter, rnd blk base, EX, A..$15.00

Little Mermaid, tall plastic dome on rnd base, NM $20.00

Lone Ranger Round-Up, Drier, 1940s, lassoing cow in glass dome on rnd base, M $100.00

Mickey Mouse, Bully, 1977, blk & wht striding Mickey in Dome, EX...$18.00

Mickey Mouse, in space suit w/arms stretched, Monogram Products, EX $45.00

Paul Bunyan & Blue Ox, plastic dome on wht ftd base, M ..$15.00

Teenage Mutant Ninja Turtles, dome w/different characters, M, ea $8.00

Yosemite Sam, plays Home on the Range, glass dome on wooden base, MIB $50.00

FIGURES

#1 Teacher, 'bookworm' atop figural red apple w/heart-shaped window displaying phrase, M....................................$10.00

Cat Playing Drum, drum is water compartment, M18 ......$12.00

Coffeepot, clear plastic w/girl & snowman inside, old, M18 .$10.00

Elephant, realistic detail, seated atop dome w/2 elephants inside against gr trees w/dk bl ground, wht oval base, M......$18.00

Orange w/gr leaves...$30.00

Salty Seaman & Captain, standing behind rnd dome w/sailing ship inside, German, M $45.00

Snowman, blk top hat, red ear muffs & lg red smile, carrot nose, tall, old, M18 ....$12.00

HOLIDAYS AND SPECIAL OCCASIONS

Birth Announcement, boy & girl babies on seesaw w/stork in middle in plastic dome, ftd base, M $8.00

Birth Announcement, It's a Boy in bl letters floating inside bottle w/bl trim, M $8.00

Birthday, boy & girl holding up cake on platform mk Happy Birthday against bl ground in plastic dome on wht ftd base, EX........$8.00

Birthday, girl in bikini popping out of cake in tall plastic dome, ftd base, M..$8.00

Birthday, Happy Birthday! lettered on side of bl 3-tiered cake w/red candles, plastic dome, wht rnd ftd base, M.........$8.00

Birthday, It's Down Hill From Here, Garfield w/floating numbers, Enesco, 1991, MIB $20.00

Champion, gold figure inside of trophy, M......................$8.00

Christmas, figural gift box w/snowman waving inside, lg red bow atop, old, rare, M18 ....$15.00

Christmas, figural bear in Santa hat & gr neck ribbon, no plaque, M18 ....$12.00

Christmas, figural boot w/Santa in sled, pine trees & red church inside, old, M18 ....$10.00

Christmas, figural Christmas tree w/lights & balls, old, M18..$15.00

Christmas, figural dog w/gift (water compartment), M18.$12.00

Christmas, figural Santa climbing out of chimney, plastic, M18 ....$12.00

Christmas, figural Santa on lamppost, M18 ....$12.00

Christmas, figural Santa w/gift atop lg oval dome, angel & deer inside, old, rare, M18 ....$15.00

Christmas, Santa & snowman on seesaw, plastic dome on ftd base, M...$25.00

Christmas, Santa on rocket, lg, M...................................$20.00

Christmas, Snowmen, NM, from $15.00 to $20.00 each.

Christmas, tree in glass dome, mk Made in USA, 4", NM, A...$45.00

Easter, rabbit sitting on fence inside egg-shaped dome atop wooden base, Midwest Imports, 1988, M $8.00

Easter, rabbit w/Easter eggs standing next to pine tree, Austrian glass dome, new, M18 ....$10.00

Easter, The Resurrection, 2 figures watch the spirit of Jesus rise from tomb against dk bl background in plastic dome, M $10.00

Graduation, figural graduation cap cocked atop dome w/Congratulations lettered inside, M.....................................$8.00

Graduation, Garfield as graduate, Congratulations on base, EX...$20.00

Halloween, haunted house on dome atop tall rnd base, Marcel Schurman/San Francisco, M...$8.00

Halloween, Trick or Treat!, witch atop haunted house w/skeletons in dome on base, M...$10.00

New Year, Let's Celebrate, champagne bottle & wht gloves in top hat next to 2 glasses in dome on rnd base, M.........$8.00

Valentine's Day, red heart in cylinder shape w/flat back, slot for personal photo, gold glitter, pk base, EX....................$15.00

Wedding, Good Luck on banner around bride & groom cutting wedding cake inside dome on wht oval ftd base, M...$10.00

Wedding, Weddingland on banner above bride & groom flanked by 2 wedding cakes inside dome, wht oval base, M ...$10.00

SOUVENIR AND COMMEMORATIVES

Aloha Hawaii, EX, $15.00.
(Photo courtesy Helen Guarnaccia)

Memphis, EX, $10.00.
(Photo courtesy Helene Guarnaccia)

Alaska, polar bear bending over stream, sm oval plastic dome, M18 ....$6.00

Atlanta, blk skyline in front of puffy bl & wht clouds, orange sun & plane, M18...$4.00

Berlin Bleldt Doch Berlin (Berlin Will Always Be Berlin), mc city scene, sm oval plastic dome, M18.........................$8.00

Blue Ridge Parkway, 2 blk bears on seesaw, gr hills & rainbow at back, sm oval plastic dome, M18......................$9.00

Cancun, Cozumel Mexico, fish on string in lg plastic dome, M18..$8.00

Cancun, Mexico, 2 pk dolphins in lg dome, M18 ....$6.00

Cape Cod, 2 sailboats in sm oval plastic dome, old, M18 ...$7.00

Cedar Point OH, view of amusement park against dk bl background in rnd dome on pedestal base, M....................$12.00

Cooper Union (NYC Building), detailed replica, clear all around, broad blk base w/gold decal, rnd, lg, M18.....$18.00

Dickeyville Grotto, Dickeyville WI, religious scene against dk bl background in plastic dome, wht base, M $10.00

Florida, salt & pepper shakers, 2 different views in pk & bl plastic TVs, M, pr $20.00

Florida, 2 pk flamingos in red dome on pk shell-shaped ashtray, gold trim, M...$45.00

Gillette Castle State Park CT, castle inside dome on 3-legged base, M18 ....$10.00

Great Smoky Mountains, bear atop sm dome, old, M18...$12.00

Holiday World, Santa Claus IN, Santa waving against name on bl background, plastic dome, M....................................$12.00

Knott's Berry Farm, scene against dk bl background in plastic dome, M $10.00

Lake George, sailboat on lake scene, lg plastic dome, M18...$6.00

Lake Tahoe, sailboats against pine trees on shoreline, NM..$10.00

Lourdes, kneeling figure praying to figure of the Virgin Mary standing in archway w/church in background, plastic, M $15.00

Mount Rushmore, Black Hills SD, plastic dome, M....................$12.00

Myrtle Beach SC, blk letters on band at bottom across sailing scene inside plastic dome, old, M18 ....$8.00

Paris, Eiffel Tower, Notre Dame & Sacre Coeur at back, glitter, lg plastic dome, M18...$7.00

Sears Tower Chicago, lg blk letters in flat bullet-shaped dome, M18 ....$1.00

Six Flags Over Georgia, calendar dome..........................$15.00

Space Needle, Seattle WA, salt & pepper shakers, pk & bl plastic, tall popsicle shape, M18, pr....................................$18.00

St Augustine FL, fish on string, glitter, low rectangular dome w/blk trim, old, M18 ....$7.00

St Thomas Virgin Islands, parrot inside sm oval plastic dome, M18..$10.00

United Nations, UN building inside heart-shaped dome, name lettered on base, M18 ....$10.00

USS Constitution, open-work ship inside plastic dome, old, M18..$12.00

USS Massachusettes, Fall River MA, lg gray battleship against bl sky panel, w/glitter, 1950s, G-, M18.........................$10.00

Wonderful World of Disney, 1960s, Mickey & Minnie w/castle in background, plastic dome, EX $50.00

Soldiers

'Dimestore soldiers' were made from the 1920s until sometime in the 1960s. Some of the better-known companies who made these small-scale figures and accessories were Barclay, Manoil, and Jones (hollow cast lead); Gray Iron (cast iron); and Auburn (rubber). They're about 3" to 3½" high. They were sold in Woolworth's and Kresge's 5 & 10 stores (most for just five cents), hence the name 'dimestore.' Marx made tin soldiers for use in target gun games; these sell for about $8.00. Condition is most important as these soldiers saw a lot of action. They're most often found with much of the paint worn off and with some serious 'battle wounds,' such as missing arms or legs. Nearly two thousand different figures were made by the major manufacturers, plus a number of others by minor makers such as Tommy Toy and All-Nu. Serious collectors should refer to *Collecting Toys* (1993) or *Toy Soldiers* (1992), both by Richard O'Brien, Books Americana.

Another very popular line of toy soldiers has been made by Britains of England since 1893. They are smaller and usually more detailed than 'dimestores,' and variants number in the thousands. O'Brien's book has over two hundred pages devoted to Britains and other foreign makers.

You'll notice that in addition to the soldiers, many of our descriptions and values are for the vehicles, cannons, animals, and cowboys and Indians made and sold by the same manufacturers. Note: Percentages in the description lines refer to the amount of original paint remaining, a most important evaluation factor.

Advisors: Sally and Stan Alekna (A1).

See also Dinky; Plastic Figures.

American Metal, bull, 98%, A1 ....$17.00
American Metal, calf, 93%, A1 ....$10.00
American Metal, doctor, wht, scarce, 98%, A1 ....$175.00
American Metal, farmer, 99%, A1 ....$19.00
American Metal, fox, gray, scarce, 99%, A1 ....$24.00
American Metal, hen, M, A1 ....$13.00
American Metal, horse, gray, 98%, A1 ....$11.00
American Metal, mule, 99%, A1 ....$12.00
American Metal, soldier, lying wounded, scarce, 97%, A1 ..$145.00
Auburn Rubber, aircraft defender, scarce, NM, A1 ....$55.00
Auburn Rubber, baseball batter, wht w/bl trim, scarce, 98%, A1 ....$59.00
Auburn Rubber, baseball fielder, wht w/bl trim, scarce, NM, A1 ....$60.00
Auburn Rubber, doctor in wht, scarce, 99%, A1 ....$47.00
Auburn Rubber, Foreign Legion, White Guard officer, yel w/red trim, 99%, A1 ....$38.00
Auburn Rubber, howitzer, red, 98%, A1 ....$45.00
Auburn Rubber, infantry private, marching, port of arms, oval base, early version, scarce, 97%, A1 ....$21.00
Auburn Rubber, infantry private, marching port of arms, sq base, early version, 99%, A1 ....$18.00
Auburn Rubber, machine gunner charging, sm early version, scarce, 98%, A1 ....$49.00
Auburn Rubber, Marmon-Harrington tank, 4½", 96%, A1..$32.00
Auburn Rubber, officer on horse, scarce, M, A1..............$52.00
Auburn Rubber, sound detector, 97%, A1 ....$38.00
Auburn Rubber, stretcher bearer, scarce, 94%, A1 ....$35.00
Auburn Rubber, US infantry private, 97%, A1 ....$13.00
Auburn Rubber, white guard officer, yel w/red trim, scarce, 99%, A1 ....$38.00
Authenticast, #500, British Musketeers (1600), 6-pc, EX (EX box), A $100.00
Barclay, AA-gun truck, w/2 men, wht tires, scarce, 94%, A1 ....$51.00
Barclay, airplane mechanic, scarce, 95%, A1..................$65.00
Barclay, animal, horse, blk mane & tail, 98%, A1..........$15.00

Barclay, armored car, 98%, A1 ....$25.00
Barclay, army motorcyclist, scarce, 93%, A1 ....$37.00
Barclay, army truck w/AA-gun, khaki, 99%, A1 ....$28.00
Barclay, aviator, gr, scarce, 98%, A1 ....$29.00
Barclay, boy in knickers, 98%, A1........................$15.00
Barclay, boy skater, 99%, A1 ....$14.00
Barclay, cadet, 97%, A1........................$18.00
Barclay, cannon, field; red spoke wheels, closed hitch, sm, 99%, A1 ....$20.00
Barclay, cannon, field; red spoke wheels, 98%, A1..........$38.00
Barclay, cannon, rubber tires, med, very scarce, 90-95%, A1 ..$53.00
Barclay, cannon (1st Barclay toy made), scarce, 99%, A1 ..$69.00
Barclay, cavalryman, blk horse, ca 1930, sm, 98%, A1.....$34.00
Barclay, cavalryman, gray horse, ca 1930, sm, 95%, A1 ...$32.00
Barclay, cow grazing, M (in orig tissue), A1......................$17.00
Barclay, cowboy, tin hat brim, 97%, A1 ....$26.00
Barclay, cowboy masked rider, no lasso, scarce, 97%, A1 .$56.00
Barclay, cowboy w/pistol, 97%, A1 ....$19.00
Barclay, cowboy w/rifle, 97%, A1 ....$19.00
Barclay, cowboy w/rifle in movable arm on rearing horse, very scarce, 94%, A1 ....$75.00
Barclay, girl on skis, NM, A1........................$27.00
Barclay, girl on sled, 99%, A1 ....$22.00
Barclay, HO scale, boy, scarce, 99%, A1........................$16.00
Barclay, HO scale, dining steward, NM, A1 ....$12.00
Barclay, HO scale, engineer, NM, A1 ....$12.00
Barclay, HO scale, hobo, 99%, A1 ....$11.00
Barclay, HO scale, mailman, 98%, A1 ....$10.00
Barclay, HO scale, oiler, M, A1........................$12.00
Barclay, HO scale, policeman, NM, A1 ....$12.00
Barclay, HO scale, porter, 99%, A1 ....$11.00
Barclay, HO scale, train conductor, NM, A1....................$12.00
Barclay, horse-drawn sleigh w/man & woman, 97%, A1 ..$84.00
Barclay, Indian chief, 97%, A1........................$17.00
Barclay, Indian w/bow & arrow, kneeling, 97%, A1........$19.00
Barclay, Indian w/rifle, midi, scarce, 96%, A1 ....$73.00
Barclay, Indian w/rifle, 97%, A1 ....$33.00
Barclay, Indian w/spear & knife, 99%, A1 ....$18.00
Barclay, knight, blk, NM, A1 ....$39.00
Barclay, knight w/pennant, 99%, A1 ....$24.00
Barclay, knight w/sword across chest, NM, A1 ....$37.00
Barclay, man & woman on park bench, summer garb, 98%, A1 ....$38.00
Barclay, man & woman on park bench, winter garb, 3-pc, 99%, A1 ....$28.00
Barclay, man pulling kids on sled, scarce, 99%, A1 ....$60.00
Barclay, man speed skater, 98%, A1........................$19.00
Barclay, marine, 95%, A1........................$18.00
Barclay, marine officer, long stride, tin hat, 94%, A1.......$31.00
Barclay, military nurse, blk hair, scarce, 98%, A1............$37.00
Barclay, milk truck, #377, red w/blk rubber tires, w/6 milk cans, 3⅝", M, A1 ....$68.00
Barclay, minister in hat, walking, very scarce, 90%, A1 ...$69.00
Barclay, minister standing holding hat, 99%, A1 ....$18.00
Barclay, officer, gr, 99%, A1........................$20.00
Barclay, officer sword, gr pot-metal helmet, 97%, A1 ......$24.00
Barclay, race car w/driver, gr, 1960s, 99%, A1 ....$20.00
Barclay, ram, M (in orig tissue), A1 ....$17.00

Barclay, sailor, in puttees, long stride, wht, 96%, A1 ....$24.00

Barclay, sailor, in puttees, short stride, bl, 97%, A1 ....$22.00

Barclay, Santa (sm) seated on sled, 97%, A1 ....$48.00

Barclay, Santa seated w/holly wreath, 97%, A1 ....$80.00

Barclay, sheep lying down, M, A1 ....$17.00

Barclay, shoeshine boy, scarce, 96%, A1 ....$23.00

Barclay, soldier, ammo carrier, 96%, A1 ....$24.00

Barclay, soldier, bazookaman, gr, 97%, A1 ....$21.00

Barclay, soldier, bomb thrower, khaki, 98%, A1 ....$22.00

Barclay, soldier, carrier pigeons, tin helmet, 95%, A1 ......$31.00

Barclay, soldier, charging, gr, 99%, A1 ....$21.00

Barclay, soldier, charging, short stride, 98%, A1 ....$28.00

Barclay, soldier, crawling w/pistol, khaki, scarce, 97%, A1..$97.00

Barclay, soldier, drummer, short stride, tin helmet, 97%, A1 ....$29.00

Barclay, soldier, flame thrower, gr, 99%, A1 ....$21.00

Barclay, soldier, kneeling & firing, gr pot helmet, 93%, A1..$69.00

Barclay, soldier, loading cannon shell, tin helmet, 95%, A1.$19.00

Barclay, soldier, machine gunner kneeling, tin helmet, 98%, A1 ....$22.00

Barclay, soldier, marching, khaki, 99%, A1 ....$16.00

Barclay, soldier, marching w/slung rifle, cast helmet, 99%, A1 ....$40.00

Barclay, soldier, marching w/slung rifle, khaki, 98%, A1 .$15.00

Barclay, soldier, parachutist landing, 98%, A1 ....$26.00

Barclay, soldier, running w/rifle, cast helmet, 98%, A1 ....$31.00

Barclay, soldier, sentry in overcoat w/rifle, 98%, A1 ....$28.00

Barclay, soldier, sniper kneeling, gr, 99%, A1 ....$27.00

Barclay, soldier, standing firing rifle, khaki, NM, A1 ....$18.00

Barclay, soldier, tommy gunner, gr pot-metal helmet, 97%, A1...$24.00

Barclay, soldier, tommy gunner, tin helmet, 96%, A1 ......$20.00

Barclay, soldier, w/bazooka, gr, 98%, A1 ....$22.00

Barclay, soldier, wounded on crutches, khaki, scarce, 99%, A1 ....$33.00

Barclay, train conductor, 99%, A1 ....$18.00

Barclay, train engineer, 99%, A1 ....$18.00

Barclay, train passenger, elderly lady in traveling costume, 95% $15.00

Barclay, train passenger, girl, 93% $10.00

Barclay, train passenger, woman w/dog, pk or bl, NM, A1, ea $16.00

Barclay, train porter w/wisk broom, M, A1 ....$28.00

Barclay, truck, beer; silver, w/6 barrels, wht tires, ca 1940, scarce, 95%, A1 ....$65.00

Barclay, truck, gas; Shell, yel, 98%, A1 ....$19.00

Barclay, truck, gas; Sinclair, gr, 99%, A1 ....$20.00

Barclay, truck, moving; Hertz, 1960s, 98%, A1 ....$18.00

Barclay, truck, side dump; yel & bl, 1960s, 98%, A1 ....$15.00

Barclay, truck, stake; mk Express, gr, 1930s, 97%, A1 .....$48.00

Barclay, VW, red, 1960s, scarce, 98%, A1 ....$24.00

Barclay, West Point cadet marching, short stride, gray, 96%, A1...$27.00

Barclay, zeppelin, very scarce, 70-75%, A1 ....$89.00

Britains, #1 Life Guards, 5-pc, G-EX (G box w/label), A $115.00

Britains, #1 Life Guards, 5-pc, M (EX Whisstock box), A $175.00

Britains, #1 Life Guards, 5-pc, NM (VG illustrated box) .$200.00

Britains, #3 5th Dragoon Guards (Princess Charlotte of Wales), 1925-41, 5-pc, VG (VG British Empire box), A $200.00

Britains, #3 5th Dragoon Guards, 5-pc, M (Fair Whisstock box), A $315.00

Britains, #6 Middlesex Regiment, dtd 1905, 8-pc, G, A $200.00

Britains, #12 11th Hussars, ca 1935, 5-pc, EX, A $100.00

Britains, #19 West India Regiment, 2nd version, 8-pc, VG (VG box), A $250.00

Britains, #19 West India Regiment, ca 1930, 9-pc, G-EX, A $275.00

Britains, #24 9th Queen's Royal Lancers, ca 1960, 4-pc, G-EX, A $100.00

Britains, #28 Mountain Artillery Team w/Quick Firing Gun, 11-pc, M (Fair illus 'Flowers' box), A $575.00

Britains, #28 Mountain Gun of the Royal Artillery, 12-pc, EX (EX repro Britains box), A $175.00

Britains, #30 Drums & Bugles of the Line, ca 1925, 8-pc, VG (VG Whisstock box), A $150.00

Britains, #30 Drums & Bugles of the Line, ca 1935, 8-pc, G-EX, A $100.00

Britains, #33 16th Queen's Lancers, 5-pc, EX, A............$185.00

Britains, #37, Band of the Coldstream Guards (metal drums), ca 1950, 21-pc, NM (G box), A $400.00

Britains, #37 Band of the Coldstream Guards, 21-pc, G-EX, A $250.00

Britains, #39, Royal Horse Artillery, ca 1955, 13-piece, EX (EX box), A, $275.00.

Britains, #47 1st Bengal Cavalry, ca 1930, 5-pc, G-EX (VG Sons of the Empire box), A..$375.00

Britains, #55F Britains Model Farm, 10-pc, NM (NM box), A $225.00

Britains, #66 Indian Army (13th Duke of Connaught's Own Lancers), 5-pc, G-EX (EX box), A..........................$115.00

Britains, #69 Pipers of the Scots Guard, 1930, marching, 7-pc, EX (EX Flowers British Soldiers box), A $200.00

Britains, #74 Royal Welch Fusiliers, dtd 1905, 8-pc, G (G printer's box w/battle honors), A $200.00

Britains, #75 Scots Guards, ca 1935, 8-pc, G-EX, A.........$75.00

Britains, #77 The Gordon Highlanders, 6-pc, M (EX Regiments box), A..$115.00

Britains, #79 Royal Navy Landing Party, 11-pc, EX (Poor box), A $140.00

Britains, #90 Coldstream Guards, 24-pc, M (M Regiments box), A..$375.00

Britains, #92 Spanish Infantry, 8-pc, EX-M (EX box), A......$1,150.00

Britains, #101 Band of the Life Guards, 12-pc, M (EX Regiments of All Nations box), A.........................$350.00

Britains, #104 City Imperial Volunteers, c date 1900, 10-pc, G, A..$350.00

Britains, #110 Devonshire Regiment 11th Foot, 7-pc, M (EX Whisstock box), A...................................$140.00

Britains, #114 Cameron Highlanders, dtd 1901, 8-pc, rare, G (G Whisstock box), A...............................$1,.00

Britains, #115 Egyptain Cavalry, ca 1960, 4-pc, EX, A.....$100.00

Britains, #117 Egyptian Infantry, standing at attention, 8-pc, EX (EX Whisstock box), A.......................$200.00

Britains, #123 The Bikanir Camel Corps, 3-pc, M (EX+ box), A..$545.00

Britains, #124 Irish Guards, 9-pc, NM (EX Whisstock box), A..$250.00

Britains, #133 US of Soviet Russia Infantry, 8-pc, M (Fair box), A..$430.00

Britains, #135 Japanese Cavalry, 1939-41, 5-pc, EX (VG Whisstock box), A........................$1,800.00

Britains, #136 Russian Cavalry, 5-pc, EX (Fair Whisstock box), A..$275.00

Britains, #136 Russian Cossacks, ca 1960, 4-pc, G-EX, A....$150.00

Britains, #138 Cuirassiers, 5-pc, EX-M (EX Whisstock box), A..$300.00

Britains, #138 French Army Cuirassiers, 5-pc, EX (G Regiments box), A..$160.00

Britains, #138 French Cuirassiers, ca 1960, 4-pc, EX, A...$100.00

Britains, #142 Zouaves, charging w/rifles, 8-pc, (EX EX Whisstock-Flowers box), A........................$175.00

Britains, #145 Royal Army Medical Corps Horse-Drawn Ambulance, ca 1930, 7-pc, G (G box), A $550.00

Britains, #147 Zulus of Africa, 8-pc, M (EX box), A $220.00

Britains, #154 Prussian Infantry, 1908, marching at the slope in review order, 8-pc, EX (EX box), A $200.00

Britains, #159 British Expeditionary Force Cavalry, 4-pc, EX (EX box), A..$350.00

Britains, #164 Arabs of the Desert, M (EX Britains Ltd box), A..$115.00

Britains, #167 Turkish Infantry, 8-pc, EX (Whisstock box), A, from $200 to $275.00

Britains, #169 Bersagliere, 1925, 8-pc, EX (EX Types of the Italian Army box), A $200.00

Britains, #173 Serbian Infantry, charging, 8-pc, EX, A ..$175.00

Britains, #179 Cowboys w/Lassos & Pistols, ca 1935, 5-pc, G-EX (G box), A..$175.00

Britains, #182 11th Hussars (Prince Albert's Own), 8-pc, G-EX, A..$100.00

Britains, #192 Zouaves, 8-pc, M (G Whisstock box), A $220.00

Britains, #193 Arabs of the Desert, 5-pc, M (EX box), A ...$440.00

Britains, #196 The Evzones, 8-pc, G (G box), A.............$45.00

Britains, #197 1st King George V's Own Gurkha Rifles/Malaun Regiment, 8-pc, EX, A..............................$150.00

Britains, #201 General Staff Officers, 4-pc, M (EX box), A ...$175.00

Britains, #201 Officers of the General Staff, 4-pc, M (EX Whisstock box), A..$160.00

Britains, #217 Argentine Cavalry, 4-pc, EX+M (EX box), A.$175.00

Britains, #225 King's African Rifles, 8-pc, EX, A $175.00

Britains, #228 US Marines, 12-pc, G (G box), A.............$70.00

Britains, #228 US Marines, 8-pc, EX-M (G Whisstock box), A..$160.00

Britains, #230 US Navy Blue Jackets, ca 1935, 8-pc, G-EX, A..$100.00

Britains, #258 British Infantry, steel helmets & gas masks, ca 1940, 8-pc, EX, A......................................$150.00

Britains, #276 US Cavalry at the Gallop, ca 1935, 5-pc, G-EX, A..$200.00

Britains, #339, Black Watch, ca 1935, 13-pc, rare, G (G Armies of the World Box), A...............................$1,600.00

Britains, #400 The Life Guards, 5-pc, M (EX Whisstock box), A..$290.00

Britains, #1253 US Navy White Jackets, ca 1935, 8-pc, G-EX, A..$125.00

Britains, #1256, Railway Station Staff, 17-piece, EXIB, A, $385.00.

Britains, #1283 Grenadier Guards, ca 1940, 9-pc, EX-M (VG Soldiers of the British Empire box), A.............$150.00

Britains, #1301 US Army Military Band, G-EX (EX box), A.$115.00

Britains, #1301 US Military Band, 12-pc, EX, A............$210.00

Britains, #1318 British Machine Gunners, ca 1940, 6-pc, EX (G Armies of the World box), A......................$175.00

Britains, #1327 Grenadier Guards Firing, display set, ca 1960, 14-pc, EX (VG box), A....................................$160.00

Britains, #1343 Horse Guards, 1930s, 5-pc, EX (G Armies of the World box), A..$300.00

Britains, #1349 North West Mounted Police, 5-pc, M (G box), A..$125.00

Britains, #1432 10-Wheel Covered Tender, NM (Fair box), A..$185.00

Britains, #1437 Italian Army Carabinieri, 7-pc, M (M box), A..$200.00

Britains, #1470 State Coach of England, 10-pc, EX (G box), A..$275.00

Britains, #1470 The State Coach, 11-pc, M (Fair box), A..$325.00

Britains, #1475 Beefeaters, Outsiders & Footman of the Royal Household, 18-pc, M (Fair box), A...................$300.00

Britains, #1510 Royal Navy Sailors, ca 1940, 8-pc, EX (VG box), A..$150.00

Britains, #1512 Army Ambulance, EX (EX box), A.......$300.00

Britains, #1525 US Biplane, 1937-40, olive drab pnt w/red, wht & bl stars, rare, EX, A.................................$5,100.00

Britains, #1542 New Zealand Infantry, marching at the slope, 8-pc, NM (EX Types of the Colonial Army box), A ..$300.00

Britains, #1711 French Foreign Legion, 7-pc, EX-M (EX box), A $150.00

Britains, #1727 Mobile Howitzer Unit, 4-pc, EX (G box), A .$520.00

Britains, #1837 Argentine Infantry, 8 pcs, rare, EX (EX Armies of the World box), A $1,800.00

Britains, #1858, British Infantry, in battle dress & steel helmets, ca 1940, 8-pc, G-EX, A $100.00

Britains, #1874 Historical Series, 10-pc, EX-M (G box), A....$920.00

Britains, #1886 Historical Series, 15-pc, M (G box), A .$920.00

Britains, #1889 Historical Series, 16-pc, EX-M (Fair box), A.$400.00

Britains, #1891 Historical Series, M (Fair box), A $920.00

Britains, #1901 Capetown Highlanders, 1953, marching at the slope, 7 pcs, EX (VG Regiments box), A.................$125.00

Britains, #1911 Officers & Petty Officers of the Royal Navy, 7-pc, EX-M (G Types of the Royal Navy box), A $185.00

Britains, #2009 Belgian Army — Le Regiment Des Grenadiers, 8-pc, EX (Fair box), A..$125.00

Britains, #2027 The Red Army Infantry Guards, 8-pc, M (EX box), A...$185.00

Britains, #2031 Australian Infantry, 8-pc, EX, A $150.00

Britains, #2035 Swedish Army — Svea Livarde, 8-pc, M (M box), A...$150.00

Britains, #2035 Swedish Life Guards, 8-pc, EX (G box), A...$200.00

Britains, #2048 British Army Mobile Artillery Unit, clockwork, 4-pc, G-EX (VG box), A...$225.00

Britains, #2051 Uruguayan Military School Cadets, 1953-59, 8-pc, M (EX Regiments box), A....................................$300.00

Britains, #2067, Sovereign's Standard of the Life Guards & Escort, 7-pc, NM (EX box), A $225.00

Britains, #2073 Royal Air Force, 1953-59, marching slope arms, 8 pcs, NM (EX Regiments box), A $150.00

Britains, #2079 Royal Company Archers, partial 12-pc set, EX...$200.00

Britains, #2084 Colour Party of the Scots Guards, 6-pc, M (M box), A...$435.00

Britains, #2091 Rifle Brigade, marching at the trail, 8 pcs, MIB, A $125.00

Britains, #2098 Republica de Venezuela Cadets de la Escuela Militar, 1955-59, 7-pc, NM (G Regiments box), A $250.00

Britains, #2111 The Black Watch Colour Party, 6-pc, M (M box), A...$490.00

Britains, #2132 Royal Army Medical Corps Stretcher Party, 8-pc, M (G Empire box), A...$210.00

Britains, #2153 Band of the Royal Marines, 1957-60, 12-pc, EX (VG box), A $600.00

Britains, #2184 Bahamas Police, 1960-61, 7-pc, rare, EX, A ..$1,200.00

Britains, #2255 United Nations Infantry, ca 1960, 7-pc, NM.$150.00

Britains, #9167 French Foreign Legion, ca 1960, 6-pc, EX (G window box), A..$100.00

Britains, #9178 US West Point Cadets, marching at the slope, 7-pc, MIB, A $100.00

Courtenay, Alain Lord of Montendre, mounted, position H-13, sgn R Courtenay, EX, A...$1,800.00

Courtenay, Erle of Warwick, position Z-5, sgn R Courtenay, EX, A $750.00

Courtenay, Thibaud de Scey, position 2, VG, A $450.00

Courtenay, King Henry V, full gold armor, movable right arm, VG, A, $250.00.

Courtenay, Thierry D'Auffay le Hardi, postion 9, VG, A..$400.00

Courtenay-Greenhill, Jaques de Vienne Sieure de Longwy, postion Z-20, sgn Peter Greenhill, EX............................$650.00

Courtenay-Greenhill, Sir John Pateshull, position Z-9, EX, A.$600.00

Dorset, #A19 General Service Wagon 24th Foot, 10-pc, NM (NM Armies of the World box), A............................$100.00

Dorset, #A58 Pontoon Wagon, G (G Armies of the World box), A $125.00

Dorset, #A66 Royal Engineers Limbered Wagon, 2-horse team, NM (NM Armies of the World box), A $65.00

Edmund's Traditional, 3rd New Jersey Cavalry Regiment (1st US Hussars), marching at the trail, NM (NM box), A......$75.00

Edmund's Traditional, 79th New York State Militia, 5 infantry marching at the slope & 1 w/sword raised, MIB, A ...$75.00

Elastolin, Knights in Armour, 22-pc, Fair-G, A $520.00

Elastolin, US Revolutionary War Soldiers in Action, 24-pc, Poor-G, A..$1,150.00

Grey Iron, Am Family at Home, delivery boy, 97%, A1 ..$19.00

Grey Iron, Am Family at Home, garage man in gr, postwar, 99%, A1 ....$21.00

Grey Iron, Am Family at Home, milkman, scarce, 98%, A1 ......$24.00

Grey Iron, Am Family at Home, old woman sitting, 98%, A1 ...$14.00

Grey Iron, Am Family at Home, woman w/basket, 97%, A1 .....$17.00

Grey Iron, Am Family at the Beach, old man in wht suit sitting, very scarce, 97%, A1 ....$62.00

Grey Iron, Am Family on the Farm, cow, brn & yel, 98%, A1.$15.00

Grey Iron, Am Family on the Farm, farmer, 98%, A1 ......$17.00

Grey Iron, Am Family on the Farm, goose, 97%, A1........$14.00

Grey Iron, Am Family on the Farm, hired hand digging, scarce, 98%, A1 ....$20.00

Grey Iron, Am Family Travels, bench, M, A1 ....$14.00

Grey Iron, Am Family Travels, boy in traveling suit, tan, 99%, A1 ....$11.00

Grey Iron, Am Family Travels, conductor, 99%, A1........$13.00

Grey Iron, Am Family Travels, girl in traveling suit, 98%, A1 ....$14.00

Grey Iron, Am Family Travels, mailman, 99%, A1 ....$16.00

Grey Iron, Am Family Travels, policeman, aluminum, rare, 99%, A1 ....$16.00

Grey Iron, Am Family Travels, porter, scarce, 97%, A1...**$19.00**

Grey Iron, cadet, 97%, A1..**$22.00**

Grey Iron, cadet officer, 98%, A1 ....**$35.00**

Grey Iron, cannon, 1st model, spring action, scarce, 98%, A1..**$51.00**

Grey Iron, clown w/arched back, red & wht, 92%, A1.....**$50.00**

Grey Iron, colonial officer, 97%, A1...........................**$28.00**

Grey Iron, Ethiopian Chief, scarce, 95%, A1 ....**$65.00**

Grey Iron, Grey Iron Company B, bugler, marching, EX+, A1 ....**$7.00**

Grey Iron, Greyklip Battery E, officer leading gun limber drawn by 4 horses & several attached soldiers, 2-pc, EX, A1 .**$32.00**

Grey Iron, Greyklip Company A, flagbearer, EX+, A1.......**$7.00**

Grey Iron, Greyklip Company A, officer, EX+, A1 ....**$7.00**

Grey Iron, Greyklip Company B, drummer, EX+................**$7.00**

Grey Iron, Greyklip Company C, set of 10 figures, EX+, A1..**$59.00**

Grey Iron, Greyklip Uncle Sam's Defenders, rifleman at attention, scarce, 96%, A1......................................**$16.00**

Grey Iron, Greyklips Company B, officer, EX+, A1...........**$7.00**

Grey Iron, Greyklips Company B, rifleman, EX+, A1 ....**$5.00**

Grey Iron, holdup man in blk, M, A1..........................**$31.00**

Grey Iron, Indian chief w/knife, 98%, A1......................**$32.00**

Grey Iron, Legion bugler, early version, 99%, A1............**$29.00**

Grey Iron, Legion colorbearer, 95%, A1........................**$34.00**

Grey Iron, pirate w/sword, gr, 97%, A1.......................**$33.00**

Grey Iron, Ranch Series, bucking bronco, blk, very scarce, 97%, A1..**$57.00**

Grey Iron, Royal Canadian Mounted Police, early version, 98%, A1..**$44.00**

Grey Iron, ski trooper, scarce, 97%, A1 ....**$55.00**

Grey Iron, soldier, wounded, on crutches, scarce, 97%, A1........**$70.00**

Grey Iron, US Doughboy, bomber crawling, postwar, 95%, A1.**$28.00**

Grey Iron, US Doughboy, charging, 95%, A1 ....**$20.00**

Grey Iron, US Doughboy, officer, early version, 96%, A1..**$19.00**

Grey Iron, US Doughboy, officer, 95%, A1 ....**$19.00**

Grey Iron, US Doughboy, shoulder arms, 98%, A1 ....**$22.00**

Grey Iron, US Doughboy, signalman, postwar, 98%, A1 .**$41.00**

Grey Iron, US marine, later version, 98%, A1.................**$24.00**

Grey Iron, US navy officer in bl, postwar, 98%, A1 ....**$24.00**

Grey Iron, US sailor in wht, postwar, 97%, A1 ....**$24.00**

Grey Iron, US sailor signalman, 97%, A1......................**$33.00**

Heyde, Chinese Boxers, 10-pc, NM, A............................**$250.00**

Heyde, English Cavalry Mounted, 12-pc, Fair-G, A.......**$230.00**

Heyde, French Infantry, missing 6 figures, VG (worn box), A..**$325.00**

Heyde, Valley Forge Display, 40-pc, Fair-Good (Fair box), A ...**$3,565.00**

Imperial, #14 65th Foot Regiment, 6 pcs, MIB, A............**$75.00**

Imperial, #58 Naval Brigade, 6 pcs, MIB, A.....................**$85.00**

Imperial, #7 South Australian Scottish Infantry, 6 pcs, MIB, A...**$125.00**

Jones, bull, 99%, A1...**$6.00**

Jones, calf, #236, 93%, A1..**$10.00**

Jones, donkey, #226, 98%, A1.......................................**$11.00**

Jones, farmer, 99%, A1...**$19.00**

Jones, fox, gray, scarce, 99%, A1.................................**$24.00**

Jones, German soldier, kneeling firing long rifle, 99%, A1 ..**$195.00**

Jones, mule, 99%, A1..**$12.00**

Jones, soldier, prone firing dbl machine gun, khaki, scarce, 94%, A1...**$105.00**

Jones, soldier, standing firing rifle, khaki, scarce, 97%, A1 ..**$120.00**

Jones, 54mm, Scot highlander of 1814, scarce, 98%, A1..**$28.00**

Jones, 54mm, 1775 British marine firing musket at angle, scarce, 98%..**$28.00**

Lineol, Italian Bersaglieri, marching at the slope, 18 pcs, EX, A...**$250.00**

Lineol, Swiss Army Band, 10-pc, G, A...........................**$160.00**

Lucotte, #401/6 1st Empire Mounted Napoleon & Six Mounted Figures, 7-pc, Fair-G (Poor box), A.....................**$1,450.00**

Manoil, anti-tank gun, wooden wheels, scarce, 96%, A1.**$71.00**

Manoil, bench, 97%, A1 ....**$14.00**

Manoil, bicycle dispatch rider, scarce, 98%, A1 ....**$47.00**

Manoil, Black man eating watermelon, scarce, 99%, A1 .**$99.00**

Manoil, bull, head turned, 97%, A1................................**$22.00**

Manoil, calf, sm, 96%, A1 ....**$15.00**

Manoil, cannon, coastal defense, variant breach & sight, late version, 98%, A1...**$21.00**

Manoil, cannon, mk M 69 USA, wooden wheels, 99%, A1.**$25.00**

Manoil, carpenter carrying door, scarce, 96%, A1 ....**$65.00**

Manoil, carpenter sawing wood, 95%, A1......................**$34.00**

Manoil, colt, maroon, scarce, 99%, A1...........................**$29.00**

Manoil, colt, tan & wht, scarce, 98%, A1.......................**$28.00**

Manoil, cow feeding, 98%, A1 ....**$20.00**

Manoil, cowgirl, no horse, 98%, A1................................**$29.00**

Manoil, doctor, wht, red cross on cap, 95%, A1 ....**$28.00**

Manoil, farm boy stacking wood, 98%, A1 ....**$27.00**

Manoil, farm tractor, loop in front, 97%, A1...................**$28.00**

Manoil, farm woman picking berries, scarce, 94%, A1 .....**$51.00**

Manoil, farm woman sweeping w/broom, 99%, A1 ....**$45.00**

Manoil, farmer at pump, 96%, A1...................................**$22.00**

manoil, farmer cutting corn, 98%, A1............................**$27.00**

Manoil, farmer pitching sheaves, NM, A1 ....**$29.00**

Manoil, girl, wht dress, 99%, A1....................................**$15.00**

Manoil, hostess, gr, scarce, 98%, A1 ....**$72.00**

Manoil, man chopping wood, 95%, A1............................**$20.00**

Manoil, mason laying bricks, scarce, 98%, A1 ....**$41.00**

Manoil, nurse w/red bowl, no hem, different veil, scarce, 94%, A1..**$42.00**

Manoil, nurse w/red bowl, 95%, A1 ....**$26.00**

Manoil, officer w/sword, NM, A1....................................**$30.00**

Manoil, pontoon boat on wheels, scarce, 92%, A1...........**$51.00**

Manoil, scarecrow, w/straw hat, 97%, A1 ....**$24.00**

Manoil, shepherd w/flute, 98%, A1................................**$35.00**

Manoil, shoe cobbler, scarce, 90%, A1 ....**$25.00**

Manoil, soldier, cannon loader, 98%, A1........................**$28.00**

Manoil, soldier, combat w/rifle, 93%, A1........................**$37.00**

Manoil, soldier, firing AA-gun, compo, very scarce, 96%, A1...**$79.00**

Manoil, soldier, firing camp AA-gun, compo, very scarce, 96%, A1...**$79.00**

Manoil, soldier, flag bearer, 97%, A1............................**$231.00**

Manoil, soldier, kneeling w/bayonet, scarce, 95%, A1 .....**$72.00**

Manoil, soldier, lying wounded, number on back, scarce, 94%, A1...**$28.00**

Manoil, soldier, machine gunner, seated, compo, scarce, 92-94%, A1..**$52.00**

Manoil, soldier, mine detector, 98%, A1 ....**$39.00**

Manoil, soldier, observer, 97%, A1 ....**$44.00**

Manoil, soldier, parachute jumper, orange harness, 97%, A1 ....$54.00

Manoil, soldier, sitting w/rifle, 94%, A1 ....$39.00

Manoil, soldier, standing firing rifle, 98%, A1 ....$31.00

Manoil, soldier, stretcher bearers, 93%, A1 ....$28.00

Manoil, soldier, trench mortar, 98%, A1 ....$32.00

Manoil, soldier, wounded on stretcher, rare, 99%, A1 ...$185.00

Mark Time, #MT17 13th Middlesex Volunteer Cyclists (Queen's Westminsters), 1899, 3-pc, MIB, A............$65.00

Marlborough, #J1 Queen Victoria in Landau, MIB, A ...$265.00

Marlborough, #MF44 Royal Horse Artillery, 4 infantry in action & 1 dog, MIB, A..$65.00

Mignot, Ancient Gaul Archers, 12-pc, M (EX box), A .$150.00

Mignot, Ancient Roman Infantry, 12-pc, M (EX box), A..$200.00

Mignot, Arabs, marching, 12-pc, MIB, A $250.00

Mignot, Band of the Legion of the North (1806), 12-pc, M (EX box), A...$275.00

Mignot, English Infantry of the Line (1812), 12-pc, M (EX box), A..$150.00

Mignot, French Army Cavalierie du Train (Supply Train Escort — 1890-1914), 12-pc, G-EX (G box), A.................$350.00

Mignot, French Cuirassiers (1890-1914), ca 1950, 12-pc, G (G box), A..$175.00

Mignot, French Grenadiers a Cheval (1812), 6-pc, M (EX box), A..$200.00

Mignot, French Marine Fusliers (1910-1914), ca 1975, 12-pc, EX-M (EX box), A $225.00

Mignot, French Napoleonic Field Artillery Caisson (1812), 5-pc, EX-M (EX box), A..$200.00

Mignot, Garde Imperiale De Russe, #228, 6-pc, M (G box), A..$350.00

Mignot, Grenadier Guards Mounted, 6-pc, M (M box), A $490.00

Mignot, Infanterie Coloniale w/Colonial Spahi Algerian Bugler, 13-pc, G-EX (G box), A $400.00

Mignot, Infantry of the line, 12-pc, M (EX box), A.......$290.00

Mignot, Legionnaires, 1906, 4 different firing positions, 12-pc, MIB, A..$350.00

Mignot, Mamelukes of the Imperial Guard (1812), 6-pc, M (EX box), A...$250.00

Mignot, Paris Fire Brigade, pumper & ladder trucks w/hand-drawn hose reel & pump, 19 figures, EX, A..........$1,650.00

Mignot, Prussian Infantry (1914), 12-pc, M (EX new-style box), A..$275.00

Mignot, Royal Deux Ponts Regiment (1779), 12-pc, M (EX box), A...$150.00

Mignot, Russian Cosacks (1890-1914), ca 1950, 6-pc, EX (G box), A..$175.00

Mignot, Russian Infantry (1914), 12-pc, M (EX new-style box), A..$200.00

Mignot, Saracen Warriors, 8-pc, G-EX (EX repro box), A ..$165.00

Mignot, Scouts of the Young Guard (1812), 6-pc, M (EX box), A..$200.00

Mignot, Sudanese Camel Battery Gun Team, ca 1930, 10-pc, Fair-G (G box), A...$800.00

Mignot, Swiss Sappers of the Guard (1810), 12-pc, M (EX box), A..$150.00

Mignot, Volontaires, #25, 12-pc, M (Fair box), A $290.00

Mignot, WWI German Fokker Triplane, pilot in gray-gr field uniform & spiked helmet, 2-pc, M (EX box), A......$425.00

Mignot-Lucotte, French Napoleonic Four-Wheeled Field Kitchen (1810), 5-pc, EX-NM (EX box), A............$300.00

Mignot-Lucotte, Napoleon's Imperial Coronation Coach, complete, rare, A, $1,000.00.

Molded Products, aviator, sq harness, 95%, A1 ....$14.00

Molded Products, Indian standing w/arms folded, scarce, 94%, A1 ....$13.00

Molded Products, marine, bl, 93%, A1 ....$11.00

Molded Products, officer on horse, WWII helmet, scarce, 98%, A1 ....$23.00

Molded Products, soldier prone w/machine gun, WWII, 95%, A1 ....$13.00

Molded Products, soldier w/parachute, 99%, A1 ....$17.00

Plantagenet, #2 Mounted English Knights of Agincourt, Richard Beauchamp, Earl of Warrick & Sir Hugh Wrottesley, MIB, A $150.00

Plantagenet, #4 Mounted English Knights of Agincourt, Thomas Montagu, Earl of Salisbury & Richard Pembridge, MIB, A $250.00

Playwod Plastics, parade soldier w/pack, 98%, A1 ....$18.00

Playwod Plastics, soldier marching in O'seas cap, 95%, A1 ..$18.00

Steadfast, #SF67 Royal Engineers Telegraph Wagon set, M (M boxes), A $400.00

Tradition, #83, Royal Scots Fusiliers (1895), EX (G box), A .$100.00

Tradition, #88, Scots Guards (1895), 6-pc, M (EX box), A..$75.00

Warren, US Army Field Artillery Gun Team, 8-pc, G-EX, A $1,000.00

Sporting Collectibles

Baseball — the great American pastime — has given us hundreds of real-life sports heroes plus a great amount of collectible memorabilia. Baseball gloves, bats, game-worn uniforms, ephemera of many types, even games and character watches are among the many items being sought out today. And there are fans of basketball, football, and hockey that are just as avid in their collecting.

As you can see, many of our listings describe Kenner's Starting Lineup figures. These small plastic likenesses of famous sports greats were first produced in 1988. New they can be purchased for $5.00 to $8.00 (though some may go a little higher), but they have wonderful potential to appreciate. As the sports stars fluctuate in popularity, so do their Starting Lineup figures. Some may occasionally sell for several hundred dollars, but on the average most from 1988 run from $25.00 to $50.00. Football and basketball series have been made as well, and in 1993 Kenner added hockey. If you're going to collect them, be critical of the condition of the packaging.

Bobbin' head dolls made of papier-mache were manufactured in Japan during the 1960s until about 1972 and were sold at ball parks, stadiums, and through the mail for about $2.98. They were about 7" high or so, hand painted and then varnished. Some of them represent sports teams and their mascots. Depending on scarcity and condition, they'll run from as low as $35.00 up to $100.00, though there are some that sell for $300.00 or so. A few were modeled in the likeness of a particular sports star; these are rare and when they can be found sell in the $500.00 to $1,000.00 range. Base colors indicate when the doll was made. During 1961 and '62, white bases were used; today these are very scarce. Green bases are from 1962 until '66, and gold bases were used from 1967 until 1972. Mascot-heads are favored by collectors, and football figures are becoming very collectible as well. One of our advisors, Tim Hunter, has prepared a *Bobbin' Head Guide*, with a rarity scale and current values. See Dealer and Collector Codes for his address.

Advisors: Tim Hunter (H13); James Watson (W8) Hartland Figures.

See also Cereal Boxes; Character Clocks and Watches; Games; Pin-Back Buttons, Wrestling Collectibles.

Andy Pafko, scorekeeper's ring, 1950s premium, brass, EX+, J5.**$100.00**
Babe Ruth, record, The Legend Comes to Life, Fleetwood, 1970s, 33 rpm, M (sealed), M17...............................$25.00
Babe Ruth, ring, gold-plated baseball w/ball & glove emb on sides, scarce, EX, A......................................$150.00
Bill Dickey, windup toy, 1940s, celluloid, NM, J6..........$150.00
Bob Feller, book, How To Pitch, Ronald Press, 1948, hardcover, EX, w/dust jacket, J5............................$20.00
Boston Celtics, radio, Sutton, player, 6", EX....................$50.00
Chicago Bears, pennant, Super Bowl XX, EX..................$20.00
Chicago Cubs, headphone radio, Univoice of Chicago, sides promote Burger King, 2" dia, EX...........................$50.00
Chicago White Sox, ring, baseball, NM, J2....................$45.00
Cleveland Indians, bank, Gibbs, 1950, player w/bat standing beside ball, 7", EX, A.....................................$200.00
Cleveland Indians, pin-back button, 1950s, Cleveland Indians Am League & baseball design, 1¾" dia, from $35 to.$45.00
Dallas Cowboys, clock radio, Bradley, 1984, 4½" sq, EX..$40.00
Detroit Tigers, doll, stuffed cloth, 12", EX, from $35 to ...$45.00
Detroit Tigers, yearbook, 1955, NM, J5...........................$50.00
Hank Aaron, pin-back button, Thanks Milwaukee, 1954-76, full-color image w/blk lettering, 2", EX, J5.................$15.00
Harlem Globetrotters, yearbook, 1963, NM, M17............$25.00
Harry Carey, book, Holy Cow!, 1989, EX, from $20 to $25.00
Jackie Robinson, bank, Save & Win w/Jackie Robinson Daily Dime Register, metal box-shape w/canted corners, 3", EX $475.00
Jackie Robinson, doll, Allied Grand Doll Mfg, 1950, jtd compo w/cloth uniform, 13", MIB $900.00
Joe DiMaggio, pin-back button, 1950s, photo on lt bl background, 1¾" dia, EX, from $50 to.............................$75.00

Joe DiMaggio, ring, Club Member, 1940s, metal with signature and embossed images, VG, A, $330.00.

Joe Garagiola, book, Baseball Is a Funny Game, 1960, w/autograph, EX, from $25 to................................$30.00
Joe Namath, doll, Ace Novelty, stuffed cloth w/49ers uniform, 25", EX...$40.00
Kansas City Chiefs, radio, football helmet, Pro Sports series, EX..$50.00
Lenny Dykstra, bat, Louisville Slugger model 125 M110, w/autograph, 34", EX...$100.00
Los Angeles Dodgers, doll, 1960s, stuffed cloth w/plastic eyes & nose, 12", EX, minimum value $35.00
Lou Gehrig, book, Boy of the Sand Lot, Riper, 1949, hardcover, EX...$25.00
Mickey Mantle, pin-back button, 1950s, photo on lt bl background, 1¾", EX, from $50 to...........................$75.00
New York Knicks, bear, Good Stuff, 1991, stuffed plush w/cloth uniform & ball, 6", NM..................................$25.00
NFL Football, toy chest, footlocker featuring Dick Butkus, Daryle Lamonica, etc, EX, J2 ....$100.00
Philadelphia Flyers, doll, stuffed cloth, EX, minimum value.$25.00
Pittsburgh Pirates, radio, player, Sutton, EX $50.00
Pittsburgh Steelers, radio, Pro-Sports Marketing, helmet shape, NM, from $35 to...$50.00
Roberto Clemente, key chain, shows 1960 Topps card, NM, from $10 to...$15.00
Roger Maris, Action Baseball, complete, NM (VG box)..$135.00
Roger Maris, pin-back button, 1950s, photo on yel background, 3" dia, EX, from $50 to $75.00
Shaquille O'Neal, poster, w/autograph, EX....................$50.00
Steve Carlton, bat, Adirondack Big Stick, w/autograph, 32", EX $75.00
Ted Williams, baseball, Official McPhail American League, w/autograph, NM...$95.00
Ty Cobb, doll, Ideal, 1911, stuffed cloth w/compo head & hands, MIB $400.00
Yogi Berra, cup, 1960s, w/Yogi Bear & Yoo Hoo advertising, wht plastic, 5", NM.....................................$50.00

BOBBIN' HEAD DOLLS

Atlanta Braves, team mascot, 1967-72, gold base...........$135.00
Atlanta Falcons, 1967, rnd gold base $75.00
Baltimore Bullets, Little Dribblers..................................$200.00
Baltimore Colts, 1966-68, realistic face, rnd gold base ...$250.00
Baltimore Orioles, team mascot, 1961-62, wht base, rare, minimum value $450.00
Boston Patriots, Type VI, lg shoulder pads, from $300 to ..$400.00
Chicago Bears, Black player, 1962, gold base.................$350.00
Chicago Bears, 1967, rnd gold base................................$100.00

Cincinnati Reds, Black player, 1962-66, gr base $1,500.00
Cleveland Indians, team mascot, 1961-62, sq wht base, rare ..$600.00
Dallas Cowboys, team mascot, 1962-66, gr base, minimum value..$180.00
Green Bay Packers, 1967, gold base, NM.......................$150.00
Harlem Globetrotters, 1962 ....$350.00
Houston Oilers, 1966-67, rnd gold base $55.00
Kansas City Chiefs, 1968, rnd gold base, from $50 to.......$75.00
Kansas State Wildcats, rnd gr base $50.00
Los Angeles Dodgers, Black player, 1962-66, gr base ..$1,200.00
Los Angeles Lakers, 1962...$225.00
Mickey Mantle, 1961-62, sq or rnd wht base, ea $600.00
Minnesota Vikings, sq gold base, from $100 to..............$150.00
New York Mets, 1960-61, sq bl base $200.00
New York Yankees, 1961-62, wht base, minimum value ..$225.00
Philadelphia Eagles, 1961-62, 1960 Champions emb on gr base,
    scarce $135.00
Roger Maris, 1961-62, sq wht base $485.00
Seattle Sonics, 1967, yel uniform...............................$225.00
St Louis Cardinals, team mascot, 1961-62, wht base, minimum
    value $500.00
Washington Redskins, Merger series, rnd gold base $225.00
Willie Mays, 1961-62, lt face, rnd wht base $400.00

HARTLAND FIGURES

Babe Ruth, NM, from $175 to....................................$200.00
Dick Groat, EX, from $800 to.................................$1,000.00
Don Drysdale, EX, from $275 to................................$300.00
Duke Snyder, EX, from $300 to.................................$325.00
Eddie Mathews, NM, from $125 to $150.00
Ernie Banks, NM, from $250 to $350.00
Harmon Killebrew, NM, from $400 to..........................$500.00
Henry Aaron, EX, from $150 to $175.00
Little Leaguer, 4", EX, from $50 to $75.00
Louie Aparacio, NM, from $250 to $350.00
Mickey Mantle, NM, from $250 to $350.00
Minor Leaguer, 4", EX, from $50 to.............................$75.00
Nellie Fox, NM, from $200 to $250.00
Rocky Colavito, NM, from $600 to $700.00
Roger Maris, EX, from $300 to $350.00
Stan Musial, EX, from $150 to...................................$175.00
Ted Williams, NM, from $225 to.................................$300.00
Warren Spahn, NM, from $150 to................................$375.00
Willie Mays, NM, from $225 to $250.00
Yogi Berra, no mask, NM, from $150 to $175.00
Yogi Berra, w/mask, NM, from $175 to.........................$250.00

KENNER STARTING LINEUP FIGURES

Charles Barkley, 1995, MIP..$15.00
Cy Young, Cooperstown, NM, D8................................$20.00
Don Mattingly, 1988, MIP $30.00
Dwight Gooden, 1990, MIP $20.00
Kareem Abdul-Jabbar, 1988, MIP, from $85 to $100.00
Ken Griffey Jr, 1991, MIP, D8, from $55 to....................$65.00
Kevin Mitchell, 1990, MIP...$15.00
Larry Bird, 1988, MIP...$125.00
Mark McGwire, 1989, MIP..$25.00

Michael Jordon, 1988, MIP, D8 ....$135.00
Ozzie Smith, 1990, MIP, D8 ....$35.00
Patrick Ewing, 1988, MIP, D8, from $40 to $50.00
Pete Rose, 1988, MIP, D8, from $50 to..........................$60.00
Reggie Miller, 1995, MIP..$35.00
Ricky Henderson, 1991, MIP $15.00
Roger Clemens, 1989, MIP, D8.....................................$35.00
Ryne Sandberg, 1989, MIP, D8....................................$65.00
Steve Sax, 1989, MIP $75.00
Troy Aikman, 1994, MIP $40.00
Wilt Chamberlain, MIP, from $40 to..............................$50.00

Star Trek

The Star Trek concept was introduced to the public in the mid-1960s via a TV series which continued for many years in syndication. The impact it had on American culture has spanned two generations of loyal fans through its animated TV cartoon series (1977), six major motion pictures, Fox Network's 1987 TV show, 'Star Trek, The Next Generation,' and two other television series, 'Deep Space 9,' and 'Voyager.' As a result of its success, vast amounts of merchandise (both licensed and unlicensed) has been marketed in a wide variety of items including jewelry, clothing, calendars, collector plates, comics, costumes, games, greeting and gum cards, party goods, magazines, model kits, posters, puzzles, records and tapes, school supplies, and toys. Packaging is very important; an item mint and in its original box is generally worth 75% to 100% more than one rated excellent.

Other Sources: P3.

See also Character and Promotional Drinking Glasses; Fast-Food Collectibles; Halloween Costumes; Lunch Boxes; Model Kits.

FIGURES

Applause, Deep Space 9, Sisko, Odo, Quark & Kira Nerys, 10",
    MIP, ea..$10.00
Applause, Generations, Kirk, Picard, Riker, Data, Worf or
    LaForge, 10", MIP, ea $10.00
Ertl, Star Trek III, Kirk, 3¾", MOC.............................$25.00
Ertl, Star Trek III, Klingon Leader, 3¾", MOC..............$30.00
Ertl, Star Trek III, Scotty, 3¾", MOC $25.00
Ertl, Star Trek III, Spock, 3¾", MOC...........................$30.00
Galoob, STNG, Data, 1st series, bl or spotted face, 3¾",
    MOC..$125.00
Galoob, STNG, Data, 2nd series, 3¾", MOC..................$40.00
Galoob, STNG, Data, 3rd series, 3¾", MOC $20.00
Galoob, STNG, Data, 4th series, 3¾", MOC $8.00
Galoob, STNG, Ferengi, 3¾", MOC..............................$12.00
Galoob, STNG, LaForge, 3¾", MOC $12.00
Galoob, STNG, Picard, 3¾", MOC $12.00
Galoob, STNG, Riker, 3¾", MOC.................................$12.00
Galoob, STNG, Tasha Yar, 3¾", MOC...........................$20.00
Galoob, STNG, Worf, 3¾", MOC..................................$12.00
Mego, 1974-76, Cheron, 2nd series, 8", MOC, from $250 to ..$300.00
Mego, 1974-76, Gorn, 2nd series, 8", MOC, from $300 to ..$350.00

Mego, 1979, Captain Kirk, 12", MIB, from $100.00 to $125.00.

Mego, 1974-76, Kirk, 1st series, 8", MOC.........................$55.00
Mego, 1974-76, Klingon, 1st series, 8", MOC..................$55.00
Mego, 1974-76, McCoy, 1st series, 8", MOC, from $150 to..$175.00
Mego, 1974-76, Spock, 1st series, 8", MOC.....................$55.00
Mego, 1974-76, The Keeper, 2nd series, 8", MOC, from $250
    to..$300.00
Mego, 1979, Motion Picture, Arcturian, 12", MIB, from $100
    to $125.00
Mego, 1979, Motion Picture, Decker, 3¾", MOC, from $20 to..$30.00
Mego, 1979, Motion Picture, Ilia, 12", MIB, from $75 to ...$100.00
Mego, 1979, Motion Picture, Ilia, 3¾", MOC, from $15 to..$20.00
Mego, 1979, Motion Picture, Kirk, 3¾", MOC, from $40 to .$50.00
Mego, 1979, Motion Picture, Klingon, 12", MIB, from $200
    to..$250.00
Mego, 1979, Motion Picture, McCoy, 3¾", MOC, from $40 to .$50.00
Mego, 1979, Motion Picture, Scotty, 3¾", MOC, from $20
    to..$30.00
Mego, 1979, Motion Picture, Spock, 12", MIB, from $100
    to..$125.00
Playmates, Generations, Admiral Kirk, MOC $25.00
Playmates, Generations, Picard, Riker, Worf, Data, Guinan, Bev
    Crusher, Dr Soran, Troi, LaForge, MOC, ea..............$20.00
Playmates, STNG, Data, Borg, Troi, LaForge or Picard, 1 st
    series, MOC, ea..$20.00

PLAYSETS AND ACCESSORIES

Command Communications Console, Mego, 1976, MIB..$150.00
Communication Set, Mego, 1974, MIB..........................$125.00
Mission to Gamma VI, Mego, 1975, rare, MIB, from $700
    to..$950.00
Telescreen Console, Mego, 1975, MIB $125.00
Transporter Room, Mego, 1975, MIB $125.00
USS Enterprise Bridge, Mego, 1975, MIB.....................$125.00

VEHICLES

Ferengi Fighter, STNG, Galoob, 1989, NRFB.................$55.00
Klingon Warship, Dinky, MIB, from $75 ....$85.00

Klingon Warship, Star Trek II, Corgi #149, MOC...........$25.00
Shuttlecraft Galileo, STNG, Galoob, 1989, NRFB.........$50.00
USS Enterprise, Motion Picture, Dinky #803, 1979, 4",
    MOC $30.00
USS Enterprise, Star Trek II, Corgi, 1982, MOC, from $18 to..$25.00

MISCELLANEOUS

Activity Set, Mix 'N Mold casting set, Captain Kirk, Mr Spock
    or Dr McCoy, MIB, ea...$65.00
Binoculars, Larami, MOC...$80.00
Book, Mission to Horatius, 1968, hardcover, VG $20.00
Book, Star Trek Quiz Book, Signet, 1977, softcover, VG...$5.00
Book & Record Set, Passage to Moauv, Peter Pan, 1979, MIP.$10.00
Bop Bag, Spock, 1975, M..$50.00
Communicators (Wrist), 1974, MIB................................$100.00
Doll, Captain Kirk, Knickerbocker, 1979, stuffed cloth w/vinyl
    head, 12", MIB...$50.00
Doll, Mr Spock, Knickerbocker, 1979, stuffed cloth w/vinyl
    head, 12", MIB...$50.00
Figure Paint Set, Motion Picture, Mr Spock, Whitling, 1979, M
    (EX+ card), H4...$10.00
Flashlight Gun, 1968, plastic, NM $50.00
Iron-On Transfers, 4 different, General Mills, 1979, M, ea...$5.00
Kite, Star Trek III, M..$25.00
Ornament, Enterprise Ship, Hallmark, 1st series, MIB...$350.00
Paint-By-Number Set, Hasbro, 1970s, MIB (sealed) $70.00
Patch, Motion Picture, Kirk & Spock, M.......................$35.00
Playing Cards, Star Trek: Wrath of Khan, MIB...............$15.00
Postcard Set, Star Trek: Motion Picture, 1979, complete,
    M..$40.00
Punch Out & Play Album, Saalfield, 1975, unused, NM, J5..$45.00
Puzzle Cube, STNG, Applause, turn cube to reveal 9 photos,
    M..$5.00
Rubber Stamp, Motion Picture, M $8.00
Silly Putty, Larami, 1979, MOC, C1................................$25.00
Sticker Book, Jeopardy at Jutterdon, Whitman, 1979, unused,
    NM..$45.00
Tablet, 1967, features Captain Kirk w/phaser rifle, unused,
    NM..$20.00
Utility Belt, complete, MIB...$100.00
Wastebasket, Motion Picture, M.....................................$35.00
Wristwatch, 1970s, NM, A..$40.00

Star Wars

The original 'Star Wars' movie was a phenomenal box office hit of the late 1970s, no doubt due to its ever-popular space travel theme and fantastic special effects. A sequel called 'Empire Strikes Back' (1980) and a third hit called 'Return of the Jedi' (1983) did just as well. As a result, an enormous amount of related merchandise was released — most of which was made by the Kenner Company. Palitoy of London supplied England and other overseas countries with Kenner's products and also made some toys that were never distributed in America. Until 1980 the logo of the 20th Century Fox studios (under whom the toys were licensed) appeared on each item; just before the second movie, 'Star Wars' creator, George Lucas, regained control of the merchandise rights, and items inspired by the last two named films can be identified by his own Lucasfilm logo. Since 1987 Lucasfilm, Ltd., has operated shops in conjunction with the Star Tours at Disneyland theme parks.

The first action figures to be introduced were Luke Skywalker, Princess Leia, R2-D2, and Chewbacca. Because of delays in production that prevented Kenner from getting them on the market in time for Christmas, the company issued 'early bird' certificates so that they could be ordered by mail when they became available. In all, more than ninety action figures were designed. Figures from the 'Power of the Force' series (1985), though of more recent vintage, are steadily climbing in value. A collector coin was included on each 'Power of the Force' card.

Original packaging is very important in assessing a toy's worth. As each movie was released, packaging was updated, making approximate dating relatively simple. A figure on an original 'Star Wars' card is worth more than the same character on an 'Empire Strikes Back' card, etc.; and the same 'Star Wars' figure valued at $50.00 in mint-on-card condition might be worth as little as $5.00 'loose.'

Especially prized are the original 12-back Star Wars cards (meaning twelve figures were shown on the back). Second issue cards showed eight more, and so on. Unpunched cards tend to be valued at about 15% to 20% more than punched cards, and naturally if the proof of purchase has been removed, the value of the card is less. (These could be mailed in to receive newly introduced figures before they appeared on the market.) A figure in a factory (Kenner) bag is valued at $2.00 to $3.00 more than it is worth loose, and an original backing card adds about $1.00 to $2.00. In our listings, you'll find many of these variations noted. These have been included for the information of potential buyers; remember, pricing is not a science — it hinges on many factors. No doubt in time the merchandise released in conjunction with the new sequel *Episode One: The Phantom Menace* will become attractive to collectors as well. Note: The figures listed below are 3¾" unless noted otherwise. For more information we recommend *Modern Toys, American Toys, 1930 to 1980,* by Linda Baker.

Advisor: George Downes (D8).

Other Sources: B3, B10, D4, D9, J2, J8, P3.

See also Character and Promotional Drinking Glasses; Coloring, Activity, and Paint Books; Fast-Food Collectibles; Lunch Boxes; Halloween Costumes; Model Kits; Trading Cards.

Key:
ESB — Empire Strikes Back
POTF — Power of the Force
ROTJ — Return of the Jedi
SW — Star Wars
* — proof of purchase removed

FIGURES

A-Wing Pilot, POTF, MOC (unpunched), H4 ....$140.00
Admiral Ackbar, ROTJ, MOC, H4.............................$25.00
Amanaman, POTF, MOC, H4.................................$100.00
Anakin Skywalker, POTF, from $30 to.........................$40.00

Anakin Skywalker, SW, w/accessories, NM, H4 ....$30.00
AT-AT Commander, ESB, NMOC, H4 ....$25.00
AT-AT Commander, ESB, w/accessories, NM, H4..........$10.00
AT-AT Commander, ROTJ, MOC (unpunched), H4.....$20.00
AT-AT Driver, ESB, w/accessories, NM, H4....................$10.00
AT-AT Driver, ROTJ, MOC*, H4.................................$32.00
AT-ST Driver, ROTJ, w/accessories, NM, H4 ....$8.00
B-Wing Pilot, POTF, MOC (unpunched) $20.00
B-Wing Pilot, ROTJ, MOC*, H4.................................$15.00
Barada, POTF, complete w/coin, NM $40.00
Ben Obi-Wan Kenobi, POTF, MOC (unpunched), H4.$130.00
Ben Obi-Wan Kenobi, SW, MOC (20-back), H4..........$170.00
Ben Obi-Wan Kenobi, SW, w/accessories, NM, H4.........$20.00
Ben Obi-Wan Kenobi, 12", MIB..............................$375.00
Ben Obi-Wan Kenobi, 1995, w/long saber, MOC (head shot),
    H4 ....$40.00
Ben Obi-Wan Kenobi, 1995, 1st series, long saber, MOC (head
    shot), H4 ....$40.00
Bespin Security Guard, ESB, Black or Caucasian, MOC
    (unpunched) $40.00
Bespin Security Guard, ESB, Black or Caucasian, w/accessories,
    NM...$8.00
Bib Fortuna, ROTJ, MOC, H4................................$20.00
Bib Fortuna, ROTJ, w/accessories, NM.......................$10.00
Biker Scout, ROTJ, MOC (unpunched), H4 ....$32.00
Boba Fett, SW, MOC (unpunched)..............................$165.00
Boba Fett, SW, w/accessories, NM, H4 ....$15.00
Boba Fett, 12", NM (VG box*), H4 ....$265.00
Boba Fett, 1995, 2nd series, ½ circle, MOC, H4 ....$45.00
Bossk, ESB, Bounty Hunter outfit, NM, H4 ....$10.00
Bossk, ESB, MOC (unpunched)................................$45.00
C-3PO, SW, w/accessories, NM, H4 ....$10.00
C-3PO, 12", M (EX+ box), H4..................................$95.00
Chewbacca, ESB, MOC (unpunched), H4 ....$40.00
Chewbacca, ROTJ, MOC, H4..................................$40.00
Chewbacca, SW, M (EX 20-back card), H4...................$100.00
Chewbacca, SW, w/accessories, NM, H4 ....$10.00
Chief Chirpa, ROTJ, MOC, H4................................$26.00
Chief Chirpa, ROTJ, MOC (unpunched), H4 ....$30.00
Classic Edition Four-Pack, 1995, 4th series, Luke, Darth, Han,
    Chewy, NRFB, H4 ....$70.00
Cloud Car Pilot, ESB, w/accessories, NM, H4 ....$18.00
Cloud Car Pilot, ROTJ, MOC*...............................$35.00
Darth Vader, ROTJ, MOC, H4.................................$40.00
Darth Vader, SW, w/accessories, NM, H4 ....$15.00
Darth Vader, 1995, 1st series, long saber, MOC, H4........$25.00
Darth Vader, 1995, 1st series, short saber, MOC, H4.......$10.00
Death Squad Commander, ESB, MOC...........................$75.00
Death Squad Commander, SW, M (EX 20-back card), H4 .$90.00
Death Star Droid, ESB, MOC $125.00
Death Star Droid, SW, w/accessories, NM, H4................$15.00
Death Star Gunner, 1995, 4th series, MOC, H4 ....$18.00
Dengar, ESB, NMOC (41-back), H4 ....$55.00
Dengar, ESB, w/accessories, NM, H4 ....$8.00
Dengar, ROTJ, MOC (unpunched), H4 ....$30.00
Dulok Scout, Ewoks, MOC.....................................$15.00
Emperor, ROTJ, MOC..$35.00
Emperor, ROTJ, w/accessories, NM, H4 ....$10.00

Emperor's Royal Guard, ROTJ, w/acccessories, NM, H4..$10.00
FX-7, ESB, MOC (unpunched), H4.................................$40.00
FX-7, ESB, w/accessories, NM, H4..............................$10.00
General Madine, ROTJ, MOC, H4................................$12.00
General Madine, ROTJ, w/accessories, NM, H4..............$8.00
Gammorean Guard, ROTJ, MOC, H4............................$18.00
Greedo, ROTJ, MOC...$30.00
Greedo, SW, MOC (21-back), H4...............................$160.00
Greedo, SW, w/accessories, NM, H4............................$10.00
Greedo, 1995, 4th series, MOC, H4.............................$18.00
Hammerhead, ESB, MOC (unpunched), H4.....................$70.00
Hammerhead, SW, w/accessories, NM, H4......................$10.00
Han Solo, ESB, Bespin outfit, w/accessories, NM, H4......$15.00
Han Solo, ESB, Hoth gear, w/accessories, NM, H4..........$15.00
Han Solo, ROTJ, Bespin outfit, MOC, H4.....................$50.00
Han Solo, ROTJ, lg head, MOC*, H4............................$85.00
Han Solo, ROTJ, sm head, Bespin outfit, M (EX+ card), H4..$50.00
Han Solo, SW, lg head, w/accessories, NM, H4..............$24.00
Han Solo, SW, sm head, w/accessories, NM, H4..............$28.00
Han Solo, 12", NM (VG box*), H4.............................$375.00
Han Solo, 1995, Stormtrooper outfit, mail-in premium, MOC, H4.................................$50.00
Han Solo, 1995, 2nd series, Hoth gear, closed hand, MOC, H4.................................$10.00
Han Solo, 1995, 2nd series, Hoth gear, open hand, MOC, H4.................................$18.00
Han Solo, 1995, 3rd series, in Freezing Chamber, MOC, H4.$12.00
ID-88, 12", complete, M, J6...................................$285.00
IG-88, ESB, w/accessories, NM, H4............................$15.00
Imperial Commander, ESB, MOC (41-back), H4.............$55.00
Imperial Commander, ESB, MOC (47-back), H4.............$30.00
Imperial Commander, ESB, w/accessories, NM, H4.........$8.00
Imperial Dignitary, POTF, MOC, H4...........................$80.00
Imperial Stormtrooper, ESB, Hoth gear, NM, H4...........$10.00
Imperial TIE Pilot, ROTJ, w/accessories, NM, H4..........$12.00
Jawa, ESB, MOC...$80.00
Jawa, POTF, MOC..$75.00
Jawa, ROTJ, MOC..$65.00
Jawa, SW, w/cloth cape & accessories, NM, H4..............$18.00
Jawa, 12", MIB...$225.00

Jawa, SW, 3¾", MOC (12-back), $175.00.
(Photo courtesy June Moon)

King Gorneesh, Ewoks, MOC (unpunched), H4..............$22.00
Klaatu, ESB, MOC, H4...$10.00
Klaatu, ROTJ, MOC, H4...$18.00
Klaatu, ROTJ, Skiff Guard outfit, w/accessories, NM, H4..$8.00
Klaatu, ROTJ, tan limbs, w/accessories, NM, H4...........$10.00
Lando Calrissian, ESB, regular, w/accessories, NM, H4....$12.00
Lando Calrissian, ESB, wht teeth, w/accessories, NM, H4.$16.00
Lando Calrissian, ROTJ, MOC (punched), H4...............$40.00
Lando Calrissian, ROTJ, Skiff Guard outfit, MOC (unpunched), H4.................................$30.00
Lobot, ESB, w/accessories, NM, H4.............................$6.00
Luke Skywalker, ESB, Bespin outfit, NM, H4................$30.00
Luke Skywalker, ESB, Hoth gear, NM, H4.....................$15.00
Luke Skywalker, ROTJ, Jedi Knight outfit, gr saber, MOC, H4.$60.00
Luke Skywalker, ROTJ, Jedi Knight outfit, w/accessories, NM, H4.................................$30.00
Luke Skywalker, SW, Bespin outfit, blond, yel saber, NM, H4..$25.00
Luke Skywalker, SW, w/accessories, NM, H4.................$22.00
Luke Skywalker, SW, X-Wing Pilot outfit, NM, H4........$12.00
Luke Skywalker, 1995, 1st series, long saber, MOC, H4...$35.00
Luke Skywalker, 1995, 1st series, short saber, MOC, H4..$10.00
Luke Skywalker, 1995, 2nd series, Dagobah outfit, long saber, MOC, H4.................................$18.00
Luke Skywalker, 1995, 2nd series, Dagobah outfit, short saber, long tray, MOC, H4.................................$15.00
Luke Skywalker, 1995, 2nd series, Dagonah outfit, short saber, MOC, H4.................................$10.00
Luke Skywalker, 1995, 2nd series, X-Wing outfit, long saber, MOC, H4.................................$25.00
Luke Skywalker, 1995, 2nd series, X-Wing outfit, short saber, long tray, MOC, H4.................................$20.00
Luke Skywalker, 1995, 2nd series, X-Wing outfit, short saber, MOC, H4.................................$10.00
Power Droid, ROTJ, MOC, H4...................................$35.00
Power Droid, SW, w/accessories, NM, H4......................$8.00
Princess Leia Organa, ESB, Bespin outfit, w/accessories, NM, H4.................................$22.00
Princess Leia Organa, ESB, Hoth gear, NM, H4............$18.00
Princess Leia Organa, ROTJ, Boushh outfit, w/accessories, NM, H4.$18.00
Princess Leia Organa, SW, w/accessories, NM, H4..........$30.00
Princess Leia Organa, 12", NM.................................$100.00
Princess Leia Organa, 12", w/accessories, VG, H4..........$60.00
Princess Leia Organa, 1995, 1st series, 2 bands on belt, MOC, H4.................................$10.00
Princess Leia Organa, 1995, 1st series, 3 bands on belt, MOC, H4.................................$16.00
Prune Face, ROTJ, M (unpunched card), H4..................$20.00
Rancor Keeper, ROTJ, MOC, H4................................$12.00
Rancor Keeper, ROTJ, w/accessories, NM, H4...............$8.00
Rebel Commander, ESB, w/accessories, NM, H4............$8.00
Rebel Commando, ESB, MOC, H4...............................$12.00
Rebel Commando, ESB, w/accessories, NM, H4.............$8.00
Rebel Commando, ROTJ, MOC, H4.............................$18.00
Rebel Soldier, ESB, MOC (unpunched), H4...................$40.00
Rebel Soldier, ESB, w/accessories, NM, H4...................$8.00
Ree-Yees, ROTJ, MOC, H4..$15.00
Ree-Yees, ROTJ, w/accessories, NM, H4......................$10.00
Romba, SW, w/coin, NM, H4.....................................$35.00

R2-D2, ESB, MOC (unpunched), H4 ....$45.00
R2-D2, POTF, MOC (unpunched), H4 ....$70.00
R2-D2, ROTJ, w/sensorscope, MOC (unpunched), H4 ...$35.00
R2-D2, SW, w/accessories, NM, H4...............................$12.00
R2-D2, 12", remote control, MIB.................................$125.00
R5-D4, SW, MOC (21-back), H4..................................$140.00
R5-D4, SW, w/accessories, NM, H4................................$8.00
Shaman, Ewoks, MOC (unpunched), H4 ....$22.00
Snaggletooth, ESB, MOC (unpunched), H4 ....$65.00
Snaggletooth, SW, MOC (21-back), H4 ....$140.00
Snaggletooth, SW, w/accessories, NM, H4 ....$12.00
Squid Head, ROTJ, w/accessories, NM, H4 ....$8.00
Star Destroyer Commander, ESB, MOC (unpunched), H4.$40.00
Star Destroyer Commander, SW, w/accessories, NM, H4...$12.00
Stormtrooper, ROTJ, MOC, H4 ....$35.00
Stormtrooper, SW, w/accessories, NM, H4 ....$10.00
Stormtrooper, 12", EX (VG box*), H4..........................$200.00
Tatooine Stormtrooper, 1995, 4th series, MOC, H4 ....$18.00
Teebo, ROTJ, MOC (unpunched), H4............................$24.00
TIE Fighter Pilot, 1995, 2nd series, MOC (w/warning sticker), H4 .$22.00
Tusken Raider, SW, w/accessories, NM $14.00
Ugnaught, ESB, MOC (unpunched), H4.........................$40.00
Ugnaught, ESB, NM, w/accessories, H4...........................$8.00
Ugnaught, ROTJ, MOC, H4 ....$28.00
Urgah, Ewoks, MOC (unpunched), H4 ....$22.00
Walrus Man, SW, MOC (unpunched 20-back), H4 ......$130.00
Walrus Man, SW, w/accessories, NM, H4 ....$10.00
Weequay, ROTJ, MOC, H4...$12.00
Weequay, ROTJ, w/accessories, NM, H4 ....$8.00
Wicket W Warrick, Ewoks, MOC (unpunched), H4 ....$25.00
Yoda, ESB, orange snake, MOC.....................................$50.00
Yoda, ESB, orange snake, NM..$20.00
Yoda, ROTJ, brn snake, MOC, H4 ....$40.00
Zuckuss, ESB, w/accessories, NM, H4 ....$8.00
Zuckuss, ROTJ, MOC (unpunched), H4 ....$30.00
4-Lom, ROTJ, MOC...$50.00
4-Lom, ROTJ, w/accessories, NM, H4 ....$10.00
8D8, ROTJ, MOC, H4 ....$25.00

PLAYSETS AND ACCESSORIES

Bespin Control Room, SW, Micro Collection, MIB, H4 .$50.00
Bespin Gantry, SW, Micro Collection, EX, H4 ....$25.00
Cloud City, EX (EX box) $300.00
Darth Vader's Star Destroyer, SW, complete, VG, H4.....$60.00
Death Star Compactor, SW, Micro Collection, MIB $85.00
Death Star Space Station, 1977, EX (EX box), F8............$50.00
Ewok Village, ROTJ, M (EX box), H4............................$70.00
Hoth Generator Attack, SW, Micro Collection, MIB, H4..$55.00
Hoth Ion Cannon, SW, Micro Collection, EX, H4..........$30.00
Hoth Ion Cannon, SW, Micro Collection, MIB, H4 ....$70.00
Hoth Turret Defense, SW, Micro Collection, EX, H4 .....$25.00
Hoth Wampa Cave, Micro Collection, MIB, from $25 to..$35.00
Imperial Attack Base, EX (EX box)................................$65.00
Jabba the Hut, NRFB (Canadian/French), H4 ....$85.00
Radar Laser Cannon, ROTJ, NMIB, H4 ....$20.00
Sy Snoodles & the Rebo Band, NRFB, H4.....................$100.00
Tripod Laser Cannon, ESB, MIB, H4 ....$20.00

VEHICLES

AT-AT, ESB, VG (VG box), H4 ....$125.00
AT-ST, SW, EX, H4...$35.00
Boba Fett's Slave I, EBS, EX (VG box), H4 ....$75.00
Boba Fett's Slave I, SW, diecast, EX, H4 ....$16.00
Boba Fett's Slave I, SW, EX (VG box), H4 ....$75.00
Darth Vader's TIE Fighter, diecast, MOC (unpunched), H4..$70.00
Darth Vader's TIE Fighter, SW, NMIB...........................$75.00
Endor Forest Ranger, NRFB, H4 ....$25.00
Ewok Assault Catapult, NRFB, H4 ....$25.00
Imperial Shuttle, ROTJ, NRFB, H4................................$250.00
Imperial TIE Fighter, SW, Micro Collection, MOC
    (unpunched), H4..$70.00
Imperial Troop Transport, EX (EX box) $65.00
Jawa Sandcrawler, SW, complete, NM $350.00
Landspeeder, SW, VG (G box), H4................................$22.00
Millennium Falcon, Micro Collection, Sears Exclusive, MIB ..$600.00

Millennium Falcon, SW, MIB, $80.00.
(Photo courtesy June Moon)

One-Man Sand Skimmer, POTF, rare, MOC, H4.............$85.00
Rebel Armored Snow Speeder, ESB, M (EX box) $70.00
Snow Speeder, diecast, EX, H4.....................................$18.00
Speeder Bike, ROTJ, NRFB, H4 ....$40.00
Star Destroyer, diecast, VG, H4 ....$16.00
TIE Fighter, SW, VG+ (VG box), H4 ....$35.00
X-Wing Fighter, diecast, VG, H4 ....$16.00
X-Wing Fighter, ROTJ, NMIB, H4................................$75.00
X-Wing Fighter, SW, M (VG box), H4 ....$35.00
X-Wing Fighter, SW, Micro Collection, EX, H4.............$35.00
X-Wing Fighter, SW, Micro Collection, VG (VG box*), H4.$70.00
Y-Wing Fighter, ROTJ, MIB, H4...................................$100.00
Y-Wing Fighter, SW, EX, H4...$55.00

MISCELLANEOUS

Bop Bag, Darth Vader, Kenner, 1978-79, inflatable vinyl, 45",
    EX...$40.00
Bop Bag, R2-D2, Kenner, 1978, inflatable vinyl, 33", EX...$40.00
Card Set, Burger King, 1980, unused, NM, A..................$25.00
Case, Darth Vader, EX, H4..$20.00

Case, SW, Kenner, 1979-80, vinyl w/2 removable plastic trays, snap closure, EX $20.00

Color 'N Clean Machine, ESB, Craftmaster, 1980, complete, unused, NM $25.00

Display, any character, diecut cb stand-ups, life-size, EX, F1, ea..$30.00

Doll, Chewbacca, Kenner, 1978-79, synthetic fur w/plastic eyes & nose, 20", EX $25.00

Doll, R2-D2, Kenner, 1978-79, stuffed cloth, w/squeaker, 10", EX..$25.00

Force Lightsaber, NM (w/orig header card), H4 ....$90.00

Laser Pistol, SW, Kenner, 1978-83, plastic, EX $40.00

Laser Rifle, ESB, Kenner, 1980, plastic, battery-op, 18½", EX ..$75.00

Movie Viewer, SW, Kenner, 1978-79, plastic w/snap-in cartridge, 7", EX...$35.00

Play-Doh Action Set, SW, Kenner, 1978-79, complete w/play mat, EX (EX box) $35.00

Play-Doh Set, ESB, complete, MIB, H4..........................$20.00

Presto Magix Transfer Set, ROTJ Battle on Endor, NRFB (sealed), H4 ....$10.00

Radio Watch, Lucasfilm/Bradley, 1982, R2-D2 & C-3PO on face, MIB...$50.00

Record Case & Records, VG+, H4..................................$10.00

Steam Powered

During the early part of the century until about 1930, though not employed to any great extent, live steam power was used to activate toys such as large boats, novelty toys, and model engines.
See also Boats; Trains.

Accessory, airship roundabout, 3 airships w/gondolas & side-mounted props, litho & pnt tin, 9", EX, A...........$1,200.00

Accessory, blacksmith & man at mixer, Bing, emb & litho tin, 5½", VG+, A...$385.00

Accessory, chimney sweep, Doll, red simulated brick chimney w/figure in blk, 4", VG, A $350.00

Accessory, clown in barrel w/hoop, pnt tin, hand-crank causes clown to spin, sq base, 6", EX, A.............................$475.00

Accessory, man at printing press, Falk, litho tin figure turns crank on wood & tin press, brn tin base, 5½", VG, A.........$700.00

Accessory, mill house, Doll, tin, features man & donkey on revolving platform, water wheel on side, sq base, 8", EX, A .$300.00

Accessory, power station, Doll, tin figure on revolving base enters & exits through doors, tall chimney, 9", EX, A..........$335.00

Accessory, thresher, Marklin, gr & red w/wooden rollers under rear cap, wire mesh bottom, 8" L, EX, A..................$475.00

Accessory, wheat sifter, Bing, red w/yel trim, side crank, bl rectangular base, 5½" L, VG, A $700.00

Carousel w/Airplane, Zeppelin & Hot Air Balloon, pnt tin, beveled base, 32", prof rstr, A............................$17,000.00

Ferris Wheel, Falk, red w/gold highlights, 6 dbl-seat chairs w/figures, 12", rstr, A...$500.00

Ferris Wheel, Germany, pnt tin w/6 bsk figures, orig tin flags, 15", VG, A...$750.00

Fire Truck w/Trailer, unknown maker, red w/brass trim, 43", EX, A..$2,400.00

Organ Grinder, Germany, figure cranks lg wheel, rectangular base, EX, A $800.00

Pickup Truck, Doll, blk & yel tin, rubber tires w/spoke wheels, chain-driven live steam mechanism, 19", EX, A ..$3,300.00

Road Roller, Weeden, brass roller & boiler, CI spoke wheels, NP flywheel, 7" L, EX, A $850.00

Steam Engine, Corliss, polished steel w/brass lubricator cups, red-spoked flywheel, gray base, 22", NM, A.........$3,850.00

Steam Engine, Doll, CI base w/brass boiler, orig burner w/attached plated door, 9", VG, A..........................$300.00

Steam Engine, Doll, horizontal boiler w/dual flywheel, NP detail to levers & rods, CI base, 11½", NM, A..................$650.00

Steam Engine, Doll, sheet metal & brass w/CI components, horizontal, 16x13x7", EX, A..$1,200.00

Steam Engine, Weeden, single cylinder, NP base, 8" L, EX, A.$850.00

Steam Plant, Doll, gr base w/yel & red trim, 13x12x2", EX, A.$275.00

Tractor, Mamod, brass boiler, tall front stack, spoke wheels, 9", VG, A..$250.00

Tractor, mk Buffalo Pitts, blk w/red spoke wheels, brass accessories, 26", EX, A..$650.00

Wishing Well, Fleishmann, crank or steam power, tin, 7", EX (EX box), A..$150.00

Windmill, Doll, hand-painted tin, simulated brick base, 19", EX, A, $600.00.

Steiff

Margaret Steiff made the first of her felt toys in 1880, stuffing them with lamb's wool. Later followed toys of velvet, plush, and wool, and in addition to the lamb's wool stuffing, she used felt scraps, excelsior, and kapok as well. In 1897 and 1898 her trademark was a paper label printed with an elephant; from 1900 to 1905 her toys carried a circular tag with an elephant logo that was different than the one she had previously used. The most famous 'button in ear' trademark was registered on December 20, 1904. 1904 and 1905 saw the use of the button with an elephant (extremely rare) and the blank button (which is also rare). The button with Steiff and the underscored or trailing 'FF' was used until 1948, and the raised script button is from the 1950s.

Steiff teddy bears, perhaps the favorite of collectors everywhere, are characterized by their long thin arms with curved wrists and paws that extend below their hips. Buyer beware: the Steiff company is now making many replicas of their old bears. For more information about Steiff's buttons, chest tags, and stock tags as well as the inspirational life of Margaret Steiff and the fascinating history of Steiff toys, we recommend *Button in Ear Book* and *The Steiff Book of Teddy Bears*, both by Jurgen and Marianne Cieslik; *Teddy Bears and Steiff Animals*, 2nd and 3rd Series, by Margaret Fox Mandel; *4th Teddy Bear and Friends Price Guide* by Linda Mullins; *Collectible German Animals Value Guide* by Dee Hockenberry; and *Steiff Sortiment, 1947 – 1995*, by Gunther Pefiffer. (This book is in German; however, the reader can discern the size of the item, year of production, and price estimation.) See also Clubs, Newsletters, and Other Publications (for Cynthia's Country Store).

Advisor: Cynthia's Country Store, Cynthia Brintnall (C14); Candelaine (G16).

See also Disney; Santa.

Baby Chick, spotted Dralon w/felt comb, plastic feet & beak, all ID, 1971, 4", NM, G16......................................$85.00
Baby Chick, spotted Dralon w/plastic feet, chest tag, 4", NM, G16...$65.00
Ball, mc mohair, remnant US Zone stock tag, 1948, 8" dia, NM, G16...$200.00
Basset Dog, mohair, swivel head, orig gr collar, chest tag, 1950s, 4½", NM, G16..$165.00
Bazi Dog, mohair, plastic eyes, orig bl collar, chest tag, 1960s, 4", NM, G16..$110.00

Bear, cinnamon mohair, shoe-button eyes, FF button, 18", EX, from $8,500.00 to $9,500.00. (Photo courtesy Cynthia Brintnell)

Bear, gold mohair, glass eyes, orig bl ribbon, raised script button, 1950s, 13", NM, G16......................................$600.00
Bear, gold mohair, glass eyes, side squeaker, FF underscored button, 1920s, 5", EX, G16......................................$975.00
Bear, Margaret Strong, cinnamon mohair, brass button & cloth stock tag, 1982-90, 9", NM, G16.............................$125.00
Bear, wht mohair, blk bead eyes, FF underscored button, 1905, 3", VG, G16..$900.00

Bear, wht mohair, fully jtd, raised script button, 1950s, 3", NM, G16..$485.00
Bear, wht mohair, glass eyes, FF underscored button, 1910, 4", NM, G16..$1,250.00
Bear, wht mohair, glass eyes, orig bl ribbon, raised script button, 1950s, 6", EX, G16......................................$500.00
Bendy Panda, mohair, all ID, 1960s, 3", NM, G16.........$325.00
Bengal Tiger, mohair, glass eyes, raised script button & chest tag, 1959-61, 5½", rare, M, G16......................$500.00
Biggie Beagle, mohair, glass eyes, orig red collar, all ID, 1950s, 4", EX, G16..$100.00
Biggie Beagle, mohair, plastic eyes, orig red collar, all ID, 1960s, 7½", M, G16..$185.00
Bird, mohair & felt w/plastic legs & beak, all ID, 1969, 4", M, G16..$150.00
Boxer Dog, mohair w/velvet chin, glass eyes, orig bl leather collar, all ID, 1954, 4", NM, G16..............................$165.00
Bully Dog, blk & cream mohair w/velvet face, glass eyes, FF underscored button, 1920s, 4", EX, G16.................$600.00
Clownie Clown, orig outfit, chest tag, 5", M, G16.........$100.00
Cockie Dog, mohair, glass eyes, orig red leather collar, chest tag, 4", EX, G16..$100.00
Coco Monkey, gray mohair w/wht fringe around face & ears, glass eyes, orig red leather collar, all ID, 5½", M, G16........$225.00
Crabby Lobster, felt w/vivid airbrushing, glass eyes, all ID, 4½", M, G16..$350.00
Dally Dog, mohair, glass eyes, swivel head, orig red collar, raised script button, 6½", NM, G16..............................$150.00
Duckling, mohair w/brn airbrushing, felt beak & feet, raised script button & stock tag, 1950s, 4½", NM, G16....$115.00
Electrola Fox Dog, velvety Dralon w/mohair ears, orig red leather collar, chest tag, 1968, 4½", rare, NM, G16..............$900.00
Fawn, mohair, glass eyes, no ID, 9", VG, G16.................$50.00
Floppy Beagle, sleeping, mohair, orig ribbon, chest tag, 8", NM, G16..$125.00
Gaty Alligator, all ID, 1968, 14", NM, G16.................$150.00
Gaty Alligator, puppet, all ID, 1950s, 9", NM, G16.......$135.00
Giraffe, mohair, plastic eyes, incised button & chest tag, 1960s, 11", NM, G16..$150.00
Gogo Chinchilla, Dralon & felt, all ID, 5½", M, G16 ...$200.00
Goldy Hamster, mohair, glass eyes, all ID, 4", NM, G16..$100.00
Goose on Wheels, wht mohair w/gray airbrushing, glass eyes, all ID, 9" L, NM, G16..$500.00
Halloween Cat, blk mohair, plastic eyes, orig ribbon, raised script button, 9½", NM, G16......................................$175.00
Halloween Cat, blk velvet & mohair, glass eyes, chest tag, raised script button & remnant stock tag, 1950s, 4", EX, G16..$165.00
Hen & Rooster, mohair w/felt heads & tails, metal legs, raised script button & stock tag, 1953, 3", NM, G16.........$265.00
Hoppy Rabbit, mohair, glass eyes, orig ribbon & bell, all ID, 1968, 9", NM, G16..$265.00
Hoppy Rabbit, mohair, plastic eyes, orig ribbon & bell, all ID, 1968, 7½", NM, G16..$165.00
Horse, mohair, plastic eyes, red bridle, all ID, 1968-76, 6½", M, G16..$125.00
Hucky Raven, mohair & felt w/metal legs, all ID, 1960, 4½", M, G16..$200.00

Hucky Raven, mohair & felt w/metal legs, all ID, 1960, 7", M, G16 ....$300.00

Jocko Monkey, long curly mohair, glass eyes, fully jtd, raised script button, 1950s, 18", NM, G16 ....$300.00

Jumbo Elephant, mohair w/red felt bib, all ID, 1968, 9", M, G16 ....$385.00

Kangoo Kangaroo, w/orig joey, all ID, 1959, 5", NM, G16.$125.00

Kid, mohair w/felt ears, gr eyes, all ID, 1950s, 4", M, G16 ..$125.00

Kitty, tiger-striped mohair, glass eyes, fully jtd, orig ribbon & chest tag, 4", EX, G16 ....$150.00

Koala Bear, fully jtd, all ID, 1955-58, 9", M, G16...........$900.00

Koala Bear, jtd head, all ID, 1959-61, 4½", M, G16.......$425.00

Lama Llama, cream mohair w/blk & brn detail, glass eyes, raised script button & chest tag, 1957, 17½", rare, M, G16 .$600.00

Lamby Lamb, lying down, woolie mohair, glass eyes, orig ribbon, all ID, 4", EX, G16..$300.00

Lizzy Lizard, velvet, glass eyes, no ID, 1959-61, 12", EX, G16.$385.00

Manni Rabbit, mohair, glass eyes, orig ribbon, all ID, 1961-64, 6½", NM $265.00

Manni Rabbit, mohair, glass eyes, w/squeaker, orig ribbon & bell, no ID, 1950s, 16", NM, G16 ....$950.00

Maxi Mole, mohair, all ID, 1964, 4", M, G16.................$135.00

Mimic Tessie Schnauzer, puppet, gray mohair, glass eyes, orig red ribbon, raised script button, 12", rare, NM, G16........$400.00

Molly Dog, puppet, mohair, glass eyes, no ID, 1950s, 9", EX, G16 ....$65.00

Molly Dog, wht mohair w/red-brn tipping, glass eyes, orig ribbon & bell, all ID, 1950s, 7", M, G16 ....$225.00

Moosy Moose, mohair & felt, glass eyes, all ID, 5", rare, NM, G16 ....$425.00

Nagy Beaver, mohair w/felt hands & feet, glass eyes, all ID, 1958, 3¾", M, G16..$100.00

Nagy Beaver, mohair w/felt hands & feet, glass eyes, all ID, 1958, 7", M, G16..$165.00

Neander Caveman, felt w/mohair suit, rubber face, orig tooth on string, all ID, 1968, 8", M, G16................................$485.00

Neander Caveman, felt w/mohair suit, rubber face, orig tooth on string, all ID, 1968-74, 5", M, G16 ....$285.00

Nelly Snail, velvet w/rubber shell, leather underbelly, glass eyes, chest tag, 6½", rare, NM, G16 ....$400.00

Niki Rabbit, mohair, glass eyes, fully jtd, orig ribbon, raised script button & stock tag, 7", M, G16......................$400.00

Original Teddy, caramel mohair, fully jtd, chest tag, 3½", M, G16 ....$325.00

Original Teddy, caramel mohair, glass eyes, fully jtd, raised script button, 1950s, 5½", VG, G16 ....$200.00

Original Teddy, dk brn mohair w/peach felt pads, glass eyes, orig red ribbon, chest tag, 1950s, 8", M, G16.................$900.00

Original Teddy, gold mohair, blk bead eyes, fully jtd, chest tag, 1950s, 3½", EX, G16..$265.00

Original Teddy, gold mohair, glass eyes, orig bl ribbon, chest tag & raised script button, 8", NM, G16......................$565.00

Original Teddy, tan mohair, all ID, 1968, 13", M, G16 .$225.00

Original Teddy, tan mohair, all ID, 1968, 9", M, G16 ...$175.00

Original Teddy, tan mohair, glass eyes, fully jtd, chest tag, 3½", NM, G16 ....$375.00

Ossi Rabbit, mohair & Dralon, incised button, 6", NM, G16..$60.00

Peggy Penguin, mohair, glass eyes, chest tag, 3", NM, G16 ...$110.00

Peky Dog, mohair, glass eyes, swivel head, all ID, 1950s, 8", M, G16 ....$225.00

Pieps Mouse, wht mohair, all ID, M, G16.......................$100.00

Pony, mohair, glass eyes, orig red leather saddle & plastic reins, chest tag, 1950s, 5", NM, G16 ....$125.00

Possy Squirrel, all ID, 1968, 3½", M, G16 ....$125.00

Rabbit, Dralon, glass eyes, chest tag, 1956-67, 6", NM, G16.$100.00

Rabbit, puppet, mohair, glass eyes, orig bl ribbon, US Zone tag, 1948, 9", EX+, G16 ....$100.00

Rabbit, puppet, mohair, plastic eyes, no ID, 9", EX, G16 .$50.00

Raccy Raccoon, mohair, glass eyes, stock tag, 6", EX, G16.$100.00

Richard Bear, gray mohair, 1983, 12", MIB, G16 ....$350.00

Schwarzbar Bear, blk mohair w/red stitched claws, fully jtd, brass button & stock tag, 6", NM, G16 ....$125.00

Siamy Cat, wht mohair w/brn tipping, glass eyes, no ID, 1950s, 5", rare, NM, G16...$300.00

Skunk, mohair & velvet, glass eyes, chest tag, 1962-63, 4¼", M, G16 ....$250.00

Snaky Snake, puppet, mohair, raised script button, 1966-67, 13", rare, EX, G16 ....$450.00

Soldier, felt w/airbrushed features, glass eyes, fully jtd, no ID, early 1900s, 14", rare, EX, G16 ....$1,975.00

Sonny Rabbit, mohair, glass eyes, orig ribbon & bell, raised script button & stock tag, 3", EX, G16 ....$100.00

Squirrel, mohair, blk plastic eyes, incised button & stock tag, 1968, 6", M, G16..$110.00

Squirrel, puppet, mohair w/felt hands & feet, glass eyes, 8½", NM, G16..$75.00

Susi Cat, mohair, plastic eyes, orig pk ribbon, all ID, 1960s, 5", NM, G16 ....$200.00

Tabby Cat, mohair, glass eyes, orig ribbon & bell, no ID, 1950s, 5½", NM, G16...$85.00

Teddy Baby, dk brn mohair, glass eyes, orig collar & bell, chest tag & raised script button, 1948, 9", rare, EX, G16 ......$1,100.00

Teddy Baby, gold mohair w/velvet muzzle & feet, glass eyes, all ID, 1950s, 3", rare, NM, G16.................................$1,650.00

Tessie Schnauzer, gray mohair, glass eyes, orig red collar, chest tag, 4½", NM, G16...$150.00

Tucky Turkey, mohair w/felt wings & tail, velvet face, glass eyes, all ID, 1952, 4¼", M, G16...$365.00

Vario Rabbit, mohair, glass eyes, raised script button & stock tag, 5", EX, G16..$100.00

Waldili Dog, mohair & felt, orig felt suit & vest, w/rifle, all ID, 1968, 8½", NM, G16...$450.00

Woolie Baby Bird, plastic feet, raised script button & stock tag, 1958, 1½", NM, G16...$50.00

Woolie Baby Duck, metal feet, raised script button & stock tag, 1950s, 1½", NM, G16...$55.00

Woolie Cat, blk & wht, gr plastic eyes, orig red ribbon, raised script button & stock tag, 3", M, G16......................$85.00

Woolie Chick, plastic feet, raised script button & stock tag, 1950s, 1½", M, G16..$50.00

Woolie Fish, gr & yel, raised script button & stock tag, 1968, 1½", NM, G16 ....$35.00

Woolie Fish, yel & brn, raised script button & stock tag, 1968, 1½", NM, G16 ....$35.00

Woolie Owl, cinnamon & cream, glass eyes, metal legs, 2 real feathers for tufts, 2", rare, NM, G16........................$250.00

Woolie Owl, incised button & stock tag, 1971, 2", NM, G16.$35.00

Woolie Parrot, plastic feet, incised button & stock tag, 1971, 2½", M, G16...$65.00

Woolie Rabbit, gray & wht, glass eyes, raised script button & stock tag, 1949-50, 2", M, G16.............................$50.00

Woolie Raven, blk w/red felt beak, metal feet, raised script button & stock tag, 2½", M, G16..........................$55.00

Wooly Bird, raised script button & stock tag, 1949, 2", NM, G16...$50.00

Xorry Fox, mohair, glass eyes, chest tag, 1950s, 4½", EX, G16.$135.00

Zicky Goat, mohair, glass eyes & wood horns, orig ribbon & bell, chest tag, 6", EX, G16 ....$100.00

Zooby Bear, brn mohair, jtd head & arms, raised script button, 11", rare, M, G16..$950.00

Zotty Bear, caramel mohair, plastic eyes, orig red ribbon, chest tag, 6½", M, G16...$300.00

Zotty Bear, tan mohair, glass eyes, orig bl ribbon, chest tag, 7", M, G16...$365.00

Strauss

Imaginative, high-quality, tin windup toys were made by Ferdinand Strauss (New York, later New Jersey) from the onset of World War I until the 1940s. For about fifteen years prior to his becoming a toymaker, he was a distributor of toys he imported from Germany. Though hard to find in good working order, his toys are highly prized by today's collectors, and when found in even very good to excellent condition, many are in the $500.00 and up range.

Advisor: Scott Smiles (S10).

Air Devil, 1926, w/pilot, 8½", EX, from $500 to $600.00

Big Show Circus Cage Wagon, complete w/marquee, 9", EX, A..$1,000.00

Boob McNutt, man in red polka-dot pants & blk jacket, rnd flat hat, 9", VG $500.00

Chek-A-Cab #69, yel & blk w/checked trim, 8½", VG .$650.00

Chicago Zeppelin, 9", G, A $275.00

Dandy Jim Clown Dancer, 1921, does the jig & plays cymbals atop circus tent, 10", EX...$600.00

Donkey Target, 1920s, donkey kicks stable boy into the air, 15", rare, EX, A...$650.00

Flivver Auto, blk, w/driver, 8", VG, A............................$175.00

Flying Airship, 1930s, aluminum w/brass propellers, 10", NMIB, from $850 to $900.00

Graf Zeppelin Jr #2, aluminum w/brass propeller, 10", EX (EX box), from $600 to...$700.00

Graf Zepplin, aluminum w/brass propeller, 16", VG (VG box)..$1,000.00

Ham & Sam, 1921, Black banjo player beside piano player, 5½", EX (EX box), from $1,000 to $1,200.00

Inter-State Bus, 1930s, gr & yel w/aluminum tires, 11", VG, from $500 to $600.00

Jackie the Hornpipe Dancer, boat advances as sailor dances on deck, 9", EX (EX box) $800.00

Jazzbo Jim, 1920s, figure plays banjo & dances atop cabin roof, 10", EX (EX box), from $700 to...............................$800.00

Jenny the Balky Mule, 1925, advances w/crazy action as farmer bounces in seat, 9½", NMIB $575.00

Jenny the Balky Mule, 1925, advances w/crazy action as farmer bounces in seat, 9½", EX $375.00

Jolly Pals, 1920, bulldog pulls monkey in cart, 8", EX $475.00

Junior Oil Tank Truck, red, gr & yel, NM.....................$850.00

Knock-Out Prize Fighters, 1921, EX (EX box), A $650.00

Leaping Lena Car, 1930, w/driver, blk w/wht lettering, 8", EX, from $400 to $500.00

Miami Sea Sled, adjustable tiller, 10", EX, from $275 to ..$325.00

Parcel Post Special Delivery Truck, orange & red w/blk roof & fenders, 11", NM $1,500.00

Play Golf, 1925, 12x7" base, NM (EX box), from $1,000 to..$1,100.00

Racer #21, 9", VG, A...$475.00

Red Flash Racer #31, w/driver, red & yel, 9½", scarce, EX, from $850 to..$900.00

Santee Claus in Sleigh, 1923, 11", EX, $1,400.00.

Standard Oil Tanker Truck, 10½", VG, A.....................$525.00

Tip Top Porter, 1925, Black man pushes 2-wheeled cart, 6½", EX (EX box), A $450.00

Travelchiks, 1925, railroad car advances as chickens peck for food on top, 7½", NM...$425.00

Wildfire Trotter, driver jumps up & down in seat as donkey cart advances, 8½", EX $250.00

Yell-O Taxi, w/driver, 8½", VG, A................................$850.00

Structo

Pressed steel vehicles were made by Structo (Illinois) as early as 1920. They continued in business well into the 1960s, producing several army toys, trucks of all types, and firefighting and construction equipment.

Advisors: Kerry and Judy Irvin (K5).

Army Ambulance #416, 17", EX..................................$275.00

Cement Mixer, 1950s, 20", EX......................................$175.00

DeLuxe Auto #12, 16", EX+, A $800.00

Deluxe Roadster, orange w/blk convertible top, wht tin tires w/spoke wheels, 14", EX, A...................................$825.00

Dump Truck #14, ca 1926, 18¼", EX, A $400.00

Earth Mover, red, 20", EX, A $125.00

End Loader #340, red w/blk rubber tires, 13", EX, A $100.00

Fire Truck, enclosed cab pulls trailer body w/extension ladder mounted on revolving base, 34", NM, A $200.00

Fire Truck, open bench seat cab, orange water tank mounted to floor, 2 ladders mounted on sides, 21", EX, A..........$550.00

Fire Truck, open bench seat w/bell on hood, hose reel & ladders mounted on body, 18", M, A $1,000.00

Gasoline Truck #912, 1950s, 13", NM............................$135.00

Packard Dump Truck #405, 1930, 18", EX $950.00

Racer #8, ca 1925, clockwork mechanism, 12", VG, A..$550.00

Ready Mix Cement Mixer #700, metallic enamel w/blk tires, NM (NM box) $250.00

Steam Shovel, 1950s, gr w/yel decals, 16", EX...............$150.00

Structo Transport Tractor Trailer, 1950s, bl & red w/yel lettering, 21", EX, D10..$200.00

Stutz Bearcat #10, 16", VG+, A $500.00

Tow Truck #910, red w/decals, complete w/accessories, 11", NM (NM box), A $200.00

Transport Tractor Trailer, 1950s, blue and red with yellow lettering, 21", EX, D10, $200.00. (Photo courtesy Dunbar Gallery)

Truck Fleet Set #725, NMIB, A......................................$600.00

US Mail Truck #928, 17", NM..$300.00

Teddy Bears

The history of old teddy bears goes way back to about 1902–1903. Today's collectors often find it difficult to determine exactly what company produced many of these early bears, but fortunately for them, there are many excellent books now available that contain a wealth of information on those early makers.

Interest in teddy bears has been increasing at a fast pace, and there are more and more collectors entering the market. This has lead to an escalation in the values of the early bears. Because most teddies were cherished childhood toys and were usually very well loved, many that survive are well worn, so an early bear in mint condition can be very valuable.

We would like to direct your attention to the books on the market that are the most helpful on the detailed history and identification of teddies. *A Collectors History of the Teddy Bear* by Patricia Schoonmaker; *Teddy Bears Past and Present (Volumes I and II)* and *American Teddy Bear Encyclopedia* by Linda Mullins; *Teddy Bears — A Complete Guide to History, Collecting, and Care,* by Sue Pearson and Dottie Ayers; *Teddy Bear Encyclopedia and*

Ultimate Teddy Bear Book by Pauline Cockrill; and *Big Bear Book* by Dee Hockenberry. The reader can easily see that a wealth of information exists and that it is impossible in a short column such as this to give any kind of a definitive background. If you intend to be a knowledgeable teddy bear collector, it is essential that you spend time in study. Many of these books will be available at your local library or through dealers who specialize in bears.

Advisor: Cynthia's Country Store, Cynthia Brintnall (C14). **See also Schuco; Steiff.**

2½", gold mohair w/glass eyes, orig collar, straw-stuffed, 1930, M, G16..$75.00

4½", gold mohair w/lg glass eyes, 1940s, EX.....................$75.00

6¾", tan mohair w/amber glass eyes, German, 1940-50, VG, G16 ....$150.00

10", gold mohair w/felt pads, embroidered nose & mouth, brn claws, excelsior stuffing, ca 1905, EX, A.................$750.00

11", gray & beige plush w/glass eyes, shaved snout, flesh-colored oval pads, straw-stuffed, 1945-52, EX......................$250.00

12", gold mohair w/glass eyes, straw-stuffed, fully jtd, Am, 1920-30, EX, G16 ....$500.00

12", yel mohair w/embroidered features, fully jtd, Ideal, VG, A.$485.00

13", yel mohair w/shoe-button eyes, embroidered nose & claws, fully jtd, G, A $300.00

13½", yel mohair w/shoe-button eyes, embroidered wool features, leatherette pads, possibly artist made, EX, A .$325.00

14¾", yel mohair w/shoe-button eyes, embroidered features, fully jtd, Ideal, 1905, VG, A...$450.00

15", brn mohair w/glass eyes, pnt details, German, 1927, EX $350.00

15", yel mohair w/embroidered features, football-shaped body, fully jtd, Ideal, 1920s, EX, A $250.00

17", blond mohair w/blk steel eyes, embroidered features, felt pads, fully jtd, 1910, VG...$525.00

17", gold mohair w/glass eyes, embroidered nose & mouth, fully jtd, Clemens, ca 1940, VG, A..................................$300.00

17", gold mohair w/glass eyes, straw-stuffed, Am, 1920-30, EX...$465.00

17", ride-on, ginger mohair w/glass eyes, embroidered features, steel frame w/wooden wheels, 1920s, EX, A $750.00

18", tan mohair with glass eyes, replaced pads and nose, pre-1915, VG, from $2,400.00 to $2,800.00.
(Photo courtesy Cynthia Brintnall)

19", gold mohair w/shoe-button eyes, fabric nose, embroidered mouth, fully jtd, Herman, early 1900s, VG, A $175.00

20", ginger mohair w/shoe-button eyes, embroidered features, fully jtd, Ideal, 1919, EX, A...............................$450.00

20½", ride-on, brn mohair w/glass eyes, metal frame w/CI wheels, 1913, EX, A $250.00

21", ride-on, tan rayon plush w/glass eyes, embroidered features, steel frame w/rubber tread & metal wheels, 1930s, G.$150.00

22", yel mohair w/embroidered features, glass eyes (1 missing), fully jtd, Ideal, 1920, EX, A...............................$450.00

25", gold mohair w/glass eyes, embroidered features, fully jtd, Ideal, 1920s, EX, A...$450.00

26½", yel mohair w/glass eyes, embroidered features, excelsior stuffing, fully jtd, 1930s, G.....................................$300.00

34", blond mohair w/glass eyes, embroidered features, fully jtd, Ideal, 1919, NM, A..$2,500.00

Tekno

The Tekno company was formed in Denmark during the late 1920s. The toy vehicles they made were of the highest quality, fully able to compete with the German-made Marklin toys then dominating the market. The earliest Tekno vehicles were made of tinplate, and though some were not marked at all, others were stamped with a number. The factory continued to expand until WWII broke out and restrictions made further building impossible. In 1940 the government prohibited the use of tinplate for toy production, and the company began instead to manufacture diecast vehicles in a smaller (1/43) scale. These were exported worldwide in great volume. Collectors regard them as the finest diecasts ever made. Due to climbing production costs and the resulting increases in retail prices that inevitably hurt their sales, the company closed in 1972. Tekno dies were purchased by Mercury Kirk Joal who used them to produce toys identical to the originals except for the mark.

#142 Scania Truck & Long Wheel Base Trailer, bl & red w/silver trailer cover, NM $50.00
#321 Falck Utility Truck, red, tinplate, G $195.00
#356 Porsche, metallic bl w/wht rubber tires, NM..........$150.00
#401 Flying Fortress, silver, US, VG $75.00
#408 VW Pickup Fire Truck, NMIB................................$135.00
#409 VW Army Bus, NM (EX box).................................$125.00
#411 VW Ambulance, MIB...$160.00
#415 Ford Tanus, Transit Ambulance, NM (EX box)....$125.00
#423 Ford VB Garbage Truck, red & gr, G.....................$45.00
#426 Volvo FB88 Lumber Semi, MIB.............................$150.00
#428 V8 Wrecking Truck, red & blk, metal tires, rare, G.$175.00
#434 Scania-Vebis Esso Tank Truck, 1965, cream & gray, NM..$50.00
#434 Volvo BP Tanker, wht & gr, M.............................$150.00
#440 Mercury, NMIB...$175.00
#443 Vespa Scooter, w/sidecar, M................................$125.00
#445 Scania Vabis Ladder Truck, red, EX.....................$100.00
#449 Scania Vabis Lumber Truck, MIB..........................$145.00
#452Y Covered Trailer, Tekno Transport, yel w/bl cover, M (G box)..$30.00
#459 Falck Zonen Fire Truck, MIB................................$175.00
#463 Harrow, NM...$15.00
#465 International Harvester Truck, MIB $80.00
#481 Ford V8 Wrecker Truck, MIB................................$190.00
#491 Gyro Coupe, NMIB $90.00
#723 Mercedes Benz 180, EX (EX box) $110.00
#724 Opel Kadett, EX (G box).......................................$55.00
#727 Junior Coupe, metallic bl, M $85.00
#731 Buick Ambulance, MIB...$145.00
#734 Chevrolet Truck, EX...$75.00
#739 Dodge Truck, w/topper, yel & red, VG................$125.00
#740 Dodge Milk & Cream Truck, bl & wht, NM.........$175.00
#741 Chevrolet Lumber Truck, EX (EX box) $75.00
#762 Motorcycle, w/sidecar, MIB..................................$100.00
#775 Small Utility Trailer, MIB.....................................$30.00
#809 Ford Thunderbird Convertible, MIB.....................$190.00
#812 Alfa Romeo 2500, NMIB $175.00
#812 Cooper Norton #1, silver, EX $60.00
#815 Travel Trailer, Sprite, NM $30.00
#824 MGA Coupe 1600, lt bl, NMIB..............................$150.00
#827 Saab 96, MIB...$130.00

#833 Ford Mustang, 1967, wht & blk w/Rallye Monte Carlo #169 decals, NM $65.00

#834GCB Ford Mustang Convertible, metallic gold w/blk interior, MIB $70.00

#834K, Ford Mustang Kit, 1967, MIB $30.00

#837 SAAB 99, wht, MIB $55.00

#838 Volvo 164, EX $45.00

#851 Scania CR 76 Bus, dk red, MIB $75.00

#914 Ford D800 Tipping Truck, red side panels, MIB......$45.00

#915 Ford D-Truck, red & silver, MIB..................$65.00

#918 Ford Beer Truck D800, NMIB $50.00

#927 E-Type Jaguar, 1960s, red & blk top, NMIB..........$100.00

#928 Mercedes 230SL Convertible, 1965, wht, EXIB $30.00

#930 Monza GT, silver, MIB.................................$65.00

#930S Corvair Monza Coupe, chrome, M....................$45.00

#931 Monza Spider, wht, MIB..............................$65.00

#933 Oldsmobile Toronado, 1965, brn & blk, MIB $180.00

#934TM Toyota 2000GT, mustard body, MIB.................$40.00

#948 Dodge Missile Launcher, M (EX box) $60.00

#951 Dodge Army Truck, covered, NM (EX box)...........$50.00

#956 Dodge Truck w/Searchlight, MIB.....................$85.00

Junior Assembly Set, MIB, $300.00.

Telephones

Novelty phones representing a well-known advertising or cartoon character are proving to be the focus of a lot of collector activity — the more recognizable the character the better. Telephones modeled after a product container are collectible too, and with the intense interest currently being shown in anything advertising related, competition is sometimes stiff and values are rising.

Advisor: Bill Bruegman (T2).

Alvin (Alvin & the Chipmunks), 1984, plastic, 15", NM..$50.00

Bart Simpson, Columbia Tel-Com, 1990s, MIB $35.00

Batmobile (Batman Forever), MIB, from $35 to..............$50.00

Beetle Bailey, MIB, from $125 to $135.00

Bugs Bunny, Warner Exclusive, MIB, P12 ....$100.00

Darth Vader, 1983, MIB, P12..................................$195.00

Ghostbusters, M, P12..$100.00

Gumball Machine, 1980s, rare, NM, P12...................$95.00

Little Orphan Annie & Sandy, Columbia Pictures, 1982, 11", EX, M17..$100.00

Mickey Mouse, Western Electric, 1976, EX..............$175.00

New Kids on the Block, Big Step Prod, 1990, MIB..........$25.00

Poppin' Fresh, Hong Kong, 1984, MIB, minimum value.$300.00

Raggedy Ann & Andy, Pan Phone, 1983, plastic, heart-shaped holder, 7½", EX $40.00

Sly Dog, 1986, MIB, P12, from $85 to $110.00

Snoopy and Woodstock, American Telephone Corporation, 1976, touch-tone, EX, $100.00.

(Photo courtesy June Moon)

Spider-Man Climbing Down Chimney, NM, from $165 to.$200.00

Strawberry Shortcake, M, J6...................................$55.00

Superman, early version w/rotary dial, M.................$500.00

Tetley Tea, man in wht boat on rnd bl base, 9", EX.......$100.00

Winnie the Pooh, sq base, M, from $225 to.................$250.00

Tonka

Since the mid-'40s, the Tonka Company (Minnesota) has produced an extensive variety of high-quality painted metal trucks, heavy equipment, tractors, and vans.

Our values are for items with the original paint. A repainted item is worth much less.

Advisor: Doug Dezso (D6).

Allied Van Lines Truck, #1089, 1962, 16", NMIB, A....$150.00

Allied Van Lines Truck, 1956, NM $300.00

Army Tractor, #250, 1964, EX $75.00

Ace Stores Delivery Truck, 1954, M, $600.00.
(Photo courtesy John Turney)

Backhoe, #422, 1963, M...$200.00
Car Carrier, 1960, complete w/3 cars, NM $350.00
Cement Truck, #620, 1963, M..$200.00
Coast to Coast Utility Truck, 1952, VG.........................$175.00
COE Low Boy & Shovel, M...$200.00
Crane & Clam, #150, 1947, EX $150.00
Dump Truck, #180, 1949-53, NM....................................$275.00
Dump Truck w/Sand Loader, #116, 1961, EX.................$200.00
Fire Jeep, #425, 1963-64, M $300.00
Gambles Pickup, 1960, EX $200.00
Gambles Semi, 1958, M $425.00
Gasoline Tanker, #33, 1958, M..$700.00
Hi-Way Side Dump Truck, 1956, EX $250.00
Holsum Bread Van, 1956, rare, NM................................$850.00
Jewel Tea Co Semi, 1954, NM..$800.00
Livestock Van, #36, 1954-57, NM $275.00
Livestock Van, #500, 1952-53, NM.................................$275.00
Log Hauler, #14, 1954-57, EX $225.00
Meier & Frank Semi, 1953, NM $600.00
MFD Aerial Ladder Truck, #700, mk No 5 on doors, 1954, NM .$400.00
Mobile Clam, #942, 1963, VG...$350.00
Mobile Dragline, #135, 1961, EX....................................$200.00
Parcel Delivery Van, #10, 1957, NM $400.00
Pickup w/Camper, gr, #530, 1965, NM...........................$200.00
Power Lift Truck & Trailer, #200, 1948, EX $150.00
RCD Fast Freight Semi, 1954, VG...................................$450.00
Rescue Squad Van, #105, 1960-61, NM $350.00
Sanitary System Service Truck, #140, 1961, rare, EX $450.00
Sportsman Pickup w/Boat on Camper Shell, #5, 1959, NM..$250.00
Stake Truck, #0860-5, 1955, NM $400.00
Stake Truck w/Tandem Platform, #30, 1959, M.............$375.00
Standard Wrecker, 1961, rare, NM..................................$600.00
Star-Kist Van, 1954, 14½", NM.......................................$400.00
State Hi-Way Dept Dump Truck, 1956, NM $275.00
State Hi-Way Dept Hydraulic Dump Truck, 1957, EX ..$200.00
State Hi-Way Dept Hydraulic Land Rover, #42, 1959, rare,
   MIB..$1,300.00
State Hi-Way Dept Road Grader, #12, 1956, M $150.00
Suburban Pumper Truck, #926, 1960, NM.....................$250.00
Thunderbird Express Semi, #37, 1960, MIB..................$600.00
Tonka Air Express Truck, #16, 1959, NM......................$400.00
Tonka Express Truck #185, 1950, rare, EX $350.00

Tonka Farms Stake Truck w/Horse Trailer, #35, 1959, NM...$350.00
Tractor & Carry-All Truck, #120, 1949-50, EX $200.00
True Value Box Van, 1954, EX.......................................$550.00
Utility Truck, 1950-51, NM..$300.00
Wrecker, #250, 1953, EX..$250.00

Toothbrush Holders

Figural ceramic toothbrush holders have become very popular collectibles, especially those modeled after well-known cartoon characters. Disney's Mickey Mouse, Donald Duck, and the Three Little Pigs are among the most desirable, and some of the harder-to-find examples in mint condition sell for upwards of $200.00. Many were made in Japan before WWII. Because the paint was not fired on, it is often beginning to flake off. Be sure to consider the condition of the paint as well as the bisque when evaluating your holdings. For more information we recommend *Pictorial Review of Toothbrush Holders* by Marilyn Cooper. Plate numbers in the following listings refer to Marilyn's book.

Advisor Marilyn Cooper (C9).

Bear w/Scarf & Hat, Japan, plate #16, 5½", from $80 to ..$95.00
Betty Boop w/Toothbrush & Cup, KFS, plate #261, 5", from $85
   to...$100.00
Big Bird, Taiwan (RCC), plate #263, 4½", from $80 to...$90.00
Bonzo, Japan, plate #22, 6", from $80 to $95.00
Candlestick Maker, Japan (Goldcastle), plate #150, 5", from $70
   to...$85.00
Cat, Japan (Goldcastle), plate #36, 6", from $70 to..........$90.00
Cat on Pedestal, Japan (Diamond T), plate #225, 6", from $150
   to...$175.00
Cat w/Bass Fiddle, Japan, plate #38, 6", from $115 to $135.00
Circus Elephant, Japan, plate #56, 5", from $85 to.........$100.00
Clown Head w/Bug on Nose, Japan, plate #59, 5", from $150
   to...$180.00
Clown Juggling, Japan, plate #60, 5", from $75 to $90.00
Dalmatian, Germany, plate #202, 4", from $170 to........$190.00
Donald Duck, WDE, bsk, plate #83, 5", from $250 to $300.00
Ducky Dandy, Japan, plate #84, 4", from $150 to...........$175.00
Dutch Boy & Girl Kissing, Japan, plate #88, 6", from $55 to...$65.00
Dwarfs in Front of Fence (Sleepy & Dopey), Japan/WDE, bsk,
   3½" $1,275.00

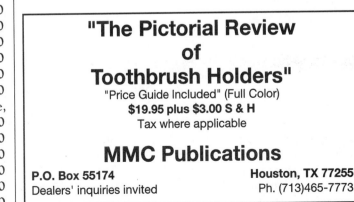

Humpty Dumpty, Pat Pending, bsk, plate #114, 5½", from $200 to $225.00

Little Red Riding Hood, Germany (DRGM), plate #210, 5½", from $200 to $225.00

Mary Poppins, Japan, plate #119, 6"..............................$150.00

Mickey Mouse, Donald Duck & Minnie, Japan/WDE, plate #121, 4½", from $300 to.....................................$375.00

Mickey Mouse & Pluto, WDE, plate #122, 4½", from $250 to...$300.00

Old Mother Hubbard, Germany, plate #3, 6", from $350 to $410.00

Penguin, Japan, plate #128, 5½", from $85 to $100.00

Pinocchio & Figaro, Shafford, plate #242, 5", from $500 to ..$525.00

Popeye, Japan, bsk, plate #244, 5" $500.00

Snow White, Walt Disney, foreign copyright, plate #246, 6", from $225.00 to $250.00.
(Photo courtesy Marilyn Cooper)

Three Bears w/Bowls, Japan (KIM USUI), plate #248, 4", from $90 to..$125.00

Three Little Pigs w/Piano, WDE, bsk, plate #250, 5", from $150 to..$175.00

Traffic Cop, Germany, Don't Forget the Teeth, plate #243, 5", from $350 to $375.00

Uncle Willie, Japan/FAS, plate #157, 5", from $85 to ...$100.00

Tootsietoys

The first diecast Tootsietoys were made by the Samuel Dowst Company in 1906 when they reproduced the Model T Ford in miniature. Dowst merged with Cosmo Manufacturing in 1926 to form the Dowst Manufacturing Company and continued to turn out replicas of the full-scale vehicles in actual use at the time. After another merger in 1961, the company became known as the Stombecker Corporation. Over the years, many types of wheels and hubs were utilized, varying in both style and material. The last all-metal car was made in 1969; recent Tootsietoys mix plastic components with the metal and have soft plastic wheels. Early prewar mint-in-box toys are scarce and command high prices on today's market.

Advisors: Kerry and Judy Irvin (K5).

Aces of the Air, complete w/4 airplanes, NM (EX cb container), A..$1,200.00

Aero-Dawn, #4660, 1934, red, NM................................$70.00

Army Bonanza Plane, 1948, blk w/decals, NM.................$45.00

Austin-Healy, 1959-64 (made in 1956), 6"......................$45.00

Auto Transport, complete w/2 convertibles, fire truck & sedan, 10", EX (EX box), A...$175.00

Autogyro, #4659, 1934, early wheel type, NM $100.00

Biplane, #4650, 1926, NM $115.00

Buck Rogers' Venus Duo-Destroyer, 1937, NM.............$115.00

Buick Station Wagon, 1955-59 (made in 1954), 6", NM.$40.00

Caterpiller Scraper, #3710, 1956-59, yel w/metal blade, 5½", NM $45.00

Cement Truck, #2543, 1970-79, red, yel & wht, 6", NM.$20.00

Chevy Bel Air, 1956-58 (made in 1955), gr, NM............$25.00

Chevy Coupe, #231, 1940-41, med aqua, NM.................$40.00

Chevy El Camino, 1960-1967 (made in 1950), red, 6", NM.$40.00

Chevy Fastback Coupe, 1947-49, red w/blk tires, NM $40.00

Chrysler New Yorker, 1953-54, bl, 6", NM....................$40.00

Chrysler Windsor Convertible, 1951-55 (made in 1950), 6", NM $100.00

CJ-3 Civilian Jeep, 1947-54, red w/blk rubber tires, 4", NM ..$25.00

CJ-5 Jeep w/Snowplow, 1961, 6", NM $45.00

Coast Guard Seaplane, 1950, silver w/decals, NM $135.00

Corvette Roadster, 1955-69, bl, 4", NM $35.00

Curtis P-40 Plane, #721, 1941, NM.............................$175.00

DC-4 Long-Range Bomber, 1941 (?), bl & wht camouflage w/decals, NM $175.00

Delta Jet, 1954-55, silver, NM......................................$35.00

Dodge Panel Truck, 1959-66 (made in 1956), tin bottom, 6", NM $80.00

Dodge Pickup, 1950-60, olive gr, open windows, 4", NM.$30.00

Doodlebug, #716, 1935-37, NM....................................$95.00

F-40 Skywing, 1956-69, blk, NM $25.00

Ferrari Racer, 1956, gr w/gold driver, 6", NM $40.00

Fire Department Set #411, 1930, complete, EX (EX box), A.$900.00

Ford Falcon, 1961-64 (made in 1960), gr, 3", NM...........$25.00

Ford Mainliner, 1953-54 (made in 1952), red, 4-door, 3", NM.$45.00

Ford Ranch Wagon, 1955-60 (made in 1954), turq, 3", NM $30.00

Ford Sedan, 1934, mint gr w/wht rubber tires, NM $75.00

Ford Sinclair Oil Tanker, 1949-52, 6", NM $60.00

Ford Texaco Oil Tanker, 1949-52, red w/silver lettering, 6", NM...$60.00

Ford Tractor, red w/silver grille & blk tires, cast seat & steering wheel, NM $55.00

Ford Trimotor Plane, #04649, 1932, NM $115.00

GMC Greyhound Bus, #3571, 1948-55, bl & silver, NM.$55.00

Graham 5-Wheel Sedan, #0513, bl-gray w/wht rubber wheels, M $150.00

Greyhound Bus, #1045, 1942-46, bl & silver, NM $55.00

High-Wing Plane, #107, 1932, NM $80.00

Hiller Helicopter, 1968-69, NM....................................$40.00

HO Series Dump Truck, #2470, 1960s, red & silver, NM ..$35.00

HO Series School Bus, #2490, 1960s, yel & blk, scarce, NM.**$45.00**

Hose Wagon, #238, 1947-48, red w/blk tires, integral driver, NM...**$40.00**

Insurance Patrol Car, #104, 1932-34, red, NM **$35.00**

International K-5 Grain Hauler, 1949-58 (made in 1947), red cab & gr trailer, NM **$45.00**

International K-5 Stake Truck, 1947, yel, closed sides, 6", NM **$45.00**

Jeepster, 1949-52 (made in 1947), yel, 3", NM................**$30.00**

Jumbo Pickup, #1019, 1936-41, yel & silver, NM **$50.00**

Jumbo Wrecker, #1027, 1937-41, gray w/wht rubber wheels, 6", NM...**$60.00**

Jumpin' Jeeper w/Honda Hitch-Up, #2523, 1970-75, NM .**$15.00**

Lancia Racer, 1956, red, w/driver, 6", NM.....................**$40.00**

Lincoln Capri, 1953-58, red & wht, 2-door, 6", NM........**$40.00**

Lockheed Constellation, 1951, silver, NM **$125.00**

Los Angeles SWAT Armoured Car, 1976-79, NM **$10.00**

Mack B-Line Cement Truck, 1959-69 (made in 1955), red & yel, 6", NM...**$45.00**

Mack B-Line Log Truck, 1960-67 (made in 1955), 9", NM..**$70.00**

Mercury Custom, 1950-52 (made in 1949), bl, 4-door, 4", NM **$40.00**

Motors Set #7200, 9 pcs, MIB, A **$900.00**

Oldsmobile 88 Convertible, 1960-68 (made in 1959), lt gr, 6", NM **$30.00**

Oldsmobile 98 w/Skirted Fenders, 1955, bl & wht, 4", rare, NM **$45.00**

Packard, 1956-59, bl & wht, 4-door, 6", NM **$40.00**

Pan American Airport Set, 12 pcs, NMIB, A.................**$750.00**

Panther Jet, 1953-55, bl, 2-pc body, NM **$35.00**

Piper Cub Plane, 1948-52, bl, NM **$25.00**

Plymouth Sedan, 1951-54 (made in 1950), bl, 4-door, 3", NM **$25.00**

Police Van, #1299, 1976-79, NM....................................**$10.00**

Pontiac Fire Chief Car, 1950-54, red, 4", NM **$50.00**

Pontiac Sedan, 1950-54, gray, 4", NM **$35.00**

Porsche Roadster, 1959-64 (made in 1956), red, 6".........**$40.00**

Racer, #23, 1927, w/driver, sm, rare, NM........................**$85.00**

Rambler Station Wagon, 1961-63 (made in 1960), bl, 4", NM **$25.00**

RC 180 Boat Transport, 1962-67, red & silver, w/3 blk & wht boats, NM **$80.00**

Rescue Helicopter, #2552, 1975-79, red & wht w/bl blades, NM..**$10.00**

Station Wagon, #239, 1940-41, gr & cream, NM.............**$45.00**

Stingin' Bug w/Snowmobile Hitch-Up, #2528, 1970-75, NM...**$15.00**

Studebaker Coupe, 1949 (made in 1947), gr, 3", NM **$55.00**

Thunderbird Coupe, 1955-60, 3", NM...........................**$25.00**

Tractor & Harrow, #2810, 1952-69, red & silver w/blk tires, NM...**$70.00**

US Army Oldsmobile Staff Car, 1958-60, blk w/star decal on top, 4", NM..**$40.00**

US Army Plane, #119, 1936, NM **$75.00**

US Army Supply Truck, #4634, 1939, open cab w/integral driver, NM...**$70.00**

US Army Tractor, #4654, 1931-32, integral driver, rare, NM...**$135.00**

US M-8 Armored Car, #2943, 1973-76, NM...................**$10.00**

Waco Dive Bomber, #718, 1937, NM.............................**$130.00**

Tops and Other Spinning Toys

Tops are among the oldest toys in human history. Homer in *The Iliad*, Plato in the *Republic*, and Virgil in *The Aeneid* mention tops. They are found in nearly all cultures, ancient and modern.

There are seven major categories: 1) The twirler — spun by the twisting action of fingers upon the axis. Examples are Teetotums, Dreidels, advertising spinners, and Tippe Tops. 2) The supported top — started with a string while the top is supported upright. These include 'recuperative,' having a string that automatically rewinds (Namurs); 'seperative,' with a top that detaches from the launcher; 'spring launched,' which is spun using a wound spring; 'pump' or 'helix,' whereby a twisted rod is pumped to spin the top; and 'flywheel-' or 'inertia wheel-powered.' 3) The peg top — spun by winding a string around the peg of the top which is then thrown. 4) The whip top — which is kept spinning by the use of a whip. 5) The yo-yo or return top. 6) The gyroscope. 7) The Diavuolo or Diabolo.

Advisor: Bruce Middleton (M20).

See also Yo-Yos.

Air Powered, Cracker Jack, Dowsy, Chicago, red, wht & bl, M, M20...**$16.00**

Air Powered, Poll Parrot Shoes, yel, NM, M20 ....**$16.00**

Aladdin Ball & Top, early 1900s, helix rod powered, EX (EX box), M20 ....**$550.00**

Autogyro Horse Race, Britains, lead & wire, flywheel mechanism, w/4 jockeys on horses, 11" L, EX, M20 ....**$1,000.00**

Circus Horse & Rider, lead w/wire & tin, horse & female rider on rods attached to base, 7", VG, M20 ....**$375.00**

Competition Award Patches, top shape, 1st, 2nd & 3rd, M, M20, ea **$50.00**

Dancing Couple, Ives, japanned & polychromed CI, w/arms entwined, she in lead bell-shaped skirt, 3½", EX, M20 ....**$135.00**

Disk, maroon & red wood flat-top w/natural wood holder, 3½" dia, EX, M20 ....**$45.00**

Disk, red & natural wood w/gr stripes, w/hdl, 4" dia, EX, M20 .**$75.00**

Game, Big Top, Marx, plastic, battery-op, MIB, M20 ......**$35.00**

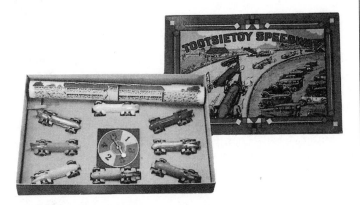

Speedway Set #5081, 1932, complete, NM (EX box), A, $1,900.00.

Game, Brownie Kick-In, MH Miller, litho tin w/Brownies, top kicks ball into indentations for score, VG (G box), M20 ....$50.00
Game, Double Diablos, Parker Bros, 1930s, EX (EX box), M20 .$60.00

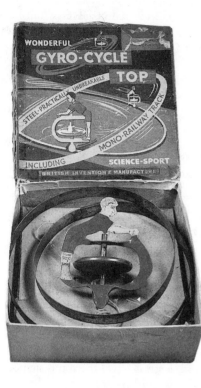

Gyro-Cycle Top, British, boy rides circular track, EX (EX box), M20, $600.00.
(Photo courtesy Bruce Middleton)

Hummer, German, litho tin, clown-head knob w/wooden hat, 8", VG, M20 ....$575.00
Hummer, inverted wood beehive-shape w/mc stripes, 2½" dia, VG, M20...$415.00
Hummer, wht celluloid ball w/mc stripes, tall, 7", EX, M20 ..$415.00
Namur, wooden ball w/brass string housing, EX, M20......$20.00
Peg Top, Duncan Chicago Twister, #329, wood, MIP, M20 ..$20.00
Peg Top, Duncan Tournament, #349, wood, MIP, M20...$20.00
Peg Top, Duncan Twin Spin #310, wood, MIP, M20.......$20.00
Peg Top, Duncan Whistler #320, wood, MIP, M20..........$20.00
Peg Top, Helix Rod Launcher, advertises Kinney Shoes, VG, M20 ....$15.00
Recuperative, natural wood w/pnt stripes, wood string housing, EX, M20, from $75 to..$100.00
Recuperative, wood, 6-sided string housing over ovoid body, G, M20..$85.00
Spinner, Alemite Motor Oil, Bakelite, Keep Yor Car Humming Like a Top, NM, M20...$25.00
Spinner, Brown-Bilt Shoes, Buster Brown, blk & red letters on yel background w/red trim, EX, M20.........................$45.00
Spinner, Cracker Jack, M, M20, from $35 to $75.00
Spinner, Derby Petroleum Products, M, M20, from $35 to .$75.00
Spinner, man w/mug of beer, Hvem Betaler on hat, litho tin, spin to see who pays, NM, M20.................................$85.00
Spinner, Nolde's American Maid Breads & Cakes, red & wht, NM, M20 ....$30.00
Spinner, OTC Trenton Oyster Crackers, bl letters on wht, M, M20...$50.00
Spinner, Robin Hood Shoes, M, M20, from $35 to.........$75.00

Spinner, shaped like a pointing spaniel, Heads I Win, Tails You Lose, NM, M20..$25.00
Spinner, Tastykake Cakes & Pies, M, M20, from $35 to..$75.00
Spinner, Tip Top Bread, plastic, NM, M20 ....$10.00
Supported, pressed board disk w/graphics of boy shooting a toy gun, M, M20 ....$60.00
Supported, Rainbow, Seneca, pnt metal 4-tooth disks inside lg disk rotating around shaft, changes color, NM, M20.$65.00
Tip Tray, Canada Dry, dimple in center to spin on, G, M20 .$20.00
Tip Tray, SS Pierce, Wine & Spirit Merchants..., dimple in center to spin on, M, M20..$60.00

Trading Cards

Modern collector cards are really just an extension of a hobby that began well before the turn of the century. Advertising cards put out by the food and tobacco companies of that era sometimes featured cute children, their pets, stage stars, battle scenes, presidential candidates, and so forth. Collectors gathered them up and pasted them in scrapbooks.

In the 20th century, candy and bubble gum companies came to the forefront. The cards they issue with their products carry the likenesses of sports figures, fictional heroes, TV and movie stars, Disney characters, Barbie dolls, and country singers!

Distinguishing a collectible trading card from other cards may be a bit confusing. Remember, trading cards are released in only two ways: 1) in a wax or foil pack, generally in multiples of twelve — twenty-four, thirty-six, or forty-eight); or 2) as a premium with another product. The only exception to this rule are sets issued as limited editions, with each set individually numbered. Cards issued as factory sets are not trading cards and have no collector value unless they cross over into another collecting area, for example, the Tuff Stuff Norma Jean (Marilyn Monroe) series. In general, from 1980 to the present, wrappers tend to fall into the 50¢ to $2.00 range, though there are some exceptions. For more information we recommend Collector's Guide to Trading Cards by Robert Reed.

Advisors: Mark and Val Macaluso (M1).

Other Sources: C1, C10, D11, F1, F8, H4, H11, H12, J6, J7, M8, M17, T2.

A-Team, Monty Gum, 1983, set of 100 ....$15.00
A-Team, Topps, 1983, 2 different packs, set of 66 w/12 stickers, ea $9.50
Akira, Cornerstone, 1994, set of 100................................$18.00
Aladdin, Skybox, 1993, set of 90.....................................$20.00
Alien, Topps, 1979, set of 84 w/22 stickers $45.00
Alien Nation, FTCC, 1990, set of 60................................$15.00
Alien 3, Star Pics, 1992, set of 80....................................$16.00
American Bandstand, Collect-A-Card, 1993, set of 100 ..$15.00
Animal Mystic, Comic Images, 1997, set of 72 ....$19.00
Babysitter's Club, Topps, 1992, set of 55 ....$15.00
Back to the Future II, Topps, 1989, set of 88 w/11 stickers ..$11.00
Barbie, Dart/Panini, 1991, series 1, set of 196.................$30.00
Batman (Movie), Topps, 1989, 2 different packs, set of 132 w/22 stickers, ea..$18.00
Battlestar Galactica, Topps, 1978, set of 132 w/22 stickers ...$55.00

Bay City Rollers, Topps, 1975, set of 66..................$75.00

Beatles, River Group, 1993, set of 220 ....$25.00

Beauty & the Beast, Pro Set, 1992, set of 75 w/10 sticker cards & 10 mirror cards $18.00

Beavis & Butthead, Fleer, 1994, set of 150 ......$35.00

Berenstain Bears, Kenwis Inc, 1992, 6 different packs, set of 72 w/5 stickers, ea $15.00

Beverly Hillbillies, Eclipse, 1993, set of 110...........$15.00

Beyond Bizarre, Comic Images, 1993, set of 90.............$12.00

Bill & Ted's Adventure, Pro Set, 1991, set of 140 ....$8.00

Black Hole, Panini, complete set........................$45.00

Bozo, Lime Rock, 1994, set of 54.....................$10.00

Cabbage Patch Kids (Astronauts), Coleco, 1989, set of 6 (1 w/ea doll) ...$90.00

Cabbage Patch Kids (Circus Clowns), Coleco, 1989, set of 6 (1 w/ea doll) $60.00

Captain America, Comic Images, 1990, set of 45 ....$25.00

Charlie's Angels, Topps, 1977, series 1, set of 55.............$55.00

Charlie's Angels, Topps, 1977, series 2, set of 66.............$45.00

Close Encounters, Crown, 1978, set of 48, postcard sz $30.00

Close Encounters, Topps, 1978, set of 66 w/11 stickers $18.00

Comic Images, Comic Images, 1996, set of 90 ....$35.00

Crazy Labels, Fleer, 1979, set of 64....................$35.00

Creature Feature, Topps, 1980, 4 different packs, set of 88 w/22 stickers, ea $39.00

Dallas, Donruss, 1981, set of 56......................$12.00

Dark Shadows, Imagine, 1993, set of 62 ....$18.00

DC Comics 3-Pack Cards, DC Comics, 1988, set of 48, 6 uncut sheets, scarce.....................$75.00

DC Comics 3-Pack Cards, DC Comics, 1990, 9 uncut sheets of 8, set of 72............................$115.00

DC Justice League, DC Comics, set of 15 ....$20.00

Deep Space 9, Skybox, 1993, set of 50 ....$20.00

Deep Space 9, Skybox, 1994, set of 100 ....$16.00

Demolition Man, Skybox, 1991, set of 100.............$18.00

Dinosaurs, Nu-Card, 1962, set of 80 ....$400.00

Dracula, Topps, 1992, set of 66 ....$35.00

Dream Machines, Champs, 1991-92, series 1 or 2, set of 100, ea..................$25.00

Dukes of Hazzard, Donruss, 1981, 3rd series, set of 44 ......$20.00

Dune, Fleer, 1984, 3 different packs, set of 132, ea...........$25.00

Elvis, River Group, 1992, 1st series, 3 different packs, set of 220, ea................$25.00

Empire Strikes Back, 2nd series, Topps, 1980, set of 132..$38.00

ET, Topps, 1982, set of 12 stickers only $20.00

Fantastic Odd Rods, Donruss, 1973, 1st series, set of 66...$45.00

Flash Gordon, MV Jasinski, 1990, 1st series, set of 36 of limited edition $30.00

Flintstones (The Movie), Topps, 1994, set of 88 w/11 stickers..................$16.00

Flintstones (The Return of), Cardz, 1994, set of 50 w/10 stickers..................$15.00

Freddie & the Dreamers, Donruss, 1965, set of 66 ....$95.00

Fright Flicks, Topps, 1988, 4 different packs, set of 90 w/11 stickers, ea..................$12.50

Gargoyles, Skybox, 1995, set of 90 w/10 stickers $25.00

Ghostbusters, Panini, 1987, set of 264 ....$35.00

GI Joe, Diamond, 1987, set of 225 ....$20.00

GI Joe, Milton Bradley, 1986, set of 192 w/12 stickers $55.00

Garbage Pail Kids, Topps, 1986, 2nd series, set of 88, $85.00.
(Photo courtesy Robert Reed)

Golden Age of Comics, Comic Images, 1995, set of 90....$39.00

Gong Show, Fleer, 1979, set of 10 stickers.....................$25.00

Gong Show, Fleer, 1979, set of 66.........................$25.00

Grease, Topps, 1st series, set of 66 w/11 stickers...............$18.00

Gremlins, Topps, 1984, set of 82 w/11 stickers...............$16.00

Gunsmoke, Pacific, 1992, set of 110...................$15.00

Happy Days, OPC, 1976, complete set..................$25.00

Happy Days, Topps, 1976, set of 44 w/11 stickers............$25.00

Harry & the Hendersons, Topps, 1987, set of 77 w/22 stickers.......................$12.00

Here's Bo, Fleer, 1981, set of 72 w/12 stickers..................$15.00

Hockey Freaks, Panini, 1992, 3 different packs, set of 100, ea ..$12.00

Home Improvement, Skybox, 1994, set of 80 w/10 stickers.$22.00

Hook, Topps, 1991, set of 99 w/11 stickers $10.00

Hunchback of Notre Dame, Skybox, 1996, set of 101 ......$20.00

In Living Color, Topps, 1992, set of 88 w/11 stickers.......$15.00

James Bond, Eclipse, 1993, 1st series, set of 110 ....$40.00

Jaws II, Topps, 1978, set of 59 w/11 stickers.........................$9.50

Judge Dredd (The Epics), Edge Entertainment, 1995, set of 90.......................$15.00

Judge Dredd (The Movie), Edge Entertainment, set of 82..$15.00

King Kong, Eclipse, 1993, set of 110 ....$20.00

King Kong, Topps, 1976, set of 55 w/11 stickers...............$35.00

KISS II, Donruss, 1978, set of 66.....................$85.00

Kung Fu, Topps, 1973, set of 55 ....$100.00

Leave It to Beaver, Pacific, 1984, set of 60.............$75.00

Lion King, AMC, 1995, set of 16 (given out at AMC theaters) $25.00

Lion King, Skybox, 1994, set of 90...................$20.00

Lone Ranger, WTW reprint, set of 48.................$50.00

M*A*S*H, Donruss, 1982, set of 66.................$29.00

Magnum PI, Donruss, set of 66.......................$12.00

Marvel Super Heroes, Crunch 'n Munch, 1995, 1st or 2nd series, set of 6 (premium in boxes), ea $15.00

Marvel Super Heroes, Topps, 1976, 3 different packs, set of 9 w/40 stickers, ea $60.00

Marvel Universe, Comic Images, 1987, 1st series, set of 90..$125.00

Masters of the Universe (Movie), Panini, 1987, set of 240..$32.00

Maverick (Movie), Cardz, 1994, set of 60 ....$19.00

Michael Jackson, Topps, 1984, set of 13 Super Stickers, 5x7" $30.00
Michael Jackson, Topps, 1984, 1st series, set of 33 w/33 stickers..$8.50
Mickey Mouse, Americana, set of 360 ....$150.00
Monster in My Pocket, Source Group, 1991, set of 48 w/24 stickers $22.00
Moonraker, Topps, 1979, set of 99 w/22 stickers $24.00
Mork & Mindy, Topps, 1978, set of 99 w/22 stickers $22.00
Mortal Kombat, Topps, 1994, set of 100 ....$11.00
Musclecards Big Engine Cars, Performance, 1991, set of 102 ..$25.00
National Lampoon, 21st Century, 1993, set of 100 ....$20.00
New Kids on the Block, Topps, 1990, 1st series, 2 different packs, set of 88 w/22 stickers, ea..................................$12.00
Nightmare Before Christmas, Skybox, 1993, set of 90......$23.00
Nintendo, Topps, 1990, 3 different packs, set of 55 w/33 stickers $7.00
Peanuts (Snoopy), Pro Sports, 1992, set of 200 ....$28.00
Pete's Dragon, Panini, 1980, complete set $45.00
Phantom (Movie), Inworks, 1996, set of 90 ....$12.00
Planet of the Apes (TV), Topps, 1975, set of 66 ....$65.00
Plasm, River Group, 1993, set of 150 ....$6.00
Power Rangers, Collect-A-Card, 1994, set of 72 w/12 stickers, Wal-Mart version $20.00
Prince Valiant, Comic Images, 1995, set of 90 ....$10.00
Raiders of the Lost Ark, Topps, 1981, set of 88 ....$20.00
Ren & Stumpy, Topps, 1994, set of 50.............................$15.00
Return of the Jedi, Topps, 1983, 1st series, set of 132 w/66 stickers $25.00
Robotech the Macross Saga, FTCC, 1986, 2 different packs, set of 60, ea..$29.00
Rocketeer, Topps, 1991, 2 different packs, set of 99 w/11 stickers, ea $10.00
Rocky Horror Picture Show, FTCC, 1980, set of 60........$18.00
Rocky IV, Topps, 1985, 2 different packs, set of 66 w/22 stickers, ea..$12.00
Roger Rabbit, Topps, 1988, set of 132 w/22 stickers........$18.00
Saturday Night Fever, Donruss, 1978, set of 66 ....$15.00
Saved by the Bell, Pacific, 1992, set of 110......................$18.00
Saved by the Bell (College Years), Pacific, 1994, set of 110...$18.00
Seaquest, Skybox, 1994, set of 100..................................$25.00
Sesame Street, Idolmaker, 1992, set of 100.....................$15.00
Shadow, Topps, 1994, set of 90 w/10 stickers $35.00
She-Ra, Panini, 1987, set of 216 ....$35.00
Simpsons, Skybox, 1994, set of 70 w/10 stickers..............$35.00
Six Million Dollar Man, Monty Gum, 1975, set of 72......$75.00
Smurf Supercards, Topps, 1984, set of 55 ....$12.00
Snow White, Skybox, 1993, set of 90................................$20.00
Space: 1999, Donruss, 1976, set of 66 ....$19.00
Spaceshots (NASA), Space Ventures, 1991, set of 110 ...$50.00
Spider-Man, Comic Images, 1988, set of 50 stickers.........$39.00
Star Trek II, Monty Gum, 1983, set of 100.....................$125.00
Star Trek III, FTCC, 1984, set of 60 cards $75.00
Stargate, Collect-A-Card, 1994, set of 100 w/12 stickers .$15.00
Stupid Smiles, Topps, 1990, set of 44................................$15.00
Superman, Drakes, 1979, set of 24....................................$75.00
Superman (Movie), Topps, 1978, 1st series, set of 77 cards .$18.00
Tarzan, Panini, set of 400 ....$60.00
Teenage Mutant Ninja Turtles, Diamond, 1989, set of 180.$17.50

Teenage Mutant Ninja Turtles (Movie), Topps, 1990, set of 132 w/11 stickers...$10.00
Terminator 2, Topps, 1991, set of 4 stickers....................$6.00
Three Stooges, FTCC, 1985, set of 60 ....$75.00
Thundercats, Panini, 1980s, set of 264............................$25.00
Tiny Toons, Cardz, 1994, set of 50 w/10 stickers $18.00
Total Recal, Pacific, 1990, set of 110 ....$20.00
Transformers, Milton Bradley, 1985, set of 192 w/24 stickers ..$60.00
Trivia Battle, Topps, 1984, set of 132 w/11 stickers.........$18.00
Truckin', Donruss, 1973, set of 44 ....$18.00
Universal Monsters, Topps, 1994, set of 100 ....$28.00
V (TV Show), Fleer, 1984, set of 22 stickers $40.00
Welcome Back Kotter, Topps, 1976, set of 44 ....$25.00

Who Framed Roger Rabbit, Topps, 1988, set of 132 with 22 stickers, $15.00.

X-Force, Comic Images, 1991, set of 90 ....$25.00
Zero Heros, Donruss, 1984, 3 different packs, set of 66, ea...$15.00

BOXES

Addams Family, Topps, 1991...$6.00
Alf, Topps, 1987..$6.00
Andy Griffith, Pacific, 1990 ....$5.00
Barbie, Dart/Panini, 1991 ....$4.00
Battlestar Galactica, Topps, 1978.....................................$20.00
Baywatch, Merlin, 1996..$5.00
Betty Boop, Eclipse, 1993 ....$5.00
Charlie's Angels, Topps, 1977..$25.00
Dallas, Donruss, 1981..$8.00
Desert Storm, Pro Set, 1991..$4.00
Dick Tracy, Topps, 1993..$7.00
ET, Topps, 1982 ....$6.00
Fievel Goes West, Impel, 1991..$40.00
Football Superfreaks, Donruss, 1974.................................$10.00
Ghostbusters II, Topps, 1989 ....$4.00
Goonies, Topps, 1986 ....$6.00

Grease, 1st series, Topps, 1978 ....$18.00
Harry & the Hendersons, Topps, 1987 ....$4.00
Honeymooners, Comic Images, 1988 ....$20.00
Indian Jones In The Temple of Doom, Topps, 1984 ....$8.00
Jaws II, Topps, 1978 ....$4.00
Jurassic Park Gold, Topps, 1993 ....$10.00
Knight Rider, Donruss, 1985 ....$6.00
Lion King, Skybox, 1994 ....$4.00
Magnum PI, Donruss, 1983 ....$5.00
Masters of the Universe, Topps, 1984 ....$6.00
Minnie & Me, Impel, 1991 ....$4.00
Monkees, Cornerstone, 1996 ....$12.00
Munsters, Dart Flipcards, 1996 ....$5.00
New Kids on the Block, 1st series, Topps, 1990 ....$6.00
Nightmare on Elm St, Comic Images, 1988 ....$4.00
Pee Wee's Playhouse, Topps, 1989 ....$10.00
Rambo, Topps, 1985 ....$6.00
Return of Superman, Skybox, 1993 ....$5.00
Robin Hood, Topps, 1991 ....$4.00
Rocketeer, Topps, 1991 ....$4.00
Scream Queen, 3rd series, Imagine, 1993 ....$5.00
Spider-Man, Comic Images, 1988 ....$6.00
Star Trek III, FTCC, 1984 ....$18.00
Superman (Movie), 1st series, Topps, 1978 ....$10.00
Terminator 2, Topps, 1991 ....$6.00
Three Stooges, FTCC, 1985 ....$6.00
V (TV Show), Fleer, 1984 ....$6.00
Winston Cup, Pro Set, 1991 ....$5.00
X-Files, Topps, 1995 ....$6.00
Zero Heores, Donruss, 1984 ....$5.00
21 Jump Street, Topps, 1988 ....$5.00

WRAPPERS

Alien Nation, FTCC, 1990 ....$.50
Bay City Rollers, Topps, 1977 ....$7.50
Betty Boop, Eclipse, 1993 ....$1.00
Boris, Comic Images, 1991 ....$1.25
Buck Rogers, Scanlens, 1979 ....$4.00
Comic Book Foldees, Topps, 1966 ....$15.00
Conan, Comic Images, 1993 ....$1.50
Dark Shadows, Imagine, 1993 ....$1.00
DC Legends, Skybox, 1995 ....$1.00
Dollman, Full Moon, 1991 ....$5.00
Empire Strikes Back, 1st series, Topps, 1980 ....$2.00
Fabulous Odd Rods, Donruss, 1968 ....$3.00
Gargoyles, Skybox, 1995 ....$1.00
Gong Show, Fleer, 1979 ....$2.00
Honeymooners, Comic Images, 1988 ....$2.00
James Bond (13 Movies), Monty Gum, 1986 ....$3.00
Jurassic Park Gold, Topps, 1993 ....$1.50
Knight Rider, Donruss, 1985 ....$1.00
Kung Fu, Topps, 1971 ....$9.00
Leave It to Beaver, Pacific, 1984 ....$3.00
Marvel Super Heros, Topps, 1975 ....$4.00
Menudo, Topps, 1983 ....$1.00
Monster Initials, Topps, 1974 ....$6.00
Munsters, Dart Flipcards, 1996 ....$1.00

Nightmare Before Christmas, Skybox, 1993 ....$1.00
Puppetmaster, Full Moon, 1991 ....$3.00
Return of the Jedi, Monty Gum, 1983 ....$2.00
Rocketship X-M, FTCC, 1979 ....$2.50
Six Million Dollar Man, Donruss, 1975 ....$4.00
Six Million Dollar Man, Monty Gum, 1975 ....$1.00
Spider-Man, Comic Images, 1992 ....$1.00
Spitting Image, Topps/Trebor, 1990 ....$1.50
Star Wars, 1st series, Topps, 1977 ....$6.00
Superman (Movie), 1st series, Topps, 1978 ....$1.00
The Saint, Sompertex, 1966 ....$25.00
Total Recall, Pacific, 1990 ....$25.00
X-Men Ultra, Fleer, 1994 ....$2.00

Trains

Some of the earliest trains (from ca 1860) were made of tin or cast iron, smaller versions of the full-scale steam-powered trains that transversed America from the east to the west. Most were made to simply be pushed or pulled along, though some had clockwork motors. Electric trains were produced as early as the late 19th century. Three of the largest manufacturers were Lionel, Ives, and American Flyer.

Lionel trains have been made since 1900. Until 1915 they produced only standard gauge models (measuring 2½" between the rails). The smaller O gauge (1¼") they introduced at that time proved to be highly successful, and the company grew until by 1955 it had become the largest producer of toys in the world. Until discontinued in 1940, standard gauge trains were produced on a limited scale, but O and 027 gauge models dominated the market. Production dwindled and nearly stopped in the mid-1960s, but the company was purchased by General Mills in 1969, and they continue to produce a very limited number of trains today.

The Ives company had been a major producer of toys since 1896. They were the first to initiate manufacture of the O gauge train and at first used only clockwork motors to propel them. Their first electric trains (in both O and #1 gauge) were made in 1910, but because electricity was not yet a common commodity in many areas, clockwork production continued for several years. By 1920, #1 gauge was phased out in favor of standard gauge. The company continued to prosper until the late 1920s when it floundered and was bought jointly by American Flyer and Lionel. American Flyer soon turned their interest over to Lionel, who continued to make Ives trains until 1933.

The American Flyer company had produced trains for several years, but it wasn't until it was bought by AC Gilbert in 1937 that it became successful enough to be considered a competitor of Lionel. They're best noted for their conversion from the standard (wide gauge) 3-rail system to the 2-rail S gauge (⅞") and the high-quality locomotives, passenger, and freight cars they produced in the 1950s. Interest in toy trains waned during the space-age decade of the 1960s. As a result, sales declined, and in 1966 the company was purchased by Lionel. Today both American Flyer and Lionel trains are being made from the original dies by Lionel Trains Inc., privately owned.

For more information we recommend *Collecting Toy Trains, An Identification and Value Guide*, by Richard O'Brien.

Advisors: Bill Mekalian (M4) and Gary Mosholder, Gary's Trains (G1).

See also Buddy L (for that company's Outdoor Railroad); **Paper-Lithographed Toys.**

AMERICAN FLYER

Accessory, #12B transformer, 250 watts, EX (EX box) **$75.00**
Accessory, #95 freight station, 12", EX, A **$200.00**
Accessory, #102 passenger station, EX (EX box), A.......**$350.00**
Accessory, #371 whistle stop set, 3 pcs, VG, A **$150.00**
Accessory, #23789 station & baggage smasher, G, A **$200.00**
Car, #751 lumber loader, VG (worn box), A..................**$175.00**
Car, #779 oil drum loader, NMIB **$150.00**
Car, #4006 hopper, red, EX (EX box) **$450.00**
Car, #4011 caboose, yel & brn, VG (VG box), A **$275.00**
Loco & Tender, #332 AC Northern, missing boiler bell, VG, A **$300.00**
Loco & Tender, #332 DC Northern, G, A **$250.00**
Loco & Tender, #343, VG, A **$350.00**
Loco & Tender, #4637 Shasta, rpl wheels, VG, A **$450.00**
Loco & Tender, #4694 w/Golden State tender, VG, A .**$500.00**
Set, #4000 loco, #4151 Bunker Hill pullmans (2), #4152 York-town observation car, VG (VG boxes), A **$900.00**
Set, blk CI loco w/blk litho tin tender, 1 red & 1 gr coach mk American Flyer, w/up, MIB, A..................................**$600.00**
Set, blk CI loco w/2 red litho tin cars mk Sunshine Special, 4½" to 5½" cars, MIB, A **$550.00**
Set, Burlington Zephyr, #9900 loco & 4 cars, silver- & blk-litho tin, VG, A **$225.00**
Set, Comet, loco & 3 cars, VG, A **$450.00**
Set, Empire Express, #4753 loco, #4140 Knickerbocker pullmans (2), #4142 Henry Hudson observation car, VG, A....**$2,500.00**
Set, Golden State, #3115 loco & 3 cars, VG (G boxes), A..**$575.00**
Set, Macy's Electric Speed Special, red, NM (G box), A.**$1,300.00**
Set, Mayflower, #4689 loco w/brass eagle, #4390 combine, #4391 & 4393 coaches, #4392 observation car, rstr, A **$1,400.00**
Set, Minnie Ha-Ha, loco & 3 cars, VG, A **$300.00**
Set, Potomac, #3116 Shasta loco, #3180 combine, #3181 coach, #3182 observation car, VG, A **$400.00**

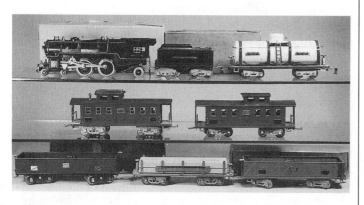

Set, Presidents Special, 1927, blue with brass detail, NMIB, A, $7,100.00.

Set, Warrior, #4693 loco w/tender, #4380 Hancock combine, #4381 coach, #4382 observation car, VG, A **$4,600.00**

LIONEL MODERN ERA 1970 – 96

Accessory, #2117 block target signal, NM **$25.00**
Accessory, #2125 whistling freight shed, NM **$50.00**
Accessory, #2145 gateman, automatic, EX **$40.00**
Accessory, #2163 block target signal, M, G1 ....**$25.00**
Accessory, #2180 road sign, MIB, G1 ....**$5.00**
Accessory, #2256 TCA station platform, NM **$25.00**
Accessory, #2312 mechanical semaphore, M, G1 ....**$15.00**
Accessory, #2317 drawbridge, MIB, G1 ....**$125.00**
Accessory, #2320 flagpole, EX, G1 ....**$20.00**
Accessory, #2792 whistle stop set, NM **$25.00**
Accessory, #8157 Santa Fe FM trainmaster, NMIB, A...**$400.00**
Accessory, #12702 control tower, EX **$75.00**
Accessory, #12719 refreshment stand, animated, MIB, G1 .**$75.00**
Accessory, #12809 billboard, animated, NM **$25.00**
Accessory, #12891 reefer tractor-trailer, MIB, G1 ....**$20.00**
Accessory, #51900 signal bridge & control panel, M **$250.00**
Car, #782 LRRC 1995 tank car, M, G1 ....**$45.00**
Car, #784 LRRC 1984 covered hopper, MIB, G1 ....**$75.00**
Car, #5700 Ozark TCA Oppenheimer reefer, NM **$50.00**
Car, #5706 Lindsay Bros reefer, EX **$25.00**
Car, #5710 Canadian Pacific reefer, EX **$25.00**
Car, #5716 Central Vermont reefer, EX............................**$25.00**
Car, #5724 Pennsylvania Railroad bunk car, EX **$20.00**
Car, #5739 B&O tool car, EX (orig box), G1 ....**$40.00**
Car, #6100 Ontario Northland hopper, EX, G1 ....**$35.00**
Car, #6138 B&O hopper, EX, G1 ....**$35.00**
Car, #6238 Burlington Northern boxcar, NM **$50.00**
Car, #7220 Illinois Central baggage car, MIB................**$100.00**
Car, #7228 Wabash baggage car, MIB **$100.00**
Car, #7232 Wabash observation car, MIB **$100.00**
Car, #7404 Jersey Central boxcar, MIB, G1....................**$50.00**
Car, #7510 Red Lobster reefer, NM **$25.00**
Car, #7518 Carson City mint car, MIB, G1 ....**$45.00**
Car, #7782 TCA Museum Carlisle Finch, MIB, G1 ....**$30.00**
Car, #8690 Lionel Lines trolley car, M, A **$100.00**
Car, #8912 LCAC 1988 Canadian Southern club car, MIB, G1 ....**$225.00**
Car, #9013 Canadian National hopper, EX, G1 ....**$15.00**
Car, #9054 JC Penney boxcar, EX, G1.............................**$20.00**
Car, #9133 Burlington Northern flatcar w/van, MIB, G1...**$40.00**
Car, #9160 Illinois Central-N5C caboose, EX, G1 ....**$30.00**
Car, #9162 Pennsylvania Porthole caboose, EX, G1 ....**$35.00**
Car, #9173 Jersey Central caboose, M..............................**$25.00**
Car, #9205 Norfolk & Western boxcar, M **$25.00**
Car, #9229 Express mail car, operating, MIB, G1 ....**$40.00**
Car, #9282 Northern flatcar w/van, operating, MIB, G1..**$40.00**
Car, #9284 Santa Fe gondola, M **$25.00**
Car, #9301 US mail car, operating, MIB, G1....................**$40.00**
Car, #9305 Santa Fe Cowboy car, operating, EX, G1 ....**$25.00**
Car, #9307 Erie gondola, animated, MIB, G1 ....**$75.00**
Car, #9312 Conrail searchlight car, EX, G1.....................**$25.00**
Car, #9321 Santa Fe tank car, MIB **$50.00**
Car, #9413 Naperville boxcar, MIB, G1 ....**$15.00**

Car, #9435 LCCA 1981 Cental of Georgia club car, MIB, G1 ....$40.00
Car, #9443 Florida East Coast boxcar, M $20.00
Car, #9621 NHL Campbell boxcar, MIB, G1 ....$25.00
Car, #9726 Erie Lackawanna boxcar, EX (orig box), G1 ..$25.00
Car, #9753 Maine Central boxcar, M $25.00
Car, #9780 Johnny Cash boxcar, MIB, G1 ....$40.00
Car, #9802 Miller High Life reefer, EX (orig box), G1 .....$30.00
Car, #9818 Western Maryland reefer, EX $25.00
Car, #13400 Lionel Lines baggage car, MIB $150.00
Car, #13402 Lionel Lines observation car, MIB $150.00
Car, #16003 Pennsylvania Railroad car, NM $25.00
Car, #16015 Amtrak observation car, NM $35.00
Car, #16042 Southern quad hopper w/coal load, NM $35.00
Car, #16043 Illinois Central combination car, M $35.00
Car, #16059 Santa Fe vista dome car, M $35.00
Car, #16103 Lehigh Valley 2-D tank car, NM $25.00
Car, #16214 Rio Grande auto carrier, MIB, G1 ....$35.00
Car, #16215 Conrail auto carrier, MIB, G1 ....$35.00
Car, #16310 Mopar Express gondola, M $35.00
Car, #16318 Lionel Lines flatcar w/reels, MIB, G1 ....$25.00
Car, #16323 Lionel Lines flatcar, MIB, G1 ....$35.00
Car, #16343 Burlington gondola w/coils, MIB, G1 ....$20.00
Car, #16352 US Military flatcar w/missile, NM $35.00
Car, #16374 D&RGW flatcar w/trailer, M $35.00
Car, #16548 Conrail caboose, EX $25.00
Car, #16640 Rutland boxcar, MIB, G1 ....$155.00
Car, #16660 fire car, MIB, G1 ....$35.00
Car, #16663 Missouri Pacific searchlight car, NM $25.00
Car, #16688 fire car w/ladders, M $65.00
Car, #16702 Amtrak bunk car, NM $25.00
Car, #16801 LRRC 1988 bunk car, MIB, G1 ....$35.00
Car, #16802 LRRC 1989 tool car, MIB, G1 ....$35.00
Car, #16803 LRRC 1990 searchlight car, MIB, G1 ....$45.00
Car, #16907 flatcar w/tractors, M $50.00
Car, #17602 Conrail Woodside caboose, M $100.00
Car, #17605 Reading caboose, M, G1 ....$40.00
Car, #17876 LCCA 1989 CN&L boxcar, MIB, G1 ....$45.00
Car, #17881 TTOS 1990 Phelps Dodge club car, MIB, G1 ..$35.00
Car, #17884 TTOS 1990 Columbus-Dayton club car, MIB, G1 ....$40.00
Car, #17898 TCA Wabash reefer, M $50.00
Car, #17900 Santa Fe Unibody tank car, MIB, G1 ....$40.00
Car, #19001 Southern Crescent dining car, MIB, G1 ....$100.00
Car, #19002 Pennsylvania Railroad dining car, M $50.00
Car, #19130 Lackawanna passenger car, set of 4, MIB ...$425.00
Car, #19203 Detroit-Toledo boxcar, MIB, G1 ....$20.00
Car, #19205 Great Northern boxcar, MIB, G1 ....$35.00
Car, #19207 Canadian Pacific rail boxcar, MIB, G1 ....$20.00
Car, #19209 Florida East Coast boxcar, MIB, G1 ....$20.00
Car, #19210, Soo-Line boxcar, NM $20.00
Car, #19215 Union Pacific boxcar, dbl-door, MIB, G1 ....$20.00
Car, #19230 Frisco boxcar, dbl-door, MIB, G1 ....$30.00
Car, #19234 New York City boxcar, NM $50.00
Car, #19239 Toronto-Hamburg-Buffalo boxcar, MIB, G1 ..$20.00
Car, #19303 Lionel Lines Quad hopper, MIB, G1 ....$25.00
Car, #19311 Southern Pacific covered hopper, MIB, G1 .$25.00
Car, #19408 Frisco gondola w/coils, MIB, G1 ....$45.00

Car, #19413 Frisco flatcar w/stakes, NM $25.00
Car, #19419 Charlotte mint car, MIB, G1 ....$45.00
Car, #19506 Thomas Newcomer reefer, MIB, G1 ....$20.00
Car, #19508 Leonardo DeVinci reefer, MIB, G1 ....$20.00
Car, #19602 Johnson tank car, MIB, G1 ....$45.00
Car, #19652 Jersey Central bunk car, M $25.00
Car, #19656 Milwaukee Road bunk car, MIB, G1 ....$45.00
Car, #19709 Pennsylvania Work caboose, MIB, G1 ....$60.00
Car, #19939 Christmas car, MIB, G1 ....$45.00
Car, #52000 Detroit-Toledo TCA flatcar w/trailer, NM ..$75.00
Car, #52010 TTOS 1993 Weyerhauser club car, MIB, G1 .$60.00
Car, #52058 Santa Fe, 100 Year Anniversary, MIB $60.00
Car #87004 Southern boxcar, lg gauge, MIB, G1 ....$45.00
Car, #87407 MKT boxcar, lg gauge MIB, G1 ....$35.00
Car, #87602 Gulf tank car, lg gauge, MIB, G1 ....$40.00
Car, #87700 Pennsylvania caboose, lg gauge, MIB, G1 ....$35.00
Loco, #8160 Burger King GP-20 diesel engine, EX, G1 .$125.00
Loco, #8466/67 Amtrak F-3 AA diesel engine, MIB, G1 .$425.00
Loco, #8485 US Marine NW-2 diesel engine, EX, G1 ...$125.00
Loco, #8568 Preamble Express F-3 diesel engine, M, A....$75.00
Loco, #8602 Pennsylvania 4-4-2 steam engine, MIB, G1 ....$85.00
Loco, #18011 & #17608 Chessie T1 & caboose, steam, MIB, G1 ....$900.00
Loco, #18303 Amtrak GG1 diesel engine, MIB, G1 ......$400.00
Loco, #18610 Rock Island 0-4-0 steam engine, MIB, G1 .$150.00
Loco, #33000 GP-9 Railscope diesel engine, MIB, G1 ...$225.00
Loco & Tender, #8310 Santa Fe 2-4-0, NM $30.00
Loco & Tender, #8369 Erie Lackawanna GP-20, NM ...$125.00
Loco & Tender, #8402 Reading 2-4-2, EX $50.00
Loco & Tender, #8506 Pennsylvania Railroad 0-4-0, M .$100.00
Loco & Tender, #8604 Jersey Central 2-4-2, M $50.00
Loco & Tender, #18011 Chessie, MIB, A $575.00
Loco & Tender, #18635 Santa Fe 2-6-4, NMIB $225.00
Loco & Tender, #18638 Norfolk & Western 2-6-4, NMIB $225.00
Set, #1050 New Englander, NM $200.00
Set, #1085 Santa Fe Express, NM $200.00
Set, #1253 Quicksilver Express, NM $300.00
Set, #1450 SS Rio Grande, MIB, G1 ....$550.00
Set, #1461 Black Diamond, NM $125.00
Set, #1632 Sante Fe Work Train, MIB, G1 ....$375.00
Set, #1663 Amtrak Lake Shore Limited, NM $250.00
Set, #1865 Chesapeake Flyer, EX $150.00
Set, #8951 Southern Pacific FM Trainmaster, NMIB $500.00
Set, #8970 Pennsylvania Railroad F-3 AA, MIB $500.00
Set, #11758 1989 SSS Desert King, MIB, G1 ....$250.00
Set, #51001 Freight Special, MIB $500.00
Set, #81006 Union Pacific Limited, lg gauge, MIB, G1 .$225.00
Set, Conrail Limited, MIB......................................$600.00
Set, Fireball Express, MIB $1,000.00
Set, Great Northern Empire Builder, MIB $1,000.00
Set, Lionelville Circus, MIB...................................$225.00
Set, New York Central, MIB $325.00
Set, Northern Pacific, Sears, MIB $225.00
Set, Rock Island & Peoria, NMIB $325.00
Set, Southern Crescent Limited, MIB.......................$700.00
Set, Union Pacific Overland Route, MIB.................$1,200.00
Set, Western Maryland, MIB $500.00

LIONEL POSTWAR

Accessory, #30 water tower, EX $125.00
Accessory, #45N automatic gateman, EX $50.00
Accessory, #110 graduated trestle, EX (orig box), G1 ......$15.00
Accessory, #118 newsstand w/whistle, VG $65.00
Accessory, #150 telegraph pole set, VG.............$50.00
Accessory, #182 magnetic crane, EX....................$200.00
Accessory, #197 rotating radar antenna, VG $75.00
Accessory, #256 freight station, EX, G1.............$65.00
Accessory, #264 lumber loading platform w/#6264 flat, EX, A $350.00
Accessory, #310 billboard set, EX (EX box), G1..............$25.00
Accessory, #334 dispatch board, operating, EX (EX box), A ..$400.00
Accessory, #342X culvert loader w/#6342 gondola, G (G box), A...$200.00
Accessory, #352 ice depot w/car, red base, VG (VG box), A ..$200.00
Accessory, #356 baggage station, operating, EX, G1 ....$75.00
Accessory, #366 minuteman cannon launcher, VG (VG box), A...$575.00
Accessory, #397 coal loader, NMIB, A $650.00
Accessory, #415 diesel fueling station, VG, A..............$175.00
Accessory, #455 oil derrick, complete w/accessories, EX (EX box), A...$450.00
Accessory, #464 sawmill, EX, G1........................$145.00
Accessory, #494 rotating silver beacon, EX, G1 ....$45.00
Accessory, #497 coal station, EX, A $200.00
Accessory, #943 exploding ammo dump, EX (EX box), A..$100.00
Accessory, #962 turnpike set, complete, NM....................$60.00
Accessory, #981 freight yard set, complete, NM...............$50.00
Accessory, #1010 transformer, 35 watts, NM....................$25.00
Accessory, #1011 transformer, 25 watts, EX, G1 ....$15.00
Accessory, #1014 transformer, 40 watts, NM....................$25.00
Accessory, #1033 transformer, 90 watts, NM....................$50.00
Accessory, #1033 transformer, 90 watts, w/whistle, EX, G1 ..$55.00
Accessory, #1044 transformer, 90 watts, w/whistle, EX (EX box), G1 ....$55.00
Accessory, #1122 automatic 027 switches, EX (EX box), G1.$35.00
Accessory, #1333 lighted station, EX, G1...........$45.00
Accessory, #2460 Bucyrus Erie crane, glossy variation w/gray cab, VG (VG box), A $500.00
Accessory, #3662 milk set, complete, EX, G1.................$65.00
Accessory, #3472 milk set, complete, EX, G1.................$55.00
Accessory, #6456 Lehigh Valley hopper, red, EX (EX box), A...$200.00
Accessory, KW transformer, 190 watts, w/whistle, EX (EX box), A...$165.00
Accessory, LW transformer, 125 watts, w/whistle, EX, G1 ..$85.00
Car, #X2454 Pennsylvania boxcar, EX $175.00
Car, #55 Tie Jector, test run, MIB......................$250.00
Car, #60 trolley car, VG (VG box), A.................$250.00
Car, #164 lumber loader, EX, A $200.00
Car, #221 Santa Fe Alco A-unit, olive, EX, A $650.00
Car, #228P Canadian National Alco, MIB, A................$450.00
Car, #346 culvert unloader, EX, A......................$325.00
Car, #1866 Western & Atlantic baggage car, NM...........$50.00
Car, #2240 Wabash F-3 AB units, EX (EX power unit box), A...$1,100.00

Car, #2321 Lackawanna FM, maroon top, G (G box), A.$500.00
Car, #2331 Virginian FM, blk & gold, G, A..................$325.00
Car, #2350 New Haven EP-5, wht N decal, EX (EX box), A...$250.00
Car, #2350 New Haven EP-5, wht-pnt N, VG (VG box), A...$375.00
Car, #2358 Great Northern EP-5, VG (VG box), A......$400.00
Car, #2379 Rio Grande F-3 AB units, G+, A.............$1,300.00
Car, #2410 Santa Fe observation car, NM.............$75.00
Car, #2429 Livingston pullman, unrun, NM (NM box), A...$350.00
Car, #2434 Newark pullman car, NM $50.00
Car, #2530 baggage car, sm doors, G, A............$150.00
Car, #3309 missile car, olive body, NM, A $600.00
Car, #3349 turbo flatcar, repro missiles, EX, G1 ....$45.00
Car, #3357 hydraulic platform boxcar, EX, G1 ....$75.00
Car, #3360 burro crane, NMIB $600.00
Car, #3361X operating log dump flatcar, EX, G1 ....$35.00
Car, #3376 zoo car, no lettering, EX (EX box), A $300.00
Car, #3410 flatcar, repro helicopter, EX, G1.....................$45.00
Car, #3435 aquarium car, gold lettering, EX (EX box), A....$600.00
Car, #3435 traveling aquarium car, yel rubber stamp, G, A .$175.00
Car, #3510 satellite car, red, unrun, EX, A $175.00
Car, #3519 flatcar, repro satellite, EX, G1 ....$55.00
Car, #3530 generator car, EX (EX box), A $150.00
Car, #3530 GM generator car, VG (VG box), A $175.00
Car, #3540 radar, VG (G box), A.........................$175.00
Car, #3562-50 gondola, yel, EX, G1....................$50.00
Car, #3620 searchlight car, NM $50.00
Car, #4454 Pennsylvania Railroad boxcar, NMIB, A.....$200.00
Car, #6014 Frisco boxcar, wht, EX, G1..............$15.00
Car, #6024 Shredded Wheat boxcar, EX, G1 .....$25.00
Car, #6044 Airex boxcar, bl, EX, G1 ....$25.00
Car, #6315 Gulf tank car, NMIB, A $150.00
Car, #6343 barrel ramp car, VG $40.00
Car, #6346 Alcoa quad hopper, EX (EX box) $65.00
Car, #6414 Evans auto loader, w/4 red cars, VG (G box), A ..$175.00
Car, #6424 flatcar, red w/wht autos, EX, G1 .....$45.00
Car, #6428 US Mail boxcar, EX (EX box), A.................$325.00
Car, #6457 lighted caboose, EX (EX box), G1.................$30.00
Car, #6464-150 boxcar, NM, A $200.00
Car, #6464-325 B&O Sentinel boxcar, NM (NM box), A ..$1,100.00
Car, #6464-350 MKT boxcar, NM (NM box), A..........$500.00
Car, #6464-450 Great Northern boxcar, unrun, NMIB, A .$250.00
Car, #6464-475 B&M boxcar, NM (NM box), A $275.00
Car, #6464-50 M&StL boxcar, EX (EX box), G1............$60.00
Car, #6464-725 New Haven boxcar, blk, unrun, EX (EX box), A...$375.00
Car, #6464-725 New Haven boxcar, orange, EX, G1 ....$75.00
Car, #6464-75 Rhode Island boxcar, NMIB, A $100.00
Car, #6464-825 Alaska boxcar, EX (worn box), A.........$250.00
Car, #6464-900 NYC boxcar, VG (VG box), A.............$125.00
Car, #6468 automobile car, bl, VG, G1 ....$35.00
Car, #6472 refrigerator car, EX, G1 ....$30.00
Car, #6477 bulk car, repro pipes, EX, G1 ....$45.00
Car, #6501 jet boat flatcar, NM (NM box), A $250.00
Car, #6512 cherry picker, EX (EX box), A $150.00
Car, #6544 missile-firing car, blk panel, VG (VG box), A..$275.00
Car, #6560 crane car, red, 8 wheels, EX, G1 ....$45.00

Car, #6562 NY Central gondola, red or gray, NM, ea $50.00
Car, #6636 Alaska quad hopper, NM.................................$50.00
Car, #6651 USMC flatcar w/cannon, olive, unrun, EX, A .$400.00
Car, #6657 Rio Grande caboose, EX (EX box), A..........$225.00
Car, #6672 Santa Fe refrigerator boxcar, bl letters, EX (EX box),
   A $425.00
Car, #6805 Atomic Energy Disposal flatcar w/load, EX (EX box),
   A $250.00
Car, #6807 flatcar w/USMC boat, unrun, EX (EX box), A..$250.00
Car, #6812 track maintenance car, NM (NM box), A...$275.00
Car, #6822 searchlight car, gray, EX (EX box), G1 ....$55.00
Loco & Tender, #614 Alaska NW2 switcher, w/dynamic brake
   unit, EX (EX box)..$350.00
Loco & Tender, #682 loco & #2046W tender, EX (EX boxes),
   A $525.00
Loco & Tender, #736 Berkshire, VG (G box), A...........$400.00
Loco & Tender, #746 Norfolk & Western, VG (VG
   box) $1,300.00
Loco & Tender, #773 Hudson, steam-powered, NM ..$1,000.00
Loco & Tender, #2023 Union Pacific Alco, NMIB.......$600.00
Loco & Tender, #2339 Wabash GP7, MIB.................$1,000.00
Loco & Tender, #2349 Northern Pacific GP-9, MIB
   (sealed) $1,500.00
Loco & Tender, #2379 Rio Grande F-3 AB, EX (EX box) ..$500.00
Set, #251 loco, #206 pullmans (2), #606 observation car, gray
   w/maroon trim, G, A...$300.00
Set, #1649 Santa Fe Alco, MIB $1,950.00
Set, #2573 Berkshire Freight, NMIB $4,200.00
Set, #51000 Hiawatha, MIB, A.................................$825.00

LIONEL PREWAR

Accessory, #46 crossing gate, EX...............................$100.00
Accessory, #47 crossing gate, VG (VG box), A $250.00
Accessory, #71 telegraph post set, VG (VG box), A......$500.00
Accessory, #76 warning bell shack, G, A.....................$125.00
Accessory, #83 flashing traffic signal, yel & red, EX, (worn box),
   A $325.00
Accessory, #92 floodlight tower, red & gray, VG (G box), A...$275.00
Accessory, #94 tension tower, silver & red, VG, A........$425.00
Accessory, #96 coal elevator, manual, NM...................$300.00
Accessory, #117 station, VG (VG box), A....................$350.00
Accessory, #120L tunnel, EX (EX box), A....................$300.00
Accessory, #121 station, VG (worn box), A..................$300.00
Accessory, #124 Lionel City station, EX, A..................$200.00
Accessory, #128 animated newsstand, EX (EX box), A .$275.00
Accessory, #129 station & #115 terrace, late colors, VG, A..$1,900.00
Accessory, #136 Lionelville station, 10", NM, A $550.00
Accessory, #155 freight shed, VG (VG box), A.............$500.00
Accessory, #280 bridge, gr, G, A.................................$85.00
Accessory, #315 trestle bridge, EX..............................$75.00
Accessory, #436 power station, EX (VG box), A $400.00
Accessory, #438 signal tower, G, A.............................$350.00
Accessory, #441 weighing station, VG $550.00
Accessory, #550 railroad figures, set of 6, MIB, A $500.00
Accessory, #810 derrick crane, VG (VG box), A...........$625.00
Accessory, #915 tunnel, cb base, VG, A $1,850.00
Accessory, #1045 watchman, EX..................................$40.00

Accessory, Hellgate bridge, pnt tin w/brass ID plates, 28", NM,
   A $4,000.00
Car, #13 cattle car, early version, EX $450.00
Car, #17 caboose, early version, EX $400.00
Car, #44K boxcar kit, NMIB, A.................................$900.00
Car, #46K hopper kit, NMIB, A..............................$1,000.00
Car, #212 gondola w/7 split barrels, VG, A $675.00
Car, #213 cattle car, terra cotta & gr, VG, A $250.00
Car, #214 boxcar, yel w/orange roof, G, A..................$600.00
Car, #218 dump car, VG, A.....................................$475.00
Car, #220 searchlight car, VG, A $250.00
Car, #426 Coral Isle observation car, EX $550.00
Car, #712 observation car, orange & olive w/woodgrain trim, G,
   A $225.00
Car, #717 caboose, VG...$425.00
Car, #814R reefer, G, A..$250.00
Car, #815 tank car, gr w/brass trim, VG, A $100.00
Car, #2602 baggage car, VG.....................................$150.00
Car, #2814 boxcar, VG (VG box), A........................$1,300.00
Car, #2955 Sunoco tank car, EX $550.00
Loco & Tender, #226, steam-powered, G, A $375.00
Loco & Tender, #253, bl-gr, rare, VG, A.....................$300.00
Loco & Tender, #254, orange, VG, A.........................$475.00
Loco & Tender, #256, orange, VG, A.........................$950.00
Loco & Tender, #260E loco & Vanderbilt tender, EX (EX box),
   A $900.00
Loco & Tender, #385, dk gunmetal, VG, A...............$1,000.00
Loco & Tender, #385E loco & #1835T tender, steam-powered,
   VG, A $300.00
Loco & Tender, #400, 2-tone bl w/wht stripe, G, A ...$1,400.00
Loco & Tender, #402E, VG, A..................................$500.00
Loco & Tender, #1511, steam-powered, VG $175.00
Loco & Tender, #1668 loco & #2689 tender, dk gray, VG, A .$175.00
Loco & Tender, #1835, steam-powered, VG, A $500.00
Set, #252 loco, #529 pullman cars (2), #530 observation car,
   terra cotta, rare, EX, A......................................$1,700.00
Set, #257 loco, #529 pullman cars (2), #530 observation car, blk
   loco w/gr & orange cars, NMIB, A $1,000.00
Set, #262 loco w/tender, #608 observation car, #607 pullman
   cars (2), gr w/blk roofs, EX, A $650.00
Set, #1523 loco, #601 passenger cars (2), #602 baggage car, dk
   gr, EX, A $300.00
Set, #8006 W Schranz & Bieber Co Special, #1664 loco,
   #2689W tender & 3 cars, G (G box), A.................$600.00

Set, Bild-A-Loco #381E, green, complete, NM, A, $6,500.00.

Set, armored tank & 2 boxcars, complete w/track, EX (EX box), A...$5,500.00

Set, Bild-A-Loco #4, unassembled, EX (EX box), A...$8,200.00

Set, Blue Streak, #249 loco w/tender, #617, #618, #619 cars, EX, A...$2,400.00

Set, City of Portland, #752 E loco, #753 coach, #754 observation car, VG (G boxes), A.................................$650.00

Set, Flying Yankee, #616 loco, #617 coaches (2) & #618 observation car, VG (VG box).....................................$475.00

Set, Lionel Jr, #1700 loco, #1701 coach, #1702 observation car, G, A...$1,000.00

Set, Northside Ltd, #253E loco, #607 pullmans (2), #608 observation car, VG, A...$525.00

Set, Rail Chief, #5344 loco, #700T tender, #792, #793 (2), #794 passenger cars, EX, A.................................$3,500.00

Set, Union Pacific, #636 loco, #637, #638 cars, 2-tone gr, VG, A...$4,400.00

MISCELLANEOUS

Bassett-Lowke, loco & tender, Princess Elizabeth #3301 & #2265, clockwork, EX, A.................................$450.00

Bing, accessory, crane, tin lattice tower w/hand-pnt box on end, mounted on wood base w/electric posts, 18½", VG, A ..$825.00

Bing, accessory, passenger station, litho tin w/electric light, 18½", VG, A...$175.00

Bing, accessory, train station, hand-pnt tin, 2 office houses w/central walkway, railed rooftop, 23" L, VG, A.....$525.00

Bing, accessory, 0 gauge station, emb tin, 15", EX, A.....$575.00

Bing, set, #5138 loco w/tender, #210 coaches (2), EX (EX box), A...$300.00

Carlisle & Finch, Railway Trolley #1, brass w/wood fr, complete w/track & ties, VG (G wooden box), A.............$2,700.00

Dorfan, set, #54 loco (metallic bl), observation car & Seattle pullman, VG (VG box), A.................................$1,000.00

Fandor, accessory, station, litho tin w/electric light, VG, A..$325.00

Girard, cars, #424, #425 & #426, 2-tone gr, EX (EX boxes), A.$2,000.00

Hafner, set, #1010 w/Pennsylvania Railroad caboose, EX (EX box), A...$300.00

Hafner, set, Century of Progress, clockwork, red & yel litho, G, A...$200.00

Hornby, accessory, #42330 platform crane, EX (EX box), A..$200.00

Hornby, accessory, Ripon station, litho tin, G, A..........$175.00

Ives, accessory, #307 dbl street lamp, VG, A.................$300.00

Ives, car, #52 Buffalo coach, VG, A.................$475.00

Ives, car, #66 tank car, red or gray, VG, ea.....................$250.00

Ives, car, #67 Pennsylvania Railroad caboose, VG, A....$375.00

Ives, car, Atlantic Coastline boxcar, litho tin, 6", VG, A..$175.00

Ives, car, Chicago & Great Western Corn Belt Route boxcar, litho tin, VG, A...$525.00

Ives, car, Chicago & Northwestern boxcar, litho tin, 6", VG, A...$250.00

Ives, car, MK&T boxcar, litho tin, 10", VG, A..............$500.00

Ives, car, Salt Lake Route boxcar, litho tin, 10", VG, A...$750.00

Ives, car, St Louis & San Francisco Automobiles boxcar, litho tin, 10", EX, A...$550.00

Ives, car, Union Pacific Furniture boxcar, litho tin, 10", EX, A .$475.00

Ives, loco & tender, #1100, clockwork, EX.....................$150.00

Ives, loco & tender, #1120R & NYC&HR tender, EX, A ..$1,000.00

Ives, loco & tender, #1122, VG, A.................................$600.00

Ives, loco & tender, #1125, VG, A.................................$250.00

Ives, loco & tender, #3200, electric, VG, A...................$825.00

Ives, loco & tender, #3217, maroon w/gold trim, VG, A..$325.00

Ives, loco & tender, #3238, gr w/red fr, electric, rare, EX, A ...$350.00

Ives, loco & tender, #3238, maroon-pnt CI, VG, A.......$450.00

Ives, set, #11, complete, EX, A.................................$1,100.00

Ives, set, #17 loco & tender w/3 passenger cars, VG, A .$225.00

Ives, set, #30 loco, #551 chair car & #550 baggage car, gr w/yel trim, EX, A...$450.00

Ives, set, #176 loco, Lehigh Valley RR tender, #7 Lehigh Valley passenger cars (2), 25", VG, A.................................$150.00

Ives, set, #258 loco w/3 cars, gr w/red nameplates, EX, A...$1,500.00

Ives, set, #258 loco w/3 passenger cars, tan w/maroon roofs, EX, A...$1,100.00

Ives, set, #1122 loco & tender, #135 & #136 passenger cars, red w/blk roofs, VG, A...$1,000.00

Ives, set, #3252 loco, #162 parlor car, #61 chair car & #60 baggage car, brn w/blk tops, EX, A.............................$550.00

Ives, set, #3258 loco, #552 parlor car & #551 chair car, gr w/red tops, EX, A...$350.00

Ives, set, #3260 loco w/2 passenger cars, orange, EX, A .$500.00

Ives, set, #32543 loco w/3 passenger cars, orange w/blk detail, VG, A...$500.00

Ives, set, #32553 loco w/3 passenger cars, bl & red, VG, A .$1,300.00

Ives, set, Empress Princess, EX (EX box), A................$6,000.00

Ives, set, Major Seagraves Special, complete, scarce, EX (EX box), A...$6,200.00

Ives, set, Miniature Railway System, roofs mk Harvard & Yale, complete w/catalog, EX (VG box), A...................$9,900.00

Ives, set, NYC&HR loco & 3 passenger cars, orange w/gr roofs, EX, A...$600.00

Ives, set, Wanamaker, EX, A.................................$2,000.00

Marklin, accessory, overhead rail crane, hand-pnt tin, complete w/track wheels, railing & ladder, 12½", NM, A...$1,300.00

Marklin, accessory, train station, hand-pnt tin, w/waiting room & telegraph office, ornate marquee on roof, 8", EX, A ..$650.00

Marklin, loco & tender, #12910, VG, A.........................$750.00

Marklin, loco & tender, steam-powered, blk w/red, gr & gold trim, 9", EX, A...$4,300.00

Marx, set, #M10000 loco w/4 cars, gr & cream, VG, A..$175.00

Marx, set, Red Mercury, loco & tender w/Cleveland coach & Detroit observation car, G, A.................................$250.00

Marx, set, #25020, #391 loco & NYC tender, 3 cars & Reading caboose, EX (EX box), A.................................$400.00

MTH, accessory, Hellgate bridge, early colors, EX, A $500.00

MTH, loco & tender, C&O H-8, steam-powered, test run, EX (EX box), A...$1,000.00

Weeden, set, Dart, steam-powered, complete w/track & ties, VG (VG wooden box), A.................................$2,300.00

Weeden, set, loco, tender & passenger coach, steam-powered, w/17 sections of track, VG (VG box), A..............$1,150.00

Williams, loco & tender, Camelback 4-6-0, 3-rail, MIB .$550.00

Williams, loco & tender, Pennsylvania Railroad E6S 4-4-2, MIB...$350.00

Williams, set, #4001 NYC Dreyfuss Hudson w/5 cars, EX (EX boxes), A...$550.00

Williams, set, Amtrak Amfleet, MIB $225.00
Williams, set, Pennsylvania Congressional GGI loco & 5 cars,
    M (EX boxes)...$650.00

Transformers

Made by the Hasbro Company, Transformers were introduced in the United States in 1984. Originally there were twenty-eight figures — eighteen cars known as Autobots and ten Decepticons, evil robots capable of becoming such things as a jet or a handgun. Eventually the line was expanded to more than two hundred different models. Some were remakes of earlier Japanese robots that had been produced by Takara in the 1970s. (These can be identified through color differences and in the case of the Diaclone series, the absence of the small driver or pilot figures.)

The story of the Transformers and their epic adventures were told through several different comic books and animated series as well as a highly successful movie. Their popularity was reflected internationally and eventually made its way back to Japan. There the American Transformer animated series was translated into Japanese and soon inspired several parallel series of the toys which were again produced by Takara. These new Transformers were sold in the U.S. until the line was discontinued in 1990.

A few years ago, Hasbro announced their plans to reintroduce the line with Transformers: Generation 2. Transformers once again had their own comic book, and the old animated series was brought back in a revamped format. So far, several new Transformers as well as recolored versions of the older ones have been released by Hasbro, and the size of the series continues to grow. Sustained interest in them has spawned a number of fan clubs with chapters worldwide.

Because Transformers came in a number of sizes, you'll find a wide range of pricing. Our values are for Transformers in unopened original boxes. One that has been opened or used is worth much less — about 25% to 75%, depending on whether it has all its parts (weapons, instruction book, tech specs, etc., and what its condition is — whether decals are applied well or if it is worn.

Advisor: David Kolodny-Nagy (K2).

Other Sources: H4, P3.

SERIES 1, 1984

Autobot Car, #TF1023, Sunstreak, yel Countach $100.00
Autobot Car, #TF1025, Bluestreak, silver Datsun $100.00
Autobot Car, #TF1027, Jazz, Porsche.............................$100.00
Autobot Car, #TF1029, Ratchet, ambulance....................$80.00
Autobot Car, #TF1031, Trailbreaker, camper $100.00
Autobot Car, #TF1033, red Countach, MIP...................$100.00
Autobot Car, #TF1035, Hound, jeep $100.00
Autobot Car, #TF1037, Mirage, Indy car $100.00
Autobot Car, #TF1039, Prowl, police car $100.00
Autobot Car, #TF1055, Camshaft, silver car, mail-in $40.00
Autobot Car, #TF1057, Downshift, wht car, mail-in, MIP ..$40.00
Autobot Car, #TF1059, Overdrive, red car, mail-in $40.00
Autobot Car, #TF1061, Powerdasher #1, jet, mail-in.......$20.00
Autobot Car, #TF1063, Powerdasher #2, car, mail-in $20.00

Autobot Car, #TF1063, Powerdasher #3, drill, mail-in $40.00
Case, #TF1069, Collector's Case $15.00
Case, #TF1071, Collector's Case, red 3-D version............$25.00
Cassette, #TF1017, Ravage & Rumble............................$40.00
Cassette, #TF1019, Frenzy & Lazerbeak.........................$40.00
Decepticon Communicator, #TF1049, Soundwave & Buzzsaw,
    tape player & gold condor $80.00
Decepticon Jet, #TF1045, Thundercracker, bl jet.............$70.00
Decepticon Jet, #TF1047, Skywarp, blk jet......................$70.00
Decepticon Leader, #TF1051, Megatron, Walther P-38...$190.00
Minicar, #TF1000, Bumblejumper (Bumblebee card) $40.00
Minicar, #TF1000, Bumblejumper (Cliffjumper card)......$40.00
Minicar, #TF1001, Bumblebee, yel VW Bug $35.00
Minicar, #TF1003, Bumblebee, red VW Bug $25.00
Minicar, #TF1007, Cliffjumper, yel race car $25.00
Minicar, #TF1009, Huffer, orange semi cab....................$20.00
Minicar, #TF1011, Windcharger, red Firebird $20.00
Minicar, #TF1013, Brawn, gr jeep $20.00
Minicar, #TF1015, Gears, bl truck $20.00

SERIES 2, 1985

Autobot Air Guardian, #TF1201, Jetfire, F-14 jet..........$140.00
Autobot Car, #TF1163, Skids, Le Car $100.00
Autobot Car, #TF1165, Red Alert, fire chief....................$70.00
Autobot Car, #TF1169, Hoist, tow truck $70.00
Autobot Car, #TF1171, Smokescreen, red, wht & bl Datsun
    S $80.00
Autobot Car, #TF1173, Inferno, fire engine $70.00
Autobot Car, #TF1175, Tracks, Corvette $80.00
Autobot Scientist, #TF1197, Perceptor, microscope $50.00
Constructicon, #TF1127, Bonecrusher (1), bulldozer.......$20.00
Constructicon, #TF1129, Scavenger (2), steam shovel $20.00
Constructicon, #TF1131, Scrapper (3), front-end loader .$20.00
Constructicon, #TF1135, Long Haul (5), dump truck......$50.00
Constructicon, #TF1135, Long Haul (5), dump truck......$20.00
Constructicon, #TF1137, Mixmaster (6), cement mixer ..$25.00
Constructicon, #TF1139, Devastator, construction gift set ..$200.00
Decepticon Jet, #TF1187, Ramjet $50.00
Decepticon Jet, #TF1189, Dirge $50.00

Decepticon Operations, #TF1203, Shockwave, $90.00.
(Photo courtesy David Kolodny-Nagy)

Deluxe Insecticon, #TF1155, Chop Shop, beetle $90.00
Deluxe Insecticon, #TF1157, Barrage $90.00
Deluxe Insecticon, #TF1161, Ransack, grasshopper $90.00
Deluxe Vehicle, #TF1193, Whirl, lt bl helicopter $70.00
Deluxe Vehicle, #TF1195, Roadster, off-road vehicle $60.00
Dinobot, #TF1177, Grimlock, Tyrannosaurus $60.00
Dinobot, #TF1179, Slag, Triceratops $60.00
Dinobot, #TF1181, Sludge, Brontosaurus $40.00
Insecticon, #TF1141, Kickback, grasshopper $25.00
Insecticon, #TF1143, Shrapnel, beetle........................$25.00
Insecticon, #TF1145, Bombshell, boll weevil $25.00
Jumpstarter, #TF1149, Topspin, spaceship.................$25.00
Minicar, #TF1102, Bumblebee, yel w/minispy $40.00
Minicar, #TF1103, Bumblebee, red VW bug $20.00
Minicar, #TF1104, Bumblebee, red w/minispy $30.00
Minicar, #TF1106, Cliffjumper, red w/minispy $30.00
Minicar, #TF1107, Cliffjumper, yel race car $20.00
Minicar, #TF1108, Cliffjumper, yel w/minispy $30.00
Minicar, #TF1109, Huffer, orange semi cab $20.00
Minicar, #TF1111, Windcharger, red Firebird $20.00
Minicar, #TF1112, Windcharger, w/minispy $30.00
Minicar, #TF1115, Gears, bl truck $30.00
Minicar, #TF1116, Gears, w/minispy $30.00
Minicar, #TF1117, Seaspray, hovercraft $20.00
Minicar, #TF1119, Powerglide, plane $15.00
Minicar, #TF1121, Warpath, tank $15.00
Minicar, #TF1123, Beachcomber, dune buggy.................$15.00
Minicar, #TF1125, Cosmos, spaceship $15.00
Triple Charger, #TF1151, Blitzwing, tank/plane $60.00
Triple Charger, #TF1153, Astrotrain, shuttle/train..........$60.00
Watch, #TF1207, Autoceptor, Kronoform watch car......$25.00
Watch, #TF1209, Deceptor, Kronoform, watch jet $25.00
Watch, #TF1211, Listen 'n Fun, w/tape & yel Cliffjumper..$35.00

SERIES 3, 1986

Aerialbot, #TF1265, Skydive (2), F-15 jet.......................$20.00
Aerialbot, #TF1267, Fireflight (3), Phantom jet $20.00
Aerialbot, #TF1271, Silverbolt (5), Concorde $50.00
Aerialbot, #TF1273, Superion, gift set.......................$200.00
Autobot Car, #TF1333, Blurr, futuristic car.....................$60.00
Autobot Car, #TF1335, Kup, pickup truck $70.00
Autobot Car, #TF1337, Hot Rod, red race car $200.00
Autobot City Commander, #TF1365, Ultra Magnus, car carrier..$70.00
Autobot City Commander, #TF1367, Reflector, Spectro, Viewfinder & Spyglass into camera, mail-in..............$60.00
Autobot City Commander, #TF1369, STARS Control Center, action cb, mail-in..$60.00
Battlecharger, #TF1311, Runamuch, Corvette.................$15.00
Battlecharger, #TF1313, Runabout, Trans Am................$15.00
Cassette, #TF1315, Ratbat & Frenzy, bat & bl robot........$30.00
Cassette, #TF1317, Rewind & Steeljaw, gold weapons, blk robot & lion..$20.00
Cassette, #TF1318, Rewing & Steeljaw, silver weapons, blk robot & lion..$25.00
Cassette, #TF1320, Ramhorn & Eject, gold weapons, rhino & gray robot $25.00

Combaticon, #TF1287, Brawl (1), tank $20.00
Combaticon, #TF1289, Swindle (2), jeep......................$20.00
Combaticon, #TF1293, Vortex (4), helicopter................$20.00
Combaticon, #TF1295, Onslaught (5), missile transport .$20.00
Combaticon, #TF1297, Bruticus, gift set $300.00
Combaticon, Blast Off (3), shuttle................................$20.00
Decepticon City Commander, #TF1363, Galvatron, laser cannon...$100.00
Heroes, #TF1329, Wreck-Car, futuristic motorcycle........$80.00
Jet, #TF1353, Scourge, hovercraft $60.00
Jet, #TF1355, Cyclonus Space Jet $60.00
Minicar, #TF1252, Wheelie, futuristic car....................$20.00
Minicar, #TF1253, Outback, brn jeep $15.00
Minicar, #TF1255, Tailgate, wht Firebird.....................$15.00
Minicar, #TF1257, Hubcap, yel race car......................$15.00
Minicar, #TF1259, Pipes, bl semi cab.........................$15.00
Motorized Autobot Space Shuttle Robot, #TF1359, Sky Lynz shuttle $90.00
Motorized Decepticon City/Battle Station, #TF1357, Trypticon, dinosaur w/Brunt, robot tank & Full Tilt................$130.00
Predacon, #TF1341, Rampage (2), tiger.......................$60.00
Predacon, #TF1343, Divebomb (3), vulture $60.00
Predacon, #TF1345, Tantrum (4), bull $60.00
Predacon, #TF1347, Headstrong (5), rhino $60.00
Predacon, #TF1351, Gnaw, futuristic shark....................$50.00
Stunticon, #TF1275, Dead End (1), Porsche $15.00
Stunticon, #TF1277, Breakdown (2), Countach $15.00
Stunticon, #TF1279, Wildrider (3), Ferrari $15.00
Stunticon, #TF1281, Drag Strip (4), Indy car.................$15.00
Stunticon, #TF1283, Motormaster (5), tractor trailer $40.00
Stunticon, #TF1285, Menasor, gift set.........................$300.00
Triple Changer, #TF1321, Springer, armored car/helicopter .$80.00
Triple Changer, #TF1323, Sandstorm, dune buggy/helicopter $60.00
Triple Changer, #TF1325, Broadside, aircraft carrier/plane ..$60.00
Triple Changer, #TF1327, Octane, tanker truck/jumbo jet ..$55.00

SERIES 4, 1987

Cassette, #TF1441, Slugfest & Overkill, Stegosaurus & Tyrannosaurus $15.00
Clone, #TF1443, Pounce & Wingspan, puma & eagle.....$40.00
Clone, #TF1445, Fastlane & Cloudraker, dragster & spaceship $40.00
Double Spy, #TF1447, Punch-Counterpunch, Fiero $40.00
Duocon, #TF1437, Battletrap, jeep/helicopter................$40.00
Duocon, #TF1439, Flywheels, jet/tank............................$20.00
Headmaster Autobot, #TF1477, Chromedome w/Stylor, futuristic car $55.00
Headmaster Autobot, #TF1479, Hardhead w/Duros, tank .$40.00
Headmaster Autobot, #TF1481, Highbrow w/Gort, helicopter...$40.00
Headmaster Base, #TF1497, Scorponok w/Lord Zarak & Fasttrack, scorpion, mini-tank..$80.00
Headmaster Base, #TF1499, Fortress Maximus w/Cerebros & Spike, Gasket, Grommet, battle station/city...........$350.00
Headmaster Decepticon, #TF1487, Mindwipe w/Vorath, bat...$35.00

Headmaster Decepticon, #TF1489, Weirdwolf w/Monzo, wolf....$35.00

Headmaster Horrorcon, #TF1493, Snapdragon w/Krunk, jet/dinosaur $40.00

Monsterbot, #TF1461, Grotusque, tiger......................................$40.00

Monsterbot, #TF1463, Doublecross, 2-headed dragon......$40.00

Monsterbot, #TF1465, Repugnus, insect...............................$40.00

Sixchanger, #TF1495, Sixshot, starfighter jet, winged wolf, lazer pistol, armored carrier, tank......................$70.00

Targetmaster Autobot, #TF1449, Pointblank w/Peacemaker, race car & gun $30.00

Targetmaster Autobot, #TF1451, Sureshot w/Spoilsport, off-road buggy & gun $30.00

Targetmaster Autobot, #TF1453, Crosshairs w/Pinpointer, truck & gun $30.00

Targetmaster Autobot, #TF1455, Hot Rod & Firebolt, race car & gun $125.00

Targetmaster Autobot, #TF1459, Blurr w/Haywire, futuristic car & gun $60.00

Targetmaster Decepticon, #TF1469, Misfire w/Aimless, space-ship & gun $30.00

Targetmaster Decepticon, #TF1471, Slugslinger w/Caliburst, twin jet & gun $30.00

Targetmaster Decepticon, #TF1475, Scourge w/Fracas, hover-craft & gun $70.00

Technobot, #TF1425, Afterburner (1), motorcycle..........$15.00

Technobot, #TF1426, Afterburner, w/decoy.....................$20.00

Technobot, #TF1427, Nosecone (2), drill tank...............$15.00

Technobot, #TF1428, Nosecone, w/decoy........................$20.00

Technobot, #TF1429, Sate (3), fighter plane $15.00

Technobot, #TF1430, Stafe, w/decoy...............................$20.00

Technobot, #TF1431, Lightspeed (4), race car...............$15.00

Technobot, #TF1432, Lightspeed, w/decoy......................$20.00

Technobot, #TF1433, Scattershot (5), spaceship $40.00

Terrocon, #TF1413, Rippersnapper (1), lizard.................$10.00

Terrocon, #TF1414, Rippersnapper, w/decoy $15.00

Terrocon, #TF1415, Sinnertwin (2), 2-headed dog..........$10.00

Terrocon, #TF1416, Sinnertwin, w/decoy.........................$15.00

Terrocon, #TF1418, Cutthroat, w/decoy...........................$15.00

Terrocon, #TF1419, Blot (4), monster $10.00

Terrocon, #TF1417, Cutthroat (3), vulture.....................$10.00

Terrocon, #TF1420, Blot, w/decoy.....................................$15.00

Terrocon, #TF1421, Hun-grr (5), 2-headed dragon..........$30.00

Terrocon, #TF1423, Abominus, gift set...............................$70.00

Throttlebot, #TF1401, Goldbug, VW bug $10.00

Throttlebot, #TF1403, Freeway, Corvette $10.00

Throttlebot, #TF1404, Freeway, w/decoy $15.00

Throttlebot, #TF1405, Chase, Ferrari $10.00

Throttlebot, #TF1406, Chase, w/decoy...............................$15.00

Throttlebot, #TF1407, Wideload, dump truck..................$10.00

Throttlebot, #TF1408, Wideload, w/decoy.......................$15.00

Throttlebot, #TF1409, Rollbar, jeep $10.00

Throttlebot, #TF1410, Rollbar, w/decoy............................$15.00

Throttlebot, #TF1411, Searchlight, race car....................$10.00

Throttlebot, #TF1412, Searchlight, w/decoy $15.00

SERIES 5, 1988

Cassette, #TF1539, Squawkalk & Beastbox, hawk & gorilla..$15.00

Cassette, #TF1541, Grand Slam & Raindance, tank & jet $15.00

Firecon, #TF1507, Cindersaur, dinosaur $10.00

Firecon, #TF1509, Flamefeather, monster bird $10.00

Firecon, #TF1561, Sparkstalker, monster.........................$10.00

Headmaster Autobot, #TF1555, Hosehead w/Lug, fire engine...$30.00

Headmaster Autobot, #TF1559, Nightbeat w/Muzzle, race car..$25.00

Headmaster Decepticon, #TF1561, Horri-Bull w/Kreb, bull.$25.00

Headmaster Decepticon, #TF1563, Fangry w/Brisko, winged wolf..$25.00

Headmaster Decepticon, #TF1565, Squeezeplay w/Lokos, crab.$25.00

Powermaster Autobot, #TF1567, Getaway w/Rev, MR2 ..$35.00

Powermaster Autobot, #TF1569, Joyride w/Hotwire, off-road buggy $40.00

Powermaster Autobot, #TF2571, Slapdash w/Lube, Indy car ..$40.00

Powermaster Autobot Leader, #TF1617, Optimus Prime w/HiQ, tractor trailer $90.00

Powermaster Decepticon, #TF1575, Dreadwing w/Hi-Test, lt gray jet $40.00

Powermaster Mercenary, #TF1613, Doubledealer w/Knok (robot) & Skar (bat), missile launcher.......................$80.00

Pretender, #TF1577, Landmine, race car w/shell..............$60.00

Pretender, #TF1579, Cloudburst, jet w/shell....................$60.00

Pretender, #TF1581m Waverider, submarine w/shell.......$40.00

Pretender, #TF1583, Skullgrin, tank w/shell....................$40.00

Pretender, #TF1585, Bomb-burst, spaceship w/shell.........$60.00

Pretender, #TF1587, Submarauder, submarine w/shell.....$40.00

Pretender, #TF1589, Groundbreaker, race car w/shell......$40.00

Pretender, #TF1591, Sky High, jet w/shell $40.00

Pretender, #TF1593, Splashdown, sea skimmer w/shell....$40.00

Pretender, #TF1595, Iguanus, motorcycle w/shell $40.00

Pretender, #TF1599, Finback, sea skimmer w/shell $25.00

Pretender Beast, #TF1601, Chainclaw, bear w/shell........$30.00

Pretender Beast, #TF1603, Catilla, sabertooth tiger w/shell..$30.00

Pretender Beast, #TF1605, Carnivac, wolf w/shell $30.00

Pretender Beast, #TF1607, Snarler, boar w/shell $30.00

Pretender Vehicle, #TF1609, Gunrunner, red jet w/vehicle shell $40.00

Seacon, #TF1513, Overbit (1), shark..............................$15.00

Seacon, #TF1515, Seawing (2), manta ray $15.00

Seacon, #TF1517, Nautilator (3), lobster.........................$15.00

Seacon, #TF1519, Skalor (4), fish...................................$15.00

Seacon, #TF1521, Tentakil (5), squid...............................$15.00

Seacon, #TF1523, Snaptrap (6), turtle..............................$35.00

Seacon, #TF1525, Pirancon, gift set...............................$200.00

Sparkbot, #TF1501, Fizzle, off-road buggy......................$10.00

Sparkbot, #TF1505, Guzzle, tank $10.00

Targetmaster Autobot, #TF1543, Scoop w/Tracer & Holepunch, front-end loader & 2 guns....................$25.00

Targetmaster Autobot, #TF1545, Landfill w/Flintlock & Silencer, dump truck & 2 guns.....................$25.00

Targetmaster Decepticon, #TF1549, Quaker w/Tiptop & Heater, tank & 2 guns $20.00

Targetmaster Decepticon, #TF1553, Needlenose w/Sunbeam & Zigzag, jet & 2 guns.................................$20.00

Tiggerbot, #TF1527, Backstreet, race car.........................$15.00

Triggercon, #TF1533, Ruckus, dune buggy $15.00

Triggercon, #TF1535, Windsweeper, B-1 bomber $15.00

Triggercon, #TF1537, Crankcase, jeep..............................$15.00

Series 6, 1989

Legends, K-Mart Exclusive, #TF1727, Bumblebee, VW bug..$30.00

Legends, K-Mart Exclusive, #TF1729, Jazz Porsche $40.00

Legends, K-Mart Exclusive, #TF1731, Grimlock, dinosaur..$40.00

Legends, K-Mart Exclusive, #TF1733, Starscream, jet......$45.00

Mega Pretender, #TF1717, Vroom, dragster w/shell $35.00

Mega Pretender, #TF1719, Thunderwing, jet w/shell.......$35.00

Mega Pretender, #TF1721, Crossblades, helicopter w/shell ..$25.00

Micromaster Base, #TF1679, Skyhopper & Micromaster, helicopter & F-15..$50.00

Micromaster Base, #TF1681, Groundshaker & Micromaster, self-propelled cannon & stealth fighter.....................$35.00

Micromaster Base, #TF1735, Skystalker, Space Shuttle Base & Micromaster Porsche $55.00

Micromaster Base, #TF1737, Countdown, Rocket Base & Micromaster Lunar Rover......................................$60.00

Micromaster Patrol, #TF1651, Off-Road Series, 4 different, ea..$20.00

Micromaster Patrol, #TF1657, Sports Car Patrol Series, 4 different, ea...$20.00

Micromaster Patrol, #TF1661, Battle Patrol Series, 4 different, ea..$20.00

Micromaster Station, #TF1675, Ironworks, semi w/construction site...$20.00

Micromaster Transport, #TF1663, Overload, car carrier ..$15.00

Micromaster Transport, #TF1665, Flattop, aircraft carrier..$15.00

Micromaster Transport, #TF1667, Roughstuff, military transport $15.00

Pretender, #TF1697, Pincher, scorpion w/shell $20.00

Pretender, #TF1699, Longhtooth, hovercraft w/shell.......$20.00

Pretender, #TF1701, Stranglehold, rhino w/shell $20.00

Pretender, #TF1705, Bludgeon, tank w/shell $30.00

Pretender, #TF1707, Doubleheader, twin jet w/shell........$20.00

Pretender Classic, #TF1709, Bumblebee, VW bug w/shell ..$40.00

Pretender Classic, #TF1711, Grimlock, dinosaur w/shell .$40.00

Pretender Classic, #TF1713, Starscream, jet w/shell.........$40.00

Pretender Classic, #TF1715, Jazz, Porsche w/shell $40.00

Pretender Monster, #TF1683, Icepick (1) $12.00

Pretender Monster, #TF1687, Wildfly (3), ...$12.00

Pretender Monster, #TF1695, Monstructor, gift set, not produced $1,000.00

Ultra Pretender, #TF1725, Roadblock, tank w/figure & vehicle.$40.00

Ultra Pretender, #TF1727, Skyhammer, race car w/figure & vehicle...$40.00

Series 7, 1990

Action Master, #TF1781, Soundwave: Soundwave (bat), Wingthing..$15.00

Action Master, #TF1785, Grimlock: Grimlock, Anti-Tank Cannon (tank gun)..$15.00

Action Master, #TF1789, Rad: Rad, Lionizer (lion).........$15.00

Action Master, #TF1793, Devastator: Devastator, Scorpulator (scorpion)..$15.00

Action Master, #TF1799, Blaster: Blaster, Flight-Pack (jet pack) ..$15.00

Action Master, #TF1809, Inferno: Inferno, Hydro-Pack (water laser backpack) $25.00

Action Master, #TF1817, Prowl: Prowl, Turbo Cycle $60.00

Action Master, #TF1821, Over-Run: Over-Run, Attack Copter..$40.00

Action Master, #TF1825, Wheeljack: Wheeljack, Turbo Racer $70.00

Action Master, #TF1829, Gutcruncher: Gutcruncher, Stratotronic Jet..$30.00

Action Master, #TF1833, Optimus Prime: Optimus Prime, Armored Convoy $80.00

Action Master, #TF1873, Skyfall: Skyfall, Top-Heavy Rhino..$20.00

Micromaster Combiner, #TF1763, Battle Swuad: Meltdown, Half-Track, Direct Hit, Power Punch, Fireshot & Vanguish $15.00

Micromaster Combiner, #TF1767, Metro Squad: Wheel Blaze, Road Burner, Oiler, Slide, Power Run & Strikedown..$15.00

Micromaster Combiner, #TF1771, Tanker Truck: Tanker Truck, Pipeline & Gusher...$15.00

Micromaster Combiner, #TF1775, Missile Launcher: Missile Launcher, Retro & Surge...$15.00

Micromaster Combiner, #TF1777, Anti-Aircraft Base: Anti-Aircraft Base, Blackout & Spaceshot.............................$15.00

Micromaster Patrol, #TF1755, Air Patrol: Thread Bolt, Eagle Eye, Sky High & Blaze Master....................................$10.00

Micromaster Patrol, #TF1759, Hot Rod Patrol, Big Daddy, Trip-Up, Greaser & Hubs..$10.00

Micromaster Patrol, #TF1761, Military Patrol: Bombshock, Tracer, Dropshot & Growl $10.00

Generation 2, Series 1, 1992 – 93

Autobot Car, #TF1863, Jazz, Porsche...............................$25.00

Autobot Car, #TF1867, Inferno, fire truck $25.00

Autobot Leader, #TF1879, Optimus Prime w/Roller, tractor trailer w/electronic sound-effect box $35.00

Autobot Minicar, #TF1881, Bumble, metallic VW bug ...$30.00

Autobot Minicar, #TF1883, Hubcap, metallic..................$20.00

Autobot Minicar, #TF1887, Seaspray, metallic hovercraft ..$15.00

Autobot Obliterator (Europe only), Spark.......................$45.00

Color Change Transformer, #TF1905, Deluge.................$15.00

Color Change Transformer, #TF1911, Gobots $15.00

Constructicon (orange version), #TF1851, Bonecrusher (1), bulldozer..$7.00

Constructicon (orange version), #TF1855, Scrapper (3), front-end loader..$7.00

Constructicon (yel version), #TF1851, Bonecrusher (1), bulldozer $6.00

Constructicon (yel version), #TF1855, Scrapper (3), front-end loader..$6.00

Decepticon Abliterator (Europe only), Colossus $45.00

Decepticon Jet, #TF1875, Starscream, gray jet w/electronic light & sound-effect box $30.00

Dinobot, #TF1869, Grimlock, bl Tyrannosaurus $25.00

Dinobot, #TF1870, Grimlock, turq Tyrannosaurus $50.00

Dinobot, #TF1873, Snarl, orig gray Stegosaurus $30.00

Dinobot, #TF1873, Snarl, red Stegosaurus........................$25.00

Small Autobot Car, #TF1899, Skram.................................$8.00

Small Autobot Car, #TF1903, Turbofire.............................$8.00

Small Decepticon Jet, #TF1889, Afterburner $8.00

Small Decepticon Jet, #TF1893, Terradive $8.00

Small Decepticon Jet, #TF1895, Windrazor......................$8.00

Generation 2, Series 2, 1994

Aerialbot, #TF1915, Skydive (1), F-15 ....$7.00
Aerialbot, #TF1919, Firefight (3), Phantom.......................$7.00
Aerialbot, #TF1923, Silverbolt (5), Concorde $18.00
Combaticon, #TF1927, Brawl (1), tank $7.00
Combaticon, #TF1931, Blast Off (3), shuttle $7.00
Combaticon, #TF1935, Onslaught (5), missile transport .$18.00
Heroes, #TF1953, Autobat Hero Optimus Prime, M (Japanese
    box)...$35.00
Heroes, #TF1953, Autobot Hero Optimus Prime $20.00
Heroes, #TF1955, Decepticon Hero Megatron.................$20.00
Laser Rod Transformer, #TF1937, Electro $15.00
Laser Rod Transformer, #TF1937, Electro, M (Japanese box) .$20.00
Laser Rod Transformer, #TF1941, Jolt.............................$15.00
Laser Rod Transformer, #TF1941, Jolt, M (Japanese box) ..$20.00
Rotor Force, #TF1945, Leadfoot......................................$7.00
Rotor Force, #TF1951, Ransack.......................................$7.00
Stunticon, BotCon '94 Exclusive, #TF1925, Breakdown (2),
    Countach $100.00
Watch, #TF1957, Superion $12.00
Watch, #TF1961, Ultra Magnus..$12.00
Watch, #TF1965, Scorpia..$12.00

Bootleg/Unlicensed Transformers

Action Master Blue Streak w/Action Master Optimus Prime's
    Vehicle, K2 ....$30.00
Action Master Jazz, gray & purple or gray & ultramarine bl, K2,
    ea $5.00
Action Master Rad, orange & purple, K2...........................$5.00
Blitzwing, plastic, K2..$6.00
Dai-Atlas (Dai-Atris), same as orig Japanese toy except for
    recolored stickers, battery-op, K2 ....$25.00
Dino King, oversized version from Victory series, K2 ....$25.00
Generation 3 Inferno, plastic, yel arms & legs, K2..............$6.00
Gumball Transformer Models, Japanese, set of 4, very rare, MIP,
    K2 ....$30.00
G2 Combaticon Blast-Off, giant size, K2 ....$10.00
Mini Max, sm version of Fortress Maximus, spike forms head, 7",
    K2 ....$15.00
Power Master Decepticon Jet, different colors than orig, K2 ..$15.00
Sky Garry, remake of robot from Star Convoy series, no micro-
    masters or shuttles, K2 ....$10.00
Star Saber, Brainmaster from Japanese Victory series, no com-
    ponets to form super robot, K2 ....$15.00
Superion, lg firearm, gold helmet, 13", K2 ....$25.00
Transformer Landross, Japanese remake, K2 ....$15.00

Trolls

The first trolls to come to the United States were modeled after a 1952 design by Marti and Helena Kuuskoski of Tampere, Finland. The first trolls to be mass produced in America were molded from wood carvings made by Thomas Dam of Denmark. As the demand for these trolls increased, several US manufacturers were licensed to produce them. The most noteworthy of these were Uneeda Doll Company's Wishnik line and Inga Scandia House True Trolls. Thomas Dam continued to import his Dam Things line. Today trolls are enjoying a renaissance as baby boomers try to recapture their childhood. As a result, values are rising.

The troll craze from the '60s spawned many items other than just dolls such as wall plaques, salt and pepper shakers, pins, squirt guns, rings, clay trolls, lamps, Halloween costumes, animals, lawn ornaments, coat racks, notebooks, folders, and even a car.

In the '70s, '80s, and '90s, new trolls were produced. While these trolls are collectible to some, the avid troll collector still prefers those produced in the '60s. Remember, trolls must be in mint condition to receive top dollar.

For more information, we recommend *Collector's Guide to Trolls* by Pat Petersen.

Advisor: Pat Peterson (P1).

Astronaut, Dam, 1964, 11", EX...............................$125.00
Astronorf, Dam, 1977, silver suit w/transparent face mask,
    orange hair, amber eyes, 9¾", NM $45.00
Ballerina, Dam, bright red hair, gr eyes, MIP $55.00
Batman, Uneeda Wishnik, 1966, orig felt outfit, 6", NM,
    T2 ....$100.00
Blue Troll w/Fangs, mk Made in Hong Kong, wht hair, amber
    eyes, 3", NM..$20.00
Boy w/Guitar, Norwegian, Nyform, pnt-on clothes, brn hair, bl
    eyes, 6", NM..$50.00
Bride-Nik, Uneeda Wishnik, 1980s reissue, orig gown & veil,
    red hair, amber eyes, 6", NM $20.00
Caveman, Dam, 1964, felt outfit, yel hair, gr eyes, 12", NM,
    from $135 to $155.00
Cheerleader, Dam, 1964, pnt-on clothes, several variations,
    2½", NM, ea $20.00
Clown, Dam, 1965, pnt-on clothes, yel eyes & red nose, 5½",
    NM, from $175 to..$250.00
Cook-Nik, Uneeda Wishnik, bendable, orig outfit, bl hair, brn
    eyes, 5", EX $20.00
Cotton Hair Troll, Dam, redressed in denim shorts & red ban-
    dana, red eyes, 12", NM...$80.00
Cowboy, Dam, felt outfit & holster w/metal six-shooters, bl hair
    & eyes, 7", NM $50.00
Doll-Faced Troll, Uneeda Wishnik, red & wht petal-shaped
    dress, red hair, pnt eyes, 7", NM...............................$20.00
Donkey, Dam, 1964, blond hair, amber eyes, 3", NM.......$35.00
Eskimo, Dam, 1965, red & wht pnt-on clothes, brn hair & eyes,
    5½", EX $75.00
Fire Chief, Treasure Trolls, bl hair & eyes, 4", M $12.00
Girl, Dam, yel felt jumper & wht shirt, yel hair, brn eyes, 7",
    NM...$50.00
Girl w/Accordion, Norwegian, Nyform, pnt-on clothes, brn hair,
    amber eyes, 6", NM..$50.00
Good Luck-Nik, Uneeda Wishnik, 1970s, M (orig tube) .$30.00
Good Night-Nik, Uneeda Wishnik, orig yel felt nightshirt, pk
    hair, amber eyes, 5", NM $20.00
Grandpa Claus, Dam, 1977, orig outfit, wht hair, brn eyes, 14",
    EX, from $100 to $125.00
Greek Soldier, Russ, silver costume w/shield & cap, yel hair, brn
    eyes, 4", NM...$15.00

Hairstylist, Russ, shirt mk #1 Hairstylist, pk hair, brn eyes, 4", M $12.00

Here Come the Judge, Uneeda Wishnik, orig outfit, orange hair, gold eyes, 6", NM $50.00

Horned Troll, Norwegian, gray rabbit fur glued to body w/red plastic heart necklace, w/suction cup, 4", NM $40.00

Horse, Dam, 1960s, red hair, amber eyes, NM $40.00

Hula-Nik, Uneeda Wishnik, purple rooted skirt, orange hair (faded), yel eyes, 5", EX $30.00

Hunt-Nik, Uneeda Wishnik, orig outfit, red hair, amber eyes, complete w/rifle, NM (orig container) $25.00

Iggy-Normous, Dam, 1964-65, wht sailor-style suit w/blk tie, blond hair, amber eyes, 12", EX, from $150 to........$175.00

Indian, Dam, felt outfit w/yel feather in blk hair, gr eyes, 7", NM $50.00

Lion, Dam, 1960s, wht mane & tail, amber eyes, 5", NM, from $125 to $150.00

Little Red Riding Hood, Russ Storybook series, bl hair, complete w/basket, 4½", NM $15.00

Lucky Nik, nodder, mk Japan, 1967, red hair, brn eyes, 5", NM.$40.00

Luv You-Nik, Uneeda Wishnik, 1980s reissue, orig outfit, red hair, amber eyes, 5", M $20.00

Mama-She-Nik, Uneeda Wishnik, yel felt dress w/gr heart design, gr ribbon in wht hair, amber eyes, 5", EX $25.00

Miss America, unmk, wht satin & net gown, pearl tiara, wht hair, amber eyes, 3", EX $25.00

Neanderthal Man, Bijou Toy Inc, 1963, leopard skin outfit, blond hair, brn eyes, 7½", NM $40.00

Norfin Boy, Dam, 1979, purple pants & bl shirt, orange hair, amber eyes, fully jtd, 18", NM $65.00

Norfin Bride, Dam, 1977, orig gown & veil, blk hair, brn eyes, 9¾", NM $40.00

Norfin Exercise Girl, Dam, 1977, bl outfit, wht hair, amber eyes, 9¾", NM $35.00

Norfin Fan Club Troll, Thomas Norfin by Dam, bl & wht outfit w/gray & red cap, M $40.00

Norfin Girl, Dam, 1979, purple dress w/wht leotards & hair bow, orange hair, amber eyes, fully jtd, 18", NM $65.00

Norfin Groom, Dam, 1977, orig tuxedo, wht hair, brn eyes, 9¾", NM $40.00

Norfin Sea P'Troll, Dam, 1977, bl & wht sailor suit, blk hair, brn eyes, 9¾", NM $35.00

Norfin Seal, Dam, 1984, amber eyes, 6½", NM $50.00

Norfin Surgeon, Dam, 1977, gr surgical suit, wht hair, brn eyes, 9¾", NM $35.00

Norfin Turtle, Dam, 1984, amber eyes, 4", NM $50.00

Nursenik, Uneeda Wishnik, 1970s, 6", MOC $50.00

Ranch-Nik, Uneeda Wishnik, 1980s reissue, orig outfit, yel hair, amber eyes, 5", M $20.00

Robin Hood, Russ Storybook series, red hair, brn eyes, complete w/bow & arrow, 4½", NM $15.00

Rock-Nik, Uneeda Wishnik, bendable, orig outfit & guitar, gr hair, brn eyes, 5", EX $25.00

Rock'n Troller, Magical World of Trolls by Largo, 4 different, 3", M, ea $12.00

Scuba Diver, Treasure Trolls, yel hair & eyes, 4", M $15.00

Shekter, mk Made in USA, 1966, wht lace diaper w/bl ribbons, wht hair, amber eyes, 3", NM $40.00

Sock-It-To-Me, Uneeda Wishnik, orig outfit, wht hair, amber eyes, 6", NM $50.00

Superman, Uneeda Wishnik, felt costume w/stretch fabric cape, wht hair, amber eyes, 5", EX $75.00

Tartan Girl, Dam, 1964, orig outfit w/matching ribbons in blk hair, amber eyes, 12", M, from $145 to $165.00

Troll Baby, Dam, 1974, wht shirt w/bl trim, blond hair, brn eyes, 10", NM, from $55 to $65.00

Uglie Elephant, mk Made in Japan, bl-pnt bodies, blk rabbit fur hair, amber eyes, 3½", NM $25.00

Uglie Giraffe, mk Made in Hong Kong, blk hair, amber eyes, NM $25.00

Viking, Norwegian, gray felt tunic w/gr cloak, brn rabbit fur hair & beard, bl eyes, 7", NM $80.00

Viking Dam, 1967, wht felt dress w/bl belt, wht hair, brn eyes, 5½", NM, from $150 to $200.00

Wizard, Treasure Trolls, lt purple hair, bl eyes, 4", M.......$15.00

MISCELLANEOUS

Bank, caveman, Creative Mfg Co, 1978, molded-on clothes, 8½", NM $35.00

Bank, cowgirl, Creative Mfg Inc, 1978, molded-on clothes, pk hair, amber eyes, 8½", NM $35.00

Bank, girl in raincoat, Dam, orange hair, bl eyes, 7", NM $50.00

Bank, Hobo, Royalty Designs, 1967, hard plastic w/felt clothes, orange hair, 8", EX, from $40 to $50.00

Bank, Santa, Dam, 1960s, hard plastic w/felt clothes, 8", rare, H4 ....$45.00

Carrying Case, Ideal, w/molded waterfall, M $25.00

Outfit, any style, MIP, ea $15.00

Pillow, Treasure Trolls Surf Patrol, 14x14", NM $10.00

Pin, Patty O'Troll, Russ, 3", MOC $5.00

Playhouse, Wishnik Mini Trolls, Ideal, 1960s, EX $25.00

Ring, several variations, EX, ea $3.00

Troll Village, EX (EX box), H4 ....$175.00

Valentine Kit, Mello Smello, complete, MIB $8.00

Wristwatch, Treasure Trolls, several variations, MOC, ea $5.00

Pirates, Dam, felt clothing, red hair, green eyes, 7", NM, $55.00 each. (Photo courtesy Pat Peterson)

View-Master and Tru-Vue

View-Master, the invention of William Gruber, was introduced to the public at the 1939–1940 New York World's Fair and the Golden Gate Exposition in California. Since then, View-Master reels, packets, and viewers have been produced by five different companies — the original Sawyers Company, G.A.F (1966), View-Master International (1981), Ideal Toys, and Tyco Toys (the present owners). Because none of the non-cartoon single reels and three-reel packets have been made since 1980, these have become collectors' items. Also highly sought after are the three-reel sets featuring popular TV and cartoon characters. The market is divided between those who simply collect View-Master as a field all its own and collectors of character-related memorabilia who will often pay much higher prices for reels about Barbie, Batman, The Addams Family, etc. Our values tend to follow the more conservative approach.

The first single reels were dark blue with a gold sticker and came in attractive gold-colored envelopes. They appeared to have handwritten letters. These were followed by tan reels with a blue circular stamp. Because these were produced for the most part after 1945 and paper supplies were short during WWII, they came in a variety of front and back color combinations, tan with blue, tan with white, and some were marbleized. Since print runs were low during the war, these early singles are much more desirable than the printed white ones that were produced by the millions from 1946 until 1957. Three-reel packets, many containing story books, were introduced in 1955, and single reels were phased out. Nearly all viewers are very common and have little value except for the very early ones, such as the Model A and Model B. Blue and brown versions of the Model B are especially rare. Another desirable viewer, unique in that it is the only focusing model ever made, is the Model D. For more information we recommend *View-Master Single Reels, Volume I*, by Roger Nazeley. Note: though the market was down by a substantial percentage at one point, it appears to have recovered, and prices are now fairly stable.

Advisor: Roger Nazeley (N4).
Other Sources: C1, P3.

Adventures of GI Joe, B-585, MIP, B10............................$35.00
Adventures of Tarzan, #975, M, B10..................................$10.00
Airplanes of the World, B-773, MIP, B10.........................$15.00
Alice in Wonderland, B-360, MIP, B10..............................$15.00
Amazing Spider-Man, H-11, MIP (sealed), B10..............$25.00
America's Man in Space, B-657, MIP (sealed), B10.........$20.00
Apollo Moon Landing, B-663, MIP, B10............................$15.00
Apple's Way, B-558, MIP (sealed), B10.............................$25.00
Archie, B-574, 1975, MIP (sealed)......................................$15.00
Aristocats, B-365, 1970, MIP, B10......................................$10.00
Bambi, B-400, MIP (sealed), B10.......................................$20.00
Banana Splits, 1970, MIP..$40.00
Barbie's Around the World Trip, B-500, MIP, B10..........$35.00
Batman, B-492, 1966, MIP, B10..$35.00
Batman (Cartoon), 1003, MIP (sealed), B10.....................$8.00
Batman Forever, 4160, MIP (sealed), B10........................$10.00

Bazooka Joe, B-563, MIP, B10..$15.00
Beetlejuice, 1074, M, B10..$8.00
Beverly Hillbillies, B-570, 1963, MIP...............................$45.00
Big Blue Marble, B-587, 1976, MIP (sealed), B10...........$25.00
Black Hole, K-35, MIP (sealed), B10.................................$30.00
Bonanza, B-471, 1964, 1st issue, MIP (sealed).................$40.00
Brady Bunch Grand Canyon Adventure, TS-015, 1971, MIP, C1..$75.00
Buck Rogers in the 25th Century, J-1, 1978, MIP...........$10.00
Bugs Bunny in Big Top Bunny, B-549, MIP, B10............$20.00
Cabbage Patch Kids, 1042, MIP, B10.................................$10.00
Captain America, H-43, MIP (sealed), B10.......................$30.00
Casper's Ghostland, B-545, MIP (sealed), B10.................$25.00
Cat From Outer Space, J-22, MIP (sealed), B10...............$20.00
Catwoman's Perfect Crime, 1966, MIP, H4.......................$40.00
Charlotte's Web, B-321, MIP, B10.....................................$15.00
Children's Zoo, B-617, MIP (sealed), B10.........................$15.00
Chip 'N Dale, 3075, MIP, B10..$10.00
CHiPs, L-14, 1980, MIP..$20.00
Christmas Story, B-282, MIP (sealed), B10.......................$20.00
Cinderella, B-313, 1953, MIP..$15.00
City Beneath the Sea, B-496, MIP, B10.............................$30.00
Daffy Duck, 1009, MIP, B10..$15.00
Daktari, B-498, MIP (sealed), B10.....................................$45.00
Davy Crockett, 1950s, MIP, A..$45.00
Dennis the Menace, B-539, MIP (sealed), B10.................$25.00
Dick Tracy (Movie), 4105, MIP (sealed), B10..................$12.00
Disney World Liberty Square, A-950, MIP (sealed), B10.$20.00
Donald Duck, B-525, 1957, MIP, B10................................$15.00
Dr Shrinker & Wonderbug, H-2, MIP, B10.......................$25.00
Eight Is Enough, K-76, 1980, MIP......................................$25.00
Family Affair, B-571, 1969, MIP..$40.00
Fantastic Voyage, B-546, MIP..$10.00
Fat Albert & the Cosby Kids, B-544, 1974, MIP..............$8.00
Fievel Goes West, 411, MIP, B10.......................................$10.00
Flash Gordon, B-583, MIP (sealed), B10...........................$20.00
Flintstones, B-514, 1962, MIP (sealed), B10.....................$20.00

Happy Days, J-13, 1978, MIP, $15.00.
(Photo courtesy Greg Davis and Bill Morgan)

Flipper, B-485, MIP, B10.................................$35.00
Flipper (Movie), 4162, MIP............................$10.00
Flying Nun, #B-495, 1967, MIP.......................$35.00
Godzilla, J-23, MIP (sealed), B10....................$20.00
Goldilocks & the Three Bears, B-317, MIP (sealed), B10..$25.00
Green Hornet, B-488, 1966, MIP.....................$75.00
Gunsmoke, Showtime & the Rat Trap, 1972, MIP (sealed), A...$25.00
Happy Days, #B-586, 1974, MIP.....................$20.00
Hardy Boys, B-547, MIP, B10.........................$20.00
Hare & the Tortoise, B-309, MIP (sealed), B10....$20.00
Hawaii Five-O, B-590, MIP (sealed), B10..........$30.00
Holly Hobbie, B-344, MIP (sealed), B10...........$20.00
Huckleberry Hound & Yogi Bear, MIP..............$20.00
Hugga Bunch, 1047, MIP, B10........................$10.00
Jetsons, L-27, 1981, MIP.................................$5.00
John Travolta, K-79, MIP, B10........................$15.00
Jungle Book, B-363, MIP, B10........................$15.00
King Kong, B-392, 1976, MIP (sealed), B10......$25.00
KISS, 1970s, MIP (sealed), A..........................$25.00
Kung Fu, B-598, 1974, MIP............................$20.00
Land of the Giants, B-494, 1968, MIP..............$60.00
Lassie Rides the Log Flume, B-489, 1968, MIP, B10........$15.00
Love Bug, B-501, 1968, MIP (sealed), B10.......$25.00
Man From UNCLE, Very Important Zombie Affair, 1960s, MIP...$75.00
Mickey Mouse, B-528, 1958, MIP....................$20.00
Mighty Mouse, B-526, 1968, MIP, B10............$20.00
Million Dollar Duck, B-506, MIP (sealed), B10....$30.00
Monkees, B-493, 1967, MIP...........................$35.00
Movie Stars, 1950, EX, A................................$25.00
Muppet Movie, K-27, MIP (sealed), B10..........$20.00
Nanny & the Professor, B-573, 1970, MIP.........$45.00
New Zoo Revue, #B567, 1974, MIP (sealed).....$20.00
Partridge Family, B-571, 1971, MIP................$35.00
Peanuts, B-536, MIP (sealed), B10..................$15.00
Pink Panther, J-12, 1978, MIP, B10................$15.00
Pinocchio, B-311, MIP, B10...........................$15.00
Popeye, B-516, 1962, MIP, B10......................$12.00
Puss in Boots, B-320, MIP, B10......................$12.00
Quick Draw McGraw, B-534, 1961, MIP...........$20.00
Raggedy Ann & Raggedy Andy, 1971, MIP.......$25.00
Ren & Stempy, 1084, MIP (sealed), B10...........$8.00
Rescuers, H-26, MIP......................................$15.00
Return From Witch Mountain, J-25, MIP (sealed), B10..$20.00
Roadrunner, B-538, MIP, B10........................$15.00
Robin Hood, B-342, MIP (sealed), B10............$25.00
Rocky & Bullwinkle, B-515, MIP, B10.............$15.00
Rookies, BB-452, MIP (sealed), B10................$30.00
Roy Rogers in Adventure Round-Up, 1956, NMIP, A.....$50.00
Rudolph the Red-Nosed Reindeer, B-870, MIP (sealed), B10..$15.00
Seven Wonders of the World, B-901, MIP, B10...............$10.00
Shaggy DA, B-368, 1976, MIP, B10.................$20.00
Six Million Dollar Man, AVB-559, MIP.............$20.00
Sleeping Beauty, B-308, 1959, MIP..................$15.00
Snoopy & the Red Baron, B-544, MIP (sealed), B10.......$20.00
Superman Meets Computer Crook, B-584, MIP (sealed), B10..$30.00
Television Stars, 1950s, NM, A........................$25.00

Treasure Island, BB-432, MIP (sealed), B10.....$25.00
Village People, 1980, MIP..............................$15.00
Welcome Back Kotter, J-19, MIP (sealed), B10....$25.00
Who Framed Roger Rabbit, K-37, 1979, MIP....$35.00
Winnie the Pooh, B-362, MIP, B10.................$15.00
Wizard of Oz, B-361, MIP, B10......................$15.00
World of Liddle Kiddles, #B-577, 1970, MIP.....$75.00
Zorro, B-469, 1958, MIP (sealed), B10............$45.00
101 Dalmatians, B-532, 1961, MIP, B10...........$12.00
20,000 Leagues Under the Sea, B-370, 1954, MIP (sealed), B10......................................$25.00

Western

No friend was ever more true, no brother more faithful, no acquaintance more real to us than our favorite cowboys of radio, TV, and the silver screen. They were upright, strictly moral, extrememly polite, and tireless in their pursuit of law and order in the American West. How unfortunate that such role models are practically extinct nowadays.

This is an area of strong collector interest right now, and prices are escalating. For more information and some wonderful pictures, we recommend *Character Toys and Collectibles, First* and *Second Series*, by David Longest and *Guide to Cowboy Character Collectibles* by Ted Hake. Other publications include *The Lone Ranger* by Lee Felbinger and *The W.F. Cody Buffalo Bill Collector's Guide* by James W. Wojtowicz. With the expection of Hake's, all are published by Collector Books.

Advisors: Donna and Ron Donnelly (D7).

See also Advertising Signs, Ads, and Displays; Books; Cereal Boxes; Character and Promotional Drinking Glasses; Character Clocks and Watches; Coloring, Activity, and Paint Books; Guns; Lunch Boxes; Premiums; Windups, Friction, and Other Mechanicals.

Annie Oakley, outfit, Pla-Master, 1950, red blouse & fringed skirt w/silkscreen of Annie on pockets, NMIB........$200.00
Bat Masterson, cane, 1958, plastic w/chrome cover, NM.$35.00
Bat Masterson, holster set w/cane & vest, Carnell, 1958, no gun, NMIB, J2..$225.00
Bat Masterson, wallet, Croyder, 1950s, NMIB, A............$75.00
Bonanza, Stardust Touch of Velvet Art, Hasbro, complete, NMIB, J2...$85.00
Buffalo Bill, outfit, Leslie-Henry, 1954, 3 pcs, NM (G box), A...$75.00
Cisco Kid, hobbyhorse, vinyl w/wood hdl, VG..............$50.00
Dale Evans, outfit, Yankeeboy, w/skirt, vest, blouse & holster, EX (EX box)..$300.00
Daniel Boone, Fess Parker Cartoon Kit, Colorforms, 1964, complete, MIB...$35.00
Davy Crockett, belt, England, elastic, w/punch-out stand-up photo, EX (EX card), A..$65.00
Davy Crockett, boots, 1950s, leather w/yel lettering on suede fringe, Davy pictured on side, EX, A......................$250.00
Davy Crockett, Camera Ensemble, Herbert-George, complete w/camera, flash attachment & bulbs, scarce, NM (EX box)......$400.00

Davy Crockett, charm bracelet, 1950s, gold-colored metal w/7 charms, NM, P4 ....$35.00

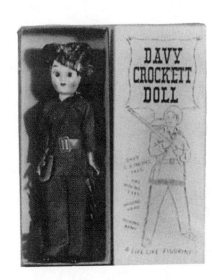

Davy Crockett, doll, plastic with hand-painted features, cloth clothes, movable head and arms, 8", NM (NM box), $150.00.

Davy Crockett, guitar, Peter Puppet/WDP, fiberboard w/decal, complete w/pick & song book, 25", EX (EX box)....$200.00

Davy Crockett, hobbyhorse, wood w/heavy bouncing springs, 23x33", EX $175.00

Davy Crockett, ring, 1960s, from gumball machine, F1 ...$15.00

Davy Crockett, sunglasses, 1950s, wht plastic w/gr lenses, w/rifles & image of Davy, EX, A $65.00

Davy Crockett, tool kit, Liberty Steel, 1955, litho tin chest complete w/tools & manual, 16", M, M17 ....$400.00

Davy Crockett, vest, 1950s, Davy w/musket on front & Davy fighting bear on bk, brn vinyl w/fringe, EX, M17 ....$100.00

Davy Crockett, wallet, 1950s, raised image of Davy in profile, EX, M17 ....$65.00

Gabby Hayes, sheriff's set, 1950s, unused, MOC, from $75 to.$100.00

Gabby Hayes, target set, EX (EX box) $195.00

Gene Autry, outfit, Leslie-Henry, 1940s, brn suede vest & chaps, red felt trim, w/images, NM (VG box), J5, from $200 to $300.00

Gunsmoke, outfit, Matt Dillon, Seneca, 1958, complete, EX (EX box) $125.00

Gunsmoke, pencil case, Hasbro, 1961, bl cb, features Matt Dillon, 4x9", EX, T2 ....$30.00

Hoot Gibson, shirt, 1930s, boy's plaid shirt w/Universal Jewel Ranch felt patch on pocket, VG+, A3 ....$150.00

Hopalong Cassidy, barette, unmk, silver-tone metal w/emb image of Hoppy, NM, C1 ....$25.00

Hopalong Cassidy, bicycle horn, w/handlebar clamp, NM...$135.00

Hopalong Cassidy, binoculars, mk Sports Glass Chicago, metal & plastic w/paper decals, EX $165.00

Hopalong Cassidy, drum, Rubbertone/Wm Boyd, 1950, 2 different images of Hoppy on drum tops, 5" dia, EX $225.00

Hopalong Cassidy, figure, chalkware, 14", NM...............$450.00

Hopalong Cassidy, film, Danger Trail, Castle Films, 1950s, 16mm, NM, P4 ....$30.00

Hopalong Cassidy, key chain w/TV viewer, Plastic Novelties, 1950, 1½", NM, A $75.00

Hopalong Cassidy, money clip, mk USA, silver w/photo flanked by name, 2", NM..$95.00

Hopalong Cassidy, necktie, Guck of Chicago, 1950s, child's, clips around neck, red w/image of Hoppy & Topper, 9", NM, A $125.00

Hopalong Cassidy, outfit, J Bard, 1950, blk pants w/red detail, blk & wht shirt w/red vinyl fringe, EX, A................$200.00

Hopalong Cassidy, pencil box, EX $135.00

Hopalong Cassidy, pennant, 1950s, image of Hoppy on Topper w/name lettered in rope effect, felt, 27", EX $95.00

Hopalong Cassidy, Picture Gun & Theater, Stephens, complete w/metal picture gun, theater & 2 slides, NM (EX box) $300.00

Hopalong Cassidy, sparkler, 1950s, plastic bust of Hoppy, push stem at bottom to produce sparks, 4", EX+, A.........$295.00

Hopalong Cassidy, spurs, metal w/name screened on leather, EX $195.00

Hopalong Cassidy, transfers, various images, 4 on sheet, 8x3", NM..$50.00

Lone Ranger, Action Arcade, 1975, NMIB, from $100 to..$125.00

Lone Ranger, bank, British, 1960s, vinyl boot-shape w/cartoon artwork of Lone Ranger on Silver, EX, A $50.00

Lone Ranger, bank, 1975, plastic figure, MIP $45.00

Lone Ranger, beanie, 1940, felt, wht image & lettering on blk w/red trim, NM, from $75 to $95.00

Lone Ranger, binoculars, 1950, red & blk plastic w/decals, red vinyl strap, EX, from $100 to $125.00

Lone Ranger, bop bag, Carlin Playthings Inc, 1980, inflatable, MIP $45.00

Lone Ranger, Cartoon Kit, Colorforms, 1966, complete, NMIB..$45.00

Lone Ranger, chair, 1981, inflatable vinyl, MIP..............$35.00

Lone Ranger, Chuckwagon Lantern, 1945, NMIB, from $175 to...$225.00

Lone Ranger, cowboy hat, 1950s, gr felt w/yel band, repeated image of Lone Ranger & Tonto, EX, J5.................$65.00

Lone Ranger, crayons, 1953, complete, NM (NM tin box), from $75 to...$100.00

Lone Ranger, doll, Dollcraft TLR, pnt compo, standing w/guns drawn, wearing chaps & felt mask, 10", NMIB.......$800.00

Lone Ranger, Electric Drawing Set, 1968, complete, NMIB, from $125 to..$150.00

Lone Ranger, figure, Lakeside, 1967, bendable, 7", MOC, J5.$65.00

Lone Ranger, figure, 1940s, chalkware w/glitter highlights, 16", NM, from $75 to...$100.00

Lone Ranger, First Aid Kit, American White Cross Inc, 1938, complete, EX...$65.00

Lone Ranger, harmonica, 1947, silverplated, NMIB, from $75 to...$125.00

Lone Ranger, horseshoe set, Gardner Games, 1950, rubber, complete, NMIB, from $175 to.................................$225.00

Lone Ranger, jail keys, Esquire, 1945, MOC, from $75 to..$100.00

Lone Ranger, Legend of; bow & arrow, 1981, MIP...........$25.00

Lone Ranger, magic slate, Whitman, 1978, cb w/lift-up erasable film sheet, EX, from $55 to......................................$75.00

Lone Ranger, Masked Rider Set, Giant Plastics Corp, 1981, complete, MIP, from $20 to..$25.00

Lone Ranger, Mysterious Prospector Playset, Gabriel, 1976, complete, scarce, NM (NM box), C1.........................$100.00

Lone Ranger, outfit, Pla-Time, 1938, complete w/chaps, vest, neckerchief, mask, rope & hat, EX (EX box), A.....$250.00

Lone Ranger, party horn, 1950, litho tin, EX...................$25.00

Lone Ranger, pencil sharpener, 1940s, bullet shape w/Merita Bread decal on front, 1", NM, J5.................................$65.00

Lone Ranger, Picture Printing Set, 1938, complete, NMIB, from $200 to..$225.00

Lone Ranger, puffy stickers, 1981, MIP............................$12.00

Lone Ranger, Punch-Out Set, 1947, complete, NMIB, from $175 to...$250.00

Lone Ranger, shirt, Tom Sawyer Apparel for Real Boys, 1950s, MIB, from $75 to..$150.00

Lone Ranger, sleeping bag, 1975, image of Lone Ranger & Tonto, NM, from $75 to...$125.00

Lone Ranger, Sports Kit, 1940, complete w/vinyl football & basketball, NMIB, from $250 to..................................$300.00

Lone Ranger, Tatto Picture Book, 1950, MIP, from $65 to.$85.00

Lone Ranger, telescope, 1946, NMIB, from $150 to......$200.00

Lone Ranger, wallet, Hidecraft, 1947, brn leather w/colorful image of Lone Ranger on Silver, NMIB, from $150 to.$175.00

Lone Ranger, Water Gun Set, HG Toys, 1981, MIB, M17.$50.00

Maverick, TV Eras-O-Picture Book, Hasbro, 1959, MIB (sealed), J2..$100.00

Range Rider, chair, 1956, wood folding-type w/image on blk fabric bk, wht fringe on bottom, 24", scarce, EX, T2......$75.00

Range Ryder, outfit, Pla-Master, 1950s, complete, MIB.$275.00

Rin-Tin-Tin, outfit, Pla-Master, 1955, Corporal Rusty 101st Cavalry, complete, scarce, EX (EX box)................$150.00

Roy Rogers, bank, Ohio Art, litho tin w/colorful image of Roy & Trigger, 8", MIP, A...$250.00

Roy Rogers, banner, 1950s, gr felt w/wht image & lettering, 28", EX, A...$185.00

Roy Rogers, camera & binoculars, Herbert George, complete w/paperwork & photo, NMIB..............................$675.00

Roy Rogers, Cowboy & Indian Kit, Colorforms, complete, NM (VG box)...$150.00

Roy Rogers, doll, 1950s, plastic w/fringed leather pants, gr checked shirt, vest & hat, 7", EX, A.........................$125.00

Roy Rogers, flashlight, Bantam, 1974, red & wht plastic, complete w/Trail Guide pamphlet, 3", NM.................$165.00

Roy Rogers, gloves, w/Sears tag, M, C10......................$145.00

Roy Rogers, harmonica, Reed, 1955, NMOC...................$95.00

Roy Rogers, moccasins, Roy & Trigger graphics, EX......$165.00

Roy Rogers, Modeling Clay Set, Standard Toykraft, complete, NM (NM box)...$125.00

Roy Rogers, outfit, Merit Playsuits, 1950s, complete, NMIB..$350.00

Roy Rogers, outfit, Yankeeboy, 1950s, tan pants, vest & folding cloth hat, EX (G box)...$275.00

Roy Rogers, pencil box, 1950s, cb w/woodgrain design, RR logo at top, 2 pull-out drawers & tray on top, EX, J5......$100.00

Roy Rogers, telescope, Herbert George, 1950s, blk w/no markings, NM (VG box), A...$225.00

Roy Rogers, wallet, 1950s, Roy & Trigger in emb letters on brn leather w/mc image, EX (VG box), A.....................$150.00

Roy Rogers, yo-yo, photo image of Roy & Trigger, EX.....$15.00

Tales of Wells Fargo, coloring set, Transogram, 1959, complete, EX (EX box), J5...$65.00

Tales of Wells Fargo, mug, 1950s, EX, A.........................$50.00

Tom Mix, belt, 1930s, orange & bl w/checkerboard design, brass buckle w/red & bl foil insert, EX, J5.....................$100.00

Tom Mix, belt, 1930s, wht plastic w/red checkerboard & cowboy design, brass buckle w/secret compartment, EX, J5..$125.00

Wild Bill Hickok, Western Bunkhouse Kit, Vornado, 1950s, complete, MIB...$65.00

Wyatt Earp, guitar, 24", EX, J2......................................$125.00

Wyatt Earp, spurs, Selcol, plastic, NMOC.......................$50.00

Zorro, cape, Carnival Creations, NMOC...........................$65.00

Zorro, charm bracelet, 1950s, pnt brass w/picture, figure, fan, castle, gun & foil, NMIB, A...$100.00

Zorro, dominoes, Halsam, complete, MIB, A....................$65.00

Zorro, figure, Lido, Zorro on horse, plastic, 6", NMOC, A...$75.00

Zorro, hat & mask, M, C10..$95.00

Zorro, key chain, flasher, WDP, 1966, EX, C10................$35.00

Zorro, Magic Paint & Water Board, MIP...........................$95.00

Zorro, pinwheel, 1950s, wood pole w/plastic 8-point star, rings as it spins, rare, EX, M17...$150.00

Windups, Friction, and Other Mechanicals

Windup toys represent a fun and exciting field of collecting — our fascination with them stems from their simplistic but exciting actions and brightly colored lithography, and especially the comic character or personality-related examples are greatly in demand by collectors today. Though most were made through the years of the '30s through the '50s, they carry their own weight against much earlier toys and are considered very worthwhile investments. Various types of mechanisms were used — some are key wound while others depend on lever action to tighten the mainspring and release the action of the toy. Tin and celluloid were used in their production, and although it is sometimes possible to repair a tin windup, experts advise against investing in a celluloid toy whose mechanism is not working, since the material is usually too fragile to withstand the repair.

Many of the boxes that these toys came in are almost as attractive as the toys themselves and can add considerably to their value.

If you especially enjoy windup and friction motorcycle toys, Sally Gibson-Downs and Christine Gentry have written a collectors' guide called *Motorcycle Toys, Antique and Contemporary*, published by Collector Books.

For more information on windups such as identification, action, value, etc., see Categories of Special Interest under Windups in the back of the book.

Advisors: Richard Trautwein (T3); Scott Smiles (S10).

See also Aeronautical; Automobiles and Other Replica Vehicles; Boats; Chein; Lehmann; Marx; Robots and Space Toys; Strauss.

AMERICAN

Acrobatic Monkeys, Wyandotte, monkey on motorcycle hits other 2 & makes them spin, litho tin, 10" dia base, NM (VG box)..$600.00

Action Ski Jumper, Wolverine, skier somersaults down ski jump, litho tin, 26" ramp, MIB, A..$300.00

Aero Speeders, Buffalo Toys, spiral action, litho tin, 9½", VG+, A...$125.00

Air-E-Go-Round, Reeves Mfg, 3 airplanes circle tower, litho tin, NMIB, A..$700.00

Artie the Clown, Unique Art, clown drives comical car w/several actions, litho tin, 9½", EX...............................$450.00

Auto-Lift, Wolverine, car goes up parking garage & travels down ramp, litho tin, 11", NM (EX box), A $500.00

Auto Speedway, Automatic Toy Co., 1930s, NM (VG box not shown), $225.00. (Photo courtesy June Moon)

Bazooka Truck, Courtland, advances w/gun sound, litho tin & plastic, friction, 7", EX (EX box), A $200.00

Billiard Players, Ranger Steel, litho tin, 15", MIB, A.....$400.00

Blue Bird Racer, Kingsbury, 1930s, w/driver, pressed steel, 18", EX (EX box), A...$1,200.00

Captain Marvel Car, Automatic Toy, 1947, litho tin, 4", NM, A.$250.00

Carousel, Wolverine, w/horses & jockeys & airplanes, litho tin, 13", NM, A..$500.00

Carousel, Wyandotte, w/4 airplanes & 4 swans, litho tin, lever action, 5", EX, A...$275.00

Casey the Cop, Unique Art, advances w/swinging arms, litho tin, 9", scarce, EX (EX box), A............................$1,400.00

Casey the Cop, Unique Art, advances w/swinging arms, litho tin, 9", scarce, NM, A...$850.00

Charlie Chaplin, att Unique Art (similar to one made by Gunthermann), litho tin, 8", VG+, A $650.00

Chrysler Speedster, Girard, 1925, w/driver, litho tin, 8½", rare, NM (EX box), A $800.00

Commando Joe, Ohio Art, soldier realistically crawls w/rifle, litho tin, 8", MIB, A...$200.00

Cow Jumped Over the Moon, Action Toys, pull string & cow jumps over the moon, wood, 10", EX (EX box), A..$100.00

Dancing Cinderella & Prince, Irwin, 1950, figures perform waltz, plastic, 5", M (EX box), from $150 to.....................$200.00

Dandy Andy Rooster, Wolverine, rooster plucks worm from tree trunk as baby chick looks on, wheeled base, tin, 10", NMIB..$850.00

Daredevil Motor Cop, Unique Art, advances, tumbles & rights itself, litho tin, 8½", rare, NM (EX box), A.........$1,300.00

Donald Duck Racer #5, 1930s, litho tin w/rubber tires, 4", rare, NM, from $600 to..$700.00

Donald Duck Rail Car, Lionel, 1935, Donald works handlebars as Pluto's head bounces, compo, 10½", EX, from $800 to..$900.00

Drum Major, Wolverine, advances & plays drum, litho tin, 13", VG, A...$250.00

Easter Bunny Delivery, Wyandotte, bunny on motorcycle w/sidecar, litho tin, 9", EX..$275.00

Easter Bunny Delivery Cycle, Wyandotte, litho tin, 9", VG, A...$250.00

Finnegan, Unique Art, cart advances in erratic motion w/baggage handler on front, litho tin, 13", NMIB, A.......$300.00

Flasho the Mechanical Grinder, Girard, 1925, workman sharpens tool on wheel, litho tin, 4½", NMIB.................$200.00

Fliver Bug, Buffalo Toys, 1937, travels in figure-8 pattern, red-pnt tin, 6½", NM (EX box)....................................$250.00

Flying Circus, Unique Art, plane & clown circle elephant, litho tin, 11", NM (G box), A.....................................$1,500.00

GI Joe & His Jouncing Jeep, Unique Art, advances as figure bounces in seat, litho tin, 7", NM (G box), A.........$450.00

GI Joe & His K-9 Pups, Unique Art, advances w/puppies in cages, litho tin, 9", EX, from $250 to $300.00

Golden Racer #1, Kingsbury, 1930s, w/driver, pnt tin w/blk rubber tires, 19", EX, A $1,000.00

Hee-Haw the Balky Mule, Unique Art, 1930, mule kicks & farmer jumps in seat, litho tin, 10", NM (EX box), A............$500.00

Hobo Train, Unique Art, dog tugs on man's pants atop train, litho tin, 8", EX, A...$350.00

Hoky & Poky, Wyandotte, 2 clowns work handlebars on handcar, litho tin, 6", NM (EX box), A............................$400.00

Home Run King, Selrite, baseball player on rectangular base, litho tin, 7", G...$450.00

Hott & Tott, Unique Art, Black banjo player standing beside piano player, litho tin, 8", EX (G box), A............$1,400.00

Humphrey Mobile, Wyandotte, 1950, figure pedals trike w/attached shack, litho tin, 8½", NM (NM box), A..$900.00

Jackie Gleason Bus, Wolverine, 1955, litho tin, 13", EX (EX box) $1,000.00

Jazzbo Jim, Unique Art, 1920s, Black man w/checked pants dances on roof of litho tin house, 10", NMIB, A.....$850.00

Jolly Juggler Clown, Wolverine, 1930s, litho tin, scarce, NM (NM box), A $600.00

Kiddy Cyclist, Unique Art, 1930s, boy pedals bike & turns handlebars, litho tin, 9", NM, A $450.00

Koolie Koal Kart, GE Carter, 1920, figure advances w/wheelbarrow, litho tin, 6½", rare, NM (NM box), from $750 to $850.00

Li'l Abner & His Dogpatch Band, Unique Art, 1945, figures around piano, litho tin, 6", NMIB, A $700.00

Li'l Abner & Lonesome Polecat Canoe, Ideal, 1951, plastic, 12", NMIB, A..$400.00

Lincoln Tunnel, Unique Art, cars travel road to tunnel as policeman directs traffic, litho tin, 24", MIB, A......$600.00

Little Red Hen, Baldwin, turn crank & she cackles & lays eggs, litho tin, 5", NM (EX box), A.................................$200.00

Loop-A-Loop, Wolverine, track shakes as cars go through loop, litho tin, 19" track, NM, A $450.00

Loop-A-Loop, Wolverine, track shakes as cars go through loop, litho tin, 19" track, EX (EX box), A $700.00

Magic Crossroads, Automatic Toy, 2 cars navigate track, litho tin, 19" base, MIB, A..$265.00

Merry-Go-Round, Wyandotte, 4 swan boats & airplanes circle base, litho tin, 5½", EX, A..$400.00

Mickey Mouse Racer #5, bl version, litho tin w/rubber tires, 4", VG, A $350.00

Never Stop Seesaw, Gibbs, boy & girl seesaw up & down tower, hand-pnt tin, 14", rare, EX (EX box), A.................$400.00

O-Look the Juggler, Irwin, 1930s, rocks back & forth while balancing balls & flags, mixed materials, 14", NMIB, A $275.00

Over & Under, Wolverine, race car travels track & automatically comes to the top, litho tin, 2½" car, EX (EX box), A $300.00

Preacher at Pulpit, Ives, Black preacher behind pulpit, wood w/compo figure, 10", EX, A.............................$3,000.00

Race Master #9, Lupor, litho tin, 11½", MIB, A $265.00

Red Devil Racer, Budwill, 1950, w/driver, red & yel w/blk balloon tires, litho tin, NM (EX box), A......................$350.00

Santa Car, Lionel, 1935, Santa works handlebars, Mickey Mouse in sack on his bk, compo, 11", NM (EX box), A..$3,400.00

Sky Rangers Tower, Unique Art, airplane & zeppelin circle tower, litho tin, 9", EX, A $800.00

Sport Coupe, Buffalo Toys, 1935, pull spiral rod out for action, litho tin, 11", NMIB, A..$500.00

Sportsman's Convertible, Wyandotte, roof slides up & down, trunk opens, pressed steel, 12", MIB, A $700.00

Sunshine Dairy Truck, 1950s, yel plastic w/red lettering, blk rubber tires, friction, NM (EX box), A $100.00

Texas Pete, 1950s, cowboy bounces up & down on rocking horse, plastic, 9", MIB, A $125.00

Toytown Estate Station Wagon, Wyandotte, litho tin w/blk rubber tires, 21", EX, A..$400.00

Traffic Policeman, 1925, Stop & Go sign turns & arm raises, litho tin, 5½", EX, A..$200.00

Trap-A-Tank, Wolverine, tanks travels up base & gets trapped in obstacles, tin w/wood tanks, 36" base, EX (G box), A.$200.00

US Mail Cart, Unique Art, litho tin w/figure on front platform, 13½", NM, A...$275.00

Woman Churning Butter, Ives, wood & tin figure w/cloth clothes on wooden box, 9", NM, A $4,500.00

FRENCH

Auto Transport, Martin, ca 1920, truck w/driver pulls 2-wheeled wagon, 10½", EX (EX box), A.............................$1,500.00

Bear Climbing Pole, Martin, wht bear climbs pole, 14", NM, from $1,200 to $1,500.00

Bimbo Clown Car, Joustra, car spins & front end lifts up, litho tin, 4½", NM, A $200.00

Black Man Pushing Fruit Cart, Martin, man leans on flat 4-wheeled cart, litho tin w/cloth clothes, 8", EX, A..$1,000.00

Black Minstrel, shakes bell & plays cymbals w/feet, pnt tin, 7", EX, A $800.00

Boy Twirling Balls, no cap, pnt tin, 8½", EX, A............$550.00

Boy Twirling Balls, w/cap, pnt tin, 10", EX, A $900.00

Bugatti Racer #3, JEP, litho tin, 8", EX, A..................$250.00

Chestnut Vendor, Martin, figure stirs chestnuts as head moves, litho tin w/cloth clothes, 7½", EX, A..............$1,800.00

Chinese Warrior w/Swords, Martin, hat mk FM, figure wields sword, pnt tin & wire, 7", VG..............................$1,000.00

Clown & Duck Roundego, clown bobs up & down as duck pops in & out of base, pnt tin, 8½", VG, A....................$800.00

Clown Trombonist, straddles base & plays trombone, plink-plunk music, pnt tin, 8½", VG, A $1,000.00

Clown Twirling Star w/8 Bells, star twirls on clown's stomach, pnt tin, rare, EX, A $2,000.00

Clown w/Duck, clown faces quacking duck that flaps wings as they move back & forth, pnt tin, 10", VG..............$600.00

Clowns on Seesaw, legs outstretched on plank attached to drum on base, plink-plunk music, pnt tin, 10", rare, G, A $1,300.00

Couple Dancing, Martin, figures dance & spin, pnt tin w/cloth clothes, 7½", EX, A..$800.00

Couple Dancing, Martin, pnt-tin w/cloth clothes (redressed), 7½", VG, A, VG, A $400.00

DeLage Convertible, JEP, operating steering & gear shift, litho tin, 13½", EX, A...$750.00

Donald Duck, 1950s, waddles around, compo-type material, 8", rare, EX, A $400.00

Donald Duck (Donald le Canard), Donald as caballero bounces around, plastic, 6½", NM (NM box), A $300.00

Fisherman, Martin, pnt tin w/cloth clothes, 7", EX, A..$1,800.00

Girl Skipping Rope, figure attached to rod on base jumps in realistic motion, pnt tin, 6", NMIB, A $1,100.00

International Circus Set, clown balances on 2 ladders, litho tin w/cloth clothes, wood ladders, MIB, A.................$1,100.00

Jeu de Course Car Race, JEP, pnt lead cars race in circle on sq base, lever activated, 8½" base, EX, A...................$550.00

Lady w/Fan, dances around as torso moves, pnt tin, 7", VG, A..$850.00

Lady w/Muff, Martin, slowly advances in rocking motion, tin w/cloth clothes, 8", VG, A...............................$1,000.00

Man Sweeping, Martin, twists & swings broom, pnt tin, wire & lead w/cloth clothes, 7", rare, VG, A $900.00

Marechal Ferrand, Martin, 2 men working forge w/anvil, pnt & litho tin, 6½", EX, A..$2,750.00

Miracle Car, 1940s style sedan, circles & stops as door opens & man comes out, litho tin, 5", NM (EX box), A $250.00

Mysterious Ball, Martin, 1915, pull string & ball w/figures travels up & down spiral ramp, tin, 14", EX, A.................$1,000.00

Oriental Soldier, Martin, free-standing figure in gold costume cap holds weapon, pnt tin, wire & lead, 8", VG, A.$800.00

Porter Pushing 2-Wheeled Cart, Martin, porter pushing cart w/lg box, inertia wheel, tin, 5", EX, A $700.00

President Town Car, JEP, w/driver, litho tin w/disk wheels, electric headlights, 18", EX, A $3,800.00

Racer #4, Pinard, red w/blk rubber tires & red spokes, side-mounted exhaust pipe & horn, electric headlamps, 12", VG, A...$1,600.00

Street Trolley, Rossignol, electric rod mounted on roof, railed platforms on ea end, litho tin, 8", EX, A $750.00

Torpedo Convertible, JEP, tin roadster w/driver, 10", NMIB, A...$2,500.00

Trolley Bus, Joustra, advances w/bell sound, litho tin w/balloon tires, 12", NM (NM box), A $450.00

Violin Player (Le Gai Violinist), Martin, man in top hat plays violin, tin w/cloth clothes, EX (EX box), A.........$1,200.00

GERMAN

Aeroplane Ride, US Zone, 3 planes spin around canopy, litho tin w/celluloid props, 8", EX, A.................................$200.00

Arabian Trotter, horse pulls sulky w/driver, tin & compo, 6½", EX (EX box), A $200.00

Barnacle Bill in Rowboat, Hoge, litho tin figure in pressed-steel boat, 14", G, A $825.00

Barney Google Riding Spark Plug, Nifty, Barney rocks back & forth as Spark Plug nods head, litho tin, 7", EX, A..$1,400.00

Bear Riding Scooter, Schuco, litho tin w/fur-covered bear, friction, 6", EX, A $1,200.00

Bimbo Clown Car, US Zone, advances on back wheels as figure lurches forward, litho tin, 4½", NM, A $125.00

Black Drummer, Schuco, plays cymbals & bass drum, litho tin w/felt clothes, 4½", EX, A..$225.00

Boat-Tail Racer, G&K, litho tin w/full-figure driver, 6½", EX, A .$400.00

Bonzo on Scooter, TW, Bonzo on 3-wheeled scooter, litho tin, 7½", NM, A..$350.00

Boy w/Performing Poodle, Gunthermann, boy holds rope as poodle jumps on wheeled platform, hand-pnt tin & lead, 6", VG, A $850.00

Cable Car, Technofix, 2 cars travel on mountain & 2 travel on road, litho tin, 18" base, NM (EX box), A...............$225.00

Charlie Chaplin, Schuco, dances around & twirls cane, litho tin w/cloth clothes, 6", NMIB, A $1,200.00

Charlie Chaplin Hat Tipper, CKO, pull string & Charlie tips hat, litho tin, 4", NM, A $300.00

Circus Elephant, US Zone, performs balancing act, litho tin, 8", NM (EX box), A $500.00

Clown & Child Performing, Gunthermann, clown plays cymbals as child spins on pedestal, hand-pnt tin, 7", G, A ...$500.00

Circus Monkey, GNK, lithographed tin with paper umbrella, 7½", EX (EX box), A, $300.00.

Clown Band, 1 clown plays drum & 1 plays cymbals, litho tin, 9" base, EX, A $800.00

Clown Carousel w/Boats & Whales, Gunthermann, rotates w/plink-plunk music, pnt tin, rare, G, A $9,500.00

Clown w/Billy Goat, clown atop rnd base tries to train billy goat on wheeled platform, hand-pnt tin, 6½", VG, A.$1,000.00

Clowns & Monkey, Gunthermann, 2 clowns swing monkey on bar, litho tin, 8", EX (EX box), A........................$1,500.00

Clowns on Seesaw, Distler, litho tin, 10½" L, VG+, A..$500.00

Construction Truck w/Extension Ladder, Schuco, red w/open bed, ladder mounted on swinging platform, 10", EX, A $850.00

Dare Devil Racer, Arnold, car spins in loop, litho tin, 4" car, NMIB, A...$500.00

Dog Race, Gunthermann, 3 greyhound dogs chase rabbit on 4-wheeled platform, litho tin, 7", VG, A $350.00

Donkey Cart, Gunthermann, donkey pulls Black man in cart, litho tin, 8½", VG, A...$450.00

Famous Juggler, clown juggles rings on hands & head, litho tin w/cloth clothes, 10½", NM (EX box), A.................$300.00

Felix the Cat on Scooter, Gunthermann, Felix on 3-wheeled scooter, litho tin, 7", NM, A..................................$1,400.00

Fighting Roosters, 1930, roosters travel back & forth on base & peck at ea other, litho tin, 10", EX, A $500.00

Fire Chief Car, Hoge, advances w/sound, pressed steel w/decal, 15", NM, A...$350.00

Fishing Fred, US Zone, fisherman rotates on base w/fish attached to line, litho tin, 6", MIB, from $400 to....$500.00

Ford Model T Roadster, Bing, 1921, w/driver, blk w/spoke wheels, mounted spare, 6½", NM, A $600.00

Fox Carrying Swan in Cage, Schuco, litho tin & plush w/cloth clothes, 5", VG, A $750.00

Friendly Cycle, Technofix, full-figure driver & passenger w/dog between them, litho tin, friction, 8", EX, A $300.00

Frog Walker, pnt tin w/lead feet, dressed in top hat & tuxedo coat w/cane, 6½", G, A $650.00

Garage & Limousine, Bing, litho tin, 5x7" garage, MIB, A .$800.00

Gordon Bennet Racer #5, Gunthermann, litho tin w/rubber tires, wood & paper bellows, 9", rare, EX, A $9,000.00

Grand Prix Racing Set, Technofix, complete w/3 cars, litho tin, 13x19" base, NM (EX box), A $300.00

Halloween Train, US Zone, train navigates circular track through tunnel, litho tin, VG (VG box), A $300.00

Handstand Clown, Issmayer, balances on hands & sways, litho tin, 7", VG, A..$250.00

Happy Clown, US Zone, vibrates around as eyes open & close, litho tin, 6", EX (G box), A......................................$300.00

Harold Lloyd Bell Toy, 1930, bell rings & face changes expressions, flat tin face, lever action, 6", EX (EX box), A .$550.00

Hen & Chick Cart, hen pulls chick on 2-wheeled cart, litho tin, 10", VG, A...$275.00

Hessmobile Tractor & Log Trailer, Hess, litho tin, complete w/stacked wood, 15½", EX (EX box), A $350.00

Howdy Doody Acrobat, Arnold, performs flips on highbar, compo figure w/cloth clothes, litho tin base, 12", VG, A $300.00

Ice Cream Vendor, man pushes cart w/2 spoke wheels, litho- & hand-pnt tin, 6", VG, from $500 to $600.00

Jack Sprat & His Wife, Gunthermann, advances & twirls, hand-pnt tin, 6½", VG, A...$450.00

Jackie Coogan, moves side to side as eyes move, litho tin, 7½", VG, A...$700.00

Jackie Ostrich Wagon, Gundka & Kelpert, ostrich pulls wagon w/girl on open bench seat, litho tin, 9½", VG, A ...$700.00

Jiggs Jazz Car, Nifty, 1920s, litho tin, 6½", scarce, NM, A .$2,400.00

Jim the Walking Trolley Man, Stock's Dienstmann, man pushes trunk in cart, litho tin, 6½", NM (NM box), A...$1,400.00

Juggler, M&K, boy juggles, hand-pnt tin w/wooden pins, 7½", VG, A...$450.00

Jumbo the Elephant, US Zone, litho tin, 4", EX (EX box), A .$500.00

Lady Chasing Mouse, Gunthermann, lady swats mouse attached to rod w/broom, hand-pnt tin, 7½", EX, A $1,100.00

Lady in Convertible, Schuco, red tin w/compo figure, 10", EX, A..$500.00

Lady w/Umbrella, Gunthermann, Black woman advances w/umbrella & basket, hand-pnt tin, 6", EX, A $500.00

Limousine, Carette, gr w/red detail, rubber tires w/spokes, w/chauffeur, EX, A $2,200.00

Limousine, Karl Bub, maroon w/blk roof & running boards, open front w/enclosed rear, w/chauffeur, 10", NM, A...$1,000.00

Mac 700 Motorcycle, Arnold, driver flips over steering wheel, litho tin, 8", NM, A...$750.00

Maggie & Jiggs, Nifty, 1924, figures travel on platform, litho tin, 7", EX, A $1,300.00

Main Street Trolley, litho tin, 9", EX, A $850.00

Mammy Dancing, Lindstrom, litho tin, 7½", VG, A $250.00

Mammy Sweeping, Lindstrom, litho tin, 8", NM (EX box), A $500.00

Man in Parachute, Muller & Kadeder, figure sails around bases, pnt & stained tin, 16", VG, A $2,500.00

Man Pulling Girl in Cart, litho tin stake cart w/spoke wheels, 7", VG, A..$400.00

Mickey Mouse Jazz Drummer, Nifty, 1934, plunger activated, litho tin, 7", rare, VG, A......................................$2,300.00

Mickey Mouse Organ Grinder (Hurdy Gurdy), Mickey playing organ w/Minnie dancing atop, 8x6", scarce, NM, A..$6,500.00

Miniature Railway, Distler, train w/station, tunnels & bridges on rnd base, litho tin, 10" dia, EX (EX box), A........$1,600.00

Motodrill Clown, Schuco, bl coat version, advances in circular motion, litho tin w/cloth clothes, 5", EX, A $1,400.00

Motodrill Clown, Schuco, gr coat version, advances in circular motion, litho tin w/cloth clothes, 5", NM (NM box), A............$2,600.00

Motodrill 1006, Schuco, travels in circles, spins out & changes directions, litho tin, 5", EX (EX box), A $500.00

Motorcycle w/Driver (Curvo 1000), Schuco, litho tin, 5", NMIB, A..$550.00

Mouse in Open Roadster, Schuco, litho tin, 6", EX, A ..$250.00

Musical Car, Schuco, advances w/musical chiming, tin, 6", MIB, A..$350.00

Paddy's Pride, pig pulling rider in 2-wheeled cart, litho tin, 8", NM (VG box), A..$2,000.00

Peacock, Hans Eberle, advances, litho tin, 10", VG, A.$300.00

Phaeton, Gunthermann, pnt & litho tin, orig driver, spoke wheels, 9", rare, EX, A $4,600.00

Phaeton w/Canopy, Carette, litho tin w/4 figures, rubber tires w/spokes, 8", rare, EX, A $4,400.00

Popeye in Rowboat, Hoge, 1930s, litho tin & pressed steel, complete w/oars, 14", rare, EX $2,500.00

Powerful Katrinka, Fontaine Fox, 1923, advances & lifts figure in wheelbarrrow, litho tin, EX, A $1,500.00

Racing Cycle #4, Technofix, advances in circular motion, litho tin, 7", NM (NM box), A..$350.00

Rolly Clown, Schuco, rocks back & forth & pushes himself w/pole, compo w/cloth clothes, 8", EX (EX box), A..$600.00

Round-About Carousel, WK, men spin in chairs w/sound, litho tin, 11", EX, A..$500.00

Rudy the Ostrich, Nifty, 1924, litho tin, 8½", EX, A.....$575.00

Santa Claus, Schuco, advances w/swinging arms, litho tin w/felt clothes & fur beard, 5", NM, A $1,000.00

Sky Rider, 1950s, 2 planes attached to rod circle above airport hangar, litho tin, 8", NM (NM box), A..................$200.00

Solisto Clown Violinist, Schuco, litho tin w/cloth clothes, 4½", VG (VG box), A..$200.00

Stunt Racer, Arnold, car circles inside loop, litho tin, 10" loop, EX (EX box), A..$350.00

Sweeping Katinka, Lindstrom, vibrates, spins & sweeps, litho tin, 8", NM (NM box), A..$300.00

Tango Dancers, Gunthermann, couple in formal attire tango, hand-pnt tin, 8", VG, A..$825.00

Telesteering Car 3000, Schuco, enameled steel, 4", EX (EX box), A..$300.00

Toonerville Trolley, Fontaine Fox, 1922, advances, stops & shakes, litho tin, 6", rare, EX (EX box) $1,200.00

Topsy Turvy Tom, Ri N, car w/roll bars & clown driver advances & flips over, litho tin, 10", MIB, A.......$2,800.00

Traffic Man (Flic), Schuco, figure rotates & lifts arm as lights change on base, 5", NM (NM box), A....................$275.00

Trip-Trapp Donkey Cart, Hans Eberle, donkey pulls farm wagon w/driver, litho tin, 11", EX, A $650.00

Turkey, US Zone, advances as tail feathers open & close & move up & down, litho tin, 6", NM (EX box), A ...$450.00

Vis-A-Vis, Gunthermann, red open-seater w/driver, tin w/wht rubber tires & blk spokes, 6½", rare, NM, A $3,200.00

Volkswagen Micro Racer, Schuco, red, 4", MIB, A........$200.00

JAPANESE

Airplane Go-Round, prewar, 6 airplanes w/figures circle base w/sound, tin & celluloid, 14", rare, EX, A $500.00

**Atom-Car, Y, lithographed tin, friction, 16",
extremely rare, EX (EX box), A, $3,200.00.**

Animal Barber Shop, TPS, cat simulates shaving a rabbit's face, litho tin, 5", MIB, A...$500.00

Anti-Aircraft Jeep, SSS, advances w/siren sound, litho tin, friction, 11", NM (EX box), A $175.00

Army Tank, H, advances w/swivel action machine gun & sound, litho tin, friction, 8", NM (EX box), A $200.00

Atom Racer #45, Marusan, 1950s, w/driver, litho tin, 8", EX (EX box), A $600.00

Babes in Toyland Soldier, Linemar, 1961, lithographed tin, 6", EX, from $325.00 to $375.00.
(Photo courtesy Scott Smiles)

Balloon Santa, Alps, 1950s, lifts balloons & rings bell, 7½", MIB, A...$200.00

Banjo Bunny, Alps, sits on stump & plays banjo, celluloid & litho tin, 8", EX (worn box), A..............................$200.00

Batman, 1989, litho tin, 8", MIB..$125.00

Batman Batmobile, Alps, 1966, litho tin, friction, 8", scarce, EX $900.00

Bear Golfer, TPS, bear hits ball across bridge into net, litho tin, 4", NM (NM box), A...$400.00

Betty Boop on Trapeze, celluloid figure on wire trapeze, 8½", NM, A...$1,300.00

Big Joe Chef, Yone, advances w/chicken on plate, litho tin, 9", MIB, A..$200.00

Big League Hockey Player, TPS, 1950s, skates w/realistic movement, litho tin, 6½", NM (NM box), A..................$650.00

Billie Boy, bellhop pushes trunk, litho tin & celluloid, 3½", scarce, EX (G box), A...$300.00

Black Boy on Tricycle, goes forward & reverse w/bell sound, litho tin & celluloid, 8½", rare, NM, A...............$1,500.00

Black Knight Jet, Y, advances w/sparking engine, litho tin, friction, 14" L, NM (EX box), A...................................$250.00

Bobo the Magician (Happy-Go-Lucky Magician), TN, lifts hat & rabbit, chick & egg appear, litho tin, NM (NM box), A..$900.00

Boy on Scooter, Occupied Japan, celluloid, M $125.00

Boy on Tricycle, prewar, advances w/bell sound, litho tin & celluloid, 7½", EX, A...$500.00

Boy w/Dog, Occupied Japan, celluloid w/cloth clothes, 5", EX, A...$100.00

Bozo, Alps, clown rocks side to side & plays drum, litho tin, 8½", NM (NM box), A...$1,000.00

Branko Mechanical Acrobat, CK, child performs acrobats on highbar, celluloid & tin, 13", MIB, A....................$200.00

Brutus, advances w/swinging arms, hand-pnt celluloid, 7", rare, EX, A...$1,400.00

Bulldog, Alps, advances & growls, cloth over tin, 8", NM, A...$125.00

Butterfly, Alps, advances & flaps wings, litho tin, friction, 5", NM (EX box), A..$165.00

Buzzy Bee, TN, litho tin & plush, MIB..........................$150.00

Calypso Joe, TPS, native rocks back & forth while playing drum, litho tin, 6", NM (NM box), A..............................$400.00

Captain America, see Marvel Super Hero Tricycle

Casper the Ghost Tank, Linemar, Casper forces tank to turn over, litho tin, 4", EX (EX box), A........................$600.00

CBS Television Truck, Ashitoy, litho tin w/cameras on top, friction, 6", VG (G box), A...$200.00

Champ on Ice, TPS, 3 bears skate w/realistic movement, litho tin, 8", NM (NM box), A...$1,100.00

Charlie McCarthy, prewar, vibrates around as mouth opens & closes, celluloid, 7", M, A...$750.00

Chirpee Chick, Alps, litho tin & plush, MIB.................$125.00

Circus Boy, TN, shuffles around, moves head & rings bell, litho tin, 6", NM (EX box), A...$500.00

Circus Bugler, TPS, rare version w/bl pants, sways side to side & plays trumpet, litho tin, 9", MIB............................$500.00

Circus Car, KO, litho tin, MIB, J6................................$200.00

Circus Motorcycle, clown on motorcycle advances & turns automatically, litho tin, 6", EX (EX box), A $300.00

Circus Parade, TPS, elephant pulls 3 performing clowns, litho tin, 11", NM (EX box), A...$400.00

Circus Plane, Yone, advances & flips over, clown pilot, litho tin, 3½", MIB...$125.00

Circus Tricycle, Occupied Japan, boy peddles tricycle w/bell sound, celluloid, 4", EX (EX box), A......................$150.00

Circus Truck, Linemar, advances as lion rocks in cage, litho tin, friction, 5½", EX (EX box), A $175.00

Cleo Clown, TPS, clown waves wand & dog jumps through hoop, litho tin, 5", NM (EX box), A......................$275.00

Climbing Pirate, TPS, pull string for action, litho tin, 5", EX (EX box), A $200.00

Clown Making the Lion Jump Thru the Flaming Hoop, TPS, litho tin, 5", NM (NM box), A..............................$300.00

Clown on Donkey, Occupied Japan, vibrates w/spinning tail, celluloid, 4½", NM, A..$100.00

Clown on Roller Skates, TPS, skates in realistic motion, litho tin w/cloth clothes, 6½", EX (EX box), A..............$450.00

Clown on Roller Skates, TPS, skates in realistic motion, litho tin w/cloth clothes, 6½", NM, A $350.00

Clown w/Monkey Whirligig, prewar, advances in circular pattern w/parasol spinning above, celluloid, 7", NM, A.........$250.00

Comet Car, advances w/sparks & sound, litho tin, friction, 7½", EX, A $300.00

Comic Locomotive, TN, advances w/twirling smoke, litho tin, MIB..$150.00

Comical Clara, TPS, body shakes & her eyes bulge out, litho tin, 5", NM (EX box), A...$550.00

Comical Driver, car advances as monkey driver rocks back & forth, litho tin, friction, 6", EX (EX box), A $200.00

Cowboy, Y, horse rocks as cowboy's hat flops, litho tin, 6½", NM (EX box), A $350.00

Cowboy Banjo Player, Linemar, plays banjo as head sways, litho tin, 5", EX, A..$150.00

Cragstan Jalopy Stock Car, NGS, advances w/siren sound, litho tin, friction, 6½", EX (EX box), A $200.00

Crawling Baby, KT, prewar, tin & celluloid w/knitted sweater, 9", NM (EX box mk Bestmaid Crawling Baby), A ..$250.00

Daily News Truck, Linemar, bl tin w/litho sign, Over Twice the Circulation..., friction, 5", NM (G box), A.............$165.00

Dance Hawaiian, SSG, girl performs hula, celluloid w/grass skirt, 6", MIB, A $165.00

Dancing Chef, Occupied Japan, Black chef travels around w/plate of food, celluloid, 5", scarce, MIB................$750.00

Dancing Couple, Ashitoy, couple perform waltz, celluloid, 5", MIB, A..$100.00

Disney Airplane, Linemar/WDP, 1950s, litho tin, friction, 8" wingspan, rare, EX (EX box), A...........................$1,600.00

Disney Flivver, Linemar, push down on Donald Duck's head for action, litho tin & celluloid, 5½", EX (EX box), A...$800.00

Disneyland Happy Birthday Carousel, Ross, litho tin, 9", EX (EX box), A..$150.00

Donald & Nephews, Linemar, Donald pulls nephews, litho tin, 11", rare, VG, A $650.00

Donald Duck & Elmer on Trapeze, Borgfeldt/WD, celluloid figures on wire trapeze, rare, A...................................$5,200.00

Donald Duck Delivery Wagon, Linemar, Donald pedals wagon mk Mickey's Delivery, tin & celluloid, M, A $650.00

Donald Duck Dipsy Car, Linemar, advances w/crazy action as Donald's head bobs, litho tin, 5½", NM (EX box) ..$800.00

Donald Duck Drummer, Linemar, advances & plays drum, litho tin, 6", NM (EX box), A $900.00

Donald Duck Fire Chief Truck, Linemar, advances in erratic motion, litho tin, 5", NM...$500.00

Donald Duck in His Convertible, Linemar, litho tin w/celluloid figure, friction, 5", NM (NM box), A $700.00

Donald Duck Riding Pluto, mk Made in Japan, figures on rocking base, celluloid & wood, 7", NM, A.................$3,000.00

Donald Duck w/Huey & Voice, Linemar, pull string & Huey moves closer & quacks, litho tin, 8", NM (EX box), A.......$1,000.00

Donald Duck Waddler, Borgfeldt, celluloid, 5½", rare, NMIB, A $2,400.00

Donald Duck, see also Disney Flivver and Walt Disney's Rocking Chair

Drummer Boy, Nifty, prewar, plays drum & head sways, celluloid, 10", EX (EX box), A..$300.00

Drunken Sailor, Occupied Japan, celluloid, 6", scarce, NM, A.$300.00

Duck Amphibious Taxi, TPS, duck pulls monkey driver & 2 squirrels, litho tin, 6", scarce, EX (EX box), A $950.00

Eagle Racer #57, IY Metal Toys, Indy-type racer mk Speed on wheels, litho tin, w/driver, 11", NM (NM box), A..$950.00

Elephant Circus Car, elephant driver juggles world globe on his nose, litho tin, friction, 7", EX (EX box), A...........$250.00

Felix the Cat Acrobat, celluloid figure w/crossed arms & legs on wire balance bar, 8½", EX, A $600.00

Ferdinand the Bull, Linemar, head moves up & down & tail spins, tin w/rubber tail, 5½", scarce, NM (EX box), A $900.00

Ferry Boat, Y, boat w/bus travels across bay, hits dock & goes back, litho tin, 17", NM (EX box), A.....................$365.00

Fire Car, SSS, w/ladder & 5 firemen, advances w/siren sound, litho tin, friction, 6½", NM (EX box), A $300.00

Fire Engine, TKK, advances w/sparks & sound, litho tin, friction, 18", EX (EX box), A $125.00

Fishing Bear, TPS, fish jumps in & out of net, litho tin, 7½", NM (EX box), A $275.00

Fishing Monkey on Whale, TPS, monkey on whale w/fishing rod attached to fish, several actions, litho tin, 9", MIB.....$400.00

Flying Fish Racing Boat, Ashitoy, w/driver, tail fin mk F-55, litho tin, 12", EX, A $185.00

Ford Fancy Antique Autos, tin, friction, 9", MIB, pr $100.00

Fred Flintstone on Dino, Linemar, advances & growls, litho tin w/vinyl-headed figure, 8", NM (NM box), A $475.00

G-Man Car, MT, advances w/sound, red w/blk rubber tires, friction, 5", MIB, A...$200.00

G-Men Car No 1, Cragstan, litho tin, friction, 4", EX (G box)..$150.00

Girl on Roller Skates, prewar, celluloid, 7", NM, A.......$500.00

Gay 90s Cyclist, TPS, 1950s, lithographed tin with cloth clothes, 7", EX, from $275.00 to $325.00.

(Photo courtesy Scott Smiles)

Girl w/Purse, prewar, celluloid, 6", NM, A $125.00
Good Flavor Ice Cream Wagon, little boy drives ice cream cart, litho tin w/celluloid figure, 4", NM, A.............$200.00
Goofy, see also Whirling Tail Goofy
Goofy Unicyclist, Linemar, litho tin w/cloth pants, 5", rare, NMIB, A $1,700.00
Goofy's Stock Car, Linemar, advances w/siren sound, litho tin, friction, 6", scarce, EX (EX box), A $850.00
Grand-Pa's New Car, Yonezawa, advances as grandpa bounces in seat, litho tin, 5", NM (NM box)............................$350.00
Grasshopper, SAN, advances w/realistic movement, litho tin, 7½", EX (EX box), A $200.00
Greyhound Line Bus, Marusan, mk New York, litho tin, friction, 13", EX (EX box), A..$475.00
Groolies Car, Yone, advances as front end jumps up & down, litho tin, 5", NM (EX box), A...............................$250.00
Happy Life, Alps, girl & duck under umbrella on sq base, several actions, litho tin & celluloid, 6", NM (NM box), A ..$700.00
Happy Skater, TPS, bear skates in realistic motion, litho tin w/cloth clothes, 5½", EX (EX box), A.....................$400.00
Happy Skater, TPS, rabbit skates in realistic motion, litho tin w/cloth clothes, 6", EX (EX box), A $400.00
Happy the Violinist, TPS, clown plays violin & sways, litho tin w/cloth clothes, 8½", EX (EX box), A.....................$250.00
Henry Eating Candy, Linemar, 1950s, litho tin, 5½", EX, A $400.00
Henry Eating Ice Cream, Linemar, 1950s, vibrates around & eats ice-cream cone, litho tin, 6", scarce, NM, A........$1,000.00

Hopping Astro, Linemar, litho tin, 4", rare, EX (EX box), A..$3,300.00
Horse Race, Occupied Japan, boy in clown suit rides horse on base, celluloid & tin, 4", EX (EX box) $200.00
Howdy Doody Band, Howdy dances as Clarabell plays the piano, litho tin, 6x5", EX, A...$1,600.00
Humpty-Dumpty Clown, prewar, clown vibrates around w/spinning umbrella overhead, celluloid, 12", rare, MIB.$1,100.00
Hurricane Racer #7, KSG, litho tin w/celluloid figure, friction, 5", EX (EX box), A...$250.00
Ice Cream Cart, Occupied Japan, man pedals cart, litho tin w/celluloid figure, 3", NM, A...............................$175.00
Ice Cream Vendor, Frankonia, 1950s, boy pedals cart, litho tin w/celluloid figure, 4", MIB, A $200.00
Indian Chief on Horse, Haji, horse bounces up & down, litho tin, 8", EX, A...$250.00
Indianapolis 500 Racer #27, litho tin, friction, 6", EX (EX box), A..$150.00
Indians in Canoe, advances as 1 figure plays tomtom & 1 oars, litho tin, friction, 9½", NM $225.00
International Auto Cycle Race, 5 motorcycles race down track, litho tin, scarce, EX, A..$700.00
Japanese Clown, vibrates around as ball goes up & down rod extended from nose, litho tin, 8", rare, NM, A........$500.00
Jiminy Cricket, Linemar, litho tin, 6", cane missing, G, A...$350.00
Joker (Batman), 1989, litho tin, 8", MIB, J5....................$65.00
Jolly Farmer w/Pig, prewar, farmer pulls pig's tail, tin & celluloid, 7½", MIB, A...$250.00

Juggling Popeye & Olive Oyl, Linemar, Popeye balances Olive Oyl in chair on his nose, litho tin, 9", EX (EX box), A ..$3,500.00

Jumping Clown, several actions, litho tin w/cloth pants & handkerchief, 6", MIB, A $350.00

Kiddy City Amusement Park, ATC, planes circle tower w/bell noise, litho tin, lever action, 9", NM (EX box), A..$200.00

Kitty Ball Romp, Occupied Japan, advances w/ball in front of him, celluloid, 8", EX (EX box), A $100.00

Ko-Ko Sandwich Man, TN, advances w/several actions, Eat at Joes sign around neck, tin w/cloth clothes, 7½", NMIB, A $175.00

Lady & the Tramp, Linemar, advances w/spinning ball, litho tin, friction, 4", NM, A..................$275.00

Lady Bug & Tortoise w/Babies, TPS, flips over to reveal lady bug & tortoise, litho tin, 7", NM (EX box), A...............$100.00

Lester the Jester, Alps, vibrates & twirls cane, litho tin w/cloth clothes, 9½", EX (EX box), A.................$525.00

Lone Ranger on Silver (unauthorized), Haji, litho tin, 9", VG...$250.00

Louie in His Dream Car, Linemar, litho tin w/celluloid figure, friction, 5", EX (EX box), A.....................$500.00

Lucky Baby Machine (Girl at Sewing Machine), Marusan, 1950s, several actions, litho tin & celluloid, 5½", NMIB, A..$575.00

Lucky Sledge, Occupied Japan, sled spins w/rosy-cheeked figure, celluloid, rare bl version, MIB, A..........................$225.00

Magic Fire Car, MT, advances w/sound & extended bumper, litho tin w/vinyl-headed animal driver, friction, 7", MIB...............................$100.00

Magician Dog Triksie, lifts hat & chick & egg appear, tin & plush w/cloth clothes, 8", EX (EX box), A $475.00

Marching Drummer Bear, Alps, advances & plays drum & cymbals, litho tin & plush, 6½", EX (EX box), A..........$150.00

Marvel Super Heroes Tricycle, Linemar, 1960s, Capt America pedals tricycle w/bell, litho tin, NMIB, from $450 to........$650.00

Mary & Her Little Lamp, prewar, Mary pulls lamb behind her, celluloid, 4", MIB, A $450.00

Mechanical Trotter, prewar, horse-drawn cart w/little boy, litho tin & celluloid, 7", EX (EX box), A.........................$300.00

Mickey Mouse, see also Rambling Mickey Mouse

Mickey Mouse & Minnie Mouse Acrobats, Nifty/Borgfeldt, prewar, figures perform on bar, celluloid, 12", NM (G box), A $1,700.00

Mickey Mouse & Minnie on See-Saw, pendulum action, celluloid figures on litho tin base, 6", EX, A....................$600.00

Mickey Mouse on Tricycle, Linemar/WDP, figure pedals trike w/rear bell, tin & celluloid, 4", MIB, A $1,400.00

Mickey Mouse Roller Skater, Linemar, skates in realistic motion, litho tin w/cloth pants, 6", EX (EX box), A............$2,200.00

Mickey Mouse Whirligig, prewar, advances on wheels as umbrella w/ball spins above, celluloid, 7", NM, A................$1,900.00

Minnie Mouse Knitting, Linemar, Minnie knitting in rocking chair, litho tin, 6½", M, A $800.00

Monkey Basketball Player, TPS, flips ball into basket, litho tin, 7½", NM (EX box), A........................$475.00

Monkey Catcher, TPS, several actions, litho tin, 6", rare, NM, A $550.00

Mouse, CK, advances in circular motion w/spinning tail, tin, 5", EX (G box), A $100.00

Mr Cragstan, Yone, advances w/sound as mouth opens & closes, litho tin, 7", scarce, NM, A................$350.00

Mr Dan the Hot Dog Eating Man, TN, 1950s, several actions, litho tin w/red cloth coat & flocked hair, 7", MIB ..$125.00

Mr Hare the Spectacle Bunny, Alps, bounces around & wipes glasses, tin & plush w/cloth clothes, 7", NM (EX box), A................................$150.00

New X Car, advances w/non-fall action, litho tin, 6", NM (EX box), A................................$185.00

Old Fashioned Ambulance Truck, Bandai, litho tin, 6½", EX (EX box), A................................$200.00

Old Fashioned City Police Car, Bandai, advances w/siren sound, litho tin, friction, 6½", EX (EX box), A.................$200.00

Old Fashioned Ford Roadster Sedan, Bandai, litho tin, friction, 6½", MIB, A................................$150.00

Old Fashioned Ice Cream Car, Bandai, litho tin, friction, 6½", NM (NM box), A................................$150.00

Old Fashioned Royal Wagon, Bandai, litho tin woody style, friction, 6½", NM (NM box), A $150.00

Old Fashioned Van Truck, Bandai, mk Express Delivery, litho tin, friction, 6½", EX (EX box), A........................$150.00

Old Timer Airplane, S&E, advances w/visible piston action, litho tin, friction, 13", NM (EX box), A.................$250.00

Olive Oyl, Linemar, head nods erratically, litho tin, 5", M, A $1,600.00

Olive Oyl Ballet Dancer, Linemar, litho tin, friction, 5", EX (EX box), A................................$850.00

Olive Oyl on Tricycle, Linemar, figure pedals trike w/bell, litho tin & celluloid, 4", EX, A.....................$2,200.00

Over the Hill, M, race car travels track & automatically goes to the top, litho tin, extends to 24", NM (EX box), A.................................$300.00

Pango-Pango African Dancer, TPS, vibrates around, litho tin, 6", MIB, A................................$300.00

Peace Corps Man, SY, advances & changes direction as bell rings, litho tin, 7", NM (EX box), A......................$250.00

Peaceful Pigeon, Ichiko, advances w/flapping wings & tail, litho tin, 8", NM (EX box), A $750.00

Perfection Bicycle Rider, CK, prewar, advances in circular motion w/ringing bell, litho tin & celluloid, 6½", NMIB, A..$375.00

Picnic Bus, SAN, advances w/siren sound, tin, friction, 9½", NM (G box), A $85.00

Piggy Cook, Y, vibrates & flips egg, litho tin, 5", NM (NM box), A $250.00

Pinocchio Walker, Linemar, litho tin, 6", NM, A..........$950.00

Playful Little Dog, Occupied Japan, vibrates in circles w/spinning tail, litho tin, 3½", NM (EX box), A...............$165.00

Playful Pluto, Linemar, vibrates around as head moves & tail spins, litho tin, 5", NM (G box), A $450.00

Pluto, see also Running Pluto

Pluto Acrobat, Linemar/Gym Toys, celluloid figure on metal trapeze, 8", EX (EX box), A $450.00

Pluto Motorcycle, Linemar, advances w/sound, litho tin, friction, 4", NM, A $250.00

Pluto the Drum Major, Linemar, rocks, plays horn & rings bell, litho tin & rubber, complete w/cane, 6", NMIB, A.$650.00

Police Paddy Wagon, SAN, advances w/siren sound, tin, friction, 9½", NM (G box), A $100.00

Popeye, advances as head moves up & down, hand-pnt celluloid, 8½", EX, A $700.00

Popeye, advances as head moves up & down, hand-pnt celluloid, 5", rare, EX, A..$900.00

Popeye & Bluto, Linemar, celluloid figures on separate litho tin 2-wheeled bases, NM, from $2,000 to $2,500.00

Popeye & Olive Oyl Playing Ball, Linemar, figures throw ball back & forth on base, litho tin, 19" base, EX (EX box), A..$2,400.00

Popeye on Tricycle, Linemar, figure pedals trike w/bell, litho tin & celluloid, 4½", EX, A $700.00

Popeye Roller Skater, Linemar, skates in realistic motion, Linemar, litho tin w/cloth pants, 6½", EX (EX box), A $1,800.00

Popeye the Basketball Player, Linemar, Popeye shoots ball through net, litho tin, 9", NMIB, A $2,500.00

Popeye Transit Co Truck, Linemar, litho tin, friction, NM, from $750 to..$850.00

Popeye Turnover Tank, Linemar, lithographed tin, 4", EX, $350.00. (Photo courtesy Jeff Bub)

Popeye Turnover Tank, Linemar, Popeye forces tank to turn over, litho tin, 4", VG, A $300.00

Popeye Unicyclist, Linemar, litho tin w/cloth pants, NMIB, from $1,000 to..$1,200.00

Popeye, see also Juggling Popeye and Tumbling Popeye

Prehistoric Dinosaur, Linemar, advances & growls, litho tin, 8", NM (EX box), A $350.00

Professor Von Drake Go-Mobile, Linemar, tin w/vinyl-headed figure, friction, 6", MIB, A $300.00

Puzzle Cat, TN, advances w/ball between paws, litho tin, friction, 6", NM (G box), A $150.00

Rabbit Playing Violin, prewar, sits on tree stump & plays violin, celluloid, 9", NM, A..$400.00

Racer #5, mk New York & Miami, litho tin, friction, M .$300.00

Rambling Mickey Mouse, prewar, waddles around w/swinging arms, celluloid, 7½", NM, A.................................$1,800.00

Reading Santa Claus, Alps, flips pages in book & nods head, tin & vinyl w/cloth clothes, 7", NM, A........................$150.00

Roly Poly Circus Clown, SK, clown rolls around in hoop, litho tin w/cloth clothes, 5½", EX (EX box), A $400.00

Running Pluto, Linemar, advances as tongue moves in & out, litho tin w/rubber tail, friction, 4", EX (EX box), A ..$500.00

Sam the Strolling Skeleton, Mikuni, advances w/swinging arms, litho tin, 5½", M, A $200.00

Sambo the Minstrel Man, Japan, prewar, monkey sits on stump & plays banjo, celluloid, 8", M (EX box), A...........$250.00

Santa Claus, Occupied Japan, advances w/step-over action, celluloid w/tin legs, 6½", NM, A................................$200.00

Santa Claus, Occupied Japan, travels around w/bell & nods head, celluloid, 4½", NM, A....................................$200.00

Santa Claus, TN, advances, waves sign & rings bell, litho tin, 7", NM (NM box), A..$300.00

Santa in Chimney, Alps, Santa goes up & down chimney w/sound, vinyl, cloth & cb, 5", NM (NM box), A ..$150.00

Santa on Skis, KSK, advances using ski poles, litho tin, 5½", NM (EX box), A $500.00

Santa on Sleigh, OKD, advances as carousel spins above, litho tin & celluloid, 6", EX (EX box), A.........................$300.00

Sea Wolf, Alps, pirate spins & looks through telescope, litho tin, 6½", NM (NM box), A..$200.00

Shy Anne Skating Indian, Linemar, skates in realistic motion w/bow & arrow, litho tin w/cloth clothes, 6", NMIB, A $350.00

Skating Chef, TPS, Black chef realistically skates around w/plate of food, litho tin, 6½", MIB, A $1,000.00

Skating Chef, TPS, Black chef realistically skates around w/plate of food, litho tin, 6½", EX, A....................................$700.00

Skip Rope Animals, TPS, dog & squirrel hold rope as baby bear jumps, litho tin, 8", EX, A....................................$125.00

Skippy the Tricky Cyclist, TPS, clown pedals unicycle, stops & turns around, litho tin w/cloth clothes, 6", NMIB, A ..$275.00

Snapping Alligator, Cragstan, snaps at jumping fish, litho tin, 12", MIB, A $200.00

Soldier w/Gun (Vilco Gun), MT, prewar, vibrates & lifts gun up & down, celluloid, 7", MIB, A.............................$1,200.00

Sports Land Amusement Park Ride, prewar, litho tin, 6½x6½" base, EX, A $500.00

Squirrel, advances w/nut, eyes roll, litho tin, 5", NM (EX box), A $150.00

SSN 25 Submarine, SAN, advances w/spinning prop, litho tin, 10", NM (EX box), A...$200.00

Super Racer #6, Linemar, tin w/plastic figure, friction, 9½", NM (EX box), A $225.00

Super Sonic Race Car No 36, MT, advances w/engine sound, litho tin, friction, 9", NM (NM box), A..................$200.00

Superman Turnover Tank, Linemar, Superman forces tank to turn over, litho tin, 4", EX, A $350.00

Surprise Santa Claus, Y, rings bell & lifts gift out of bag, litho tin w/vinyl face & cloth clothes, 8", NM (EX box), A .$200.00

Suzy Bouncing Ball, TPS, girl realistically bounces ball, litho tin w/vinyl head, 5½", NM (EX box), A.......................$150.00

Swimmer, prewar, realistic swimming motion, celluloid w/tin arms, 6", NM (EX box), A $250.00

Tap Dancer, Occupied Japan, Black man taps in front of Lenox Ave sign, tin & celluloid w/cloth clothes, 8", NM, A $300.00

Teacup Merry-Go-Round, 3 bears in seats circle on base as umbrella spins above, tin, plastic & plush, 8", NMIB, A $185.00

Telephone Santa Claus, Alps, Santa answers phone w/different sounds, tin w/vinyl face & cloth clothes, 7", M, A..**$125.00**

Three Little Pigs Acrobats, Borgfeldt, celluloid figures on wire bar, 11", rare, EX, A **$1,200.00**

Tin Lizzy w/Driver, Linemar, flapper girl driving car w/comical sayings allover, tin & celluloid, friction, 5", NMIB, A.......**$500.00**

Troy Ruttman Jet Racer, Marusan, 1955, w/driver, litho tin w/rubber tires, friction, 8", EX (EX box), A.............**$500.00**

Trumpet Player, TN, Black man stands on base & plays trumpet, litho tin w/cloth clothes, 10½", NM, A **$400.00**

Tumbling Popeye, Linemar, Popeye does somersaults, litho tin, 5", EX (EX box), A **$1,800.00**

Unicycle Clown, clown w/flag & parasol spins inside drum, litho tin, 6", M, A **$700.00**

USA Military Vehicle Group, Cragstan, tin, friction, set of 5, NMIB, A..**$250.00**

Vacationland Airplane Ride, Y, boats circle base w/planes flying overhead, litho tin, 6", EX (EX box), A **$125.00**

Vacationland Express, Y, train circles carnival as plane flies overhead, litho tin, 5½" sq base, MIB, A **$150.00**

Walt Disney Carousel, Linemar, litho tin w/celluloid figures, 7", MIB, A **$3,200.00**

Walt Disney's Rocking Chair, Linemar, Pluto rocks Donald in chair, litho tin & celluloid, NMIB, from $650 to....**$850.00**

Western Ranger (Lone Ranger), K, horse gallops along, litho tin, 5", EX (EX box), A **$250.00**

Whirling Tail Goofy, Linemar, litho tin w/rubber tail, 5½", NM, A **$400.00**

Wimpy, Linemar, hopping action w/nodding head, litho tin, 5", scarce, NM (NM box), A..**$8,000.00**

Wimpy on Tricycle, Linemar, pedals tricycle w/bell, litho tin & celluloid, 4", EX, A **$1,000.00**

Wonder MG Car, SAN, advances on platform w/spinning umbrella, litho tin, 12", EX (EX box), A **$350.00**

SPANISH

Bears on Motorcycle, Rico, mk RSA, big bear driver w/2 sm bear passengers, litho tin, 9", EX, A **$1,600.00**

Boat w/Revolving Airplane, Espana, planes fly as boat advances, litho tin, 9", EX, A **$575.00**

Charlie Chaplin, 1950s, figure in famous pose w/valise labeled Juguetes Roman, plastic, 6½", EX **$100.00**

Disneylandia, Nibo, 1950s, 2 vehicles navigate track, litho tin w/plastic station house in center, 11x18", NMIB, A .**$350.00**

Donald Duck Walking Car, advances as Donald's head bobs, litho tin w/celluloid figure, 5½", MIB, A.................**$300.00**

Goofy Walking Car, advances as Goofy's head bobs, litho tin w/celluloid figure, 5½", MIB, A **$475.00**

Harley-Davidson Police Motorcycle, Sanchis, red & wht plastic w/driver in bl uniform, 10", EX (EX box), A **$300.00**

Laurel & Hardy w/Picnic Basket, RS Isla Toys, 1930s, head pops out of basket, plunger action, litho tin, 6", NM, A..**$2,800.00**

Louie Walking Car, advances as Louie's head bobs, litho tin w/celluloid figure, 5½", MIB, A **$250.00**

Negro Danzante (rare variation of Pango-Pango African Dancer), litho tin, 6", EX (EX box), A..................**$275.00**

Wrestling Collectibles

TV wrestling has spawned a new segment of super heroes, and every fan has his favorite. Right now interest is high, and manufacturers of kids' toys and games see to it that the market is well stocked with memorabilia featuring these colorful warriors.

Advisor: George Downes (D8).

See also Action Figures.

Belt, World Wrestling Federation, aqua w/WWF logo on plastic buckle, EX, F1 ....**$10.00**

Doll, Hulk Hogan, Ace Novelty, 1991, stuffed plush w/Python Power lettered on bandana, 2½-ft, EX, F1 ....**$25.00**

Doll, Hulk Hogan, Ace Novelty, 1991, stuffed plush w/Python Power lettered on bandana, 3½-ft, EX, F1 ....**$50.00**

Figure, Big Boss Man, PVC, 3", EX, F1...............................**$5.00**

Figure, Ultimate Warrior, PVC, 3", EX, F1 ....**$5.00**

Finger Puppet, Big John Studd, LJN, MOC, D8 ....**$15.00**

Finger Puppet, Hillbilly Jim, LJN, MOC, D8...................**$15.00**

Finger Puppet, Roddy Piper, LJN, MOC, D8 ....**$15.00**

Game, World Wrestling Federation Superstars, Milton Bradley, complete, EX (EX box)...**$25.00**

Kite, Ultimate Warrior, Spectra, 1990, plastic, 4½", MIP, F1..**$15.00**

Photo Pin, Incredible Hulk, glossy cb figure, Hulk Rules, 1990, MOC, M17 ....**$12.00**

Ring, World Championship Wrestling, w/4 electronic sounds & removable steel cage, 13½x13⅓", MIB, F1 ....**$40.00**

Sparkle Art Kit, Hulk Hogan, Colorforms, 1991, complete, MIB, F1 ....**$12.00**

Sticker Album w/Decoder, Hulk Hogan's Rock 'N Wrestling, Diamond Pub, 1986, 32 pgs, EX, F1 ....**$20.00**

Video Game, Hulk Hogan, Micro Games of American, 1995, hand-held, EX, F1 ....**$15.00**

Wyandotte

Though the Wyandotte Company (Michigan) produced toys of all types, included here are only the heavy-gauge pressed-steel cars, trucks, and other vehicles they made through the 1930s and '40s.

See also Aeronautical; Boats; Character, TV, and Movie Collectibles; Windups, Friction, and Other Mechanicals.

Ambulance, #340, w/swinging rear door, 11", EX...........**$175.00**

Auto Carrier w/Steam Shovel, 22½", VG, A **$300.00**

Car Carrier, orange w/yel wheels, no cars, 21", EX, A....**$200.00**

Circus Truck & Trailer, Greatest Show on Earth on backplate, 11", EX, A..**$500.00**

Dump Truck, #326, 1931, NM..**$350.00**

Fire Truck w/Water Pump & Hose, mk #5, complete w/extension ladder, 10", NM (EX box), A **$200.00**

Gasoline Truck, early, red w/chrome detail, blk rubber tires, 11", EX, A **$250.00**

Construction and Steam Shovel Truck, 1940s, white, blue, and yellow, NM, $450.00. (Photo courtesy Jeff Bub)

Cord Roadster, #600, 1936, yellow with red top, 13", EX (G box), A, $700.00.

LaSalle Sedan w/Trailer, 1930's, 25½", VG $425.00
Official AAA Service Car, 1930s, 12", EX $300.00
Painter's Truck, #126, red, wht & bl w/Jiffy's Painting & Decorating decal, 10", NM (EX box), A $325.00
Racer, red streamline body w/sleek fenders, wht rubber tires, battery-op headlights, 8½", EX (EX box), A $600.00
Service & Wrecker Truck, red, wht & gr w/yel wheels, 11½", NM (NM box), A $500.00
Toytown Estate Wagon, EX $200.00

Yo-Yos

Yo-yos are starting to attract toy collectors, especially those with special features such as Hasbro's 'Glow-Action' and Duncan's 'Whistler.' For more information we recommend *Lucky's Collector's Guide to 20th Century Yo-Yos, History and Values* written by our advisor Lucky J. Meisenheimer, M.D. He is listed under (M3) in the Coded Dealers and Collectors section.

All Western Plastics, Roy Rogers & Trigger, 1940s, M $18.00

Alox Flying Disc, 1950s, wood w/gold die stamp or pnt seal, M, ea $25.00
Avon, Teenage Mutant Ninja Turtles, MIP $5.00
Cayo Whistling Ka-Yo, 1930s, tin w/wood-grain finish, blk paper sticker, VG $100.00
Cheerio Genuine Pro #99, 1950s, wood w/die stamp, M .. $50.00
Cheerio Glitter Spin, 1947, wood w/4 rhinestones, gold foil sticker w/blk & red print, M $200.00
Cheerio Official Pro 99, wood w/foil sticker, EX, M3 .... $80.00
Cheerio Tournament Practice #25, 1940s-50s, wood w/airbrushed stripe, gold foil sticker w/blk & red print, M $70.00
Cheerio Tournament Practice #99, 1940s-50s, wood w/airbrushed stripe, silver foil sticker w/red & blk print, M $80.00
Chico Olympic Tournament, 1959, wood, gold foil sticker w/blk print, M $45.00
Dell Big D Trickster, 1960s, plastic w/swirled colors, M ... $25.00
Dell Fireball, 1960s, plastic satellite model, M $30.00
Duncan Advertising, Coca-Cola, 1950s, wood w/die stamp, 2 styles, M, ea $120.00
Duncan Advertising, Red Goose Shoes, 1950s, wood w/die stamp, M $25.00
Duncan Cattle Brand, late 1970s, MOC, M3 .... $12.00
Duncan Chief #44, 1950s, wood, foil sticker w/red & bl graphics, M $125.00
Duncan Colorama, 1960s, plastic w/paper inserts, M $60.00
Duncan Competition, 1970s, plastic w/diamond design & maple decal, M $25.00
Duncan Genuine Beginner #44, 1930s, wood w/gold die stamp or yel-pnt seal, M, ea $35.00
Duncan Genuine Junior, 1930s, wood w/die stamp, VG .. $25.00
Duncan Glow Imperial, 1960s, plastic w/gold indented stamp, M $25.00
Duncan Jeweled Tournament, 1940s, wood w/4 rhinestones, gold die stamp, M $100.00
Duncan Junior, 1970s, plastic w/pnt image of Duncan Yo-Yo man, M $15.00
Duncan Little Ace, 1960s, plastic w/gold die stamp, M $30.00
Duncan Mardi Gras, 1960s, plastic w/silver or gold die stamp, M, ea $75.00
Duncan O-Boy, 1930s, red-& blk-pnt wood w/silver stamp, M $50.00
Duncan Official Mickey Mouse Club, 1960s, plastic w/paper inserts, MIP $45.00
Duncan Pearlessence Tournament #888, 1950s, wood w/metallic pearl pnt, silver or gold die stamp, M, ea $100.00
Duncan Pony #22, 1950s, clear plastic w/concentric circles, M . $50.00
Duncan Professional, 1970s, plastic w/diamond design, M ... $15.00
Duncan Shrieking Sonic Satellite, 1960s, wood w/2-tone metal flake pnt, gold die stamp, M $35.00
Duncan Super #77, 1950s, wood w/airbrushed stripe, silver die stamp, M $75.00
Duncan Super Heroes, 1970s, plastic, any character, M, ea .. $25.00
Duncan Whistling Yo-Yo, 1930s, litho tin, M, M3 .... $150.00
Duncan World Class, 1979, translucent red plastic w/silver print, M $8.00
Duncan 8-Ball, 1960s, blk plastic, M $25.00
Festival Be a Sport Series, 1970s, MIP, M3 .... $25.00
Festival Disney Series, Goofy, 1970s, MOC, M3 .... $20.00

Festival Disney Series, Mickey, Pluto or Donald, 1970s, MOC, M3, ea $20.00
Festival Dragonfly, 1964, plastic, M $15.00
Festival Screamer, 1954, litho tin checked design w/paper sticker, M $60.00
Fli-Back #65, red- & bl-pnt wood w/gold die stamp, M $35.00
Fli-Back Genuine Tournament Championship, 1960, wood w/air-brushed stripe or swirled pnt, gold foil sticker, M, ea..$100.00
Fli-Back Orbit Beginner, red- & bl-pnt wood w/space capsule & stars, gold die stamp, M $25.00
Flores Beginner, 1920s, wood w/blk-pnt seal, M.............$350.00
Goody Genuine Champion Filipino Twirler, 1930s, wood w/air-brushed stripe & 3 jewels, pnt seal, M $150.00
Goody Genuine Master Filipino Twirler, 1930s, wood w/air-brushed stripe & 1 jewel, pnt seal, M.......................$100.00
Goody Joy-O-Top, 1930s, wood w/pnt seal, M $100.00
Hallmark Peanuts Characters, 1960s-70s, wood w/paper sticker, any character, M, ea $20.00
Hasbro Glow Action, 1968, MOC, M3 ....$20.00
Hi-Ker Spin Master, 1950s, wood w/glitter pnt, gold die stamp, M..$75.00
Lumar Beginner #34, 1930s, litho tin w/spiral pattern, M..$150.00
Medalist Genuine Trophy, translucent plastic w/gold stamp, M..$35.00
Royal Champion Junior, wood w/gold die stamp, M.........$35.00
Royal Deluxe Tournament, wood w/paper sticker, M.......$75.00
Royal Master Official Championship, wood w/crown logo, M..$75.00
Royal Monarch, translucent plastic w/gold foil die stamp, M..$25.00

Royal Tops Mfg. Co. King Size, wood with airbrushed stripe and crown logo, NM, $50.00. (Photo courtesy Christopher Cook)

Royal Thunderbird, 1959, wood w/paper sticker, MIP......$75.00
Spectra Star, Freddy Krueger, 1980s, MOC, M3 ....$8.00
Spectra Star, Ghostbusters, 1980s, MOC, M3 ....$8.00
Spectra Star, Pee Wee Herman, 1980s, MOC, M3...........$10.00
Union Wadding, Mickey Mouse, 1960s, plastic, MOC, P4 ..$20.00
World's Fair, 1939, decal seal, NM, M3 ....$45.00

Dealer and Collector Codes

Most of our description lines contain a letter/number code just before the suggested price. They correspond with the names of the following collectors and dealers who sent us their current selling list to be included in this addition. If you're interested in buying an item in question, don't hesitate to call or write them. We only ask that you consider the differences in time zones, and try to call at a convenient time. If you're corresponding, please send a self-addressed, stamped envelope for their reply. **Because our data was entered several months ago, many of the coded items will have already sold,** but our dealers tell us that they are often able to restock some of the same merchandise over and over. Some said that they had connections with other dealers around the country and might be able to locate a particular toy for you. But please bear in mind that because they may have had to pay more to restock their shelves, they may also have to charge a little more than the price quoted in their original sales list. We must stress that these people are not appraisers, so please do not ask them to price your toys.

If you have lists of toys for sale that you would like for us to use in the next edition, please send them to us at the address below as soon as possible. We will process incoming lists as they arrive and because our space is limited, the earlier you send it, the better. Please do not ask us to include you in our Categories of Special Interest unless you contribute useable information. Not only are we limited on available space, it isn't fair to those who do. If you would like to advertise with us but cannot contribute listings, display ads are available (see page 484 for rates). We will hold a previously assigned dealer code over for you who are our contributors/advisors from year to year as long as we know you are interested in keeping it, but if we haven't heard from you by February 1, we will reassign that code to someone else. Because the post office prefers your complete 9-digit zip code, please send us that information for our files.

Direct your correspondence to: **Huxford Enterprises, Inc., 1202 7th St., Covington, IN 47932**

(A1)
Stan and Sally Alekna
732 Aspen Lane
Lebanon, PA 17042-9073
717-228-2361
fax 717-228-2362

(A3)
Avalon Comics
Larry Curcio
P.O. Box 821
Medford, MA 02155
617-391-5614

(A4)
Bob Armstrong
15 Monadnock Rd.
Worcester, MA 01609
508-799-0644
e-mail: raahna@oldpuzzles.com
www.oldpuzzles.com

(A5)
Geneva Addy
P.O. Box 124
Winterset, IA 50273

(A7)
Tatonka Toys
Matt and Lisa Adams
1234 Harbor Cove
Woodstock, GA 30189-5467
770-516-6874
e-mail: mattradams@earthlink.net

(B1)
Richard Belyski
P.O. Box 124
Sea Cliff, NY 11579
516-676-1183
e-mail: peznews@juno.com

(B2)
Larry Blodget
Box 753
Rancho Mirage, CA 92270

(B3)
Bojo
Bob Gottuso
P.O. Box 1403
Cranberry Twp., PA 16066-0403
Phone or fax 724-776-0621
e-mail: bojo@zbzoom.net

(B5)
Martin and Carolyn Berens
Collection Connection
P.O. Box 18552
Fairfield, OH 45018
Phone or fax 513-851-9217

(B6)
Jim Buskirk
3009 Oleander Ave.
San Marcos, CA 92069
760-599-1054

(B8)
Stanley A. and Robert S. Block
P.O. Box 51
Trumbull, CT 06611
203-261-3223 or 203-775-0138

(B10)
Ditto Enterprises
Tom Bremer
P.O. Box 49
Newark, NY 14513
Phone or fax 315-331-7688
e-mail: Dittoent@aol.com
members.aol.com/dittoent/
    catalogpage.index.html

(B11)
Sue and Marty Bunis
RR 1, Box 36
Bradford, NH 03221-9102

(B12)
Bromer Booksellers, Inc.
607 Boylston St.
Boston, MA 02116
617-247-2818; fax 617-247-2975

(B14)
Scott Bruce
P.O. Box 481
Cambridge, MA 02140
e-mail: scott@flake.com

(C1)
Casey's Collectible Corner
HCR Box 31, Rt. 3
N Blenheim, NY 12131
607-588-6464
e-mail: caseysco@aol.com
www.csmonline.com/caseys

(C2)
Mark E. Chase
Collector Glass News
P.O. Box 308
Slippery Rock, PA 16057
412-946-2838; fax 412-946-9012
www.glassnews.com

(C3)
Ken Clee
Box 11412
Philadelphia, PA 19111
215-722-1979

(C6)
Cotswold Collectibles
P.O. Box 716, Dept. SC
Freeland, WA 98249
360-331-5331; fax 360-331-5344
www.whidbey.net/-cotswold

(C9)
Marilyn Cooper
P.O. Box 55174
Houston, TX 77255
713-465-7773
Author of *The Pictorial Review of Toothbrush Holders*

(C10)
Bill Campbell
1221 Littlebrook Lane
Birmingham, AL 35235

205-853-8227; fax 405-658-6986
e-mail: billanne@bellsouth.net

(C11)
Me and Dad's Toys
Sally and Jim Christoffel
409 Maple
Elburn, IL 60119
708-365-2914
e-mail: jimc@elnet.com

(C12)
Joel J. Cohen
Cohen Books and Collectibles
P.O. Box 810310
Boca Raton, FL 33481
561-487-7888; fax 561-487-3117
e-mail: cohendisney@prodigy.net
www.cohendisney.com

(C13)
Brad Cassity
1350 Stanwix
Toledo, OH 43614
419-389-1100

(C14)
Cynthia's Country Store
The Wellington Mall #15-A
12794 W Forest Hill Blvd.
Wellington, FL 33414
561-793-0554; fax 561-795-4222 (24 hr)
e-mail: cynbears@aol.com
www.thecrier.com/ccs

(C15)
Rosalind Cranor
P.O. Box 859
Blacksburg, VA 24063

(C17)
John and Michele Casino
633 Franklin Ave., Suite #169
Nutley, NJ 07110
973-759-2520
e-mail: Ostfront@aol.com

(D2)
Marl Davidson (Marl & B)
10301 Braden Run
Bradenton, FL 34202
941-751-6275; fax 941-751-5463
www.marlbe.com

(D3)
Larry DeAngelo
516 King Arthur Dr.
Virginia Beach, VA 23464
757-424-1691

(D4)
John DeCicco
57 Bay View Dr.
Shrewsbury, MA 01545
508-797-0023
e-mail: jctoygift@aol.com
www.Johns-Toys.com

(D6)
Doug Dezso
864 Patterson Ave.
Maywood, NJ 07607
201-488-1311

(D7)
Ron and Donna Donnelly
Saturday Heroes
6302 Championship Dr.
Tuscaloosa, AL 35405

(D8)
George Downes
Box 572
Nutley, NJ 07110
201-935-3388
e-mail: gad@advanix.net
www.advanix.net/~gad

(D9)
Gordy Dutt
P.O. Box 201
Sharon Center, OH 44274-0201
330-239-1657; fax 330-239-2991
www.gremlins.com/kitbuilders

(D10)
Dunbar's Gallery
Leila and Howard Dunbar
76 Haven St.
Milford, MA 01757
508-634-8697; fax 508-634-8696

(D11)
Larry Doucet
2351 Sultana Dr.
Yorktown Heights, NY 10598
914-245-1320

(E1)
Larry Egelhoff
4175 Millersville Rd.
Indianapolis, IN 46205
317-846-7228

(F1)
Anthony Balasco
P.O. Box 19482
Johnston, RI 02919
401-946-5720; fax 401-942-7980
e-mail: figinc@aol.com
www.ewtech.com/figures

(F2)
Paul Fideler
20 Shadow Oak Dr., Apt. #18
Sudbury, MA 01776
617-386-0228 (24 hours)

(F3)
Paul Fink's Fun and Games
P.O. Box 488
59 S Kent Rd.
Kent, CT 06757
860-927-4001
www.gamesandpuzzles.com

(F4)
Mike and Kurt Fredericks
145 Bayline Cir.
Folsom, CA 95630
916-985-7986

(F5)
Fun House Toy Co.
G.F. Ridenour
P.O. Box 343
Bradfordwoods, PA 15015-0343
724-935-1392 (fax capable)
www.funhousetoy.com

(F7)
Finisher's Touch Antiques
Steve Fisch, proprietor
10 W Main St.
Wappingers Falls, NY 12590
914-298-8882; fax 914-298-8945

(F9)
Donald Friedman
660 W Grand Ave.
Chicago, IL 60610
708-656-3700 (day) or 312-226-
4741 (evening & weekends)
fax 708-656-6292

(G1)
Gary's Trains
186 Pine Springs Camp Road
Boswell, PA 15531
814-629-9277

(G2)
Mark Giles
510 E Third St.
Ogalala, NE 69153
308-284-4360

(G6)
Carol Karbowiak Gilbert
2193 14 Mile Rd. 206
Sterling Height, MI 48310

(G7)
PAK-RAT
Andy Galbus
900 8th St. NW
Kasson, MN 55944-1079
507-634-2093
e-mail: lhpakrateans.net

(G8)
Joan Stryker Grubaugh
2342 Hoaglin Rd.
Van Wert, OH 45891
419-622-4411; fax 419-622-3026

(G16)
Candelaine (Candace Gunther)
1435 Wellington Ave.
Pasadena, CA 91103-2320
626-796-4568; fax 626-796-7172
e-mail: Candelaine@aol.com.

(H1)
The Hamburgs
Happy Memories Antique Toy Co.
P.O. Box 1305
Woodland Hills, CA 91365
818-346-9884 or 818-346-1269
fax 818-346-0215

(H3)
George Hardy
1670 Hawkwood Ct.
Charlottesville, VA 22901
804-295-4863; fax 804-295-4898
e-mail: georgeh@comet.net
www.comet.net/personal/georgeh/

(H4)
Jerry and Ellen L. Harnish
110 Main St.
Bellville, OH 44813
Phone or fax 419-886-4782
after 7 PM Eastern time

(H6)
Phil Helley
Old Kilbourne Antiques
629 Indiana Ave.
Wisconsin Dells, WI 53965
608-254-8770

(H7)
Jacquie and Bob Henry
Antique Treasures and Toys
Box 17
Walworth, NY 14568
315-597-4719
e-mail: Jhenry5792@aol.com or
jacqueline.henry@mci2000.com

(H8)
Homestead Collectibles
Art and Judy Turner
P.O. Box 173-TC
Mill Hall, PA 17751-0173
717-726-3597
e-mail: jturner@cub.kcnet.org

(H9)
Pamela E. Apkarian-Russell, The
Halloween Queen
C.J. Russell & The Halloween
Queen Antiques
P.O. Box 499
Winchester, NH 03470
603-239-8875

(H10)
Don Hamm
P.O. Box 2996
Kissimmee, FL 34742

(H11)
N.F. Huber, the SNO-PEA Trader
Norman Huber, Buyer
931 Emerson St.
Thousand Oaks, CA 91362-2447
805-497-0119; fax 1-800-SNOOPY2

(H12)
Roslyn L. Herman
124-16 84th Rd.
Kew Gardens, New York 11415
718-846-3496; 718-846-8491

(H13)
Tim Hunter
4301 W. Hidden Valley Dr.
Reno, NV 89502
702-856-4357; fax 702-856-4354
e-mail: thunter885@aol.com

(I2)
Terri Ivers, Terri's Toys and Nostalgia
206 E. Grand Ave.
Ponca City, OK 74601
580-762-8697 or 580-762-5174
fax 580-765-2657
e-mail: toylady@poncacity.net

(I3)
Dan Iannotti
212 W. Hickory Grove Rd.
Bloomfield Hills, MI 48302-1127
248-335-5042
e-mail: modernbanks@ameritech.net

(J1)
Bill Jackameit
972 Kelsey Dr.
Charlottesville, VA 22903
804-923-3398 (Mon.–Thurs., 7
pm–9 pm EST)
e-mail: wj2d@sprintmail.com
www.freeyellow.com/members/bj
diecast

(J2)
Character Company
Ed Janey
1756 65th St.
Garrison, IA 52229-9644
319-477-8888
e-mail: edjaney@aol.com
www.characterco.com

(J3)
Dana Johnson Enterprises
P.O. Box 1824
Bend, OR 97709-1824
503-382-8410

(J5)
Just Kids Nostalgia
310 New York Avenue
Huntington, NY 11743
516-423-8449; fax 516-423-4326
e-mail: justkids25@aol.com

(J6)
June Moon
245 N Northwest Hwy.
Park Ridge, IL 60068
847-825-1411 (24-hr phone); fax
847-825-6090
e-mail: junemoonstr@aol.com
www.toymarket.com/junemoon

(J7)
Jim's TV Collectibles
P.O. Box 4767
San Diego, CA 92164
Phone/fax 619-462-1953

(J8)
Jeff and Bob's Fun Stuff
7324 Reseda Blvd #168
Reseda, CA 91335
818-705-3368

(K1)
K-3 Inc.
Bendees Only; Simpson Mania
2335 NW Thurman
Portland, OR 97210
503-222-2713

(K2)
David Kolodny-Nagy
May through Jan:
3701 Connecticut Ave. NW #500
Washington, DC 20008
202-364-8753

(K3)
Ilene Kayne
1308 S Charles St.
Baltimore, MD 21230
410-685-3923
e-mail: kayne@clark.net

(K4)
Debby and Marty Krim
P.O. Box 2273
W Peabody, MA 01960
978-535-3140; fax 978-535-7522

(K5)
Kerry and Judy's Toys
1414 S. Twelfth St.
Murray, KY 42071
270-759-3456
e-mail: kjtoys@apex.net

(K6)
Keith and Donna Kaonis
60 Cherry Ln.
Huntington, NY 11743
516-261-8337; fax 516-261-8235

(L1)
Jean-Claude H. Lanau
740 Thicket Ln.
Houston, TX 77079
713-497-6034 (after 7 pm, CST)

(L2)
John and Eleanor Larsen
523 Third St.
Colusa, CA 95932
916-458-4769 (after 4 pm)

(L4)
Tom Lastrapes
P.O. Box 2444
Pinellas Park, FL 34664
813-545-2586

(L6)
Kathy Lewis
187 N Marcello Ave
Thousand Oaks, CA 91360
805-499-8101

(L7)
Terry and Joyce Losonsky
7506 Summer Leave Ln.
Columbia, MD 21046-2455
301-381-3358

(M1)
Mark and Val Macaluso
3603 Newark Rd.
Marion, NY 14505
315-926-4349; fax 315-926-4853

(M2)
John McKenna
801-803 W Cucharres
Colorado Springs, CO 80905
719-630-8732

(M3)
Lucky J. Meisenheimer, M.D.
7300 Sandlake Commons Blvd.,
Suite 105
Orlando, FL 32819
407-352-2444; fax 407-363-2869
e-mail: LuckyJ@MSN.com
www.yo-yos.net

(M4)
Bill Mekalian
550 E Chesapeake Cir.
Fresno, CA 93720; 209-434-3247

(M5)
Mike's General Store
52 St. Annes Rd.
Winnipeg, Manitoba, Canada R2M-2Y3
204-255-3463; fax 204-253-4124

(M7)
Judith A. Mosholder
186 Pine Springs Camp Road
Boswell, PA 15531
814-629-9277

(M8)
The Mouse Man Ink
P.O. Box 3195
Wakefield, MA 01880
781-246-3876; fax 781-245-4511
e-mail: mouse_man@msn.com
www.mouseman.com

(M9)
Steven Meltzer
1255 2nd St.
Santa Monica, CA 90401
310-656-0483

(M10)
Gary Metz
P.O. Box 1430
Salem, VA 24153

(M11)
Michael and Polly McQuillen
McQuillen's Collectibles
P.O. Box 50022
Indianapolis, IN 46250-0022
317-845-1721
e-mail: buttons@oaktree.net

(M12)
Helen L. McCale
Holly Hobbie Collector
1006 Ruby Ave.
Butler, MO 64730-2500

(M14)
Ken Mitchell
710 Conacher Dr.
Willowdale, Ontario
Canada M2M 3N6
416-222-5808 anytime

(M15)
Marcia's Fantasy
Marcia Fanta
427 S. 33rd St. SE
Tappen, ND 58487-9411
701-327-4441
e-mail: fantbck@daktel.com

(M17)
Mrs. Miller's Memorabilia
70a Greenwich Ave., Box #116
New York, NY 10011
212-614-9774
(leave message)
e-mail: mmm@photobbs.com

(M18)
Nancy McMichael
P.O. Box 53262
Washington DC 20009

(M19)
Model Auto
P.O. Box 79253
Houston, TX 77279
713-468-4461; fax 713-468-6970
(phone evenings; fax anytime)

(M20)
Bruce Middleton
5 Lloyd Rd.
Newburgh, NY 12550
914-564-2556

(M21)
Peter Muldavin
173 W 78th St., Apt. 5-F
New York, NY 10024
212-362-9606
members.aol.com/kiddie78s/

(N1)
Natural Way/dba Russian Toy Co.
820 Massachusetts
Lawrence, KS 66044
913-841-0100

(N2)
Norman's Olde & New Store
Philip Norman
126 W Main St.
Washington, NC 27889-4944
252-946-3448

(N3)
Neil's Wheels, Inc.
Box 354
Old Bethpage, NY 11804
516-293-9659; fax 516-420-0483

(N4)
Roger Nazeley
4921 Castor Ave.
Philadelphia, PA 19124
215-743-8999 or 215-533-6110
extension 221
e-mail: vmreelguy2@aol.com
(will answer all messages)

(P1)
Pat Peterson
1105 6th Ave. SE
Hampton, IA 50441

(P2)
Dawn Parrish
20460 Samual Dr.
Saugus, CA 91350-3812
661-263-TOYS

(P3)
American Pie Collectibles
John and Sheri Pavone
29 Sullivan Rd.
Peru, NY 12972
518-643-0993 Toll Free 888-
458-2200; fax 518-643-8152

e-mail: apc1@worldnet.att.net
www.serftech.com/apc
Mastercard Visa Discover

(P4)
Plymouth Rock Toy Co.
38 Russell St.
Plymouth, MA 02360
508-746-2842 or 508-830-1880
(noon to 11 PM EDT); fax 508-830-0364
e-mail: plyrocktoy@aol.com

(P5)
Gary Pollastro
5047 84th Ave. SE
Mercer, WA 98040
206-232-3199

(P6)
Judy Posner
P.O. Box 2194
Englewood, FL 34295
e-mail: judyandjef@aol.com
www.judyposner.com

(P8)
Diane Patalano
P.O. Box 144
Saddle River, NJ 07458
201-327-2499

(P10)
Bill and Pat Poe
220 Dominica Circle E
Niceville, FL 32578-4085
850-897-4163; fax 850-897-2606
e-mail: McPoes@aol.com

(P11)
The Phoenix Toy Soldier Co.
Bob Wilson
16405 North 9th Place
Phoenix, AZ 85022
602-863-2891

(P12)
Michael Paquin, That Toy Guy
72 Penn Blvd.
E Lansdowne, PA 19050
610-394-8697 (10 am – 10 pm
EST); fax 610-259-8626 (24 hr)
e-mail: Mike@thattoyguy.com
www.thattoyguy.com

(P13)
Lorraine Punchard
8201 Pleasant Ave. South
Bloomington, MN 55420
612-888-1079

(R2)
Rick Rann, Beatlelist
P.O. Box 877
Oak Park, IL 60303
708-442-7907

(R3)
Jim Rash
135 Alder Ave.
Egg Harbor Twp., NJ 08234-9302
609-646-4125 (evenings)

(R4)
Robert Reeves
104 Azalea Dr.
St. Mathews, SC 29135
803-578-5939
(leave message)

(R5)
Reynolds Toys
Charlie Reynolds
2836 Monroe St.
Falls Church, VA 22042
703-533-1322

(R6)
David E. Riddle
P.O. Box 13141
Tallahassee, FL 32308
904-877-7207

(S1)
Sam Samuelian, Jr.
700 Llanfair Rd.
Upper Darby, PA 19082
215-566-7248

(S5)
Son's a Poppin' Ranch
John Rammacher
1610 Park Ave.
Orange City, FL 32763-8869
904-775-2891
e-mail: sap@bitstorm.net
www.bitstorm.net/sap

(S6)
Bill Stillman
Scarfone & Stillman
  Vintage Oz
P.O. Box 167
Hummelstown, PA 17036
717-566-5538

(S7)
Nate Stoller
960 Reynolds Ave.
Ripon, CA 95366
209-599-5933
e-mail: multimotot@aol.com
www.geocities.com/heartland/
plains/6385

(S10)
Scott Smiles
848 SE Atlantic Dr.
Lantana, FL 33462-4702
561-582-4947
e-mail: ssmiles664@aol.com

(S13)
Refried Jeans
David Shedlock
115 E 17th St.
515-791-2551 or 888-429-4326
(no Sunday call please)

(S14)
Cindy Sabulis
P.O. Box 642
Shelton, CT 06484
203-926-0176
e-mail: toys4two@snet.net
www.dollsntoys.com

(S16)
Bill Smith
56 Locust St.
Douglas, MA 01516; 508-476-2015

(S18)
The Silver Bullet
Terry and Kay Klepey
P.O. Box 553
Forks, WA 98331
360-327-3726
e-mail: slvrbllt@olypen.com

(S19)
Craig and Donna Stifter
P.O. Box 6514
Naperville, IL 60540; 630-789-5780

(S20)
Pat and Kris Secor
P.O. Box 158
Clarksville, AR 72830
501-754-5746

(S21)
Robin Stine
P.O. Box 6202
Toledo, OH 43614
419-385-7387
e-mail: doogerbear@Aol.com

(S22)
Carole & Richard Smyth
Carole Smyth Antiques
P.O. Box 2068
Huntington, NY 11743

(S24)
Mark and Lynda Suozzi
P.O. Box 102
Ashfield, MA 01330
Phone or fax 413-628-3241
(9am to 5pm)
e-mail: marklyn@valinet.com
marklynantiques.com

(S25)
Steve Stevenson
11117 NE 164th Pl.
Bothell, WA 98011-4003
206-488-2603; fax 206-488-2841

(T1)
Tom Duncan, Tom's Treasures
746 Kennedy St. P.O. Box 1654
Jackson, MI 49206
e-mail: toms.1@mcione.com

(T2)
Bill Bruegman, Toy Scouts, Inc.
137 Casterton Ave.
Akron, OH 44303
330-836-0668; fax 330-869-8668
e-mail: toyscouts@toyscouts.com
www.toyscouts.com

(T3)
Richard Trautwein
Toys N Such
437 Dawson St.
Sault Ste. Marie, MI 49783
906-635-0356
e-mail: r.traut@portup.com

(T5)
Bob and Marcie Tubbs
6405 Mitchell Hollow Rd.
Charlotte, NC 28277
704-541-5839

(T6)
TV Collector
P.O. Box 1088
Easton, MA 02334
508-238-1179 or fax by pre-set
agreement

(V1)
Norm Vigue
3 Timberwood Dr. #306
Goffstown, MA 02072
603-647-9951

(V2)
Marci Van Ausdall
P.O. Box 946
Quincy, CA 95971
916-283-2770
e-mail: dreams707@aol.com

(W1)
Dan Wells Antique Toys
7008 Main St.
Westport, KY 40077
270-225-9925; fax 270-225-0019
e-mail: dwatcatDan@aol.com

(W2)
Adrienne Warren
1032 Feather Bed Lane
Edison, NJ 08820; 732-381-1616
e-mail: adrienne.w@worldnet.att.net

(W4)
Randy Welch
27965 Peach Orchard Rd.
Easton, MD 21601-8203
410-822-5441

(W5)
Linda and Paul Woodward
14 Argo Drive
Sewell, NJ 08080-1908
609-582-1253

(W6)
John D. Weatherhead
5224 S. Guerin Pass
New Berlin, WI 53151
414-425-8810; fax 414-425-7844

(W7)
Larry White
108 Central St.
Rowley, MA 01969-1317

(W8)
James Watson
25 Gilmore St.
Whitehall, NY 12887
518-499-0643; fax 518-499-1772

(Y1)
Henri Yunes
971 Main St., Apt. 2
Hackensack, NJ 07601
201-488-2236

(Y2)
Mary Young
Box 9244
Dayton, OH 45409
937-298-4838

Categories of Special Interest

If you would like to be included in this section, send us a list of your 'for sale' merchandise. These listings are complimentary to those who participate in the preparation of this guide by doing so. Please understand that the people who are listed here want to buy and sell. They are not appraisers. Read the paragraph under the title *Dealer and Collector Codes* for more information. If you have no catalogs or lists but would like to advertise with us, see the display ad rate sheet on 484.

Action Figures
Also GI Joe, Star Wars and Super Heroes
John DiCicco
57 Bay View Dr.
Shrewsbury, MA 01545
508-797-0023
24-hour fax 508-852-0066
e-mail: jctoygift@aol.com
www.johns-toys.com

Captain Action, Star Wars, Secret Wars, and other character-related Western, TV, movie, comic, or paperback tie-ins
George Downes
Box 572
Nutley, NJ 07110; 201-935-3388
e-mail: gad@advanix.net
www.advanix.net/~gad

Figures
Anthony Balasco
P.O. Box 19482
Johnston, RI 02919
401-946-5720; fax 401-942-7980
e-mail: figinc@aol.com
www.ewtech.com/figures

GI Joe, Captain Action, and other character-related TV, advertising, Marx and Mego figures; send $2 for sales catalog
Jerry and Ellen Harnish
110 Main St.
Bellville, OH 44813
Phone or fax 419-886-4782

Advertising
M&M Toppers
Ken Clee
P.O. Box 11412
Phil., PA 19111; 215-722-1979

Gary Metz
P.O. Box 1430
Salem, VA 24153

Also general line
Mike's General Store
52 St. Annes Rd.
Winnipeg, Manitoba, Canada
R2M 2Y3
204-255-3463; fax 204-253-4124

Advertising figures, novelty radios, Barbies, promotional watches, character toys, and more
Michael Paquin, That Toy Guy
72 Penn Blvd.
E Lansdowne, PA 19050
610-394-8697 (10 am – 10 pm EST); fax 610-259-8626 (24 hrs)
e-mail: mike@thattoyguy.com
www.thattoyguy.com

Coca-Cola and Pepsi-Cola toys
Craig and Donna Stifter
P.O. Box 6514
Naperville, IL 60540
630-789-5780

Automobilia
Especially model kits, promotional model cars, books and literature
Model Auto
P.O. Box 79253
Houston, TX 77279
713-468-4461; fax 713-468-6970
(phone evenings; fax anytime)

Banks
Ertl; sales lists available
Homestead Collectibles
Art and Judy Turner
P.O. Box 173-TC
Mill Hall, PA 17751-0173
717-726-3597
e-mail: jturner@cub.kcnet.org

Modern mechanical banks: Reynolds, John Wright, James Capron, Book of Knowledge, Richards, Wilton; sales lists available

Dan Iannotti
212 W. Hickory Grove Rd.
Bloomfield Hills, MI 48302-1127
248-335-5042
e-mail: modernbanks@ameritech.net

Also children's sadirons, Black Americana dolls and memorabilia
Diane Patalano
Country Girls Appraisal and
   Liquidation Service
P.O. Box 144
Saddle River, NJ 07458
201-327-2499

Penny banks (limited editions): new, original, mechanical, still, or figural; also bottle openers
Reynolds Toys
Charlie Reynolds
2836 Monroe St.
Falls Church, VA 22042-2007
703-533-1322
reynoldstoys@erols.com

Antique tin and iron mechanical penny banks; no reproductions or limited editions; cast-iron architectural bank buildings in Victorian form. Buy and sell list available upon request
Mark and Lynda Suozzi
P.O. Box 102
Ashfield, MA 01330
Phone or fax 413-628-3241 (9 am – 5 pm). Mail order and shows only
e-mail: marklyn@valinet.com
marklynantiques.com

Specializing in still banks, safe banks and antique safes
Larry Egelhoff
4175 Millersville Rd.
Indianapolis, IN 46205
317-846-7228

Barbie and Friends
Wanted: Mackies, holiday, and porcelain as well as vintage Barbies; buying and selling ca 1959 dolls to present issues
Marl Davidson (Marl & B)
10301 Braden Run
Bradenton, FL 34202
941-751-6275; fax 941-751-5463
www.marlbe.com

Battery-Operated
Tom Lastrapes
P.O. Box 2444
Pinellas Park, FL 34664
813-545-2586

Also general line
Mike Roscoe
3351 Lagrange
Toledo, OH 43608
419-244-6935

Beatles Memorabilia
Buying and selling old and new memorabilia; 1 piece or collection
Bojo
P.O. Box 1403
Cranberry Township, PA 16066
Phone or fax: 724-776-0621
e-mail: bojo@zbzoom.net

Books
Little Golden Books, Wonder Books, many others; 20-page list available
Ilene Kayne
1308 S Charles St.
Baltimore, MD 21230
410-685-3923
e-mail: kayne@clark.net

Specializing in Little Golden Books and look-alikes
Steve Santi
19626 Ricardo Ave.
Hayward, CA 94541; 510-481-2586

Author of *Collecting Little Golden Books, Volumes I* and *II*. Also publishes newsletter, *Poky Gazette*, primarily for Little Golden Book collectors

Breyer
Carol Karbowiak Gilbert
2193 14 Mile Rd. 206
Sterling Heights, MI 48310

Bubble Bath Containers
Including foreign issues; also character collectibles, character bobbin' head nodders, and Dr. Dolittle; write for information or send SASE for Bubble Bath Bulletin
Tatonka Toys
Matt and Lisa Adams
1234 Harbor Cove
Woodstock, GA 30189-5467
770-516-6874
e-mail: mattradams@earthlink.net

Building Blocks and Construction Toys
Anchor Stone Building Blocks by Richter
George Hardy
1670 Hawkwood Ct.
Charlottesville, VA 22901
804-295-4863; fax 804-295-4898

California Raisins
Ken Clee
Box 11412
Philadelphia, PA 19111
215-722-1979

California Raisins (PVC); buying collections, old store stock, and closeouts
Larry DeAngelo
516 King Arthur Dr.
Virginia Beach, VA 23464
757-424-1691

John D. Weatherhead
5224 S. Guerin Pass
New Berlin, WI 53151
414-425-8810
fax 414-425-7844

Candy Containers
Jeff Bradfield
Corner of Rt. 42 and Rt. 257
Dayton, VA 22821
703-879-9961

Also Tonka, Smith-Miller, Shafford black cats, German nodders
Doug Dezso
864 Patterson Ave.
Maywood, NJ 07607
201-488-1311

Cast Iron
Pre-war, large-scale cast-iron toys and early American tinplate toys
John McKenna
801-803 W Cucharres
Colorado Springs, CO 80905
719-630-8732

Victorian bell toys, horse-drawn wagons, fire toys, carriages, penny banks, pull toys, animated coin-operated machines. Buy and sell, list available upon request, mail order and shows only
Mark and Lynda Suozzi
P.O. Box 102
Ashfield, MA 01330
Phone/fax 413-628-3241
(9 am – 5 pm)
e-mail: marklyn@valinet.com
marklynantiques.com

Cereal Boxes and Premiums
Scott Bruce, Mr. Cereal Box
P.O. Box 481
Cambridge, MA 02140
e-mail: scott@flake.com

Character and Promotional Glasses
Especially fast-foods and sports glasses; publisher of Collector Glass News
Mark Chase
P.O. Box 308
Slippery Rock, PA 16057
412-946-2838
fax 412-946-9012
www.glassnews.com

Character Clocks and Watches
Also radio premiums and decoders, P-38 airplane-related items from World War II, Captain Marvel and Hoppy items, Lone Ranger books with jackets, selected old comic books, toys and cap guns; buys and sells Hoppy and Roy items
Bill Campbell
Kirschner Medical Corp.
1221 Littlebrook Ln.
Birmingham, AL 35235
205-853-8227
fax 405-658-6986
e-mail: billanne@bellsouth.net

Character Collectibles
Dolls, rock 'n roll personalities (especially the Beatles), related character items and miscellaneous toys
BOJO
Bob Gottuso
P.O. Box 1403
Cranberry Twp., PA 16066
Phone or fax 724-776-0621
e-mail: bojo@zbzoom.net

1940s–'60s character items such as super heroes, TV and cartoon items, games, playsets, lunch boxes, model kits, comic books, and premium rings
Bill Bruegman
Toy Scouts, Inc.
137 Casterton Ave.
Akron, OH 44303
216-836-0668; fax 216-869-8668
e-mail: toyscouts@toyscouts.com
website: www.toyscouts.com

Hanna-Barbera, Warner Bros, Disney, vintage TV and 'toons; also collectible dolls of the '60s and '70s
John and Michele Casino
633 Franklin Ave., Suite #169
Nutley, NJ 07110; 973-759-2520
e-mail: ostfront@aol.com

TV, radio, and comic collectibles; sports and non-sports cards; silver and golden age comics
Casey's Collectible Corner
HCR Box 31, Rt. 3
N Blenheim, NY 12131
607-588-6464
e-mail: caseyco@aol.com
www.csmonline.com/caseys

Disney, especially books and animation art
Cohen Books and Collectibles
Joel J. Cohen
P.O. Box 810310
Boca Raton, FL 33481
561-487-7888; fax 561-487-3117
e-mail: cohendisney@prodigy.net
www.cohendisney.com

Early Disney, Western heroes, premiums and other related collectibles
Ron and Donna Donnelly
Saturday Heroes
6302 Championship Dr.
Tuscaloosa, AL 35405

Dick Tracy collectibles; free appraisals of DT items with SASE and photo or detailed description
Larry Doucet
2351 Sultana Dr.
Yorktown Heights, NY 10598
914-245-1320

Rocketeer memorabilia
Don Hamm
P.O. Box 2996
Kissimmee, FL 34742

Snoopy/Peanuts classics, new and old
N.F. Huber, The SNO-PEA Trader
931 Emerson St.
1000 Oaks, CA 91362
805-497-0119; fax 1-800-SNOOPY-2

Any and all, also Hartland figures
Terri Ivers
Terri's Toys & Nostalgia
206 E. Grand Ave.
Ponca City, OK 74601
580-762-8697 or
580-762-5174
fax 580-765-2657
e-mail: toylady@poncacity.net

Characters from comic strips/comic books, related memorabilia
Jeff and Bob's Fun Stuff
7324 Reseda Blvd #168
Reseda, CA 91335
818-705-3368

TV characters and shows, original network stills from 1955–85, soundtrack albums from 1950–90
Jim's TV Collectibles
P.O. Box 4767
San Diego, CA 92764
Phone or fax 619-462-1953

Games, models, action figures, dolls, general line; especially Nightmare Before Christmas
June Moon
245 N Northwest Hwy
Park Ridge, IL 60068
847-825-1411 (24-hour phone)
fax 847-825-6090
Open 2 to 6 PM Tues – Sat
e-mail: junmoonstr@aol.com
www.toymarket.com/junemoon

TV, Western, Space, Beatles; auction as well as set-price catalogs available
Just Kids Nostalgia
310 New York Ave.
Huntington, NY 11743
516-423-8449
fax 516-423-4326
e-mail: justkids25@aol.com

Especially bendy figures and the Simpsons
K-3 Inc.
Bendees Only; Simpson Mania
2335 NW Thurman
Portland, OR 97210
503-222-2713

Auction house with consignments welcomed; specializing in western Hartlands, airplanes, boats, cars, trucks, robots, windups, battery-ops, dolls, character items, and playset figures
Kerry and Judy's Toys
1414 S. Twelfth St.
Murray, KY 42071
270-759-3456
e-mail: kjtoys@apex.net

Disney and other character collectibles
Kathy and Skip Matthews
Second Childhood Antiques &
Collectibles
1154 Grand Ave.
Astoria, OR 97103; 503-325-6543

Any and all, also gum cards,
sports, movie posters, etc.
Mrs. Miller's Memorabilia
70a Greenwich Ave., Box 116
New York, NY 10011
212-614-9774 (leave message)
e-mail: mmm@photobbs.com

Especially Disney; send $5 for
annual subscription (6 issues) for
sale catalogs
The Mouse Man Ink
P.O. Box 3195
Wakefield, MA 01880
781-246-3876; fax 781-245-4511
e-mail: mouse_man@msn.com
www.mouseman.com

Especially pottery, china, ceramics,
salt and pepper shakers, cookie jars, tea
sets and children's china; with special
interest in Black Americana and Disneyana; illustrated sale lists available
Judy Posner
P.O. Box 2194
Englewood, FL 34295
e-mail: judyandjef@aol.com
www.judyposner.com

Buying, selling, and trading original
Beatles and Monkees memorabilia
Rick Rann, Beatlelist
P.O. Box 877
Oak Park, IL 60303; 708-442-7907

Also battery-ops, character clocks,
and novelties
Sam Samuelian, Jr.
700 Llanfair Rd.
Upper Darby, PA 19082
215-566-7248

Lone Ranger collector, buy and
sell; publisher of Silver Bullet
Newsletter (see Clubs, Newsletters,
and Other Publications)
The Silver Bullet
Terry and Kay Klepey
P.O. Box 553
Forks, WA 98331; 360-327-3726
e-mail: slvrbllt@olypen.com

Wizard of Oz memorabilia; quar-
terly mail/phone bid auctions avail-
able for $2; always buying Oz
Bill Stillman
Scarfone and Stillman Vintage Oz
P.O. Box 167
Hummelstown, PA 17036
717-566-5538

Especially tinplate toys and cars,
battery-op toys, and toy trains
Richard Trautwein, Toys N Such
437 Dawson St.
Sault Ste. Marie, MI 49783
906-635-0356
e-mail: r.traut@portup.com

TV, movie, rock 'n roll, comic
character, commercials, radio, theater, etc., memorabilia of all kinds;
Send $4 for sale catalog. We are
not interested in buying items. All
inquiries must include SASE for
reply unless ordering catalog
TV Collector
P.O. Box 1088
Easton, MA 02334
508-238-1179 or fax by pre-set
agreement

Games, premiums, cartoon person-
alities, Dick Tracy, Popeye, Buck
Rogers, Flash Gordon, Tarzan,
Lone Ranger, and others
Norm Vigue
3 Timberwood Dr., #306
Goffstown, MA 03045
603-647-9951

Especially ceramic figures,
Garfield, Muppets, Kliban,
Snoopy, Ziggy, Smurfs, Raggedy
Ann, Strawberry Shortcake, Care
Bears, Monsters, Enesco, Holt
Howard, etc.; lists available
Adrienne Warren
1032 Feather Bed Lane
Edison, NJ 08820
732-381-1616 (EST)
e-mail: adrienne.w@worldnet.att.net

Children's Play Dishes
Author of book
Lorraine Punchard
8201 Pleasant Ave. South
Bloomington, MN 55420
612-888-1079

Chinese Tin Toys
Also buying and selling antiques,
old toys, and collectibles; custom
refinishing and quality repairing
Finisher's Touch Antiques
Steve Fisch, proprietor
10 W Main St.
Wappingers Falls, NY 12590
914-298-8882; fax 914-298-8945

Comic Books
Also Western pulps, Big Little Books,
magazines, Mad and other humor
publications; large catalog available
Avalon Comics
Larry Curcio
P.O. Box 821
Medford, MA 02155; 617-391-5614

Also Sunday comics, books, pulp
magazines, premiums, character collectibles, non-sports cards, and more
Ken Mitchell
710 Conacher Dr.
Wilowdale, Ontario
Canada M2M 3N6
416-222-5808 (anytime)

Cracker Jack
Author of Cracker Jack Toys and
Cracker Jack, The Unauthorized
Guide to Advertising Collectibles
Larry White
108 Central St.
Rowley, MA 01969-1317

Dakins
Jim Rash
135 Alder Ave.
Egg Harbor Twp., NJ 08234-9302

Diecast
Especially Dinky; also selling inexpensive restorable diecast as well as
reproduction parts and decals for
many diecast brands
Paul Fideler
20 Shadow Oak Dr., Apt. #18
Sudbury, MA 01776
617-386-0228 (24 hours)
fax 617-386-0159 (24 hours)

Especially English-made toy vehicles
Mark Giles
510 E Third St.
Ogalala, NE 69153
308-284-4360

Especially Matchbox and other
small-scale cars and trucks
Bill Jackameit
972 Kelsey Dr.
Charlottesville, VA 22903
804-923-3398 (Monday–Thurs-
day, 7 pm–9 pm EST)
e-mail: wj2d@sprintmail.com
www.freeyellow.com/members/bj
diecast

Especially Matchbox, Hot Wheels,
Majorette
Dana Johnson Enterprises
P.O. Box 1824
Bend, OR 97709-1824; 503-382-8410
Author/publisher of Matchbox
Blue Book, Hot Wheels Blue Book,
and Collecting Majorette Toys
(prices updated yearly)

Especially Dinky; also obsolete
French, German, Italian, and
English-made vehicles
Jean-Claude Lanau
740 Thicket Ln.
Houston, TX 77079
713-4971-6034

Matchbox of all types including
Dinky, Commando, Convoys,
Harley-Davidson, Indy/Formula 1,
and Looney Tunes; also Corgi,
Hartoy, Hot Wheels, Tomica, and
Tyco slot cars
Neil's Wheels, Inc.
Box 354
Old Bethpage, NY 11804
516-293-9659; fax 516-420-0483

Ertl, banks, farm, trucks, and construction
Son's a Poppin' Ranch
John Rammacher
1610 Park Ave.
Orange City, FL 32763-8869
904-775-2891
e-mail: sap@bitstorm.net
www.bitstorm.net/sap

All types; also action figures such
as GI Joe, Johnny West, Matt
Mason, and others
Robert Reeves
104 Azalea Dr.
St. Mathews, SC 29135
803-578-5939 (leave message)

Especially Soviet-made toys
(marked USSR or CCCP)
David E. Riddle
P.O. Box 13141
Tallahassee, FL 32308
905-877-7207

Hot Wheels
Steve Stevenson
11117 NE 164th Pl.
Bothell, WA 98011-4003
206-488-2603
fax 206-488-2841

Hot Wheels, Matchbox, and all
obsolete toy cars, trucks, and airplanes
Dan Wells Antiques Toys
7008 Main St.
Westport, KY 40077
502-225-9925; fax 502-225-0019
e-mail: dwatcatDan@aol.com

Dolls
Strawberry Shortcake dolls, acces-
sories, and related items
Geneva Addy
P.O. Box 124
Winterset, IA 50273
515-462-3027

Hard plastic and composition,
Ginny and accessories, pincushion
dolls, doll dishes; catalogs available
Roslyn L. Herman
124-16 84th Rd.
Kew Gardens, NY 11415
718-846-3496 or 718-846-8491

Chatty Cathy and Mattel
Kathy Lewis
187 N Marcello Ave.
Thousand Oaks, CA 91360
805-499-8101
Author of book: *Chatty Cathy Dolls,
An Identification and Value Guide*

Ad dolls, Barbie Dolls and other Mattel dolls, premiums, character memorabilia, modern dolls, related items
Marcia Fanta, Marcia's Fantasy
427 33rd St. SE
Tappen, ND 58487-9411
701-327-4441
e-mail: fantbck@daktel.com

*Gerber Baby dolls; author of book
($44 postpaid)*
Joan S. Grubaugh
2342 Hoaglin Rd.
Van Wert, OH 45891
419-622-4411; fax 419-622-3026

Holly Hobbie dolls and collectibles
Kathe Conley
51 Spencer Rd.
Airville, PA 17302; 717-862-3162
fax per Winchester Group; 410-866-3125

Holly Hobbie dolls and collectibles
Helen L. McCale
1006 Ruby Ave.
Butler, MO 64730-2500

*Liddle Kiddles and other small dolls
from the late '60s and early '70s*
Dawn Parrish
20460 Samual Dr.
Saugus, CA 91350-3812
661-263-TOYS

Dolls from the 1960s–70s, including Liddle Kiddles, Barbie, Tammy, Tressy, etc. Co-author of The Collector's Guide to Tammy, the Ideal Teen (Collector Books)
Cindy Sabulis
P.O. Box 642
Shelton, CT 06484
203-926-0176
e-mail: toys4two@snet.net
www.dollsntoys.com

Betsy McCall
Marci Van Ausdall
P.O. Box 946
Quincy, CA 95971
916-283-2770
e-mail: dreams707@aol.com

Celebrity and character dolls
Henri Yunes
971 Main St., Apt. 2
Hackensack, NJ 07601
201-488-2236

Dollhouse Furniture
Renwal, Ideal, Marx, etc.
Judith A. Mosholder
186 Pine Springs Camp Road
Boswell, PA 15531; 814-629-9277

Dollhouses
*Tin and fiberboard dollhouses and
plastic furniture from all eras*
Bob and Marcie Tubbs
6405 Mitchell Hollow Rd.
Charlotte, NC 28277
704-541-5839

Elvis Presley Collectibles
Rosalind Cranor
P.O. Box 859
Blacksburg, VA 24063
Author of books: *Elvis Collectibles, Best of Elvis Collectibles*

Fast Food
Allan Bradley Music (BMI)
Allan Licht
484 S. Grand
Orange, CA 92866
714-633-2628
Also '50s & '60s toys; Batman;
Superman; '60s & '70s cereal boxes

Specializing in McDonald's®
Me and Dads Toys
Sally and Jim Christoffel
409 Maple
Elburn, IL 60119; 630-365-2914
e-mail: jimc@elnet.com

*All restaurants and California
Raisins*
Ken Clee
Box 11412
Philadelphia, PA 19111
215-722-1979

McDonald's® *only, especially older
or unusual items*
John and Eleanor Larsen
523 Third St.
Colusa, CA 95932
916-458-4769

McDonald's®
Terry and Joyce Losonsky
7506 Summer Leave Lane
Columbia, MD 21046-2455
410-381-3358
Authors of *Illustrated Collector's
Guide to McDonald's*® *Happy
Meals*® *Boxes, Premiums, and Promotionals* ($9 plus $2 postage),
McDonald's® *Happy Meal*® *Toys in
the USA* and *McDonald's*® *Happy
Meal*® *Toys Around the World*
(both full color, $24.95 each plus
$3 postage), and *Illustrated Collector's Guide to McDonald's*®
McCAPS® ($4 plus $2 postage)

Source for catalog: McDonald's®
*Collectibles and Other Fast-Food
Toys and Memorabilia*
Bill and Pat Poe
220 Dominica Circle E
Niceville, FL 32578-4085
850-897-4163; fax 850-897-2606
e-mail: McPoes@aol.com
Send $3.00 for catalogs (2 each
year, in January and July); see
Clubs, Newsletters, and Other
Publications for information on
McDonald's® club

Fisher-Price
Brad Cassity
1350 Stanwix
Toledo, OH 43614
419-389-1100

Games
*Victorian, cartoon, comic, TV,
and nostalgic themes*
Paul Fink's Fun & Games
P.O. Box 488
59 S Kent Rd.
Kent, CT 06757
860-927-4001
website: gamesandpuzzles.com

Paul David Morrow
1045 Rolling Point Ct.
Virginia Beach, VA 23456-6371

Circa 1900 to modern
Bill Smith
56 Locust St.
Douglas, MA 01516
508-476-2015

GI Joe
Also diecast and Star Wars
Cotswold Collectibles
P.O. Box 716, Dept. SC
Freeland, WA 98249
360-331-5331; fax 360-331-5344
www.whidbey.net/-cotswold

Guns
*Pre-WWII American spring-air BB
guns, all Red Ryder BB guns, cap
guns with emphasis on Western six-
shooters; especially wanted are pre-
WWII cast iron six-guns*
Jim Buskirk
3009 Oleander Ave.
San Marcos, CA 92069
760-599-1054

*Parts for 1940 cast-iron and 1950
diecast guns: steer-head grips, 2-pc. silver or silver and brass bullets for
Nicholas paint 6-shooter and spitfire rifle*
ED Drew
7530 146th Ave. NE
Redmond, WA 98052
206-885-7378

Specializing in cap guns
Happy Memories Antique Toy Co.
The Hamburgs
P.O. Box 1305
Woodland Hills, CA 91365
818-346-9884 or 818-346-1269
fax 818-346-0215

*Also model kits, toy soldiers and
character toys, and watches; character watch service available*
Plymouth Rock Toy Co.
38 Russell St.
Plymouth, MA 02360
508-746-2842 or 508-830-1880
(noon to 11 pm EDT)
fax 508-830-0364
e-mail: plymouthrocktoy@aol.com

Hartland Plastics, Inc.
Author of book
Gail Fitch
1733 N. Cambridge Ave.
Milwaukee, WI 53202

Specializing in Western Hartlands
Kerry and Judy's Toys
1414 S. 12th St.
Murray, KY 42071
270-759-3456
e-mail: kjtoys@apex.net

Specializing in Hartland Sports Figures
James Watson
25 Gilmore St.
Whitehall, NY 12887
518-499-0643
fax 518-499-1772

Halloween Collectibles
Also postcards
Pamela E. Apkarian-Russell
C.J. Russell and The Halloween
Queen Antiques
P.O. Box 499
Winchester, NH 03470
603-239-8875

Lunch Boxes
*Also Little House on the Prairie
items and TV collectibles of the
'50s and '60s*
PAK-RAT
Andy Galbus
900 8th St. NW
Kasson, MN 55944-1079
507-634-2093
e-mail: lhpakrateans.net

Norman's Olde and New Store
Philip Norman
126 W Main St.
Washington, NC 27889-4944
252-946-3448

Also characters such as cowboys, TV shows, cartoons, and more
Terri Ivers, Terri's Toys
206 E. Grand Ave.
Ponca City, OK 74601
580-762-8697 or 580-762-5174
fax 580-765-2657
e-mail: toylady@poncacity.net

Marbles
Block's Box is the longest continuously running absentee marble auction service in the country; catalogs issued
Stanley A. & Robert S. Block
P.O. Box 51
Trumbull, CT 06611
203-261-3223 or 203-926-8448;
e-mail: bblock@well.com
www.pages.prodigy.com/
    marbles/mcc.html
Prodigy: BWVR62A

Marionettes and Puppets
Steven Meltzer
1255 2nd St.
Santa Monica, CA 90401
310-656-0483

Marx
Figures, playsets, and character toy; send 3 33¢ stamps for extensive sales lists
G.F. Ridenour, Fun House Toy Co.
P.O. Box 343
Bradfordwoods, PA 15015-0343
724-935-1392 (fax capable)
www.funhousetoy.com

Model Kits
Specializing in figures and science fiction
Gordy Dutt
P.O. Box 201
Sharon Center, OH 44274-0201
330-239-1657 or 330-239-2991
Also action figures, monsters (especially Godzilla and Japan automated toys), Star Trek, and non-sports cards

From and of science fiction, TV, movies, figures, space, missiles, comics, etc.
John F. Green Inc.
1821 W. Jacaranda Pl
Fullerton, CA 92633
714-526-5467; 800-807-4759

Character, space, monster, Western, radio and cereal premiums and toys; GI Joe, Captain Action, tin toys and windups
Ed Janey, Character Company
1756 65th St.
Garrison, IA 52229
319-477-8888
e-mail: edjaney@aol.com
website: www.characterco.com

Also plastic toys and radio, movie or TV tie-ins, movie posters
John and Sheri Pavone
29 Sullivan Rd.
Peru, NY 12972
518-643-0993 Toll Free 888-458-2200; fax 518-643-8152
e-mail: apc1@worldnet.att.net
www.serftech.com/apc
Mastercard Visa Discover

Non-Sport Trading Cards
Send $1 for our 40-page catalog of non-sport cards ca 1970 to date; dealers send large SASE for our 10-page wholesale and closeout list
Mark and Val Macaluso
3603 Newark Rd.
Marion, NY 14505
315-926-4349; fax 315-926-4853

Paper Dolls
Author of books
Mary Young
Box 9244
Dayton, OH 45409
937-298-4838

Paper Lithographed Toys
Rare 18th-, 19th-, and 20th-century games, paper dolls, books, etc.
Bromer Booksellers, Inc.
607 Boylston St.
Boston, MA 02116
617-247-2818; fax 617-247-2975

Antique McLoughlin games, Bliss and Reed boats, toy wagons, Ten Pin sets, cube blocks, puzzles, and Victorian doll houses. Buy and sell; lists available upon request. Mail order and shows only
Mark and Linda Suozzi
P.O. Box 102
Ashfield, MA 01330
Phone or fax 413-628-3241 (9am to 5pm)
e-mail: marklyn@valinet.com
website: marklynantiques.com

Pedal Cars
Also specializing in Maytag collectibles
Nate Stoller
960 Reynolds Ave.
Ripon, CA 95366
510-481-2586
e-mail: multimotot@aol.com
www.geocities.com/heartland/pla
ins/6385

Pez Candy Dispensers
Richard Belyski
P.O. Box 124
Sea Cliff, NY 11579
e-mail: peznews@juno.com

Plastic Figures
Also Dakins, cartoon and advertising figures, and character squeeze toys
Jim Rash
135 Alder Ave.
Egg Harbor Twp., NJ 08234-9302
609-649-4125

Playsets
Also GI Joe, Star Trek and dinosaurs
Mike and Kurt Fredericks
145 Bayline Circle
Folsom, CA 95630-8077

Political Toys
Michael and Polly McQuillen
McQuillen's Collectibles
P.O. Box 11141
Indianapolis, IN 46201
317-322-8518
e-mail: buttons@oaktree.net

Promotional Vehicles
'50s and '60s models (especially Ford); also F&F Post Cereal cars; author of 2 books on promotional model cars, both available directly from him
Larry Blodget
Box 753
Rancho Mirage, CA 92270
619-862-1979

Puzzles
Wood jigsaw type, from before 1950
Bob Armstrong
15 Monadnock Rd.
Worcester, MA 01609
508-799-0644
e-mail: raahna@oldpuzzles.com
www.oldpuzzles.com

Specializing in advertising puzzles
Donald Friedman
660 W Grand Ave
Chicago, IL 60610
Day phone: 708-656-3700;
evenings and weekends: 312-226-4741; fax 708-656-6292

Radio Premiums
Also Fisher-Price; lists available
Pat and Kris Secor
P.O. Box 158
Clarksville, AR 72830
501-754-5746

Radios
Authors of several books on antique, novelty, and transistor radios
Sue and Marty Bunis
RR 1, Box 36
Bradford, NH 03221-9102

Ramp Walkers
Specializing in walkers, ramp-walking figures, and tin windups
Randy Welch, Raven'tiques
27965 Peach Orchard Rd.
Easton, MD 21601-8203
410-822-5441

Records
78 rpm children's records and picture disks; buys, sells, and trades records as well as makes cassette recordings for a small fee
Peter Muldavin
173 W 78th St., Apt. 5-F
New York, NY 10024
212-362-9606
kiddie78s@aol.com
members.aol.com/kiddie78s/

Russian and East European Toys
Wooden Matrioskha dolls, toys of tin, plastic, diecast metal; military theme and windups
Natural Way/DBA Russian Toy Co.
820 Massachusetts
Lawrence, KS 66044
913-841-0100

Specializing in Russian toys
David E. Riddle
P.O. Box 13141
Tallahassee, FL 32308
904-877-7207

Sand Toys
Authors of book; send $25 plus $3 for postage for a signed copy. NY residents please add 8¼% sales tax.
Carole and Richard Smyth
Carole Smyth Antiques
P.O. Box 2068
Huntington, NY 11743

Schoenhut
Publishers of Inside Collector and Antique Doll World
Keith and Donna Kaonis
60 Cherry Ln.
Huntington, NY 11743
516-261-8337; fax 516-261-8235

Slot Cars
Especially HO scale from the 1960s to the present; also vintage diecast
Joe Corea
New Jersey Nostalgia Hobby
401 Park Ave.
Scotch Plains, NJ 07076
908-322-2676; fax 908-322-4079

Specializing in slots and model racing from the '60s–'70s; especially complete race sets in original boxes
Gary Pollastro
5047 84th Ave. SE
Mercer, WA, 98040; 206-232-3199

Snow Domes

Broad assortment from states, cities, tourist attractions, novelties, also glass domes; list available
Nancy McMichael
P.O. Box 53262
Washington DC 20009
Editor of *Snow Biz*, quarterly newsletter, see Clubs, Newsletters, and Other Publications

Soldiers

Barclay, Manoil, Grey Iron, Jones, dimestore types and others; also Syrocco figures
Stan and Sally Alekna
732 Aspen Lane
Lebanon, PA 17042-9073
717-228-2361; fax 717-228-2362

Recasts, conversions, diorama work; price list available
Bryan and Val Davis
3132 E. Prince Rd.
Tucson, AZ 85716
520-323-2598 (9 am – 7 pm, MST)

Auburn, Airfix, Atlantic, etc; also Marx plastic figures, playsets and accessories; lists available with SASE
Phoenix Toy Soldier Co.
Bob Wilson
16405 North 9th Place
Phoenix, AZ 85022
602-863-2891

Sports Bobbin' Head Dolls

Tim Hunter
4301 W. Hidden Valley Dr.
Reno, NV 89502
702-856-4357
fax 702-856-4354
e-mail: thunter885@aol.com

Star Wars

Also vehicles, model kits, GI Joes, games, ad figures, View-Master, non-sports cards, Star Trek, advertising, antiques, fine art, and much more
June Moon
Jim and Nancy Frugoli
245 N Northwest Hwy
Park Ridge, IL 60068
847-825-1411 (24-hr phone); fax 847-825-6090
Open 2 to 6 PM Tues – Sat
e-mail: junmoonstr@aol.com
www.toymarket.com/junemoon

Steiff

Also Schucos and children's things
Candelaine (Candice Gunther)
1435 Wellington Ave
Pasadena, CA 91103-2320
626-796-4568; fax 626-796-7172
e-mail: candelaine@aol.com.

Especially limited editions, '50s and antique. Other teddies and reference books.
Cynthia's Country Store
The Wellington Mall #15-A
12794 W Forest Hill Blvd
Wellington, FL 33414
561-793-0554; fax 561-795-4222
www.thecrier.com/ccs
e-mail: cynbears@aol.com

Particularly bears; also Schucos and dolls
Bunny Walker
Box 502
Bucyrus, OH 44820; 419-562-8355

Tonka

Also candy containers and German nodders
Doug Dezso
864 Patterson Ave.
Maywood, NJ 07607; 201-488-1311

Toothbrush Holders

Also Pez
Marilyn Cooper
P.O. Box 55174
Houston, TX 77255

Tops and Other Spinning Toys

Yo-yos, advertising spinners, gyroscopes, spinning games, Victorian figural tops; any unique spinning toy. Buy, sell, trade
Bruce Middleton
5 Lloyd Rd.
Newburgh, NY 12550; 914-564-2556

Toy Mall

General line (toys on 2nd floor)
Bo-Jo's Antique Mall
3400 Summer Avenue
Memphis, TN 38122; 901-323-2050

Trains

Lionel, American Flyer and Plasticville
Gary's Trains
186 Pine Springs Camp Road
Boswell, PA 15531
814-629-9277

Also Fisher-Price, Tonka toys and diecast vehicles
Bill Mekalian
550 E Chesapeake Cir.
Fresno, CA 93720; 209-434-3247

Buying American Flyer S gauge. Toys of all types for sale. Satisfaction guaranteed; color photos with SASE; shipping extra. No return calls on sold items; phone until midnight
Linda and Paul Woodward
14 Argo Drive
Sewell, NJ 08080-1908
609-582-1253

Transformers

Specializing in Transformers, Robotech, Shogun Warriors, Gadaikins, and any other robot; want to buy these MIP — also selling
David Kolodny-Nagy
May through Jan: 3701 Connecticut Ave. NW, Apt #500
Washington, DC 20008
202-364-8753
For copy of BotCon Transformer Comic Book, *Comic Smorgasbord Special*, send $3 + $1.50 for single issues, $2.50 each for 10 or more + $2. Also available: *Transformers: BotCon '94 Ten-Year Retrospective* (130+ pages) at $15 + $2

Trolls

Pat Peterson
1105 6th Ave. SE
Hampton, IA 50441

View-Master

Also games, slot cars, Pez, lunch boxes, Halloween costumes, dolls, premiums, TV Guides, Mad magazines
Ditto Enterprises
Tom Bremer
P.O. Box 49
Newark, NY 14513
Phone or fax 315-331-7688
e-mail: Dittoent@aol.com
members.aol.com/dittoent/
   catalogpage.index.html

Roger Nazeley
4921 Castor Ave.
Phil., PA 19124
215-743-8999 or 215-533-6110
extension 221;fax 215-288-8030
e-mail: vmreelguy2@aol.com

Windups

Especially German and Japan tin toys, Cracker Jack, toothbrush holders, radio premiums, pencil sharpeners, and comic strip toys
Phil Helley
Old Kilbourne Antiques
629 Indiana Ave.
Wisconsin Dells, WI 53965
608-254-8770

Also pressed steel toys, battery-ops, candy containers, dolls and children's things, games, soldiers, Noah's ark, space, robots, etc.
Jacquie and Bob Henry
Antique Treasures and Toys
Box 17
Walworth, NY 14568-0017
315-597-4719
e-mail: jhenry5792@aol.com or jacqueline.henry@mci2000.com

Fine character windups; also Black Americana
Stephen Leonard
Box 127
Albertson, LI, NY 11507
516-742-0979

Also friction and battery operated; fast-food toys, displays
Antique Toy Information Service
Send: SASE, good photos
(35mm preferred)
and $9.95 per toy to:
Scott Smiles
848 SE Atlantic Dr.
Lantana, FL 33462-4702
561-582-4947
e-mail: ssmiles664@aol.com

Yo-Yos

Lucky J. Meisenheimer, M.D.
7300 Sand Lake Commons Blvd.
Suite 105
Orlando, FL 32819
407-352-2444; fax 407-363-2869
e-mail: LuckyJ@msn.com
www.yo-yos.net
Author of book, *Lucky's Collectors Guide to 20th Century Yo-Yos*. To order call 1-877-969-6728. Cost is $29.95 + $3.20 postage.

Clubs, Newsletters, and Other Publications

There are hundreds of clubs, newsletters, and magazines available to toy collectors today. Listed here are some devoted to specific areas of interest. You can obtain a copy of many newsletters simply by requesting a sample.

Action Figure News & Toy Review
James Tomlinson, Editor
556 Monroe Turnpike
Monroe, CT 06458
203-452-7286; fax 203-452-0410

Action Toys Newsletter
P.O. Box 31551
Billings, MT 59107
406-248-4121

American Game Collectors Assn.
49 Brooks Ave.
Lewiston, MA 04240

American International Matchbox
Collectors & Exchange Club
News-Monthly
Dottie Colpitts
532 Chestnut St.
Lynn, MA 01904
617-595-4135

Anchor Block Foundation
908 Plymouth St.
Pelham, NY 10303
914-738-2935

Antique Advertising Association
P.O. Box 1121
Morton Grove, IL 60053
708-446-0904

Antique & Collectors Reproduction News
Mark Cherenka
Circulation Department
P.O. Box 71174
Des Moines, IA 50325
800-227-5531. Monthly newsletter showing differences between old originals and new reproductions; subscription: $32 per year

Antique Trader Weekly
Kyle D. Husfloen, Editor
P.O. Box 1050
Dubuque, IA 52004
Subscription $32 (52 issues) per year

The Autograph Review newsletter
Jeffrey Morey
305 Carlton Rd.
Syracuse, NY 13207
315-474-3516

Autographs & Memorabilia
P.O. Box 224
Coffeyville, KS 67337; 316-251-5308. 6 issues per year on movie and sports memorabilia

Barbie Bazaar magazine
5617 Sixth Ave., Dept NY593
Kenosha, WI 53140
414-658-1004; fax 414-658-0433
6 issues for $25.95

Barbie Talks Some More!
Jacqueline Horning
7501 School Rd.
Cincinnati, OH 45249

The Baum Bugle
The International Wizard of Oz
Club
Fred M. Meyer
220 N 11th St.
Escanaba, MI 49829

Berry-Bits
Strawberry Shortcake Collectors
Club
Peggy Jimenez
1409 72nd St.
N Bergen, NJ 07047

Beyond the Rainbow Collectors
Exchange
P.O. Box 31672
St. Louis, MO 63131

Big Little Times
Big Little Book Collectors Club
of America
Larry Lowery
P.O. Box 1242
Danville, CA 94526
415-837-2086

Bobbing Head Doll newsletter and
price guide
Tim Hunter
4301 W. Hidden Valley Dr.
Reno, NV 89502
e-mail: thunter885@aol.com

Bojo
P.O. Box 1403
Cranberry Township, PA 16066-0403
724-776-0621 (9 am – 9 pm EST)
Issues fixed-price catalog containing Beatles and Rock 'n' Roll memorabilia

Buckeye Marble Collectors Club
Betty Barnard
472 Meadowbrook Dr.
Newark, Oh 43055
614-366-7002

Canadian Toy Collectors Society
Gary A. Fry
P.O. Box 636
Maple, Ontario, Canada L6A 1S5

Candy Container Collectors of
America
P.O. Box 352
Chelmsford, MA 01824-0352
or Jeff Bradfield
90 Main St.
Dayton, VA 22821

The Candy Gram newsletter
Candy Container Collectors of
America
Douglas Dezso
864 Paterson, Ave.
Maywood, NJ 07607
201-845-7707

Captain Action Collectors Club
P.O. Box 2095
Halesite, NY 11743
516-423-1801
Send SASE for newsletter info

Cast Iron Toy Collectors of America
Paul McGinnis
1340 Market St.
Long Beach, CA 90805

Cat Collectors Club
33161 Wendy Dr.
Sterling Heights, MI 48310
Subscription: $18 per year

Cat Talk
Marilyn Dipboye
31311 Blair Dr.
Warren, MI 48092; 810-264-0285

Century Limited
Toy Train Collectors Society
160 Dexter Terrace
Tonawanda, NY 14150
716-694-3771

Coca-Cola Collectors Club
International
P.O. Box 49166
Atlanta, GA 30359
Annual dues: $25

Collecting Tips Newsletter
c/o Meredith Williams
P.O. Box 633
Joplin, MO 64802
417-781-3855 or 417-624-2518
12 issues per year focusing on
fast-food collectibles

Collector Glass News
P.O. Box 308
Slippery Rock, PA 16057
412-946-2838; fax 412-946-9012
www.glassnews.com
6 issues per year focusing on
character glasses, $15 per year

Collectors Life
Beth Savino
c/o The Toy Store
7856 Hill Ave.
Holland, OH 43528
419-865-3899 or 800-862-8697

The Cookie Jar Collectors Club
News
Louise Messina Daking
595 Cross River Rd.
Katonah, NY 10536
914-232-0383
fax 914-232-0384

Cookie Jarrin' With Joyce: The
Cookie Jar Newsletter
R.R. 2, Box 504
Walterboro, SC 29488

Cynthia's Country Store
Wellington Mall #15A
12794 West Forest Hill Blvd.
West Palm Beach, FL 33414
Phone or fax 407-793-0554
Specializing in Steiff new, discontinued, and antique. Publishes quarterly Steiff and bear-related newsletter and limited edition yearly price guide. $15 per year for both. Call or fax for information or if you have any questions. Also specializes in pieces by R. John Wright, other bear manufacturers, toy soldiers, and some old toys. Many Steiff color catalogs and books available.

Dark Shadows Collectibles Classified
Sue Ellen Wilson
6173 Iroquois Trail
Mentor, OH 44060
440-946-6348
For collectors of both old and
new series

Dionne Quint Collectors Club
(see also *Quint News*)
Jimmy Rodolfos
P.O. Box 2527
Woburn, MA 01888
617-933-2219

Doll Castle News Magazine
P.O. Box 247
Washington, NJ 07882
908-689-7042; fax 908-689-6320
Subscription: $16.95 per year or
$31.95 for 2 years; issued 6 times
a year, serves general interests of
doll and miniature collectors as
well as dollmaking

Doll Investment Newsletter
P.O. Box 1982
Centerville, MA 02632

Doll News
United Federation of Doll Clubs
P.O. Box 14146
Parkville, MO 64152

*Dollhouse & Miniature Collectors
    Quarterly*
Sharon Unger, Editor
P.O. Box 16
Bellaire, MI 49615
$20.00 for 4 issues per year, 45-
50 pages of information, buy &
sell ads, pricing information

Dunbar's Gallery
76 Haven St.
Milford, MA 01757
508-634-8697
fax 508-634-8698
Specializing in quality advertising, Halloween, toys, coin-operated machines; holding cataloged auctions occasionally, lists
available

The Ertl Replica
Ertl Collectors Club
Mike Meyer, Editor
Hwys 136 & 20
Dyersville, IA 52040
319-875-2000

Fiend Magazine
1205 B Commercial Park Dr
Tallahassee, FL 32303
www.fiendmagazine.com
Runs collector's columns and
tracks collectible yo-yo prices.
To order call 1-888-284-8548.
Subscription rate is $16/year for
4 issues.

The Fisher-Price Collectors Club
This club issues a quarterly
newsletter packed with information and ads for toys. For more
information write to:
Fisher-Price Club
c/o Jeanne Kennedy
1442 N. Ogden
Mesa, AZ 85205

*FLAKE, The Breakfast Nostalgia
    Magazine*
P.O. Box 481
Cambridge, MA 02140
617-492-5004. Bimonthly illustrated issue devoted to one hot
collecting area such as Disney,
etc., with letters, discoveries,
new releases, and ads; single
issue: $4 ($6 foreign); annual:
$20 ($28 foreign); free 25-word
ad with new subscription

Friends of Hoppy Club and
    Newsletter
Laura Bates
6310 Friendship Dr.
New Concord, OH 43762-9708
614-826-4850

Game Times
American Game Collectors Assn.
Joe Angiolillo, Pres.
4628 Barlow Dr.
Bartlesville, OK 74006

*Garfield Collectors Society
    Newsletter*
c/o David L. Abrams, Editor
744 Foster Ridge Rd.
Germantown, TN 38138-7036
901-753-1026

Gas Toy Collector
P.O. Box 440818
Houston, TX 77244-0818
Membership: $15 per year; sam-
ple issue $1.00

Gene Autry Star Telegram
Gene Autry Development Assn.
Chamber of Commerce
P.O. Box 158
Gene Autry, OK 73436

Ginny Doll Club News
Jeanne Niswonger
305 W Beacon Rd.
Lakeland, FL 33803
813-687-8015

*Gone With the Wind Collectors
Club Newsletter*
8105 Woodview Rd.
Ellicot City, MD 21043
301-465-4632

Good Bears of the World
Terri Stong
P.O. Box 13097
Toledo, OH 43613

Grandma's Trunk
P.O. Box 404
Northport, MI 49670
Subscription: $8 per year for 1st
class or $5 per year for bulk rate

Headquarters Quarterly, for GI
Joe Bodnarchuk, Joe Collectors
62 McKinley Ave.
Kenmore, NY 14217-2414

Hello Again, Old-Time Radio
    Show Collector
Jay A. Hickerson
P.O. Box 4321
Hamden, CT 06514; 203-248-
2887; fax 203-281-1322. Sample
copy upon request with SASE

Highballer for Toy Train collectors
c/o Lou Bohn
109 Howedale Dr.
Rochester, NY 14616-1543

Hobby News
J.L.C. Publications
Box 258
Ozone Park, NY 11416

*Hopalong Cassidy Fan Club Inter-
national*
Laura Bates
6310 Friendship Dr.
New Concord, OH 43762
614-826-4850; Subscription: $15
(USA) or $20 (Canada and over-
seas); includes quarterly newsletter and information on annual
Cambridge, Ohio, festival

Hopalong Cassidy Newsletter
Hopalong Cassidy Fan Club
P.O. Box 1361
Boyes Hot Springs, CA 95416

Ideal Doll & Toy Collectors Club
P.O. Box 623
Lexington, MA 02173
617-862-2994

*International Wizard of Oz Club
Inc.*
P.O. Box 95
Kinderhook, IL 62345

John's Collectible Toys and Gifts
    catalog
John DeCicco
57 Bay View Dr.
Shrewsbury, MA 01545
www.johns-toys.com
$4.00 per issue. To order call toll
free 1-800-505-Toys

Kitbuilders Magazine
Gordy's
Box 201
Sharon Center, OH 44274-0201
330-239-1657
fax 330-239-2991
www.gremlins.com/kitbuilders
Covering vintage plastic figure
and sci-fi kits from the late 50's

to the early 70's. Plus, today's
new plastic, resin and vinyl
releases. $20/year US; $24/year
US first class; $45/year foreign;
$32/year Canada; $6 single
copy/US; $12/foreign;
$8/Canada

*Madame Alexander Fan Club
    Newsletter*
Earl Meisinger
11 S 767 Book Rd.
Naperville, IL 60564

Marble Mania
Marble Collectors Society of
    America
Stanley Block
P.O. Box 222
Trumbull, CT 06611
203-261-3223

Marl & B catalog
Marl Davidson
10301 Braden Run
Bradenton, FL 34202
941-751-6275
fax 941-751-5463
www.marlbe.com
subscription: US $25/year;
Canada $30/year; foreign
$40/year; sample copy US
$7.95/foreign $12.95. Released 4
times a year.

Martha's Kidlit Newsletter
Box 1488A
Ames, IA 50010.
A bimonthly publication for chil-
dren's books collectors. Subscrip-
tion: $25 per year

Matchbox USA
Charles Mack
62 Saw Mill Rd.
Durham, CT 06422
203-349-1655

McDonald's® *Collecting Tips*
Meredith Williams
Box 633
Joplin, MO 64802
Send SASE for information

McDonald's® Collector Club
Joyce Terry Losonsky
7506 Summer Leave Ln.
Columbia, MD 21046-2455
301-381-3358
Authors of *Illustrated Collector's
Guide to McDonald's*® *Happy
Meal*® *Boxes, Premiums, & Pro-
motions*© ($9 plus $2 postage),
and *Illustrated Collector's Guide to
McDonald's Mccaps* ($3 plus $2),
both available from the authors.

Florida Sunshine Chapter,
McDonald's® Collectors Club
Bill and Pat Poe, founders and
current chapter officers (President and Treasurer)
220 Dominica Circle E.
Niceville, FL 32578-4085
850-897-4163; fax 850-897-2606
e-mail: McPoes@aol.com
Club membership: $15 for individual; $20 family/couple; $7
junior; out of state $15; International $20. Annual show in
February of each year in central
Florida area. *The Sunshine Express*
newsletter published monthly.

*McDonald's® Collector Club
  Newsletter*
c/o Tenna Greenberg
5400 Waterbury Rd.
Des Moines, IA 50312
515-279-0741

McDonald's® Collector Club
Sharon Iranpour, President
24 San Rafael Dr.
Rochester, NY 14618
716-381-9467; fax 716-383-9248
e-mail: siranpour@aol.com
Membership $15 per year/individual; $20 per year/family
Benefits include dated lapel pin,
quarterly newletter and an annual
members directory. For more
information send LSASE to:
McDonald's® Collector Club
1153 S. Lee St. Suite 200
Des Plaines, IL 60016

Model & Toy Collector Magazine
Toy Scouts, Inc.
137 Casterton Ave.
Akron, OH 44303
330-836-0668; fax 330-869-8668
e-mail: toyscouts@toyscouts.com
www.toyscouts.com

Modern Doll Club Journal
Jeanne Niswonger
305 W Beacon Rd.
Lakeland, FL 33803

The Mouse Club East (Disney
  collectors)
P.O. Box 3195
Wakefield, MA 01880
e-mail: mouse_man@msn.com
www.mouseman.com
Family membership: $25 (includes
newsletters and 2 shows per year)

The Mouse Club (newsletter)
Kim and Julie McEuen
2056 Cirone Way
San Jose, CA 95124
408-377-2590; fax 408-379-6903

Movie Advertising Collector (magazine)
George Reed
P.O. Box 28587
Philadelphia, PA 19149

NAOLH Newsletter
National Assn. for Outlaw &
  Lawman History
Hank Clark
P.O. Box 812
Waterford, CA 95386;
209-874-2640

NAPAC Newsletter
National Assn. of Paper and
  Advertising Collectors
P.O. Box 500
Mt. Joy, PA 17552
717-653-4300

National Fantasy Fan Club
(for Disney collectors)
Dept. AC, Box 19212
Irvine, CA 92713
Membership: $20 per year,
includes newsletters, free ads,
chapters, conventions, etc.

National Headquarters News
Train Collectors Assn.
300 Paradise Ln.
Strasburg, PA 17579

*Old Toy Soldier
The Journal for Collectors*
209 N Lombard Ave.
Oak Park, IL 60302
708-383-6525
fax 708-383-2182
Subscription: $35 per year for 6
issues (1st class U.S. mail); current sample copy available by
sending $3. Written for collectors
by collectors, this magazine shares
useful information on military
and civilian toy figures and the
companies that produced them

On Line With Betsy McCall
Marci Van Ausdall
P.O. Box 946
Quincy, CA 95971
Subscription: $10/yr. for 4 issues

Paper Collectors' Marketplace
470 Main St., P.O. Box 128
Scandinavia, WI 54977
715-467-2379
Subscription: $19.95 (12 issues)
per year in USA; Canada and
Mexico add $15 per year

Paper Doll News
Emma Terry
P.O. Box 807
Vivian, LA 71082

The Pencil Collector
American Pencil Collectors Soc.
Robert J. Romey, Pres.
2222 S Millwood
Wichita, KS 67213
316-263-8419

Pepsi-Cola Collectors Club Newsletter
Pepsi-Cola Collectors Club
Bob Stoddard
P.O. Box 1275
Covina, CA 91722
714-593-8750
Membership: $15

Pez Collector's News
Richard and Marianne Belyski,
  Editors
P.O. Box 124
Sea Cliff, NY 11579
Phone or fax 516-676-1183
e-mail: peznews@juno.com

Piece by Piece
Frances Main, Editor
P.O. Box 12823
Kansas City, KS 66112-9998
For Springbok puzzle collectors;
subscription: $8 per year

Plastic Figure & Playset Collector
5894 Lakeview Ct. E
Onalaska, WI 54650

*The Pokey Gazette, A Little Golden
  Book* collector newsletter
Steve Santi
19626 Ricardo Ave.
Hayward, CA 94541
510-481-2586

The Prehistoric Times
Mike and Kurt Fredericks
145 Bayline Circle
Folsom, CA 95630; 916-985-7986
For collectors of dinosaur toys; 6
issues (1 yr), $19

The Prize Insider Newsletter, for
  Cracker Jack collectors
Larry White
108 Central St.
Rowley, MA 01969-1317
978-948-8187

The Puppet Collector's Newsletter
Steven Meltzer
1255 2nd St.
Santa Monica, CA 90401
310-656-0483

Quint News (see also Dionne
  Quint Collectors Club)
Dionne Quint Collectors
P.O. Box 2527
Woburn, MA 01888
617-933-2219

Record Collectors Monthly
(newspaper)
P.O. Box 75
Mendham, NJ 07945
201-543-9520
fax 201-543-6033

Roy Rogers-Dale Evans Collectors Assn.
Nancy Horsley
P.O. Box 1166
Portsmouth, OH 45662

Schoenhut Collectors Club
For membership information:
Patricia J. Girbach
1003 W Huron St.
Ann Arbor, MI 48103-4217

*The Shirley Temple Collectors
  News*
8811 Colonial Rd.
Brooklyn, NY 11209
Dues: $20 per year; checks
payable to Rita Dubas

The Silent Film Newsletter
Gene Vazzana
140 7th Ave.
New York, NY 10011
Subscription $18, send $2.50 for
sample copy

The Silver Bullet
Terry and Kay Klepey
P.O. Box 553
Forks, WA 98331
360-327-3726
e-mail: slvrbllt@olypen.com
Subscription $15 per year, sample issue $4; back issues available; also licensed mail-order
seller of memorabilia and
appraiser

Smurf Collectors Club
24ACH, Cabot Rd. W
Massapequa, NY 11758
Membership includes newsletters. LSASE for information

Snow Biz
c/o Nancy McMichael
P.O. Box 53262
Washington, DC 20009
Quarterly newsletter (subscription $10 per year) and collector's club, annual meeting/swap
meet

Still Bank Collectors Club of
  America
Larry Egelhoff
4175 Millersville Rd.
Indianapolis, IN 46205
317-846-7228

The Sno-Pea Trader catalog/price
  guide
Send $3 to:
N.F. Huber, Dept. TSF
931 Emerson St.
1000 Oaks, CA 91362-2447
805-497-0119
Subscriptions available $12/year
— refundable with purchase

The Survivors
For membership information:
Send name and address along
with SASE or e-mail address to:
Liane Elliot
6202 34th St. NW
Gig Harbor, WA 98335-7205
e-mail: tetra@eskimo.com

The Television History Magazine
William J. Flechner
700 E Macoupin St.
Staunton, IL 62088
618-635-2712

Toy Collector Club of America
  (for Ertl toys)
P.O. Box 302
Dyersville, IA 52040
800-452-3303

Toy Dish Collectors
Abbie Kelly
P.O. Box 351
Camillus, NY 13031
315-487-7415

*Toy Gun Collectors of America
  Newsletter*
Jim Buskirk, Editor and Publisher
3009 Oleander Ave.
San Marcos, CA 92069
760-599-1054
Published quarterly, covers cap
guns, spring air BB guns and
other toy guns. Dues: $17 per
year; SASE for information

Toy Shop
700 E State St.
Iola, WI 54990
715-445-2214
Subscription (3rd class) $23.95
for 26 issues

Toy Trader
100 Bryant St.
Dubuque, Iowa 52003
1-800-364-5593
Subscription in US $24 for 12 issues

Toychest
Antique Toy Collectors of
  America, Inc.
2 Wall St., 13th Floor
New York, NY 10005
212-238-8803

Toys & Prices magazine
700 E State St.
Iola, WI 54990-0001
715-445-2214; fax 715-445-4087
Subscription: $14.95 per year

The Trick or Treat Trader
CJ Russell and the Halloween
  Queen Antiques
P.O. Box 499, 4 Lawrence St.
and Rt. 10
Winchester, NH 03470
Subscription is $15 a year for 4
issues or $4 for a sample

Trainmaster (newsletter)
P.O. Box 1499
Gainesville, FL 32602
904-377-7439 or 904-373-4908
fax 904-374-6616

Troll Monthly
5858 Washington St.
Whitman, MA 02382
800-858-7655 or 800-85-Troll

Turtle River Farm Toys
Rt. 1, Box 44
Manvel, ND 58256-9763

The TV Collector
Diane L. Albert
P.O. Box 1088
Easton, MA 02334-1088
508-238-1179
Send $4 for sample copy

View-Master Reel Collector
Roger Nazeley
4921 Castor Ave.
Phil., PA 19124
215-743-8999
e-mail: vmreelguy2@ad.com

Western & Serials Club
Rt. 1, Box 103
Vernon Center, NM 56090
507-549-3677

The Working Class Hero (Beatles
  newsletter)
3311 Niagara St.
Pittsburgh, PA 15213-4223
Published 3 times per year; send
SASE for information

The Wrapper
Bubble Gum & Candy Wrapper
  Collectors
P.O. Box 573
St. Charles, IL 60174
708-377-7921

The Yellow Brick Road Fantasy
  Museum & Gift Shop
Rt. 49 and Yellow Brick Rd.
Chesterton, IN 46304
219-926-7048

Yo-Yo Times
P.O. Box 1519-SCT
Herndon, VA 22070

DON'T MISS YOUR CHANCE
TO REACH THOUSANDS OF TOY COLLECTORS

TO RESERVE YOUR AD SPACE FOR THE NEXT EDITION
PLEASE CONTACT HUXFORD ENTERPRISES *IMMEDIATELY*

RATES
(Ad Size)

FULL PAGE   7½" wide x 9¾" tall – $750.00

HALF PAGE   7½" wide x 4½" tall – $400.00

QUARTER PAGE   3½" wide x 4½" tall – $250.00

EIGHTH PAGE   3½" wide x 2¼" tall – $150.00

(or business card)

*NOTE: The above rates are for **camera ready copy only** – Add $50.00 if we are to compose your ad. These prices are net – no agency discounts allowed. Payment in full must accompany your ad copy.*

All advertising accepted under the following conditions:

1. The Publisher will furnish advertising space in sizes and at rates as set forth in this rate sheet upon full payment in advance of its annual advertising deadline as set forth herein.

2. Submission of Copy. The publisher shall have the right to omit any advertisement when the space allotted to Advertiser in a particular issue has been filled. In addition, the Publisher reserves the right to limit the amount of space the Advertiser may use in any one edition.

3. Content and Design. Publisher reserves the right to censor, reject, alter, or refuse any advertising copy at its sole discretion or disapprove any advertising copy in accordance with any rule the Publisher may now have, or may adopt in the future, concerning the acceptance of advertising matter, but no intentional change in advertising copy will be made without the prior consent of the Advertiser.

4. Publisher's Liability for Deletions. Publisher's liability for failure of the Publisher to insert any advertisement in their books shall be limited to a refund of the consideration paid for the insertion of the advertisement or, at Advertiser's option, to such deleted advertisement being inserted in the next edition.

5. Copyright and Trademark Permission. Any Advertiser using copyrighted material or trademarks or trade names of others in its advertising copy shall obtain the prior written permission of the owners thereof which must be submitted to the Publisher with the advertising copy. Where this has not been done, advertising will not be accepted.

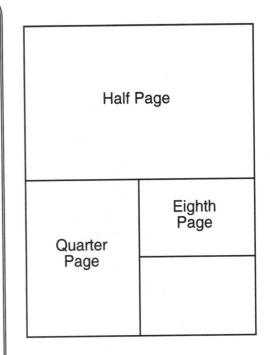

Make checks payable to:

HUXFORD ENTERPRISES
1202 7th St.
Covington, IN 47932

Antique Toys and Collectibles

Auctions held in our galleries at Christie's East,
219 East 67th Street, New York, New York 10021.
For further information, please contact the Collectibles
Department at 212 606 0543. For auction catalogues,
please telephone Christie's Publications at
800 395 6300.

A rare tinplate Marklin Ferris Wheel, circa 1890s, 21 in. high.
Sold at Christie's New York, June 1994, for $55,200.

Principal auctioneer: Cathy Elkies

CHRISTIE'S
EAST

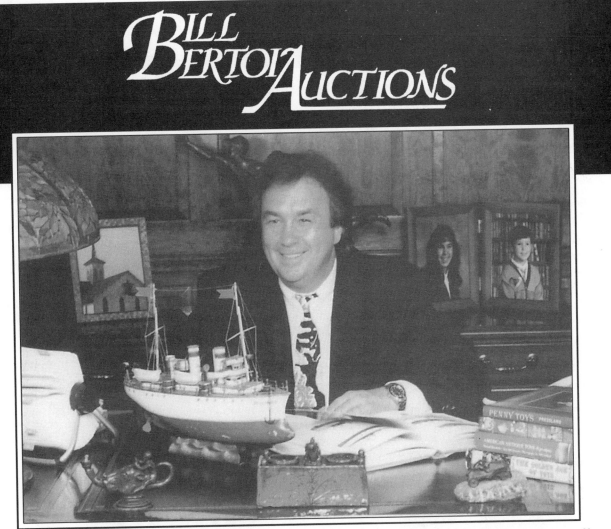

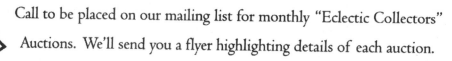

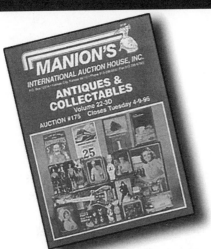

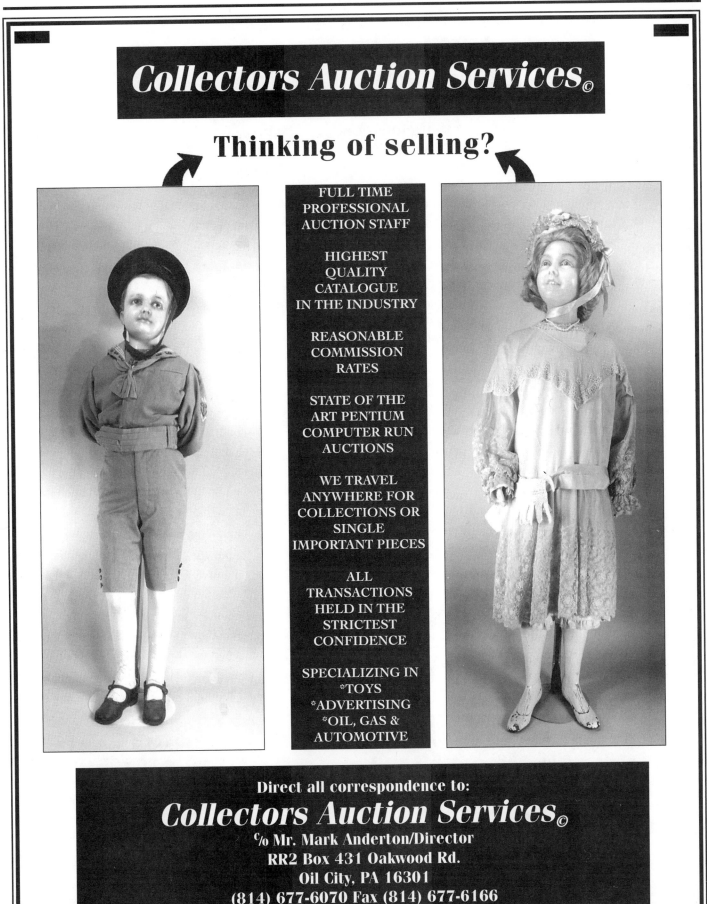

Index to Advertisers

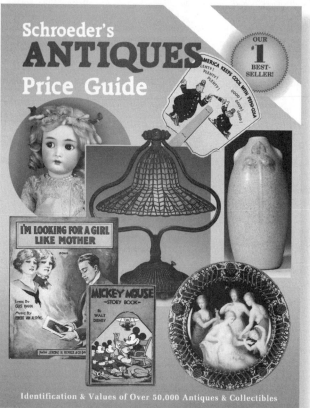